Library of Congress Cataloging-in-Publication Data

Dagel, John F.
   Diesel engine and fuel system repair / John F. Dagel, Robert N. Brady.—5th ed.
      p. m.
   Includes index.
   ISBN 0-13-092981-6
   1. Diesel motor—Maintenance and repair. 2. Diesel motor—Fuel systems—Maintenance
and repair. I. Brady, Robert N. II. Title.

TJ799 .D33 2001
621.43'68—dc21

2001024940

Editor in Chief: Stephen Helba
Editor: Edward Francis
Production Editor: Christine M. Buckendahl
Production Coordinator: Carlisle Publishers Services
Design Coordinator: Robin G. Chukes
Cover Designer: Linda Fares
Cover photo: International Stock
Production Manager: Brian Fox
Marketing Manager: Jamie Van Voorhis

This book was set in Palatino by Carlisle Communications, Ltd., and was printed and bound by Courier
Kendallville, Inc. The cover was printed by The Lehigh Press, Inc.

Prentice-Hall International (UK) Limited, *London*
Prentice-Hall of Australia Pty. Limited, *Sydney*
Prentice-Hall Canada, Inc., *Toronto*
Prentice-Hall Hispanoamericana, S.A., *Mexico*
Prentice-Hall of India Private Limited, *New Delhi*
Prentice-Hall of Japan, Inc., *Tokyo*
Prentice-Hall Singapore Pte. Ltd.
Editora Prentice-Hall do Brasil, Ltda., *Rio de Janeiro*

10 9 8 7 6 5 4 3
ISBN 0-13-092981-6

Diesel Engine and Fuel System Repair

Fifth Edition

John F. Dagel

Robert N. Brady

Vancouver Community College
Department Head, Diesel Technician Program,
and President of Hi Tech Consulting Ltd.

Prentice Hall

Upper Saddle River, New Jersey
Columbus, Ohio

Especially for Linda, Alanna, Alicia, Scott, Tracy, and Adele!

To all of the creative individuals who have allowed me to gain knowledge and skills from their benchmark experiences and to the many motivated students, friends, and SAE colleagues within the diesel and automotive industry who have shared their standards of excellence. This book is a reflection of a diversity of backgrounds of truly remarkable people who provided me with their time and support. I trust that the finished product meets your high standards and expectations.

Special Note

No textbook of this kind can be written for potential technicians without the support and cooperation of many unique individuals, colleagues, companies, and corporations. Constructive criticism, reviews, and feedback from prior users of the first four editions of this book have been of great assistance. I have within the confines of this book, and where most appropriate to the greatest cross section of users, attempted to include the most up-to-date information and as many suggestions as possible in this fifth edition.

Some suggestions for specific overhaul data and information related to component rebuild and testing of mechanical and electronic fuel injection system parts are best obtained by contacting the equipment manufacturer. This highly technical and specialized area is best handled and addressed through a professional association such as the Association of Diesel Specialists (ADS), whose members are employed to specifically overhaul, rebuild, and test fuel injection and other components with the assistance of complex and costly equipment. If you review the various Automotive Service Excellence (ASE) and Trade Qualification (TQ) skills tasks and tests lists for a certified service technician in the medium/heavy truck, commercial transport (truck and bus), heavy-duty equipment, marine, industrial, or agricultural specialty areas, it is not a prerequisite for the technician to have specific skills for each area. Typical service technicians are expected to have the skills and knowledge to remove and reinstall, diagnose, perform minor adjustments to on-engine fuel systems, troubleshoot, analyze failure, maintain, and repair or replace faulty parts and components where needed.

The information in this textbook is not designed to supplant the excellent information in original equipment manufacturer (OEM) service literature or service training programs through the local distributor or factory service training schools. To obtain specific details about a certain area, it is always best to refer to the engine manufacturer's own service manuals, slide training programs, videos, or CD-ROMs. Instructors in the specialty content areas of medium/heavy trucks and diesel-powered equipment have access to a diversified selection of software and hardware to assist them in developing courses and programs that address the task lists required to challenge ASE or TQ type certification. If you download ASE's preparation guides from its website (www.asecert.org), you will find no reference or necessity for potential service technicians to prepare to certify in the area of overhaul, testing, or adjustment of mechanical or electronic fuel injection pumps, mechanical or electronic unit injectors, mechanical or electronic governors, or nozzle rebuilds. They do, however, have to be capable of pop-testing nozzles and unit injectors for correct cracking or popping pressures and correct spray patterns. When special equipment is available, some technicians may be taught to flow-test individual unit injectors for recommended fuel volume, but again it is not an ASE or TQ necessity.

Vocational/technical and college students, and aspiring service technicians who choose to use this textbook, will find appropriate and diversified information related to subjects directly referenced in both the ASE and TQ testing areas. However, no theoretical course of study alone can prepare students to develop standards of excellence without matching this new-found knowledge to a well-planned, hands-on skills application of the diversified content areas in which they hope to challenge themselves and gain certification. The Service Technicians Society (STS) and ASE offer various publications to help you study for certification in the different ASE content areas. Learn to access the many appropriate websites that offer numerous topics to broaden your scope of learning and to inform you about new developments. Learn to apply and share knowledge with your fellow service technicians; study, retain, and apply knowledge and skills learned from experienced service technicians. Exchange knowledge by becoming an active member in professional organizations such as STS, and set a goal to become a certified Blue Seal ASE or a Red Seal Trade Qualification Interprovincial (TQ-IP) Canada-wide recognized professional technician. Attend local and national meetings of STS and other appropriate technical societies. Dedicate your future career to lifelong learning by availing yourself of the many company and OEM training programs and local community college courses open to you. A highly motivated service technician with first-class technical and human resource development skills is the catalyst to fulfilling the current shortage of qualified personnel. Such persons are likely to be tomorrow's supervisors, service

managers, fleet maintenance superintendents, factory service representatives, technical training instructors, company owners, and possible future engineers. In essence, they are key to the success of the diversified diesel industry.

The many diagrams throughout this book appear through the kindness and support of various OEMs who are strongly supportive of well-trained and technologically up-to-date service technicians. Without their support, this book could not have been presented in its current format. Note that courtesy lines accompany each diagram for the name of the specific company and product features.

In addition, thank you to ASE for allowing me to describe the various content areas and skills tasks for the different certification tests that they offer to improve the skills of technicians, particularly in the diesel field. Thanks also to SAE's Service Technicians Society for its role in encouraging the high standards of today's and tomorrow's technicians. To anyone associated with the diesel industry from technicians to salespeople, your everyday actions contribute to the economic development of the industry.

Many thanks!

R. N. (Bob) Brady

About the Author

Robert N. (Bob) Brady has been involved in the automotive, heavy-duty truck/bus, and equipment field since 1959, having served a recognized indentured apprenticeship as both an automotive and heavy-duty truck/bus and equipment technician. He is a certified automotive, commercial transport, and heavy-duty equipment technician. A graduate of Stow College of Engineering, where he majored in the Thermodynamics of Heat Engines, he holds a degree in Mechanical Engineering Technology. He also holds a degree in Adult Education.

His experience includes positions as a shop foreman and service manager for a number of major heavy truck companies and OEMs, as well as a Fleet Maintenance Superintendent with a large North American truck fleet. Other experience includes positions as Manager of National Technical Training, Canada; Sales Application Engineer; Field Service Engineer for Detroit Diesel Corporation; Diesel Engineering and Diesel Mechanic/Technician college instructor; and Department Head of the program at Vancouver Community College, where he also served a two-year term as President of the Faculty Association.

He is a full member of SAE International (Society of Automotive Engineers), for which he has served as the chair of the British Columbia Section. Under his leadership in 1989–90, the section received an SAE Award of Merit for outstanding technical meetings. At the International level of SAE, he served three years on the worldwide Sections Board as Vice-Chair and then Chair. Other activities in SAE at the Sections-Board level included chairing the Executive Committee, the Administrative Committee, the Brazil Ad Hoc Committee, and the International Sections and Affiliates Committee. He has also served as a member of the Sections Evaluation and Awards Committee. He served as a Regional Coordinator, where he worked with the B.C., Alberta, and Manitoba Sections in Canada, and was an acting RC for the NW/Spokane-Intermountain, Washington, and Oregon sections. He also served as a member of SAE's Total Quality Committee. He was elected to SAE's worldwide International Board of Directors, serving from 1994 through 1996, and was one of two SAE board of directors appointed to the Ad Hoc Committee that in March 1996 initiated the development and organization of the STS (Service Technicians Society), an affiliate of SAE International.

In 1987 he established his own company, HiTech Consulting Ltd., which specializes in technical training program design/implementation aimed specifically at heavy-duty, on- and off-highway equipment. He has delivered specialized training courses for engineers, service technicians, and maintenance personnel at a number of companies and corporations. Other functions include fleet maintenance and failure analysis programs as well as equipment specing. He has appeared as an expert witness in a number of cases involving patent infringement and engine/equipment failure.

He is the author of fourteen textbooks for Prentice Hall dealing with automotive fuel injection and electronics/computers, diesel, and heavy-duty trucks. A member of the TWNA (Truck Writers of North America), he writes monthly technical/maintenance articles for two of Canada's major newspaper/magazines: *Trucknews*, Canada's National Trucking Newspaper and Equipment Buyer's Guide, and *Grainews*, a national farmer's monthly newspaper distributed in both Canada and the United States, where his monthly articles deal with truck and equipment maintenance.

Contents

1 Introduction

Overview

The diesel engine industry is highly diversified, exposing the potential service technician to approximately 5000 different applications in which the diesel engine is used as the primary power source. The different application areas are generally categorized as follows:

- Automotive (cars, vans, pickups)
- Medium/heavy-duty truck/tractor/trailer
- Public transit (city and intercity buses)
- Marine
- Off-highway equipment (construction, logging, mining, road building, oil field, etc.)
- Agricultural
- Locomotive or self-powered railcars

Within this textbook we offer broad coverage of the mechanical and electronic details of diesel engine and fuel systems including their function, operation, repair, overhaul, maintenance, diagnosis, and troubleshooting. Due to space limitations we cannot include details on the special equipment that is used in each of the above categories. The key to a successful career in the diesel industry, however, is to fully comprehend and understand the function and operation of the main power plant in each of these applications, which rests with the diesel engine itself. Take time to preview the table of contents for this book to find the subjects and topics described herein.

A number of well-written texts on the market deal with specific categories of the diesel engine and their types of applications. If you are interested in medium/heavy-duty trucks, power trains, systems, and service, refer to Robert N. Brady's 950-page textbook of the same name, published by Prentice Hall, Inc., Upper Saddle River, New Jersey 07458. See the Library of Congress Catalog, International System of Book Numbering (ISBN) 0-13-181470-2, or contact a local bookstore. Original equipment manufacturers (OEMs) publish outstanding textbooks dealing specifically with their own equipment. Use these texts to broaden your knowledge of particular models of machinery.

TECHNICIAN PROFESSIONALISM AND IMAGE

Recent and ongoing technological changes in automotive, heavy-duty truck, bus, and equipment technology have advanced to such a degree that the "new breed" of technician needs to be familiar with a variety of advanced technologies to be able to function as a highly skilled, trained, and dedicated professional. Evolving technology is responsible for causing changes in the type of individual who is able to perform automotive and heavy-duty truck service. Many vocational schools and colleges now offer two-year bachelor programs that include management training in addition to the needed technical skills and computer training to enter and succeed within the industry. Instructors at the various schools and colleges can provide the needed catalyst to motivate and encourage students and technicians to reach for that higher standard of excellence and to improve the image of service technicians in the eyes of the general public.

Technician certification is a vital part of improving professionalism and image. The mechanical and electronic advances that now permeate every facet of heavy-duty trucks, engines, and equipment demand that a new breed of service repair and diagnostic technician be created. In a fairly recent study by the U.S.

1

General Accounting Office in Washington, D.C., after analyzing the collected data of the skills and capabilities required to successfully achieve benchmark industry standards, both heavy-duty truck technicians and automotive technicians were adjudged to require skills equivalent to that for computer programmers and X-ray technicians.

Professionalism has three key dimensions: qualifications, individual attitude and a philosophy of one's own standards, and a perception of industry benchmark standards and customer expectations. Although certification is not mandatory at this time in the United States in the areas of automotive and heavy-duty truck maintenance, general public and customer demands have placed an ever increasing emphasis on quality and standards from maintenance, repair, and diagnostic technicians. All major OEMs currently spend hundreds of millions of dollars annually on creating training programs offered at both the factory and local level to ensure that their distributor and dealer personnel are continually kept abreast of the latest technological advancements in their products.

In Canada, provincial certification is required in the automotive, heavy-duty equipment, commercial transport, and autobody repair sectors. Certification is obtained through 8000 hours of experience during a recognized and structured apprenticeship, or by being able to prove that equivalent experience has been accumulated to allow a challenge of the TQ test. Some provinces have recently enacted legislation to prohibit anyone who is not qualified in a specific area of expertise from practicing in this area.

Technicians must be provided with an opportunity to stay abreast of current technology, which changes faster than most people outside of the industry can imagine. In the United States, several avenues are open to automotive and heavy-duty truck mechanics and technicians to elevate their knowledge and expertise. The two most recognized organizations now in existence that offer technicians an opportunity to voluntarily improve their professionalism and certification are the National Institute for Automotive Service Excellence (NIASE), more commonly known as ASE, and the Service Technicians Society (STS), which was created in February 1996 as an affiliate of the Society of Automotive Engineers (SAE) International. ASE has offered voluntary testing and certification for 25 years for both automotive and heavy-duty truck technicians in a variety of specialty areas.

10 Reasons to Become ASE-Certified

Everybody knows that MD following an individual's name means Medical Doctor. And most people know that CPA signifies Certified Public Accountant. Associations and professions use certification to recognize qualified and competent individuals. The certification process is one of the single most important steps in career development. Here are the top ten reasons an automotive professional should consider becoming ASE-certified.

1. **Certification grants you professional credentials.** Since it recognizes your individual accomplishments, ASE's certification serves as an impartial, third-party endorsement of your knowledge and experience on a national, even international basis.

2. **Certification demonstrates your commitment to the automotive service and repair profession.** Receiving ASE certification shows your peers, supervisors and, in turn, the general public, your commitment to your chosen career and your ability to perform to set standards.

3. **Certification enhances the profession's image.** ASE's certification program seeks to grow, promote and develop certified professionals, who can stand "out in front" as examples of excellence in the automotive service and repair industry.

4. **Certification reflects achievement.** ASE certification is a reflection of personal achievement because the individual has displayed excellence in his or her field by meeting standards and requirements established by the entire automotive industry.

5. **Certification builds self-esteem.** ASE certification is a step toward defining yourself beyond a job description or academic degree while gaining a sense of personal satisfaction.

6. **Certification can improve career opportunities and advancement.** ASE certification can give you the "edge" when being considered for a promotion or other career opportunities. ASE certification clearly identifies you as an employee who has demonstrated competency in specific technical specialty areas based on accepted industry standards.

7. **Certification may provide for greater earnings potential.** Many automotive professionals who have become ASE certified experience salary and wage increases based on their certification status. ASE-certified professionals are in high demand throughout North America.

8. **Certification improves skills and knowledge.** Typically, achieving ASE certification requires training, study and "keeping up" with changing technology. ASE certification showcases your individual competence by confirming proficiency and knowledge.

9. **Certification prepares you for greater on-the-job responsibilities.** Since ASE certification is a clear indicator of your willingness to invest in your own pro-

fessional development. Certified professionals are aware of the constantly changing technology and environment around their profession and possess the desire to anticipate and respond to change.

10. **Certification offers greater recognition from peers.** As an ASE-certified professional, you can expect increased recognition from your peers for taking that extra step in your professional development.

CAREER ADVANCEMENT

The diesel industry offers both challenging and rewarding opportunities for tomorrow's technician. Once you have attained certification as a service technician you can progress into one of the following careers:

- Master mechanic/technician (any equipment category)
- Lead hand or shop foreman
- Fleet supervisor
- Service manager
- Service/sales
- OEM service representative
- Fleet or equipment management
- OEM service engineer
- Technical training instructor (private or community college)
- Parts sales
- Factory service representative or application engineer
- Business owner

Financial Rewards

The financial rewards available to you are limited only by your education, experience, motivation, and commitment to excellence. Because learning is a lifelong challenge, you will more than likely have to supplement your service technician knowledge and education with a variety of courses in human resource development (HRD), which involves sales and management training as a means to successful promotion in the future. Most dynamic companies and corporations today offer excellent in-house training for their employees on a regular basis.

Typical financial rewards for an apprentice or beginner can vary widely between Canadian provinces and U.S. states. Another factor is the exchange rates between different currencies. The hourly rate for beginners, however, is approximately $10 (U.S.), rising to about $22 when certified. In the United States, certification can be attained in two years by passing the ASE test. Pay rate will also be affected if a shop is a union facility. Currently in Canada, an apprentice will earn

about 65% of the journeyman rate, receiving an increase of about 5% every additional six months. At the completion of the apprenticeship in the year 2001, service techs can expect a salary of approximately $28 to $30 (Canadian) per hour.

Working regular hours, a U.S. certified service technician can expect yearly earnings of between $35,000 and $40,000. In a busy shop of a major equipment dealer/distributor, overtime can be a normal demand. Working overtime permits a service tech to earn between $60,000 and $80,000 (U.S.) per year. Such personnel as shop supervisors, service managers for major engine and equipment dealers, and fleet maintenance directors can expect salaries as high as $85,000 to $140,000 (U.S.) per year plus benefits.

ASE CERTIFICATION

In Canada and in other countries worldwide, mandatory trade apprenticeships of between four and five years is common to gain certification as a journeyman. Throughout the training and learning period the apprentice must attend classes at a vocational/ technical school or college where a combination of theory and hands-on instruction is then tested before the apprentice is certified in each specific trade skills area. In the diesel field these skills include:

- Heavy-duty equipment mechanic/technician (off-highway equipment)
- Commercial transport mechanic/technician (truck and bus)
- Diesel engine specialist

Generally this technical training is accommodated either through regular day-release classes, or by attending instruction modules of between four and six weeks or longer throughout each subsequent year of the apprenticeship. At the completion of the apprenticeship, candidates must pass a TQ test to receive a Department of Labor trade certificate.

In the United States an apprenticeship such as described is currently not required to gain certification; however, the widely accepted method by industry is to voluntarily become certified through a series of tests administered by the NIASE (ASE). This choice provides an industry-recognized avenue for automotive and medium/heavy truck diesel technicians to challenge themselves and become certified in one or more areas of the trade, and thus earn the most valuable credentials as recognized throughout the United States. ASE encourages you to take these tests and to join the proven professionals who wear the ASE blue seal patch of excellence (see Figure 1–1).

FIGURE 1–1 *Well-known logo's of these two major technician societies. (Courtesy of STS and ASE.)*

There are currently eight tests in the medium/heavy truck technician certification series. If you can pass one or more tests, and have at least two years of relevant hands-on work experience, then you will become certified as an ASE medium/heavy truck technician. In addition, if you pass either the gasoline engines test (T1) or the diesel engines test (T2), and tests T3, T4, T5, T6, and T8 as listed below, you will earn certification as a master medium/heavy truck technician. Beginning in January 2001, the HVAC (T7) test will also be required for master status.

Medium/Heavy Truck Tests
ASE offers testing in the following areas:

- Gasoline engines (Test T1)
- Diesel engines (Test T2)
- Drivetrain (Test T3)
- Brakes (Test T4)
- Suspension and steering (Test T5)
- Electrical/electronic systems (Test T6)
- Heating, ventilation, and air-conditioning (HVAC) systems (Test T7)
- Preventive maintenance inspection (PMI) (Test T8)

ASE has also introduced a recertification test series for 'school-bus' technicians. The first tests to be offered in this series are brakes (S4), suspension and steering (S5), and electrical/electronic systems (S6).

ASE Master Technician Certified Status
Effective January 1, 2001, the gasoline engines (T1) test may no longer be used to help fulfill the master requirement. Certification in diesel engines (T2) will be required. While T1 will continue to be offered, it will no longer count toward master status. In addition, to obtain master status, the heating, ventilation and air conditioning systems (T7) test will also be required for master status. These changes reflect current industry standards.

ASE DIESEL ENGINES TASK LIST

To assist potential technicians in their preparation for the T2 diesel engines test, the ASE provides a task list at its website (www.asecert.org). Within the various chapters of this textbook we also provide detailed information to help you successfully complete the ASE T2 test. Details of ASE tasks A through H follow, with the accompanying chapter in this book where you can find data and information to help prepare yourself to score high on the T2 test.

T2 Test—Content Task Lists
Part A: General Engine Diagnosis (15 ASE questions). Refer to Chapter 5 for subject information.

Part B: Cylinder Head and Valve Train Diagnosis and Repair (5 ASE questions). Refer to Chapter 9 for subject information.

Part C: Engine Block Diagnosis and Repair (5 ASE questions). Refer to Chapters 5 and 6 for subject information.

Part D: Lubrication and Cooling Systems Diagnosis and Repair (9 ASE questions). Refer to Chapters 11 and 12 for subject information.

Part E: Air Induction and Exhaust Systems Diagnosis and Repair (9 ASE questions). Refer to Chapter 13 for subject information.

Part F: Fuel System Diagnosis and Repair.
1. Mechanical Components (9 ASE questions)
2. Electronic Components (11 ASE questions) Refer to Chapters 15 through 18 for subject information.

Part G: Starting System Diagnosis and Repair (4 ASE questions). Refer to Chapter 26 for subject information.

Part H: Engine Brakes (3 ASE questions). Refer to Chapters 13, and 21 through 23 for subject information.

Diesel Engines—ASE T2 Test Specifications
Subject matter in the ASE T2 test covers the following content areas.

Content area	Questions in test	Percentage of test
A. General engine diagnosis	15	21%
B. Cylinder head and valve train diagnosis and repair	5	7%
C. Engine block diagnosis & repair	5	7%

D. Lubrication and cooling systems diagnosis and repair — 9 — 13%

E. Air induction and exhaust systems diagnosis and repair — 9 — 13%

F. Fuel system diagnosis and repair — 20 — 29%
   1. Mechanical components (9)
   2. Electronic components (11)

G. Starting system diagnosis and repair — 4 — 6%

H. Engine brakes — 3 — 4%

Total 70* 100%

Note: ASE advises potential challengers of the T2 test that it could contain up to 10 additional questions for statistical research purposes only. Your answers to these questions will not affect your score, but because you do not know which questions they are, answer all questions in the test. The five-year recertification test will cover the same content areas as those listed here; however, the number of questions in each content area will be reduced by approximately 50%. Additional ASE certification areas include automobile, truck equipment, school bus, collision repair/refinish, engine machinist, and advanced level specialties.

Note that a breakdown of the individual ASE T2 Diesel Engine Tests task list topics is provided on page 4, and is supplemented at the beginning of chapters 6 through 24 of this textbook to introduce and provide the reader with goals and objectives to assist with study habits. Various end-of-chapter review questions, plus sample ASE diesel engine T2 test questions, will help you in preparing to write for ASE certification.

ASE L2 Test

The ASE L2 test involves electronic diesel engine diagnosis specialist certification. For details on content, tasks lists, and the test, refer to Chapter 18.

If you fail a test, you may arrange to retake it during another scheduled test time. Results are confidential and cannot be released without your written permission.

Test Know-How

To successfully pass the various ASE tests, you will need both knowledge and skills in the areas in which you will challenge, including the following capabilities.

- Basic technical knowledge tests your knowledge of system identification, what and how a system functions and operates, and the correct procedures and precautions to use during repairs and readjustments.

- Correction or repair knowledge tests your understanding and reasoning ability to logically apply industry-standard repair procedures and proper precautions during disassembly, assembly, overhaul, and reconditioning operations, as well as during major inspections and necessary adjustments. It also demonstrates your ability to logically use shop and diagnostic troubleshooting manuals and the various precision tools of the trade.

- Testing and diagnostic knowledge and skill tests your ability to recognize and diagnose system faults by using the accepted measurement and testing equipment available to trace the symptoms related to a particular condition and to confirm the causes or faults.

Details of ASE Test Content Areas

For detailed information about ASE certification test areas, contact ASE at the address given at the end of this chapter. The various ASE certification areas in which an aspiring technician can certify are shown in the following tables.

Gasoline Engines—T1 Test Specifications

Content area	Questions in test	Percentage of test
A. General engine diagnosis	11	18%
B. Cylinder head and valve train diagnosis and repair	5	8%
C. Engine block diagnosis and repair	5	8%
D. Lubrication and cooling systems diagnosis and repair	4	7%
E. Ignition system diagnosis and repair	7	12%
F. Fuel and exhaust systems diagnosis and repair	7	12%
G. Battery, starting and charging systems diagnosis and repair	6	10%
H. Emissions control systems diagnosis and repair	16	10%
I. Computerized engine controls diagnosis and repair	9	15%
Total	**60**	**100%**

Diesel Engines—T2 Test Specifications

Content area	Questions in test	Percentage of test
A. General engine diagnosis	15	21%
B. Cylinder head and valve train diagnosis and repair	5	7%
C. Engine block diagnosis and repair	5	7%
D. Lubrication and cooling systems diagnosis and repair	9	13%
E. Air induction and exhaust systems diagnosis and repair	9	13%
F. Fuel system diagnosis and repair 1. Mechanical components (9) 2. Electronic components (11)	20	29%
G. Starting system diagnosis and repair	4	6%
H. Engine brakes	3	4%
Total	**70**	**100%**

Drive Train—T3 Test Specifications and Task List

Content area	Questions in test	Percentage of test
A. Clutch diagnosis and repair	13	26%
B. Transmission diagnosis and repair	15	30%
C. Drive shaft and univeral joint diagnosis and repair	11	22%
D. Drive axle diagnosis and repair	11	22%
Total	**50**	**100%**

Brakes—T4 Test Specifications and Task List

Content area	Questions in test	Percentage of test
A. Air brakes diagnosis and repair 1. Air supply & service systems (17) 2. Mechanical/foundation (11) 3. Parking brakes (5)	33	55%
B. Hydraulic brakes diagnosis and repair 1. Hydraulic system (8) 2. Mechanical system (6) 3. Power assist units and miscellaneous (4)	18	30%
C. Air and hydraulic antilock brake system (ABS) and automatic traction control (ATC)	5	8%
D. Wheel bearings diagnosis and repair	4	7%
Total	**60**	**100%**

Suspension and Steering—T5 Test Specifications and Task List

Content area	Questions in test	Percentage of test
A. Steering system diagnosis and repair 1. Steering column (3) 2. Steering units (6) 3. Steering linkage (3)	12	24%
B. Suspension system diagnosis and repair	13	26%
C. Wheel alignment diagnosis, adjustment, and repair	13	26%
D. Wheels and tires diagnosis and repair	9	18%
E. Frame service and repair	3	6%
Total	**50**	**100%**

Electrical/Electronic Systems—T6 Test Specifications and Task List

Content area	Questions in test	Percentage of test
A. General electrical system diagnosis	11	22%
B. Battery diagnosis and repair	6	12%
C. Starting system diagnosis and repair	8	16%
D. Charging system diagnosis and repair	8	16%
E. Lighting systems diagnosis and repair 1. Headlights, parking, clearance, tail, cab, and dash lights (3)	6	12%

2. Stoplights, turn signals, hazard light, and back-up lights (3)

Content area	Questions in test	Percentage of test
F. Gauges and warning devices diagnosis and repair	6	12%
G. Related systems	5	10%
Total	**50**	**100%**

Heating, Ventilation, and Air Conditioning (HVAC) Systems—T7 Test Specifications and Task List

Content area	Questions in test	Percentage of test
A. HVAC systems diagnosis, service, and repair	6	15%
B. A/C system and component diagnosis, service, and repair	16	40%
1. A/C system— general (6)		
2. Compressor and clutch (5)		
3. Evaporator, condenser, and related components (5)		
C. Heating and engine cooling systems diagnosis, service, and repair	6	15%
D. Operating systems and related controls diagnosis and repair	8	20%
1. Electrical (5)		
2. Air/vacuum/ mechanical (2)		
3. Constant/automatic temperature control (1)		
E. Refrigerant recovery, recycling, handling, and retrofit	4	10%
Total	**40**	**100%**

Preventive Maintenance Inspection (PMI)—T8 Test Specifications and Task List

Content area	Questions in test	Percentage of test
A. Engine systems	13	26%
1. Engine (2)		
2. Fuel system (3)		
3. Air induction and exhaust system (2)		

Content area	Questions in test	Percentage of test
4. Cooling system(4)		
5. Lubrication system (2)		
B. Cab and hood	7	14%
1. Instruments and controls (2)		
2. Safety equipment (1)		
3. Hardware (2)		
4. Air conditioning and heating (HVAC) (2)		
C. Electrical/electronics	10	20%
1. Battery and starting systems (4)		
2. Charging system (4)		
3. Lighting system (2)		
D. Frame and chassis	17	34%
1. Air brakes (4)		
2. Hydraulic brakes (2)		
3. Drivetrain (3)		
4. Suspension and steering systems (3)		
5. Tires and wheels (3)		
6. Frame and 5th wheel (2)		
E. Drive test	3	6%
Total	**50**	**100%**

Medium/Heavy Truck Dealership Parts Specialist—P1 Test Specifications and Task List

Content area	Questions in test	Percentage of test
A. Communications skills	7	10%
B. Sales skills	11	16%
C. Vehicle systems	44	63%
1. Brakes (8)		
2. Electrical systems (6)		
3. Drive train (7)		
4. Suspension and steering (7)		
5. Cab/sleeper heating and air conditioning (4)		
6. Engines (12)		
a. General/major components (4)		
b. Fuel system (2)		
c. Cooling system (2)		
d. Lubrication system (2)		
e. Air induction and exhaust systems (2)		
D. Inventory Management	8	11%
Total	**70**	**100%**

Medium/Heavy Truck Aftermarket Parts Specialist—P3 Test Specifications and Task List

Content area	Questions in test	Percentage of test
A. General operations	4	9%
B. Communications and sales skills	8	18%
C. Inventory management	3	7%
D. Specific vehicle systems	30	66%
Option 1: Brakes		
a. Air brake systems (15)		
b. Hydraulic brake systems (9)		
c. Wheel end systems (6)		
Option 2: Suspension and steering		
a. Air suspension systems (10)		
b. Mechanical suspension system (10)		
c. Steering axle assembly (5)		
d. Steering gear & linkage system (5)		
Total	**45**	**100%**

SERVICE TECHNICIANS SOCIETY

Although the skill level needed to successfully maintain, repair, diagnose, and troubleshoot equipment used in automotive, heavy truck, off-highway, railroad, marine, and aircraft applications has grown exponentially with the major technological advancements in recent years, the perceived image of service technicians has not improved substantially in the eyes of the general public. The establishment of the Service Technicians Society (STS) in 1996 by the Society of Automotive Engineers (SAE) was designed to offer technicians training and access to the latest technological information by creating local STS chapters that are organized and governed by elected STS members who then liaise with OEMs, dealers, and community colleges. The STS logo is shown in Figure 1–1.

A current online database system and monthly magazine should be utilized to continue to improve on the skills and professional image of technicians by way of the following:

- Credibility
- Training
- Technical information
- Industry standards
- Customer education
- Networking opportunities

STS was formed through SAE to support the maintenance, dismantling, disposal, and recycling of mobility technologies, and has a vision statement that describes the STS as "an organization of individuals dedicated to advancing the skills, education, and image of technicians that service vehicles and systems for the mobility community."

STS will encourage and support voluntary certification and testing through the long established NIASE. STS will work toward distribution of technical information on today's and tomorrow's vehicles, provide information from various sources including the internet, training programs, and networking opportunities on regional, national, and international levels, and support bringing the technician closer to the engineering community—leading to more effective communications between serviceability and design improvements. STS will be governed on a national basis but with strong local focus through a board of governors, president, and various operating divisions in liaison with SAE.

In summary, STS will offer programs that aim to

- Enhance the stature and professional image of technicians
- Enhance the skills of technicians
- Promote a technical information exchange
- Provide data, information, and processes that promote levels of competence
- Develop a body of knowledge, recommended practices, and a system to disseminate this information
- Gain the support of the public, industry, educational organizations, and government
- Support environmental responsibility

STS member benefits will include

- Discounts on STS and SAE publications, training, and education programs
- A membership card, certificate, and shoulder patch
- The STS newsletter
- Affiliation with other STS members through a local chapter
- STS home page on the internet
- Special discounts on rental cars, office equipment and supplies, copy products, health care, insurance, hotel and travel discount programs, and overnight delivery service
- Sponsorship; members are encouraged to sponsor friends and associates into STS membership. Programs to recognize sponsorship activity are in place.

Address all contacts and inquiries for STS/SAE and ASE to:

Service Technicians Society
400 Commonwealth Drive
Warrendale, PA 15096-0001
U.S.A.
Tel: 800-STS-9596
Fax: 412-776-2644
Website: www.sts.sae.org

National Institute for Automotive Service Excellence
13505 Dulles Technology Drive
Suite 2
Herndon, VA 22071-3421
U.S.A.
Tel: 800-ASE-8822
Fax: 703-713-0727
Website: www.asecert.org

2

Diesel Engine Operating Fundamentals

Overview

In this chapter we discuss the operating fundamentals of both two- and four-stroke-cycle diesel engines. This discussion will provide you with a solid foundation on which to pursue and understand the other technological and engineering characteristics relative to the successful operation of the diesel engine. Direct-injection (DI) and indirect-injection (IDI) designs are described as well as important characteristics of valve timing and relative piston positions during engine operation. We study the advantages and disadvantages of two-cycle and four-cycle engines, and the different firing orders commonly used by engine OEMs.

Although there is no specific ASE or TQ test area dealing with the information in this chapter, it is imperative that any aspiring certified service technician be fully conversant with the operation of both two- and four-stroke-cycle engines, the different firing orders used, and how valve timing affects engine performance. In Chapters 9 and 10, when you study the cylinder head and valve train, your basic understanding of valve timing acquired within this chapter will help to clarify the important task of proper camshaft/valve timing and the necessity for correct valve clearance (lash) adjustment. Valve lash adjustment is described in Chapters 20 through 23 of this book. End-of-chapter questions are supplied to permit you to self-test your newly acquired knowledge.

DIESEL ENGINE CLASSIFICATIONS

Diesel engines can be classified by two major characteristics: their operating cycle design and the type of combustion chamber they employ. By this we simply mean that the engine can operate on either the two- or four-stroke-cycle design. In addition, either one of these types of engines can be designed to operate on what is commonly referred to as the direct-injection (DI) open-combustion-chamber concept, or alternatively, on the indirect-injection (IDI) closed-combustion-chamber design. All heavy-duty high-speed diesel engines now in use operate on the direct-injection principle. Figure 2–1 briefly illustrates the difference between DI and IDI combustion-chamber design; combustion chambers are discussed in more detail in Chapter 4.

An understanding of the operation of two- and four-stroke-cycle diesel engines will facilitate your efforts when troubleshooting engines and fuel systems. The operating characteristics of each type of design will exhibit problems common only to that style of engine. The majority of high-speed diesel engines manufactured today are of the four-stroke-cycle design, so we begin with a study of its basic operating cycle. The fundamental operation of both four-stroke-cycle gasoline and diesel engines is the same: They require two complete revolutions of the engine crankshaft, or 720°, to complete the four piston strokes involved in one complete cycle of events.

FOUR-STROKE-CYCLE OPERATION

There are two major differences between a gasoline and a diesel engine:

1. A diesel engine requires a much higher compression ratio, because with no spark plug to initiate combustion, the heat generated by compressing the air in the cylinder is what causes the high-pressure injected diesel fuel to ignite.

2. On the intake stroke of a diesel engine, only air is supplied to the cylinder, whether the engine is natu-

Direct injection (a) defines the category where the fuel is injected directly into the combustion chamber volume formed between the cylinder head and the top of the piston. Mixing is achieved by using a multi-hole fuel injection nozzle and/or causing the intake air to swirl. High injection pressures are required (18,000–30,000 psi) (124110–206850 kPa) for fine atomization which promotes good contact between air and fuel.

Indirect Injection (b) occurs where fuel is injected into a pre-chamber which communicates with the cylinder through a narrow passage. During the compression stroke, air enters the pre-chamber, which is usually about one half of the total compression volume. Mixing is achieved by spraying fuel into the turbulent air in the pre-chamber (generally with a single-hole pintle nozzle) where ignition occurs. The burning air-fuel mixture then enters the cylinder where it mixes with the remaining air to complete the combustion. This chamber has a small throat area so that inflow and exit velocities are high. Low injection pressures (5000–14,000 psi) (34475–96530 kPa) are used and the chamber is not as sensitive to the degree of fuel atomization.

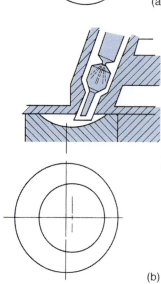

(a)

(b)

FIGURE 2–1 *(a) Principle of DI (direct-injection) and (b) principle of IDI (indirect-injection) combustion chamber design.*

rally aspirated or turbocharged. In a gasoline engine a mixture of air and gasoline is taken into the cylinder on the intake stroke and then compressed. A spark plug then initiates combustion of this premixed fuel charge.

The four piston strokes in a four-stroke-cycle diesel engine are commonly known as (1) the intake stroke, (2) the compression stroke, (3) the power or expansion stroke, and (4) the exhaust stroke. Figure 2–2 illustrates the four piston strokes in schematic form in a direct-injection engine. Next we consider the sequence of events involved in one complete cycle of operation of the four-stroke-cycle engine.

Intake Stroke

During the intake stroke, the exhaust valves are closed but the inlet valves are open; therefore, the downward-moving piston induces a flow of air into the cylinder. This air pressure will be less than atmospheric which is 14.7PSI (101.3kPa) at sea level on a naturally aspirated engine, whereas on a turbocharged or blower-equipped engine, this air pressure will be higher than

atmospheric. Basically, the intake stroke accounts for 180° of piston movement, which is one half of a crankshaft revolution. During this time the piston has completed one complete stroke down the length of the cylinder. The weight or percentage of air that is retained in the cylinder during this time is known as volumetric efficiency (VE). In most naturally aspirated engines that rely only on piston movement to inhale air, VE is between 85 and 90% of atmospheric pressure. In turbocharged or gear-driven blower engines, the VE is always greater than atmospheric or 100%; therefore, VE values between 120 and 200% are common on these engines. The power output of any engine depends on the cylinder air charge at the end of the intake stroke. The engine crankshaft and flywheel have rotated through approximately 180°.

Compression Stroke

During the compression stroke, both the intake and exhaust valves are closed as the piston moves up the cylinder. The upward-moving piston causes the trapped air

4 CYCLE

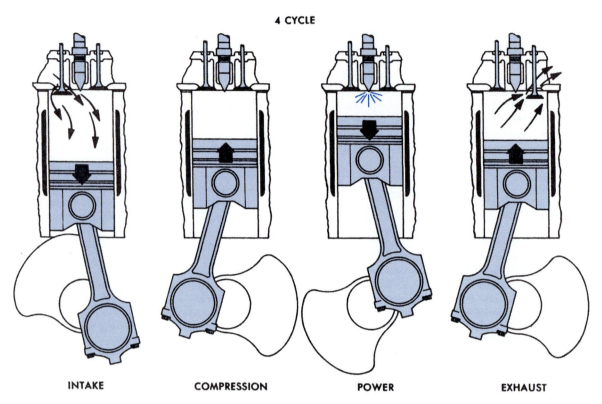

INTAKE   COMPRESSION   POWER   EXHAUST

FIGURE 2–2 *Sequence of individual piston and valve events for a four-stroke-cycle diesel engine.* (Courtesy of Detroit Diesel Corporation.)

to be placed under compression to approximately 450 to 550 psi (3103 to 3792 kPa) and 1000 to 1200°F (538 to 649°C) as a mean average. Both pressures and temperatures vary based on the actual engine design and compression ratio. Cylinder compression pressures and temperatures are affected by the ambient air temperature, turbocharger boost pressure, engine compression ratio, valve timing, and engine speed and load. Consequently, some engines may exhibit compression pressures into the 600s, with their air temperature being at the high end of the previous figures as quoted. Just before the piston reaches the top of the cylinder, high-pressure diesel fuel is injected into this hot air mass and fuel is ignited, causing a substantial pressure and temperature rise within the combustion chamber. Fuel is injected continually to maintain this high pressure, with the number of degrees of injection being related to engine load and speed as well as to the specific model and type of engine being used. Once again the piston has completed approximately 180° of crankshaft rotation. Added to the crankshaft rotation from the intake stroke, the engine crankshaft and the flywheel have now rotated through approximately 360° or one full turn of rotation within the cycle of events.

Power or Expansion Stroke

The combustion chamber of the cylinder is formed between the space that exists between the top of the piston (crown) and the cylinder head. The pressure released by the burning fuel in the combustion chamber forces the piston down the cylinder. The peak cylinder firing pressures on today's high-speed heavy-duty truck engines can range between 1800 and 2300 psi (12,411 to 15,856 kPa), with temperatures between 3000 and 4000°F (1649 to 2204°C) for very short time periods. This motion is transferred through the piston, the piston pin, and the connecting rod to the engine crankshaft and flywheel. Therefore, the straight-line motion of the piston is converted to rotary motion at the crankshaft and flywheel from the connecting rod. The length of the power stroke is controlled by how long the exhaust valves remain closed. Basically, the piston has moved down the cylinder from the top to the bottom and in so doing traveled through approximately 180°. Therefore, added to the already completed intake and the compression strokes, the crankshaft and flywheel have rotated through approximately 540° of the cycle of events.

Exhaust Stroke

The engine camshaft has now opened the cylinder exhaust valves; therefore, the exhaust gases, which are at a higher pressure than atmospheric, will start to flow out of the open exhaust valves. The upward-moving piston will positively displace these burned gases out of the cylinder as it moves from the bottom of its stroke to the top. This involves another 180° of crankshaft and flywheel rotation, which will complete the cycle of events within 720°, or two complete revolutions. Four piston strokes were involved to achieve one power stroke from this individual cylinder. The sequence of events will be repeated once again.

Valve Timing

During the four-stroke cycle of events just described, the opening and closing of the intake and exhaust valves are accomplished by the action of the gear-driven and rotating engine camshaft. Each engine manufacturer determines during the design phase just how long each valve should remain open to obtain the desired operating characteristics from that specific engine model. One simplified example of the sequence of events that occurs during a four-stroke-cycle engine's operation for one cylinder of a turbocharged engine is shown in a basic schematic in Figure 2–3.

> NOTE   The valve timing diagram shown in Figure 2–3 represents 720° of crankshaft rotation. For simplicity, two complete circles have been superimposed on one another.

To ensure complete scavenging of all the exhaust gases from the cylinder at the end of the exhaust stroke and prior to the start of the intake stroke, the engine manufacturer actually has the camshaft open the intake valve before the upward-moving piston has completed its exhaust movement. The action of the burned gases flowing out of the exhaust valve ports allows a ram-air effect to occur once the intake valve is opened. This ensures complete removal of the exhaust gases. When the piston has reached top dead center (TDC) on its exhaust stroke and the piston starts to move down on its intake stroke, the exhaust valves remain open to ensure complete scavenging of any remaining exhaust

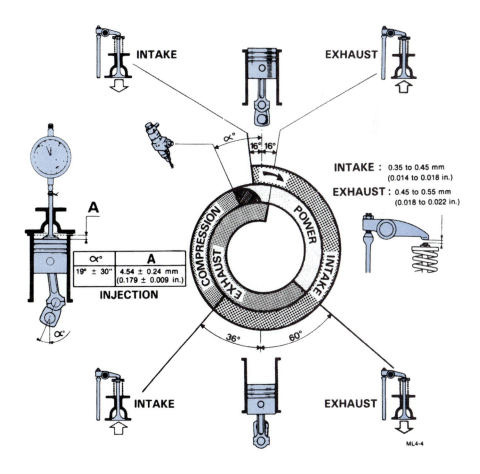

FIGURE 2–3 Typical four-stroke-cycle diesel engine polar valve timing diagram showing the relative piston strokes for intake, compression, power, and exhaust. Specific degrees are also shown for the duration of each stroke as well as the actual start of fuel injection BTDC (before top dead center). (Courtesy of Caterpillar, Inc.)

gases caused by the inrushing air through the intake valve ports. The exhaust valves are closed a number of degrees after top dead center (ATDC) by the camshaft lobe action. The fact that the intake valves are opened before the piston reaches TDC on its exhaust stroke and the exhaust valves do not close until the piston is moving down on its intake stroke creates a condition known as *positive valve overlap*, which simply means that both the intake and exhaust valves are open at the same time for a specified number of crankshaft rotation degrees. For example, if the intake valves open 16° before top dead center (BTDC) and the exhaust valves do not close until 16° ATDC, the valve overlap condition is said to be 32°.

The downward-moving piston would reach bottom dead center (BDC) and start its upward stroke for the compression cycle. However, note in Figure 2–3 that the intake valves do not close until a number of degrees after bottom dead center (ABDC). This ensures that a full charge of air will be retained in the cylinder. Remember that the greater the air retained at the start of the compression stroke, the greater the engine's volumetric efficiency and power output capability. Simply put, VE is the difference in the weight of air contained in the cylinder with the piston at BDC with the engine stopped versus what it would be with the piston at BDC with the engine running.

The compression stroke begins only when the intake valves close (exhaust valves are already closed). Fuel is injected BTDC by the fuel injector or nozzle, depending on the type of fuel injection system used. Again, the start of fuel injection is determined by the engine manufacturer, based on the load and speed requirements of the engine. Fuel injection will begin earlier (farther away from TDC) with an increase in speed and load, whereas it will begin later (closer to TDC) under low speed and load conditions.

When the piston is forced down the cylinder by the pressure of the expanding and burning gases (air and fuel), the power stroke will continue until such times as the engine camshaft opens the exhaust valves. In the simplified diagrams shown in Figures 2–2 and 2–3, the exhaust valves open before bottom dead center (BBDC) to allow the burned gases to start moving out and through the exhaust ports, exhaust manifold, exhaust piping, and muffler. When the piston turns at BDC and starts to come back up the cylinder, it will positively expel all burned exhaust gases from the cylinder. As the piston approaches TDC, the camshaft once again opens the intake valves for the cylinder, and the sequence of events is repeated over again.

Figure 2–3 illustrates one example of the duration of degrees involved in each piston stroke of a typical four-stroke-cycle Mack MIDS06.20.30 Midliner truck diesel engine. Such a diagram is commonly referred to as a *polar valve timing diagram*, since both TDC and BDC are always shown. The positions of both TDC and BDC are similar to that of the north and south poles on a globe of the earth, hence the technical term *polar valve timing.* Keep in mind that the actual number of degrees varies between engine makes and models. Typical stroke degrees for a high-speed diesel engine may include the following four conditions:

1. *Intake stroke.* Valves open at 16° BTDC and close at 36° ABDC; total duration is 232° of crankshaft rotation.
2. *Power stroke.* Starts at TDC and continues until the exhaust valves open at 60° BBDC; total duration is 120°.
3. *Compression stroke.* Occurs when the intake valves close at 36° ABDC until TDC; total duration is 144°.
4. *Exhaust stroke.* Valves open at 60° BBDC and close at 16° ATDC; total duration is 256° of crankshaft rotation.

Piston Positions

The sequence of events just described represents the cycle of events in one cylinder of a multicylinder engine. In a six-cylinder four-stroke-cycle engine application, for example, six cylinders are in various stages of events while the engine is running. The technician must understand what one cylinder is doing in relation to another at any given position of the crankshaft, because often when timing an injection pump to the engine or when adjusting exhaust valves or timing unit injectors, a specific sequence of adjustment must be followed. Knowing the firing order of the engine and what piston/cylinder is on what stroke can save time when performing timing and valve adjustments. We mentioned earlier that the sequence of one cycle occurs within two complete revolutions of the crankshaft, or 720° of rotation of the engine. Therefore, in a six-cylinder four-stroke-cycle engine each piston would be 120° apart in the firing stroke. Simply put, we would have six power strokes occurring within two crankshaft revolutions on a six-cylinder engine.

To demonstrate such an example, refer to Figure 2–4, which simplifies the complete cycle of events and where each piston would be and on what stroke when piston 1 is at TDC starting its power stroke. For simplicity we have shown the 720° of crankshaft rotation in two individual circles as well as in one sketch that shows both circles superimposed on top of one another, which is the commonly accepted method in the

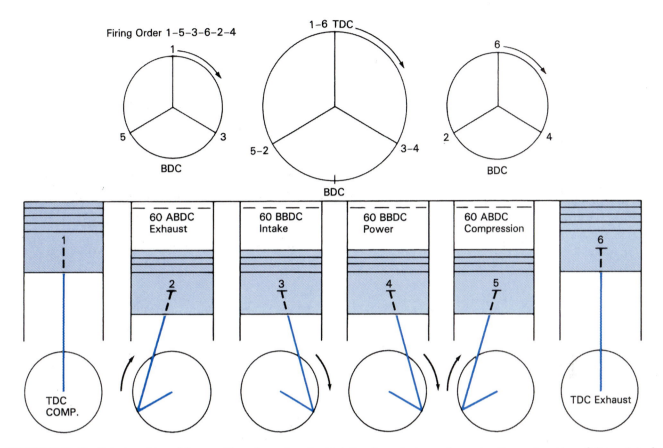

FIGURE 2–4 Relative piston firing positions for a six-cylinder inline four-stroke-cycle engine throughout two full crankshaft turns (720° of crankshaft rotation with a firing order of 1–5–3–6–2–4).

industry. The example shows a firing order of 1–5–3–6–2–4 for an engine that rotates clockwise (CW) when viewed from the front.

TWO-STROKE-CYCLE OPERATION

The largest manufacturer of two-stroke-cycle high-speed heavy-duty diesel engines in the world is Detroit Diesel, now owned by Daimler-Chrysler. Although there are two-stroke-cycle engines that do not employ valves but operate on ports only, Detroit Diesel two-stroke-cycle engines employ a set of intake ports located around the center of the cylinder liner, with conventionally operated pushrod-type exhaust valves at the top of each cylinder. The operation of the two-stroke-cycle engine is illustrated in Figure 2–5, which depicts the layout of a V-configuration engine. The only difference between the V and inline two-stroke Detroit Diesel engines is in the basic cylinder arrangement.

In a four-stroke-cycle engine, 720 crankshaft degrees or two complete revolutions, plus four piston movements, are required to complete the intake, compression, power, and exhaust strokes. On a two-stroke-cycle engine, this sequence of events is completed in only one complete turn of the crankshaft, or 360° of rotation involving only two piston movements. This is accomplished basically by eliminating the separate intake and exhaust strokes, which are a necessary part of four-stroke-cycle operation. During the intake and exhaust piston movements of the four-stroke cycle, the engine basically acts as an air pump by drawing air in and pumping burned exhaust gases out.

To achieve the elimination of these two specific strokes in the two-cycle engine requires the use of a gear-driven, positive-displacement blower assembly, commonly known as a Roots-type blower. This blower supplies the airflow necessary for several actions:

- Scavenging of exhaust gases from the cylinder.
- Cooling of internal engine components, such as the cylinder liner, the piston, and exhaust valves. Approximately 30% of the engine cooling is achieved by airflow from the blower and turbocharger.

FIGURE 2–5 Two-stroke-cycle V-configuration diesel engine principle of operation. (Courtesy of Detroit Diesel Corporation.)

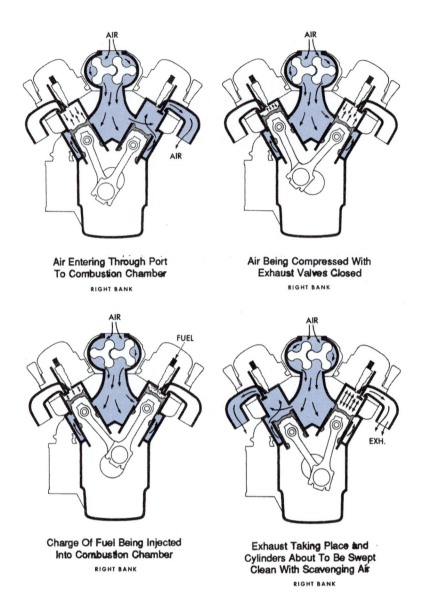

Air Entering Through Port
To Combustion Chamber
RIGHT BANK

Air Being Compressed With
Exhaust Valves Closed
RIGHT BANK

Charge Of Fuel Being Injected
Into Combustion Chamber
RIGHT BANK

Exhaust Taking Place and
Cylinders About To Be Swept
Clean With Scavenging Air
RIGHT BANK

- Combustion purposes.
- Crankcase ventilation by controlled leakage of air past the oil control rings when the piston is at TDC.

Most models of Detroit Diesel two-stroke-cycle engines are equipped with both a gear-driven blower and an exhaust-gas-driven turbocharger. The blower supplies a positive displacement of air, which is required at idle and light-load operation since the turbocharger does not receive a high enough exhaust gas pressure/flow to cause it to supply sufficient air to the engine. The blower is capable of producing approximately 4 to 7 psi (27 to 48 kPa) throughout the engine speed range. Under heavy loads the turbocharger boost will increase and supply between approximately 40 and 50 in. of mercury (in. Hg) or between 20 and 25 psi (140 to 172 kPa) to the intake ports in the cylinder liners. When the engine is operating under load, a bypass valve built into the gear-driven blower end plate opens and allows the air pressure on both sides of the blower (inlet and outlet) to equalize. In this way the horsepower required to drive the blower is reduced, and basically the airflow is being supplied by the exhaust-gas-driven turbocharger.

Two-stroke-cycle Detroit Diesel engines are equipped with exhaust valves only, with four per cylinder being used for better scavenging purposes. The cylinder liner is arranged so that it has a series of ports cast and machined around the liner circumference approximately halfway down its length. These ports act basically as intake valves.

The engine block is designed so that all liners are surrounded by an *air box* that runs the length of the block. The air box is somewhat like a plenum chamber, where the blower air is pumped in to ensure that there will always be an adequate volume for the four functions listed. Any time that a piston in a cylinder has uncovered the liner ports, the air box pressure is free to flow into and through a cylinder. The operational events are described next.

Scavenging

During scavenging the liner ports are uncovered by the piston and the exhaust valves are open. The angled ports in the liner provide a unidirectional flow of pressurized air into and through the cylinder to scavenge the exhaust gases through the open exhaust valves. This action also cools the internal components, such as the piston, liner, and valves, with approximately 30% of engine cooling provided by this airflow. This leaves the cylinder full of clean, cool fresh air for combustion purposes when the piston covers the liner ports.

Compression

Compression begins when the piston moves up from BDC and covers the previously open liner intake ports. The exhaust valves are timed to close a few degrees after this occurs, to ensure positive scavenging along with a positive charge of fresh air for combustion purposes.

Power

The initial start of fuel injection varies between series of engines and the year of manufacture; however, generally speaking, this is between 12 and 15° BTDC, with the engine running at an idle speed between 500 and 600 rpm. Advancement of injection occurs automatically through throttle movement via a helical cut injector plunger in non-DDEC-equipped engines, or electronically in DDEC (Detroit Diesel Electronic Control) systems as the engine speed is increased.

When the unit injector sprays fuel into the combustion chamber, there is a small delay before ignition occurs; then the intense heat generated by combustion of the fuel increases both the temperature and pressure of the air/fuel charge. Injection continues for a number of degrees and the resultant force of the high-pressure gases drives the piston down the cylinder on its power stroke. The length of the power stroke in Detroit Diesel two-stroke-cycle engines will vary slightly, but at 90 to 95° ATDC, the exhaust valves will start to open. Compare this with a power stroke of between 120 and 140° on a four-stroke-cycle engine; but although the power stroke is shorter on

the two-cycle engine, there are twice as many of them. When the piston is at TDC, a regulated amount of air box pressure is designed to leak past the oil control ring drain holes of the piston to ensure positive crankcase ventilation.

Exhaust

Exhaust occurs when the exhaust valves start to open by camshaft and rocker arm action. The power stroke, therefore, effectively ends at this point, as the burned gases escape into the exhaust manifold either to drive a turbocharger or to flow freely to a muffler. The exhaust valves have to open before the piston uncovers the liner ports; otherwise, the higher pressure of the exhaust gases would blow back into the air box against the much lower blower pressure.

Once the piston crown uncovers the liner ports, usually about 60° BBDC, the air box pressure is higher than the exhaust pressure and scavenging begins again. This continues until the piston has reached BDC and starts back up in the cylinder and ends when the piston has again recovered the liner ports to start the compression stroke once more.

Therefore, every upstroke of the piston in a two-stroke-cycle engine is basically a compression stroke, and every downstroke is a power stroke. The intake and exhaust events occur only during the time that the exhaust valves and liner ports are open. Scavenge blowthrough (liner ports open) takes place through approximately 120° of crankshaft rotation, although keep in mind that the exhaust valves open at about 90 to 95° ATDC and close several degrees after the piston has recovered the liner ports as it moves upward. The exhaust valves are therefore open for approximately 155 to 160° of crankshaft rotation.

Valve Timing

The polar valve timing diagram shown in Figure 2–6 illustrates one example of the various degrees of port opening, valves opening, and closure for a two-stroke-cycle non-DDEC-equipped V92 engine. The specific year of manufacture of the engine, the particular engine series, specific model, and application as well as the fuel delivery rate can result in different degrees of valve timing as well as injection duration.

If you compare this valve timing diagram with that shown in Figure 2–3 for the four-stroke-cycle engine, you will see that there are substantial differences in the duration of the various strokes and the number of crankshaft degrees involved. A thorough understanding of the differences between the two- and four-stroke operating cycles will serve you well when considering their operation and when attempting to troubleshoot the engine in some cases.

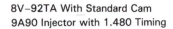

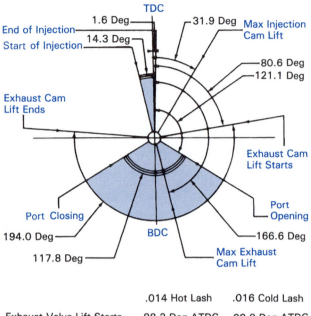

.014 Hot Lash   .016 Cold Lash

	.014 Hot Lash	.016 Cold Lash
Exhaust Valve Lift Starts–	98.2 Deg ATDC	98.9 Deg ATDC
Exhaust Valve Lift Ends–	246.0 Deg ATDC	243.0 Deg ATDC

Max. Injection Cam Lift– .2755
Max. Exhaust Cam Lift – .3270

FIGURE 2–6 *Example of a typical two-stroke-cycle diesel engine polar valve timing diagram. (Courtesy of Detroit Diesel Corporation.)*

Piston Positions

In Figure 2–4 we considered an example of the relative piston positions for a six-cylinder four-stroke-cycle engine. This diagram allowed us to visually interpret where each piston is in relation to the others as well as what stroke each piston is on. Now assume that in the two-stroke-cycle Detroit Diesel engines we are to consider where each piston is at a given time and what stroke it is on. Most of us would simply assume that since the sequence of events occurs in 360 crankshaft degrees, we can divide the degrees by the number of cylinders and we would know where each piston was. If we were to consider an 8V-71 or 92 series model, logic would tell us to divide 360° by 8 = 45°. This conclusion would be reasonable if the engine were a 90°V configuration; in fact, however, these engines have a 63.5° angle between the banks. Therefore, the firing impulses between two cylinders must add up to 90°. Figure 2–7 illustrates how Detroit Diesel does this on these series of engines for a right-hand rotation model with a firing order of 1L–3R–3L–4R–4L–2R–2L–1R. Keep in mind that the manufacturer determines the engine rotation from

the front and identifies the left and right cylinder banks from the flywheel end, although it numbers the cylinders on each bank from the front of the engine. If we assume that cylinder 1 on the left bank is at TDC compression, the other cylinders would be spaced 26.5°, 63.5°, 26.5°, and so on, throughout the firing order. By referring to Figure 2–6, which illustrates a typical example of a two-stroke 8V-92TA (turbocharged and aftercooled) engine polar valve timing diagram, you can determine exactly what stroke each piston is on in Figure 2–7.

COMPARISON OF TWO- AND FOUR-STROKE-CYCLE DESIGNS

Although the two-stroke-cycle engine has twice as many power strokes as that of its four-cycle counterpart, it does not produce twice the power output at the engine crankshaft or flywheel. This is due, in part, to the fact that the length of the power stroke is much shorter in the two-stroke than in the four-stroke engine. Average power stroke length in the two-cycle engine can be between 90 and 95 crankshaft degrees, while the four-cycle engine tends to have a power stroke of between 120 and 140°.

The two-stroke-cycle engine, however, generally delivers more power for the same weight and cylinder displacement, or the same basic horsepower, from a smaller-displacement engine size. We can compare the power differences as follows:

1. In a four-stroke-cycle engine, there is a longer period available for the scavenging of exhaust gases and the separation of the exhaust and inlet strokes. In addition, with a shorter valve overlap period versus the port/valve concept in the two-stroke engine, there tends to be a purer air charge at the start of the compression stroke in a four-cycle engine than in a conventional blower-air-supplied two-stroke engine. However, once a turbocharger is added to the two-stroke engine, the airflow delivery rate is increased substantially; therefore, two-stroke-cycle engines such as Detroit Diesel's 71 and 92 series engines equipped with both a blower and a turbocharger match the characteristics of the four-stroke engine.

2. Both four- and two-stroke-cycle engines have pumping losses. The four-stroke-cycle losses occur during the intake and the exhaust strokes, whereas in the two-stroke-cycle engine the power losses required to drive the gear-driven blower reduce the net engine power output. In addition, two-stroke engines require a much larger airflow capacity to operate since the purpose of the airflow is to (a) scavenge the burned exhaust gases from the cylinder in a short interval (usually be-

FIGURE 2–7 *Example of the firing order and piston positions in degrees between each cylinder for a Detroit Diesel two-stroke-cycle 63.5° design V-type diesel engine with a right-hand (CW from front) rotation and a firing order of 1L–3R–3L–4R–4L–2R–2L–1R. Note that the left bank and right bank are determined from the rear or flywheel end of the engine block. Cylinders are numbered from the front to rear on each bank.*

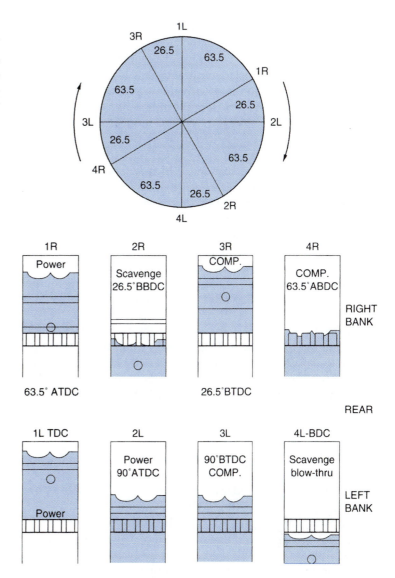

tween 100 and 150°); (b) cool the internal engine components, such as the cylinder liner, the piston crown, and the exhaust valves (approximately 30% of the cooling of a two-stroke-cycle engine is done by airflow); (c) supply fresh air for combustion purposes; and (d) provide air leakage for positive crankcase ventilation.

3. Pumping losses occur in a four-stroke-cycle engine during the intake and exhaust strokes. Equivalent losses to drive the gear-driven blower exist in the two-stroke engine, plus as much as 40% of the engine friction. However, this has been reduced substantially in current Detroit Diesel two-cycle engines by the use of a bypass blower to reduce pumping losses once the turbocharger boost increases to a predetermined level. Generally, on a nonturbocharged two-cycle engine the blower power loss is less than the four-cycle pumping losses when the engines are operating at less than 50% of their rated speed. From 50% up to rated speed, how-

ever, the four-cycle engines' pumping losses tend to be about two-thirds that for the two-cycle engine. Two-cycle engines that employ both a turbocharger and a bypass blower—such as Detroit Diesel 71, 92, and 149 series engines—have changed this ratio substantially.

4. The thermal (heat) loading on the piston, valves, cylinder head, and cylinder liner tend to be lower on a four-stroke-cycle engine because the power stroke occurs only once every two crankshaft revolutions versus once per revolution on a two-stroke engine.

5. It is easier to lubricate the pistons, rings, and liners in a four-cycle engine, due to the absence of ports that are required in the two-cycle liner.

6. The two-cycle engine tends to have a slightly higher fuel consumption curve due to its double-power-stroke principle throughout the same 720° for a four-cycle engine.

7. Generally, the two-stroke-cycle engine can produce more power per cubic inch (cubic centimeter) of displacement than that for a four-cycle engine when high-power applications are required, such as in high-output marine and off-highway mining trucks. In heavy-duty on-highway truck applications, one example is the Detroit Diesel 8V-92TA-DDEC model rated at 500 bhp (373 kW) at 2100 rpm from 736 in^3 (12.1 L). This same engine can pump out up to 765 bhp (571 kW) in high-output marine applications, which is more than 1 hp/in^3 of displacement. The Cat 3406E at 500 bhp has a displacement of 893 in^3 or 14.6 L, while the Cummins N14 at 500 bhp has a displacement of 855 in^3 (14 L). Mack's six-cylinder E7 model at 454 bhp (339 kW) from 728 in^3 (12 L), however, is a good example of high power from small displacement in a four-stroke-cycle engine.

8. The compression ratio (CR) on four-stroke engines tends to be lower than that on an equivalent-rated two-cycle engine. Consider that the Caterpillar 3406E engine has a CR of 16.25:1; the Cummins N14 has a CR of 16.2:1, Detroit Diesel's series 60 12.7-L and series 50 each have a CR of 15:1 while its two-cycle 92 has a CR of 17:1. However, Volvo's VE D12 electronically controlled six-cylinder four-stroke model has a CR of 17.5:1.

9. The brake mean effective pressure (BMEP) which is the average pressure exerted on the piston crown during the power stroke, is generally lower on a two-cycle engine. Consider that a Detroit Diesel 92 series engine rated at 450 bhp (336 kW) at 2100 would have a BMEP of 115 psi (793 kPa); the same engine at 500 bhp (373 kW) would have a BMEP of 128 psi (883 kPa). Compare this with the four-stroke-cycle engine models in the same general power rating category. The Caterpillar 3406E rated at 475 bhp (354 kW) at 1800 rpm would have a BMEP of 234 psi (1613 kPa), and at the peak torque point of 1200 rpm, its BMEP climbs to 295 psi (2037 kPa). A Cummins N14 at 500 bhp at 2100 rpm would develop a BMEP of 221 psi (1524 kPa). A Detroit Diesel series 60 12.7 L rated at 370 bhp (276 kPa) at 1800 rpm would develop a BMEP of 210 psi (1460 kPa); the same engine at 470 bhp (351 kW) would have a BMEP of 229 psi (1579 kPa). Mack's E7-454 bhp (339 kW) model has a BMEP of 274 psi (1890 kPa), while its E9 V8 rated at 500 bhp (373 kW) develops a BMEP of 209 psi (1440 kPa). Volvo's latest six-cylinder electronically controlled VE D12 rated at 415 bhp (310 kW) at 1900 rpm develops a BMEP of 234 psi (1612 kPa). As you can see, four-cycle engines tend to have BMEPs almost twice that for the two-cycle engines rated at the same horsepower. You may have noticed that the smaller the four-cycle engine displacement, the higher the BMEP value will be. In Chapter 3 we discuss in more detail and describe how to determine the BMEP of any engine.

10. The brake specific fuel consumption (BSFC) of a two-stroke-cycle engine tends to be higher than that for a comparably rated four-cycle engine. BSFC is simply the ratio of fuel burned to the actual horsepower produced. Engine manufacturers always show their projected BSFC for an engine at different loads and speeds in their sales literature. Later in this chapter we discuss BSFC in more detail; examples of BSFC for several well-known engine makes and models are illustrated and discussed. Electronically controlled heavy-duty diesel engines are capable of returning fuel economy superior to mechanical models, which confirms that these engines have a higher *thermal efficiency* (heat efficiency) as well as the ability to meet the stringent exhaust emissions regulations of the U.S. Environmental Protection Agency (EPA).

We can summarize the two cycles by considering that the piston operation is divided into closed and open periods. The *closed period* occurs during the power stroke and the *open period* during the time the inlet and exhaust strokes are occurring. Consider the following sequence:

Two-Stroke Cycle

- Closed period
  a–b: compression of trapped air
  b–c: heat created by the combustion process
  c–d: expansion or power stroke
- Open period
  d–e: blowdown or escape of pressurized exhaust gases
  e–f: scavenging of exhaust gases by the blower and/or blower–turbocharger combination
  f–g: air supply for the next compression stroke

All of the above events occur within 360°, one complete turn of the engine crankshaft/flywheel.

Four-Stroke Cycle

- Closed period
  a–b: compression of trapped air
  b–c: heat created by the combustion process
  c–d: expansion or power stroke
- Open period
  d–e: blowdown or escape of pressurized exhaust gases
  e–f: exhaust stroke
  f–g: inlet and exhaust valve overlap
  g–h: induction stroke
  h–i: compression

All of these events require 720° of crankshaft/flywheel rotation, in contrast to the 360° in the two-cycle engine.

ENGINE FIRING ORDERS

The number of cylinders and the engine configuration (inline versus V) and the directional rotation of the engine determine the actual firing order. In Chapter 7 we discuss the purpose and function of crankshaft counterweights, engine balance shafts, and vibration dampers in the overall balance of a running engine. Every cylinder in an engine produces what are commonly referred to as *disturbing forces* that act along the axis of each cylinder as a result of the acceleration and deceleration of the rotating connecting rod and piston assembly as the individual cranks rotate through 360°.

The actual firing order of an engine, and therefore the position of the individual cranks on the shaft, can be established today by computerized analysis. The following parameters must be considered:

- Main bearing loads when adjacent cylinders fire in sequence
- Engine balance
- Torsional vibrations of the crankshaft
- In some special cases, the airflow interference in the intake manifold

Figure 2–8 illustrates typical firing orders used for various engines with differing numbers of cylinders

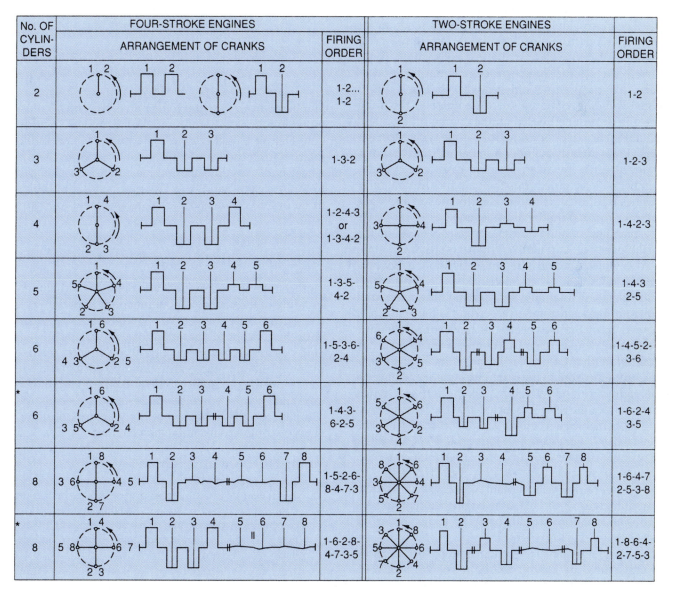

FIGURE 2–8 *Typical crankshaft throw arrangements for both four- and two-stroke-cycle models for engines with between two- and eight-cylinder designs.*

for both two- and four-stroke-cycle engines. Two-stroke crankshaft arrangements tend to be more complicated than those in a four-cycle engine, because the two-stroke engine must fire all cylinders in one crankshaft rotation (360° versus 720°). It is common in four-cycle engines to repeat, or "mirror," the two halves of the crankshaft to eliminate coupling forces (equal masses positioned opposite one another). This also often allows a number of firing orders to be obtained from a single crankshaft arrangement. The discussion of crankshaft balance and the forces involved is a specialized area in its own right, so we will not delve into details here. In many current high-speed V-configuration engines the desired firing order is often achieved by employing offset con-rod (connecting rod) journals on the same throw of the crankshaft.

The most widely used six-cylinder firing order for a CW-rotation (from the front) two- or four-stroke cycle engine is 1–5–3–6–2–4. If the engine rotation is reversed, such as for some twin-engine marine applications, a typical firing order might be 1–4–2–6–3–5. When V-engine configurations are employed, the firing order is determined based on the engine rotation and whether it is a two- or four-stroke-cycle type. Most engine OEMs identify cylinder numbering from the front of the engine; however, in some cases the cylinder number is determined from the rear. In addition, on V engines most manufacturers identify the left and right cylinder banks from the flywheel end.

Standard rotation on many engines is based on the SAE (Society of Automotive Engineers) technical standard in which rotation is determined from the flywheel end. Normally, this is counterclockwise (CCW) which results in a CW rotation when viewing the engine from the front. Opposite rotation according to the SAE is still viewed from the flywheel end; however, the engine crankshaft would rotate CCW when viewed from the front. Note that Caterpillar numbers its engine cylinders from the front to the rear, with cylinder 1 being on the right side and cylinder 2 on the left side when viewed from the rear. This means that the left and right engine banks on a V model are determined from the flywheel end. For example, a four-cycle V12 Caterpillar 3512 engine model with a standard SAE rotation would have a firing order of 1–12–9–4–5–8–11–2–3–10–7–6; the cylinder numbering system would appear as illustrated in Figure 2–9. This same engine running in SAE opposite rotation would have a firing order of 1–4–9–8–5–2–11–10–3–6–7–12.

A two-stroke-cycle V configuration, such as those manufactured by Detroit Diesel in V6, V8, V12, V16, and V20 models, determines left and right cylinder banks from the flywheel end, with the cylinders being

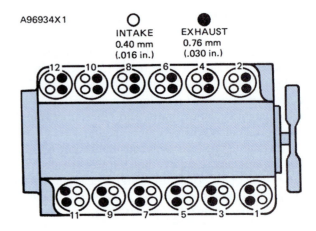

CYLINDER AND VALVE LOCATION

FIGURE 2–9 Cylinder and valve locations for a model 3512 (V12) four-stroke-cycle engine. (Reprinted courtesy of Caterpillar, Inc.)

numbered from the front to rear on each bank, as illustrated in Figure 2–10 for a series of V models. In addition, Detroit Diesel engines determine the crankshaft rotation from the front of the engine, *not* from the flywheel end. Anytime the engine rotation is changed from CW (right hand) to CCW (left hand), the engine firing order is always different, as indicated in Figure 2–10.

SUMMARY

This chapter has provided you with a solid understanding of the concept of operation for both two- and four-stroke-cycle engines. You have also been provided with the concept of operation for both IDI and DI engine designs. Knowing engine firing orders, relative piston positions, and valve timing information will contribute to your ability to set and adjust both the intake and exhaust valve clearances and to discuss and compare the advantages and disadvantages of different types of internal combustion engines.

SELF-TEST QUESTIONS

1. Technician A says that the piston strokes in a four-stroke-cycle diesel or gasoline engine involve intake, compression, power, and exhaust. Technician B says that the order is compression, intake, power, and exhaust. Who is correct?

2. Technician A says that a four-stroke-cycle diesel engine requires 720° (two full turns) of crankshaft rotation to produce one power stroke. Technician B says that two

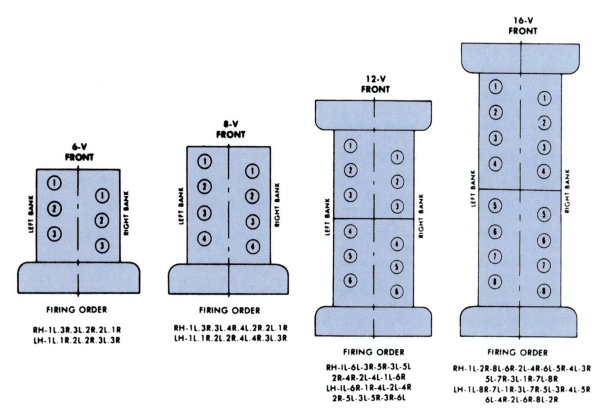

FIGURE 2–10 *Engine cylinder designation and firing orders for two-stroke-cycle V6, V8, V12, and V16 models.* (Courtesy of Detroit Diesel Corporation.)

power strokes are produced within 720°. Which technician is correct?

3. Technician A says that during the intake stroke on a gasoline engine, both air and fuel are mixed. Technician B says that only air is inhaled into the cylinder. Who is correct?

4. Technician A says that on a diesel engine, only air is inhaled on the intake stroke. Technician B says that both air and fuel are taken into the cylinder on the intake stroke. Who is right?

5. Technician A says that the term *volumetric efficiency* (VE) refers to the weight of air retained in the cylinder at the end of the intake stroke. Technician B says that it is the pressure of the air at the end of the compression stroke. Which technician is correct?

6. Technician A says that in naturally aspirated engines, the VE will always be less than 100%. Technician B says that the engine would starve for air if this were the case, and therefore it must have at least a VE of 100% (atmospheric pressure).

7. Technician A says that atmospheric pressure at sea level is approximately 14.7 psi (101.3 kPa). Technician B says that it is closer to 16 psi (110.3 kPa). Who is correct?

8. Technician A says that the VE in turbocharged engines is always greater than atmospheric pressure, or higher than 100%. Technician B says that no engine can run at VEs in excess of 100%, due to frictional losses. Which technician is correct?

9. Technician A says that typical cylinder pressures at the end of the compression stroke (prior to injection of fuel) range between 1000 and 1200 psi (6895 to 8274 kPa). Technician B says that they would be closer to the range 450 to 600 psi (2758 to 4137 kPa). Which technician is correct?

10. Technician A says that typical compression temperatures range between 1000 and 1200°F (538 to 649°C). Technician B says that they would be closer to 2000°F (1093°C). Who is correct?

11. Technician A says that peak cylinder firing pressures in electronically controlled high-speed heavy-duty diesel engines range between 1200 and 1400 psi (8274 to 9653 kPa). Technician B believes that they are closer to 1800 and 2300 psi (12,411 and 15,856 kPa). Who is correct?

12. Technician A says that the intake valves open at BTDC and close at ABDC. Technician B says that they open at TDC and close at BDC. Who is correct?

13. Technician A says that the term *positive valve overlap* indicates that both the intake and exhaust valves are open for a given number of degrees before and after TDC. Technician B says that both the intake and exhaust valves are open before and after BDC. Which technician is correct?

14. Technician A says that a polar valve timing diagram indicates the duration of all strokes. Technician B says that it only indicates the duration of the power stroke. Who is correct?

15. Technician A says that two-stroke-cycle DDC engine models employ both intake and exhaust valves. Technician B says that only exhaust valves are used in these engines since the cylinder liners are designed with a row of intake ports. Which technician is correct?

16. Which of the following two strokes are eliminated from a two-stroke-cycle engine?
    a. intake and exhaust
    b. compression and exhaust
    c. intake and compression
    d. compression and power

17. Technician A says that in a two-stroke-cycle DDC engine, every upstroke of the piston produces compression, and every downstroke produces power. Technician B says that this is impossible since the engine would not run without both an intake and an exhaust stroke. Which technician is correct?

18. Technician A says that a two-stroke engine has a longer power stroke in crankshaft degrees than that of a four-cycle engine model. Technician B says that the four-stroke-cycle engine has a longer power stroke. Which technician is correct?

19. A typical firing order for a six-cylinder four-stroke-cycle engine would be
    a. 1–5–2–4–6–3
    b. 1–5–3–6–2–4
    c. 1–4–2–6–3–5

20. Technician A says that in a two-stroke-cycle DDC engine, the gear-driven blower is used to supply the air required for both the scavenging and intake strokes. Technician B says that the blower is used to supercharge the engine. Which technician is correct?

21. Technician A says that a supercharged engine is any engine that has pressurized air added to it or any engine that uses a turbocharger or blower. Technician B disagrees and says that to supercharge an engine, you must close the valves early enough to trap the high-pressure turbo or blower air in the cylinder; therefore, a supercharged engine is any engine that takes air into the cylinder at higher than atmospheric pressure and then compresses it. Which technician is correct?

22. Technician A says that all DDC two-cycle engines must be supercharged since they employ a gear-driven blower. Technician B disagrees and says that the blower air is simply used to scavenge exhaust gases and supply fresh air for combustion purposes. Which technician is correct?

23. Technician A says that approximately 30% of the engine cooling in a two-stroke-cycle DDC engine is achieved by blower airflow. Technician B believes that possibly 10% cooling might be achieved by blower airflow. Which technician is correct?

24. Technician A says that on two-cycle DDC engines, the blower supply air pressure is between 20 and 25 psi (138 to 172 kPa). Technician B says that it ranges between 4 and 7 psi (28 to 48 kPa). Who is correct?

25. Technician A says that average turbocharger boost pressures on both two- and four-cycle heavy-duty high-speed diesel engines range between 40 and 50 in. (102 to 127 cm) of mercury, or approximately 20 to 25 psi (138 to 172 kPa). Technician B says that it is closer to 8 to 10 psi (55 to 69 kPa). Who is correct?

26. Technician A says that scavenge blowthrough of the cylinder liners in two-stroke-cycle DDC engines occurs when the piston is approximately 40° ABDC. Technician B says that it occurs approximately 60° BBDC until about 60° ABDC, for a duration of 120°. Which technician is correct?

27. Technician A says that two-cycle DDC 71 and 92 series V-configuration engines are designed with a 63.5° angle between the banks. Technician B says that they are 90° Vs. Who is correct?

28. Technician A says that the average duration of a two-stroke-cycle engine power stroke is about 90 to 95°. Technician B says that they are closer to between 120 and 140°. Who is correct?

29. Technician A says that pumping losses occur in all two-stroke-cycle engines during the intake and exhaust strokes. These losses occur in a four-stroke-cycle engine according to technician B. Who is correct?

30. Technician A says that the compression ratio tends to be higher on four-cycle engines than on two-cycle models. Not so, says technician B; it is the other way around. Who is correct?

31. Technician A says that the BMEP is lower on two-cycle engines than on four-cycle models. Technician B says that it is the exact opposite to technician A's statement. Who is correct?

32. Technician A says that the BSFC tends to be higher for a two-cycle engine. Not so, says technician B; the four-cycle engine uses more fuel than the two-stroke engine. Who is correct?

33. True or False: Standard engine rotation according to SAE (Society of Automotive Engineers) standards is counter-clockwise from the flywheel end.

34. Technician A says that the cylinder number for most engines is determined from the front end of the engine. Technician B says that cylinder numbers are always determined from the flywheel end. Which technician is correct?

35. Technician A says that most OEMs determine the left and right banks on a V-configuration engine from the flywheel end. Technician B says that they are determined from the front. Who is correct?

36. True or False: The duration of the power stroke in crankshaft degrees is longer on a two-cycle diesel engine than it is on a four-cycle engine.

37. Draw a circle and sketch in the duration of each individual stroke for a four-stroke-cycle diesel engine. Show the start and end of injection at an idle speed as well as the positive valve overlap condition that exists.

38. Repeat the process described in Question 37 for a two-stroke-cycle diesel engine.

39. Sketch and show the relative piston firing positions for a six-cylinder CW-rotation four-stroke-cycle engine with a firing order of 1–5–3–6–2–4 using the degrees created in Question 37, and describe where each piston is and what stroke it is on.

40. Repeat the process that was described in Question 39 for a two-stroke-cycle engine.

41. List the advantages and disadvantages of a two-stroke-cycle engine in comparison to an equivalent four-cycle model.

42. Technician A says that current heavy-duty high-speed DI diesel engines employ single-hole pintle-type injection nozzles. Technician B says that they employ multi-hole nozzles/injectors for better fuel distribution and penetration. Who is correct?

3 Understanding Horsepower and Related Terms

Overview

In this chapter we discuss the technical concepts and basic engineering knowledge needed by a diesel technician in everyday service operations, and how a thorough understanding of these concepts will assist in reading and interpreting OEM engine performance brochures. We will compare gasoline engine to diesel engine performance, and determine why different makes or models of engines perform at different levels. In addition, we will determine why both horsepower and torque, individually and together, play major roles in the overall performance of heavy-duty truck, industrial, off-highway, mining, logging, agricultural, locomotive, or marine equipment. You will learn why horsepower cannot be multiplied, but torque can; why different engine applications determine the classification of horsepower; why engine fuel consumption differs between different engines; and why diesel engines are more thermally efficient than gasoline engines.

When owner-operators and fleet maintenance personnel query about specific engine or equipment operating performance, fuel economy, and so forth, your acquired knowledge gained from the information in this chapter will prepare you to describe logically the hows and whys of engine operation. This knowledge will be invaluable as you progress through this book, and will offer you added expertise in diesel engine operation. End-of-chapter questions will assist in self-checking your new acquired knowledge.

UNDERSTANDING POWER TERMS

In this section, English and metric equivalents have been used as much as possible. Use the English/metric conversion chart (Table 3–1) to review or convert from either system. After using the chart for a short period of time, you will find that you will remember many of the more common conversion factors.

Think about *energy, force, work, power, horsepower,* and *torque*. If these terms are confusing to you as a beginning technician, you are not alone. Many technicians and people who work with diesel-powered vehicles every day have the same problems.

Energy

The *first law of thermodynamics* states that energy can be neither created nor destroyed. Only the form in which energy exists can be changed; for example, heat can be transformed into mechanical energy. All internal combustion engines apply the same principle by burning a fuel within the cylinder to produce heat. The high-pressure gases created due to combustion force the piston down the cylinder on its expansion or power stroke. The heat energy is converted into mechanical energy through the piston and connecting rod, which in turn rotates the engine crankshaft and flywheel to supply the power needed.

The *second law of thermodynamics* states that heat cannot be completely converted to another form of energy. For example, in an engine, mechanical energy can be produced from a fuel, because heat passes only from a warmer to a colder body. The reverse of this process is possible only if energy is supplied.

Force

Force can be defined as push or pull on an object (See Figure 3–1A). As the diesel fuel within the engine cylinder is burned, it expands and exerts force on the piston head (Figure 3–1B). This force causes the piston to move downward and exerts force onto the engine

TABLE 3–1 Metric conversion chart

Common metric prefixes

kilo (k) = 1000	milli (m) = 0.001
centi (c) = 0.01	micro (μ) = 0.000001

Multiply	By	To get	Multiply	By	To get
Length					
inches (in.)	25.4	millimeters (mm)		0.03937	inches (in.)
inches (in.)	2.54	centimeters (cm)		0.3937	inches (in.)
feet (ft)	0.3048	meters (m)		3.281	feet (ft)
yards (yd)	0.9144	meters (m)		1.094	yard (yd)
mile (mi)	1.609	kilometers (km)		0.6214	mile (mi)
microinch (μin.)	0.0254	micron (μm)		39.37	microinch (μin.)
micron (μm)	0.000001	meters (m)		1,000,000	micron (μm)
microinch (μin.)	0.000001	inches (in.)		1,000,000	microinch (μin.)
Area					
square inches (in^2)	645.16	square millimeters (mm^2)		0.00155	square inches (in^2)
square inches (in^2)	6.452	square centimeters (cm^2)		0.155	square inches (in^2)
square feet (ft^2)	0.0929	square meters (m^2)		10.764	square feet (ft^2)
Volume					
cubic inches (in^3)	16,387.0	cubic millimeters (mm^3)		0.000061	cubic inches (in^3)
cubic inches (in^3)	16.387	cubic centimeters (cm^3)		0.06102	cubic inches (in^3)
cubic inches (in^3)	0.01639	liters (L)		61.024	cubic inches (in^3)
quarts (qt)	0.94635	liters (L)		1.0567	quarts (qt)
gallons (gal)	3.7851	liters (L)		0.2642	gallons (gal)
cubic feet (ft^3)	28.317	liters (L)		0.03531	cubic feet (ft^3)
cubic feet (ft^3)	0.02832	cubic meters (m^3)		35.315	cubic feet (ft^3)
Weight/force					
ounces (av) (oz)	28.35	grams (g)		0.03527	ounces (av) (oz)
pounds (av) (lb)	0.454	kilograms (kg)		2.205	pounds (av) (lb)
U.S. tons (t)	907.18	kilograms (kg)		0.001102	U.S. tons (t)
U.S. tons (t)	0.90718	metric tons (t)		1.1023	U.S. tons (t)
Power					
horsepower (hp)	0.7457	kilowatts (kW)		1.341	horsepower (hp)
Torque/Work Force					
inch-pounds (lb-in.)	0.11298	newton-meters (N · m)		8.851	inch-pound (lb-in.)
foot-pounds (lb-ft)	1.3558	newton-meters (N · m)		0.7376	foot-pound (lb-ft)
Speed					
miles/hour (mph)	1.609	kilometers/hour (km/h)		0.6214	miles/hour (mph)
kilometers/hour (km/h)	0.27778	meters/sec (m/s)		3.600	kilometers/hr (km/h)
miles/hour (mph)	0.4470	meters/sec (m/s)		2.237	miles/hour (mph)
Pressure					
pounds per square inch (psi)	0.069	bar		14.50	pounds per square inch (psi)
pounds per square inch (psi)	6.895	kilopascal (kPa)		0.14503	pounds per square inch (psi)

Subtract	From	To get	Multiply	By	To get
Temperature					
32	Fahrenheit (°F) and divide by 1.8	Celsius (°C)		1.8 and add 32	Fahrenheit (°F)

Fuel consumption

$$\frac{235}{\text{miles per gallon (mpg) U.S.}} = \text{liters/100 kilometers (L/100 km)}$$

$$\frac{282}{\text{miles per gallon (mpg) Imp.}} = \text{liters/100 kilometers (L/100 km)}$$

$$\frac{235}{\text{liters/100 kilometers (L/100 km)}} = \text{miles per gallon (mpg) U.S.}$$

$$\frac{235}{\text{liters/100 kilometers (L/100 km)}} = \text{miles per gallon (mpg) Imp.}$$

(a)

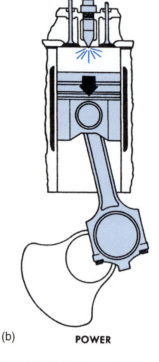

(b)   **POWER**

FIGURE 3–1 *(a) The horse is applying force against a large rock, but the rock is not moving. Therefore, no work is being done. (b) Injected fuel creates high pressure on the piston crown to rotate the crankshaft. (Courtesy of the American Association for Vocational Instructional Materials.)*

crankshaft connecting rod, causing the crankshaft to turn. The amount of force is controlled by the amount of fuel burned. It can be seen then that the chemical burning of fuel provides the mechanical energy that creates force so that the engine can do work.

Work

Work is done when a force travels through a distance (Figure 3–2). If force is exerted and no movement occurs, no work is being done. Work is also done in "braking" or slowing down a vehicle such as a tractor or truck.

Force and *distance* can easily be measured in most cases, so the amount of work can be calculated by using the following formulas:

- English measurement

$$\begin{aligned} \text{work} &= \text{force (pounds)} \times \text{distance (feet)} \\ &= 330 \text{ pounds} \times 100 \text{ feet} \\ &= 33{,}000 \text{ foot-pounds} \end{aligned}$$

- Metric measurement

$$\text{work (joules)} = \text{force (newtons)} \times \text{distance (meters)}$$
$$(1 \text{ N} = 4448 \text{ pounds-force})$$
$$330 \text{ ft-lb} \times 4.448 = 1468 \text{ N}$$
$$\begin{aligned} \text{work} &= 1468 \text{ newtons} \times 30.5 \text{ meters} \\ &= 44{,}774 \text{ joules (J) or newton-meters} \\ &\quad (\text{N} \cdot \text{m}) \end{aligned}$$

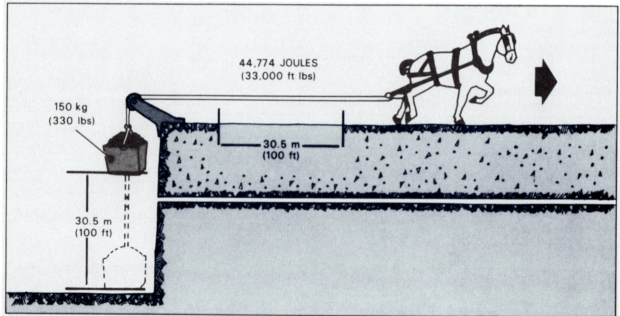

FIGURE 3–2 *If a force moves an object from a state of rest, then we can say that work has been done (force moved through a distance). (Courtesy of the American Association for Vocational Instructional Materials.)*

Work, along with energy and force, is the beginning of determining power. Since the only kind of work we have discussed so far has been accomplished by pulling or pushing, we need to look at another kind of work, that which is developed by rotating motion such as an engine crankshaft. The amount of work done is still determined by multiplying the force in pounds times the distance the weight is moved in feet.

Power

The term *power* is used to describe how much work has been done in a given period of time. The rate at which work can be done is measured in terms of power, or how many units of work (ft-lb) have been done in a unit of time. We can show this simply as

$$\text{power} = \frac{\text{work}}{\text{time}}$$

Normally, power is expressed as how many foot-pounds of work is done per minute. If enough work is performed in a given period of time, we can start to compare it with the word *horsepower*, which is used to describe the power output of all internal combustion engines (see Figure 3–1B). A detailed description of horsepower follows.

Horsepower

What is horsepower? The term is peculiar to the U.S. customary system. In the SI system, *watt* is the term used for power.

1 horsepower = 746 watts

The term *horsepower* was introduced by James Watt when he observed how much power one horse could develop. He found that a medium-size draft horse could pull 330 pounds a distance of 100 feet in 1 minute. This became a standard *unit of measure*, one that he used to rate his steam engine. By multiplying 330 lb times 100 ft, he set 33,000 ft-lb/min as defining 1 horsepower. The formula for horsepower thus is

$$\text{horsepower} = \frac{\text{force (pounds)} \times \text{distance (feet)}}{\text{time (minutes)} \times 33,000}$$

Thus, 1 horsepower is the ability to do 33,000 ft-lb of work in 1 minute, or 550 ft-lb of work in 1 second (33,000 divided by 60 seconds equals 550).

Note that in Figure 3–2 the horse is lifting a 330-lb weight to a height of 100 ft in 1 minute. Using the formula, the number of horsepower represented is determined as follows:

$$\text{horsepower} = \frac{330 \text{ lb} \times 100 \text{ ft}}{1 \text{ min} \times 33,000}$$
$$= 33,000$$
$$= 1$$

In Figure 3–3a the horse is dragging at the rate 100 ft/min a weight that requires 330 lb of pull to move it. In this example it is not necessary to know the value of the weight. The pulling force is determined by how difficult the weight is to pull. You apply the horsepower formula as follows:

$$\text{horsepower} = \frac{330 \text{ lb} \times 100\text{ft}}{1 \text{ min} \times 33,000}$$
$$= \frac{33,000}{33,000}$$
$$= 1$$

This is typical of how you determine the *drawbar horsepower* of a tractor.

In Figure 3–3b, force by pulling is replaced by a shaft turning (rotating force). This is the way power is measured at the engine flywheel and at the power take-off (PTO) shaft of tractors. If we assume that it takes 1 minute to lift the 330-lb weight to a height of 100 ft, you can determine horsepower as follows:

$$\text{horsepower} = \frac{330 \text{ lb} \times 100 \text{ ft}}{1 \text{ min} \times 33,000}$$
$$= \frac{33,000}{33,000}$$
$$= 1$$

Let us consider the work that is produced by moving a weight of 100 lb (45.36 kg) through a distance of 10 ft (3 m) in a time of 4 seconds (sec or s). The power expended would be

$$\text{power} = \frac{\text{work}}{\text{time}} = \frac{1000 \text{ ft-lb}}{4 \text{ sec}} = 250 \text{ ft-lb/sec}$$

How much horsepower have we expended in doing this work? One horsepower is considered as being 550 ft-lb/sec, 33,000 ft-lb/min, or 1,980,000 ft-lb/hr. Therefore, we can compute horsepower as follows:

$$\text{horsepower} = \frac{250 \text{ ft-lb/sec}}{550 \text{ ft-lb/sec}} = 0.45 \text{ hp (0.33 kW)}$$

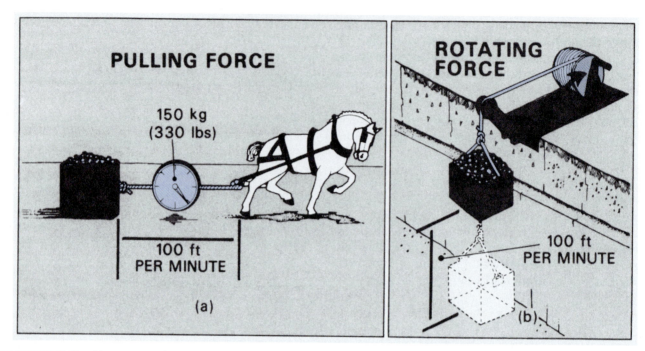

FIGURE 3–3 Horsepower is measured by the amount of work accomplished, and can be performed by lifting or, as shown in this two-part diagram, (a) pulling or (b) creating rotary force. In example (a) of the diagram it takes this horse 1 minute to move (pull) the 330-pound (149.7 kg) load a distance of 100 feet (30.5 m), so we could say that this horse has created 1 horsepower. In reality, however, 1 horsepower is calculated out to 33,000 ft-lb of work per minute, or 550 ft-lb of work per second. (Courtesy of the American Association for Vocational Instructional Materials.)

If this work were expended continually for a period of 1 min, the energy produced would be

$$\text{power} = \frac{\text{work}}{\text{time}} = \frac{1000 \text{ ft-lb}}{1 \text{ min}} = 1000 \text{ ft-lb/min}$$

and the horsepower produced would be

$$\text{horsepower} = \frac{1000 \text{ ft-lb/min}}{33,000 \text{ ft-lb/min}} = 0.030 \text{ hp}$$

You can see that if work is performed at a slower rate, less horsepower is produced; therefore, we can safely say that the word *horsepower* is an expression of how fast work can be done. In an internal combustion engine this work is produced within the cylinder due to the expanding gases. The faster the engine speed, the quicker the work is produced.

Metric Horsepower

In the metric system, power is expressed by the word *kilowatt* (kW), used initially to express the power of electrical machinery, where 1 hp is considered equal to 746 watts (W) in the English equivalent. (A watt is an ampere × a volt; an ampere is a measure of volume/quantity and a volt is a measure of electrical pressure.) Since 1 kW equals 1000 W, we can show 1 electrical hp as being equivalent to 0.746 kW. Conversely, 1 kW equals 1.341 hp. This 746 W of measurement is an American equivalent; in the metric system 1 hp is considered as being 735.5 W, or 75 kg · m/s. The German abbreviation for this unit of measurement is PS (*Pferdestärke*), where 1 PS (European horsepower) = 0.986 hp. The French equivalent is CV (*cheval vapeur*), where 1 ch = 1 PS = 0.07355 kW. This means that metric horsepower is approximately 1.5% less than the American unit of measurement! Other measures that you will encounter have been established by the International Standardization Organization (ISO), Deutsches Institut für Normung—German Institute for Standardization (DIN), and Society of Automotive Engineers (SAE), headquartered in Warrendale (Pittsburgh), Pennsylvania.

Horsepower Formulas

Work is done when a force is exerted over a distance. This can be defined mathematically as work equals distance (D) multiplied by a force (F). As horsepower is a measure of the rate (speed) at which the work is done, we can show this mathematically as

$$\text{horsepower} = \frac{D \times F}{33,000}$$

where the 33,000 is a constant figure determined by the analysis and observation of James Watt, as mentioned, when he studied the average rate of work for a horse with respect to the work of his steam engine. He determined that the average horse could produce a work rate equal to 33,000 ft-lb/min (0.7457 kW/min), which he equated to 1 hp/min, or 550 ft-lb/sec (0.0124 kW/s).

Horsepower is generally considered as being one of two types:

1. *Brake horsepower* (bhp). This is the actual useful horsepower developed at the crankshaft/flywheel. It can be determined by a known formula, but certain data must be readily available, such as the dynamometer information (weight on a brake arm × distance). Without the dynamometer information, this type of horsepower cannot be readily determined unless the engine is run on a dynamometer with suitable horsepower, torque, and speed gauges. Many dynamometers also have a formula and data included on a riveted plate to allow you to compute the engine power being produced.

2. *Indicated horsepower* (ihp). This is the power developed within a cylinder based on the amount of heat released but does not take into account any frictional losses. The cylinder's mean indicated pressure can be monitored by installing a special test gauge to record the maximum firing pressure. If a maximum pressure indicator gauge is available and the cylinder pressure is known, you can factor out indicated horsepower using a formula.

Horsepower Performance Curves

One easy way to show engine performance curves is to view an OEM sales specification sheet. These sheets include graphs indicating the horsepower, torque, and fuel performance curves for various engine models. Figure 3–4 shows several engine ratings for Detroit Diesel's four-stroke-cycle, 12.7 L series 60, electronically controlled heavy-duty truck engine. By picking an engine rpm along the horizontal line of each graph, we can draw a vertical line upwards until it bisects the horsepower curve and the torque curve, where we can

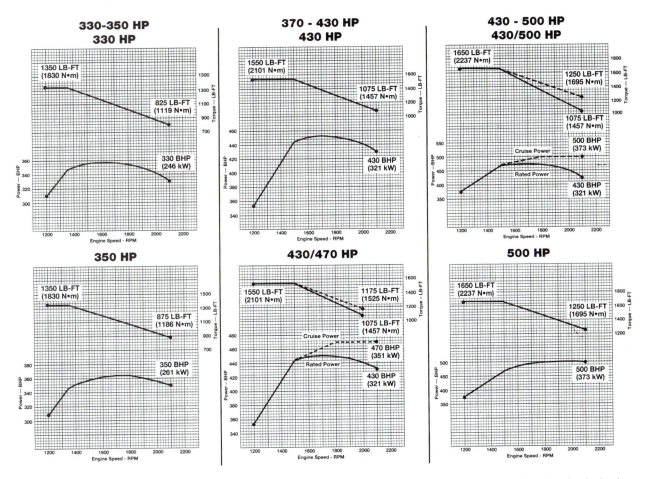

FIGURE 3–4 Example performance curve graphs for a variety of series 60 electronic engines showing both the horsepower and torque developed at given engine speeds under load. (Courtesy of Detroit Diesel Corporation.)

read the respective values desired. Note the ratings as shown. They are achieved through electronic programming of the engine electronic control module (ECM). On the 430/470 and 430/500 bhp (321/373 kW) models, the engine can be programmed to provide a lower power setting at rated speed, climbing to the higher power setting from 1500 rpm. This feature allows the operator to run the vehicle in a cruise mode at a lower engine speed, which also provides a lower brake specific fuel consumption, but with a higher horsepower at this lower speed. Both engine models also offer a constant horsepower setting from 2100 rpm down to 1800 rpm, while the vehicle operates in the cruise control mode. Programming electronic engines to produce their best power at a lower speed results in a gear-fast-run-slow concept (lower numerical axle ratio). This, coupled with higher power and torque curves, provides better vehicle performance overall. Some of the performance graphs in Figure 3–4 illustrate a fairly flat power line, commonly known as a constant horsepower curve, since there is no loss of power with a reduction in engine speed for several hundred rpm.

> **NOTE** Horsepower is related to BMEP but is also influenced by both the speed of the engine and the cylinder/engine displacement. Horsepower cannot be multiplied.

Figure 3–5 illustrates the performance curve and relative information for the Caterpillar 3406E electronically controlled unit injector truck engine. Figure 3–6 illustrates an engine performance curve for a Cummins N14-460E electronically controlled heavy-duty truck engine. Note in this example and others that the engine brake horsepower performance curve is tailored so that the maximum power and best fuel economy are achieved at a speed within the operating range where most driving is done on a heavy-duty truck application. Cummins refers to the point on the engine performance curve where this occurs as the "command point." In Figure 3–7 note how the engine horsepower begins to drop as the operator revs the engine beyond 1700 rpm. Also note in Figure 3–6 that the engine torque starts to decrease fairly quickly beyond 1500 rpm and the fuel consumption starts to increase. This design feature "forces" the truck driver to use a *progressive shift pattern,* which means that the engine is accelerated only high enough to get the vehicle rolling; then a shift is made to the next higher gear. By using this shifting technique, not only does the higher engine *torque* move the vehicle gradually up to road speed, but it also keeps the engine within the most fuel-efficient curve, as you can see from the BSFC line in Figures 3–5 and 3–6. Most heavy-duty electronically controlled diesel engine-mounted ECMs are programmed to provide this type of operational response. The fuel consumption and torque curves are discussed later in the chapter.

The performance curves of brake horsepower we have been discussing are typical of most of the newer electronically controlled unit injector heavy-duty truck engines manufactured by Caterpillar, Cummins, Detroit Diesel, Mack, Isuzu, and Volvo. On mechanically governed and injected engines, however, the horsepower generally tends to decrease with a reduction in engine speed (rpm) from the full-load-rated setting as the engine rpm is reduced due to an increasing load, since the rate/speed of doing the work is slower. Electronic controls provide tremendous flexibility for tailoring engine performance that is not possible with mechanical controls. Proper selection of turbocharging and air-to-air-charge cooling, high top piston rings, piston bowl geometry, and the use of low-sulfur diesel fuel all help to provide this improvement in engine performance and reduce the exhaust emissions so that they can comply with the EPA-mandated limits.

Regardless of the type of horsepower calculated, most diesel technicians in the field choose to use the following simplified formula to determine horsepower, particularly when the engine torque and speed are known:

$$\text{hp} = \frac{\text{torque} \times \text{rpm}}{5252}$$

Brake Horsepower

The formula for brake horsepower can be stated as

$$\text{bhp} = \frac{2 \times \pi \times r \times \text{rpm} \times w}{33,000}$$

where π (*pi*) = 3.1416

r = distance between the centerline of the engine crankshaft and the application of a weight on a brake arm, in feet or meters

rpm = speed of the engine, in revolutions per minute

w = effective weight on a brake arm, in pounds or kilograms

Indicated Horsepower

The commonly accepted formula to determine indicated horsepower is

$$\text{ihp} = \frac{P \times L \times A \times N}{33,000}$$

3406E

Truck Engine Performance

475 (354) @ 1800 rpm

DM0479-00

1750 Peak Torque
50 State

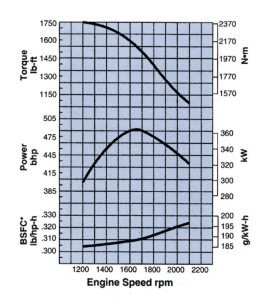

| | | Rated | English | | | Maximum | | | Rated | Metric | | | Maximum |

| | **475 hp** | | | | | **485 hp** | | | **354 kW** | | | | **362 kW** |

Engine Speed rpm	Engine Power w/o fan hp	Engine Torque lb ft	Engine BMEP psi	S Fuel Consum lb/hp-h	Fuel Rate gph	Engine Speed rpm	Engine Power w/o fan kW	Engine Torque N•m	Engine BMEP kPa	S Fuel Consum g/kW-h	Fuel Rate l/hr
2100	431	1078	182	.324	20.0	2100	322	1462	1254	197	75.6
2000	447	1173	198	.322	20.5	2000	333	1590	1364	196	77.7
1900	461	1275	215	.319	21.0	1900	344	1729	1483	194	79.5
1800	475	1387	234	.316	21.3	1800	354	1880	1613	192	80.8
1700	485	1499	253	.311	21.5	1700	362	2033	1745	189	81.3
1600	485	1593	269	.309	21.3	1600	362	2160	1854	188	80.8
1500	472	1653	279	.309	20.8	1500	352	2241	1923	188	78.9
1400	455	1705	288	.307	20.0	1400	339	2312	1984	187	75.7
1300	430	1738	293	.306	18.7	1300	321	2356	2022	186	70.9
1200	400	1751	295	.304	16.9	1200	298	2374	2037	185	64.0

Engine Speed rpm	Intake Manif Temp °F	Intake Manif Pres in-Hg	Intake Air Flow cfm	Exh Manif Temp °F	Exh Stk Temp °F	Exh Gas Flow cfm	Engine Speed rpm	Intake Manif Temp °C	Intake Manif Pres kPa	Intake Air Flow m³/min	Exh Manif Temp °C	Exh Stk Temp °C	Exh Gas Flow m³/min
2100	110	45.4	1164	911	671	2441	2100	43	153	33.0	488	355	69.2
2000	114	47.2	1168	938	695	2498	2000	45	159	33.1	503	368	70.8
1900	114	49.2	1161	965	717	2537	1900	45	166	32.9	518	381	71.9
1800	113	51.3	1143	993	741	2547	1800	45	173	32.4	533	393	72.2
1700	113	53.1	1108	1018	765	2519	1700	45	179	31.4	548	407	71.4
1600	112	54.1	1055	1041	790	2452	1600	44	182	29.9	561	421	69.5
1500	110	53.6	988	1061	815	2343	1500	43	181	28.0	571	435	66.4
1400	107	51.7	906	1080	840	2198	1400	41	174	25.7	582	449	62.3
1300	103	48.1	811	1099	871	2011	1300	39	162	23.0	593	466	57.0
1200	98	41.7	688	1121	914	1767	1200	36	140	19.5	605	490	50.1

Conditions

This engine performance data is typical of the engines approved by the Environmental Protection Agency (EPA) and the California Air Resources Board (CARB) for the calendar year 1994. This engine is approved for use in Canada. This data may change, subject to EPA and CARB approved engineering changes

* Brake Specific Fuel Consumption

Tolerance

Curves represent typical values obtained under lug conditions. Ambient air conditions and fuel used will affect these values. Each of the values may vary in accordance with the following tolerances.

Exhaust Stack Temperature	± 75°F ± 42°C	Power BSFC*	±3% ± 010 lb/hp-h ± 6 g/kW-h
Intake Manifold Pressure-Gage	± 3 in. Hg ± 10 kPa	Fuel Rate	± 5%
Torque	± 3%		

FIGURE 3–5 Truck engine performance curve and operating data for a 475 hp (354 kW) model 346E electronic engine. (Reprinted courtesy of Caterpillar, Inc.)

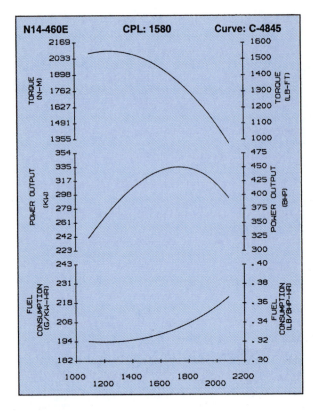

FIGURE 3–6   One performance curve for an N14-460E (855 in³) displacement electronically controlled Celect engine. (Courtesy of Cummins Engine Company, Inc.)

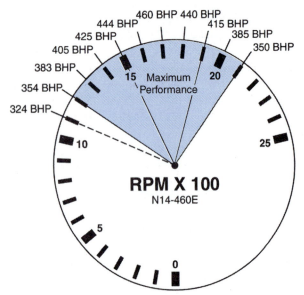

FIGURE 3–7   Performance graph of typical horsepower output versus engine speed for an N14-460E electronic engine. (Courtesy of Cummins Engine Company, Inc.)

where P = indicated brake mean effective pressure
L = length of the piston stroke, in feet
A = area of the piston crown, in square inches
N = number of power strokes per cylinder per minute

In two-stroke-cycle engines, N is the number of cylinders $\times$ rpm, while for four-stroke-cycle engines, N is the number of cylinders $\times$ rpm/2, since there are only half as many power strokes in the four-cycle engine. Using the formula, let us determine the ihp developed from a four-cycle six-cylinder engine with a bore of 5.4 in. (137 mm) and a stroke of 6.5 in. (165 mm) that develops an indicated mean effective pressure (IMEP) of 234 psi (1613 kPa) when operating at 1800 rpm.

$$\text{ihp} = \frac{PLAN}{33,000} = \frac{234 \times 6.5 \times 22.9 \times 1800 \times 6}{12 \times 33,000 \times 2}$$
$$= 474.96 \ (354 \text{ kW})$$

The number 12 in the formula is needed to convert the piston stroke into feet; however, if the stroke were 6 in. (152.4 mm) we could simply enter it on the upper line as 0.5 and remove the number 12 from the lower line. The answer, 474.96 ihp, is actually the horsepower listed for the Cat 3406E electronically controlled unit injector engine shown in Figure 3–5.

If we were to use the same formula but apply it to a two-stroke-cycle engine such as a Detroit Diesel 6V-92 series engine with a bore of 4.84 in. (123 mm), a stroke of 5 in. (127 mm), and a BMEP of 137 psi (944.6 kPa) running at 2100 rpm, what would be the ihp?

$$\text{ihp} = \frac{PLAN}{33,000} = \frac{137 \times 5 \times 18.39 \times 2100 \times 6}{12 \times 33,000}$$
$$= 400.81 \ (299 \text{ kW})$$

Some people prefer to use these optional formulas for determining indicated horsepower:

- Two-stroke cycle

$$\text{ihp} = \frac{PLANK}{23,000 \times 12} \text{ or } \frac{PLANK}{396,000}$$

- Four-stroke cycle

$$\text{ihp} = \frac{PLANK}{33,000 \times 12 \times 2} \text{ or } \frac{PLANK}{792,000}$$

where N is the rpm and K is the number of cylinders.

Horsepower Ratings

Now that we are familiar with how to determine horsepower, let us discuss horsepower ratings applied to engines when installed in various applications. If you consider the same model engine in different applications, the horsepower ratings may not be the same because of the loads and speed variation that an engine is subjected to during a typical working day. An engine in a heavy-duty on-highway truck tends to be exposed to an *intermittent–continuous duty cycle* as the operator revs the engine up and down during upshifting and downshifting of the transmission as a result of the geography and terrain in which the vehicle is operating. On the other hand, a diesel generator set is designed to start and run at a fixed speed, possibly with a fixed load or an alternating load based on the demands for electrical power. Consequently, the horsepower (kW) rating for the gen-set (generator set) would be lower than that for the truck, because it is possible that the gen-set engine might run 24 hours a day, 7 days a week for a month or longer. To ensure optimum engine life and fuel economy, as well as factoring in some possible temporary overload capability into the gen-set application, most OEMs will derate this engine to 70% of maximum-rated horsepower.

NOTE All current heavy-duty diesel engines are equipped with either an engine identification plate or a series of stick-on decals attached to the rocker cover(s) that list the horsepower output at rated speed. In addition, an EPA compliance sticker confirms that the engine meets the mandated exhaust emissions limits for the year in which the engine was manufactured. Other information on these decals indicates the engine model, family and displacement, fuel injector delivery rate, initial injection timing, and intake and exhaust valve clearances. All specifications—even on U.S.-built engines—are now adopting the metric standard of measurement.

Basically, there are seven general classifications of horsepower ratings with which you should be familiar.

1. *Rated horsepower* is the net horsepower available from the engine with a specified injector fuel rate and engine speed, which is guaranteed within ±5% of that shown in OEM sales literature according to the SAE standard ambient conditions, elevation, and air density. This is usually stated in the literature, such as 77°F (25°C) and 29.31 in. Hg (99 kPa) barometer (dry).

2. *Intermittent rated horsepower* is used for variable speed and load applications where full output is required for short intervals. To obtain optimum life expectancy, the average load should not exceed 60% (turbo) and 70% (nonturbo) of full load at the average operating speed. Typical examples for this rating are a crew boat, crane, shovel, railcar, railyard switcher, front-end loader, earthmoving scraper, and off-highway rear-dump truck.

3. *Intermittent maximum horsepower* is a rating used for applications in which maximum output is desirable and long engine life between overhauls is of secondary importance, or in which the average load does not exceed 35% of the full load at the average operating speed. Typical examples include a bow thruster used for docking purposes on marine vessels, standby gen-set, and standby fire pump.

4. *Continuous horsepower* is a rating given to an engine running under a constant load for long periods without a reduction in speed or load. This rating gives the range of optimum fuel economy and longest engine life. The maximum speed for this rating is generally shown on a performance curve chart. The pump or injectors may have reserve capacity for momentary overload demands. The average load should not exceed the continuous rating of the engine. Typical examples include a stationary air compressor, quarry-rock crusher, marine dredge, gen-set, and mud pump in oil-well drilling applications.

5. *Intermittent continuous horsepower* is a rating used for applications that are primarily continuous but have some variations in load and/or speed. Average fuel consumption at this rating should not exceed that of the continuous rating. The injectors or pump may have reserve capacity for momentary overload demands. Typical applications include a steering bow thruster on marine vessels, workboat, portable air compressor, dredge, gen-set, railroad locomotive, and bottom-dump earthmoving truck.

6. *Shaft horsepower* is the net horsepower available at the output shaft of an application, for example, the horsepower measured at the output flange of a marine gearbox.

7. *Road horsepower* is a rating of the power available at the drive wheels, for example, on a truck after losses due to the transmission, driveline, and so on.

Engine Torque

Torque can be defined as an effort that produces or tends to produce rotation. Generally, this effort is produced by force acting on a lever. Torque, a twisting and turning force that is developed at the engine crankshaft, is a measure of the engine's capacity to do work. Torque is expressed in pound-feet (lb-ft), or newton-meters (N · m) in the metric system. Smaller quantities of torque can be expressed in pound-inches (lb-in.) or N · m.

When measuring torque, the length of the lever arm and force applied are important. To obtain torque, multiply pounds of force times the length of the lever arm.

To further develop your understanding of torque, note the differences in torque shown in Figure 3–8. To determine the torque in Figure 3–8a, use the following formula:

$$\text{torque} = \text{force} \times \text{length of lever arm}$$

- US: torque = 330 lb × 1 ft
  = 330 foot-pounds
- SI: torque = 1468 N × 0.305 m
  = 447.7 newton-meters

If the length of the lever arm is doubled as in Figure 3–8b, the result is

- US: torque = 330 × 2
  = 660 foot-pounds
- SI: torque = 1468 N × 0.61 m
  = 895.5 newton-meters

If 330 foot-pounds of torque is all that is needed, you can reduce the amount of force because the length of the lever arm has been increased (Figure 3–8c).

- US: torque = 165 × 2
  = 330 foot-pounds
- SI: torque = 734 N × 0.61 m
  = 447.7 newton-meters

Torque produced at the engine flywheel is developed by energy from the burning fuel, which has expanded and produced force. This force causes the engine piston to move downward and transmit force through the connecting rod to the crankshaft connecting rod journal on the crankshaft throw. The throw then becomes the lever that transmits the force to the engine crankshaft, causing it to turn and develop torque.

As you accelerate the engine in a truck or tractor under load, notice that the engine block has a tendency to turn in the direction opposite to the flywheel.

Figure 3–9 illustrates how this happens. In Figure 3–9a the engine is not running and remains level on its mounts. With the engine running and a light load applied to the engine flywheel, the engine tips slightly to the left in the direction opposite to the flywheel rotation. As the load on the engine is increased, the engine leans farther to the left as a result of the increased torque.

Figure 3–10 illustrates the conditions related to the development of torque, which is produced by a force (expanding high-pressure gases) pushing down on top of the piston crown. This force is measured in pounds per square inch (or in the metric system of measurement, kilopascal). The force on the piston is transferred through a lever (length and throw of the connecting rod), which in turn is connected to the crankshaft journal. The force exerted on the top (crown) of the piston decreases as the piston moves down the cylinder; this energy is used up in rotating the crankshaft. Torque depends on BMEP and engine cylinder displacement; therefore, BMEP is the average pressure exerted on each square inch (square millimeter) of the piston

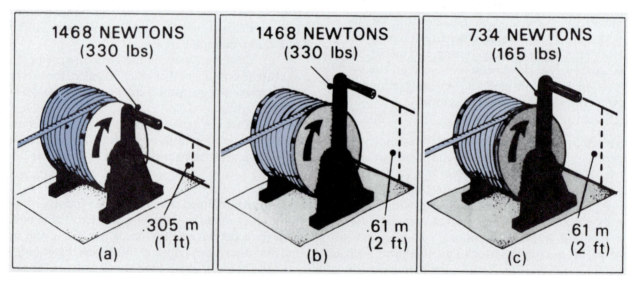

FIGURE 3–8 Torque is expressed as a "twisting or turning force" around a fulcrum point. As illustrated, torque is determined by multiplying the force in pounds or kilograms by the length of the lever arm in feet or meters. (Courtesy of the American Association for Vocational Instructional Materials.)

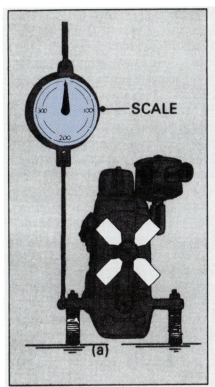

FIGURE 3–9   Development of torque. (a) There is no torque applied in a stopped engine as shown by the zero needle position. (b) With light load applied to a running engine, torque will increase slightly as shown on the scale. (c) When the load applied to the engine is increased, the torque will become greater and is registered as a higher value on the scale. This greater twisting and turning force causes the engine to shift further to the left as shown. (Courtesy of the American Association for Vocational Instructional Materials.)

crown throughout the actual power stroke within the cylinder multiplied by the area of the piston crown. This force (F) = area × BMEP.

The length of the connecting rod (lever) is shown in Figure 3–10. Torque can therefore be described as the force (F) multiplied by the length of the lever (L) and is best defined as

$$\text{torque } (T) = \frac{\text{hp} \times 5252}{\text{rpm}}$$

The number 5252 is a mathematical constant derived from the basic horsepower (kilowatt) formula:

$$\text{hp} = \frac{DF}{33{,}000T}$$

An easy way to understand torque is to consider that as a heavy-duty truck is forced to move up a hill and the road speed and engine speed are decreased by the grade, the horsepower (rate of doing work) is slower but the engine torque increases with a reduction

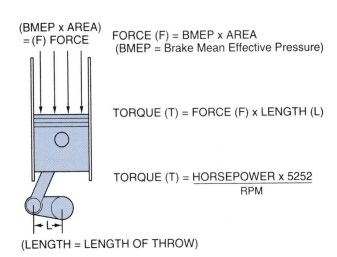

(BMEP x AREA) = (F) FORCE

FORCE (F) = BMEP x AREA
(BMEP = Brake Mean Effective Pressure)

TORQUE (T) = FORCE (F) x LENGTH (L)

TORQUE (T) = $\dfrac{\text{HORSEPOWER x 5252}}{\text{RPM}}$

(LENGTH = LENGTH OF THROW)

FIGURE 3–10   Characteristics involved in determining engine crankshaft torque.

in speed. Therefore, it is the torque that keeps the crankshaft turning and actually pulls the truck up the hill. Similarly, when a tandem-axle dump truck is up to its axles in mud, it is not horsepower that pulls it out (high horsepower occurs at elevated speed, so revving the engine simply results in wheel slippage with no appreciable movement); once again it is the torque.

An attempt to move a heavily loaded truck from a parked position on a hill involves *gradeability* (percentage of hill steepness). What the vehicle needs is the ability to produce enough torque or *work power* to get moving and stay moving at a slow vehicle speed. Therefore, the engine torque multiplied through the transmission and rear-axle ratios determines the truck's ability to overcome resistance to soft terrain or an uphill working position. For example if a truck transmission gear ratio was 5:1 in a given selected gear, and the axle ratio was 4:1, then the overall gear multiplication ratio would be 20:1; therefore the engine torque input to the road wheels would be multiplied × 20. The horsepower however *can not* be multiplied since its rating is engine speed dependent. Review the HP and Torque curves shown in Figures 3–4, 3–5, 3–6 and 3–11 for clarification of the difference between torque and horsepower.

We can determine the torque produced in a given engine if we know some of the other specifications of the engine. The formula for torque,

$$T = \frac{5252 \times hp}{rpm}$$

is the simplest method to use when you want to determine the torque from an engine at a certain operational speed. From our earlier discussion of horsepower, we know that heavy-duty electronically controlled engines are designed to produce their best power and fuel consumption at a midrange rpm value. Figure 3–6 is one example, a Cummins N14 Celect engine rated at 460 hp at 1700 rpm. What is important here is that the torque drops off fairly quickly as the engine speed is increased beyond this range. On the other hand, as the rpm is reduced, the torque increases until at 1200 rpm it reaches its *peak torque point*, which in this example is 1550 lb-ft (2101 N · m). The later model N14-460E+ was recalibrated to produce 1650 lb-ft (2237 N · m) at 1200 rpm.

Refer now to Figure 3–5 which lists the operational data for the 3406E Caterpillar engine rated at 475 bhp at 1800 rpm. Using our torque formula we can confirm if the horsepower and torque are as stated in the figure. Let us see if the torque at full-load-rated speed and the peak torque point check out by using the formula

$$T = \frac{5252 \times hp}{rpm} = \frac{5252 \times 475}{1800}$$
$$= 1386 \text{ lb-ft } (1879 \text{ N} \cdot \text{m})$$

Another method is commonly used and can be applied to determine the torque from two- and four-stroke-cycle engines if the engine displacement and BMEP are known.

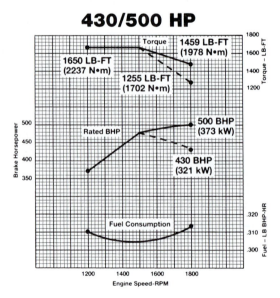

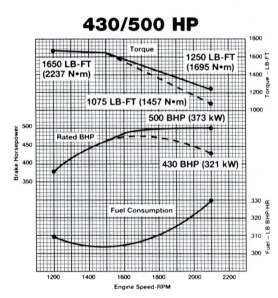

FIGURE 3–11 Examples of BSFC (brake specific fuel consumption) curves for two series 60 engines rated at the same split 430/500 hp(321/373 kW). (a) Graph shows engine governed at 1800 rpm MFL speed; (b) graph shows engine governed for 2100 rpm MFL speed. (Courtesy of Detroit Diesel Corporation.)

- Two-stroke cycle

$$T = \frac{\text{BMEP} \times \text{displacement}}{75.4}$$

- Four-stroke cycle

$$T = \frac{\text{BMEP} \times \text{displacement}}{150.8}$$

In both of these formulas the numbers 75.4 and 150.8 are constants derived from a mathematical procedure.

Once again refer to Figure 3–5 and determine the torque at rated and peak torque speeds using the four-stroke-cycle engine formula.

$$\text{Torque at rated speed } (T) = \frac{\text{BMEP} \times \text{displacement}}{150.8}$$

$$= \frac{234 \times 893}{150.8} = 1385.68 \text{ lb-ft } (1879 \text{ N} \cdot \text{m})$$

$$\text{Peak torque at 1200 rpm } (T) = \frac{\text{BMEP} \times \text{displacement}}{150.8}$$

$$= \frac{295 \times 893}{150.8} = 1747 \text{ lb-ft } (2369 \text{ N} \cdot \text{m})$$

As you can see from these calculations, there are minor variations in the final answer, but we have determined that these formulas do work.

Torque Rise

You will encounter the term *torque rise* often in reference to most of today's electronically controlled diesel engines, particularly with respect to heavy-duty on-highway truck applications. This term simply expresses as a percentage the increase in engine torque as the engine speed is reduced from its maximum full load rpm or rated speed. For example, an engine develops 1000 lb-ft (1356 N · m) of torque at its rated speed of 2100 rpm, and this torque increases to 1500 lb-ft (2034 N · m) when the rpm is reduced to 1200 rpm (known as the peak torque point); the rate of torque rise is equal to 50%. If this 50% torque increase is divided by the 900 rpm drop from rated to peak torque rpm, this engine develops 5.55% torque rise for every 100 rpm decrease. Such a situation might occur when a heavy-duty truck is forced to climb a hill without the operator downshifting the transmission or changing the throttle position. Before the introduction of electronically controlled unit injector and pump-line-nozzle systems, OEMs employed various mechanical devices, such as *torque springs* or two belleville washers within the governor, which could be adjusted to tailor the actual rate of torque rise of the engine. This function can now be programmed into the ECM on the engine to allow fine control of both the horsepower and torque curves. If the engine has been tailored for a high rate of torque rise with a decrease in engine speed, the operator downshifts the transmission less often. The engine, in truck jargon, "is able to hang on to the load a lot longer," such as when moving up a hill.

We can use the following formula to determine torque rise:

$$\text{torque rise} = \frac{\text{peak torque} - \text{torque at rated speed}}{\text{torque at rated speed}}$$

In Figure 3–5 note that the 3406E Caterpillar electronically controlled engine rated at 475 hp (354 kW) at 1800 rpm produces a torque of 1387 lb-ft (1880 N · m). The torque increases to 1751 lb-ft (2374 N · m) at 1200 rpm. Therefore, we can determine the torque rise of this engine:

$$\text{torque rise} = \frac{1751 - 1387}{1387} = \frac{364}{1387} = 26.24\%$$

BMEP Formula

BMEP, the brake mean effective pressure, is the average pressure exerted on the piston crown during the working or power stroke. This factor is often described in terms of the performance capability of an engine model, because the BMEP is a measurement of how efficiently an engine is using its piston displacement to do work. Torque depends on BMEP and engine cylinder displacement. Horsepower is a value related to BMEP but it is also influenced by engine speed and displacement. Therefore, for a constant BMEP condition, torque increases in direct relation to the piston displacement of the engine. BMEP is actually difficult to define accurately since it is a parameter that does not specifically exist. It is the *theoretical* mean effective pressure developed during each power stroke, which would in turn develop a power equal to a given horsepower or kilowatt figure.

BMEP is also equal to the IMEP (indicated mean effective pressure) times the mechanical efficiency of the engine. The BMEP must be calculated after the bhp or torque of the engine is known, and it can be determined using the conventional ihp formula stated earlier in this chapter. In the following formula, the BMEP (P_b) and bhp are used in place of IMEP (P_i) and ihp.

$$\text{bhp} = \frac{P_b L A n}{33,000} \quad \text{or} \quad P_b \frac{33,000 \text{ bhp}}{L A n}$$

where P_b = BMEP = brake mean effective pressure in psi or kPa

L = piston stroke, in feet or meters

A = piston crown area, in square inches or square millimeters

N = number of power strokes per minute

The total piston displacement (*D*) in cubic inches (or cubic centimeters or liters) of an engine is equal to the area of one piston times the stroke times the number of cylinders. So the formula can be simplified somewhat for both two- and four-stroke-cycle engines as follows:

- Four-stroke cycle

$$P_b = \frac{792,000 \text{ bhp}}{DN}$$

- Two-stroke cycle

$$P_b = \frac{396,000 \text{ bhp}}{DN}$$

where *D* is the total piston displacement of the engine, in either in^3 or cm^3, and *N* is the engine speed in rpm.

For example, using the formula above for a four-stroke-cycle Cummins engine with a displacement of 855 in^3 (14,011 cm^3, 14.011 L) developing 460 bhp at 1800 rpm, the BMEP would be

$$P_b = \frac{792,000 \text{ bhp}}{DN} = \frac{792,000 \times 460}{855 \times 1800}$$
$$= 236.72 \text{ psi (1632 kPa)}$$

Using the same dimensions for a two-stroke-cycle engine, the BMEP would be

$$P_b = \frac{396,000 \text{ bhp}}{DN} = \frac{396,000 \times 460}{855 \times 1800}$$
$$= 118.36 \text{ psi (816.1 kPa)}$$

Note that the two-stroke-cycle engine has a BMEP close to half that of a four-cycle model, even when running at the same horsepower setting. This is due to the fact that approximately only half as much fuel is injected for each power stroke in the two-stroke model as in the four-stroke model. Keep in mind, however, that the two-cycle model has about twice as many power strokes as the four-cycle engine. For example, a 400 hp Detroit Diesel 92 series engine running at full load would have approximately 90 mm^3 of fuel injected for each stroke of the injector plunger. The four-cycle engine set at the same horsepower rating would have approximately 180 mm^3 of fuel injected on every stroke of the injector plunger. This does not mean that the two-cycle model is more fuel efficient than the four-cycle model. Generally, the two-cycle engine tends to be a little more thirsty than its four-stroke counterpart.

More simplified formulas can be used to determine BMEP if the engine torque and the engine displacement are known, for example:

- Two-stroke cycle

$$BMEP = \frac{75.4 \times \text{torque}}{\text{displacement}}$$

- Four-stroke cycle

$$BMEP = \frac{150.8 \times \text{torque}}{\text{displacement}}$$

Refer again to Figure 3–5. You will see that the BMEP at the rating and speed of 475 hp (354 kW) at 1800 rpm is 234 psi (1613 kPa). Take careful note that in any engine as the engine rpm is reduced under full-load operation toward the peak torque point, the BMEP increases accordingly. In the 475 hp (354 kW) 3460E engine, notice that the BMEP climbs to 295 psi (2037 kPa) at 1200 rpm. Using our formulas, let us determine if the BMEP is as listed for both the rated and 1200 rpm peak torque speeds.

- Rated speed (1800 rpm)

$$BMEP = \frac{150.8 \times \text{torque}}{\text{displacement}}$$
$$= \frac{150.8 \times 1387}{893}$$
$$= 234.22 \text{ psi (1614.96 kPa)}$$

- Peak torque speed (1200 rpm)

$$BMEP = \frac{150.8 \times 1751}{893} = 295.6 \text{ psi (2039 kPa)}$$

Compare these answers with the values listed in Figure 3–5, and you will see that they agree.

Piston Speed Formula

The speed of the piston within the cylinder is to some degree a measure of the wear rate within the cylinder and the wear rate of the piston ring. Piston speed can be determined by the following formula:

$$\text{piston speed} = \frac{L \times \text{rpm} \times 2}{12} \text{ or } \frac{\text{stroke (in.)} \times \text{rpm}}{}$$

The number 2 appears in the first formula because the piston moves up and down for each crankshaft revolution. The number 12 is to convert the speed to feet per minute. In the second formula we have simply substituted the number 6 and removed the 2. In either case, the formula produces the same result. If an engine had a stroke of 6.5 in. (165 mm), what would its piston speed be in feet per minute (meters per minute) with the engine running at 1800 rpm?

$$\frac{L \times rpm \times 2}{12} = \frac{6.5 \text{ in. (165 mm)} \times 1800 \times 2}{12}$$
$$= 1950 \text{ ft/min (594 m/min)}$$

BSFC Formula

BSFC, brake specific fuel consumption, is always listed on engine manufacturers' sales literature and is usually shown in either lb/bhp-hr or g/kWh (grams/kilowatt-hour). One lb/hp-hr is equal to 608.277 g/kWh. Figure 3–5 illustrates an example of the BSFC for a Caterpillar 3406E model heavy-duty truck engine rated at 475 hp (354 kW) at 1800 rpm and a peak torque at 1200 rpm of 1750 lb-ft (2373 N · m). As you can readily see on the graph for BSFC, fuel consumption is approximately 0.316 lb/hp-hr (192 g/kWh) for a fuel rate of 21.3 U.S. gallons (80.8 L/h) when running at 1800 rpm. At the peak torque rating of 1200 rpm, the fuel rate is 0.304 lb/hp-hr (185 g/kWh) for a fuel consumption rate of 16.9 U.S. gallons (64 L/h). This same chart lists the various other important specifications and operating conditions for this engine rating, which can actually produce a maximum horsepower rating of 485 bhp (362 kW) at approximately 1650 rpm, for example, during a cruise-control mode.

In the OEM's sales data for BSFC in Figure 3–5, the U.S. gallons per hour, or fuel rate in liters per hour, is determined as follows. Let us consider the example listed with an engine speed of 1800 rpm and 475 hp (354 kW), where the BSFC is shown as 0.316 lb/hp-hr (192 g/kWh). If we multiply 475 × 0.316, we get 150.1 lb/hr of fuel consumed, which is listed in the chart as being equivalent to 21.3 U.S. gallons/hr (80.8 L/h). If we divide 150.1 lb by 21.3, the weight of the fuel per U.S. gallon is 7.046 lb (3.196 kg). Table 14–1 indicates that this fuel has an American Petroleum Institute (API) gravity rating of approximately 36. The API rating of the fuel determines its heat value and therefore the British thermal unit (Btu) of heat content available from a pound or a gallon.

Based on the foregoing information, we can use the following formula to determine BSFC:

$$BSFC = \frac{\text{pounds of fuel per hour}}{\text{bhp}}$$
$$= \frac{150.1}{475} = 0.316 \text{ lb/hp-hr (192 g/kWh)}$$

If manufacturers' information is not readily available, the BSFC could be determined by noting the fuel injection rate listed on the engine decal. If we were to assume that this was 249.36 mm^3 per stroke of the injector, we could multiply this times the number of engine power strokes over a 1-hour period. In the 3406E Cat engine described in Figure 3–5, we can calculate the total power strokes as follows:

$$\frac{1800 \times 6 \times 60}{2} = 324{,}000 \text{ power strokes per hour}$$

A cubic millimeter is 1/1000 of a cubic centimeter; therefore, each injector will deliver 0.24936 cm^3 per stroke (249.36 mm^3). To determine the fuel used, multiply 324,000 × 0.24936 cm^3, which equals 80,792 cm^3 or 80.792 L/h, or 21.34 U.S. gallons/hr. The data listed in Figure 3–5 have been rounded off to show 80.8 L/h (21.3 U.S. gallons/hr).

Refer again to the information for the 3406E engine in Figure 3–5. Notice that the BSFC actually decreases, or improves, as the engine speed is reduced by load down to its peak torque of 1200 rpm (fewer injection cycles) where it is shown to be 0.304 lb/hp-hr (185 g/kWh). Usually this occurs because the volumetric efficiency of the engine tends to increase with a reduction in engine speed due to the fact that the intake valves are open for a longer time at this lower speed and the intake manifold temperature is also usually lower.

Two-stroke-cycle engines tend to be a little more thirsty than their four-stroke-cycle counterparts. The two-stroke engine, however, is generally a faster accelerating and decelerating engine because of its power stroke every 360° (versus 720° in the four-stroke cycle). In addition, most two-stroke engines produce equal or greater horsepower from a smaller-displacement engine. Often, they tend to be more compact and lighter, but there are exceptions when we factor in the latest design of four-cycle models that use new lightweight materials and electronic controls. We already know what a typical electronic four-cycle engine (Caterpillar 3406E) will consume in fuel through reference to Figure 3–5. In Figure 3–11 we show the BSFC curves for a 430/500 hp series 60 with one model rated for 1800 rpm, and the other for 2100 rpm. Now let us consider the BSFC for an equivalent two-stroke engine such as the DDC 92 series with electronic controls and in the same basic horsepower rating category as the four-stroke series 60 and the 3406E from the BSFC chart in Figure 3–5.

Information for one model of two-stroke 8V-92TA DDEC engine rated at 500 bhp at 2100 rpm indicates a BSFC of approximately 0.378 lb/hp-hr (0.230 g/kWh). To be fair, this engine produces 475 bhp at a speed of approximately 1740 rpm, with a BSFC of approximately 0.344 lb/hp-hr (209 g/kWh). At the peak torque speed of 1200 rpm, the 92 series engine has a BSFC of 0.348 lb/hp-hr (212 g/kWh) versus 0.304 (185) for the 3406E and 0.303 (184) for the series 60. What this means is that if all engines were run at the speeds that produced this 470 to 475 bhp (351 to 354 kW) for 1 hour on a dynamometer under carefully controlled and equal conditions, we might expect each engine to consume the following amounts of fuel:

- Detroit Diesel 475 bhp 8V-92TA DDEC at 1740 rpm = 475 × 0.344 = 163.4 lb/hr (74.11 kg) divided by its API 36 gravity rating of approximately 7.046 lb/U.S. gallon; this engine will burn 23.19 U.S. gallons/hr (87.78 L).
- DDC series 60 at 470 bhp at 1800 rpm = 470 × 0.310 = 145.7 lb/hr (66.08 kg) divided by an API rating of 36 at 7046 lb/U.S. gallon; this engine will burn 20.67 U.S. gallons/hr (78.27 L).
- Caterpillar 3406E at 475 bhp at 1800 rpm = 475 × 0.316 = 150.1 lb/hr (68.08 kg) divided by an API 36 fuel rating of 7.046 lb/U.S. gallon; the fuel consumption rate is 21.3 U.S. gallons/hr (80.63 L).

As you can see, the two-stroke-cycle engine would burn 2.92 U.S. gallons/hr (11.05 L) more than its Detroit Diesel series 60 counterpart, and 1.89 U.S. gallons/hr (7.15 L) more than the 3406E Caterpillar engine.

SPECIAL NOTE   The BSFC curves shown at full-load conditions in OEM sales literature are *not* true indicators of fuel-tank mileage or fuel consumption over a 1-hour period, because the engine spends only a portion of time operating on the full-load curve. A significant amount of time is spent at various part-load conditions; therefore, full-load BSFC curves cannot be used to accurately reflect fuel-tank mileage or economy. Nevertheless, published figures can be used to approximate what the fuel economy might be under varying operating conditions—if the operator has a record of a typical daily operating cycle.

If an engine is being operated on a gaseous fuel such as liquid natural gas (LNG) or compressed natural gas (CNG), the BSFC is determined by the following formula:

$$BSFC = \frac{ft^3 \text{ of gas burned} \times \text{heating value} \times 60}{\text{length of test (min)} \times bhp}$$

For example, if an engine rated at 300 bhp (224 kW) used a gaseous fuel with a heating value of 1100 Btu/ft^3 (31 m^3), and consumed 400 ft^3 (11.3 m^3) of gas in 15 min, what would be its BSFC?

$$BSFC = \frac{400 \times 1100 \times 60}{15 \times 300} = \frac{26,400,000}{4500}$$
$$= 5867 \text{ Btu/bhp-hr}$$

Thermal Efficiency

Thermal efficiency (TE) represents the *heat efficiency* of an internal combustion engine. Diesel and gasoline engines can consume either a liquid or a gaseous fuel that is normally injected into the combustion chamber. The heat that is released as the fuel burns creates the high-pressure gases required to force the piston down the cylinder and rotate the engine crankshaft. The API fuel rating determines the Btu heat content contained within a given volume of fuel (see Table 14–1).

Let us determine the TE of the 3406E Caterpillar engine rated at 475 hp (354 kW) listed in Figure 3–5. We know from the information in the chart that at 1800 rpm this engine consumes 0.316 lb/hp-hr (192 g/kWh); therefore, if we multiply the horsepower by the fuel, we have 475 × 0.316 = 150.1 lb/hr (68 kg/h) of fuel consumed. We need to know the heat value of the fuel used, and we can determine this from Table 14–1; earlier we determined under the BSFC for this engine that it was in fact using an API fuel rated at 36. Each pound of this fuel contains a low heat value (LHV)—see Chapter 14 for a description—of approximately 18,410 Btu; therefore, if we multiply the Btu value by the total fuel consumed in 1 hour, which was 150.1 lb, the total heat released into the engine combustion chambers was 150.1 × 18,410 = 2,763,341 Btu/hr. Divide this total heat released by the available horsepower of 475 and we can determine that to produce each horsepower in this engine required 5817.56 Btu (2,763,341 ÷ 475 hp). Mathematical information indicates that a perfect engine requires 2545 Btu/hp-hr, so if we divide 2545 by 5817.56, which is what our engine used, we find that we have a thermal efficiency of 43.74%. If we were to use the high heat value (HHV) figure for this fuel, we would have a TE of 40.99%. In other words, for every dollar of fuel that we poured through this engine, we received approximately a LHV TE of 43.74 cents of a return at the flywheel.

All of the step-by-step procedures just described can be pulled into a simplified BTE (brake thermal efficiency) formula:

$$BTE = \frac{2545}{BSFC \times Btu/lb}$$

Using this formula, we can calculate the 3406E engine TE as follows using the LHV for this 36 API fuel of 18,414 Btu/lb:

$$BTE = \frac{2545}{0.316 \times 18,414} = \frac{2545}{5817.56} = 43.74\%$$

Keep in mind that these TE percentages have been determined under controlled test lab conditions as shown in Figure 3–5. In actual field operating conditions where changing speeds and loads are experienced along with ambient air temperatures and other factors, the TE may be lower. Notice in Figure 3–5 that for the 3406E engine the BSFC is quoted as being accurate within ±010 lb/hp-hr (±6 g/kWh), and the fuel rate is listed as being acceptable within ±5% of that shown. This means that the TE for the LHV could be as low as 40.99% less 5% (2.04%) = 38.95%, or for the HHV rating, 43.74% less 5% (2.187%) = 41.55%. These are impressive figures for TE. All of the latest electronically controlled DI (direct-injection) unit injector diesel engines from Caterpillar, Cummins, Detroit Diesel, Mack, and Volvo have thermal efficiencies in the same basic range. See the next section for more information on thermal efficiency.

Heat Losses

Let us continue to use the TE example for the 3406E Caterpillar engine rated at 475 hp (354 kW). If we assume that our TE was in fact 43.74%, it means that we lost 100 − 43.74 = 56.26% of the heat that was released into the cylinders. Where did this heat loss go? This heat loss can be related to four factors:

1. Cooling system (approximately 23 to 27%)
2. Exhaust system (approximately 23 to 27%)
3. Friction losses (approximately 7 to 9%)
4. Heat radiation (approximately 3%)

If we assume that we lost 23% to the cooling system, 23% to the exhaust (turbocharger driven), 7.26% to friction, and 3% to radiation, the total accounts for our heat losses of 56.26%. We calculated that this engine needed 5817.56 Btu to prouder 1 hp-hr and that 2545 Btu of this was needed to produce that 1 hp-hr. Therefore, by multiplying each of the system's heat loss per-

centages by 5817.56, we expended the heat injected into the engine as follows:

Cooling   = 5817.56 × 0.23   = 1338 Btu
Exhaust   = 5817.56 × 0.23   = 1338 Btu
Friction   = 5817.56 × 0.0726 = 422.35 Btu
Radiation = 5817.56 × 0.03   = 174.52 Btu
            1 horsepower/hr = 2545 Btu
            Total Btu of heat = 5817.87 Btu

The heat losses chosen for the 3406E Cat engine are examples only and are not specific to this engine. Nevertheless, they can be considered as fairly typical for high-speed heavy-duty electronically controlled unit injector diesel engines in use today.

Engine Speed Droop

All diesel engines use mechanical (weights versus a spring) or electronic (magnetic pickup) governors to control the idle and maximum speeds, or all speed ranges when desired. Unless the engine is equipped with an *isochronous* or *zero-droop* governor, the engine speed is always lower when operating under load than when it is running with no load. This speed difference is described in Chapter 16. The difference between these two operating speed conditions commonly referred to as *governor droop*, can be determined as follows:

$$\frac{speed}{droop} = \frac{rpm\ at\ MNL\ speed - rpm\ at\ MFL\ speed}{rpm\ at\ MFL\ speed}$$

NOTE   MNL = maximum no-load speed, often referred to as *high idle*; MFL = maximum full-load speed, often referred to as *rated*.

Joule's Equivalent

A common measure for determining the amount of work available from an engine based on its fuel heat value in Btu is Joule's equivalent, which states that 1 Btu is capable of releasing the equivalent of 778 ft-lb of work, or 1 ft-lb = 0.001285 Btu. Therefore, the horsepower-hour (kWh) is the measure of 1 hp for a 1-hr period. Since we know that the amount of work required to produce a horsepower is equal to 550 lb-ft/sec, 33,000 ft-lb/min, or 1,980,000 ft-lb/hr, we can determine that a perfect engine with no heat losses would require 2545 Btu/hr to produce 1 hp by using the following formula:

$$1\ hp/hr = \frac{1,980,000}{778} = 2545\ Btu$$

Gasoline versus Diesel Engines

The thermal efficiency, or heat efficiency, of a diesel engine is superior to that of the spark-ignited gasoline (Otto cycle) engine. As we know from information discussed earlier in this chapter, the diesel engine employs compression ratios much higher than those of a gasoline engine. This is necessary to create a high enough cylinder air temperature for the injected diesel fuel to vaporize and start to burn. The much higher combustion pressures and temperatures allow a greater expansion rate and more energy to be extracted from the fuel. Tremendous improvements have occurred in gasoline spark-ignited engines, particularly in the 1990s when fuel consumption improvements due to changes in engine component design, combustion improvements, and electronic control of distributorless ignition and fuel injection systems have resulted in thermal efficiencies in the area of 32 to 35%, and as high as 39%. Gasoline engines tend to return better fuel economy when held at a steady speed, such as during highway driving, but they suffer in city-driving cycles because of the intake manifold air-throttling effect and pumping losses that occur at lower speeds.

Diesel engines, on the other hand, do not suffer from a throttled air supply and operate with a stratified air charge in the cylinder under all operating conditions. The net result of the unthrottled air in the diesel engine is that at idle rpm and light loads, the air/fuel ratio in the cylinder is very lean (90:1 to 120:1). This excess air supply lowers the average specific heat of the cylinder gases, which in turn increases the indicated work obtained from a given amount of fuel.

To comply with EPA exhaust emissions standards, automotive gasoline engines have to operate close to a *stoichiometric* air/fuel ratio, which is approximately 14:1. In other words, about 14 kg of air is required to completely combust 1 kg of fuel. Another way to look at this is that approximately 10,000 L of air is required to burn 1 L of gasoline. Even under full-load operating conditions the diesel engine operates with an excess air factor of at least 10 to 20%, which usually results in air/fuel ratios in the region 20:1 to 25:1. To meet exhaust emissions standards the gasoline engine relies on an exhaust-gas oxygen sensor to constantly monitor the "richness" or "leanness" of the exhaust gases after combustion. This oxygen sensor signal sends update information continuously to the on-board ECM (electronic control module) to allow operation in what is commonly known as a *closed-loop* operating mode. Failure of the oxygen sensor results in the engine falling back into an *open-loop* mode (no signal to the ECM), and the ECM automatically resorts to a "limp-home" condition that allows the engine to run but at a reduced performance. Because of their excess air factor of operation, most diesel engines at this time do not need an exhaust-gas oxygen sensor, or a catalytic converter, although some light- and midrange mechanically controlled truck engines are equipped with converters (see the section "Exhaust Emissions Limits" in Chapter 4, Table 4–2).

Another advantage that the diesel engine enjoys over its gasoline counterpart is that the diesel fuel contains about 11% more Btu per unit volume than that in gasoline. Therefore, the diesel engine would have a better return per dollar spent on fuel.

Mechanical Efficiency

The mechanical efficiency (ME) of an internal combustion engine is determined by comparing the actual usable hp (bhp) to the cylinder hp (ihp). The higher the mechanical efficiency of the engine, the lower the fuel consumption. The ME of an engine can be determined from the following formula:

$$ME = \frac{bhp}{ihp}$$

If an engine produced 280 bhp with an ihp of 350, its ME would be

$$\frac{bhp}{ihp} = \frac{280}{350} = 80\%$$

Volumetric Efficiency

The power that can be extracted from an internal combustion piston engine is related to the amount of air that can be consumed or fed into the engine cylinders and retained. The higher the percentage of air retained, the larger the quantity of fuel that can be injected and burned to completion.

VE (volumetric efficiency) is the weight of air retained in the engine cylinder at the start of the compression stroke. In naturally aspirated (NA) nonturbocharged or blower-equipped engines that rely on atmospheric air pressure to force its way into the cylinder, the resistance to airflow caused by the intake ducting (such as the diameter, number of bends, length, and air-cleaner restriction) and intake manifold design lower the VE. The VE of an NA engine is therefore always less than atmospheric pressure (14.7 psi or 101.35 kPa) at sea level. Most NA engines have a VE in the region of 85 to 90% of atmospheric pressure, or between 12.49 and 13.23 psi (86.1 to 91.2 kPa).

When a turbocharger or gear-driven blower is added to a two- or four-stroke-cycle engine, the VE can be greater than atmospheric pressure (that is, 100%).

The critical factor in determining the cylinder air pressure before the start of the compression stroke is the timing of the intake valve closing on a four-stroke-cycle engine or the liner port and exhaust valve closing on a two-stroke-cycle Detroit Diesel engine. As an example refer to Figure 3–5, which lists operating conditions for Caterpillar's 3406E engine. Note that at 1800 rpm under full load this engine has an intake manifold pressure of 51.3 in. Hg. This is equivalent to 25.2 psi (173.7 kPa) and is supplied by the exhaust gas-driven turbocharger on this four-cycle engine. As the engine speed is reduced under load, note that the turbocharger boost pressure at the peak torque point of 1200 rpm reduces to 41.7 in. Hg (20.5 psi or 141.2 kPa). The reason behind this is that with a slower-running engine, the exhaust-gas flow rate has decreased to 1767 cubic feet per minute (cfm), or 50 cubic meters per minute (cm^3/min), from 2547 cfm (or 72 cm^3/min) at 1800 rpm. Therefore, although the engine cylinder receives air at a pressure well above atmospheric, the valve timing is the final determining factor of what the trapped cylinder air pressure will be. On turbocharged engines, this can range anywhere between 130 and 200% higher than atmospheric.

People often talk about an engine as being "supercharged" and believe that as soon as an engine is fitted with a turbocharger or gear-driven blower that it automatically becomes so. Keep in mind that in technical classifications the intake valve timing on a four-cycle engine and the port and exhaust valve timing on a two-cycle model determine if the engine is actually supercharged. If the cylinder air pressure at the start of the compression stroke is higher than atmospheric, the engine is basically supercharged. The degree of supercharging, however, is directly related to the actual cylinder air pressure charge.

Engine Displacement and Compression Ratio

Although there are many electronically controlled unit injector diesel engines on the market today with similar horsepower (kW) ratings, the torque developed by some of these engines is higher or lower than that of others in some instances. The displacement of the engine cylinders and the compression ratio are factors that can affect the developed torque at a given engine speed.

Displacement

The displacement of an engine can be determined from OEM sales or service literature. In the absence of this information, a cylinder's displacement can be determined by the following formulas. To determine the cubic inch or cubic centimeter displacement of a cylinder,

we need to know the bore and stroke dimensions. For example, let us assume that an engine has a bore and stroke of 5.12 × 6.30 in. (130 × 160 mm). The first thing we need to do is compute the area of the piston crown from the known bore size of 5.12 in. (130 mm). Use this formula: area = πR^2, where $\pi = 3.1416$ and R is the radius of the bore squared. In our example, area = 3.1416 × 2.56 × 2.56 = 20.58 in^2 (132.83 cm^2). Now if we multiply the area of the piston by the stroke, we can determine the cylinder volume or displacement: 20.58 × 6.30 in. = 129.7 in^3 (2125.39 cm^3, or 2.125 L).

If the engine were a six-cylinder model, we would have an engine displacement of 6 × 129.7 = 778 in^3 (12,752 cm^3, or 12.7 L). Using the same formula for the 3406E engine in Figure 3–5, we would find a piston crown area of 22.9 in^2 (148 cm^2) multiplied by a stroke of 6.5 in. (165 mm) for a cylinder displacement of 148.85 in^3 (2349.2 cm^3). Since it is a six-cylinder engine, the total engine displacement is 893.1 in^3 (14.6 L).

To determine the *airflow requirements* of an engine, we need to be able to calculate the approximate volume of air required per minute in either cubic feet per minute (cfm), or cubic meters per minute (m^3/min) in the metric system of measurement. This can be determined by knowing the volume swept by all the pistons during one stroke for each cycle, which can be determined simply by knowing the number of cylinders times the area of the piston crown in square feet (square meters) times the stroke in feet (meters) times the number of cycles per cylinder per minute:

$$\text{engine displacement per minute} = N \times A \times S \times n \text{ (cfm)}$$

where N = number of cylinders
  A = piston area, in ft^2 (m^2)
  S = stroke, in ft (m)
  n = cycles per min for one cylinder
    = rpm for two-cycle engines
    = rpm/2 for four-cycle engines

Let us assume that we want to calculate the airflow requirements for the 3406E engine discussed in Figure 3–5, which is a six-cylinder four-stroke-cycle engine with a bore of 5.4 in. (137 mm), a stroke of 6.5 in. (165 mm), and horsepower (kW) rated at 1800 rpm:

engine displacement per minute

$$= \frac{6 \times \pi}{4 \times 0.45^2 \times 0.541} \times \frac{1800}{2}$$
$$= 6 \times 0.7854 \times 0.202 \times 0.541 \times 900 = 464 \text{ cfm}$$

This airflow requirement is for a nonturbocharged engine model. Once we turbocharge the engine and add an air-to-air aftercooler system and electronic fuel injection controls to meet the mandated limits for exhaust emissions, the engine airflow requirement demands generally increase by turbocharger boost pressure ratios on the order of 2:1 and 3:1 in high-speed high-output models. In the case of the 3406E engine, note in Figure 3–5 that the specification for intake airflow calls for 1143 cfm (32.4 m³/min) at 1800 rpm. Note also that the exhaust gas flow rate at 1800 rpm with the engine producing 475 bhp (354 kW) is quoted as 2547 cfm (72 m³/min). Therefore, the 3406E engine actually requires an airflow rate that is 1143 cfm divided by 464 cfm (from the simplified formula calculation), which yields a ratio difference for this turbocharged and aftercooled engine that is 2.463 times greater than that for a naturally aspirated engine of the same displacement.

An alternative method to determine the airflow requirements is to use this formula:

$$\frac{\text{cubic inch displacement} \times \text{rpm}}{3456}$$
$$\times \text{volumetric efficiency} = \text{cfm}$$

Inserting the same data for the 3406E engine results in the following:

$$\frac{893 \times 1800}{3456} = 465 \text{ cfm} \times \text{VE} = \text{demand flow air}$$

We know from the specification sheet that this engine requires 2.46 times the air that a naturally aspirated model would require. In Chapter 13 we discuss the airflow requirements for two- and four-stroke-cycle engines in more detail.

Compression Ratio

Compression ratio (CR) is used to compare the difference in cylinder volume when the piston is at BDC and when the piston is at TDC. Figure 3–12 is a CR comparison of a low-compression gas engine and a diesel engine. Most gasoline engines operate with CR values between 8:1 and 10.5:1, whereas diesel engines operate with much higher CR values, averaging between 14:1 and 17.5:1 on most current high-speed heavy-duty electronically controlled models of the DI (direct-injection) design. However, a number of IDI (indirect-injection) models run CRs as high as 23:1. Figure 3–12 indicates that the volume of air in the cylinder for the gasoline engine has been compressed to one-sixth its volume with the piston at TDC; in the diesel example, the volume has been reduced to one-sixteenth its volume with the piston at TDC.

The higher CR in diesel engines is one of the reasons why diesel engines are more thermally efficient than their gasoline counterparts. Higher CR results in greater expansion of the gases in the cylinder after combustion; therefore, a higher percentage of fuel energy is converted into useful work. Since a diesel engine does not use a spark plug for ignition of the fuel charge, the high CR raises the trapped cylinder air to a temperature that is above the self-ignition point of the injected diesel fuel. Typical CRs are 15.0:1 for the Detroit Diesel series 50 8.5 L and series 60 12.7 L (16:1 for the series 60 11.1 L model); 16.2:1 for the Cummins N14, and 16.25:1 for the 3406E Caterpillar model. Since we know that the engine displacement for the 12.7 L series 60 is 778 in³/6 = 129 in³ (2114 cm³) divided by the CR of 15.0:1, the clearance volume (CV) between the piston crown and the underside of the cylinder head at TDC would be 129 divided by 15 = 8.6 in³ (141 cm³). The se-

FIGURE 3–12 This example of how CR (compression ratio) is estimated shows that a gasoline engine operates with a much lower CR than a diesel engine.

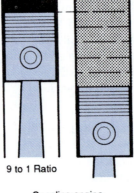

9 to 1 Ratio

Gasoline engine

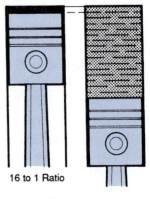

16 to 1 Ratio

Diesel engine

ries 60 11.1 L model CV is 7 in³ (115.5 cm³). For the N14, with a displacement of 855 in³ (14 L), the CV is 8.79 in³ (144 cm³). The 3406E, with a displacement of 893 in³ (14.6 L) would have a CV of 9.16 in³ (150.2 cm³).

Keep in mind that both the engine torque and the horsepower of an engine are related to engine displacement, BMEP, and speed. Thus the different torque figures that are listed on OEM sales sheets for engines of the same speed and horsepower settings are controlled by the variables of engine displacement, BMEP, valve timing, injector timing, turbocharger boost, air inlet temperature, air swirl, fuel injection spray-in pressure, distribution, and so on.

Compression Temperature

Engine compression ratio has a bearing on the final temperature of the cylinder air charge before injection of fuel. The temperature of the compressed air (boost) flowing from the turbocharger on high-speed heavy-duty engines at full-load operating conditions is usually in the region of 300°F (149°C). This air temperature drastically lowers the denseness of the air charge and affects the power output of the engine and its ability to meet mandated exhaust emissions standards. Therefore, an air-to-air aftercooler (ATAAC) is widely used on heavy-duty highway trucks; and industrial, off-highway, and marine engines employ jacket water aftercooling (JWAC) systems. These systems are described in Chapters 12 and 13. The ATAAC system lowers the turbo boost air to between 100 and 110°F (38 and 43°C). Typical high-speed heavy-duty diesel engines generate compression pressures in the range 450 to 500 psi (3103 to 3792 kPa), which create cylinder air temperatures in the region of 900 to 1000°F (482 to 538°C).

The relationship of temperature and pressure during the compression cycle can be considered to be in the region of about 2:1 and 3:1; the figure can be higher or lower depending on the engine compression ratio, air turbulence created during the upward movement of the piston, and of course the turbocharger boost ratio and the temperature of the air entering and being trapped within the cylinder. Final pressures and temperatures created during the power stroke are relative to the compression pressures and the quantity of fuel injected based on the load/speed of the engine. Engines operating with boost pressure ratios in the region of 3:1 and ATAAC experience BMEPs between 180 and 295 psi (1241 to 2034 kPa) on most four-stroke-cycle engines for rated speed and peak torque rpm outputs, respectively. Because of their double power stroke, two-cycle engines have BMEP that are normally about 100 psi (690 kPa) lower than that of an equivalent four-stroke model. Keep in mind, however, from the infor-

mation shown in Figure 3–5, that peak cylinder pressures experienced in current high-speed heavy-duty engines can be between 1800 and 2300 psi (12,411 to 15,856 kPa).

HEATING VALUE EQUIVALENTS

Typical heat value equivalents and their metric units for some of the more commonly used fuels are listed next.

Fuel	Imperial units	Metric units
Diesel	162,000 Btu/gallon	0.0377 GJ/L
Gasoline	146,000 Btu/gallon	0.0340 GJ/L
Propane	110,000 Btu/gallon	0.0255 GJ/L
	21,570 Btu/lb	0.0515 GJ/kg
Natural gas	1000 Btu/ft³	0.0372 GJ/m³
Coal	8500 to 15,000 Btu/lb	20 to 35 GJ/tonne
Electricity	3412 Btu/kWh	0.0036 GJ/kWh

GJ represents gigajoules, used to describe the metric quantity in billions (giga).

These heat values in Btu are average readings only and will vary in actual heat content of the gas or crude oil used. In the case of diesel fuel, refer to Table 14–1, which shows Btu heat values based on the fuels' API rating.

ISO STANDARDS

Many manufactured products now contain a decal indicating that the component or item has been manufactured to ISO 9000 standards. This rating system is the core quality gauge for frontline parts makers to meet a set of industry-specific sets of standards. ISO 9000 means global quality standards. Although *ISO* stands for International Standardization Organization, the term is used as a variant of the Greek word *isos*, meaning equal, and is pronounced *ice-oh*. The choice of the number 9000 was arbitrary. The North American manufacturing industry does not want variations in supplier standards within a country or between countries; rather, the industry demands consistency of an agreed-on standard at all levels. Since most ISO standards will be common, suppliers and OEMs will save time and money.

We have discussed the ISO 9000 standards, but there are others. The ISO standards can be grouped into the following categories:

- ISO 9000: an overview and introduction to the other standards, including definitions of terms and concepts related to quality that are used in the other standards

- ISO 9001: comprehensive general standard for quality assurance in product design, development, manufacturing, installation, and servicing
- ISO 9002: standards that focus on manufacturing and installation of products
- ISO 9003: standards that cover final inspection and testing
- ISO 9004: guidelines for managing a quality control system; more details on managing the quality systems that are called for in the other standards; intended for use in auditing quality systems

SUMMARY

The information provided within this chapter gives you a solid foundation from which to discuss the detailed engineering operating concepts of a diesel engine. These concepts will help you to compare various types and models of engines, and to see how the design features of a specific engine can be altered to improve its overall performance in a given application.

SELF-TEST QUESTIONS

1. Tech A says that HP can be multiplied by directing it through a transmission. Tech B disagrees and says that only torque can be multiplied. Who is correct?
2. The first law of thermodynamics states that energy can be neither created nor destroyed. True or False?
3. Force can be defined as a push or a pull on an object. True or False?
4. Technician A says that the term *thermal efficiency* is an expression of the mechanical efficiency of the engine, whereas technician B says that it is an indicator of the heat efficiency of the engine. Who is correct?
5. Thermal efficiency of a diesel truck engine generally runs between
   a. 24 and 28%
   b. 30 and 34%
   c. 34 and 38%
   d. 38 and 42%
6. Typical fuel performance figures for current high-speed heavy-duty diesel engines average between
   a. 0.380 and 0.395 lb/bhp-hr (231 to 240 g/kWh)
   b. 0.350 and .0370 lb/bhp-hr (213 to 225 g/kWh)
   c. 0.315 and 0.340 lb/bhp-hr (192 to 207 g/kWh)
   d. 0.300 and 0.315 lb/bhp-hr (183 to 192 g/kWh)
7. One gallon of U.S. fuel is equal to
   a. 4.256 L
   b. 3.900 L
   c. 3.785 L
   d. 3.600 L
8. True or False: Btu means British thermal unit.
9. How many Btu are required to produce 1 hp in a perfect engine over a 1-hr period?
   a. 2040
   b. 2250
   c. 2415
   d. 2545
10. Technician A says that the term *work* is computed by multiplying the force times the distance. Technician B disagrees. Who is correct?
11. Technician A says that horsepower keeps the piston moving and is a measure of how fast work can be done by the engine. Technician B says that torque is the ability to move a load or do work. Who is correct?
12. Horsepower is accepted as being a given amount of work developed in a given period. In English-speaking countries this is generally accepted as being equal to
    a. 28,000 ft-lb/min
    b. 33,000 ft-lb/min
    c. 35,550 ft-lb/min
    d. 37,300 ft-lb/min
13. Torque is a twisting and turning force that is developed at the
    a. piston
    b. connecting rod
    c. crankshaft
    d. flywheel
14. True or False: A constant-horsepower engine maintains a steady horsepower over a wider speed band than does a conventional diesel engine.
15. Technician A says that all diesel truck engines develop their greatest torque value at about 65% of their rated speed under full loads, for example, 1200 rpm versus 1950 rpm. Technician B says that the greatest torque is developed at the rated speed and horsepower setting, for example, 1950 rpm and 400 hp. Which technician is correct?
16. Technician A says that torque is what pulls a truck up a hill with a decrease in speed. Technician B says that horsepower is what pulls the truck up the hill as the engine and road speed drop off. Who is correct?
17. Technician A says that a high-torque-rise diesel engine will allow fewer transmission shifts to be made over a conventional diesel engine–equipped truck. Technician B says that there is no difference as long as the engine speed is kept at the rated value. Who is correct?
18. Technician A says that torque in the metric system is expressed in newton-meters (N · m), whereas technician B says that it is expressed in kilopascals (kPa). Who is correct?
19. Horsepower is expressed in kilowatts in the metric system of measurement, with 1 kilowatt equal to 1000 watts. Technician A says that 1 hp is higher in value than 1 kW. Technician B says that 1 hp is less than 1 kW. Is technician A or technician B correct?
20. A horsepower is equivalent to
    a. 0.674 kW
    b. 0.746 kW
    c. 0.940 kW
    d. 1.341 kW

21. Technician A says that brake mean effective pressure (BMEP) is the average pressure developed on the piston crown during the power stroke, whereas technician B says that it is the maximum pressure developed when the injected diesel fuel ignites. Who is correct?

22. Many heavy-duty highway-truck diesel engines use aftercooling to increase the horsepower of the engine. Technician A says that aftercooling reduces the exhaust heat loss of the engine and allows more heat for power. Technician B says that aftercooling lowers the temperature of the pressurized air from the turbocharger so that a denser charge is supplied to the engine cylinders, thereby producing more power. Is technician A or technician B correct?

23. Technician A says that the exhaust temperatures developed at the full-load-rated rpm speed of an engine will be lower than that produced at the peak torque engine speed. Technician B disagrees. Who is correct?

24. Technician A says that the exhaust temperatures on a two-stroke-cycle engine tend to be slightly higher than those produced on an equivalent-horsepower four-stroke-cycle engine at rated rpm. Technician B says that he has this reversed; exhaust temperatures are cooler on the two-stroke-cycle engine. Who is correct?

25. To convert cubic inches to cubic centimeters, multiply by
    a. 6.895
    b. 12.7
    c. 16.387
    d. 22.32

26. A Caterpillar 3176 model engine has a displacement per cylinder of 1.7 L. How many in^3 is this? Give the engine's total displacement in in^3 and L.

27. How many cubic centimeters make 1 L?

28. How many millimeters make 1 in.?

29. How many cubic inches make 1 L?

30. Determine the total in^3 displacement of a six-cylinder engine with a bore of 5.5 in. (139.7 mm) and a stroke of 6 in. (152 mm); then convert this answer to cm^3 and L.

31. One micron is equal to one millionth of a meter. This can be expressed in decimal form as
    a. 0.03937 in.
    b. 0.003937 in.
    c. 0.0003937 in.
    d. 0.00003937 in.

32. To convert engine torque from lb-ft to its metric equivalent, by what should you multiply?

33. Describe briefly the definition of a supercharged engine.

34. Typical full-load-rated horsepower air temperature leaving the outlet side of the turbocharger on high-speed diesel engines is approximately

    a. 65.5°C (150°F)
    b. 93°C (200°F)
    c. 149°C (300°F)
    d. 204°C (400°F)

35. True or False: VE (volumetric efficiency) refers to the weight of air contained in the cylinder with the piston at BDC stopped versus what it would be at BDC running.

36. True or False: Ihp (indicated horsepower) refers to usable power at either the engine crankshaft or flywheel.

37. Technician A states that 1 hp is considered equal to 33,000 lb-ft (44,741 N · m) of work per minute. Technician B states that it is equivalent to 550 lb-ft (746 N · m) of work per second. Is only one technician correct or are both correct?

38. One Btu (kJ/kg) of released heat within a combustion chamber is capable of producing the following amount of mechanical work:
    a. 710 ft-lb (963 N · m)
    b. 758 ft-lb (1028 N · m)
    c. 778 ft-lb (1055 N · m)
    d. 876 ft-lb (1188 N · m)

39. Technician A states that current high-speed DI diesel engines develop peak firing pressures between 1200 and 1400 psi (6895 to 8274 kPa). Technician B says that this is too low and that peak pressures run between 1800 and 2300 psi (12,411 to 15,858 kPa). Who is correct?

40. Determine the following information for a six-cylinder four-stroke-cycle engine running at 1800 rpm:
    a. ihp; then convert it into kW; bore of 5.5 in. (140 mm) and a stroke of 6 in. (152 mm); a BMEP of 237 psi (1634 kPa)
    b. piston speed in feet/minute (m/min); then convert it to mph and km/h
    c. torque in lb-ft; then into N · m
    d. convert BMEP to its metric equivalent of kPa
    e. thermal efficiency using a fuel consumption rate of 0.316 lb/bhp-hr (g/kWh) with a calorific value of 19,100 Btu/lb (kJ/kW)

41. Determine the BMEP of a 365-bhp (272-kW) four-stroke-cycle engine using the formula

$$BMEP = \frac{792,000 \times bhp}{D \times N}$$

where D is the total piston displacement of the engine in in^3 and/or cm^3. Employ the displacement from your answer in question 40; $N = 2100$ rpm.

42. If an engine develops a torque of 1650 lb-ft (2237 N · m) at 1200 rpm, what horsepower (kW) would it produce?

43. If an engine develops 470 bhp (351 kW) at 1800 rpm, what torque would it produce in lb-ft and N · m?

4 Combustion Systems

Overview

In this chapter we introduce and describe the fundamentals of internal combustion for diesel engines. As a result of contemporary environmental concerns, and the stringently mandated Environmental Protection Agency (EPA) exhaust emissions limits, combustion systems have undergone major changes to improve their efficiency and also to comply with these EPA regulations. Such technological advances include new turbochargers, carefully contoured inlet and exhaust manifolds, piston crown design changes, overhead camshaft engines with new cam lobe profiles, very-high-pressure fuel injection, two-stage fuel injection in some engines, electronic controls and sensors, exhaust gas recirculation, particulate traps and catalytic-type converters, very low diesel fuel sulfur content, and the use of alternative fuel sources. We discuss the characteristics of air and fuel, and the engine combustion processes. The information and knowledge gained in this chapter will be of help when troubleshooting and diagnosing complaints of poor engine operation and performance faults. By understanding the combustion phases, unusual exhaust smoke color at the exhaust stack can often be traced to poor combustion within one or more engine cylinders, whether the engine is equipped with mechanical or electronic controlled fuel injection.

ASE CERTIFICATION

Within the various ASE medium/heavy truck tests, diesel engines, tasks lists, and the T2 test, exhaust emissions problems are generally related to some phase of fuel combustion within the engine. Content areas related to combustion can be found in the following subsections of this ASE preparation guide.

A. General Engine Diagnosis

B. Cylinder Head and Valve Train Diagnosis and Repair

E. Air Induction and Exhaust Systems, Diagnosis, and Repair

F. Fuel System Diagnosis and Repair

Each of these content area tasks lists is described in Chapter 1, and then later detailed in their respective chapters (see Chapters 9, 10, 13, and 18 through 25).

THE COMBUSTION PROCESS

The combustion phase of engine operation is the period during which the high-pressure diesel fuel is injected into the compressed air mass in the cylinder, then ignited to produce a high temperature and high-pressure rise in the combustion chamber. The pressure created by the expanding gases forces the piston down the cylinder. The chemical energy released from the burning diesel fuel and air mixture is then converted to mechanical energy through the piston, connecting rod, and crankshaft to power the flywheel.

TYPES OF COMBUSTION CHAMBERS

The vintage of a diesel engine and its OEM determine the type of combustion chamber used. The types of combustion chambers are of three main designs:

1. Precombustion chamber (PC)
2. Turbulence or energy cell
3. Direct injection (DI) used in all current high-speed, heavy-duty diesel engines.

For many years mechanical fuel-injected and governed engines employed either the precombustion or turbulence chamber design. Both of these systems allowed use of an electrically heated glow plug to facilitate ease of starting, particularly in cold-weather operation. Heavy-duty diesel engines with both types of systems employed pistons that had a lower compression ratio than that used in direct-injection models. They also used lower injection pressures than the DI models. Both the PC and turbulence chamber models due to their design features were less reliant on higher-grade fuels and would emit lower exhaust emissions when using these lower-grade fuels than would a DI engine model. However, they were harder to start than a higher-compression-ratio DI engine, and if one or more glow plugs were faulty, both hard starting and rough combustion would be evident until the engine reached normal operating temperature. In addition, the PC and turbulence chamber engines tended to consume between 10 and 15% more fuel than the DI model engine. In automotive diesel engines, due to the need for power output and performance somewhat similar to a gasoline engine, high compression ratios of between 21 and 23:1 were required; therefore, the PC chamber model was chosen initially due to its quieter operation; however, many modern automotive diesel engines now employ the DI design concept, with some models also employing a glow plug simply to facilitate quick and rapid starts in cold weather along with smoother operation. One example using this DI and glow plug design concept is the International 7.3 L/444 in³ hydraulically actuated electronic unit injector (HEUI) engine model used in both Ford and International truck products.

Precombustion Chambers

The precombustion chamber (Figure 4–1) differs from the energy cell in that fuel is injected into the prechamber rather than the main chamber as in the case of the energy cell. The precombustion chamber will contain approximately 20 to 35% of the combustion chamber's total top dead center (TDC) volume. Prechambers are connected to the main chamber by a direct passageway.

Precombustion chambers are used in some modern diesel engines and exhibit advantages such as acceptable exhaust emissions and adaptability to various grades of fuel; they also require less atomization of injected fuel. Disadvantages include hard starting and less efficiency. Most prechamber engines are equipped with a cylinder-type glow plug for easier starting.

Components

1. A single- or two-piece chamber either screwed into the cylinder head or held in place by the injection nozzle

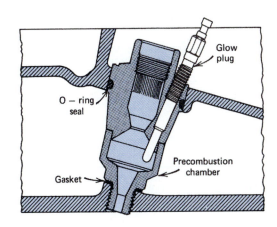

FIGURE 4–1 Precombustion chamber screwed into the cylinder head along with an electrically heated glow plug to facilitate combustion. (Courtesy of Caterpillar, Inc.)

2. A piston head designed with a concave section
3. In many cases a glow plug that is threaded into the nozzle body or holder and protrudes into the prechamber

Precombustion Chamber Operation

As the piston reaches the top of its compression stroke, heated air is trapped in the main chamber and in the prechamber. At this point fuel is injected into the precombustion chamber. Although the mixture (fuel and air) in the prechamber is excessively rich at the point of injection, burning begins and the rapidly expanding fuel and air rush through the connecting passageway into the main chamber, where burning is completed. As can be seen, the fuel and air mixture rushing from the prechamber into the main chamber causes a high degree of turbulence and creates a mixture of air and fuel that will burn evenly and cleanly.

Type of Injection Nozzle or Injector Used

Precombustion chamber engines use a single- or double-hole nozzle, since atomization requirements are not great. Nozzle opening pressure also can be greatly reduced.

Turbulence Chambers

A turbulence chamber (Figure 4–2) is very similar to a precombustion chamber in that it is a separate, smaller chamber connected to the main chamber. It differs in that it usually contains approximately 50 to 75% of the TDC cylinder volume and is connected to the main chamber with a passageway that may run at right angles to the main chamber.

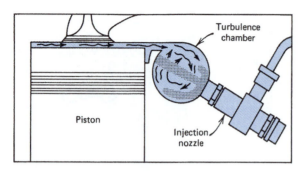

FIGURE 4–2 *Basic concept of a turbulence chamber design.*

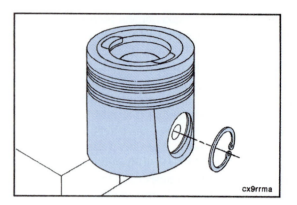

FIGURE 4–3 *In-bowl combustion chamber formed by the shape of the piston crown. Often referred to as the MAN design, as it was perfected by this engine company. This piston design is more popular in both European and Japanese medium/heavy diesel engines. North American engines favor the Mexican hat piston crown design shown in Chapter 8. (Courtesy of Cummins Engine Company, Inc.)*

Components

1.   Turbulence chambers may be an integral part of the cylinder head or, like the precombustion chamber, may be a separate part that is installed into the cylinder head.

2.   They usually have flat-top pistons, since the fuel and air mixture does not strike the piston at a right angle when it leaves the chamber. In most cases the passageway is designed so that the fuel and air mixture will enter the chamber parallel to the top of the piston or at a 15 to 20° angle.

3.   Engines with this type of turbulence chamber may use a cylinder glow plug for ease in starting.

Turbulence Chamber Operation

As the piston reaches the top of its compression stroke, air is trapped in the turbulence chamber and the main combustion chamber. Fuel is injected into the turbulence chamber, where burning occurs immediately, and the resulting expansion forces the air and fuel mixture into the main chamber with considerable force and speed. Because of the design of the passageway connecting the chamber with the main combustion chamber, the fuel and air mixture enters the main chamber at an angle and creates a high degree of turbulence in the main chamber. This turbulence aids in mixing the fuel with the air, enabling complete combustion.

Type of Injection Nozzle or Injector Used

A single- or double-hole nozzle is used in most turbulence chamber engines. This chamber is somewhat similar in operation to the precombustion chamber. A high degree of atomization is not required. Nozzle opening pressure is usually in the range 1800 to 2000 psi (127 to 141 kg/cm^2).

Direct Injection

Although the IDI design was used for many years in some diesel engines, the DI system is dominant in today's heavy-duty high-speed diesel engines. In the DI system the fuel is injected directly into an open combustion chamber formed by the shape of the piston crown or bowl and the underside of the cylinder head fire deck. In the typical DI system shown in Chapter 2 (Figures 2–1a and 2–2), the injection nozzle is located in the cylinder head and extends directly into the engine cylinder. Note that the piston crown is shaped in such a manner that, in effect, it will form the combustion chamber when the piston approaches TDC and fuel is injected.

Two main piston crown designs are used today in DI diesel engines:

1.   The Mexican hat–shaped piston shown in Figure 2–1 is the basic shape used by Detroit Diesel, Caterpillar, Cummins, and Mack, with minor variations among them.

2.   The in-bowl piston shape (Figure 4–3) is often referred to as the MAN system, since much research was undertaken by this German engine company in perfecting this shape. Others who use this type of piston crown shape in their light- and medium-duty engines include Perkins, Caterpillar, Cummins, and Detroit Diesel in their 8.2 L four-stroke-cycle engines.

Piston-Induced Swirl or Squish

As the intake valve closes and the piston starts upward on its compression stroke, the design on the piston—the Mexican hat—forces the trapped air to rotate or swirl rapidly by the time the piston reaches the end of its compression stroke. Highly atomized fuel is then injected into the combustion chamber containing the rapidly swirling heated air, and combustion occurs immediately.

Type of Injection Nozzle or Injection Used

A multihole injection combustion chamber design in Figure 2–1a is needed to distribute the fuel throughout the cylinder and to atomize it. Nozzle opening pressures are usually in the average range 2500 to 4000 psi (176 to 281 kg/cm^2). Electronic engines currently use unit injectors that open between 5000 and 5500 psi.

COMBUSTION DYNAMICS

Pressure–Volume Curve

Figure 4–4 will help you understand the processes that occur within the engine cylinder and combustion chamber. The figure illustrates what actually transpires during the two most important strokes in a four-stroke-cycle diesel engine. The pressure–volume (PV) diagram represents the piston from a position corresponding to 90° BTDC (before top dead center) as it moves up the cylinder on its compression stroke to 90° ATDC (after TDC) on its power stroke. The vertical lines in the diagram represent cylinder pressure, which can vary substantially between makes and models of engines.

Typical cylinder pressures within the cylinder and combustion chamber at the start of injection would be approximately 550 to 600 psi (3793 to 4137 kPa) and the compressed air would be anywhere between 900 and 1100°F (482 to 593°C). Both the pressures and temperatures can, of course, vary with different compression ratios and engine design characteristics. Once the

diesel fuel has been injected and starts to burn, peak cylinder pressures can run between 1800 and 2300 psi (12,411 to 15,859 kPa), with temperatures peaking to between 3500 and 4000°F (1927 to 2204°C) on high-speed heavy-duty truck direct-injected diesel engines.

In Figure 4–4 the dashed line represents the increase in cylinder pressure BTDC and prior to fuel being injected when the engine is cranked over on the starter motor. For our close study of the actual four phases of combustion, we are concerned with the solid black line shown on the PV diagram. When the fuel is injected at point A, the liquid-atomized fuel leaving the injector spray tip must vaporize and mix first to initiate combustion, due to the heat contained within the compressed air charge. The higher the cylinder pressure and temperature, the faster the fuel will vaporize and the quicker ignition will begin.

The ignition delay period extends from point A to point B; normal ignition delay periods range from 0.001 to 0.003 second. When the injected fuel ignites at point B, a rapid rise in both pressure and temperature occurs within the cylinder. This phase is known as the *uncontrolled burning* or *flame propagation* period. The uncontrolled burning period ends at point C, which is followed by a controlled combustion period from point C to point D as the remaining fuel is injected. This action creates a gradual increase in cylinder pressure. The engine manufacturer determines through engineering analysis the actual rate of injection for this period. The

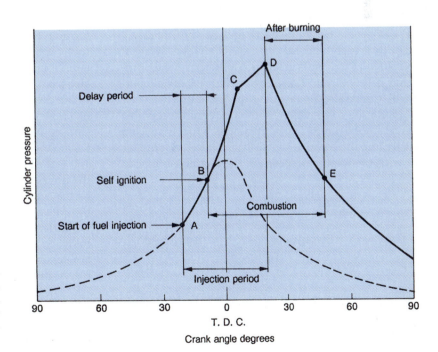

FIGURE 4–4 Graph of a pressure–volume (PV) curve representing the compression and power stroke operating principles 90° BTDC and 90° ATDC. (Courtesy of Zexel USA, Technology and Information Division.)

actual rate of injection is simply the quantity or volume of diesel fuel injected in terms of either the injection pump camshaft angle degrees (multiple-plunger inline pump) or the engine camshaft angle degrees in a unit injector fuel system.

Note that between points B and C the piston has actually attained its TDC position and is being pushed down the cylinder by the pressure of the expanding gases. In this example the fuel injection duration ends at point D, with the piston being approximately 18 to 20° ATDC. The last droplets of fuel that were cut off at point D and any remaining unburned fuel particles will continue to burn between points D and E, thereby creating an afterburning period that produces the pressures to keep the piston moving on its power stroke. Note, however, that if the afterburning period takes too long due to poor mixing of the fuel and air, combustion temperatures will increase, with a subsequent decrease in the engine's thermal efficiency (heat efficiency). Thermal efficiency is discussed in more detail in Chapter 3. One other problem of a long afterburn period is the generation of soot in the exhaust, as a result of incomplete combustion.

In the diesel engine, air only is drawn into the cylinder and subsequently compressed during the upward-moving piston compression stroke. Table 4–1 lists the properties of air. The diesel engine always operates with an excess air/fuel ratio due to the unthrottled entry of air. A diesel engine mechanically or electronically regulates the fuel flow and is therefore a leaner-burning engine than its gasoline counterpart. At an idle rpm, the diesel engine tends to operate at an extremely lean air/fuel ratio with the excess air running between 600 and 1000%; at the high-speed end of the operating range, the diesel still has an excess air/fuel ratio of about 10 to 15% over its gasoline counterpart when producing its maximum horsepower. This excess air percentage can be shown as: excess air = lambda (λ) + 1.1 to 1.15, for the combustion to remain within acceptable exhaust smoke limits. The point at which fuel is injected directly into the compressed air varies between engines and with the load and speed on the engine, similar to

the way the spark plug firing point varies in a gasoline engine through the advance mechanism.

Compression ratios in the automotive precombustion chamber diesel engine average between 20 and 23:1, with resultant compression pressures from as low as 275 to 490 psi (1896 to 3378 kPa). Heavy-duty high-speed DI diesel engines used in highway trucks with compression ratios between 14 and 17:1, which are turbocharged and air-to-air aftercooled, obtain average compression pressures between 435 and 600 psi (2999 to 4137 kPa) and compression temperatures before fuel is injected of between 700 and 900°C (1292 to 1652°F). Peak cylinder pressures and temperatures after the fuel is injected range anywhere between 1200 psi (8274 kPa) to as high as 2300 psi (15,858 kPa) on direct-injected high-speed heavy-duty diesel engines. Temperatures can peak as high as 2204°C (4000°F).

The fuel injection pressures will depend on the type of system used, with pump-line-nozzle systems being incapable of delivering as high an injection pressure as the compact unit injector system. The fuel pressure required to open the nozzle needle valve in a pump-line system generally ranges between 1800 and 3950 psi (12,411 to 27,235 kPa), although there are some that are capable of slightly higher pressure peaks. When this high-pressure fuel, also termed *nozzle lift* or *release pressure*, is forced through the tiny holes in the tip, there is a fuel pressure increase similar to placing your thumb over a garden hose without a nozzle. The result is an increase in spray pressure and a reduction in volume so that spray-in pressure ranges between 18,000 and 19,600 psi (124,110 to 135,142 kPa). The number of holes in the spray tip and their diameter determine the fuel droplet size. Both have an impact on fuel vaporization times, combustion rate, and exhaust emissions levels. Generally, the fuel droplets range in size from 10 to 100 microns (μm) for a typical light distillate diesel fuel. Recall that 1 micron is one millionth of a meter; it can be written as a decimal: 0.00003937 in. Consequently, the fuel droplet size in inches would be 0.0003937 in. for a 10 μm droplet and 0.003937 in. for a 100 μm fuel droplet size. The final pressure at which the nozzle or unit injector needle valve opens depends on the compressive force of the needle valve spring and the area on which the increasing fuel pressure operates. However, many holes or orifices in the tip are usually between 0.005 and 0.010 in. (0.127 to 0.254 mm) in diameter on multiple-hole nozzles used in high-speed heavy-duty diesel engines.

The unit injector system is capable of producing spray-in pressures between 26,000 and 30,000 psi (179,270 to 206,850 kPa). The speed of penetration of the fuel leaving the injector tip can approach velocities

TABLE 4–1 *Percentage and ratio of nitrogen and oxygen by both volume and weight in atmospheric air*

	By volume		By weight	
	Percent	Ratio	Percent	Ratio
Nitrogen	79	3.76	76.8	3.32
Oxygen	21	1.00	23.2	1.00
Total	**100**		**100**	

as high as 780 mph (1255 km/h), which is faster than the speed of sound. The fact that the pump-line-nozzle systems cannot obtain as high a pressure for injection and control of exhaust emissions has forced fuel injection manufacturers to move toward adoption of the superior unit injector system. Detroit Diesel Corporation, which has always used unit injectors, has now been joined by Caterpillar, Cummins, Volvo, Deere and Robert Bosch in using this type of injection system.

The injected fuel (atomized) is basically in a liquid state; therefore, for ignition to take place, the fuel must vaporize (known as distillation temperature). This means that the fuel must penetrate the air mass (high-pressure air/high temperature) to allow the fuel molecules to mix with the oxygen molecules within the combustion chamber. Unlike a gasoline engine, where the air/fuel mix has already taken place during the intake and compression strokes, the diesel fuel must achieve this after injection. For the fuel actually to reach a state of ignition, there is a time delay from the point of injection to the point of ignition. This time delay is approximately 0.001 second and results in a slower-igniting fuel. The longer this time delay before the initial fuel that was injected takes to ignite, the greater the volume of injected fuel that will be collected within the combustion chamber. When this volume of fuel does ignite, there is a pressure increase within the combustion chamber. A time delay of longer than approximately 0.003 second would be an excessively long ignition delay period and would therefore result in a rough-running engine (knocking). This knocking occurs at the start of combustion in a diesel engine instead of at the end of combustion in a gasoline engine.

In a DI diesel engine, fuel that is injected and mixed during the ignition delay period will have a direct effect on the shape of the cylinder/combustion chamber pressure rise pulse. Fuel that is burned before the cylinder pressure reaches its peak value controls the peak height value developed within the cylinder. In other words, the peak rate of heat release determines the rapid rise in cylinder pressure that occurs immediately after ignition of the fuel. The peak in the heat release results from the rapid combustion of the diesel fuel, which was injected and premixed with the high-temperature cylinder air during the delay period. This rapid pressure rise after ignition contributes to the noise from the diesel combustion process that is characteristic of all diesel engines. A reduction in the cetane number of the diesel fuel being used increases the ignition delay period and contributes to a noisier combustion sound.

Fuel that is premixed during the ignition delay period, and therefore the peak rate of heat release and the peak rate of cylinder pressure increase in the combustion chamber, depends on the ignition delay and the quantity of fuel injected and mixed with the air. Ignition delay is affected by five factors:

1. The duration in crankshaft degrees of the actual delay period from the start of fuel injection until the fuel vaporizes and ignites, more commonly known as *ignition delay*

2. The temperature and pressure of the intake air

3. Engine compression ratio

4. The heat absorbed by the open-cylinder air charge during the intake stroke and during the closed compression stroke from various surrounding engine surfaces

5. The cetane number of the fuel; the higher the rating, the shorter the ignition delay period

Ignition lag will increase if the injection timing is either very late or very early, because the fuel will be injected into an air mass that has lost a lot of its compression heat (late timing) or not yet attained it through early injection timing. Since the injector will continue to inject fuel into this already burning mass, the pressure will rise to a peak pressure as the piston attains the TDC position. As the piston starts down into its power stroke, this additional injected fuel maintains a steady pressure as it starts to burn, thereby providing the diesel engine with the term *constant-pressure cycle*. In some engines, the fuel is cut off just BTDC, others may cut off fuel at TDC, while still others may not cut fuel off until after TDC. Because of the fact that diesel fuel continues to be injected into the already burning fuel of the combustion chamber as the piston moves down the cylinder on its power stroke, the cylinder pressure is said to remain constant during a number of degrees.

With the gasoline engine, the instantaneous ignition concept produces a very rapid rise in cylinder pressure with a very fast burn rate, resulting in a hammerlike blow on the piston crown. In the diesel cycle, the pressure rise is sustained for a longer period, resulting in a more gradual and longer push on the piston crown than that in the gasoline engine. Rudolf Diesel's original concept more than 100 years ago was that his engine would continue to have fuel injected during the power stroke and that no heat losses would occur in his uncooled engine. This concept was known as an *adiabatic diesel engine*, which in the true sense of the term meant that there would be no loss of heat to the cylinder walls while the piston moved up on its compression stroke. In addition, no cooling system would be used, resulting in the transfer of waste heat to the exhaust for a gain in thermal efficiency. Since no cooling system would be required, no frictional losses would occur through having to use a gear-driven water pump, and so on. We know this was impossible to achieve; however, Diesel's original idea of producing a true constant-pressure cycle, although never achieved, did attain some measure of success in the engines that now bear his name.

No internal combustion engine today operates on either a true constant-pressure or constant-volume cycle under varying operating conditions, because they all require a few degrees of crankshaft rotation to complete combustion with a subsequent rise in cylinder pressure.

FUEL INJECTION TIMING

Engine manufacturers determine the best fuel injection timing point by experimentation in a test cell with the engine on a dynamometer. Actual fuel injection timing is then determined after consideration of the following factors:

- Horsepower output
- Fuel consumption
- Engine noise
- Exhaust gas denseness due to incomplete combustion (black soot)
- Exhaust gas temperatures
- Exhaust gas emissions with respect to NO_x (nitric oxides), HC (hydrocarbons), CO (carbon monoxide), CO_2 (carbon dioxide), and PM (particulate matter)

The actual start of fuel injection varies among makes and models of engines due to design differences; at an idle speed the variance can be anywhere between 5 and 15° BTDC. As the engine speed is increased and a greater volume of fuel is injected, timing must be advanced to allow the fuel to burn to completion because of the now-faster-moving piston, since there will be less time available. Consider that in an engine having a piston stroke of 6 in. (152.4 mm), at an idle speed of 600 rpm the speed of the piston will be 2 × 6 in., since the piston will move up the cylinder once and down the cylinder once for every 360° or each complete turn of the crankshaft. Therefore, piston speed can be determined by the following formula:

$$\text{piston speed} = \frac{2 \times \text{stroke length} \times \text{rpm}}{12}$$

So at a 600 rpm idle speed, the piston will travel 600 ft/min, or 60 × 600 in 1 hr. In 1 hr the piston travels

36,000 ft; if we divide by 5280 ft we can determine its speed in miles per hour, which in this case is 6.81 mph (11 km/h). At a maximum engine speed of 2100 rpm, the piston will travel at 2100 ft/min or 23.86 mph (38.39 km/h). If the start of fuel pressurization within the fuel injection pump barrel was to occur at the same number of degrees BTDC at the high-speed as at the low-speed setting, then, as you can see in Figure 4–5, the piston would be closer to the top of its stroke before fuel injection actually began, while running at the higher speed. The start of fuel injection has therefore been retarded (begins later in the compression stroke of the upward-moving piston) at the higher speed. It becomes necessary to advance the start of fuel injection (inject fuel earlier) in the cylinder with an increase in engine speed. Figure 4–5 shows the actual beginning of fuel pressurization (beginning of compression) within the pumping plunger and barrel bore. In an inline multiple-plunger injection pump that uses long fuel lines to transfer the fuel from the pump to the injector and nozzle, there is also a time delay required to create a high enough pressure in this long column of fuel before the nozzle will open and allow fuel injection to begin. This is important to understand since the speed of the engine/pump affects the actual start of injection.

Figure 4–6 illustrates a typical inline injection pump plunger and barrel assembly with the spring-loaded delivery valve assembled above the barrel. The connecting high-pressure fuel line and fuel nozzle are shown on the right side. Once the upward-moving plunger has closed the fuel supply and discharge ports in the barrel, trapped fuel is placed under pressure or compression. The fuel must be at a high enough pressure to overcome the fuel line residual pressure and the spring-loaded delivery valve above the barrel. T_1 is the time from the start of fuel pressurization/compression until the delivery valve actually opens. T_2 in the diagram is the time required for transmission of the high-pressure fuel inside the fuel pipe to the nozzle. T_2 is determined by the speed of the pressure wave transmission and the pipe length. In most high-speed diesel engines using inline pumps, this pressure wave transmission speed is approximately 1350 to 1400 m/s (4429 to 4593 ft/sec), which is a fuel speed of between 3020 and 3132 mph (4860 to 5040 km/h). Note that T_2 remains constant regardless of injection pump speed. The time required for the residual pressure in the injection pipe to reach a high enough level that it can open the nozzle delivery valve is pressure T_3. Keep in mind that nozzle release pressures are adjustable by either an internal screw adjustment or by the use of shims. In both cases you effectively change the compressive force of the nozzle valve spring. This allows the same nozzle to be used in more

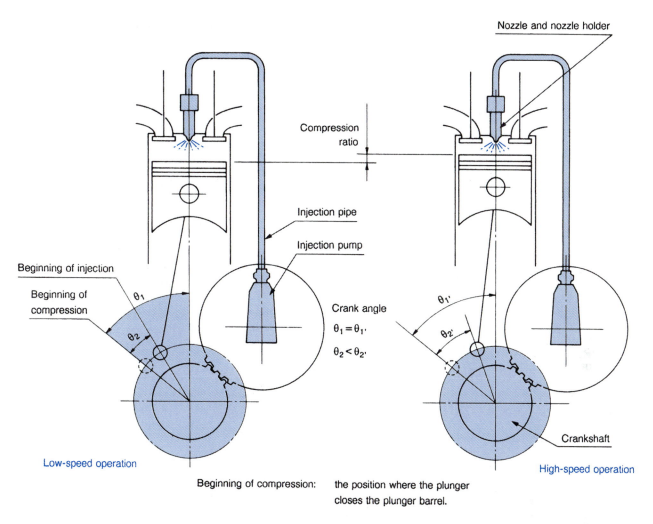

Nozzle and nozzle holder

Compression ratio

Injection pipe

Injection pump

Beginning of injection

Beginning of compression

θ_1

θ_2

Crank angle

$\theta_1 = \theta_1'$

$\theta_2 < \theta_2'$

θ_1'

θ_2'

Crankshaft

Low-speed operation

High-speed operation

Beginning of compression: the position where the plunger closes the plunger barrel.

Beginning of injection: the position where the fuel oil is injected from the nozzle into the cylinder.

FIGURE 4–5 *Graphical representation of how the start of fuel injection into the combustion chamber must be advanced as the engine speed/load is increased. (Courtesy of Zexel USA, Technology and Information Division.)*

than one particular model of engine. Pressure T_3 decreases as the injection pump speed increases, and increases (longer lag time) when the residual pressure in the fuel line decreases.

The injection lag time in a unit injector fuel system is shorter than that in an inline pump system, because there is no long fuel line as a result of the fuel pressure being developed within the body of the unit injector. To give you an appreciation of just how short a time is involved in the fuel injection period, refer to Figure 4–7 which illustrates the time in milliseconds (thousandths of a second) required to complete the injection period in a typical high-speed diesel engine running at different rpm levels.

If an engine idling at 500 rpm requires 15° of engine crankshaft rotation to inject its desired quantity of fuel, the actual time to complete this process will be 5 milliseconds. If injection started at 15° BTDC at 2000 rpm, the time available for injection drops to approximately 1.75 milliseconds. The same engine running at a speed of 2000 rpm starting injection at 30° BTDC will have only 3 milliseconds for the completion of the injected fuel to burn, which includes the actual injection time and the mixing of the atomized fuel with the compressed air charge, plus the vaporization of the fuel followed by burning. Advancement of the start of fuel injection can be obtained through either mechanical or electronic means.

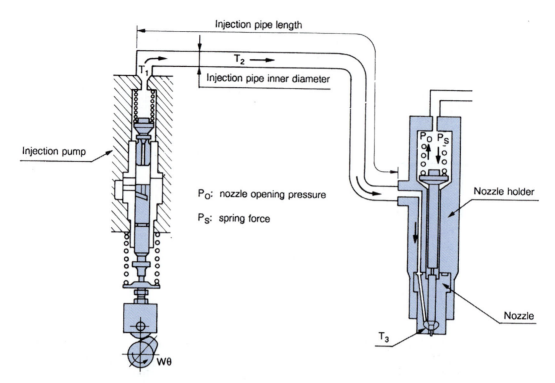

FIGURE 4–6   Representation of the three major areas that create injection lag in a port and helix design fuel injection pump. (Courtesy of Zexel USA, Technology and Information Division.)

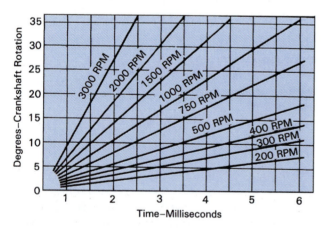

FIGURE 4–7   Graph illustrating the extremely short time period in thousandths of a second that is available for fuel injection purposes related to engine speed, and the point at which injection begins BTDC. (Courtesy of Zexel USA, Technology and Information Division.)

RETARDED VERSUS ADVANCED TIMING

The reason why a variable injection/engine timing system is required on today's heavy-duty diesel engines, particularly in on-highway vehicles, is the stringent ex-

haust emissions legislation mandated through the EPA in the United States was designed to reduce pollutants in the air that we breathe. In addition to limiting the exhaust emissions from the engine exhaust stack, however, the engine manufacturers want to improve the fuel economy and performance of their products. The two main culprits that EPA wants controlled are hydrocarbons and nitrogen oxides.

Just what are hydrocarbons? Unburned or partially burned fuel in the combustion chamber results in hydrocarbons—basically soot produced from the carbon in the diesel fuel. Nitrogen oxides, on the other hand, are what create the yellowish-brown smog that is so noticeable in cities such as Los Angeles. Nitrogen oxides are created when combustion chamber temperatures exceed 3000°F (1649°C), due to oxygen and nitrogen combining during this high-temperature phase. Since both oxygen and nitrogen are constituent parts of the air that we breathe, it is pretty hard to avoid these conditions completely.

EXHAUST EMISSIONS LIMITS

Both gasoline and diesel engines in North America are manufactured to comply with the U.S. EPA exhaust emissions standards for the year in which they are produced. For heavy-duty on-highway diesel engines, these exhaust emissions fall into various categories that deal with hydrocarbons, carbon monoxide, nitrogen oxides, and particulate matter.

Exhaust gases have several major constituents.

- Carbon dioxide (CO_2), although nonpoisonous, does contribute to *global warming*. Complete combustion produces CO_2 and water.
- Carbon monoxide (CO) is a colorless, odorless, and tasteless gas. Inhalation of as little as 0.3% by volume can cause death within 30 minutes. The exhaust gas from spark ignition engines at an idle speed has a high CO content. For this reason, *never* allow the engine to run in enclosed spaces such as a closed garage.
- Oxides of nitrogen (NO_x) have two classes. Nitrogen monoxide (NO) is a colorless, odorless, and tasteless gas that is rapidly converted into nitrogen dioxide (NO_2) in the presence of oxygen. NO_2 is a yellowish to reddish-brown poisonous gas with a penetrating odor that can destroy lung tissue. NO and NO_2 are customarily treated together and referred to as oxides of nitrogen (NO_x).
- Hydrocarbons (HC) of many different types are present in exhaust gas. In the presence of nitrogen oxide and sunlight, they form oxidants that irritate the mucous membranes. Some hydrocarbons are considered to be carcinogenic. Incomplete combustion produces unburned hydrocarbons.
- Particulate matter (PM), in accordance with U.S. legislation, includes all substances (with the exception of unbound water) that under normal conditions are present as solids (ash, carbon) or liquids in exhaust gases.

Federal emissions standards for diesel truck and bus exhaust in g/bhp-hr and on- and off-highway diesel engines are shown in Table 4–2.

Future EPA regulations also extend into off-highway diesel equipment and marine applications. California, which has the strictest internal combustion engine exhaust emissions in the world, usually sets standards that are then followed by the EPA. California has enacted emission levels that extend to utility engines such as lawn mowers and garden equipment (gas or diesel). Separate standards are in place for handheld engines. Nonhandheld engines have to meet two standards (three for diesels): total hydrocarbon plus nitrogen oxide level, carbon monoxide level, and for diesels, a particulate matter limit.

The California Air Resources Board (CARB) has laws in place covering all types of internal combustion engines in all types of applications; retrofitted engines as well. The CARB requires certification test procedures and emission standards for heavy-duty (40 hp, 30 kW, and over) construction and farm equipment.

To reduce exhaust emissions from diesel engines, particularly heavy-duty on-highway models, engine advancements and after-treatment technologies have been adopted to ensure that all engines are in compliance with EPA standards. Exhaust emissions standards have become more stringent over the years. Most heavy-duty on-highway engines are able to meet the regulations through higher injection pressures, high top ring pistons, tailored intake and exhaust systems, and closely designed turbochargers using air-to-air-charge cooling systems. In addition, in October 1993 in the United States, legislation reduced the allowable sulfur content in diesel fuel to 0.05%, which has also helped in reducing emissions because 98% of the sulfur is combusted to sulfur dioxide and the rest is combusted to sulfates. This low-sulfur fuel still leaves about 0.01 g/bhp-hr sulfate in the raw exhaust. Diesel fuel contains molecules with between 8 and 15 carbon atoms, and engine lube oils tend to have molecules with more than 15 carbon atoms; diesel fuel and engine lube oil differ in molecular size.

SUMMARY

Your knowledge acquired through details given in this chapter will provide you with a thorough understanding of the phases of combustion within the diesel engine. This knowledge will help you when troubleshooting an engine with unusual exhaust smoke color, poor fuel economy, hard starting, and rough running.

TABLE 4–2   United States and the European Union exhaust emissions standards through 2008

U.S.A.

Heavy-Duty Highway Engines, g/bhp-hr

Year	HC	CO	NMHC +NO$_x$	NO$_x$	PM	HCHO
1990	1.3	15.5	–	6.0	0.60	–
1991	1.3	15.5	–	5.0	0.25	–
1993	1.3	15.5	–	5.0	0.25 (0.10)[a]	–
1994	1.3	15.5	–	5.0	0.10 (0.07)[a]	–
1996	1.3	15.5	–	5.0	0.10 (0.05★)[a]	–
1998	1.3	15.5	–	4.0	0.10 (0.05★)[a]	–
2004[c]	–	15.5	2.4[b]	–	0.10 (0.05★)[a]	–
2007[d]	0.14[e]	15.5	–	0.2	0.01	0.016

★ – in-use PM standard 0.07
a – urban bus standard
b – manufacturers can choose a 2.5 g/bhp-hr NMHC+NO$_x$ standard with a 0.5 g/bhp-hr NMHC cap
c – October 2002 for EPA Consent Decree signers
d – proposed standard; phased-in schedule 25% in 2007, 50% in 2008, 75% in 2009 and 100% in 2010
e – NMHC

U.S.A.

Off-Road Diesel Engines, g/kW·hr (g/bhp·hr)

Engine Power	Tier	Model Year	NO$_x$	HC	NMHC + NO$_x$	CO	PM
kW < 8	Tier 1	2000	–	–	10.5 (7.8)	8.0 (6.0)	1.0 (0.75)
(hp < 11)	Tier 2	2005	–	–	7.5 (5.6)	8.0 (6.0)	0.80 (0.60)
8 <= kW < 19	Tier 1	2000	–	–	9.5 (7.1)	6.6 (4.9)	0.80 (0.60)
(11 <= hp < 25)	Tier 2	2005	–	–	7.5 (5.6)	6.6 (4.9)	0.80 (0.60)
19<= kW < 37	Tier 1	1999	–	–	9.5 (7.1)	5.5 (4.1)	0.80 (0.60)
(25 <= hp < 50)	Tier 2	2004	–	–	7.5 (5.6)	5.5 (4.1)	0.60 (0.45)
37 <= kW < 75	Tier 1	1998	9.2 (6.9)	–	–	–	–
(50 <= hp < 100)	Tier 2	2004	–	–	7.5 (5.6)	5.0 (3.7)	0.40 (0.30)
	Tier 3	2008	–	–	4.7 (3.5)	5.0 (3.7)	–★
75 <= kW < 130	Tier 1	1997	9.2 (6.9)	–	–	–	–
(100 <= hp < 175)	Tier 2	2003	–	–	6.6 (4.9)	5.0 (3.7)	0.30 (0.22)
	Tier 3	2007	–	–	4.0 (3.0)	5.0 (3.7)	–★
130 <= kW < 225	Tier 1	1996	9.2 (6.9)	1.3 (1.0)	–	11.4 (8.5)	0.54 (0.40)
(175 <= hp < 300)	Tier 2	2003	–	–	6.6 (4.9)	3.5 (2.6)	0.20 (0.15)
	Tier 3	2006	–	–	4.0 (3.0)	3.5 (2.6)	–★
225 <= kW < 450	Tier 1	1996	9.2 (6.9)	1.3 (1.0)	–	11.4 (8.5)	0.54 (0.40)
(300 <= hp < 600)	Tier 2	2001	–	–	6.4 (4.8)	3.5 (2.6)	0.20 (0.15)
	Tier 3	2006	–	–	4.0 (3.0)	3.5 (2.6)	–★
450 <= kW < 560	Tier 1	1996	9.2 (6.9)	1.3 (1.0)	–	11.4 (8.5)	0.54 (0.40)
(600 <= hp < 750)	Tier 2	2002	–	–	6.4 (4.8)	3.5 (2.6)	0.20 (0.15)
	Tier 3	2006	–	–	4.0 (3.0)	3.5 (2.6)	–★
kW = 560	Tier 1	2000	9.2 (6.9)	1.3 (1.0)	–	11.4 (8.5)	0.54 (0.40)
(hp = 750)	Tier 2	2006	–	–	6.4 (4.8)	3.5 (2.6)	0.20 (0.15)

★ – Tier 3 PM standard to be proposed and adopted in the 2001 review

TABLE 4–2 (continued).

European Union

A – Steady-state test cycle, g/kWh

Tier	Date & Category	Test Cycle	CO	HC	NO$_x$	PM
Euro I	1992, <85 kW	ECE R-49	4.5	1.1	8.0	0.612
	1992, >85 kW		4.5	1.1	8.0	0.36
Euro II	1996.10		4.0	1.1	7.0	0.25
	1998.10		4.0	1.1	7.0	0.15
Euro III	*1999.10, EEVs only*	*ESC*	*1.5*	*0.25*	*2.0*	*0.02*
	2000.10	ESC	2.1	0.66	5.0	0.10 0.13★
Euro IV	2005.10		1.5	0.46	3.5	0.02
Euro V	2008.10		1.5	0.46	2.0	0.02

EEV – voluntary standards for "enhanced environmentally friendly vehicles"
★ - for engines of less than 0.75 dm^3 swept volume per cylinder and a rated power speed of more than 3000 min^{-1}

European Union

B – Transient test cycle, g/kWh

Tier	Date & Category	Test Cycle	CO	NMHC	CH$_4$[a]	NO$_x$	PM[b]
Euro III	*1999.10, EEVs only*	*ETC*	*3.0*	*0.40*	*0.65*	*2.0*	*0.02*
	2000.10	ETC	5.45	0.78	1.6	5.0	0.16 0.21[c]
Euro IV	2005.10		4.0	0.55	1.1	3.5	0.03
Euro V	2008.10		4.0	0.55	1.1	2.0	0.03

EEV – voluntary standards for "enhanced environmentally friendly vehicles"
a - for natural gas engines only
b - not applicable for gas fueled engines at the year 2000 and 2005 stages
c - for engines of less than 0.75 dm3 swept volume per cylinder and a rated power speed of more than 3000 min-1

European Union

Off-Road Diesel Engines, g/kWh

Net Power	Date	CO	HC	NO$_x$	PM
Stage I					
130–560 kW	1999.01	5.0	1.3	9.2	0.54
75–130 kW	1999.01	5.0	1.3	9.2	0.70
37–75 kW	1999.04	6.5	1.3	9.2	0.85
Stage II					
130–560 kW	2002.01	3.5	1.0	6.0	0.2
75–130 kW	2003.01	5.0	1.0	6.0	0.3
37–75 kW	2004.01	5.0	1.3	7.0	0.4
18–37 kW	2001.01	5.5	1.5	8.0	0.8

SELF-TEST QUESTIONS

1. Technician A says that the most popular type of combustion chamber design for heavy-duty high-speed diesel truck engines is the IDI (indirect-injection) or PC (precombustion chamber) design. Technician B disagrees and says that the DI (direct-injection) design is the most widely used type of combustion system. Which technician is correct?

2. Which of the following combustion chamber designs offers the best fuel economy when used in midheavy and heavy-duty diesel truck engines?
   a. swirl chamber design
   b. precombustion chamber design
   c. direct-injection design

3. Technician A says that a glow plug is not required for startup of a precombustion chamber design engine. Technician B disagrees, stating that it is the direct-injection engine type that does not require the use of a glow plug system for startup. Who is right?

4. The MAN M-type combustion chamber design is one whereby
   a. the combustion chamber bowl is contained within the crown of the piston
   b. the combustion chamber is in fact a small antechamber contained within the cylinder head
   c. the combustion chamber is located to the side of the main chamber

5. Technician A says that current cylinder firing pressures in high-speed heavy-duty engines average 1000 to 1200 psi (6895 to 8274 kPa). Technician B says this is too low and that pressures between 1800 and 2300 psi (12,411 to 15,858 kPa) are more common. Who is correct?

6. Technician A says that fuel injection pressures now in use in heavy-duty highway truck engines range between 19,000 and 28,000 psi (131,005 to 193,060 kPa). Technician B says this is impossible because such pressures would blow the engine apart. Is technician A or technician B correct?

7. Technician A says that the diesel engine operates on the constant-volume principle. Technician B disagrees, saying that the diesel engine operates on the constant-pressure cycle. Who is correct?

8. When the diesel fuel is injected into the combustion chamber, it is broken down into very fine particles. The term to describe this process is
   a. vaporization
   b. injection
   c. cetane explosion
   d. atomization

9. Ignition delay in a diesel engine is
   a. the time lag from initial injection to actual ignition
   b. the time required to raise the fuel pressure high enough to overcome the compression pressure in the cylinder
   c. the time delay required for the glow plug to reach its red-hot state
   d. the time lag for the injected vaporized fuel actually to atomize

10. Technician A says that a long ignition delay period would result in a rough-running engine. Technician B says that a long ignition delay period would result in an engine knocking sound, due to the high pressures created within the combustion chamber. Who is correct?

11. Technician A says that combustion in a diesel engine can take place only when the carbon and hydrogen molecules are atomized, whereas technician B says that the carbon and hydrogen must mix with the oxygen in the combustion chamber in a vaporized state to initiate successful combustion. Who is correct?

12. Air used in a diesel engine for combustion is made up of oxygen and nitrogen. Technician A says that by volume, there is more nitrogen than oxygen in a given amount of air. Technician B says that there has to be more oxygen to sustain combustion. Which technician knows his or her basic chemistry?

13. Technician A says that a by-product of combustion is carbon dioxide (CO_2), whereas technician B says that carbon monoxide (CO) is formed as a by-product of combustion. Who is right?

14. Technician A says that a diesel engine operates with an air/fuel ratio of approximately 20 to 25:1 under full load, whereas technician B states that it is closer to 90 to 100:1 under all conditions of operation. Who is correct?

15. List and describe briefly the four stages of combustion that occur in a diesel engine to achieve complete burning of the injected fuel.

16. List the main factors that affect the ignition delay period in the combustion chamber.

17. Technician A says that the letters EPA mean "European Protection Association," whereas technician B says that they mean "Environmental Protection Agency." Who is correct?

18. List the four main culprits that EPA wants controlled as a by-product of the combustion process in the exhaust of heavy-duty diesel engines.

19. Technician A says that when an engine is running at normal injection timing (nonadvanced), the injection of fuel will be later than it would be when running in an advanced timing mode. Technician B says that under normal timing, the fuel is injected earlier in the injection cycle. Who is correct?

20. True or False: During advanced injection timing, the fuel is injected earlier (piston is farther away from TDC). This means that the air pressure and temperature in the cylinder are lower, resulting in an increased ignition delay period.

21. Technician A says that during normal injection timing a lower nitrogen oxide content is produced at the exhaust but a higher percentage of hydrocarbons is produced. Technician B says that this is incorrect; instead, at normal injection timing there is a higher nitrogen oxide content but a lower hydrocarbon content. Who is correct?

22. True or False: Sulfur dioxide, which is a by-product of combustion, is caused by the sulfur content of the diesel fuel.

5 Engine Disassembly Considerations

Overview

In this chapter we discuss the prior reasoning involved when determining if an engine requires disassembly and overhaul or simply requires repair and replacement of specific component parts. Various factors must be considered before removing an engine from a piece of equipment, from both a cost and an equipment downtime standpoint. Other considerations include weighing the cost of rebuilding in-house versus jobbing it out to a specialist shop, and installing a rebuilt swing engine compared with trading the unit in on a newer model due to age, accumulated hours, or number of miles/kilometers on the equipment. A review of the engine/equipment repair file and costs associated with its accumulated hours/miles may determine that its running costs are no longer economical.

Many fleets schedule an engine for an in-frame overhaul at a specific mileage, or when conditions so warrant. In many cases, fleets rely upon regular engine oil analysis reports to track and determine the internal condition of the engine, and to key in on what specific engine components are showing high wear characteristics. Refer to information in Chapter 11 on lubrication systems for more details on how to interpret a lube oil analysis report. Of course, major failure of an engine leaves little doubt as to the repairs needed.

Engine disassembly is a very important part of being a proficient diesel technician; teardown should be accomplished rapidly but not haphazardly. Much can and should be learned about the engine during teardown, such as: Did it fail prematurely? Was failure operator or maintenance oriented? Also, by the time teardown is complete, the technician should have a good idea of what parts will be needed for repair or rebuilding the engine. It can be seen, therefore, that engine teardown or disassembly is one of the most important parts of engine overhaul. The decision to disassemble an engine for overhaul should be based on fact, not assumptions, and must be made by the technician before any disassembly takes place. To assist in making this decision the engine should be run or operated in some manner, preferably with a dynamometer.

The physical size and application/installation of a diesel engine will determine the best process to employ during repair. Often it is not possible to completely remove the engine from its application/installation because of its size, such as the very large slow-speed engines used in large marine or industrial applications. These engines are overhauled in place by removal of component parts as necessary. In addition, in some pleasure craft, workboat marine applications, or mobile equipment such as heavy-duty trucks, maintenance management personnel may choose to complete an in-frame overhaul rather than a major overhaul that requires complete removal of the engine from its application. If the engine assembly can be removed from its application, a more thorough cleaning, inspection, and repair can be performed.

Engine Diagnosis and Inspection before Disassembly

Discuss the engine operation with the operator. Is the engine being overhauled as a matter of routine because of mileage or hours, or is it being overhauled because of a particular problem such as oil consumption or engine noise? In discussing the engine operation with the operator you may discover that the engine does not need an overhaul; it is possible that an incorrect assumption has been made by the owner or operator. An example of this is excessive engine oil consumption, which may be caused by many things besides worn piston rings.

63

A thorough check of the following items should be made before the engine is overhauled:

1. *Engine valve seals* (if used). Seals may be broken, worn out, or improperly installed.
2. *Engine front and rear main seals.* Check for leakage during operation.
3. *Air systems and air compressor* (if used). Check air tank for oil accumulation.
4. *Engine turbocharger*
   a. Remove the pipe or hose that connects the turbocharger to the intake manifold. Oil accumulation in this pipe indicates a turbo seal leak.
   b. Oil dripping out the exhaust side of the turbocharger indicates a turbo seal leak.
5. *Engine blower*
   a. Remove air inlet pipe to blower (Detroit Diesel two-cycle engines).
   b. Blower rotors should not be wet with oil; if they are, oil seal leak is indicated.

After discussing the engine to be overhauled with the owner/operator, the technician should make a test run to determine if there are any unusual engine conditions that will require special attention during overhaul. The engine should be checked for the following:

1. *Engine noises.* Noises such as rod bearing noise or piston slap are generally removed during a complete overhaul. Other noises that come from timing gears and piston pin bushings should be noted so that they are completely checked during engine overhaul.
2. *Engine oil pressure.* Engine oil pressure must be considered one of the vital signs of engine condition. For example, if engine oil pressure is low, particular attention must be given to the following items during engine rebuild:
   a. Oil level
   b. Oil filters
   c. Oil pump pickup
   d. Oil pump
   e. Crankshaft journal size and condition
   f. Pressure relief valves
   g. Oil filter bypass valves
   h. Oil cooler bypass valves
   i. Camshaft journals and camshaft bearings
3. *Engine temperature.* If the engine temperature is abnormal (higher or lower) during operation, the following items should be given a close check during engine overhaul:
   a. Coolant level
   b. Gauge condition
   c. Radiator flow and condition
   d. Water pump condition

   e. Thermostats and shutters (if used)
   f. Thermostat seals
4. *Engine operation.* Check engine operation for the following:
   a. Excessive smoke
      - Air cleaner may be restricted.
      - Injectors or injection nozzles are clogged or incorrectly adjusted.
      - Fuel system may be improperly calibrated.
   b. Low power, no smoke
      - Fuel starvation is indicated.
      - Pump may be improperly calibrated.
      - Fuel filter may be dirty or clogged.

If you review the ASE medium/heavy truck tests preparation guide, diesel engines task list, and T2 test, part A, as follows, you will be better able to determine the existing mechanical condition of the engine. Typically the test will include 15 questions from this area.

ASE General Engine Diagnosis Considerations

1. Verify the complaint, and road/dyno test vehicle; review driver/customer interview and past maintenance documents (if available); determine further diagnosis.
2. Inspect engine assembly and compartment for fuel, oil, coolant, or other leaks; determine needed repairs.
3. Inspect engine compartment wiring harness, connectors, seals, and locks; determine needed repairs.
4. Listen and diagnose engine noises; determine needed repairs.
5. Check engine exhaust emissions, odor, smoke color, opacity (density), and quantity; determine needed repairs.
6. Perform fuel system tests; check fuel contamination and consumption; determine needed repairs.
7. Perform air intake system restriction and leakage tests; determine needed repairs.
8. Perform intake manifold pressure tests; determine needed repairs.
9. Perform exhaust back pressure and temperature tests; determine needed repairs.
10. Perform crankcase pressure test; determine needed repairs.
11. Diagnose no cranking, cranks but fails to start, hard starting, and starts but does not continue to run problems; determine needed repairs.
12. Diagnose surging, rough operation, misfiring, low power, slow deceleration, slow ac-

celeration, and shutdown problems; determine needed repairs.

13. Isolate and diagnose engine-related vibration problems; determine needed repairs.

14. Check cooling system for protection level, contamination, coolant type and level, temperature, pressure, conditioner concentration, filtration, and fan operation; determine needed repairs.

15. Check lubrication system for contamination, oil level, temperature, pressure, filtration, and oil consumption; determine needed repairs.

16. Check, record, and clear electronic diagnostic codes; monitor electronic data; determine needed repairs.

17. Perform visual inspection for physical damage and missing, modified, or tampered components; determine needed repairs.

Engine Condition and Failure Analysis

In order to avoid a repeat in-service engine failure condition, a number of systematic checks should be performed to determine the cause(s). The fundamentals of failure analysis should include the following checks:

1. A preliminary investigation, including observation, inquiry, and a review of engine history.
2. Prepare the failed parts for close examination.
3. Determine the type and cause of failure.
4. Correct the failure and cause(s).
5. If the engine is still under an OEM warranty gather the following information:
   - the engine model and serial number
   - what happened
   - where it happened
   - when it happened
   - why it happened

After completing the various checks and tests described above, including those listed in the ASE task list 2, compare available options in a cost analysis and then make a final decision. If the decision is to actually disassemble and overhaul/repair the engine assembly, then follow the engine OEM's disassembly procedures in an organized, step-by-step fashion. It is also important to exercise care and caution when pulling apart major components for several reasons, including

- Personal safety
- The cause of further damage to parts, particularly if the parts can be reused and are still within wear

tolerance specs. Therefore match and mark parts and components so they can be reinstalled in the same position and location.

- Failure analysis of components to determine the cause(s) of failure to thus prevent a reoccurrence. This step is of great importance if the engine or component part is still under warranty.
- Conservation of time and effort. Organized disassembly allows logical and quick determination of what parts and components need to be replaced. If the customer demands a written report on the condition of and the costs required to repair the engine, you can do this with ease.
- Proper parts cleaning procedures and inspection/measurement where required.
- Failure of an engine/component which is under warranty. Always label and identify parts and their location on and in the engine. Specific parts include pistons, rings, liners, fuel injectors, valves, shell bearings, etc. This will assist the factory service representative or field service engineer to determine the reason(s) for failure and whether the cause is related to a warrantable condition.

Types of Engine Overhaul

Engine overhaul usually falls into one of two categories: overhaul with the engine in the vehicle or overhaul with the engine removed from the vehicle.

In many large fleets, it is customary to stock one or more overhauled engines, so that when required, an engine can be removed from a piece of equipment and quickly replaced with a like model. In this way, equipment downtime is kept to a minimum, and the efficiency of the equipment is maintained. This practice is common in long-distance on-highway trucks and in mobile mining equipment applications. In these cases the engine is usually mounted on a subframe assembly that facilitates quick and easy removal. The removed engine can then be systematically disassembled and overhauled to an as-new condition.

Overhaul with the Engine in the Vehicle

Very often engines are overhauled (in the frame major) with the engine left in the vehicle.

Advantages

1. Time is saved by not having to remove the engine.
2. The vehicle serves as a place to mount the engine so that it can be worked on without additional stands or brackets.
3. Cost to the customer is reduced. As much as 16 hours (two days' working time) may be saved by not removing and reinstalling the engine.

Disadvantages

1. All engine seals and gaskets are harder to replace, such as front and rear main seals.
2. It is harder to inspect some engine components such as the camshaft.
3. The block is not thoroughly cleaned as it would be if it were removed from the vehicle and cleaned in a chemical tank. In particular, the water jacket would be cleaned much better if it were cleaned in a chemical tank.
4. The technician may have to climb up on a crawler tractor (for instance), causing considerable inconvenience and awkward work access.

Overhaul with the Engine Removed from the Vehicle

Most complete overhauls are done with the engine removed from the vehicle.

Advantages

1. The engine can be completely disassembled and all gaskets and seals replaced.

2. The engine can be mounted on an engine stand, which provides easy access (Figure 5–1).

Disadvantages

1. It takes more time than in-the-vehicle overhaul.
2. Heavy lifting stands and brackets are required to remove engine from the vehicle.

Engine Removal

The engine shall be removed from and re-installed in the vehicle in accordance with approved service procedures. Care should be taken to recover all fluids and gasses from the engine prior to removal. All fluids and gasses shall be stored or disposed of in accordance with Federal, State and local EPA and municipal regulations.

These procedures are intended to supplement the service manual.

1. Remove hood, side panels, or tilt the cab if engine is in a cab-over truck.
2. Visually inspect the engine for oil and water leaks. This may help you in making a repair decision later.

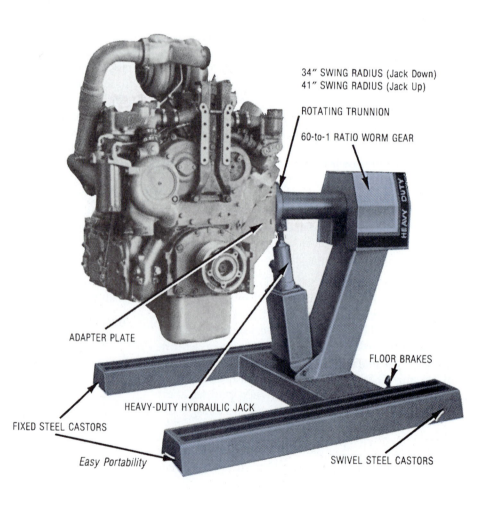

34″ SWING RADIUS (Jack Down)
41″ SWING RADIUS (Jack Up)

ROTATING TRUNNION

60-to-1 RATIO WORM GEAR

HEAVY DUTY

ADAPTER PLATE

FLOOR BRAKES

HEAVY-DUTY HYDRAULIC JACK

FIXED STEEL CASTORS

Easy Portability

SWIVEL STEEL CASTORS

FIGURE 5–1 *Heavy-duty engine mounting/rotator stand for overhaul of a diesel engine. (Courtesy of Kent-Moore Division of SPX Corporation.)*

3. Steam clean or pressure wash the engine and vehicle in the engine area.

4. Drain the coolant from the radiator and engine block. Dispose of used antifreeze according to safety regulations.

5. Remove the radiator and all connecting hoses if required.

6. Disconnect any oil lines that lead to oil filters or gauges. Drain and dispose of used engine oil.

7. Disconnect all air lines that lead to the engine.

8. Disconnect the transmission or remove as required. Refer to your instructor.

9. Remove the intake and exhaust pipes.

10. Disconnect all electrical connections from the vehicle to the engine. Most technicians identify the electrical connections in some manner so that after the engine is reinstalled there is no question about where to hook them up. This can be done with various colors of spray paint, masking tape, or tags. Any method that you have available will save considerable time later.

11. Remove any other items that in your opinion may get in the way of engine removal, including linkages and any engine accessories.

12. Attach a lifting chain or bracket to the engine.

13. Move the hoist over the engine and connect the chain to the hoist (see Figure 5–2).

NOTE   Make sure that the hoist and chain have sufficient capacity to lift the engine being removed.

---

14. Lift the engine from the vehicle.

NOTE   If the transmission is not removed, place a support under the transmission to prevent it from falling.
Remove the engine.

---

15. Place the engine on the floor with blocks to level it or on an engine rotator stand in preparation for disassembly as per Figure 5–1.

Engine Disassembly

Since engine disassembly with the engine removed from the vehicle is the most complete disassembly procedure, it will be discussed in detail in this section. If the engine is to be disassembled in the vehicle, the procedures need only be altered to omit the engine components that are not going to be removed, such as the crankshaft. If the engine has not been cleaned by steaming or high-pressure washer previous to re-

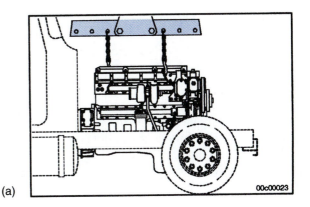

(a)

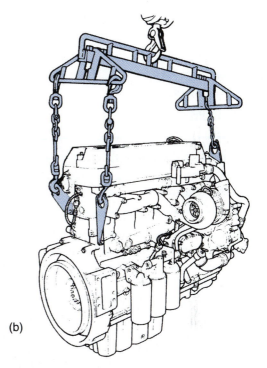

(b)

FIGURE 5–2   (a) Using a spreader bar and chain falls to safely sling an engine in a heavy-duty truck prior to its removal. (Courtesy of Cummins Engine Company, Inc.) (b) Recommended sling arrangement for safely lifting a heavy-duty diesel engine using chain falls and a spreader bar. (Courtesy of Detroit Diesel Corporation.)

moval, it should be cleaned at this time. Place the engine on a suitable stand or cart for disassembly.

NOTE   The following disassembly procedure is general in nature and should be used with the engine service manual.

CAUTION   Do not disassemble the engine in a manner that damages component parts.

To aid you in becoming a professional technician, many visual checks that you should make as a matter of practice have been included in the following disassembly procedures.

Rocker Covers

Remove the bolts from the cover and then remove the cover; place the bolts back into the cover. Note the condition of the oil clinging to the underside of the rocker cover. A white scum or film of oil clinging to the cover may indicate water leakage into the engine by any of the following:

1. Cracked block
2. Cracked head (other than combustion chamber area)
3. Leaking sleeve seal rings (if wet-type sleeve engine)
4. Leaking oil cooler

Intake Manifold

NOTE   On some engines the fuel injection lines may have to be removed before the intake manifold can be removed.

---

1. Remove the capscrews or bolts that hold the intake manifold on, and remove the intake manifold.
2. Inspect the manifold for accumulation of dust or oil.
   a. Dust or dirt in the manifold would indicate a faulty air cleaner or inlet pipe. (Check it closely before engine reassembly!)
   b. A wet, oily film in the intake manifold would indicate leaking turbocharger or blower seals. If the engine is not equipped with a turbo or blower, the air cleaner could be overfull (oil bath type of air cleaner).
3. Check the manifold for cracks (visual).

Remove the Rocker Arms or Rocker Box Assemblies and Pushrods

1. See Figure 5–3.
2. Inspect the rocker arm assemblies for worn bushings by disassembling the rocker arm assembly and visually inspecting the bushing and shaft. See Figure 5–4.
3. Inspect pushrods for straightness.

Water Manifold and Thermostat Housing (if Used)

1. Remove the bolts that attach it to the engine head or block.
2. Inspect the water manifold for cracks or rusted spots that may cause water leakage.

Turbocharger (if Used)

1. Remove the turbocharger hold-down bolts and any other support brackets.
2. Remove oil inlet and return lines.
3. Inspect turbo outlet for traces of oil film. (This may indicate that the turbo needs an overhaul.)

Exhaust Manifold

1. On some engines, lock plates (plates that hold the bolts in place) will have to be straightened before the manifold-retaining bolts can be removed.
2. Check the manifold for cracks.

Injection Nozzles or Injectors and Fuel Lines

1. On engines using injection nozzles, remove the fuel lines from the nozzles and injection pump. Place plastic shipping caps or plugs on all openings to prevent the entry of dirt.
2. Inspect the fuel lines for worn spots that may cause leakage.
3. Loosen and remove the nozzle hold-down capscrew or screws; some Bosch and Lucas/Delphi injectors are threaded and thus screw into the cylinder head.
4. Grasp the nonthreaded type of nozzle and attempt to turn it back and forth, pulling up at the same time. This will remove many nozzles.
5. If stud bolts are used to hold the nozzle in, it cannot be turned; in this case, use a pry bar or similar tool. Wedge it under the nozzle to move it upward out of the cylinder head. Visually inspect nozzle for damage to the tip.

CAUTION   Care must be used in prying the nozzle upward, as damage to the nozzle could result. (Pencil nozzles manufactured by Stanadyne Diesel Systems are easily bent and extreme care must be taken.)

---

   a. Since nozzles are often stuck in the cylinder head, a puller or slide hammer must be used to pull them.
   b. Some nozzles require special pullers. Consult the manufacturer's service manual for more information.
6. Remove the unit injectors on engines so equipped.
   a. Loosen and remove hold-down capscrew or nut.
   b. Use a rolling head pry bar or special removal tool. Remove injector by pulling or prying it upward.
   c. Visually inspect injector tip for damage. Make sure that injector openings are all capped or

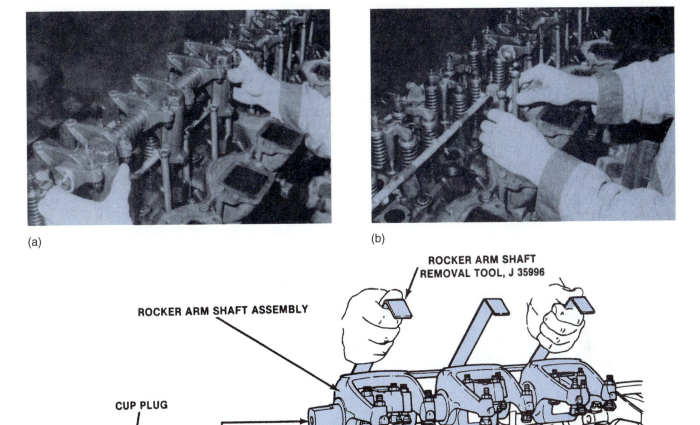

(a)

(b)

ROCKER ARM SHAFT
REMOVAL TOOL, J 35996

ROCKER ARM SHAFT ASSEMBLY

CUP PLUG

OUTBOARD
END

(c)

FIGURE 5–3 (a) Removal of rocker arm assemblies—3406 Cat engine. (b) Removal of pushrods—3406 Cat engine. (Courtesy of Caterpillar, Inc.) (c) Using special tooling J 35996 to remove three rocker arm assemblies simultaneously from an overhead camshaft series 60 engine. (Courtesy of Detroit Diesel Corporation.)

plugged, and store injectors in a place where they will not be damaged.

Water Pump

1. Remove drive belts if used.
2. Check the drive belts for cracks.
3. Remove capscrews that hold the water pump to block or cylinder head and remove the water pump.
4. Visually check the water pump impeller for erosion.
5. If the fan was bolted to the water pump drive pulley, check it closely for cracks and bent blades.

All Accessories

Remove fuel filter housings, hoses, and oil and water filters attached to the engine.

Injection Pump

1. Prior to removal, center the rack on CAT PLN systems (see chapter 23, Figure 23–9). On Bosch PLN systems, rotate the crankshaft to place No. 1 piston at TDC—compression.
2. Remove all bolts that hold the injection pump to the engine and remove pump.

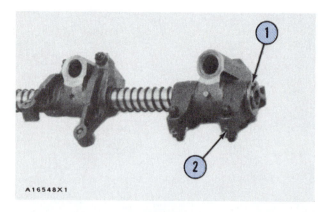

A16548X1

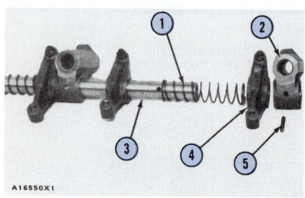

A16550X1

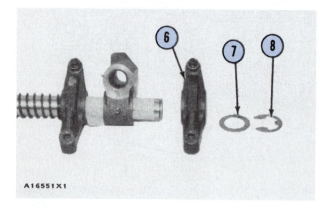

A16551X1

FIGURE 5–4 Component parts identification for a rocker arm assembly for a 3400 series Cat engine. (Courtesy of Caterpillar, Inc.)

3. Visually inspect the pump for broken mounting flange and stripped or cross-threaded fittings.

Cylinder Head or Heads

1. Before you remove the cylinder head, open and/or remove drain plugs to make sure that all coolant has been drained from the block. Although the cooling system radiator or heat exchanger may have been drained before the engine was removed from the vehicle or equipment, some coolant may have remained in the block.

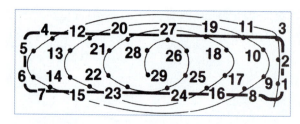

FIGURE 5–5 One example of a cylinder head loosening sequence for studs, bolts, or nuts.

2. Loosen all cylinder head hold-down bolts. (See Figure 5–5 for a typical sequence.)

3. Lift out the cylinder head bolts, checking each for erosion and rust. Eroded or rusted bolts should not be reused.

4. Lift the cylinder head from the block as follows:

   a. Use a lifting bracket and hoist (Figure 5–6).
   b. Manually: Single (DDC149, DD/MTU, Cat, Mercedes-Benz, Cummins) or two-cylinder heads (Cummins, Mack, Cat) can be lifted off by hand or by a sling.

5. Inspect the cylinder head combustion chamber surface closely for:

   a. Cracks
   b. Pitting
   c. Signs of gasket leakage

NOTE   If the head is badly cracked or pitted, now is the time to make a decision about replacement or repair. See chapter 9 for more details.

6. Inspect the cylinder gasket closely, especially around water holes. Areas that are blackened or burned out may indicate a warped head or block.

7. Inspect the top of piston for injection nozzle tracks or pitting.

NOTE   Fuel injected into the cylinder generally leaves light carbon or soot tracks on the pistons. This "track" or pattern indicates how well the injection nozzle or injector tip is aligned and if any plugged holes exist. See Figure 2–1a for an example.

8. Place the cylinder head on blocks or cardboard to protect it from damage.

9. If you wish to disassemble the cylinder head at this time, refer to Chapter 9 before further engine disassembly.

(a)

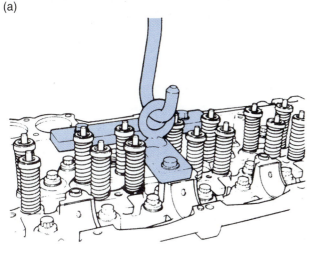

(b)

FIGURE 5–6 *(a) Using a chain fall and lifting hooks to remove a cylinder head from the engine block. (Courtesy of Caterpillar, Inc.) (b) Use of a special lifting bracket bolted to the cylinder head for safe removal. (Courtesy of Detroit Diesel Corporation.)*

Clutch and Flywheel

1. Before removing the clutch pressure plate and clutch disc, mark the pressure plate by placing "match marks" on the pressure plate and flywheel. Match marking is usually done with a center punch and a hammer or a metal marker pen.

2. Remove the bolts that secure the pressure plate to the flywheel.

3. Lift the pressure plate and clutch disc from the flywheel using proper lifting equipment.

4. Inspect the pressure plate for:
   a. Cracks, distortion, or warpage with a straightedge
   b. Wear on release fingertips and loose release finger pivot pins

5. Inspect the clutch disc (follow OSHA asbestos dust regulations). Lining is worn excessively if the riv-

ets that hold it on the disc are flush with the lining surface. On new clutch plates the rivets will be recessed about 1/16 in. (1.6 mm).

6. Match-mark the flywheel (if not marked by manufacturer). Match marking of the flywheel is done by marking the flywheel and crankshaft if accessible. If the crankshaft cannot be reached with the flywheel installed, sometimes a punch mark can be put on the flywheel and flywheel dowel pin. Many flywheels are marked or so designed at the factory for correct assembly in one of the following ways:
   a. Offset bolt holes
   b. Offset dowel pin holes
   c. Match marks or timing marks. In any event, match-marking the flywheel ensures that you will reinstall it the same way it was installed previously. If there is any doubt about flywheel timing when reinstalling the flywheel, double check the engine service manual.

7. Loosen the flywheel attaching bolts and remove the flywheel. See Chapter 7 for proper removal procedures.

CAUTION If the flywheel does not have dowel pins, use caution when removing the last bolt, since the flywheel may fall on the floor and injure you or a fellow worker.

---

8. Check the flywheel for the following:
   a. Cracks
   b. Warpage or distortion (use a straightedge)
   c. Pilot bearing fit (pilot bearing should be a hammer tap fit into the flywheel)
   d. Bolt holes for oblong-shaped and missing or stripped threads (pressure plate bolt holes)
   e. Starter ring gear for damaged or missing teeth

Oil Pan

1. Remove the bolts that secure the engine oil pan to block.

2. Remove the oil pan.

NOTE The oil pan gasket may cause the oil pan to stick to the engine block, requiring you to wedge a small screwdriver or putty knife between the block and the oil pan to break it loose. Use caution when prying on the pan to prevent damage to block or oil pan. Striking the pan with a rubber mallet can help dislodge the pan without damage.

Oil Pump and Pickup Screen (Refer to Chapter 11)

1. Unlock the oil pump bolts that hold the oil pump to the engine block.
2. Remove the oil pump hold-down bolts and remove the pump.
3. Inspect the screen for blockage.
4. Inspect the pickup tube for cracks or bends.

NOTE Some engine models such as the 14 L Cummins have an externally mounted oil pump. This type of oil pump can be removed without removing the pan. (See Chapter 11.)

At this time turn the engine over to allow further disassembly to take place (refer to Figure 5–1). If the engine is mounted on an engine stand, simply rotate the engine by turning the crank on the engine stand. If the engine is situated on the floor, lift the engine with a hoist to tip it over or lay it down.

CAUTION When lifting or moving the engine with a hoist, get someone to help you. Make it safe. Use correctly rated slings.

Vibration Damper (See Chapter 7)

The vibration dampers on most engines require a special puller for removal.

1. Remove the bolt or bolts that secure the crank shaft damper to the crankshaft.
2. Select the correct puller for removal or as indicated by your instructor.

CAUTION Most dampers have puller holes to allow them to be removed. Connect the puller only at this point, or serious damage to the damper may result. Do not remove it by striking with a hammer!

3. After removal of the damper, check it visually for:
   a. Worn areas where engine front seal rides
   b. Nicks or marks on the flywheel part of damper
4. For further information and checks to be made on the damper, refer to Chapter 7.

Timing Gear Cover

1. Remove the bolts that hold the timing gear cover to the engine block. (See Chapter 10.)
2. Remove the timing cover by tapping it with a plastic hammer.

3. If the cover cannot be removed by tapping with a plastic hammer, a screwdriver may be wedged between the cover and block to "break" it loose.

CAUTION Care must be exercised when wedging or driving a screwdriver between the cover and the block, as damage to the cover may result.

Flywheel or Bell Housing (See Chapter 7)

1. Remove the bolts from the flywheel housing.
2. Remove the housing and inspect it for cracks.

NOTE Most flywheel housings are aligned to the block with dowel pins and may require the use of a plastic hammer to jar them loose. If the hammer does not loosen the housing, you may have to use a bar or a screwdriver to pry it off.

CAUTION Care must be used when prying the housing off, or damage to the housing may result.

NOTE If the engine block is not on an engine stand, enabling you to rotate the engine, have someone help you tip it over or use a hoist. The engine block can be in the horizontal or vertical position when removing the pistons. If the engine block is mounted on an engine stand, it can be rotated easily so that pistons can be removed (Figure 5–1).

1. Before attempting to remove the pistons, the carbon and/or ridge should be removed from the top of the cylinder bore. If only carbon is at the top of the bore, it can be removed easily with emery paper or a carbon scraper. If a ridge is worn at the top of the cylinder, a ridge reamer must be used to remove it (refer to Chapter 6).

NOTE Most diesel engines using sleeves have very little or no ridge, regardless of the time on the engines. This is a result of the lubricating quality of diesel fuel, and since sleeves are generally replaced during a major overhaul, ridge removal is necessary only on engines that do not have sleeves.

2. Check the rod bearing caps and rods for match marks. If the rods have not been factory marked, mark them with a punch or number marking set to ensure that the rod cap and rod are placed together during inspection and reassembly.

3. Remove the rod cap bolts and remove the rod caps (Figure 5–7). See also Chapter 8.

4. Push the piston and rod assembly out with a wooden driver or plastic hammer handle (Figure 5–8).

CAUTION Do not attempt to drive connecting rod and piston assemblies out with a metal driver. Serious damage to the connecting rod may occur.

---

5. Keep bearings with rods for inspection.

FIGURE 5–7 Removing connecting rod cap. (Courtesy of Caterpillar, Inc.)

FIGURE 5–8 Removing the piston and con-rod assembly from the cylinder bore. (Courtesy of Caterpillar, Inc.)

Main Bearing Caps and Crankshaft

1. Place the engine block upside down to facilitate safe crankshaft removal.

2. Remove the main bearing bolts.

3. Check the main bearing caps for match marks or numbers. If the caps are not marked, use a punch or number marking set and mark the caps in relationship to the block to ensure that the caps are reinstalled in the same position!

4. After match-marking or checking the factory marks, remove the main bearing caps (Figure 5–9).

NOTE In many cases the main bearing caps have an interference fit with the block and will require a slight tap with a plastic hammer to remove. If this does not remove the cap, insert a main bearing bolt into the cap partway and tip sideways on the bolt. This will cause the cap to tip. Continue working the cap from side to side in this manner to allow you to remove it easily. Use slide hammers on caps equipped with tapped holes.

---

5. After the main bearing caps have been removed, inspect the main bearings in an effort to detect any unusual wear patterns that may indicate problems with the block or crankshaft. For a detailed explanation of bearing failures, see Chapter 7.

6. Remove the crankshaft using a lifting hook and hoist (Figure 5–10) or web slings.

FIGURE 5–9 Removing a main bearing cap. (Courtesy of Caterpillar, Inc.)

FIGURE 5–10 *Removing the crankshaft assembly with rubber hose–protected hook ends.*

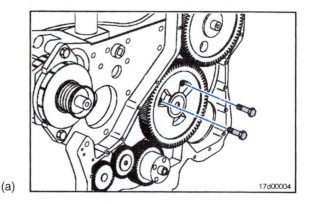

(a)

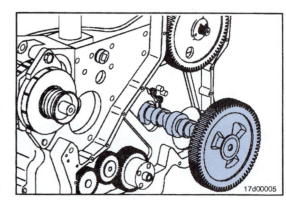

(b)

FIGURE 5–11 *(a) Remove the cap screws from the camshaft thrust plate. Note: Because both the ISC and ISL engine models' camshaft thrust plate extends more than 180° around the camshaft, the thrust plate can only be removed from the camshaft after removing the cam gear from the camshaft. (b) Remove the camshaft and thrust plate as a unit from the engine block. (Courtesy of Cummins Engine Company, Inc.)*

> **NOTE** In cases when a small inline or V8 engine is being worked on, the crankshaft can be removed easily by hand. Have someone help you lift the shaft straight up and out.

7.   Lay the crankshaft on the floor to support it or stand it on end and secure it to a workbench or other solid structure.

> **NOTE** If the crankshaft is to be laid on the floor, it should be placed on a clean piece of plywood and in an area where no damage can occur.

8.   Visually inspect the crankshaft for ridging and roughness.

An evaluation should be made at this time regarding the condition of the crankshaft, since it may have to be sent out for inspection and grinding, which takes a considerable amount of time. This decision should be made now to prevent holding up reassembly of the engine at a later date. See Chapter 7 for more detailed information on how to check and evaluate the condition of the crankshaft.

Camshaft and Timing Gears

1.   Remove the bolts that secure the camshaft retainer to the block and remove the camshaft (Figure 5–11).

2.   Visually inspect the camshaft for worn lobes or bearing journals.

3.   Inspect the timing gear or gears for wear.

Cam Followers or Cam Follower Boxes

1.   Remove cam followers by lifting them from the bores in the block (3406 Cat engine). Note that some engines such as the Cummins N14 and 'C' models require follower removal before the camshaft.

> **NOTE** Most engines (except Cummins and Detroit Diesel) with in-block camshafts have cam followers that ride in holes bored in the block and can be removed simply by lifting them out of the bore. Cummins N14 engines have the cam followers anchored to a plate called a box, which is bolted to the side of the engine. To remove this box requires the removal of the six bolts that hold it in place. Overhead camshafts employ roller followers. Refer to Chapter 10, Figure 10–3.

2.   Visually inspect the cam followers for wear, pitting, and flaking. For more detailed information on checking cam followers, see Chapter 10.

Other Brackets and Miscellaneous Items

To prepare the block for cleaning and inspection, all other brackets and soft plugs and cylinder liner sleeves (for cylinder sleeve removal instructions, see Chapter 6) should be removed before placing the block in the chemical tank.

ENGINE CLEANING PROCEDURES

All U.S. states and Canadian provinces currently have in place regulations about the disposal of hazardous chemicals. The concerned diesel technician today should be familiar with the local laws concerning the use and disposal of any cleaning agent that is commonly used in maintaining diesel-powered equipment, regardless of the application. Failure to follow the regulations can result in serious environmental damage as well as danger to the user. Substantial monetary fines are levied against companies and individuals who fail to follow responsible disposal practices.

The skilled diesel technician must be aware that to prevent damage to certain components, the correct cleaning method and chemicals must be used. Adopting the wrong cleaning method or agent can be as harmful as no cleaning at all. Bearing races and rollers, polished shafts, or gear teeth exposed to moisture, acids, or caustic solutions during the cleaning process can quickly water spot, stain, rust, or corrode. Returning such parts to the engine can cause rapid wear and premature failure. The methods discussed herein are general in nature and should not be considered an all-encompassing guide for cleaning and degreasing components. Specific cleaning methods and cleaning agents required for a particular component or assembly are usually available from commercial chemical cleaning companies; information is also available in the service literature of engine manufacturers.

SAFE WORK HABITS WHEN CLEANING

Read carefully WHHIS (workplace hazardous materials information systems) regulations. Some alkalis, detergents, and solvents can irritate the skin or be harmful to the eyes. Adequate ventilation is a must when working around and with cleaning chemicals. When working with potentially harmful substances, carefully read and heed the cautions and warnings on the product labels. *Always* wear safety equipment such as safety glasses, a face shield, gloves, and apron. Exercise extreme care when spraying to prevent injury to other personnel and to avoid an accident. Components such as cylinder liners, oil cooler cores, and radiators usually require special treatment when cleaned.

Steam Cleaning

Steam cleaning should be done only to remove heavy deposits of dirt and grease from exterior surfaces of the engine block and major drive components. Heavy grease deposits should first be scraped and brushed away. Internal engine components should not be steam cleaned, because the process may remove the protective oil film and cause the parts to water spot and rust. During an in-frame overhaul, if no other cleaning agent is readily available, steam cleaning may be done but cautiously, and all parts should be thoroughly flushed, blown-dry with compressed air, and quickly relubricated to prevent rusting.

Pressurized Oil Sprays

Oil-based mineral solvents and fuel oils under pressure can be used to flush varnish, sludge, and dirt from cylinder block internal passages and surfaces of component part housings. Drain holes or other openings through which these solvents can be flushed must be adequate to carry away dirt and flushing oils. All flushing oils must be drained completely from the components to prevent contamination from lubricants added to the reassembled components.

Heated Solvents

Many smaller engine and drive assembly components can be thoroughly and safely cleaned by flushing, soaking, or mechanically agitating them in heated petroleum solvents. Oils and solvents used for this purpose, however, must be capable of being heated to the required temperature without producing safety or health hazards from volatile or harmful vapors. Naphtha, white gas, varnish remover, and similar solvents obviously should not be heated under any circumstances.

Small parts such as bearings and gears can be suspended on metal wires, or placed in wire baskets, and submerged in the heated solvent tank to soak off grease, varnish, and sludge. Mechanical agitation of the solvent or parts will increase the effectiveness of the cleaning solvents. Extremely tough scale and varnish can be brushed loose. Exercise care to keep loose brush bristles out of assembled parts.

After cleaning all parts, machined and polished surfaces of components, bores, housings, and their internal parts should be protected from rust and corrosion with a coating of oil or light grease. Small parts can be kept in shallow pans and covered with oil until needed. Larger parts should be coated with grease or oil and wrapped in polyethelene film or oil-proof paper.

Hot Tank Cleaning

Hot tank cleaning is a method commonly used for all ordinary cast iron or steel engine parts, and is usually required when heavy scale buildup is evident within the engine block coolant passages. However, many companies that rebuild engines now employ glass or walnut beads to clean off engine blocks. The engine block is placed in an enclosure with a rotating table. The doors of the enclosure are then securely closed and the table is rotated with the engine bolted securely in place. The engine block or parts are bombarded by the beading agent to clean the part effectively without having to use chemicals.

Generally, a hot tank can be filled with a variety of commercially available cleaning chemicals; selection and strength are determined by the type of metal to be cleaned. One of the most commonly used cleaning agents for both cast iron and steel parts consists of a commercial heavy-duty alkaline solvent with a tank big enough to accept the largest engine block or component part to be cleaned. To increase the effectiveness of the cleaning process, the engine block can be lowered onto a steel grade below the level of the alkaline; then the solvent is heated to approximately 160°F (71°C) and a mechanically driven device moves the grate backward and forward to create an agitating action. In some cases, air can also be injected into the solution.

The time required to clean a component part in the alkaline solvent hot tank is determined by the degree of scale and so forth that has to be removed and the type of chemical being used. It can be as short as 20 minutes or as long as an overnight soak. For example, cylinder blocks and cylinder heads that are heavily scaled may require extra cleaning by agitating the parts in a bath of inhibited commercial pickling acid and leaving them in the acid until the bubbling action stops, which is usually between 20 and 30 minutes.

CAUTION When using commercial pickling acid, take care to prevent electrolysis between dissimilar metals such as aluminum, copper, and other nonferrous metals with the cast iron or steel engine block or head(s). These metals should be removed from the parts before they are treated with acid. Two examples are aluminum square head plugs and the injector copper tubes that are used within the cylinder head area.

After the bubbling action stops, lift the parts, allow them to drain, then reimmerse them for another 10 minutes. Repeat as necessary to completely remove all scale from the block or head coolant passages. Rinse all parts thoroughly in clean, hot water or with steam. Neutralize any remaining acid by immersing the parts in an alkali bath. Finally, rinse the parts in clean, hot water or with steam; dry the parts with compressed air; and oil all machined surfaces to prevent rusting.

Cold Tank Solvent Cleaning

Cold tank solvent cleaning can be used for most of the steel and aluminum parts of the engine. Make sure that the strength of the chemical solvent will not attack tin-coated parts such as those found on some pistons and/or liners. Cold tank cleaning is also good for removing the rustproofing compound from service replacement parts. In addition to solvents, diesel fuel oil can also be used for cleaning purposes, particularly when working with injector components. To clean a part using the cold tank method, follow these three steps:

1. Immerse and agitate the part in a suitable tank.
2. Use a soft-bristle brush to go over and through oil and water passages so that all deposits are removed.
3. When parts are thoroughly clean, rinse them in clean fuel oil and allow them to air dry, or carefully use compressed air for this purpose.

TIP   NEVER spin ball and roller bearings at high-speed with compressed air.

Cleaning Aluminum Parts

Aluminum parts can be cleaned safely in diesel fuel or in a detergent solution, but *never* one containing an *alkali*. Detergents can be used at room temperature, in a heated tank with mechanical agitation, or in a steam cleaner. To detergent-clean aluminum parts, follow these five steps:

1. Prepare a solution of heavy-duty detergent in a hot tank, cold tank, or a steam cleaner.
2. Agitate the parts in the detergent or steam clean with the detergent–water solution until all grease and dirt are removed.
3. Rinse the parts thoroughly in a tank of hot water, with a high-pressure hot water rinse, or with steam.
4. Dry all parts with compressed air.

5. If further cleaning is required, perform each of the following steps:
   a. Brush on a commercial, chlorinated solvent suitable for aluminum and leave it on the part for several hours.
   b. Steam clean the part with a solution of detergent and water.
   c. Rinse the part in clean water and dry with compressed air.

QUALITY ASSURANCE

These Standards for quality and test procedures embrace every kind of repair of internal combustion compression ignition engines—from the repair of individual engine parts to a rebuilt engine with the goal of restoring the established properties and characteristics of the engine.

Technical Prerequisites

The following equipment must be available for the proper execution of quality-assured engine repairs:

- Cleaning equipment capable of cleaning all areas of the engine parts.
- Cylinder sizing machinery for oversizing and honing of cylinders and the installation of cylinder sleeves.
- Crankshaft grinders and polishing surface finishing equipment.
- Align boring or line honing equipment for the treatment of main and cam bearing bores.
- Connecting rod equipment for the treatment of the connecting rods, including equipment to accurately gage bore diameter, roundness and taper. (honing, boring, straightening, etc.)
- Surface grinder or milling machine.
- Crankshaft straightening press.
- Head straightening equipment.
- Hydraulic press.
- Valve seat and guide equipment.
- Valve seat finishing equipment to include accurate gauging, designed for this purpose, to determine valve seat concentricity. Vacuum testing may be used in conjunction with, but not exclusively to determine machining accuracy of the finished seat.
- Equipment for the treatment of engine valves.
- Thermal equipment for fitting of parts.
- Non-destructive test equipment, for example, magnetic particle inspection, liquid penetrant testing, etc.
- Hardness testing equipment in Rockwell C or Skelgraf.

- Spring pressure test equipment.
- Precision measuring instruments for inside and outside diameters and depths with a minimum accuracy of $\pm$ 0.0001" or .0025mm, i.e. micrometers, dial indicators, cylinder bore gauges.
- Radius gauges, straight edge, surface analyzer, torque wrenches.

Technical Resources

Reference materials to establish and verify manufacturers' engine specifications. As published by the Original Engine Manufacturer, the replacement parts manufacturer or the AERA's Technical Committee.

Reconditioned Component

A component which has been found to be beyond acceptable industry standards, but which is rendered suitable for normal service by acceptable machining techniques.

Replacement Components

Replacement components are defined as items that are acquired from manufacturers or suppliers who can demonstrate fitness for purpose and who can support their products with written warranty. Replacement parts defined as those parts not designed for re-use such as gaskets, bearings, piston rings, soft plugs, o-rings and seals.

Shall

The term, shall, indicates that a statement is mandatory.

Should

The term, should, indicates a recommendation.

Inspection

Inspection refers to non-destructive testing, including visual, measurement, magnetic particle inspection, pressure testing, hardness testing, and surface finish analysis.

SUMMARY

This chapter completes the general disassembly of the engine. If the recommended visual inspections were made as the engine was disassembled, you should know the general condition of the engine and you have some idea of what parts will be needed to repair it. At this time further component inspection and repair check should take place so that a complete parts listing can be compiled. Components such as cylinder head, oil pump, and fuel injection pumps are covered separately in other chapters of this book.

SELF-TEST QUESTIONS

1. True or False: When degreasing or cleaning dirty engines and equipment, you can dump or drain oil and filters into a city drain.

2. Technician A says that heavy-duty ball or roller bearing assemblies can be cleaned safely by submerging them into a hot tank of caustic solution. Technician B disagrees strongly, saying that this can cause water spotting and acid etching of the components and should not be attempted; it is better to wash the components carefully in a clean solvent. Who is correct?

3. After a ball or roller bearing has been cleaned, technician A says that it is acceptable to spin the bearing with compressed air to ensure that all dirt particles have been removed. Technician B says that this action can severely damage the bearing and in some cases cause the bearing to disintegrate. Which technician knows safe work habits?

4. Technician A says that regardless of what type of cleaning agent is being used, you should always work in a well-ventilated area and wear safety glasses, an eye shield, gloves, and an apron. Technician B says that this is necessary only when using a caustic solution in a hot tank. Who is correct?

5. Technician A says that you should never heat naphtha, white gas, varnish remover, and similar solvents under any cleaning condition. Technician B says that as long as you do not exceed 200°F (93°C) there is no danger. Who is correct?

6. Technician A says that after any cleaning procedure, all machined surfaces should be oiled lightly to prevent rust and corrosion from forming. Technician B says that this is a bad idea because the oil tends to attract dust. Who is correct?

7. True or False: A common hot tank cleaning solution for use with both cast iron and steel parts consists of a commercial heavy-duty alkaline solvent solution.

8. Technician A says that when using a commercial pickling acid in a hot tank it is not necessary to remove nonferrous metals such as copper and aluminum engine parts. Technician B says that if you do not remove these parts, an electrolytic action between dissimilar metals will cause them to be eaten away. Who is correct?

9. True or False: The time required to clean a component part of scale accumulation depends on the strength of the cleaning solution.

10. True or False: After hot tank cleaning all parts should be thoroughly rinsed with clean hot water or steam and dried with compressed air, and machined surfaces should be lightly oiled.

11. True or False: Aluminum parts should never be cleaned in a solution containing alkali.

12. Technician A says that an in-frame engine overhaul is just as effective as a complete rebuild that involves removing the engine from its application. Technician B says that you cannot achieve as successful a job of internal cleaning of the engine block with an in-frame repair. Who is correct?

13. If an engine block is to be steam cleaned externally for any reason, technician A says that the engine should always be running to allow equal distribution of the heat from the engine block. Technician B says that this is unsafe: Steam heat applied to an aluminum injection pump housing can result in severe distortion of the housing; internal plunger-to-barrel clearances can be affected, thereby causing scuffing or scoring. Which technician knows safe working procedures best?

14. Technician A says that when disassembling an engine, you should follow a systematic procedure that allows you to minimize damage to components and to get to other components as required. Technician B says that it does not matter how you pull the engine apart, because most components will be replaced anyway. Who is correct?

15. To facilitate and assist the technician in determining the possible cause for an engine failure, technician A says that all mating parts should be carefully labeled and identified. In addition, care should be taken not to scratch, score, or damage the parts during disassembly. Technician B says that this is not necessary—why waste time since new parts will be installed. Which technician has better standards of excellence?

16. Technician A says that all engine parts that are not already marked by the manufacturer should be match-marked to allow reinstallation in the same position. Technician B says that this does not matter since all parts will be cleaned anyway and position does not make any difference. Which technician is correct?

17. On a separate sheet of paper, list the four major procedural steps required in a failure analysis.

The Cylinder Block and Liners

Overview

In this chapter we describe the main function and features of the major structural part of the diesel engine—the engine block which can be a one-piece casting, or consist of several sections bolted together. Blocks are designed to retain the engine crankshaft, camshaft, and cylinder kits (piston, rings, con-rods, liners). Blocks are machined as (1) a "parent bore" where the piston runs directly in the block, (2) a dry liner where no water/coolant contacts the outside of the cylinder liner, or (3) a wet-liner design where coolant contacts the outside diameter of the cylinder liner assembly. We discuss the necessary disassembly, inspection, and cleaning of the cylinder block and the service repair tasks required at major overhaul. Rebuild of a cylinder block can involve what is commonly referred to as either "a short block" or "a long block." A short block has been reassembled with new cylinder kits, crankshaft, camshaft, auxiliary balance shafts, bearings, oil seals, and gear train. The long block includes these components, plus installation of the oil pump, flywheel housing on diesel engines, harmonic balancer, cylinder heads, and valve train assembly. In some cases the flywheel may be included from the engine rebuild specialist shop.

ASE TEST SPECIFICATIONS

As an industry standard guide for inspection and repair of the diesel engine block, let us look at the ASE medium/heavy trucks test preparation guide, specifically diesel engines T2 test, item C, which deals with engine block diagnosis and repair. The following list highlights the areas required for inspection and assembly of this major component. From this list, ASE testing will require five correct answers.

C. Engine Block Diagnosis and Repair (5 ASE questions)

1. Remove, inspect, service, and install pans, covers, vents, gaskets, seals, and wear rings.
2. Disassemble, clean, and inspect engine block for cracks; check mating surfaces for damage or warpage and surface finish; check condition of passages, core, and gallery plugs; inspect threaded holes, studs, dowel pins and bolts for serviceability; service/replace as needed.
3. Pressure test engine block for coolant leakage; determine needed repair.
4. Inspect cylinder sleeve counterbore and lower bore; check bore distortion; determine needed service.
5. Inspect and measure cylinder walls or liners for wear and damage; determine needed service.
6. Replace/reinstall cylinder liners and seals; check and adjust liner height.
7. Inspect in-block camshaft bearings for wear and damage; replace as needed.
8. Inspect, measure, and replace/reinstall in-block camshaft; measure/adjust end play.
9. Clean and inspect crankshaft and journals for surface cracks and damage; check condition of oil passages; check passage plugs; measure journal diameters; determine needed service.
10. Inspect and replace main bearings; check cap fit and bearing clearances; check and adjust crankshaft end play.
11. Inspect, reinstall, and time the drive gear train (includes checking timing sensors, gear

wear, and backlash of crankshaft, camshaft, auxiliary, drive, and idler gears; service shafts, bushings, and bearings).

12. Clean, inspect, measure, or replace pistons, pins, and retainers.

13. Measure piston-to-cylinder wall clearance.

14. Check ring-to-groove clearance and end gaps; install rings on pistons.

15. Identify piston and bearing wear patterns that indicate connecting rod alignment or bearing bore problems; check bearing bore and bushing condition; determine needed repairs.

16. Assemble pistons and connecting rods and install in block; replace rod bearings and check clearances; check condition, position, and clearance of piston cooling jets (nozzles).

17. Inspect and measure, and service/replace crankshaft vibration damper; determine needed repairs.

18. Inspect, install, and align flywheel housing.

19. Inspect flywheel/flexplate (including ring gear) and mounting surfaces for cracks, wear, and runout; determine needed repairs.

ASE CYLINDER BLOCK SPECIALIST

In addition to the ASE diesel engines T2 test, item C, for certification as an ASE cylinder block specialist, engine machinist test preparation guide, test M2, also provides technicians with an opportunity to increase their knowledge and level of expertise of repair and service of diesel engine blocks. The cylinder block specialist test specifications consist of the following areas:

Cylinder Block Specialist—M2 Test Specifications

Content area	Questions in test	Percentage of test
A. Cylinder block disassembly and cleaning	5	8%
B. Cylinder block crack repair	4	7%
C. Cylinder block machining	22	37%
D. Crankshaft inspection and machining	12	20%
E. Connecting rods and piston inspection and machining	9	15%
F. Balancing	3	5%
G. Cylinder block preparation	5	8%
Total	**60**	**100%**

In this chapter we concentrate specifically on the engine block and the recommended ASE content areas A, B, C, and G as described from test M2, and additional chapters within this book will focus on test M2 content areas D, E, and F.

ASE M2 Task List—Cylinder Block Specialist

The following task list for test M2 shows the breakdown of the areas and components with which you must become familiar, and also indicates how many questions must be answered to pass and be certified in this area.

Cylinder Block Specialist—M2 Task List

A. **Cylinder Block Disassembly and Cleaning (5 ASE questions)**

1. Inspect block and attached components for damage.

2. Remove sensors, external components, and ID tags as needed; identify locations.

3. Remove main bearing caps, inspect main bearing caps and saddles; identify locations and mark as needed.

4. Remove and inspect camshaft bearings and auxiliary/balance shaft bearings/bushings; identify locations.

5. Remove and inspect cylinder liners as needed.

6. Remove core plugs; identify locations as needed.

7. Remove gallery plugs; identify locations as needed.

8. Verify engine make and model; record serial and casting number(s).

9. Remove engine studs as needed; identify locations.

10. Clean cylinder block

B. **Cylinder Block Crack Repair (4 ASE questions)**

1. Determine extent of crack and evaluate for repair.

2. Determine crack repair method by location of the crack; repair using accepted industry procedures.

C. **Cylinder Block Machining (22 ASE questions)**

1. Detail cylinder block; inspect mating surfaces.

2. Inspect block for cracks.

3. Inspect block for structural integrity and porosity; repair as needed.

4. Inspect block deck following manufacturer's recommendations for warpage, finish and heights; record measurements and resurface as needed.

5. Inspect cylinder bores for taper, out-of-round, and perpendicularity (squareness); bore or sleeve cylinders as needed.

6. Inspect counterbore diameter, counterbore depth, concentricity to lower bore, and lower bore condition; repair as needed.

7. Inspect main bearing caps and block mating surfaces for condition and fit.

8. Install main bearing caps and measure housing bore diameter and alignment; measure thrust width; correct bore as needed.

9. Measure camshaft and auxiliary/balance shaft bearing housing bores and alignment; repair as needed.

10. Hone cylinder bores or liners, finish to manufacturers' specifications.

11. Inspect threaded holes; repair as needed.

12. Inspect lifter bores; repair as needed.

13. Identify fastener type, condition, and suitability for reuse.

14. Locate specifications and use proper methods for tightening fasteners.

G. Cylinder Block Preparation (5 questions)

1. Clean cylinder block using industry-accepted methods.

2. Lay out all parts and components to be assembled.

3. Install cam bearings, auxiliary/balance shaft bushings and bearings; verify size, fit, alignment, location, and position.

4. Install core plugs, oil gallery plugs, sensors, external components, and ID tags as needed.

5. Install liners; verify height, fit, and O-ring position as required.

ASE Test M3 Engine Assembly Specialist

ASE offers a certification test for a technician to certify as an engine assembly specialist. The content area for this specialty is as follows:

Assembly Specialist—M3 Test Specifications

Content area	Questions in test	Percentage of test
A. Engine disassembly, inspection, and cleaning	10	17%
B. Engine preparation	11	18%
C. Short block assembly	17	28%
D. Long block assembly	14	23%
E. Final assembly	8	13%
Total	**60**	**100%**

ASE Engine Assembly Specialist Task List M3

Details of the content areas, knowledge, and hands-on expertise needed to challenge and pass this test are listed in the following informational charts and the actual number of questions that an aspiring technician would have to answer correctly to become certified as an engine assembly specialist.

> **NOTE** For detailed information about cylinder liners, pistons, rings, cam bearings, camshafts, connecting rods, main and con-rod bearings, flywheels and housings, harmonic balancers, and so forth, see the specific chapters in this book that deal with these components.

Assembly Specialist—M3 Task List

A. Engine Disassembly, Inspection, and Cleaning (10 questions)

1. Verify engine make and model; inspect engine for damage; interpret available technical and customer information.

2. Remove and inspect engine fluids; dispose of in approved manner.

3. Remove sensors, external components, studs, and ID tags as needed; identify locations.

4. Note timing marks as needed, remove fuel system, ignition system, supercharger and/or turbocharger.

5. Remove, clean, and inspect manifolds, coolers, housings, and gaskets.

6. Mark as needed, and remove harmonic balancer/pulley and flywheel.

7. Remove, clean, and inspect all pans and covers.

8. Remove and inspect valve train, cylinder heads, gaskets, and related components.

9. Remove valve lifters; identify locations.

10. Note timing marks, inspect and remove timing and retaining components.

11. Remove oil pump, remove and inspect drive and pickup assembly.

12. Check all connecting rod and main bearing caps for correct position and numbering; mark in accordance with manufacturer's recommended procedures.

13. Remove and inspect connecting rod and piston assemblies.

14. Remove and inspect main bearing caps; remove crankshaft from bearing saddles.

15. Remove and inspect main and connecting rod bearings; identify locations.
16. Remove and inspect camshaft and accessory (auxiliary/balance) shafts.
17. Remove and inspect accessory (auxiliary/balance) bearings/bushings; identify locations.
18. Remove and inspect camshaft bearings; identify locations.
19. Remove and inspect cylinder liners as needed.
20. Remove core plugs; identify locations as needed.
21. Remove gallery plugs; identify locations as needed.
22. Remove engine studs and fasteners; identify locations.
23. Clean cylinder block.

B. Engine Preparation (11 questions)
1. Clean cylinder block, crankshaft, and related components for final assembly.
2. Lay out all parts and components to be assembled; verify for application, reuse, and sizes.
3. Install camshaft bearings, auxiliary/balance shaft bushings/bearings; verify location, position, and fit.
4. Install core plugs, oil gallery plugs, oilers/piston cooling nozzles, and wear sleeves.
5. Verify cylinder liner height, fit, and O-ring position as required.

C. Short Block Assembly (17 questions)
1. Install cylinder liners as required.
2. Install mushroom-style valve lifters.
3. Install camshaft, auxiliary/balance shafts, and related components.
4. Install main bearings, oil seals, and crankshaft, following recommended procedures.
5. Install main bearing caps and check crankshaft bearing clearance and end play; check for snout, gear(s), and flange run out.
6. Install timing components; verify correct timing positions, gear backlash, and end play.
7. Assemble piston on connecting rod; verify correct position and alignment.
8. Check piston ring end gap; install piston rings following manufacturers' recommendations.
9. Install piston and connecting rod assembly according to manufacturers' recommendation and verify piston height.
10. Check connecting rod bearing clearances and connecting rod side clearances.

D. Long Block Assembly (14 questions)
1. Inspect oil pump assembly; service as needed.
2. Check for pump drive gear run out; install oil pump, drive, and pickup assembly.
3. Replace check valves, fittings, dowel pins, and adapters as needed.
4. Install ID tags, pans, covers, and housings.
5. Check flywheel housing for run out; correct as necessary. (This task applies to diesel engines only.)
6. Check harmonic balancer assembly according to manufacturers' recommendations; replace as needed; install.
7. Install cylinder head assemblies.
8. Install lifters/cam followers as needed.
9. Install pushrods and valve train components; verify valve lash setting.

E. Final Assembly (8 questions)
1. Install manifolds and intercoolers as needed.
2. Set timing; install injection pump, injectors, supercharger, and/or turbocharger; install ignition system.
3. Assemble, test, and install lubricating and oil cooling system.
4. Install remaining components.
5. Install flywheel.
6. Test short block or complete assembly.

CYLINDER BLOCK STRUCTURE

The high-speed, heavy-duty cylinder block manufactured from a cast-iron alloy with a fairly high silicon content can best be described as the main structural part of the engine because it acts as the foundation and backbone to which all other components are attached. One example of a modern, high-speed heavy-duty diesel engine cylinder block is illustrated in Figure 6–1 for Cummins ISX/Signature series models. This engine employs dual overhead camshafts located in the cylinder head. A wet-type cylinder liner and seal rings for a Detroit Diesel series 60 single overhead camshaft engine is shown in Figure 6–2. All other engine parts are bolted or connected to the cylinder block in some way.

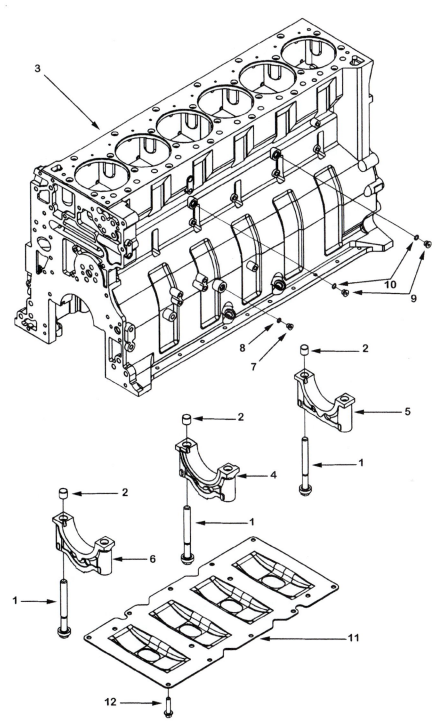

FIGURE 6–1 ISX and Signature series engine models cylinder block component identification. (Courtesy of Cummins Engine Company, Inc.)

Ref No.	Part Number	Part Name	Req	Remarks
		CYLINDER BLOCK		
		OPTION BB1724		No auxillary drive provision. Apex/Signature.
	3800452	Block, Cylinder		
1	3678506	Screw, Hex Flange Head Cap	14	
2	3678507	Dowel, Ring	14	
3	(4026532)	Block, Cylinder	1	
4	3680246	Cap, Main Bearing	1	
5	3688547	Cap, Main Bearing	1	
6	3688549	Cap, Main Bearing	5	
7	3678610	Plug, Threaded	1	
8	3678603	Seal, O Ring	1	
9	3678921	Plug, Threaded	2	
10	3678912	Seal, O Ring	1	
11	3680425	Plate, Cyl Blk Stiffening	1	
12	3680781	Screw, Hex Flange Head Cap	10	

FIGURE 6–1   (continued).

Contained within the cylinder block are the following:

1. Coolant passages and water jacket
2. Holes or bores for the piston and sleeve assembly
3. Bores or supports for the cam bushings and camshaft
4. Main bearing bores that hold the main bearings and support the crankshaft
5. Drilled or cored passageways for the engine lubrication system
6. Holes or bores in the water jacket that allow insertion of the freeze or expansion plugs
7. Many drilled and tapped holes utilizing various types of threads that allow the cylinder head or heads and other engine parts to be bolted or connected to it with some type of fastener or bolt

DIESEL ENGINE CYLINDER BLOCKS

Diesel engine cylinder blocks may be one of four types: wet sleeve, dry sleeve, bored without a sleeve (parent bore), or air cooled.

Wet Sleeve Block

A *wet sleeve* or liner is designed with a number of machined bores in which the cylinder sleeves are inserted (Figure 6–2). Coolant will be circulated around the cylinder sleeve or liner. The coolant is prevented from leaking into the crankcase of the engine by O-ring seals at the bottom of the liner. At the top of the block is a counterbore cut for the lip or flange of the liner to fit onto and prevent coolant leakage. The uppermost part of this lip may be slightly larger than the lower part. This larger diameter provides an interference fit with the block when the sleeve is installed.

Figure 6–3 illustrates three different types of wet liners. Figure 6–3a shows a widely used conventional wet liner with a press-fit flange at the top, and the respective location of the various seal rings. Figure 6–3b shows a Caterpillar 3176B, C10, and C12 engine model midstop liner that is supported in the engine block approximately halfway down its length. This design is finding much wider acceptance in several major engine models, including Cummins—in particular the dual-overhead camshaft ISX and Signature series (see Figure 6–3c). A midstop type liner is also used by Mack/RVI in its E7 inline six-cylinder engine model.

Advantages of Wet Liners

1. The major advantage is the contact of coolant directly with the sleeve, enabling rapid and positive heat transfer from the combustion chamber to the coolant.
2. Sleeves are easily removed and installed during engine rebuild to bring the cylinder block back to like-new condition.
3. Cylinder sleeves may be replaced individually if they become worn or damaged prematurely.

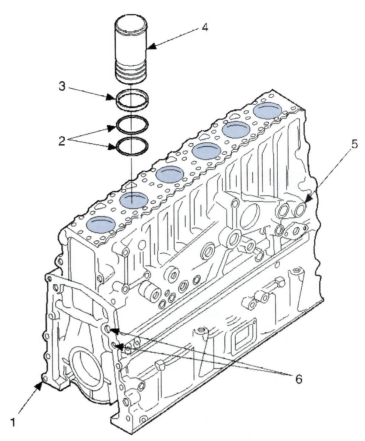

FIGURE 6–2 *Series 60 cylinder block and liner component identification. (Courtesy of Detroit Diesel Corporation.)*

1. Cylinder Block
2. D-rings
3. Crevice Seal
4. Cylinder Liner
5. Integral Coolant Inlet Manifold
6. Oil Galleries

Disadvantages of Wet Liners

1. The major disadvantages are the problems encountered in maintaining a coolant seal between the bottom of the sleeve and the block. The seals used (O-ring and crevice seals) sometimes do not have the same longevity as might be expected from the engine.

2. This seal leakage generally occurs at the bottom of the sleeve and contaminates the lube oil.

Dry Sleeve Block

A *dry sleeve* block (Figure 6–4) is designed with a bored or honed hole in the block that allows no coolant contact with the cylinder sleeve. The sleeve is inserted into the block bore where it can be either a "slip or press-fit." A counterbore is bored into the block to accommodate the sleeve flange and to help position the sleeve as in the wet sleeve type. The sleeve is held in place by the cylinder head gasket and cylinder head bolted onto the block.

Advantages of Dry Liners

1. The dry sleeve type does not have coolant in contact with the cylinder sleeve, since the sleeve is fitted into a bored hole in the block. This is a major advantage in that sealing the sleeve at the bottom is not required.

2. There is no lube oil contamination as a result of the leaking of coolant by the sleeve seals.

3. The block can be brought back to like-new condition easily by the installation of new sleeves.

4. Cylinder sleeves may be replaced individually if they become worn prematurely or damaged.

Disadvantages of Dry Liners

1. Since the coolant is not in direct contact with the sleeve, heat transfer from the combustion chamber to the coolant water is not as rapid as it would be with a wet-type sleeve.

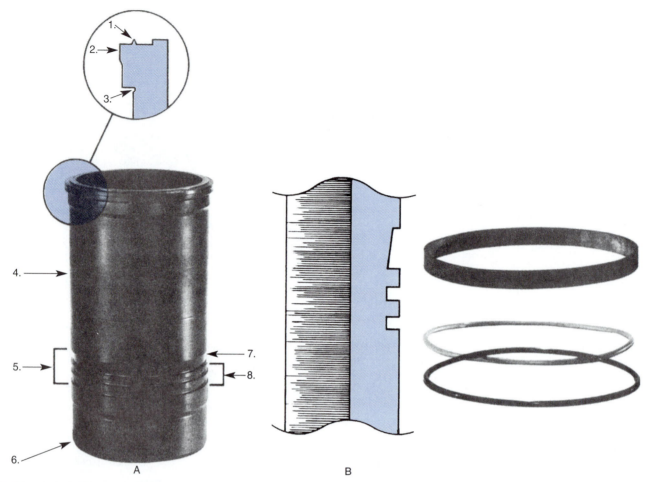

FIGURE 6–3A Features of a typical wet cylinder liner assembly and the seal rings required to retain the engine coolant within the block passages: 1. bead; 2. press fit; 3. relief; 4. liner wall; 5. sealing area; 6. chamfer; 7. crevice seal groove; 8. packing ring grooves. (Courtesy of Cummins Engine Company, Inc.)

Liner Seat

Crankcase Pilots

FIGURE 6–3B Midstop cylinder liner design employed by Cat in its 3176 and 10 and 12 L engine models. (Reprinted courtesy of Caterpillar, Inc.)

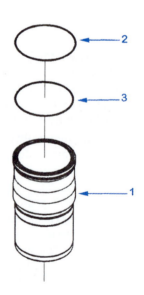

FIGURE 6–3C Cylinder liner kit for Signature and ISX series engine models: 1. cylinder liner; 2. O-ring seal; 3. O-ring seal. (Courtesy of Cummins Engine Company, Inc.)

Ref No.	Part Number	Part Name	Req	Remarks
		CYLINDER LINER KIT		
		OPTION BB1724		
	3800453	Kit, Cylinder Liner	1	
1	(3681046)	Liner, Cylinder	6	
2	3678737	Seal, O Ring	6	
3	3678738	Seal, O Ring	6	

FIGURE 6–3 (continued).

FIGURE 6–4 Dry press-fit cylinder liner showing the liner flange shim required to obtain the correct flange protrusion. (Courtesy of Mack Trucks, Inc.)

2. This slow heat transfer may result in short engine life and cylinder damage.

No-Sleeve Block

A *parent-bore* or *no-sleeve* block, such as the Cat 3116 or 3126 engine model, has holes bored for the cylinder with the pistons and piston rings inserted directly into this hole. No provision in the block for wet- or dry-type sleeves is made, but a damaged block can be bored to accept a sleeve.

Advantages of a Parent Bore

1. The major advantage is the initial cost of construction in that the machining and fitting of sleeves is not required.
2. No provision has to be made for O-ring grooves and no contact area is needed.
3. The block can be made lighter because of thin cylinder wall construction.

Disadvantages of a Parent Bore

1. A major disadvantage of this type of block is that during rebuild or repair of the engine a worn cylinder must be rebored or honed.
2. Reboring requires special equipment and the engine must be disassembled completely.
3. Reduced engine block life.

Air-Cooled Block

An *air-cooled* block is similar to a parent-bore block in that it does not have cylinder sleeves but bored holes for the piston. It has no coolant passageways or water jackets; fins have been added to the cylinder block to dissipate heat. Cooling then is accomplished by the passage of air around the fins.

Advantages of Air Cooling

1. It is much lighter in weight because the water jackets have been eliminated.
2. No coolant is required, which in itself eliminates problems that go with liquid-cooled engines, such as leakage, freezing, rust formation, and inadequate cooling.
3. This eliminates the need for a radiator, water pump, and thermostat.

Disadvantages of Air Cooling

1. It generally does not have sleeves, making replacement or reboring necessary if one cylinder becomes worn or damaged.
2. It has no coolant with which to operate hot water heaters used in trucks, and in tractors with cabs.
3. It needs some type of cooling fan, usually belt driven.
4. Cooling fans around cylinders can become clogged by dirt and engine oil, creating an overheated cylinder.

DISASSEMBLY, INSPECTION, AND CLEANING OF THE CYLINDER BLOCK

At this point all major components and accessories should have been removed from the block. Further disassembly should include removal of the following:

1. *Oil galley or passageway plugs*
2. *All cover plates (oil and water)*
3. *Expansion plugs (soft plugs).* Removal of expansion plugs can be accomplished quickly and easily by:
    a. Driving a sharp punch or chisel through them
    b. Twisting or turning them sideways
    c. Prying them from block with a bar, using caution not to damage the block, which will prevent a new plug from sealing
    d. Inspecting the expansion plugs after removal in an attempt to determine if the engine coolant was being properly maintained

NOTE   If expansion plugs show signs of high corrosive action within the cooling system, check the water filter or conditioner.

4. *Oil pressure relief valves*
    a. Remove the valve and spring.
    b. Make sure that the valve moves freely in its bore and that the spring is not broken. (See Chapter 11.)

Removing the Cam Bushings

Removal of cam bushings or bearings should not be attempted without special bushing drivers, or damage to the cam bearing bore in the block may result. Two types of bushing installation and removal tools are common in most shops: the solid nonadjustable type (Figure 6–5a) made to fit one size bushing or the adjustable type (Figure 6–5b) which can be adjusted to fit any size bushing within a given range.

Before removal of the cam bushings, inspect them to determine if normal wear has occurred or if some malfunction or lubrication problem exists. Also check all oil supply holes before removal of the bushings so that no question exists about the proper alignment when installing the bushing. The cam bushings should be removed as follows:

1. Select the correct-size bushing driver.
2. Place the bushing driver into the bushing to be removed.

(a)

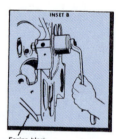

(b)

FIGURE 6–5   (a) Fixed size (nonadjustable) cam bushing removal and installation tools. (b) Adjustable-type camshaft bushing removal and installation tools.

3. Place the driver guide cone on the driving bar and insert the assembly into the block and bushing driver.

4. Make sure that the guide cone is held securely into another bushing or bushing bore so that no misalignment of driving bar can occur.

5. Hold the bar with one hand and strike it on the driving end with solid, firm hits with a large hammer.

6. Drive the bushing until it clears the block bore.

7. Repeat the procedure to remove all cam bushings.

BLOCK FLOWCHART INSPECTION

To comply with and determine repairs according to ASE cylinder block task list items, refer to Figure 6–6, which illustrates in simplified flowchart order the various step procedures to determine if repair or replacement of the engine block is actually necessary. Information following this flowchart describes in detail how to check, inspect, and test the various components listed therein.

Removing the Cylinder Sleeves/Liners

Cylinder sleeves must be pulled or pushed out of the block with a sleeve puller. The most common type of sleeve puller in use is similar to the one shown in Figure 6–7. Always match-mark the liner-to-the-block before removal to allow reinstallation in the same cylinder and position if it is to be reused!

Pulling Wet Sleeves from the Block

1. Select the adapter plate that will fit the sleeve.

2. Make sure that the plate fits snugly in the sleeve (to prevent cocking) and that the outside diameter of the puller plate is not larger than the sleeve outside diameter. (An adapter plate larger than the sleeve may damage the block.)

3. Attach the adapter plate to the through bolt.

NOTE   If the adapter plate is the type that can be installed from the top of the sleeve, it will have a cutaway or milled area on each side (Figure 6–7). This, and the swivel on the bottom of the through bolt, allows the plate to be tipped slightly and inserted from the top, eliminating the need to install the adapter plate in the bottom of the sleeve and then insert the through bolt and attach the nut.

4. After the adapter plate and through bolt have been installed in the sleeve, hold them firmly in the sleeve with one hand and install the support bracket with the other hand.

5. Screw the through-bolt nut down on the through bolt until it contacts the support bracket. This will hold the adapter plate and through bolt snugly in place.

CAUTION   Before tightening the sleeve puller nut, make sure the sleeve puller supports or legs are positioned on a solid part of the block. Tighten the nut with the ratchet; the sleeve should start to move upward. If it does not and the puller nut becomes hard to turn, stop and recheck your puller installation before proceeding.

By using an air-impact wrench to rotate the hex nut on top of the tool, quick liner removal is assured. A tool such as this allows the technician to pull six stubborn wet liners in less than four minutes. By means of adapters, this tool can be made to fit a wide variety of diesel engine cylinder liners.

6. On wet sleeves, after the sleeve has been pulled from the block far enough to clear the O-rings, tip or swivel the sleeve puller adapter plate and remove the sleeve puller assembly.

7. The sleeve can now be lifted out by hand.

NOTE   Engines with tight-fitting dry sleeves may require a special hydraulic puller.

Pulling Dry Sleeves with a Hydraulic Puller

1. Select an adapter plate to fit the sleeve. (See note in "Pulling Wet Sleeves from the Block.")

2. Assemble the through-bolt plate and hydraulic ram.

3. Adjust the through-bolt nut so that the adapter plate fits snugly in the sleeve and the hydraulic ram sits firmly on the supports or legs.

CAUTION   Make sure that the legs or supports are positioned on a solid part of the block to prevent cracking the block.

4. Stroke the hydraulic hand pump connected to the hydraulic ram.

5. Make sure that the puller plate is seated correctly in the sleeve.

6. Operate the hand pump until the sleeve is removed.

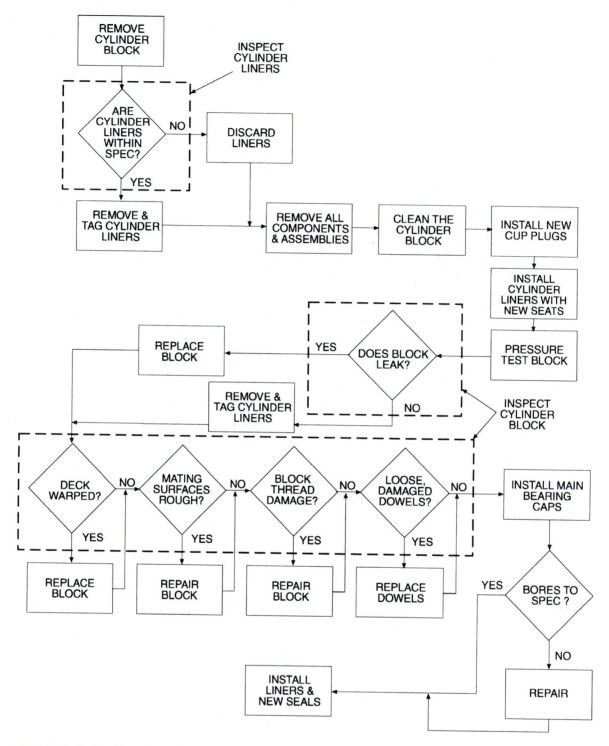

FIGURE 6–6 Diagnostic flowchart for repair and replacement of the engine cylinder block. (Courtesy of Detroit Diesel Corporation.)

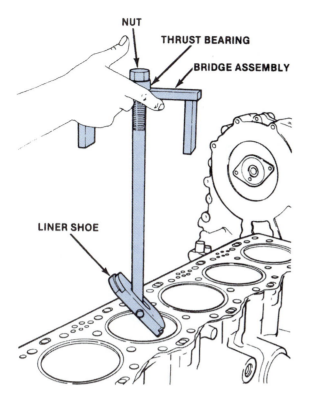

FIGURE 6–7 *Pivoting shoe type of cylinder liner puller with its bridge assembly and puller screw, Kent Moore P. N. J35791. (Courtesy of Detroit Diesel Corporation.)*

NOTE   If the sleeve does not move upward after considerable hydraulic pressure has been applied, it may be necessary to tap the sleeve adapter plate from the bottom, using a bar and hammer to break it loose.

CAUTION   Under no circumstances should a hydraulic ram or hand pump be overloaded by using an extension handle on the hand pump. This may cause a hydraulic hose to burst, resulting in serious injury to the operator from high-pressure hydraulic fluid escaping.

---

7.   Pump the hydraulic hand pump until the puller cylinder has moved its full length.

8.   If the sleeve cannot be moved using this procedure, try using an electric welder and weld several beads vertically inside the full length of the sleeve from top to bottom. This heating and cooling of the sleeve may shrink it enough to allow removal.

9.   In some cases, press-fit dry sleeves cannot be removed successfully using any one or all of the procedures as outlined. If this is the case, the cylinder block must be taken to an automotive machine shop and the sleeve bored out.

Once the liner has been removed, write the cylinder number on its outer surface with a liquid metal marker or Dykem, and tag any shims from below the liner flange to ensure that they will be used with the same liner. This will allow you to retain the same cylinder liner protrusion or intrusion, depending on the type of liner used. Should the liner be removed due to failure, use match marks and numbers so that upon closer inspection, the technician or factory service representative can determine the cause of failure.

Cylinder Liner Inspection Flowchart

When reviewing the ASE tasks lists items to determine the condition of individual cylinder liners, refer to the flowchart in Figure 6–8. More specific details of this process follow in the next section.

Inspecting the Cylinder Liner

When a wet cylinder liner has been removed at major overhaul or because of leaking liner seal rings, consider whether the liner might be used again. If so, it must be thoroughly cleaned and then inspected. After removing the liner seal rings, wash the liner in detergent soap and warm water and clean the inside diameter with a stiff nonmetallic brush to remove dirt and impurities. Use a high-quality steel wire brush to clean the liner flange seating area. If the outside diameter of the liner is scaled from coolant, check the thickness of the scale buildup. Use a wire brush on the liner to remove the scale, because a strong caustic solution could leave stains on the machined inside diameter of the liner. Then use a steam cleaner or solvent in a tank to clean the liner. Dry the liner with compressed air and lightly lubricate the machined surfaces to prevent any possibility of rusting. This also allows the oil to work its way into the surface finish.

SERVICE TIP   If the liners are not going to be inspected or used right away, always store them in an upright position until ready for use. Experience has shown that liners left on their sides for any length of time can become egg shaped and distorted, thereby making reinstallation in the block bores very difficult—sometimes even impossible.

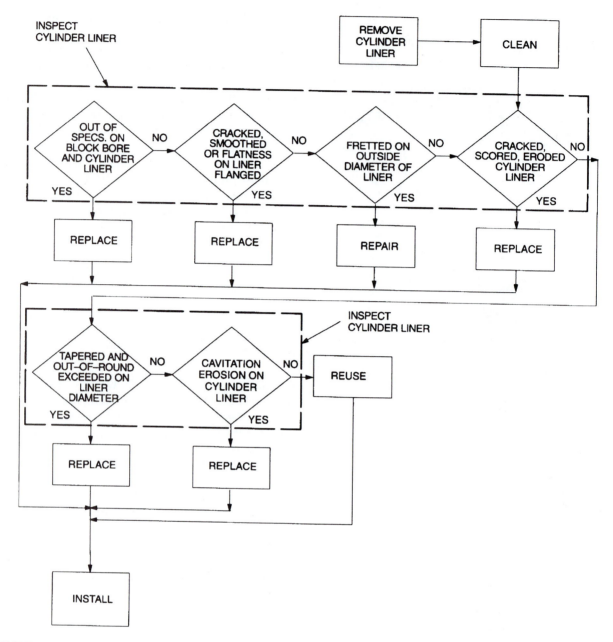

FIGURE 6–8   Cylinder liner repair and replacement flowchart diagnosis. (Courtesy of Detroit Diesel Corporation.)

Once a liner has been cleaned thoroughly, closely inspect it to determine if it has the following characteristics:

1. *Surface finish and/or crosshatch irregularities.* Refer to Figure 6–9a and check for a moderate polish. A moderate polish means a bright mirror finish exists only in areas that are worn and some traces of the original hone marks, or an indication of an etch pattern, are still visible. Figure 6–9b illustrates a near-mirrorlike finish in the worn area with no traces of the original

hone marks or an etch pattern. Replace the liner if a heavy polish is visible over 20% of the piston ring travel area (Figure 6–9c) or if 30% of the ring travel area has both a moderate and a heavy polish while the other half shows a heavy polish (Figure 6–9d).

2. *Scuffing, scoring, gouging, or low spots on the inside diameter.* If your fingernail catches in a scratch, the liner should be replaced.

3. *Taper, wear, and ovality on the inside diameter of the liner by using a precision dial bore gauge at various*

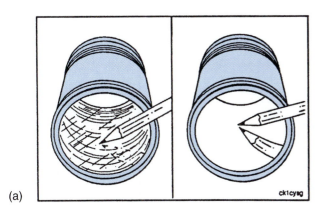

(a)

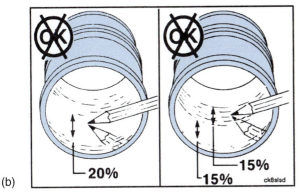

(b)

FIGURE 6–9   (a) Surface shows signs of moderate polish, but some traces of the original hone marks and etch pattern are visible. (b) Surface exhibits a mirrorlike finish with no traces of the original hone or etch marks. (c) Surface shows a heavy polish present over 20% of the piston ring travel area. (d) Surface shows both moderate and heavy polish over 30% of the piston ring travel area, and one half (15%) is heavy polish. (Courtesy of Cummins Engine Company, Inc.)

points, as shown in Figure 6–10. If the taper and out-of-round exceed the engine OEM's specs, replace with a new liner. Also check the outer seal ring and crevice seal grooves for minor burrs or sharp edges. Smooth these with emery cloth. Severe burrs or pitting requires liner replacement.

4.   *Signs of cracking, particularly at the flange, and around the port belt area of two-stroke-cycle engines.* (It may be necessary to employ a nondestructive magnetic particle, fluorescent magnetic particle, and a black light, or a fluorescent penetrant method similar to that described for checking an engine block or crankshaft, if cracks cannot be seen clearly with the naked eye.)

5.   *Additional flange irregularities.* Check for smoothness and flatness on the top and bottom surfaces.

6.   *A smooth and flat hardened liner insert, if used below the flange.* Replace the insert if it shows signs of indentations.

7.   *Cavitation erosion, severe corrosion, or pitting on the outside surface of wet liners.* This problem is caused by poor cooling system maintenance. An example of erosion on the outside of a liner can be seen in Figure 6–11. If cavitation erosion is uncorrected, it will eventually create pinholes through the liner wall surface. When the engine is running, the turbocharger boost pressure, the exhaust gases, and the combustion gases can blow coolant out of the radiator or heat exchanger and result in oil in the coolant. When the engine is shut down, coolant can enter the oil through the cylinder and also cause a hydrostatic lock when the coolant is placed under pressure by the upward-moving piston. This can cause a bent con-rod. Reject the liner if deep pits are visible or if the corrosion cannot be removed with a fine emery cloth.

8.   *Dark spots, stains, or low-pressure areas on the outside diameter of dry liners.* This indicates poor liner-to-block contact.

9.   *Shiny areas on the outside diameter or flange area.* These usually indicate liner movement (wet or dry type).

10.   *Fretting on the outside diameter of the liner, particularly below the ports on two-cycle engines.* This is the result of slight movement of the liner during engine operation, causing block metal to adhere to the liner. These metal particles can be removed from the surface of the liner with a coarse, flat stone.

SYSTEMATIC OVERVIEW OF ENGINE BLOCK CHECKS

Prior to preparing to determine the overall condition of the block, with the aid of both short text and diagrams carefully review what is required to rebuild a fitted or short block assembly.

Rebuilding A Fitted or Short Block Assembly

Cylinder Block

The cylinder block shall be disassembled and all oil and water galley plugs and all bearings removed and thoroughly cleaned inside and out. Where fitted, bolt-on piston cooling nozzles and cylinder liners shall be removed. The cylinder block, including all threaded holes, shall be inspected as appropriate to ensure suitability for reuse.

a.   The block deck surface shall be checked for deck height and surface flatness (See Fig. 6–12), to ensure it meets manufacturers' and replacement part manufacturers specifications.

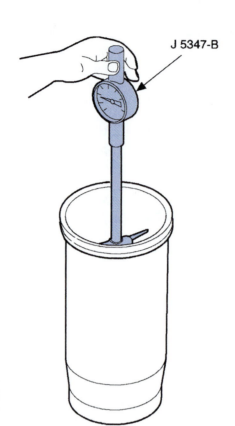

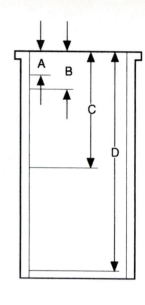

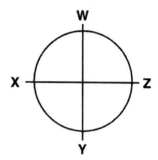

FIGURE 6–10 Series 50/60 cylinder liner dial indicator measurement diagram. (Courtesy of Detroit Diesel Corporation.)

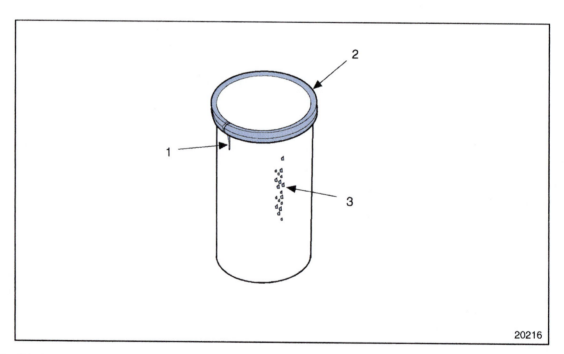

20216

1. Cracks

2. Cylinder Liner

3. Erosion

FIGURE 6–11 Example of pitting of a wet cylinder liner due to cavitation erosion: 1. cracks; 2. cylinder liner; 3. erosion. (Courtesy of Detroit Diesel Corporation.)

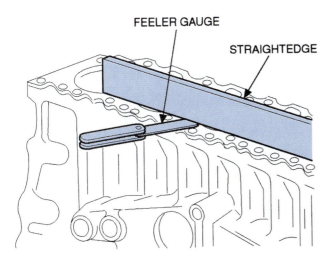

FEELER GAUGE

STRAIGHTEDGE

FIGURE 6–12 *Checking the top deck of the engine block with a straightedge and feeler gauge for warpage or distortion. (Courtesy of Detroit Diesel Corporation.)*

1. In certain instances, such as engines with removable liners, the surface may not require machining, but in such instances liner recesses shall be checked and trued as required (See Figure 6–17), and the sealing surfaces shall be verified to conform to acceptable industry standards.
2. All other gasket or sealing faces on the block shall be checked for reuse or serviceability and corrected if necessary using industry acceptable machining methods. See Figure 6–18.

b. The main bearing housing bore shall be checked for the following
   1. Proper fit of cap to block
   2. All housing bores having the correct inside diameter (See Fig. 6–13).
   3. All bores in a straight plane in a proper location (See Fig. 6–14).
   4. Thrust location to be checked and verified
   5. Complete crankcase check; may require liner honing (Fig. 6–22).

c. All bore type blocks shall have cylinder bores checked for reuse. Similar to Fig. 6–10. Either boring to oversize as per Figure 6–21 or installing sleeves back to standard can reclaim bores not meeting specification for size, surface finish, and crosshatch as recommended by the manufacturer. All these types of blocks shall be pressure tested.

d. All blocks with replaceable type liners shall have liner "o"ring sealing areas checked for pits (See Fig. 6–11), including chamfer where crevice seal Fig. 6–2 is used, and bore concentricity compared to the upper 'pilot bore' area Fig. 6–24. Counter bores are to be checked as per Fig. 6–16 including depth and squareness. Parent bores shall be checked for accordance with manufacturer specifications.

All cylinders that dimensions are outside of manufacturer's specifications are to be:

a. Replaced with new sleeves manufactured from proper materials and finished to original or ring manufacturers' specification.
b. Or resized and finished honed as per Figure 6–20 to within the recommended limits of oversized with an appropriate surface finish and crosshatched angle as defined by the piston ring manufacturers' specification. See Figure 6–29 and 6–30.

Assembly Procedures

Engine Assembly

During assembly of the short block the following procedures shall be observed:

a. All components shall be thoroughly cleaned.
b. All expansive plugs shall be replaced. See Fig. 6–23. All other plugs may be reused if qualified by inspection.
c. All applicable mating surfaces shall be lubricated with an appropriate lubricant and surfaces susceptible to storage corrosion shall be treated with suitable rust inhibitor.
d. Cylinder block shall be reassembled using the following new or reconditioned parts as determined in Chapter 7 and Chapter 8.
   1. Main, connecting rod, camshaft and auxiliary shaft bearings and bushings.
   2. Pistons, pins and rings
   3. Gaskets, expansion plugs and seals.

Long Block Assembly

A long block assembly is a combination of a short block as described and a cylinder head as described and assembled as in Chapter 9.

> **NOTE** All relevant bolts, nuts and screws, etc. shall be tightened to specifications as determined by the manufacturer, and all running clearances shall be checked and corrected during assembly.

Inspecting the Cylinder Block

After all sleeves have been removed, a preliminary visual inspection should be made to determine if the block can be repaired and reused or if it requires replacement. See Figure 6–6. Items to check at this point are:

1. Visual cracks in water jacket internally and externally
2. Cored or drilled passageways for cracks
3. Main bearing and cylinder head bolt holes for cracked or broken threads
4. Block top surface for excessive erosion around water holes, head gasket wear, or cracks
5. Main bearing caps and saddles for cracks

After determining that the block will be reusable, all gasket material and heavy accumulation of grease or oil should be scraped or wiped off. It is common practice at this time to soak the block in a hot or cold tank of cleaning solution, which should remove all carbon, grease, scale, and lime deposits. After the block is removed from the tank, it can be cleaned with a steam cleaner, high-pressure washer, or water hose. During steaming of all passageways, oil galleys, and water jackets, use a stiff bristle brush or other suitable device to dislodge all foreign material that may be lodged or caked in the block. Finally, pressure check the block for cracks similar to that shown in Figure 9–9 for a cylinder head.

NOTE Special attention should be given to the removal of scale or sludge accumulations within the water jackets because they will act like insulation and prevent heat from traveling into the coolant water. Poor heat transfer may cause scuffing or scoring of the cylinder and rings and excessive oil consumption. Consideration of what caused the sludge formation should be given at this point. Is it a normal accumulation, or has the cooling system maintenance been neglected?

It is recommended that after the block has been steamed it be sprayed with a light coat of preservative or rust preventive oil or solution.

FINAL INSPECTION, TESTING, RECONDITIONING, AND ASSEMBLY

At this time it is suggested that the block be placed on a suitable engine stand so that it can be rotated and tilted to allow access to all areas. If an engine stand is not available, a clean workbench will be sufficient.

NOTE It is also suggested that the block be checked with an electric crack detector if it is available. Every attempt should be made at this point to ensure that the block is not cracked, since in the following steps the block is being readied for reassembly.

Checking the Block-Top Surface for Warpage

The cylinder block top must be checked for straightness throughout its length and for erosion around water outlets, using the following procedures.

NOTE Erosion can be checked only after the block has been thoroughly cleaned.

1. Clean the top machined surface of the block by hand with sandpaper or with an electric or air-driven sander.
2. To determine the extent of erosion damage, use a new head gasket. Lay the gasket on the block. Visually check to see whether erosion will interfere with the gasket sealing.
3. If the erosion around water holes is excessive, the block-top surface must be resurfaced or the water holes sleeved. No further checks can or should be made until the top surface has been resurfaced. (Resurfacing or machining the block-top surface requires special equipment and should not be attempted in a general repair shop.) Most automotive machine shops have equipment to perform the resurfacing operation. If the water holes are to be sleeved, refer to the engine service manual for the correct procedure.
4. If the top surface has not been resurfaced and is considered usable because of lack of erosion, it should be checked for straightness both lengthwise and crosswise as well as diagonally.
5. Using an accurate straightedge, check the block by setting the straightedge on the top of the block (Figure 6–12).
6. Hold the straightedge with one hand. Using a 0.0015 to 0.002 in. (0.04 to 0.05 mm) feeler gauge, try to insert the feeler gauge between the block and straightedge. Most engine manufacturers recommend that if

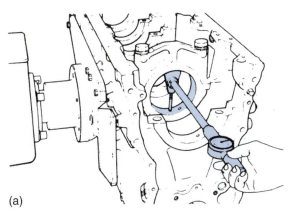

(a)

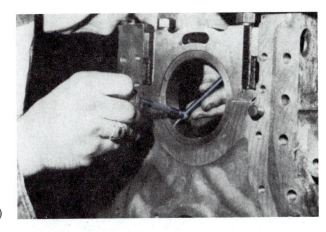

(b)

FIGURE 6–13 (a) Measuring the cylinder block crankshaft main bearing bores with a precision dial bore gauge. (b) Checking the main bearing bore with a telescoping gauge. (Courtesy of Detroit Diesel Corporation.)

the block is warped 0.004 in. (0.10 mm) or more, it should be remachined.

7. Inspect and tap all bolt holes to ensure that the threads are clean and usable.

Checking the Main Bearing Bore Size and Alignment

Checking the main bearing bore is a very important step in engine or block rebuild. The main bearing bore should be checked for correct diameter and out-of-roundness using either a dial bore gauge or telescoping holegauge, as shown in Figure 6–13. In addition to this check, many manufacturers recommend the use of a master bar (Figure 6–14) to check the main bearing bore alignment.

FIGURE 6–14 Using a master bar to check the main bearing bore alignment. (Courtesy of Cummins Engine Company, Inc.)

NOTE Some technicians do not make main bearing bore alignment checks on engines that have a tendency to have a problem with bore alignment. The main bearing bore is simply redone whenever the engine is rebuilt, as a matter of routine. With this in mind, check with your instructor or someone who has had experience with engine rebuilding. If in doubt about main bearing bore alignment, send the block to a shop that has the capability to check and/or bore the main bearing bores.

Checking and/or Reconditioning the Cylinder Sleeve Counterbore

1. The block counterbore and packing ring area must be cleaned of all rust, scale, and grease and should not have any rough, eroded areas that might cut or ruin a sleeve, O-ring, or crevice seal.

a. Check the sleeve counterbore closely for cracks; if cracks are found, the block can be salvaged by resleeving the counterbore. Resleeving the counterbore should be attempted only by experienced technicians using the correct equipment.

2. Cleaning the block packing ring area and liner flange counterbore lip can be done by hand with a small piece of crocus cloth, wet–dry sandpaper, or emery paper of 100 to 120 grit (Figure 6–15).

3. The block counterbore top depth must be measured to ensure that sleeve protrusion will be correct after the sleeve is installed. The counterbore should also be uniform in depth around the circumference of the bore.

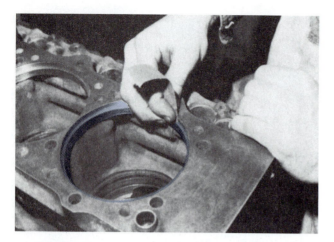

FIGURE 6–15 *Cleaning the cylinder liner flange block counterbore with emery cloth prior to liner installation. (Courtesy of Cummins Engine Company, Inc.)*

4. Measurement of the block counterbore should be done with a depth micrometer or dial indicator mounted on a machined sled fixture (Figure 6–16). If a depth micrometer is used, make sure that the micrometer is held firmly on the block surface when making measurements.

5. The counterbore depth should be checked in at least four positions around the circumference of the counterbore to determine if the depth is within specifications. The counterbore depth should not vary more than 0.001 in. (0.025 mm) at all four positions. Counterbore slope will cause liner flange cracking!

6. After measuring the counterbore depth, the sleeve lip or flange should be measured with an outside micrometer.

NOTE   Use a new sleeve for this measurement or check the service manual specification.

The block counterbore depth can then be subtracted from this figure to obtain an estimated sleeve protrusion of 0.001 to 0.005 in. (0.025 to 0.127 mm).

7. If the counterbore does not meet the manufacturer's specifications, it should be reworked. On many engines, reworking the counterbore is a simple operation that can be accomplished easily if the correct tools are available. The counterbore tool is designed to fit into the block and recut the counterbore to a uniform depth (Figure 6–17). If the block counterbore cannot be reworked within your shop, many automotive machine shops can perform this type of work. Since correct sleeve protrusion determined by block counterbore depth and condition is vitally important to correct head gasket sealing, the block counterbore must be correct before engine reassembly can continue.

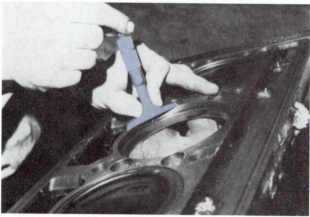

(a)

(b)

FIGURE 6–16 *(a) Measuring the block liner flange counterbore with a depth micrometer. (b) Checking the counterbore depth with a dial indicator mounted on a sled gauge. (Courtesy of Detroit Diesel Corporation.)*

NOTE   After recutting, the counterbore depth has been increased in depth. As a result, the sleeve protrusion will not be correct. This can be remedied by placing shims of the proper thickness on the sleeve to make up for the metal that has been removed from the block. Not all sleeves fit in the block with protrusion. Some engine sleeves when installed are below the top surface of the block. Check the sleeve position according to the manufacturer's specifications.

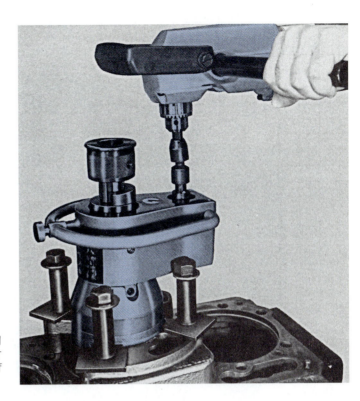

FIGURE 6–17 Using a power-driven Porta-Matic tool for an in-frame repair of a cracked or damaged cylinder liner counterbore area of the cylinder block. (Courtesy of Kent Moore Division, SPX Corporation.)

After you have completed the checks as outlined, the block is ready for reassembly.

Block Machining

Cylinder block checks, inspection, and measurements may indicate the following problems:

1. Warpage of the top deck
2. Cylinder bores distorted (taper, ovality, wear). Parent bore engines do not employ a cylinder liner; the piston rides directly in the cylinder block bore.
3. Cylinder liner block counterbore slope or damage
4. Lower block bore damage at the base of the liner seal ring area on wet liners
5. Camshaft bore damage
6. Crankshaft bore misalignment
7. Erosion around water passage holes
8. Blower mounting pad distortion (two-cycle engine models)

Any of these conditions would necessitate the need for machining of the top deck, power honing or boring of the cylinder liner parent bores, machining and sleeving of the liner counterbore or lower bore area, or camshaft or crankshaft line boring/honing of the crankshaft main bearing caps. This requires special equipment such as that shown in Figure 6–18 to remachine the top of the block.

NOTE The amount of material that can be removed from the top surface of the engine block is limited to the engine manufacturer's specs. If too much material is removed, the distance from the centerline of the crankshaft to the top of the block will be reduced. Consider that with an overhead camshaft design such as that used by Caterpillar in its 3406E, Detroit Diesel in its series 60, and John Deere—all of which use a SOHC—and Cummins with its ISX and Signature DOHC, the camshaft is mounted in the cylinder head so resurfacing of the block affects the position of the camshaft and its gear in relation to either an adjustable idler gear or to the gear train itself. Insufficient gear backlash can result. In a cylinder block with an in-block camshaft, removing too much material from the top surface of the block could also result in a piston coming into contact with the cylinder head or valves. The block machinist should always stamp the amount of stock removed from the top surface of the block in a nonsealing area. One common location to do this is shown in Figure 6–19 on a pad just above the pan rail mounting surface.

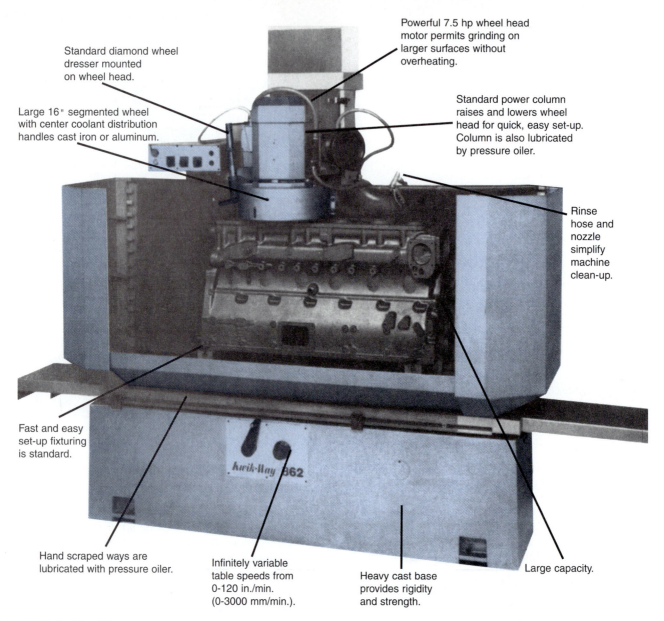

Standard diamond wheel dresser mounted on wheel head.

Large 16" segmented wheel with center coolant distribution handles cast iron or aluminum.

Powerful 7.5 hp wheel head motor permits grinding on larger surfaces without overheating.

Standard power column raises and lowers wheel head for quick, easy set-up. Column is also lubricated by pressure oiler.

Rinse hose and nozzle simplify machine clean-up.

Fast and easy set-up fixturing is standard.

Hand scraped ways are lubricated with pressure oiler.

Infinitely variable table speeds from 0-120 in./min. (0-3000 mm/min.).

Heavy cast base provides rigidity and strength.

Large capacity.

FIGURE 6–18 Diesel engine block securely mounted and precision leveled to allow a grinding and milling machine to resurface the top deck of the block. This same machine can be used to resurface the cylinder head. (Courtesy of Kwik-Way Manufacturing Co.)

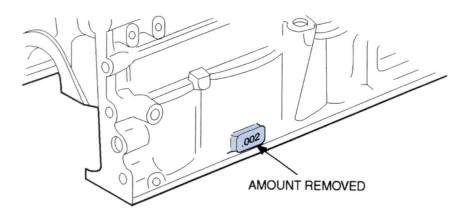

.002

AMOUNT REMOVED

FIGURE 6–19 Location to stamp or record the amount of stock removed from a resurfaced cylinder block assembly. (Courtesy of Detroit Diesel Corporation.)

NOTE Caterpillar 3126 Engine blocks with heights less than 12.667 in. (321.75 mm) require the use of the 119-2948 head gasket. The gasket is 0.010 in./0.25 mm thicker than the standard head gasket. The thicker head gasket allows the block deck to be resurfaced below what would be possible with the standard head gasket. The increased material removed from the block deck causes the pistons to project higher above the block surface at top center (TC). The thicker head gasket keeps the pistons from hitting the cylinder head and valves.

NOTE The 119-2948 head gasket should not be used unless the block has been resurfaced below the minimum specified measurement. Using the 119-2948 head gasket when it is not needed will result in a lower compression ratio and may cause hard starting and excessive white smoke.

Figure 6–20 shows the equipment needed either to power-hone the block liner bores, or to rebore the cylinder bore to accept an oversized-outside-diameter cylinder liner. In dry liners, a damaged block bore

FIGURE 6–20 Power honing machine used to hone a cylinder block bore to accept either an oversized outside-diameter liner or piston assembly. (Courtesy of Kwik-Way Manufacturing Co.)

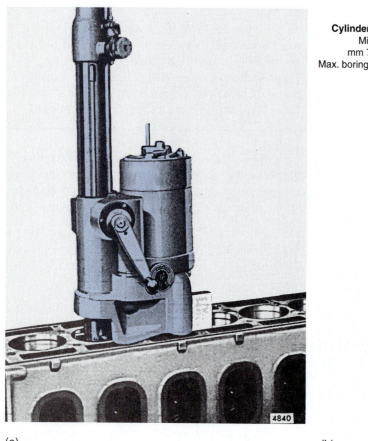

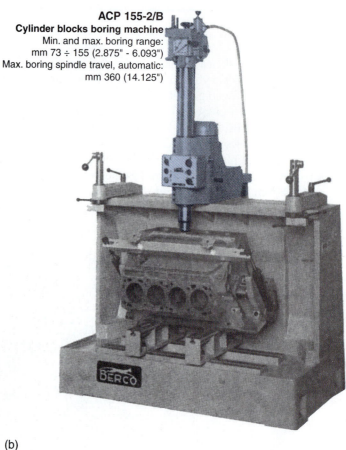

ACP 155-2/B
Cylinder blocks boring machine
Min. and max. boring range:
mm 73 ÷ 155 (2.875" - 6.093")
Max. boring spindle travel, automatic:
mm 360 (14.125")

(a)   (b)

FIGURE 6–21   (a) Portable boring bar for in-frame or out-of-frame reconditioning purposes. (b) Out-of-frame boring of cylinder block. (Courtesy of Detroit Diesel Corporation.)

larger than the biggest available outside-diameter liner can be resalvaged by machining the bore oversize, fitting a press-fit sleeve into the block, then power-honing or boring the sleeve back to the standard outside diameter of the new liner (Figure 6–21). In addition, if the cylinder liner counterbores (top of block) are damaged, they can also be remachined using the cutter tool shown in Figure 6–17, and if necessary, a press-fit sleeve can be installed. If the crankshaft bores are out of alignment, either machining or power honing with the tooling shown in Figure 6–22 can be employed. Normally, the main bearing caps must be machined flat at the parting line first, then the power hone run through the bores after torquing the retaining bolts to specifications.

Installing the Cam Bushing

Installation of cam bushings requires a special bushing driver or drivers, as described in the removal section (see Figure 6–5).

CAUTION   Particular attention must be given to bushing alignment during installation to ensure lubrication to various parts of the engine. Many engines pump oil to the cam bushings and then to the rocker arms via a drilled passageway. Alignment of the bushing oil feed hole with the passageway is critical.

Before bushing installation, check all cam bushing bores in the block for nicks, scratches, and rust. Most bushing bores are tapered or chamfered slightly on one or both sides to make bushing installation easier. Make sure that the taper has no nicks or burrs that may damage the new bushing. Select bushings and determine their proper location in the block. Cam bushings may be of different widths and of different internal and external diameters in any one given engine.

1. Place the bushing on the driver without the driver bar.

FIGURE 6–22 *Use of special crankshaft line honing repair tools to correct for misalignment. (Courtesy of Sunnen Products Company.)*

2. Place the bushing and driver in front of the hole or bore into which the bushing is supposed to be driven.

3. Make sure that the bushing is aligned with the block oil holes.

4. Mark the bushing driver in line with the lube hole in the bushing.

5. Mark the block in line with the lube hole in the bushing bore, using a Magic Marker or similar device.

6. Insert a driving bar with a driving cone into the bushing and driver.

7. Tap the driving bar lightly to start the bushing into the bore, recheck alignment, and then drive the bushing into place with firm, solid hits with the hammer.

CAUTION   When driving cam bushings into a block, use care to prevent the bushing from tipping sideways; this could ruin the bushing.

Cam bushings can also be installed using a puller tool (Figure 6–5). This tool is very similar to the one mentioned previously; the main difference is that the bushings are not driven in with a hammer but pulled in. The driving rod or through bolt has been threaded and the bushings can be pulled or pushed in place by tightening a nut screw onto the threaded through bolt. This particular type of puller has an advantage because very little or no damage is done to the cam bushing, which sometimes happens when a driving-type installer is used.

Installing the Galley Plugs, Expansion Plugs, Cover Plates, and Oil Pressure Relief Valves

---

NOTE   Select a suitable sealer such as Permatex, pipe joint sealer, or 3-M compound.

---

1. Apply sealer to the galley plugs in small amounts and tighten the plugs securely.

FIGURE 6–23 *Installation of cylinder block cup plugs using a plug driver.*

2.   Apply sealer to the expansion plugs and, using a driver, drive into the block with a hammer.

a.   Cup plugs can be driven in with a bushing or seal driver that just fits into the plug (Figure 6–23).

b.   A convex plug can be expanded when in place by striking with a ball peen hammer and driver to deflect it into position.

Block Bore Diameter

The cylinder block must be checked with a dial bore gauge to determine if taper and out-of-round (ovality) readings are within worn limit specifications. The number of readings taken and their spacing throughout the block bore length depend on whether the block has been designed as a parent bore (no liner), a dry liner, or a wet liner. In dry liner engines, or engines with a parent bore, measure the bore diameter throughout its length at five or six places and at 90° to each other for taper and ovality dimensions and compare with service manual specs. On a four-stroke-cycle wet liner engine, dial reading checks are taken at three positions, A, B, and C, as illustrated in Figure 6–24 for a series 50 or 60 DDC model.

In blocks using either dry or wet liners, any physical damage to the liner surface usually requires installation of a new cylinder liner. In DDC two-stroke-cycle series 71 engines, a dry slip-fit liner is used; so if the

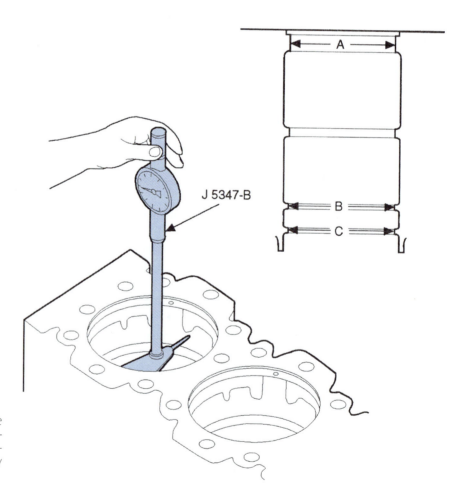

FIGURE 6–24 Using a bore gauge to measure the maximum cylinder block bore diameters after cleaning and descaling the block. (Courtesy of Detroit Diesel Corporation.)

liner inside diameter is lightly scuffed or scored, or the liner outside diameter exhibits some discoloration (dark spots), contact is not occurring. The cylinder block can be lightly cleaned with a fixed hone to accept a 0.001 in. (0.0254 mm) oversize-outside-diameter liner. If boring is required, oversize-outside-diameter liners are readily available from DDC in 0.005, 0.010, 0.020, or 0.030 in. (0.125, 0.254, 0.508, or 0.762 mm) outside diameter *only*. No liners with larger inside diameter are available; therefore, a standard-diameter piston is always used.

In some light- and medium-duty diesel engines, no cylinder liners are used, and the piston operates directly within the engine block (parent bore). Visually inspect the block bore for any signs of scuffing or scoring; if there are signs, the block bore may have to be power-honed or bored to take an oversize piston. If the block bore requires boring beyond the largest size of oversize piston available, a replacement press-fit sleeve could be obtained to salvage the block. The block must be bored to accept the outside diameter of the sleeve (allow a press fit of 0.002 to 0.003 in. or 0.0508 to 0.0762 mm). Then rebore the inside diameter of the sleeve after pressing it into the block to bring it back to the replacement piston size. The boring tool should be kept sharp to reduce fracturing of the surface material. A minimum of .003" of stock on diameter, must be left in the cylinder bores for removal with a rigid type hone.

Honing versus Reboring

Any service technician involved in major engine repairs must be well versed in the various techniques of honing the cylinder block bore and liner, including knowing when to hone and when to correct the block bore by remachining with a boring tool. In all cases, the initial use of a cylinder hone is simply to remove minor imperfections from the block or liner inside diameter before employing a dial gauge to determine bore or liner condition for reuse with respect to diameter, out-of-round condition, and taper. Cylinder liners that fall outside specifications should be replaced automatically with new liners. Honing can also be done to break any cylinder wall glaze, so that new piston rings can be seated on a nonpolished surface.

A hone or ridge reamer is also required to remove any minor ridge at the top of the block bore or cylinder liner formed by the old piston ring travel. Attempting to hand-hone a cylinder block to accept oversize liners in excess of 0.001 in. (0.0254 mm) or oversize pistons, which generally are available in 0.010, 0.020, and 0.030 in. (0.254, 0.508, and 0.762 mm) sizes, can be done correctly only by using a boring bar. A portable boring bar such as the one illustrated in Figure 6–21a can be used to perform an in-frame repair; or at major engine overhaul, the block assembly can be mounted and clamped into a floor-mounted model such as the one illustrated in Figure 6–21b. An optional method that is widely used to prepare a cylinder block to accept oversize-outside-diameter liners, or oversize pistons in a parent bore block, is to use a power hone similar to the one illustrated in Figure 6–20.

Attempting to enlarge a cylinder bore with a hand hone powered by an air or electric drill motor would require considerable time; in addition, the hone would tend to follow the existing imperfections in the block bore. If reboring is necessary in any parent block bore, or to accept an oversize-outside-diameter liner, only remove enough material to clean up the bore and to accept the first oversize piston or liner available; in this way, future reboring at major overhaul is possible. If you are boring to accept an oversize piston, determine from service information just what piston-to-block clearance is specified. For example, if the piston-to-liner clearance for an aluminum piston is specified as being between 0.006 and 0.007 in. (0.152 to 0.177 mm), bore to within 0.002 to 0.003 in. (0.050 to 0.076 mm) or slightly less to allow finishing by honing the block bore. This would allow you to obtain the proper crosshatch pattern and surface finish on the cylinder wall.

Some engine manufacturers do not offer oversize-diameter pistons for some of their engines. One example is the Caterpillar 3116 truck engine. Caterpillar determined that it was not practical to rebore the blocks for oversize pistons. In this case the procedure to salvage a cylinder block with major cylinder bore damage is to bore the cylinder oversize and employ a press-in sleeve, which can then be rebored to produce the correct-size bore while leaving enough material to allow for a properly honed crosshatch pattern.

CYLINDER HONES

A power honing machine (see Figure 6–20) can be used for cylinder block reconditioning. Although major tool and equipment suppliers offer hones in a variety of styles, there are three basic types of hand-operated hones used to recondition cylinder block bores or liners:

1. A spring-loaded hone (Figure 6–25) can be adjusted to suit different bore sizes. This type of hone tends to follow the contours of a worn bore due to the spring pressure exerted on the stones; therefore, it is used to quickly deglaze a bore or a liner. Do not use this type of equipment when attempting to hone a just-completed cylinder block bore to achieve the correct piston-to-liner clearance and the correct surface finish crosshatch pattern.

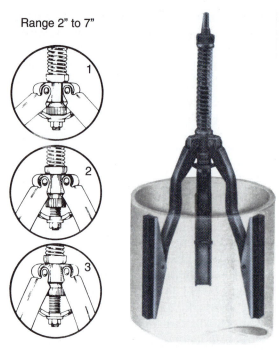

Range 2" to 7"

3-Stone Glaze Breaker Hone
ADJUSTABLE TENSION

Full range 2" to 7" diameter. Fully adjustable for both diameter and tension. Rugged construction. Flexible drive shaft. Equipped with three 220 grit stones recommended for ring seating.

Spreader Limiter permits easy insertion in the cylinder bore or when changing from cylinder to cylinder.
1. Spread Limiter adjustment nut shown in position to allow hone to open to full capacity.
2. Spread Limiter adjustment shown turned up on shaft to limit arm diameter to open to about half capacity of the hone.
3. Spread Limiter adjustment nut turned up on shaft to limit the arm's diameter to open for a smaller diameter job.

FIGURE 6–25 Spring-loaded adjustable cylinder liner hone used to lightly clean or deglaze a liner or block bore. (Courtesy of Hastings Manufacturing Co.)

2. A ball-type hone or flexi-hone (Figure 6–26) is also used mainly to create effective cylinder wall deglazing or to clean a used liner by lightly roughening up the surface to facilitate new piston ring seating.

3. A fixed-type hone (Figure 6–27) can be set to a specific diameter by rotating a knurled knob above the stones until the expanding mechanism (stones) make firm but light contact with the cylinder wall. This type is used to hone a cylinder or block bore after reboring to achieve the correct crosshatch pattern and desired piston-to-liner clearance.

Reasons for Honing

It is not necessary to hone a new cylinder liner to modify its inside-diameter surface finish. The liner has already undergone a machine-honing process at the factory, and any change to the crosshatch pattern will adversely affect the seating of the piston rings. When reusing liners, some engine manufacturers support honing and others are opposed to it. By way of background information, Detroit Diesel, Mack, and a number of major European and Japanese diesel engine manufacturers are in favor of honing used liners if they

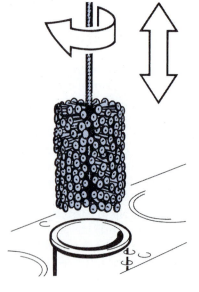

FIGURE 6–26 Ball-type hone, or flexi-hone, used mainly to deglaze cylinder liners or to clean a used liner or block bore to provide a good surface finish for seating of new piston rings.

(a)

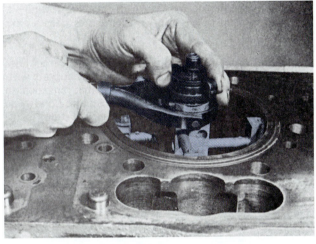

(b)

FIGURE 6–27 (a) Installing an adjustable hone set into the cylinder liner or block bore. (b) Adjusting the hone to a fixed position within the cylinder liner to obtain a specific crosshatch finish of a liner or block bore after machining or boring. (Courtesy of Sunnen Products Company.)

are to be reused. There are several reasons why many engine manufacturers recommend honing a liner prior to reuse:

- To break any glaze and to obtain the correct surface roughness so that the piston rings can seat against the cylinder wall as quickly as possible with minimum wear; otherwise, the piston ring seating time will be lengthened or piston rings may fail to seat correctly.
- To obtain a surface structure that allows optimum adhesion of the lube oil, so that a film of oil is maintained between the piston rings and the liner.
- To create a crosshatch pattern on the inside diameter of the liner. This will optimize the distribution and removal of oil from the cylinder wall when the piston moves down. Too steep a crosshatch pattern can lead to excessive oil consumption, whereas too narrow a pattern can lead to scuffing of the rings, inadequate lubrication, and damage to the cylinder kit.
- Any deep ridge at the top of the liner would invariably render the liner unfit for further use. You may need to use a ridge reamer (Figure 6–28) to remove this ridge before attempting to pull the piston and rings from the liner or block bore in a press-fit liner. A small ridge formed at the top of the liner by the piston rings can be removed with a hone; if it is not removed, interference with the travel of the new rings may result in actual compression ring breakage.

Ridge Reamers

QUICK-CUT–FEED UP
This extra-sturdy, extra-durable ridge reamer will handle all modern engines with bores including canted and most short stroke types. Tool sits solidly in the cylinder, with holding blades maintaining hook wall contact for smooth cut. Cutter head guide plate locks on both sides. Tungsten carbide Saf-T-Blade will not overcut, chatter or dig in. Smooth cutting action of this ridge reamer is attained by fine-thread feed-up. Accuracy maintained by heavy, heat-treated center bolt. Steel collar on center bolt protects threads from wrench damage. Three position setting of spring-loaded cutter head permits change from one cylinder to another without adjusting cutter head assembly.

Clamshell package

FIGURE 6–28 Clamshell adjustable design ridge reamer tool used to cut and remove a wear ridge within a cylinder liner or block bore to facilitate piston and ring removal. (Courtesy of Hastings Manufacturing Company.)

Holding Fixture

You cannot effectively hone a liner when it is outside the engine block without using a suitable holding fixture. Ideally, a scrap cylinder block makes the best fixture! If you choose to install the liner in a cylinder block that is to be reused, the block should be dismantled and then cleaned thoroughly after the liner honing process. The type of hone recommended and the stone grit required to successfully hone a liner depend on the liner material used. Cast iron liners, hardened cast iron, steel, and even aluminum cylinders dictate the honing stones and materials that should be used. Major manufacturers of hones and stones for all facets of the automotive and diesel industry, such as Sunnen Products Company, include with their products honing instructions for reconditioning cylinders and liners. Refer to these directions along with the engine manufacturer's service manual procedure prior to honing. For best results, thoroughly wash out all cylinders before honing.

Liner Surface Finish

Correct honing procedures produce a cylinder liner surface finish that exhibits a crosshatch pattern similar to that illustrated in Figure 6–29 which shows a 20 to 25° and a 40 to 50° example. This illustration is magnified many times for instructional purposes. Each engine manufacturer specifies in its service manual what angle of crosshatch pattern and what surface finish are desired. Surface finish is usually stated as being in the region of 20 to 35 RMS (root mean square), which is simply a mathematical term indicating the average irregularity in millionths of an inch (0.000001 in.). This angle of surface finish is usually referred to as a *microinch finish* because the actual surface finish on the liner inside diameter would appear to the naked eye similar to that shown in Figure 6–29b.

The actual microinch surface finish is controlled by the proper selection of honing stone used—the grit. Reference to Figure 6–30 lists a stone-set selection chart for different grit having stones to produce a specific surface finish. A two-step process should be used regardless of the type of rings being installed. Rough stones of 180–220 grit should be used to remove all but .0005" of stock on diameter. The final .0005" of stock should be removed with 280 grit stones. Cast iron and chrome rings require a surface finish of 20–20 RA and moly rings require a surface finish of 15–25 RA. Keep in mind that the rougher the stone grit used, the larger will be the microinch surface finish. Consider the finish on a liner or sleeve surface from the following information:

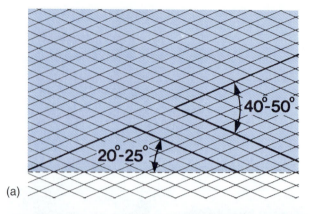

(a)

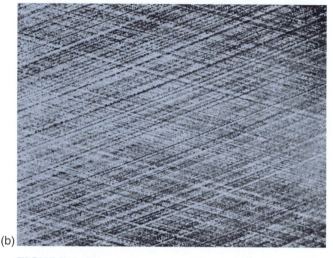

(b)

FIGURE 6–29   (a) Example of how to identify a cylinder liner or block bore surface finish crosshatch pattern in degrees. (b) Actual example of how the crosshatch pattern would appear in a correctly honed block bore or liner surface pattern. (Courtesy of Cummins Engine Company, Inc.)

Liner material	Stone type used					
	70 grit	150 grit	220 grit	280 grit	400 grit	600 grit
	Liner microinch surface finish					
Cast iron	100	32	20	12	6	3
Hardened sleeve	25	20	—	12	5	1
Steel sleeve	—	35	—	20	7	2

Hone Driving Power and Adjustment

When using a hone, the drive motor (air or electric) must be set to rotate the assembly in a clockwise direction at speeds between 250 and 450 rpm. The size of drive motor required depends on the diameter of stones being used. It is advisable to use a 1/2 in. (12.7 mm) capacity drill motor for bore sizes up to 3 in. (76.2

STONE SET SELECTION TABLE FOR SUNNEN CYLINDER HONES

For Use in Cylinder Hone Models	DIAMETER RANGE	When Used In	Roughing Stone Set (70 Grit)	Finishing Stone Set (150 Grit)	Med. Finishing Stone Set (220 Grit)	Polishing Stone Set (280 Grit)	Fine Finish Stone Set (400 Grit)	Extra-Fine Stone Set (600 Grit)▲
SN Midget	1.75 to 2.0 (44 to 51 mm)	Cast Iron	SN-100	SN-200	......	SN-500	S18-J87	....
JN Junior	2.0 to 2.2 (51 to 56 mm)	Cast Iron Hardened Sleeves	JN-100 JN-130	JN-200 JN-230	JN-300	JN-500 JN-530	T20-J87 T20-J85	....
	2.2 to 2.4 (56 to 61 mm)	Cast Iron Hardened Sleeves	JN-101 JN-131	JN-201 JN-231	JN-301	JN-501 JN-531	U22-J87 U22-J85	....
	2.4 to 2.6 (61 to 66 mm)	Cast Iron Hardened Sleeves	JN-102 JN-132	JN-202 JN-232	JN-302	JN-502 JN-532	V24-J87 V24-J85	....
AN Standard and Heavy Duty	2.5 to 2.7 (63 to 70 mm)	Cast Iron	AN-115	AN-215	......	AN-515	G25-J87	....
	2.7 to 4.1 (69 to 104 mm)	Cast Iron Hardened Sleeves Steel	AN-100 AN-130	AN-200 AN-230 AN-200A	AN-300	AN-500 AN-530 AN-500A	M27-J87 M27-J85 M27-J87	MM33-C05 MM33-C05 MM33-C05
	3.5 to 5.5 (89 to 139 mm)	Cast Iron Hardened Sleeves Steel	AN-101 AN-131	AN-201 AN-231 AN-201A	AN-301	AN-501 AN-531 AN-501A	N37-J87 N37-J85 N37-J87	NN40-C05 NN40-C05 NN40-C05
	4.7 to 15.0 (119 to 381 mm) Use this series of Stone Sets with Master Holder Sets and Stone Support (order below)	Cast Iron Hardened Sleeves Steel	AN-106 AN-136	AN-206 AN-236 AN-206A	AN-306	AN-506 AN-536 AN-506A	W47-J87 W47-J85 W47-J87	WW51-C05 WW51-C05 WW51-C05
Approximate Surface Finish in Microinches (AA)		Cast Iron Hardened Sleeves Steel	100 25	32 20 35	20	12 12	6 5 7	3 1 2

▲ Range on these sets as follows MM33—3.3 to 4.1", NN40—4.0" to 5.6", WW51—5.1 to 9.2
Shipping weight of all Stone Sets: Approximately 1-1.4 lbs. (1.2 kg) per Set

HONING ALUMINUM CYLINDERS
Sunnen Cylinder Hones are ideal for reconditioning aluminum cylinders. When honing aluminum, Sunnen Honing Oil must be used.
The general recommendation is as follows:

REGULAR ALUMINUM
FOR ROUGHING use the 150 grit stone set, the same type as for cast iron cylinders.
FOR FINISHING use the 280 grit stone set, the same type as for cast iron cylinders.

HIGH-SILICON ALUMINUM ALLOYS
(such as used in Chevrolet Vega 2300 engine)
High-silicon aluminum alloys require special honing techniques. Write to the Automotive Sales Department for honing instructions and fully detailed information.

FIGURE 6–30 Cylinder honing stone set selection table. (Courtesy of Sunnen Products Company.)

mm), a 5/8 in. (16 mm) motor for up to 4.75 in. (121 mm), and a 3/4 in. (19 mm) motor for bore sizes larger than 4.75 in. (121 mm).

A ball-type hone offers no adjustment, but it does come in a range of sizes to suit different-diameter bores and liners. Some spring-loaded hones can be adjusted, and all fixed hones are equipped with an adjustment knob to allow expansion of the stones until they have a firm but light drag on the cylinder wall. Figure 6–27a illustrates placement of a fixed, adjustable Sunnen hone into the cylinder or liner. The pinion is raised about 1/4 in. (6 mm), then turned counterclockwise to set the stones to the approximate diameter of the cylinder and liner. Push the pinion down until it engages with the outside gear on the hone body. Expand the combination of two stones and two guides firmly against the cylinder liner wall by turning the hone ring wrench clockwise (Figure 6–27b). While making this adjustment, the tops of the stones and guides should not extend more than 1/2 in. (12.7 mm) out of the top of the liner.

Honing Process

Honing stones can be used either dry or wet. When used dry, stones cut faster; when used wet, a honing oil must be used. Metal removal can be achieved faster in a cast iron liner when dry honing is done; honing oil is recommended when a 280-, 400-, or 600-grit stone is used. Honing oil should always be used when honing steel or aluminum. Use a squirt can or brush to apply a continuous flow to the stones and cylinder. If a recommended honing oil is not readily available, smear vegetable shortening liberally on the cylinder and the stones.

It is important to inspect liners thoroughly before honing to avoid wasting time on those that are damaged severely or are worn and in an out-of-round condition beyond acceptable service manual specifications. The smaller the amount of material that can be removed from the used liner to clean it up lightly, the better. However, avoid casual roughing up of the cylinders, since too coarse a crosshatch pattern will show deep scratches that will permit leakage between the rings and cylinder wall as well as wearing the new rings excessively. If wear limits published in the engine service manual are exceeded after honing, new rings will not have sufficient wall tension due to the size increase, and new liners will be required.

The purpose of honing a used cylinder liner is simply to deglaze the surface with minimal removal of metal. The intent is not to enlarge the bore size. Consequently, it takes very little effort and time to accomplish this procedure. Always exercise care when honing to avoid removing excess material from the cylinder or liner.

With the honing tool fixture (with the correct stone grit) inserted into and adjusted to the cylinder or liner bore size, connect the top of the hone driveshaft to a drive motor. Using the chuck key, tighten the chuck securely.

SERVICE TIP Support the drive motor on an overhead support bracket similar to the one illustrated in Figure 6–31. This tool allows you to adjust a stroking rod to prevent the hone from moving too far through the cylinder at the bottom; otherwise, the stones can strike the lower end of the block-strengthening struts, resulting in breakage of the stones and damage to the hone.

To achieve optimum results, check with your equipment supplier for assistance in determining the proper speed and load settings during your honing process. Types of abrasives and honing oils will also affect cylinder finish, burnishing and tearout, all of which will have adverse affects on oil control.

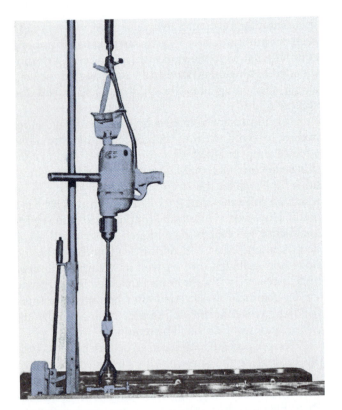

FIGURE 6–31 *Use of a special honing fixture to support a heavy-duty variable-speed drill motor used to drive the honing stones. (Courtesy of Cummins Engine Company, Inc.)*

Surface speed is extremely important in attaining the objectives of honing. The two principal motions, rotation and reciprocation, must be selectively adjusted and interrelated to obtain the maximum efficiency. Pressure control is an important element in maintaining the desired shearing action. The proper flow of coolant is necessary to remove loose abrasive particles and metal chips from the faces of the honing stones and to maintain a reasonably cool temperature over the work area.

Engine tests have substantiated the fact that bore finish is an important factor in internal combustion engine oil economy and engine life. Your greatest gain in adopting good bore finish specifications will not only be an improvement in oil consumption averages, but a reduction in the range of oil consumption from engine to engine.

The speed at which you manually push/pull (stroke) the drive motor and hone the cylinder up and down will determine the finished crosshatch angle. The stone grit determines the RMS surface finish. You need to use short up-and-down overlapping strokes equal to about one stroke per second. Detroit Diesel recommends a 120 grit stone set when honing its four-stroke-cycle series 50 and 60 engine cylinder liners, while Mack recommends a stone set between 150 and 250 grit to "glaze bust" its dry liners. Cummins recommends a 280 grit stone set to deglaze and clean the cylinder bores of its B series engines that do not use a liner. Cummins further recommends that a fine-grit ball hone and a mixture of equal parts of mineral spirits and SAE 30W engine oil be used.

Remember these two steps when honing. First, on used liners or bores, always start stroking at the bottom or least worn section of the liner or bore using short strokes to concentrate honing in the smallest diameter of the cylinder. Gradually lengthen the stroke as metal is removed and the stones make contact higher up the cylinder. Allow the stones to extend about 1/2 in. (13 mm) from the cylinder at the top of its stroke.

Second, work the hone up and down the full length of the liner with the drive motor running at between 300 and 400 rpm. Do this a few times (about 15 seconds maximum) or after about 10 full strokes of the hone. The result should be a crisscross pattern that produces hone marks on an axis stated by the engine manufacturer in the respective engine service manual. For example, DDC states that the liner should be honed to produce between a 22 and 32° crisscross (crosshatch) pattern in its series 50 and 60 cylinder liners, while Mack recommends that a diamond crisscross pattern of a 20 to 35 µin. RMS finish be achieved. On Cummins B series engines that use no liner, the block bore finish should be honed to produce a correctly deglazed surface and crosshatched appearance with the lines at a 15 to 25° angle with the top of the cylinder block (or a 30 to 50° included angle). When bringing the drive motor to a stop, do not allow the hone to come to a stop in the same position. Keep it moving so that no one area of the bore ends up with too narrow a crosshatch pattern. In addition, to avoid vertical scratches up and down the length of the cylinder, relieve the tension on the hone before removing it from the cylinder. Otherwise, these vertical scratches can form a path for combustion gases to blow by.

Cleaning the Liner or Block after Honing
The cast iron filings and residue from the honing stones are very abrasive and damaging to piston rings and other internal engine components. These abrasives must be completely removed from the block before engine assembly.

A chemical solution of caustic compounds or a detergent with hot water must be used for cleaning. *Do not* use kerosene or other petroleum liquids as these will tend to seal in the loose abrasives instead of removing them. After honing, wash the inside surface of the liner with a solution of household laundry detergent and scrub with a stiff nonmetallic bristle brush to remove as much of the honing debris as possible. Rinse with hot water and blow dry. After the bore is dry, coat it with clean engine oil and allow it to soak in for 10 minutes. Wipe the lube oil from the bore with a clean white cloth or white paper towel. If the cloth or towel shows evidence of gray or darker stains, honing debris is still present on the cylinder liner surface. Repeat the oil application and wiping procedure until no evidence of stain appears on the cloth or towel. Use a brass or steel wire brush to clean the top of the liner flange.

NOTE If you are honing an engine block with no liner (that is, where the piston runs directly in the block bore), after the honing procedure is complete and before engine reassembly, thoroughly clean the cylinder block, oil galleries, and cylinder bores using a solution of strong detergent and water. Incomplete cleaning will lead to piston seizure or rapid wear of the cylinder bores or sleeves, pistons, and rings.

Installing a Wet Liner
A wet liner can be installed on its own or as part of a cylinder pack that includes the assembled piston, piston rings, and connecting rod. (The cylinder pack is described in detail in Chapter 8).

If the measurements of the outside diameter and thickness of the liner flange area are outside specifications, the liner will have to be replaced. If the cylinder block counterbore is damaged, remachine it and/or install a sleeve. Many engine manufacturers supply liners of oversized flange diameter and thickness to allow reuse of an engine block. For example, in the Cummins NT-855 (14 L) engine series, you can obtain liners with a 0.020 in. (0.51 mm) larger outside-diameter flange and liners with a 0.010 in. (0.25 mm) thicker flange. You can install a wet liner into the cleaned block bore minus any of the seal rings, pull the liner into position and secure it in place with liner hold-down clamps, and check the flange protrusion. Then you can add or delete liner flange shims to obtain the correct specifications.

Procedure for Wet Liner Installation
1. Engine manufacturers suggest that you lubricate the liner crevice and seal rings shown in Figure 6–3a. Pay particular attention to the lubricant recommended by the engine OEM, because some specify vegetable oil whereas others suggest clean engine oil, due to the type of seal ring material. In some engines the seal rings are installed on the liner, but in others they are located in machined grooves within the cylinder block bore area. Using the wrong type of lubricant can adversely affect the sealing capability of the rings by causing swelling of the material. Following is a general example of how liner seal lubricant recommendations can differ.

- Cummins N14 and ISX/Signature engines: vegetable oil (See Figure 6–32.)
- Cummins L10 engines: 15W-40 engine oil
- Caterpillar 3176 engines: clean engine oil
- Caterpillar 3406 engines: liquid soap on early engine O-ring seals; engine oil on the crevice seal and later engine model O-rings
- Detroit Diesel two-stroke 92 engines: clean engine oil
- Detroit Diesel series 50/60 engines: clean petroleum jelly
- Mack E7: ethylene glycol (See Figure 6–33.)

Always check the service manual for the proper type of liner seal ring lubricant to use.

CAUTION Many engine manufacturers oppose the use of hydrogenated vegetable shortening as a seal lubricant because of the adverse effects that it has on the seal ring material.

FIGURE 6–32   Lubrication of cylinder liner O-ring seals with vegetable oil prior to assembly. (Lube will change based on seal material used.) In this example for a Cummins ISX/Signature engine liner, the O-ring seals are black (top) and green (lower liner groove). (Courtesy of Cummins Engine Company, Inc.)

2.   Some engine manufacturers suggest that you apply a bead of room-temperature vulcanizing (RTV) sealant on either the cylinder block counterbore or on the underside of the liner flange. The diameter of the bead should be between 3/64 in. (0.047 in., or 1.19 mm) and 1/16 in. (0.0625 in., or 1.58 mm). Figure 6–34 illustrates where to apply this sealer bead. Note that the liner *must* be installed within five minutes, maximum, after bead installation; otherwise, the RTV sealer will have dried out and may not seal effectively.

3.   Insertion of the cylinder liner into the block can follow two methods based on the make and model of engine. Some manufacturers suggest that the piston, rings, and con-rod first be loaded into the cylinder liner with special tooling to provide a cylinder kit, which makes for a simple installation procedure of these major components. Detroit Diesel is one manufacturer that uses this concept in its two-cycle engines. Caterpillar recommends this same concept in some of its engine models, with the 3176B, C10, C12 engines being three examples (see Chapter 8 for details.) In some engines, special cylinder kit installation tooling is available to make this job fairly simple. The second method is to install each cylinder liner into the engine block before the piston and con-rod. Regardless of the method adopted, if used liners are to be reinserted into the block, install them as per the correct cylinder numbered Dykem mark applied during removal. In addition, the liner-to-block orientation mark applied earlier should be aligned. Some manufacturers, however, suggest that the used liner-to-block orientation mark be rotated 90° from its original position (Cummins ISX and Signature) in the block bore. Manually insert the liner carefully

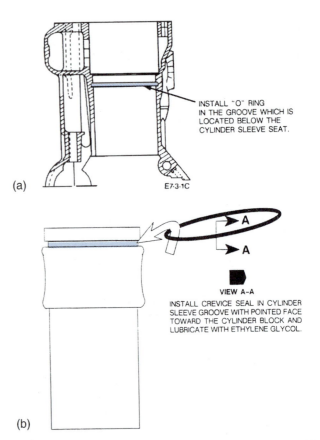

(a)

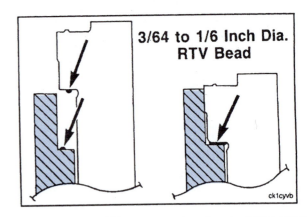

(b)

FIGURE 6–33   (a) Mack E7 six-cylinder engine wet/dry liner O-ring groove. (b) Location of cylinder liner crevice seal groove. (Courtesy of Mack Trucks, Inc.)

FIGURE 6–34   Where to apply a bead of RTV (room-temperature vulcanizing) sealant between the cylinder liner flange and engine block counterbore. (Courtesy of Cummins Engine Company, Inc.)

into the block bore (align the previous match marks to the block) and push it down squarely as far as you can.

4.   Using a properly sized cylinder liner diameter driver and handle, gently tap the liner all the way into the block counterbore. When the liner reaches bottom

you will hear a dull thud. If you have a suitable liner installer similar to that illustrated in Figure 6–35, you can pull the liner squarely into position, or use a liner driver tool, shown in Figure 6–36. This allows you to recheck the liner protrusion with a dial gauge (Figure 6–37), which clearly shows where cylinder liner protrusion is measured in relation to the top machined surface of the engine block. If a liner press is not available, once the liner has been driven home, you may have to install a cylindrical liner clamping plate bolted to the cylinder block upper deck to ensure that the liner is completely bottomed in the block counterbore. Recheck the liner protrusion with either a dial sled gauge, or a straightedge and feeler gauges, at four points 90° apart. If the protrusion is not within the service manual specifications, try reshimming; or, the liner may have to be repulled and both the liner flange and block counterbore rechecked for possible problems.

FIGURE 6–36   Driving a cylinder liner into place with a special driver tool. (Courtesy of Cummins Engine Company, Inc.)

FIGURE 6–37   Employing two cylinder liner hold-down clamps while using a sled-mounted dial gauge to check liner protrusion after installation. (Courtesy of Cummins Engine Company, Inc.)

5.   Some engine manufacturers recommend that once protrusion has been checked, you should use a feeler gauge to measure the clearance between the liner and its lower bore to ensure that no distortion has occurred during installation. Figure 6–38 illustrates this particular check where one manufacturer's spec calls for a clearance of 0.002 to 0.006 in. (0.05 to 0.15 mm).

6.   Take a dial bore gauge and recheck the liner inside diameter for out-of-roundness at five points throughout the liner length. Then take another set of readings at a 90° axis to the first.

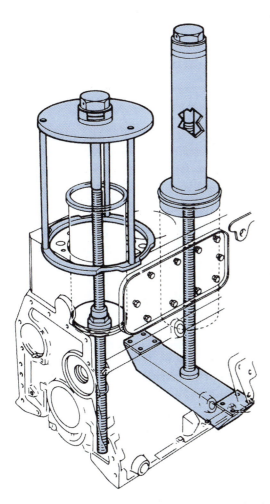

FIGURE 6–35   Special installation tooling used to install a cylinder liner assembly into the engine block when a press fit or interference fit is used.

FIGURE 6–38 *Using a feeler gauge around the bottom circumference of a wet cylinder liner after installation to check for any signs of liner distortion due to rolled or twisted seal rings. (Courtesy of Cummins Engine Company, Inc.)*

7.   If the liner protrusion, lower liner block check with the feeler gauge, or the liner bore out-of-round condition are not within specs, repull the liner and check for possible rolled or twisted seal rings, or clean the liner flange or cylinder block counterbore.

8.   On Detroit Diesel two-stroke-cycle engines, once the liner has been installed, use a liner hold-down clamp and check the distance (intrusion) of the liner below the cylinder block machined surface. Figure 6–39 illustrates that these engines employ a hardened steel insert in the block counterbore on which the liner flange sits and an individual cylindrical sealing gasket that sits on the liner flange. When the cylinder head is torqued down, this gasket is compressed and acts as a seal between the combustion chamber, liner, head, and block.

Installing a Dry Slip-Fit Liner

Detroit Diesel's two-stroke 71 series engine model has a dry cylinder liner that is a slip-fit design in the engine block bore. The service manual specification calls for a liner-to-block bore clearance of between 0.0005 and 0.0025 in. (0.0127 to 0.0635 mm) on used parts. Before removing a liner from the block, match-mark it with a metal marker to ensure that when it is reinstalled it will be inserted into the same position. If the cylinder block has to be lightly honed at overhaul, Detroit Diesel supplies 0.001 in. (0.0254 mm) oversize-outside-diameter liners to allow a closer fit to the block bore. If, however, the cylinder block has to be rebored oversize, oversize-*outside-diameter-only* liners will be required. These liners are available in 0.001, 0.005, 0.010, 0.020, and 0.030 in. oversize (0.0254, 0.127, 0.254, 0.508, and 0.762 mm). Take careful note that the liners are *only* available in

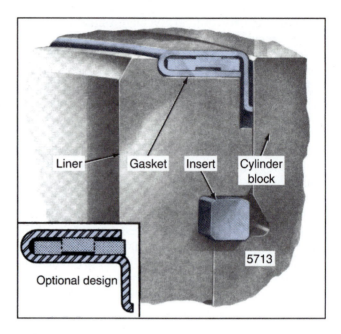

FIGURE 6–39 *Location of a cylinder liner-to-block hardened steel insert and individual sealing gasket used on DDC two-stroke cycle 71 series engines that use a dry slip-fit liner. (Courtesy of Detroit Diesel Corporation.)*

oversized outside diameter, and *no* oversized pistons are available! If a liner is replaced, it can be reused with a used or a new standard-diameter piston assembly. Liner-to-block clearances after reboring should fall within 0.0005 to 0.0015 in. (0.013 to 0.038 mm). The oversize dimension of the liner is etched on its outside diameter.

Installing a Dry Press-Fit Liner

Dry liners that are press fit or interference fit into the cylinder block are between 0.0004 and 0.0008 in. (0.010 to 0.020 mm) larger on their outside diameter than the block bore. Follow these steps to achieve proper installation of the liner:

1.   Select a hydraulic or mechanical press and suitable guide adapters that can be inserted across the liner at the top. Figure 6–35 is a mechanical installer arrangement. The left side of the figure shows removal of the liner; the right side shows the tooling required to press the liner back into place.

2.   Refer to Figure 6–4 and make sure that any shims from under the liner flange that were removed when it was pulled from the block bore are reinstalled into the block counterbore prior to installation.

3.   Position the liner squarely with the machined surface of the top of the engine block. Although this can be determined visually, if you use a small try square placed at 90° intervals around the liner outside diame-

ter prior to installation, you can lightly hand bump the liner to square it up.

4. Apply a small amount of light lube oil to the top edge of the block bore if necessary. Be careful—excessive amounts can create heat transfer problems between the outside diameter of the block bore and the liner during normal operation.

5. Carefully press the liner into the block bore. Then check the liner flange protrusion height above the machined surface of the block as illustrated in Figure 6–37. Obtain this specification from the engine service manual. Then you can lay a small straightedge across the top of the liner and gauge the protrusion with a feeler gauge, although the use of a dial indicator mounted on a sled gauge as illustrated is preferable. Securely hold the liner in position during the protrusion check with two cylinder liner hold-down clamps, which are shown in Figure 6–37. Liner protrusion is needed to allow the cylinder head gasket to seal correctly. If the liner protrusion is not within published specs, you will have to pull it back out. By using different liner-to-block counterbore shims, proper protrusion can be achieved. However, you may have to clean or remachine the counterbore to square it up again.

NOTE Press-fit dry-liner installation can be made easier by chilling the liner. Pack in dry ice for 35 to 45 minutes to allow it to cool before installation. If you choose this method, *be very careful* to avoid serious injury when handling dry ice or parts that have been chilled. Dry ice can cause skin burns and eye injury if not handled properly. Always wear safety gloves and goggles. Never seal dry ice in an airtight container because it may cause the container to explode or burst. Follow these two steps:

1. When removing the liner from the dry ice, *do not* wrap a shop cloth or towel around it, because it may stick to the liner surface.

2. Using safety gloves, quickly insert the liner into the block bore; make sure that it is square to the top of the block. Then pull the liner into position as shown in Figure 6–35 (right-hand side) or by using a hydraulic press.

Final Testing of the Block for Water Leaks after Sleeve (Wet Type) Installation

Testing the cylinder block for water leaks before final assembly is recommended by some manufacturers.

NOTE This procedure is rarely used in the field, since if the block is in good condition and the sleeves are installed correctly, water leaks rarely occur.

Methods of checking blocks for water leaks are dictated primarily by the test equipment available. Two methods are listed here. Select the method that is recommended by the engine manufacturer.

1. Fill the block with antifreeze after sleeves and expansion plugs have been installed. Install sheet rubber gaskets below the steel bolted test strips. Pressurize with compressed air and check for leaks (Figure 6–40).

2. Pressurize the block water jacket with air and immerse the block in a tank of hot water. Check for bubbles. Any area leaking air should be checked. The block should now be ready for further assembly of engine parts and complete engine assembly.

Dry-liner engines should have a maximum air pressure applied to them of 40 psi (276 kPa), whereas wet-liner engines should never have air pressure in excess of 20 psi (138 kPa) applied to them. Allow the air pressure to be maintained for at least 2 hours. At the end of the test period, carefully inspect the outside diameter

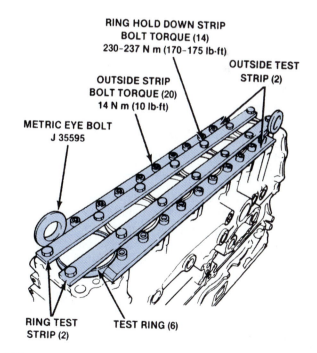

FIGURE 6–40 *Bolted steel test strips/gaskets location on a series 60 engine block to effectively perform a pressure check. (Courtesy of Detroit Diesel Corporation.)*

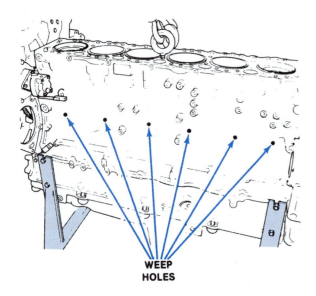

WEEP HOLES

FIGURE 6–41 *Location of series 50/60 cylinder-block-located weep holes to indicate coolant leakage past the upper liner O-ring seal. (Courtesy of Detroit Diesel Corporation.)*

of wet-liner flanges and the underside of the block on Cummins or Caterpillar engines for any signs of liner O-seal ring leakage. Note, however, that on Detroit Diesel series 50 and 60 engines (see Figure 6–41) coolant weep holes with rubber plugs located alongside the engine block allow any coolant that leaks past the top liner seal ring to exit at the holes. Check the various oil passages, crankcase, and exterior of the block for any signs of water and antifreeze leakage, which would confirm that either the block is cracked or a liner seal ring is leaking. Most manufacturers recommend that a cracked block be replaced with a new one. There are, however, methods that are sometimes used to repair a small crack that is not located in an area close to either the cylinder liner or cylinder head sealing surfaces.

> **NOTE** If a block is to be stored for a time before further engine assembly, it should be protected from rusting by first covering any openings and then painting the block. A heavy coat of oil or grease should be applied to the inside of cylinder liners as a rust preventive and preservative measure.

SUMMARY

The information gleaned from the detailed service descriptions described in this chapter will permit you to systematically perform an inspection, analysis, and repair of the engine cylinder block and liners at major overhaul. This skill will broaden your understanding of the importance of the block and its components, and assist you in both the service/repair and effective troubleshooting of the engine.

SELF-TEST QUESTIONS

1. Technician A says that most high-speed diesel engine cylinder blocks are made from aluminum alloy. Technician B disagrees, stating that gray cast iron alloys with a fairly high silicon content ensure superior durability. Who is correct?

2. Technician A states that all high-speed diesel engines employ one-piece cylinder blocks. Technician B says that a number of larger high-speed engines employ two- and even three-piece bolted blocks. Who knows the product information best?

3. Technician A says that when cylinder block bores become worn, the block should be replaced. Technician B says that the block can be rebored or a new cylinder sleeve (liner) can be used. Who is correct?

4. Technician A says that when overhauling an engine, it is very important to remove any scale buildup from the internal coolant passages to prevent overheating during operation. Technician B says that as long as you steam clean these passages thoroughly, there should be no problem. Which technician has higher standards of excellence?

5. Technician A says that it is not necessary to pressure test a cylinder block at major overhaul if no visible cracks are apparent during inspection when you are using nondestructive testing methods. Technician B says that you should always perform a pressure check to confirm that no cracks exist, since you cannot always detect hairline cracks using the nondestructive method. Which technician is correct?

6. True or False: All machined surfaces of an engine block should always be checked with a straightedge and a feeler gauge for any signs of distortion.

7. True or False: Cylinder block crankshaft bore alignment should be checked at major overhaul even if no bearing damage is evident.

8. True or False: If a cylinder block crankshaft bore is misaligned, the block should be replaced.

9. True or False: Signs of fretting at the main bearing cap parting line are indicative of movement of the main bearing cap.

10. True or False: A dry cylinder liner is always press fit in the block bore.

11. Technician A says that a dry press-fit cylinder liner can normally be pressed in the block bore by hand. Not so says technician B; a hydraulic press is necessary to install it. Which technician is correct?

12. Technician A says that to recondition a cylinder block bore, either an adjustable/fixed power hone (see Figure 6–20) can be used, or a boring bar can be used. Technician B says that a boring bar should be used to enlarge the block bore and that a hone should be used only to finish the bore crosshatch. Which technician is correct?

13. List the conditions for which cylinder block counterbores should always be checked.

14. Damaged cylinder liner block counterbores can be remachined to repair them, according to technician A. Technician B says that the block would have to be replaced. Who is correct?

15. Technician A says that when remachining of the top deck of the cylinder block is necessary, you are limited to how much metal can be removed and should be guided by the dimension from the centerline of the crankshaft to the top of the deck. Technician B says that you can remove as much metal as necessary from the top deck surface; simply employ a thicker cylinder head gasket to offset the removed deck metal. Which one of these technicians would you follow?

16. Cylinder block camshaft bores can also be remachined at engine overhaul if necessary, according to technician A. Technician B says that the block would require replacement. Who is right?

17. To determine if the cylinder block bore is within the allowable limits regarding wear, ovality, and taper, use
    a. a precision dial indicator
    b. inside calipers
    c. an inside micrometer
    d. a tape measure

18. List the three most commonly used types of cylinder liners.

19. True or False: All cylinder liners are press fit in the cylinder block bore.

20. Which current high-speed heavy-duty diesel engine manufacturer employs telltale weep holes along the side of its engine block to indicate that coolant is leaking past the first liner seal O-ring?

21. Technician A says that cylinder liners should not only be numbered but should be match-marked before removal to ensure that they are reinstalled in the same cylinder bore. Technician B says that numbering is required, but it doesn't matter where you reinsert the liner. Which technician is correct, and why?

22. Technician A says that liners should be stored horizontally before and after inspection. Technician B says that they should be stored vertically (standing up); otherwise, they can become egg shaped or distorted after a period of time. Which technician is correct?

23. What condition is indicated by a very high glasslike polish on the inside surface of a liner?

24. Technician A says that to repair the condition in question 23 successfully, you need to rebore the block or liner. Technician B says that by using a fine-grit ball hone and a mixture of equal parts of mineral spirits and 30 weight engine oil you can correct this condition. Which technician is correct?

25. When inspecting a used cylinder liner bore, a bright mirror finish in certain areas is indicative of
    a. wear
    b. glazing
    c. scuffing
    d. scoring

26. Liners should always be checked with a dial bore gauge to determine what three conditions?

27. Cavitation corrosion on the outside surface of a wet-type liner is usually caused by what operating condition(s)?

28. Dark spots, stains, or low-pressure areas on the outside diameter of dry liners generally indicate what type of a condition?

29. Shiny spots or areas on the outside diameter or flange area of a cylinder liner are usually indicative of
    a. movement during engine operation
    b. overheating
    c. coolant leakage
    d. distortion

30. Cracking of a cylinder liner flange can usually be attributed to
    a. sloping counterbores in the block
    b. liner movement
    c. overheating
    d. light-load operation

31. True or False: A liner crosshatch pattern can be established to produce any surface angle finish.

32. Cylinder liner glaze must be broken using
    a. emery cloth
    b. glass beading
    c. reboring
    d. cylinder hone

33. List the three basic types of cylinder hones that are widely used.

34. Technician A says that a honing stone of any grade grit can be used to finish the desired crosshatch pattern on the inside diameter of a block bore or liner assembly. Not so, says technician B; the type of block or liner material determines the grit of stone that would be used. Who is correct?

35. True or False: Honing stones should always be used dry.

36. If a cylinder block bore requires that an oversized liner be used, technician A says that a boring machine must be employed. Technician B says that a power hone could also be used. Are both technicians correct in their statements?

37. True or False: In question 36, if a boring machine is used, you still need to employ a fixed hone to produce the correct liner surface crosshatch pattern.

38. Technician A says that too steep a crosshatch pattern on a block bore or liner surface would result in scuffing and tearing of the new piston rings. Technician B believes that it would result in pumping oil. Which technician is correct?

39. Technician A says that too shallow a crosshatch pattern in a block bore or liner would result in pumping oil, while technician B says that too shallow a crosshatch angle in a block bore or liner surface would result in tearing and scuffing of the rings. Which technician is correct?

40. True or False: To achieve the desired crosshatch pattern in the block bore or liner, the speed at which you stroke the honing stones up and down is the key factor.

41. True or False: Honing debris is best removed by submerging the liners in a tank with hot caustic solution.

42. Describe how you would best remove all traces of honing dust from a liner or block bore.

43. Technician A says that liners should always be clamped down prior to checking the liner flange protrusion limit. Technician B says that this isn't necessary since most liners are press fit at the flange area anyway. Which technician is correct?

44. Too much cylinder liner protrusion would result in (possibly more than one correct answer)
    a. liner movement
    b. cracking of the liner flange
    c. cracking of the cylinder head
    d. head gasket leakage

45. Insufficient cylinder liner protrusion would result in (possibly more than one correct answer)
    a. liner movement
    b. head gasket leakage
    c. liner distortion
    d. liner flange cracking

46. To correct for insufficient liner protrusion, what remedy would you use?

47. If too much liner protrusion existed, what remedy would you use?

48. True or False: Wet cylinder liner seals should usually be lubricated prior to liner installation in the block. If your answer is *true*, what lubricant would you use? If your answer is *false*, why so?

49. Some engine manufacturers suggest that you apply a thin bead of RTV sealant to what two areas of the cylinder liner during installation?

50. After you install a wet-type cylinder liner, the lower inside bore of the liner indicates some distortion. What condition do you think might cause this problem?

51. Technician A says that cylinder liners are available in both oversized inside and outside diameter. Technician B disagrees, stating that all cylinder liners retain a standard inside bore diameter and are oversized only on their outside diameter. Which technician is correct?

52. True or False: Most cylinder liners require removal and installation by use of a special liner puller.

7

Crankshafts, Main Bearings, Vibration Dampers/Pulleys, Flywheels, and Flywheel Housings

Overview

This chapter deals with the largest rotating component, and one of the most expensive items in the engine: The crankshaft, and the individual components that support it, balance out its static and dynamic vibrations and permit easy transmission of its rotating torque to a power coupling for effective use. The crankshaft's function and operation are closely interlinked with the connecting rods, pistons, vibration damper, and flywheel to effectively transfer the chemical energy released within the combustion chambers to useful work (mechanical energy) at the rotating flywheel that is bolted to the crankshaft rear flange. Reciprocating motion (either back and forth, or up and down as in a vertical engine) of the piston is delivered through the connecting rod and journals, where it is converted into rotary motion at the crankshaft main journals. We will discuss the cleaning, inspection, repair, and service of these important components to provide you with both the technical theoretical knowledge and suggested hands-on tasks required to interface with the ASE testing requirements discussed herein.

ASE T2 TEST SPECIFICATIONS

As an industry standard guide for inspection and repair of the engine crankshaft and its mating components described in the overview, let us look at the ASE medium/heavy trucks T2 tests preparation guide tasks lists. Part C of the T2 tasks list for engine block diagnosis and repair indicates that items 9, 10, 11, 17, 18, and 19 identify the checks needed for the crankshaft, main bearings, gear train, vibration damper, and the flywheel and housing.

C. Engine Block Diagnosis and Repair (5 ASE questions)

9. Clean and inspect crankshaft and journals for surface cracks and damage; check condition of oil passages; check passage plugs; measure journal diameters; determine needed service.

10. Inspect and replace main bearings; check cap fit and bearing clearances; check and adjust crankshaft end play.

11. Inspect, reinstall, and time the drive gear train. (Includes checking timing sensors, gear wear, and backlash of crankshaft, camshaft, auxiliary, drive, and idler gears; service shafts, bushings, and bearings.)

17. Inspect and measure, and service/replace crankshaft vibration damper; determine needed repairs.

18. Inspect, install, and align flywheel housing.

19. Inspect flywheel/flexplate (including ring gear) and mounting surfaces for cracks, wear, and runout; determine needed repairs.

ASE M2 AND M3 TEST SPECIFICATIONS

In addition to the knowledge required in the ASE T2 tests, the ASE engine machinist test M2, part D, provides greater information on the required skills needed to challenge the crankshaft inspection and machining area of the cylinder block specialist. The ASE M3 section, assembly specialist, describes the important areas and items involved in this testing area. The following ASE tasks lists indicate the appropriate items that you should study and be capable of demonstrating hands-on skills knowledge.

D. **Crankshaft Inspection and Machining (12 ASE questions)**

1. Inspect crankshaft for damage; determine needed repairs.
2. Identify crankshaft by make, model, and casting number.
3. Remove oil gallery plugs and crankshaft attachments as needed.
4. Clean crankshaft.
5. Inspect crankshaft for cracks; repair as needed.
6. Check crankshaft for straightness; check flange, seal surface, and snout runout; repair as needed.
7. Check journals for hardness as needed; compare to manufacturer's specifications and repair as needed.
8. Inspect all threaded areas for damage, repair as needed.
9. Check all snout, journals, flanges, flywheel, and pilot areas for size and condition; inspect seal surfaces for wear; inspect for thrust wear and fillet (radius) condition; repair as needed.
10. Remove dowels as needed.
11. Inspect gears, keyways, and keys; remove and replace as needed.
12. Identify, remove, and inspect counterweights and bolts; mark locations as needed.
13. Chamfer/debur oil holes and polish crankshaft journals; verify journal size and surface finish according to manufacturer's specifications.

Task List Assembly Specialist (Test M3)

A. **Engine Disassembly, Inspection, and Cleaning (10 ASE questions)**

1. Verify engine make and model; inspect engine for damage; interpret available technical and customer information.
6. Mark as needed, and remove harmonic balancer/pulley and flywheel.
14. Remove and inspect main bearing caps; remove crankshaft from bearing saddles.
15. Remove and inspect main and connecting rod bearings; identify locations.

B. **Engine Preparation (11 ASE questions)**

1. Clean cylinder block, crankshaft, and related components for final assembly.
2. Lay out all parts and components to be assembled; verify for application, reuse and sizes.

C. **Short Block Assembly (17 ASE questions)**

4. Install main bearings, oil seals, and crankshaft, following recommended procedures.
5. Install main bearing caps and check crankshaft bearing clearance and end play; check for snout, gear(s), and flange runout.
6. Install timing components; verify correct timing positions, gear backlash, and end play.

D. **Long Block Assembly (14 ASE questions)**

5. Check flywheel housing for runout; correct as necessary. (This task applies to diesel engines only.)
6. Check harmonic balancer assembly according to manufacturers' recommendations.

E. **Final Assembly (8 ASE questions)**

5. Install flywheel.

CRANKSHAFT STRUCTURE AND FUNCTION

The crankshaft in a diesel engine is used to change the up-and-down motion of the pistons and connecting rods to usable rotary motion at the flywheel. It is called a crankshaft because it is made with cranks or throws (an offset portion of the shaft), with a rod journal (that connects rod-bearing surfaces) machined or manufactured on the end. Different designs and different throw arrangements are used, determined by the number of engine cylinders and engine configurations, such as inline or V design. On one end, generally the rear of the shaft, a flywheel (a heavy metal wheel) will be bolted. Attached to the opposite end will be the vibration damper. High-speed engine crankshafts are usually manufactured from a one-piece forged alloy steel billet.

Underslung crankshafts are supported in medium- and high-speed engines by a series of seven main bearing caps in a six-cylinder engine (see Figure 6–1, items 4, 5, and 6). In big-bore slow-speed engines, the large and massive crankshaft is lowered into and supported in the "bed" of the engine; therefore, no main bearing caps are used. Figure 7–1 illustrates a crankshaft for a two-cycle high-speed Detroit Diesel

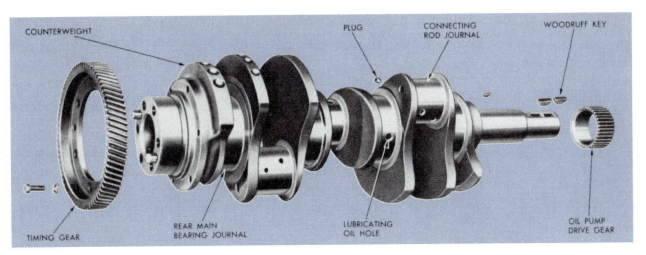

FIGURE 7–1   *Typical heavy-duty diesel engine crankshaft identification. (Courtesy of Detroit Diesel Corporation.)*

engine featuring a bolted timing gear at the rear end that meshes with and drives an idler gear to transfer motion to the camshaft gears on a V configuration, or to one camshaft and a balance shaft on an inline model. The smaller gear at the front end of the crankshaft is used to drive the engine oil pump assembly. Figure 7–2 illustrates the crankshaft for a four-stroke-cycle Cummins ISX/Signature DOHC 15 L engine model. The engine gear train on these models is located behind the engine front cover; therefore, the small gear numbered as item 4 in the diagram transfers motion to the engine gear train. Item 2, the crankshaft adapter, has a series of threaded bolt holes to which the crankshaft pulley and vibration damper are bolted. Because these engine models are electronically controlled, note that item 5 in the diagram is a speed ring indicator used to generate an electrical signal to the engine speed and position sensor. This signal is transmitted to the engine ECM. In this same diagram, items 7 and 8 are the crankshaft main bearings (upper and lower) and item 9 is the crankshaft thrust washers used to control end float.

Within the diesel engine the pressure developed during operation by the burning fuel and air is trapped in the cylinder by the pistons and rings that are connected to the crankshaft by the connecting rods. The crankshaft then transmits this pressure or power to the flywheel for use outside the engine. To increase this power and produce torque, the crankshaft has been designed with the addition of cranks or throws. These throws extend from the centerline of the shaft outward. The distance that they extend outward is determined by the engine manufacturer and is called the stroke of the crankshaft. The crankshaft will have one throw for every cylinder in an inline engine and one throw for

every two cylinders in a V-design engine. Throw arrangement or spacing plays a very important part in helping to balance the engine. Figure 7–3 shows typical throw arrangements found in engines used today.

Since the crankshaft must rotate at different speeds over a wide speed range, it must be balanced precisely to avoid vibration. In addition, counterweights must be added to offset the inertia forces generated by the up-and-down movement of the piston-and-rod assembly. Most crankshafts will be constructed with counterweights on them, whereas others may be bolted on.

The crankshaft must be solidly supported in the block to absorb the power from the engine cylinders. This is done by the use of upper and lower shell-type main bearings, commonly called friction-type bearings constructed as shown in Figure 7–4, which fit into machined bores or saddles in the block. Since the main and rod bearings are friction-type bearings, adequate pressure lubrication must be maintained at all times.

Lubrication for the crankshaft and main bearings is provided by engine oil supplied by the oil pump to the oil galleries that are connected to the main bearings. After reaching the bearings, it flows through drillings in the crankshaft to the rod-bearing journals. It then provides lubrication for the rod bearings and is allowed to drip off into the oil pan.

Mounted on the rear of the crankshaft is the flywheel. This flywheel helps to smooth out the power impulses developed within the engine and provides a place for the attached transmission clutch (a transmission connecting and disconnecting device).

Since the crankshaft now has a heavy flywheel mounted on the back, the free or front end must have a torsional (twisting) vibration damper to prevent

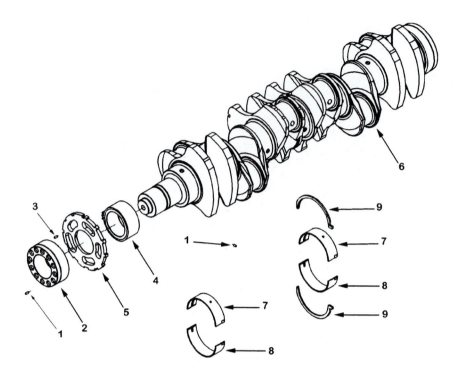

Group No. 01.02		Crankshaft		Option No. BB1724
Ref No.	**Part Number**	**Part Name**	**Req**	**Remarks**
		CRANKSHAFT		
		OPTION BB1724		
	3608889	Assembly, Crankshaft	1	
1	3068935	Dowel, Pin	2	
2	3680503	Adapter, Crankshaft	1	
3	3680505	Dowel, Pin	1	
4	3680542	Gear, Crankshaft	1	
5	3681194	Ring, Speed Indicator	1	
6	(3608888)	Crankshaft, Engine	1	
	3800298	Set, Main Bearing (std)		
7	3678555	Bearing, Main	7	
8	3678556	Bearing, Main	7	
9	3680202	Bearing, Crankshaft Thrust	4	

FIGURE 7–2   Signature/ISX engine model crankshaft and major component identification. (Courtesy of Cummins Engine Company, Inc.)

twisting of the crankshaft by power impulses that create dangerous vibrations as they occur in the engine. This damper is smaller in size than the flywheel and is especially designed to prevent crankshaft breakage that may result from torsional vibrations created in the engine during operation.

The flywheel, crankshaft, main bearings, and vibration damper make up the team that transmits the power developed within the engine to the load. During engine overhaul, these components require careful, detailed inspection and reconditioning if they are to give many hours of trouble-free service.

Unfortunately, components such as the vibration damper and flywheel sometimes receive at best only a casual inspection during a major rebuild and, as a result, bring about premature engine failure. It is recommended that all the components be checked and reconditioned as described in this chapter.

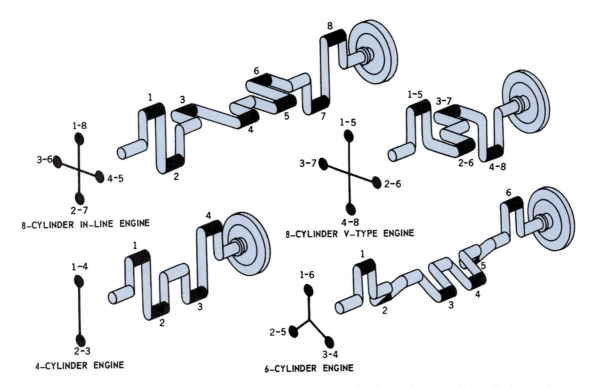

FIGURE 7–3   Examples of common crankshaft throw arrangements for four-, six-, and eight-cylinder engines.

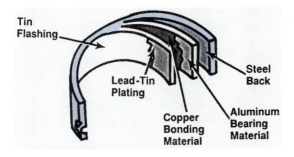

FIGURE 7–4   Construction concept of a five-layer precision shell bearing. (Courtesy of Clevite Engine Parts, Dana Corporation.)

CRANKSHAFT CLEANING AND INSPECTION

The flowchart in Figure 7–5 shows important items to know when repairing or replacing a crankshaft. We discuss some of these details in this section.

Before any measurements are made on the crankshaft, it should be thoroughly cleaned in a large solvent tank. If a hot chemical tank is used for crankshaft cleaning, make sure that the chemicals used will not etch or damage the polished journal surfaces. Before placing the crankshaft in the solvent or hot tank you should:

1. Remove all oil passageway plugs.
2. Remove all seal wear sleeves if present.
3. Remove transmission pilot bearing or bushing (if mounted in crankshaft).

After removal from hot tank, the crankshaft should be cleaned further by:

1. Using a stiff bristle brush to clean oil passageways and drillings
2. Using a steam cleaner or high-pressure washer to clean the entire shaft
3. Using compressed air to blow out all oil passageways and blow dry entire crankshaft

Visual Inspection

The crankshaft should be visually inspected at this time for the following:

1. Check for cracked or worn front hub woodruff key slots.
2. Check the rod and main bearing journals visually for excessive scoring and bluing.
3. Check the crankshaft dowel pin holes for:
   a. Cracks
   b. Size (oversize or oblong)
4. Check the dowel pins for wear or damage and snug fit into crankshaft.

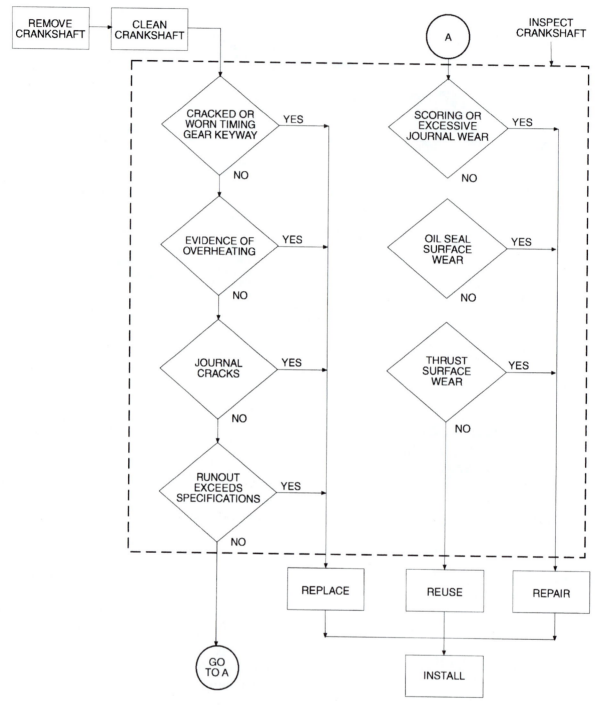

FIGURE 7–5 *Diagnostic flowchart to aid in repair/replacement of the crankshaft. (Courtesy of Detroit Diesel Corporation.)*

5. Check around all oil supply holes for cracks.
6. Check the area on the shaft where the oil seals ride (front and rear). If the wear sleeve is not used and the shaft has a deep groove in it, the groove should be smoothed out with emery paper, and a wear sleeve and oversize seal installed.

7. Inspect the condition of the crankshaft gear(s) for signs of wear, damaged or broken teeth, or signs of the gear "walking" around its press-fit seating area. Some engines use a crankshaft timing drive gear that is bolted to a flange on the rear of the crankshaft, such as the one shown in Figure 7–1 for two-stroke-

cycle Detroit Diesel engine models; however, some manufacturers press these gears into position on the crankshaft (for example, Caterpillar 3176/3176B and the C10 and C12 models). If this gear is to be replaced at any time, it should be heated prior to removal; or use a hydraulic puller to remove it. Prior to installation, always use crocus cloth to remove any scuffing or minor irregularities on the crankshaft mounting surface. Preheat the gear to no more than 410°F (210°C) for no longer than one hour.

NOTE   If at this point you find that the crankshaft is unfit for further use or needs reconditioning, try to determine what caused the crankshaft wear or damage so that the problem can be remedied before a new or reground shaft is installed.

The following steps should be used to determine what may have caused the damage to the crankshaft and main bearings:

8. Inspect both the main and connecting rod bearings, using the illustrations later in this chapter as a guide.
9. Check the bearings and shaft for evidence of insufficient lubrication.
10. Check the bearings and shaft for evidence of improper assembly.
11. Check the block line bore as outlined in the block section (see Figures 6–13, 6–14, and repair according to Figure 6–22).
12. If the crankshaft was broken, carefully check the vibration damper.

NOTE   If the crankshaft does not appear to be worn or damaged beyond repair, the following checks should be made to accurately determine if the shaft needs to be reconditioned.

Inspection by Measurement

Accurate measurement of crankshaft rod and main bearing journals must be made with a micrometer in the following manner:

1. *Out of roundness.* Check by measuring in at least two different places around the journal diameter with a micrometer as shown in Figure 7–6A. Usually if the journal diameter is

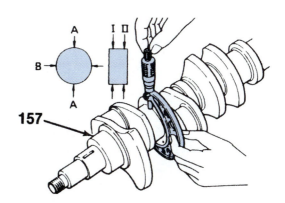

157. Crankshaft

FIGURE 7–6 *(a) Using an outside micrometer to accurately measure the crankshaft journals for taper, ovality, and wear. (Reprinted courtesy of Caterpillar, Inc.)*

0.001 to 0.002 in. (0.025 to 0.050 mm) smaller (less) than manufacturer's specifications, the crankshaft should be reground.

NOTE   The manufacturer's specifications should be checked for allowable crankshaft wear.

2. *Journal taper.* Check by measuring the connecting rod and main bearing journal diameter with a micrometer. Measure near one edge of the journal next to the crank cheek and then move across the journal, checking the diameter in the middle and opposite edge. If the diameters are different and in excess of OEM specs, the crankshaft must be reground.
3. *Crankshaft thrust surfaces.* The crankshaft thrust surfaces should be checked for:
   a. Scoring (visually)
   b. Measurement with an inside micrometer (Figure 7–6B).

NOTE   Thrust surfaces may be reconditioned or reground if they are scored or rough. Most shops that are equipped to regrind crankshafts can perform this repair. It must be remembered that after the thrust surface has been reground, an oversize thrust bearing set will be required.

If the crankshaft is to be reconditioned, it should be taken to an automotive machine shop that specializes in this type of work. It is recommended that a shop be selected that can grind the fillets (area between the

FIGURE 7–6 (b) Checking crankshaft thrust bearing surfaces width with an inside micrometer; you can also use a telescoping gauge. (Courtesy of Cummins Engine Company, Inc.)

crank cheek and journal) in addition to the crankshaft journals and that can make some type of magnetic or flourescent penetrant check for cracks.

> **NOTE** Crankshafts that are ground undersize in the connecting rod and main bearing journals are marked on the front counterweight. See Figure 7–7. If the crankshaft is marked, check the bearing shell part number to make sure the correct bearing size is used.

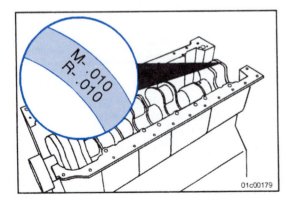

FIGURE 7–7 Example of a reground crankshaft indicating that both the 'main' and 'con-rod' journals have been ground 0.010" (0.254 mm) undersize. (Courtesy of Cummins Engine Company, Inc.).

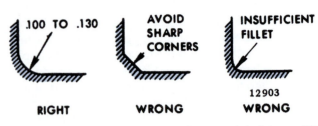

FIGURE 7–8 Enlarged view of the crankshaft journal fillet area radius showing right and wrong fillet radii finishes. (Courtesy of Detroit Diesel Corporation.)

> **CAUTION** All diesel engine crankshaft journals must be fillet ground at the cross-section to relieve stresses and prevent breakage of the crankshaft (Figure 7–8). See OEM specifications.

Crack Detection

One of several methods may be employed by repair shops to check for cracks in a crankshaft. In most cases, crack detecting will be done by the shop doing the grinding. Explanation of two popular methods used is given at this point in case a repair shop does not have the equipment and capability to perform the checks.

Magnetic Particle Method

The magnetic particle method uses some type of electrical magnet to magnetize either a small section or the whole crankshaft at a time. A fine metallic powder is then sprayed on the crankshaft. If the crankshaft is cracked, a small magnetic field forms at the crack and the metal particles are concentrated or gathered at this point.

Spray Penetrant Method

The spray penetrant method uses a dye, which is sprayed on the crankshaft and the excess wiped off. The shaft is then sprayed with a developer that draws the penetrant out of the cracks, making them visible.

REPAIR OR REPLACEMENT OF CRANKSHAFT MAIN BEARINGS

ASE tasks required for diagnosis of crankshaft main bearings is illustrated in the flowchart in Figure 7–9. Greater details on these individual inspection areas are provided in the following section.

MAIN BEARING DEFECTS AND REMEDIES

Main bearings are generally replaced with new ones during a major engine overhaul or rebuild. As indi-

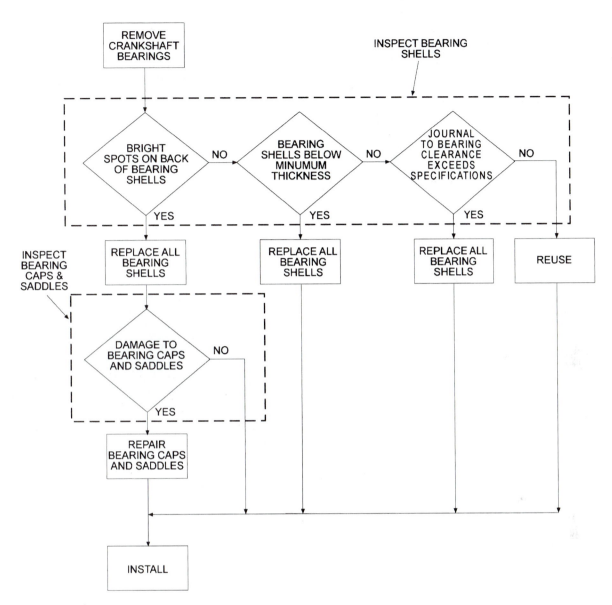

FIGURE 7–9 *Diagnostic flowchart to aid in repair/replacement decisions for the crankshaft main shell bearings. (Courtesy of Detroit Diesel Corporation.)*

cated earlier in this chapter, the bearings should be inspected closely for wear and damage to determine if some abnormal condition such as low oil pressure or main bore misalignment exists within the engine that must be corrected before the engine is reassembled.

The following information and illustrations should be used when inspecting main bearings to determine if the bearing wear is normal or if conditions exist within the engine that may cause premature bearing failure. Premature bearing failures are caused by:

- Dirt: 44.9%
- Misassembly: 13.4%
- Misalignment: 12%
- Insufficient lubrication: 10.8%
- Overloading: 9.5%
- Corrosion: 4.2%
- Other: 4.5%

Surface Fatigue (Figure 7–10)

Appearance.   Small irregular areas of surface material are missing from the bearing lining.

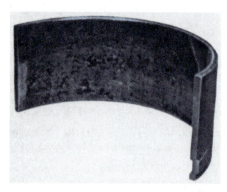

FIGURE 7-10 *Shell bearing surface showing effects of surface fatigue. (Courtesy of Clevite Engine Parts, Dana Corporation.)*

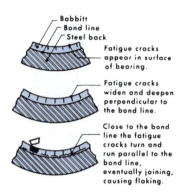

FIGURE 7-11 *Shell bearing cross section showing internal damage caused by fatigue. (Courtesy of Clevite Engine Parts, Dana Corporation.)*

Damaging Action. Heavy pulsating loads imposed on the bearing by a reciprocating engine cause the bearing surface to crack due to metal fatigue, as illustrated in Figure 7–11. Fatigue cracks widen and deepen perpendicular to the bond line. Close to the bond line, fatigue cracks turn and run parallel to the bond line, eventually joining and causing pieces of the surface to flake out.

Possible Causes. Bearing failure due to surface fatigue is usually the result of the normal life span of the bearing being exceeded.

Corrective Action.

1. If the service life for the old bearing was adequate, replace with the same type of bearing to obtain a similar service life.

2. If the service life of the old bearing was too short, replace with a heavier-duty bearing to obtain a longer life.

3. Replace all other bearings (main, connecting rod, and camshaft), as their remaining service life may be short.

4. Recommend that the operator avoid "hot rodding" and lugging, as these tend to shorten bearing life.

Foreign Particles in the Lining (Figure 7–12)

Appearance. Foreign particles are embedded in the bearing. Scrape marks may also be visible on the bearing surface.

Damaging Action. Dust, dirt, abrasives, and/or metallic particles present in the oil supply embed in the soft babbitt-bearing lining, displacing metal and creating a high spot (Figure 7–13).

A high spot may be large enough to make contact with the journal, causing a rubbing action that can lead

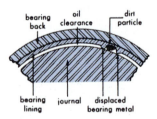

FIGURE 7-12 *Foreign particles embedded in a shell bearing. (Courtesy of Clevite Engine Parts, Dana Corporation.)*

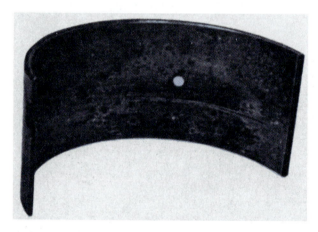

FIGURE 7-13 *Shell bearing cross section showing how dirt particles are embedded in the bearing material. (Courtesy of Clevite Engine Parts, Dana Corporation.)*

to the eventual breakdown and rupture of the bearing lining. Foreign particles may embed only partially and the protruding portion may come in contact with the journal and cause a grinding wheel action.

Possible Causes. Three factors can lead to bearing failure due to foreign particles.

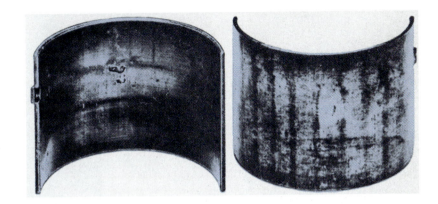

FIGURE 7–14   *Results of a shell bearing being installed with dirt on the backside. (Courtesy of Clevite Engine Parts, Dana Corporation.)*

1. Improper cleaning of the engine and parts prior to assembly
2. Road dirt and sand entering the engine through the air-intake manifold
3. Wear of other engine parts, resulting in small fragments of these parts entering the engine's oil supply

Corrective Action.

1. Install new bearings, being careful to follow proper cleaning procedures.
2. Grind journal surfaces if necessary.
3. Recommend that the operator have the oil changed at proper intervals and have air filter, oil filter, and crankcase breather-filter cleaned as recommended by the manufacturer.

Foreign Particles on the Bearing Back (Figure 7–14)

Appearance.   A localized area of wear can be seen on the bearing surface. Also, evidence of foreign particle(s) may be visible on the bearing back or bearing seat directly behind the area of surface wear.

Damaging Action.   Foreign particles between the bearing and its housing prevent the entire area of the bearing back from being in contact with the housing base (Figure 7–15). As a result, the transfer of heat away from the bearing surface is not uniform and causes localized heating of the bearing surface, which reduces the life of the bearing.

Also, an uneven distribution of the load causes an abnormal high-pressure area on the bearing surface, increasing localized wear on this material.

Possible Causes.   Dirt, dust, abrasives, and/or metallic particles either present in the engine at the time of assembly or created by a burr-removal operation can become lodged between the bearing back and bearing seat during engine operation.

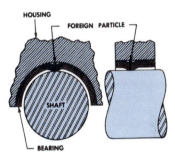

FIGURE 7–15   *Cross section of a shell bearing showing dirt under the bearing. (Courtesy of Clevite Engine Parts, Dana Corporation.)*

Corrective Action.

1. Install new bearings following proper cleaning and burr-removal procedures for all surfaces.
2. Check the journal surfaces and regrind if excessive wear is discovered.

Insufficient Crush (Figure 7–16)

Appearance.   Highly polished areas are visible on the bearing back and/or on the edge of the parting line.

Damaging Action.   When a bearing with insufficient crush is assembled in an engine, it is loose and therefore free to work back and forth within its housing. Because of the loss of radial pressure, there is inadequate contact with the bearing seat, thus impeding heat transfer away from the bearing. As a result, the bearing overheats, causing deterioration of the bearing surface.

Possible Causes.   There are four possible causes of insufficient crush:

1. Bearing parting faces were filed down in a mistaken attempt to achieve a better fit, thus removing the crush.
2. Bearing caps were held open by dirt or burrs on the contact surface.

FIGURE 7–16 *Shell bearing showing the effects of insufficient crush. (Courtesy of Clevite Engine Parts, Dana Corporation.)*

3. Insufficient torquing occurred during installation. (Be certain bolt does not bottom in a blind hole.)
4. The housing bore was oversize or the bearing cap was stretched, thus minimizing the crush.

Corrective Action.

1. Install new bearings using correct installation procedures (never file parting faces).
2. Clean the mating surfaces of bearing caps prior to assembly.
3. Check the journal surfaces for excessive wear and regrind if necessary.
4. Check the size and condition of the housing bore and recondition if necessary.
5. Correct the shim thickness (if applicable).

Shifted Bearing Cap (Figure 7–17)

Appearance. Excessive wear areas can be seen near the parting lines on opposite sides of the upper and lower bearing shells.

Damaging Action. The bearing cap has been shifted, causing one side of each bearing half to be pushed against the journal at the parting line. The resulting metal-to-metal contact and excessive pressure cause deterioration of the bearing surface and above-normal wear areas.

Possible Causes. Following are five factors that can cause a shifted bearing cap:

1. Using too thick a socket wall to tighten the bearing cap. In this case, the socket crowds against the cap, causing it to shift.
2. Reversing the position of the bearing cap.
3. Inadequate dowel pins between bearing shell and housing (if used), allowing the shell to break away and shift.
4. Improper torquing of cap bolts, resulting in a "loose" cap that can shift positions during engine operation.
5. Enlarged cap bolt holes or stretched cap bolts, permitting greater-than-normal play in the bolt holes.

FIGURE 7–17 *Damage caused to a shell thrust bearing by a shifted or misaligned bearing cap. (Courtesy of Clevite Engine Parts, Dana Corporation.)*

Corrective Action.

1. Check journal surfaces for excessive wear and regrind if necessary.
2. Install the new bearing, being careful to use the correct-size socket to tighten the cap and the correct-size dowel pins (if required).
3. Alternate torquing from side to side to ensure proper seating of the cap.
4. Check the bearing cap to ensure its proper position.
5. Use new bolts to prevent overplay within the bolt holes.

Distorted Crankcase (Figure 7–18)

Appearance. A wear pattern is visible on the upper or lower halves of the complete set of main bearings. The degree of wear varies from bearing to bearing depending on the nature of the distortion. The center bearing usually shows the greatest wear.

Damaging Action. A distorted crankcase imposes excessive loads on the bearing with the point of greatest load being at the point of greatest distortion. These excessive bearing loads cause excessive bearing wear. Also, oil clearance is reduced and metal-to-metal contact is possible at the point of greatest distortion.

Possible Causes. Alternating periods of engine heating and cooling during operation are a prime cause of crankcase distortion. As the engine heats, the crankcase expands; and as it cools, the crankcase contracts. This repetitive expanding and contracting causes the crankcase to distort in time.

Distortion may also be caused by extreme operating conditions (for example, hot-rodding and lugging) or improper torquing procedure for cylinder head bolts.

Corrective Action.

1. Determine if distortion exists by use of Prussian blue or visual methods.
2. Align bore the housing (if applicable).
3. Install new bearings.

Bent Crankshaft (Figure 7–19)

Appearance. A wear pattern is visible on the upper and lower halves of the complete set of main bearings. The degree of wear varies from bearing to bearing depending upon the nature of the distortion. The center bearing usually shows the greatest wear.

Damaging Action. A distorted crankshaft subjects the main bearings to excessive loads, with the greatest load being at the point of greatest distortion (Figure 7–20). The result is excessive bearing wear. Also, the oil clearance spaces between journals and bearings are reduced, making it possible for metal-to-metal contact to occur at the point of greatest distortion.

FIGURE 7–18 Shell bearings damaged by a distorted engine block/crankcase. (Courtesy of Clevite Engine Parts, Dana Corporation.)

FIGURE 7–19 Shell bearings damaged by a bent crankshaft. (Courtesy of Clevite Engine Parts, Dana Corporation.)

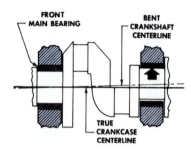

FIGURE 7-20   Cross section of how a bent crankshaft will fit into the saddle of the engine block main bearing bores. (Courtesy of Clevite Engine Parts, Dana Corporation.)

Possible Causes. A crankshaft is usually distorted due to extreme operating conditions, such as hot-rodding and lugging.

Corrective Action.

1. Determine if distortion exists by means of Prussian blue or visual methods.
2. Install a new or reconditioned crankshaft.
3. Install new bearings.

Out-of-Shape Journal (Figure 7-21)

Appearance. In general, if a bearing has failed because of an out-of-shape journal, an uneven wear pattern is visible on the bearing surface. Specifically, however, these wear areas can be in any one of three patterns: Figure 7-21a shows the wear pattern caused by a tapered journal. Figure 7-21b shows the wear pat-

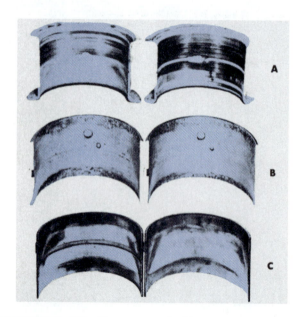

FIGURE 7-21   Damage to shell bearings as a result of out-of-round crankshaft journals. (Courtesy of Clevite Engine Parts, Dana Corporation.)

FIGURE   7-22   Various crankshaft journal shapes caused by wear. (Courtesy of Clevite Engine Parts, Dana Corporation.)

tern caused by an hourglass-shaped journal. Figure 7-21c shows the pattern of a barrel-shaped journal. See also Figure 7-22.

Damaging Action. An out-of-shape journal imposes an uneven distribution of the load on the bearing surface, increasing heat generated and thus accelerating bearing wear. An out-of-shape journal also affects the bearing's oil clearance, making it insufficient in some areas and excessive in others, thereby upsetting the proper functioning of the lubrication system.

Possible Causes. If the journal is tapered, there are two possible causes.

1. Uneven wear at the journal during operation (misaligned rod)
2. Improper machining of the journal at some previous time

If the journal is hourglass or barrel shaped, this is always the result of improper machining.

Corrective Action. Regrinding the crankshaft can best remedy out-of-shape-journal problems. Then install new bearings in accordance with proper installation procedures.

Fillet Ride (Figure 7-23)

Appearance. When fillet ride has caused a bearing to fail, areas of excessive wear are visible on the extreme edges of the bearing surface (Figure 7-24).

Damaging Action. If the radius of the fillet at the corner where the journal blends into the crank is larger than required, it is possible for the edge of the engine bearing to make metal-to-metal contact and ride on this oversize fillet. This metal-to-metal contact between the bearing and fillet causes excessive wear, leading to premature bearing fatigue.

Possible Causes. Fillet ride results if excessive fillets are left at the edges of the journal at the time of crankshaft machining.

Corrective Action.

1. Regrind the crankshaft, paying particular attention to allowable fillet radii (Figure 7-8).

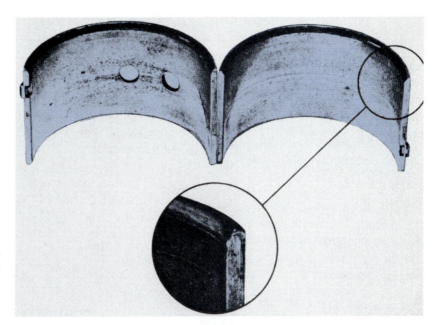

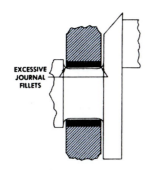

EXCESSIVE
JOURNAL
FILLETS

FIGURE 7–23 *Shell bearing damage caused by crankshaft journal fillet wear or incorrect fillet radius; also see Figure 7–8. (Courtesy of Clevite Engine Parts, Dana Corporation.)*

FIGURE 7–24 *Cross section of a crankshaft and shell bearing showing fillet ride due to improper fillet radii during grinding. (Courtesy of Clevite Engine Parts, Dana Corporation.)*

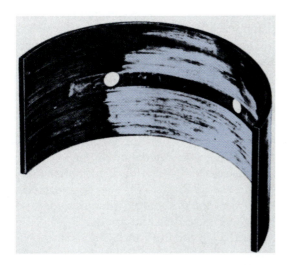

FIGURE 7–25 *Shell bearing damage caused by oil starvation. (Courtesy of Clevite Engine Parts, Dana Corporation.)*

NOTE   Be careful not to reduce fillet radius too much, since this can weaken the crankshaft at its most critical point.

2.   Install new bearings.

Oil Starvation

Appearance.   When a bearing has failed due to oil starvation, its surface is usually very shiny. In addition, there may be excessive wear of the bearing surface due to the wiping action of the journal (Figure 7–25).

Damaging Action.   The absence of a sufficient oil film between the bearing and the journal permits metal-to-metal contact. The resulting wiping action causes premature bearing fatigue (Figure 7–26).

Possible Causes.   Any one of the following conditions could cause oil starvation:

1.   Insufficient oil clearance—usually the result of utilizing a replacement bearing that has

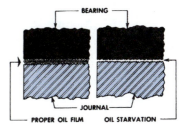

BEARING

JOURNAL

PROPER OIL FILM   OIL STARVATION

FIGURE 7–26 *How oil starvation would damage the bearing and journal during engine operation. (Courtesy of Clevite Engine Parts, Dana Corporation.)*

too great a wall thickness. In some cases the journal may be oversize.

2. Broken or plugged oil passages, prohibiting proper oil flow.

3. A blocked oil suction screen or oil filter.

4. A malfunctioning oil pump or pressure relief valve.

5. Misassembling main bearings blocking off an oil supply hole.

Corrective Action.

1. Double-check all measurements taken during the bearing selection procedure to catch any errors in calculation.

2. Check to be sure that the replacement bearing you are about to install is the correct one for the application (that it has the correct part number).

3. Check the journals for damage and regrind if necessary.

4. Check the engine for possible blockage of oil passages, oil suction screen, and oil filter.

5. Check the operation of the oil pump and pressure relief valve.

6. Be sure that the oil holes are properly indexed when installing the replacement bearings.

7. Advise the operator about the results of engine lugging.

Misassembly

Engine bearings will not function properly if they are installed wrong. In many cases misassembly will result in premature failure of the bearing. Figures 7–27 to 7–29 show typical assembly errors most often made in the installation of engine bearings.

FIGURE 7–27 View showing that the shell bearing lugs have not been correctly nested or seated in the bearing cap or saddle. (Courtesy of Clevite Engine Parts, Dana Corporation.)

FIGURE 7–28 Oil starvation will result if the two bearing shell halves are installed in the wrong position. (Courtesy of Clevite Engine Parts, Dana Corporation.)

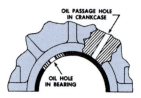

FIGURE 7–29 Results of installing a bearing shell backwards will block the oil passage hole. (Courtesy of Clevite Engine Parts, Dana Corporation.)

SPUN MAIN BEARINGS

On some high-speed, high-torque engines, spun main bearings can be traced to main bearing cap fretting (metal galling) due to the failure of the main bearing capscrews to provide sufficient clamping load for extreme-duty-cycle engine applications. This fretting at the block/main bearing cap interface will result in an oval shape and an overall decrease in the main bearing bore size. This can cause a decrease in the oil film thickness between the crankshaft main bearings and journals and can spin the main bearings in the caps and saddles of the engine block. Some engine manufacturers recommend that the flat surfaces of the main bearing cap, and where the flat surface of the cap contacts the mating flats on the block, have Loctite 620 or equivalent applied. This provides an additional 70% to the shear strength of the main bearing cap-to-block joint. On Cummins M11/ISM models, this OEM recommends that you first thoroughly clean the main bearing cap mounting surfaces on the block with a solvent-based degreaser, then dry the mounting surfaces with a clean, lint-free cloth. Mask the crankshaft mains prior to spraying Loctite Primer-N to the cap and saddle flat surfaces. Allow the primer five minutes to dry.

Refer to Figure 7–30 and apply a bead of Loctite 620 between 0.118 and 0.197 inch (3 and 5 mm) wide to the four locations of each main bearing cap as shown. Do not allow any sealant to enter the main bearing shell

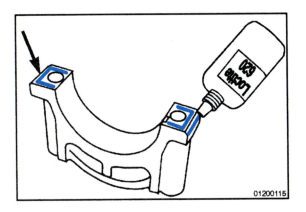

FIGURE 7–30 Applying a thin bead of Loctite 620 to the four locations of each main bearing cap. (Courtesy of Cummins Engine Company, Inc.)

inside diameter. The main bearing capscrews must be tightened within 15 minutes of applying the Loctite 620. Do not fill the crankcase with oil for at least three hours to allow the Loctite 620 to cure or set.

MAIN BEARING SPECIFICATIONS AND CRANKSHAFT TOLERANCES

Shell bearings are manufactured so that in their free state (not installed in place) they actually form an oval or off-center shape. Figure 7–31a illustrates the bearing in its *free state*, or free spread, where the shell OD (outside diameter) at the mating faces is slightly larger than the bearing bore diameter. This difference in diameter ensures that the bearing will not move during engine operation; it also ensures good contact between the bearing backing and the cap or saddle seating surface. Figure 7–31b illustrates that the bearing shells sit slightly higher than the main bearing split parting line. The purpose of this design concept, known as *bearing*

crush, is that when the main bearing or con-rod bolts are torqued to specifications, the crush on the bearing ensures that the bearing shells are tightly seated in their bores formed by the cap and saddle.

Main bearings for many high-speed engines are supplied in standard 0.001, 0.010, 0.020, 0.030, and 0.040 in. sizes.

TIP   0.001" undersize bearings can be used when the crankshaft journals have been lightly polished to remove minor scratches and imperfections!

Some engine manufacturers do not recommend that the crankshaft be ground; as a result, no undersize bearings are supplied. After the crankshaft has been reconditioned, the correct-size main bearings must be selected to give the recommended running or oil clearance. For example, a crankshaft may be ground to a 0.020 undersize (the correct main bearing then is a 0.020 undersize). Shell bearing sizes are stamped or etched on the backside.

If specifications are not available for the crankshaft on which you are working, the following general specifications may be referred to when you are measuring the crankshaft.

General specifications for main bearings and crankshaft tolerances are as follows:

1. Crankshaft finish: 20 μin or more.
2. Diameter tolerance:
   a. 0.0005 in. for journals up to 1 1/2 in. in diameter
   b. 0.001 in. for journals 1 1/2 to 10 in. in diameter
3. Out of round: 0.002 in. maximum. (Never use a medium out-of-round journal with a maximum out-of-round bore.)

FIGURE 7–31 (a) Design concept of a shell bearing results in a larger "free-spread" when the bearing is out of the bearing cap or saddle, (b) The installed shell bearing provides slight extension above the parting line in order to provide bearing crush. This crush ensures that the bearing will be forced into contact with its seat in the cap or saddle when torqued down. (Courtesy of Detroit Diesel Corporation.)

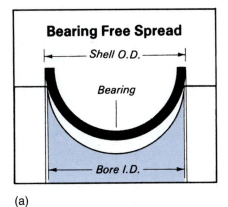

(a)

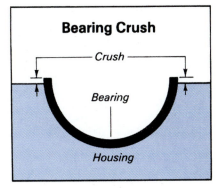

(b)

4. Taper should not exceed:
   a. 0.0002 in. for journals up to 1 in. wide
   b. 0.0004 in. for journals from 1 to 2 in. wide
   c. 0.0005 in. for journals 2 in. and wider
5. Hourglass or barrel-shaped condition: use same specifications.
6. Oil holes must be well blended into journal surface and have no sharp edges.

MAIN BEARING AND CRANKSHAFT INSTALLATION

It is assumed that the cylinder block has been checked, cleaned, and reconditioned. If not, refer to block reconditioning in Chapter 6 before attempting to install main bearings or crankshaft.

1. Put the cylinder block on a clean workbench or engine stand in the inverted position.
2. Install the main bearing top half (shells) of proper size carefully in cylinder block, making sure that the bearing locating lug is aligned correctly with the matching slot in the block or cap (Figure 7–32).

CAUTION Ensure that all main bearing feed holes are lined up with holes in the main bearings. Also make sure that the block and bearings are clean.

---

3. Install the rear main bearing seal into the block if a split seal is used.
4. Blow out all oil passageways and remove/clean any protective grease or preservative from crankshaft.
5. Install crankshaft using a lifting sling or bracket as in Figure 7–33.
6. If the timing gears and camshaft are installed in the block, index the timing mark on the crankshaft gear with the appropriate mark.
7. Main bearing clearance should be checked at this time, which is best done by using a special extruded plastic thread that is referred to by its trade name of *Plastigage*. This product is readily available from major parts suppliers. Plastigage is available in four thicknesses; choose one based on the desired oil clearance that you are checking. Each box of Plastigage contains 12 envelopes of a given color and size. Bearing clearances for a given engine can be found in the service manual. Plastigage is widely used in four main sizes, which are identified by the color-coded packets green, red, blue, and yellow:

- Green = 0.001 to 0.003 in. (0.025 to 0.076 mm)
- Red = 0.002 to 0.006 in. (0.051 to 0.152 mm)
- Blue = 0.004 to 0.009 in. (0.102 to 0.229 mm)
- Yellow = 0.009 to 0.020 in. (0.23 to 0.51 mm)

Plastigage offers a fast and accurate method of checking the clearances of both main and con-rod bearings. To use Plastigage correctly, make sure it is at room temperature; then follow these steps:

1. If the engine is turned upside down, lay a strip of Plastigage equivalent to the width of

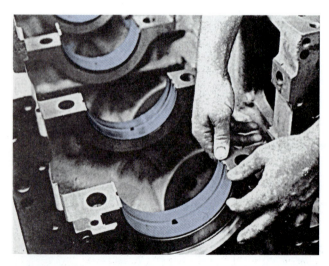

FIGURE 7–32 Installation of the upper bearing shells into the engine block. Take care not to touch the bearing shell surface, and ensure that the bearing alignment tangs are correctly located to retain the bearing shell. (Courtesy of Cummins Engine Company, Inc.)

FIGURE 7–33 Lifting the engine crankshaft with a sling covered with rubber hose over the bent hook ends to avoid any journal damage.

the bearing journal across it and parallel to the crankshaft centerline.

2. If the main bearing clearances are being checked with the engine in position in its equipment, support the weight of the crankshaft and the flywheel by means of a jack under the counterweight adjoining the bearing being checked; otherwise, a false reading will be obtained.

3. Cut or tear off a length of the paper envelope that contains the Plastigage to the bearing width required. Avoid squeezing the envelope during this action, because if the Plastigage is compressed, a false reading may result or the Plastigage may become stuck to the envelope.

4. Carefully roll or remove the strip of Plastigage from the envelope by cutting with a pair of scissors or a knife.

5. Wipe any oil from the bearing shell or journal.

6. Place the Plastigage across the full width of the bearing journal or bearing shell as shown in Figure 7–34a.

7. Reinstall the bearing cap and tighten the bolts to the recommended torque value.

8. Loosen the bolts and carefully remove the bearing cap.

9. Lay the Plastigage envelope, which is printed with a series of graduations, alongside the flattened Plastigage as shown in Figure 7–34b until one of the numbered graduations equals the Plastigage width. One side of the envelope is graduated in thousandths of an inch, while the opposite side is in metric dimensions.

10. If the bearing clearance is too small or too large, try to determine the cause(s). Too small a clearance can be caused by high spots behind the bearing shell in the cap or saddle; therefore, check for nicks, burrs, or dirt behind the bearing. Too large a clearance may be due to worn bearings, worn journals, or use of the wrong size of bearings on a reground crankshaft.

11. Remove Plastigage by flooding it with clean engine oil and scraping it from a journal with a fingernail. Do not scratch or etch a bearing surface (nonhardened). Plastigage will self-destruct during engine operation.

12. Lubricate all bearing shells before installation over the crankshaft journals; apply clean engine oil to the journals.

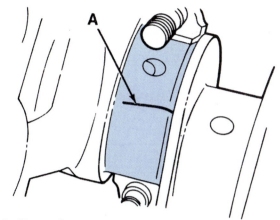

A. Place Gaging Plastic Parallel to Crankshaft

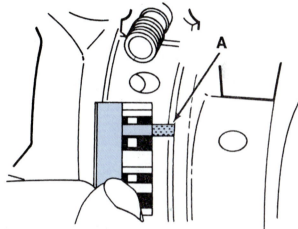

B. Measure Widest Point of Gaging Plastic With Graduated Scale

FIGURE 7–34 *(a) Placing a strip of Plastigage (plastic wire) lengthwise across the crankshaft bearing journal. (b) Using the Plastigage paper packet measuring strip to determine the bearing to crankshaft journal clearance. (Reprinted courtesy of Caterpillar, Inc.)*

13. Install the crankshaft lower thrust washer halves into position on the main bearing cap that is machined to accept them. To help hold the washers in place during installation, apply petroleum jelly on the backside of the washer.

14. With all bearing caps in position, apply either clean engine oil or International Compound No. 2 or equivalent to the bolt threads and the underside of the bolt heads (some manufacturers recommend SAE 140W oil under the bolt head). Some high-speed engine models employ *main bearing cap stabilizers,* similar to

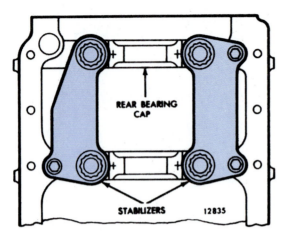

FIGURE 7–35 *Main bearing cap stabilizer brackets used to prevent flexing of the caps during engine operation on a high-speed heavy-duty two-stroke-cycle engine model. (Courtesy of Detroit Diesel Corporation.)*

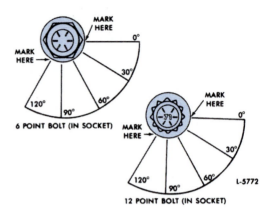

FIGURE 7–36 *One example of a main bearing cap torque-turn method used to correctly tighten the retaining bolts to specs. (Courtesy of Detroit Diesel Corporation.)*

those illustrated in Figure 7–35, to prevent flexing of the caps during engine operation. These are commonly used by Detroit Diesel on its two-stroke-cycle engines: the stabilizers are standard items on 8 and 12V-71 and on 6, 8, 12, and 16V-92 engine cylinder blocks. The main bearing cap bolts pass through holes in these stabilizers, which are also bolted to tapped holes in the block machined oil pan mounting pad area.

15. Prior to drawing all bolts snug, if main bearing cap *side bolts* are used, thread them into position through the block bolt holes. Snug all cap bolts; then rap them individually with a fiber or plastic hammer or mallet to ensure that the caps are fully seated.

SERVICE TIP Always begin by tightening the center main bearing bolts and working progressively toward each end of the crankshaft. After tightening each set of cap bolts, manually rotate the crankshaft to check that no bind exists. If you do not do this, and the crankshaft fails to rotate after all cap bolts have been tightened, you will not know what caps are creating the binding problem.

16. Check the final torque. The final torque depends on the size of bolt being used. In addition, the bolts should be torqued up in stages and never tightened to the maximum value in one step. Many engine manufacturers rec-

ommend what is commonly referred to as a bolt *torque-turn method*. Figure 7–36 illustrates one example of this procedure; it involves tightening the bolts to a specified torque value, then marking the heads of the bolts to the cap with paint or a line. You then mark the socket being used with two marks 120° apart. Each bolt is rotated from this point a given number of degrees that places the bolt at the correct torque value. Refer to the specific engine service manual specs for this information.

17. When all bolts have been torqued to specs, manually rotate the crankshaft to check that it turns freely with no bind. If any bind exists, you will have to loosen off each set of main bearing cap bolts one at a time to determine where the problem exists and to correct the problem. The problem may be due to metal nicks, burrs, or scores between the cap and bearing or cap and saddle.

18. Now check the amount of crankshaft end float or freedom of movement. Follow these steps:

■ Pry the crankshaft assembly either to the front or rear of the block with a suitable metal bar placed between one of the bearing caps and crank weights.

■ Refer to Figure 7–37 and install a dial indicator gauge on the end of the block with the gauge extension rod against the end of the crankshaft. With the pry bar, exert pressure against the crank in the direction of the dial to allow you to set the gauge to zero.

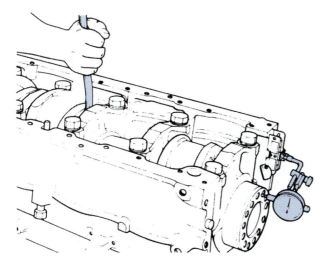

FIGURE 7–37   *Using a small pry bar to force the crank-shaft toward a dial indicator to determine the crankshaft end play. (Courtesy of Detroit Diesel Corporation.)*

- Pry the crankshaft away from the dial gauge and carefully note the reading on the face of the gauge. This is the amount of end play or end float of the crankshaft assembly, which is required to allow for self-centering of the crank and con-rods during engine operation due to heat expansion and due to the thrust loads experienced on the flywheel. The amount of end play varies between engines. On high-speed diesel engines, this normally is in the region of 0.004 to 0.018 in. (0.10 to 0.457 mm).
- If the end play is less than specs, loosen the cap screws slightly and shift the crankshaft toward the front and then the rear of the engine. Retorque the cap bolts in sequence once again; recheck the end clearance.
- If end clearance is insufficient, or too much, carefully check that the correct thickness of thrust washers is being used. If the crank thrust surfaces have been reground, thicker thrust washers are required.

SERVICE TIP   It is acceptable to use different thicknesses of thrust washers on each side of the main bearing cap to obtain the necessary end play. For example, you may use standard-thickness thrust washers (upper and lower) on one side and 0.010 in. oversize washers (upper and lower) on the opposite side, or any combination that will provide the correct crankshaft end float.

- If main bearing cap side bolts are used, torque these to specifications now. Recheck the crankshaft end float again. If main bearing bolt flat metal locks are used, bend one end of the lock around the cap and the other end against one flat surface of the nut or bolt head.

In-Frame Bearing Removal

When engine bearings wear, particularly the main bearings, engine lube oil pressure decreases, because the oil that flows from the engine main oil gallery flows directly to the crankshaft and passes through the drillings in the crankshaft to the main bearings. Oil then flows through intersecting crank oil passages to feed the con-rod bearings. Worn main bearings allow a large volume of oil to exit between the sides of the main bearings and the crank journal, where the oil drops into the oil pan. Consequently, the overall oil pressure decreases and the con-rod and other lubricated components within the engine suffer due to oil starvation.

During normal engine life, between overhauls, it may become necessary to replace the crankshaft main bearings while the crankshaft and engine are still in the equipment. Reasons for replacement may be bearing failure from deterioration (acid formation) of the oil or loss of oil. Some engine manufacturers indicate that to achieve longer life between rebuilds, the main bearings should be replaced in-frame at specific mileage (kilometer) intervals. Upper shell bearing removal can be performed successfully by inserting a *roll-out pin* into the crankshaft main journal oil hole, and slowly rotating the crankshaft over in its normal direction of rotation to carefully remove the upper main bearing from its saddle. Figure 7–38 illustrates a roll pin being inserted, and Figure 7–39 illustrates a special Kent-Moore upper main bearing shell remover/installer tool set recommended for Detroit Diesel series 50 and 60 engine models. The kit includes a dummy main bearing cap, a dummy main bearing shell tool, and the roll pin. This same tool can be used to effectively remove the No. 6 main bearing thrust washers on the series 60 engine.

The new upper main bearing shell can then be rolled into position using the special tooling just described. If special tooling is not available, select a cap-screw/bolt that will fit into the oil hole of the crankshaft, but *grind* the bolt head so that it is thin enough to prevent jamming the bolt as you rotate the crankshaft, or to prevent grooving or scoring of the block bearing saddle area. You can also grind a circular contact area into the bolt head area to assist in proper bearing removal.

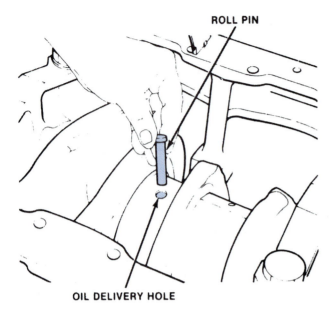

OIL DELIVERY HOLE

FIGURE 7–38 *Installing a special roll pin into the crank-shaft main bearing journal hole to allow rolling the upper shell bearing in or out with the crankshaft in position in the engine block. (Courtesy of Detroit Diesel Corporation.)*

CRANKSHAFT SEALS

A circular oil seal contained within a housing is located at both the front and rear machined sealing surfaces of the crankshaft. Each seal is first pressed into the front timing cover and then the flywheel housing. These seals are designed with a unidirectional, hydrothread-type primary sealing lip and a secondary (dust) sealing lip as shown in Figure 7–40. An internal garter spring ensures proper seal lip tension. One or both of the seals can ride upon a thin-wall hardened steel sleeve to pre-vent a wear ridge from occurring on the crankshaft ma-chined surface. Some engine OEMs automatically use these sleeves when the engine is manufactured, to pre-vent the development of a wear groove on the crank-shaft sealing surface; however, some OEMs do not use a sleeve at the time of manufacture. Consequently, if a seal leaks due to high mileage or high hours of opera-tion, a hardened sleeve will need to be installed onto the worn area of the crankshaft sealing surface. Then an oversize inside-diameter seal must be fit over the wear sleeve outside diameter. On engines that are equipped with a sleeve and seal at the time of manu-facture, both are packaged as a combination unit should replacement be necessary at any time.

When these seals require replacing at overhaul, simply remove by pressing them from their respective bore in the gear case cover or flywheel housing. Note, however, that should these seals leak during engine

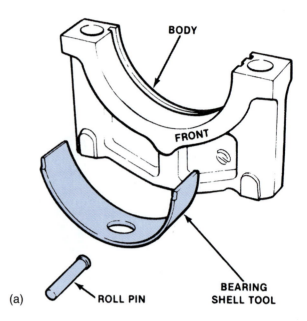

(a)

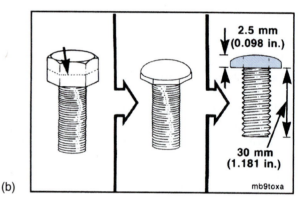

(b)

FIGURE 7–39 *(a) Kent-Moore J36187 main bearing shell removal tool. (Courtesy of Detroit Diesel Corporation.) (b) Example of how to make a bearing roll-out pin by grind-ing a bolt head for use in a Cummins ISC or QSC 8.3 L en-gine model. (Courtesy of Cummins Engine Company, Inc.)*

operation, they can be replaced without removing the housings by using special tooling. To replace the front oil seal, remove the crankshaft pulley and vibration damper; to replace the rear seal with the transmission, PTO, marine gear, or torque converter removed, also remove the engine flywheel.

Rear Seal Removal
There are several methods available to remove the front or rear seal from its housing bore, but the se-quences in each are similar.

1.   Refer to Figure 7–41 and drill two or three holes evenly spaced around the circumferential face of the seal housing.

2.   Thread self-tapping screws into the drilled holes and attach two body repair–type slide hammers

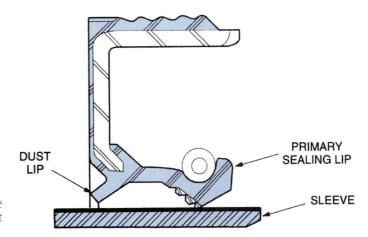

FIGURE 7–40 *View of a rear crankshaft oversize inside-diameter oil seal and sleeve. (Courtesy of Detroit Diesel Corporation.)*

DUST LIP

PRIMARY SEALING LIP

SLEEVE

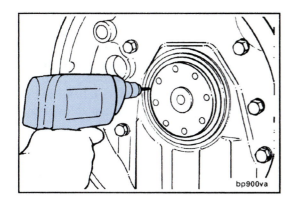

FIGURE 7–41 *Using a small electric drill and bit to drill two or three holes evenly spaced around the circumference of the crankshaft seal prior to removal. (Courtesy of Cummins Engine Company, Inc.)*

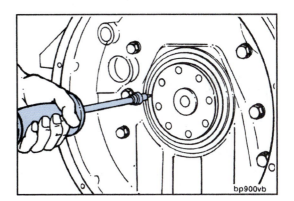

FIGURE 7–42 *Self-tapping screws threaded into the previously drilled seal holes to permit the installation of a slide hammer–type puller(s) to facilitate oil seal removal. (Courtesy of Cummins Engine Company, Inc.)*

onto each screw head (see Figure 7–42). Using the slide hammer, pull the seal from its bore.

3. Optionally install oil seal removal tool J 35993 (Kent-Moore) shown in Figure 7–43 over the butt end of the crankshaft.

4. If the hardened oil seal sleeve, which is press fit over the crankshaft, is worn, then it can be removed using Kent-Moore sleeve remover tool J 37075 shown in Figure 7–44. To use this tool, first install its hardened sleeve into the flywheel housing bore. Using a socket and breaker bar, next rotate the tool in three different locations (2-, 4-, and 8-o'clock positions) until the sleeve stretches sufficiently so that it can be slipped off the end of the crankshaft. Crocus cloth can be used to clean any high spots or minor imperfections from the crankshaft sleeve surface. If a wear sleeve requires removal and no special tooling is available, then the sleeve can be removed in the following ways:

- Use a sharp center punch and stake a series of marks around the outside diameter of the old

sleeve. This action will usually result in sufficient stretching of the sleeve inside diameter so that it can be pulled free from the crankshaft butt end.

- Use a small sharp chisel and carefully nick or split the old sleeve to remove it. Be careful to not mar the sealing surface on the crankshaft.

- Try cutting the sleeve with a small hardened tungsten-carbide cutter or fine-tooth hacksaw blade. Once again, take care to not damage the crankshaft sealing surface.

NOTE   When you receive a new seal and sleeve, do not separate the components; otherwise seal lip damage can result. These two items are designed to be installed as a unit assembly. Read the seal package directions to determine whether it needs to be prelubricated, because many of these seal/sleeve packages are already prelubricated.

J–35993
CRANKSHAFT OIL SEAL REMOVER
Application Series: 50 50G 60 92 8.2L

How Used: Permits removal of oil seal from front or rear of crankshaft without damage to seal bore or crankshaft. Requires small drill motor, preferably variable speed. Can also be used on 8.2L and 92 Series rear oil seals.

(a)

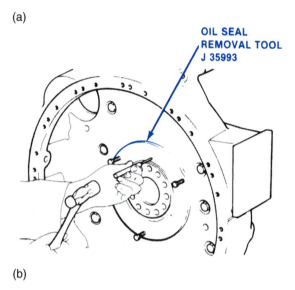

OIL SEAL
REMOVAL TOOL
J 35993

(b)

FIGURE 7–43   (a) Oil seal removal tool J35993. (Courtesy of Kent-Moore Tool Div., SPX Corporation.); (b) Removing seal from flywheel housing. (Courtesy of Detroit Diesel Corporation).

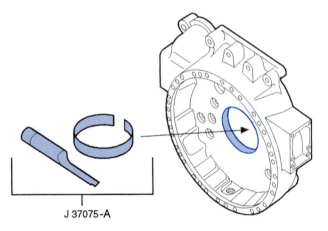

J 37075-A

FIGURE 7–44   Oil seal sleeve removal tool J 37075. (Courtesy of Kent-Moore Tool Div., SPX Corporation.)

5.   Figure 7–45 illustrates the Kent-Moore J 35686-4 and J 35686-10 seal/sleeve installation components with the seal and sleeve assembly in place on the guide studs supplied with the kit. A seal pilot supplied with the new seal/sleeve kit protects the seal during installation.

6.   Figure 7–46 shows the tightening of a hex nut with a ratchet and socket to smoothly pull the seal/sleeve into position, and thus, efficiently install the wear sleeve to the crankshaft and the seal into the flywheel housing gear case bore. Some OEM seal/sleeve installers require you to install a seal pilot protector, followed by an alignment tool that must then be tapped with a hammer at the 3-, 6-, 9-, and 12-o'clock positions to drive the seal into position.

7.   Figure 7–47 illustrates using a special driver set used on Cummins engines to install a wear sleeve onto the end of the crankshaft. Apply a thin coat of clean 15W-40 engine oil to the inside diameter of the tool and also onto the crankshaft seal surface. Position the chamfered edge of the sleeve onto the end of the crankshaft, and with the installer tool squarely positioned in place, alternately tighten each one of the capscrews until the driver bottoms against the end of the crankshaft.

VIBRATION DAMPERS

Vibration dampers used on diesel engines are designed to help dampen the torsional vibrations created within the crankshaft when the engine is running. The vibration damper is usually connected or mounted onto the free end of the crankshaft opposite the flywheel. It may be made up of two round steel cast rings bonded together by a rubber element or employ a flywheel encased within a viscous silicone fluid (Figure 7–48).

Bonded Rubber Dampers
The inner hub unit of the damper construction is hublike to fit the crankshaft, while the outer unit or ring is designed to fit over the hub with the rubber element in between. The entire assembly is held together by the molded rubber.

Inspecting a Bonded Rubber Damper
Although vibration dampers appear to be a solid unit that requires little if any inspection, they must be checked before use on a rebuilt engine. Some rubber element dampers have index marks that should be checked for mark alignment. If the marks do not line up, the damper should be replaced.

It should also be checked for wobble (lateral runout) after it has been mounted on the crankshaft. (A

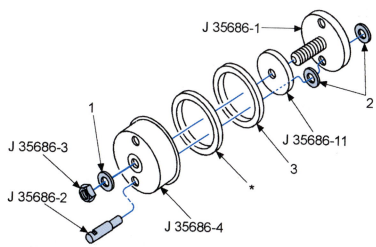

* USE J 35686-10 COLLAR FOR FEDERAL MOGUL® OIL SEAL
INSTALLATION (NO COLOR)
USE J 35686-20 COLLAR FOR CR® OIL SEAL INSTALLATION (WHITE COLOR)

FIGURE 7–45 *Stack-up and identification of parts for tool J 35686-A to install a rear crankshaft oil seal assembly. (Courtesy of Detroit Diesel Corporation.)*

1. Washer
2. Washer
3. Crankshaft Seal

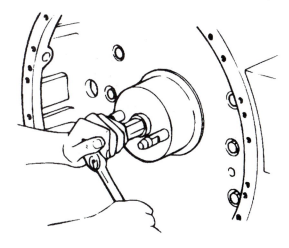

FIGURE 7–46 *Using special tooling J 35686-A with a socket and ratchet to pull in/install the rear crankshaft oil seal/sleeve into the flywheel housing. (Courtesy of Detroit Diesel Corporation.)*

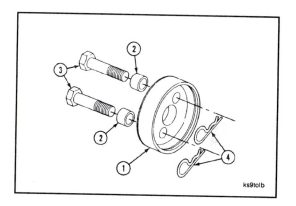

Ref. No.	Description	Qty.
1	Driver	1
2	Spacer	2
3	Capscrew M14x1.5x60 mm	2
4	Hair Pin Cotter	2

FIGURE 7–47 *Crankshaft oil seal installation tool set and component identification. (Courtesy of Cummins Engine Company, Inc.)*

dial indicator is used on the inner surface.) If wobble exceeds the manufacturer's specifications, a new damper should be installed.

Viscous Dampers

The viscous damper, Figure 7–48b, is of a two-piece design. The fluid in the housing provides the resistance so that the flywheel unit absorbs the twisting mo-

tion of the crankshaft. During operation, the outer damper shell, which is bolted to the crankshaft, rotates at the same speed. The rotating motion is transferred to the internal flywheel through the highly viscous fluid. Based on the frequent speed changes to which

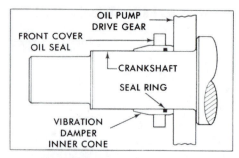

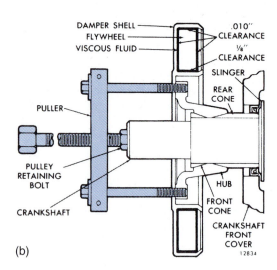

FIGURE 7–48   (a) Typical viscous vibration damper parts. (b) Special puller tooling to safely remove a viscous damper from the crankshaft. (Courtesy of Detroit Diesel Corporation.)

the engine is subjected, there is substantial slippage between the solid inner flywheel and the outer housing/shell. Therefore, the flywheel will be driven during engine acceleration and will actually freewheel during engine deceleration periods. The difference in rotative speed between the two rotating elements decreases the vibration amplitude emanating from the crankshaft to the slower-moving internal flywheel,

thereby reducing these otherwise harmful effects to the rotating crankshaft. The following information will support inspection of a viscous damper assembly.

Inspecting a Viscous Damper
Viscous dampers should be checked for nicks, cracks, or bulges. Bulges or cracks may indicate that the fluid has ignited and expanded the damper case.

NOTE Many engine manufacturers recommend that the viscous dampers be replaced during a major engine overhaul or rebuild. The manufacturer's suggestions and recommendations concerning replacement should be followed closely in this area to prevent crankshaft breakage.

To check a viscous damper assembly with the engine stopped, clean the housing with a good solvent cleaner. Do not steam clean it, because this can alter the internal silicone fluid temperature. Replace the damper if any of the following conditions are found:

- Visually inspect the housing for any signs of dents, nicks, deep scratches, raised surfaces, or other physical damage.
- Look carefully around the mounting bolt area for signs of cracking.
- Check the rolled lip at the outer circumference of the damper where there is usually a raised lip. If the back is flush with the outer edge, the damper has internal damage.
- Check for signs of fluid leakage.
- Refer to Figure 7–49A and use emery cloth to remove paint at four positions on both sides of the damper 90° apart. Check the thickness of the damper about 1/8 in. (3.175 mm) from its outer diameter at these four places. Variations in thickness should not be greater than 0.010 in. (0.254 mm).
- Check the damper for runout using a dial indicator for eccentricity by placing the gauge against the outer circumference. Rotate the damper through 360°. Readings should not exceed 0.004 in./1 in. (0.1 mm/25.4 mm) of damper diameter.
- Check the damper for wobble by setting a dial indicator against the front face of the housing. Push the crankshaft rearward to avoid any false reading from crankshaft end float. The readings should not exceed 0.007 in./1 in. (0.177 mm/25.4 mm) of damper radius.
- Remove the damper from the engine. Never strike a viscous damper with a hammer; many dampers have drilled and tapped holes to allow use of a suitable puller assembly similar to that illustrated in Figure 7–48B.
- Shake the damper back and forth. If a metallic rattling sound is heard, a loss of fluid is indicated and the damper must be replaced.
- Refer to Figure 7–49B and spray the damper with spot-check developer (type SKD-NF or equivalent). Place the damper in a temperature-controlled oven with the rolled lip side down and heat the damper at 200°F (93°C) for at least 30 minutes. Remove the damper from the oven using protective gloves. Check for any signs of fluid sweating or leaks.
- Check for loose or deteriorated engine mounts.

CAUTION Loose engine mounts allow the engine to move during operation, which can cause damage to the vibration damper by adding an extra couple to the damper action. If severe damage to the viscous damper is found, it is possible that crankshaft damage has occurred. Therefore, it is wise to remove the crankshaft for inspection. If the engine is being overhauled, this inspection would be performed routinely. When an in-frame overhaul is being done, the crankshaft should be checked very carefully!

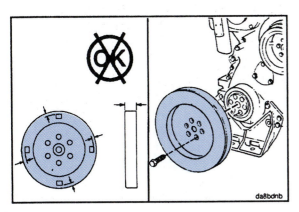
(a)

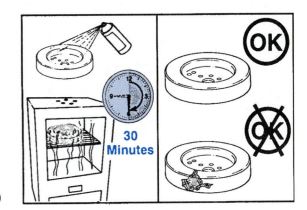
(b)

FIGURE 7–49 (a) Removing paint from the viscous damper at four points and checking the thickness with an outside micrometer. After reinstalling the damper, check it for wobble and runout using a precision dial indicator; (b) Cleaning and spraying the viscous damper housing with spot-check developer. Then place the damper into a temperature-controlled oven for 30 minutes. After removal, check it for signs of fluid sweat or leaks. (Courtesy of Cummins Engine Company, Inc.)

Eccentricity Check

Clean the outside surface of the vibration damper. To measure damper eccentricity (out of round), install the dial indicator onto the gear cover as indicated in Figure 7–50A. Rotate the crankshaft with the accessory driveshaft one complete revolution (360 degrees), and record the total indicator movement. Replace the vibration damper if the eccentricity exceeds 0.28 mm [0.011 in].

Wobble Check

To measure wobble (face alignment), install the dial indicator as shown in Figure 7–50B. Push the crankshaft to the front or rear of the engine and set the indicator to "0" (zero). Rotate the crankshaft one complete revolution (360 degrees) while maintaining the position of the crankshaft either toward the front or rear of the engine. Record the total indicator movement. Replace the damper if wobble exceeds 0.28 mm [0.011 in].

Crankshaft Pulley Inspection

Bolted to the front of the engine crankshaft is a pulley of the rigid design, as shown in Figure 7–51A. Today's high-speed diesel engines generally have multiple belts or a poly-V-type belt driven from the pulley used to transfer crankshaft rotary motion to water pumps, fan pulleys, alternator pulleys, power steering pumps, air-conditioning compressors, and air compressors. These pulleys should be closely inspected to determine if they are cracked, broken, or out of alignment with their mating pulleys. Bent flanges or rough belt grooves can quickly destroy belts. Bent or damaged pulleys, elongated retaining bolt holes, worn dowel pins, or locating flanges, if apparent, can create severe torsional vibrations and should always be replaced. Inspect the machined mating surface at the back side of the crankshaft pulley where it couples to the front of the viscous vibration damper to ensure that no galling or metal burrs appear. This situation can cause runout leading to severe crankshaft vibration. A loose, misaligned, or bent pulley can lead to severe crankshaft damage, including a cracked crankshaft, if not replaced.

Another cause of severe vibration, short belt life, or belts rolling out of their grooves can usually be traced to misalignment between one or more pulleys. Check for this problem using a straightedge between pulleys in conjunction with a spirit level bubble protractor. A unique tool from Cummins Performance Tools, kit no. 3163524, is shown in Figure 7–51B. This laser-powered and extremely accurate pulley alignment tool can be used on any make and model of engine. By attaching the tool to any exposed pulley with the aid of the toolkit-supplied elastic connectors, the laser is then turned on and aimed at the next pulley in the system. By viewing the laser light beam, the technician can quickly and effectively determine if the pulley is out of alignment.

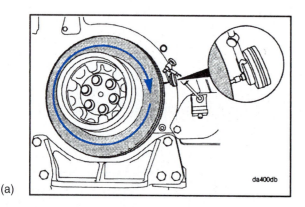

(a)

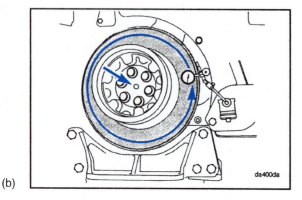

(b)

FIGURE 7–50 *(a) Checking damper eccentricity with the use of a dial indicator. (b) Checking damper face alignment (wobble) using a dial indicator. (Courtesy of Cummins Engine Company, Inc.)*

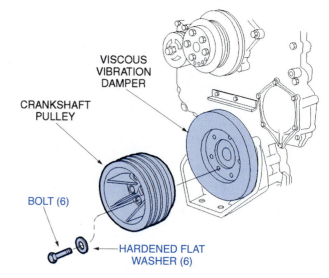

VISCOUS VIBRATION DAMPER

CRANKSHAFT PULLEY

BOLT (6)

HARDENED FLAT WASHER (6)

FIGURE 7–51 *(a) Series 60 engine crankshaft pulley retaining hardware. (Courtesy of Detroit Diesel Corporation.)*

Performance Tools

Pulley Alignment Tool

" Finally... a tool that can verify your engine pulleys are in perfect alignment. Helps prevent jumping belts and premature wear...less down time, too. "

FIGURE 7–51 (b) Cummins p.n. 3163524 laser-powered pulley alignment tool. (Courtesy of Cummins Engine Company, Inc.)

FLYWHEELS

The engine flywheel is a component that, like the vibration damper, sometimes does not get a close inspection during an engine rebuild. The flywheel has several important functions to perform.

PURPOSES OF FLYWHEELS

The engine flywheel illustrated in Figure 7–52A is generally manufactured from cast iron or cast steel. It is de-

signed for multiple purposes such as those described next.

1. The engine flywheel is fitted with a ring gear shrunk onto the circumference of the assembly. The starter motor drive gear engages this ring gear to rotate the engine crankshaft to start the engine.

2. The flat machined surface or face of the flywheel serves as a power transfer mounting point for various elements:

- Heavy-duty friction clutch disc (standard transmission)

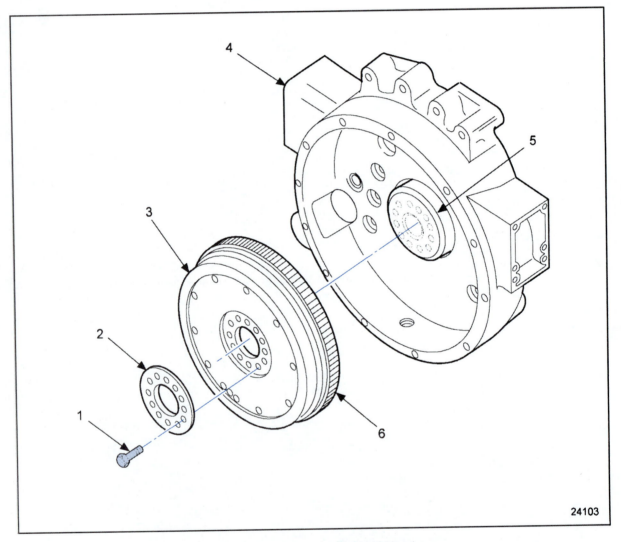

1. Bolt (12)
2. Scuff Plate
3. Flywheel
4. Flywheel Housing
5. Crankshaft
6. Ring Gear

FIGURE 7–52   (a) Typical flywheel and housing component parts. (Courtesy of Detroit Diesel Corporation.)

- Clutch pressure plate (standard transmission)
- Flex disc for an automatic or powershift transmission
- Bolted and toothed ring to accept a rubber drive flex plate for hydraulic marine gear
- Drive ring attachment for a power generator
- Mounting surface for a power takeoff (PTO)
- Mounting surface for a multiple-belt/chain drive pulley
- Direct bolting surface for a drive plate and universal joint
- Engine balancing
- Provision of momentum to keep the engine running under heavy load between firing impulses
- Place to mount the clutch pilot bearing

3. The mass of the rotating flywheel produces a high centrifugal force to provide energy for operating the engine between power impulses. The amount of energy absorbed and returned by the flywheel is relative to the work developed, which is based on the number of engine cylinders, whether the engine is a two- or four-stroke cycle, the power of the engine, and the engine's speed of rotation. The flywheel reduces the variation in the rotative speed of the crankshaft during individual cylinder power impulses. On a two-stroke-cycle engine, the number of degrees between each cylinder power stroke will be closer than on an equivalent four-stroke-cycle engine. During the exhaust, intake, and compression strokes of a four-stroke-cycle engine, and on the compression stroke of a two-cycle engine, the energy stored in the flywheel on the power stroke keeps the engine rotating. Obviously, the greater the number of cylinders, the less energy the flywheel has to store to keep the engine rotating at a steady speed. Therefore, the actual diameter and weight of the flywheel used on any engine depend on the number and the size of the cylinders, the engine rpm, and the allowable speed fluctuation desired. On engine applications that operate at varying speeds throughout the governed operating range, if quick acceleration or engine response is required, a light flywheel is desirable (for example, on a parallel diesel gen-set application where the frequency must be kept very close).

FLYWHEEL DESIGNS AND SAE SIZE

Some flywheels are designed with a flat machined surface; whereas others employ what is commonly referred to as a *pot-type* design. Various threaded bolt holes are located around the flywheel to allow bolting of drive assemblies. Closer inspection of the flywheel will reveal that there are a number of drilled holes spaced unevenly around the assembly. These holes are to provide for static and dynamic balance. Also in pot-type flywheels, a series of circumferential holes are drilled around the flywheel to allow any dirt or dust accumulations to be centrifuged out when the engine is running. These holes also allow airflow through the flywheel for cooling purposes, for example, when using a clutch drive.

Flywheel diameters and the spacing of the various bolt holes are not all the same. An acceptable industry standard for flywheels is that provided by the SAE. Figure 7–52B illustrates how the various flywheel dimensions for high-speed heavy-duty diesel engines are determined. Note that the large-diameter flywheel is assigned an SAE number of double zero (00), and the smallest flywheel dimension shown is a No. 6. This same numbering sequence is used for the flywheel housing assembly on the engine. For example, you cannot install a 00 flywheel into a No. 2 SAE housing, since the flywheel is physically too large to fit into the bore of the housing, as you can see from the chart.

FLYWHEEL TIMING MARKS

Flywheel rims are usually scribed on all four-stroke-cycle engines to assist the diesel technician with setting valves, starting cylinder positions on large slow-speed direct-air-start engines, respective cylinder TDC positions, and fuel injection pump timing degree marks BTDC. High-speed two-stroke-cycle engines such as those manufactured by Detroit Diesel do not have flywheel timing marks, because technicians are not required to align any injection pump (they use unit injectors) or to set the valves or injectors during a tune-up procedure.

Figure 7–53 illustrates flywheel rim timing marks. The TDC or the degree marks on the flywheel are aligned with a stationary pointer; in some engines slotted marks on the flywheel are aligned with a bolted-on degree marker plate. The flywheel timing marks are visible through an inspection cover hole on the flywheel housing. Some four-stroke-cycle engines also employ engine timing marks on the crankshaft pulley located at the front of the engine, plus injection pump timing marks that are visible after removing an inspection cover from the pump housing.

REMOVING AND INSPECTING THE FLYWHEEL

The engine flywheel is an extremely heavy component. When removing it, use a suitable safety sling or specially adaptable flywheel lifting tool that can be bolted

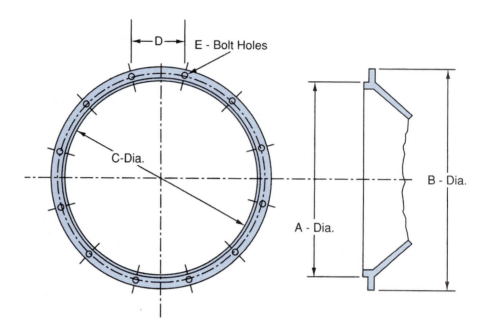

SAE No.	A	B	C	D	E	
					No.	Size
00	31	34 3/4	33 1/2	6 17/32	16	17/32
0	25 1/2	28	26 3/4	5 13/64	16	17/32
1/2	23	25 1/2	24 3/8	6 5/16	12	17/32
1	20 1/8	21 3/4	20 7/8	5 13/32	12	15/32
2	17 5/8	19 1/4	18 3/8	4 3/4	12	13/32
3	16 1/8	17 3/4	16 7/8	4 3/3	12	13/32
4	14 1/4	15 7/8	15	3 57/64	12	13/32
5	12 3/8	14	13 1/8	5 1/64	8	13/32

FIGURE 7–52 (b) SAE (Society of Automotive Engineers) flywheel and flywheel housing sizes and bolt pattern dimensions.

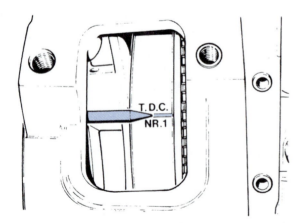

FIGURE 7–53 Example of flywheel timing marks that can be aligned with the stationary pointer when checking injection-pump-to-engine timing, or when placing the No. 1 piston at TDC, and/or when setting and adjusting the intake and exhaust valves.

into position, and attach a chain hoist or overhead crane as shown in Figure 7–54a to safely support its weight. Remove all of the flywheel retaining bolts except for one, as shown in Figure 7–54b. Install two flywheel guide studs with slotted heads; then remove the flywheel after removing the single retaining bolt. Many flywheels are supported on the rear crankshaft flange by two hardened dowel pins. You may have to lightly tap the flywheel to loosen it from these dowels, or use a heel bar to pry it loose without damaging the ring gear.

A flywheel is usually removed when the engine is given a major overhaul or when the machined flat face surface has been damaged, for example, due to a slipping clutch or drive member. Another reason to remove the flywheel is to replace a damaged starter motor ring gear (see Figure 7–52). Carefully inspect the contact surfaces of both the rear of the crankshaft and

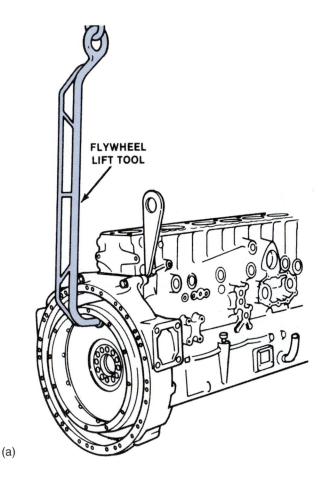

(a)

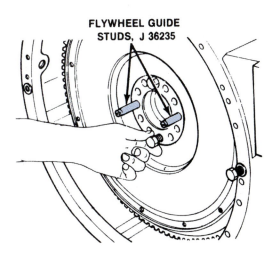

(b)

FIGURE 7–54   (a) Using a special lifting tool to either remove or install the flywheel safely; (b) using two guide studs threaded into the rear mounting flange of the crankshaft to facilitate removal or installation of the flywheel assembly. (Courtesy of Detroit Diesel Corporation.)

the flywheel for any signs of nicks, burrs, high spots, or scoring or signs of possible overheating, which will be visible as discoloration. The rear of the crankshaft is generally a hardened surface, so you may have to use a small finger grinder to remove any high spots, although a smooth file or rough-grade emery cloth will often do the job. Any radii on the flywheel surface or crankshaft flange should be maintained during any cleanup procedure.

Inspect the flat machined surface of the flywheel, particularly when a heavy-duty clutch is involved. Minor heat checks are acceptable, but use a straight-edge and a feeler gauge or a dial indicator and sled gauge to determine what warpage exists on this surface. Severe discoloration is an indication of excessive heat buildup caused by a slipping clutch friction disc. The flat machined clutch surface may be reground providing that the following two conditions are met:

1. There should be no cracks within 0.200 in. (5 mm) from the inner or outer edge, unless they are minor heat checks.
2. No more than the recommended metal should be ground from the flywheel face. Check the service manual for the allowable minimum flywheel thickness.

If the flat machined surface is damaged, the flywheel face can be remachined on a flywheel grinder (Figure 7–55). The amount of metal removed should only be sufficient to provide a new, clean, flat surface. If too much material is removed, the induction hardened surface will be penetrated and short face life will result. Often the engine service manual specifies a minimum flywheel thickness dimension after any regrind procedure. If this dimension is exceeded, then a new flywheel will be required.

Refer to the following typical acceptable limits when grinding flywheels:

Flat Type

6, 7, 8 in. (152, 178, 203 mm)	Limit = 0.020 in. (0.5 mm)
9, 10 in. (229, 254 mm)	Limit = 0.030 in. (0.75 mm)
11, 12 in. (279, 305 mm)	Limit = 0.040 in. (1 mm)
13, 14 in. (330, 356 mm)	Limit = 0.060 in. (1.5 mm)
15, 15.5 in. (381, 394 mm)	Limit = 0.090 in. (2.29 mm)

Recess Type

13, 14, 15 in. (330, 356, 381 mm)	Limit = 0.090 in. (2.29 mm)

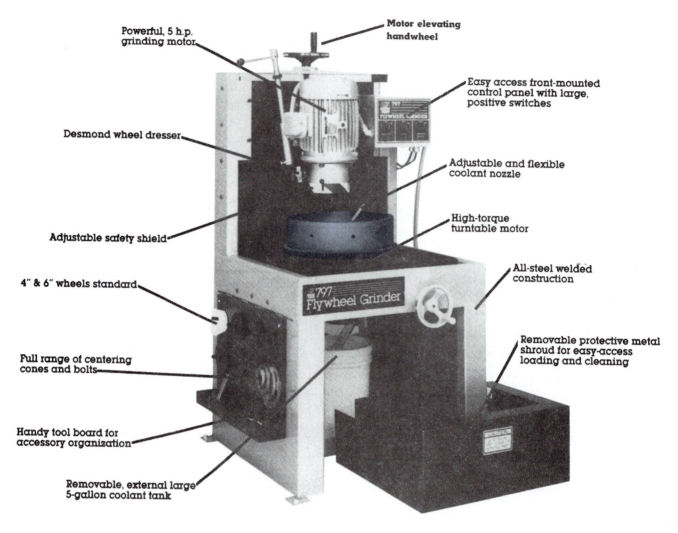

Powerful, 5 h.p. grinding motor

Motor elevating handwheel

Easy access front-mounted control panel with large, positive switches

Desmond wheel dresser

Adjustable and flexible coolant nozzle

Adjustable safety shield

High-torque turntable motor

4" & 6" wheels standard

All-steel welded construction

Full range of centering cones and bolts

Removable protective metal shroud for easy-access loading and cleaning

Handy tool board for accessory organization

Removable, external large 5-gallon coolant tank

FIGURE 7–55   *Grinding a heavy-duty diesel engine flywheel clutch surface. (Courtesy of Kwik-Way Manufacturing Co.)*

NOTE   Flywheel thickness is normally measured from the crankshaft bolt surface to the clutch or PTO disc friction surface. After any regrinding, to ensure that there is no clutch disc hangup, always place the clutch driven disc in or onto the flywheel and check the clearance between the disc hub damper springs, and the clearance between the heads of the crankshaft bolts.

RING GEAR REPLACEMENT

The steel flywheel ring gear that is driven by the starter motor drive pinion is press fit (shrunk) onto the rim of the flywheel. Figure 7–56 illustrates the ring gear and the machined lip on the flywheel over which it is pressed.

Ring Gear Removal

To remove the ring gear, lay the flywheel flat and support it on blocks as shown in Figure 7–57 so that the ring gear faces down. *Always* wear eye protection when attempting to remove or install a ring gear. The ring gear can be removed with a suitable brass punch and hammer by working around the circumference of the gear to avoid possible cocking and binding. Alternatively, you can use a sharp hand chisel to cut the ring gear between two of the teeth. A third method you can employ is an oxyacetylene torch to cut the ring gear between one-half to three-fourths of the way through, while exercising extreme care that the flame does not touch the flywheel. This action will expand and weaken the ring gear, which can then be easily tapped from its seat on the flywheel assembly.

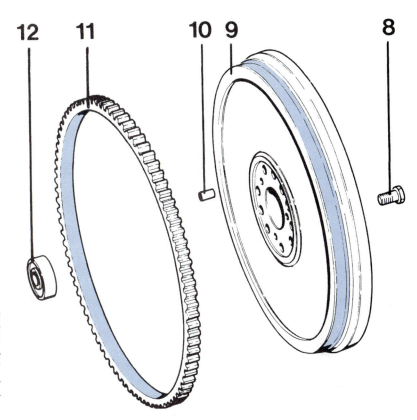

FIGURE 7–56 *Example of how the starter motor ring gear (11) is attached to the engine crankshaft flywheel (9) typically by a shrink-fit procedure onto a stepped flange area. Bolt (8), dowel pin (10), and sealed ball bearing (12) to pilot and support a transmission shaft. (Courtesy of Cummins Engine Company, Inc.)*

FIGURE 7–57 *Using a hammer and punch to remove the flywheel ring gear while supporting the flywheel on two wooden blocks. (Courtesy of Cummins Engine Company, Inc.)*

Ring Gear Installation

Before installing a new ring gear, clean the rim area using emery cloth; if nicks, burrs, or scores are evident, carefully use a small-mill smooth file. Closely inspect the new ring gear to ensure that it is the same as the removed unit. Many flywheel ring gears are manufactured with a chamfered tooth side, but some do not have a chamfer. If a chamfer is evident, the ring gear

must be installed so that the chamfer on the teeth faces the starter motor drive gear pinion as it engages it.

Follow these steps to install a ring gear:

1. Support the flywheel upside down on a solid flat surface.

CAUTION To install a new ring gear, use either an oxyacetylene torch or temperature-controlled oven to expand the ring gear enough to drop over the flywheel rim. Since the ring gear and teeth are hardened, excessive heat can withdraw the temper from the teeth causing them to wear rapidly. The engine service manual usually states the maximum temperature to use when heating the ring gear, for example, Cummins 14 L—600°F (316°C) maximum; Cummins C engine—260°F (127°C); and Detroit Diesel series 92, 50, and 60 engines—400°F (204°C). Be sure to check the service manual. If using an oven, heat the new ring gear for one hour!

2. To ensure that you do not exceed the temperature for expanding the ring gear, use a heat-indicating crayon (Thermomelt or Tempilstik),

which is similar to a wax-type crayon. A label on the crayon indicates its melting temperature. Although you can lay a small piece of the crayon on the ring gear, it is acceptable to simply mark the ring gear in several places around its circumference. Use the torch to move around the ring gear so that even heat distribution is ensured during the heating operation.

3. Place the ring gear on a flat metal surface. While wearing welding gloves, heat the ring gear uniformly with an oxyacetylene torch by moving the torch around the circumference. Do not allow the end of the flame to lick directly onto the ring gear.

4. Pay close attention to the crayon markings. When they start to become fluid, the ring gear has been heated sufficiently. Use a pair of large tongs to lift and place the ring gear into position over the flywheel rim, ensuring that the chamfered teeth are facing in the proper direction. Quickly tap the ring gear squarely into position until it bottoms gently against the flywheel shoulder. Should the ring gear not drop into position (become severely cocked), remove it, reheat it, and try again.

5. Allow the ring gear and flywheel to cool. Do not pour cold water over the ring gear to cool it, because this can change the structural properties of the metal.

PILOT BEARING REPLACEMENT

Many engine applications such as those bolted to a heavy-duty truck transmission require that a sealed (pilot) ball bearing shown in Figure 7–56 be pressed into the center bore of the flywheel assembly. In some engines, a split-tube-type retainer is driven into the end of the crankshaft to prevent the pilot bearing from entering the crankshaft cavity. The purpose of this bearing is to support and align the transmission input shaft. In other applications, a bushing may be used in place of a bearing. If it is necessary to remove this bearing, it can be replaced without removing the flywheel from the crankshaft. The bearing can be removed easily by using a special slide hammer puller similar to the one illustrated in Figure 7–58. By turning the slide hammer threaded rod in or out, the two small jaws can be expanded to suit the inside bore size of the pilot bearing. Then by using the slide hammer, the bearing is removed with little effort. The replacement bearing can be driven into place with a suitable installer.

FIGURE 7–58   Slide-hammer-type flywheel pilot bearing puller. (Courtesy of Kent-Moore Tool Division, SPX Corporation.)

FLYWHEEL INSTALLATION

During flywheel installation, use the same tooling that was described to remove it. Normally, the flywheel bolts onto the rear of the crankshaft in only one direction to ensure that the respective timing marks are aligned properly. If the flywheel bolt holes are not offset to guide you during installation, manually rotate the engine over to place the No. 1 cylinder on TDC on its compression stroke. Install the flywheel so that the No. 1 TDC scribe mark on the rim is aligned with the stationary pointer visible through the flywheel housing inspection cover hole, similar to that illustrated in Figure 7–53. If no dowel pins are used on the rear face of the engine crankshaft, to facilitate flywheel installation, refer to Figure 7–54 and install two guide studs threaded into the crankshaft at the 3- and 9-o'clock positions. Using the lifting arrangement shown in Figure 7–54, lift the flywheel into position and slide it over the guide studs or onto its dowel pins. If a scuff plate similar to the one illustrated in Figure 7–52 is used, install a new one. If a new one is not available, reverse the scuff plate and install two bolts 180° apart and tighten them to 50 lb-ft (68 N · m) to hold the flywheel in place while you remove the guide studs and the lifting tool. Replace bolt lock plates if used.

Most manufacturers specify that you should lightly lubricate the threads of the flywheel retaining bolts as well as the underside of the bolt head contact area with 15W-40 engine oil. If the bolt holes are "blind" (do not run right through), however, do not use excessive amounts of lubricant since this can create a hydrostatic lock in the hole. If you use a bolt lubricant such as International Compound No. 2 or equivalent, apply it to the bolt threads so that they are completely filled with compound and wipe off the excess. Also, apply this same compound to the underside of the bolt heads or hardened washers. Lubricating the bolts ensures that a minimum friction is created, thereby resulting in an accurate torque tightening value.

SERVICE TIP   Some high-speed engine manufacturers recommend what is known as a *torque-turn method* when tightening the flywheel bolts. This procedure provides a more consistent clamping load on the bolts. See Figure 7–36 for an example.

In addition, many engine manufacturers now state that flywheel mounting bolts are considered *one-use items* and thus cannot be reused. New mounting bolts must be installed when attaching the flywheel. Using old bolts can lead to either a loss of torque or bolt breakage during engine operation, resulting in serious engine damage.

Follow these five steps to install the flywheel:

1. After the flywheel is lifted into position over the two guide studs, install two bolts and torque them to 50 lb-ft (68 N · m).

2. Install all remaining bolts, lubricated as described, and snug them.

3. Remove the two bolts installed in step 1 and lubricate them with International Compound No. 2 or equivalent.

4. Using an accurately calibrated torque wrench, tighten each bolt to 50 lb-ft (68 N · m) using a star or diagonally opposite pattern sequence.

5. Mark the heads of the bolts to the flywheel with chalk; rotate each bolt the recommended number of additional degrees as specified in the service manual. One manufacturer's torque-turn method indicates that once the 50 lb–ft torque is achieved, the bolts would be rotated an additional 120°, or the equivalent of two flats on a six-point bolt head.

FLYWHEEL RUNOUT

Once the flywheel has been installed, it is important to carefully check its concentricity (running true) and face runout. This can be done by means of a dial indicator attached to the flywheel housing. Attach the dial indicator by using a magnetic base type or by using a bolt to hold the indicator bracket to the flywheel housing.

Always use a dial indicator as shown in Figure 7–59 to check flywheel-to-housing runout specs after torquing the retaining bolts. A misaligned flywheel can cause vibration problems, as well as clutch drag, pilot bearing, and transmission input shaft front support bearing problems. Misalignment can be caused by use

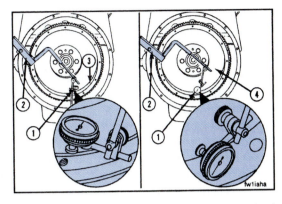

FIGURE 7–59   Use a dial indicator to accurately check both the flywheel and housing runout. (Courtesy of Cummins Engine Company, Inc.)

of the incorrect torquing sequence; worn support dowels; a worn, galled, or irregular mounting flange; and a damaged bore in the flywheel. You can often correct runout simply by loosening the retaining bolts and retightening them, or loosening the bolts and repositioning the flywheel.

In Figure 7–59 the dial gauge is set up to check the bore runout of the flywheel to the flywheel housing. The contact tip of the indicator has been preloaded against the inside diameter of the flywheel bore, and the gauge has been set to zero. The service manual will specify the maximum allowable runout, which is usually stated as total indicator reading (TIR). This means that if the TIR is given as a maximum of 0.010 in. (0.25 mm), then the total of the plus and minus readings on the dial gauge must not exceed this specification. If the TIR does exceed the spec, loosen the flywheel bolts, remove the flywheel, and closely inspect the flywheel-to-crankshaft mounting surface for dirt, scores, nicks, or damage. Also, closely check the dowel pins (if used) in the rear of the crankshaft flange for signs of wear. Replace them if they are worn. Reinstall the flywheel and repeat the dial indicator reading procedure.

Also mount a dial indicator against the flat machined surface of the flywheel. The gauge tip should be approximately 5.5 in. (140 mm) from the centerline of the crankshaft for a high-speed diesel engine, or approximately in the mid-travel area of the clutch surface. This check is used to determine the axial (end to end) runout of the flywheel. To accurately determine this axial runout, push the flywheel fully forward; otherwise, the normal crankshaft end float will create an erroneous reading. With the crankshaft in the fully forward position, zero the dial indicator tip against the machined surface of the flywheel. Manually rotate the flywheel and compare the reading obtained with that stated in the service manual for the engine. Once again, if the reading exceeds specifications, remove the flywheel and determine the cause. In the absence of manufacturers' specifications, use the following: A 16 in. (406 mm) diameter flywheel would have an average acceptable TIR runout of approximately 0.0008 in. (0.203 mm). Allowable runout would increase by approximately 0.002 in. (0.05 mm) for each additional 2 in. (51 mm) diameter of the flywheel. Therefore, a 32 in. (813 mm) diameter flywheel would have an allowable TIR runout of approximately 0.016 in. (0.406 mm).

Flywheels used in heavy-duty trucks that employ a mechanical clutch use a pilot bearing, which is shown as item 12 in Figure 7–56. After flywheel installation, mount a dial indicator gauge to check the bore runout of the clutch pilot bearing. Compare the obtained reading to the service manual specifications.

FLYWHEEL HOUSING

The flywheel housing is generally bolted to the rear of the engine and encloses the flywheel assembly. It is designed to provide the mounting surface for the bolted engine mounts, and it is machined to accept the installation of the press-fit rear crankshaft oil seal in its centerbore area. In addition, the housing provides the structural mounting surface to which is bolted a transmission, marine gear, pump, gen-set, torque converter, and so forth. Accessory drive items such as a vehicle alternator, air compressor, and hydraulic pump may also be mounted to the flywheel housing and driven by a gear or belt drive from the rear gear train if used. The engine starter motor is bolted to the forward side of the flywheel housing, which is generally a one-piece casting manufactured from either cast iron or aluminum. Figure 7–52a illustrates a flywheel housing.

Removal of Flywheel Housing

The flywheel housing can be removed with the engine in position in its application; however, the transmission or drive unit would have to be removed first. The engine must be supported securely by a jack or stands or slung to an overhead crane. As an example, assume that the engine is mounted into an engine overhaul stand such as the one illustrated in Figure 5–1. First, the flywheel has to be removed to access the flywheel housing. The number of bolts that you have to loosen varies between different makes and models of engines. Before removing the housing, it is generally helpful to thread in several long guide studs to the rear of the engine block or mounting plate surface. This facilitates pulling the housing away from the block squarely, since some housings are positioned over several dowel pins. It is advisable to sling the housing during removal, unless it is small and light enough for you to handle manually. Many housings are equipped with tapped threaded holes to facilitate the installation of eyebolts, to which a chain-fall or bracket-and-web sling can be attached.

Inspection of Flywheel Housing

After cleaning any dirt, grime, and old gasket material from the flywheel housing, inspect the housing for signs of stress cracks, particularly at the engine mount bolt area as well as the area to which the transmission is bolted. At the time of a major overhaul, the crankshaft rear oil seal should be removed and replaced. Inspect the oil seal bore for any signs of damage that might lead to oil leakage. All flat surfaces of the flywheel housing should be checked for any signs of severe distortion or warpage. If any bolt holes show signs of thread damage, you may have to install a heli-coil, a Tap-lok insert, or a Rexnord-type *Keensert* (which is similar to a Tap-lok unit).

Installation of Flywheel Housing

Some flywheel housings are mounted directly to the rear face of the engine block. Others are bolted to an adaptor plate that has already been bolted to the engine block, such as those used on Detroit Diesel two-stroke-cycle engine models in which the flywheel housing on these engines forms the complete rear cover for the rear-mounted gear train. A gasket may be used between the housing and block. Alternatively, you can apply a continuous 1/16 in. (1.6 mm) bead of gasket eliminator (RTV-type sealant or equivalent) as illustrated in Figure 7–60 prior to housing installation. Some engines may require a wider bead than this, but seldom would you need more than a 1/8 in. (3.175 mm) bead. These types of sealants usually cure fairly quickly—within 5 to 10 minutes after application. Therefore, do not apply the sealant until you are ready to install the flywheel housing. If the flywheel housing has a new rear crankshaft oil seal installed in it, always use a seal protector during housing installation to prevent possible damage or rolling of the seal lip.

Use two long guide studs to ensure that the flywheel housing is installed squarely. Install all necessary bolts (lubricated) and torque them in sequence according to instructions in the service manual. Figure 7–61 illustrates one example of how to tighten the flywheel housing bolts. Once the flywheel housing has been securely bolted in place, install two dial indicators as illustrated in Figure 7–62, with the gauges supported on a base post threaded into the bolt holes of the flywheel. These gauges are required to check the bore

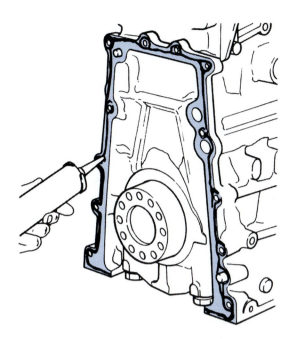

FIGURE 7-60 Installation of gasket eliminator to the rear of the engine block for a series 60 engine. (Courtesy of Detroit Diesel Corporation.)

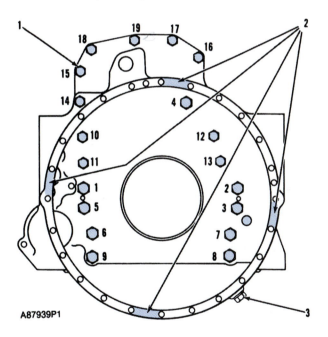

A87939P1

FIGURE 7-61 Torquing sequence for the flywheel housing bolts for a 3406E Cat engine. Item 2 indicates that the flywheel face runout should be checked at four main points with a dial indicator. (Reprinted courtesy of Caterpillar, Inc.)

concentricity and face runout of the flywheel housing to ensure that a square fit exists between the engine drivetrain and the drive option (for example, transmission, PTO, or marine gear). If the flywheel has not yet

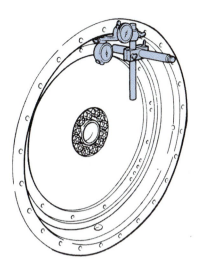

FIGURE 7-62 Measuring flywheel housing bore concentricity and bolting flange runout. (Courtesy of Detroit Diesel Corporation.)

been installed, you can simply attach the dial gauge base to one of the holes in the rear crankshaft flange area and use dial gauge extension rods to allow the gauge tips to contact the reading areas. The top gauge in the diagram has its tip preloaded and zeroed against the flat bolted flange surface of the housing to check for runout. The lower of the two gauges has its tip bearing against the inside bore of the flywheel bell housing.

Manually pry the crankshaft toward one end of the block to ensure that end play does not affect any of the readings. Take dial gauge readings at four places 90° apart and compare them with the service manual specs. If the flywheel housing readings exceed the specs, remove the housing and check for dirt, metal particles, or anything that might prevent the housing from seating fully or squarely.

SUMMARY

The components discussed in this chapter are major items related to the successful operation of a diesel engine. Therefore it cannot be emphasized enough that a complete and extensive check/measurement should always be made of these components. Failure to do so can result in embarrassing and costly premature engine failure. Thus, a technician must not simply become a "parts replacer", but, like a doctor, must be capable of correctly diagnosing these parts to avoid any possibility of premature failure after overhaul. If you pay particular attention to the information and data within this chapter this will enable you to avoid having to rework an engine after performing a complete and costly repair/overhaul.

SELF-TEST QUESTIONS

1. Technician A says that there is generally one more main bearing journal than there are cylinder numbers. Technician B says that the crankshaft must have the same number of main bearing journals and cylinders. Who is correct?

2. True or False: Crankshaft counterweights are employed to produce greater torque when the engine is running.

3. True or False: Most high-speed engine crankshafts are manufactured from a one-piece forged alloy steel billet.

4. True or False: The crankshaft fillet radius is used to relieve the stresses at each journal by spreading the load across a greater cross-sectional area.

5. What washers maintain crankshaft end float or end play?

6. Give three ways to minimize flexing of main bearing caps during engine operation.

7. Technician A says that crankshaft oil passages can be cleaned effectively by removing the Allen-head screws and using a stiff-bristle brush pushed and pulled through the oil hole drillings. Technician B says that it is better to submerge the crankshaft in a tank of hot caustic solution. Who is correct?

8. On a separate sheet of paper, list the various checks and tests that you would perform on a crankshaft at overhaul.

9. Technician A says that minor imperfections on crankshaft journals can be removed only by regrinding. Technician B says that this can be done by polishing the crankshaft in a metal lathe using fine emery cloth and diesel fuel as a lubricant. Which technician is correct?

10. When a crankshaft is reground, technician A says that you would want to use *oversized* bearings to account for the metal that has been removed. Technician B says that you would want to use *undersized* bearings in this case. Which technician understands the philosophy behind this procedure?

11. True or False: If the crankshaft thrust surfaces have been reground, you usually have to employ thicker thrust washers to maintain the correct end float.

12. Technician A says that to maintain crankshaft end float within specs, it is acceptable to use either thicker or thinner thrust washers on either side of the crankshaft. Technician B says that this cannot be done; instead, the same thickness thrust washers are required on both sides of the thrust surfaces. Which technician is correct?

13. Generally, a high-speed crankshaft is reground to a diameter that is smaller by one of three sizes. List the three sizes.

14. Most high-speed engine manufacturers specify that the maximum amount of metal that can be removed from a crankshaft journal be limited to
    a. 0.762 mm (0.030 in.)
    b. 1.000 mm (0.03937 in.)
    c. 1.500 mm (0.060 in.)

15. When measuring a crankshaft journal with a micrometer, it should be checked at how many different positions and how many axes?

16. True or False: To determine taper on a crankshaft journal, you should compare the readings from one axis with those of another.

17. True or False: To determine ovality on a crankshaft journal, you should compare readings along one axis.

18. True or False: If either a front or rear crankshaft oil seal surface is badly worn, the crankshaft can be repaired using a Speedi-Sleeve and an oversized oil seal assembly.

19. True or False: To determine if the crankshaft webs are misaligned or overflexed, a dial indicator inserted between the webs can be used.

20. Crankshafts can be checked for signs of cracks using what three nondestructive methods?

21. When installing a crankshaft with new bearings that are properly lubricated and main bearing caps torqued to spec, technician A says that if the crankshaft rotates freely, you do not need to check each individual bearing for the proper clearance. Is this an acceptable service procedure? Explain why or why not.

22. Crankshaft bearing clearance can be accurately checked by using
    a. wire solder
    b. Plastigage
    c. layout ink
    d. Prussian blue

23. The majority of high-speed diesel engines employ main and con-rod bearings that are generally referred to as
    a. ball bearings
    b. roller bearings
    c. shell bearings
    d. needle bearings

24. True or False: Normally, the size of a shell bearing is stamped on the back face of the bearing assembly.

25. Shell bearings are prevented from spinning during engine rotation by the use of a
    a. locating tang
    b. dowel pin
    c. retaining bolt

26. Shell bearings dissipate their heat by being compressed into the cap or saddle; this is known as
    a. free diameter
    b. bearing crush
    c. press fit
    d. slip fit

27. True or False: All shell bearings can be installed in either the upper or lower position without any problems occurring.

28. True or False: Upper main shell bearings can be removed and replaced during an in-frame overhaul by the use of a roll pin.

29. When inspecting shell bearings at overhaul, bright or shiny spots appearing on the back side of the bearing are usually indicative of
   a. overheating
   b. bearing shell movement
   c. insufficient bearing clearance
   d. too much bearing clearance

30. Excessive main bearing clearance will result in
   a. low oil pressure
   b. high oil pressure
   c. aeration of the oil
   d. engine vibration

31. Severe scratches or scoring on the surface of a shell bearing is usually indicative of
   a. lack of oil
   b. overheating
   c. metal-to-metal contact between the bearing and journal
   d. dirt or foreign particles in the oil

32. The most common cause of shell bearing damage can usually be attributed to
   a. overloading
   b. dirt and foreign particles
   c. corrosion
   d. lack of lubrication

33. Technician A says that many new crankshaft oil seals are precoated with a special lubricant and should not, therefore, have the lip prelubricated with oil. Technician B says that you should always coat the oil seal lip with clean engine lube oil. Who is correct?

34. The most effective type of engine crankshaft vibration damper on high-speed diesel engines is the
   a. single-rubber type
   b. double-rubber type
   c. viscous type

35. Flywheels and housings are available in different diameters that are manufactured to meet standards set by which one of the following associations?
   a. ASTM
   b. API
   c. SAE
   d. ISO

36. True or False: No. 1 size flywheel is smaller than a No. 4.

37. Technician A says that the starter ring gear is usually pinned or bolted to the flywheel assembly. Technician B says that the ring gear is a shrink fit to the flywheel. Who is correct?

38. Technician A says that to replace the flywheel ring gear you have to remove the flywheel from the crankshaft. Technician B says that you simply have to unbolt it and replace it with a new ring gear. Who is correct?

39. Technician A says that a scuff plate used on a flywheel is designed to prevent scuffing of the machined surface by a clutch assembly. Technician B says that the scuff plate is used as a self-locking plate for the retaining bolts. Who is correct?

40. True or False: One of the functions of the mass contained in the flywheel is to store energy and return it to the crankshaft during engine operation. This maintains a steady engine speed between the firing impulses of the cylinders.

41. Technician A says that all engine flywheels contain engine timing marks to facilitate in-service checks. Technician B disagrees, saying that two-cycle Detroit Diesel engines do not use any flywheel timing marks, since they are not necessary when a unit injector fuel system is used. Who is correct?

42. True or False: All flywheels are mounted on the rear of the engine and supported on dowel pins, and bolted onto the rear of the engine crankshaft.

43. Technician A says that many engine flywheels can be installed in only one position to align the retaining bolt holes. Technician B says that flywheels can be installed in any position, because the bolt holes are always drilled the same center-to-center distance apart. Who is correct?

44. True or False: If a flywheel is capable of being installed in any of several positions, you should manually rotate the crankshaft over to place the No. 1 piston at TDC; then install the flywheel so that the No. 1 TDC mark is aligned with the stationary pointer.

45. True or False: Slight discoloration and a series of small cracks on the machined surface of a flywheel that employs a heavy-duty clutch or PTO requires that the flywheel be replaced.

46. Technician A says that a worn flywheel pilot bearing can be replaced without having to remove the flywheel from the engine crankshaft. Technician B says that this is not possible; you must remove the flywheel assembly. Who is correct?

47. True or False: Using excessive heat on a flywheel ring gear can destroy the surface hardness of the teeth.

48. Technician A says that to prevent overheating a flywheel ring gear, you can use a heat-indicating crayon or install the ring gear into a temperature-controlled oven. Technician B says that heat should never be applied to a flywheel ring gear. Who is correct?

49. Technician A says that it is advisable to thread two guide studs into the rear of the crankshaft mounting flange when installing the flywheel and to use a suitable lifting bracket and sling to facilitate installation. Technician A says that it is easier to manually lift the flywheel into position and rotate it to line up the bolt holes. Which technician knows safer work habits?

50. True or False: Many engine manufacturers recommend that flywheel bolts be changed at major overhaul regardless of the visible condition of the bolts.

51. Technician A says that flywheel retaining bolts that thread into "blind" holes should be heavily lubricated prior to installation. Technician B says that this can cause a hydrostatic lock in the hole; therefore, only a

light coating of oil should be used on the threads, plus a small amount of oil under the bolt head. Who is correct?

52. Technician A says that when flywheel retaining bolts are to be tightened, they should be pulled up in increments using a diagonal tightening sequence until the correct torque is obtained. Technician B says that most high-speed engine manufacturers specify that the flywheel bolts be tightened using the torque-turn method, which is more accurate. Which technician is correct?

53. True or False: Flywheel housing concentricity or runout should always be checked with a dial indicator gauge after tightening the retaining bolts.

54. Technician A says that a flywheel housing bore that is not concentric after installation can cause oil leakage from the rear oil seal. Technician B disagrees, saying that this could not happen since the oil seal is press fit in the bore. Which technician is correct?

55. After flywheel installation, what runout checks would you perform using a dial indicator?

56. Technician A says that excessive flywheel runout can lead to complaints of engine vibration and heavy-duty

clutch problems. Technician B says that this is not possible if the flywheel is torqued to the right spec. Who is correct?

57. True or False: Distortion of the machined flywheel face surface could cause clutch slippage.

58. Technician A says that if the rear crankshaft oil seal which is press fit in the flywheel housing bore leaks, the flywheel must be removed to replace the seal. Technician B says that the problem can be solved in place by drilling two small holes in the seal housing, inserting two self-tapping screws, and using a slide hammer to remove the seal. Which technician is correct?

8

Pistons, Piston Rings, and Connecting Rod Assembly

Overview

This chapter deals with the three components that together function to transfer the chemical heat of combustion into mechanical energy at the rotating crankshaft. The piston crown is acted upon by the high-pressure expanding gases of combustion to drive it down the cylinder on the power stroke. To seal the high-pressure gases within the combustion chamber and engine cylinder, a set of closely fitted piston rings is required. Piston energy is transferred to the piston pin, which is in turn attached to the connecting rod. The con-rod acts as a mechanical lever to transfer reciprocating motion (up and down) from the piston, through the con-rod, to the crankshaft journal to produce rotary motion at the flywheel.

In today's technologically advanced high-speed heavy-duty electronically controlled diesel engines, peak cylinder pressures can average between 1800 and 2300 psi (12,411 and 15,858 kPa). To handle such high pressures, many of these engines now use two-piece piston assemblies, although many medium/midrange engines still use one-piece trunk-type piston designs. Information in this chapter describes the structure, function, and operation of these important components, and details on the inspection, cleaning, and service repair tasks necessary to ensure a smooth-running engine and effective sealing of combustion gases within the cylinder.

ASE DIESEL ENGINES TESTS

As an industry standard guide for inspection and repair of the piston, piston rings, and con-rod described in the chapter overview, let us look at the ASE medium/heavy trucks T2 tests preparation guide tasks lists. In section C of engine block diagnosis and repair,

items 12 through 16 list the tasks to be performed on these components. Review this T2 list shown in Chapter 1 to ensure that you gain both the theoretical knowledge and the hands-on skills required to challenge this ASE test module. Details on these tasks are contained within this chapter.

C. **Engine Block Diagnosis and Repair (5 ASE questions)**
12. Clean, inspect, measure, or replace pistons, pins, and retainers.
13. Measure piston-to-cylinder wall clearance.
14. Check ring-to-groove clearance and end gaps; install rings on pistons.
15. Identify piston and bearing wear patterns that indicate connecting rod alignment or bearing bore problems; check bearing bore and bushing condition; determine needed repairs.
16. Assemble pistons and connecting rods and install in block; replace rod bearings and check clearances; check condition, position, and clearance of piston cooling jets (nozzles).

ASE ENGINE MACHINIST TESTS

In the ASE M2 task list, subsections E (connecting rods and piston inspection and machining) and F (balancing) list the individual task list areas in which you require both a theoretical and hands-on knowledge to be able to challenge this ASE test certification area. See the website, www.asecert.org, which lists these specific areas. Details on these tasks are contained within this chapter.

E. **Connecting Rods and Piston Inspection and Machining (9 ASE questions)**

1. Separate piston and connecting rod; verify assembled position, and remove small end bushing if needed.
2. Clean and visually inspect connecting rods; verify matched set.
3. Inspect connecting rod, cap, and bolts for cracks as required by manufacturer.
4. Evaluate connecting rod fasteners for condition and suitability for reuse.
5. Measure width of large end of connecting rod; compare with manufacturer's specifications.
6. Measure connecting rod housing bore diameter and compare with manufacturer's specifications; repair as needed.
7. Measure connecting rod small end bore diameter; compare with manufacturer's specifications; repair as needed.
8. Install and size small end bushing according to manufacturer's recommended procedure.
9. Inspect connecting rod for bend, twist, and center-to-center distance according to manufacturer's recommended procedure; repair as needed.
10. Evaluate pistons and pins for reuse as needed.
11. Assemble piston on connecting rod; verify correct position.
12. Compare or verify piston compression heights and configuration.
13. Identify type and install piston pin retainer according to manufacturer's recommended procedures.

F. **Balancing (3 ASE questions)**

1. Weigh, compare, and equalize piston weights as needed.
2. Weigh, compare, and equalize connecting rod weights as needed.
3. Determine internal versus external crankshaft assembly balance and correct to manufacturer's tolerance.

ASE ASSEMBLY SPECIALIST TESTS

In the ASE M3 assembly specialist tasks lists area, refer to subsection A, engine disassembly, inspection, and cleaning (items 12, 13, and 15); see also subsection C, short block assembly (items 7 through 10). Informational details on these tasks are contained within this chapter.

A. **Engine Disassembly, Inspection, and Cleaning (10 ASE questions)**

12. Check all connecting rod and main bearing caps for correct position and numbering; mark in accordance with manufacturers' recommended procedures.
13. Remove and inspect connecting rod and piston assemblies.
14. Remove and inspect main bearing caps; remove crankshaft from bearing saddles.
15. Remove and inspect main and connecting rod bearings; identify locations.

C. **Short Block Assembly (17 ASE questions)**

7. Assemble piston on connecting rod; verify correct position and alignment.
8. Check piston ring end gap; install piston rings following manufacturers' recommendations.
9. Install piston and connecting rod assembly according to manufacturers' recommendation and verify piston height.
10. Check connecting rod bearing clearances and connecting rod side clearances.

PISTON STRUCTURE AND FUNCTION

The piston rings, piston pin, and connecting rod assembly make up what are considered the major parts in a reciprocating diesel engine (Figure 8–1). The piston and ring assembly provides the plug or seal for the pressure developed by the burning fuel and air within the cylinder. The piston pin attaches the piston and ring assembly to the connecting rod, which in turn is connected to the crankshaft. Power developed within the cylinder is transferred to the crankshaft by this assembly.

The piston, piston rings, and connecting rod assembly is one of the most unique and important assemblies within the diesel engine. Probably no other part of the diesel engine is subjected to the extreme heat, pressure, and force that are encountered by the piston, which is the central or main part of this assembly. During normal engine operation the piston is subjected to temperatures of 1200 to 1300°F (650 to 700°C), while during shutdown it may be at ambient temperature (temperature surrounding engine, or atmospheric temperature).

To accept this extreme temperature change many times through its normal lifetime without failing, the

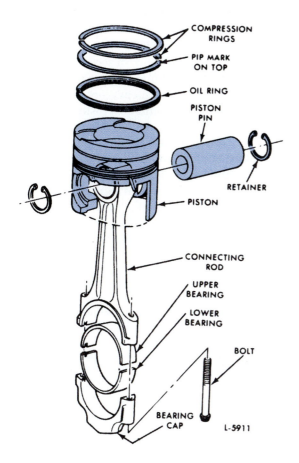

FIGURE 8–1 Trunk-type piston details and relative location of component parts. (Courtesy of Detroit Diesel Corporation.)

piston must be made from a very durable material. Some diesel engine pistons are made from aluminum alloy, a mixture of copper, silicon, magnesium, manganese, iron, and lead. An exception to this is Detroit Diesel two-stroke-cycle pistons, which are constructed from pearlitic malleable iron and plated with tin.

NOTE   Aluminum is most commonly used in four-stroke-cycle diesel engines because of its ability to transfer heat quickly, thereby allowing the piston to run cooler than one made from cast iron. In addition, aluminum is much lighter, making the total reciprocating weight within the engine less; this decreases the inertia (the tendency of a body in motion to stay in motion). Inertia is generated at the top and bottom of the piston stroke by rapid start and stop. Less inertia helps to create a better-balanced and smoother-running engine.

Some diesel engine pistons are a one-piece trunk type (Figure 8–2), although many diesel engines now use the crosshead or articulated type of piston. This design almost eliminates any side or thrust load on the piston, thereby decreasing wear and increasing ring life.

The trunk type of piston is made up of piston head, piston pin boss (bearing area), ring grooves, groove lands, and piston skirt. Because trunk-type aluminum pistons are constructed with more metal in the

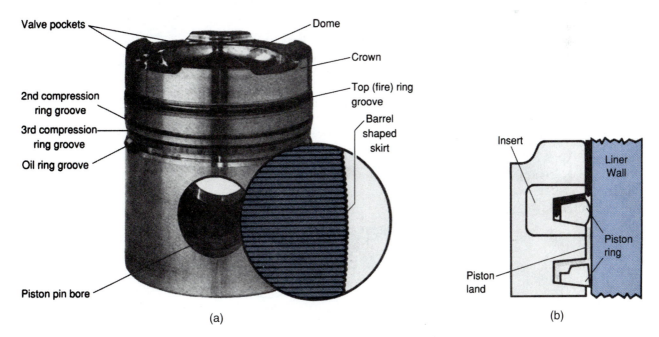

(a)   (b)

FIGURE 8–2 (a) One-piece trunk-type aluminum alloy piston; (b) nomenclature of piston areas. (Courtesy of Cummins Engine Company, Inc.)

piston pin boss area to support the piston pin, provision must be made for the uneven expansion that results from this design. To ensure that the piston will be round after expansion from the heat of combustion, aluminum pistons can be cam ground or egg shaped (elliptical).

Figure 8–3 illustrates a SCFR trunk-type aluminum-silicon alloy piston from a Cummins C series engine used in on-highway truck applications of 250 bhp (186 kW) and above, with high peak torque above 700 lb-ft (949 N·m). A major production advantage of squeeze casting is that the piston can subsequently be machined using conventional tooling. The ceramic alumina fiber mesh reinforcement increases piston strength, reliability, and durability. The ceramic fibers have a polycrystalline structure consisting of alumina, zirconia, carbon, boron nitride, boron carbide, and silicon carbide. The aluminum fiber material is subjected, while still in a viscous (liquid) condition and prior to final solidification, to a process equivalent to that used in the forging process.

Ceramic-fiber-reinforced aluminum alloy, or CFA, pistons are now being used in both indirect- and direct-injection diesel engines. The CFA material extends from the top of the piston down to below the top compression ring, as well as extending inward some distance toward the center of the crown. Tests indicate that the wear and seizure resistance of CFA pistons has been vastly improved compared with aluminum pistons and is equal to or superior to the Ni-resist insert that is still widely used in the top and/or second compression ring lands of many aluminum alloy pistons. In addition, the thermal (heat) conductivity of the CFA piston is better than an aluminum alloy piston using a Ni-resist insert; therefore, the overall operating temperatures of the CFA piston tend to run slightly cooler.

Industrial and automotive/truck applications for the same Cummins engines rated below 250 bhp (186 kW) and 700-lb-ft (949 N·m) have gravity cast pistons with an anodized coating on the piston crown.

In summary, CFA aluminum alloy pistons have the following advantages over a comparable cast-iron model:

- Lighter weight therefore lower inertia forces
- Faster heat dissipation
- Good bearing surface (frictional) and quieter running.

TWO-PIECE PISTON DESIGNS

As U.S. EPA exhaust emissions standards became increasingly more stringent throughout the 1980s, heavy-duty high-speed diesel engine manufacturers such as

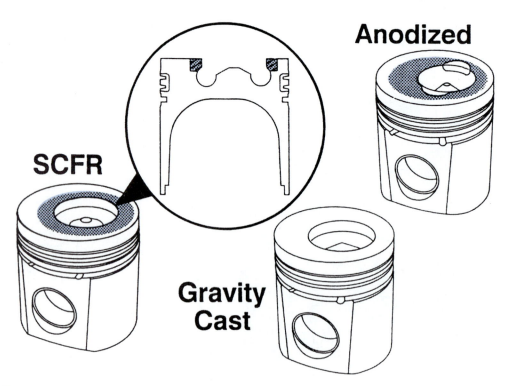

FIGURE 8–3 SCFR (squeeze cast fiber reinforced), anodized, and gravity cast one-piece trunk-type aluminum alloy pistons for use in various horsepower rating C model engines. (Courtesy of Cummins Engine Company, Inc.)

Caterpillar, Cummins, Detroit Diesel, and Mack realized they had to make changes to meet on-highway truck emissions standards of the 1990s. They would have to redesign not only the fuel injection systems (higher injection pressures and electronic controls) but also the pistons within the cylinders. Aluminum alloys were reaching the limits of their capability to withstand the increased temperatures, pressures, and stresses created within the combustion chamber and cylinder during the power stroke. Two-piece pistons began to emerge in all of the high-speed heavy-duty on-highway truck engines; Detroit Diesel and Mack had already employed this concept for more than 20 years in a number of their engine models.

Research indicated that aluminum alloy pistons with top ring land heights of less than 4% of the piston diameter using single or double Ni-resist (Alfin process) ring carriers could withstand the higher pressures, temperatures, and stresses experienced in high-speed heavy-duty diesel engines. Consequently, both ferrous metal and aluminum alloy pistons in these heavier-duty applications have their compression ring and fire ring very close to the top of the piston crown to reduce the dead-air-space volume above the top piston ring. Another major change in pistons as a result of tighter exhaust emissions regulations is the redesign of the piston bowl geometry and size to provide optimum combustion conditions through increased air motion. The purpose of this change is to take advantage of better fuel atomization from the higher injection pressure injectors now in use, particularly on electronically controlled engines.

Major engine manufacturers at this time tend to employ one-piece trunk-type aluminum-silicon alloy pistons in their lower horsepower engines. Higher power models, such as those found in heavy-duty Class 8 truck applications employing electronically controlled fuel injection systems, use the stronger and superior performance two-piece unit with a steel-crown to withstand the higher pressures and heat generated. For example, Caterpillar uses a one-piece aluminum piston for the lower horsepower ratings in both its 3116 and 3406E engines; in its higher rated 3116 and 3406E (435 hp, 325 kW, and higher) engines, as well as its 3176B, C10 and C12 model truck engines, it employs a two-piece articulated piston that has a forged steel crown and aluminum alloy skirt. A Cat 3176B engine articulated piston is illustrated in Figures 8–7a and 8–7b. Cummins also employs an articulated piston in its higher power ISL engine, and the newer ISM and N14 Celect models. Figure 8–4 illustrates a crosshead piston design used by Cummins in its ISX and Signature series engine models.

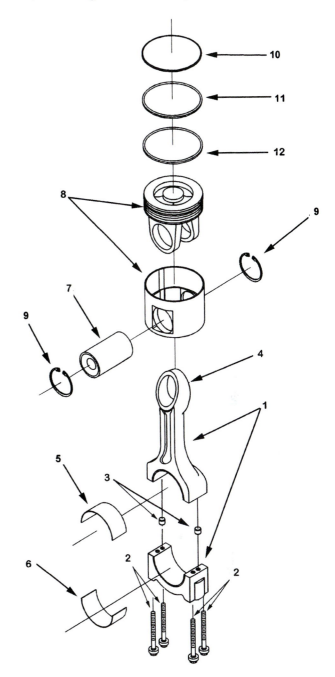

FIGURE 8–4 Two-piece Signature engine articulated piston and con-rod assembly with identification of the various parts. (Courtesy of Cummins Engine Company, Inc.)

Advantages of Two-Piece Pistons

The two-piece piston design has been in use for many years in large-bore, slow-speed two-stroke-cycle marine engines such as those of Sulzer, B&W, GMT, and Mitsubishi. Detroit Diesel was the first high-speed diesel engine manufacturer to employ the crosshead piston design in its engines. In the early 1970s, Detroit Diesel used the design in its 92 series two-stroke-cycle

Ref No.	Part Number	Part Name	Req
	3681343	Rod, Engine Connecting	
1	(3678570)	Rod, Engine Connecting	6
2	3678574	Screw, Connecting Rod Cap	24
3	3678739	Dowel, Ring	12
4	(3679314)	Bushing	6
	3800297	Kit, Rod Brg	
5	(3678573)	Bearing, Connecting Rod	1
6	(3678591)	Bearing, Connecting Rod	1
7	(3678590)	Pin, Piston	6
	3800941	Kit, Engine Piston	6
8	(3681738)	Piston, Engine	1
9	3064305	Ring, Retaining	2
	3800609	Set, Piston Ring	6
10	(4026512)	Ring, Compression Piston	1
11	(3681047)	Ring, Compression Piston	1
12	(3680725)	Ring, Oil Piston	1
	3800609	Set, Piston Ring	
	(3681046)	Liner, Cylinder	1
	(3681738)	Piston, Engine	1
	(3678590)	Pin, Piston	1
	3064305	Ring, Retaining	2
	3678737	Seal, O Ring	1
	3678738	Seal, O Ring	1
	3800609	Set, Piston Ring	1

FIGURE 8–4 (continued).

engines; then the company expanded use into its other series of two-stroke-cycle (53, 71, and 149 series) and four-stroke-cycle designs (series 50 and 60 engines). The DDC two-piece piston has an all-steel crown and skirt in the two-piece crosshead design. The malleable iron dome has greater strength than aluminum at operating temperatures and provides ring groove surfaces with very low wear rates, which are the result not only of material differences but also of reduced dome motion inherent in the crosshead design. The iron piston skirt is tin plated to provide lower seizure susceptibility than a conventionally fitted aluminum piston while using a smaller skirt-to-liner clearance. This reduced clearance results in less noise due to piston slap and less liner excitation for reduced susceptibility to wet liner cavitation damage (pitting of the external liner surface).

Use of surface treatments has increased, for example, hard anodizing of the piston crown to resist thermal cracking and graphite coating of the aluminum skirt to achieve better resistance to scuffing. EUI engine two-piece articulated pistons consist of a forged steel crown with pressed-in bore bushings and a forged aluminum skirt. The steel crown has excellent high temperature strength and the ability to withstand much higher cylinder pressure and thermal loads than can an aluminum piston. Consider that heavy-duty electronic engines have peak cylinder firing pressures of 2200 psi

(15.2 mPa) plus, compared with 1700 to 1800 psi (11,722 to 12,411 kPa) capability of typical aluminum pistons that are used in midrange model engines.

In 1991, Cummins and Mack adopted two-piece crosshead pistons similar to those used by DDC and Caterpillar, although Mack had used a two-piece all-aluminum crosshead design for a number of years during the 1970s. Some of the major piston manufacturers now supply two-piece articulated pistons designed to cover bores of from 4 in. (100 mm) to 6.6 in. (170 mm) for high-speed diesel engines. Articulated pistons consisting of a steel crown and an aluminum skirt seem to be one of the most suitable designs to withstand the engine performance requirements of the 2000's.

The two-piece pistons are strictly for high-output performance engines and are constructed to separate piston guiding and sealing functions within the cylinder so that both parts, the crown (dome) and the skirt, are connected via the piston pin as shown in Figure 8–4. The current trend is to move away from an all-aluminum one-piece or two-piece piston to a two-piece iron-aluminum alloy design. This takes the form of a cast or forged steel crown and a cast or forged aluminum skirt. Forged pistons can withstand more severe operating conditions in heavy-duty diesel engines. The piston crown uses a variety of high-strength materials, including nodular cast iron, steel cast, or forged steel to transmit combustion gas pressure via the pin and connecting rod. This concept is necessary due to the higher cylinder temperatures and pressures now found in the combustion chambers of electronically controlled diesel engines that employ higher injection pressures and higher BMEPs (brake mean effective pressures) to comply with the strict EPA exhaust emissions standards. Peak cylinder temperatures of as high as 4000°F (2204°C), and peak pressures of 1800 to 2300 psi (12,411 to 15,858 kPa), require the piston head (crown) to be mechanically stronger and more heat resistant than it was in the past.

Construction of Two-Piece Pistons

The crosshead piston shown in Figure 8–5a illustrates the various parts of this type of piston. Note that a metal oil seal ring is used between the crown and skirt to prevent any excess oil used for under-piston cooling from flooding the cylinder above the oil control ring area. The actual crown and skirt are held together by the piston pin, which passes through the holes in the skirt and the mating holes in the extension struts of the crown. Because of the design characteristics of the crosshead piston, some models do not use the conventional eye- or hole-type connecting rod; instead, a con-rod such as that illustrated in Figure 8–5a is employed. The con-rod is bolted directly to the piston pin, which also has a lube oil tube passing through it to deliver pressurized lube oil from the rifle-drilled con-rod to the underside of the piston crown for cooling purposes.

The piston dome and skirt can each react independently to normal stresses developed during engine operation. When the engine is running, the forces of the combustion chamber gases acting on top of the piston are absorbed directly by the piston pin after passing through the crown and struts and the large surface area of the slipper bearing (bushing). Because the skirt is separate from the crown, it is free from vertical load distortion and it receives less heat transfer from the crown, thereby allowing less thermal distortion. As the piston is forced down the cylinder, the con-rod swings off to the side as it rotates the engine crankshaft. During this action, the biggest part of the sidewise or thrust load is taken by the piston skirt; the crown area, which is separate or independent from the skirt, takes only a small portion of these side loads. The minimal side thrust on the crown ensures that the piston ring life will be extended, because as the piston is forced downward, the crown is not pushed sideways under the compression rings at the same time as they are pushed down hard against the bottom of their grooves during the actual power stroke.

Both crosshead and articulated pistons have the following major advantages over a one-piece trunk-type piston assembly:

- Piston-liner clearances are more tightly controlled due to the isolation of the skirt from the crown.
- The piston skirt maintains its designed shape better, thereby minimizing piston slap and lower engine noise.

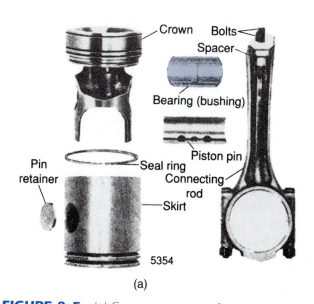

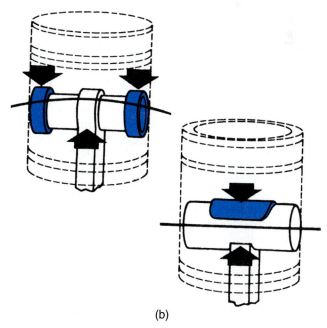

(a)   (b)

FIGURE 8–5   (a) Component parts of a two-stroke-cycle DDC crosshead piston assembly. (b) Comparison of the bending stresses imposed on a piston pin of a single-piece trunk-type piston versus that for a two-piece crosshead or articulated piston assembly. (Courtesy of Detroit Diesel Corporation.)

- Piston ring and groove wear is reduced as a result of less piston crown motion.
- Increased lubrication and cooling of the piston crown occur due to the "cocktail shaker" action of the lube oil.
- Improved pin and bearing life occurs due to the increased slipper bearing area and less bending stress on the piston pin. This advantage can be clearly seen in Figure 8–5b, which illustrates the bending stresses imposed on the piston pin in a conventional trunk-type piston and shows how the crosshead and articulated piston design eliminates this bending stress.
- The two-piece piston is able to direct the force directly down to the connecting rod through the pin. Since both up and down forces are centered at the same point, the tendency of the pin to bend is eliminated.

Even though the articulated and crosshead two-piece pistons have major advantages over the one-piece model, they are more expensive to manufacture, and are generally heavier, thereby creating higher inertia forces. Because of their backward and forward (reciprocating) motion, all pistons generate inertia loads (the tendency of a body, in this case the piston assembly, to want to keep moving in the same direction when it reaches the bottom of its stroke).

PISTON CROWN SHAPES

Piston crown shape is a critical factor in the reduction of diesel exhaust emissions. Major reductions in diesel emissions are possible by incorporating into the piston combustion bowl a feature commonly referred to as a *re-entrant chamber*, where the sides of the bowl slant inward toward the central axis of the piston as illustrated in Figure 8–6. This piston bowl design improves mixing and turbulence of the air and fuel in the combustion space, which leads to a cleaner exhaust stream from all emissions. Tests have shown, however, that there is a progressive and significant deterioration in piston life as the bowl shape becomes more re-entrant (the outer angle of the bowl becomes more severe). This flank angle should not exceed 15° to the vertical unless the piston is cooled by an oil gallery or reinforced.

Experience has proven that piston bowl shape, piston cooling, and piston material are major influences on crown life. Direct-injection heavy-duty truck diesel engines use a variety of piston crown shapes. Some employ high-air-swirl deep-bowl systems (Figure 8–3) with moderate injection pressures, whereas others favor quiescent shallow-bowl systems with

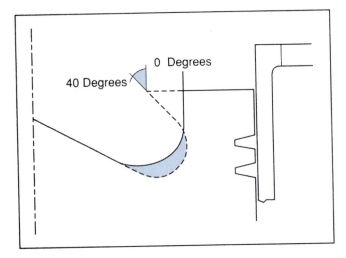

FIGURE 8–6   Design concept of a re-entrant bowl piston crown.

much higher injection pressures. Research and development indicate that at this time both U.S. and European exhaust emissions regulations can be met using the quiescent combustion system with an optimized electronic unit injector. The actual shape of the piston crown determines to a great extent the amount of swirl imparted to the trapped cylinder air during the compression stroke.

Some engine manufacturers have adopted a bowl-in-crown design similar to that illustrated in Figure 8–3; this design is more commonly used on lower-horsepower engine models with one-piece trunk-type aluminum alloy pistons. Figure 8–7 illustrates one design of high-speed heavy-duty diesel engine piston crown used by a number of major engine manufacturers including Caterpillar, Cummins, Detroit Diesel, and Mack in their heavy-duty on-highway truck engines. Known as a concave design, it is also referred to as a *Mexican hat* shape because it resembles a sombrero. This piston offers the following major advantages:

- It reduces the risk of burning the center of the piston crown by direct flame impingement of fuel from the injector.
- It permits diffusion of the fuel spray further into the air mass for quicker and better mixing of injected fuel.
- It allows better relief from internal stresses in the metal due to expansion caused by heat.
- It allows considerably more squish effect of the injected fuel into the combustion chamber because of the high degree of swirl imparted to the air during the compression stroke.

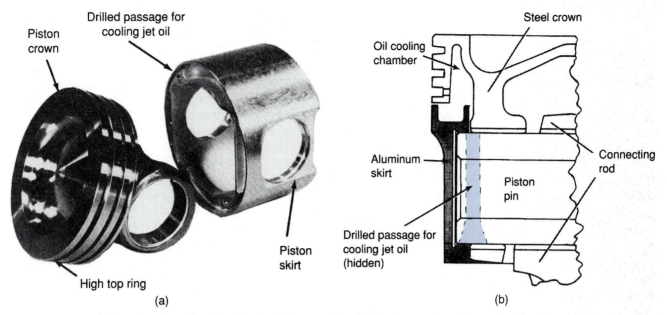

FIGURE 8–7   (a) Section through a Cat 3176 engine model articulated two-piece piston showing the piston skirt oil supply cooling passage to the crown. (b) Cross section of the same piston assembly highlighting the oil flow-up into the piston crown area. (Reprinted courtesy of Caterpillar, Inc.)

PISTON OPERATING TEMPERATURES

Temperatures within the combustion chamber depend on a number of factors, but they can range between 2500°F and over 3500°F (1371 to 1927°C). Some of the newer high-speed electronically controlled engines can approach peak cylinder temperatures of 4000°F (2204°C). These high temperatures last for a very short time; the heat generated is dissipated to the surrounding cylinder head fire deck and valves as well as to the cylinder liner. The piston is forced down the cylinder by the expansion of the high-pressure gases on the power stroke; therefore, the piston metal and crown operating temperatures vary in different makes of engines depending on the speed and horsepower they produce. Figure 8–8 illustrates typical piston operating temperatures. An uncooled cast-iron piston can absorb as much as 15 to 18% of the heat created by the burning gases, leading to temperatures in the center of the crown in excess of 1000°F (538°C). In an uncooled aluminum piston, temperatures can run between 550 and 700°F (288 to 371°C).

Careful consideration must be given to the clearance of the piston within the cylinder. Excessive clearance will allow the piston to pound or knock against the cylinder wall after engine startup until the piston becomes hot. Too little clearance can cause scoring of the piston when it is hot because no clearance remains

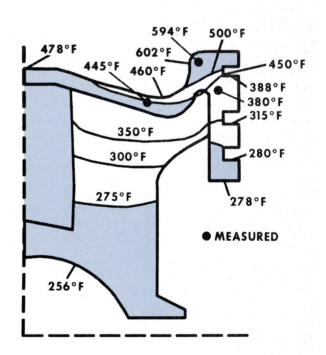

FIGURE 8–8   Typical operating temperatures in the piston crown of a two-piece crosshead piston for a DDC series 50/60 four-stroke-cycle engine. (Courtesy of Detroit Diesel Corporation.)

for lubricating oil between the piston and cylinder wall. It can be seen then that a clearance that gives little or no piston noise during cold operation and provides lubrication clearance during hot operation is the clearance desired. This clearance is generally built into the piston by the manufacturer. For example, a 4 in. (101.60 mm) diameter cylinder might be fitted with an aluminum piston 0.001 to 0.002 in. (0.025 to 0.05 mm) smaller in diameter than the cylinder. Clearance between the piston and cylinder depends a great deal on the diameter of the piston and the type of material, as a large piston must have more room for expansion when it becomes hot during engine operation.

The head of the piston or crown contains (depending on engine design) the cylinder combustion chamber. The combustion chamber is designed to aid in mixing the fuel and air together so that complete combustion (burning of the fuel) can occur.

> **NOTE**   Complete combustion in a diesel engine is the ultimate goal of all engine manufacturers. How well it is achieved depends on factors such as the design of the combustion chamber, injection nozzle opening pressure, injection nozzle hole size, and compression ratio. This subject is discussed in detail in Chapter 4.

The piston pin boss (bearing area) is the part of the piston that provides the support for the piston pin that connects the piston to the connecting rod. The piston boss is made as part of the piston and supported also by ribs or bars on the inside of the piston.

Guiding and supporting the piston within the cylinder is the piston skirt (side wall of the piston below the ring area). When combustion occurs and force is exerted on the piston, it is held straight in the cylinder by the piston skirt in contact with the cylinder wall.

> **NOTE**   In reality, piston skirts do not make contact with the cylinder wall, since a film of lubricating oil is maintained between wall and piston at all times during engine operation.

Cut in the piston immediately below the head are the ring grooves. These ring grooves are designed or shaped the same as the rings that are fitted into them. Many aluminum pistons have an iron or Ni-resist insert in the top ring groove. The Ni-resist area of the piston, in which the ring groove is cut, will be made from a harder metal such as nickel-chrome-iron to increase the wear qualities of the ring groove.

Installed into the ring grooves to aid the piston in reducing power loss due to blowby are the piston rings (circular, springlike steel devices) (Figure 8–1). Between each ring, supporting them, are the ring lands.

Piston rings are designed with an uninstalled or free diameter larger than the cylinder bore, so that when the ring is installed, radial pressure is applied to the cylinder wall.

The piston will normally have several different types of rings on it. Here are three examples:

1. *Compression ring* (top position). The top or compression ring seals the compression and pressure from combustion in the combustion chamber.

2. *Combination compression and oil scraper ring* (second groove). This second ring is generally a combination compression and oil scraper ring, aiding in controlling combustion loss and oil control.

3. *Oil control ring* (third or fourth groove depending on how many rings are on the piston). The oil control ring is designed to control the flow of oil onto the cylinder wall on the upstroke of the piston for lubrication and scrape the oil back off on the downstroke.

Not all pistons will have three rings. The number of rings is determined by the engine manufacturer, taking into consideration factors such as bore size, engine speed, and engine configuration (inline or V). Figure 8–9 shows several different pistons with their respective ring combinations.

One of the most critical wear areas in the engine is the piston rings and pistons because they are subjected to the tremendous heat of combustion and possible dirt-laden air supplied to the cylinder. To ensure a long, trouble-free period of operation, particular attention must be given to regular oil, oil filter, and air filter changes. In addition, it is important during engine overhaul or rebuild that strict attention be paid to detail and manufacturer's recommendations to ensure that a quality job can be done.

As stated earlier in this chapter, the pistons and ring combination are connected to the connecting rod by the piston pin, which is held in place by the retainer rings. The piston pin bushing is supported in the end of the connecting rod by a bushing made from brass, bronze, steel, or aluminum. The connecting rod is composed of very strong steel alloy shaped like an I-beam with a hole in one end for the piston pin (Figure 8–10). The other end of the rod has a larger hole or bore with a removable cap so that the rod may be connected to the rod journal. Installed in this hole will be a sleeve-type friction bearing comprised of two halves, one half in the connecting rod and the other half in the rod cap. Connecting rod bearings are specially designed to meet

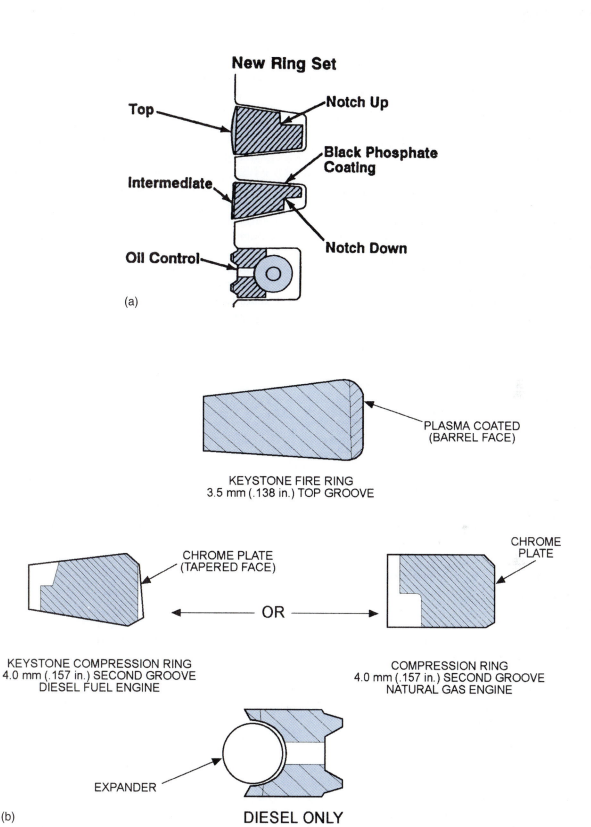

FIGURE 8–9 (a) Example of a three-ring arrangement used in Cummins L10, M11, and N14 engine models. (Courtesy of Cummins Engine Company, Inc.) (b) comparison of typical piston ring packs (DDC) in series 50 and 60 engines. (Courtesy of Detroit Diesel Corporation.)

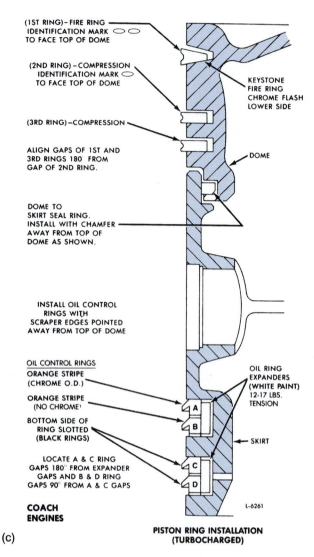

(1ST RING)-FIRE RING
IDENTIFICATION MARK
TO FACE TOP OF DOME

(2ND RING)-COMPRESSION
IDENTIFICATION MARK
TO FACE TOP OF DOME

(3RD RING)-COMPRESSION

ALIGN GAPS OF 1ST AND
3RD RINGS 180 FROM
GAP OF 2ND RING.

DOME TO
SKIRT SEAL RING.
INSTALL WITH CHAMFER
AWAY FROM TOP OF
DOME AS SHOWN.

INSTALL OIL CONTROL
RINGS WITH
SCRAPER EDGES POINTED
AWAY FROM TOP OF DOME

OIL CONTROL RINGS
ORANGE STRIPE
(CHROME O.D.)

ORANGE STRIPE
(NO CHROME)

BOTTOM SIDE OF
RING SLOTTED
(BLACK RINGS)

LOCATE A & C RING
GAPS 180° FROM EXPANDER
GAPS AND B & D RING
GAPS 90° FROM A & C GAPS

KEYSTONE
FIRE RING
CHROME FLASH
LOWER SIDE

DOME

OIL RING
EXPANDERS
(WHITE PAINT)
12-17 LBS.
TENSION

SKIRT

COACH
ENGINES

(c)

L-6261

PISTON RING INSTALLATION
(TURBOCHARGED)

FIGURE 8–9   (continued). (c) Example of the piston ring stackup used by DDC in its V92 two-stroke-cycle transit bus engines.

the following requirements imposed on them during engine operation:

1. *Fatigue resistance.* The bearing must be able to withstand intermittent loading to which it may be subjected.

2. *Conformability.* The bearing material must be able to creep or flow slightly to compensate for any unavoidable misalignment between the shaft and bearing.

3. *Embeddability.* The ability of the bearing material to absorb foreign abrasive particles that might otherwise scratch the shaft that the bearing is supporting.

4. *Surface action.* The ability of a bearing to resist seizure if the bearing and shaft make contact during engine operation. This situation may occur when an

extreme load squeezes the oil film out of the clearance space between the shaft and bearing.

5. *Corrosive resistance.* A bearing characteristic that resists chemical corrosion caused by acids that are the by-product of combustion.

6. *Temperature strength.* How well the bearing will carry its load at engine-operating temperature without flowing out of shape or breaking up.

7. *Thermal conductivity.* The ability of a bearing material to absorb heat and transfer it from the bearing surface to the housing. An important factor in bearing longevity.

Con-rods employ an upper and lower shell bearing as shown in Figure 8–10. They are constructed in the same manner as crankshaft main bearings, and are manufactured from similar materials to that shown in Chapter 7, see Figure 7–4. Failure analysis can be con-

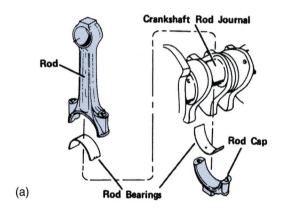

Crankshaft Rod Journal

Rod

Rod Cap

Rod Bearings

(a)

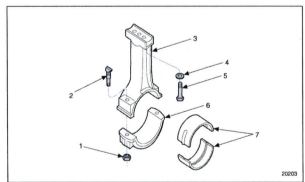

(b)

1. Connecting Rod Nut (2)	5. Piston Pin Bolt (2)
2. Notched Bolt	6. Connecting Rod Bearing Cap
3. Connecting Rod	7. Bearing Shells
4. Spacer	

FIGURE 8–10   (a) Typical trunk-type piston con-rod, upper and lower precision shell bearings, and cap, and their location to the crankshaft journal. (Courtesy of Cummins Engine Company, Inc.) (b) Details of a cross-head or articulated piston connecting rod assembly. (Courtesy of Detroit Diesel Corporation.)

sidered common to that discussed in Chapter 7, see Figures 7–10 through Figure 7–29. Rod bearing shells are smaller in overall diameter than are main bearings, but they are held in the cap and saddle with a small tang. In some engines the upper con-rod bearing shell has an oil hole to permit pressurized oil flow up through the length of the rifle-drilled con-rod to deliver cooling oil to the underside of the piston crown. You can generally identify the upper and lower shell bearings by looking at the backside of the shell, which identifies it as being the 'upper' or 'lower' shell, plus the bearing size (STD. = standard, 0.010″, 0.020″, or 0.030″ undersize). All of the service precautions that apply to a main shell bearing discussed in Chapter 7 should be considered when dealing with con-rod bearings.

The rod bearing is lubricated by engine oil supplied under pressure through a drilling in the crankshaft journal (Chapter 11). Since there is clearance between the connecting rod bearing and the crankshaft journal, the oil used for lubrication is allowed to leak off into the oil pan or crankcase area of the engine.

PISTON REMOVAL FROM THE BLOCK

The piston, rings, and con-rod assembly can be removed from the block of high-speed heavy-duty engine models by the following two methods.

1. First drain the engine oil and coolant from the block and remove the oil pan and cylinder-head assembly. Loosen off the con-rod cap retaining nuts/bolts and push the piston and con-rod from the cylinder liner, or the parent block bore. Then remove the cylinder sleeve/liner as described in Chapter 6.

2. Repeat the same procedure as in method 1, but remove the piston, con-rod, and cylinder liner as a unit (cylinder pack or kit). This process can be performed using the special tooling shown in Figure 8–11. Refer also to the following section.

Remove Cylinder Pack

As mentioned, in some engines it is possible to remove the piston, con-rod, and cylinder liner as a complete assembly from the cylinder block bore, usually referred to as removing the *cylinder pack* or *kit.* Considerable time is saved during an in-frame overhaul when all of these components are replaced as a preassembled set. This procedure is also used when the liner is a dry-type slip-fit design in the block bore or a wet liner retained by O-ring seals, because in many cases when removing the piston and con-rod without using cylinder liner hold-down clamps, the liner will pop out of the block bore. You might want to remove the cylinder pack from engines such as the 3176, C10, C12 and the 3406 Cat, the Cummins NT-855 (14L), and Detroit Diesel two- and four-stroke-cycle models.

1. Match-mark the cylinder liner to the engine block, so that if the liner is to be reused it will be reinstalled in the same position in the same cylinder. Also

FIGURE 8–11 Using an expandable rubber plug-type puller inserted into a wet cylinder liner to enable withdrawal of the complete cylinder kit consisting of the liner, piston, and con-rod assembly. (Courtesy of Kent-Moore Tool Division, SPX Corporation.)

take note of the piston for any numbers or distinguishing marks that indicate "front" and so forth on the crown.

2.   Manually rotate the engine crankshaft to place the con-rod for the cylinder to be removed at the BDC position. This will facilitate removal of the con-rod cap.

3.   Use special tooling (Figure 8–11) to pull both the piston and liner as a unit from various engine models such as Cat, Cummins, and Detroit Diesel. The tool set includes a large expandable rubber plug sandwiched between two steel end plates. The large threaded rod that is securely attached to the lower round steel plate extends up to three large nuts, which are threaded onto the assembly. The first nut above the top plate of the rubber plug is used to expand the plug until it is tight in the liner bore. The second nut up is the puller unit that, when tightened as shown in the diagram, will withdraw the cylinder kit from the block bore. The top nut is used to lock the handle in place so that you can hold onto the assembly while rotating the puller nut. The handle can then be used to lift the cylinder kit from the engine. Alternatively, you can loosen off the center nut first, withdraw the steel crab, then pull the cylinder kit. During initial installation of the large expandable rubber plug into the cylinder liner bore, the piston would be positioned at BDC. Some models of cylinder pack pullers can have the puller nut rotated clockwise by the aid of a deep socket and air-impact wrench to quickly and effectively pull the liner, piston, and connecting rod from the block bore as an assembly. Take care during this process, however, that the con-rod does not come into contact with the crankshaft journal and score it as it moves upward. (For details on how to remove the press-fit cylinder liner on its own, see Chapter 6.)

PISTONS AND PISTON RINGS

Inspection Flowchart
To assist in recognizing piston and ring damage when using ASE tasks lists, use the flowchart shown in Figure 8–12.

Cleaning Pistons and Components
When cleaning, always wear goggles and protective clothing. Do not clean pistons and rods in an acid tank.

On lightly carboned pistons, attempt to clean the components with diesel fuel oil. If the fuel oil doesn't remove the carbon deposits, use an approved chemical solvent that will not harm the tin plate on ferrous metal pistons. However, avoid using a chemical solvent on the bushing area of the piston pin bore. On aluminum alloy pistons, wash the pistons and rods in a strong solution of laundry detergent in hot water, or select a cleaning solvent that is approved for use with this material and that can be used either hot or cold. Soak the pistons in a hot soapy solution for up to 30 minutes before using a nonmetallic brush to remove carbon deposits. If a cold cleaner solution is being used, soaking the pistons overnight usually loosens any carbon deposits.

SERVICE TIP   Never use a metal-wire brush to clean aluminum alloy pistons; this type of brush will scratch and score the skirt as well as the piston ring grooves.

Similarly, do not attempt to clean aluminum alloy piston ring grooves or the piston pin bores with glass beads or walnut shells, because this action can damage the skirt, pin bore surface finish or prevent the rings from seating correctly in the ring grooves. If the piston is fitted with Ni-resist ring groove inserts, then blasting with walnut shells may be done safely if the machine pressure is raised only enough to remove the carbon. Take care also not to concentrate the spray in one area (including the piston crown) for an extended period of time.

On ferrous metal piston domes, a wire brush can be used safely on both the piston dome and compression ring grooves to remove carbon; however, never use a wire brush on the piston skirt, particularly on Detroit Diesel pistons since they are tin coated (this applies to both the one-piece trunk-type and two-piece crosshead pistons). Removing this protective layer can result in scuffing, then scoring, of the skirt when it is operating in the cylinder liner.

Detroit Diesel approves glass beading of the piston crown dome using Mico Bead Glass Shot MS-M, 0.0029 to 0.0058 in. (0.073 to 0.147 mm), using air pressure of 552 to 689 kPa (80 to 100 psi). Make certain that no glass beads remain in the piston dome after cleaning! In addition, do not allow the glass beading to contact any area of the piston pin bushing. Avoid refinishing or polishing the piston pin.

After any cleaning solution has been used, whether on ferrous metal or aluminum alloy pistons, wear safety glasses and wash the pistons in a strong solution of laundry detergent in hot water. Some engine manufacturers allow steam cleaning of their aluminum alloy pistons. In both cases, dry off all components by using compressed air while wearing safety goggles. Make sure that all oil drain holes in the piston grooves are open and clean, as well as the oil supply cooling holes in the skirt and crown.

Cleaning the Ring Grooves
1.   A ring groove cleaner (Figure 8–13) can be used to clean all the carbon from the ring grooves (only

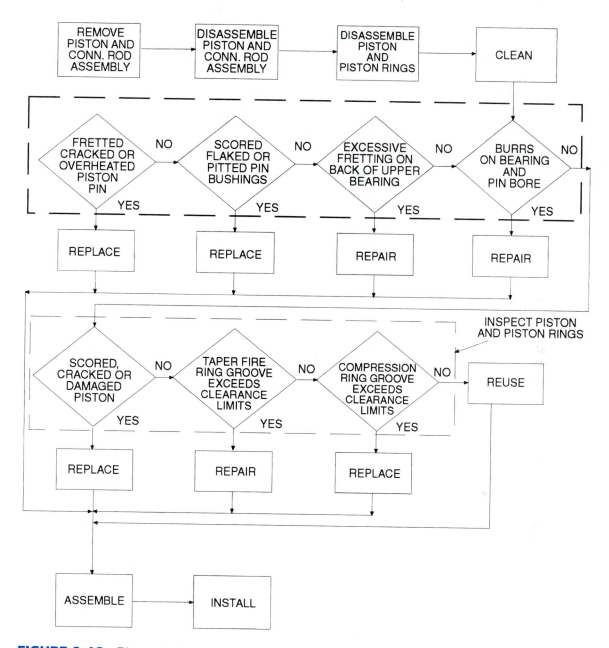

FIGURE 8–12 *Diagnostic flowchart to assist in either the repair or replacement of the piston and rings.* (Courtesy of Detroit Diesel Corporation.)

if recommended in the service manual) so they can then be checked for wear.

2. Select the tool bit that fits the ring groove and install the cleaner on the piston in the ring groove.

3. Operate the groove cleaner by twisting or turning it around the piston.

4. Clean the grooves until all carbon has been removed.

CAUTION Care must be exercised when using the groove cleaner to prevent any metal from being removed from the bottom of the ring grooves or piston surface by continuing to turn the cleaner after all the carbon has been cleaned away.

FIGURE 8–13   Adjustable-diameter piston ring carbon groove cleaner tool.

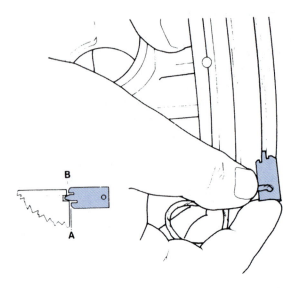

FIGURE 8–14   Checking a piston fire (top) ring groove for wear with a set of special keystone gauges sized for a specific make/model of engine. If the gauge shoulder contacts the piston at position A or B, replace the piston due to ring groove wear. (Courtesy of Detroit Diesel Corporation.)

Many engine manufacturers recommend, however, using a piece of an old compression ring that has been lightly ground to a bevel edge, or has been broken in half and then filed or ground square since the used ring is of the correct width for this purpose. Take care not to scratch or groove the ring sealing surface in the piston groove; this can cause carbon to form as well as possibly create a sticking ring. Any carbon left in the ring grooves will reduce piston ring clearance and prevent new rings from making good seals.

Measuring the Ring Groove

The ring grooves can now be checked for wear to determine if the pistons will be reusable. Use the following procedure:

1.   Check the top and second keystone ring grooves with a ring groove gauge if available (Figure 8–14).

2.   If a ring groove gauge is not available, a new ring and a feeler gauge may be used. If the ring and groove are straight, the ring need not be installed on the piston. If the ring and groove are of the keystone type, the ring must be installed on the piston and the ring pushed flush with the piston ring land. Using a 0.006-in. (0.015-mm) feeler gauge, try to insert the gauge between the ring and piston ring land (Figure 8–15). If the feeler gauge can be inserted and removed easily, the ring groove is worn excessively and the piston must be replaced.

Removing the Piston from the Con-Rod

Once it has been determined that the piston ring grooves are in usable condition, the piston can now be removed from the connecting rod for further checking. The piston may be removed as follows:

1.   Remove the piston pin retaining rings using a pair of circlip pliers.

NOTE   When removing Detroit Diesel (two-stroke) piston pin retainers (a thin spring steel-like cap holds the pin in); see Figure 8–5a. A hole should be made in the retainer with a small chisel or center punch; then carefully pry the pin retainer from the piston. The pin can now easily be pushed from the piston and rod by hand.

CAUTION   Piston pins must never be driven from an aluminum piston without first heating the piston to approximately 200°F (93°C) in hot water. If this procedure is not followed, serious damage to the piston may result. After the piston is heated, the piston pin can be tapped out using a driver and a hammer. Detroit Diesel iron pistons will not require heating and the piston pin can easily be pushed from the piston after removal of the piston pin retainers.

Visual Inspection of the Piston

Place the piston and rod assembly in a vise and clamp it securely.

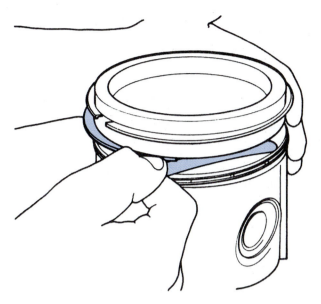

FIGURE 8–15 *Using a feeler gauge to check/measure piston ring to groove side clearance. (Courtesy of Detroit Diesel Corporation.)*

NOTE   It is recommended that a vise with brass or aluminum jaw protectors or a rag be used to protect the rod when it is clamped into the vise.

Make a visual inspection of the piston rings, land, and skirt area to determine if the piston is reusable. The piston should be checked for:

1. Scored skirt area
2. Cracked skirt
3. Uneven wear (skirt area)
4. Broken ring lands
5. Stuck or broken rings
6. Worn piston pin bores
7. Burned or eroded areas in head

Piston skirt scoring can be caused by any of the following: engine overheating, excessive fuel settings, improper piston clearance, insufficient lubrication, or improper injection nozzle or injector spray pattern.

Piston cracking or ring land breakage can be caused by excessive use of starting fluid, excessive piston clearance, or foreign objects in the cylinder.

Piston skirt wear can be caused by normal engine operation, dirty lubricating oil, too little piston clearance, or dirty intake air.

Piston burning or erosion can be caused by plugged nozzle or injection orifices, excessive engine load during cold operation, and water leakage into the cylinder.

Piston pin bearing bore wear can be caused by normal engine operation, dirty engine oil, or insufficient lubrication.

Pistons with stuck rings may be the result of overheating, insufficient lubrication, or excessive fuel settings.

After inspecting the piston as described determine what caused the piston damage (if any). The condition that caused the piston damage must be corrected before the engine is reassembled.

If the piston fails this inspection, remove it from the rod and discard (see section on rod removal). If the decision is made to use the piston again, it should be left on the rod for now.

PISTON SCUFFING IDENTIFICATION

When a new piston is fitted or installed into a cylinder liner, or a parent bore in the cylinder block, many technicians believe that a new piston with its rings neatly packaged from the factory should simply be a drop-in item, particularly when new cylinder packs are installed. This is normally true, and 99.9% will have no service problems. If a lone new piston (not a cylinder pack or kit) with new rings is to be installed, however, it is necessary for the technician to ensure that the piston-to-liner clearance or parent block bore clearance is checked to ensure that piston scuffing does not occur. Scuffing is the condition that occurs in a new engine that we can equate with a scuff on a polished leather shoe or the paint on a car after polishing, where it removes the original finish. In a piston, a very light scuff will generally not create a problem, but a more heavy scuff can remove small particles of metal from the piston skirt. These particles can lead to scoring, and scoring can then lead to seizure. Scuffing is more common to trunk-type (one-piece) pistons than to two-piece crosshead or articulated-type pistons on which the skirt and crown are independent of one another.

Causes of Scuffing

Several causes can lead to piston scuffing, particularly by a technician who does not perform a series of checks/tests and by outside forces due to poor maintenance. These causes are as follows:

- Clearance
- Hot intake air
- Hydrostatic lock
- Top of piston meltdown
- Combustion cracks in the bowl area
- Dustouts

Clearance

A general reason for scuffing can be traced to piston-to-liner clearances that are on the low end of the specification, or a high spot in the block bore. Problem scuffs that are traceable to a lack-of-clearance condition will show up as light to very light vertical lines that appear across the complete piston skirt. These lines are highly polished, and on aluminum skirt pistons will have a soft texture. Note that the ring lands zone is normally undamaged due to the taper that exists from the top of the skirt to the top of the piston thus allowing for expansion when hot.

Hot Intake Air

In turbocharged engines, three types of aftercoolers are used to reduce the boosted air temperature: the jacket water aftercooler (JWAC), the advanced liquid charge cooler (ALCC), and the air-to-air aftercooler (ATAAC), with this last model being the most efficient of the three. See Chapters 12 and 13 for more details on these aftercoolers. Hot air ingested into the cylinders on the intake stroke will fail to reduce the piston crown and top ring land area temperature to acceptable levels. This hotter-running piston material will eventually lead to erosion of the piston above the top ring area.

Hydrostatic Lock/Breakage

A hydrostatic lock is the condition that exists when liquid becomes trapped between the cylinder head and the piston crown. This liquid could be due to lube oil, fuel oil, or coolant. A leaking cylinder head gasket could also be the fault, as well as a cracked head, worn valve stems and guides, a dribbling injector spray tip, and so forth. When the piston moves upward on its compression stroke, extremely high hydraulic pressures are created. These high pressures will crack the piston crown (even splitting it in half), damage the ring lands (break-

age), and bend the connecting rod assembly. Of course these conditions can cause major engine failure.

Piston Crown Meltdown

When inspection reveals that the top (crown) of the piston has melted down, this can usually be traced to severe overheating possibly due to a plugged piston lube oil cooling nozzle or an overfueling condition.

Cracks in Piston Bowl Area

When visible cracks appear in the combustion bowl of the piston, this can usually be traced back to mistimed injection (advanced), high exhaust back pressure, or constant overloading and excessive heat. On turbocharged engines, the wastegate could be set too high.

Engine Dustout Conditions

The term *dustout* refers to the entrance of unfiltered air/dust/dirt/grime being allowed to enter the engine cylinders. This can occur due to a tear in the air filter element, to leaking air cleaner and joint O-rings, through elbows and joints that have split due to overtightening of hose clamps, or through a pin hole or burn due to routing these too close to hot engine exhaust surfaces. Generally the wear pattern on the second compression ring will indicate a polished appearance across the full-face width of the ring where any blackened areas will appear more polished than normal. These polished areas will begin at the bottom of the ring and move upward on the tapered face of the ring. The edges of the ring may appear razor sharp, and the cylinder block bore will show indications of ridges usually about 0.50 in. (12.7 mm) below the fire deck of the block.

Scuffing Examples

Figure 8–16 illustrates an example when scuffing occured due to a lack of oil between the piston skirt and

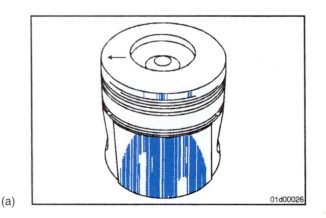

(a)

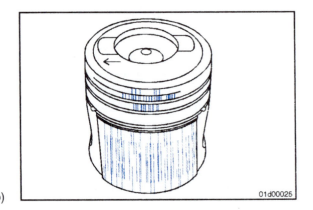

(b)

FIGURE 8–16   (a) Identification marks confirming a lack of oil caused a heavy scuffing failure on the thrust side of the piston assembly. (b) Same type of failure as in (a), but on the nonthrust side of the piston skirt and crown. (Courtesy of Cummins Engine Company, Inc.)

the cylinder wall on the thrust side. The scuff will tend to start in the area of the piston pin bosses where more metal is used to support the pin. In aluminum cam-ground pistons, the boss area has greater clearance when cold (thrust side), eventually expanding when hot to form a true circle of the skirt to block bore. A tight initial clearance will lead to the scuff condition and it will progress down the piston skirt. The scuffed surfaces will move from a highly polished pressure condition to dark-colored (brown/black) fairly smooth smears on the skirt. The top ring land is undamaged due to the piston ring land taper that exists, and therefore will show no signs of failure. This type of scuff failure is lighter than one due to a lack of engine coolant.

Figure 8–17 illustrates a scuff failure caused by a lack of oil, but specifically to the off or antithrust side of the piston skirt where the severity of the score marks will not be as great as those that might occur on the thrust side of the piston. The scuff will appear as oil deposit marks fairly light in texture and not too rough to

the touch, with very little to no scoring on this side of the skirt, although discoloration will be evident and less black in color than a thrust-side scuff.

Figure 8–18 illustrates a view of the underside of the piston crown where you will be able to see a lacquering or oil deposit condition caused by high piston operating temperatures usually traceable back to a lack of pressurized lube oil from a misaligned or clogged/plugged oil cooling nozzle. The discoloration will normally appear as brown or black patches extending outward from the underside of the piston crown. In Figure 8–19 we can see the results of a piston skirt thrust-side scuff condition traceable back to a lack of engine coolant. This will cause scuffing around most of the skirt circumference if the engine has been operated for a long enough time with low to no coolant. The vertical scuff lines on the skirt will always be darker and rougher than those caused by a lack-of-oil scuff condition shown earlier in Figure 8–16. Due to the rougher scuff and tearing of piston skirt material, some

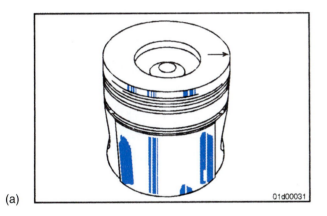

(a)

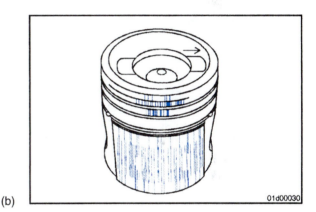

(b)

FIGURE 8–17 (a) Identification marks of a scuff failure due to a lack of oil to the off, or antithrust, side of the piston skirt. (b) Greater scuff marks on the thrust side of the piston. (Courtesy of Cummins Engine Company, Inc.)

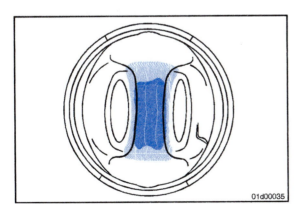

(a)

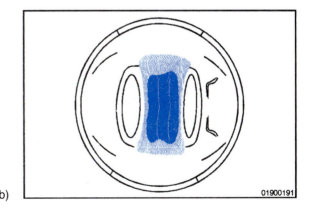

(b)

FIGURE 8–18 (a) A lack of oil scuff; view of the underside of the piston crown showing either a lacquering or an oil deposit condition caused by high oil temperatures. (b) Discoloration normally appears as dark patches (brown or black) extending outward from the underside of the crown. (Courtesy of Cummins Engine Company, Inc.)

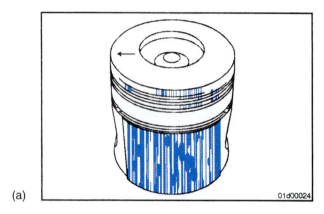

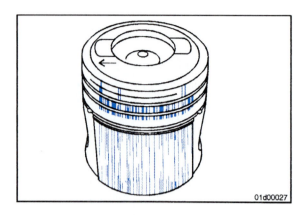

(a)   (b)

FIGURE 8–19   (a) A piston thrust-side lack of coolant scuff generally extends around most of the piston skirt circumference. (b) The rougher and darker scuff marks will cause metal tearing and some damage in the piston ring land areas. (Courtesy of Cummins Engine Company, Inc.)

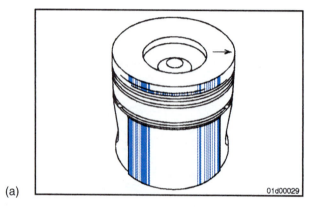

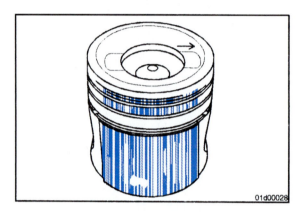

(a)   (b)

FIGURE 8–20   (a) Piston nonthrust-side lack of coolant failure identifed by two vertical score columns, one on each side of the piston pin. (b) In some cases this failure can appear across a larger skirt surface area. (Courtesy of Cummins Engine Company, Inc.)

of the metal will tend to travel upward and cause some damage in the piston ring land areas. The rings will also show scuff damage, more so on the bottom ring, decreasing in circumferential wear damage toward the top ring. The inside of the skirt will tend to appear black on the thrust side. Minimal scuffing may also be noticeable at the center of the skirt due to the actual designed shape of the piston with a possibility of a scuff on one side of the skirt only. Fretting (galling) around the entire circumference of the piston skirt is not unusual on one-piece trunk-type pistons. On two-piece crosshead or articulated piston designs, it is possible to see four-point scuffing rather than complete circumferential scuffing as appears on the trunk-type pistons.

Piston scuff due to a lack of coolant that occurs on the nonthrust side of the skirt—although somewhat similar to that for the thrust side described in Figure 8–19 will appear as shown in Figure 8–20. Here two vertical score columns appear, one on each side of the

piston (wrist) pin area. In some cases, however, these score marks can appear across a larger skirt surface area than do the two columns. Inspection of the underside of the piston crown will normally be clean and free of any signs of oil deposits as shown in Figure 8–21.

PISTON RINGS INSPECTION DETAILS

NOTE   Leaving the piston on the rod will provide a means for holding the piston during the cleanup and inspection to follow.

Rings can be easily removed by using a ring installation removal tool (Figure 8–22). Normally, pistons and rings are discarded and replaced with new ones during

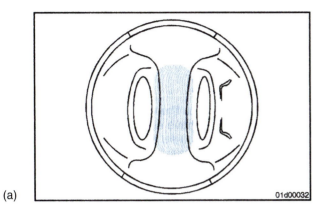

(a)

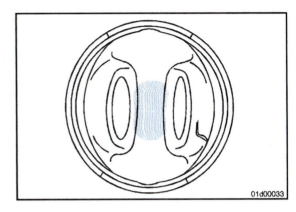

(b)

FIGURE 8–21   *Piston undercrown lack of coolant scuff. In both cases the underside of the piston crown will normally be clean and free of any signs of oil deposits. (Courtesy of Cummins Engine Company, Inc.)*

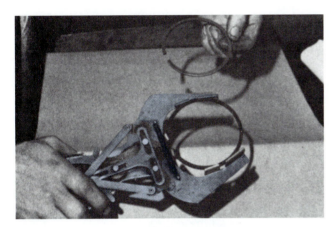

FIGURE 8–22   *Adjustable piston ring installation and removal expander tool.*

a high-mileage or hours major overhaul, but there are exceptions. For example, a new engine with very few hours on it may be disassembled because of excessive oil consumption. Engine manufacturers recommend replacing the rings only, not the pistons. Pistons can be used again in an engine assuming that they pass all of the necessary checks listed in Figure 8–12.

Piston Ring Condition Analysis

Short ring life can be attributed to a number of causes. They include overheating, (oil, coolant or aftercooler air), incomplete combustion, high exhaust back-pressure, high air inlet restriction, improper piston-to-liner clearances, incorrect ring end gap or side clearances, wrong type or grade of engine oil, dust out due to unfiltered air entering the engine cylinders, installation of new rings without staggering the ring end gaps correctly, ring installation upside down, and abrasive dirt in components when initially installing the new rings. Several worn ring examples follow:

1. Figure 8–23, Item A illustrates a new ring face condition, while Item B shows a worn compression ring caused by ingested abrasive dirt or metal. In B the chromium plated ring face has been worn away. Typical causes for this type of failure can usually be traced back to poor cleaning habits during engine repair or overhaul. For example when a cylinder block has been rebored and honed, or when a used cylinder liner has been deglazed, thorough cleaning is a must. See Chapter 6 for information on proper cleaning procedures for blocks and liners. DO NOT use emery cloth or sandpaper to remove the carbon ridge from the top of used cylinder liners since the aluminum oxide or silicon particles can cause serious engine damage. Also do not use any abrasives in the ring travel area which will damage the liner surface as well as the rings. To clean carbon from the cylinder liner, use a

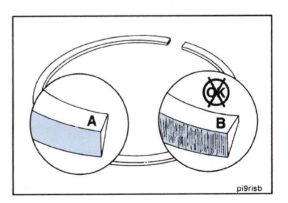

FIGURE 8–23   *Item A illustrates a new piston ring face. Item B shows abrasive wear on the ring face. (Courtesy of Cummins Engine Company, Inc.)*

fine fibrous abrasive pad such as a Scotch Brite 7448 model or equivalent, along with solvent to remove the carbon.

2. Figure 8–24, Item A illustrates a new ring face, while Item B shows a scuffed and scored ring face which is indicated by heavy scratches, metal discoloration and voids in the ring surface. Typically this condition can be traced back to ring-to-liner oil film breakdown. This leads to metal scuffing, which in turn leads to scoring as metal particles are torn from mating surfaces (liner to ring face). Oil film breakdown can be the result of engine overheating, crankcase oil dilution, poor oil/filter change period maintenance, or piston cooling nozzle plugging/restriction to flow.

3. Figure 8–25, Item A illustrates a new oil control ring condition, while Item B shows that oil ring plugging of the grooves has occurred.

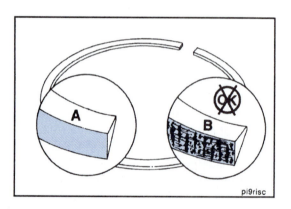

FIGURE 8–24 *Item A shows a new ring face. Item B shows severe ring face scuffing and scoring. (Courtesy of Cummins Engine Company, Inc.)*

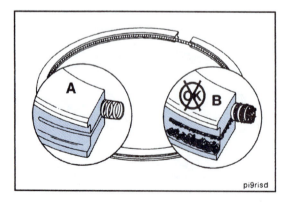

FIGURE 8–25 *Item A shows a normal oil ring condition. Item B shows oil ring plugging by deposits. (Courtesy of Cummins Engine Company, Inc.)*

This condition will restrict the oil drain back to the oil pan when the piston moves down the cylinder, therefore excessive oil will not only flood the cylinder wall, but also the ring belt area. This condition can be caused by:

- low engine operating temperature
- excessive idling periods
- excessive light load operation
- cooling system malfunction
- extended oil and filter change intervals
- wrong grade of engine oil
- use of poor quality engine oil

INSPECTING THE CONNECTING RODS

The connecting rod bearings should be removed from the rod and rod cap in preparation for inspection. After removal of bearings the rod cap should be installed on the rod and cap bolts torqued to specifications. After torquing the cap, the rod should be checked. When the con-rod is separated from the piston, make a careful check according to the flowchart in Figure 8–26.

Measuring the Rod Small End Bore for Out-of-Roundness with a Snap Gauge and Outside Micrometer

1. Place a snap or telescoping gauge into the rod bore and determine the bushing diameter (Figure 8–27).

2. Remove the snap gauge and use the outside micrometer to measure the snap gauge size.

3. This measurement is the bushing size expressed in thousandths of an inch.

Completing the Rod Inspection

The rod big end bore should be measured with a snap gauge and inside micrometer in the same manner that the small end bore was measured. If the rod big end bore does not meet specifications, it should be reconditioned or replaced.

NOTE   Major rod reconditioning, such as honing the big end bore and checks for cracks using a magna-flux machine, is generally not attempted in a general repair shop because this procedure requires special equipment.

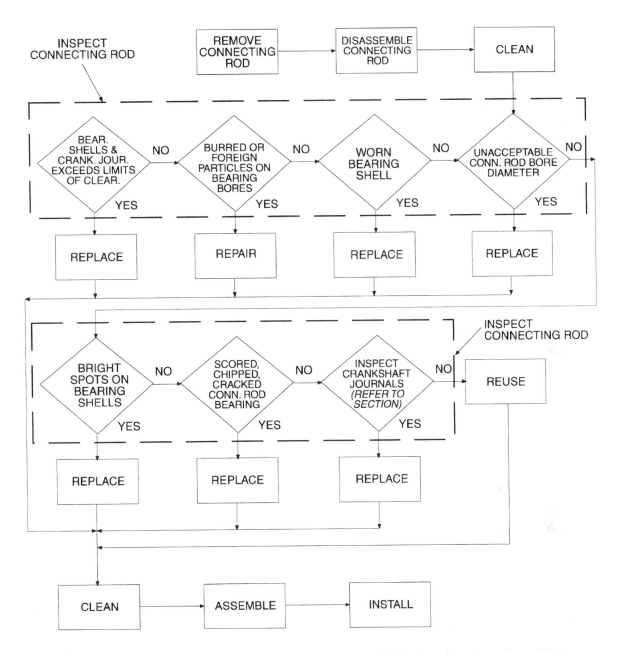

FIGURE 8–26 Diagnostic flowchart to determine when to repair/replace the connecting rod. (Courtesy of Detroit Diesel Corporation.)

CHECKING ROD BORE OVALITY

Closely inspect the con-rod bearing cap and saddle area for any signs of dark spots, which usually indicate poor contact of the precision shell bearing. Also check for color discoloration throughout the rod; this could indicate overheating, which affects rod strength. Look for signs of bluing at either the top or bottom end of the rod, and replace the rod if it is severely discolored.

With the con-rod and cap assembled (no bearings) and torqued to specs, use a dial bore or telescoping gauge to measure the distortion and ovality of the rod bore. Closely inspect the rod and cap at the split parting line for any signs of fretting, which would signify bearing cap movement. Signs of movement or rod bore ovality may require that the rod be replaced. Check the engine manufacturer's service literature. The bearing cap and saddle can be parted (machined flat) on a cap

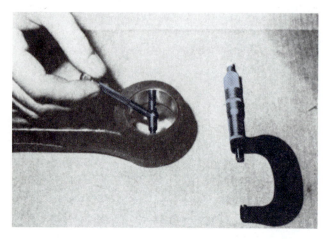

FIGURE 8–27 *Using a telescoping gauge and outside micrometer to measure the con-rod piston pin bushing diameter.*

CAUTION Some engine manufacturers are opposed to parting and remachining the con-rod since when metal is removed, the weight of the rod as well as the clearance height of the piston to cylinder head fire deck are changed. Thus the cylinder compression and injector spray distribution throughout the combustion chamber are altered. Always check the engine service manual closely to determine if remachining is an acceptable practice. Detroit Diesel is one major engine manufacturer that cautions against any such remachining of its connecting rods.

and rod grinder similar to the one shown in Figure 8–28. Grinding the parting surface of the bearing caps leaves all the rod cap bores *undersize* when the caps are bolted back in place. Con-rods can be power honed back to a stock bore size on a machine similar to the one illustrated in Figure 8–29.

Most manufacturers suggest that rod bolts be replaced at each major overhaul, or at least that the self-locking nuts be replaced. Inspect the rod bolts for signs of fretting (movement), thread damage, or bolt stretch, and compare them to a new bolt. If new nuts are used, install them in the proper direction so that the hardened machined face bottoms against the rod cap.

The rod can be checked for straightness using a rod alignment device (Figure 8–30 and 8–31). If the rod is not straight, it should be replaced or reconditioned.

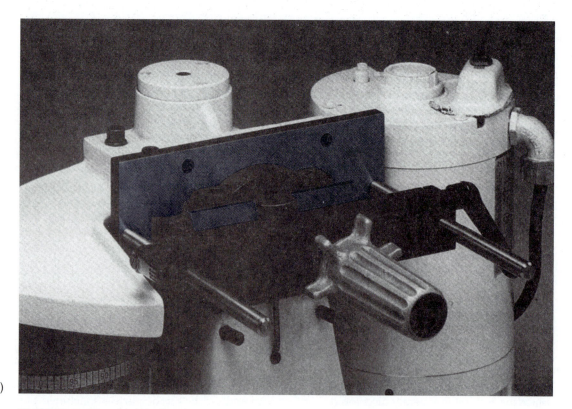

(a)

FIGURE 8–28 *(a) Grinding the con-rod cap at the flat machined surface. (Courtesy of Sunnen Products Company, St. Louis, MO.)*

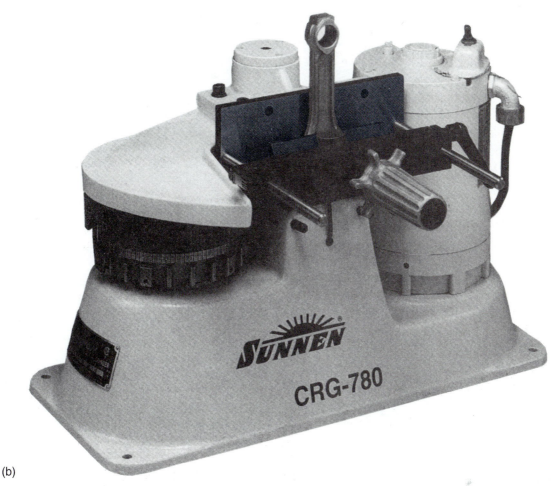

(b)

FIGURE 8–28 *(b) Grinding the mating flat surface of the con-rod using a cap and rod grinder, model CRG 780 (con-rod grinder).*

PISTON PIN INSPECTION

The piston pin should be measured with an outside micrometer at both ends and in the middle (Figure 8–32). The measurement should agree with the manufacturer's specifications. If not, the pin should be replaced.

NOTE   This check may be omitted if new sleeves and pistons are being installed, since most sleeve and piston kits contain a new piston pin.

FINAL ASSEMBLY OF PISTONS, PISTON RINGS, AND CONNECTING RODS

1.   Install the piston on the rod by inserting the piston pin though the rod and piston. Then install the piston pin retainer rings or circlips.

NOTE   The piston pin can be inserted through an aluminum piston very easily by hand if the piston has been preheated to 200°F (93°C) using hot water.

2.   Install the piston pin retainers.

NOTE   After driving the solid piston pin retainers into Detroit Diesel or some Caterpillar trunk- or crosslead-type pistons, it is critical that an inspection be made to ensure that it will seal oil out of the combustion chamber. A special vacuum pump and adapter can be used for this purpose. Do not make only a visual inspection (Figure 8–33).

3.   Using a rag or some other suitable protector for the rod, clamp the piston and connecting rod assembly into a vise.

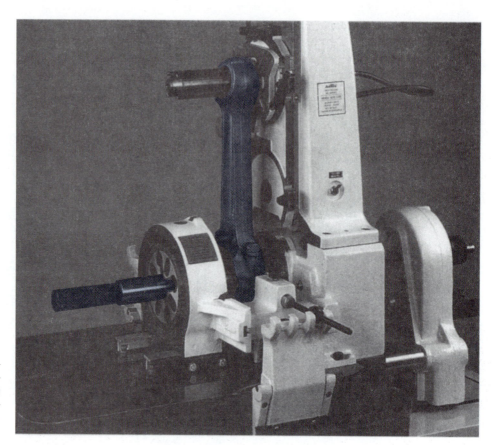

FIGURE 8–29 Power honing the big end of the reassembled con-rod and cap on a model PM-300 machine. (Courtesy of Sunnen Products Company, St. Louis, MO.)

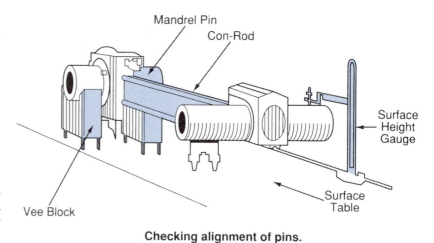

FIGURE 8–30 Checking the con-rod for straightness on a surface table with an adjustable pin and sled gauge using a pin or mandrel.

Checking alignment of pins.

4. Allow the piston to rest on the vise jaws, in preparation for piston ring installation onto the piston.

5. Before installing the piston rings on the piston, it is good practice to check the rings in the cylinder for correct end gap.

NOTE Insufficient ring end gap will not allow the ring to expand when heated and may cause ring scuffing and scoring, resulting in compression loss, excessive blowby, and oil consumption.

FIGURE 8–31 Model R1-9000 electronic gauge assembly for checking a con-rod for twists and bends. (Courtesy of Sunnen Products Company.)

6.   Insert rings vertically one at a time into the cylinder with the end gap up. Tip the ring into the horizontal position and place a piston without rings head first into the cylinder bore, pushing it down onto the ring, leveling it.

7.   With a feeler gauge, measure the gap between the ends of the ring (Figure 8–34). The ring gap should be within specifications provided by the manufacturer. A general specification for the ring end gap is 0.004 in. (0.1 mm) for every 1 in. (25 mm) of cylinder diameter.

FIGURE 8–32 Using an outside micrometer to measure the diameter of the piston pin.2

If the ring gap does not meet specifications, check the ring set to ensure that the correct set is being used. All rings in the set should be checked as indicated on the previous page.

8.   Carefully read the instructions included with the packaged piston rings before attempting to install them.

> NOTE   Installation of piston rings on the piston is a very important step and allows no room for error. Follow instructions to the letter in this critical area.

9.   The following instructions are general but are very similar to the instructions included with most ring sets.
   a. With the piston and rod assembly clamped in a soft-jaw vise, place the oil ring expander (if used) (Figure 8–35) in the piston groove where the oil ring will be installed.

> CAUTION   On two-piece oil rings, do not allow the expander (a spring device that fits under the ring, holding it out against the cylinder wall) ends to overlap. This could cause broken rings or excessive oil consumption during or after installation!

> NOTE   Since the oil control ring, or rings, is the ring nearest the bottom of the piston, it should be installed first. If the top rings were installed first, it would be impossible to install the lower rings unless they were installed from the bottom up. Although this can be done, most technicians pre-

(a)   5362

(b)   5748

FIGURE 8–33 (a) Installing a solid piston pin retainer into a two-stroke-cycle DDC engine using a special installer tool. (b) Using a hand-operated vacuum pump to check that the solid piston pin retainer is properly seated and does not leak. (Courtesy of Detroit Diesel Corporation.)

fer to install the rings on the piston starting with the lowest ring and working upward, installing the top ring last.

   b. Select the oil ring that fits into the lowest groove on the piston and carefully inspect it to

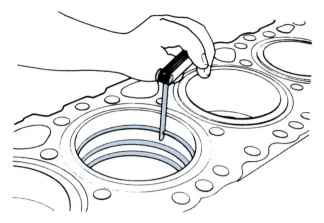

FIGURE 8–34 *Measuring the piston ring end gap with a feeler gauge after installing the rings into the cylinder and squaring them up with a piston inserted upside down into the cylinder bore. (Courtesy of Detroit Diesel Corporation.)*

the top. Square or rectangular shaped rings may not have any taper or mark and can be installed either way.

c. Place the ring in a ring installation tool (see Figure 8–22). Expand the ring so that it will slide down over the piston easily and install it over the ring expander. Place the ring end gap at a 90° angle from the expander butt joint.

CAUTION Do not expand the ring any more than is absolutely needed to slide it over the piston, as this may permanently warp, damage, or break the ring.

---

d. After installation of the oil ring, select and install the ring immediately above it, paying close attention to the top mark.

e. Continue installing the remaining rings, using the installation instructions as a reference, until all rings are installed.

determine which side goes up. This can be easily determined if the ring is marked with a dot or "top" (Figure 8–36). If the ring is not marked, refer to the installation instructions. Some oil rings may be tapered, with the taper installed to

This completes assembly of the piston, rings, and rod assembly. The assembly is now ready to be installed in the engine (see the following section). If assembly is

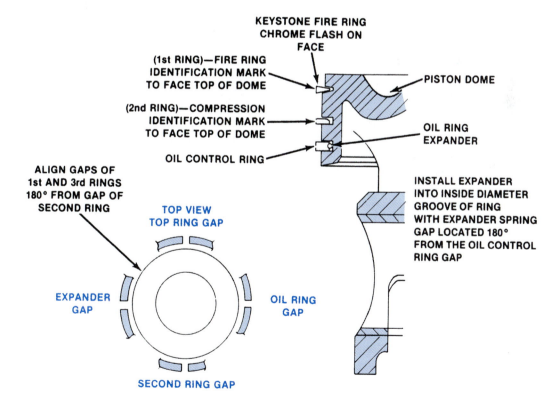

FIGURE 8–35 *Specific example of the piston rings placement and ring identification for a series 50 or 60 DDC engine. (Courtesy of Detroit Diesel Corporation.)*

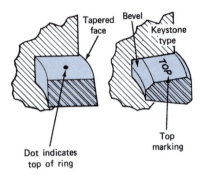

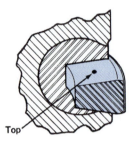

FIGURE 8–36 Always check both sides of the piston ring for a dot or the word top indicating which way to install the ring on the piston.

FIGURE 8–37 One type of piston ring compressor tool which uses a sprung steel adjustable band to act as a clamp to fit different diameter pistons. (Courtesy of Kent-Moore Tool Division, SPX Corporation.)

FIGURE 8–38 Heavy-duty clamp piston ring compressor. (Courtesy of Kent-Moore Tool Division, SPX Corporation.)

not to be installed in the engine immediately, it should be placed in a rack or in some suitable place so that no damage to rings or piston will result.

Installing the Piston and Connecting Rod Assembly

Installation of the piston and rod assembly into the sleeve or cylinder bore requires a special tool called a ring compressor. The ring compressor is a device that fits around the piston and compresses the rings so that they may be inserted into the cylinder or sleeve without breakage or damage. Ring compressors are usually of the compression (Figure 8–37), clamp type (Figure 8–38), or tapered sleeve type (Figure 8–39).

A sleeve-type ring compressor resembles an engine sleeve but has a taper cut into one end. When the piston and rod assembly is inserted into the sleeve, the rings contact the taper and are compressed into position as the piston is pushed into the compressor. This type of ring compressor can be made for any engine by obtaining and machining a taper on one end of an old sleeve. This type of ring compressor is preferred by many technicians, since it is easier to install on the piston and eliminates the possibility of ring breakage during piston installation into the cylinder. The primary disadvantage is that it will work for only one engine or cylinder size, requiring the technician who works on many engines to have a ring compressor for each one.

After selection of a ring compressor, the piston and rod assembly may be installed in the following steps:

1. With the piston and rod assembly clamped in the vise, remove the rod bolts and rod cap from the connecting rod.

2. Determine what size rod bearing must be used from earlier measurement of the crankshaft rod journal with a micrometer. Select and insert the bearing top half into the connecting rod, paying particular attention to the bearing locating lug and the slot in the connecting rod (Figure 8–40).

CAUTION Make sure that a final check is made of the rod bearing insert to ensure that it is the correct size. Size markings are found on the back of the rod bearing insert. Standard-size bearings may or may not be marked indicating their size: 0.010 in., 0.020 in. (0.25 mm, 0.50 mm).

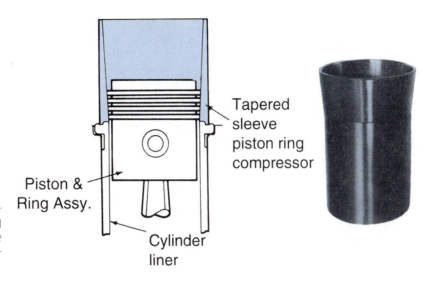

FIGURE 8–39 *Special machined taper sleeve type of piston ring compressor sized and available for a specific engine make/model. (Courtesy of Kent-Moore Tool Division, SPX Corporation.)*

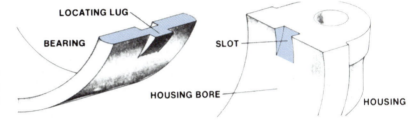

FIGURE 8–40 *Always align the shell bearing locating lug with the matching slot in the con-rod and cap. (Courtesy of Clevite Engine Parts, Dana Corporation.)*

3. Lubricate the rod bearing with engine oil or light grease.

4. Lubricate rings and pistons liberally with engine oil.

5. Position rings around piston so that the gaps do not line up. A common recommendation is to stagger ring gaps 90 to 180° apart around the piston (refer to Figure 8–35).

NOTE Positioning the rings in this manner will prevent excessive blowby during the initial startup that would result if all the ring gaps were in line.

6. If a clamp or band ring compressor is to be used, expand it and place on the piston (Figure 8–41).

7. If a tapered sleeve ring compressor is being used, the piston and rod assembly must be removed from the vise and inserted into the sleeve compressor (Figure 8–42).

8. After installation of the ring compressor on the piston and rod assembly, it can now be inserted into the cylinder sleeve or cylinder bore; the rod number should face the camshaft on six-cylinder engines and the outside of blocks on V8 engines. The rods are numbered to indicate which cylinder they fit into.

CAUTION Before inserting the piston and rod assembly in the cylinder bore, the crankshaft should be positioned so that the rod journal of the pistons being installed is in the bottom dead-center position.

NOTE Some engine manufacturers (Detroit Diesel and Cat 3176) recommend installing the piston and rod assembly into the sleeve before the sleeve is installed into the block (Figure 8–43).

9. Using a hammer handle, tap or push down on the piston, inserting it into the cylinder (Figure 8–41).

CAUTION When pushing the piston into the cylinder, make sure that the rod is lined up with the rod journal. Failure to do this may result in damage to the rod journal by the rod. If the rod bolts are in the rod, it is a good practice to put a plastic cap or piece of rubber hose on each bolt to protect the rod journal.

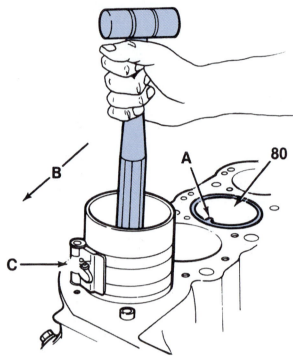

80. Piston
   A. "Front" Mark
   B. Front of Engine
   C. Piston Ring Compressor Tool   W-00508

FIGURE 8–41 *Use a thin sprung-steel adjustable band-clamp ring expander to compress the rings, then gently push the piston assembly into its bore using a wooden/plastic hammer handle until the piston is free of the tool. (Reprinted courtesy of Caterpillar, Inc.)*

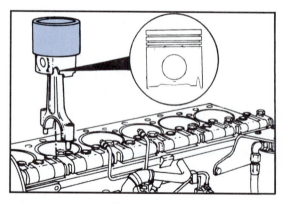

FIGURE 8–42 *Preparing to install the piston/rings already assembled in a special ring compressor into the cylinder liner bore. Ensure that any piston I.D. letters/numbers, and the numbered side of the con-rod, are facing the proper direction in the engine block. (Courtesy of Cummins Engine Company, Inc.)*

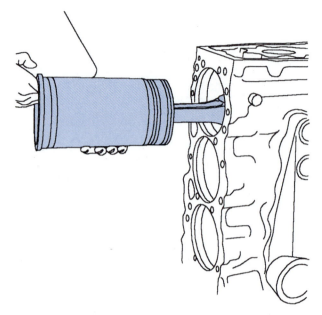

FIGURE 8–43 *Installation of a cylinder kit/pack as an assembly into the engine block bore. (Courtesy of Detroit Diesel Corporation.)*

10.   After the piston and rod assembly is in place with the rod and bearing firmly seated on the rod journal, the rod bearing clearance should be checked using Plastigage (Figure 7–34).

NOTE   Plastigage is thin plastic thread that can be broken into the correct length and placed on the rod journal or in the rod cap on the bearing. When the rod cap is installed and torqued, the plastic thread is flattened out to the clearance between the rod journal and rod bearing. The cap is then removed, and the width of the Plastigage compared to various widths imprinted on the package that contained the Plastigage. See the example in Chapter 7, Figure 7–34B. By this comparison the rod bearing clearance can be determined. Carefully clean the Plastigage from the rod journal and bearing.

11.   Lubricate the rod bearing with the lubricant recommended by the manufacturer. This can be clean engine oil, Lubriplate 105 or its equivalent. Install the rod cap, making sure that the number on the rod and cap match and are on the same side (Figure 8–44).

In some engines a unique number (**not** cylinder number) is stamped on the connecting rod and matching cap. See Figure 8–44B. When the rods and caps are installed in the engine, the numbers on the rods and

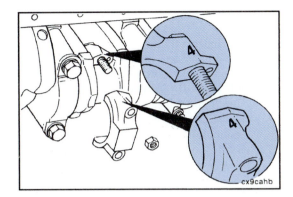

(a)

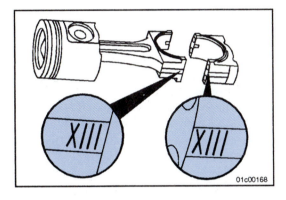

(b)

FIGURE 8–44   (a) Location of con-rod numbered or lettered I.D. marks. (b) Location of con-rod alpha characters. (Courtesy of Cummins Engine Company, Inc.)

caps **must** match and be installed on the same side of the engine.

CAUTION   The rod cap alpha characters must match the alpha characters on the connecting rod and must be installed with the characters aligned to prevent damage to the connecting rods and crankshaft.

---

12.   Torque the rod cap bolts to specifications and, if used, lock the lock plates. Then with a feeler gauge, check for the correct rod side clearance between the connecting rod and the crank journal flange or between both rods on a Vee engine configuration. *Turn the crankshaft after each rod and piston assembly has been installed to make sure that it moves freely.* If the crankshaft does not turn after torquing the rod cap, recheck the rod for alignment-bearing clearance and rod side clearance to determine the problem. Install all rods and rod caps in the same manner, as described. Install liner retainer clamps on top of the block to prevent possible liner movement when turning the crankshaft.

Recheck all rod torques and numbers, making sure that rods and pistons are in the correct cylinders and rod caps are matched to the correct rod. After this final check the engine is ready for further assembly.

SUMMARY

This chapter has covered the correct procedures for removing, checking, cleaning, and reassembling pistons, connecting rods, and piston rings. If you have any further questions concerning the piston and connecting rod assembly, consult the engine service manual or your instructor.

SELF-TEST QUESTIONS

1.   Describe the major purpose of a piston.
2.   A trunk-type piston is a
     a.   one-piece assembly
     b.   two-piece assembly
3.   Many heavy-duty high-speed engines in use today employ two-piece pistons. What are they called?
4.   Technician A says that a trunk-type piston exerts less side thrust on the piston rings and cylinder wall than does a two-piece piston design. Technician B says that the two-piece piston design accomplishes this much better. Which technician understands piston design better?
5.   List the advantages of a two-piece piston design over a single-piece design.
6.   The top of the piston is usually referred to as the
     a.   crown
     b.   skirt
     c.   slipper bearing
     d.   boss area
7.   Aluminum alloy pistons normally employ a Ni-resist insert at the top and sometimes the second ring belt area. Describe this material and state the reason for its use.
8.   Technician A states that when two-piece piston assemblies are used the crown is manufactured from a forged aluminum alloy to allow for greater expansion and better sealing, while the skirt is made from forged steel. Technician B says the reverse: The crown is steel and the skirt is aluminum alloy. Which technician is correct?
9.   True or False: Since aluminum weighs approximately one-third that of cast iron and steel, an aluminum piston would be one-third of the weight of an equivalent steel model.
10.   High-speed heavy-duty direct injection diesel engines normally employ pressurized under-piston lube oil cooling, according to technician A. Technician B says that this would result in unacceptable lube oil temperatures; therefore, an air intake system aftercooler is used

instead. Which technician knows basic engine design theory better?

11. The letters SCFR mean that a piston, in addition to being manufactured from aluminum alloy, is
    a. special chrome ferrous reinforced
    b. squeeze-cast fiber reinforced

12. The advantage of using SCFR in the manufacture of a piston is to
    a. improve fatigue strength
    b. provide better piston-to-liner clearance
    c. provide linger piston ring life
    d. improve piston scuffing characteristics

13. One of the coatings that is sometimes used on pearlitic malleable iron piston skirts to improve scuff resistance is
    a. tin
    b. solder
    c. chrome
    d. copper

14. One of the coatings sometimes used on aluminum alloy piston skirts to improve scuff resistance is
    a. graphite
    b. tin
    c. solder
    d. powdered cast iron

15. True or False: Two-piece pistons generally have a piston pin bearing that is referred to as a slipper bearing.

16. Current high-speed heavy-duty diesel engines tend to employ a piston crown that is shaped similar to a
    a. saucer
    b. Mexican hat (concave)
    c. bowl in crown

17. List the advantages of using the piston design selected in your answer for question 16.

18. Some heavy-duty high-speed diesel engines use a piston crown shape that is known as a *re-entrant chamber.* What are the advantages of this design?

19. Technician A says that the average operating temperature in the center of the piston crown of a heavy-duty high-speed diesel engine is in the range of 475 to 600°F (246 to 315°C). Technician B says that the temperature has to be higher than this and suggests that it is closer to 1000 to 1200°F (538 to 649°C). Which technician is closer to reality?

20. True or False: The thermal (heat) conductivity of steel is slower than that of aluminum; consequently, a higher cooling oil flow is required to prevent oil aging when a steel crown is used.

21. Piston pin retainers are generally of what type?

22. Technician A says that two-stroke-cycle DDC engines employ solid piston pin retainers because the oil control rings are located toward the base of the piston skirt. Technician B says the solid retainers are strictly to prevent the fully floating piston pin from striking the ports in the cylinder liner. Which technician knows theory better?

23. True or False: Pistons should always be identified as to cylinder number to ensure they will be replaced in the same position.

24. Technician A says that the best way to clean a piston of carbon at overhaul is to glass bead the complete assembly. Technician B disagrees, saying that this procedure would remove any protective coating from the piston skirt and should be avoided. Technician B says crushed walnut shells in a glass-bead-type machine are better for cleaning carbon from the piston ring belt area. Which technician is correct?

25. Aluminum alloy pistons employing fully floating piston pins should be preheated to facilitate piston pin hand insertion or removal, according to technician A. Technician B disagrees, saying that the pin should be pressed or hammered in or out. Which technician is correct?

26. True or False: The term *fire ring* in relation to a piston ring means that it is the top ring on the piston.

27. True or False: The purpose of placing the top ring very close to the piston crown on high-speed heavy-duty engines is to reduce the dead air space that exists with lower-positioned rings. This results in more effective combustion.

28. True or False: Piston rings should always be removed using a special piston ring expander.

29. Most high-speed heavy-duty diesel engines now employ rings shaped in a
    a. keystone design
    b. rectangular design
    c. square design
    d. bevel-faced design

30. The advantage of using the ring in your answer to question 29 is that it tends to minimize
    a. combustion gas blowby
    b. ring sticking
    c. pumping oil
    d. ring scuffing

31. The ring in your answer to question 29 generally has sides that are
    a. flat
    b. oval
    c. tapered
    d. convex

32. Name the two main piston ring clearances.

33. Piston ring wear groove gauges are generally used to check the following design of piston ring:
    a. square
    b. rectangular
    c. bevel faced
    d. keystone

34. An insufficient piston ring gap can result in
    a. ring breakage
    b. combustion blowby
    c. piston land damage
    d. scoring of the liner
    e. all of the above

35. True or False: Insufficient piston ring side clearance can result in ring sticking.

36. Technician A says that during piston ring installation, you must look for a dot, part number, the word *top*, or a

black phosphate coating to determine how to install the ring. Technician B says that the ring can be installed in any direction without any problems. Which technician is correct?

37. Technician A says that the purpose of an oil control ring is to prevent oil from being burned in the combustion chamber. Technician B says that it is designed to distribute oil across the face of the cylinder wall on the upstroke and to scrape it off on the downstroke. Which technician is correct?

38. List the causes that might lead to surface scuffing of the piston ring and cylinder liner.

39. Technician A says that piston rings must be staggered around the piston so that their gaps are not aligned. Technician B says that since the rings rotate during engine operation, it doesn't matter where you place the individual ring gaps. Which technician is better trained?

40. Technician A says that on some pistons the design of the crown makes it necessary that the piston be installed facing in only one direction. Technician B says that pistons can be installed in any position. Which technician is correct?

41. Technician A says that the cylinder liner must be installed into the block bore before the piston and rings can be installed. Technician B says that on many engines the piston and liner can be installed as a complete assembly. Which technician is correct?

42. What is the purpose of rifle-drilling some connecting rods?

43. True or False: Technician A says that all con-rods are balanced, so you should never mix the caps and rods on an engine. Technician B says that since all rods are balanced, it wouldn't make any difference. Who is correct?

44. True or False: Rod bolts or nuts should be replaced automatically at each major overhaul.

45. Dark spots in the bearing cap or saddle area of a con-rod are usually indications of
    a. bearing movement
    b. poor bearing contact
    c. insufficient bearing-to-journal clearance
    d. too much bearing-to-journal clearance

46. Shiny areas at the parting line of the con-rod cap to rod are indicative of
    a. cap movement
    b. bearing movement
    c. insufficient bearing clearance
    d. too much bearing clearance

47. If a con-rod is honed at its crank journal end, does this have any effect on the compression ratio in that cylinder?

48. List the procedure(s) that can be used at the time of overhaul to determine if a con-rod is twisted or bent.

49. One of the more common conditions that leads to bending of a con-rod is
    a. a hydrostatic lock (water in the cylinder)
    b. overspeeding of the engine
    c. uneven cylinder balance
    d. trapped fuel or oil in the cylinder

50. What might cause the condition to the answer you chose in question 49?

51. Technician A says that the top and bottom bearings of the con-rod are identical. Not so, says technician B, and if the wrong bearing is used, the oil hole through the rifle-drilled con-rod can be blocked. Is there any validity in technician B's statement of concern?

52. True or False: Con-rod bearings can be identified in regard to size and position by etched or stamped numbers on the backside.

53. What gauge should you use to check con-rod bearing clearances?

54. True or False: When installing con-rods and pistons into an engine cylinder, the numbered sides of the rod and cap should always face one another.

55. Technician A says that once a con-rod has been installed over the crankshaft journal and its bolts have been torqued to spec, you should always check the rod side clearance with a feeler gauge. Technician B says that as long as the engine crankshaft can be rotated manually, this check is not necessary. Which technician is correct?

56. Technician A says that the numbers on the con-rod of an inline engine are usually designed to face a specific side of the engine block, such as the camshaft or oil cooler side. Technician B says the way the numbers face makes no difference. Which technician is correct, and why?

57. In engines using two-piece crosshead or articulated pistons, the con-rod has an open saddle at the piston pin end. How are the piston and pin attached to the rod?

58. Technician A says that if the crankshaft con-rod journals are in need of regrinding to a smaller diameter, the main bearing journals also have to be reground to the same size. Not so says technician B; only the rod journals need to be reground. Which technician is correct?

9 The Cylinder Head and Components

Overview

This chapter will provide you with details of the purpose and function of the cylinder head assembly. Various designs are discussed as are the service repair tasks required to ensure successful performance of the engine intake and exhaust systems. In addition, we analyze specialized equipment needed to perform these various service and repair functions. The individual components of the cylinder head and the necessary service/repair tasks are also important topics.

ASE CERTIFICATION

ASE offers two major areas in which the service technician can become certified in cylinder head diagnosis, service, and repair. First, in the ASE medium/heavy truck test diesel engines (test T2) area, a technician must have the knowledge and expertise to successfully answer five questions in the T2, part B content area. The following chart lists the areas of expertise required in the cylinder head and valve train diagnosis and repair content.

B. Cylinder Head and Valve Train Diagnosis and Repair (5 ASE questions)

1. Remove, inspect, disassemble, and clean cylinder head assembly(s).
2. Inspect threaded holes, studs, and bolts for serviceability; service/replace as needed.
3. Measure cylinder head deck-to-deck thickness, and check mating surfaces for warpage and surface finish; inspect for cracks/damage; check condition of passages; inspect core, gallery, and plugs; service as needed.
4. Test cylinder head for leakage using approved methods; service as needed.
5. Inspect valves, guides, seats, springs, retainers, rotators, locks, and seals; determine serviceability and needed repairs.
6. Inspect and replace injector sleeves and seals; measure injector tip or nozzle protrusion where specified by manufacturer.
7. Inspect, clean, and/or replace precombustion chambers where specified by manufacturer; determine needed repairs.
8. Inspect and/or replace valve bridges (cross-heads) and guides; adjust bridges (crossheads).
9. Clean components; reassemble, check, and install cylinder head assembly as specified by the manufacturer.
10. Inspect pushrods, rocker arms, rocker arm shafts, electronic wiring harness, and brackets for wear, bending, cracks, looseness, and blocked oil passages; repair/replace as needed.
11. Inspect and adjust/replace cam followers.
12. Adjust valve clearance(s).
13. Inspect, measure, and replace/reinstall overhead camshaft and bearings; measure and adjust endplay and backlash.

ASE Engine Machinist Tests

ASE also allows a technician to become certified as a cylinder head specialist by challenging the engine machinist test M1. The following chart lists the content area for this specialty, and the number of questions related to the test.

Test Specifications Cylinder Head Specialist (Test M1)

Content area	Questions in test	Percentage of test
A. Cylinder head disassembly and cleaning	11	20%
B. Cylinder head crack repair	5	9%
C. Cylinder head inspection and machining	29	53%
D. Cylinder head assembly	10	18%
Total	**55***	**100%**

ASE Task List—Cylinder Head Specialist

To successfully challenge the ASE M1 certification test, the technician must demonstrate knowledge and expertise in the following skill tasks list areas.

Task List Cylinder Head Specialist (Test M1)

A. Cylinder Head Disassembly and Cleaning (11 ASE questions)

1. Inspect cylinder head for damage and missing related components.
2. Remove sensors, external components, studs, and identification tags as needed; identify locations.
3. Remove, clean, and inspect housings and covers.
4. Remove and inspect precombustion chambers, nozzle adaptors, and injector assemblies as needed.
5. Remove core plugs; identify locations.
6. Remove gallery plugs and restrictors, relief valves, fittings, and adaptors; identify locations.
7. Remove, disassemble, and inspect valve train components; identify locations.
8. Inspect and remove timing and retaining components.
9. Remove and inspect oil pump and distributor drive assemblies as needed.
10. Check all camshaft bearing caps for correct position and numbering; mark in accordance with manufacturer's recommended procedures.
11. Remove and inspect camshaft carriers, camshaft bearing caps, and camshaft.
12. Remove and inspect camshaft bearings; identify locations.
13. Remove and inspect valve springs, rotators, retainers, locks, seals, shims, and seats; identify locations.
14. Measure and record installed valve stem height and/or valve protrusion/ recession; measure lash adjustment shims.
15. Remove and inspect valves; identify locations.
16. Clean cylinder head and related components.
17. Verify engine make and model.

B. Cylinder Head Crack Repair (5 ASE questions)

1. Evaluate head for repair.
2. Determine extent of crack.
3. Determine crack repair method by location of the crack; repair using accepted industry procedures.

C. Cylinder Head Inspection and Machining (29 ASE questions)

1. Detail cylinder head; inspect mating surfaces.
2. Inspect cylinder head for cracks.
3. Inspect cylinder head for structural integrity and porosity; repair as needed.
4. Inspect cylinder head for warpage, gasket surface finish, and thickness; record measurements and repair according to industry-accepted procedures.
5. Inspect threaded holes and fasteners; repair or replace as needed.
6. Measure valve guide wear; repair as needed.
7. Inspect valve seat condition; repair as needed.
8. Inspect injector area, measure injector tip; protrusion/recession; repair as needed. (Applies to diesel cylinder heads only.)
9. Inspect precombustion chamber and nozzle adaptor fit and location; repair as needed. (Applies to diesel cylinder heads only.)
10. Inspect fire ring grooves; repair as needed. (Applies to diesel cylinder heads only.)
11. Inspect and measure lifter (lash adjuster, camshaft follower) bores; repair as needed.
12. Inspect and measure valves; repair or replace as needed.
13. Measure valve stem installed height and/or valve protrusion/recession; adjust or repair as needed.

14. Inspect, measure, and test valve springs; replace as needed.
15. Inspect valve spring retainers, rotators, and locks; replace as needed.
16. Inspect other valve train components (rocker arms, cam followers, camshafts, studs, etc.); repair or replace as needed.
17. Inspect and measure camshaft bores; repair as needed.
18. Perform industry-recommended updates as appropriate.

D. Cylinder Head Assembly (10 ASE questions)
1. Clean cylinder head and related parts.
2. Install camshaft bearings, if required; check camshaft fit.
3. Lay out all parts for assembly.
4. Install valves and seals.
5. Check valves for seating.
6. Install camshaft and related parts.
7. Check valve lash where appropriate; adjust if required.
8. Align and install precombustion chambers; evaluate height.
9. Pressure-test cylinder head assembly as required.
10. Install gallery plugs and restrictors, relief valves, fittings, and adaptors in correct locations.

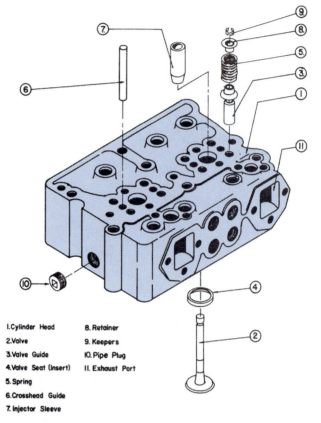

1. Cylinder Head
2. Valve
3. Valve Guide
4. Valve Seat (Insert)
5. Spring
6. Crosshead Guide
7. Injector Sleeve
8. Retainer
9. Keepers
10. Pipe Plug
11. Exhaust Port

FIGURE 9–1 Cylinder head and components designed to cover two cylinders of an N14 (855 in³) six-cylinder engine. (Courtesy of Cummins Engine Company, Inc.)

CYLINDER HEAD STRUCTURE AND FUNCTION

Diesel engine cylinder heads are similar in structure to the one shown in Figure 9–1. The cylinder head's main function is to provide a head or cap to the engine cylinder. Cylinder heads may be found in different configurations depending on the number of cylinders they cover. Different configurations are designed to deal with such factors as weight, warpage, and ease of handling. It is common to find cylinder heads that are designed for one, two, three, four, and six cylinders.

The diesel engine cylinder head shown in Figure 9–1 is designed to cover two cylinders, and is used with an in-block camshaft, roller lifters, and pushrods to actuate the rocker arms and to open and close the valves. Some engines employ an overhead camshaft(s) supported in the cylinder head. Overhead camshafts eliminate the necessity for pushrods and provide a more positive opening and closing of the valves as well as direct activation of the injector follower. In addition, engine compression brake activation is a simpler task. The cylinder head illustrated in Figure 9–2 is for a dual overhead camshaft Cummins 15 L (912 in³) displacement ISX/Signature electronically controlled engine. The diagram shows the various cylinder head components required for its successful function and operation. Other electronically controlled engines currently using single overhead camshafts supported in the cylinder head include Detroit Diesel's series 50 and 60 models (the first engine OEM to adopt this design on its heavy-duty high-speed electronic engines), Caterpillar's 3406E, and Volvo's six-cylinder truck engine.

NOTE In this chapter we will not deal with overhead camshafts. Refer to Chapter 10 for details on camshafts, followers, pushrods, and rocker arms.

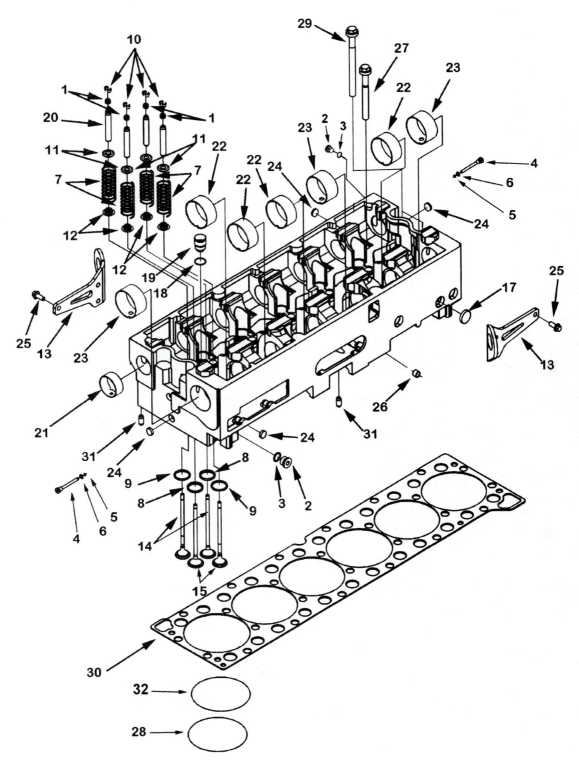

FIGURE 9–2 One-piece dual overhead camshaft design cylinder head assembly used on the six-cylinder Cummins Signature and ISX electronic engine models. (Courtesy of Cummins Engine Company, Inc.)

Ref No.	Part Number	Part Name	Req	Remarks
		CYLINDER HEAD		
		OPTION PP2628		
		OPTION PP2629		
		OPTION PP2630		
	4026542	Head, Cylinder		
1	3606766	Seal, Valve Stem	24	
2	3678611	Plug, Threaded	3	
3	3678606	Seal, O Ring	1	
4	3679354	Plug, Threaded	6	
5	3678603	Seal, O Ring	1	
6	3679122	Seal, O Ring	1	
7	3679551	Spring, Valve	24	
8	3679537	Insert, Valve	12	
9	3681071	Insert, Valve	12	
10	3680883	Collet, Valve	48	
11	3680884	Retainer, Valve Spring	24	
12	3680318	Guide, Valve Spring	24	
13	3680656	Bracket, Lifting	2	
14	3680759	Valve, Exhaust	12	
15	3680760	Valve, Intake	12	
16	(4026541)	Head, Cylinder	1	
17	3015865	Plug, Expansion	7	
18	3678536	Seal, Rectangular Ring	6	
19	3412352	Sleeve, Injector	6	
20	3680867	Guide, Valve Stem	24	
21	4026423	Bushing	7	
22	3680580	Bushing	4	
23	3680581	Bushing	3	
24	3813247	Plug, Expansion	21	
25	3910495	Screw, Hex Flange Head Cap	6	M12 X 1.75 X 30.
26	3911678	Dowel, Ring	2	
27	3678506	Screw, Hex Flange Head Cap	22	
28	3678751	Seal, Combustion	6	
29	3678804	Screw, Hex Flange Head Cap	4	
30	3412424	Gasket, Cylinder Head	1	
31	3901846	Dowel, Pin	2	
32	3412426	Seal, Combustion	6	

FIGURE 9–2   (continued).

The diesel cylinder head consists of several components, of which their major functions are as follows:

1. A single-piece casting that may cover one or more cylinders

2. Individual valve guides pressed into the head casting that function to guide and support the valve stem during engine operation as they open and close.

3. Intake and exhaust ports cast within the cylinder head to permit the smooth flow of air and exhaust gases to and from the head through both the intake and exhaust valves.

4. Cast and machined bores in the cylinder head to support/locate the injection nozzle or unit injectors. Some injection nozzle bodies are threaded into the cylinder head. Unit injectors are typically located in either a copper or stainless steel tube in the head. These tubes are normally surrounded by engine coolant to control the operating temperature of the injector assembly.

5. Cast passages to permit the circulation of pressurized coolant from the cylinder block into and through the cylinder head. Some heads employ pressed-in copper water directional nozzles to direct increased coolant flow to and around the casting area of the various valve support locations. Expansion plugs at strategic coolant passages are used for seal-

ing. These can be removed at overhaul when cleaning the coolant passages (descaling). Some one-piece heads contain one or more coolant thermostats and housings.

6. Individual special steel alloy valve seat inserts that the valve face sits on

7. With indirect-injection-type engines, individual precombustion chambers and glow plug access holes

8. Machined bolt holes to allow head-to-block retention

9. Rocker arm support pedestals and threaded holes

10. Fuel and oil passages cast within the head and sealed with threaded plugs where necessary.

11. On electronic engines, various sensors installed to or onto the cylinder head

12. Machined mounting surfaces and threaded passages to allow retention of the intake and exhaust manifolds

In modern diesel engines, cylinder head service must be an important part of major engine overhaul. Cylinder head service is sometimes performed hastily and with little consideration of the important functions the cylinder head must perform. Along with the cylinder and rings, the cylinder head aids in the development of compression and oil control. It is recommended then that the cylinder head service be performed with care and accuracy to provide long hours of trouble-free engine operation. If the cylinder head is being repaired, if a routine major overhaul is being done, or if the head has experienced a premature valve failure, all the following service recommendations should be performed.

SERVICE RECOMMENDATIONS

Disassembling the Cylinder Head

Assume that the cylinder head or heads have been removed from the engine and are ready to be disassembled and reconditioned. If not, refer to Chapter 5 on engine disassembly. Before disassembly of cylinder head, all loose grease and dirt should be removed by using either a steam cleaner or high-pressure washer.

CAUTION All injectors or injection nozzles should be removed before the head is steamed or washed.

Repair or Replacement of Cylinder Head

Prior to attempting to perform major repairs of the cylinder head and/or its components such as the valves, valve guides, roller followers, and injector tubes, it is wise to perform a close visual inspection to determine if the head is in fact reusable. Any visible cracks will generally render the head unfit for further use. In addition to the ASE cylinder head specialist tasks listed earlier in this chapter, review the flowchart shown in Figure 9–3 and use it as a guide to determine whether to reuse the cylinder head. Greater details of the individual flowchart highlights are described in the following sequences.

NOTE There are some situations when small cracks in the cylinder head are not damaging or detrimental to the operation of the engine. Each engine design may have some peculiarity in this regard. If the technician does not have experience with a particular model of cylinder head, it must be taken to a shop or repair station that has been rebuilding or servicing cylinder heads of that type. Figure 9–4 shows a cracked cylinder head that is no longer usable.

Cracked cylinder heads are often repaired by welding or pinning, and in many cases they have proven to be dependable. A firm that has considerable experience should be selected if the cylinder head is to be repaired, since a rebuilt head that does not stand up in service may ruin the rest of the engine by allowing coolant to leak into the engine lube oil. If a cracked head is discovered during a major rebuild, the head should be replaced with a new one. The increased cost will be offset in the long run by increased engine life and dependability. If there is some question about rebuilding or replacing a cylinder head, check with your instructor.

The valve springs, keepers, and retainer should be removed with a valve spring compressor. Many types of compressors can be used, but the most common one in the field is the C-clamp type (Figure 9–5).

1. With the valve spring compressor in the open position, place it on the valve and valve spring.

2. Adjust the spring end jaws with the adjusting screw so that the jaws clamp snugly on the valve spring retainer.

3. Compress the spring by closing the valve spring compressor.

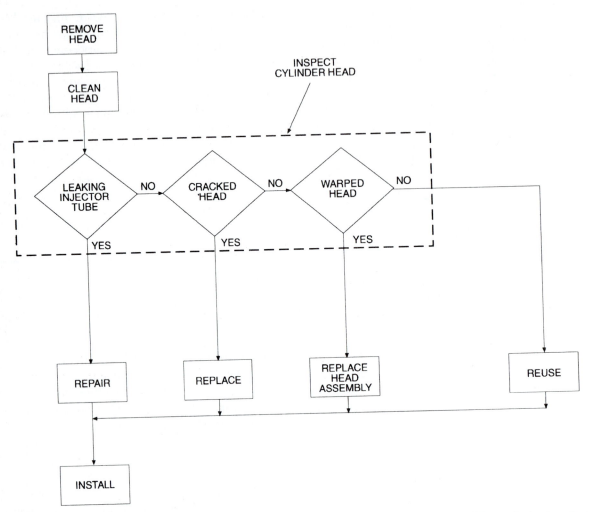

FIGURE 9–3   Diagnostic flowchart used to determine either the repair or replacement of the cylinder head assembly. (Courtesy of Detroit Diesel Corporation.)

NOTE   It may be impossible to break the retainer loose from the retaining clips and compress the spring with the force exerted by the valve spring compressor. A slight tap with a hammer on the retainer while attempting to compress the spring will aid in loosening the retainer.

4.   When the valve spring retainer is loosened, compress the spring far enough to remove keepers and retainer.

5.   Loosen the compressor and remove the spring and valve from the cylinder head.

6.   Visually inspect the valves and valve seats for signs of damage and wear.

7.   Remove any other part or parts from the cylinder head, such as water plates, thermostat housings, and brackets.

Precombustion Chamber Inspection

Prechambers require some special attention when the engine is being serviced, since they are a part of the cylinder head. Many of them are fitted into the water jacket and have O-rings and copper gaskets that must be replaced whenever the chamber is removed. Special tools are required to remove and/or replace most prechambers. Check your service manual or ask your instructor for the proper procedures.

Cleaning the Cylinder Head

Always use proper safety goggles and protective clothing when cleaning and using compressed air to blow been removed, further cleaning may be necessary. If, however, the cylinder head is being removed, disassembled, and overhauled (valves, seats, and injector tubes, etc.) it is generally advisable to descale the coolant passages in the head by submerging the head in a hot solvent, acid, or alkaline solution as shown in Figure 9–6A. Prior to doing this however, you should scrape the old head gasket from the head machined deck surface. Be careful not to scratch or nick this surface. Use a Scotch-Brite 7448 pad and diesel fuel or solvent as shown in Figure 9–6B for this purpose. Clean the exhaust and intake manifold gasket surfaces in the same manner. Clean carbon deposits from the valve pockets with a high quality steel wire wheel installed in a drill or a die grinder. Clean the head capscrews using a petroleum-based solvent in conjunction with a wire brush, a soft wire wheel, or use a non-abrasive bead blast to remove deposits from the shank and the threads. Thoroughly clean the capscrews in solvent after using a bead blaster.

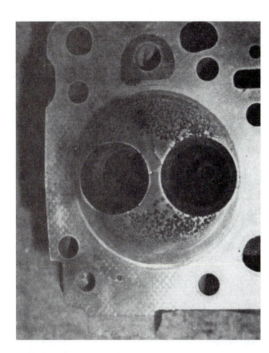

FIGURE 9–4 View of a cracked cylinder head which also shows the effects of water that has been in the combustion chamber.

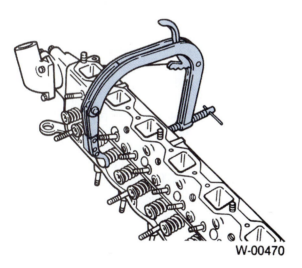

FIGURE 9–5 Compressing the individual valve retainer springs by using a large, adjustable C-clamp tool for either spring/valve removal or installation.

dry components. Two general methods can be followed to clean the cylinder head. If the head is being removed to replace a leaking head gasket, or to access and replace a cylinder kit (piston, rings, liner, con-rod), and the head is not to be disassembled, then steam cleaning of the external surfaces of the head and rocker cover(s) before removal is common. Once the head has

(a)

(b)

FIGURE 9–6 (a) Cleaning the cylinder head in a tank of hot soapy water, solvent, acid or alkaline solution. (b) Scraping old gasket material from the cylinder head and engine block; use a Scotch-Brite 7448 pad with solvent and diesel fuel for further cleaning. (Courtesy of Cummins Engine Company, Inc.)

Also keep in mind that the cylinder block deck should be thoroughly cleaned. Plug or cover all of the coolant and oil passages in the block deck using suitable plastic plugs. Refer to Figure 9–6A and use a gasket scraper to clean the block deck particularly if the head gasket is stuck to the deck as shown. Also use a Scotch-Brite 7448 pad and solvent to remove residual gasket material from the deck surface.

Testing and Checking the Cylinder Head for Cracks

At this time the cylinder head must be checked for cracks that may not have been detected during visual inspection. Cylinder head cracks can be caused by several factors: improper torque sequence used in securing head to block during assembly, difference in cylinder sleeve height or protrusion, or overheating.

Overheating is a primary cause of cylinder head cracks that are usually found in the combustion chamber between the valves or between a valve and an injector or nozzle. A buildup of scale from the cooling system of 1/16 in. has the insulating effect equal to 4 in. of cast iron. Therefore, if a cylinder head shows signs of cracking, it will be necessary to inspect and service the cooling system to prevent a recurrence. The three most common methods available to perform this check are described next.

Electromagnetic Crack Detector

An electromagnetic crack detector is a U-shaped device that is set on the surface of the cylinder head and energized with an electrical power source (Figure 9–7). Metal filings are sprinkled around the detector and, if the head has a crack, the crack will attract the metal filings, making the crack visible.

Pressure Testing

Plates or plugs to cover all water inlets and outlets must be available to pressure test a cylinder head. After plates have been bolted on, connect air pressure to the head with appropriate fittings and immerse in a tank of water. Any cracks will be pinpointed by the air bubbles escaping from them. Identify the source of the bubbles to make sure they are not coming from the plates or the plugs being used to seal the head. Particular attention must be given to the area around the valve seats and injector sleeves. Mark the leaking sleeves for replacement.

The pressure checking method is widely used since it is fairly easy to perform and is very effective not only in determining if a crack(s) exists but also if there are coolant leaks at the injector sleeves. Different heads require special blank-off plates and gaskets, although many service technicians employ sheet rubber or neo-

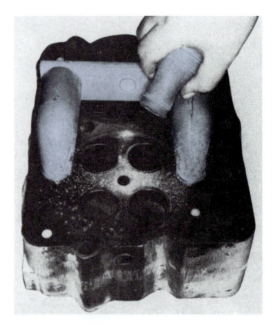

FIGURE 9–7 One method used to check a cylinder head for cracks employs an electromagnetic tester. (Courtesy of Cummins Engine Company, Inc.)

prene gaskets and steel plates to seal off the various coolant passages (Figure 9–8A). One of the blank-off plates must be drilled and tapped to accept a compressed air fitting, such as at the sealing plate bolted in place over the thermostat housing cover opening with a quick-couple connector for an air hose attachment.

Figure 9–8b illustrates another pressure test example where two metal test strips and gaskets are assembled to the cylinder head. The test strips are bolted to the head using the cylinder head bolts and nuts. If the cylinder head has been descaled, install all of the re-

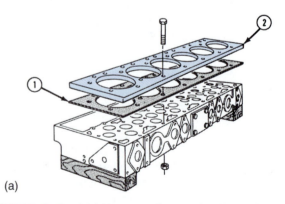

(a)

FIGURE 9–8 (a) Using a sealing gasket (1) and a thick steel plate (2) bolted to the underside of an L10 cylinder head in preparation for pressure testing. (Courtesy of Cummins Engine Company, Inc.)

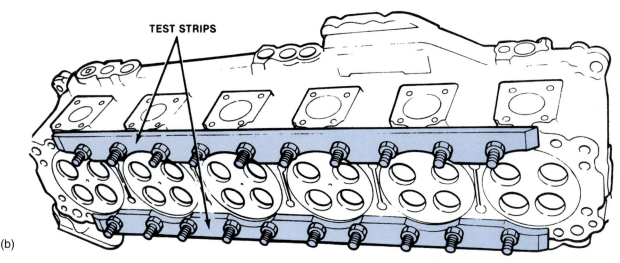

TEST STRIPS

(b)

FIGURE 9–8 (continued). (b) Steel test plates and sealing gaskets bolted to the underside of a DDC series 60 cylinder head in preparation for a pressure test to determine if leaks or cracks exist. (Courtesy of Detroit Diesel Corporation.)

moved plugs. If new plugs are used, they are usually precoated with a sealer. If the old plugs are being reused, coat the plugs with Loctite, pipe sealant, or Teflon tape and torque them to the spec listed in the service manual. If new cup plugs or frost plugs are used, coat them with a good grade of nonhardening sealant such as Loctite 620 or equivalent. Similarly, if injector sleeves (tubes) have been removed, new ones have to be installed prior to the pressure check.

Minor variations will exist between engines and models, so follow these basic steps in the pressure check method:

1. Install the coolant passage blank-off plates along with a compressed air fitting into a coolant passage.

2. Install dummy injectors into position in each injector bore sleeve (tube). If dummy injectors are not readily available, use old scrap ones torqued into place. If an injector sleeve holding tool kit similar to the one illustrated in Figure 9–9a for a Cummins L10 engine model is available, install and tighten these components in place for each cylinder as shown.

3. Use one of these two methods to check the cylinder head.

   a. Submerge the head in a tank of preheated water usually at a temperature of 180 to 190°F (82 to 93°C). Apply the recommended air pressure to the coolant water jacket for at least 20 minutes (Figure 9–9b).

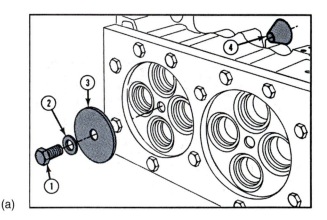

(a)

(b)

FIGURE 9–9 (a) Installation of special injector retaining sleeve tooling to an L10 engine model cylinder head prior to pressure checking: 1, capscrew; 2, flat washer; 3, ST-1179-4 anvil; 4, ST-1179-2 mandrel. (b) L10 cylinder head submerged in a tank of hot water with a fitting attached to a compressed-air line supply; signs of air bubbles indicate a cracked head, assuming that no leaks are evident at the sealing plates or gaskets. (Courtesy of Cummins Engine Company, Inc.)

b. If a tank is not available, fill the coolant jackets with a mixture of antifreeze and water; bolt the blank-off plates into position; apply the recommended regulated air pressure to the air fitting and leave it under pressure for 1 to 2 hours to allow the antifreeze mixture to penetrate any cracks.

NOTE   The air pressure applied to the cylinder head will vary depending on the type of injector and sleeve used. On replaceable sleeves (tubes) that are surrounded by coolant, the recommended air pressure is between 30 and 40 psi (207 to 276 kPa). However, some designs of cylinder heads suggest air test pressure of between 80 and 100 psi (552 to 690 kPa). *Always* closely check the engine manufacturer's service literature to ensure that you do not exceed the recommended pressure.

---

4.   Air bubbles appearing when the head is submerged in a tank of heated water are indicative of cracks (Figure 9–9b). Closely inspect the area to ensure that any leak is not from one of the gaskets and blank-off plates. If so, the head may be distorted and require remachining.

5.   Note any signs of leakage of antifreeze mixture which would indicate a crack in the cylinder head.

Dye Penetrant

Dye penetrant is a crack-detecting method that requires no special equipment with the exception of a can of spray-type penetrant and a can of spray developer. When using the dye penetrant, spray the area to be checked and wipe off or remove all excess dye. Spray on the developer. It will draw the dye penetrant from the crack, making it visible.

Of the three types of crack detection discussed here, the electromagnetic and dye penetrant would be used in areas where they can be seen. The pressure testing method should be used where there is a possibility of a crack in an area that cannot be seen, such as valve ports, combustion chambers, and all other areas not visible.

Although cylinder heads can be repaired by welding, and a number of specialty shops offer this service, most engine manufacturers suggest that all cracked heads be replaced.

Testing the Cylinder Head for Warpage

Individual cylinder heads used to cover only one or two cylinders are fairly short in overall length, therefore they can be checked for warpage with a steel straightedge and a feeler gauge in a free-state (nonbolted condition). Longer cylinder heads such as those used to cover six-cylinder engines may indicate longi-

tudinal warpage after they are unbolted from the engine block. Unless the Service manual specifies a head holding fixture should be used, check the head for warpage in its free-state, and use the published longitudinal and transverse warpage measurements listed in the manual as your guide. Remachine/plane the head firedeck surface to return it to serviceable condition. Make sure that the minimum head thickness is still within published specs after machining.

If the Service Manual specifies that a head holding fixture should be used, follow the process shown in Figure 9–10A which shows a six-cylinder head from a DDC Series 60 engine clamped to a special fixture to 'normalize-and-clamp' the head to from its locating surfaces (datums). If the head during this test with a straightedge and feeler gauge checks within warpage specs, it should be okay. If however, it is machined, check it for straightness as shown in Figure 9–10B of this diagram. Once it is removed from the holding fixture, the head will resume its original shape until it is once again bolted to the engine block and torqued to the appropriate specs in sequence.

Checking and/or Replacing the Valve Guide

After the cylinder head has been checked or resurfaced and is considered usable, the valve guides should be checked for wear as follows: Check the guide inside diameter with a snap, ball, or dial gauge in three different locations throughout the length of the guide (Figure 9–11).

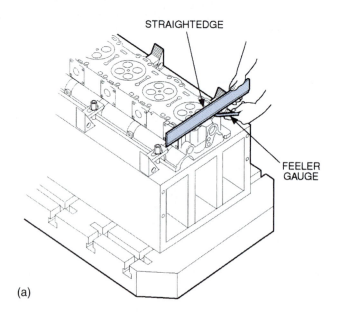

(a)

FIGURE 9–10 (a) Checking a cylinder head for warpage by using a feeler gauge and a straightedge. (Courtesy of Detroit Diesel Corporation.)

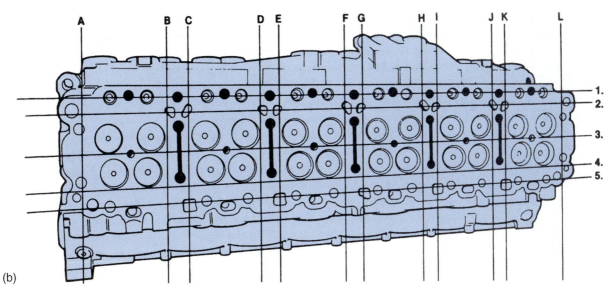

(b)

FIGURE 9–10 (continued). (b) Checks should be made at the points indicated in the illustration. (Courtesy of Detroit Diesel Corporation.)

Small Hole Gages

Extra long for gaging deep and shallow holes, slots and similar work.

J 26900-14
Set of 4 Small Hole Gages

- Gaging surface is a full-round with a flat bottom; permits use in smallest of shallow holes, slots and grooves, etc.
- Knurled knob at end of handle is used for size adjustment. Hole size is obtained by measuring over the contact points with a micrometer.
- Gauging surface is fully hardened to insure long tool life.
- Supplied 4 gages in a fitted case.

Range		Overall Length	Probe Depth (L)
English	Metric		
.125" - .200"	(3-5MM)	3 5/8"	.880:
.200" - .300"	(5-7.5MM)	3 7/8"	1.200"
.300" - .400"	(7.5-10MM)	4"	1.600"
.400" - .500"	(10-13MM)	4 1/4"	1.600

(a)

FIGURE 9–11 (a) Small hole gauges have a split ball at one end that can be expanded by turning the upper knurled part of the handle. These gauges are typically used to measure both intake and exhaust valve guides for wear. The ball end dimension is then checked by using an outside micrometer. (Courtesy of Kent-Moore Tool Division, SPX Corporation.)

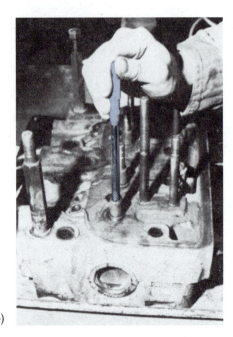

(b)

FIGURE 9–11 *(continued). (b) Inserting a small hole (ball) gauge into a valve guide. Adjust for a slight drag as you move it up and down. Remove the gauge and measure the diameter with an outside micrometer.*

NOTE   Experienced technicians can usually determine if the valve guide is worn excessively by inserting a new or unworn valve into the guide within approximately 1/4 in. (7 mm) of the cylinder head or valve seat and moving it from side to side. The method of measurement used will be determined by the technician's experience and the degree of accuracy desired.

SPECIAL NOTE   If you suspect excessive valve guide wear, but want to confirm this before removing the cylinder head, follow these steps: Remove the rocker cover(s), rotate the engine to TDC on one cylinder at a time, depress the valve spring, and remove the valve locks (keepers) and spring. Refer to Figure 9–12 and place a dial indicator tip against the valve stem. Rotate and rock the valve to determine the stem-to-guide wear and compare it with the service manual specifications.

With the cylinder head removed and disassembled, use a small valve guide bore cleaning brush of nylon or wire construction attached to a drill motor to remove all gum, varnish, or carbon deposits. Then carefully inspect the guide for signs of cracks, chip-

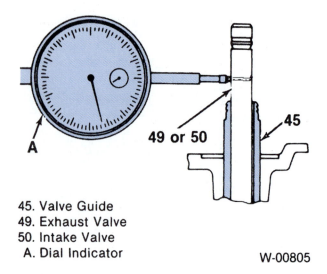

45. Valve Guide
49. Exhaust Valve
50. Intake Valve
A. Dial Indicator

W-00805

FIGURE 9–12   *An alternate method of checking valve stem-to-guide clearance with the cylinder head still bolted to the engine block is to place a dial indicator as illustrated against the valve stem while rocking the valve back and forth. (Reprinted courtesy of Caterpillar, Inc.).*

ping, scoring, or excessive wear. Use a small hole (ball) adjustable gauge (see Figure 9–11B) within the guide bore and adjust the gauge to produce a slight drag; then remove the gauge, check it with an outside micrometer, and compare the dimension with the service manual specs. Check the guide diameter in three places (top, middle, and bottom) and the measurements at 90° to one another. Check the diameter of the valve stem with an outside micrometer to the published specs, and compare the valve stem diameter with that of its mating guide to determine the actual valve stem-to-guide wear. Clearances beyond worn limits require that the valve guide be replaced on most diesel engines. However, some engine manufacturers (mainly light-duty automotive) offer oversized-outside-diameter valve stems to bring the clearance within specs.

One method that can be used with integral guides is to *knurl* the inside diameter of the guide with special equipment, or to bore the worn guide and install a bronze valve guide liner. In both cases, a reamer is used to resize the guide after this procedure. Knurling is a process that basically cuts a spiral screw thread within the bore of the guide. Figure 9–13 illustrates the procedure that can be used to bore and install a bronze guide liner as well as how to use the optional guide spiral (knurling) and finish ream the guide insert.

Replacement valve guides are press fit within their mating bore in the cylinder head. To remove the valve guides, you can use one of several methods: a hammer and properly sized shouldered punch, a mechanical threaded guide puller, a hydraulic press, or an air-

Installation Procedure

I.D. FINISHING METHODS

BALL BROACH   **SPIRAL & FINISH REAM**

BORING GUIDE OVERSIZE
Select proper tooling and bore out old guide. Both H.S. and Carbide Boring Tools are available

INSTALLING "BRONZE LINER' IN GUIDE
Lube guide, push guide-liner into holder, select guide driver and hammer into place.

TRIMMING BRONZE LINER
Insert tool point into the seam, push down to guide top and turn once to remove excess material.

FINISH SIZE OPERATION
To finish I.D., select appropriate Ball Broach and drive through guide. Flex-hone with high RPM drill.

OPTIONAL GUIDE SPIRAL
For closer than normal stem to guide clearance, spiraling is suggested for added lubrication.

FINISH SIZE OPERATION
To finish ream, lubricate reamer with bronze-lube and run through guide. Both H.S. and Carbide Reamers are available.

FIGURE 9–13 *Installation and finishing procedures required for successful and accurate reconditioning of a worn valve guide by the insertion of a precision wear sleeve. (Courtesy of Hastings Manufacturing Co.)*

impact hammer and chisel arrangement similar to that illustrated in Figure 9–14. Removal or installation of the guide with the air chisel hammer requires that you employ special tools that must be held vertical to the cylinder head and forced tight against the guide to prevent pounding of the end of the guide.

Drive or press the guide out of the cylinder head, making sure that the driver is driven or pressed straight (Figure 9–15). If it is not pressed straight, damage to the valve guide or cylinder head may result. After the guide has been removed, check the guide bore for scoring. Use a stiff-wire brush similar to that used to clean the inside of the guide; run the brush through the bore in the cylinder head to remove any minor imperfections. A badly scored guide bore may have to be reamed out to accommodate the next-larger-size guide. After guide bore is checked, select the correct guide (intake or exhaust) and insert it in guide bore.

NOTE Guide insertion can be made easier by the use of a press-fit lubricant such as that supplied by Sunnen Manufacturing Company.

Insert the chamfered end of the new valve guide into its bore from the top side of the cylinder head. Then make sure that you have the correct guide installer, as shown in Figure 9–16, and use the air-impact chisel to drive the guide into place in the cylinder head from the top side.

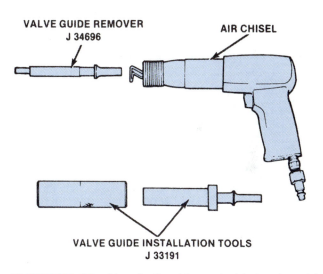

VALVE GUIDE REMOVER
J 34696

AIR CHISEL

VALVE GUIDE INSTALLATION TOOLS
J 33191

FIGURE 9–14 *Use of a Kent-Moore air chisel and special adapter tools required to remove or install a valve guide from the cylinder head. (Courtesy of Detroit Diesel Corporation.)*

NOTE If you do not have the correct guide installation tools, take extreme care when installing a new guide. Do not drive the guide too far into the head bore. Either measure the height of a guide that is still in place or refer to the service manual to ensure that you install the new guide to its specified height above the cylinder head using a vernier caliper as shown in Figure 9–17.

FIGURE 9–15 *An alternate method of removing a valve guide from a cylinder head is to use a hydraulic press.*

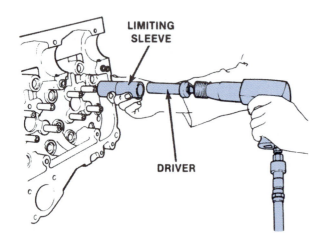

FIGURE 9–16 *Using a special air chisel and tooling to install a new valve guide into the cylinder head. (Courtesy of Detroit Diesel Corporation.)*

In some engines employing aluminum alloy cylinder heads, a nonferrous valve guide is used. Often, this means that you must heat the head in boiling water or a temperature-controlled oven to safely remove the guide. To install the new guide safely, the head can be preheated and the guide chilled before installation.

Many manufacturers recommend that a new guide be hand reamed after installation to ensure that the guide inside diameter did not change during the installation process.

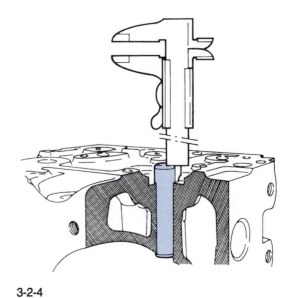

FIGURE 9–17 *Using a vernier caliper on the cylinder head to measure the installed height of a new valve guide.*

NOTE   Some engine manufacturers have guides that are made by a special process to make them wear longer; these guides should not be reamed. Check engine manufacturer's recommendation closely in this area.

Checking and Reconditioning the Valve Seat

After guides have been replaced or reconditioned, valve seat checking and reconditioning should be done. Valve seats must be checked for looseness by tapping the seat lightly with the peen end of a ball peen hammer. A loose seat will produce a sound different from the sound produced while tapping on the cylinder head. In some cases a loose seat can be seen to move while tapping on it. If the seat is solid, check it for cracks and excessive width. If the seat passes all checks, it should be reconditioned as outlined, using a specially designed valve seat grinder.

Reconditioning or Grinding the Valve Seat

First select the proper mandrel pilot.

NOTE   The mandrel pilot is selected by measuring the valve stem with a micrometer or caliper or by referring to the manufacturer's specifications. With experience, pilot selection is easily done by a visual check.

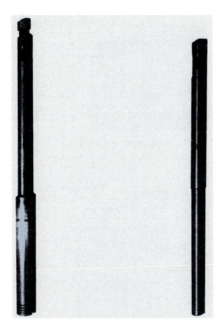

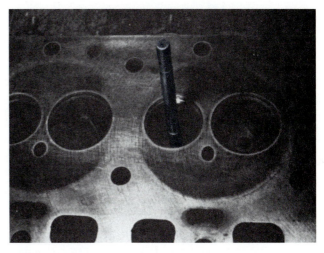

FIGURE 9–19   View of a tapered valve guide pilot inserted into the valve guide.

FIGURE 9–18   (a) Expandable type of valve guide pilot; (b) tapered style of valve guide pilot. These are required to support a valve seat grinding tool.

Pilots are usually one of two types full-measure, expandable or tapered. An expandable pilot (Figure 9–18a) is inserted into the guide and then expanded by tightening the expanding screw on the pilot until it is tight in the guide. Expandable pilots are not considered as accurate as tapered pilots and should be used only when a tapered pilot is not available. Some technicians prefer expandable pilots because they compensate for guide wear better than does a tapered pilot; by expanding into the guide, the pilot tightens and adjusts to the guide size or wear. A tapered pilot (Figure 9–18b) does not have an expanding screw and relies on the taper of the pilot to tighten it into the guide.

After the pilot has been selected and inserted into the guide (Figure 9–19), the grinding wheel or stone must be selected. Selection of the grinding wheel is made by determining the valve seat angle, diameter, and the seat material.

1.   Use a *concentric grinder*, one in which the grinding stone contacts the full-seat face width.

2.   Use an *eccentric grinder* and stone, similar to Figure 9–20, which is designed so that the rotating grinding wheel contacts the seat at only one point at any time as it rotates around the seat. A micrometer feed on the handle of the drive motor permits very fine adjustment of the amount of material to be removed.

3.   Use an adjustable seat cutter of tungsten carbide blades that can cut thousands of seats before showing wear and can produce a very fine surface finish. This system is superior to a grinding stone, which

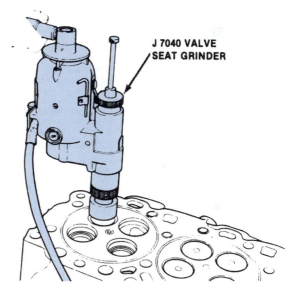

FIGURE 9–20   Grinding a valve seat insert within the cylinder head using an electric motor–driven "eccentric" valve seat grinder and stone. (Courtesy of Detroit Diesel Corporation.)

requires refacing and or replacing much more frequently.

Although the concentric and eccentric valve seat grinders have been used for many years, they do have some drawbacks. The concentric valve seat stone grinder that contacts the full-seat circumference at one time tends to retain the fine grinding dust during the grinding process and can actually pound these filings back into the seat. Consequently, it does not produce as fine a seat surface finish as the eccentric grinder shown in Figure 9–20, which contacts only one part of the seat

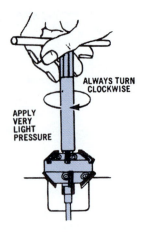

FIGURE 9–21   *Using a valve seat insert cutter tool to restore a worn seat face. (Courtesy of Neway Manufacturing, Inc.)*

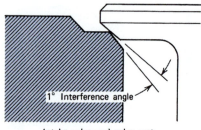

Intake valve and valve seat

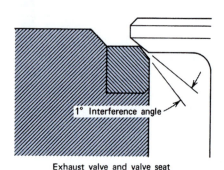

Exhaust valve and valve seat

FIGURE 9–22   *Location and determination of an interference angle between the valve seat insert in the cylinder head and the valve face.*

at any given time as it rotates off center around the valve seat. The eccentric grinder does, however, take longer to grind the seat than does a concentric grinder. Both concentric and eccentric valve seat grinders employ grinding stones and holders that are threaded onto the end of the drive motor chuck. Stones are readily available in a wide variety of diameters and seat angles. Stones can be reground using a diamond-point tool attachment when worn. Stones are available in different grits and colors; their makeup is relative to the type of material to be ground. Cast-iron heads and regular steel inserts usually employ a gray stone, whereas hardened Stellite inserts require a white stone.

The main advantage of a seat cutter with a tungsten carbide blade shown in Figure 9–21 is that it does not require regular resharpening as a grinding stone does. It retains seat-to-guide concentricity much better, and it can grind thousands of seats with one set of blades, which are replaceable when required. This type of seat cutter can cut a seat in the same time that it takes to dress a stone, plus it cuts in far fewer revolutions and produces a true flat seat at an exact angle with a superior finish.

NOTE   To establish an interference angle between valve and valve seat, one must be ground at a different angle to provide a sharp or narrow seat to valve contact. For example, seat ground at 45° with valve ground at 44° (Figure 9–22).

This interference angle with its narrow contact area aids in seating the valve during starting by helping to cut through the carbon particles that may accu-

mulate on the valve seat. Interference angles are not recommended for valves that have rotators, as the rotating valve will remove any carbon that may accumulate on the seat or valve face.

The important part of the valve seat grinding process is to ensure that the insert, when finish ground, will produce the desired valve seat contact width along with the proper location on the valve face. The width required on the valve face-to-seat contact area is determined by the overall valve head diameter and is specified by the engine manufacturer in the service literature. For example, a 2 in. (50.8 mm) diameter valve might call for a face width of 0.060 to 0.090 in. (1.5 to 2.25 mm). The seat face contact should start at about the midpoint of the valve face and move toward the head of the valve but stop short of the rim (margin). To achieve this accurately, often you must use a *three-angle cutting sequence* on the valve seat insert in the cylinder head by employing three stones (cutters) ground or adjusted to these three separate angles. This allows you to perform what is commonly referred to as *overcutting* or *undercutting,* to position the seat on the desired location of the valve face. In addition, the cutting sequence allows you to obtain the recommended face seat width accurately.

To effectively produce a three-angle valve seat, the technician can employ a 15°, 30°, and 60° cutter set.

This tooling is designed to produce a three-angle cut using a carbide tip tool that cuts all three valve seat angles at once. The tooling allows manual operation by hand or an electric cutting motor drive assembly. It features a carbide pilot and articulated spindle holder with a ball-mounted spindle for self-aligning tooling.

When cutting a three-angle valve seat as shown in Figure 9–23, note that area 4 has been cut with a 60° cutter or stone, while area 3 has been cut with a 15° stone. Item 1 in the diagram is the *minimum* valve seat width, which in this example is 0.060 in (1.5 mm); item 2 is the *maximum* seat width of 0.090 in. (2.25 mm). Both items 1 and 2 have a 30° angle. Once the seat has been initially cut or ground to 30°, it should not require recutting if the service technician applied the 15° and 60° cutters or stones very gently to obtain the desired seat width and location on the valve face when checked with Prussian blue paste.

If you are using a grinding stone, refer to Figure 9–20, which illustrates an eccentric seat grinder supported on a valve guide pilot. By adjusting the drive motor micrometer handle, the stone will automatically be lowered onto the seat, and the internal drive mechanism will allow the stone to slowly rotate around the seat until it has finished the rotation. If you are using a concentric grinding stone, you control how hard the stone contacts the seat (downward pressure) and for how long. Therefore, be very careful that you do not remove too much stock from the seat. Start the drive

motor and lightly and quickly allow the stone to contact the seat; then inspect it to see how much material has been removed. Carefully continue to grind the seat until it is cleaned up completely.

If you are using a valve seat cutter with tungsten carbide blades, you can select a cutter of the same basic diameter as the valve head that has been set to the correct angle. Refer to Figure 9–21 and place the cutter over the valve guide pilot. Slowly lower the cutter to the valve seat face, since dropping it can damage the cutter blade and seat. Place a T-handle or motor-driven power unit over the hex drive of the cutter, and while maintaining a centered light downward pressure, rotate the cutter clockwise through several complete revolutions. Carefully remove the cutter and inspect the seat surface as shown in Figure 9–24 to determine the condition of the surface finish. This procedure will allow you to gauge just how much material needs to be removed to square up the seat.

Whether you are using a grinding stone or a cutter arrangement, once the seat has been cleaned to satisfaction, remove the tooling, apply Prussian blue paste to the valve as shown in Figure 9–25, and inspect the

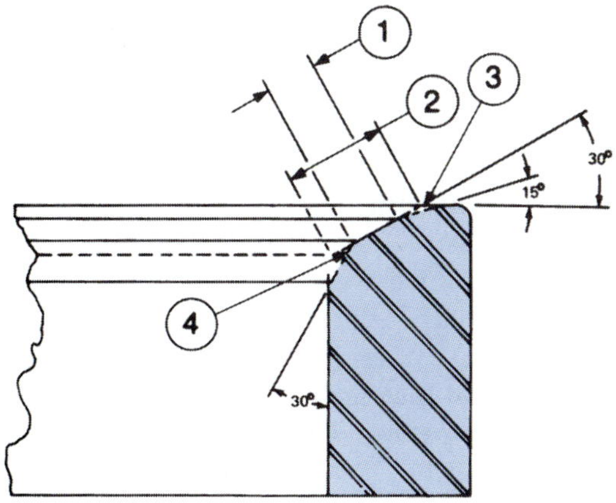

FIGURE 9–24 Close inspection of the valve seat insert to determine how much material needs to be cut/removed to clean up and produce a new seat. (Courtesy of Neway Manufacturing, Inc.)

FIGURE 9–23 Illustration of a 30° valve seat insert. The minimum seat width is shown as item 1; item 2 shows the maximum recommended seat width. The seat width and its location to the valve face can be achieved by using a 15° stone or cutter to remove metal from the top side at position 3, a method known as undercutting, because the angle is less than the recommended 30°. Position 4 at the throat area can be overcut by using a 60° stone or cutter bit if required. (Courtesy of Cummins Engine Company, Inc.)

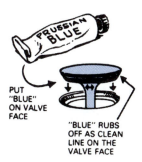

FIGURE 9–25 Use of Prussian blue paste spread lightly across the valve face. Bounce the valve once on its seat, then carefully remove it from the guide and check the impression on the seat to determine the contact area width and location. (Courtesy of Neway Manufacturing, Inc.)

valve face for the seat width and location. Normally, if you have used only one stone (cutter) set to the recommended angle (30°, for example), the seat width will normally be too wide. You will have to *overcut* or *undercut* to raise or lower the seat location and to achieve the desired seat width.

Figure 9–26 illustrates that by using a stone (cutter) with a steeper angle (overcutting 60°, for example), you can successfully raise the bottom edge of the seat contact surface, since the removed material no longer contacts the valve face. This is known as a *bottom narrowing cut*.

Figure 9–27 illustrates that by using a narrower stone (cutter)—undercutting 15°, for example—you can remove valve seat insert material from the top edge of the seat contact surface area, thereby lowering the top edge of the valve face seat. This is known as a *top narrowing cut*.

If the top and bottom narrowing cuts have been performed very lightly and with adequate care, the seat will be centered between both cuts as illustrated in Figure 9–28. If the seat width is too narrow, you will have to use the 30° stone (cutter) again. If the seat is too wide, or the seat location is too high or too low, you may have to overcut or undercut to achieve the correct seat location and width.

Always confirm the seat width and location by use of Prussian blue paste on the valve face as described

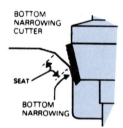

FIGURE 9–26   Overcutting a valve seat insert by using a 60° cutter to raise the bottom edge of the valve face seat contact surface. (Courtesy of Neway Manufacturing, Inc.)

FIGURE 9–27   Undercutting a valve seat insert by using a 15° cutter to lower the valve face seat contact surface. (Courtesy of Neway Manufacturing, Inc.)

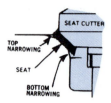

FIGURE 9–28   Centering of the valve seat insert to the valve face contact surface by narrowing both the top and bottom seat areas. (Courtesy of Neway Manufacturing, Inc.)

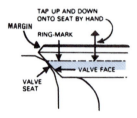

FIGURE 9–29   Determining the contact location of the valve seat insert by tapping the valve onto the seat by hand. After removal, check the Prussian blue paste as described in Figure 9–25 to determine seat width and actual location. (Courtesy of Neway Manufacturing, Inc.)

earlier. Refer to Figure 9–29 and gently tap the valve up and down. Apply finger pressure to the top of the valve head and to the stem tip until you have achieved a clean valve face seat contact area. If an *interference angle* is being used, the valve face seat contact area will appear as a *ring mark* or narrow line, rather than the wider seat that occurs when no interference angle is used. The ring mark should appear about one-third of the way down the valve face from the rim (margin). If the mark is too high, cut the top narrowing angle slightly to lower the mark. If the mark is too low, cut the seat angle at the bottom to raise the mark. If an open spot appears on the valve face seat contact area and it is greater than 0.5 in. (12.7 mm), reuse the seat stone (cutter) over the pilot and gently attempt to blend it in by turning the stone (cutter) by hand only. Small noncontact spots on the valve seat face tend to peen themselves into a full-face contact pattern within a very short time after initial engine startup.

After any valve seat cutting (grinding) procedure, install a small dial gauge on a pilot (as illustrated in Figure 9–30) with its extension point resting against the valve seat. Set the gauge to zero and gently rotate it at least one complete turn to determine the runout that exists between the valve guide and seat insert. This will indicate if the valve seat is concentric to the guide; although stated in the engine service manual specs, the maximum reading is usually 0.002 in. (0.05 mm), but

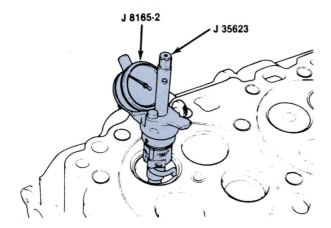

FIGURE 9–30 Using a special dial gauge and adapter to check the concentricity (runout) of the valve guide to the valve seat insert. (Courtesy of Detroit Diesel Corporation.)

check the engine service manual specs. Excessive runout readings can be traced to a worn valve guide or grinding equipment that has not been set up or used properly.

SPECIAL NOTE Any time that the valve seats or the valves have been reground, it is very important that you check the *valve head recess* which can be done by using a dial indicator mounted onto a sled gauge as illustrated in Figure 9–31. Always check the engine service manual to determine the allowable dimension. If the valve head is too low in its seat, *valve guttering* will occur. In other words, the valve will fail to open wide enough and may result in a restriction to both the air inlet and exhaust gas flow to and from the combustion

chamber and cylinder. Rough engine operation will result along with low power, poor fuel economy, smoke at the exhaust stack, incomplete combustion, and carbon buildup around the neck of the valves. In some cases when both a new valve and seat insert are being used, the seat insert *may* require grinding to lower the valve head sufficiently to avoid contact with the piston crown. This situation can occur when a cylinder head fire deck has been resurfaced and new standard thickness inserts have been installed. Reduced thickness inserts of 0.010, 0.020, and 0.030 in. (0.254, 0.5, and 0.75 mm) should be installed to handle the same amount of material ground from the fire deck. Note that maximum values for valve *protrusion* and *intrusion* are specified. If the valve sits too high above the fire deck, regrind the seat insert. If it sits too far below the fire deck, replace the insert. If the valve head rim (margin) is too thin, replace the valve.

Replacing the Valve Seat

If it is determined that the valve seat must be replaced because of cracks or excessive width, the following procedure should be used:

1. Using a removing tool (Figure 9–32), remove the seat carefully to prevent damage to the cylinder head.

NOTE Use extreme caution when removing the valve seat. Damage to the cylinder head in the valve seat area may render the head unfit for further use.

FIGURE 9–31 Using a dial indicator mounted on a flat surface sled gauge to determine the valve head protrusion or intrusion and compare it with specs. (Courtesy of Detroit Diesel Corporation.)

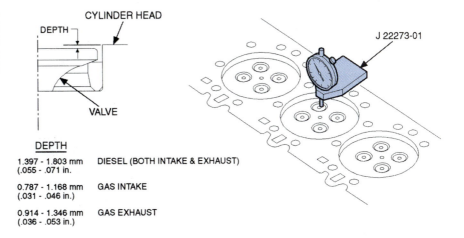

DEPTH	
1.397 - 1.803 mm (.055 - .071 in.)	DIESEL (BOTH INTAKE & EXHAUST)
0.787 - 1.168 mm (.031 - .046 in.)	GAS INTAKE
0.914 - 1.346 mm (.036 - .053 in.)	GAS EXHAUST

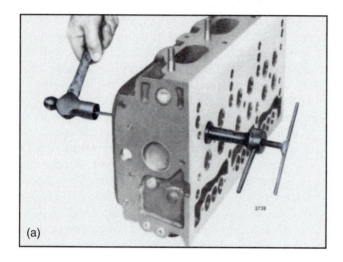

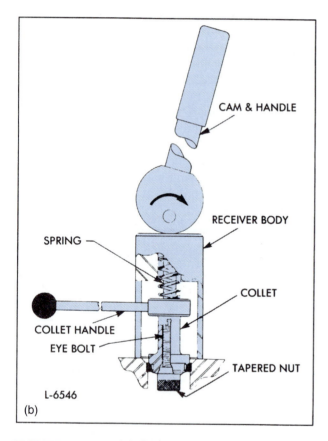

FIGURE 9–32 (a) Removing a valve seat insert—Method 1. (b) Using special Kent-Moore tooling to remove a valve seat insert from the cylinder head. (Courtesy of Detroit Diesel Corporation.)

2. Clean the valve port and seat area with a carbon brush and compressed air.

> NOTE   It is recommended that after removal of a valve seat, the seat counterbore be enlarged to allow installation of an oversized seat. Although this practice is used most often, with additional experience the technician will be able to determine the type of cylinder heads that will allow the successful replacement of valve seats without enlargement of the counterbore. A slightly oversized valve seat (0.005 to 0.010 in., 0.013 to 0.25 mm) is generally available and may be used to ensure a good seat fit in the counterbore if the counterbore is not recut.

> CAUTION   Valve guides must be in good condition or replaced before any attempt to cut valve seat counterbore or replace valve seats.

3. If it is decided to enlarge the valve seat counterbore or to cut a counterbore in a head not originally equipped with valve seats, a cutting tool or reseater similar to the one shown should be used (Figure 9–33). Many types of counterbore cutting tools are available. Follow operating instructions of cutter being used to eliminate damage to the cylinder head.

Installing the Valve Seats

1. After the valve seat counterbore has been enlarged or considered usable, select a mandrel pilot for the insert that will fit snugly in the valve guide.

FIGURE 9–33 Using special tooling to cut/machine the cylinder head valve seat counterbore to accept a new oversize valve seat insert.

2. Obtain a new valve seat insert that will fit the counterbore using the engine parts manual as reference or using the chart supplied with the valve seat insert cutting tool set.

3. Visually inspect the counterbore, making sure that it is free from metal particles and rough edges. Select a driver that has an outside diameter slightly smaller than the seat.

4. Place a ring insert over the driver pilot onto the cylinder head counterbore.

5. Place the driver onto the pilot, and with a hammer drive the valve seat into the counterbore using sharp, hard blows.

NOTE Alternative methods of valve seat installations are (1) shrinking valve seats by cooling and then driving them in, or (2) warming the cylinder head in hot water and then installing the seat.

CAUTION Safety glasses should be worn during this operation, as valve seat inserts are very brittle and may shatter, causing eye damage.

6. Some OEM's recommended that the seat be staked or knurled in place (Figure 9–34). If a knurling or staking tool is not available, a 0.25 in. (7 mm) round-end punch may be used to stake the insert around its outer circumference.

NOTE If the seat is cast iron, no knurling or staking is necessary, as the seat has the same coefficient of expansion as the cylinder head. Seats that are made of steel alloy require staking, as their expansion rate does not match that of cast iron. As a result, they may fall out during engine warm-up.

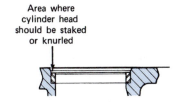

Area where
cylinder head
should be staked
or knurled

FIGURE 9–34 *Areas of cylinder head that should be staked with a sharp center punch, or knurled in order to hold a valve seat insert.*

Valve Inspection, Cleaning, and Refacing

Prior to undertaking the time and effort to service the intake and exhaust valves, review the ASE diesel engines T2 test, part B tasks list, and the ASE cylinder head specialist M1 test tasks list shown at the beginning of this chapter. Follow these tasks lists and use them as general guides for valve servicing. To further assist in inspection/service decisions, refer to the valves repair/replacement flowchart shown in Figure 9–35. Greater details of valve servicing procedures are described in the following paragraphs.

Valve Inspection

A decision must be made at this time to replace or reface the valves (Figure 9–36). To determine if the valves are reusable, they should be inspected for the following:

1. Carbon buildup on the underside of the head. A buildup of carbon could indicate that oil has been leaking into the combustion chamber between the valve stem and the valve guide.

2. Stretched stem or cupped head. Valves that are badly cupped or stretched should not be reused, as they could break and ruin the engine. Cupped or stretched valves are usually caused by excessive heat, excessive tappet clearance, engine overspeeding, or weak valve springs.

3. Nicks or marks in the head. Valves with nicks or marks in the head indicate the valve was in a cylinder that had metal particles in it. Metal particles in a cylinder usually come from broken piston rings, broken pistons, or broken valves. Replace all valves that show any sign of damage.

4. Burned or pitted area in face. Burning or pitting can be caused by tight valve lash adjustment, dirty inlet air, or engine overfueling.

5. Worn keeper (collet) grooves (recesses).

6. Scored or worn stem (Figure 9–36). Stem diameter should be checked with micrometer.

7. Margin width.

8. Worn stem end.

Valve Cleaning

1. If the valve passes all the checks listed above, it must be cleaned thoroughly using a wire buffing wheel.

CAUTION Do not press the valve against the wire wheel too hard, as damage to the valve may result. Safety glasses must be worn during valve buffing.

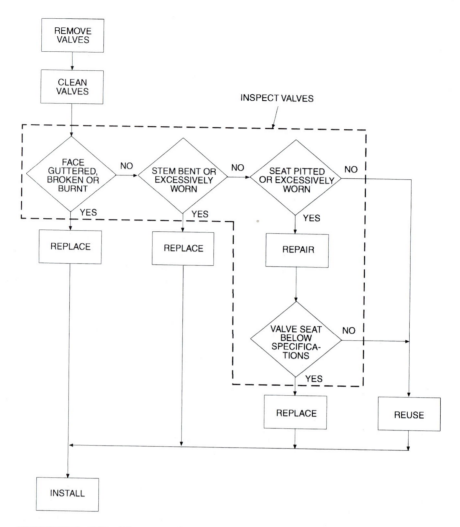

FIGURE 9–35   *Diagnostic flowchart used to determine whether to repair or replace the intake or exhaust valves. (Courtesy of Detroit Diesel Corporation.)*

A much preferred method of valve cleaning is the glass bead blaster, if it is available.

2.   After cleaning, the valve must be checked for warpage. Experienced technicians usually check valves for warpage by inserting them into the valve-refacing machine. If the valve is warped, it can easily be seen and heard when the valve is moved up to the grinding wheel.

Valve Refacing

Valve refacing is done on a valve-refacing machine similar to the one shown in Figure 9–37.

1.   Determine at what angle the valve face is ground by visual inspection or by checking the manufacturer's specifications.

2.   Adjust valve chuck head to correspond with the valve face angle (Figure 9–37). If an interference

angle is recommended by the engine manufacturer, set the valve chuck head at that angle at this time. Although the valve is generally ground with an interference angle, some manufacturers recommend grinding the valve seat to establish the interference angle.

3.   With the valve-grinding machine stopped, install and adjust the grinding wheel dresser so that it will just touch the grinding wheel (Figure 9–37). Start the machine and move the diamond dresser back and forth across the face of the grinding wheel until the wheel surface is smooth and flat all the way across. Remove the dressing attachment.

CAUTION   Safety glasses must be worn during valve refacing.

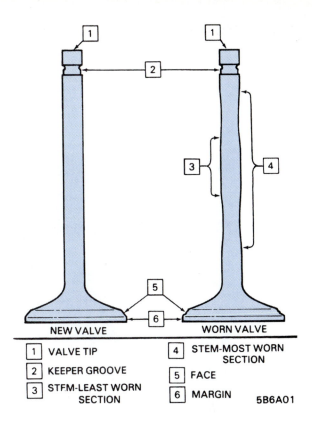

FIGURE 9–36 Typical areas to inspect for valve wear at major cylinder head overhaul. (Courtesy of Neway Manufacturing, Inc.)

1	VALVE TIP	4	STEM-MOST WORN SECTION
2	KEEPER GROOVE	5	FACE
3	STEM-LEAST WORN SECTION	6	MARGIN

5B6A01

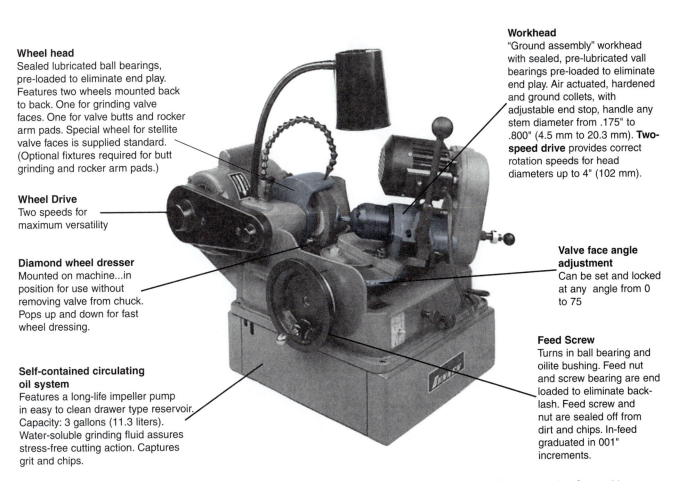

Wheel head
Sealed lubricated ball bearings, pre-loaded to eliminate end play. Features two wheels mounted back to back. One for grinding valve faces. One for valve butts and rocker arm pads. Special wheel for stellite valve faces is supplied standard. (Optional fixtures required for butt grinding and rocker arm pads.)

Wheel Drive
Two speeds for maximum versatility

Diamond wheel dresser
Mounted on machine...in position for use without removing valve from chuck. Pops up and down for fast wheel dressing.

Self-contained circulating oil system
Features a long-life impeller pump in easy to clean drawer type reservoir. Capacity: 3 gallons (11.3 liters). Water-soluble grinding fluid assures stress-free cutting action. Captures grit and chips.

Workhead
"Ground assembly" workhead with sealed, pre-lubricated vall bearings pre-loaded to eliminate end play. Air actuated, hardened and ground collets, with adjustable end stop, handle any stem diameter from .175" to .800" (4.5 mm to 20.3 mm). **Two-speed drive** provides correct rotation speeds for head diameters up to 4" (102 mm).

Valve face angle adjustment
Can be set and locked at any angle from 0 to 75

Feed Screw
Turns in ball bearing and oilite bushing. Feed nut and screw bearing are end loaded to eliminate back-lash. Feed screw and nut are sealed off from dirt and chips. In-feed graduated in 001" increments.

FIGURE 9–37 Model VR-6500 precision valve refacer machine is used to grind metal from the valve face with a rotating grinding wheel (stone). (Courtesy of Sunnen Products Company.)

219

Air-actuated hardened and ground collets speed production, assure pinpoint chucking of valves.

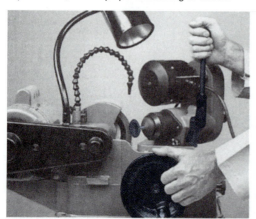

Valve butt chamfering attachment (standard) removes sharp edges after grinding process.

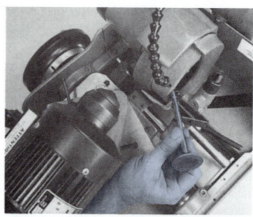

Valve butt grinding attachment (optional) has quick action cam lock and micrometer feed.

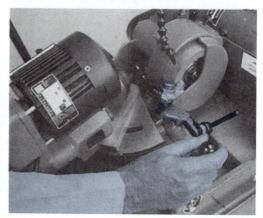

Rocker arm grinding attachment (optional) grinds pad parallel to the bore of shaft type rocker arms.

FIGURE 9–38 *Four of the common grinding jobs that can be performed to a valve and rocker arm using the model VR-6500 valve refacer machine. (Courtesy of Sunnen Products Company.)*

4. Place the valve in the machine chuck (Figure 9–38) and adjust the valve stop so that the valve will be positioned in the chuck on the uppermost portion of the machined area on the stem.

5. Tighten the chuck on the valve stem.

6. With the machine stopped and grinding stone backed slightly away from valve face, adjust the valve table stop nut (Figure 9–37) so that the stone does not touch the valve stem.

7. Start the machine; adjust cooling oil flow with adjusting valve on coolant hose or pump so that an adequate flow of oil is established. Move the grinding wheel toward the valve until it just touches. Move the valve back and forth across the face of the stone with table control lever, moving the stone closer to the valve with the stone feed control as the valve is ground (Figure 9–39).

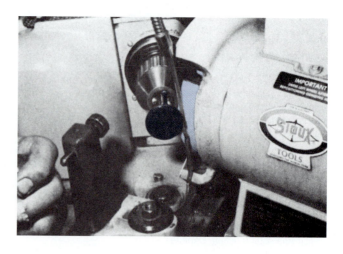

FIGURE 9–39 *Close-up of the grinding procedure of a worn valve face.*

8. When the valve appears to be ground or refaced so that it is smooth and free from pits and/or burned spots, back the stone away from the valve and move the valve table and valve clear of grinding stone, using controls mentioned previously.

> **CAUTION** Do not move the valve table away from the grinding stone until the stone has been backed away from the valve, as damage to the valve face may result.

9. Visually check the valve carefully for pits and face condition. If the valve face still has pits and wear marks, continue grinding until the valve face is completely smooth and free of burned spots and pits.

> **CAUTION** Do not remove the valve from the chuck until the grinding or refacing is completed. Once the valve is removed from the chuck, it is impossible to reinstall it in the same position. As a result, the valve will require additional grinding, which would have been unnecessary if it had remained in the chuck. Following removal of the valve from the machine chuck, check the valve margin (Figure 9–36).

> **NOTE** The valve margin is the distance from the valve head or top to the valve face. This margin must be held within the manufacturer's specifications to prevent premature burning and subsequent failure. If it is not within the manufacturer's specifications, the valve should be replaced.

Refacing the Valve Stem End

After the valve has been refaced, the stem end of the valve should be ground to ensure that it is flat. Use the following procedure:

1. Start the machine; using the dressing diamond, dress the stone (Figure 9–37).
2. Clamp the valve in the holding bracket.
3. With the valve-grinding machine operating, move the valve across the stone, removing only enough metal to "true" up or flatten the end of the valve (Figure 9–38, bottom left).
4. Remove the valve from the holder and install a taper or chamfer tool in holder. Start the machine and grind the taper (Figure 9–38, top right).

> **NOTE** The taper does not have to be very large; 1/32 to 1/16 in. (0.79 to 1.59 mm) is considered sufficient.

Checking the Valve Springs

Valve springs are very important to the life of the valve as well as to efficient engine operation. They must be checked before reassembling the cylinder head. The valve spring should be checked for straightness, tension, and breaks by using the following tools and methods:

1. *Straightness.* Use a T-square or similar device (Figure 9–40).
2. *Tension and free length.* Insert the valve spring in a spring tension gauge to test unloaded or free length and tension at loaded length (Figure 9–41).
3. *Breaks.* By visual inspection check the valve spring carefully after it is cleaned for cracked or broken coils. If any evidence of breaks or cracks is indicated, the valve spring must be replaced.

Valve Rotators and Keepers

Valve rotators can be one of two types, either the free release or mechanical, positive type. Valve rotators are attached to the valves to make them rotate during engine operation. This rotation ensures that no carbon will collect on the valve face or seat and cause valve burning.

The free valve or release type of rotator is designed so that every time the valve is opened and closed, the valve has no spring tension on it (Figure 9–42). This release of spring tension allows the valve to be rotated by

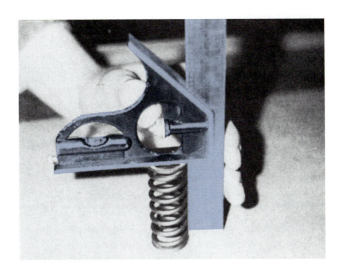

FIGURE 9–40 *Checking the squareness of a valve spring using a small T-square.*

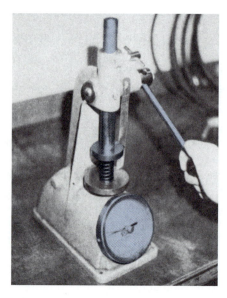

FIGURE 9–41 *Checking a valve spring for its compressed length using a special spring tester.*

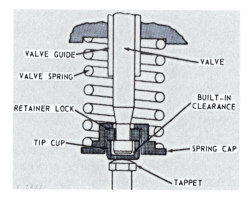

FIGURE 9–42 *Components of a free valve rotator.*

the outgoing exhaust gases or engine vibration. The free valve rotator must be visually checked closely for wear during reassembly and all worn parts replaced.

The positive rotator is a mechanical device that mechanically rotates the valve every time it is opened and closed by the rocker arm. The positive-type rotator can be checked by tapping with a plastic hammer after the valve spring rotator and keepers have been installed. (Tapping with a hammer simulates engine operation.)

NOTE   Although all valve rotators may pass the tests or checks and be considered usable, it is good practice during a major engine overhaul to replace all valve rotators to ensure a long period of trouble-free operation.

The valve keepers must be checked closely for wear and replaced if any wear is evident.

Preparing for Cylinder Head Assembly
After the cylinder head has been given a final cleaning (rinsed with cleaning fluid and blown off with compressed air), it should be placed in or on a suitable stand for final assembly.

Checking the Valve Seat-to-Valve Contact
Install the valves in the head one at a time and check seat-to-valve contact with one of the following methods:

1. *Prussian blue.* When Prussian blue is being used to check valve seating, apply the bluing to the valve face (Figure 9–25). Insert the valve into the valve guide and snap it lightly against the seat. Remove the valve and inspect the face. The bluing should have an even seating mark around the valve face. If not, the valve seat is not concentric and must be reground.

2. *A lead pencil or felt-tip marking pen.* When a lead pencil or felt-tip marker is being used to check the valve-to-seat contact, place pencil marks about 0.125 in. (3 mm) apart around valve face (Figure 9–43). Place the valve in the guide and snap or rotate it against the valve seat. Remove the valve and inspect the marks made on the face. If the valve-to-seat contact is good, all marks will be broken. If all marks are not broken, the valve seat is not concentric and it must be reground. After checking the valve-to-seat contact, make sure that the lead is wiped from the valve.

NOTE   Lapping or seating of the valve with a lapping compound is not required if the valve and seat have been ground properly. Lapping is not recommended by most engine manufacturers.

Checking the Valve Head Height
If the valve head height (distance the valve protrudes above or below the machined surface of the cylinder

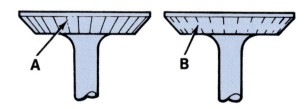

FIGURE 9–43 *(a) Placing a series of lead pencil marks across the valve face prior to face-to-seat contact seat checking. (b) Inspecting the valve face-to-seat contact area after proper contact.*

head) has not been checked previously, it should be checked at this time, as follows:

1. Place a straightedge across the cylinder head and use a feeler gauge to measure the distance between the valve head and the straightedge. Compare this reading with the manufacturer's specifications.

2. As indicated, some valves may protrude above the surface of the cylinder head; if this is the case, place the straightedge across the valve and use a feeler gauge to measure the distance from the valve head to the cylinder head machined surface.

Selecting the Valve Seats

After all valves and seals have been checked, the next step in the head assembly is to determine what type of valve seals (if any) are to be used.

NOTE   Some engines do not use valve seals because the valve guides have been tapered to prevent oil loss at this point.

Valve seals fit around the valve and prevent oil from running down the valve stem into the combustion chamber, causing oil consumption. Valve seals come in many types and configurations. If the cylinder head was originally equipped with valve seals, the engine overhaul gasket set will generally contain the valve seals. If the cylinder head was not originally equipped with valve seals, select either the positive or umbrella type of valve seal for intake and exhaust valves.

NOTE   Although some cylinder heads may have been equipped with valve seals, it may be desirable to select a more modern or positive type of seal for installation on the cylinder head.

The most common types of seals are the rubber umbrella or Teflon insert type that clamps onto the valve stem (Figure 9–44). Umbrella oil deflectors will generally not require guide top machining. Positive seals will require machining if the cylinder head was not originally equipped with them. A valve guide machining tool must be used to machine the guide.

Valve Guide Machining and Seal Installation

1. Select the correct cutting tool by referring to the seal manufacturer's application data.

2. Install the cutting tool in a 0.5 in. electric drill and machine the top of the guide, using firm pressure on the drill to prevent cutting a wavy or uneven top on the guide (Figure 9–45).

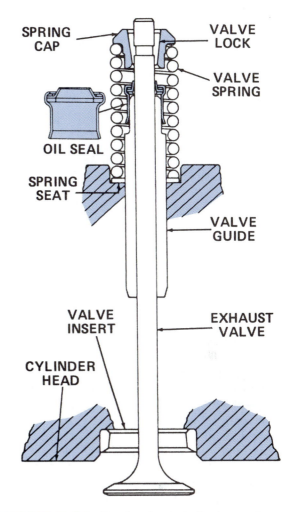

FIGURE 9–44   *Details of a typical valve, spring, seal, and valve seat insert. (Courtesy of Detroit Diesel Corporation.)*

FIGURE 9–45   *Machining a valve guide, or bore in the cylinder head to accept a new positive valve seal.*

NOTE The guide should be machined to the height specified in the instruction sheet provided by the seal manufacturer.

After all guides are machined, all metal chips must be thoroughly cleaned from the cylinder head.

3.   Blow out all intake and exhaust ports with compressed air to ensure that no chips or particles remain.

4.   Install valves and valve seals.

Testing and Replacing the Injector Sleeves

Many diesel engine cylinder heads have a copper sleeve into which the injector is installed. This copper sleeve is installed directly into the water jacket and must be sealed at the top and bottom. If leakage occurs at the copper sleeve, water may leak into the combustion chamber. As a result, the sleeve seal must be checked carefully during cylinder head repair for water leakage. Leakage testing of the injector sleeves will involve pressurizing the coolant passageways as outlined under pressure testing of the cylinder head.

If it is found that the injector sleeves leak and they are to be replaced, the following procedure should be followed:

1.   Remove the injector sleeve following the manufacturer's instructions. Most engine manufacturers provide specially designed tools to install and remove the injector sleeves (Figure 9–46).

2.   Before sleeve installation is attempted, the bore in the cylinder head that the sleeve fits into must be thoroughly cleaned, using compressed air or by sanding with emery paper.

NOTE Many cylinder heads use O-rings in the sleeve bore to help seal the sleeve to the cylinder head. During cleaning of the sleeve bore, make sure that the O-ring grooves are cleaned.

3.   Install the new sleeve on the installation tool and insert a sleeve and installation tool in the cylinder head. Some sleeves are simply driven in place (Figure 9–46), while others must be rolled over on the combustion chamber side and reamed (Figure 9–47) after installation. Refer to the OEM service manual.

4.   After injector sleeves have been installed, it is recommended that the cylinder head be pressure checked to ensure that a leaktight seal has been established to prevent water leakage around the sleeves.

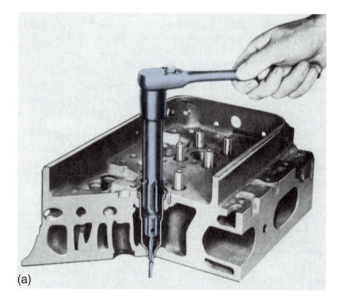

(a)

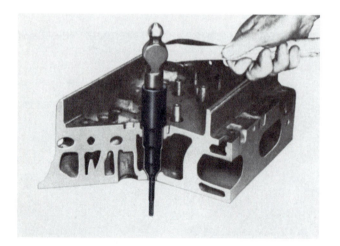

FIGURE 9–46 Driving a new injector copper sleeve into the cylinder head using a special tool. (Courtesy of Detroit Diesel Corporation.)

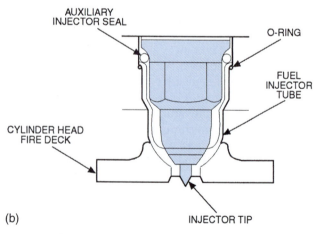

(b)

FIGURE 9–47 (a) Using special tooling to cut/ream the injector copper tube after installation. (Courtesy of Detroit Diesel Corporation.) (b) Injector copper tube and sealing arrangement in the cylinder head.

5. After a new injector sleeve has been installed, injector tip protrusion should be checked and compared with the manufacturer's specifications. Injector tip protrusion is the distance the injector tip protrudes below the surface of the cylinder head gasket surface. Too much or too little protrusion may cause the injector spray to strike the piston in the wrong place or strike the cylinder wall. This incorrect positioning of the injector spray can cause incorrect cylinder operation (combustion).

Cylinder Head Assembly
During cylinder head assembly the following procedures shall be observed:

1. All components shall be thoroughly cleaned.
2. All applicable mating surfaces shall be lubricated with an appropriate lubricant and surfaces susceptible to storage corrosion shall be treated with a suitable rust inhibitor.
3. All overhead camshaft and auxiliary shaft bearings/bushings shall be replaced as required to restore correct clearance.
4. All seals and gaskets shall be replaced.

Final Cylinder Head Assembly
Complete the head assembly using the following procedures:

1. Install a spring over the valve and valve seal.
2. Install a spring retainer on the valve spring.
3. Using the valve spring compressor, compress the spring just far enough to install keepers (Figure 9–5).
4. If the cylinder head is to be stored for some time before it is installed, the intake and exhaust ports must be plugged or covered with tape to prevent anything from getting into them until final engine assembly.

Assembling the Cylinder Head onto the Engine
The assembly of the cylinder head or heads onto the engine block will involve many different procedures that are peculiar to a given engine. The following procedures are general in nature and are offered to supplement the manufacturer's service manual.

1. Before attempting to install the cylinder head, make sure that the cylinder head and block surface are free from all rust, dirt, old gasket materials, and grease or oil.

NOTE   Before placing the head gasket on the block, make sure that all bolt holes in the block are free of oil and dirt by blowing them out with compressed air.

2. Select the correct head gasket and place it on the cylinder block, checking it closely for an "up" or "top" mark that some head gaskets may have on them.

NOTE   In most cases head gaskets will be installed dry with no sealer, although in some situations an engine manufacturer may recommend applying sealer to the gasket before cylinder head installation. Take particular note of the recommendations in the service manual or ask your instructor.

3. After placing the head gasket on the block, place water and oil O-rings (if used) in the correct positions.

Some head gaskets will be a one-piece solid composition type, while others will be made of steel and composed of several sections or pieces. Detroit Diesel two-cycle engines, for example, use a circular ring that fits on top of the cylinder sleeve to seal the compression (see Figure 6–39). In addition to this sleeve seal are numerous O-rings that seal the coolant and lubricating oil, making up the head gasket.

NOTE   The installation of some head gaskets requires the use of threaded guide studs that are screwed in the head bolt holes to hold the head gasket in place during head installation. Guide studs can be made from bolts by sawing off the heads and grinding a taper on the end. Most modern engines will have dowels or locating pins in the block to aid in holding the cylinder head gasket in place during cylinder head assembly.

4. After gasket and all O-rings are in place, check the cylinders to make sure that no foreign objects have been left in them, such as O-rings and bolts.
5. Place head or heads on the cylinder block carefully to avoid damage to the head gasket.
6. On in-line engines with three separate heads that do not use dowel pins, it may be necessary to line up heads by placing a straightedge across the intake or exhaust manifold surfaces.
7. Clean and inspect all head bolts or capscrews for erosion or pitting. Clean bolts that are very rusty and dirty with a wire wheel.

CAUTION   Do not force or push the threaded part of the bolt into the wire wheel, as damage to the threads may result.

NOTE   Any bolt that shows any signs of stretching or pitting should be replaced. A broken head bolt can ruin a good overhaul job.

8.   Coat bolt threads and heads with light oil or International Compound No. 2 and place the bolts or capscrews into the bolt holes in the head and block.

CAUTION   Before placing bolts into the engine, be sure that each bolt has a washer (if used). Some engines do not use washers under the head bolts. Check to be sure that you have the correct bolt and/or washer combination.

9.   Using a speed handle wrench and the appropriate-size socket, start at the center of the cylinder head and turn the bolts down snug, which is until the bolt touches the head and increased torque is required to turn it.

10.   When all bolts have been tightened this far, continue to tighten each bolt one-fourth to one-half turn at a time with a torque wrench until the recommended torque is reached.

NOTE   Bolt tightening must be done according to the sequence supplied by the engine manufacturer when available (Figure 9–48). If sequence is not available, tighten the head starting with the center bolts, working outward toward the ends in a circular sequence.

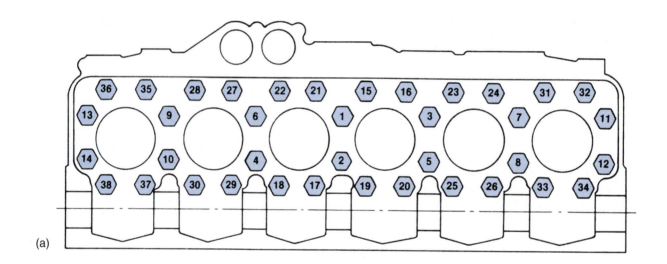

(a)

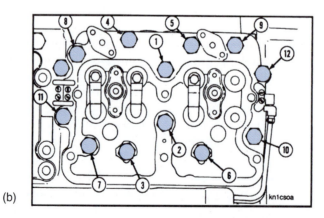

(b)

FIGURE 9–48   (a) Example of a cylinder head bolt tightening sequence for a series 60 DDC engine model. (Courtesy of Detroit Diesel Corporation.) (b) Cylinder head bolt tightening sequence for a Cummins N14 engine. (Courtesy of Cummins Engine Company, Inc.)

SUMMARY

Details within this chapter have provided you with information and knowledge necessary to successfully service/repair the cylinder head assembly. This will increase your level of expertise in successfully diagnosing, analyzing, and effectively troubleshooting performance complaints of this major engine component.

SELF-TEST QUESTIONS

1. Technician A says that the term *four-valve head* refers to an engine with a total of four valves within the cylinder head. Technician B says the term means that each cylinder covered by the head contains four valves. Who is correct?

2. Technician A says that the term *crossflow cylinder head* means that the intake manifold is on one side while the exhaust manifold is on the opposite side. Technician B says that the term means that the inlet air enters one side of the head, flows across the piston crown, and flows back out of the same side to induce swirl to the exhaust gases during the valve overlap cycle. Which technician is correct?

3. Technician A says that all DDC two-stroke-cycle engines only use exhaust valves. Technician B says that all engines need both intake and exhaust valves to operate. Which technician knows engine operating theory best?

4. True or False: Most unit injectors are inserted into a copper or stainless steel injector tube within the cylinder head to allow for adequate cooling of the injector assembly.

5. The shape of the intake and exhaust valves in diesel engines is commonly referred to as a
   a. reed valve
   b. poppet valve
   c. gate valve
   d. rotating valve

6. How do intake and exhaust valves manage to dissipate their absorbed heat?

7. Technician A says that both the intake and exhaust valves are retained in place in the cylinder head by the use of split locks (keepers). Technician B says that the spring retainer performs this function. Who is correct?

8. Technician A says that faulty valve stem seals will result in combustion blowby, low compression, and hard starting. Technician B says that oil will be pulled down the valve guide, resulting in burning of oil and blue smoke in the exhaust gas. Which technician is correct?

9. Technician A says that worn valve guides can cause a rocking action as the valve opens and closes, resulting in poor valve face-to-seat contact and early valve failure from burning. Technician B says that oil pulled down the guides will cause blue smoke in the exhaust gas. Are both statements correct?

10. Technician A says that worn valve guides can sometimes be repaired by a knurling procedure. Technician B says that when worn, all valve guides must be replaced. Who is correct?

11. Technician A says that if a cylinder head does not contain replaceable valve guides, when the head is worn it must be replaced. Technician B says that the head can be machined to accept press-fit valve guide assemblies. Which technician is correct?

12. True or False: Valve seat inserts are shrink fit in the cylinder head.

13. Technician A says that all valves should be marked at removal to ensure that they will be replaced into the same guide position upon reassembly. Technician B says that it doesn't matter where they are placed after repair. Which technician is correct?

14. Technician A says that cylinder head bolts should be loosened off in the reverse order that they were torqued in, which is from the outside of the head toward the center. Technician B disagrees, saying that you should always start by loosening the head bolts from the center and working outward. Which technician is correct?

15. Technician A says that when remachining the fire deck of the cylinder head, you are limited to how much metal can be taken off. Therefore, refer to the engine manufacturer's specs for the minimum head thickness. Technician B says that it doesn't matter how much metal you remove; you can always use a thicker cylinder head gasket. Which technician knows the overhaul procedure best?

16. True or False: Heavy coolant scale buildup can result in cylinder head cracking due to overheating.

17. List the four methods that can be used to check a cylinder head for signs of cracks at engine overhaul.

18. True or False: Cylinder head flatness can be checked by visually looking at the surface condition.

19. Technician A says that valve guide wear can be determined without removing the cylinder head by following a set procedure, which includes using a dial indicator. Technician B says that the only way to determine valve guide wear is to remove and disassemble the cylinder head assembly. Which technician is correct?

20. To check valve face-to-seat contact, the best method to use is to lightly coat the face with
   a. blue layout ink
   b. Prussian blue paste
   c. Never-seize
   d. line pencil marks

21. Technician A says that the best way to remove valve seat inserts is to use a small, sharp chisel and a hammer to split them. Technician B says that you should employ a special puller assembly. Which technician is correct?

22. Technician A says that when installing new valve seat inserts, you can heat the head in a temperature-controlled oven and chill the insert for best results, or use a guided installer and press or tap (hammer) the insert

into place. Technician B says that you can simply drive the insert into the head with a hammer by working around the outer circumference of the insert. Who is correct?

23. Technician A says that valve face seat contact width and placement are very important when regrinding valves and seats. Technician B says that it doesn't matter where the seat contact is as long as a good, wide seat exists to help to dissipate valve head heat. Which technician has a better understanding of the valve and seat grinding procedure?

24. True or False: The terms *overcutting* and *undercutting* refer to the procedure used when it is necessary to use a grinding stone or cutter with a larger or smaller angle.

25. The term *three-angle grinding* is often used by high-performance cylinder head rebuild shops. Describe what this term means.

26. What kinds of problems would exist if a valve had too much head protrusion?

27. What kinds of problems would exist if a valve had too much intrusion?

28. Too wide a valve seat face contact surface usually results in what types of problems?

29. Too narrow a valve seat face contact area usually results in what kinds of problems?

30. Technician A says that if a cylinder head has worn valve guides, these should be replaced before attempting to regrind the valve seat inserts. Technician B says that replacement will have no bearing on the finished valve seat grind quality, because either a grinding stone or cutter will be used. Which technician understands the factors behind a good valve seat reconditioning procedure?

31. Technician A believes that using a grinding stone produces a better valve seat insert finish than using a valve seat cutter with blades. What do you think? Give your reasons.

32. How would you check a valve to determine if it is bent when you cannot see that it is bent?

33. After regrinding a valve face, you discover that the head margin is too thin. What types of problems would occur if you reused the valve?

34. What is an interference angle between a valve and its seat insert? Does this feature provide any advantages?

35. Technician A says that all valves should be lapped into their seats after grinding to produce a smooth finish. Technician B says that lapping should only be used, and very lightly, if a sealing test indicates poor seat-to-face contact. Which technician is correct?

36. Technician A says that to check for tight valve face-to-seat sealing, you can employ a vacuum pump and suction cup over the valve head, or you can turn the cylinder head on its side and fill the intake and exhaust ports with diesel fuel and check for signs of fluid leakage. Technician B says that you should seal off both the intake and exhaust ports on the cylinder head with bolted plates drilled to take a compressed air fitting to check for effective valve seat sealing. Which technician knows the correct procedure?

37. List the checks required on all valve springs when performing a cylinder head rebuild.

38. Technician A says that cylinder head gaskets are designed to be installed one way only. Technician B says that they can be installed in any direction since there is no top or bottom. Which technician is correct?

39. Technician A says that cylinder heads should be retorqued from the ends of the heads working toward the center. Technician B says that you should start the torquing sequence from the center of the head and work outward in a CW direction. Which technician knows the procedure best?

40. Technician A says that cylinder head retaining bolts should be lightly coated with clean engine oil or International Compound No. 2 or equivalent on the threads, as well as underneath the hex head to provide for a more uniform torque loading of the bolt. Technician B says that you should flood the cylinder block oil hole with clean engine oil to ensure that proper torque is achieved. Which technician is correct, and why?

41. Overtorquing of a cylinder head can result in
    a. bolt breakage
    b. head distortion
    c. head cracking
    d. coolant leakage into the cylinder
    e. all of the above

42. Undertorquing of a cylinder head can result in
    a. head gasket leakage
    b. head cracking
    c. valve breakage
    d. injector seizure

43. Technician A says that cylinder head nuts and bolts should be taken to their final value in one step after snugging up. Technician B says that you should torque these up in incremental values using two to three steps because this procedure will provide a more even torque. Which technician is correct?

10

Camshaft, Cam Followers, Pushrods, Rocker Arms, and Timing Gear Train

Overview

Information presented in this chapter will provide the service technician with the necessary knowledge associated with the ASE T2, M2, and M3 tasks lists tests, or the TQ (Trade Qualification) tests commonly used in Canada. The material specifically describes the engine valve/injector actuation components, often called the overhead, that are required to open and close the intake and exhaust valves, and operate the unit injector assembly on both mechanical unit injector (MUI) and electronic unit injector (EUI) equipped engines. The most important component in this group is the camshaft. With in-block camshafts shown in Figure 10–1, flat/mushroom lifters or roller follower designs, with a pushrod, are required to transfer motion through a rocker arm to open the valves and actuate the unit injectors. With overhead camshaft engines shown in Figure 10–2 for a single overhead camshaft, no pushrods are necessary to actuate either the valves or the unit injector; however, rocker arms are still required to transfer camshaft motion to these assemblies. See also Figure 9–2 which illustrates a dual overhead camshaft cylinder head assembly.

In some light automotive engines such as the VW diesel, the single overhead camshaft lobes act directly on flat bucket tappets to open the intake and exhaust valves. Since the camshaft must open and close the intake/exhaust valves at the correct number of degrees before and after TDC to provide the proper duration—and create the very high fuel injection pressures at the precise moment during the compression stroke (mechanical or electronic engines)—the camshaft must be timed to the engine gear train to ensure that this important function occurs at the proper time. After reading and completing this chapter you will need to apply

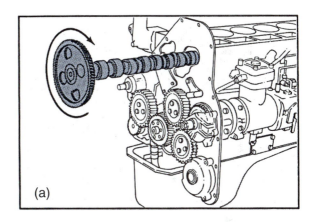

(a)

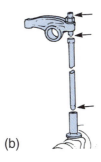

(b)

FIGURE 10–1 (a) Typical location of an in-block camshaft design for a Cummins L10 engine showing its drive gear in relation to the engine gear train. (b) Flat-type cam follower, pushrod, and rocker arm assembly used with an in-block camshaft design. (Courtesy of Cummins Engine Company, Inc.)

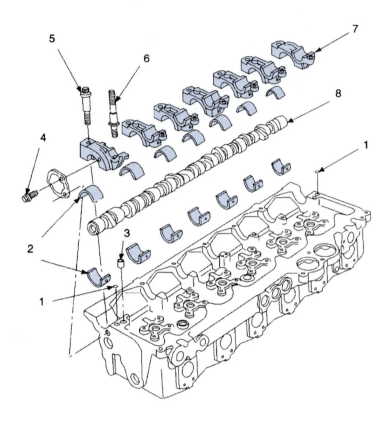

FIGURE 10–2 *Exploded view of a DDC series 60 overhead camshaft design and its components. (Courtesy of Detroit Diesel Corporation.)*

1. Round Dowel (2)
2. Bearing Shells
3. Bolt
4. Camshaft Cover
5. Bolt, Camshaft Cap (13)

6. Stud, Camshaft Cap (2)
7. Camshaft Cap
8. Camshaft
9. O-ring Seal (2)
10. Cylinder Head

the knowledge to perform and retain the art of diagnosis, troubleshooting, hands-on repairs, and adjustments to these components to thus master the skills required to challenge and pass ASE or TQ testing.

ASE CERTIFICATION

The components discussed in this chapter fall under the ASE medium/heavy truck test diesel engines (test T2) area, as well as the engine machinist tests for the cylinder block specialist—test M2, and assembly specialist—test M3.

Since the information contained in this chapter deals with camshafts, cam followers, pushrods, rocker arms, and the timing gear train, we list only those items from the ASE T2, M2, and M3 tasks lists areas appropriate to the following topics.

ASE Diesel Engines

Task List T2

Part B—Cylinder Head and Valve Train Diagnosis and Repair (5 ASE questions)

10. Inspect pushrods, rocker arms and shafts, electronic wiring harness and brackets for wear, bending, cracks, looseness, and blocked oil passages; repair and replace as needed.
11. Inspect, adjust/replace cam followers.
12. Adjust valve clearances.
13. Inspect, measure, and replace/reinstall overhead camshaft(s) and bearings; measure and adjust end play and backlash.

Part C—Engine Block Diagnosis and Repair (5 ASE questions)

8. Inspect, measure, and replace/reinstall in-block camshaft; measure/adjust end play.

11. Inspect, reinstall, and time the drive gear train. (Includes checking timing sensors, gear wear, and backlash of the crankshaft, camshaft, auxiliary gearing, and drive and idler gears; service shafts, bushings, and bearings.

ASE Engine Machinist— Cylinder Block Specialist

Task List M2

Part A—Cylinder Block Disassembly and Cleaning (5 ASE questions)

4. Remove and inspect camshaft bearings and auxiliary/balance shaft bearings/ bushings; identify locations.

Part C—Cylinder Block Machining (22 ASE questions)

9. Measure camshaft and auxiliary/balance shaft bearing housing bores and alignment; repair as required.

12. Inspect lifter bores; repair as necessary.

ASE Machinist—Assembly Specialist

Task List M3

Part A—Engine Disassembly, Inspection, and Cleaning (10 ASE questions)

4. Rotate engine to place No. 1 cylinder at TDC compression.
   Note engine OEM's timing marks between all gears so marked; remove the fuel injection pump noting the timing marks; remove the supercharger/blower and turbocharger.

9. Remove all valve lifters (flat or roller follower type), and identify each lifter's location for reinstallation in the same position if reusing during assembly.

10. Note timing marks, inspect and remove timing/retaining components.

16. Remove and inspect the camshaft (in-block or overhead), plus the auxiliary balance shaft(s) if used.

17. Remove and inspect accessory (auxiliary/balance shaft) bearings/bushing; identify bushing locations for reinstallation in the same position if reusing during assembly.

18. Remove and inspect camshaft bearings; identify locations.

Part B—Engine Preparation (11 ASE questions)

3. Install camshaft bearings, auxiliary/balance shaft bushings/bearings; verify location, position, and correct fit.

Part C—Short Block Assembly (17 ASE questions)

2. Install mushroom-type lifters.

3. Install camshaft, auxiliary/balance shaft(s), and related components.

6. Install timing gear components, verify correct timing positions, and check gear backlash and end play.

Part D—Long Block Assembly (14 ASE questions)

8. Install lifters/cam followers as appropriate.

9. Install in-block camshaft pushrods and associated valve train components; check and verify valve lash settings.

SYSTEM STRUCTURE AND FUNCTION

During engine operation the camshaft (a long shaft with cams on it), cam followers, pushrods, and timing gears (Figure 10–1) work together to open and close the intake and exhaust valves. As the valves open and close, intake air is admitted into the cylinder on the intake stroke and exhaust gases are allowed to move out of the cylinder on the exhaust stroke, allowing the engine to breathe. In addition to providing the mechanism to operate the valves, the camshaft and timing gear train may also be utilized to operate the fuel transfer pump (sometimes called a lift pump), injection pump, and the engine oil pump. The onblock camshaft shown in Figure 10–1 fits into the engine block in bores (drilled holes) fitted with sleeve-type bearings or is mounted in bearing supports on top of the cylinder head (overhead camshaft engines; Figure 10–2). Lubrication is provided by splash in some engines, whereas in others it is provided to the cam bushings or bearings under pressure from the oil pump.

The camshaft in a diesel engine is used to operate the intake and exhaust valves. In most diesel engines this camshaft will have two lobes per cylinder to operate the intake and exhaust valves.

NOTE: On unit injector engines such as Detroit Diesel, Cat, Volvo, and Cummins, an additional lobe or cam on the camshaft is used to operate the injector. In these engines the camshaft will have three lobes per cylinder, as in Figure 10–3, which illustrates an overhead camshaft design.

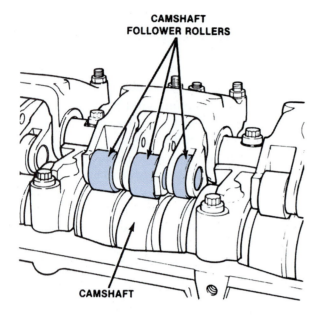

CAMSHAFT FOLLOWER ROLLERS

CAMSHAFT

FIGURE 10–3 *DDC series 60 engine overhead camshaft roller followers; the left-hand roller actuates the exhaust valves, the center follower actuates the injector, and the right-hand follower actuates the intake valves. (Courtesy of Detroit Diesel Corporation.)*

Figure 10–4 illustrates the two camshafts used by Cummins in their 15 L (912 in³.) displacement, inline six-cylinder dual overhead camshaft (DOHC) ISX and Signature series engine models. The first cam (large diameter) drives the fuel injector rocker arms required to create the very-high pressure fuel injection for clean, responsive power. The cam lobes are extra wide for longer life and higher-pressure capacity. The second camshaft (smaller diameter) operates both the intake and exhaust valves, but also includes a dedicated set of lobes for the operation of the integrated (Intebrake) engine compression brake.

Working with the camshaft to operate the valves are:

1. *Cam followers.* Sleevelike plungers that fit into bored holes in the block and ride on the camshaft. They are also called lifters (Figure 10–5).

2. *Pushrods.* Long, hollow, or solid rods that fit into the cam followers on one end with the other end fitting into a ball socket arrangement on the rocker arm (Figure 10–5).

3. *Rocker arms and rocker arm shaft* (Figure 10–6). The rocker arms provide the pivot point between the pushrod and valve or injector. Generally mounted on a shaft that is supported by brackets bolted to the cylinder head, the rocker arms are pushed up on one end by the pushrod and rock on the shaft much like a lever. The opposite end pushes the valve down against the spring pressure, allowing air into the cylinder or exhaust gases out. Most rocker arms have an adjusting

FIGURE 10–4 *Dual overhead camshaft design and component identification for the Cummins Signature/ISX engines. (Courtesy of Cummins Engine Company, Inc.)*

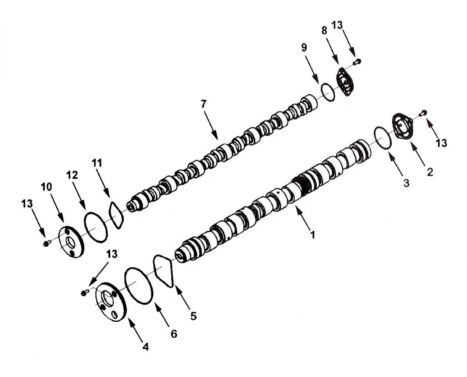

Ref No.	Part Number	Part Name	Req	Remarks
		CAMSHAFT		
		OPTION PP2628		
		OPTION PP2629		
1	3681710	Camshaft	1	
2	4026588	Cover, Camshaft	1	
3	4026523	Seal, Rectangular Ring		
4	3679929	Support, Camshaft Thrust	1	Injector
5	3679931	Gasket, Camshaft Cover	1	Injector
6	3679933	Seal, O Ring	1	Injector
7	3412284	Camshaft	1	
8	4026587	Cover, Camshaft	1	
9	4026522	Seal, Rectangular Ring		
10	3679930	Support, Camshaft Thrust	1	Valve
11	3679932	Gasket, Camshaft Cover	1	Valve
12	3679934	Seal, O Ring	1	Valve
13	3902460	Screw, Hex Flange Head Cap	8	M10 X 1.50 X 25.

FIGURE 10–4   (continued).

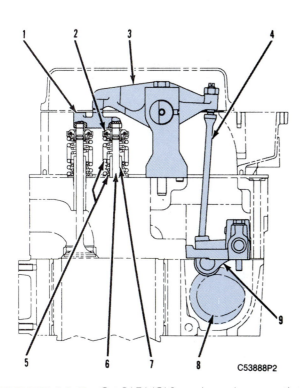

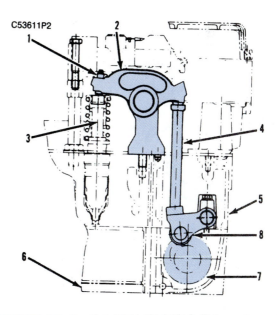

FIGURE 10–6   Cat 3176/C10/C12 EUI engine, electronically controlled but mechanically actuated, unit injector operating mechanism: 1. adjusting nut; 2. rocker arm assembly; 3. electronically controlled unit injector; 4. pushrod; 5. cylinder head; 6. spacer block; 7. camshaft; 8. lifter. (Courtesy of Cummins Engine Company, Inc.)

FIGURE 10–5   Cat 3176/C10 engine valve operating mechanism: 1. intake bridge; 2. rotocoil; 3. intake rocker arm; 4. pushrod; 5. valve springs (inner and outer); 6. intake valve; 7. valve guide; 8. camshaft; 9. lifter. (Reprinted courtesy of Caterpillar, Inc.)

screw and locknut that are used to adjust the clearance from rocker arm to valve (tappet).

Figure 10–7 illustrates the overhead rocker lever components arrangement supported on their respective rocker shafts, as required with the Cummins

ISX/Signature DOHC engine models. Each cylinder has four rocker levers consisting of:

- The exhaust valves rocker lever (bottom row in diagram; roller followers driven from the smaller-diameter camshaft). There are two exhaust valves per cylinder where each rocker arm contacts a valve crosshead mechanism to accomplish the opening task.

- The intake valves rocker lever (bottom row in diagram; roller followers driven from the smaller-diameter camshaft). There are two intake valves per cylinder where each rocker arm contacts a valve crosshead mechanism to accomplish the opening task.
- The injector rocker lever (upper row in diagram; driven from larger-diameter camshaft).
- The engine compression brake rocker lever (driven from smaller-diameter camshaft).

On ISX/Signature Series engines, the control system is split into two banks. The front bank controls cylinders 1, 2, and 3, while the rear bank controls cylinders 4, 5, and 6. Therefore, the four rocker lever shafts employed are:

1. front valve and brake rocker lever shaft
2. rear valve and brake rocker lever shaft
3. front injector rocker lever shaft
4. rear injector rocker lever shaft

Overhead Camshaft Inspection Flowchart

To assist with the recommended ASE tasks lists chart for the camshaft, Figure 10–8 lists in "flowchart" form the important items that should be closely inspected to determine repair or replacement. Although this particular flowchart is for an overhead camshaft assembly, it can be applied to an in-block type of camshaft. More specific details of what to look for during camshaft inspection are provided in the following section.

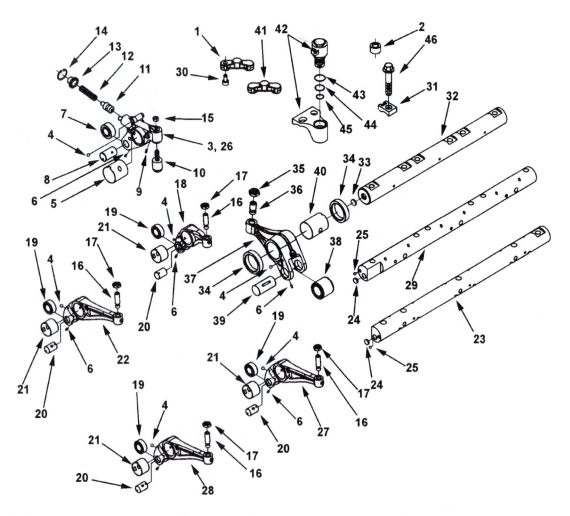

FIGURE 10–7   Exploded view of the rocker arms and components identification for a Signature/ISX engine model. (Courtesy of Cummins Engine Company, Inc.)

Ref No.	Part Number	Part Name	Req	Remarks
		ROCKER LEVER		
		OPTION RL1731		Use with Jacobs engine brake.
				Detent control valve centering mechanism.
				Application: Automotive and Industrial.
1	3412261	Crosshead, Valve	6	
2	3412351	Spacer, Mounting	2	
	3413135	Assb. Rocker Lever	1	
	3413098	Lever, Engine Brake	3	
3	3413127	Lever, Engine Brake	1	
5	3413133	Bushing	1	
7	3679914	Roller, Cam Follower	1	
8	3680173	Pin, Cam Follower Roller	1	
9	3871558	Plug, Pipe	1	
10	3413128	Piston, Engine Brake Slave	1	
11	3413129	Valve, Check	1	
12	3413130	Spring, Compression	1	
13	3413131	Cover, Actuator	1	
14	3413132	Ring, Retaining	1	
15	3679921	Nut, Regular Hexagon Jam	1	
	3679891	Lever, Rocker	3	
16	3679033	Screw, Rkr Lever Adjusting	1	
17	3679694	Nut, Regular Hexagon Jam	1	
18	(3679890)	Lever, Rocker	1	
4	3067941	Plug, Ball	1	
19	3679336	Roller, Cam Follower	1	
20	3679487	Pin, Cam Follower Roller	1	
21	3679488	Bushing	1	
6	3679504	Pin, Roll	1	
	3680667	Lever, Rocker	3	
16	3679033	Screw, Rkr Lever Adjusting	1	
17	3679694	Nut, Regular Hexagon Jam	1	
22	3680666	Lever, Rocker	1	
4	3067941	Plug, Ball	1	
19	3679336	Roller, Cam Follower	1	
20	3679487	Pin, Cam Follower Roller	1	
21	3679488	Bushing	1	
6	3679504	Pin, Roll	1	
23	3681421	Shaft, Rocker Lever	1	
24	(3680954)	Plug, Drive	2	
25	(3680955)	Plug, Ball	2	
	3413136	Assembly, Rocker Lever	1	
	3413098	Lever, Engine Brake	3	
26	3413127	Lever, Engine Brake	1	
4	3067941	Plug, Ball	1	
5	3413133	Bushing	1	
6	3679504	Pin, Roll	1	
7	3679914	Roller, Cam Follower	1	
8	3680173	Pin, Cam Follower Roller	1	
9	3871558	Plug, Pipe	1	
10	3413128	Piston, Engine Brake Slave	1	
11	3413129	Valve, Check	1	
12	3413130	Spring, Compression	1	
13	3413131	Cover, Actuator	1	
14	3413132	Ring, Retaining	1	
15	3679921	Nut, Regular Hexagon Jam	1	
	3679893	Lever, Rocker	3	
16	3679033	Screw, Rkr Lever Adjusting	1	
17	3679694	Nut, Regular Hexagon Jam	1	

FIGURE 10–7 (continued).

Ref No.	Part Number	Part Name	Req	Remarks
27	(3679892)	Lever, Rocker	1	
4	3067941	Plug, Ball	1	
19	3679336	Roller, Cam Follower	1	
20	3679487	Pin, Cam Follower Roller	1	
21	3679488	Bushing	1	
6	3679504	Pin, Roll	1	
	3680670	Lever, Rocker	3	
16	3679033	Screw, Rkr Lever Adjusting	1	
17	3679694	Nut, Regular Hexagon Jam	1	
28	(3680669)	Lever, Rocker	1	
4	3067941	Plug, Ball	1	
19	3679336	Roller, Cam Follower	1	
20	3679487	Pin, Cam Follower Roller	1	
21	3679488	Bushing	1	
6	3679504	Pin, Roll	1	
29	3681423	Shaft, Rocker Lever	1	
24	(3680954)	Plug, Drive	2	
25	(3680955)	Plug, Ball	2	
30	3413137	Guide, Valve Crosshead	6	
31	3679427	Clamp, Retaining	4	
	(3680153)	Assembly, Rocker Lever	1	
32	3679418	Shaft, Rocker Lever	1	
33	3019630	Plug, Drive	2	
34	3679935	Spacer, Thrust Ring	6	
	3680169	Lever, Rocker	3	
35	3680057	Nut, Regular Hexagon Jam	1	
36	3680058	Screw, Rkr Lever Adjusting	1	
37	(3680168)	Lever, Rocker	1	
4	3067941	Plug, Ball	3	
6	3679504	Pin, Roll	1	
38	3679868	Roller, Cam Follower	1	
39	3679869	Pin, Cam Follower Roller	1	
40	3679870	Bushing	1	
41	3680475	Crosshead, Valve	6	
	(3680664)	Assembly, Rocker Lever	1	
32	3779418	Shaft, Rocker Lever	1	
33	3019630	Plug, Drive	2	
34	3679935	Spacer, Thrust Ring	6	
	3800942	Kit, Solenoid		
42	4026536	Valve, Engine Brake	3	
	4026538	Solenoid	1	
43	4026537	Seal, Rectangular Ring	1	
44	3871218	Seal, Rectangular Ring	1	
45	3871638	Seal, Rectangular Ring	1	
46	3681221	Screw, Hex Flange Head Cap	24	

FIGURE 10–7 (continued).

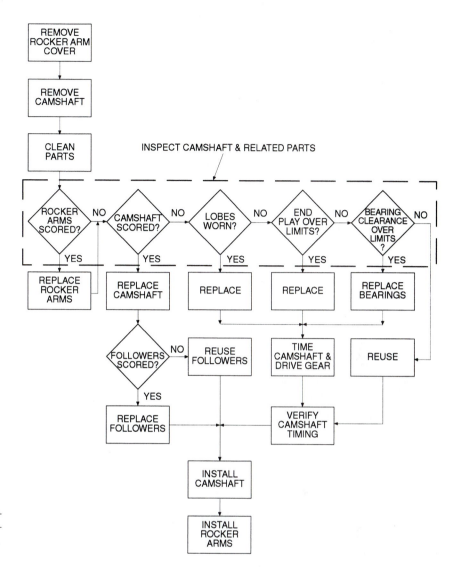

FIGURE 10-8 Diagnostic flow-chart to determine repair or replacement of the camshaft and related parts. (Courtesy of Detroit Diesel Corporation.)

CAMSHAFT CLEANING AND INSPECTION

The power required to turn the camshaft and operate the valves is supplied by the crankshaft through the timing gear train. The time when the valves open and close is called valve timing and is controlled by the timing gears (the cam lobes and their placement on the camshaft). This valve timing becomes a critical part of the engine design, as engine fuel efficiency, power, and smooth operation are dependent upon it. Because valve timing is so important in the operation of the engine, all component parts related to it must be checked during an engine overhaul.

It is assumed at this time that the camshaft has been removed. Since the camshaft is an internal engine part that constantly runs in lubricating oil within the engine, it requires little cleanup. Generally, it can be cleaned by rinsing in a cleaning solvent of the type used in a shop cleaning tank or by steaming with a steam cleaner.

NOTE If the camshaft has oil galleries or oil passageways, clean them with a wire brush and compressed air.

After cleaning, blow dry with compressed air. Then visually inspect the shaft, cam lobes, and bearing surfaces. This visual inspection must include the following:

1. Inspection of the cam lobes for pitting, scoring, or wear

2. Inspection of cam bearing journals for scoring, bluing, or wear

3. Inspection of cam drive gear keyway for cracks or distortion

---

NOTE Detroit Diesel two-cycle engines use a unique camshaft-bearing (bushing) arrangement (Figure 10–9) made up of two bearing halves that when fitted together around the camshaft journal make up the camshaft bearing. Holding the bearing together until it and the camshaft are installed into the block is a spring ring. After installation in the block, the bearing is secured with a setscrew. See the engine repair manual or consult your instructor for correct removal procedures.

If the camshaft does not pass this visual inspection, it must be discarded and replaced with a new one. If the camshaft does pass visual inspection, it must be inspected further, using a micrometer to measure the cam lobes and bearing journals. Measure the cambearing journals as shown in Figure 10–10 using a micrometer and comparing the measurement to specifications supplied by the engine manufacturer. Since engine manufacturers recommend many different ways to check camshaft lobes, consult the service manual before making the cam lobe measurement. In addition, to perform an accurate check, you must have a thorough understanding of cam lobe design. Study the cam lobe shown in Figure 10–11 before making any checks.

Listed below are several procedures that can be used to check a cam lobe:

1. Measure with a micrometer from heel to toe with the outside micrometer to determine if the cam is worn sufficiently to affect lift. (Refer to specifications.)

2. Measure with a micrometer at the base circle, then heel to toe, and subtract the base circle from the heel–toe measurement to determine the cam lift.

3. Measure the cam lobe for wear using a feeler gauge and piece of hard square stock slightly longer than the lobe width. Lay the stock across the cam lobe and attempt to insert the feeler gauge as shown (Figure 10–12). The cam lobe should not be worn in excess of 0.003 in. (0.076 mm).

4. Measure the cam lobe from heel to toe and compare with specifications.

5. Some engine manufacturers recommend placing the camshaft in V blocks and using a dial indicator to check runout.

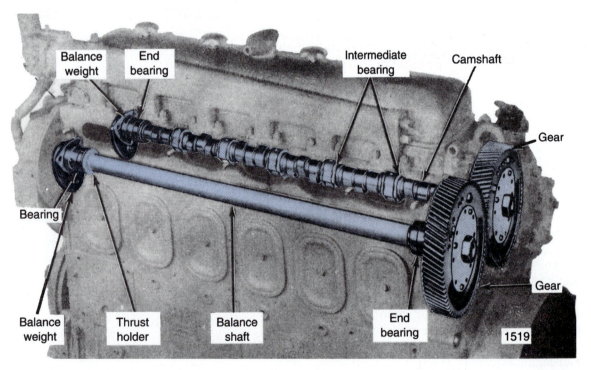

FIGURE 10–9 Location of both the camshaft and balance shaft for a two-stroke cycle DDC inline 6-71 engine model. (Courtesy of Detroit Diesel Corporation.)

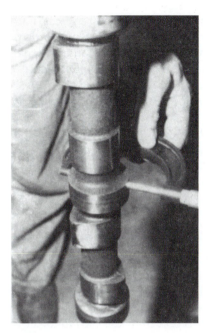

FIGURE 10–10 *Using an outside micrometer to measure the camshaft journal diameters.*

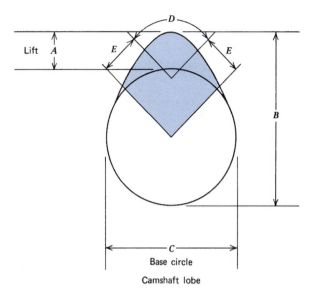

FIGURE 10–11 Example camshaft lobe design. A = lift, B = lift plus base circle dimension, C = base circle, D = nose, E = flank.

FIGURE 10–12 *Checking cam lobes using a feeler gauge and square stock. (Courtesy of Detroit Diesel Corporation.)*

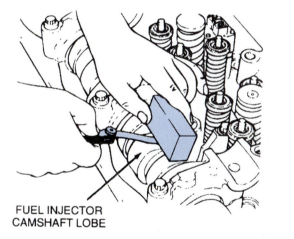

FUEL INJECTOR
CAMSHAFT LOBE

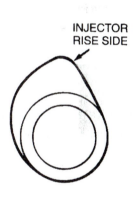

INJECTOR
RISE SIDE

NOTE If the equipment is not available to do step 5, perform a close check on the camshaft runout by inserting the camshaft into its bore in the block. If the camshaft turns freely without binding, you can assume that it is straight.

When the foregoing checks have been completed and the camshaft is considered usable, closely check each lobe for roughness or burrs on the cam lobe surface. These small surface imperfections can be removed by sanding with a fine crocus cloth.

Inspecting with the Camshaft in the Engine

In some situations it may become necessary to check the cam lobe lift with the camshaft installed in the engine. This can be done by using a dial indicator in the following manner:

1. Remove the rocker arm assembly and place the dial indicator on the engine as shown in Figure 10–13, with the plunger of indicator on the pushrod.

2. Turn the engine until the pushrod has bottomed (dial indicator will stop moving). This indicates that the cam follower is on the base circle or heel of the cam lobe. Zero the indicator at this point.

FIGURE 10–13 *Measuring camshaft lobe lift on an engine by use of a dial indicator centered into and zeroed in the pushrod cup/ball end.*

3. Turn the engine until the dial indicator needle stops moving in one direction (clockwise, for example) and begins to move in the opposite direction. This indicates that the cam follower has moved up on the cam to the point of highest travel and is starting to drop off (or recede).

> NOTE   It may be necessary to back the engine up for a quarter-turn and then turn it back in the direction of rotation to reestablish the point of maximum rise.

4. Record the dial indicator travel from zero to maximum rise. This represents the cam lobe lift and should be compared with the manufacturer's specifications.

5. If the cam lobe lift is less than the manufacturer's specifications, the camshaft must be replaced.

Valve/Injector Operating Mechanism Inspection Flowchart

The intake and exhaust valves and unit injectors can be operated by roller tappets/followers in contact with the camshaft lobes, then via pushrods and rocker arms in in-block camshafts. With overhead camshafts, roller followers and rocker arm assemblies are used to actuate the valves and injectors. Figure 10–14 is a flowchart

that can be used as a general guide when inspecting and determining needed repairs or parts replacement of the valve and injector operating mechanism. More specific details of an inspection procedure follow.

CAM FOLLOWER INSPECTION

As explained previously, the cam followers are round, sleeve-shaped devices that ride on the camshaft lobes in a bored guide hole in the block or are attached to the rocker arms as shown in Figures 10–3 and 10–7. The followers guide and support the pushrods in en-block engines.

> NOTE   Some cam followers (See figure 10–15A) have a roller attached to the end of the sleeve. This roller rolls on the camshaft lobes and aids in the reduction of friction (Figure 10–15B) shows the connection from the cam follower up to the rocker arms.

Sleeve-type cam followers must be checked on the thrust face for pitting and scoring. Roller-type cam followers must be disassembled so that a check of the roller, roller bushing, and roller pin can be performed. Consult the engine repair manual before attempting to disassemble roller and pin from a cam follower. Most manufacturers recommend special procedures and fixtures for removal of the pin and roller. If this procedure is not followed, damage to the cam follower may result.

If roller bushing and pin are worn excessively or beyond the manufacturer's specifications, they should be replaced with new ones.

> NOTE   The foregoing procedures apply in general to overhead valve engines (those with pushrods and cam followers). Some diesel engines may have overhead camshaft arrangements. Engines with this type of arrangement will have different cam followers that require different checking procedures. Consult the service manual when working on these engines.

PUSHROD INSPECTION

The long metal rod or tube that rides in the cam follower and extends upward to the rocker arm is a very important part of the valve operating mechanism. In normal service very few problems are associated with

FIGURE 10–14 Diagnostic flowchart to determine repair or replacement of the camshaft, valve, and injector operating mechanism. (Courtesy of Detroit Diesel Corporation.)

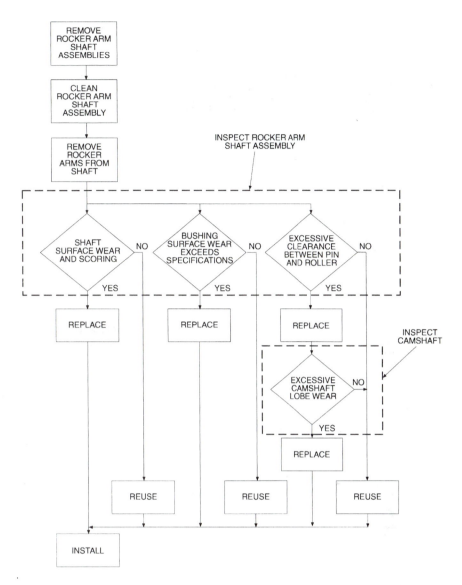

the pushrod. Pushrod damage generally occurs when the rocker arms are incorrectly adjusted or the engine is overspeeded.

When the pushrods are removed as a result of engine service, they should be checked for the following:

Straightness by rolling on a flat surface or with a straightedge
Ball and socket wear, usually with a magnifying glass or as recommended by the manufacturer

NOTE: Hollow push tubes used in some Cummins engines should be checked to determine if they are full of oil by tapping them lightly on a

hard surface. A hollow sound should result. If not, the tube is full of oil and indicates that the ball pressed into the tube is loose. Replace the push tube if this condition is found.

NOTE: Straightening of push tubes is discouraged. Bent ones should be replaced with new. Push tubes must be checked for wear, breaks, or cracks where the ball socket on either end has been fitted into the tube. Place rods or tubes in the engine, making sure that they fit into the cam followers or tappets correctly.

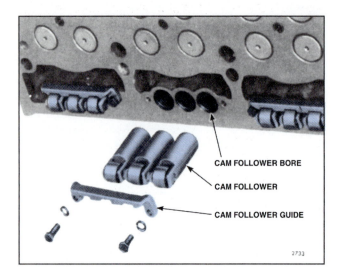

FIGURE 10-15 *Exploded view showing the valve and MUI (mechanical unit injector) operating mechanism used on two-stroke-cycle 53, 71, and 92 series DDC engines. (Courtesy of Detroit Diesel Corporation.)*

ROCKER ARM INSPECTION

Rocker arms should be inspected and checked as outlined.

Checking and Installing the Rocker Arm

The rocker arm assembly or rocker arm is one component part of the engine that is occasionally overlooked during a diesel engine overhaul. Some technicians have the mistaken assumption that rocker arms wear very little or not at all. This is not true. Rocker arm wear may account for increased engine oil consumption. Oil consumption occurs because the increased clearance allows an excessive amount of oil to splash or leak on the valve stem. This oil will run down the valve and end up in the combustion chamber.

Rocker Arm Checks

The rocker arms and rocker arm assembly should be visually checked for the following:

1. Rocker arm bushing wear
2. Rocker arm shaft wear

Although some manufacturers may give a dimension for the shaft and bushing, the decision to replace should not rest entirely on dimension. The appearance of the shaft and bushing is a factor in determining if a replacement should take place. Look for:

1. *Scoring.*
2. *Pitting.* It must also be kept in mind that a bushing may be acceptable now but not after an additional 2000 hours of operation.
3. *Magnetic inspection.* Some manufacturers recommend that the rocker arms be checked for cracks using a magnetic-type tester. If equipment is available, it is recommended that this check be made.

Installing and Adjusting the Rocker Arm

Place rocker arm assembly or housing on engine, making sure that rocker arm sockets engage the pushrods.

NOTE Rocker arm assemblies on some engines may be built into a separate housing called a rocker box. These box assemblies will require the installation of gaskets between them and the cylinder head.

CAUTION If rocker arm or tappet adjusting screws were not loosened during engine disassembly, they should be loosened at this time. This ensures that no damage will result to the valves or valve train when the rocker arm assembly is pulled in place with the hold-down bolts.

Install rocker arm hold-down bolts and torque them to specifications.

NOTE Some rocker arms may be held in place with bolts that serve as head bolts in addition to holding the rocker arms. These bolts will be tightened to the same torque as the head bolts.

Checking the Valve Crossheads (Bridges) and Guides

Valve crossheads are used on some types of diesel engines that use *four-valve heads.* Four-valve heads used on four-stroke-cycle engines have two intake and two exhaust valves per cylinder. Two-stroke-cycle engines such as Detroit Diesel use four exhaust valves in each cylinder. The crosshead is a bracket or bridgelike device that allows a single rocker arm to open two valves at the same time (Figure 10–5 and 10–16).

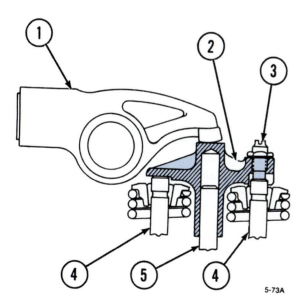

5-73A

FIGURE 10–16 *Close-up view of a four-valve head showing: 1. the rocker arm used to actuate two valves simultaneously; 2. yoke/bridge or crosshead; 3. yoke adjusting screw; 4. valve stem; 5. yoke guide pin. (Courtesy of Mack Trucks, Inc.)*

The crossheads (bridge) must be checked for wear as follows:

1. Check the crosshead for cracks visually and with magnetic crack detector if available.
2. Check the crosshead inside diameter for out-of-roundness and excessive diameter.
3. Visually check for wear at the point of contact between rocker lever and crosshead.
4. Check the adjusting screw threads for broken or worn threads.
5. Check the crosshead guide pin for diameter with micrometer.
6. Check the crosshead guide pin to ensure that it is at right angles to head-milled surface.
7. If the guide pin requires replacement, check the engine service manual for the correct procedure.

VALVE ADJUSTMENT

Valve lash adjustment can be performed only when the valves are in a fully closed position or on the base circle of the camshaft. By following the engine firing order, all valves and unit injectors can be adjusted on four-stroke engines in two complete crankshaft revolutions (720°); on two-stroke-cycle engines, all valves and injectors can be adjusted in one full turn (360°) of the crankshaft. All later-model engines have several decals attached to the engine or rocker cover(s) that indicate U.S. EPA emissions certification as well as the intake and exhaust valve clearances and the injector setting information.

The procedure required to check or set both the valves and injectors on different makes of engines can be considered common; the position of the valves and injectors and *specific* setting processes, however, do vary. First we will discuss a general procedure, then specific procedures for a number of well-known high-speed heavy-duty diesel engines, many of which are using electronically controlled unit fuel injectors. On engines that have nozzles rather than unit-type injectors, either a distributor-type or inline multiple-plunger injection pump is used. Therefore, no adjustment is required to the nozzle while it is in the engine, although the nozzle popping pressure can be adjusted by the use of shims or a setscrew during nozzle service.

General Procedure

Valves can be checked and adjusted by rotating the engine over in its normal direction of rotation and choosing one of the following methods for four-stroke-cycle engines.

1. Visually determine when the inlet valve starts to open and the exhaust valve has just closed. This procedure is commonly referred to as the *rocking motion of valve adjustment*. For example, consider an inline six-cylinder engine with a conventional firing order of 1–5–3–6–2–4. The valves to be adjusted on a given cylinder can be determined as follows:

Rocking Cylinder	Cylinder/Valves to Be Adjusted
6	1
2	5
4	3
1	6
5	2
3	4

Figure 10–17 illustrates a feeler gauge installed between the end of the rocker arm and the valve stem on a two–valve-head engine. On four–valve-head models, the clearance is checked between the rocker arm and the valve bridge pallet surface. To accomplish valve adjustment, loosen off the locknut at the rear of the rocker arm; then rotate the slotted screw either CW or CCW until the desired lash is achieved. Tighten the nut to specs while securely holding the adjusting screw. The next cylinder intake and exhaust valves can then be adjusted by rotating the engine manually another 120°, or one-third of a turn. Continue this process until all valves have been adjusted.

2. Again let us consider an inline six-cylinder engine. On a two–valve–head model there are 12 valves (6 intake and 6 exhaust). On a four–valve-head model there are 24 valves (12 intake and 12 exhaust); two valves

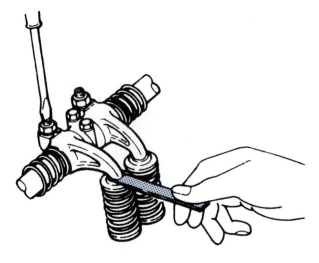

FIGURE 10–17 *Location of feeler gauge placement to check the clearance between the rocker arm pallet and valve stem on a two–valve/head engine. (Reprinted courtesy of Caterpillar, Inc.)*

(one set), however, are opened at once through the bridge mechanism. If we use what is commonly referred to as the *thirteen system* (front to rear of engine), we can easily set both the intake and exhaust valves as follows:

> Starting from the front of the engine, note that the valves or valve sets (2) are numbered consecutively 1 through 12 for either a two- or four-valve head.
>
> To set any valve clearance, visually determine when any valve is fully open while rotating the engine manually.
>
> Assume that valve 5 is fully open. To obtain a count of 13, we check and adjust the valve clearance on valve 8. Similarly, if valve 9 is fully open, we check and adjust valve 4. By following this procedure, we can quickly check and adjust all valves.

On a four-cylinder four-stroke engine, a *nine system* is used to check and adjust the valve clearances.

TECH TIP Go-no-go feeler gauges provide a more accurate clearance feel than straight single-dimension feeler gauges, as they do not depend on individual technician feel as to how tight or how loose the gauge is when pulled between the rocker arm and bridge mechanism. Go-no-go feeler gauges are manufactured with a stepped design where the first 0.5 in. (12.7 mm) length of the gauge is of a size two-thousandths smaller than the step-up portion of the gauge. For example, if a valve clearance spec is quoted as being 0.016 in. (0.406 mm), you would select a 0.015 to 0.017 in. (0.381 to 0.431 mm) go-no-go feeler gauge. When the valve lash clearance has been adjusted correctly, the 0.015 in. end of the gauge should pass freely between the end of the rocker arm and bridge, while the 0.017 in. end should not; this ensures that there is a definite 0.016 in. clearance. You will actually feel the larger part of the gauge bump against the pallet surface of the rocker arm when you attempt to push it through. If you adjust the clearance to allow the thicker end of the go-no-go gauge to pass through with very little drag, once the locknut has been tightened, you will find that the clearance is usually correct. Once you have used go-no-go gauges, you will find it hard to use anything else to set valve clearances. After a short period of usage, you will find that you can set valve clearances faster and more accurately with this type of a gauge.

Valve and Injector Adjustment

All of the intake and exhaust valves should now be adjusted along with the mechanical or electronic unit injector assembly timing height. The correct sequence to use will depend on the engine make and its firing order. Refer to the information contained in Chapters 21, 22, and 23, which describe in detail how best to adjust valve clearances and injector timing heights.

After valve and injector adjustment, install the rocker arm covers. New gaskets should be used on the cover or covers and glued to the cover with a gasket adhesive. Install the intake manifold, exhaust manifold, generator or alternator, thermostat housing, and any other accessory that could not be installed before the heads were installed. After this final assembly, recheck all hose connections and electrical connections to ensure that all connections are completed and tight.

INSPECTION, REPLACEMENT, AND ASSEMBLY OF THE TIMING GEAR TRAIN

The timing gear train will include all gears that drive the camshaft and will generally include the crankshaft gear, idler gear, and camshaft gear. Figures 10–18 through 10–20 illustrate three gear train examples. All gears in the timing gear train should be checked when the camshaft or cam gear is serviced, because any wear on an associated gear in the train may have an adverse effect on the camshaft gear and/or engine timing. In addition, worn gears may cause a knocking noise in the engine or fail after a few hours of operation.

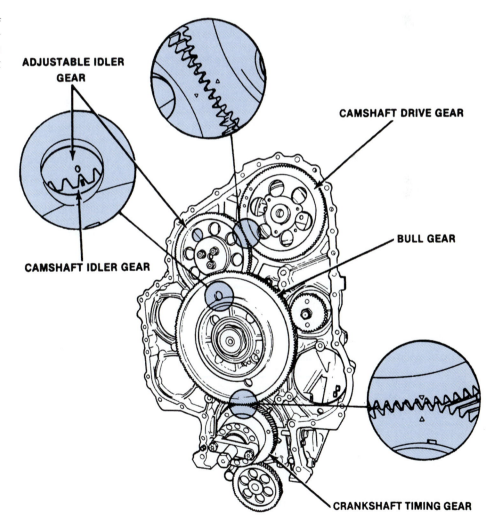

FIGURE 10–18 *View of the individual gears and their timing marks for a series 60 DDC engine. (Courtesy of Detroit Diesel Corporation.)*

ADJUSTABLE IDLER GEAR

CAMSHAFT DRIVE GEAR

CAMSHAFT IDLER GEAR

BULL GEAR

CRANKSHAFT TIMING GEAR

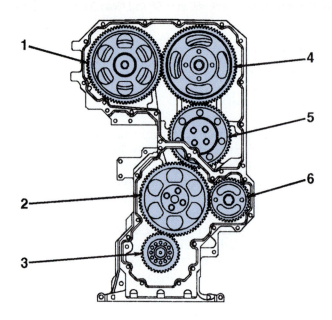

Table 1, Complete Gear Train

1. Valve camshaft gear
2. Lower idler gear
3. Crankshaft gear
4. Injector camshaft gear
5. Adjustable idler gear
6. Accessory gear

FIGURE 10–19 *Exploded view of the gear train and housing and component identification for the Signature/ISX engine models. (Courtesy of Cummins Engine Company, Inc.)*

Inspecting the Timing Gears

The timing gears should be visually inspected for the following:

- Chipped teeth
- Pitted teeth
- Burred teeth

NOTE   Often a close visual inspection of the timing gears will reveal a slight roll or lip on each gear tooth caused by wear. A gear worn with this type of wear should be replaced.

Removing the Camshaft Gear

If the camshaft gear is to be replaced, it must be removed from the camshaft using either a press or a puller. If a press is to be used, follow these general rules:

1.   Ensure that the gear is supported on the center hub next to the shaft to prevent cracking or breaking.

246

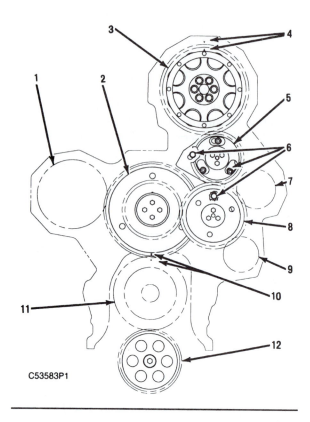

(1)   Water pump gear.

(2)   Cluster gear. Tighten four cluster gear bolts to a torque of .... 28 ± 7 N•m (21 ± 5 lb ft)
Tighten five cluster gear stubshaft bolts to a torque of .... 50 ± 10 N•m (37 ± 7 lb ft)

(3)   Camshaft gear. Tighten six camshaft bolts to a torque of .... 240 ± 40 N•m (176 ± 29 lb ft)

(4)   Align timing marks.

(5)   Adjustable idler gear assembly. Set distance between the centers of the camshaft gear and the adjustable idler gear to obtain a backlash of .... .250 ± .076 mm (.0010 ± .0030 in)
Tighten the three adjustable idler gear bolts to a torque of .... 28 ± 7 N•m (21 ± 5 lb ft)

NOTE: See Testing And Adjusting for the correct procedures to set the camshaft gear backlash.

(6)   Tighten two bolts and five nuts to a torque of .... 47 ± 9 N•m (35 ± 7 lb ft)

(7)   Air compressor gear.

(8)   Idler gear assembly. Tighten three idler gear bolts to a torque of .... 28 ± 7 N•m (21 ± 5 lb ft)

(9)   Fuel transfer pump gear.

(10) Align timing marks.

(11) Crankshaft gear.

(12) Oil pump drive gear. Tighten oil pump drive gear to a torque of .... 50 ± 10 N•m (37 ± 7 lb ft)

FIGURE 10–20 *Gear train timing group for a Cat 3406E engine with component identification. (Reprinted courtesy of Caterpillar, Inc.)*

2. Place a shaft protector on the end of the camshaft to protect the shaft.

3. Press shaft from gear (Figure 10–21).

CAUTION Safety glasses should be worn when the press is being used, and the engine service manual should be checked to determine if any special pullers, supports, or procedures are to be used.

NOTE If failure of the timing gear train has occurred, it is very important at this point to determine what may have caused it; for example, lack of lubrication, gear misalignment or overloading, wrong gear for the application, or normal wear. Make sure that you know what caused the failure before you reassemble the gear train.

Replacing the Camshaft Gear

Replacement of the camshaft gear on the camshaft requires strict attention to detail, because damage to the gear and camshaft may result if proper procedures are not followed. After consulting the engine service manual, the following general procedures must be followed when assembling the camshaft gear to the camshaft:

1. Install a new key in the camshaft keyway.

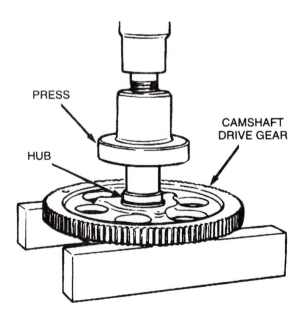

FIGURE 10–21 *Supporting the series 60 camshaft drive gear to press out the support hub safely. (Courtesy of Detroit Diesel Corporation.)*

NOTE Some engines may require offset keys to advance the camshaft timing. (Check your service manual carefully.)

2. Check and install the thrust plate or wear washer, if used. Some engines will not require a wear washer, since the back of the camshaft gear rides directly against the block.

NOTE If not done previously, the thrust plate or wear washer should be checked for wear visually and with a micrometer.

3. If the gear is to be pressed on the shaft, apply grease to the end of the shaft.

4. Support the camshaft in an arbor press to prevent damage to the camshaft. This can be done by using two flat pieces of metal on the press table. Insert the camshaft between them until the shoulder of the camshaft rests firmly on them.

5. Set the gear on the shaft, paying close attention to alignment with a woodruff key.

6. Select a sleeve or piece of pipe that will fit over the shaft and place it on the gear.

NOTE This sleeve or pipe must have an inside diameter at least 0.0625 in. (1.58 mm) larger than the camshaft diameter.

7. Press the gear onto the camshaft until the gear contacts the shoulder of the camshaft.

8. If the gear is to be heated and then installed on the camshaft, the following procedure is to be followed:

NOTE Heating of the gear is recommended by some engine manufacturers. Consult your service manual.

a. Heat the camshaft gear to 300 to 400°F (150 to 200°C), using an oven or a heating torch.

NOTE A 400°F Tempilstick may be used to check the gear temperature. If a Tempilstick is not available, a piece of soft solder of 50% lead and 50% tin melts at approximately 350 to 400°F (175 to 200°C) and can be used to check gear temperature. Touch the gear with the Tempilstick or solder to check the temperature.

b. With a plier or tongs, place the gear on the camshaft. Tap slightly with a hammer to ensure that it is installed all the way onto the camshaft.

c. Install the retaining nut, if used.

CAUTION   Gear should not be overheated and should be allowed to cool normally. *Do not* use cold water to cool the gear, as it may shrink the gear and cause it to break.

---

9. When camshaft and gear are assembled, the camshaft can be inserted into the block and timing marks indexed or lined up (Figure 10–18).

NOTE   If camshaft bushings have not been replaced and are worn, refer to "Installing the Cam Bushing" in Chapter 6.

---

10. Check timing gear backlash to ensure that the gears have the correct clearance between the gear teeth. Too little clearance will cause a whining noise, whereas too much clearance may cause a knocking noise.

NOTE   Two methods of checking gear backlash are acceptable: the dial indicator method and the feeler gauge method.

---

11. If the dial indicator method is to be used, attach the dial indicator to the engine block by clamping or with magnetic base.

12. Position the indicator plunger on a gear tooth and zero indicator.

13. Rock the gear forward and back by hand, observing the dial indicator movement. (Figure 10–22).

NOTE   Gear backlash is measured between mating gears only, so that one gear must remain stationary during checking.

---

14. If the feeler gauge method is to be used in checking, select feeler ribbons of the correct thickness as indicated in the engine repair manual. If, after insertion of a correct-thickness feeler gauge, there is still gear backlash, the gears are worn excessively and must be replaced.

FIGURE 10–22   *Checking camshaft gear backlash with the aid of a dial gauge.*

15. After the camshaft and timing gears have been installed and all timing marks checked, recheck all retaining bolts for proper torque; lock all lock plates if used.

16. If an oil slinger is used, install it on the crankshaft.

NOTE   It is a good practice at this point to review and check the oil supply system for the timing gears. Most engines lubricate the timing gear train with splash oil; others may employ pressure lubrication through a nozzle or oil passage. If a complete engine overhaul is being performed, all passageways should have been checked during block cleaning and inspection. *Double-check it now,* before the front cover is installed.

Installing the Front Timing Cover

When a final check has been made of the timing mark alignment, lock plates, bolt torques, and oil slinger installation, the engine is ready for installation of the front cover.

1. If not done previously, clean the cover thoroughly and remove the old crankshaft oil seal and cover gasket.

2. Install a new seal into the front cover using a seal driver. See Chapter 7.

3. Glue a new cover gasket onto the cover with a good gasket sealer.

NOTE   On some engines the camshaft will have a retaining device of some type other than a plate that is bolted to the block to hold the camshaft in place. It may be a thrust plate in the cover or a spring-loaded plunger in the end of the camshaft. This (hold-in device) must be checked carefully before installation of the front cover for the proper adjustment or installation procedures.

4.   Install the front cover, starting it onto the dowel pins (if used) and tapping in place. Install and tighten the bolts.

5.   Install the vibration damper or front pulley in this manner:

a.   Install the woodruff key in the crankshaft slot if used.

b.   Start the damper or pulley on the shaft, making sure that the slot in the pulley lines up with the woodruff key in the crankshaft.

c.   Install the retaining bolt with a washer into the end of the crankshaft and tighten, pulling the damper in place.

NOTE   Some dampers may not slide onto the shaft far enough so that the retaining bolt can be started into the crankshaft. If this condition exists, a long bolt may be used to pull the damper in place.

CAUTION   Do not drive on the damper with a hammer, as damage may result that would cause it to have excess runout or be out of balance. See Chapter 7 for more details.

6.   Install all other components, such as water pump, alternator, and fan brackets.

SUMMARY

This chapter has presented a detailed explanation of cam lobe nomenclature and valve timing to assist you in understanding the function of the camshaft and timing gear train. In addition, information concerning camshaft, cam followers, pushrods, rocker arms, and timing gear train inspection and assembly has been provided to assist you in repair or replacement of the timing gears and camshaft components. If questions still exist concerning the procedures and recommendations, consult your instructor.

SELF-TEST QUESTIONS

1.   Technician A says that camshafts on high-speed heavy-duty diesel engines are generally belt or chain driven. Technician B says that camshafts are gear driven on high-speed heavy-duty diesel engines. Who is correct?

2.   Technician A says that the camshaft on electronically controlled unit injector diesel engines is only required to operate the intake and exhaust valves, since the injector is controlled from the ECM. Technician B disagrees, stating that the camshaft is needed to operate the injector plunger to create the high pressures required for injection. Which technician is correct?

3.   Technician A says that the highest point on the camshaft is generally referred to as the *nose;* technician Be says that it is called the *base circle.* Who is correct?

4.   True or False: A camshaft that is located within the engine block rather than in the cylinder head is known as an *overhead camshaft.*

5.   Technician A says that the camshaft on a four-stroke-cycle engine is driven at half the speed of the crankshaft, while on a two-cycle engine it is driven at the same speed. Technician B disagrees, stating that the camshaft on the two-cycle must turn twice crankshaft speed since there is a power stroke every crankshaft revolution. Who is correct?

6.   Technician A says that on two-stroke-cycle DDC71 and 92 engine models, only one camshaft is used to operate the valves and injectors, similar to that commonly found on V8 gasoline engines. Technician B disagrees, saying that each cylinder bank has its own camshaft assembly. Who is right here?

7.   Technician A says that when an in-block camshaft lobe is suspected of being worn, you can check it by placing a dial indicator gauge on top of the valve spring retainer and setting the rocker arm for zero lash (or on the injector follower), rotating the engine over, and comparing the cam lift to specs. Technician B says that you need to remove the camshaft from the block to check its worn lobe condition. Who is correct?

8.   Technician A says that inline model two-stroke DDC engine models have a balance shaft driven from the oil pump drive gear. Technician B disagrees, saying that the balance shaft is located on the side of the block opposite the camshaft. Who is correct?

9.   True or False: The valve bridge (crosshead, yoke) is designed to allow two valves to be opened at the same time.

10.   Technician A says that valve bridges require occasional adjustment. Technician B disagrees, stating that no adjustment is provided or required. Which technician is correct?

11 Lubrication Systems and Lube Oil

Overview

The lubrication system is an extremely important contributor to the overall successful operation and longevity to overhaul of the diesel engine. In this chapter we describe the various types of lube oils used in heavy-duty high-speed diesel engines, and the importance of regular maintenance and oil analysis. We describe the purpose, function, and operation of the major components of the lube system that require regular maintenance and possible repair at overhaul. Details of the necessary repairs are described to provide you with the knowledge necessary to challenge ASE or TQ test certification.

ASE CERTIFICATION

ASE offers within the medium/heavy truck tests certification area, a diesel engines T2 test. Part D of the content deals with lubrication and cooling systems diagnosis and repair with nine test questions related to lube/cooling systems, accounting for 13% of the test specifications T2 test. To assist you with identifying what tasks need to be studied, and the appropriate hands-on skills required for lube systems, we look at Part A and Part D of the T2 content tasks lists. In Part A of the diesel engines tasks lists area, item 15 states:

> Check the lubrication system for contamination, oil level, oil temperature, pressure, filtration, and oil consumption; determine needed repairs.

In Part D of the diesel engines tasks lists content area, the following items relate to lube systems:

1. Verify engine oil pressure and check operation of the pressure sensor, pressure gauge, and sending unit.

2. Inspect, measure, repair/replace the oil pump, drives, inlet pipes, and screens.

3. Inspect, repair/replace the oil pressure regulator valve(s), bypass valve(s), and filters.

4. Inspect, clean, test, reinstall/replace the oil cooler, bypass valve, oil thermostat, lines, and hoses.

5. Inspect and clean the turbocharger oil supply and return lines; repair and replace as necessary.

Within this chapter we provide detailed information to support a course of study in preparation for challenging the ASE content in the T2 test.

LUBRICATION SYSTEM FUNCTION

Most diesel engine lubrication systems are similar to the one shown in Figure 11–1. The system is composed of oil galleries, oil cooler, oil filter, oil pump, and oil pan or oil sump.

The oil pan or sump will be filled with engine oil. This oil is supplied by the lubrication system throughout the engine to all points of lubrication during engine operation. Without this supply of pressurized oil the engine would quickly be destroyed.

The diesel engine lubrication system provides pressurized lubrication throughout the engine during operation to reduce friction. Other functions of the lube system are:

1. *Dissipate (get rid of) engine heat.* The heat generated by friction within the engine must be controlled to avoid engine damage.

2. *Clean; prevent rust and corrosion.* By-products of combustion (water, acids) must be removed from the

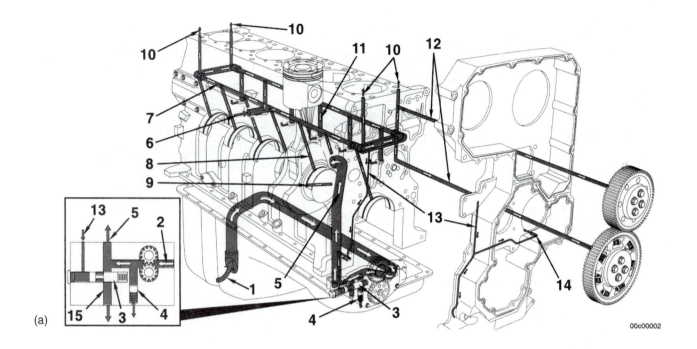

1. Lubricating Oil Flow from Oil Pan through Suction Tube
2. Flow from Suction Tube to Oil Pump
3. Pressure Regulator
4. High-Pressure Relief Valve
5. Flow from Oil Pump to Oil Cooler/Filter Head Housing
6. Oil Return from Oil Cooler/Filter Head Housing to Main Oil Rifle
7. Main Oil Rifle
8. Flow to Main Bearing
9. Flow from Main Bearing to Crankshaft
10. Flow to Cylinder Head
11. Flow to Piston Cooling Nozzle
12. Flow to Idler Gears
13. Oil Transfer from Main Oil Rifle
14. Flow to Air Compressor
15. Rifle Sensing Regulator Dump to Inlet.

FIGURE 11–1 (a) Lube oil system flow diagram through the Cummins Signature/ISX engine. (Courtesy of Cummins Engine Company, Inc.)

engine by the lube system and lube oil so that parts such as pistons, rings, and bearings remain clean throughout the engine life. In addition, the lube oil must prevent rust and corrosion from occurring, especially during long periods of engine shutdown.

3. *Provide a seal between the piston rings and cylinder wall or cylinder sleeve.* The piston and ring assembly would not be capable of providing a gas-tight seal without the aid of the lube oil provided by the lube system. Excessive blowby would result if this seal did not exist, resulting in the loss of compression and a poor-running engine.

4. *Absorb thrust or shock loads.* As the engine operates, many parts throughout the engine are subjected to shock- or thrust-type loads that must be absorbed or reduced to prevent engine noise and damage. An example of this would be the force exerted on the connecting rod journal by the connecting rod and piston assembly during the engine power stroke. At full load this force may be as much as 5000 psi ($350 \text{ kg}/\text{cm}^2$). Without the cushioning effect of lube oil, the rod bearings would be destroyed quickly.

5. *Reduce friction.* The lube system reduces friction by providing and maintaining an oil film between all moving parts. The oil film between two sliding surfaces (such as the rod bearing and the crankshaft journal) has two characteristics that make us realize how very important the lubrication of engine parts is.

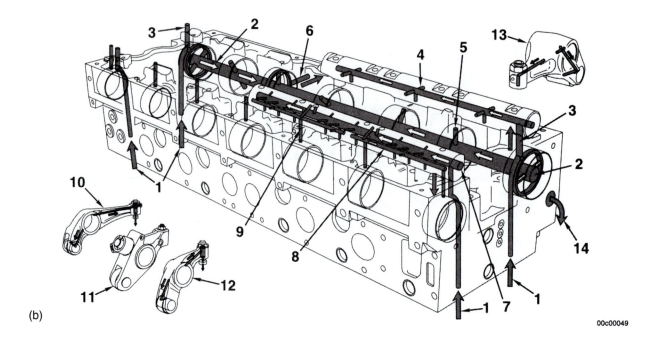

1. Lubricating Oil Flow from Cylinder Block to Cylinder Head
2. Flow around Grooved Head to Drilled Camshaft and Rocker Lever Shafts
3. Flow to Injector Rocker Lever Shafts
4. Flow to Injector Rocker Levers
5. Flow to Injector Camshaft Journal Bearings
6. Flow to Fuel Pump
7. Flow to Valve Rocker Lever Shaft

8. Flow to Valve Rocker Levers
9. Flow to Valve Camshaft Journal Bearings
10. Intake Valve Rocker Lever
11. Engine Brake Lever
12. Exhaust Valve Rocker Lever
13. Injector Rocker Lever
14. Oil Drain from Overhead (Front and Rear).

FIGURE 11–1   (continued). (b) Oil flow through the cylinder head. (Courtesy of Cummins Engine Company, Inc.)

a. Oil molecules shaped like very small ball bearings slide over one another freely.
b. The oil molecules adhere to the bearing and crankshaft surfaces more readily than to each other.

Figure 11–2 shows the resulting effect. The top layer of oil molecules clings to the surface of the moving metal and moves with it. In so doing, it slides over the second layer of oil molecules to some degree, but does exert some drag that causes the second layer to move, but at a much slower rate. In like manner, the second layer slides over and drags the third layer at a slower speed. This continues through all the layers of oil molecules until the bottom layer is reached. The bottom layer clings to the stationary piece of metal and remains stationary. This action by the lubricant greatly reduces friction and increases bearing life.

SYSTEM COMPONENTS

Lubrication system components vary greatly in design, but little difference exists between component function from engine to engine. A typical full-force-feed system will have the following components:

1. *Reservoir* (oil pan), generally located at the bottom of the engine to hold and collect engine oil. Oil is distributed to the various lubrication points from this pan by the oil pump.

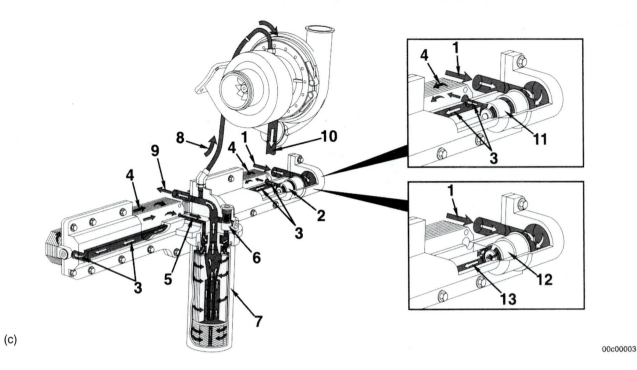

(c)

00c00003

1. Lubricating Oil Flow from Oil Pump
2. Thermostat
3. Oil Cooler Bypass Flow
4. Flow through Oil Coolers
5. Flow Return to Filter Head
6. Filter Bypass Valve
7. Oil Filter

8. Flow to Turbocharger
9. Flow to Main Oil Rifle
10. Oil Drain from Turbocharger
11. Thermostat Open - Oil Flows through Oil Coolers
12. Thermostat Closed - Oil Flows Directly to Oil Filter
13. Flow to Oil Filter.

Lubricating Oil System

Oil Pressure at Idle (minimum allowable at 93°C [200°F] oil temperature) .... 69 kPa [10 psi]

Oil Pressure at No-Load Governed Speed (**automotive and industrial only**) .... 241 to 276 kPa [35 to 40 psi]

Oil Capacity of Standard Engine:
    Combination Full-Flow/Bypass Filter Capacity .... 3.78 liters [1 gal]
    Oil Pan Capacity:
        Automotive and Industrial
        High .... 41.6 liters [11 gal]
        Low .... 37.9 liters [10 gal]
        Power Generation (for oil pan option OP1493)
        High .... 94.6 liters [25 gal]
        Low .... 83.3 liters [22 gal]
    Oil Change Capacity (oil pan and filter filled to capacity):
        Automotive and Industrial .... 45.4 liters [12 gal]
        Power Generation (for oil pan option OP1493) .... 98.4 liters [26 gal]

Total Lubricating Oil System Capacity Including Filter:
    Automotive and Industrial .... 45.4 liters [12 gal]
    Power Generation (for oil pan option OP1493) .... 98.4 liters [26 gal]

Oil Pressure Range:
    Cold Engine .... Up to 900 kPa [130 psi]
(d)   Warm Engine .... 241 to 276 kPa [35 to 40 psi]

FIGURE 11–1 *(continued). (c) Oil flow through the filter and oil coolers, and to and from the turbocharger. (d) Lube oil system specification for the Signature/ISX engines. (Courtesy of Cummins Engine Company, Inc.)*

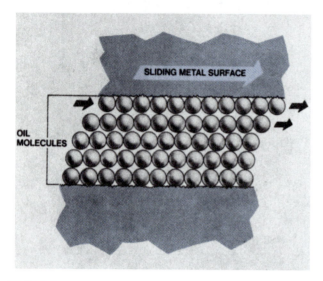

FIGURE 11–2 *Concept of how oil molecules prevent metal-to-metal contact between two surfaces. (Courtesy of Clevite Engine Parts, Dana Corporation.)*

2. *The pickup screen or suction strainer* (Figure 11–3), is located on the inlet side of the pump to prevent large dirt particles or other foreign material from entering the pump. This strainer in many engines is nothing more than fine metal screen; in others it may be a cloth or fabric strainer.

3. *Oil pump,* considered the heart of the lubrication system. A sufficient flow of oil to maintain oil pressure to all lubrication points must be supplied by this positive-displacement pump. Engine lube oil pumps for high-speed diesel engines are generally of two types:

a. *External gear pumps* (Figure 11–4) are most commonly used. This pump consists of two meshed gears, one driving the other, a body or housing in which they are enclosed, and an inlet and outlet. As the gears are turned, oil is drawn in the inlet side and is carried in the space between the teeth and the pump housing. As the gears continue to turn, the oil is carried around to the outlet port of the pump and forced out by the meshing of the gear teeth.

b. *Internal gear or crescent pumps* (Figure 11–5), often called gerotor pumps (combination gear and rotor), are designed with one gear rotating inside another gear. The smaller gear drives the larger-diameter gear and is offset from the center of the large gear so that the gear teeth are in mesh. As the gears turn, oil is picked up and carried by the space between the large gear teeth. When the gears come into mesh, the oil is forced out the pump outlet by the intermeshing of gears.

NOTE   As the impeller turns, oil is trapped in the space between the vane and pump body. Continued turning forces the oil into a progressively smaller area and finally discharges it out of the pump outlet.

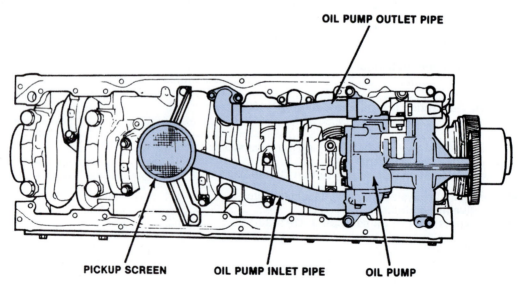

FIGURE 11–3 *View of the underside of a DDC series 60 engine with the oil pan removed. Note the inlet and outlet pipes to and from the oil pump. (Courtesy of Detroit Diesel Corporation.)*

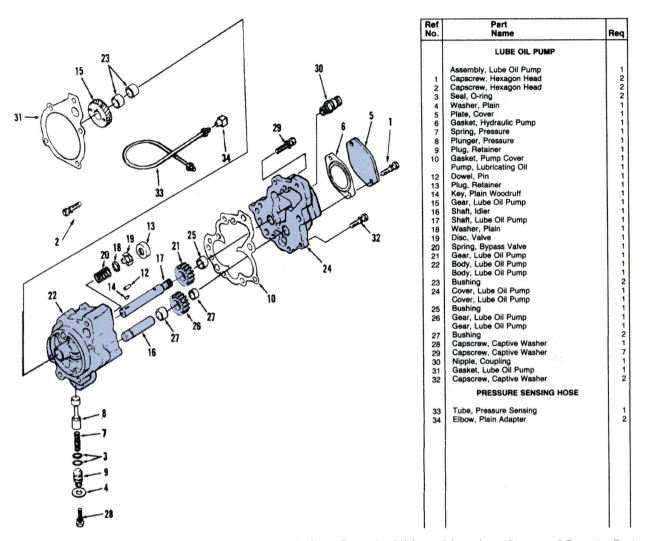

Ref No.	Part Name	Req
	LUBE OIL PUMP	
	Assembly, Lube Oil Pump	1
1	Capscrew, Hexagon Head	2
2	Capscrew, Hexagon Head	2
3	Seal, O-ring	2
4	Washer, Plain	1
5	Plate, Cover	1
6	Gasket, Hydraulic Pump	1
7	Spring, Pressure	1
8	Plunger, Pressure	1
9	Plug, Retainer	1
10	Gasket, Pump Cover	1
	Pump, Lubricating Oil	1
12	Dowel, Pin	1
13	Plug, Retainer	1
14	Key, Plain Woodruff	1
15	Gear, Lube Oil Pump	1
16	Shaft, Idler	1
17	Shaft, Lube Oil Pump	1
18	Washer, Plain	1
19	Disc, Valve	1
20	Spring, Bypass Valve	1
21	Gear, Lube Oil Pump	1
22	Body, Lube Oil Pump	1
	Body, Lube Oil Pump	1
23	Bushing	2
24	Cover, Lube Oil Pump	1
	Cover, Lube Oil Pump	1
25	Bushing	1
26	Gear, Lube Oil Pump	1
	Gear, Lube Oil Pump	1
27	Bushing	2
28	Capscrew, Captive Washer	1
29	Capscrew, Captive Washer	7
30	Nipple, Coupling	1
31	Gasket, Lube Oil Pump	1
32	Capscrew, Captive Washer	2
	PRESSURE SENSING HOSE	
33	Tube, Pressure Sensing	1
34	Elbow, Plain Adapter	2

FIGURE 11–4   Oil pump (externally mounted) details for a Cummins N14 model engine. (Courtesy of Cummins Engine Company, Inc.)

FIGURE 11–5   Gerotor design oil pump assembly.

4.   *Filters.* Oil filters generally are one of two common types: partial or full flow (Figure 11–6).

a.   *Partial or bypass.* The partial flow filter, as the name implies, filters only a certain percentage of the oil (approximately 30 to 40%). It is connected to the engine oil gallery in such a manner that oil does not have to pass through the filter before entering the engine. In fact, oil flows through the filter and then back to the oil pump or oil pan. Most engine manufacturers no longer use this type of filter because of its low cleaning efficiency.

b.   *Full flow.* Most modern diesel engines use the full-flow filter. In this filter all oil pumped by the oil pump must pass through the oil filter before it enters the engine oil gallery. Since

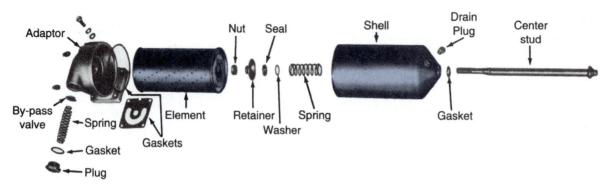

FIGURE 11–6   *Details of a full-flow oil filter of the shell and element design. (Courtesy of Detroit Diesel Corporation.)*

100% of the oil is filtered before it is used for lubrication, this filter's efficiency in dirt removal is much greater, resulting in its widespread use.

Either type of filter, partial or full flow, may be a shell and element type (Figure 11–6) with a replaceable element or a replaceable type of metal can (Figure 11–7) that has the element sealed into it, commonly referred to as a *spin-on* model. The replaceable cartridge for the element type may be constructed in one of two different ways:

a. Cotton waste (an absorbent or depth type of filter), which absorbs impurities in the oil.

b. Treated pleated paper (more common). The treated paper filter element is considered an adsorbent (or surface) type. It filters from the oil passing through it all dirt particles larger than the porous holes in the paper.

NOTE   As the filter continues to catch dirt, it becomes more efficient, since the collection of dirt particles on its surface allows increasingly smaller particles to pass through it. Eventually, however, the filter becomes completely plugged and must be replaced with a new cartridge.

---

5. *Pressure regulator and bypass valves.* Pressure within the lubrication system must be regulated as the viscosity of the oil changes. Also, because of temperature changes, filters such as the full-flow filter must have an automatic bypass system to prevent engine damage in the event that the filter becomes clogged.

Both of these requirements are fulfilled by both a pressure regulator valve and a bypass valve. Design of these valves may be one of two common types:

a. Ball (spring loaded)

b. Plunger (spring loaded) (Figure 11–6)

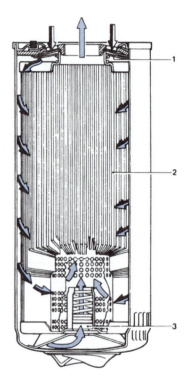

FIGURE 11–7   *Typical oil flow through a spin-on type of full-flow oil filter assembly: 1. nonreturn valve; 2. treated and pleated paper element filter media; 3. pressure relief valve which opens when the filter is plugged, allowing oil to bypass the filter and enter the lube system unfiltered.*

The main job of the pressure-regulating valve is to prevent excessive oil pressure within the system; in a sense, it becomes a safety valve or limiting valve. Oil pumps are designed to maintain sufficient flow at normal engine temperature and speed. As a result, when oil temperature is low and viscosity is high, excess pressure will be developed. A regulating valve is then used to dump off the excess flow to maintain correct pressure.

Since most modern diesel engines have a full-flow filter, a bypass valve is designed into the filter or filter base so that the engine receives a sufficient oil supply at all times in the event that a filter cartridge or element becomes plugged. This "safety device" is in the normally closed position during engine operation unless the filter becomes clogged.

6. *Oil coolers* (warmers). Oil coolers in many diesel engines are of the oil-to-water type. Coolers of this type resemble a small radiator enclosed in a housing. Water is pumped around the copper core or element and oil is circulated through it (Figure 11–8).

In most situations during engine operation, the oil is hotter than the coolant water, resulting in heat trans-

fer from oil to water, keeping the oil at a safe operating temperature. Normal oil temperature in most engines will be about 220 to 230°F (104 to 110°C).

Cooling is not the main job of the oil cooler at all times. During operation following a cold start, engine water will reach operating temperature much sooner than engine lube oil. In this situation the oil cooler warms the oil rather than cools it.

Supplementary Components

1. *Pressure gauge or indicator light*. The oil pressure gauge is calibrated in pounds per square inch (psi) or in kilopascal (kPa). It is used by the operator to determine if the engine oil pressure is correct. Pressure gauges can be one of two types:

   a. *Mechanical.* The mechanical type (sometimes called the Bourdon type) (Figure 11–9) is con-

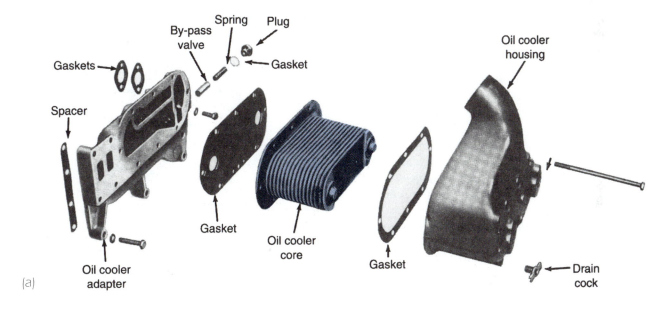

(a)

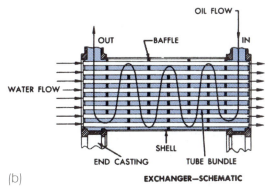

(b)

FIGURE 11–8 (a) Details of a plate-type oil cooler assembly. (b) Typical lube oil flow through a tube-type oil cooler. (Courtesy of Detroit Diesel Corporation.)

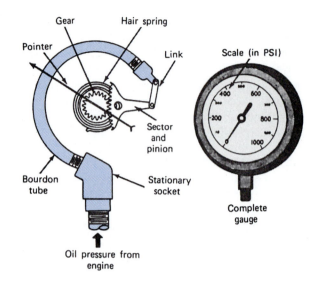

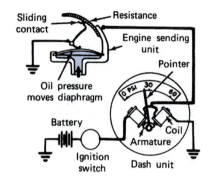

FIGURE 11–10 Electric-type oil pressure gauge.

FIGURE 11–9 Bourdon-type oil pressure gauge.

nected to an oil pressure gallery by a tube that transmits the pressure to the gauge mounted on the operator's instrument panel.

b. *Electrical.* The electrical type (Figure 11–10) is made up of an indicating gauge (similar to the one used on the Bourdon tube), which is a wire and pressure-sending unit screwed into the engine oil gallery at a convenient takeoff port. Engine oil pressure pushing against the diaphragm in the sending unit moves a sliding wiper arm across a resistor (Figure 11–11), changing the resistance value of the sending unit, since the sending unit provides the ground for the gauge circuit. The amount of current passing through the gauge, which causes needle movement, will be determined by the amount of ground that the sending unit is providing.

Many modern engines employ an indicating light system in place of a pressure gauge. Making up the system are an indicator light, electrical wire, and sending unit. In this system, the sending unit inserted into the oil gallery is a pressure-operated switch that operates the lamp circuit. During engine shutdown with no oil pressure, the sending unit is closed, providing a ground for the lamp circuit. With the ignition switch in the ON position, power is supplied to the lamp to illuminate it. After the engine is started and oil pressure opens the sending unit by pushing against the diaphragm, the lamp circuit ground is lost and the light goes out, indicating to the operator that the engine has oil pressure. This system has a built-in disadvantage in that it gives the operator no indication of the amount of oil pressure being developed.

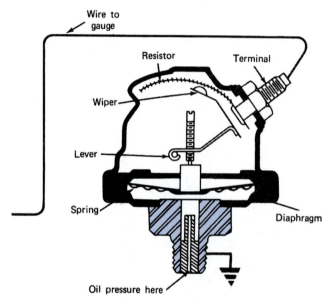

FIGURE 11–11 Schematic of an electrical oil pressure sending unit.

2. *Dipstick.* The most simple and widely used method of checking the oil in the crankcase is the dipstick. The dipstick is constructed of a long piece of flat steel that fits into a tube inserted into the engine oil pan from the top, allowing easy operator access.

ENGINE LUBE OIL

The lubrication system is not complete without lube oil. Lube oil is a petroleum product made up of carbon and hydrogen along with other additives to make a lubricant that can meet the specifications supplied by engine manufacturers. In general, to meet the following requirements, diesel engine lube oil must:

1. be viscous enough at all engine temperatures to keep two highly loaded surfaces apart;

2. remain relatively stable at all engine temperatures;

3. act as a coolant and cleaner; and

4. prevent rust and corrosion.

Hundreds of commercially available engine oils are produced worldwide, and labeling terminology and grading differ among suppliers. Some marketers of engine lube oils may claim that their lubricant is suitable for all makes of diesel engines. Such claims should be checked with the recommendations of a specific engine's manufacturer. Engines manufactured in North America require a lube oil that is selected based on SAE viscosity grade and API (American Petroleum Institute) service designations, although OEM and U.S. military specifications are also often quoted. In Europe, military specifications and the CCMC (The Comité des Constructeurs du Marché Commun) represent the requirements of European lube oil manufacturers for engine oil quality. In North America both the SAE and API standards are displayed, and only oils meeting these recommended properties should be considered as suitable for a given engine. Figure 11–12 illustrates a typical oil can symbol that indicates the lube oil meets an enhanced level of lubricant performance of the API CF-4 category. Heavy duty diesel oil has since moved to the CG-4 and CH-4 ratings level.

NOTE   To conform with this change, it is now recommended that heavy-duty electronically controlled diesel engines operating on low-sulfur fuel (0.05%) use API CG-4 or CH-4 rated lube oils.

The recommended lube oil viscosity grade continues to be 15W-40 for heavy-duty high-speed on-highway truck engines manufactured by all of the major OEMs. CG-4 and CH-4 lube oil has the following advantages:

- Better control of engine deposits and prevention of corrosive wear
- Reduced oil consumption and improved oil viscosity control
- Control of combustion soot dispersancy, oxidation, and lube oil shear

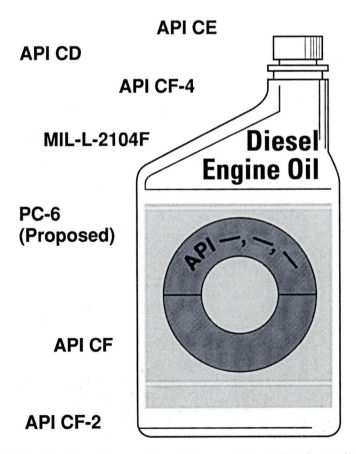

API CD
API CE
API CF-4
MIL-L-2104F
PC-6 (Proposed)
API CF
API CF-2

Diesel Engine Oil

API —, —, —

API Symbol:

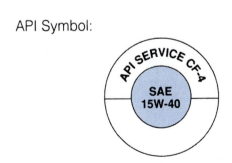

API SERVICE CF-4
SAE 15W-40

FIGURE 11–12 API and SAE symbols on a typical lube oil container. (Reprinted with permission from Chevron Research and Technology Company, a Division of Chevron USA Inc.; copyright Chevron Research Company.)

Viscosity of Oils

Oils are classified by a numbering system to indicate basic viscosity grading. For example, in Figure 11–12 note that the oil is a 15W-40 grade, which is a multiviscosity lubricant. The 15W indicates that the oil has a viscosity of 15 when cold (W = winter). The 40 indicates that when the oil is hot, its additives allow it to thicken to an equivalent viscosity of 40 weight oil. Some oils may be labeled as a single-weight lubricant such as 30, 40, or 50. Various alphabetical letters have appeared on oil containers for years; these letters have changed as lubricating oils have improved. Letters on an oil can such as SA, SB, SC, SD, SE, SF, or SG signify that the oil has been designed for S (spark ignition) internal combustion engines. Diesel engine lubricant containers have the letters CA, CB, CC, CD, CD-11, CE, CF, or CG to signify that the oil is intended for a C (compression ignition) type of diesel engine.

Engine oil viscosity was first defined by Isaac Newton as a measure of the resistance offered when one layer of the fluid moves relative to an adjacent layer. The higher the viscosity or thickness of the fluid film, the greater is the internal resistance to motion. Newton discovered that the viscosity of a fluid or lube oil will remain constant if both the temperature and pressure are held constant. Within an engine subjected to changing operating conditions, however, these two "constants" are regularly subjected to change. Most single-grade lube oils such as a 30, 40, or 50 are sometimes referred to as being Newtonian, whereas multi-grade oils are non-Newtonian because they do not obey the basic law, as we shall see. Several factors affect lube oil viscosity:

- Composition of the refined oil with its additives
- Operating temperature of the oil
- Pressure (loads) between two lubricated parts

The American Society for Testing and Materials (ASTM) created a method to provide a number called the viscosity index (VI). The VI is related to the amount of change for a given oil compared with two reference oils over a range of 104 to 212°F (40 to 100°C). On the ASTM scale, most engine oils have a VI of 90 or more, although it is not uncommon for light, multigrade oils to have a VI approaching 200 due to the additive packages used with them. Single-weight oils are more successful in some engine designs than others, but they have the disadvantage of having a much higher drag when cranking the engine over in cold-weather operation. Non-W grades of lube oil are based only on their viscosities at 212°F (100°C). Multiviscosity oils are formulated to meet the W-grade criterion of a relatively thin oil at a particular low temperature, yet meet the

standards for a thicker, non-W-grade oil at a higher temperature, usually 212°F (100°C).

Three major characteristics of multi-viscosity engine lube oils are as follows:

1. *Viscosity:* resistance to flow of a liquid. The molecules of a more viscous oil have greater cohesion (stick together more firmly) than a less viscous oil. The higher the number given to the oil, the greater its viscosity (resistance to flow) will be. Temperatures also greatly affect the viscosity of an oil. Hotter oil will flow more rapidly than colder oil.

2. *Pour point:* lowest temperature at which an oil will still be thin enough to pour.

3. *Flash point:* temperature at which the oil will be sufficiently vaporized to ignite.

Oil Recommendations

Engine manufacturers recommend engine oils based on their experience with oil viscosities. Manufacturers do not always specifically state that a certain *brand name* lube oil be used. Rather, the key is that the oil brand selected meet the minimum specs stated in the engine manufacturer's technical data.

Although some OEMs offer engine oils under their own name, any brand name engine oil can be used as long as it meets the standards and specifications specified by the engine manufacturer regarding sulfated ash and so on. Always refer to the engine service manual, operator manual, or lube oil spec sheets to ensure that the oil you choose for a certain engine make and model does in fact comply with the specs of the OEM. Failure to do so could have a detrimental effect on engine oil consumption and engine life and may void the existing warranty for the engine.

Some typical lube oil recommendations as specified by engine manufacturers follow:

- *Caterpillar:* Cat diesel engine oil CF-4, CE/SG (15W-40, 10W-30), CD11 (15W-40), CD/SD (10W, 30, 40). For Cat natural gas engine operation use NGEO (natural gas engine oil) SAE 30 or 40.
- *Cummins:* Cummins Valvoline Premium Blue SAE 15W-40, CE, CF-4, SG, Cummins NTC-400, and Cummins NTC-444. Cummins Premium Blue 2000 SAE 15W-40 meeting Cummins Engineering Standard 20066, 20071 and 20076 are recommended.
- *Mack:* Bulldog Premium EO-L (engine oil lube) meeting the T-8 engine test.
- *Detroit Diesel:* DDC manufactures two- and four-stroke-cycle engines; therefore, its recommended lube oil viscosities are that a single-weight lube oil be used in its two-cycle models. SAE 40 is typically used in series 71 and 92 engines; for 149 series and

high-output 71 and 92 engines, SAE 50 is recommended. For series 50, 55, and 60 engines, 15W-40 oil is the base oil, and current engines have a decal on the rocker cover recommending the use of a 15W-40 Mobil Delvac 1300 Super product. In all DDC engines, any engine oil that meets the company's specifications for CG-4 lubricants can be used.

To avoid possible engine damage, do not use single-grade (monograde) lubricants in Detroit Diesel four-cycle series 50, 55, and 60 engines, regardless of API classification.

Synthetic Lube Oils

The history of synthetic oils dates back to World War II when they were developed to meet the critically high standards of the aviation industry. Synthetic oils have been used in various forms for diesel truck applications since the early to mid-1960s, particularly for differentials and transmissions. Because of their superior cooling quality and service life much longer than that of mineral oils, they have found favor in severe-duty service off-road operations for diesel engines. Although more expensive than mineral oils, synthetic lubricants can be the ideal choice under heavy loads and steep operating grades. Synthetic oil is a far more refined, purer product than mineral oil, which is one reason it costs more. In addition, synthetic oil tends to be stickier than mineral oil and provides a better oil wedge between gear teeth on differentials and transmissions. As stricter emissions standards become a fact of life, synthetic engine oils are on the horizon for heavy-duty diesel engines as well as for gasoline-powered passenger cars.

Exhaust Emissions and Lube Oil

Electronically controlled diesel engines now operate in an era dominated by low-emissions fuels. Engine lube oil plays an important role in meeting stringent exhaust limits. Engine oils are being formulated to handle the side effects of EPA mandates.

Low-sulfur fuel (0.05%), which was introduced in October 1993, allows the engine to burn cleaner but also affects key engine parts. To meet the strict standards for diesel particulate emissions, engine manufacturers have changed their piston designs by moving the rings closer to the top of the piston crown; thus the crevice volume (area above the top ring and piston crown) is reduced, but the rings are subjected to hotter temperatures. To protect the engines, lubricants have to control deposits at elevated temperatures. Since the top piston rings now operate in a much hotter environ-

ment, top ring groove deposits may increase, as well as oil viscosity. Improved additive packages help to minimize these new deposit configurations, thereby reducing wear and oil consumption. Improved oxidation inhibitors keep the oil viscosity within its designed grade level for longer periods.

To reduce nitrogen oxide emissions, many new engines use retarded injection timing, a feature that can substantially increase soot loading in the oil film on the cylinder walls. Advanced dispersancy additives help to keep this extra load of soot suspended instead of attaching internally to key engine parts. When the oil is drained, the soot is removed with the used oil. Dispersed soot is what makes the engine oil "black," and it can also cause the oil to thicken in time. Dispersancy-type oil additives provide reduced abrasive wear, fewer plugged filters, cleaner engines, and excellent pumpability during cold-weather startup. Much of the particulate exhaust emissions in the newer diesel engines consist of unburned oil escaping through the exhaust gases.

The new characteristics of the widely used 15W-40 oils in high-speed heavy-duty engines also offer fleets the possibility of extending oil drain intervals without suffering any loss of performance. An oil drain interval of 30,000 miles (48,279 km) is not uncommon in many of today's newer engines. Accumulated mileages of between 800,000 and 1,000,000 miles (1,287,440 to 1,609,300 km) are becoming standard practice between overhauls. The 15W-40 multiviscosity oil is also designed to be compatible with oil oxidation catalysts that will be required on many high-speed diesel engines throughout the 2000's.

The main elements of these new engine oils is that there is only 1% ash content, which is held in check by ashless dispersants, and that the total base number (TBN) is 9. TBN is an indication of the depletion rate of the oil's additive package. Low ash in lube oils is key to reducing deposits in the piston top ring groove area; any such deposits can cause ring sticking, blowby, and high oil consumption.

Oil Change Intervals

During use, engine lubricating oil undergoes deterioration from combustion by-products and contamination by the engine. Certain components in a lubricant additive package are designed to deplete with use. For this reason, regardless of the oil formulation, regular oil drain intervals are necessary. These intervals may vary in length, depending on engine operation, fuel quality, and lubricant quality. Generally, shorter oil drain intervals extend engine life through prompt replenishment of the protection qualities in the lubricant.

Should it be determined that the oil drain interval is unacceptably short, then the selection of a lubricant with a TBN (per ASTM D 2896) above 10 may be appropriate. Experience has shown, however, that a higher TBN oil with a longer oil change interval is not as effective in protecting the engine from wear. Use the intervals listed until the best practical oil drain interval can be established by oil analysis.

Proper drain intervals for engine oil require that the oil be drained before the contaminant load becomes so great that the oil's lubricating function is impaired or heavy deposits of suspended contaminants occur. Oil and filter change intervals are usually recommended by each engine manufacturer for various operating conditions. This information is usually contained in service manual literature as well as operator manuals (engine, vehicle, equipment) and is provided simply as a general guide. Engine operating environments, speeds, loads, idling time, ambient air temperature, grades encountered with mobile equipment, and airborne dust all affect the lube oil life cycle.

Regardless of the type of oil used, it is always wise to have a schedule for oil sampling in a fleet operation to determine the best mileage (hours, time) at which to change the engine lube oil and filter(s). Another method for determining the oil and filter change interval if no service literature is available is to use miles (kilometers), hours, or months—whichever comes first. On industrial and marine engine applications, oil change intervals are normally based on accumulated engine hours; the type of application, loads, and speeds play a large part in determining the recommended oil drain period. The type of diesel fuel used and the sulfur content also are relevant. Because of the many factors involved, the change interval can range from as low as 50 hours to 500 hours or six months maximum.

As can be seen from the preceding information, the lube system and the lube oil in it deserve more than a casual consideration, especially in oil selection. Engine oil must be changed at regular intervals to keep the internal engine parts clean, since in most cases dirt is the engine's primary enemy. Keep the engine clean and it will not wear out.

In addition, the lube system must be closely inspected during an engine overhaul if it is to function correctly for many hours of operation. All too often the components of the system are taken for granted and overlooked during engine overhaul. The result in many cases is a newly overhauled engine with less oil pressure than it should have. It is recommended that all lubrication system components be checked thoroughly during engine overhaul.

WASTE OIL DISPOSAL

Over 1 billion gallons of waste oil is generated annually in the United States alone. Waste oil has now been legislated as a hazardous waste material and must be disposed of according to the local, state, provincial, and federal laws. Collection and recycling companies pick up used oil and try to recycle it to a rerefining manufacturer. Many major engine manufacturers are now permitting the use of rerefined oils in their engines, provided that the rerefined oils meet the SAE viscosity and API specifications for new oils.

ASE T8 Task List

To become an ASE master service technician, one of the areas that you must be proficient in is the Preventive Maintenance Inspection (PMI) test specifications and task list, or Test T8 area. There are two questions related to the engine lubrication system within the T8 test area, including knowing how to perform the following checks/tests:

1. Change engine oil and filters; visually check the oil for diesel fuel or coolant contamination; inspect and clean magnetic drain plugs.
2. Take an engine oil sample.

The following information describes the interpretation of lube oil diluted or contaminated with either diesel fuel or engine coolant, as well as how to take an oil sample correctly.

LUBE OIL DILUTION

During normal daily checks of the engine lube oil by the operator or service technician, unusual oil color is an indication of an internal problem with the engine. The color of diluted engine oil depends on whether the oil is being contaminated by diesel fuel or engine coolant. In Figure 11–13 note that thin black oil is an indication of diesel fuel in the oil. Such contamination can originate at injector O-ring seals or from fuel lines or fuel studs located underneath the valve rocker cover areas. In extreme cases a cracked cylinder head may be the culprit. Don't confuse dark-colored lube oil with thin oil diluted by fuel. Normal engine lube oils turn dark when they are doing their job properly; the contaminants from unburned fuel (carbon particles) cause this change. The detergent or dispersant additives within the oil are designed to handle this contamination. A quick method to check for fuel contamination is to pull the dipstick and feel the oil viscosity between your fingers. In addition, smell the oil between your

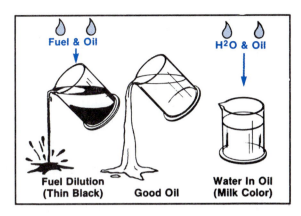

FIGURE 11–13 *Visual lube oil color when diluted with either diesel fuel or engine coolant. (Courtesy of Cummins Engine Company, Inc.)*

fingers; if it is diluted with diesel fuel, you can normally smell it.

When the oil appears milky white or grey in color, usually there is coolant in the lube oil. Coolant can originate from a leaking cylinder head gasket, engine oil cooler, air aftercooler, wet cylinder liner seals, cracked wet-type liner, cracked cylinder head or block, or leaking core plugs in the cylinder head assembly. Keep in mind that during engine operation, the lube oil pressure is higher than the coolant pressure. A leak in the oil cooler will show as oil in the coolant; however, after engine shutdown, as the engine cools, the residual pressure in the cooling system will cause coolant to seep through the leak path and into the lube oil system.

Drawing an Oil Sample

Any drained oil sample must be secured in the proper manner to avoid the entrance of outside contaminants that would affect analysis. Most oil sampling labs provide a container and often the required equipment for drawing an oil sample. Oil samples should always be taken from an engine which is at normal operating temperature, since this will ensure that any contaminants and trace wear metals are still in suspension within the oil and have not had time to deposit themselves internally within the engine block. It is also important to thoroughly clean the area around which the oil sample will be drawn.

Ideally, oil samples can be taken from the engine crankcase or oil pan. This can be done by removing the drain plug in most engines; however, on applications such as marine units, oil can be sucked from the dipstick tube using a suitable pump system. Exercise caution here to allow at least a liter of oil to drain from the engine before you collect the sample; this usually min-imizes the possibility of picking up debris from the bottom of the oil pan or from the dipstick tube. Whatever type of container is being used for the oil sample must be clean; otherwise, any contaminants added to the oil will create false interpretations of the lab results. Make sure that you seal the container and label it with the engine serial number; total hours or miles (kilometers) of accumulated engine operating time; the number of hours, miles (kilometers), or time interval since the last oil change; and the sample date.

OIL ANALYSIS

An oil analysis program involves saving at least a liter of drained oil in a clean sealed container with the engine serial number, number of hours or miles (kilometers), and the make and weight of oil clearly identified on the container. Many equipment companies, marine organizations, and heavy-duty truck fleets use an oil analysis program to monitor the condition of the crankcase oil. Engine lube oil analysis is conducted primarily to determine the overall condition of the lube oil, but it also reveals the state of the internal components of the engine. Oil analysis can be relied on to assist effective engine maintenance only if proper sampling is conducted over a relatively long period of time. In this way, varying engine operating conditions and applications allow a fleet to determine a practical oil drain interval.

The oil sample can detect undesirable contaminants such as diesel fuel, combustion soot, coolant, salt, airborne sand, dirt or dust, and trace wear metals from internal components. Contaminant identification allows maintenance personnel to take corrective action to eliminate their causes or to determine when component repair or engine overhaul is required. To determine a baseline value, or average mathematical change point for the oil, the first three or four samples taken from the engine (drained at the same hours, miles, kilometers, or time interval) should be monitored closely.

INSPECTION AND OVERHAUL OF COMPONENTS

It is assumed that the oil pump has been removed from the engine at this time. If not, refer to Chapter 6 on engine disassembly.

Oil Pump Disassembly

1. Remove the pump cover from the pump body (external gear-type pump). See Figure 11–4.
2. Inspect the cover for wear.

NOTE   If the cover is worn, it should be machined or replaced with a new cover.

3.   Remove the idler gear and driven gear from the pump housing.

NOTE   In most cases the idler gear can be lifted from its supporting shaft (idler shaft) and removed. The drive gear will be keyed to the driveshaft with a woodruff key (half moon) or roll pin (spring steel pin) and may have to be pressed from the shaft. If the drive gear must be pressed from the driveshaft, the driveshaft should be removed from the pump body before attempting to remove the gear. In many cases the pump drive shaft will have the oil pump drive gear pressed onto it. This must be removed before the driveshaft and drive gear can be removed from the pump housing. (Check your engine service manual or with your instructor.)

4.   Check the idler and drive gear closely for pitted and worn teeth. Teeth should be checked closely.
5.   Check the gear width (parallel with the center hole) with a micrometer.
6.   Check the driveshaft diameter at the bushing contact with a micrometer. This diameter should meet the manufacturer's specifications.
7.   Check the pump housing internally for wear.
8.   Check the driveshaft bushing (if used) with a snap gauge. Compare with specifications.

NOTE   Some pumps have replaceable bushings that can be renewed. Others require replacement of the pump body. If bushings are to be replaced in the pump body, check the service manual closely for installation and boring instructions.

9.   Check all mating surfaces (such as where the cover fits onto the pump body). Surfaces should not be nicked or burred. If there are nicks or burrs, remove them with a small, flat file.

CAUTION   Care must be exercised when filing on a pump body, as it can easily be ruined. If the body is warped excessively, replace it with a new one.

Oil Pump Reassembly (General)

After all parts have been inspected, repaired, or replaced, the pump can be reassembled.
1.   Insert the oil pump driveshaft with the driven gear installed on it into the pump body.

NOTE   To install the pump drive gear, the pump driveshaft must be supported on the opposite end while the pump drive gear is installed. You must do this before the pump cover is installed.

2.   Support the driveshaft on the drive gear end and press the pump drive gear in place.

CAUTION   Make sure that the woodruff key or roll pin is installed, securing the gear to the shaft, to prevent gear from turning on the shaft during operation.

3.   Install the idler gear on the idler shaft.
4.   Turn the driveshaft, checking for binding or interference as the shaft is turned.

NOTE   Any binding is usually caused by nicks on gears. Remove the gears and file or stone off nicks.

5.   When the pump driveshaft and gears have been rotated without binding, pump cover-to-gear clearance should be checked with Plastigage as follows:
    a.   Place Plastigage across the face of the gears.

NOTE   Plastigage is a thin plastic thread that can be broken into the correct length and used to check the clearance between two closely fitted parts. See Figure 7–34 for an example.

    b.   Install the cover and tighten to specifications.

CAUTION   Do not turn the pump drive gear with Plastigage on it.

    c.   Remove the cover and check the width of the Plastigage against the Plastigage envelope to determine the clearance between the cover and gears.

d. If the clearance is excessive or does not meet specifications, it must be corrected by replacing the gears or pump as needed. [General specifications for oil pump gear-to-cover clearance are 0.003 to 0.005 in. (0.076 to 0.127 mm).]

NOTE   Many oil pumps will contain a bypass or regulating valve that should be checked during pump overhaul as outlined later in the chapter.

Gerotor-Type Oil Pump Inspection

Cummins ISC, QSC 8.3, and the ISL model engines use a gerotor pump. During inspection visually look for signs of damage or overheating (parts discoloration). Refer to Figure 11–14a–d and perform the checks shown. Compare all clearances with service manual specifications.

Inspection and Repair of Oil Pressure Regulation and Bypass Valves

Because of different systems' designs and requirements, the regulator or bypass valves may be located in the engine or oil pump (see items 3 and 4 in Figure 11–1a). Regardless of where they are located or what their function is, all valves must be disassembled and inspected as follows:

1. Remove the valve spring cap retainer.

2. Remove the spring, inspect for worn or twisted coils, and check the free length and spring pressure with a spring tester.

3. If the valve is the plunger type, check the plunger and plunger seat for scoring and wear. Replace all valves that show excessive wear.

4. Ball valves should be checked for pitting and wear and replaced if found defective.

5. Check the valve seat visually for pitting and uneven wear.

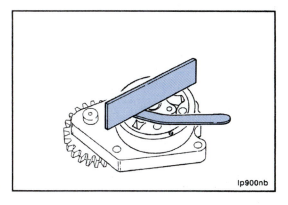
(a)

(b)

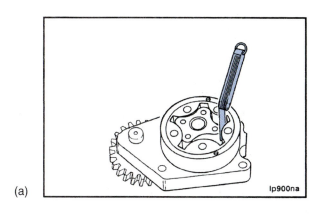
(c)

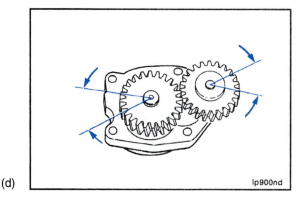
(d)

FIGURE 11–14   Cummins ISC, QSC 8.3, and ISL engines gerotor design lube oil pump. (a) Measuring the tip clearance of a gerotor-type lube pump with a feeler gauge; (b) measuring the clearance of the gerotor planetary to the body bore; (c) measuring the clearance of the gerotor drive/gerotor planetary to port plate; (d) measuring the drive gear to driven gear backlash (use either a feeler gauge or a dial gauge). (Courtesy of Cummins Engine Company, Inc.)

NOTE   Some valve seats are replaceable and can be replaced without replacing the valve assembly. Other types of valves will require replacement of the entire valve body or pump assembly, which includes the valve seat.

Checking the Oil Filter Housing or Mounting

Regardless of the type of filter used, element or cartridge type, the base or filter mount must be checked carefully during engine overhaul as follows:

1.   If a bypass valve is incorporated into the housing, it should be removed and checked as outlined in the regulator valve section (see Figure 11–1c, item 6).

2.   Check the housing for cracks.

3.   Check all gasket surfaces for straightness and nicks.

4.   If using an element filter, which uses a can or shell with a center bolt, make sure that the center bolt threads are usable.

5.   Make sure that springs, gaskets, and spacers (as outlined in the service manual or parts book) are in place in element-type filters.

6.   Check the can for signs of collapse on the closed end.

7.   Check for cracks around the bolt hole and elsewhere.

8.   Check housing passageways, making sure that all are open and free of obstructions.

Oil Cooler Testing and Repair

Since oil and water both flow through the oil cooler simultaneously, it becomes very important that mixing of oil and water at this point does not occur due to a leak or crack in the cooler. Two types of coolers are found on modern diesel engines—plate type and tube type. Many variations of these basic types will be found. Figure 11–1c, item 4, shows two plate-type coolers.

NOTE   Complete servicing of the oil cooler should be done on a routine basis during a major engine overhaul. In addition, the cooler may occasionally fail between engine overhaul periods. Indications of cooler failure are oil in the water or water in the oil pan. In either case the following service instructions will apply.

Servicing of the oil cooler assembly should include complete disassembly and cleaning of the core section with a solution recommended by the engine manufacturer. In most cases the cooler core can be cleaned using an oakite-type solution or muriatic acid.

CAUTION   Some cores contain aluminum, a nonferrous metal that cannot be cleaned as outlined above. In this type of situation, use a normal parts-cleaning solution. After cleaning, inspect all parts as follows.

1.   Check the core visually for

a.   Cracks or breaks in welded joints

b.   Bulges or bent tubes

2.   If the core does not pass visual inspection, replace it with a new one.

3.   If the core passes visual checks, it should be checked by pressurizing with air in the following manner:

a.   If a test fixture is available, mount the core in the fixture in preparation for testing.

NOTE   If a test fixture is not available, a plate or plates can be made to test the cooler core. In general, the plate should be designed so that air pressure can be supplied to one side (oil or water) of the cooler only (Figure 11–15).

b.   After the plates have been attached to the core, pressurize it with 35 to 40 psi (2.5 to 2.8 kg/cm^2) and immerse it in water.

c.   Inspect carefully for air leaks.

4.   If core passes all the checks outlined above, clean the housing and install new O-rings or gaskets and reassemble the core to the cooler.

NOTE   Generally, cooler assembly will be a simple matter of installing the core in the cooler housing, using new gaskets or O-rings. An exception to this is the Cummins tube-type cooler, which requires indexing (timing) in the housing during assembly. Figure 11–16 is an example of index marking.

5.   Before the cooler assembly is installed onto the engine, the bypass valve should be checked as outlined under the regulator valve section.

6.   Using new gaskets, mount the cooler on the engine and tighten all bolts.

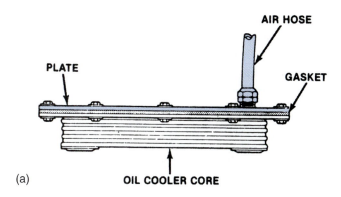

(a)

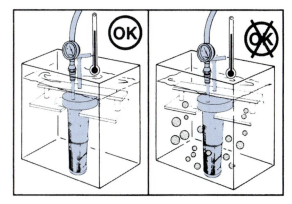

(b)

FIGURE 11–15   (a) Preparing a plate oil cooler for pressure checking. (Courtesy of Detroit Diesel Corporation.) (b) Submerging a tubular oil cooler core into a container of heated water to check for signs of air bubbles from the compressed air supply. (Courtesy of Cummins Engine Company, Inc.)

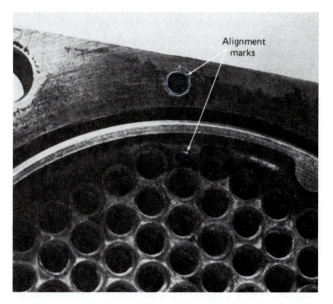

FIGURE 11–16   Tubular oil cooler index markings. (Courtesy of Cummins Engine Company, Inc.)

SYSTEM TESTING

Testing the lube oil system involves testing the pressure at various engine speeds and temperatures. In general, testing is done at the following times:

1.   *After an engine overhaul.* The lube system must be thoroughly checked and monitored during engine startup and rebuild. Proper oil pressure is vital to long engine life.

2.   *Lube system problems between engine overhauls.* Many times low lube oil pressure will occur long before the engine is due for a major rebuild. The cause of the problem can be found only by testing and checking the lube system.

3.   *Before an overhaul.* Many technicians like to check lube oil pressure before the engine is disassembled for rebuild as an indication of what to be especially alert for during rebuild. (For example, if lube pressure is low, the clearances throughout the engine should be carefully checked and held within recommendations.)

TESTING AND TROUBLESHOOTING THE LUBE SYSTEM

To accurately test and determine the condition of a lubrication system, the following procedure is recommended:

1.   Test the oil level and check the oil for correct weight, viscosity, and possible dilution. If any doubt exists about the condition of the lube oil, it should be replaced before proceeding with further tests.

2.   Change the lube oil filter and inspect the old filter for metal particles.

NOTE   If a can type of spin-on filter is used, it may be necessary to cut it apart to check for metal particles. If the filter is filled with many particles of bearing material, it is a good possibility that a worn or damaged bearing is causing the low oil pressure. In most cases the engine bearings should be checked before proceeding with further testing of the lube system.

3.   Warm the engine thoroughly by driving the vehicle or by loading the engine on a dynamometer.

4.   Install a master pressure gauge somewhere in the system where it will indicate system pressure.

CAUTION   Make sure that the gauge is calibrated/scaled to handle the highest expected oil pressure, or damage to the gauge may result.

5. Discuss the complaint with the customer if the condition is customer oriented. Make a mental note of causes that may be creating problems.

6. Determine from the engine service manual what correct oil pressure should be and at what speed testing should be done. [Many engines require a minimum of 40 psi (2.8 kg/cm^2) at either rated load or high idle, for example], refer to OEM specs.

7. Run the engine and check the oil pressure.

8. If the engine oil pressure meets specifications, no further checks need be made. If not, proceed with step 9.

9. If the oil pressure was too low or too high, an attempt should be made to determine what the cause might be.

NOTE   Some engines will have a pressure regulator adjustment for oil pressure. If your engine is so equipped, make the adjustment to bring the oil pressure into the specified range.

---

10. If the oil pressure cannot be adjusted and does not meet specifications, the system pressure regulating valve should be checked.

NOTE   The order and the type of checks that will be made are largely dependent on the technician and the condition of the engine. For example, a newly rebuilt engine would be tested knowing that all clearances and regulator valves were checked during assembly. A key item to look for in rebuilt engines is improperly installed or incorrect gaskets at such places as the oil filter base, oil pump mounting, blower mounting, and other places where pressure oil could be routed incorrectly. In contrast to this would be an engine that had been performing correctly with good oil pressure for many hours and then developed low oil pressure. Troubleshooting of this engine must be approached with the idea that it was correct at one time, but wear or malfunction of some part has created a low-pressure situation.

---

11. If the pressure regulator valve and spring are in good condition, check all the bypass valves used on oil filters and oil coolers.

12. Check the oil pump. In most cases the engine oil pan will have to be removed to gain access to the oil pump.

13. If no problem exists with the oil pump, the main and rod bearings should be checked by removing the caps and checking the bearings for wear, scoring, and clearance with Plastigage.

14. If the main and rod bearing clearances are all right, check the camshaft bushings.

NOTE   Since checking the camshaft bushings requires an extensive amount of engine teardown, a decision should be made at this time about the engine condition. Perhaps a complete engine overhaul should be done at this time. This decision would be dependent on the overall general condition of the engine, number of hours in use, and the owner's wishes.

---

15. At this time most of the points within the engine that contribute to low oil pressure have been indicated. If the problem has not been remedied, a thorough study of the engine lubrication system should be undertaken, considering any peculiarity the engine being worked on may have.

ENGINE PRELUBRICATION

When an engine is completely disassembled, all parts are cleaned, dried, and inspected. When the engine is reassembled with used or new parts, the engine oil galleries must be filled with oil, and all lubricated components such as crankshaft bearings and thrust washers, camshafts, roller followers, rocker arms, pushrods, and oil pumps must be liberally coated with engine oil to ensure that a dry-start condition does not occur. Tests of various engines that have not been prelubed indicate that it can take from 30 to 60 seconds for the pressurized lube oil to reach all areas of an engine after initial start-up of a new engine and longer if the engine has been stopped or stored for long periods in cold ambient conditions.

During the reassembly process that follows replacement of major parts or engine overhaul, certain load-bearing components require prelubrication. This is to ensure that they receive adequate lubrication between initial engine start-up and the complete pressurizing of the lube system by the lube oil pump. In any engine assembly operation, the primary prelubricant is clean engine oil of the correct grade as recommended by the engine manufacturer. Usually, this is 15W-40 multigrade for many heavy-duty four-stroke-cycle engines and straight 40 oil on two-stroke Detroit Diesel engines. Some engine manufacturers recommend liberal use of special lubricants, such as Lubriplate or equivalent, during component assembly.

Failure to prelubricate parts while rebuilding the engine or prior to initial start-up can result in severe wear and damage to the components and engine downtime. Many major tool and equipment suppliers offer engine *prelubers,* which consist of an air- or electric-motor-driven pump and oil reservoir tank that can be filled with clean engine oil.

Figure 11–17 illustrates a prelubricating electric-motor-driven pump sitting on top of an oil barrel with its suction hose extending down into the reservoir. A flexible hydraulic hose can be connected between the pump outlet side and the engine main oil gallery or suitable tap point, so that when the unit is switched on pressurized lube oil can be sent through all oil passages to actively fill and prelubricate all component parts within the engine.

The prelube procedure has several steps:

1. Remove the valve rocker cover(s).
2. Remove a main oil gallery plug from the engine block; if no plug is accessible, remove the oil pressure gauge sensing unit or the sensor on an electronically controlled engine.
3. Refer to Figure 11–17 and connect the hydraulic hose and connector from the preluber to the engine block main oil gallery or oil filter head. On Cummins 14L engines, you can prime the lube system by removing the pipe plug from the external oil pump cover. On some engines it may be easier to remove the 1/2 in. (12.7 mm) pipe plug from the oil filter head above the full-flow oil filter such as that illustrated in Figure 11–17.

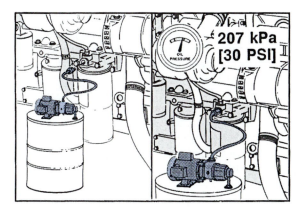

FIGURE 11–17 *Using a small electric motor–driven pump to pressure prelubricate the engine lube system after an overhaul, and prior to cranking and initial startup. (Courtesy of Cummins Engine Company, Inc.)*

4. Fill the preluber reservoir with the recommended grade of lubricant for the engine. Refer to the service manual.
5. With the prelube pump regulated to 25 to 35 psi (172 to 241 kPa), allow oil to flow into the engine. Generally, the preluber is equipped with a bypass regulating valve to control the maximum delivery pressure.
6. When oil is visibly flowing from the rocker arms, the engine oil galleries are primed. Manually rotate the engine over one-half turn to ensure that the oil penetrates all areas. In addition, if the oil pressure gauge is connected, once the gauge registers pressure, you know that the system is primed.
7. On turbocharged engines, disconnect the oil supply line at the turbo center bearing housing and fill the housing cavity with approximately a 1/2 L (pint) of the same grade of engine lube oil. Be sure to manually rotate the turbo wheel during this procedure to coat all internal surfaces with oil; then reinstall the supply line, but leave it between one-half to one-full turn loose.
8. Allow the prelube oil to drain to the crankcase for at least 5 minutes; then add the remaining quantity of engine oil to bring the level to the full mark on the dipstick. Pour this oil slowly over the rocker arms, followers, and camshaft pocket areas to ensure that all of the component parts are adequately lubricated.
9. Disconnect the preluber and plug the main oil gallery.
10. Crank the engine with the governor control in the no-fuel position on mechanical engines until oil pressure starts to register on the gauge.
11. Prior to starting the engine, make sure that the fuel system has been bled of air and that the engine can be *shut down* for any reason. It is sometimes wise to have a suitable blanking plate that can be placed over the air inlet system to kill (stop) the engine should it not shut off in the normal manner.
12. Once the engine cranks, or as soon as it starts, be prepared to tighten up the turbocharger oil supply line, which was left loose in step 7, as soon as oil flow is visible. If no oil flow is apparent to the turbocharger within 20 to 30 seconds, shut the engine off and determine the cause.

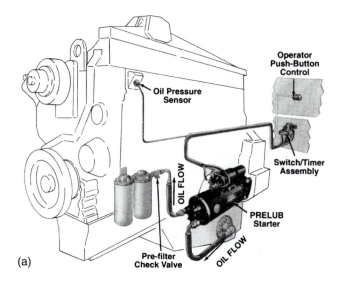

(a)

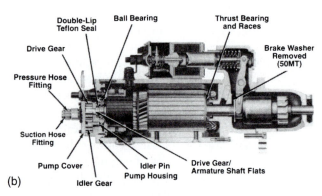

(b)

FIGURE 11–18 (a) Schematic showing a prelube starter motor and oil flow. (b) Sectional view of a prelube starter motor assembly. (Courtesy of Delco Remy America, Anderson, IN.)

STARTER MOTOR PRELUBE SYSTEMS

To provide heavy-duty diesel engines with adequate lubrication prior to engine startup, particularly in cold climates, PRELUB starter and remote mount motors can be used as shown in Figure 11–18a. This arrangement assures engine oil pressure prior to each engine start—automatically. Designed with a powerful and compact gear pump assembled into the end of the starter motor as shown in Figure 11–18b, the starter motor will automatically fill the engine oil filters, and lubricate critical wear surfaces such as the crankshaft, camshaft, turbocharger and valve rockers prior to engine cranking. Available from Delco Remy America and RPM Industries, this PRELUB option is available on 42-MT, 50-MT and 41-RM starter motor models for construction, mining, stationary power, transit and coach, marine, heavy-duty on-highway, compressors, rental fleet protection, and locomotive engine applications.

SUMMARY

This chapter has covered the lube oil and system requirements in a diesel engine. The function, operation, testing, and overhaul or replacement of each component are covered in sufficient detail to allow you to understand, test, and repair the system. When troubleshooting, it is very important to view the lube oil, lube system, and its components as a complete unit, using common sense and a systematic simple-to-complex method of checking to isolate and repair problems.

SELF-TEST QUESTIONS

1. Lube oils in North America are manufactured to various standards set down by these organizations. What do the letters represent?
   a. SAE
   b. API
   c. ASTM

2. Technician A says that letters appearing on any oil container that begin with S indicate a diesel engine lubricant. Technician B says that the letter C indicates a diesel engine lubricant, since the letter S is used for gasoline spark-ignited engines. Which technician is correct?

3. True or False: Oil viscosity rating is a measure of the oil's resistance when one layer of the fluid moves relative to an adjacent layer.

4. Multiviscosity oils are identified by an alphabetical letter following the first number. This letter is
   a. C
   b. F
   c. S
   d. W

5. True or False: The viscosity of multigrade oils is based on their ability to meet an ASTM W-grade standard of a relatively thin oil at a particular low temperature, while also meeting the standards for a thicker non-W-grade oil at a higher temperature, usually 212°F (100°C).

6. The most frequently recommended oil grade for use in heavy-duty high-speed four-stroke-cycle engines such as those of Caterpillar, Cummins, Detroit Diesel, Volvo, Mack, and Navistar is
   a. 5W-20
   b. 10W-30
   c. 10W-40
   d. 15W-40

7. Name the two spring-loaded valves within the lube oil system that control normal and maximum operating pressures.

8. What prevents starvation of lube oil to the engine if and when the full-flow oil filter(s) becomes plugged?

9. If the engine oil cooler becomes plugged, what device would still allow oil to flow to the engine components?

10. True or False: Most oil pumps are gear driven from the crankshaft.

11. The word *gerotor* describes an oil pump that is a combination of
    a. gear and rotor
    b. piston and gear
    c. piston and rotor
    d. dual gears

12. High-speed diesel engine full-flow oil filters are generally rated for a micron filtration size of approximately
    a. 30
    b. 25
    c. 20
    d. 10

13. True or False: Thin black oil is an indication of fuel in the oil?

14. True or False: Milky discoloration of the oil is an indication of coolant in the oil?

15. Name the two types of engine oil coolers that are used on heavy-duty diesel engines.

16. Technician A says that a leaking oil cooler core during engine operation will result in water in the oil. Not so, says Technician B, who believes that lube oil would enter the cooling system instead. Who is correct and state your reasons why.

17. Describe how you would perform a pressure check on an oil cooler core.

18. Describe how you would prelubricate an engine.

12 Cooling Systems

Overview

The cooling system, in conjunction with the lube system, maintains the operating temperature of the engine components to the most efficient temperature under all loads and speeds. Proper coolant treatment protects the internal components of the engine to minimize and protect the wet cylinder liners from cavitation erosion, pitting, and internal coolant passages scale buildup and accumulation. Specific features of various types of cooling systems are discussed and highlighted, along with a description of the purpose, function, and operation of the various components. Details are provided on the necessary maintenance checks and testing and repair/replacement of the major components to permit you to challenge the various ASE or TQ tests.

ASE CERTIFICATION

ASE offers within the medium/heavy truck tests certification area, a diesel engines T2 test. In the general engine diagnosis content area, Part D deals specifically with cooling systems diagnosis and repair, in which a total of nine questions accounting for 13% of the T2 test deal with a combination of both lube and cooling systems. The ASE T2 tasks list for Part D includes items 6 through 14, as follows:

6. Inspect and reinstall/replace pulleys, tensioners, and drive belts; adjust drive belts; check alignment.

7. Verify coolant temperature and check the operation of both temperature and coolant level sensors, temperature gauge, and sending unit.

8. Inspect and replace thermostat(s), bypass passages, housing(s), and seals.

9. Flush and refill the cooling system; bleed all entrapped air from the system; recover and recycle used coolant as per local safety regulations.

10. Inspect, repair/replace the coolant conditioner/filter; check valves, lines, and fittings.

11. Inspect, repair/replace water pump, hoses, and idler pulley(s).

12. Inspect and clean the radiator, pressure cap, and tank(s); determine required and appropriate service.

13. Inspect, repair/replace the fan hub, fan, fan clutch, mechanical and electronic fan controls, fan thermostat, and fan shroud.

14. Inspect, repair/replace radiator shutter assembly and controls.

Also within Part A and Part C of this same content area are several items that reference the skills and knowledge necessary to challenge the T2 cooling systems test. In Part A of the content area, the following numbered items under the subheading "General Engine Diagnosis" deal with these procedures:

2. Check for coolant leaks and determine necessary repairs.

14. Check cooling system for protection level, contamination, coolant type and level, temperature, pressure, conditioner concentration, filtration, and fan operation; determine necessary and appropriate repairs.

In Part C of the T2 tasks list, item 3 states the following:

3. Pressure-test the engine block for coolant leakage; determine necessary and appropriate repair(s).

Within this chapter we provide detailed information to support a course of study in preparation for challenging the ASE content in the T2 diesel engines test content area.

COOLING SYSTEM FUNCTION

All internal combustion engines require treated water within a radiator system, heat exchanger, keel cooler, or cooling tower to prevent the engine from overheating and boiling over. Documented studies have shown that more than 40% of all engine problems are directly or indirectly related to improper maintenance of the cooling system.

The basic function of a cooling system is to dissipate a portion of the heat created within the engine combustion chamber. Heat absorbed by the pistons, rings, liners, cylinder heads, and cylinder block during engine operation that is not directly converted into useful power at the flywheel must be handled by the cooling system. A properly designed cooling system must maintain the coolant operating temperature within a fairly narrow band to ensure proper combustion, minimize blowby, and allow the engine lube oil to function correctly. Tests have proven that wear on cylinder walls can be up to eight times greater with a coolant temperature of 100°F (38°C) compared with one of 180°F (82°C). Normal engine operating temperatures are generally controlled by one or more temperature regulators or thermostats. Typical coolant temperatures under loaded engine conditions fall within 180 to 200°F (82 to 93°C).

Engine Block Coolant Flow

The flow of treated coolant through an engine block will vary between different makes and models, but can be considered generic in most cases. Figure 12–1 illustrates the flow of coolant through the engine block of a Cummins ISX/Signature series DOHC 15-L inline six-cylinder engine model. Hot coolant leaving the thermostat housing is directed to a radiator on mobile equipment applications such as heavy-duty truck/tractors, or to a heat exchanger and expansion tank for industrial or marine applications. A typical example of the cooling system specs for this particular engine is listed in Table 12–1.

Component Description, Operation, and Function

All liquid-type cooling systems have the same basic components except for the temperature controls, such as fan clutches, shutters, and thermostats. A typical liquid cooling system will have the following components:

1. *Radiator.* A device that performs two important functions:
   a. Provides a storage tank for the engine coolant.
   b. Provides a surface where engine heat can be dissipated to the surrounding air.
      (1) Radiator cores (the radiator surface that dissipates the heat) are generally tube and fin type (Figure 12–2).
2. *Water jackets.* Water jackets surround the engine block and provide a storage area for the coolant. They also provide a place for the coolant to circulate through the block and pick up the excess engine heat.
3. *Water pump.* A centrifugal nonpositive-displacement pump used to pump the water through the block (water jacket) and radiator. It may be driven by a gear or pulley and belt arrangement.
4. *Thermostat.* A temperature-controlled valve that regulates the flow of coolant through the engine and radiator. This flow regulation maintains engine temperature.
5. *Fan and fan drives.* The fan is mounted on the water pump drive pulley hub or on a separate fan hub driven by a V- or serpentine belt. It provides air movement across the radiator so that heat can be dissipated. On some diesel engines (especially trucks), the fan can be driven by a fluid clutch, which is controlled by the temperature of the air passing over it. Depending on the temperature, the fan will run fast or slow.

> **NOTE** Viscous fan drives reduce fan speed when the engine and coolant water are cold, while electric clutch fan drives disconnect the fan from the drive hub entirely and the fan is not driven at all when the engine is cold.

Clutch fan drives save fuel and horsepower, since the fan does not run at all, or its speed is substantially reduced when the engine is cold.

6. *Temperature gauge.* A gauge that tells the operator what the engine coolant temperature is. It can be one of two types:
   a. *Electric.* An electric temperature gauge has a sending unit threaded into the water jacket or manifold to sense engine temperature. This sending unit provides the ground for the gauge circuit that includes the indicator gauge. Current is supplied to the circuit from the battery via the ignition switch. When the

Flow Diagram, Cooling System

General Information

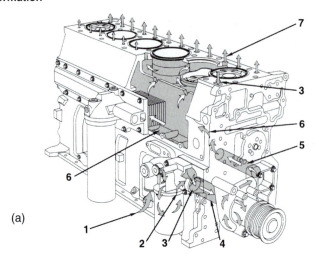

(a)

1. Coolant Inlet
2. Coolant Flow from Coolant Filter
3. Coolant Bypass Flow from Thermostat
4. Coolant Flow to Water Pump

5. Coolant Flow from Water Pump
6. Coolant Flow past Oil Cooler
7. Coolant Flow to Cylinder Head.

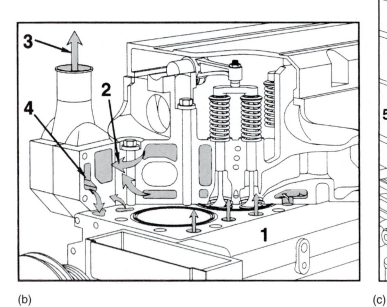

(b)

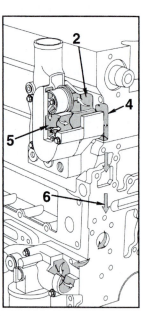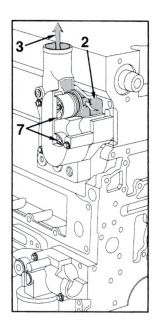

(c)

1. Coolant Flow from Cylinder Block to Cylinder Head
2. Coolant Flow from Cylinder Head to Thermostat Housing
3. Coolant Flow to Radiator
4. Coolant Bypass Passage

5. Coolant Bypass Flow to Water Pump
6. Coolant Bypass Closed
7. Thermostats

FIGURE 12–1 (a) Engine coolant flow through the block of a Cummins Signature/ISX model. (b) Coolant flow from the block to the cylinder heads and to the thermostat housing. (c) Close-up view of the engine coolant flow to the thermostat housing and bypass passage with a closed thermostat, and to the radiator when the thermostat is open. (Courtesy of Cummins Engine Company, Inc.)

TABLE 12–1 *Cooling system specifications chart for the Cummins Signature/ISX engine models*

Specifications

Cooling System

Coolant Capacity (engine **only**) .... 24 liters [25 qt]

Standard Modulating Thermostat Range .... 82 to 93°C [180 to 200°F]

Maximum Coolant Pressure
(exclusive of pressure cap - closed thermostat at the maximum no-load governed speed) .... 227 kPa [33 psi]

Coolant Alarm Activation Temperature **(automotive and industrial only)** .... 110°C [230°F]

Maximum Allowable Top Tank Temperature:
  Automotive and Industrial .... 107°C [225°F]
  Power Generation:
    Standby .... 110°C [230°F]
    Prime .... 104°C [220°F]

Minimum Recommended Top Tank Temperature .... 70°C [158°F]

Minimum Allowable Drawdown or 10 Percent of System Capacity (whichever is greater) .... 2.4 liters [2.5 qt]

Minimum Recommended Pressure Cap:
  Automotive and Industrial .... 50 kPa [7 psi]
  Power Generation .... 69 kPa [10 psi]

Minimum Fill Rate (without low-level alarm) .... 19 liters/min [5 gpm]

Maximum Deaeration Time .... 25 minutes

Fan on Coolant Temperature **(automotive and industrial only)** .... 95°C [203°F]

Fan on Intake Air Temperature **(automotive and industrial only)** .... 66°C [150°F]

Shutter Opening Temperature **(automotive and industrial only)**:
  Coolant .... 85°C [185°F]
  Intake Air .... 66°C [150°F]

Winterfronts - **Automotive Only** .... Air passage area 775 cm² [120 in²]

coolant is cold, the sensing unit provides no ground for the circuit; when it heats up, a ground is provided, causing current to flow in the gauge circuit and to indicate a reading on the gauge.

  b. *Expansion.* The Bourdon expansion gauge unit is made up of a gauge, a long copper or steel tube with a protective cover, and a sensing unit or bulb that fits in the block or water manifold. The tube and gauge expansion unit are filled with a liquid that expands rapidly when heated. When the coolant warms up, the sensing unit and the liquid in it warm up and the gauge mechanism is operated, showing coolant temperature.

  7. *Shutters.* Shutters are louverlike panels that are mounted in front of the radiator and, when closed, prevent airflow across the radiator. This restricted airflow decreases warm-up time after a cold engine start and provides a means for regulating water temperature during engine operation. Most shutters are air closed and spring opened, while some may be operated by a thermostat through direct linkage.

  8. *Radiator cap.* A cap that maintains a given pressure within the cooling system. This pressure allows coolant temperatures to run hotter without boiling. (Every pound of pressure exerted on the coolant increases the boiling point by 3.5°F). Included in the cap is a vacuum valve that allows air to enter the system when the coolant cools and contracts. If the cap did not have a vacuum valve, pressure inside the radiator might fall so low that outside air pressure might cause the radiator and hoses to collapse.

  9. *Water conditioner and filter.* A filter containing an element that conditions the coolant and prevents it from becoming too acidic. An over-acid coolant can cause cavitation that can erode the sleeves and cylinder block.

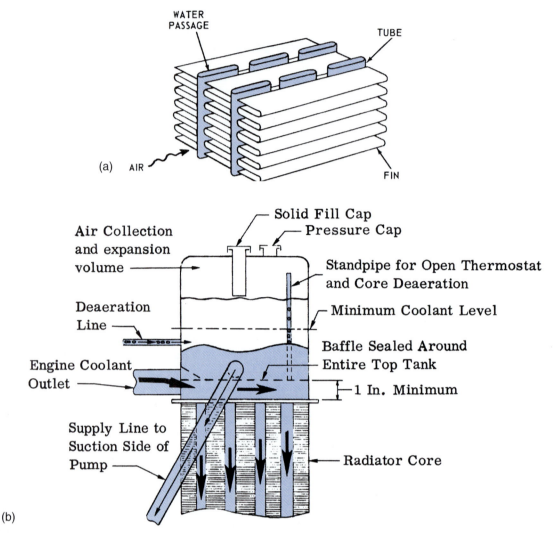

FIGURE 12–2   (a) Tube-and-fin radiator design; (b) typical heavy-duty downflow tube-and-fin radiator highlighting the baffled top tank arrangement. (Courtesy of Detroit Diesel Corporation.)

10.   *Coolant.* The coolant is generally a water and antifreeze mixture. Even in climates where freezing is not a problem, antifreeze and water are the most popular coolant because of the antifreeze's rust-inhibitor capabilities. Antifreeze and water are generally installed in the cooling system in a 50:50 ratio.

11.   *Shutterstat.* The shutterstat is an air control valve that is operated by coolant temperature and controls the air supply to the shutter operating cylinder.

12.   *Hoses.* The hoses that direct the flow of water from the block to the radiator are made from neoprene, a rubberlike material, and may be of the molded type, straight type, or flexible type. The straight-type hose can be used where a straight line exists between the two hose connections. If the hose has to make a bend, a

molded or flexible hose must be utilized. Lower radiator hoses, the ones that connect the lower water pump elbow with the lower radiator connections, usually have a coiled wire in them so that they do not collapse or suck shut during operation.

13.   *Clamps.* Many different types of clamps are used when attaching the hoses to the radiator and block inlet and outlets.

ENGINE HEAT LOADS

Heat dissipated to the coolant at rated power and peak torque engine speeds is used to define the heat load that must be dissipated by the cooling system, either to a radiator or heat exchanger system such as that found in industrial and marine applications. The energy distribution from combustion of the injected fuel can be split into four categories:

1. Useful work or power available after frictional losses
2. Exhaust gases (which recapture some heat energy to drive a turbocharger)
3. Cooling system (which recaptures some energy, for example, as an in-cab heater and defroster)
4. Heat radiation from the engine

Exact heat loads vary in specific makes of engines. In modern electronically controlled engines, thermal efficiency (TE), or the heat efficiency and useful work from the engine, approaches 40 to 42%. Typical heat rejection values for today's engines can range from as high as 14,000 Btu (10,440 kW) per minute in high-output electronically controlled engines to as little as 4000 Btu (2,983 kW) per minute in low-horsepower engines. Average heat rejection to the cooling system is usually in the range of 30 to 35 Btu/hp-min for a basic engine. The addition of accessories to the coolant system, such as transmission and marine gear oil coolers, can increase the cooling system heat load to between 40 and 50 Btu/min.

Assume that an engine is rated at 450 bhp (335.6 kW) with a heat load of 14,000 Btu (10,440 kW) per minute. If we divide the heat load by 450 bhp (335.6 kW), the cooling system would have to absorb 31 Btu/hp-min. In a smaller engine rated at only 150 bhp (112 kW) with a heat load of 4000 Btu/min, the cooling system has to absorb 27 Btu/hp (0.471 kW) per minute. As you can see, there is little difference between the cooling system heat absorption requirements of the smaller and the larger rated engines. For example, the 3176B Caterpillar inline six-cylinder four-stroke-cycle engine which has electronically controlled unit injectors is a 10.3-L (629 in^3) displacement engine. Although initially designed for heavy-duty truck applications, it is now used in a variety of applications. Total heat rejection on this engine is 27 Btu/hp-min, with 17 Btu from the engine cooling jacket and 10 Btu from the ATAAC (air-to-air aftercooler) charge air system.

Thermal efficiency (or heat efficiency) simply means that if the engine has a 42% TE, for every $1 of fuel injected into the combustion chamber, there is a 42-cent return at the flywheel as usable power. This means that approximately 58% of the heat developed from combustion is wasted and dissipated to the cooling, exhaust, friction, and radiation areas. If we assume that our example engine is rated at 450 bhp (335.6 kW) and

the cooling system handles 14,000 Btu (10,440 kW) per minute, in 1 hour the cooling system has to handle 60 × 14,000 = 840,000 Btu. If we divide this figure by 450 bhp (335.6 kW), the cooling system load is 1866.66 Btu/hp-hr.

From the discussion in Chapter 3 we know that a perfect engine incurring no heat losses would require enough injected fuel to release 2545 Btu of heat within the cylinder to produce 1 hp (0.746 kW) over a 1-hour period. If this 2545 Btu/hp-hr represents usable power with a 42% TE value, we can factor out the remaining Btu heat losses. If the engine has a fuel consumption of 0.310 lb/bhp-hr (188.5 g/kWh), at a rating of 450 bhp (335.6 kW) in 1 hour the engine consumes 450 × 0.310 = 139.5 lb (63.27 kg) of fuel. If the fuel has an API rating of 38, it weighs 6.95 lb/U.S. gallon (3.15 kg/3.78 L). The engine consumes, therefore, 20.07 U.S. gallons/hr (75.97 L/h). A 38 API fuel contains 137,000 Btu HHV (high heat value) per U.S. gallon, so in 1 hour the total heat released into the engine cylinders is 137,000 × 20.07 = 2,749,590 Btu. If we divide this total heat released by the power rating of 450 bhp (335.6 kW), the engine requires 6110.2 Btu to produce 1 hp over a 1-hour period. We know that only 2545 Btu of this heat was actually useful power; therefore, 6110.2 − 2545 = 3565.2 Btu was lost to the cooling system, exhaust, friction, and radiation. The 1866.66 Btu/hp-hr is equal to 30.54% of the total heat used (6110.2 Btu). Added to the 42% TE, we have now accounted for 42 + 30.54 = 72.54% of the fuel heat released into the combustion chamber. This means that the remaining 27.46% of dissipated heat losses was accounted for by the exhaust and friction and radiation area, which represents 1698.54 Btu.

COOLANT FLOW DETERMINATION

Although the service technician is seldom required to determine the water flow through an engine, it is helpful to appreciate what the coolant flow demands are on various diesel engines. A reduction in coolant flow from a faulty water pump, a restricted radiator caused by scale buildup or plugging, collapsed top and bottom hoses, and faulty thermostats can all affect the flow rate through the engine water jackets.

Let's say we were asked to consider the rate of water flow in gpm (gallons per minute) or lpm (liters per minute) required to cool an engine rated at 450 bhp with a heat rejection rate to the cooling water of 1500 Btu/bhp/hr (25 Btu/bhp/min) with a water inlet temperature to the engine of 170°F (76.6°C), and a thermostat outlet temperature of 195°F (90.5°C). We need to apply a known formula to determine the cooling flow rate solution:

$$gpm = \frac{bhp \, (Btu \, per \, bhp \, per \, hour)}{(t1 - t2) \, 500}$$

where $t1$ is the outlet temperature and $t2$ is the coolant inlet temperature.

$$gpm = \frac{450 \, (1500)}{(195 - 170) \, 500} = \frac{450 \, (1500)}{(25) \, 500} = \frac{675,000}{12,500}$$

$$= 54 \text{ U.S. gpm (204.5 L)}$$

Using the same formula, if the same engine rated at 450 bhp had a heat rejection rate of 2000 Btu/bhp/hr (33.3 Btu/bhp/min) and the same water inlet and outlet temperatures, the water flow requirements through the engine would be 72 U.S. gpm (272.5 L). On a 3000 bhp engine with a heat rejection rate of 1800 Btu/bhp/hr (30 Btu/bhp/min) and the same water inlet and outlet temperatures, the required coolant flow rate through this engine would be 432 U.S. gpm (1635 L).

RADIATORS

A radiator is a form of heat exchanger that is designed to allow hot coolant from the engine to flow through a series of tubes or cores to dissipate its heat. The heat is dissipated by air being drawn through the radiator fins when the vehicle is stationary by an engine-driven suction fan; when the vehicle is moving, ambient ram (forced or pushed) air passes through the radiator. When a radiator is used on a stationary piece of equipment such as a portable air compressor, a *blower fan* pulls ambient air from below the unit and forces it through the radiator core in the opposite direction to what occurs on a car, truck, or piece of mobile equipment capable of being driven at a reasonable speed. There are three main types of radiators in use:

1. In a *downflow* design, the coolant flows from the top to the bottom of the radiator core. The effect of gravity in this type of system generally minimizes the restriction to the suction side of the water pump. Typical heavy-duty class 8 diesel trucks employ radiators with a frontal area ranging from 1000 to 1700 in^2 (6451 to 10,967 cm^2) depending on the engine power rating and the required heat loads.

2. In another design the hot coolant from the thermostat housing enters either the top or bottom of the radiator first and circulates through a series of tubes and liquid-tight baffles in a crossflow, downward, or upward loop. The number of passes of the coolant through these types of radiators depends on the heat transfer level required. Figure 12–3 illustrates a two-pass heavy-duty radiator, and Figure 12–4 illustrates a two-pass

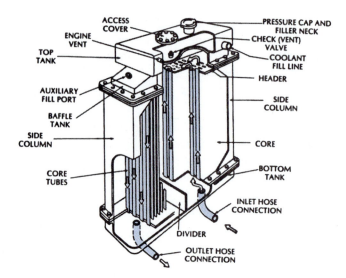

FIGURE 12–3 Coolant flow through a two-pass heavy-duty radiator. (Courtesy of Cummins Engine Company, Inc.)

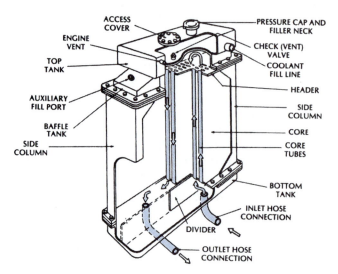

FIGURE 12–4 Coolant flow through a heavy-duty two-pass counterflow radiator. (Courtesy of Cummins Engine Company, Inc.)

counterflow design. A greater number of coolant passes increases the velocity of the coolant. In recent years, a two-pass design commonly referred to as low-flow cooling (LFC) has been used by Cummins on a number of its truck engines. Figure 12–5 illustrates the basic flow from the engine to and through this system for a 14-L engine. The main difference between an LFC system and a traditional system is that the LFC design has a reduced coolant flow rate through the radiator and usually operates with a higher-pressure cap, since system pressures can exceed 40 psi (276 kPa). The two-pass LFC radiator directs the engine coolant down one side of the core and up the other to increase tube velocity and keep the

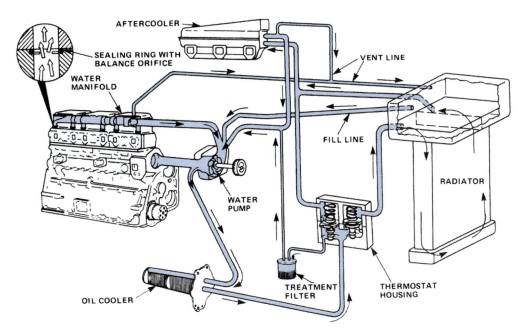

FIGURE 12–5 Coolant flow through a Cummins NTC 14-L engine low-flow cooling system. (Courtesy of Cummins Engine Company, Inc.)

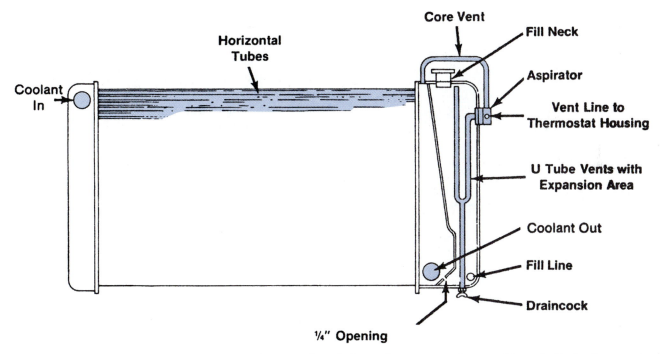

FIGURE 12–6 Identification of components for a crossflow design radiator system. (Courtesy of Cummins Engine Company, Inc.)

coolant in the radiator as long as possible. This results in a lower-temperature coolant to the water-cooled engine aftercooler, which lowers the charge temperature of the pressurized air flowing from the turbocharger to the engine. This in turn provides a denser air charge to the cylinders, resulting in improved fuel economy and lower exhaust emissions. The LFC system is generally

not required on engines employing AAACs (air-to-air aftercoolers).

3. In a *crossflow* design the coolant enters the radiator along one of the side headers and flows horizontally through the core to the opposite side. Figure 12–6 illustrates a typical crossflow radiator design for an inline engine. In V-type engines two thermostat

housings would be connected together, or alternatively, have two outlets to the radiator. The crossflow design allows a lower overall hood height, which is often necessary with aerodynamic truck styling.

RADIATOR SHUTTERS

Some heavy-duty trucks and tractors have a venetian-blind type of mechanism mounted directly in front of the radiator core. This device is known as a *shutter assembly,* and it is designed to control cooling airflow across the radiator. Certain truck models may install the radiator shutters behind the radiator core. Figure 12–7 illustrates both types of systems. Both shutter assemblies have horizontal vanes, but some crossflow radiator designs employ vertical vanes. The shutter assembly is designed to maintain and control the operating temperature of the engine coolant within a given range. It is commonly used on trucks operating in cold ambient conditions.

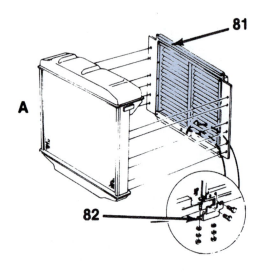

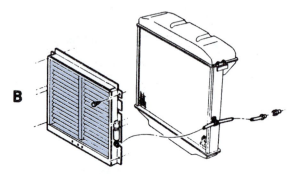

FIGURE   12–7 *Heavy-duty truck radiator shutter arrangement, showing (a) the shutter assembly located behind the radiator core, and (b) the shutters located in front of the radiator core. (Reprinted courtesy of Caterpillar, Inc.)*

CAUTION Shutters are commonly used on trucks that employ JWAC systems. Shutters should not be used on engines equipped with AAAC systems unless the installation provides for mounting the shutter between the AAAC core and the radiator core. Mounting a shutter assembly in front of the AAAC core will result in hot air from the turbocharger compressor entering the engine. This can cause short valve and piston life as well as poor fuel economy and a reduction in engine power.

Shutters are only used in conjunction with a clutch fan. With the shutters in the closed position, a fan would be highly stressed in attempting to pull air through a closed radiator core. To prevent this condition from occurring, a thermally operated fan clutch is used, which can be disengaged until the radiator shutters are opened. The actual engine coolant temperature at which the shutters and thermatic fan engage depends on the opening temperature of the engine coolant thermostat. The basic sequence of events for a heavy-duty class 8 truck equipped with 180°F (82°C) coolant thermostats, shutters, and a thermatic clutch fan is presented in Table 12–2. The vanes, or individual blinds, of the shutter assembly are connected by mechanical rod linkage so that they can be opened or closed to suit engine operating temperature conditions.

The power unit that rotates the vanes is an air cylinder which operates on compressed air from the vehicle air brake reservoir. The shutters are either fully open or fully closed. To prevent overheating of the engine in the event of a system malfunction, the shutters are normally held open by spring pressure and closed by air pressure.

FAN CLUTCHES

Since fans are only required for between 5% and 10% of the operational time of the engine, there are a number of automatic engagement and disengagement types on the market for trucks and equipment. Thermatically controlled fan clutches can save up to 10% fuel consumption and up to 10% horsepower. These fan clutches are designed to operate based on air, springs, or engine oil controlled from an engine coolant temperature sensor. Note that some thermatic fans rely on radiator air temperature directed against the heat-sensing center hub of the fan. Figure 12–8A illustrates that regardless of clutch type, the actual fan hub pulley is driven by a multiple-belt arrangement from the engine crankshaft front pulley. Although the fan hub

TABLE 12–2 Heavy-duty truck cooling system chart indicating the modulated operating temperatures for various components when using 180°F (82°C) begins-to-open thermostat. (Courtesy of Cummins Engine Company, Inc.)

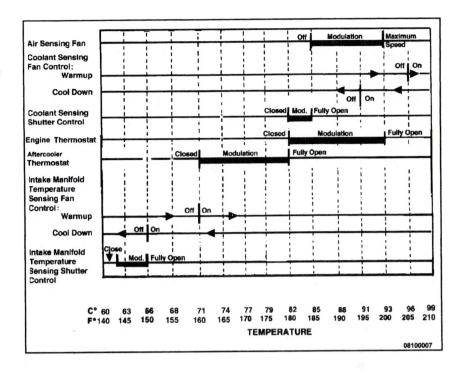

FIGURE 12–8 (a) Features of a 'spring-engaged/air pressure disengaged' Bendix fan clutch assembly. (Courtesy of Allied-Signal Truck Brake Systems Company).

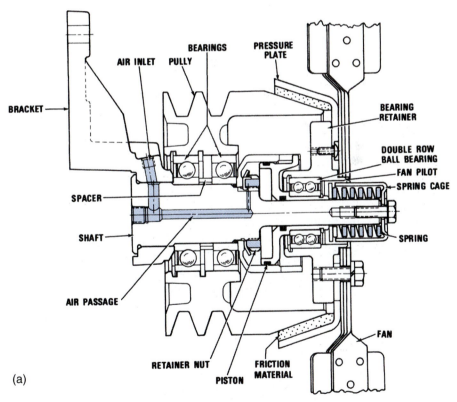

(a)

rotates, the power required to drive it is marginal when the fan clutch is not engaged. During this disengaged position, the fan blades do not rotate. When the fan clutch is engaged, the fan blades rotate as their belt-driven hub engages with the fan clutch portion of the assembly. Fan drives without a clutch require maintenance of only shaft bearings. Fan drives with a clutch engagement mechanism require bearing, clutch facing, seal, and air or electrical supply maintenance. Some of the more popular fan clutches on the market are

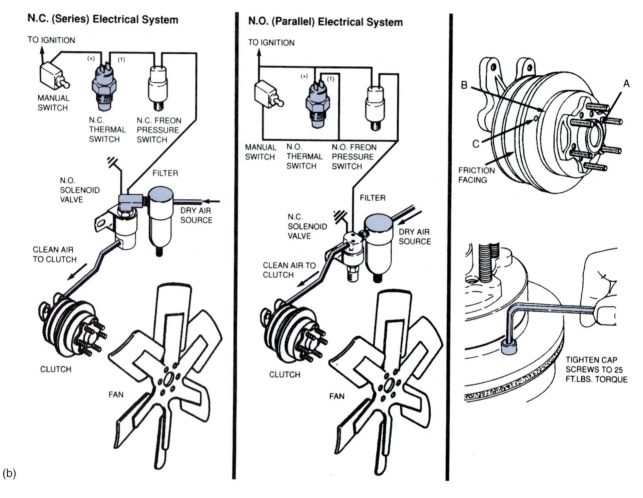

FIGURE 12–8 (continued). (b) Schematic of an 'air-pressure engaged/spring disengaged' fan clutch assembly. Note the location of the two fan clutch hub access holes (Item C) to permit the insertion of two 5/16-18 NC × 1" long Grade 8 socket head screws to engage the fan clutch in an emergency caused by fan clutch, or control system malfunction. (Courtesy of Horton Manufacturing Co., Inc.)

manufactured by Bendix, Rockford, Horton, Facet, Kysor/Cadillac, Eaton, Evans, and Schwitzer.

The electrical circuit used with a fan clutch system can be either a NC (normally closed) or NO (normally open) type of switch (see Figure 12–8B). Two optional control systems are available:

1. Combination of basic control and an optional air-conditioning control system
2. Combination of basic control system and a manual bypass system with a dash-mounted indicator light and optional air-conditioning control. The dash indicator light indicates to the driver when the fan is engaged.

Electromagnetic Fan Clutch

A number of mid-range truck engines employ an electromagnetic fan clutch energized from the 12-volt ve-

hicle electrical system. Cummins uses this type of fan clutch on their B-series engines. This type of clutch is generally used on mobile applications that benefit from ram air cooling as the vehicle moves along the road. Stationary engine applications tend to have frequent fan cycling that may result in unacceptable clutch life.

As with air spring applied clutches, the fan pulley is always being driven from a poly-vee, or vee drive belts from the engine crankshaft pulley. However, if the electromagnet circuit is open, the fan drive hub will not rotate. Rather than plumbing a compressed air line into the rear of the fan hub, a two-wire harness is employed. The fan clutch electrical circuit can be closed to engage the fan from either the coolant temperature sensor, or the freon switch pressure sensor when used with air conditioning units. The most common temperature switch used is set to close at 195°F (91°C). Note that the temperature must be set above the opening point of the thermostat. When battery voltage is applied to the fan hub, the electromagnet engages the fan drive, A typical draw is generally about 4.9 amps at 12 volts. The fan is either fully engaged, or fully disengaged. A manual override switch to allow the operator to manually engage the clutch can be installed into the circuit with its control switch (on/off) located into the vehicle instrument switch cluster.

THERMOSTATS

Purpose and Function

Although the radiator or heat exchanger system absorbs and dissipates the rejected heat to the cooling system, to maintain a steady coolant temperature under all operating conditions, all internal combustion engines employ temperature-controlled thermostats

(stats) or regulators. The thermostat(s) is normally located within a bolted housing at the top front of the engine block as illustrated in Figure 12–9. To perform effectively, a stat must operate as follows:

- Start to open at a specified temperature
- Be fully open at a specified number of degrees above the *start-to-open* temperature
- Allow a specified amount of coolant under pressure to flow when the stat is fully open
- Block all coolant flow to the radiator when in the closed position

As you can see in Figure 12–9b, all engine coolant flows through a bypass pipe (hose) back to the suction side of the water pump at temperatures below the opening point of the stat. Additional coolant requirements of the pump during this period are supplied

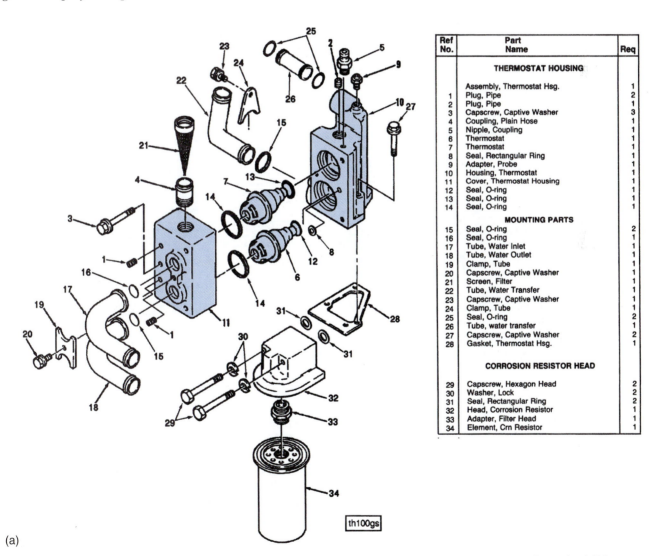

Ref No.	Part Name	Req
	THERMOSTAT HOUSING	
	Assembly, Thermostat Hsg.	1
1	Plug, Pipe	2
2	Plug, Pipe	1
3	Capscrew, Captive Washer	3
4	Coupling, Plain Hose	1
5	Nipple, Coupling	1
6	Thermostat	1
7	Thermostat	1
8	Seal, Rectangular Ring	1
9	Adapter, Probe	1
10	Housing, Thermostat	1
11	Cover, Thermostat Housing	1
12	Seal, O-ring	1
13	Seal, O-ring	1
14	Seal, O-ring	1
	MOUNTING PARTS	
15	Seal, O-ring	2
16	Seal, O-ring	1
17	Tube, Water Inlet	1
18	Tube, Water Outlet	1
19	Clamp, Tube	1
20	Capscrew, Captive Washer	1
21	Screen, Filter	1
22	Tube, Water Transfer	1
23	Capscrew, Captive Washer	1
24	Clamp, Tube	1
25	Seal, O-ring	2
26	Tube, water transfer	1
27	Capscrew, Captive Washer	2
28	Gasket, Thermostat Hsg.	1
	CORROSION RESISTOR HEAD	
29	Capscrew, Hexagon Head	2
30	Washer, Lock	2
31	Seal, Rectangular Ring	2
32	Head, Corrosion Resistor	1
33	Adapter, Filter Head	1
34	Element, Crn Resistor	1

th100gs

(a)

FIGURE 12–9   (a) Exploded view of the component parts of the thermostat housing used on Cummins N14 (855 in³) model engines. (Courtesy of Cummins Engine Company, Inc.).

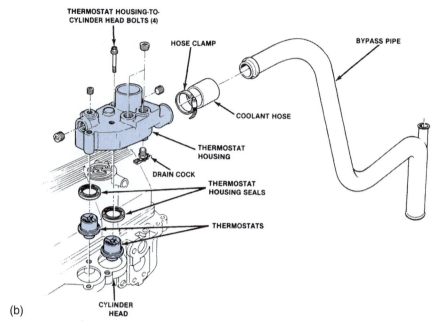

THERMOSTAT HOUSING-TO-
CYLINDER HEAD BOLTS (4)

HOSE CLAMP

BYPASS PIPE

COOLANT HOSE

THERMOSTAT
HOUSING

DRAIN COCK

THERMOSTAT
HOUSING SEALS

THERMOSTATS

CYLINDER
HEAD

(b)

FIGURE 12–9   (continued). (b) Thermostats and related parts for a series 60 DDC engine model. (Courtesy of Detroit Diesel Corporation.)

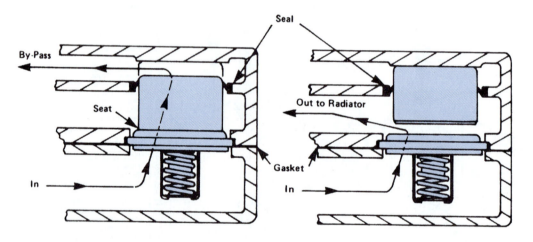

Seal

By-Pass

Seat

Out to Radiator

Gasket

In   In

FIGURE 12–10   Coolant flow to the bypass pipe and to the radiator in both the cold and hot positions when using a fully blocking type of thermostat. (Courtesy of Cummins Engine Company, Inc.)

through a makeup or fill line. When the engine coolant reaches the stat opening temperature, engine coolant flows through the open stat to the top radiator hose as shown in Figure 12–10 to the baffle area of the radiator top tank. This hot coolant then passes through the radiator tubes where it gives up its heat to the airflow moving through the radiator fins.

Types

Depending on the cooling system design three basic types of thermostats can be used in diesel engines: full blocking, nonblocking, and partial blocking. Let us examine each one of these types.

Figure 12–11 illustrates the full-blocking type of stat. Figure 12–10 depicts the actual flow of coolant through the stat to the radiator HE (heat exchanger) as well as the bypass circuit. During engine warm-up, all engine coolant flows through the bypass circuit, thereby preventing any coolant from being exposed to heat loss by flowing through the radiator or HE. This provides for a faster warm-up period. As the thermostat begins to open, increasing amounts of engine

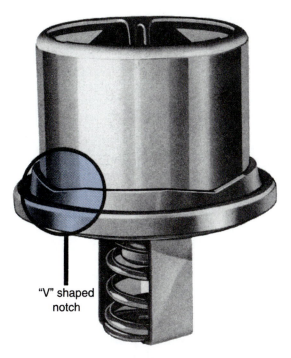

FIGURE 12–11 Weir type of the fully blocking–type thermostat design. (Courtesy of Detroit Diesel Corporation.)

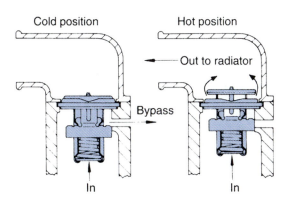

FIGURE 12–12 Coolant flow through a partial blocking type of thermostat. (Courtesy of Detroit Diesel Corporation.)

FIGURE 12–13 Partial or semiblocking (shielded) thermostat design. (Courtesy of Detroit Diesel Corporation.)

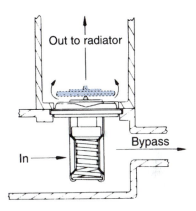

FIGURE 12–14 Coolant flow through a nonblocking (choke or poppet) thermostat. (Courtesy of Detroit Diesel Corporation.)

coolant flow to the radiator or HE, and bypass flow is correspondingly reduced. At approximately 15 to 20°F (8 to 11°C) above the opening temperature of the stat, the bypass opening is fully blocked and the total flow of coolant is directed into the radiator or HE.

The partial blocking type of stat shown in Figure 12–12 directs coolant to a bypass passage connected to the water pump when cold (closed), but directs all coolant flow to the radiator or HE when hot (open). Figure 12–13 illustrates a partial blocking, or shielded stat assembly as it would actually appear.

Figure 12–14 illustrates a nonblocking (choke or poppet type) thermostat which will always bypass some coolant down the bypass line to the water pump while the stat is open or closed.

Construction and Operation

Engine coolant is corrosive even when properly maintained and treated with antifreeze and Supplemental Coolant Additives (SCAs). Stats, therefore, are normally made from brass or brass-coated materials. The stat consists of a brass cup filled with a heat-expansive, waxlike material (sometimes referred to as beeswax) retained within the cup by an elastomeric seal. The stat valve is connected to a piston that is held on the elastomer by a spring. Figure 12–15 illustrates the basic construction and operation of a thermostat.

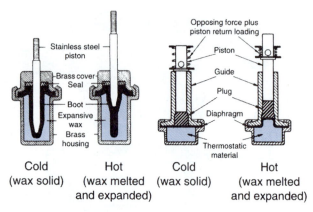

FIGURE 12–15 *Construction and operation of a typical thermostat assembly. (Courtesy of Detroit Diesel Corporation.)*

A stat can be vented or nonvented. The *vent* refers to the deaeration capability of the cooling system. The design of the cooling system determines whether the stat is vented. In a vented system, venting is accomplished by drilling a small hole in the stat valve or notching the valve at its seat (see the design shown in Figure 12–11). Nonvented stats should only be installed in cooling systems of the positive deaeration type. This is usually the case if one or more deaeration lines (hoses) extend from the stat housing area to the radiator or HE top tank.

Designs
Engine manufacturers employ various types of stats and locate one or more within a housing similar to that shown in Figure 12–9. For example, in the Cummins optimized JWAC and LFC radiator cooling system, two stats are used within a common housing; one stat is a bypass type and the other is a radiator type. At engine startup, the bypass stat is wide open and the radiator stat is closed. Coolant flows through the stat housing to the JWAC aftercooler inlet to allow the gradually warming coolant to heat the intake air for more efficient combustion. When the coolant temperature reaches 160°F (71°C), flow to the aftercooler decreases as the bypass stat begins to close. At coolant temperatures below 175°F (79°C), there is no coolant flow through the radiator core; all of the coolant flows through the bypass stat to the aftercooler. Take careful note that at 175°F (79°C) the radiator stat begins to open and some coolant begins to flow to the radiator; therefore, between 175 and 185°F (79 to 85°C), the two stats operate together to control the flow and temperature of coolant flow to the aftercooler and the radiator.

At engine coolant temperatures above 185°F (85°C), the bypass stat to the JWAC is fully closed. The radiator stat continues to open until it is fully open at 195°F (91°C) or higher and all engine coolant flows to and through the radiator as illustrated in Figure 12–5. The maximum allowable coolant temperature in these engines is 212°F (100°C). Depending on the Cummins engine model in use, 10 to 20 U.S. gpm (38 to 76 L) of coolant flows through the radiator stat to the low-flow radiator.

Removal and Inspection
In cases of engine or coolant overheating, many service personnel remove the thermostats. This should only be done, however, as a temporary measure to allow possible relocating of the vehicle or equipment when all else fails. Stat removal normally should *not* be done. Operating an engine without a stat is not recommended because the engine will run too cool, thereby causing condensation of water and incomplete combustion, which results in corrosive acids and sludge forming in the lube oil. This can restrict lube oil flow and accelerate engine wear. In addition, poor combustion causes rough idling and increased amounts of exhaust pollutants and white smoke (water vapor). When using full- or partial-blocking stats that fail to open fully (or stick closed), the bypass system will remain open and prevent a sufficient flow of coolant to the radiator or HE. As a result, the engine coolant temperature may rise even higher.

Opening Temperature and Distance
Each stat is designed and constructed to start to open at a specific temperature, which is stamped on the stem or housing area. The stat control section moves through a set distance to its fully open position. For example, Figure 12–13 shows that this stat should move through a distance of 23.36 ± 0.76 mm (0.920 ± 0.030 in.). Failure of the stat to open fully will restrict the engine coolant from reaching the rad or HE. For example, a 180°F (82°C) stat would have a start-to-open temperature in the range of 177 to 183°F (81 to 83°C) and should be fully open at approximately 197°F (92°C).

Operational Check
Never apply direct flame heat to a stat to cause it to open. Do not allow the stat to sit directly against the bottom of a metal container filled with water during the test. Ideally, the stat should be suspended in a container of clean water as shown in Figure 12–16 along with a suspended thermometer. Some stat test kits include a small drive motor that spins a propeller to agitate the water constantly. If this is not available, stir the water during the heating process.

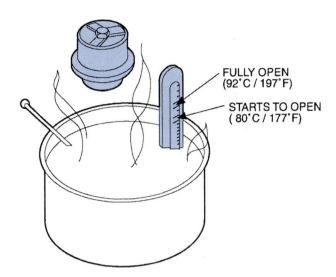

FULLY OPEN
(92°C / 197°F)

STARTS TO OPEN
(80°C / 177°F)

FIGURE 12–16 *Typical test equipment needed to perform an accurate test of a thermostat assembly. (Courtesy of Detroit Diesel Corporation.)*

Follow these steps as part of your operational check of a thermostat:

1. Note the temperature stamped on the stat.
2. Carefully record the temperature at which the stat starts to open. It may take 10 minutes for some stats to reach their full open condition.
3. Carefully watch the thermometer; the stat should be *fully open* at approximately 15 to 20°F (8 to 11°C) above the stamped value on the stat.
4. Using vernier calipers, carefully measure the distance that the stat has moved from closed to open. Figure 12–13 shows one example of a stat opening distance. Refer to the engine service literature for the spec relative to your engine make and model.
5. Replace a stat that fails to open at the correct temperature or fails to open fully.

Stats can become damaged from an overheated engine condition, which may be due to restriction to coolant flow through the radiator or HE (scale, hardened gel), collapsed or weak hoses, slipping fan belts, coolant leaks, or aerated coolant. Stats that are stuck open prevent the engine from reaching its normal operating temperature. A stat that does not open, or only opens partially, can cause engine overheating. Prior to replacing stats, make sure that the stat housing seating/seal and gasket areas are cleaned of rust and scale buildup. When installing a new seal (Figure 12–9), make certain that the seal is installed in the proper direction and use a seal driver so that the seal is not kinked or installed off square when driven into the housing(s). Apply a small amount of clean engine oil to lubricate the seal lips before pushing the stats into

position. Some engines employ horizontally installed stats and seals, whereas others have vertically installed ones. When installing the stat housing gasket, be careful not to apply excessive amounts of gasket cement. Cement can damage the seal lip or accumulate on the stat. If a stat housing drain cock or vent cock is used, apply a coating of Loctite Pipe Sealer with Teflon or equivalent to the threads.

COOLANT

Water tends to be the major constituent in all engine cooling systems. Any water, whether of drinking quality or not, produces a corrosive environment within the cooling system. If the mineral content of the water is over 300 ppm hardness or the corrosive chemicals are over 100 ppm chloride or sulfate, the water is unfit for use in the cooling system and will invariably allow deposits of scale to form on all of the internal cooling surfaces. Therefore, all water used in a cooling system must be chemically treated and tested on a regular basis to ensure that it is suitable for continued use. Generally, most engine manufacturers state that coolant solutions must meet the following requirements:

- Provide for adequate heat transfer
- Provide a corrosion-resistant environment in the cooling system
- Prevent formation of scale or sludge deposits in the cooling system
- Be compatible with cooling system hose and seal materials
- Provide adequate freeze protection during cold-weather operation and boil-over protection in hot weather

SCAs (supplemental coolant additives) have been used in coolant systems since the mid-1950s. Coolants used in current systems consist of antifreeze, water, and SCAs; these three ingredients combine to protect the engine and cooling system components. SCAs are formulated to provide protection against deposits, corrosion, and pitting that is not provided by the chemicals in the antifreeze. SCAs extend the life of antifreeze by adding to and replenishing the chemicals that tend to deplete after about 3 to 6 months or 30,000 miles (48,279 km) of normal operation. Keep in mind, however, that SCAs *do not* extend the freeze protection of the antifreeze.

The type of SCAs now being used in heavy-duty diesel engine coolants employ water-soluble polymers and detergents that often are not included in automotive antifreezes. All antifreezes create a percentage of salts (inhibitors) that can increase the percentage of electrolytes. The process is similar to that in batteries, in that the salts cause an increase in electrical activity that leads to greater corrosion potential between the dissimilar metals used in engines and radiators. To reduce corrosion that occurs as a result of the difference in electrical potential between two parts, many heavy-duty trucks and equipment with aluminum radiators have a ground strap or wire that runs from the radiator to the vehicle frame.

Coolant Glossary of Terms

Antifreeze: Pure glycol (typically 95%) with an inhibitor package added. Antifreeze can not be used by itself, it must be mixed with water before being put into the engine's cooling system.

Azole: These chemicals provide copper and brass protection. The two most common are MBT (Mercaptobenzothiazole) and TT (or TTZ) (Tolyltriazole).

Borate: a very soluble pH buffer used in premium antifreezes.

Coolant: Antifreeze mixed with water, or water mixed with an additive package for use in warm climates.

Conventional Coolant: Ethylene glycol that contains a corrosion inhibition package consisting of inorganic inhibitors such as silicate, phosphate, nitrate, and azoles.

Fully Formulated antifreeze or coolant. A modern product that contains all of the necessary inhibitors for both diesel and gasoline powered engines. (TMC RP-329 or TMC RP-330 specifications)

Ethylene Glycol: The most common base used in the manufacturing of antifreeze.

Nitrite: The primary inhibitor for wet sleeve liner pitting protection. It also protects against rust.

Nitrate: A corrosion inhibitor that provides solder and aluminum protection.

pH: A measure of the alkalinity of the coolant.

Reserve Alkalinity: A measurement of the number of milliliters of acid that is required to reduce the pH of a coolant sample to 5.5. A quality control tool.

Silicate: The primary conventional inhibitor for aluminum. In heavy duty coolants, lower (less than 250 ppm) silicate concentrations are generally preferred.

Phosphate: An inexpensive pH buffer. Phosphate is used in some antifreeze brands. It is not permitted in coolant used to protect Mercedes, BMW, Volkswagen MTU or Detroit Diesel engines.

Propylene Glycol: A less toxic, but more costly, alternative to Ethylene Glycol.

CYLINDER LINER PITTING

One of the most serious problems that can occur in a wet-type cylinder liner is *liner pitting* (see Figure 12–17). The liner metal is actually eaten away.

The definition of liner pitting is *cavitation-accelerated corrosion*. Pitting is caused by high-pressure combustion gases that tend to cause a rocking motion on the piston skirt when it is driven down the cylinder. This is usually referred to as *piston slap* (not to be confused with the slap noise that occurs in a worn cylinder) and is more pronounced on a one-piece design than on a two-piece crosshead or articulated design. Piston slap subjects the liner to intense vibration at a high frequency, which results in cavitation (vapor bubble formation and collapse) of the coolant surrounding the outer wall of the liner. The high-frequency vibration causes the pressure in the layer of coolant next to the liner to change drastically. Although the liner wall movement is very small, when it moves away from the coolant the pressure decreases, and bubbles that consist of both coolant vapor and air form. As the liner moves back toward the coolant, surface pressure again increases and the bubbles formed under low pressure now collapse, or implode, exerting forces as high as 60,000 psi (413,700 kPa) on the liner surface. These tremendous shock waves from bubble collapse hammer the liner and result in a highly stressed surface that is susceptible to corrosion. When an engine is not running, the static conditions create corrosion of the cast iron liner through heavy rust deposits, which eventually slow the corrosion process. In a running engine however, the rust and corrosion products are literally blasted away from the liner surface.

A wet liner can be perforated in less than 80,465 km (50,000 miles) if the coolant chemistry is not maintained

FIGURE 12–17 *A cylinder liner showing an acceptable degree of pitting, and a severely pitted, nonreuseable liner. (Courtesy of Cummins Engine Company, Inc.)*

properly. Coolant can then enter the engine crankcase or the cylinder area and cause destruction of the engine. Wet-liner corrosion can be prevented by using a GM-6038-M permanent-type antifreeze and a mixture of SCAs that contain nitrites or a mixture of nitrite, molybdate, and chromate. These prevent liner pitting by promoting a thin, tough, protective oxide layer on the liner surface. As the coolant film is broken by the collapse of a cavitation bubble, the protective film is rapidly reformed. This isolates the liner from the water, oxygen, and coolant impurities that cause the corrosion.

FILL-FOR-LIFE COOLANT

A number of major antifreeze suppliers now offer a "Fill-For-Life," fully formulated antifreeze. It is maintained by a 'need release' additive contained inside a spin-on coolant filter. One of these major companies is The Penray Companies who offer a variety of coolant system cleaners and treatment products. Using the Penray Need-Release membrane filter technology (see a filter example in Figure 12–18). The internal membrane within the coolant filter senses the corrosivity of the coolant and releases the correct amount of treatment to keep the system protected continuously. Fleets

have proven that with this technology, the initial coolant will last as long as 600,000 miles (965,580 km) with both improved engine and water pump reliability. Generally the need-release filter requires replacing approximately every 120,000 miles (193.116 km). Other antifreezes are referred to as Extended Life prediluted 50/50 mix, and are silicate free. These antifreezes also provide long life maintenance on a single extender top-up additive being required. To work effectively, a Fill-For-Life coolant must conform to the American Trucking Associations, The Maintenance Council (TMC) RP (Recommended Practice), RP 329 for fully formulated ethylene glycol (EG), or RP 330 for fully formulated propylene glycol (PG).

ANTIFREEZE

The antifreeze (AF) used in diesel engines can be of the ethylene glycol (EG) type or the aqueous propylene glycol (PG) type. PG is essentially EG with a methyl group attached to one end, and its chemistry is similar to that of EG. PG is propylene oxide combined with water to form the glycol.

One of the major advantages of PG is that the U.S. Food and Drug Administration has classified it as generally regarded as safe (GRAS). EG, however, is frequently responsible for poisoning cats and dogs who are drawn to its sweet taste. Consider also that 32 fluid ounces (950 milliliters) of ingested PG can be fatal to a 150 lb (68 kg) person, while less than 4 fluid ounces (100 mL) of EG is fatal. In the United States, the Clean Air Act considers EG a hazardous air pollutant. In addition, the U.S. Occupational Safety and Health Administration (OSHA), which regulates workplace safety, has placed an 8-hour average exposure standard for EG at 50 ppm. On the other hand, PG has not been considered dangerous enough to require safety legislation standards. In the face of increasing environmental concerns regarding EG, the adoption of PG-based antifreezes can be expected in heavy-duty diesel trucks and equipment.

All AFs must be disposed of in a safe manner. Most local regulations consider used AF a hazardous waste due to the heavy metals that accumulate. Because of their high biochemical oxygen demands, neither EG or PG can be disposed of in sewer systems. Check with local, state, provincial, or federal agencies for the proper disposal guidelines. Take careful note that both EG and PG antifreeze can now be cleaned and recycled, and both are biodegradable. A variety of portable AF recycling machines are available from most major equipment and tool suppliers.

Tests have shown that PG used with the same SCA package that is used with EG provides extra cavitation

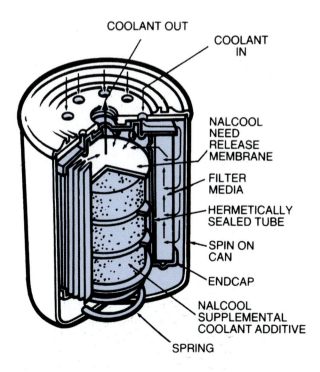

COOLANT OUT

COOLANT IN

NALCOOL NEED RELEASE MEMBRANE

FILTER MEDIA

HERMETICALLY SEALED TUBE

SPIN ON CAN

ENDCAP

NALCOOL SUPPLEMENTAL COOLANT ADDITIVE

SPRING

FIGURE 12–18 Cutaway view of a typical coolant system filter assembly containing SCAs (supplemental coolant additives). (Courtesy of The Penray Companies.)

TABLE 12–3 Selection guide for cooling system freeze protection[a]

	2[b]	3	4	5	6	7	8	9	10	11	12	13	14	15	16	17	18
7[c]	6[d]	−17°	−54°														
8		−7°	−34°	−62°													
9		0°	−21°	−50°													
10		4°	−12°	−34°	−62°												
11		8°	−6°	−23°	−47°	−62°											
12		10°	0°	−15°	−34°	−57°											
13		13°	3°	−9°	−25°	−45°	−62°										
14		15°	6°	−5°	−18°	−34°	−54°										
15		16°	8°	0°	−12°	−26°	−43°	−62°									
16		17°	10°	2°	−8°	−19°	−34°	−52°	−62°								
17		18°	12°	5°	−4°	−14°	−27°	−42°	−58°								
18		19°	14°	7°	0°	−10°	−21°	−34°	−50°	−62°							
19		20°	15°	9°	2°	−7°	−16°	−28°	−42°	−56°							
20			16°	10°	4°	−3°	−12°	−22°	−34°	−48°	−62°						
21			17°	12°	6°	0°	−9°	−17°	−28°	−41°	−54°	−62°					
22			18°	13°	8°	2°	−6°	−14°	−23°	−34°	−47°	−59°					
23			19°	14°	9°	4°	−3°	−10°	−19°	−29°	−40°	−52°	−62°				
24			19°	15°	10°	5°	0°	−8°	−15°	−24°	−34°	−46°	−58°				
25			20°	16°	12°	7°	1°	−5°	−12°	−20°	−29°	−40°	−52°	−62°			
26			21°	17°	13°	8°	3°	−3°	−9°	−16°	−25°	−34°	−45°	−57°			
27				17°	14°	9°	4°	0°	−6°	−13°	−22°	−30°	−38°	−50°	−62°		
28				18°	15°	10°	6°	1°	−5°	−11°	−18°	−27°	−34°	−44°	−55°	−62°	
29				18°	15°	11°	7°	3°	−2°	−8°	−15°	−23°	−30°	−38°	−48°	−58°	
30				19°	16°	12°	8°	4°	0°	−6°	−12°	−19°	−26°	−34°	−43°	−53°	−62°

Source: Peterbilt Motors Company, Division of PACCAR.

Ethylene glycol-base antifreeze	25%	33%	40%	50%	60%
Protects to:	10°	0°	−12°	−34°	−62°

[a]Ethylene glycol-base antifreeze required.

Note: 60% ethylene glycol-base antifreeze and 40% water by volume gives maximum protection. *Never* use concentrated ethylene glycol-base antifreeze, as it will freeze at approximately 0°F.

[b]Gallons of ethylene glycol-base antifreeze required.

[c]Cooling system capacity in gallons.

[d]Degrees of temperature in Fahrenheit.

corrosion protection equivalent to at least 20 to 40%. Thus it offers significant advantages to users of heavy-duty diesel engines.

Antifreeze is used for boil-over protection, freeze protection, and some corrosion protection. AF solutions should be used year-round to provide a stable environment for seals and hoses. The freeze protection value depends on the concentration of AF used. A 40% AF-to-water mix offers freeze protection to about $-10°F$ ($-23°C$), while a 60% AF-to-water mix offers protection to about $-65°F$ ($-55°C$). Never use more than a 67% maximum AF–water solution; more than that can adversely affect coolant freezing and boiling temperatures, increase silicate levels, and reduce heat transfer. A 50% glycol mix is considered optimal. Table 12–3 illustrates various cooling system capacities in U.S. gallons and the freeze protection offered when using EG-type AF, based on the volume of AF that is added to the system. The cooling system capacity is generally listed in the engine or vehicle service literature. When adding or topping off coolant, never use a 100% AF solution as makeup coolant or straight water; always mix AF with water to provide the same concentration as the initial fill. Otherwise, dilution or possible overconcentration of the system coolant can occur.

Heavy-duty diesel engine antifreeze consists of a number of chemicals and is formulated with a balance of nitrite, nitrate, borate, small amounts of sodium silicate, and azoles to protect soft metals. These additives provide a very effective corrosion inhibitor, particularly for aluminum components. As sodium silicate depletes over time, it can "drop out" of the coolant solution through a process called catalytic polymerization. In this process, individual silicate molecules unite in the presence of engine heat and form larger particles that precipitate in the form of gel, which can plug coolant passages.

TESTING THE COOLANT

Fleet service technicians are charged with the responsibility of maintaining the cooling system. Typical coolant should be maintained with a 50 to 67% antifreeze precharged with 3% Pencool; then a Need Release filter should be installed to safeguard the system. This coolant mix will establish a recommended inhibitor level for cost-effective protection. Two technologies are dominant in heavy-duty diesel engine cooling systems today:

1. Pencool, distributed through the Power Fleet Division, Penray Companies, Inc., is the pri-

mary supplemental coolant additive (SCA) used by Caterpillar and Detroit Diesel.
2. DCA-4 (diesel coolant additive, fourth generation) is the primary SCA used by Cummins, which owns Fleetguard.

SPECIAL NOTE   Since most heavy-duty diesel engines employ either the Penray Pencool or Fleetguard SCA products, a conversion factor of recommended SCA levels from Pencool to Fleetguard DCA units, and vice versa, is required. One DCA unit is equivalent to 2.0 volume percent Pencool measured as 800 ppm (parts per million) nitrite.

The SCAs must be checked closely and analyzed to ensure that the coolant mix is within levels recommended by engine manufacturers. Control of the SCAs is one of the major reasons for field and lab analysis of heavy-duty diesel engine coolants; therefore, it is very important that the diesel technician understand this test procedure.

Most SCAs are formulated for use with both EG and PG antifreeze. Nevertheless, if using PG, check with the SCA supplier to make sure that its package will work with PG. Remember, using an SCA package that is not suitable for PG will result in coolant dropout.

Overconcentration of SCAs causes a high level of solids to gather in the cooling system. Chemical deposits at the water pump seal weep hole are usually an indication of overconcentration. Underconcentration of SCAs can result in pitting of liner surfaces. Checking for overconcentration of SCAs can be done by testing reserve alkalinity and conductivity, but checking usually requires special kits or a coolant sample taken to a lab for analysis. Overconcentration of SCAs can lead to these conditions:

- Deposits on heat transfer surfaces and fouling of the cooling system with precipitated additives
- Water pump seal leaks
- Plugging of coolant passages from solder bloom/corrosion or silicate gelation

To effectively test the condition of the coolant for glycol and nitrite as well as total dissolved solids (TDS), a number of coolant test kits are available commercially. These kits allow the technician to test the coolant for proper SCA concentration as well as TDS and pH level, which is a measure of the degree of alkalinity or acidity of the coolant. The optimum pH is generally within the range 7.5 to 11.0. A reading below 7.5

pH indicates acidity, while one above 11.0 pH indicates an alkaline concentration. Consider the following cooling pH scale:

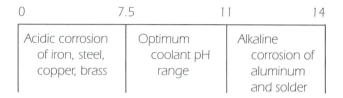

0	7.5	11	14
Acidic corrosion of iron, steel, copper, brass	Optimum coolant pH range	Alkaline corrosion of aluminum and solder	

Acids can form when glycol degrades or gases bleed past gaskets into the coolant. The Nalcool/Penray two-way test strip kit includes directions on the strip container to guide the technician on how to interpret and compare the nitrite and glycol content, as well as the acidity or alkaline level of the coolant. After dipping a test strip into the coolant and removing it, the color change on the test strip is compared with the colored blocks on the container to determine coolant SCA condition. Another test kit is used to check for mercaptobenzothiazole (MBT) and nitrite in a coolant sample. Directions in this container describe how to draw a small sample of coolant and how to mix the solutions in the various plastic bottles until a specific color change to the coolant is noted. Record the number of drops of solution required to cause a coolant color change; then refer to the directions to determine if additional SCAs need to be added. If you are using a Cummins Fleetguard test kit, note that this same procedure will indicate how many DCA-4s are required. Too much SCA can lead to silicate dropout, while too little SCA can create corrosion and cavitation. A total dissolved solids (TDS) tester can quickly indicate the solid particle percentage in the coolant when dipped into the radiator top tank by measuring the conductivity between two probes of the tester. The level of dissolved solids in the coolant water should generally not exceed 340 ppm (20 grams per gallon). The higher a coolant's TDS, the greater the amount of corrosion and scale buildup that will occur.

SCALE BUILDUP

All engines radiate a great deal of heat, which is normally removed by the coolant as it flows through the engine. Scale or rust developed in the coolant passages acts as an insulator and blocks heat transfer. Scale occurs when magnesium and calcium (always present in tap water) are deposited on the heated metal surfaces inside the cooling system. Normally, scale occurs where temperatures are highest, such as at the cylinder head and the outside of wet liners, as well as in heat exchanger or radiator cores. Depending on the water used (hardness, alkalinity, acidity, and so on), scale tends to form a hard white crust. Scale deposits on the outside of a wet liner can cause it to expand unevenly, and the liner metal can actually bulge inward in the areas of hot spots. As the pistons and rings move up and down within the liners, irregular ring and liner wear occur. This causes metal scuffing to take place between the rings, pistons, and the liner surface. Eventually, metal scoring occurs, which is an advanced stage of scuffing. The tearing metal creates stuck or broken rings, piston damage, and possible piston-to-liner seizure. Cylinder head cracking is another inevitable result.

COOLANT FILTERS

Many heavy-duty engines employ coolant filter conditioners that have two basic functions: to provide the most effective way of controlling the addition of SCAs and to provide the benefits of mechanical filtration. These filters, which are the bypass type, are plumbed into the system so that coolant under pressure from the engine block enters the inlet side of the filter assembly and returns to a low-pressure side of the coolant system (back toward the suction side of the water pump). Two shutoff valves allow the technician to prevent any coolant loss from the block when changing the coolant filter.

Figure 12–18 illustrates a typical coolant filter for a heavy-duty high-speed engine. This particular Need Release filter assembly, which is manufactured by Penray/Pencool, is designed to release the correct amount of SCAs into the coolant during engine operation to provide complete cooling system protection for up to 1 year or 120,000 miles (193,116 km). As the chemically balanced SCAs (inhibitors) within the coolant deplete, the metal alloy membranes within the filter cartridge detect the need for additional corrosion protection. Before the system reaches a corrosive condition, the *Need Release membranes* release the exact amount of treatment necessary to adjust the system to the proper level of corrosion protection.

FLUSHING THE SYSTEM

The cooling system should be flushed at a recommended time interval as stated by the engine manufacturer in the service literature. Suggested mileage or time was discussed in the "Antifreeze" section of this chapter. After draining and flushing the system, follow the manufacturer's recommendation for precharging the cooling system.

CAUTION   Service personnel often back, or reverse, flush the cooling system. In this procedure a pressurized water hose is connected to the bottom radiator hose or heat exchanger to force liquid out of the top hose outlet. This reverse flushing procedure should only be considered a salvage operation. Back flushing can loosen scale formations that cause the cooling system to clog at a later date during the operation.

Each time that the antifreeze is changed, the coolant system should be cleaned (flushed) with Penray 2001, Fleetguard Restore, or an equivalent to ensure that the system is thoroughly clean before adding Pencool or equivalent, followed by a water antifreeze mix. Follow these steps when flushing the system:

1.   Thoroughly power flush the complete cooling system using a flushing kit. Limit the air pressure to 138 kPa (20 psi) because excess pressure applied to the water can damage the radiator, thermostat, and water pump seals. Back, or reverse, flushing the cooling system can be considered a salvage operation if after using a commercially available chemical cleaner the radiator core is still partially dirty. Figure 12–19 illustrates how to reverse flush the radiator core using hot water forced through the system in the opposite direction to normal coolant flow.

CAUTION   Reverse flushing can cause small loosened scale particles to damage internal seals within the water pump and thermostat areas. It is better to remove the radiator and have it repaired at a radiator shop.

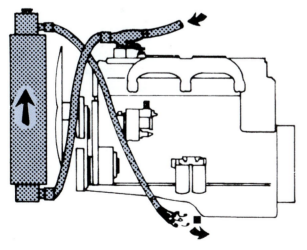

FIGURE 12–19 Hookup procedure used to reverse flush, or back flush, a radiator core. (Courtesy of Cummins Engine Company, Inc.)

2.   Add 2 L of Penray 2001 or equivalent for every 30 L of water. If using Fleetguard Restore, add 1 U.S. gallon (3.8 L) for each 10 to 15 U.S. gallons (38 to 57 L) of water.

3.   Start and run the engine for 1.5 to 2 hours. This can be done in the shop or yard area, or the vehicle can be road tested to ensure circulation of the cleaner from all cooling system surfaces and passages.

4.   Allow the engine to cool, then drain the cooling system and flush it with fresh water, or fill the system with clean fresh water and run the engine for 5 minutes at high idle with the coolant temperature above 185°F (85°C).

NOTE   If the cooling system has already started to overheat due to severe gelling problems, a longer cleaning period may be required. Proceed to step 5 if this is the case.

5.   Perform steps 1 and 2. Then leave the cleaner, such as Penray 2001 or equivalent, in the cooling system for 250 hours, 30 days, or 16 to 20,000 km (9942 to 12,428 miles), whichever comes first. Nalprep 2001 will not harm cooling system metals, seals, or hoses. It will not cause deterioration of cooling system sealants as some high PH cleaners will.

6.   Completely drain the coolant from the engine and flush with fresh water as in step 4. Add Pencool 3000 (with Stabil-Aid) or equivalent; then add a mixture of antifreeze and water to the cooling system. On a Cummins engine, install a new *initial charge* coolant filter and a 50-50 mix of antifreeze to ensure the correct DCA-4 concentration.

PRESSURE CAPS

There are two descriptive terms that you may come across when dealing with cooling systems regardless of whether a radiator or heat exchanger system is being used. The first term is air-to-water (A/W) differential and is the difference between engine *coolant out*, or the top tank temperature, and the ambient air temperature. For example, with a stabilized top tank temperature of 185°F (85°C), and with air entering the radiator at 100°F (38°C), the differential is 85°F (29°C). The second term is air-to-boil (ATB) and represents the ambient air temperature at which top tank boiling occurs. The boiling point should always be considered as 212°F (100°C). For example, consider the same engine operating at 185°F (85°C) with air at 100°F (38°C): 212°F (100°C) − 185°F (85°C) = 27°F (15°C) + 100°F (38°C ambient = 127°F (53°C) air-to-boil.

All cooling systems are able to handle a specific heat load from a given engine and are designed to prevent engine overheating at sea level without the use of a pressure cap. A pressure cap, illustrated in Figure 12–20 is used to protect against boiling at above baseline elevations. System pressure is required to maintain water pump performance at elevated coolant temperature, to prevent loss of coolant at low-boiling-point altitudes, and to reduce coolant loss due to after boil at engine shutdown. Each pound of pressure applied to the cooling system raises the boiling point of the coolant by approximately 3°F (1.7°C); therefore, a 7 lb (48 kPa) pressure cap on a cooling system will raise the boiling point of the coolant from 212°F (100°C) at sea

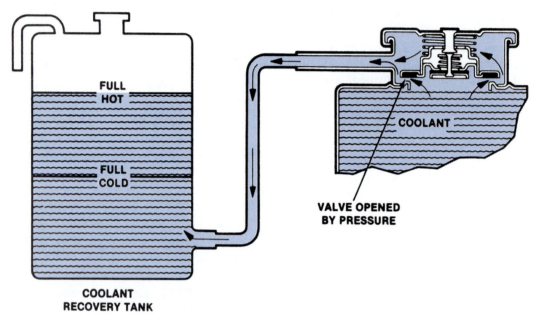

FIGURE 12–20   Process of radiator pressure cap opening and directing expanded coolant to a recovery tank. (Courtesy of Detroit Diesel Corporation.)

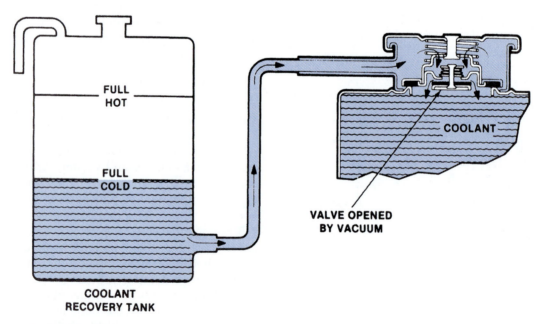

FIGURE 12–21   Opening of radiator cap vacuum valve as the engine cools to allow coolant to be recovered from the expansion tank, thereby preventing collapse of the radiator hoses. (Courtesy of Detroit Diesel Corporation.)

level to 232.5°F (111°C). For each 1000 ft (305 m) in altitude, the boiling point decreases by approximately 1.25°F (0.5°C). The opening pressure for all pressure caps is stamped or inscribed on the top of the cap in psi (kPa). For example, a number 12 indicates a 12 psi (83 kPa) cap.

Figure 12–20 illustrates a typical pressure cap for a cooling system. When the coolant pressure acting on the underside of the pressure cap seal against the spring becomes high enough, the valve unseats and hot coolant is normally routed to a surge tank to prevent any loss of coolant. When the spring pressure is greater than that developed in the cooling system, the valve closes. When an engine is shut down and the coolant starts to lose its temperature, it contracts, thereby reducing the pressure within the radiator, surge tank, or bottle and cooling system. To prevent collapse of hoses and other nonsupported components, a second and smaller valve within the pressure cap assembly opens as this vacuum is created. Figure 12–21 illustrates the action of this small valve, which usually opens at approximately 5/8 lb (4.3 kPa). The vacuum created as the fluid cools, sucks fluid from the radiator overflow line, which is normally connected to a separate surge tank or plastic bottle, and replenishes the radiator coolant volume.

To check the operating condition of the pressure cap, refer to Figure 12–22 which shows a hand tester installed on the cap. Pump up the pressure to the value stamped on the cap and note the rate of decrease on the gauge. If the pressure does not hold for approximately 10 seconds, replace the cap.

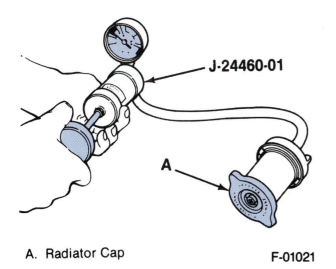

A. Radiator Cap

F-01021

FIGURE 12–22 *Using a pressure pump to determine the opening pressure of the radiator cap.*

PRESSURE CHECKING THE COOLING SYSTEM

When coolant loss or overheating is a problem, the cooling system can be pressurized to help determine the location of the leak and to determine the causes of overheating under various operating conditions. Check the following areas:

Components that leak	Reasons for overheating
Hoses and clamps	Thermostat problem
Radiator cap	Aeration
Head and gasket	Shutter control thermostat
Water pump	Thermatic (thermally
Cylinder liner O-rings	activated) fan thermostat
or counterbore	Clogged radiator fins
Radiator, oil cooler,	Plugged radiator tubes
aftercooler and	Faulty water pump
heater cores	(slipping belt, broken
	impeller, or spinning of
	the impeller on its shaft)

A pressure check of the system can be performed in the following situations:

- During an engine rebuild when wet liners are replaced and before the oil pan is installed to check that the liner O-rings are not leaking
- During engine service when coolant is found in the engine oil and the liner O-rings may be the cause
- Suspected leak of a cylinder head water seal ring or gasket
- Suspected leak of an injector sleeve
- Suspected leak of fluid by the external engine cooling system components
- Checking the radiator or heat exchanger pressure cap for its opening pressure as well as the vacuum portion of the cap when the engine is shut down

Figure 12–22 illustrates a standard cooling system pressure tester kit, which consists of a special graduated pressure gauge mounted to a hand-operated pump, a radiator filler neck adapter, a pressure cap adapter, a rubber filler neck plug, and a hose assembly. Some models of cooling system analyzer kits come with a temperature probe to allow the technician to check the exact temperature of the cooling system while under pressure. The kit also allows troubleshooting of thermostat openings, thermatic fan operating range, and electronic temperature sensors, and it monitors new and rebuilt engines through warm-up cycles. The cooling system is easily checked for pressure by hooking up the shop-regulated air supply to a pressure probe and dialing in the desired test pressure. Unlike a hand-operated pump test system, by using shop air the cooling system can be left pressurized for an extended period of time to find difficult and intermittent leaks. In addition, with the kit pressure probe, the cylinder head can be diagnosed for cracks, blown head gaskets, and leaking piston sleeves.

Attach the hand pump shown in Figure 12–22 to the radiator expansion/surge tank cap neck to check the cooling system for suspected leaks. Build up the system pressure by viewing the gauge until it registers the release pressure stamped on the radiator cap. The system should hold pressure for about 2 minutes; if it does not, check for signs of external or internal leaks.

Aeration Check

Air trapped in a cooling system can cause overheating as well as cause the water pump to become *air bound*. Air may be trapped in the cooling system when the system has been refilled after draining or flushing the system. When refilling a system, always open the vent cocks, particularly around the thermostat housing(s). Run the engine at an idle speed until a steady stream of coolant flows from the vent cocks, then close them. Air can also enter the cooling system because of a low coolant level in the radiator or expansion tank, through a suction leak on the inlet side of the water pump or loose hose connections, or by combustion gases escaping into the coolant.

To check a system for aerated coolant, remove the system pressure cap and replace it with a nonpressurized cap. You can use an old rad cap that has had the spring and the pressure relief valve removed to allow free flow of engine coolant from the rad or expansion tank connection. Figure 12–23 illustrates a solid rad cap

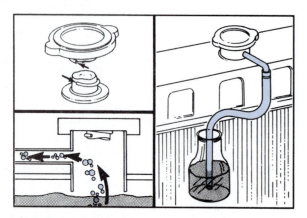

FIGURE 12–23 Installation of a nonpressurized radiator cap, clear container, and hose attached to the overflow connection to determine if aerated coolant is present. (Courtesy of Cummins Engine Company, Inc.)

in place with an overflow hose connected and submerged in a clear container of water. Proceed as follows:

1. Run the engine until it attains normal operating temperature.
2. Ideally, connect the engine to a dynamometer. If the engine is in a truck, place the engine on a chassis dynamometer. This is necessary so that the engine can be fully loaded to check if air bubbles might be caused by a leaking cylinder head gasket, and so on.
3. Refer to Figure 12–23 and check for signs of air bubbles in the clear container.

At rated speed and load, continuous air bubbles in the container indicate aeration is being induced through one of the following causes: leaking cylinder head gasket, jacket water aftercooler core leakage, air compressor head or head gasket leakage, (since most heavy-duty units are cooled by coolant from the engine), defective fan or shutter air control valves (compressed air leakage), cracked cylinder head, cracked cylinder liner, or incorrect cylinder liner protrusion after overhaul.

Air leaks suspected to be induced by the cooling system can usually be traced by installing short pieces of thick, heavy-duty, round, clear plastic sections into the system supply and discharge lines and checking for air bubbles.

EXPANSION TANKS AND HEAT EXCHANGERS

In stationary gen-set or marine engine applications, the radiator and fan cooling system is replaced by an expansion tank (ET) and heat exchanger (HE) core. The ET is a large cast-iron receptacle that acts as a header tank; it is similar to the top tank and/or ET used in a radiator and fan system (Figure 12–24). Note that the expansion tank on high-performance marine engines illustrated in Figure 12–24 is used in conjunction with deaerators on 3408/3412 Caterpillar engines. The deaerators shown in Figure 12–25 are designed to remove tiny air bubbles from the coolant. Excessive air bubbles can lead to water pump cavitation and reduced coolant flow; therefore, proper deaeration is mandatory. This is achieved by means of two swirl chamber air separator housings on V-model engines from each cylinder bank. These deaerators allow a much smaller expansion tank to be used, and they are designed to operate on the principle of a centrifuge. As the hot coolant enters the chamber, it begins to swirl and forces the coolant to the outside and onto the heat exchanger. The air bubbles move to the center of the

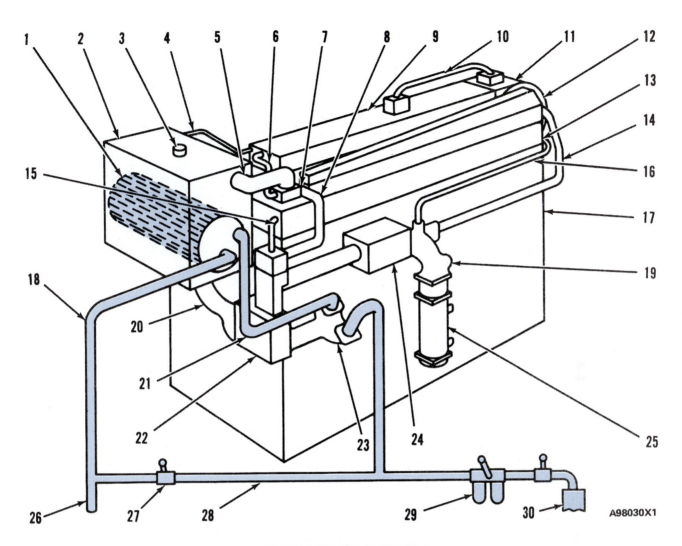

COOLING SYSTEM SCHEMATIC

1. Heat exchanger. 2. Expansion tank. 3. Pressure cap. 4. Vent line. 5. Outlet line. 6. Outlet line. 7. Regulator housing. 8. Aftercooler inlet line. 9. Water cooled manifold. 10. Outlet line. 11. Water cooled turbocharger. 12. Aftercooler housing. 13. Cylinder head. 14. Aftercooler outlet line. 15. Internal bypass (shunt) line. 16. Turbocharger inlet line. 17. Cylinder block. 18. Outlet line. 19. Bonnet. 20. Inlet line. 21. Inlet line. 22. Water pump. 23. Sea water pump. 24. Engine oil cooler. 25. Auxiliary oil cooler. 26. Outlet for sea water circuit. 27. Bypass valve. 28. Bypass line. 29. Duplex strainer. 30. Inlet for sea water circuit.

FIGURE 12–24 Flow path through a marine engine heat exchanger cooling system equipped with a JWAC (jacket water aftercooling) feature to reduce the temperature of the turbocharger boost air pressure. (Reprinted courtesy of Caterpillar, Inc.)

deaerator and exit through a short hose to the expansion tank as can be seen in Figure 12–25.

Directly below the ET is a tubular-type heat exchanger assembly with an engine-driven raw water pump connection (Figure 12–24). The coolant pump flow through the 3606 engine is quoted as being 228 U.S. gallons per minute (880 L) at 1000 rpm engine speed; for the 3616 model, it is 546 U.S. gallons per minute (2100 L) at 1000 rpm engine speed. The ET has a filler cap that may or may not contain a spring-loaded

pressure cap. An overflow tube is generally plumbed into the ET; the tube can be routed to a receptacle, or it may vent directly into the bilge on a marine installation. The ET provides a means of filling the engine cooling system as well as providing space for fluid expansion of the coolant as its temperature rises.

In the HE system, the engine is filled with a fresh water coolant mixture similar to that used in a radiator system. To cool the hot, fresh engine coolant, raw seawater, city water, or lake water can be pumped through

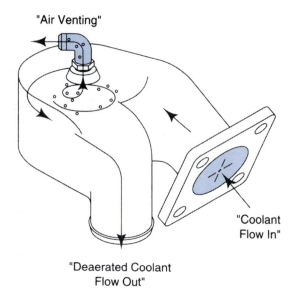

FIGURE 12–25 Swirl chamber design of a coolant deaeration housing used with a heat exchanger cooling system. (Courtesy of Caterpillar, Inc.)

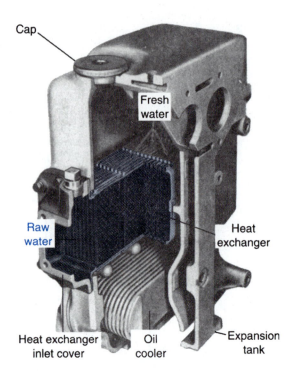

FIGURE 12–26 Cutaway view of a combination heat exchanger and expansion tank arrangement which also shows either an engine or a hydraulic marine gear oil cooler assembly. (Courtesy of Detroit Diesel Corporation.)

the HE core in a direction opposite to the flow of the fresh water. The raw water is circulated by the action of a gear- or belt-driven raw water pump (described later in this chapter). The sealed HE ensures that both the engine coolant and raw water flows never mix, since they are plumbed through separate tubing or cores. This can be seen in Figure 12–26 where the hot engine coolant flows from the cylinder head water manifold through the thermostat(s) to the ET. The coolant then flows vertically through the cells of the HE core. The raw water flowing horizontally between the cells of the HE core lowers the temperature of the engine coolant as it passes through the cells. This engine coolant can then flow over a marine gear oil cooler and the engine oil cooler to lower the operating temperature of these two lubricants. The coolant is then directed into the suction side of the engine fresh water pump and is circulated through the engine block and cylinder head.

Smaller-horsepower (kW) high-speed marine installations have a cellular-type HE assembly that is usually contained within the expansion tank. Some larger applications may employ a tubular type of HE that is bracket mounted alongside the engine. To ensure proper filling of the HE cooling system, an air-bleed hose must be installed between the top of each thermostat housing and the top of the expansion tank.

Two raw water pumps on large V-model engines supply the raw water flow to and through the HEs. The warm raw water is then plumbed overboard on a marine application. In some industrial HE applications, a raw water cooling tank is used to recirculate the raw city water to and through the HE system to minimize water usage.

Zinc Electrodes

To counteract electrolysis or galvanic action within the cooling system, zinc electrodes are normally screwed into and located in the HE inlet cover and the raw water pump(s) inlet elbow. Most electrodes can be identified by their square brass head, which allows removal with a wrench. These electrodes act as sacrificial elements within the cooling system; that is, the electrolysis tends to corrode them rather than the other metal components within the cooling system.

Electrodes should be removed at given service intervals and inspected after cleaning with a wire brush. If an electrode is worn excessively, it should be replaced. To determine the condition of a used electrode, strike it sharply against a hard metal surface; a weakened electrode will break.

Cleaning the Heat Exchanger Core

As with a radiator cooling system, after many hours of operation, scale deposits can accumulate within the core of the heat exchanger, thereby reducing its efficiency. Soft water plus a good grade of antifreeze should be used as an engine coolant. At major engine overhaul, or if the heat exchanger fails to maintain the fresh engine coolant within its designed range, the HE may require cleaning. Follow these steps:

1. Drain the cooling system.
2. Remove the heat exchanger housing and/or core.

> **NOTE** To prevent drying and hardening of accumulated foreign substances, the HE core must be cleaned as soon as possible after removing it from service. The core can be cleaned at a commercial facility that has an ultrasound cleaning system, or use step 3 as follows.

3. Immerse the HE core in a scale solvent consisting of one-third muriatic acid and two-thirds water to which 0.5 lb (0.226 kg) of oxalic acid has been added to each 2.5 U.S. gallons (9.5 L) of solution.
4. Remove the core when foaming and bubbling stops, which normally is about 30 to 60 seconds.
5. Flush the core thoroughly with clean hot water under pressure.

RAW WATER PUMPS

When a heat exchanger cooling system is used on an industrial or marine installation, a water pump(s) is required to circulate cooling raw water through the HE core. Most raw water pumps (RWPs) are gear driven on diesel engines, but it is possible for these units to be belt driven. The RWP drive location varies in different makes and models of engines. Figure 12–27, a view across the center of the RWP, shows the normal flow of raw water. Note that both the inlet and outlet passages are located on the top of the pump housing. Because these pumps are widely used in marine applications with saltwater, the pump housing is usually manufactured from a bronze or brass material, and the impeller is manufactured from a rubber or neoprene material. In applications where the vessel may be running in frigid waters, a special impeller material must be used to avoid cracking of the impeller blades.

Figure 12–28 is a cutaway view of a typical RWP manufactured by Jabsco. The pump driveshaft (213) is supported by a prelubricated, shielded, double-row ball bearing (222). An oil seal (247 and 249) prevents oil leakage from the bearing compartment and a rotary seal (256) prevents water leakage along the shaft. A rubber/neoprene impeller (220) is splined to the end of the driveshaft (213) and is self-lubricated by the

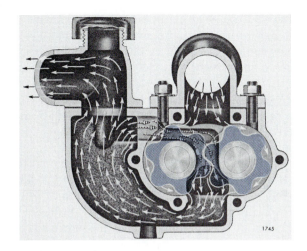

FIGURE 12–27 View across the center of a Jabsco raw water pump illustrating the normal flow of water and recirculation of the priming water through the channel at the rear of the pump housing. (Courtesy of Detroit Diesel Corporation.)

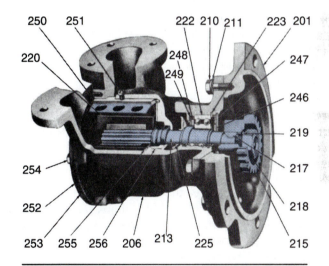

201. Adaptor – pump	225. Oil slinger – shaft
206. Housing – pump	246. Washer – felt
210. Bolt – housing to adaptor	247. Seal – bearing
211. Lock washer	248. Washer – felt
213. Shaft – drive	249. Seal – bearing
215. Gear – drive	250. Cam – offset
217. Key – woodruff	251. Bolt – cam
218. Nut – gear retaining	252. Cover
219. Lock washer	253. Gasket – cover
220. Impeller	254. Bolt – cover
222. Ball bearing	255. Wear plate
223. Retainer – bearing	256. Seal assy.

FIGURE 12–28 Identification of the components of a Jabsco raw water pump. (Courtesy of Detroit Diesel Corporation.)

pumped water. Never run the pump any longer than required for the pump to prime itself; otherwise, impeller damage can occur. A wear plate (255) in the impeller compartment prevents wear of the pump housing and can be reversed if wear on the plate becomes excessive. A slot machined in the outer periphery of the wear plate registers with a dowel in the pump housing, thereby preventing the plate from rotating with the shaft assembly.

The flexible impeller allows these pumps to be operated in either a clockwise or counterclockwise direction. The pump end cover is marked with an arrow and the letters RH or LH to show the outlet port for either of these rotations. Once the pump has been operated in one direction, attempting to reverse its rotation will result in the impeller cracking at the base of the individual blades (vanes). Within the pump housing is an offset cam (250) designed to direct the flow within the housing. This cam causes the impeller to take up a set curvature during pump operation. Any time you attempt to manually rotate the engine over, keep this caution in mind: Turning the engine opposite its normal rotation more than about one-eighth of a turn can result in impeller damage. If you have to rotate the engine in a direction opposite to its normal rotation beyond this limit, disconnect the RWP from the engine.

The seal parts of a RWP may be replaced without removing the pump from the engine as follows:

1. Remove the pump cover screws and take off the cover and gasket.

2. Using two pliers, grasp an impeller blade at each side and pull the impeller from the shaft. The spline plug will come out with the impeller.

3. Insert two wires with a hook fashioned into each end and insert between the pump housing and the seal with the hooks over the edge of the carbon seal. Pull the seal assembly from the shaft.

4. Remove the seal and gasket in the same manner if they require replacement.

5. Assemble the carbon seal, seal ring, and washer in the correct relative positions and slide them over the shaft and against the seal seat. Make sure the seal ring is contained snugly within the ferrule.

6. Install the Marcel washer (deformed one) next to the flat washer.

7. Compress the impeller blades to clear the offset cam and press the impeller onto the splined shaft; then install the spline plug.

8. Manually rotate the impeller several turns in the direction that it will normally run to position the blades correctly.

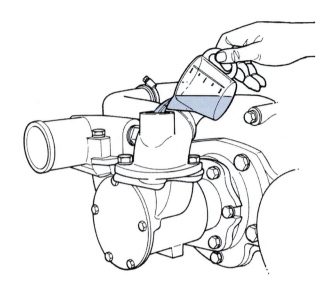

FIGURE 12–29 *Priming a new or rebuilt raw water pump prior to starting the engine. (Courtesy of Detroit Diesel Corporation.)*

9. Install a new gasket between the pump housing and cover.

10. Prime the JABSCO raw water pump by removing the pipe plug or zinc provided in the pump outlet elbow and pouring at least a pint of water into the pump. Reinstall the plug or zinc. See Figure 12–29!

11. Prime the GILKES raw water pump by disconnecting the water supply hose from the top of the priming section. Fill the pump with water and replace the hose.

KEEL COOLING SYSTEMS

In many marine applications where dirty raw water makes the use of a heat exchanger system impractical, a keel cooling system such as that illustrated in Figure 12–30 can be used. This cooling system is similar to the HE system just described: however, the heat transfer of the engine freshwater coolant occurs in a nest of tubes that are mounted to the hull of the ship below the waterline rather than in the HE core mounted in the engine ET. The ET used can be the same as that for an HE system.

In this example, when the thermostat(s) is open, the engine coolant flows to the keel cooling tubes or coils where it transfers its heat to the surrounding seawater. The return coolant is drawn through the vertical pipes and the ET by the engine water pump. When the thermostat(s) is closed, coolant entering the stat housing is bypassed directly to the engine water pump inlet

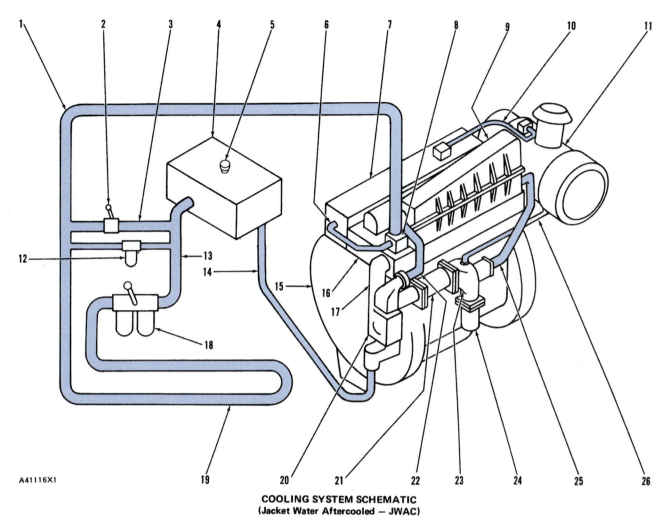

COOLING SYSTEM SCHEMATIC
(Jacket Water Aftercooled — JWAC)

1. Outlet line. 2. Bypass valve. 3. Bypass line. 4. Expansion tank. 5. Pressure cap. 6. Outlet line. 7. Water cooled manifold. 8. Regulator housing. 9. Aftercooler housing. 10. Outlet line. 11. Water cooled turbocharger. 12. Bypass filter. 13. Inlet line. 14. Inlet line. 15. Cylinder block. 16. Cylinder head. 17. Internal bypass (shunt) line. 18. Duplex strainer. 19. Keel cooler tubes. 20. Water pump. 21. Engine oil cooler. 22. Aftercooler inlet line. 23. Bonnet. 24. Auxiliary oil cooler. 25. Aftercooler outlet line. 26. Turbocharger inlet line.

FIGURE 12–30 *Schematic of a marine keel cooling system with an expansion tank (pressurized); it also features a water-cooled turbocharger center housing, plus JWAC (jacket water aftercooling) to reduce the T/C boost pressure air temperature entering the intake manifold. (Reprinted courtesy of Caterpillar, Inc.)*

where it remixes with the coolant from the water-cooled exhaust manifold jacket. The coolant is then circulated through the engine cylinder block and head. A percentage of the coolant leaving the head is routed through pipes or hoses to the hollow core exhaust manifold to minimize heat radiation into the engine room. This hot coolant leaving the exhaust manifold is then routed to the expansion tank. Since no engine coolant passes to the keel cooler with closed thermostats, a fairly rapid warm-up of the engine is assured.

SUMMARY

This chapter has highlighted the function and operation of the cooling system and its associated components. The cooling system is one of the most important and expensive engine and equipment downtime areas due to improper and regular maintenance. In this chapter, the reader is given the knowledge and skills to effectively maintain, service, and troubleshoot various types of engine cooling systems.

SELF-TEST QUESTIONS

1. Technician A says that typical coolant system temperatures should be between 140 and 165°F (60 to 74°C). Technician B disagrees, stating that normal coolant temperature should be between 185 and 200°F (85 to 93°C). Which technician do you believe?

2. Describe by approximate percentage the heat losses from an engine from the injected fuel used to produce power.

3. Technician A says that in a perfect engine with no heat losses 3300 Btu (966 W) is needed to produce 1 hp (0.746 kW) per hour. Technician B states that a perfect engine requires 2545 Btu/hp (746 W) per hour. Which technician knows heat engine theory better?

4. The average heat rejection to the cooling system in current high-speed high-output engines is approximately
   a. 30 to 35 Btu/hp (9 to 10 W/kW per minute)
   b. 40 to 50 Btu/hp (12 to 15 W/kW per minute)
   c. 50 to 60 Btu/hp (15 to 18 W/kW per minute)
   d. 60 to 70 Btu/hp (18 to 20 W/kW per minute)

5. True or False: Electronically controlled diesel engines are more thermally efficient than mechanically controlled models.

6. What does the chemical symbol pH represent in relation to coolant? Allowable pH is generally within the range
   a. 3.5 to 5
   b. 5 to 7
   c. 7.5 to 11
   d. 12 to 16.5

7. What is the purpose of using SCAs in a cooling system?

8. Describe what actually causes wet-type cylinder liner pitting. What can be done to minimize this condition?

9. Name the two common types of permanent antifreeze used in modern engines.

10. Which one of the two antifreezes listed in your answer for question 13 is considered by the U.S. EPA to be a hazardous air pollutant?

11. True or False: Antifreeze is considered to be a nonhazardous waste.

12. Technician A says that used antifreeze must be disposed of once it is drained from an engine. Technician B says that all types of antifreeze can be cleaned and recycled. Which technician is aware of current technology?

13. Which one of the two types of antifreeze listed in your answer to question 9 offers improved protection against cavitation corrosion, particularly in wet liner engines?

14. Technician A says that too great a concentration of antifreeze can result in gelling of the coolant. Technician B believes that in very low ambient operating conditions, the greater the percentage of antifreeze used the better. Which technician is correct?

15. The maximum recommended concentration of antifreeze should never exceed
    a. 50%
    b. 57%
    c. 63%
    d. 67%

16. What additive in antifreeze acts as a corrosion inhibitor?

17. When maintenance personnel talk about silicate *dropout* in a coolant, what actually transpires and what problems occur from this action?

18. True or False: Antifreeze protection level can be checked quickly by using a hydrometer or a refractometer similar to that for a battery.

19. List the problems associated with using an antifreeze concentration above the maximum recommended level.

20. True or False: Chemical deposits at the water pump seal weep hole are usually an indication of possible overconcentration of SCAs.

21. True or False: SCA concentration must be checked regularly with a kit to determine the condition of the coolant.

22. Scale buildup within a cooling system insulates and blocks heat transfer. What chemicals in tap water promote scale buildup?

23. One of the most effective ways to control coolant system SCAs is
    a. using a coolant filter
    b. flushing the system regularly
    c. changing the antifreeze mixture twice a year
    d. using a thermostat with a high opening temperature

24. Describe what the term *reverse flushing* means.

25. What is the main reason for using a radiator pressure cap (other than to prevent a loss of coolant)?

26. True or False: Each radiator or cooling system pressure cap has the opening pressure stamped on the cap.

27. What prevents the radiator or cooling system hoses from collapsing when the engine is stopped and the coolant begins to cool, thereby creating a partial vacuum?

28. How can a radiator pressure cap be checked to determine if it is operating correctly?

29. True or False: All radiators in use today are of the downflow type.

30. What major engine manufacturer employs LFC (lowflow cooling) systems on some of its engines?

31. True or False: All radiators employ one-pass coolant flow.

32. What types of problems does aerated coolant cause?

33. Describe how you would check a cooling system to determine if coolant is being aerated.

34. What are the three common types of thermostats used in diesel engines?

35. Describe how a thermostat actually opens and closes.

36. Operating an engine without a thermostat is not recommended. Give the reasons why.

37. What is the purpose of using thermostat seals, and what problems exist if they leak?

38. Describe how you would check a thermostat for effective operation. List the specific checks to confirm whether a thermostat is good or bad.

39. Why would a truck or stationary engine application use shutterstats?

40. Describe briefly how a shutterstat system operates.

41. Provide an example of the opening temperatures for a heavy-duty truck engine that employs a thermostat, a shutterstat, and a thermatic fan.

42. True or False: All thermatically operated fans use air pressure to function.

43. Technician A says that thermatic fans must have their hub belt driven from the engine crankshaft. Technician B says that no belt drive is necessary. Which technician is correct?

44. Technician A says that a Bendix and Kysor/Cadillac thermatic fan hub assembly is applied by spring pres-sure; technician B says the assembly is applied by air pressure. Who is correct?

45. True or False: A thermomodulated fan hub assembly relies on coolant temperature within the engine block to activate it.

46. True or False: Marine engine applications use raw seawater routed through the engine cooling system and plumb freshwater through the heat exchanger to cool the hot, raw seawater.

47. True or False: Raw water pumps usually employ a special rubber or neoprene type of impeller.

48. The purpose of zinc electrodes in marine engine cooling systems is to
    a. counteract electrolysis
    b. prevent scale buildup
    c. maintain the correct pH control level
    d. prevent silica dropout in the antifreeze

49. Describe briefly how a marine engine keel cooling system operates.

13 Air Inlet and Exhaust Systems

Overview

In this chapter we discuss and describe in detail the importance of both the air induction and exhaust systems to the efficiency of the combustion system. A discussion of how the individual components of these two systems contribute to air and exhaust flow into and from the cylinders is provided. Also included is information and detailed descriptions of the maintenance, troubleshooting, repair/replacement, and analysis of these two systems components. Specific diagrams and features are presented to clarify the purpose, function, and operation of the major components.

Both mechanical and electronically controlled medium/heavy-duty truck diesel engines can be equipped with either an exhaust brake or an engine compression brake. Both of these components are designed to act as a vehicle auxiliary braking device to provide longer brake service life to overhaul and to act as a backup braking source. Most heavy-duty truck diesel engines employ a compression brake designed to release the high-pressure compressed air from the cylinder at the end of the compression stroke. This venting of the high-pressure air through the exhaust system is what provides the proverbial rat-a-tat noise when applied. Jacobs Engine Brake Company, with their patented Jake Brake, has been supplying these types of brakes since the early 1960s and now supplies their product to all major engine OEMs, with Caterpillar, Cummins, Detroit Diesel, and Mack being major users. Cummins C-brake (compression brake) is simply a Jake-sourced product. Pac-Brake (Pacific Diesel Brake), Volvo, Mercedes-Benz, and Mack/RVI with their own Dynatard are other users of this type of auxiliary braking device. Exhaust flow braking devices located externally in the exhaust piping can be sourced from a number of OEMs, with Jacobs and Williams Controls being two of the well-known suppliers. In addition, an electric driveline retarder (Telma), also distributed by a number of dealers worldwide, is an auxiliary driveline retarder used widely on passenger buses and trucks, particularly in Europe.

We discuss the components required for these various systems in this chapter. At its completion, in conjunction with appropriate hands-on skill task demonstrations in a shop environment, you will be prepared to challenge the various ASE or TQ (Trade Qualification) test content areas.

ASE CERTIFICATION

ASE offers within the medium/heavy truck tests certification area, a diesel engines T2 test. In the general engine diagnosis content tasks list area, Part E—Air Induction and Exhaust Systems Diagnosis and Repair, are nine questions on the T2 test related to these two systems, representing 13% of the T2 test. There are a total of nine tasks listed under Part E, as follows:

Part E Task List

1. Inspect, service/replace air induction piping, air cleaner and element; check the air inlet restriction (AIR).

2. Inspect, repair/replace the turbocharger, wastegate, and piping system.

3. Inspect, repair/replace the intake manifold, gaskets, temperature and pressure sensors, and connections.

4. Inspect, test, clean, repair/replace the aftercooler/intercooler, or charge air cooler assembly.

304

5. Inspect, repair/replace exhaust manifold(s), piping, mufflers or silencers, scrubbers if used, exhaust back pressure (EBP) regulators, catalytic converters where used, and mounting hardware.

6. Inspect, repair/replace preheater/inlet air heater, or glow plug system and controls.

7. Inspect, repair/replace ether/starting fluid system and controls.

Part A Task List

In Part A of the T2 task lists content area, General Engine Diagnosis, items 5 through 10 are addressed:

5. Check engine exhaust emissions, odor, smoke color, opacity (denseness), and quantity; determine necessary and appropriate repairs/corrections.

7. Perform air intake system restriction and leakage tests; determine necessary repairs.

8. Perform intake manifold pressure tests and determine necessary repairs.

9. Perform exhaust back pressure (EBP) and temperature tests; determine the necessary repairs.

10. Perform crankcase pressure tests; determine necessary repairs.

Part H Task List

Part H of the ASE medium/heavy truck tests, diesel engines test T2 content area describes the various tasks lists for engine brakes. The appropriate ASE test content area requires you to answer three questions accounting for 4% of the diesel engines T2 test. The tasks required for this area include the following:

1. Inspect, test, adjust engine/exhaust brakes.

2. Inspect, test, adjust, repair/replace engine exhaust brake control circuits, switches, and solenoids.

3. Inspect, repair/replace engine exhaust brake housing, valves, seals, springs, lines, and fittings.

Within this chapter we provide detailed information to support a course of study in preparation for challenging the ASE content in the T2 diesel engines test content area.

THE AIR SUPPLY

All internal combustion engines need an adequate supply of air that is clean, dry, filtered, fresh, and cool. Damp air contains less oxygen than dry air, thus it re-

duces engine power. The power loss is usually negligible unless conditions of very high humidity are encountered in warm countries. On naturally aspirated (nonturbocharged) and particularly on turbocharged engines, air is as necessary to successful operation as is the quality of the fuel used. Lack of sufficient airflow to an engine can result in these conditions:

- High air inlet restriction
- Low turbocharger or blower boost pressure
- Higher exhaust temperatures
- Incomplete combustion
- Lower fuel economy
- Lack of power
- Smoke at the exhaust stack
- Increased exhaust emissions
- Shorter valve and piston life
- Noisier operation
- Increased lube oil use

Heavy-duty diesel engines with electronically controlled unit injectors are designed to provide minimum exhaust emissions, superior fuel economy, and high power outputs. Most of these engines are equipped with a variety of engine sensors. The air inlet system is equipped with one or more of the following sensors: ambient air pressure sensor for altitude compensation, intake manifold temperature sensor, and turbocharger boost pressure sensor. These three sensors can quickly determine a problem and cause the engine ECM to reduce speed and power. The sensors are normally mounted on the intake manifold. See Chapters 18, 21, 22, and 23 for specific OEM examples and sensor locations.

Black exhaust smoke pouring from any engine, particularly from a mechanically governed one, is a direct indication of either air starvation or engine overfueling. Unburned fuel does not all flow from the exhaust stack. Some of it actually washes down the cylinder wall and causes lube oil dilution. Some unburned fuel changes to carbon, which can stick to pistons, rings, and valves as well as plug the orifice holes in the injector tip.

Unfiltered air can rapidly wear out an engine—a condition often referred to as *dusting out* an engine. This condition is particularly noticeable when an engine has been overhauled, but after a short period of time loses compression and power and emits heavy smoke at the exhaust stack. Tests by major diesel engine manufacturers have shown that as little as 2 tablespoons of dirt can dust out an engine within a very short time. All air contains small particles of dirt and abrasive material that are not always visible to the naked eye. Dirty intake air is the main cause today for

TABLE 13–1 *Air intake system specs for Cummins Signature/ISX engine models*

Signature Series	Specifications
Section 10 - Air Intake System - Group 10	Page 10-3

Specifications

Air Intake System

⚠ CAUTION ⚠

Engine intake air must be filtered to prevent dirt and debris from entering the engine. If air intake piping is damaged or loose, unfiltered air will enter the engine and cause premature wear.

Maximum Temperature Rise between Ambient Air and Engine Air Inlet (ambient above 0°C [32°F]):
Automotive and Industrial .... -1°C [30°F]

Maximum Inlet Restriction (clean filter) Normal-Duty Element:
Automotive and Industrial .... 250 mm H_2O [10 in H_2O]
Power Generation .... 381 mm H_2O [15 in H_2O]

Maximum Inlet Restriction (dirty filter) .... 635 mm H_2O [25 in H_2O]

Maximum Allowable Pressure Drop across Charge Air Cooler:
Automotive and Industrial:
psi .... 14 kPa [2 psi]
Hg (mercury) .... 102 mm Hg [4 in Hg]

(Courtesy of Cummins Engine Company, Inc.)

wear on pistons, rings, liners, valves, and other internal engine components.

All OEMs publish specifications for every engine system (fuel, lube, oil, cooling, intake, and exhaust). These specs must be adhered to at all times if the engine system is to function and operate as designed. An example of specs for the air intake system for the Cummins ISX/Signature series DOHC 15-L electronically controlled engines is listed in Table 13–1. When an engine lacks power, runs rough, and overheats, a possible engine system problem is the air or exhaust system. More details on engine troubleshooting can be found in Chapter 25.

INTAKE AND EXHAUST SYSTEM FLOW

Four-Cycle Engines

Figure 13–1 illustrates the flow of the air in a turbocharged engine. The pressurized air flows into the cylinders through the open intake valve. The exhaust gases flow from the cylinder through the open exhaust valve(s) through the manifold and piping to the muffler assembly. This same airflow pattern is typical of turbocharged *intercooled* high-output heavy-duty engine models.

The intake charge is routed through a cast intake manifold bolted to the cylinder head. The manifold is designed and contoured to provide a minimum restriction to the airflow. In addition, most high-performance diesel engines employ four valve heads (two intake and two exhaust) in what is known as a crossflow head design where the air enters one side of the cylinder head and exits on the opposite side. This configuration provides for very short, unobstructed intake and exhaust ports for efficient airflow, low pumping losses, and reduced heat transfer, so the engine breathes more freely and runs cooler.

Two-Cycle Engines

The largest engine manufacturer of two-cycle heavy-duty engines is Detroit Diesel. The two-stroke-cycle engine differs from the four-cycle model in that it does not use intake valves. All poppet-type valves contained in the cylinder head are *exhaust only*; usually there are four valves per cylinder on high-speed heavy-duty models.

Basic airflow through a V-design DDC engine is illustrated in Figure 2–5. Note that a gear-driven blower is used to force the pressurized air into an *air-box* which completely surrounds each cylinder. The cylinder liner contains a row of helically shaped ports to create high air turbulence as air flows into the cylinder. These ports serve as the intake system. The conventional intake and exhaust strokes of four-stroke-cycle engines are eliminated in the two-cycle engine. Every piston upstroke is compression, and every downstroke is power.

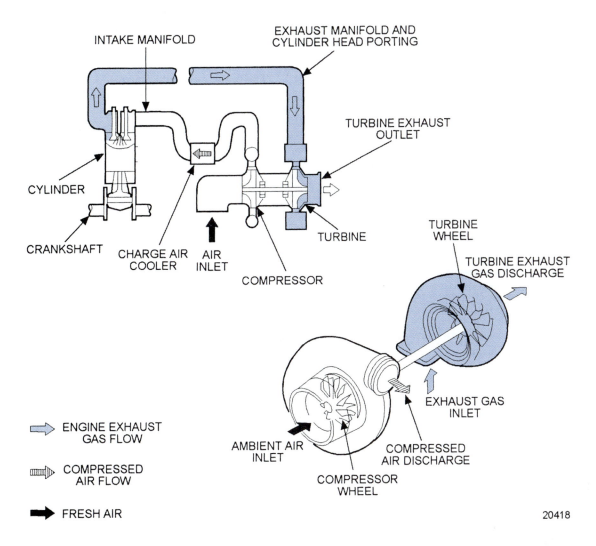

FIGURE 13–1 *Schematic of the air and exhaust flow for a heavy-duty high-speed turbocharged and intercooled diesel engine. (Courtesy of Detroit Diesel Corporation.)*

The major function of the blower in two-stroke engines is to supply air at pressures between 4 and 7 psi (27 to 48 kPa) to the engine air box area, which acts as a reservoir for a header of charged air. Remember, in a two-cycle engine the intake and exhaust strokes are physically eliminated, so pressurized air is needed and is used for several purposes:

- Supply fresh air for combustion
- Cool the cylinder liner, piston crown, and exhaust valves
- Scavenge waste exhaust gases from the cylinder
- Allow a controlled amount of air leakage past the piston oil control rings when at TDC to provide for positive crankcase ventilation

AIR CLEANERS

A large number of different air cleaner (filter) models are in use. We can categorize them into three general types: oil bath (seldom used), single-stage dry element, and two-stage dry element.

The oil bath air cleaner is seldom used now because it is less efficient at lower engine speeds when the airflow entering the engine is lower. This lower airflow reduces the agitation of the oil within the air cleaner sump and, therefore, does not trap airborne dust or dirt as well. In addition, overfilling an oil bath air cleaner can result in engine oil pullover, which causes engine overspeed. In cold weather, the oil can freeze; the result is high air inlet restriction and/or poor dust/dirt trapping ability. Operating a piece of equipment at steep angles can result in air restriction problems and possible oil pullover. An oil bath air cleaner must be serviced more frequently than a dry type, and the process is more time consuming. In addition, the oil bath air cleaner offers a higher initial restriction to airflow.

Dry Air Cleaners

The major advantage of a dry air filter is that it allows much longer periods between service intervals. Up to 100,000 miles (160,930 km) is not uncommon on heavy-duty on-highway trucks. The dry filter is capable of trapping dust or dirt with equal efficiency throughout the speed range. The filter element is made from treated paper that has been pleated and assembled into a continuous V-form throughout its circumference. In some filter models, this pleated paper element can be opened to a full length of 40 to 60 ft (12 to 18 m). The dry filter element increases in efficiency as the dirt load builds up a cake or bed in the valley of the V pleats—

upward from a minimum efficiency of 99.5% to as high as 99.99%—and remains constant throughout the engine speed range.

The paper element is surrounded and protected by a perforated steel mesh screen (shell). Dry filters are available in either a cylindrical or square/rectangular panel shape. Figure 13–2 illustrates a Donaldson dual-filter element—composite, dry and horizontally mounted—which has primary and secondary units. In composite filters, dirty air enters through the inlet opening, where it travels through a plastic ring of vanes (called a precleaner) around the outside of the element. These vanes are designed to create a *cyclonic twist* to the air to throw the heavier dust and dirt particles outward by centrifugal force and downward into the dust cup area. The dust cup is held in place by a large heavy-duty clamp. On the composite heavy-duty, vertical-tube type shown in Figure 13–3, dirty air passes through the inlet and flows onto a series of tubes that are vertically mounted inside the air cleaner. The hard-plastic tubes contain vanes, which create a cy-

FIGURE 13–2 (a) Dual (two-stage) air cleaner/filter, which is a composite, dry, and horizontally mounted unit featuring a vacuator valve to expel 90% of the air inlet laden dust or dirt by a centrifuge design; (b) same air filter assembly but in an exploded view. (Courtesy of Donaldson Co., Inc.)

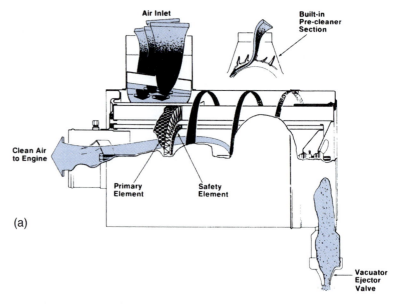

(a)

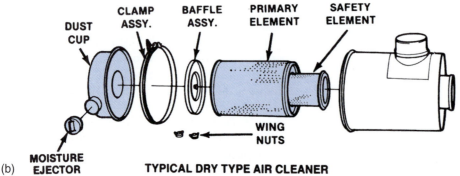

(b)   TYPICAL DRY TYPE AIR CLEANER

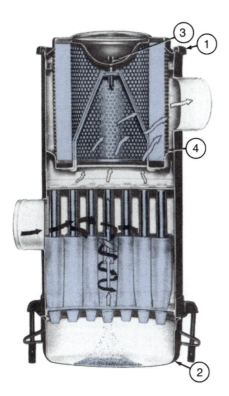

FIGURE 13–3 *Vertically mounted composite cyclonic type of heavy-duty air cleaner. 1, Top cover; 2, dust cup or reservoir; 3, wing bolt; 4, filter element. (Courtesy of Donaldson Co., Inc.)*

clonic twist similar to that described for the single and dual elements. Centrifugal action throws the heavier dust or dirt particles to the outside of the tube, where they drop downward to the removable dust cup. The clean air then passes upward through the center of the tubes and into the air filter, where minute dust and dirt particles can be removed.

An optional dust removal design is shown in Figure 13–2. In addition to the cyclonic action described, the dust that has been spun outward along the wall of the cleaner is directed toward a *vacuator* dust ejector. This filter design can be mounted horizontally, as shown, or vertically with the Vacuator located at the base of the dust cup.

Precleaners and Screens

In heavy dust conditions, for example in situations involving off-highway trucks and equipment, precleaners such as those shown in Figure 13–4 are often used. These precleaners reduce the frequency of service by spinning the dust-laden air outward as shown in Figure 13–4. This dust is trapped and stored in a heavy-duty, hard, clear plastic bowl and cover assembly. When the dirt reaches the level indicated by a painted arrow on the bowl, remove the cover by loosening the wing nut, lift off the plastic body, and empty the dust.

Many engines and equipment operate in areas where coarse or fuzzy materials such as chaff, lint, or

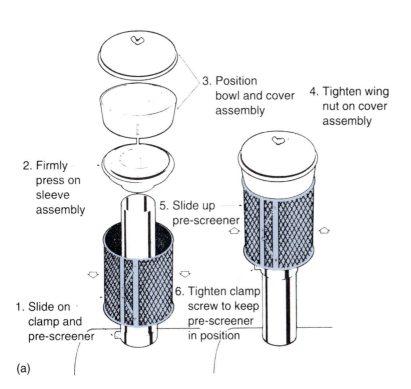

3. Position bowl and cover assembly

4. Tighten wing nut on cover assembly

2. Firmly press on sleeve assembly

5. Slide up pre-screener

1. Slide on clamp and pre-screener

6. Tighten clamp screw to keep pre-screener in position

(a)

FIGURE 13–4 *(a) Features of a snap-on pre-screen for a heavy-duty air cleaner assembly; (b) airflow diagram highlighting the spinning action imparted to the incoming air in the precleaner assembly to centrifuge and trap the dust/dirt within the clear plastic bowl and cover assembly. (Courtesy of Donaldson Co., Inc.)*

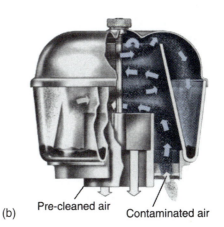

Pre-cleaned air   Contaminated air

(b)

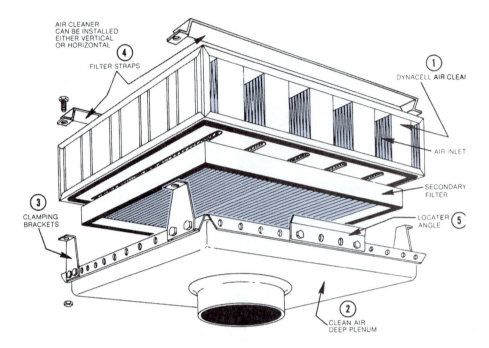

leaves are continually airborne. To prevent any of this material from entering the engine, a snap-on pre-screener can be used (Figure 13–4). In equipment applications using dry filters that fight forest fires or operate in municipal garbage dumps where sparks from burning debris are often airborne, a fine prefilter screen is necessary. This screen prevents sparks from being pulled into the air cleaner and damaging the plastic cyclonic tubes.

Many heavy-duty Class 8 on-highway trucks have air cleaner assemblies mounted on the engine intake manifold (Figure 13–5). Another very popular air cleaner for on-highway and stationary industrial engine applications is the ECO series manufactured by the Farr Company. Figure 13–6 illustrates this model, which is a spin-on disposable unit. The air filter has a tapered offset cone design and can be mounted either horizontally or vertically. This design feature ensures that airflow distribution and dirt loading are uniform throughout the core, resulting in lower overall restriction, between three to five times longer filter life, and better fuel economy. The air inlet shown at the top can also be at the side if desired.

Cartridge Panel Air Cleaners

In the cartridge panel air cleaner shown in Figure 13–7 the filter element is square or rectangular in shape rather than round. These types of filters are more commonly used on larger equipment such as mining trucks, graders, and bottom-dump scrapers, where extremely heavy dust and dirt conditions are regularly

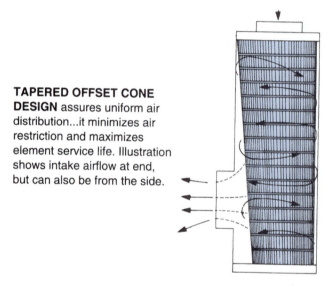

TAPERED OFFSET CONE DESIGN assures uniform air distribution...it minimizes air restriction and maximizes element service life. Illustration shows intake airflow at end, but can also be from the side.

FIGURE 13–6 Design of an Ecolite air cleaner with a tapered offset cone filter assembly. (Courtesy of Farr Company.)

encountered. Most of these designs employ an exhaust gas aspirator assembly, which is also illustrated in Figure 13–7. This system directs exhaust gas flow through the piping to the aspirator funnel which creates a constant suction to the base of the dustbin located at the bottom of the centrifugal air cleaner panel. Heavily laden dusty air is spun outward as shown in Figure 13–8a by the shape of the deflector vanes at the inlet tubes, and 90% of the dirt is drawn off through the

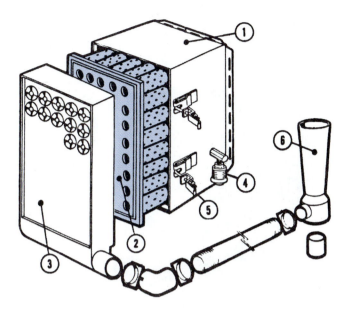

Mounting flanges are an integral part of all Series-D housings.

BASIC TWO-STAGE KIT INCLUDES

1. Air Cleaner Housing
2. Pamic Filter
3. Pre-Cleaner
4. Service Indicator
5. Fasteners
6. Aspirator Kit

FIGURE 13–7 *Component parts of a two-stage dry air cleaner featuring an exhaust gas aspirator to withdraw and expel up to 90% + of the dust-laden intake air. (Courtesy of Farr Company.)*

dustbin which is constantly subjected to the exhaust aspirator suction. Protecting the exhaust system from rain, fog, and other moisture is important to prevent corrosion of the exhaust piping. Either a balanced rain cap or smooth elbow-design raincap should be used on the end of the aspirator as illustrated in Figure 13–8b. An optional dust ejector system shown in Figure 13–9 uses a supply of vehicle compressed air to bleed airflow through a nozzle in the Rotopamic or ultraheavy-duty model precleaner panel.

In applications where moisture is a continuing problem (for example, on marine applications or in coastal logging equipment), a moisture eliminator pre-screen can be used. The moisture eliminator is fitted in front of the filter cartridge to attract moisture and dust.

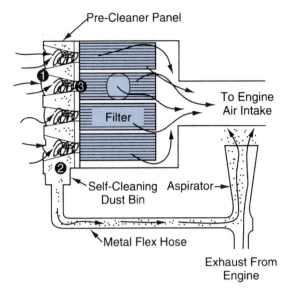

(a)

❶ Air enters pre-cleaner panel and is spun to remove 90% of dust particles.

❷ The separated dust falls into dust bin and is drawn out through aspirator.

❸ Pre-cleaned air now enters Pamic after-cleaner for second-stage cleaning.

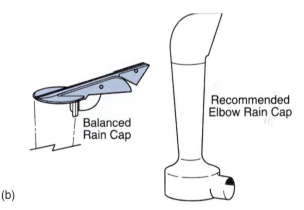

(b)

FIGURE 13–8 *(a) Operational schematic of the two-stage Rotopamic heavy-duty air cleaner equipped with an exhaust gas aspirator; (b) outlet options for the Rotopamic heavy-duty air cleaner exhaust gas aspirator unit. (Courtesy of Farr Company.)*

The coils of the eliminator cause the moisture-laden air to be trapped and drain by gravity to the base of the precleaner eliminator, which has a series of horizontal slots to allow the accumulated water to drain.

In heavy-duty off-highway equipment applications such as 170- and 200-ton mining vehicles, multiple air cleaners are required to handle the large airflow requirements of engines rated at 1600 to 2300 hp (1194

FIGURE 13–9 *Features of a compressed air aspirator bleed-tube option used with a heavy-duty Rotopamic air cleaner assembly. (Courtesy of Farr Company.)*

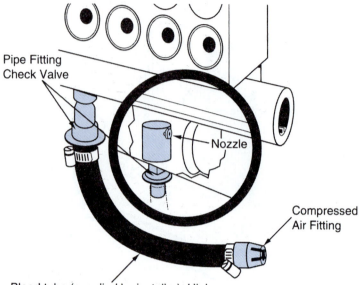

Pipe Fitting
Check Valve

Nozzle

Compressed Air Fitting

Bleed tube (supplied by installer). High temperature silicone hose capable of handling positive pressure is recommended.

FIGURE 13–10 *Example of four ultraheavy-duty dry air cleaner assemblies on the front of a large mining truck. (Courtesy of Farr Company.)*

to 1716 kW). Figure 13–10 illustrates four ultraheavy-duty (UHD) Farr air cleaners mounted on the forward bulkhead of a typical mining truck. These particular air cleaner models offer three stages of filtration for large trucks, drill rigs, shovels, and so on. The first stage of UHD filtration occurs through the *superclone* precleaner. This precleaner operates similarly to the one shown in Figure 13–8 where up to 93% of the dirt and 90% of any water entering the system are removed. The UHD air cleaner uses a small amount of vehicle-compressed air to provide bleed airflow for self-cleaning action in the precleaner section, which is located in the swing-away heavy-gauge forward metal grid that pro-

tects the precleaner section (see Figure 13–9). The compressed air source can be supplied from the air compressor, the pressure side of the turbocharger, or the airbox of naturally aspirated two-cycle engines. The second stage employs a primary filter to remove 99.9% of the dirt that gets through the precleaner (see Figure 13–8a). The third-stage safety filter is designed to trap the small amount of dirt or dust that may get past the primary filter, so that the total system efficiency of 99.99% will be maintained.

Servicing the UHD air cleaner simply involves loosening the three latches on the side of the air cleaners to open the swing-away protective grate door. The primary element is held in place by two vertical straps. After loosening off the bolt at the top and bottom of each strap, swing the strap away. Insert the fingers of both hands into the access holes of the air cleaner element and pull it straight out. Thoroughly wipe out the housing with a clean cloth. If the safety element requires changing (normally only at engine overhaul), note that it is held in place by a bolt and tab at each corner. Each bolt has a safety wire through its head to discourage unnecessary tampering. Cut the safety wires and remove the bolts. Grasp the element and pull it straight out of the housing.

In applications that operate in conditions of severe dust, it is extremely important to ensure that all ducting and piping to the air cleaner and engine are dust tight. Leaky connections, holes in piping, or other system faults must be avoided. Since only a couple of tablespoons of dust wear an engine out, several air cleaner manufacturers offer *dust detector kits* that are installed to engine duct work in the actual air cleaner.

Restriction Indicators

The most effective methods of determining when to service a dry filter element are by measuring the air inlet restriction (AIR) with a water manometer or by employing an air cleaner service indicator. Both gauges operate when there is a vacuum condition, that is, when the pressure within the air cleaner and ducting on the suction side of the turbocharger is less than atmospheric pressure. Consequently, a vacuum gauge can also be used to monitor AIR.

The restriction indicator gauge can be attached to the air cleaner housing or remotely mounted on the dash area of a heavy-duty truck or piece of equipment. A small-bore plastic tube connects the indicator with a fitting on the ducting at the engine. Figure 13–11A illustrates a common type of restriction indicator (Filter Minder). This model contains a clear plastic window so that when the air filter becomes plugged, the restriction (vacuum) pulls a small float gauge into view within the small inspection window. Once the system has been serviced, the gauge can be reset by pushing a small release button on the bottom of the gauge. The restriction gauge shown actually allows the operator or technician to visually determine the degree of AIR based on the graduated scale on the Filter Minder gauge. Restriction gauges are calibrated in inches of water and are available for different maximum settings.

Automatic Air Filter Restriction Compensation

On electronically equipped and controlled heavy-duty diesel engines automatic air filter plugging compensation is achieved by using both a turbocharger inlet pressure sensor in conjunction with an atmospheric pressure sensor. In the illustration shown in Figure 13–11B, the filter differential pressure calculation formula is explained. Automatic filter compensation means that the engine is protected against the effects of high air inlet restriction from plugged filters especially in off-road equipment that operates in severe dust conditions. In the example shown in the diagram, the automatic engine power derate starts when the air filter restriction exceeds 30 in. of water (30" H_2O), or 6.25 kPa. The engine power is derated by the engine electronic ECM at the rate of 2% per 1 kPa, with a maximum derate of 20 percent. At the 30 in. restriction level, the ECM will log a fault code in ECM memory and activate a warning light in the equipment cab. When more than one air filter is used, if only one filter is plugged, the Cat ET (Electronic Technician) service tool and Caterpillar Monitoring System will display the highest air pressure of the two filters. Therefore the engine power derate is also based on the highest air pres-

5" to 10"
Normal clean filter. (Initial restriction varies with each system design.)

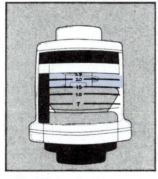

15" to 18"
The filter element is loading up with contaminants, but still has much useful life left. Fuel consumption is probably increasing.

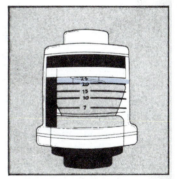

20" to 25"
The filter element should be replaced. The engine is probably using more fuel with slight loss of power. This upper limit will vary depending on whether equipment is diesel or gasoline fueled, and your fuel consumption experience.

(a)

FIGURE 13–11 (a) Graduated Filter Minder air restriction indicator which reads in inches of water (H_2O) to indicate visually to the operator or service technician the degree of air filter plugging. (Courtesy of Farr Company.)

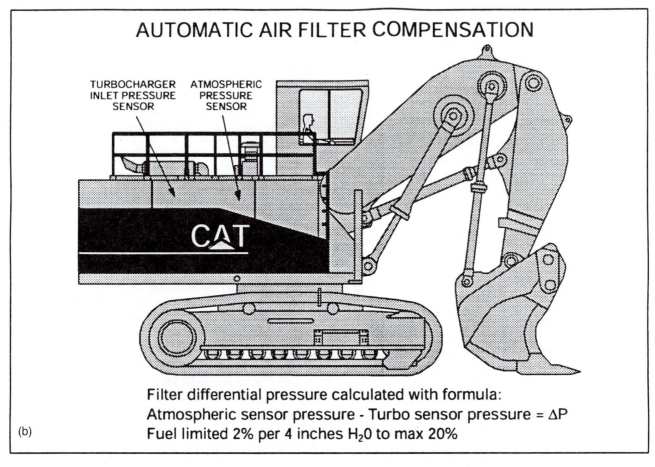

AUTOMATIC AIR FILTER COMPENSATION

TURBOCHARGER
INLET PRESSURE
SENSOR

ATMOSPHERIC
PRESSURE
SENSOR

CAT

Filter differential pressure calculated with formula:
Atmospheric sensor pressure - Turbo sensor pressure = ΔP
Fuel limited 2% per 4 inches H$_2$0 to max 20%

(b)

FIGURE 13–11   (continued). (b) Principle of automatic air filter restriction electronic engine compensation system. (Reprinted courtesy of Caterpillar, Inc.)

sure of the two filters. For more information on the Cat ET and Monitoring System, refer to Chapter 23, Caterpillar Fuel Systems.

Servicing Air Cleaners

Nothing will wear out an engine faster than unfiltered air entering the system. The finest lapping compound in the world is a combination of fine dust mixed with oil on the cylinder walls. Think also of the continuous rubbing action of the piston rings against the liner surface and you can readily appreciate the rapid wear condition that is present.

Although oil bath air cleaners are *seldom* found on modern diesel engines, you may be faced with servicing one of these older assemblies. The oil sump must be removed and the dirty oil disposed of safely. The oil sump can be washed in solvent, and the internal wire-mesh filter assembly can be washed in solvent and blown dry with an air hose. Using a steam cleaner tends to pack dirt tighter into the wire-mesh screen.

Check all gaskets and seals for an air- and oil-tight fit. Refill the oil reservoir with the same grade of oil that is used in the engine. Do not overfill the air cleaner sump; check the sump for the oil level full mark. Overfilling an oil bath air cleaner can cause oil pullover and engine overspeed.

On dry-type filters, check the manufacturer's specifications and service recommendations closely prior to service, since not all dry filter elements can be washed. A filter restriction indicator lets you know when the filter and system require servicing. When restriction readings indicate that the filter element is plugged, perform the following procedure:

1.   Clean off the access cover before removing any clamps or bolts.

2.   Remove the necessary clamps, bolts, or wing nuts to gain access to the air cleaner filter. Dust cups should be dumped when they are two-thirds full by removing the large clamp at the base of the filter housing. Precleaners can be dumped when the dust reaches the

level indicated on the clear heavy-duty plastic bowl (Figure 13–4). On cleaners equipped with the Donaldson vacuator valve (Figure 13–2), make sure the valve is not damaged or plugged. Is the cup joint sealing?

3. On heavy-duty air cleaners that have cyclonic tubes, light dust plugging can be removed as illustrated in Figure 13–12 by using a stiff-fiber brush. If heavy plugging with fibrous material is evident, remove the lower body section for cleaning with compressed air and warm water at a temperature not exceeding 160°F (71°C). Avoid steam cleaning cyclonic tubes because the heat can melt the plastic.

4. Remove the filter by loosening off the large wing nut that retains it. On square and rectangular models, there are usually four or more large external wing nuts. On cartridge-type filters, carefully insert several fingers into the tube holes and work the element free from the housing as shown in Figure 13–13.

5. On reusable dry filter elements, take care not to pound, tap, or rap the dust out of them as severe damage can result. Dust and loose dirt can be removed by directing compressed air through the element in the opposite direction to normal airflow.

CAUTION Do not allow the air nozzle to touch the element paper directly since this can rupture it. Keep the nozzle at least 2 in. (51 mm) away from the filter element. Reduced air pressure should be used, in the range of 50 to 60 psi (345 to 414 kPa), although some manufacturers allow up to 100 psi (690 kPa).

6. Thoroughly clean the filter with warm water. Many filter manufacturers offer a sudsy cleaning solution that can be mixed with warm water for cleaning purposes. The filter element should be soaked for at least 15 minutes in a large receptacle of the cleaning solution. Rinse it in clean warm water; then use a pressure air hose with a maximum of 40 psi (276 kPa) to remove excess water. Refer to Figure 13–14.

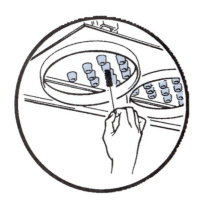

FIGURE 13–12 Using a stiff-bristle brush to clean out the cyclonic tubes of a heavy-duty air cleaner assembly. (Courtesy of Donaldson Co., Inc.)

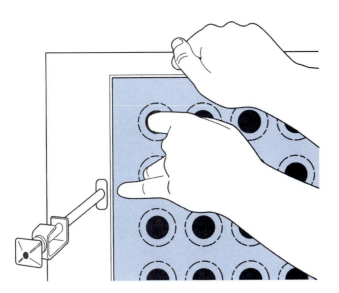

FIGURE 13–13 Removal of the molded air filter element from a heavy-duty Pamic or Rotopamic cartridge-type air cleaner assembly. (Courtesy of Farr Company.)

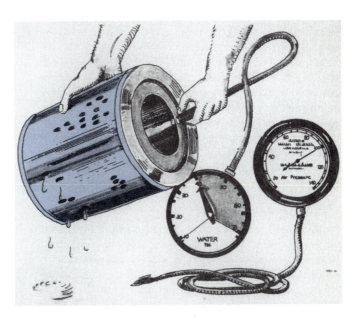

FIGURE 13–14 Using a pressurized air nozzle to remove excess warm freshwater that was used to rinse the dry air filter element after cleaning in a special sudsy solution. Never use more than 40 psi (276 kPa) of air pressure, and never place the air nozzle directly against the filter to avoid tearing (rupturing) the paper element. (Courtesy of Donaldson Co., Inc.)

7. Once a filter element has been cleaned, dry it using warm flowing air at a maximum temperature of 160°F (71°C). This can be accomplished by setting the filter on a drying rack or placing it in a temperature-controlled oven.

8. Once the filter has been dried, inspect it for rips or tears. This step is very important. The best method is to place the filter over a vertically mounted lightbulb and rotate it slowly. You can also use a Trouble-light, as illustrated in Figure 13–15, to look for signs of damage.

9. Check all air cleaner system seals and gaskets and replace if damaged. Look for dust trails, which indicate leaky gaskets. Many heavy-duty round air filters have a soft rubber compressible seal glued to one or both ends. This seal can permanently compress (set) so that it flattens out; the result is that when the air cleaner cover is installed, it does not produce a dust-tight seal. Compare the height of this seal with that of a new filter element. If the seal is badly set, replace the filter element. If starting aid fittings are used, inspect them to make sure they are tight and free of leaks.

10. On square or rectangular cartridge-type air filters, the filter elements are encased in a heavy molded rubber or neoprene casing. When the filter is changed, therefore, a new seal is assured automatically. Prior to installing the new filter, always clean out the air cleaner housing using a damp cloth to pick up any dirt or dust. Do not blow pressurized air into the housing unless a safety element is in position; otherwise, dirt may enter the turbocharger and/or engine intake manifold. Figure 13–13 illustrates the replacement of a rectangular cartridge-type filter element.

11. On air cleaner systems employing exhaust gas aspirators, ensure that the aspirator tube (piping) is not plugged. Plugging of these tubes can cause exhaust gas recirculation to melt the cyclonic tubes in the filter assembly. If components are melted, it is also possible that the assembly is located too close to an exhaust pipe. In addition, engine exhaust can rapidly plug dry filter elements, so make sure that exhaust gases are directed above and away from the air inlet system.

Remember that using a badly restricted (plugged) filter element results in excessive fuel consumption, loss of power, increased engine operating temperature, and shortened cylinder kit life. Using a damaged filter element results in rapid piston, ring, and cylinder wear and severe damage to the engine.

AIR DUCTING INSPECTION

The air induction piping functions with the air cleaner to carry clean air into the turbocharger and engine. In addition to servicing the air cleaner filter assembly, it is extremely important to check the piping hoses, elbows, and clamps for looseness, tears, or ruptures. Ignoring these components can lead to unfiltered air entering the system and destroying the engine in a very short time. Every time you service the air filter, inspect the intake ducting (piping) and elbows. Typical piping and connecting hose are illustrated in Figure 13–16a. Molded heavy-duty rubber elbows, which are approximately 0.25 in (6.25 mm) thick with ribbed reinforcement, are widely used and secured by T-bolt hose clamps. Metal tubing should be spaced at least 0.75 in. (19 mm) apart from the hose clamps.

FIGURE 13–15 *Using a Trouble-light inserted inside the air filter element to check for signs of paper damage, tears, or ruptures. (Courtesy of Donaldson Co., Inc.)*

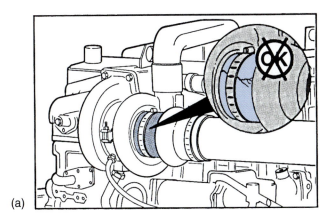

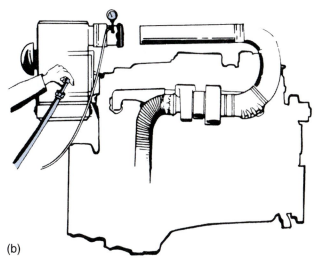

FIGURE 13–16 *(a) Inspection of air inlet ducting heavy-duty rubber elbows for signs of cracking, looseness, or damage; (b) sealed air inlet ducting being pressurized (low psi) to check for signs of air leaks. (Courtesy of Cummins Engine Company, Inc.)*

To check heavy-duty elbows and hoses, depress the hose where it is secured by the clamp and visually inspect it for signs of cutting or cracking as shown in Figure 13–16a. If you suspect that the tubing is not airtight, disconnect it at both the air cleaner outlet and the turbocharger inlet. Install heavy plastic shipping caps or light metal blanking plugs at each end and clamp them into position. Drill and tap one sealing plate, or use the air inlet restriction pipe plug, to adapt an air pressure fitting. Connect a hand pump or use a low-pressure regulator at a wall valve to limit the pressure to 2 psi (14 kPa). Apply liquid spray soap or use a brush and apply sudsy soap solution to each joint. Air bubbles indicate a leak. The same tooling described for checking AAAC Types on page 319 can also be adapted to check the piping/ducting located between the air filter housing and the inlet side of the

turbocharger assembly for signs of leaks which would allow unfiltered air to enter the system.

If you suspect that the air cleaner assembly is pulling in unfiltered air, remove the dry filter element and install a dummy one, or install a prewrapped one for the test. Refer to Figure 13–16b. Clamp a rubber sheet tightly over the air cleaner inlet and outlet connections. Prepare an air fitting connection on the air cleaner, or clamp a used tire tube with its Schrader valve over the inlet or outlet connection. Use liquid spray soap on the inlet and outlet connections as well as at the dust cup of the cleaner. Apply 2 psi (14 kPa) maximum and look for signs of air bubbles, which would indicate a leak. Clean the inside of piping and flexible connectors before replacing them on the engine.

AFTERCOOLERS

As the U.S. EPA exhaust emissions standards have become stringent, an area of engine design that has received more attention involves the temperature of the air that leaves the turbocharger and enters the engine intake manifold. One of the most important components in use today on electronically controlled high-speed heavy-duty diesel engines is the turbocharger-pressurized-air *aftercooler*.

Ideal air temperature for operating engines is usually in the region of 95 to 100°F (35 to 38°C). An engine rated at 250 hp (187 kW) would lose approximately 10 hp (7.5 kW) if the intake air temperature were allowed to rise to 130°F (54°C). The higher the ambient air temperature, the greater the expansion of the air; therefore, a loss of engine power always results. Depending on the rise in ambient air temperature and the engine design features, an engine can lose between 0.15 and 0.7% horsepower per cylinder for every 10°F (6°C) rise beyond 90°F (32°C), or approximately 1% power loss for each 10°F (6°C) of intake temperature rise above 90°F (32°C).

There are four basic types of aftercoolers:

1. Intercooler–aftercooler combination often used on high-output marine engines. This system uses raw sea or lake water to cool the intercooler, while the aftercooler is cooled by fresh engine coolant.
2. JWAC (jacket water aftercooler).
3. ALCC (advanced liquid charge cooling).
4. AAAC (air-to-air aftercooler).

The terms *intercooler* and *aftercooler* are interchangeable descriptions used by engine manufacturers. The word *inter* means in between the turbocharger and engine intake manifold; the word *after* means that a cooler is located after the pressurized air leaves the cold end of the turbocharger. Both words indicate that the pressurized turbocharger air is cooled by directing it through a cooler system, which can be either air or water cooled. Figure 13–1 shows the general location of an intercooler, and Figure 13–17 shows a charge air cooler system mounted in front of the radiator. Pressurized turbocharger air that is directed through the charge air cooler core is cooled by forced air as a vehicle moves along the highway. Most heavy-duty highway trucks powered by Caterpillar, Cummins, Detroit Diesel, Mack, and Volvo engines now use a system similar to that shown in Figure 13–17, where the charge air cooler is mounted in front of the radiator assembly. Some very-high-output marine engine applications employ both an intercooler and an aftercooler. The pressurized turbocharger air is intercooled before it enters the gear-driven blower. Once it passes through the blower, it is directed through an aftercooler and into the airbox of two-stroke-cycle engines.

Water Aftercooling

Water-type inlet air aftercoolers employ fresh engine coolant routed through its water jacket to reduce the temperature of the pressurized air flowing through it from the turbocharger. A JWAC is capable of lowering the full-load engine turbocharger boost air from a temperature of about 300°F (149°C) down to approximately 200°F (93°C). The ALCC system is capable of lowering the turbo boost air temperature down to approximately 165°F (74°C).

Air-to-Air Aftercooling

The most efficient and widely used turbocharger boost air aftercooler on heavy-duty trucks and buses is the AAAC, or ATAAC as some engine manufacturers refer to it. The engine turbocharger is driven by hot pressurized exhaust gases flowing from the exhaust manifold into the turbine side. These gases drive the turbine wheel at speeds in excess of 100,000 rpm, where they then leave the system at the exhaust piping and flow

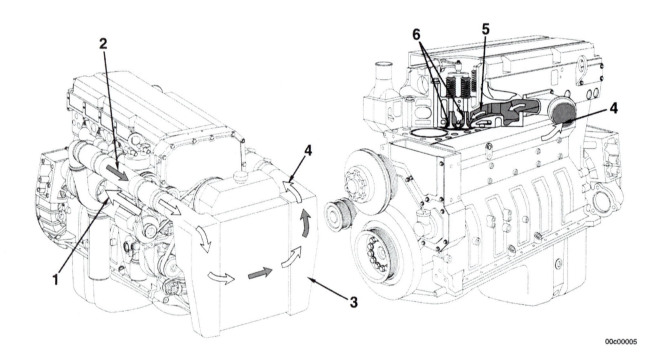

00c00005

1. Intake Air Inlet to Turbocharger
2. Turbocharger Air to Charge Air Cooler
3. Charge Air Cooler

4. From Charge Air Cooler to Intake Manifold
5. Intake Valve Port
6. Intake Valves.

FIGURE 13–17   *Air intake system flow diagram for an ATAAC (air-to-air aftercooler), often referred to as a charge air cooler, through a Cummins Signature type engine model. (Courtesy of Cummins Engine Company, Inc.)*

through the muffler system. Inlet air is pulled through the air cleaner, compressed, and heated by the compressor wheel (cold side); then it is pushed through the AAAC core and it then moves to the engine intake manifold.

Cooling of the pressurized intake air increases combustion efficiency, which in turn lowers fuel consumption, increases horsepower, and helps to minimize exhaust emissions. The AAAC system increases the engine fuel economy by approximately 4% over a JWAC engine. Today, high BMEPs, high torque rise, and maximum engine power are being developed at midrange engine speeds, particularly on heavy-duty truck engines. Without the AAAC, the pressurized air leaving the turbocharger under full-load operation, at temperatures as high as 300°F (149°C), and entering the cylinder would result in short valve and piston crown life, since there would be insufficient cooling airflow. In addition, the reduction in air density would lower the mass air charge for the combustion process resulting in a loss of power. This problem would be more severe on a two-stroke-cycle engine model where approximately 30% of the engine cooling is performed by the mass airflow rate.

Figure 13–17 illustrates a typical AAAC located in front of the radiator. Ambient air is moved across the aftercooler core and then the radiator core by means of the engine fan and also by the ram-air effect created when a truck is moving along the highway at vehicle speed. Consequently, the use of radiator shutters and/or snap-on winterfronts should be avoided. Any airflow restriction to the aftercooler core can cause higher exhaust temperatures, power loss, excessive fan usage, and a reduction in fuel economy. In cases where heavy-duty trucks operate in extremely cold weather conditions and a winterfront must be used, it should never be closed completely. Generally, a minimum of 20% airflow to the AAAC core must remain. When used with a viscous fan assembly, there should be at least a 8 in. (203 mm) diamond permanently open in the winterfront. This opening should be centered on the radiator, not at the top, bottom, or other off-center position. If more than one opening is used in the winterfront, these should be the same size at the top and bottom, or on the left and right sides, to produce a balanced airflow across the AAAC core as well as the fan blades. Winterfronts should always be completely removed when operating in ambient air temperatures above 40°F (4.5°C). Also, never install a winterfront directly against the AAAC core or radiator core or shutter. Install it in front of the truck grill with at least 2 in. (51 mm) of air space between the winterfront and the AAAC or radiator core to ensure sufficient bypass cooling in the event that the winterfront is not fully opened

in warming temperatures. When winterfronts are fully open, the airflow passage should be equal to or greater than 40% of the radiator core area.

Pressurized turbocharger air flowing through the AAAC core assembly dissipates its heat to the cooler ram air entering the grill at the front of the vehicle. This design of aftercooler reduces the turbocharger air temperature from 300°F (149°C) to between 100 and 110°F (38 and 43°C) before it flows into the intake manifold. Note that the AAAC has no water or coolant running through it. The aftercooler core consists of a series of tubes surrounded by metal fins somewhat similar to a radiator. The fins disperse the cooling air much more effectively around the tubes through which the turbocharger boost air flows. On a heavy-duty truck, flexible rubber elbows, couplings, and hose clamps are used to secure the duct work to the turbocharger, aftercooler inlet and outlet, and also at the intake manifold.

Heavy-duty electronically controlled diesel engines employ a number of sensors to accurately control the exhaust emissions levels, fuel consumption, and engine power. A number of sensors are used for the air system. An ambient air pressure (barometric pressure) sensor, an intake manifold air temperature sensor, and a turbocharger boost sensor are commonly used to monitor the airflow system. These three sensors are usually mounted directly on the intake manifold or mounted on brackets close to the intake manifold.

Checking AAAC Types

The AAAC does not have coolant flowing through it, so it can be checked using the test equipment illustrated in Figure 13–18. The core of the aftercooler should be kept free of bugs, dust, dirt, and antifreeze spilled from the radiator cooling system. Antifreeze forms a sticky substance that can attract dust and dirt. When cleaning the aftercooler core, always blow air through the core from the back side, since blowing it from the front will push it farther into the aftercooler core and the radiator core when mounted on the vehicle. Regulate the air supply to 25 to 30 psi (172 to 207 kPa) when cleaning the core. Examine the core fins for external damage, debris, and corrosion from road salt.

ATAAC Aftercooler Core Leakage Check

Low engine power complaints could be due to a leak somewhere in the A/C (aftercooler core). If the low power complaint is accompanied by low turbo boost pressure, black smoke, and/or a high exhaust temperature condition (operator can notice this on the pyrometer gauge mounted in the instrument panel if so equipped), check the downstream piping side from the turbocharger, and the A/C for signs of leakage. Using the special tool kit shown in Figure 13–18a, disconnect

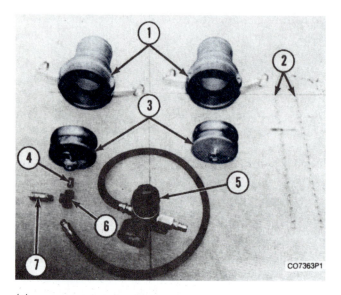

(a)

FT1984 Air to Air Aftercooler Test Group
(1) Coupler. (2) Chain. (3) Dust plugs. (4) Nipple. (5) Regulator and valve
assembly. (6) Tee. (7) Relief valve.

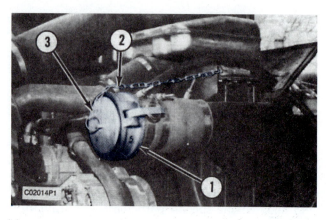

(b)

Tooling Installed (typical example)
(1) Coupler. (2) Chain. (3) Dust plugs.

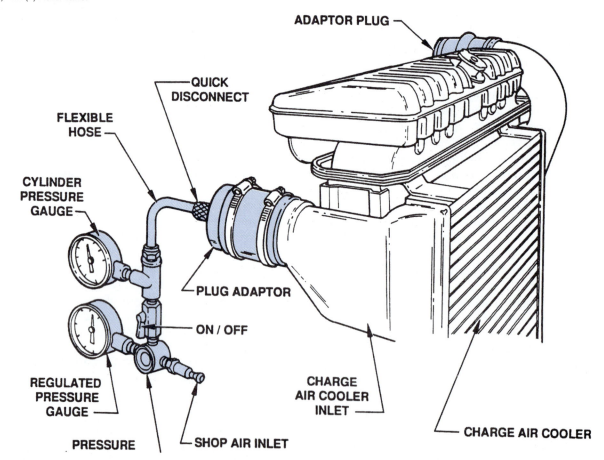

(c)

FIGURE 13–18 (a) ATAAC after cooler core pressure test toolkit. (b) Example of ATAAC aftercooler *special tooling installed. (Reprinted courtesy of Caterpillar, Inc.)* (c) Schematic of a charge air cooler pressure test hookup. *(Courtesy of Detroit Diesel Corporation.)*

the ducting from both the inlet and outlet sides of the A/C and connect the tooling as shown in Figure 13–18b. The purpose of the small chains (Item 2) in this diagram is for safety purposes. Should the couplers (Item 1) come loose during a pressure test, this safety chain will prevent the coupler from projecting into a vehicle/component, or more importantly into someone's face. Attach the loose end of the chain to a secure fitting such as the radiator top tank bolt as shown in the diagram, or a similar fixed point. With the tooling attached as shown in Figure 13–18c, connect a compressed air shop hose to the identified fitting.

SAFETY TIP   The applied test air pressure should not exceed the truck/engine OEM's specs. If heavy duty 'hump shaped' hoses are used (see example in Figure 13–18b), install additional hose clamps around these to prevent hose bulge when the air pressure is applied.

Many ATAAC's are often sourced from the same manufacturer, so maximum applied test air pressure can be considered common for most heavy duty trucks. You can check the engine service manual specs for normal maximum turbo boost pressure under full load operating conditions, and use this as a guide. Typically the test pressure should be regulated between 25 and 30 psi (172 to 205 kPa) maximum unless stated otherwise in the service manual.

SERVICE TIP   Connect the regulator and control valve assembly on the outlet side of the aftercooler. DO NOT stand in front of either one of the dust plugs (Item 3 in Figure 13–18a).

Test Procedure

1. With the test tooling securely connected as per Figure 13–18c, make sure that the pressure regulator control knob (Item 5 in Figure 13–18a) is turned out all the way CCW to prevent a rush of excess air pressure into the A/C should the shop compressed air supply not be equipped with its own regulator assembly.
2. Open the ON/OFF valve shown in Figure 13–18c.
3. Turn the regulator valve in CW until the air supply pressure registers between 25–30 psi (172 to 205 kPa), then shut off the air supply.

4. Visually inspect and listen for any signs of compressed air leakage. (Soapy water can be applied to all connections to determine where a small leak may exist by watching for bubbles).
5. Additionally the A/C system pressure should not drop more than 5 psi (35 kPa) in 15 seconds.
6. If leaks are detected, either install all new hoses, or have the A/C repaired or replaced.
7. Shut-off the shop compressed air supply.
8. Disconnect the compressed air hose and all special tooling from the aftercooler.

On heavy-duty trucks that employ air brakes, the engine-driven air compressor often draws its air supply from the engine intake manifold. The system air dryer can also be checked for correct operation while pressure checking the aftercooler core as just described. Use shop air to recharge the truck air brake reservoirs to 120 psi (827 kPa) so that you can force the air compressor governor to the unloaded position. This will allow charge air pressure to be directed to the air dryer through the air compressor. If the air dryer is leaking, it should be repaired as soon as possible.

TURBOCHARGERS

The key factor to increasing the power output of a given displacement engine model is to trap a greater airmass and density of charge air in the cylinders. The main advantage of using a turbocharger (TC) assembly is that it allows more air to be packed into the engine cylinders, thereby increasing the volumetric efficiency (VE). The higher the VE, the greater is the quantity of fuel that can be injected and burned to completion. This results in a more thermally efficient engine, and one that can produce substantial increases in both engine power and torque characteristics over its naturally aspirated or nonturbocharged sibling.

There are several methods by which the mass of trapped air within the engine cylinders can be increased. One method is to use an engine gear-driven assembly similar to the Roots blower, which is widely used by Detroit Diesel and the General Motors Electro-Motive Division on their two-stroke-cycle engine models. The power requirements needed to drive the blower are not required, however, when an exhaust-gas-driven turbocharger is used. Virtually all of the exhaust energy leaving the cylinders is available to drive the TC turbine wheel shown in Figure 13–1. Only about 5% is lost to heat transfer of the surrounding components, and even less is lost when water-cooled exhaust manifolds are employed as in marine engine applications. The blower does have the advantage of producing a positive airflow at lower speeds and light loads, when the pressure and flow rate of the engine exhaust gases are lower than at rated full-load speed. The response time of the TC is generally slower than a gear-driven blower due to the small time lag involved when additional fuel must be injected until the higher pressure and flow of exhaust gases are available to drive the turbine.

Either one of these systems delivers boost air to the engine cylinders that is in excess of atmospheric pressure. The greater the air charge that can be retained within the engine cylinders at the start of the compression stroke, then the larger is the fuel volume that can be injected to produce a higher horsepower (kW). The pressure of the trapped air within the cylinders is controlled by the TC airflow capacity and, most important, by the intake and exhaust valve timing. The basic term for an engine that uses any device to increase the cylinder air charge is *supercharged*. A supercharged engine is an engine that takes air under pressure into the cylinders during the intake stroke and then compresses it. The degree of supercharging depends on the valve timing, since this controls when the intake valves close as the piston moves up the cylinder from BDC. Generally, gear-driven blowers are referred to as superchargers, whereas the exhaust-driven TC is simply called by the descriptive term *turbocharger*. Keep in mind, however, that both devices are capable of supplying air pressure to the engine cylinders that is higher than atmospheric pressure.

Each TC model is designed for a given displacement engine. The performance of a TC is defined by the pressure ratio, mass airflow rate, and the efficiency characteristics of both the compressor and turbine, as well as the mechanical efficiency of the bearing support assembly of the rotating components. The TC identification tag riveted on the center housing usually indicates the name of the manufacturer, the model and part number, and an *A/R* ratio—the area over the radius of the turbine housing. The letter *A* is the area of the exhaust gas inlet to the turbine wheel, and the letter *R* is the radius of the spiral of the turbine housing. This *A/R* number is very important because each number indicates that a slightly different housing is determined by turbocharger efficiency, airflow through the engine, engine application and speed range, and engine load (the unit injector size, or on inline injection pumps, the rack setting dimension).

Typical TC pressure ratios for high-speed diesel engines usually fall within the range of 2 to 2.5:1. The engine TC maximum boost pressures are determined by using a mercury (Hg) manometer connected to the inlet manifold (described later in this chapter). This is usually stated in inches of Hg at full-load-rated speed in the engine service manual.

Turbocharger Types

The two main types of turbocharging are the constant-pressure turbocharging (CPTC) model and the pulse turbocharging (PTC) model. In the CPTC system, the exhaust ports from all cylinders are connected to a single exhaust manifold whose volume is large enough to provide a near constant pressure feed to the TC turbine housing inlet. This system has the advantage of providing a near constant gas flow rate; therefore, the TC can be matched to operate at optimum efficiency at specified engine operating conditions, particularly on applications that run at fairly constant loads and speeds. The disadvantage is that the energy entering the turbine is low because the pulsing energy of the gases leaving each cylinder in firing order sequence is damped out through the single exhaust manifold assembly. This represents a loss of potential energy to the turbine.

The majority of high-speed heavy-duty diesel engines in use today, particularly the electronically controlled unit injector models of Caterpillar, Cummins, and Detroit Diesel, favor the pulse turbocharging design. In addition, they employ specially designed exhaust manifolds to increase the efficiency of the exhaust gases flowing into the TC turbine housing. Figure 13–19 illustrates the DDC series 50 and 60 pulse recovery exhaust manifold, which improves TC efficiency at low engine speeds.

Pressure waves are generated in the manifold by the exhaust gases rushing past the valves as they begin to open. The length of these passages is tuned to create a response within the manifold that directs the pressure waves to the hot turbine wheel where some of the kinetic energy is recovered. Tuned TCs also improve white smoke cleanup by producing higher engine intake air boost pressure at lower engine speeds, as well as improved TC bearing temperature control. In addition, turbocharger designs are usually of the type described as a single-stage radial flow compressor, and a radial flow turbine with both components mounted to the same shaft.

Figure 13–1 illustrates a typical TC system and the air and exhaust flow passages to and from the engine cylinders. Basically, the TC consists of a housing, illustrated in Figure 13–20, that is a bolted unit with both a turbine and a compressor housing. The turbine end of the TC is often referred to as the hot side because the exhaust gases enter here. The compressor end is often referred to as the cold end, because this is where the intake air from the air cleaner system enters the housing.

In the center housing of the TC is a one-piece support shaft that has a vaned turbine and compres-

FIGURE 13–19 Turbocharger with a pulse recovery exhaust manifold used with the DDC series 50 8.5-L four-cylinder DDEC-equipped engine model. (Courtesy of Detroit Diesel Corporation.)

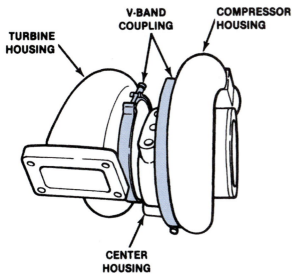

FIGURE 13–20 Three major components of a typical high-speed heavy-duty engine turbocharger assembly. (Courtesy of Detroit Diesel Corporation.)

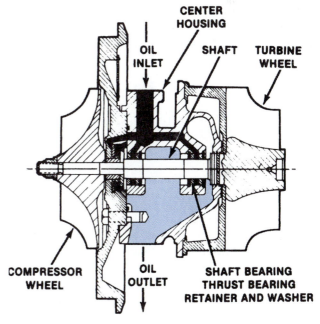

FIGURE 13–21 Sectional view of a turbocharger identifying the major components and showing the pressurized inlet oil flow into the center housing, then draining through the bottom to the oil outlet routed to the oil pan. (Courtesy of Detroit Diesel Corporation.)

sor wheel pressed onto each end. The compressor wheel is usually retained by a self-locking nut, and the turbine wheel is often part of the support shaft assembly. The rotating components are supported within the TC housing by bearings (bushings) that are pressure lubricated by engine oil directed to the center housing by a hydraulic or steel-braided hose. This allows a constant reservoir of oil to be maintained in the center housing. The pressurized oil supply actually results in the rotating shaft and components

being supported on an oil film during high-speed engine operation. Therefore, the term *floating bearings* is often used to describe this type of system. Figure 13–21 illustrates these floating bearings on the support shaft. The bearings also act as thrust surfaces to absorb the thrust loads as the rotating assembly changes position during engine operation. Figure 13–22 illustrates the TC lubrication supply and drain lines, whereas Figure 13–21 shows the actual pressurized oil flow within the TC center housing. The large drain line allows hot oil to return to the engine crankcase. On some TC models, oil drains directly through a passageway in the engine block or through the blower end plate on some DDC two-stroke-cycle engines where the TC is mounted directly to the gear-driven blower.

The easiest way to understand TC operation is to view it as a large air pump. The hot pressurized exhaust gases leaving the exhaust manifold are directed into the turbine area. As these gases expand through the housing to the atmosphere, they cause rotation of the turbine wheel and shaft. The compressor wheel mounted on the opposite end of the support shaft is driven at the same speed. This speed of rotation averages about 100,000 rpm; speeds may be higher or lower depending on the design characteristics of the TC assembly. The compressor wheel draws air in through the air cleaner system, compresses it, and delivers it to the engine intake manifold on four-stroke-cycle models. On two-stroke-cycle DDC engines, the TC delivers its airflow to the gear-driven engine Roots

blower. The TC responds to engine airflow demands by reacting to the flow of exhaust gases. As the power demands of the engine increase and the operator depresses the throttle, the exhaust gas flow increases, causing an increase in the speed of the rotating components. Since the TC relies on exhaust gas flow, there is always a small time lag between the additional injected fuel and the actual TC response. This time has been reduced to almost an unnoticeable point on new TCs by use of smaller and lighter rotating components that are often made of ceramics rather than aluminum alloy metals. Many diesel TCs employ engine coolant passages cast within the center housing to assist in maintaining the lube oil below the coking temperature. Otherwise, hot oil (particularly after engine shutdown) can actually boil and create carbon buildup within the lube oil passages and eventual plugging of the lube oil supply to the TC support bearings.

When air is pressurized, its temperature increases and its mass (density) decreases accordingly. Either JWAC or AAAC systems are widely employed on modern engines to reduce the temperature of the pressurized air entering the engine intake manifold or the two-stroke-cycle airbox.

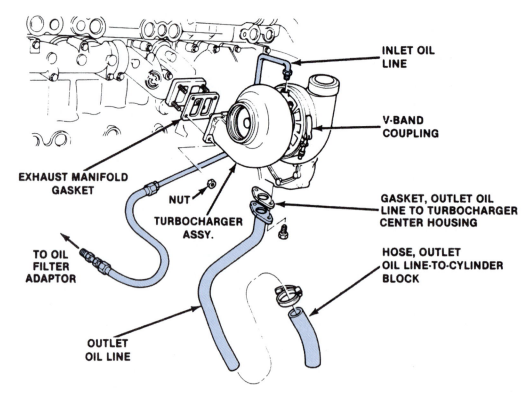

FIGURE 13–22 *Location of the turbocharger oil supply and drain lines for a heavy-duty high-speed series 60 engine model. (Courtesy of Detroit Diesel Corporation.)*

Wastegate Turbochargers

Many current high-speed on-highway truck diesel engines have wastegate turbochargers. Examples are the 5.9-L Cummins engine used in the Dodge Ram pickup truck, the 7.3-L Navistar engine used in Ford and Navistar trucks, and the 6.5-L GMC V8 diesel. Heavier-duty engines using this TC include the Cat 3116 and the Cat 3406E—ratings of 435 bhp (325 kW) and higher. Engines rated below 435 bhp use a fixed, nonceramic wheel that spins 6% faster than the 3406C engine model TC. A wastegate TC is designed to improve engine low-end performance and transient response, limit peak cylinder pressures, lower heat rejection and turbo speed, and reduce exhaust emissions. In addition, use of a wastegate allows very close matching to either an overdrive or manual transmission used in vehicles. The wastegate system can be adjusted to limit the maximum amount of boost depending on specific application needs, and the system provides improved throttle response at both the low-end and midrange loads.

An example of the location of a turbocharger wastegate can be seen in Figure 13–23. A hose is connected to the body of the wastegate from the cold end of the outlet of the turbo assembly. Pressurized air (turbo boost) is routed into the wastegate control housing where it works against a spring-loaded diaphragm and linkage connected to the housing at the hot side (exhaust gas outlet) of the turbocharger. When the air pressure exceeds the spring setting in the control housing, the wastegate linkage shifts a small butterfly-type valve within the exhaust manifold porting area. This routes the exhaust gas flow around the turbine wheel, thereby bypassing, or wasting, the heat energy around the turbine housing and back into the upstream side of the exhaust manifold piping. When the boost pressure within the intake manifold of the engine is reduced, the spring within the turbo wastegate control housing automatically reopens the wastegate valve to redirect the hot exhaust gases back into the turbine wheel area of the turbo, allowing boost to once again be delivered to the engine. There is usually an adjustable pushrod, as shown in Figure 13–23B, that must be set to ensure that the butterfly valve within the wastegate remains in either the fully open or fully closed position.

Some electronically controlled diesel engines now employ wastegated turbochargers that are controlled directly from the ECM. One example is the wastegate used by Cummins on their 15-L DOHC ISX and Signature models. Two solenoids are used to allow a four-step wastegate control system to effectively control turbocharger boost in stepped sequences. This permits maximum engine performance and fuel economy under varying loads, speeds, and operating conditions. Figure 13–23a illustrates the component parts of the Cummins ISX/Signature wastegate turbocharger, and Figure 13–23b shows the wastegate in both its open and closed conditions. When open, exhaust gases are routed directly around the hot end (turbine) of the turbocharger to limit its speed, and therefore its boost pressure. The effective stroke of the wastegate bypass valve and therefore the amount of hot gases bypassed is controlled by the ECM.

Too much or too low a turbocharger boost can lead to engine and power problems. This can often be traced back to a 'wastegate' that has not been correctly adjusted, particularly after turbocharger overhaul, or when an exchange or new unit has been installed. Assuming that the correct A/R ratio turbo has been installed, refer to Figure 13–24 and connect the tooling shown. Refer to the specific engine and turbocharger model specs to determine at what pressure the regulator valve (Item 5) should be set in order to check that the wastegate opens when it should. If not, adjust the wastegate linkage until the proper opening spec is obtained.

Turbocharger Back Pressure Device

Another unique design feature in use on some turbochargers in high-speed diesel engines is the exhaust gas back pressure device. It is being used on the International 7.3-L T 444E V8 engine that employs hydraulically actuated electronic unit injectors. Since this is a direct-injection design engine, less heat is rejected to the coolant than in an indirect-injection engine. To provide rapid warm-up in cold ambient conditions, an exhaust gas back pressure device is employed within the turbocharger (Figure 13–25). This device consists of a butterfly valve that is controlled and actuated by a solenoid and actuator piston. The butterfly valve is powered hydraulically with engine oil supplied to the turbocharger bearings. The valve is only operational at idle and light load, when engine temperature and ambient temperature are low; therefore, once the engine is warmed up, the device is turned off. At temperatures below approximately 38°F (3°C), the device is activated by the electronic control unit on the vehicle, which is a variant of Ford Motor Company's EEC-IV control module. A signal from the control module opens an oil passage to charge the actuator cylinder, which in turn moves the actuator piston and closes the butterfly valve located in the exhaust outlet area of the turbocharger to restrict the exhaust flow. This action increases the exhaust back pressure and consequently the pumping effort required by the engine. This back

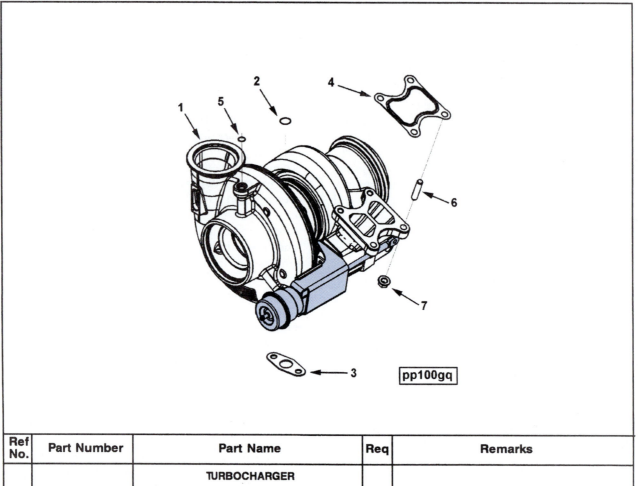

Ref No.	Part Number	Part Name	Req	Remarks
		TURBOCHARGER		
		OPTION PP10146		
				HX60W: 600 HP (S600 and QS15) Application: Automotive And Industrial Crankcase breather type: Open.
	3800770	Kit, Turbocharger	1	
1	(3592544)	Turbocharger	1	
2	3679139	Seal, O Ring	1	
3	3680324	Gasket, Flange	1	
4	3680465	Gasket, Turbocharger	1	
5	3883963	Seal, O Ring	1	
6	3095798	Stud	4	
7	3818824	Nut, Hexagon Flange	4	M10 X 1.50.

(a)

FIGURE 13–23 (a) Turbocharger and components for a Cummins 600 hp (448 kW) Signature series engine model equipped with a wastegate to limit turbocharger boost pressure. (Courtesy of Cummins Engine Company, Inc.)

pressure is monitored by a pressure sensor in the exhaust manifold. Thus, an electronic closed-loop strategy ensures that the exhaust back pressure is held at levels that will not affect driveability under varying speed, load, and acceleration conditions over a limited range of engine temperatures.

Turbocharger Maintenance

Properly maintained TCs should provide trouble-free service between engine overhauls. The three key maintenance items that affect the life of a turbocharger are excessive AIR (air inlet restriction), high EPB (exhaust back pressure), and lubrication of bearings. Un-

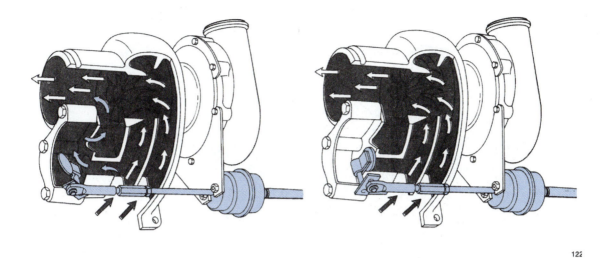

(b)   **Wastegate OPEN**   **Wastegate CLOSED**

FIGURE 13–23   (continued). (b) Signature/ISX engine turbocharger with the wastegate open, and the wastegate closed. (Courtesy of Cummins Engine Company, Inc.)

filtered air entering the TC can cause fine lapping of the rotating components, and high AIR can cause lube oil to be drawn past the seals. On mechanically governed engines, high AIR and high EBP can create incomplete combustion which leads to carbon buildup on the rotating turbine wheel. This, in turn, can create an imbalance condition of the rotating components and the turbine blading may actually come into contact with the housing. On electronically controlled diesel engines, the various intake system sensors prevent the engines from being overfueled as a result of a high AIR condition.

Leaks at the TC exhaust gaskets can prevent the rotating components from reaching the proper speed under load. This, in turn, reduces the boost pressure to the engine cylinders. Leaking gaskets or intake manifold seal rings on the outlet side of the TC compressor wheel can create a high-pitched whistle, particularly under load as the boost pressure forces its way past these areas.

TC inspection is best performed with the engine stopped and the intake ducting removed. Check for dirt and dust buildup on the compressor wheel impeller and in the housing. Excessive signs of dirt suggest that the air inlet ducting is not airtight, so perform the checks discussed earlier in this chapter and shown in Figure 13–16. You can also disconnect the exhaust piping to inspect the hot end of the turbo. Pay particular attention to the condition of the carbon buildup on the turbine vanes. Light carbon usually is indicative of

light-load operation and/or excessive periods of idling. Do not attempt to remove carbon buildup from the vanes without removing the TC from the engine and disassembling it. Any signs of physical damage to either the compressor or turbine wheels are sufficient reason for immediate removal and replacement of these rotating assemblies. If damaged TC blading disintegrated during engine operation and the parts were inhaled into the engine cylinders, complete engine failure might be the result.

With the engine stopped, rotate the turbine wheel by hand to check for smooth and free operation. Any tight spots or signs of turbine or compressor wheel contact with their respective housings require TC removal and disassembly. Also examine the TC compressor intake area for signs of oil leaks. If oil is found, both the *axial* and *radial* clearances of the rotating assembly should be checked. These checks can be performed by means of a dial indicator gauge assembly mounted over the TC as illustrated in Figures 13–26a and 13–26b. When checking the TC radial clearance with a dial gauge, use an offset gauge plunger as shown so that it comes into contact with the shaft through the oil inlet hole. Grasp the TC main shaft and slowly move it up and down while reading the dial gauge. To check the axial clearance (end to end), install and preload the dial gauge so that its pointer rests against the end of the shaft as shown in Figure 13–26b. Push and pull the shaft backward and forward to record the end play.

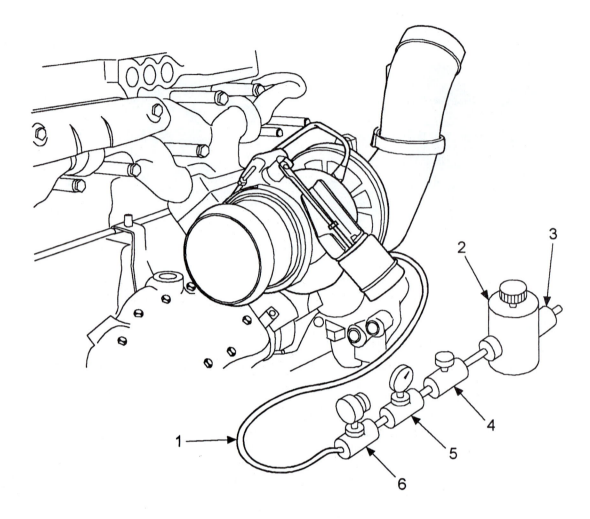

1. Hose to Wastegate Actuator	4. Supply Air Shutoff Valve
2. Vent Valve	5. Pressure Regulator
3. Pressure Gage	6. Shop Air Supply

FIGURE 13–24 Tool hookup to check that the turbocharger wastegate calibration is set to 'open' at the correct pressure setting. (Courtesy of Detroit Diesel Corporation.)

Compare the radial and axial readings obtained to the specifications listed in the TC or engine service manual literature. Both of these clearances are fairly small on high-speed engine TCs. Radial clearances are usually in the range 0.006 to 0.021 in. (0.15 to 0.53 mm); axial clearances usually run between 0.001 to 0.014 in. (0.025 and 0.35 mm), although specific models may allow greater clearances than these. If a dial indicator is not readily available, radial clearance can be checked by using a wire-type feeler gauge between the vanes and housing. Hold the TC shaft toward the feeler gauge to check this dimension.

When a suspected oil leak at the TC seal from the hot end (turbine) cannot be confirmed on a stopped en-

gine, a commercially available fluorescent tracer liquid additive can be mixed with the engine lube oil. Normally, add one unit of the tracer to each 10 U.S. gallons

CAUTION Under certain engine and turbocharger running test conditions, it may be necessary to remove the inlet ducting. If this is the case, refer to Figure 13–27 and always install a TC inlet shield to prevent the possibility of foreign objects or loose clothing being pulled into the rotating components. Never run a TC engine with this shield removed since serious personal injury can result.

Butterfly Valve

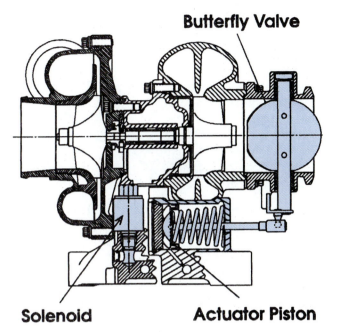

Solenoid   **Actuator Piston**

FIGURE 13–25 *Concept of an exhaust back pressure device used on the Navistar/International 7.3-L T444E V8 HEUI (hydraulically actuated electronic unit injector) engine model. (Reprinted with permission of the Society of Automotive Engineers, Inc., 2001.)*

4. Stop the engine.

5. Allow the turbocharger to cool and remove the exhaust pipe from the hot end (turbine) of the housing.

6. Use a high-intensity black light to inspect the turbine outlet for oil.

7. A dark-blue glow usually indicates a raw fuel leak, whereas a yellow glow indicates a lube oil leak.

8. Remove the TC oil drain line and check it carefully. Lube oil leaks may be traced back to restrictions within this drain line. Clean any restrictions and/or replace a damaged or collapsed drain line or hose.

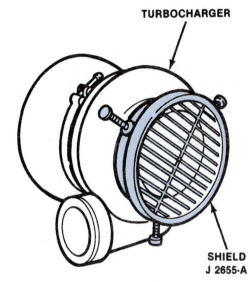

TURBOCHARGER

SHIELD
J 2655-A

FIGURE 13–27 *Installation of a turbocharger safety shield. Always use while running the engine when the air inlet piping/ducting is disconnected. (Courtesy of Detroit Diesel Corporation.)*

(38 L) of engine lube oil. Refer to the packaging for specific directions.

To test a TC seal for leakage, follow these steps:

1. Start and run the engine until normal operating temperature is reached.

2. Stop the engine and add the recommended amount of fluorescent tracer to the engine oil.

3. Start and operate the engine at low idle for 10 minutes.

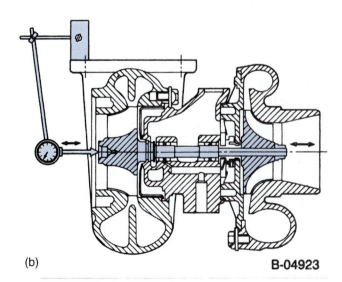

A. Oil Feed Port
B. Oil Drain Port

(a)   B-04922

(b)   B-04923

FIGURE 13–26 *(a) Mounting a dial indicator gauge to check the turbocharger bearing radial clearance. (b) Mounting a dial indicator gauge to check the turbocharger rotating assembly axial (end) play. (Courtesy of Detroit Diesel Corporation.)*

9.   Check for restrictions in the engine breather or tube, because high crankcase pressure can also cause the TC seals to leak.

Turbocharger Removal and Disassembly

Removal of the TC from the engine is a fairly straight-forward process. Refer to Figure 13–22 and note that the TC hot-end housing flange is bolted to a mating flange on the engine exhaust manifold. A gasket is located between the mating surfaces. The cold end of the TC is usually connected to the air inlet piping or ducting by use of a heavy-duty thick-walled rubber hose and clamp arrangement. In addition, the various lube oil supply and drain lines must be disconnected. Carefully sling the TC with a suitable lifting tackle prior to removing the retaining bolts that hold it to the exhaust manifold.

If it is necessary to disassemble the TC assembly, always match-mark the hot and cold ends of the housing to the center housing assembly to allow reinstallation of the components in the same position. Figure 13–28 illustrates the three main TC components split apart after either loosening off the special band clamps or removing the bolts on some models. Most service facilities simply replace a damaged TC with a new or rebuilt one, since special equipment is required to overhaul and rebalance the rotating components. If, however, the TC is to be disassembled, the self-locking retaining nut on the compressor wheel end of the assembly must be removed and the back side of the compressor wheel must be supported on a hydraulic press: Use an old nut over the threads while applying pressure to it so that the shaft and turbine wheel assembly pop from the compressor wheel. Special pliers are usually required to remove the snap rings to reach the seals and bearings (bushings). In some cases a series of small bolts at the center housing must also be removed to access these components.

Carefully inspect all disassembled components. Compare all dimensions of the parts with those in the service manual. Replace all worn or damaged components. When reassembling the TC, make sure to align the match marks that were applied during the disassembly procedure.

Reinstall the TC assembly onto the engine using the reverse procedure of removal. Always use new self-locking nuts to retain the TC to the exhaust manifold. Remember that a new or rebuilt TC must be prelubricated before engine startup. Refer to Figure 13–29 and pour clean engine oil into the bearing housing cavity while turning the rotating assembly by hand to lubricate all of the internal components. With the turbo guard shown in Figure 13–27 in position, start the engine and run at an idle speed; do not use a wide-open throttle (WOT) condition. It is also usually good prac-

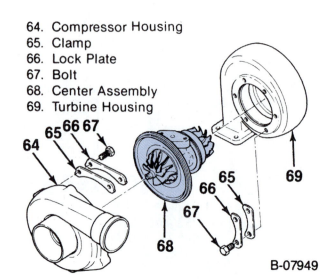

64. Compressor Housing
65. Clamp
66. Lock Plate
67. Bolt
68. Center Assembly
69. Turbine Housing

B-07949

FIGURE 13–28 *Disassembled view of the three main components of a turbocharger. (Courtesy of Detroit Diesel Corporation.)*

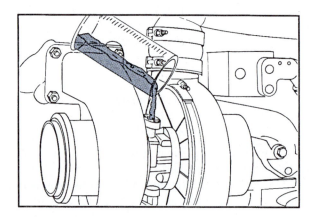

FIGURE 13–29 *Priming a new or rebuilt turbocharger by pouring clean engine oil into the reservoir of the center housing prior to engine startup. (Courtesy of Cummins Engine Company, Inc.)*

tice to leave the oil supply line slightly loose on engine startup, until you can confirm that a steady flow of lube oil is reaching the TC center housing. If no lube oil is evident within 30 seconds maximum, shut the engine down and determine the cause.

Once the engine has warmed up, carefully listen for any unusual metallic rattles or scraping sounds. After the engine has been stopped, the TC should coast freely and smoothly to a stop. Any signs of a jerky or sudden stop should be investigated and corrected.

Troubleshooting Turbochargers

Generally, when a turbocharged engine lacks power, emits black smoke, or shows signs of oil (blue smoke) at the exhaust stack, the turbocharger may not be at fault. Often the cause is TC related, but other factors can cause or contribute to these symptoms. Spend a few minutes first in checking possible causes before you start to remove the TC from the engine.

One of the easiest and most useful methods is to listen, look, and feel as described next.

Listen

Since the turbocharger is a standard item on most heavy-duty diesel engines manufactured today, most of us know what a normal-running turbocharger sounds like. Unusual TC operating sounds that you should be aware of include these:

1. A high-pitched whine, particularly under load, can be created by an exhaust gas leak or by a leak in the air induction piping between the TC and the engine intake manifold.

2. A sharp high-pitched scream is generally indicative of worn bearings or possibly that the turbine or compressor wheel is rubbing on its housing.

3. A cycling up and down in sound pitch can indicate air starvation or blockage in the air inlet duct system, a restricted air cleaner, or a buildup in dirt on the compressor wheel or diffuser vanes within the TC housing.

Look

One of the most important tools for troubleshooting is sight. Disconnect the exhaust and inlet piping from the TC housing assembly. Then make the following visual determinations:

1. Use either a flashlight or Trouble-light and carefully look into the turbine and compressor end of the TC. Are there any signs of rubbing marks (polishing) on either the wheels or the housing?

2. Are any of the blades (vanes) on the turbine or compressor wheels bent or damaged?

3. Is there heavy dirt buildup on the compressor wheel? This would indicate unfiltered air, possibly coming from a leak in the air ducting, or poor filter maintenance intervals.

4. Check for signs of heavy carbon or soot buildup on the vanes of the turbine wheel. This is indicative of incomplete combustion or burning oil (possibly from TC seals).

5. If heavy oil accumulations are noticeable, check for the possible source. Oil may be from TC seals, although oil in the compressor inlet may not necessarily be coming from the TC seals. Also check that the engine air compressor is not pumping oil.

6. Oil at the turbine end usually indicates an engine fault rather than a TC problem. Check the exhaust manifold for signs of engine oil accumulations, which may be from worn or broken rings on the pistons or worn valve guides. On two-stroke-cycle DDC models,

leaking blower seals could contribute to the oil accumulations as well as leaking solid piston pin retainers or operation of the engine for long idle periods or under light-load conditions.

7. Turbochargers generally use metal piston seal rings rather than lip seals that are used on crankshafts. Therefore, the oil sealing on the TC is known as dynamic sealing. Oil slingers keep the oil away from the seal ring areas. Check these common causes of leaking TC seals: excessive engine idling, plugged crankcase breather system (high crankcase pressure), sludge buildup or accumulations within the center housing of the TC, high air inlet restriction conditions, plugged or kinked TC oil drain line, damage to the TC bearings or wheels, and worn piston rings in the engine (blowby).

Heavy carbon buildup on the turbine wheel can be cleaned once the end housing has been removed to allow access. Use a noncorrosive cleaning solvent and a soft-bristle brush. Avoid the use of a wire brush, screwdriver, or gasket scraper which could scratch, damage, or nick the blades. It is important that carbon be thoroughly removed; if not, an imbalance condition could lead to the wheel striking the housing once the engine is started. If the TC has to be completely disassembled to clean the carbon, a glass-beading machine can be used. Make sure that you use only the recommended material for cleaning, for example, walnut shells.

Feel

To avoid personal injury, make sure that the engine is stopped and the TC has been allowed to cool off. Then perform the following checks:

1. Slowly rotate the turbo wheels by hand. They should turn easily and smoothly.

2. Push inward against each wheel one at a time as you rotate it by hand. Once again, it should rotate smoothly and freely.

3. Determine if there are any signs of rubbing or scraping; these indicate a major problem.

4. Determine if the TC rotates smoothly and freely; if it does not, a major problem is indicated.

5. After replacing a new or rebuilt TC, always prelube the turbo as shown in Figure 13–29. Check the intake and exhaust system ducting (piping) for any signs of foreign objects. Check the TC oil supply and return line and the air filter ducting to ensure that all connections are airtight. Do the same on the exhaust system.

Figure 13–30 lists typical operational conditions that you may experience when dealing with turbochargers along with possible causes and suggested corrections.

Engine lacks power	Black exhaust smoke	Excessive engine oil consumption	Blue exhaust smoke	Turbocharger noisy	Cyclic sound from turbocharger	Oil leak from compressor seal	Oil leak from turbine seal	CAUSE	CORRECTION
•	•		•	•		•		Clogged air filter element	Replace element according to engine service manual recommendations
	•	•	•	•	•	•		Obstructed air intake duct to turbo compressor	Remove obstruction or replace damaged parts as required
•	•		•					Obstructed air outlet duct from compressor to intake/manifold	Remove obstruction or replace damaged parts as required
•	•		•					Obstructed intake/manifold	Refer to engine service manual & remove obstruction
				•				Air leak in duct from air cleaner to compressor	Correct leak by replacing seals or tightening fasteners as required
•	•	•	•	•				Air leak in duct from compressor to intake/manifold	Correct leak by replacing seals or tightening fasteners as required
•	•	•	•	•				Air leak at intake/manifold engine inlet	Refer to engine service manual & replace gaskets or tighten fasteners as required
•	•	•	•	•		•		Obstruction in exhaust manifold	Refer to engine service manual & remove obstruction
•	•					•		Obstruction in muffler or exhaust stack	Remove obstruction or replace faulty components as required
•	•		•			•		Gas leak in exhaust manifold to engine connection	Refer to engine service manual & replace gaskets or tighten fasteners as required
•	•		•			•		Gas leak in turbine inlet to exhaust manifold connection	Replace gasket or tighten fasteners as required
				•				Gas leak in ducting after the turbine outlet	Refer to engine service manual & repair leak
		•	•			•	•	Obstructed turbocharger oil drain line	Remove obstruction or replace line as required
		•	•			•	•	Obstructed engine crankcase vent	Refer to engine service manual, clean obstruction
		•	•			•	•	Turbocharger center housing sludged or coked	Change engine oil & filter, overhaul or replace turbo as required
•	•							Fuel injectors incorrect output	Refer to engine service manual — replace or adjust faulty component(s) as required
•	•							Engine camshaft timing incorrect	Refer to engine service manual & replace worn parts
•	•	•	•			•	•	Worn engine piston rings or liners (blowby)	Refer to engine service manual & repair engine as required
•	•	•	•			•	•	Internal engine problem (valves, pistons)	Refer to engine service manual & repair engine as required
•	•	•	•	•	•	•	•	Dirt caked on compressor wheel and/or diffuser vanes	Clean using a *Non-Caustic* cleaner & *Soft Brush*. Find & correct source of unfiltered air & change engine oil & oil filter
•	•	•	•	•		•	•	Damaged turbocharger	Analyze failed turbocharger, find & correct cause of failure, overhaul or replace turbocharger as required

FIGURE 13–30 Typical turbocharger troubleshooting chart. (Courtesy of Detroit Diesel Corporation.)

APPEARANCE OF BEARINGS

Slight wear or scratches	Moderate to heavy gooving on O.D. only	Moderate to heavy grooving on O.D. & I.D.	Extruded, or pounded. (May be stuck in ctr. hsg.)	Smooth undersized O.D.	Cracked or broken	Deep groove around center of O.D.	Oil holes fully or partially closed	Oil holes plugged with carbon	I.D. Polished looking O.D.	Polished & worn oversize	Melted (aluminum bearing)	CONDITION	PROBABLE CAUSE
•												Normal Use	Acceptable operating & maintenance procedures
	•											Contaminated oil (dirt in oil)	Engine oil & oil filter(s) not changed frequently enough, unfiltered air entering engine intake, malfunction of oil filter bypass valve
		•		•								Severely contaminated (dirty oil)	
			•	•	•							Pounded by eccentric shaft motion	Foreign object damage, coked or loose housing, excessive bearing clearance due to lube problem
				•				•				Center housing bearing bores, rough finish	Incorrect cleaning of center housing during overhaul of turbo. (Wrong chemicals, bores sand or bead blasted)
					•							Metal or large particle oil contamination	Severe engine wear. i.e., Bearing damage, camshaft or lifter wear, broken piston
						•				•		Lack of lube, oil lag, insufficient lube	Low oil level, high speed shutdowns, lube system failure, turbo plugged with hose fitting sealants
							•					Coking	Hot shutdowns, engine overfueled, restricted or leaking air intake/inlet
					•				•	•		Fine particles in oil (contaminated oil)	See contaminated oil
									•			Rough bearing journals on shaft	Bearing journals not protected from sand or bead blast cleaning during overhaul

GLOSSARY OF TERMS

ALIGNMENT — Proper position of parts.

BURR — Sharp metal.

COLD END — Compressor end of turbocharger.

CONTAINER — A box used to hold material.

DISCOLORATION — Change in color.

DISSIPATED — Dispersing or dispelling of heat.

DO NOT REUSE — Excessive damage - part requires replacement or possible remanufacturing.

EROSION — Gradual wear of material.

EXCESSIVE — Too much.

GLASS BEADING — Procedure used to clean parts where air under pressure is used to force small glass particles at a high rate of speed against the surface of the part.

HOT SHUTDOWN — Shutdown at high rpm will cause the turbocharger to continue spinning after the lubricant supply from the oil pump has stopped. Bearings will not be adequately lubricated or cooled.

HOT SIDE — Turbine side of turbocharger.

NICK — Small notch.

PITTING — Wear that causes holes in the material.

POLISH — To clean and smooth the surface.

REUSE — Parts that require inspection and reconditioning according to published specifications.

ROTATING UNIT — Compressor wheel-shaft-turbine assembly.

RUBBING — Contact between two parts.

SEVERELY — To a large degree.

SLIGHTLY — To a small degree.

STRAIGHTEN — Make straight.

WARP — To twist or bend out of shape.

FIGURE 13–30 (continued).

EXHAUST MUFFLERS AND PARTICULATE TRAPS

Mufflers used on diesel engines can vary tremendously in physical size and design. Their purpose, however, is the same: to allow the escaping exhaust gases, which are under pressure, to expand within the muffler, thereby reducing the noise emitted as they exit into the atmosphere. Exhaust noise is caused by sound pressure waves that cause small changes in atmospheric pressure. The frequency, or pitch, of sound pressure waves is measured in cycles per second. Typical noise levels from a heavy-duty highway truck or trailer are usually within the 80 to 86 decibels (dB range).

Two typical muffler designs are illustrated in Figure 13–31. In the straight-through design, baffles located between the inlet and outlet cause the pressurized exhaust gases to follow a given path through connecting tubes. In the reverse-flow muffler design, the gases flow through connecting tubes. The muffler can be mounted either horizontally or vertically, as is the case on many heavy-duty on- and off-highway trucks and equipment.

Sometimes a small, round *spark arrestor* is added to the pipe exiting from the muffler assembly. This spark arrestor traps most incendiary sparks, thereby reducing any fire hazard, which is important in logging equipment, for example. The venting of glowing carbon particles blown out with the exhaust gases can retain sufficient heat to ignite surrounding materials. Stainless steel vanes inside the inlet tube spin exhaust gases and solid particles. Centrifugal force throws particles to the periphery of the tube where they move in an ascending spiral. When the particles pass the end of the inlet tube, they are thrown out of the gas stream into the outer chamber of the spark arrestor where they fall through a baffle and are collected in the carbon trap where they remain until the unit is serviced. The trap can be serviced by removing a clean-out plug located on the underside of the body. Any crust that has been formed over the hole can be broken with a screwdriver. Start the engine and run it at high idle to blow collected

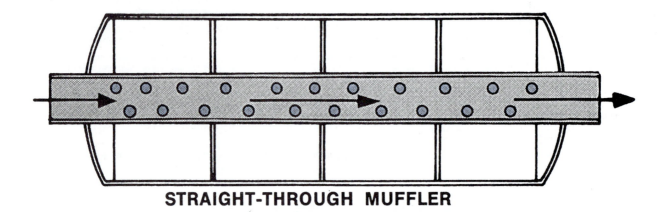

STRAIGHT-THROUGH MUFFLER

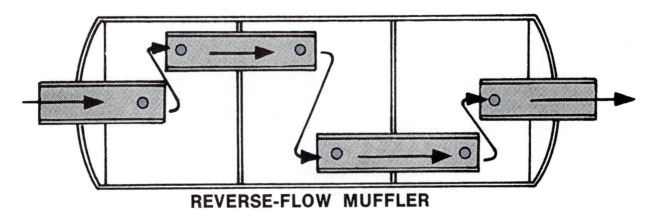

REVERSE-FLOW MUFFLER

FIGURE 13–31   Exhaust gas flow through two typical muffler assemblies.

particles out of the clean-out hole. Replace the plug when finished.

A rather widely used exhaust silencer is the *COWL* spiral silencer manufactured by Phillips & Temro (Figure 13–32). The exhaust gases are routed through an aluminum-coated 14- or 16-gauge cold-rolled steel housing. This type of a silencer is much more compact than the conventional exhaust muffler system and offers superior noise reduction. The COWL silencer consists of a spiral passage of constant cross-sectional area. The spiral is partially lined with noise absorbing stainless steel wool. The exhaust gases can pass from one spiral passage to another through bleed holes within the spiral body. Since sound waves travel in straight lines at a speed much higher than the speed of the exhaust gases passing through the silencer, they are continually bounced off the smooth wall of the spiral. Some of these sound waves are reflected into the wool-covered wall, where they are diffused. Other sound waves pass through the bleed holes, progressively attenuating the sound by wave cancellation as the gases pass through the multiple turns of the spiral. Any contaminants flowing into the silencer are centrifugally forced to the smooth outer surface and pass through the silencer, thus ensuring that no buildup of deposits occurs.

GEAR-DRIVEN BLOWERS

Figure 2–5 illustrates airflow through the engine of a V-model DDC engine. On larger models, two blowers are used, and on the DDC 20V-149 engine model three blower assemblies are needed since this engine consists of a V6–V8–V6 arrangement bolted together. The major function of the blower in two-stroke engines is to supply air at pressures between 4 and 7 psi (27 to 48 kPa) to the engine *airbox* area, which acts as a reservoir for a header of charged air. Remember, in a two-cycle engine the intake and exhaust strokes are physically eliminated, so pressurized air is needed and is used for several purposes:

- Supply fresh air for combustion
- Cool the cylinder liner, piston crown, and exhaust valves
- Scavenge waste exhaust gases from the cylinder
- Allow a controlled amount of air leakage past the piston oil control rings when at TDC to provide for positive crankcase ventilation

Blower Construction

The basic construction of the blower illustrated in Figure 13–33 consists of an aluminum housing, two end plates, and two aluminum three-lobe rotors supported on ball and roller bearings within the end plates. As the blower rotates, air is trapped between the lobes and the housing to produce a positive air displacement into the engine airbox. Figure 13–33 illustrates the major parts of a typical blower assembly used on a DDC V92 series engine. The blower is mounted on a machined pad on top of the engine block between both cylinder heads and is bolted in position. A splined shaft driven from

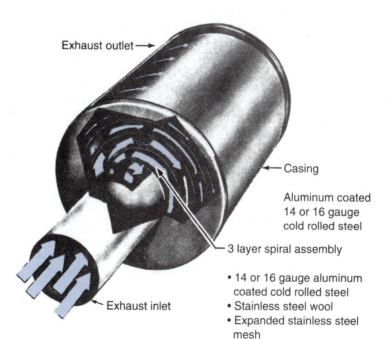

Exhaust outlet

Casing

Aluminum coated 14 or 16 gauge cold rolled steel

3 layer spiral assembly

- 14 or 16 gauge aluminum coated cold rolled steel
- Stainless steel wool
- Expanded stainless steel mesh

Exhaust inlet

FIGURE 13–32 *Features of a COWL spiral exhaust silencer assembly. (Courtesy of Temro Division, Budd Canada, Inc.)*

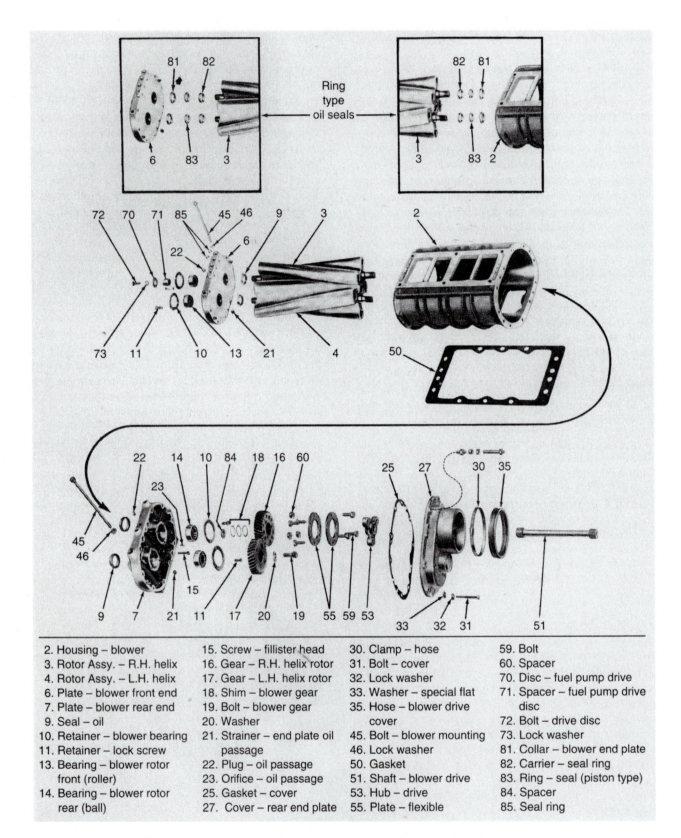

2. Housing – blower	15. Screw – fillister head	30. Clamp – hose	59. Bolt
3. Rotor Assy. – R.H. helix	16. Gear – R.H. helix rotor	31. Bolt – cover	60. Spacer
4. Rotor Assy. – L.H. helix	17. Gear – L.H. helix rotor	32. Lock washer	70. Disc – fuel pump drive
6. Plate – blower front end	18. Shim – blower gear	33. Washer – special flat	71. Spacer – fuel pump drive
7. Plate – blower rear end	19. Bolt – blower gear	35. Hose – blower drive	disc
9. Seal – oil	20. Washer	cover	72. Bolt – drive disc
10. Retainer – blower bearing	21. Strainer – end plate oil	45. Bolt – blower mounting	73. Lock washer
11. Retainer – lock screw	passage	46. Lock washer	81. Collar – blower end plate
13. Bearing – blower rotor	22. Plug – oil passage	50. Gasket	82. Carrier – seal ring
front (roller)	23. Orifice – oil passage	51. Shaft – blower drive	83. Ring – seal (piston type)
14. Bearing – blower rotor	25. Gasket – cover	53. Hub – drive	84. Spacer
rear (ball)	27. Cover – rear end plate	55. Plate – flexible	85. Seal ring

FIGURE 13–33 Exploded view illustrating the component parts of a gear-driven blower assembly for a DDC two-stroke-cycle engine. (Courtesy of Detroit Diesel Corporation.)

336

the rear of the engine (gear train end) is also splined into a blower drive gear at the rear end of the right-hand rotor. The blower is driven at approximately twice engine speed. On mechanically governed engines, the front end plate of the blower supports and drives the fuel transfer pump as well as the governor assembly. On DDEC two-cycle engine models, the blower front end plate simply supports the fuel pump, since all engine governing is controlled from the engine ECM.

Blower Operation

The airflow rates of blowers depend on their physical size and speed of rotation. Typical engine airflow rates depend on displacement and speed. The power required to rotate a gear- or belt-driven blower can be substantial; for example, average power is between 25 and 30 hp on many high-speed automotive truck engines when running at maximum rated speed. To reduce this parasitic power loss, Detroit Diesel uses a bypass blower arrangement on its two-stroke-cycle engine models, which are also equipped with a turbocharger assembly. Recall that a turbocharger only provides pressurized airflow once the engine is running and under load. It is necessary, therefore, on two-cycle engines to employ a gear-driven blower so that a positive air displacement can be supplied to the engine for starting purposes and light-load operation. Once the engine is placed under load, the hot pressurized exhaust gases allow the turbocharger to supply all the necessary air requirements for the engine, and the gear-driven blower becomes unnecessary.

The principle employed by DDC to disengage the blower is a *bypass valve*. This bypass valve and its location are shown in Figure 13–34 and the concept of operation is illustrated in Figure 13–35. The spring-loaded bypass relief valve contained within the rear end plate of the blower is held closed during engine startup and also during low-rpm and light-load conditions. When the engine speed is increased and load is applied, the turbocharger boost air pressure increases to raise the air pressure within the engine airbox area. On 6V and 8V-92 model DDC engines, when this air-box pressure reaches approximately 6 psi (12 in. Hg/305 mm manometer fluid displacement) or 41 kPa, the spring-loaded bypass valve opens. Under this valve-open condition, turbocharger boost air is free to bypass the blower rotors and enter the engine airbox. The blower is gear driven, so it will continue to rotate, but since the bypass valve is wide open, all the required air pressure is being supplied from the turbocharger assembly and the pressure rise across the blower (inlet to outlet) is greatly reduced. During this bypass mode

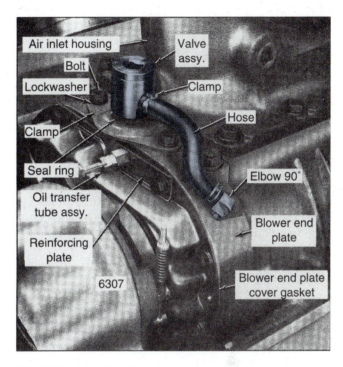

FIGURE 13–34 Location of the gear-driven blower bypass valve assembly located in the blower end plate for a two-stroke-cycle DDC engine. (Courtesy of Detroit Diesel Corporation.)

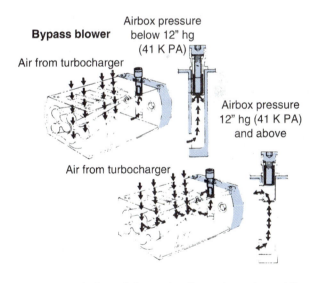

FIGURE 13–35 Schematic illustrating the airflow through a mini-bypass gear-driven blower assembly. (Courtesy of Detroit Diesel Corporation.)

of operation (reduced pumping losses) the blower requires very little power to drive it; therefore, a substantial improvement occurs in brake specific fuel consumption.

Blower Removal

The blower must be removed if a major overhaul of the engine is to be performed or if the blower assembly requires major servicing. The blower assembly has either lip-type oil seals (item 9) or hook-type piston seal rings (item 83, Figure 13–33) in both the front and rear end plates. These seals are required to prevent pressurized lube oil on V engines, or drain oil on inline models, which lubricate the rotor support bearings from entering the blower rotor housing. In addition, they prevent blower air pressure from entering the engine crankcase and creating high crankcase pressure. If the seals are suspected of leaking, check them as follows:

1. Make sure that the engine is stopped.
2. Remove the air inlet housing from the blower.
3. Remove the blower safety screen if used.
4. Start and run the engine at idle. Exercise extreme care to prevent any loose clothing or foreign objects from entering the blower.
5. If the seals are leaking, use a Trouble-light or flashlight and look into the housing; you will see oil spiral along the length of the rotors.

In addition to the seal check, note if there are signs of rotor-to-rotor contact throughout their length. Contact is an indication that the bearings (items 13 and 14 in Figure 13–33) are worn and/or that excessive gear backlash might exist in the drive and driven gears. Perform one more check before removing the blower. With the engine stopped, grasp one blower rotor and push the other one downward, then let it go; it should spring back slightly. This indicates that the blower drive hub and flex coupling are operating correctly. Any looseness detected in the rotors during this check indicates damage to the blower drive hub assembly.

When removing a DDC blower assembly, remember that minor variations will exist between a mechanically governed engine and an electronically controlled one, since there are no injector control tubes or fuel rods in the DDEC system. Nevertheless, the basic removal procedure can be considered common for most engines.

MARINE ENGINE APPLICATIONS

Air Silencers

Many marine applications, such as workboats, tugs, and logging boom boats, are equipped with conventional types of air cleaners. In certain applications they may even employ a *moisture eliminator*, described earlier in this chapter. Some pleasure craft may also employ some form of air filter/cleaner system; however, many marine applications often use what is commonly called an *air silencer*. These may take the form of a rectangular device or be similar to the system illustrated in Figure 13–36. Although servicing is not required on the air silencers shown, the air cleaner has to be removed to perform other service operations. Some silencers contain a perforated steel partition welded into place parallel with the outside faces, thereby dividing the silencer into two sections. Between the outer wall and the perforated partition (internal), sound-absorbent flameproof felted cotton waste is used.

The air separator filter element (or closed crankcase vapor collector) illustrated in Figure 13–36 is now common in pleasure craft marine applications. To operate efficiently, air separator filters and vacuum limiters must be maintained properly. Generally, there are three service intervals recommended for these systems:

1. Every 250 hours of engine service, clean and reoil the air separator filter elements and vacuum limiters.
2. Every 500 hours of engine operation, or once a year, replace the filter elements. The vacuum limiter can be replaced every two years or every 1000 hours of engine operation.
3. Clean and reoil filter elements and vacuum limiters any time that the restriction gauge shows red, or if so equipped, anytime that the restriction indicator gauge reaches its designed limit.

Servicing of these elements is similar to that for dry-type heavy-duty air filters. Once the precleaner element has been removed from the air separator, tap it

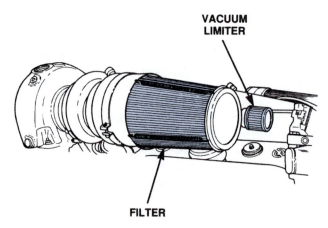

FIGURE 13–36 *Marine application showing an air silencer, and the location of the air separator and vacuum limiter. (Courtesy of Detroit Diesel Corporation.)*

gently to dislodge any large embedded dirt particles. Then gently clean the outside of the element with a soft-bristle brush. To clean the element, obtain and spray a commercially available liquid such as Walker solution onto the element and allow it to soak in for at least 20 minutes. *Never* use gasoline, steam, high-pressure water, compressed air cleaners, caustic solutions, strong detergents, or cleaning solvents. If you do, filter damage is more than likely to occur. Rinse the element with clean, fresh water from the inside toward the outside. Shake off excess water after rinsing and allow the element to dry in ambient air. *Do not* use compressed shop air to dry the element since this may rupture it. Also, avoid using temperature-controlled ovens or heat dryers to dry the element because heat will shrink the cotton filter. Finally, reoil the element by squeezing Walker air filter oil out of the application bottle and into the valley of each filter pleat; make only one pass per pleat. Do not use a fluid such as engine oil, diesel fuel, WD-40, transmission fluid, or other lightweight oil because they can damage the filter element. Allow the oil to soak into the element for approximately 15 to 20 minutes; then reoil any dry (white) spots on the element. Reinstall it.

Clean the vacuum limiter after removing the complete assembly (do not detach the filter element). Use the same service procedure as that for the air filter element.

Water-Cooled Exhaust Manifolds

A water-cooled exhaust manifold is necessary because of the high heat radiation from the engine of marine applications into the engine room. Basically, the manifold consists of an integral casting that contains a hollow jacket surrounding the regular exhaust manifold. This type of a manifold is, therefore, substantially larger in diameter than a conventional air-cooled design. Figure 13–37 illustrates one example of a water-cooled exhaust manifold for either an industrial or marine application. Note that both an inlet line and outlet line are connected at opposite ends of the manifold to allow constant coolant circulation through the integral water jacket that surrounds the manifold. The coolant flow is directed from the engine water jacket system under pressure, with a constant bypass into the exhaust manifold(s). The coolant leaves the forward end of the exhaust manifold and is discharged toward the thermostat housing area where the hot coolant can circulate through an expansion tank and heat exchanger or keel-cooled system. A drain plug is normally located below the exhaust manifold to allow water drainage when required; another drain plug allows moisture condensed from exhaust gases to be drained.

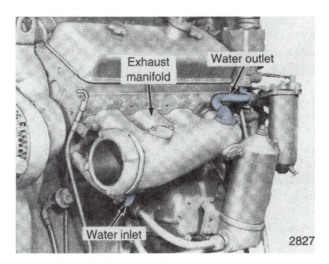

FIGURE 13–37 *Example of a water-cooled exhaust manifold commonly used on marine and industrial engine applications. (Courtesy of Detroit Diesel Corporation.)*

TROUBLESHOOTING USING MANOMETERS

All internal combustion engines require an adequate supply of clean filtered air to operate. Once combustion takes place, the exhaust gases exit the cylinders and normally expend their stored energy in driving a turbocharger. So both the *inlet* and the *exhaust* systems must be fairly free-flowing to avoid possible restrictions to either the air supply or the exhaust gases. Engine models operate at a given rpm where they are designed to produce a specific rated horsepower. If the airflow into the engine is affected in any way, not only will poor combustion result, but a number of other problem areas can surface: visible exhaust smoke, carbon deposits within the cylinders, high exhaust temperatures, a lack of power, and poor fuel economy.

The engine manufacturer usually places a limit on the amount of AIR that the engine can handle without a loss in performance. This restriction within the air system occurs at maximum airflow requirement operating conditions of rated full load. On a naturally aspirated engine, the maximum airflow occurs at the maximum no-load or high-idle speed without regard to engine power. On turbocharged engines, the maximum airflow only occurs at the full-load (rated) engine speed, since the rotative speed of the turbocharger only produces maximum boost under this operating condition. Most engine manufacturers suggest a maximum restriction of between 20 to 25 in. (510 and 635 mm) of water for diesel engines; the allowable level is printed in the service manual or literature.

Generally, the maximum allowable AIR for naturally aspirated engines is 20.0 in. (510 mm) of water; for turbocharged engines, 25 in. (635 mm) is fairly standard. Excessive restriction affects the flow of air to the cylinders. On mechanically governed engine models, this will result in poor combustion and lack of power; the engine will tend to overheat; the exhaust, coolant, and oil temperatures will climb; and fuel economy will increase. On electronically controlled engines, the turbo boost sensor will limit the unit injector pulse-width modulated (PWM) signal, thereby limiting the amount of fuel delivered. This will result in a controlled loss of engine power and speed. If the engine oil temperature drifts outside of the preset parameters, a further reduction in engine power will occur. Excessively high oil temperatures will result in an automatic engine shutdown.

Manometer Use

When dealing with air inlet and exhaust systems, a number of air restriction (vacuum) and air pressure values can be determined by using both a water (H_2O) and mercury (Hg) *manometer* assembly. A manometer allows the service technician to determine the following engine operating conditions quickly and accurately:

- AIR (air inlet restriction): H_2O manometer
- Turbocharger boost pressure (two or four cycle): Hg manometer
- ABP (airbox pressure on a two-cycle only): Hg manometer
- EBP (exhaust back pressure): Hg manometer
- Crankcase pressure: H_2O manometer

These manometers consist of a slack or solid tube formed into a U-shape as illustrated in Figure 13–38. A sliding scale allows the technician to calibrate the gauge to *zero* before use. At the top of each tube is a screw valve that allows the water or mercury within the tube to be retained when not in use and when transporting the manometers in service trucks or toolboxes. Before using a manometer, both valves at the top of the U-shaped tubes must be screwed open (one-half to one turn) to allow atmospheric air pressure to balance the fluid within each side of the tube.

Note in Figure 13–38 that the liquid within the two manometer tubes takes opposite shapes. Mercury, which is heavier than water, will not wet the inside of the tube and it forms what is commonly called a *convex miniscus*. Water, on the other hand, does wet the inside of the tube and forms a *concave miniscus*. Therefore, when zeroing in the manometer prior to use, open both valves at the top of each tube and carefully move the sliding scale until the zero (0) on the ruler is opposite the fluid. During a manometer test, read the water type by sighting horizontally between the bottom of the concave water surface and the scale. Read a mercury manometer by sighting horizontally between the top of the convex mercury surface and the scale. Both sides of the displaced fluid are added together when using a full-scale model where the distance on the scale is equal to that found on a ruler or tape measure. On half-scale manometer models, read only one side of the displaced fluid scale.

If one column of fluid travels farther than the other disregard. Minor variations within the inside diameter of the tube (particularly when heavy-duty clear plastic models are used) are the cause. The accuracy of the reading will not be impaired. Depending on the partic-

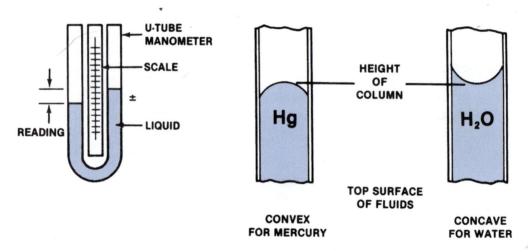

FIGURE 13–38 Comparison of the fluid column height for both a mercury (Hg) and a water (H_2O) manometer. (Courtesy of Detroit Diesel Corporation.)

ular make and model of engine, the connection tap point for the manometer fitting will vary, but it is common for most engines. Check the AIR, EBP, ABP, and turbo boost at the following recommended positions:

1. Figure 13–39 illustrates where the AIR can be checked. AIR is checked using a water manometer at a point between 4 and 8 in. (101 and 203 mm) away from the turbocharger air inlet by removing a small pipe plug screwed into the inlet piping. Install a suitable brass fitting to which you can connect a small flexible rubber hose; the opposite end should fit over one of the open manometer valves. Note that the manometer has been *zeroed* by opening both valves and moving the sliding scale. If possible, operate the engine on a chassis or engine dyno at WOT and full-rated horsepower. Refer to Figure 13–40, which illustrates the water displacement on both sides of the manometer. On full-scale manometers, add both sides together; on a half-scale manometer, read only one side. A loss of 1 psi (6.8895 kPa) of suction air pressure due to restriction in a system would be equivalent to a displacement of 27.7 in. (704 mm) on the H_2O manometer. Therefore, when the engine manufacturer's limit of say, 25 in. (635 mm) H_2O of restriction is reached, this means that the air pressure within the air inlet ducting to the suction side of the turbocharger is 0.9 psi (6.2 kPa) lower than atmospheric pressure. Compare your reading with that listed in the service manual.

2. Check turbocharger boost pressure using a Hg manometer. Remove a small plug located in the intake manifold or at the outlet side of the turbocharger assembly. Install a suitable brass fitting with a small-bore rubber hose connected between the fitting and the manometer. Repeat the same procedure as described for the AIR check and compare your results with the

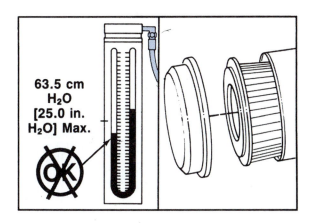

FIGURE 13–40 Fluid displacement in a water manometer during a running test to check the air inlet restriction. In this example, the maximum allowable restriction is quoted as being 25 in. (63.5 cm) H_2O. Add both sides of the manometer together when using a full-scale model; read only one side when using a half-scale manometer. (Courtesy of Cummins Engine Company, Inc.)

service manual specs. Failure to fully load the engine during this test will result in a low turbocharger boost reading. On two-stroke-cycle DDC engine models, ABP can be checked using an Hg manometer by connecting a tight-fitting rubber hose over one end of the engine block airbox drain tube and the opposite end to the manometer valve. EBP is checked using an Hg manometer connected into a brass fitting installed in the exhaust piping approximately 6 in. (152 mm) from the exhaust outlet from the turbocharger. Always use a brass fitting and make sure that the pipe plug that is installed into the hot exhaust at the completion of the test is *brass* not steel, since a steel plug will tend to freeze in position. Figure 13–41 illustrates an Hg manometer connected to the exhaust system to measure the EBP. Repeat the same procedure described for the AIR check and compare your results with specs.

3. Engine crankcase pressure can be checked using an H_2O manometer connected to one of several sources. You can place a small-bore tight-fitting hose over the oil level dipstick shroud; if the shroud extends below the oil level in the pan, however, you will not be able to record a reading. You can usually gain access to and remove a small pipe plug located in the side of the engine block above the pan rail. On some engine makes and models, the oil filler cap can be removed from a rocker cover, and an expandable rubber plug can be installed and tightened into position. A small connection on the adaptor plug can be used to connect a small-bore rubber hose to the H_2O manometer. Once again, a more accurate reading can be obtained by running the engine or vehicle on a dynamometer.

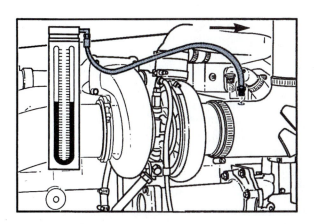

FIGURE 13–39 Water manometer hookup to the air inlet ducting on the suction side of the turbocharger to check the air inlet restriction. (Courtesy of Cummins Engine Company, Inc.)

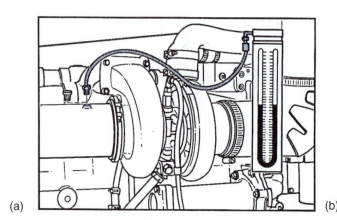

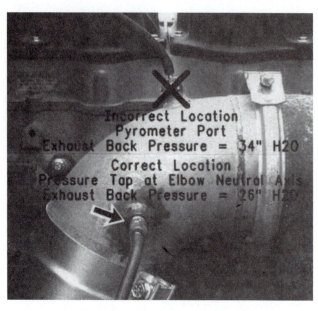

FIGURE 13–41 (a) Connection between the exhaust manifold and a Hg (mercury) manometer required to measure engine exhaust back pressure. (Courtesy of Cummins Engine Company, Inc.) (b) Illustration shows that on a T/C engine the exhaust back pressure tap point should be located on the inside and not the outside bend of an elbow. (Reprinted courtesy of Caterpillar, Inc.)

Manometer Specifications

Each engine manufacturer lists the allowable specifications for its engine manometers in the service manuals. These values are normally listed for a given engine rpm and also in inches of water or mercury. For example, you might find the following engine operating conditions listed for a given turbocharged engine:

	1800 rpm	2100 rpm
Air inlet restriction [kPa (in. Water)]		
Full-load maximum, dirty air cleaner	5 (20)	Same
Full-load maximum, clean air cleaner	3 (12)	Same
Air inlet manifold pressure [kPa (in. Hg)]		
Minimum at full load	159 (47)	152 (45)
Crankcase pressure [kPa (in. Hg)]	0.5 (2)	Same
Exhaust back pressure [kPa (in. Hg);]		
Maximum value, full load	10.1	(3)

Often it is necessary to convert the manometer reading into other units of measurement. Use the following pressure conversion values:

1 in. (25.4 mm) water	= 0.0735 in. Hg/1.86 mm Hg
1 in. (25.4 mm) water	= 0.0361 psi/0.248 kPa
1 in. (25.4 mm) mercury	= 13.60 in. H_2O/345.44 mm H_2O
1 in. (25.4 mm) mercury	= 0.491 psi/3.385 kPa
1 psi (6.895 kPa)	= 27.70 in. H_2O/703.6 mm H_2O
1 psi (6.895 kPa)	= 2.036 in. Hg/52 mm Hg
Note: 1 psi	= 6.895 kPa; 1 kPa
	= 0.145 psi

Causes for High or Low Manometer Readings

After you perform an AIR check, a turbocharger boost check, an EBP check, or a crankcase pressure check, you may find that the manometer values you obtained are higher or lower than those listed in the engine service manual. The only value that could be both high or low is the turbocharger boost value. The typical causes for high manometer readings in the AIR, EBP, and crankcase pressure operating conditions are described next.

High Air Inlet Restriction

High AIR results in poor combustion, lack of power, poor fuel economy, and higher than normal exhaust temperatures, particularly on two-stroke-cycle DDC engine models where approximately 30% of the engine cooling is achieved by airflow through the ported cylinders. The following conditions are typical of those that might cause high AIR:

- Plugged or dirty air cleaner (precleaner or main element)
- Too small an air filter assembly (improperly sized to pass the required ft^3/min of air)
- Intake piping diameter too small
- Intake piping too long
- Intake piping containing too many elbows or bends
- Crushed intake piping (hole free)
- Damaged air cleaner assembly
- Collapsed rubber hoses in intake piping
- Water-soaked paper filter element (employ a moisture eliminator assembly when operating in heavy rainfall and high humidity areas)
- Coal dust plugging in mine sites (short filter life; use two-stage filters and exhaust gas aspirators)

Low Turbocharger Boost Pressure

Many of the causes of low turbocharger boost pressure are similar for two- and four-stroke-cycle engines. Some causes, however, are unique to the two-stroke-cycle models because they employ a gear-driven blower assembly in addition to the exhaust-gas-driven turbocharger. Strategically placed small pipe plugs on the engine can be accessed to isolate the TC boost pressure from the airbox pressure on two-cycle engines such as the DDC models. Reasons for low boost pressure can usually be traced to the following conditions:

- Anything that creates a high AIR condition
- High EBP condition
- Exhaust gas leaks feeding to turbo from engine
- Leaking fittings, connections, or intake manifold gasket from outlet side of turbo (usually accompanied by a high-pitched whistle under load due to pressurized air leaks)
- Plugged turbocharger safety screen if used on the inlet or outlet side
- Plugged or damaged air system aftercooler
- Possible turbocharger internal damage (visually check the condition of the turbine and compressor blading vanes for damage with the engine stopped)
- Leaking gasket between direct-mounted TC and the blower housing on a DDC two-cycle engine
- Low airbox pressure on a two-cycle DDC engine caused by any of the foregoing conditions plus leaking hand-hole inspection covers on the block, leaking cylinder block-to-end-plate gaskets, a clogged blower inlet screen, or a partially stuck closed emergency air system shutdown valve

- Defective or damaged blower on a two-cycle DDC engine
- High airbox pressure on a DDC two-cycle engine usually traced to high exhaust back pressure or partially plugged cylinder liner ports (normally related to carbon buildup)

High Exhaust Back Pressure

A slight pressure in the exhaust system is normal, but excessive EBP will seriously affect operation of the engine. Some of the causes of high EBP are these:

- Stuck rain cap at the end of a vertical exhaust stack
- Crushed exhaust piping
- Crushed or damaged muffler
- Too small a muffler
- Exhaust piping diameter too small
- Exhaust piping too long
- Exhaust piping with too many elbows or bends
- Excessive carbon buildup in exhaust system
- Obstruction in exhaust system or piping

High Crankcase Pressure

Crankcase pressure indicates the amount of compression leakage and/or airbox pressure leakage between the piston rings. All engines operate with a slight crankcase pressure, which is highly desirable since low pressure prevents the entrance of dust as well as keeps any dust or dirt within suspension so that it can flow through the crankcase and be trapped in the engine breather system. Any signs of engine lube oil escaping from the engine breather tube, crankcase ventilator, dipstick tube hole, crankshaft oil seals, or airbox drain tubes on two-cycle DDC engines may be a positive indicator of high crankcase pressure. Causes of high crankcase pressure can usually be traced to the following conditions:

- Too much oil in crankcase (check level after adequate drain-back time after engine shutdown)
- Plugged crankcase breather or tube system
- High EBP
- Excessive cylinder blowby (worn rings, scored liner, cracked piston, or a hole)
- On two-stroke DDC engine models, loose piston pin retainers, worn or damaged blower oil seals, leaking cylinder block-to-end-plate gaskets, or a defective blower.

EXHAUST BRAKE DEVICES

An exhaust gas pressure engine retarding device is a widely used option found on many light- and medium-duty truck applications, both gasoline and

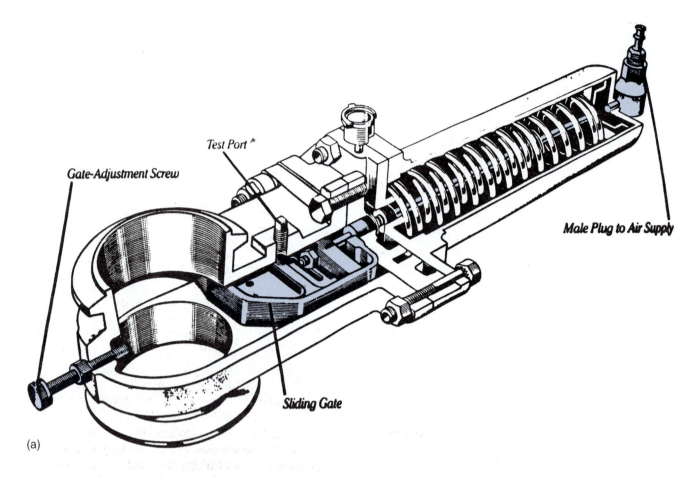

Gate-Adjustment Screw

Test Port

Male Plug to Air Supply

Sliding Gate

(a)

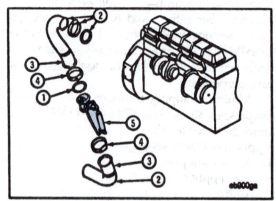

(b)

1. Gasket 2. Original Equipment 3. Exhaust Sleeve 4. V Clamp 5. EXTARDER Assembly

FIGURE 13–42 (a) Sliding gate design exhaust valve brake; (b) butterfly-type design exhaust valve brake. (Courtesy of Cummins Engine Company, Inc.)

diesel powered. The two common types currently in use are illustrated in Figure 13–42. The device shown in Figure 13–42a uses a sliding-gate type of valve, while the model in Figure 13–42b employs a butterfly valve assembly.

EXHAUST BRAKES

One popular model of engine exhaust brake is the Williams (Dana Corporation) sliding-gate-type valve illustrated in Figure 13–42a, a butterfly-type exhaust brake valve can be seen in Figure 13–42b. In both cases the brake valve is located between the engine exhaust manifold and the muffler.

Accelerator synchronization is employed so that the exhaust brake is applied as the throttle is released. An isolating switch in the vehicle cab allows the driver to turn off the exhaust brake if not required.

The exhaust brake, like the Jacobs engine brake, can be used to assist in upshifting the transmission on those engines that have an inherently slow deceleration time, since the accelerator synchronization will rapidly decelerate the engine to allow a shift while maintaining a higher road speed.

WILLIAMS EXHAUST BRAKE

Basic Controls

The brake-actuating controls of the Williams exhaust brake are electric-over-air, with the brake unit welded or bolted into the present exhaust system. Actuation and release time for a typical exhaust brake is 2/10 (0.20) second. The brake is normally controlled by the use of a dash-mounted rocker switch with either an ON or OFF position. Actual activation of either the sliding-gate or butterfly-type exhaust valve to the closed position for braking purposes is done by compressed air from the vehicle's accessory air supply circuit. With the dash-mounted toggle or rocker switch in the ON position, the brake is automatically applied whenever the accelerator is in the idle position. Anytime the throttle pedal is depressed past the idle position, the brake is automatically released. This occurs due to the electrical circuit being broken, which de-energizes the solenoid that is used to control the compressed air flow to the exhaust valve mechanism.

Minimum operating pressure to control exhaust brake operation is usually 85 psi (586 kPa), with 150 psi (1034) kPa) being the allowable maximum. In Figure 13–42a, this air pressure compresses the internal return spring within the exhaust brake cylinder to move the sliding gate valve into position. When the accelerator is depressed, the brake releases and the internal return spring withdraws the gate valve to restore full exhaust flow with no restriction. The material used in the construction of the exhaust brake is usually ductile iron, the operating cylinder is anodized aluminum, and the piston seal is viton. The action of the sliding gate is self-cleaning, and the seals require no lubrication.

Principle of Operation

When the exhaust brake is activated, it will restrict the flow of gases leaving the engine and create a back pressure between 30 and 60 psi (207 and 414 kPa) depending on the following five characteristics:

1. The design of the engine and the braking pressure it can develop
2. The engine displacement
3. The speed of the engine
4. The vehicle gearing ratios
5. The actual placement and location of the exhaust brake valve in relation to the exhaust manifold and turbocharger

When the brake is in use, it transforms the engine into a low-pressure air compressor, since it is driven only by the action of the road wheels. In reality, with the brake ON, the exhaust gases in each cylinder, which are expelled through the normally open exhaust valve, will be restricted. On each succeeding exhaust stroke there will be an increase in this exhaust back pressure in the

manifold to retard the normal piston movement up the cylinder. Coupled with normal piston-to-liner friction, a retarding effect is transmitted to the vehicle road wheels.

The exhaust brake, which is installed as shown in Figure 13–42, restricts engine exhaust flow when it is activated, thereby slowing the vehicle by increasing the pressure acting on the upward-moving pistons during the regular exhaust stroke. This action tends to transform the engine into a low-pressure air compressor.

The brake is installed in the exhaust pipe downstream from the turbocharger and before the catalytic converter and muffler. The exhaust brake valve can be actuated by either a pneumatic cylinder with air from the onboard air system of the vehicle for trucks equipped with air brakes or by an auxiliary 12V electric air system supply. Typical exhaust brake actuation and release time is approximately 2/10 (0.20) second. ON/OFF controls are normally mounted on the dashboard and activated through a rocker switch. When the rocker switch is placed in the ON position, the accelerator pedal is in the idle position, the clutch pedal is up (clutch engaged), the exhaust brake circuit is activated, and compressed air flows to the actuating cylinder to move either the sliding-gate or butterfly valve to the closed position. If the accelerator pedal is depressed past the normal idle position, the brake will be released automatically by breaking the electrical circuit to the brake actuating controls. Some exhaust brake manufacturers offer either hand or foot controls where the normal service brake is synchronized with the use of the exhaust brake. In addition, exhaust brake actuation can be wired to illuminate the stoplights of the vehicle during operation.

Minimum supply pressure of the exhaust brake compressed air is generally 85 psi (586 kPa) to overcome the force of the valve return spring. Maximum supply pressure is usually set at the same value as that for the air compressor governor, thereby limiting excessive supply pressure. Material used in the construction of the exhaust brake is usually ductile iron; in the operating cylinder the common material is anodized aluminum.

The exhaust brake restriction created affects the degree of braking that occurs. On butterfly-type valves, a factory drilled orifice (size depends on engine make and model) is used to maintain exhaust back pressure within limits set by the OEM. For example, this is limited to below 60 psi (414 kPa) on Cummins six-cylinder B5.9 engines and to below 65 psi (448 kPa) on Cummins six-cylinder C8.3 engine models. The Caterpillar 3116 engine is limited to 55 psi (379 kPa), the Detroit Diesel series 60 is limited to 45 psi (310 kPa), and the International DTA-466 is limited to 28 psi (193 kPa). The braking horsepower generated depends on several factors:

- Engine design and the allowable back pressure it can withstand
- Engine displacement
- Speed of the engine during exhaust brake activation
- Transmission and axle gear ratios
- Placement and model of exhaust brake in use

To obtain maximum performance from the exhaust brake, the truck operator should select a gear that will cause the engine to operate at its normal governed rpm, consistent with the road conditions and engine rpm limits.

CAUTION   When driving on wet, slick, or icy roads, keep the exhaust brake control switch in the OFF position.

When an exhaust brake with an automatic transmission (such as an Allison model) is used, maximum braking will occur only if the transmission is equipped with a torque converter lockup clutch. The brake can still be used in an automatic transmission without a lockup clutch; however only 70 to 75% efficiency will be obtained due to the normal hydraulic slippage that occurs within the torque converter.

The engine intake and compression strokes will occur as normal with the exhaust brake ON; during the power stroke, however, little or no torque is transmitted to the engine crankshaft since the throttle is at an idle position or zero fuel delivery.

Valve overlap (timing) will affect the amount of compression lost back through the inlet valve, but this does not normally create a problem. Maximum braking pressure usually occurs between 1500 and 2300 rpm on most midrange diesel truck engines. This maximum braking pressure is obtained in the higher rpm range when the driver selects a gear to maintain this condition within the safe operating range of both the engine and gearing. Hand or floor pedal control of the brake is also available from some manufacturers; the foot control is very popular in Europe. The foot brake is synchronized with the use of the exhaust brake. The usual method is to actuate the exhaust brake by means of a solenoid-operated control valve that is dash switch-controlled and is wired to the vehicle's stop light switch.

ENGINE COMPRESSION BRAKES

Over a 50-year period, many people attempted to design an engine brake on a diesel engine that would make use of the high-compression air as some form of braking device. The idea basically was to convert the engine into an air compressor when power was not required, but braking was.

The person who finally succeeded in doing this was Clessie M. Cummins, original founder of the Cummins Engine Company in the United States. In 1934, he experienced brake fade while driving a fully loaded vehicle down a hill and vowed to invent some form of auxiliary engine braking for diesel engines.

The first brake of this type was installed in the United States in 1960. Since that time it has been tremendously successful and is used extensively on diesel engines in North America, with its popularity constantly increasing in other areas of the world through Jacobs in Europe and in Japan.

The brake's name comes from the fact that it is manufactured by the Jacobs Manufacturing Company, which is well known for its production of drill and lathe chucks, and so on, and is now a part of the Chicago Pneumatic Tool Company.

The Jake brake, as it is commonly known, is widely used on the following diesel engines:

- Caterpillar
- Cummins
- Detroit Diesel Corporation
- Mack

Since 1961, more than a million Jake brake retarders have been specified and installed—and proven in more than 900 billion miles of driving. Over 85% of the engine brakes currently installed in heavy-duty trucks in North America were produced by Jacobs.

Figure 13–43 illustrates the simple concept of Jake brake operation for a heavy-duty four-stroke-cycle diesel engine through the intake, compression, power, and exhaust strokes:

Intake Stroke Figure 13–43(1A). The intake valve is opened, and air is pulled into the cylinder.

Compression Stroke Figure 13–43(2A). Air is compressed, with corresponding increase in pressure and temperature. Near top dead center, the Jake brake's slave piston opens the exhaust valve, and the compressed air mass (representing potential energy) is released through the exhaust system (note black arrows in Figure 13–43[2A]). No combustion occurs, since the Jake operates only when the engine is in a "no fuel" mode.

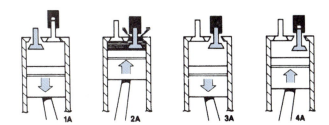

FIGURE 13–43 Simplified concept of the basic operation of a Jacobs engine compression brake: (a) intake valve open; (b) relieving compressed air by opening the exhaust valves, which is the noise heard when the brake is ON; (c) no power is produced; (d) remaining air is forced out of the cylinder. (Courtesy of Jacobs Vehicle Equipment Company.)

Power Stroke Figure 13–43(3A). No positive power is produced, since the compressed air mass was released via the exhaust system during the modified compression stroke. The energy required to return the piston to its bottom position is now derived from the momentum of the vehicle. It is this two-step process—elimination of the compressed air and use of vehicle momentum to move the piston—that develops the Jake brake's retarding capabilities.

Exhaust Stroke Figure 13–43(4A). Any remaining air is forced out of the cylinder.

In addition to the well-known Jake brake, Cummins Engine Company did at one time also offer a compression brake commonly known as the C-brake. This brake is basically a Jake brake with minor design and operational changes. Mack offers an engine compression brake on their own diesel engines known as a Dynatard model, and although there is some change in its design versus the Jake, it also operates in a similar fashion. Pacific Diesel Brake is another manufacturer that offers an engine compression brake, known as the Pac-Brake, for Cat, Cummins, Detroit Diesel, and Mack engines. Other diesel engine OEMs who offer their own compression brakes include Volvo, Scania, and Mercedes-Benz; all these brakes have operational characteristics similar to those of a Jake brake.

Brake Controls Schematic

The controls used with the Jake brake will vary between a mechanically governed and an electronically controlled engine. Figure 13–44 illustrates a schematic

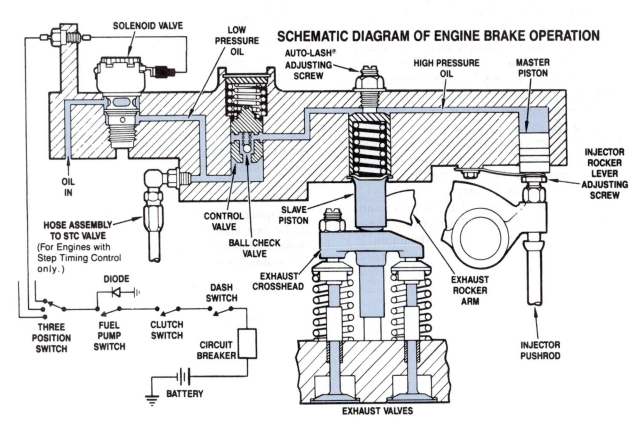

FIGURE 13–44 Operational schematic of a Jake brake on a four-cycle Cummins N14 mechanically governed engine (PT fuel system.) (Courtesy of Jacobs Vehicle Equipment Company.)

of a Jake brake system for a mechanical non-Celect-equipped N14 Cummins engine. Note the following:

1. *A dash-controlled switch.* This is an ON/OFF switch manually activated by the truck driver.

2. *A clutch switch on a standard transmission–equipped truck.* When the clutch is engaged (foot of the pedal), the switch contacts are closed, thereby completing the circuit.

3. *A fuel pump switch located alongside the PT fuel pump throttle lever.* Note that on different model OEM engines, this switch is generally located so that it can be opened and closed by throttle pedal linkage movement.

4. *A three-position dash-mounted switch* to allow the driver to select either two-, four-, or six-cylinder braking on a six-cylinder engine.

For the Jake electrical circuit to function, all of these various switches must be ON. Therefore, to complete the circuit to the engine brake solenoids located under the valve rocker covers, the following conditions must be met:

- Dash control switch ON
- Throttle pedal in the idle position
- Clutch pedal released (up) to engage the clutch
- The three-position switch in any position: 1, 2, or 3

In an electronically controlled engine, the Jake brake signal is normally arranged to interface with and receive its control signals from the electronic control module (ECM). Figure 13–45 illustrates the Jake brake schematic for a model 3406E Cat heavy-duty truck engine. Note that the main difference between this system and that shown in Figure 13–44 for the mechanical engine is that the solenoid valve (item 1 in Figure 13–45) is controlled from the lead wire (2) which is connected to the ECM brake logic controller.

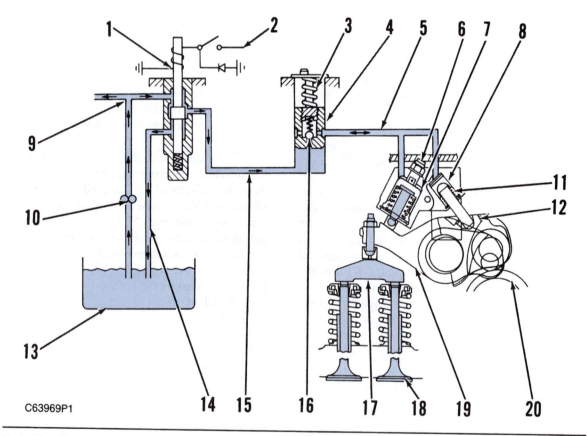

C63969P1

Master-Slave Circuit Schematic
(1) Solenoid valve. (2) Lead wire (from Jake Brake logic to solenoid valve). (3) Spring.(4) Control valve. (5) High pressure oil passage. (6) Slave piston adjustment screw. (7) Slave piston. (8) Master piston. (9) Rocker arm shaft oil passage. (10) Engine oil pump. (11) Spring. (12) Injector rocker arm. (13) Engine oil pan. (14) Oil drain passage. (15) Low pressure oil passage. (16) Ball check valve. (17) Exhaust valve bridge. (18) Exhaust valve. (19) Exhaust valve rocker arm. (20) Camshaft.

FIGURE 13–45 *Jake brake operational schematic, 3406E Cat electronic engine.* (Reprinted courtesy of Caterpillar, Inc.)

Brake Operation

The brake consists of electrically operated solenoid valves mounted above each engine cylinder as illustrated for both the mechanical and electronically controlled engine models. To achieve engine *compression braking,* the cylinder exhaust valves are opened by a *slave piston* located directly above the valve bridge or exhaust valve crosshead, or the rocker arm in the case of the 3406E engine model. Opening of the exhaust valves near the top of the normal engine compression stroke releases the high-pressure air to the exhaust manifold and into the atmosphere. At the same time, fuel to the injector is cut off, with the result that there is no return of energy to the engine piston on the power stroke, and therefore a net energy loss, which is taken from the rear wheels of a truck to provide the braking action, since the power expended to compress the cylinder air is not returned to the engine crankshaft.

Let's describe the complete operation of the Jake brake for the system illustrated in Figure 13–45, the 3406E electronically controlled electronic unit injector engine. On this engine, only the valves and valve mechanism for the exhaust side of the cylinders are used, with only one of the two exhaust valves for each cylinder being used during engine braking. The Jake controls allow either one, two, or three brake housings to be activated, resulting in two-, four-, or six-cylinder progressive braking.

Pressurized engine oil is fed from the rocker arm shaft supports to the solenoid valve (1) when it is activated by a signal from the ECM Jake logic. The solenoid valve movement closes the oil drain passage back to the crankcase and allows pressurized engine oil into the low-pressure oil passage (15) where it flows to the control valve (4) and pushes it up in its chamber against the force of the return spring (3). A groove in the valve (4), in alignment with the high-pressure oil passage (5), directs oil to the slave piston (7) and the master piston (8). The small check ball (16) is forced open allowing the high-pressure oil passage (5) and the chambers behind both the slave and master piston assemblies to be filled. This resultant oil pressure will force the master piston downward until it comes into contact with the cylinder injector rocker arm (12). During the cylinder compression stroke, camshaft lift of the injector rocker arm pushes the master piston (8) upward to increase the pressure of the trapped oil and close the small ball check valve (16). Continued movement of the master piston by camshaft rotation results in the trapped engine oil in passage (5) forcing the slave piston (7) down against the exhaust rocker arm (19) of the same cylinder with sufficient force to open the exhaust valve(s) on that specific cylinder just before the

piston reaches TDC (top dead center). This action requires approximately 0.33 of a second to operate.

The greatest degree of braking will occur when the vehicle is running down a hill on a closed throttle, with the road wheels being the driving member to allow the engine to run at its rated speed (i.e., 2100 rpm). The percentage of braking available will depend on the make of engine and the model of engine compression brake used. As an example, a Cat 3406E rated at 460 hp (343 kW) will obtain approximately 400+ braking horsepower when running at its rated speed. The individual cylinder compression braking occurs in the firing order sequence of the engine. Some engine models feature a slave piston for each exhaust valve to improve response and decrease the load applied back to the camshaft during braking.

When the solenoid valve (1) is de-energized, the engine oil supply passage is closed by the internal spring pushing the valve upward to uncover the drain passage (14) to the sump. This permits the oil below the control valve (4) to drain, and the spring (3) pushes the valve to the bottom of its bore. High-pressure oil in the passage (5) will drain into the chamber above the control valve piston (4) where the oil vents to the atmosphere from the chamber outside of the Jake brake housing located under the valve rocker cover. A spring (11) will push the master piston (8) to a released position away from the injector rocker arm (12). This release action takes approximately 0.10 second.

Electronically Controlled Engines

Electronically controlled unit injector engines such as those manufactured by Caterpillar, Cummins, Detroit Diesel, and Volvo, when equipped with a Jake brake, incorporate internal ECM controls that are programmed to operate the engine compression brake. The Jake brake selection switch (1, 2, or 3 position) outputs are connected to the engine ECM's digital input ports. The latest models offer six positions for individual control of all six cylinders (Cummins Signature models). This feature can include automatic progressive brake application in the form of two, four, or six cylinders during cruise control. This is particularly helpful when a fully loaded vehicle is descending a steep grade. In addition, automatic thermatic fan engagement can be triggered from the ECM to provide additional dynamic engine braking when the engine brake is in the high mode (all cylinders braking) to provide additional engine braking of approximately 40 hp (30 kW).

Electronically controlled diesel engines can also be equipped with a deceleration light option to warn others behind that the vehicle is slowing down. A digital output is switched to ground whenever the throttle is closed (0%) and the cruise control is inactive. This digital output from the ECM can be used to drive a deceleration light or a small relay that drives the deceleration lights. Similarly, a light can be wired into the system to illuminate on the dash whenever the engine brake is active.

Figure 13–46 illustrates a typical Jake brake wiring hookup for an N14 Cummins Celect (electronic) engine. Note that each cylinder head is wired to provide two-, four-, or six-cylinder braking. This wiring arrangement is similar on both L10 and M11 Cummins Celect engine models, with the major difference being that the Jake brake is configured to allow either three- or six-cylinder braking. Figure 13–47 illustrates a wiring arrangement for use on a series 60, 11.1-L and 12.7-L Detroit Diesel DDEC-equipped models. The wiring hookup for the four-cylinder series 50 is similar,

with the exception that only two Jake brake housings are employed rather than three.

Jake Brake Adjustment—3406E

The clearance between the slave piston and rocker arm (or valve bridge/crosshead on some engines) must be adjusted to ensure that the Jake brake will operate correctly. Figure 13–48a shows the Jake brake adjusting component location on the 3406E engine. To adjust the slave piston clearance correctly, proceed as follows:

1. Manually rotate the engine to place number 1 piston at TDC compression (intake and exhaust valves fully closed). This is best done by removing the cover plate on the forward side of the flywheel housing shown in Figure 13–49 along with the timing bolt access plug. Note that the upper bolt retaining the access cover can be used as the timing bolt for the flywheel.

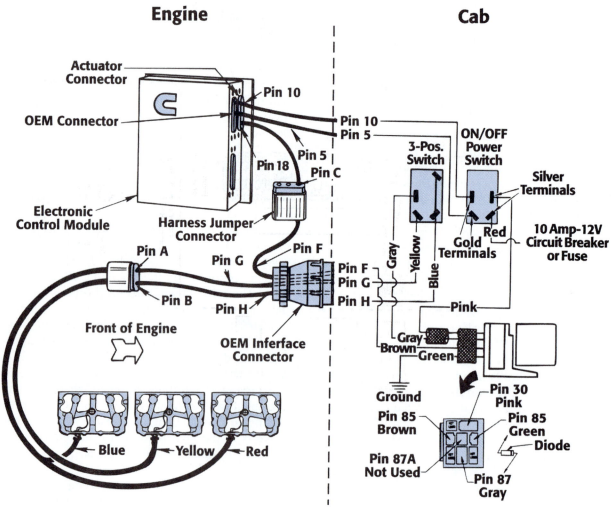

FIGURE 13–46   N14 Cummins Celect electronic engine Jake brake engine wiring diagram example. (Courtesy of Cummins Engine Company, Inc.)

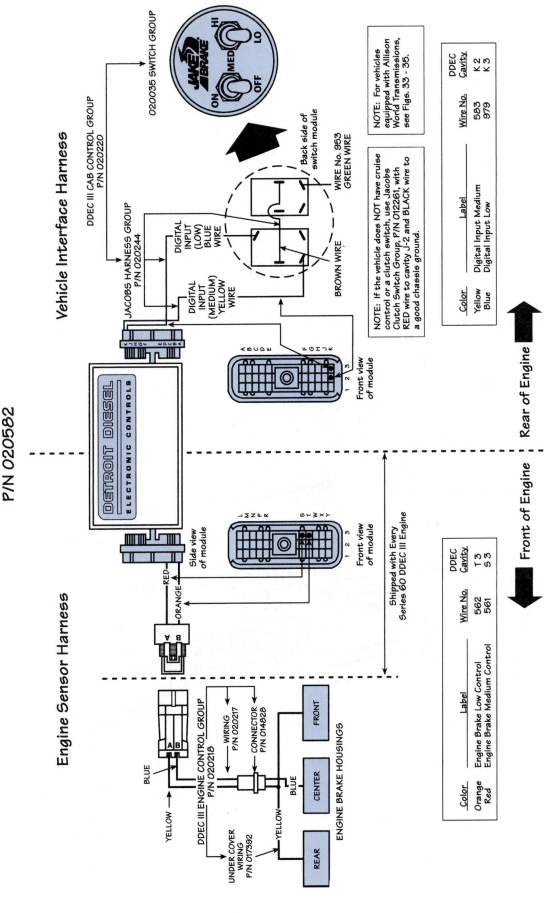

FIGURE 13–47 Series 60 DDEC III electronic engine Jake brake schematic. (Courtesy of Detroit Diesel Corporation.)

Jake Brake
(1) Adjusting screw /locknut. (2) Slave piston. (3) Rocker arm.

(a)

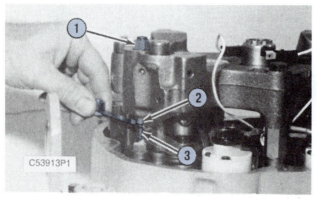

Jake Brake
(1) Adjusting screw / locknut. (2) Slave piston. (3) Actuating pin
(within the bridge adjusting screw assembly).

(b)

FIGURE 13–48 (a) 3406E Cat electronic engine Jake brake components; (b) adjusting 3176B/C10 Jake brake slave piston clearance. (Reprinted courtesy of Caterpillar, Inc.)

2. Refer to Figure 13–50 and insert Cat special tool 9S9082 into the access hole to facilitate turning the flywheel over.

3. Insert a 0.5 in. (12.7 mm) ratchet into the turning tool as shown in Figure 13–51 and rotate the engine counterclockwise (viewed from flywheel end) or clockwise (viewed from the front of the engine) until the timing bolt can be turned freely in the flywheel threaded hole. This will put number 1 piston at TDC compression.

4. Check that the intake and exhaust valves for cylinder number 1 are closed and that the rocker arms can be moved up and down by hand. If not, remove the timing bolt from the flywheel and rotate the flywheel another full turn, or 360°.

5. Refer to Figure 13–48a and insert a 0.027 in. (0.69 mm) feeler gauge between the slave piston (2) and rocker arm (3).

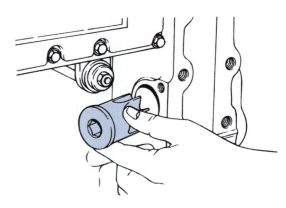

FIGURE 13–50 Inserting flywheel ring gear barring tool into the access hole in the flywheel housing. (Reprinted courtesy of Caterpillar, Inc.)

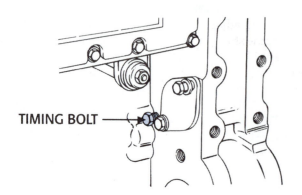

FIGURE 13–49 Cat 3406E engine timing bolt location on the forward side of the flywheel housing. (Reprinted courtesy of Caterpillar, Inc.)

TIMING BOLT

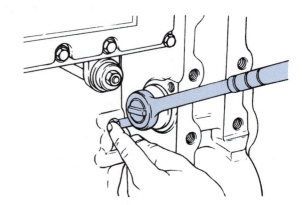

FIGURE 13–51 Installing a 0.5 in. square drive ratchet into the special flywheel turning tool to bring number 1 piston to TDC compression. (Reprinted courtesy of Caterpillar, Inc.)

6. If slave piston clearance is incorrect, loosen off the slave piston adjusting screw locknut and rotate the adjustment screw (1) clockwise until the feeler gauge drag is correct. Tighten the locknut to 26 lb-ft (35 N · m) and recheck the drag. Readjust as required.

7. Repeat steps 5 and 6 for cylinders 3 and 5.

8. Remove the timing bolt from the flywheel; rotate the engine flywheel through another 360° and reinstall the timing bolt. This will place number 6 piston at TDC compression.

9. Adjust the slave piston-to-rocker arm clearance for cylinders 2, 4, and 6. Remove the flywheel timing bolt.

Use the same basic procedure for the Cat 3176 models as that described for the 3406E (see Figure 3–48b). The slave piston clearance for the 3176 (7LG, 2YG) or C-12 (1YN) truck engines is 0.020 in. (0.508 mm). The slave piston lash setting for 3176B (9CK), C-10 (2PN) truck engines is 0.025 in. (0.64 mm); this setting is effective with 3176B (9CK28128) and C-10 (2PN1096) engine serial numbers. All earlier 3176B model (9CK) engines should have the Jake slave piston adjustment reset to 0.025 in. (0.064 mm) from 0.020 in. (0.51 mm) at the first opportunity.

TECH TIP This change does not affect the Jake brake slave piston lash settings on non–B series 3176 (7LG, 2YG) or C-12 (1YN) truck engines.

Rotate the engine crankshaft until cylinder 1 is at TDC compression and check and adjust the slave piston on cylinders 1, 3, and 5; with cylinder 6 at TDC compression, check and adjust the slave piston on cylinders 2, 4, and 6. The key feature in checking and setting the Jake brake slave piston clearance is that the engine cylinder exhaust valves must be fully closed (on the base circle of the engine camshaft).

DDC Series 60 Jake Adjustment

Figure 13–52 illustrates the components of a Jake brake housing assembly for a series 60 engine model. The Jake brake slave piston clearance to exhaust valve actuating mechanism must be properly adjusted to prevent poor engine brake performance and serious engine damage (exhaust valves being held off of their seat during normal engine operation) and to ensure that the exhaust valves will be opened at the correct number of degrees BTDC to provide maximum compression braking.

Set both the valve clearance and injector timing height, and proceed to check and adjust the Jake brake slave piston clearance as follows:

1. Make sure that the engine is stopped and cold and that the oil temperature is at 140°F (60°C) or lower. Exhaust valves must be closed on the cylinder that the slave piston clearance is to be set on. This can be determined with the rocker cover removed by checking that the rocker arm roller is on the base circle of the overhead camshaft.

2. The slave piston clearance for all series 60 models (both 11.1-L and 12.7-L models) should be 0.026 in. (0.660 mm). The one exception to this is the pre-1991 12.7-L model 6067WU40 using the 760/760A Jake model. It should be set for a clearance of 0.020 in. (0.508 mm).

3. Refer to Figure 13–53 and back out the leveling screw in the Jake slave piston assembly until the end of the screw is beneath the surface of the bridge in the slave piston assembly. See also the parts view in Figure 13–52 for guidance.

4. Insert a 0.026 in. (0.660 mm) feeler gauge between the solid side of the bridge (the side without the leveling screw) and the exhaust rocker arm adjusting screw as shown in Figure 13–53.

5. Rotate the slave piston adjusting screw (Power Lash assembly) clockwise until a light drag is felt on the feeler gauge. Or if using a go-no-go gauge, adjust until the forward part of the gauge passes through with no drag, and you feel the bump as the thicker part butts up.

6. Hold the screw and tighten the locknut to 25 lb-ft (35 N·m). Recheck the adjustment and reset it if necessary.

7. Repeat the adjustment procedures in steps 3 through 6 for the remaining engine cylinders. Manually bar the engine over to position each set of exhaust valves in the closed position for correct Jake slave piston adjustment.

Cummins N14 Jake Adjustment

Check and adjust the Jake slave piston clearance with the engine stopped and cold—stabilized water temperature at 140°F (60°C) or lower. Ensure that the exhaust valves on the cylinder to be checked are in their closed position. Figure 13–54 illustrates a specially shaped 0.023 in. (0.584 mm) thick Jake feeler gauge part number 017685. This special gauge allows you to check quickly cylinders 1, 3, and 5 on one end of the gauge and cylinders 2, 4, and 6 at the other end. Proceed as follows:

1. Rotate the engine CW from the front and align the valve set (VS) marks A, B, or C (A = 1 and 6, B = 5 and 2, C = 3 and 4) on the accessory drive pulley with the front gear train housing mark.

Engine Brake Model	Packaged Hsg. P/N	Description
765	017537	Housing assembly, 12 VDC, S/L
765	019974	Housing assembly, 24 VDC, D/L
760A	017751	Housing assembly, 12 VDC, S/L
760A	018972	Housing assembly, 24 VDC, S/L

Ill. No.	Part No.	Part Name	Qty./ Hsg.
1	012991	Retaining ring	3
2	016505	Washer	5
3	001519	Stop spring	2
4	018179	Spring	2
5	016557	Collar	2
6	011930	Control valve	2
7	016440	Solenoid valve, 12 V, single lead	1
7	016441	Solenoid valve, 24 V, single lead	1
7	016442	Solenoid valve, 24 V, dual lead	1
8	001081	Upper seal ring	1
9	001082	Center seal ring	1
10	001083	Lower seal ring	1
11	012990	Spring	1
12	012983	Accumulator piston	1
13	020382	POWER-LASH® assembly	2
14	011395	Hex nut	2
15	001492	Screw	2
16	017658	Flat spring, **760A/765**	2
16	016535	Flat spring, **760**	2
17	017565	Master piston, **765**	2
17	012981	Master piston, **760/760A**	2
18	011426	Adjusting screw	2
19	016766	Hex nut	2
20	017048	Slave piston	2
21	016771	Bridge*	2
22	019576	Torsion spring	2
23	019740	Buttonhead screw, **760A/765**	2
23	012996	Buttonhead screw, **760**	2
24	019741	Washer	2

* Use P/N 016884 Bridge for Model 760 with S/N below E-24052.

Model 760 Only

25	001021	Ball	1
26	011720	Ball check spring	1
27	008888	Pipe plug	1

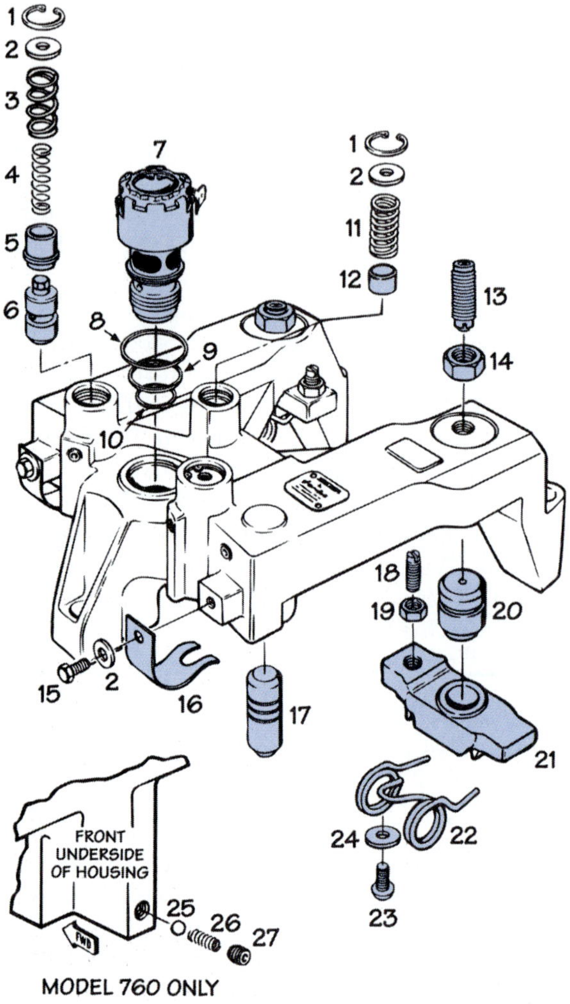

FRONT UNDERSIDE OF HOUSING

MODEL 760 ONLY

FIGURE 13–52 Exploded parts view for Model 760, 760A, and 765 Jake brake housing. Note: For a view of the later Model 790 Jacobs "flatbrake," refer to Figure 21–27. Both are used on series 60 Detroit Diesel DDEC 111/IV engines. (Courtesy of Jacobs Vehicle Equipment Company.)

2. Determine which cylinder of the two is in position to allow a slave piston check (exhaust valve rocker arms should have clearance in them); determine by grasping and moving the rocker arm up and down or by checking the valve crosshead to see if it is loose.

3. Refer to Figure 13–55, which illustrates the placement of the special gauge (use a feeler gauge if no special gauge is available). The special gauge, when used, must be positioned so that it is under both feet of the slave piston.

4. Refer to Figure 13–56, which illustrates the components of one of the Jake brake housings. Rotate the slave piston adjusting screw (Auto Lash) CW or CCW until a slight drag is felt on the feeler gauge.

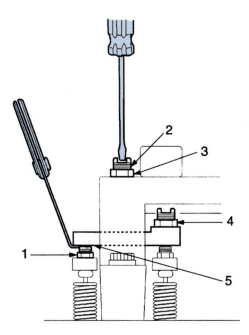

FIGURE 13–53 Components involved in setting/adjusting the Jake brake slave piston assembly on a series 60 engine. (Courtesy of Detroit Diesel Corporation.)

1. Exhaust Valve Adjusting Screw
2. Slave Piston Screw (Power Lash Assembly)
3. Locknut
4. Leveling Screw
5. Bridge

FIGURE 13–54 Special Jake brake feeler gauge for use with a Cummins N14 engine model. (Courtesy of Jacobs Vehicle Equipment Company.)

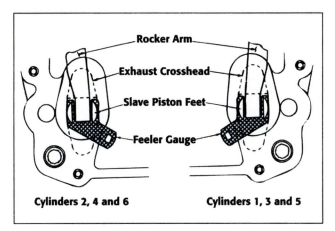

Rocker Arm

Exhaust Crosshead

Slave Piston Feet

Feeler Gauge

Cylinders 2, 4 and 6   Cylinders 1, 3 and 5

FIGURE 13–55 Feeler gauge placement under the feet of the Jake brake slave piston. (Courtesy of Jacobs Vehicle Equipment Company.)

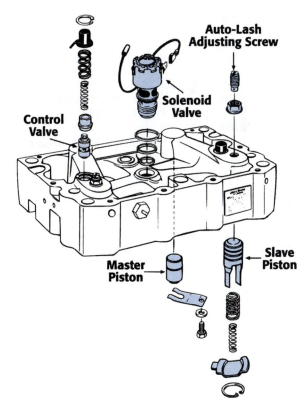

Auto-Lash Adjusting Screw

Solenoid Valve

Control Valve

Master Piston

Slave Piston

FIGURE 13–56 Parts for a Cummins N14 Jake brake housing. (Courtesy of Jacobs Vehicle Equipment Company.)

5. Hold the adjusting screw and torque the lock-nut to 25 lb-ft (35 N·m). Recheck the slave piston setting and readjust if required.

6. Rotate the engine crankshaft to place the next VS mark in position and check and reset the next cylinder slave piston as per steps 1 through 5.

Use the same basic procedure to check and adjust the slave piston clearance on the L10 and M11 models. Slave piston clearance is 0.015 in. (0.381 mm) for the Jake Model 411 used with the M11 engine model, while it is 0.015 in. (0.381 mm) for the L10 with step timing control (STC) and the L10 Celect when equipped with the 404D Jake model on 1991 and later L10 engine models.

Mack Engines

On Mack six-cylinder engines, rotate the engine CW from the front to place the number 1 piston at TDC compression. Look at the timing degree pointer above the crankshaft vibration damper until the TDC mark is correctly aligned as shown in Figure 13–57. Grasp and move the intake and exhaust valve rocker arms up and down. If no clearance exists, the valves on the number 6 cylinder will have clearance indicating that number 6 is at TDC compression. You can start here, or rotate the engine another full turn (360°) to bring number 1 to TDC compression. Adjust the Jake slave piston clearance for 0.080 in. (2.05 mm) for 1991 and later E6 and E7 model engines using the 680A and 680B Jake brake models respectively. Figure 13–58 illustrates placement of the slave piston clearance gauge. Once the number 1 cylinder Jake slave clearance has been set, follow the engine firing order of 1–5–3–6–2–4. This can be achieved by turning the flywheel 120° to set number 5, then an additional 120° to check and adjust the remaining cylinder Jake slave piston clearance.

(a)

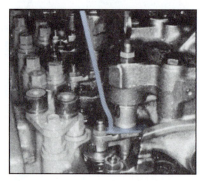
(b)

FIGURE 13–58 (a) Jake brake slave piston clearance gauge location for a Model 680A on a Mack E6 engine; (b) Jake brake slave piston clearance gauge location for a model 680B on a Mack E7 engine. (Courtesy of Jacobs Vehicle Equipment Company.)

Jake Brake Troubleshooting

Regular preventive maintenance is recommended by Jacobs to maximize the performance of their different models of Jake brakes. The mileage and hours accumulated will determine the specific scheduled maintenance requirements. Table 13–2 lists suggested preventive maintenance that should be undertaken by fleets.

Problems with the Jake are generally related to either a mechanical or electrical condition. If you refer to Figure 13–44 and Figure 13–45 for both a mechanical and electronic diesel engine, typical complaints usually fall into the following categories:

1. Jake solenoid valve stuck in the ON position, which will result in a no engine start condition

2. Brake will not operate. Check electrical system or possible ECM problems in an electronic engine.

3. Brake slow to operate or weak braking action. Check for incorrect slave piston clearance adjustment, a damaged solenoid valve seal ring,

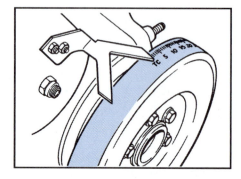

FIGURE 13–57 Front damper timing mark locations for a Mack six-cylinder engine. (Courtesy of Mack Trucks, Inc.)

TABLE 13–2 Jake brake preventive maintenance chart

Part	12 months 100,000 miles 3000 hours	36 months 300,000 miles 9000 hours	60 months 500,000 miles 15,000 hours
Wiring, terminal connections	I	I	I
Clutch/throttle/buffer	A	A/R	A/R
Safety valve screw assembly	I	I	R
Solenoid valves		I	R
Reset/Auto-Lash® assembly		I	I/R
Crosshead/bridges/ valve stem caps		I	I/R
Injector/exhaust rocker arms screws	I	I	I/R
Master piston/fork assembly		I	I/R
Slave pistons			I
External hose assembly	I	I/R	I/R
Housings		I	I
Fuel pipes	I	I/R	I/R
Hold-down bolts		I	R
Accumulator springs*		I	R
Solenoid harness*		R	I/R
Solenoid seal rings		R	I/R
Control valve springs*		R	I/R
Control valves*		R	I/R
Oil seal rings*	I	R	I/R
Master piston return springs*	I	R	I
terminal lead out*	I	R	I
Crosshead pin assembly*	I	R	I

I = inspect/correct as required
A = adjust
R = replace
*Contained in tune-up kits.
Source: Jacobs Vehicle Equipment Company.

a stuck master piston, or switch operation or solenoid valve breakdown. The engine brake oil plugs may also be leaking, or the engine lube oil may be aerated or low.

4. One or more cylinders fail to brake or the engine stalls. Check for a broken control valve spring, sticking solenoid valve(s), damaged solenoid seal rings, or plugged solenoid exhaust port.

5. Engine misses or loses power. Check for slave pistons adjusted too tight or not enough clearance between the exhaust crosshead and rocker arm.

6. Sudden drop in lube oil pressure. The oil inlet connector seal may be missing or damaged, or the upper solenoid valve seal may be missing or damaged; check for diluted engine lube oil, or a lube system malfunction.

Jake Solenoid Replacement

Refer to Figures 13–52 and 13–56, which show the location of the Jake solenoid. To remove a solenoid, remove the electrical wire connection first, then on older brake models, use the special Jake service tool part number 011494 shown in Figure 13–59. On newer brake solenoid models use a 7/8 in. 12-point socket to loosen or tighten the solenoid in the cylinder head bore. Check to see that the solenoid oil screen is free of debris and dirt. Wash the solenoid valve with approved cleaning solvent. Use a brush to clean the oil screen. Clean and dry the valve with compressed air. Replace the oil screen, if necessary. New solenoid retainers and screens are available. If the solenoid seals are damaged, remove and replace them with new ones as shown in Figure 13–60.

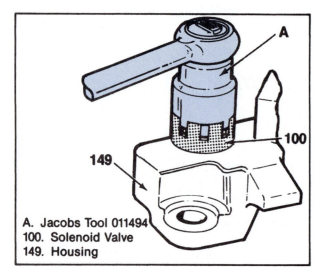

A. Jacobs Tool 011494
100. Solenoid Valve
149. Housing

FIGURE 13–59 *Removing an engine brake solenoid valve with a special Jake brake socket. (Courtesy of Jacobs Vehicle Equipment Company.)*

UPPER SEAL
CENTER SEAL
LOWER SEAL

FIGURE 13–60 *Engine brake solenoid valve seal ring replacement. (Courtesy of Jacobs Vehicle Equipment Company.)*

ELECTRIC RETARDER

The use of an electric vehicle retarder has been fairly extensive in Europe for a number of years. Designed for use on trucks, buses, and all types of heavy-duty on-and off-road vehicles powered by diesel or gasoline engines, the electric retarder offers noise-free braking alone or in conjunction with the vehicle air brakes. Power for the electric retarder is supplied either from a vehicle's 12- or 24-volt system. Figure 13–61 shows the basic design of the retarder unit.

Principle of Operation

Mounted within the cast steel frame of the electric retarder are a number of electromagnets (16 coils, 8 on each side). The frame is bolted to the chassis and frame rails. When the retarder is activated, these electromagnets exert a strong drag force on the two rotors of the electric retarder. The drag force is transmitted directly to the vehicle drive (propeller) shaft, thereby creating a retarding force on the driveline through the eddy current principle.

The eddy current principle can be easily understood by considering the electric retarder as a large generator; no power is being taken out of it by external wiring, however. The rotor assembly is driven by the transmission output shaft; therefore, as this assembly rotates within the magnetic influence of the coils surrounding it, currents are generated due to the action of this rotor assembly cutting across the lines of force, somewhat similar to a power generator.

This magnetic force acting on the rotor assembly has no place, however, for the current to flow from the rotor; therefore, it recirculates via paths not influenced by the magnets. These currents, known as eddy currents, create a magnetic reactive force that tends to stop the rotation of the rotor assembly.

Since the electrical energy generated cannot be taken away, it reflects itself in the form of heat that is dissipated by the air flow created by the turbine vanes cast on the rotors.

Controls

A master control switch on the vehicle dashboard (ON/OFF) is generally left in the ON position whenever the vehicle is in use. The power transfer to the electromagnets can be progressively controlled by a multiposition steering column or dash-mounted lever, and also the vehicle brake pedal. If the control is mounted at the brake pedal, the electric retarder is engaged within the free-play range of the pedal travel so that braking is achieved before the service brakes come on.

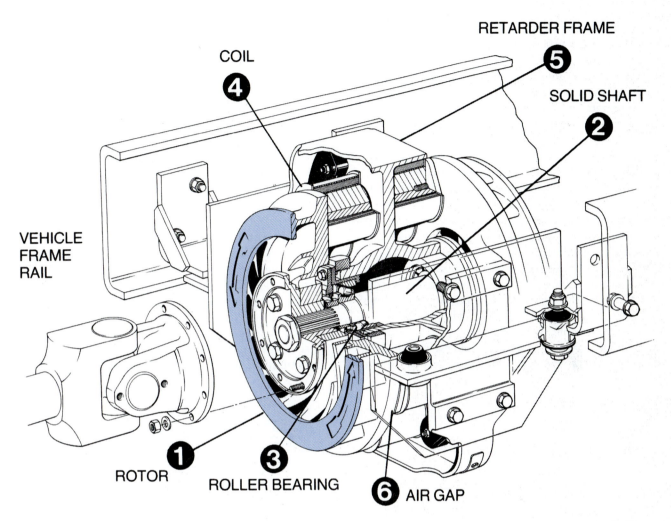

RETARDER FRAME

COIL

4

5

SOLID SHAFT

2

VEHICLE
FRAME
RAIL

ROTOR

1

3

ROLLER BEARING

6 AIR GAP

FIGURE 13–61   Concept of an electric retarder assembly bolted to the vehicle frame with the driveline (propshaft) bolted to it.

A multiposition control switch allows a progressive number of electromagnets to be activated to vary the degree of braking desired by the driver as road conditions dictate. The multiposition control switch also offers the feature of an automatic time delay that will gradually increase the rate of deceleration (retarding) without the driver having to engage each switch position progressively until the desired retarding level is reached. A low-speed detector is available to automatically de-energize the retarder whenever the vehicle operates below 5 mph (8 km/h).

The amperage draw to the retarder will vary with both the switch position and whether it is a 12- or 24-volt system. Average current consumption of an electric retarder is between 10 and 16 ampere-hours depending on the gross vehicle weight and the terrain.

USE OF STARTING FLUIDS

In very cold ambient operating conditions, particularly when an engine has been cold-soaked overnight or for several days, the temperature at the end of the compression stroke is often too low to allow vaporization of the injected and atomized diesel fuel. For example, when the ambient temperature drops from 80°F (27°C), to −20°F (−29°C), the air temperature at the end of the compression stroke can be lowered by between 200° to 300°F (93° to 149°C). Engine compression ratio, cranking speed, and combustion chamber design all affect the temperature drop at the end of the compression stroke. In cold weather, a combination of reduced cylinder compression temperatures and low cranking speeds severely affect the vaporization point of the diesel fuel.

For example, a typical no. 2 diesel fuel grade has an end boiling, or 100% vaporization point, of approximately 675°F (357°C). Obtaining this temperature would be hard under the operating conditions just discussed. Ethyl ether, or starting fluid, has an auto-ignition temperature of approximately 356°F (180°C); therefore when injected into the intake manifold of a diesel engine, it will initiate the cylinder combustion process within a reasonable time period after engine cranking. Although ethyl ether can facilitate starting in cold weather, excess amounts inhaled into the engine cylinders by an overzealous operator or service technician using a can of aerosol spray can wreak havoc with internal engine components. Using starting fluids in an uncontrolled manner can dispense as much as 12 cc of ether per second and cause severe damage. Ether used in this way can blow a cylinder head gasket, crack a piston or cylinder head, bend connecting rods, break cylinder head bolts, and damage cylinder liners. Uncontrolled amounts of ether also tend to act as a drying agent to the upper cylinder lubricant, resulting in lockup, or cause flaming in the cylinder area. In two-stroke-cycle diesel engines, loading of the cylinder block air box during ether injection, along with the rapid combustion that occurs, can blow the air box cover gaskets along the side of the engine block as the cylinder liner ports open and vent this combustible mixture into the air box.

To avoid the dangerous conditions caused by uncontrolled use of an ether aerosol spray can, a number of diesel starting fluid systems are designed to automatically control a measured (metered) shot of starting fluid that can enter the engine air intake manifold at any one time. Two manufacturers are Phillips & Temro Industries (Zerostart cold-weather starting products) and KBI (Kold Ban International, Ltd.). Generally, about 6 cc of starting fluid is needed in the air intake stream, metered over 3 to 5 seconds, to start a typical 800 cu in. (13.1L) high-speed heavy-duty diesel engine. Compare this amount to the uncontrolled introduction of ether by an operator from an aerosol spray—12 cc per second over a 3 second time period. This results in 36 cc of ether in the engine, or approximately six times the amount required to start the engine in low-temper-

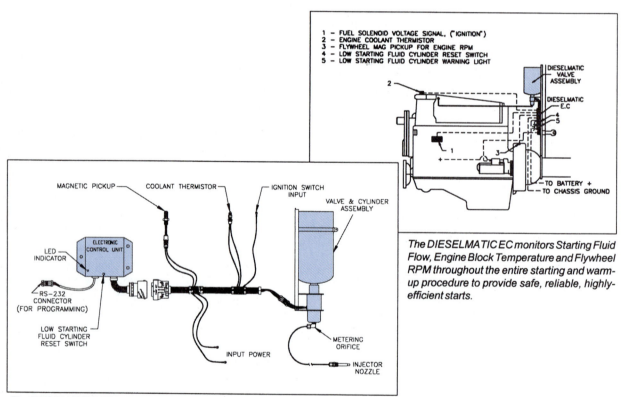

The DIESELMATIC EC monitors Starting Fluid Flow, Engine Block Temperature and Flywheel RPM throughout the entire starting and warm-up procedure to provide safe, reliable, highly-efficient starts.

The DIESELMATIC EC insures that starting fluid will be injected into the engine in only the proper amount and only at the proper time.

FIGURE 13–62 KBI Dieselmatic electronically controlled starting fluid system with electrical accessories and hookup kit for use on heavy-duty on-highway, off-road industrial, construction, and agricultural equipment. (Courtesy of Kold Ban International Ltd., Lake in the Hills, IL.)

ature conditions. High-pressure starting fluid systems have an excellent safety record and have been endorsed, specified, and recommended by virtually all of the leading diesel engine manufacturers worldwide.

In electronically controlled heavy-duty high-speed diesel engines, the ECM can be employed to safely start diesel engines in cold ambient operating conditions. Figure 13–62 is a schematic of the electronically controlled engine starting fluid injection system offered by KBI. Basically, this system taps into the power of the engine microprocessor and various sensors. By monitoring input signals from the engine or vehicle ignition switch, the engine speed sensor magnetic pickup, the coolant system thermistor (temperature and resistance), and an optional exhaust gas temperature sensor, the ECM activates the Dieselmatic pressurized starting cylinder to open the metering orifice. The starting fluid within the cylinder is approximately 148 psi (1020 kPa) at 20°C (68°F), and when exposed to atmospheric pressure, the propellants contained in the fluid begin to boil off and force the liquid starting fluid and vapors through a 1/8 in. (3.175 mm) nylon tube line to an injector nozzle located on the pressure side of the turbocharger, which is most often the intake manifold. A precisely controlled amount of vaporized starting fluid permits an optimal engine start condition and smooth warm-up, while eliminating white smoke and other detrimental effects otherwise associated with cold-start conditions. Major advantages of using the KBI cold-start electronically controlled system, include these:

- Decreases engine starter motor cranking time
- Eliminates additional cranking cycles on cold-soaked engines
- Reduces engine vibration caused by uneven combustion chamber firing through ECM sensor monitoring during the warm-up period, and provides precise, metered quantities of starting fluid until the engine is running smoothly
- Minimizes lube oil dilution that normally occurs due to nonvaporized diesel fuel by reducing the time period that combustion chamber misfire exists
- Substantially reduces (along with the ECM controls) white exhaust smoke caused by partially burned fuel droplets from misfiring cylinders
- Indicates when the starting fluid cylinder is low by activating a low cylinder dash-mounted warning light.
- Eliminates operator abuse through fully automatic controls that cannot be overridden
- Offers a replacement and recyclable spin-on high-pressure cylinder.

SUMMARY

The air inlet and exhaust systems are two of the most important systems in the engine, since they control the induction and supply of air to the engine cylinders, and permit hot exhaust gases to flow freely to the turbocharger assembly in order to provide the needed boost of pressurized air to the cylinders to produce combustion power. This chapter has highlighted the function and operation of both systems, and has provided details on the service, maintenance, repair and effective troubleshooting diagnosis needed to ensure consistent engine performance.

SELF-TEST QUESTIONS

1. List the problems associated with lack of sufficient airflow to an engine.
2. On electronically controlled high-speed heavy-duty diesel engines, list the various sensors used to monitor air system operating conditions.
3. List the four functions of the airflow on a two-stroke-cycle DDC engine.
4. What does the term *dusting-out* of an engine mean?
5. Technician A says that as little as 2 tablespoons of unfiltered air can severely damage an engine. Technician B says that it would take several pounds. Which technician is correct?
6. Technician A says that oil bath air cleaners have been almost totally replaced by dry designs. Technician B says that there are more oil bath air cleaners in use than there are dry types. Which technician is up to date?
7. True or False: Dry air filters cannot be cleaned when service is required.
8. Technician A says that ultraheavy-duty air cleaner systems used in mining and off-highway equipment employ a three-stage cleaning process. Technician B believes that it is only a two-stage cleaning process. Which technician is correct?
9. The purpose of an air system restriction indicator is to warn the operator or service technician of
   a. high exhaust back pressure
   b. high turbo boost pressure
   c. high crankcase pressure
   d. high air inlet restriction
10. The maximum allowable air system flow restriction on high-speed heavy-duty diesel engines is normally within the range of
    a. 10 to 15 in. water
    b. 10 to 15 in. mercury
    c. 20 to 25 in. water
    d. 20 to 25 in. mercury
11. Technician A says that when servicing dry-type air filters or when drying a cleaned filter, it is acceptable to

use up to 120 psi (827 kPa) of air pressure. Technician B says that this much air pressure would rupture the paper element; instead, air pressures should normally be reduced to a level between 50 and 60 psi (345 to 414 kPa). Which technician is correct?

12. Describe the best method to inspect a dry air filter element for signs of holes or tears.

13. List the sequential steps that you would employ to fully service a heavy-duty dry-type filter assembly.

14. Technician A says that some models of two- and three-stage air filter assemblies employ either an exhaust gas aspirator or a pressurized air supply to help to remove up to 90% of the initial stage of air filtration. Technician B says that exhaust gases would burn the filter and that air pressure would rupture the element. Which technician is correct?

15. List the engine problems that would be associated with continuing to operate with a high air inlet restriction condition.

16. Describe how you would inspect and check the air inlet ducting for signs of unfiltered air.

17. List the problems that can occur to the engine through excessive use of starting fluid, particularly in cold-weather operation.

18. Technician A says that an intercooler and aftercooler are basically designed to cool the turbocharger boost air before it enters the intake manifold. Technician B says that an intercooler is designed to cool the air charge, while an aftercooler is used to cool the exhaust gases. Which technician understands the purpose and function of the coolers?

19. Describe the three basic types of aftercoolers/intercoolers and the features of each.

20. Name the most common type of aftercooler used on heavy-duty high-speed engines in on-highway vehicles.

21. Describe a situation where both an intercooler and aftercooler might be employed on the same engine and discuss the function and purpose of each.

22. True or False: In an AAAC system the use of fully closed winterfronts should be avoided in cold-weather operation. Describe the reasons for your answer.

23. Technician A says that approximately 10% of the cooling on a DDC two-stroke-cycle engine is achieved by turbo blower airflow. Technician B says that it is closer to 30%. Which technician knows the product best?

24. True or False: If an AAAC system is employed, radiator shutterstats cannot be used.

25. Describe the method that you would use to check an AAAC core for possible leakage on a truck application.

26. Technician A says that most heavy-duty high-speed engine turbochargers are designed to rotate at speeds close to, and in some cases in excess of, 100,000 rpm. Impossible, says technician B; at this elevated speed the turbocharger would disintegrate. Which technician is correct?

27. The turbocharger is
   a. exhaust gas driven
   b. gear driven
   c. belt driven
   d. chain driven

28. What does the term *supercharged engine* mean?

29. True or False: All DDC two-stroke-cycle engines that employ a Roots blower are supercharged.

30. DDC engines that use Roots blowers are normally
   a. belt driven
   b. chain driven
   c. exhaust gas driven
   d. gear driven

31. True or False: Roots blowers can produce a more positive airflow at a lower speed than can a turbocharger.

32. Describe what the term *A/R ratio* means in relation to a turbocharger.

33. What is the basic conceptual difference between a constant-pressure TC and a pulse turbocharger?

34. Typical engine full-load turbocharger boost pressures on heavy-duty high-speed engines usually range between
   a. 10 and 12 psi (69 to 83 kPa)
   b. 17 and 22 psi (117 to 152 kPa)
   c. 28 and 30 psi (193 to 207 kPa)
   d. 36 and 42 psi (248 to 289 kPa)

35. Technician A says that the turbocharger rotating components are supported on pressure-lubricated ball bearings. Not so, says technician B; they use pressure-lubricated bushings. Which technician is correct?

36. Technician A says that a TC wastegate is employed to bypass exhaust gas flow around the turbine wheel to limit the maximum amount of boost pressure. Technician B believes that the wastegate is used to recirculate exhaust gases to lower combustion chamber temperatures and therefore improve exhaust gas emissions. Which technician is correct?

37. Can a TC wastegate be adjusted to control its opening pressure?

38. Describe how a TC wastegate differs from a TC back pressure device that is used on the Navistar 7.3 L 444E V8 engine model.

39. List the three key maintenance items that affect the life of a turbocharger.

40. A TC with no physical signs of damage has a high-pitched whine noise while the engine is under load. This is probably due to
   a. lack of oil to the TC bearings
   b. leaking intake or exhaust piping (hoses) on the outlet side of the TC
   c. high exhaust gas back pressure
   d. high air inlet restriction

41. A sharp high-pitched scream from a TC is usually indicative of one or more of the following problems:
   a. exhaust gas leakage

b. turbo boost air leakage

c. worn TC bearings

d. turbine or compressor wheel rubbing on the housing

42. A speed cycling sound from a TC could indicate which one or more of the following problems:
    a. high air inlet restriction
    b. high exhaust back pressure
    c. dirt buildup on the compressor wheel

43. With the engine stopped and the intake and exhaust piping removed from the TC, how would you check if the TC bearings were worn?

44. You are using a fluorescent tracer liquid engine oil additive to inspect a TC at the hot exhaust outlet side along with a black light. A yellow glow would indicate a(n)
    a. raw fuel leak
    b. engine oil leak
    c. coolant leak from a cracked cylinder head
    d. high-pressure air leak

45. Following the same procedure as in question 44, a dark-blue glow usually indicates a(n)
    a. raw fuel leak
    b. engine oil leak
    c. coolant leak
    d. high-pressure air leak

46. Describe in list form how you would disassemble a turbocharger assembly and the necessary precautions required.

47. When a new or rebuilt turbocharger is installed back onto the engine, what should be done before cranking and immediately after engine startup?

48. Signs of oil at the TC inlet side could be caused by leaking oil seals according to technician A. Technician B says that they may be caused by an air compressor pumping oil. Is only one of the technicians correct, or are both correct?

49. True or False: Signs of engine oil at the turbine (hot end) of the TC usually indicate an engine fault rather than a TC seal problem.

50. List the most common causes of leaking TC seals.

51. The type of blower assembly used by DDC in its two-stroke-cycle engines is known as a
    a. Roots type
    b. pulse type
    c. constant-pressure type
    d. supercharger

52. True or False: Rotors used in DDC blowers never touch each other or the housing since they are supported on fully floating bearings.

53. True or False: Signs of oil flowing along the blower rotors when the engine is running are indicative of leaking blower oil seals.

54. The DDC blower assembly on current model engines employs a bypass blower design. Describe what this actually means and how it operates.

55. Average air delivery pressure available from the gear-driven blower on DDC two-cycle engines is in the range
    a. 4 to 7 psi (27 to 48 kPa)
    b. 8 to 12 psi (55 to 83 kPa)
    c. 15 to 19 psi (103 to 131 kPa)
    d. 21 to 24 psi (145 to 165 kPa)

56. True or False: Signs of rotor-to-rotor lobe contact on a DDC blower usually indicate that the blower bearings are worn.

57. Technician A says that the DDC two-cycle engine blower is usually gear driven at the same speed as the engine crankshaft. Technician B believes that the blower is driven at approximately twice engine speed. Which technician is right?

58. Describe the service required on a marine engine air separator and vacuum limiter filter assemblies.

59. True or False: Most marine engines employ dry-type exhaust manifolds.

60 What two types of manometers are widely used to troubleshoot diesel engines?

61. List what engine system checks you could perform with manometers and indicate the type of manometer you would use for each check.

62. True or False: Fluid displacement in an H_2O manometer is equal to 2.036 in. (52 mm) for every 1 psi (6.895 kPa) of air pressure applied to it.

63. True or False: Fluid displacement in an Hg manometer is equal to 27.7 in. (704 mm) for every 1 psi (6.895 kPa) of pressure applied to it.

64. List the causes of a high AIR condition.

65. List the causes of low TC boost pressure.

66. List the causes of low ABP on a DDC two-stroke-cycle engine.

67. List the causes of high EBP.

68. List the causes of high crankcase pressure.

69. Technician A says that power for an electric retarder is supplied from the vehicle's own 12- or 24-volt electrical system. Technician B says that the electric retarder produces its own electrical power as it rotates. Which technician is right?

70. Technician A says that an electric retarder operates on the principle of magnetic braking. Technician B says that it depends on the generation of eddy currents. Who is right?

71. Technician A says that selective engagement (braking power) is possible on an electric retarder. Technician B says that the retarder is either full-on or full-off. Who is right?

72. Technician A says that an exhaust brake can only be used on gasoline engines. Technician B says that both gasoline and diesel engines can use an exhaust brake. Which technician is right?

73. Technician A says that an exhaust brake operates on the principle of bypassing exhaust gas pressure around the

engine turbocharger to reduce boost pressure. Technician B says that the exhaust gas flow from the engine is restricted by use of a valve to increase the exhaust back pressure against the pistons, thereby converting the engine into a low-pressure air compressor driven by the forward momentum of the vehicle. Which technician understands the concept of operation better?

74. Technician A says that engagement and disengagement of the exhaust brake are normally achieved by the use of compressed air directed to an actuating cylinder. Technician B says that it is controlled by an electrical solenoid. Who is right?

75. Technician A says that the Jacobs engine brake was perfected by Clessie M. Cummins, founder of Cummins Engine Company. Technician B says that it was designed by Mack Trucks, Inc. Who is right?

76. Technician A says that the Jake brake is designed to open the exhaust valves just before TDC on the cylinder compression stroke. Technician B says that the exhaust and intake valves are opened just after TDC. Who is right?

77. Technician A says that injection of diesel fuel is cut off when the Jake brake is activated. Technician B disagrees. Who is right?

78. Technician A says that the Jake brake controls are activated by compressed air. Technician B says that the system is controlled by an electrical circuit. Who is right?

79. On a manual-gearshift transmission, technician A says that once the dash control switch for the Jake brake is turned on the brake will be activated. Technician B says that both the clutch pedal and throttle pedals must be in the up position to complete the circuit. Who is right?

80. Once the Jake brake is activated, technician A says, compressed air will open the exhaust valves. Technician B says that an electrical solenoid is activated to permit engine oil pressure to open the exhaust valves. Who is correct?

81. Technician A says that the Jake brake can be used for an unlimited period of time. Technician B says that you are limited to 5 minutes. Which technician is correct?

82. Technician A says that the Jake brake slave piston must be adjusted for the Jake to operate correctly. Technician B says that you have to adjust the master piston clearance. Which technician is correct?

83. Technician A says that the adjustment in question 82 will be the same dimension for every model of Jake brake. Technician B says that this clearance will vary among different models. Who is right?

84. Technician A says that when adjusting the Jake activating piston in question 82, the engine exhaust valves must be in the fully closed position (piston at TDC compression). Technician B says that the intake and exhaust valves should be in the rocking position (intake opening and exhaust closing). Which technician is correct?

85. Technician A says that the Jake brake clearance in question 82 is achieved by placing a feeler gauge between the activating piston and the intake valve bridge or crosshead on four–valve head engines. Technician B says that the feeler gauge is placed between the exhaust valve and bridge. Which technician is correct?

86. Adjustment of the Jake brake activating mechanism is obtained by loosening off a locknut and rotating a screw, according to technician A. Technician B says that it is achieved by loosening off the valve rocker arm locknut and rotating the screw accordingly. Which technician is correct?

87. Technician A says that to check if a Jake solenoid is operating correctly, with the engine idling you can manually push down the solenoid above the cylinder(s); if the Jake fails to operate, then an electrical problem is indicated. Technician B says that a mechanical problem is more likely to be the cause. Who is right?

88. Technician A says that each Jake brake solenoid contains two seal rings. Technician B says that there are three O-rings used. Who is right?

89. Technician A says that a regular adjust-or-replace check of the Jake brake clutch, throttle, and buffer should be performed at each 12-month or 100,000-mile (160,930-km) period. Technician B says that this should be performed initially at this mileage, and also at 36 months or 300,000 miles (483,000 km), and at 60 months or 500,000 miles (805,000 km). Who is right?

90. Technician A says that on electronically controlled diesel engines, when the cruise control system is activated, if the vehicle speed exceeds the cruise setting, such as when the vehicle descends a long steep grade, the Jake brake can be programmed to automatically engage two, four, or six cylinders, followed by activation of the cooling fan to provide additionally needed braking to ensure that the vehicle speed does not exceed its cruise setting. Technician B says that once the cruise speed is exceeded, the operator must slow the vehicle speed by applying the service air brakes. Which technician is correct?

Diesel Fuel, Filters, and Fuel/Water Separators

Overview

In this chapter, instead of discussing the different types and concepts of the various diesel fuel injection systems in use, we provide a solid foundation for the importance of properly selected diesel fuel. The correct fuel also determines the ability of an engine to comply with the U.S. Environmental Protection Agency **(EPA)**, the Canadian EPA **(CEPA)**, and the European Economic Community **(EEC)** exhaust emissions regulations. Mandated low sulfur diesel fuel that contains no more than 0.05% by weight, or 500 ppm (parts per million), has been in use in North America since October 1, 1993, as one method to minimize sulfur dioxide emitted into our atmosphere. This rate is expected to be lowered to 0.005% by weight, or 50 ppm, in approximately 2002, to allow diesel engines to meet the next round of stringent and mandated EPA exhaust emissions standards.

A properly selected fuel grade of clean, water-free diesel fuel has always been paramount to obtaining long life from injection equipment. This is even more true with the use of electronically controlled diesel engines that function and operate with very high injection pressures. This chapter concentrates on diesel fuel grades and the important characteristics related to diesel fuel, fuel filtration and filters, fuel filter water separators, and cold-weather heaters.

ASE CERTIFICATION

Within the **ASE medium/heavy truck tests** preparation guide, **T2 tasks list Part F, fuel system diagnosis and repair,** reference is made under **mechanical fuel system components,** item 2, which provides the following tasks list description:

2. Inspect, clean, test, repair/replace fuel transfer (lift) pump, pump drives, screens, fuel/water separators/indicators, filters, heaters, coolers, ECM cooling plates, and mounting hardware.

Greater details of the other major T2 task list items for Part F are best found by referring to the individual fuel system types and makes within this book. However, the information within this short chapter will provide you with important knowledge that can be equally applied to any type of fuel injection system.

DIESEL FUEL OIL GRADES

Diesel fuel oil is graded and designated by the American Society for Testing and Materials (ASTM); its specific gravity and high and low heat values are also listed by the American Petroleum Institute (API). Each individual oil refiner and supplier attempts to produce diesel fuels that comply as closely as possible with the ASTM and API specifications. Because of different crude oil supplies, the diesel fuel end product may be on either the high or low end of the prescribed heat energy scale in Btu per pound or per gallon. Therefore, diesel fuel oils available from one supplier may vary slightly from those provided by another. At this time, only two recommended grades of fuel are considered acceptable for use in high-speed heavy-duty trucks and buses in North America. These are the No. 1D and No. 2D fuel oil classifications. The No. 1D fuel is a lighter distillate than a No. 2D; however, No. 1D fuel has less heat energy per gallon than a No. 2D grade. The No. 1D fuel also costs more per gallon to produce than a No. 2D grade. For this reason, No. 1D tends to be used more widely in city bus applications, whereas the heavier No. 2D fuel grade with its greater energy (Btu per gallon) content is widely used in heavy-duty high-speed truck diesel engine applications.

Grade No. 1D

The No. 1D fuel rating comprises the class of volatile fuel oils from kerosene to the intermediate distillates. Fuels within this classification are suitable for use in high-speed engines in service that involves frequent and relatively wide variations in loads and speeds, and also in cases where abnormally low fuel temperatures are encountered, because the No. 1D fuel provides easier starting qualities in cold-weather operation. Therefore, for heavy-duty high-speed diesel truck operation in continued cold-weather environments, No. 1D fuel may allow better operation than the heavier distillate No. 2D.

Grade No. 2D

The No. 2D fuel rating includes the class of distillate gas oils of lower volatility. They are suitable for use in high-speed engines in service that involves relatively high loads and uniform speeds, or in engines that do not require fuels having the higher volatility or other properties specified for grade No. 1D. No. 2D fuel is more widely used by truck fleets, due to its greater heat value per gallon, particularly in warm to moderate climates. Although the No. 1D fuel has better properties for cold-weather operation, many fleets still prefer to use the No. 2D grade in the winter. They employ fuel heater/water separators to provide suitable starting as well as fuel additive conditioners, which are added directly to the fuel tank.

Classifications of diesel fuels below grades No. 1D and 2D are not considered acceptable for use in high-speed automotive or truck engines; therefore, they will not be discussed here.

On a volume basis, typical No. 2D fuel has about 13% more heating value in Btu per gallon than does gasoline; No. 1D fuel, which is a lighter distillate and therefore less dense than No. 2D, has approximately 10% more Btu content per gallon than gasoline.

Fuel Grade and Engine Performance

Selection of the correct diesel fuel is a must if the engine is to perform to its rated specifications. Generally, seven factors must be considered in the selection of a fuel oil:

1. Starting characteristics
2. Fuel handling
3. Wear on injection equipment
4. Wear on pistons
5. Wear on rings, valves, and cylinder liners
6. Engine maintenance
7. Fuel cost and availability

Several other considerations are also relevant to the selection of a fuel oil:

1. Engine size and design
2. Speed and load range
3. Frequency of load and speed changes
4. Atmospheric conditions

SPECIFIC GRAVITY OF A FUEL

The lighter a fuel's specific gravity (SG), the less heat value per gallon it will have. Conversely, the heavier the SG of a diesel fuel oil, the greater will be its energy content in Btu per gallon. SG is the ratio of the diesel fuel's weight to the weight of an equivalent volume of water; usually this is designated as "sp. gr. 60/60°F," which indicates that both the diesel fuel and water are weighed and measured at 60°F (15.5°C). API measures diesel fuel with a special hydrometer and assigns a gravity degrees API rating to it. An example of the type of chart used to show various API-rated fuels is shown in the left-hand column of Table 14–1. The specific gravity shown in the second column from the left indicates the weight of an Imperial gallon of fuel compared with an Imperial gallon of water, which weighs 10 lb. The third column shows the weight in pounds of a U.S. gallon of fuel.

Diesel Fuel Quality Tester

Often the cause of a lack-of-power complaint can be attributed directly to the quality of the fuel being used in the engine. Many hours can be spent in analyzing and troubleshooting performance complaints, only to find that nothing is out of adjustment and the engine is mechanically sound. Remember, the wrong grade of fuel can affect the horsepower developed by the engine. To determine if diesel fuel quality should be considered as a possible problem area when diagnosing a lack-of-power complaint, use a simple *diesel fuel quality tester*, which is basically a hydrometer. Figure 14–1 illustrates such a tester.

HEAT VALUE OF A FUEL

The fourth and fifth columns from the left-hand side of Table 14–1 illustrate the *high* heat values in Btu per pound and also in Btu per gallon. The sixth and sev-

TABLE 14–1   Typical high and low heat values for API (American Petroleum Institute) rated diesel fuels

Gravity (°API)	Specific gravity at 60°F	Weight fuel (lb/gal)	High heat value		Low heat value	
			Btu/lb	Btu/gal	Btu/lb	Btu/gal
44	0.8063	6.713	19,860	133,500	18,600	125,000
42	0.8155	6.790	19,810	134,700	18,560	126,200
40	0.8251	6.870	19,750	135,800	18,510	127,300
38	0.8348	6.951	19.680	137,000	18,460	128,500
36	0.8448	7.034	19,620	138,200	18,410	129,700
34	0.8550	7.119	19,560	139,400	18,360	130,900
32	0.8654	7.206	19.490	140,600	18,310	132,100
30	0.8762	7.296	19,420	141,800	18,250	133,300
28	0.8871	7.387	19,350	143,100	18,190	134,600
26	0.8984	7.481	19,270	144,300	18,130	135,800
24	0.9100	7.578	19,190	145,600	18,070	137,100
22	0.9218	7.676	19,110	146,800	18,000	138,300
20	0.9340	7.778	19,020	148,100	17,930	139,600
18	0.9465	7.882	18,930	149,400	17,860	140,900
16	0.9593	7.989	18,840	150,700	17,790	142,300
14	0.9725	8.099	18,740	152,000	17,710	143,600
12	0.9861	8.212	18,640	153,300	17,620	144,900
10	1.000	8.328	18,540	154,600	17,540	146,200

FIGURE 14–1   Diesel fuel quality hydrometer tester. (Courtesy of Kent-Moore Tool Division, SPX Corporation.)

enth columns list the Btu/lb and the Btu/gallon for the *low* heat values of the fuel. In North America, the thermal efficiency or heat efficiency of an internal combustion engine that uses liquid fuel is determined on the basis of the high heat value (HHV) of the fuel used. This means that the products of combustion are cooled to their original temperature, water vapor is condensed, and the total heat released is known as the gross or HHV of the fuel. High heat value is termed in Btu/lb for liquid fuel and in Btu/ft^3 for gaseous fuels such as propane and compressed natural gas. However, if the water vapor from combustion is not condensed, the latent heat of vaporization (an indication of the cooling effect when liquids are vaporized) of the water is subtracted to give the fuel's net or low heat value (LHV). The heat value of any given diesel fuel fluctuates based on its specification as a No. 1D or a No. 2D grade. In addition, the heat energy value of the fuel varies slightly between a summer and a winter blend, even from the same refining supplier. Since the diesel fuel grade recommended by The Maintenance Council, American Trucking Associations

(TMC/ATA) for heavy-duty high-speed diesel engines in highway truck/tractors is grade No. 2D, we will use this as a generally accepted fuel energy equivalent. A No. 2D grade diesel fuel with an API gravity rating number of 36 at 60°F (15.5°C) would be as shown in Table 14–1.

The greater the Btu content per gallon of fuel, the greater the energy that can be released in the combustion chamber when that fuel is ignited. Consider that each Btu of fuel energy is capable of releasing the equivalent of 778 ft-lb of mechanical work. Therefore, if we multiply the total Btu/gal by this figure, we can determine the available work output that can be produced by the release of this heat energy. The total number of lb-ft of energy can then be divided by 33,000 ft-lb, which represents 1 hp/min. From this calculation we can equate just how much horsepower can be extracted from each gallon of diesel fuel.

Let us compare an API 34 fuel designation shown in Table 14–1, which has approximately 139,400 Btu/U.S. gallon with an API 36 with 138,200 BTU/U.S. gallon. The API 34 fuel can release 108,453,200 lb-ft of work output, while the API 36 fuel can release 107,519,600 lb-ft of work output. If we divide both totals by 33,000 lb-ft, which represents the work required to produce 1 hp/min, the API 34 fuel can produce an equivalent of 3286 hp divided by 60 to convert the total to horsepower developed in an hour, since all engines are computed on their ability to produce horsepower over a 1 hr period, we obtain 55 hp/hr. The API 36 fuel with its lower Btu heat content per gallon would produce slightly less at 54.3 hp/hr. However, on a 400-bhp engine, for example, that might consume 0.325 lb/hp-hr of diesel fuel, the engine would burn 130 lb of fuel in 1 hr. This figure is obtained by multiplying 0.325 × 400. If we divide the total fuel consumed in an hour by the weight of fuel per gallon, the API 36 fueled engine would consume 18.48 U.S. gal/hr, while the API 34 fueled engine would consume 18.26 U.S. gal/hr. Therefore, the engine running on the API 34 fuel would save 0.22 U.S. gal/hr. Projected over a 10-hr day, this is a savings of 2.2 U.S. gal. If the truck operates 7 days a week, we would save 15.4 U.S. gal/week. In a year, we would save 52 × 15.4 = 800.8 U.S. gal. Keep in mind, however, that we have to allow for heat, friction, and radiation losses from the engine, as well as the driving habits of the operator and the terrain and ambient temperatures in which the truck operates. However, taking two trucks with identical specifications, all things being equal, the truck engine using the API 34 fuel should return slightly better fuel economy than the one using API 36. For more details on thermal efficiency of an engine, refer to the section on thermal efficiency in Chapter 3.

FUEL FILTRATION

No matter how carefully fuel is handled, contaminants find their way into fuel during transfer, storage, or even inside vehicle tanks. Indeed, water, an engine's primary enemy, condenses directly from the air during normal daily heating and cooling cycles. In addition to water, solid and semisolid (microbiological) particulate contamination is prevalent. Rust, sand, and other small particles routinely find their way into diesel fuel. Sometimes larger identifiable objects such as pebbles, leaves, and paint chips are present. The most common culprits of plugged fuel filter elements, however, are oxidized organic semisolid contaminants such as gums, varnishes, and carbon. To be effective, fuel filtration devices must provide adequate solid-particle retention efficiencies while maintaining large capacities for the natural organic contaminants found in diesel fuel.

In addition to contaminant challenges, there is the potential for paraffin wax crystal formation in the fuel during cold-weather operations. These crystals form (at the cloud point of a fuel) and cause filters to plug just as if they were fouled by contamination.

Water: An Engine's Worst Enemy

Water is commonly found in diesel fuel due mainly to condensation, handling, and environmental conditions. Water contamination, although ever present, is more pronounced in humid areas and marine applications. The presence of water in diesel fuel systems may cause the following problems:

- Water causes iron components to rust and form loose aggregated particles of iron oxide that contribute to injector wear.
- At the interface of water and diesel fuel, microbiological growth occurs rapidly under proper conditions. These microbes form a sludge that can actually hinder filter effectiveness and injection performance.
- Water contamination combines with various forms of sulfur contamination to form sulfuric acid. This strong acid can damage injection systems and engine components.
- Water inhaled by the injection system can displace lubrication provided by the fuel oil itself, causing galling and premature wear.

Typical primary filtration devices do not have the capability to remove water, so they leave the engine prey to pump and injector damage and reduced efficiency. It is essential, therefore, to effectively separate water from the fuel prior to the final stages of solid-particulate filtration. In the absence of a water separator, standard primary elements become waterlogged and ineffective. When waterlogged, they are especially susceptible to waxing in cold temperatures.

An *upstream* water separator can significantly enhance the performance and life of primary filter elements. Frequent replacement of primary filters is required when the volume of contaminants is significant. In such cases, engine damage may result because filters are not immediately available for replacement, or operators are not aware of the need to replace them. Therefore, upstream filtration capacity, water separation capability, and a 30-μm rating can, when properly applied, as much as triple the service life of the filtration system.

In addition to keeping dirt particles out of the diesel fuel, water in the fuel must be avoided. Water will cause severe lack of lubrication, leading to possible seizure of injection system components. In some cases water can cause the injector tip to be blown off, due to the high engine temperatures encountered in the combustion chamber, which leads to the water exploding as it passes through the injector tip orifices, causing serious engine damage. This condition is more pronounced in direct-injection diesel engines with multiple-hole nozzles. Because of the noncompressibility factor of water and the extremely high injection pressures created, water must not be allowed to enter the diesel fuel system. Even when the engine is not running, water in the fuel system can rust precision-fitted parts, thereby causing serious problems. Clean fuel should contain no more than 0.1% of sediment and water. Auxiliary filtering equipment must be used when sediment and water exceed 0.1%; therefore, it is advisable to use a fuel/water separator. Another problem of water in the fuel is, of course, that it can lead to fuel-line freeze-up in cold-weather operation.

Most diesel fuel systems today employ a fuel return line that runs back to the fuel tank; this line carries warm fuel that has been used to cool and lubricate the injection pump and nozzles. When this warm fuel settles in the tank, condensation can form, leading to water vapor. To minimize water vapor, many fleets fill their fuel tanks up at night to displace any warm air in the tank. To prevent fuel-line freeze-up due to minute water particles in the fuel, a fuel/water filter and optional heater can be used, as well as the addition of commercially available supplemental additives containing methyl carbitol or butyl cellosolve as per the manufacturer's instructions.

Water is found in diesel fuel in three forms: absorbed, emulsified, and in a free state. Of the three, water in a free state is by far the easiest to remove from diesel fuel. This free water is generally removed from the diesel fuel by using a mechanical filter employing the process of centrifugal force. Pleated paper separator systems provide filtration and water separation, and although they perform much better than a mechanical separator, they are not as good as the true *coalescing filter*. Fuel/water filters operate on the principle of *coalescence* to remove emulsified and coarsely dispersed water from the fuel oil. The dictionary defines *coalesce* as "to cause to grow together, to unite so as to form one body or association."

Emulsified droplets of water are very small and thus take considerable time to separate from the fuel by gravitational means. On the other hand, coarsely dispersed water droplets are large enough to separate by gravitational means in a short period of time. In the process of coalescing, droplets of water enter the filter assembly where they form into large droplets or globules and become large enough to settle in the fuel/water separator sump by gravitational means. Smaller droplets are trapped in the filtering element. Factors affecting the design and performance of a coalescing element are viscosity, specific gravity, solubility, surfactants (surface-active agents) and additives, concentration of contaminants, the degree of emulsification, solids content, and filter pressure drop.

FUEL FILTERS

The use of a suitable filtration system on diesel engines is a must to avoid damage to the closely fitted injection pump and injector components. These components are manufactured to tolerances of as little as 0.0000984 in. (0.0025 mm); therefore, insufficient fuel filtration can cause serious problems. Six principal filter element media have been used for many years:

1. Pleated paper
2. Packed cotton thread
3. Wood fibers
4. Mixtures of packed cotton thread and wood fibers
5. Wound cotton or synthetic yarn
6. Fiberglass

Filtering ability varies among type of engines and manufacturers. On high-speed diesel engines, a primary filter and a secondary filter are generally employed. The primary filter is capable of removing dirt particles down to about 30 μm and the secondary down to 10 to 12 μm, although final filters with a rating of 3 to 5 μm are now more prevalent on truck diesel applications operating in severe-duty service. A micron is 1/1,000,000 of a meter, or 0.00003937 in.; therefore, 25.4 μm = 0.001 in. Figure 14–2 illustrates an example of how you can appreciate how small a micron actually is in comparison to the thickness of a human hair! Fuel filters that employ wound cotton thread, pleated paper, or fiberglass media are typically rated only as low as 10 μm; therefore, current truck diesel engines often employ additional filtration in the form of either a fuel/water separator or injector filter. Some engines use only one fuel filter, but with a screen in the fuel tank to remove any larger dirt particles.

Pleated paper elements are made of resin-treated paper with controlled porosity. These fine pores hold solid contaminants but not water. Other factors related to the type of filtering media are the pressure drop across the filter and price of the replacement unit. Pleated paper elements are generally the lowest priced, and wound cotton yarn elements are more expensive. Fiberglass and cotton thread and wood fiber elements are usually the most expensive, but they offer the best protection and longest service life.

The degree of filtration is obviously related to the type and grade of fuel that has to pass through the filter; therefore, fuel filters are available with filter ratings from as high as 60 to 70 μm down to an ultrafine 0.5 to 3 μm. The makeup of typical filters used in midrange and heavy-duty diesel fuel filters is as follows:

- Nominal 15 to 20 μm rating, consisting of 60% superfine wood fiber and 40% white cotton thread
- Nominal 10 to 15 μm rating, consisting of 40% wood fiber and 60% white cotton thread
- Nominal 5 to 10 μm rating, consisting of 85% white cotton thread and 15% synthetic thread
- Nominal 3 to 5 μm rating, consisting of 50% cotton thread and 50% cotton linters
- Nominal 0.5 to 3 μm rating, consisting of ultrafine 60% ground paper and 40% fine wood chips

The fuel system can be equipped with either a primary or a secondary fuel filter, depending on whether a fuel filter/water separator is employed. When a primary filter is used, it is usually manufactured from a cotton-wound-sock type of material and is designed to handle dirt removal down to 25 to 30 μm in size. On the other hand, the secondary filter is made from specially formulated and treated paper and is usually designed to remove dirt particles down to between 10 and 12 μm in size. For severe heavy-duty operating conditions, however, the secondary fuel filter will remove particles down to between 3 and 5 μm in size.

Filter Change Intervals

The engine application and environmental conditions determine the best change interval for both primary and secondary fuel filters. Often filters are changed at a specific accumulated mileage, number of hours, time period, or amount of fuel consumed by the engine. Each engine or equipment manufacturer specifies this in its operator and service manuals. For example, the specification may be to change filters every 10,000 miles (16,000 km), 250 hours, or 6 months—whichever comes first.

In cases where low engine power is noticed, with no unusual color exhaust smoke, a fuel pressure gauge can be installed in the inlet and outlet sides of the secondary filter head to determine if the filter is plugged. On the primary filter, a restriction check can be made of the fuel system on the suction side. This can be done by connecting an Hg (mercury) manometer or vacuum gauge to the outlet side of the primary filter head. See Figure 21–4. Refer to Figures 13–38 through 13–41, which illustrate the use of manometers. Normally there is a small pipe plug that can be removed from the filter head so the vacuum gauge or manometer brass fitting can be installed. A small-bore rubber hose is then connected to the fitting, with the opposite end attached to the manometer. Start and run the engine at the recom-

How small is a Micron?

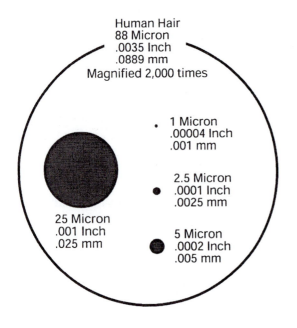

Human Hair
88 Micron
.0035 Inch
.0889 mm
Magnified 2,000 times

1 Micron
.00004 Inch
.001 mm

2.5 Micron
.0001 Inch
.0025 mm

25 Micron
.001 Inch
.025 mm

5 Micron
.0002 Inch
.005 mm

25,400 Microns = 1 Inch

FIGURE 14–2 Micron size comparison to a human hair. (Reprinted courtesy of Caterpillar, Inc.)

mended rpm, which is usually toward the high end of the speed range, and compare the reading on the manometer or vacuum gauge to the specs. For example, on both Caterpillar and Cummins engines, typical maximum allowable restriction is usually limited to 4 in. Hg on a clean system and 8 in. Hg with a dirty fuel filter. Detroit Diesel engines allow 6 in. Hg maximum on a clean system and 12 in. Hg on a dirty system. Values higher than this are indicative of fuel starvation due to plugged or collapsed hoses, hoses too small or kinked, plugging at the fuel tank inlet/suction pickup line, or a plugged filter. Also check for loose connections or fittings to determine if air is being drawn into the system.

When changing fuel filters, keep in mind that two types are commonly used: the S & E (shell and element) model or the SO (spin-on) type. The S & E model employs a steel canister that is retained in place by a bolt; the SO type is hand tightened. Fuel and lube oil filters are similar in external appearance and in liquid flow. Figures 11–6 and 11–7 illustrate an SO and an S & E lube oil filter. With the S & E type, the filter must be disassembled, washed in clean solvent, and reassembled with a new filter element and necessary gaskets. In the SO type, once the filter has been removed, it is discarded or recycled and a new unit is used. Figure 14–3 illustrates what to do before installing a new SO filter:

1.   Clean the filter head of any dirt.
2.   Apply a light coating of clean engine oil to the captive filter seal.
3.   Pour clean filtered diesel fuel into the element to prime it.
4.   Install the filter by hand and tighten it according to the directions on the attached label, which usually indicate that the filter should be rotated an addi-

tional one-half, two-thirds, or one full turn after the gasket makes contact.
5.   With S & E filters, use a torque wrench to correctly tighten the retaining bolt.
6.   Inspect the filter for fuel leaks after starting the engine.

NOTE   If the engine runs rough after changing a fuel filter, it is likely that air has been trapped in the fuel system. Bleed all air from the filter by loosening off the bleed screw. In the absence of a bleed screw, individually loosen all external injector fuel lines (see Figure 25–6) until all air has been vented from the system and a steady flow of fuel is visible.

FUEL FILTER/WATER SEPARATORS

Due to the very fine tolerances of the injection components in today's diesel engines, not only is it necessary to ensure that a supply of clean fuel is maintained but also that no trace of water is allowed to enter the fuel injection system. For this reason, most diesel automotive, heavy-duty truck, stationary, and marine engine applications employ fuel filters with built-in water separators. Figure 14–4 is a typical schematic for a heavy-duty diesel fuel system with a fuel filter/water separator that functions as a *primary* filtration system. Additional fuel filters serve as secondary filters with a finer dirt removal capability. Depending on the engine

FIGURE 14–3 *Applying a coat of clean engine lube oil to the filter gasket O-ring; priming the fuel filter with clean filtered fuel. (Courtesy of Cummins Engine Company, Inc.)*

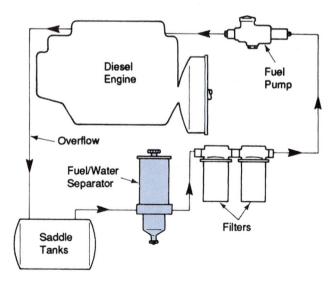

FIGURE 14–4 *Typical installation arrangement for using a fuel filter/water separator.*

FIGURE 14–5 *Fuel flow through a Racor Turbine Series fuel filter/water separator assembly. (Courtesy of Racor Division of Parker Hannifin Corporation.)*

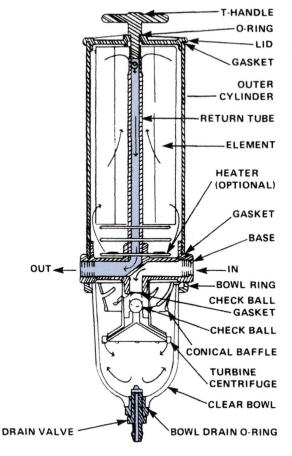

HOW THE RACOR FILTER/ SEPARATOR WORKS

The three stages of the Racor filter/separator work in series to progressively clean the diesel fuel. Because virtually all water and particles of solid contamination are removed in the primary and secondary stages, the effective life of the fine micron replaceable element (the third stage) is 2-3 times longer than standard filters.

Primary Stage (Separation)

In the primary stage, liquid and solid contamination down to 30 micron are separated out by centrifugal action created by the turbine centrifuge. There are no moving parts in this highly efficient design. Because the contamination is heavier than the fuel, it falls to the bottom of the clear bowl.

Secondary Stage (Coalescing)

This stage functions when minute particles of liquid contamination (lighter than the fuel) remain in suspension and flow up with the fuel into the lower part of the filter/separator shell. Here the minute particles tend to bead on the inner wall of the shell and the bottom of the specially treated replacement element. As the beads accumulate, they become larger and heavier and eventually fall to the bottom of the filter/separator bowl.

Final Stage (Filtration)

In this stage, the fuel flows through the replacement element where the minute solids are removed.

size and the application, filters can be of the SO or bolted-canister type.

Although there are many manufacturers of fuel filter/water separators, the concept of operation in all cases is to separate the heavier water from the lighter diesel fuel, usually by centrifugal action of the incoming fuel within the specially shaped housing. Figure 14–5 illustrates the flow of diesel fuel into, through, and out of the heavy-duty filter/water separator for a Racor Turbine series model:

1. In the primary stage, liquid and solid contaminants down to 30 μm are separated out by centrifugal action created by the turbine centrifuge. Dirt and water, both being heavier than the fuel, tend to fall to the bottom of the clear bowl.

2. In the secondary stage, any minute particles of liquid contamination (lighter than the fuel) remain in suspension and flow up with the fuel into the lower part of the filter/separator shell where the minute particles tend to bead on the inner wall of the shell and the bottom of the specially treated filter element. Any accumulation of the water beads (heavier) will allow them to fall to the bottom of the filter/separator bowl.

3. In the final filtration stage, the fuel flows through the replaceable filter element where the minute solids, down to a 2 μm particle size, are removed to a 96% rating.

Filter replacement in this model is achieved by loosening off the large T-handle on top of the assembly and opening the drain valve to remove accumulated water and fuel contaminants from the clear bowl. The filter can then be replaced.

In some models of fuel filter/water separators, the first stage of the filter assembly directs the diesel fuel through a tube of fine nylon fibers that are designed to *coalesce* any water. The fuel containing emulsified water passes through the coalescer element. The element retards the flow of water droplets, allowing them to combine to form larger drops of water. The larger drops of water emerging from the coalescer then gravitate to the filter reservoir at the bottom of the filter. The fuel then passes through the second stage of the filter assembly paper element, which is specially treated to restrict passage of small water droplets.

Another widely used filter assembly is the Davco Fuel Pro illustrated in Figure 14–6. This single filter sys-

FIGURE 14–6 Features of a Fuel Pro® 382 model fuel filter water separator. (Courtesy of Davco Manufacturing Corporation.)

Features

1 Self-Priming Port
If engine loses prime—*just spin off cap, pour in fuel, and restart engine with clean "filtered" fuel.*

2 Clear Cover
See when to change filters. See air leaks in fuel. *5 year warranty.*

3 Secondary Filter
(primary location) 7-micron media with waterproof coating.

4 Fluid Heat Base Utilizes return fuel or engine coolant to warm fuel as required. Reliable thermostatic control of fuel temperature for faster winter starts. Optional 120V-370 watt and 12/24V-250 watt heaters are available.

5 Check Valve Large inlet (1/2 NPTF) may replace more restrictive fittings.

6 Drain Valve
Brass "self-venting" ball valve.

7 Integral Bracket

Optional Unheated Version Available

tem replaces both the primary and secondary fuel filter assemblies, thereby reducing filter usage by 75%. This filter model has now been adopted by several major diesel engine OEMs, who market the Fuel Pro with their own brand name on it. In this unique heavy-duty filter model, a clear cover on the upper half of the assembly allows the operator or maintenance technician to see the filter condition, and to check for signs of air in the incoming fuel, as shown in Figure 14–7. In addition, as filter restriction increases through dirt entrapment in the filter pores, dirt collects on the filter from the bottom up and the fuel level rises on the clear filter cover, indicating the remaining life to the next service interval. Any water in the fuel falls to the bottom of the

FIGURE 14–7 *Graphic representation of increasing fuel filter restriction and possible air leakage problem in the clear filter bowl mounted on top of a Fuel Pro model. (Courtesy of Davco Manufacturing Corporation.)*

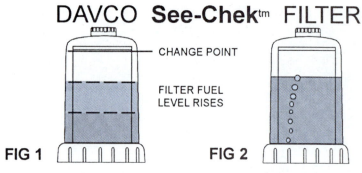

DAVCO See-Chek™ FILTER

CHANGE POINT

FILTER FUEL LEVEL RISES

FIG 1

Restriction (Δ P) remains as low as possible throughout filter life.

FIG 2

Air is visable for instant maintenance check.

filter assembly where it can be drained away using the rugged no-leak quick-drain valve at the base. Within the filter housing, a thermostatically controlled electric preheater warms the fuel to prevent waxing and gelling in cold ambient operating conditions. The standard fuel preheater is rated at 250 W, 17 A. An optional 150-W 10-A model is also available. Many electric fuel heaters employ a positive temperature coefficient (PTC) ceramic heating element. A snap-disc thermostat in the heater assembly controls the operating temperature of the diesel fuel.

For severe cold-weather operation, a Fuel Pro EF features two heat sources: electric preheat and a fluid heat tube (engine coolant). Figure 14–8 illustrates this combination heater system.

An optional engine coolant heater tube installed within the filter housing can also be used. The flow of engine coolant through this type of system is illustrated in Figure 14–8. A thermostat shuts off either the electric or engine coolant heater once the engine reaches a predetermined operating temperature. A check valve within the inlet port prevents fuel drainback when the engine is shut down. This feature prevents loss of fuel prime and hard starting conditions after shutdown. The check valve also prevents fuel losses when the filter assembly is changed.

In the aluminum housing used with the Davco filter assembly, heat radiation from the filter is greater in warm weather than it is in some other filter housings. This reduces the temperature of the fuel and results in cooler fuel entering the system and in engines that run better with more power.

FIGURE 14–8 *Features and plumbing arrangement for a Fuel Pro Model 321 that employs engine-heated coolant running through the fuel filter body. (Courtesy of Davco Manufacturing Corporation.)*

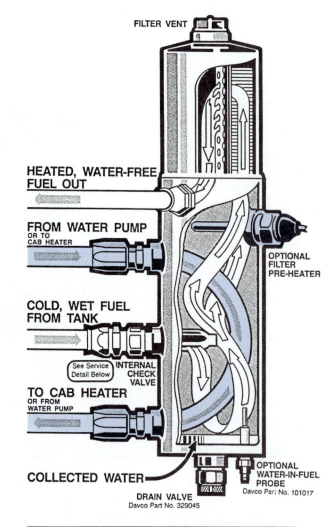

FILTER VENT

HEATED, WATER-FREE FUEL OUT

FROM WATER PUMP
OR TO CAB HEATER

OPTIONAL FILTER PRE-HEATER

COLD, WET FUEL FROM TANK

See Service Detail Below

INTERNAL CHECK VALVE

TO CAB HEATER
OR FROM WATER PUMP

COLLECTED WATER

DRAIN VALVE
Davco Part No. 329045

OPTIONAL WATER-IN-FUEL PROBE
Davco Part No. 101017

BODY
NOT A KIT PART

BALL

SPRING

RETAINER

BALL CHECK-VALVE SERVICE
USE DAVCO KIT 101132

Another diesel fuel preheater system used on many heavy-duty truck applications is the *hot joint system*. This system is used with dual saddle-type fuel tanks that employ a balance line between the tanks on either side of the vehicle (Figure 14–9). The system prevents freeze-up at the fuel tank fitting in cold ambient operating temperatures, which would create serious engine starting problems. The hot joints can be wired to operate with an ON/OFF toggle switch (used with a 4-min timer) or a thermoswitch. Each of the hot joints is typically pro-

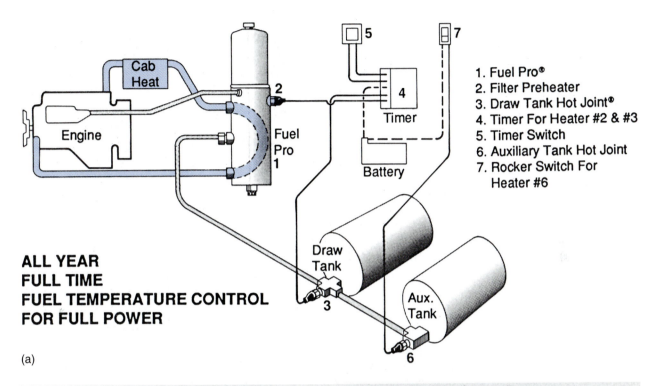

1. Fuel Pro®
2. Filter Preheater
3. Draw Tank Hot Joint®
4. Timer For Heater #2 & #3
5. Timer Switch
6. Auxiliary Tank Hot Joint
7. Rocker Switch For Heater #6

**ALL YEAR
FULL TIME
FUEL TEMPERATURE CONTROL
FOR FULL POWER**

(a)

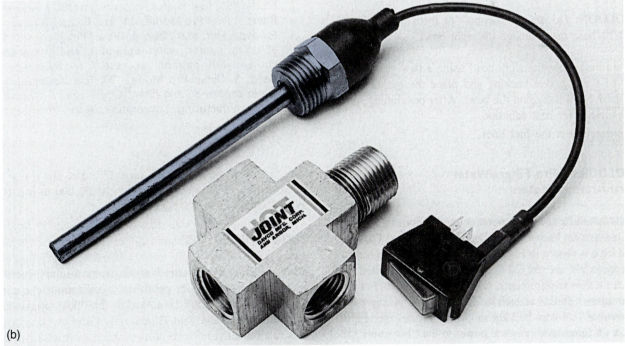

(b)

FIGURE 14–9   (a) Typical fuel system schematic showing the diesel Fuel Pro and hot joints location on a heavy-duty truck equipped with saddle tanks; (b) components of the Davco hot joint assembly. (Courtesy of Davco Manufacturing Corporation.)

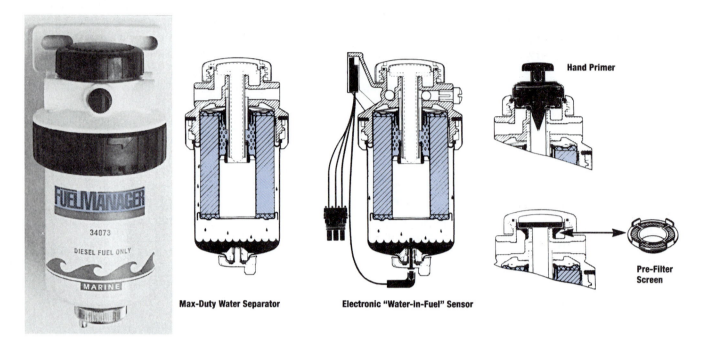

Max-Duty Water Separator   **Electronic "Water-in-Fuel" Sensor**

Hand Primer

Pre-Filter Screen

FIGURE 14–10   Engine Fuel Manager diesel fuel filtration system. (Courtesy of Stanadyne Diesel Systems.)

tected by use of individual 15-A fuses or circuit breakers. If the ACC/IGN circuit will not handle 15-A, a 20-A relay can be used. An optional top-tank-mounted hot joint is also available. The hot joint heat probe shown in Figure 14–9b is thermostatically controlled for automatic operation from 40 to 60°F (4.5 to 15.5°C).

Figure 14–10 shows the *Fuel Manager* diesel filtration system. It includes an electronic water-in-fuel detection system to warn the operator or technician of excess water accumulation in the filter system. On diesel cars, pickup trucks, and light-duty trucks, this water sensor causes a light to illuminate on the vehicle dashboard. In many applications the operator can then simply activate a pushbutton drain valve located in the filter cover assembly or employ a mechanical lever system to automatically drain the accumulated water from the base of the filter assembly. The lamp extinguishes once the water has been drained, since the water acts as a ground system whereas the diesel fuel is more of an insulator.

FUEL HEATERS

Hot Line Fuel Heater

Some heavy-duty class 8 trucks and truck/tractors employ an advanced solid-state electric fuel heater that is actually constructed within the fuel line from the fuel tank to the filter assembly. Figure 14–11 illustrates this

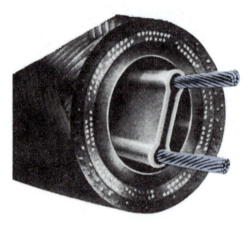

FIGURE 14–11   Close-up view of a Racor Thermoline diesel fuel line heater construction. (Courtesy of Racor Division Parker Hannifin Corporation.)

type of fuel heater system which is commonly called a *hot line system* (or a Thermoline, manufactured by the Racor Division of the Parker Hannifin Corporation). Figure 14–12 illustrates the wiring system used with a hot line system on a vehicle with a single fuel tank; a dual-saddle-tank system is also available. In a dual-tank arrangement, two hot line heaters are used (one for each tank) and a three-way dash-mounted selector switch is activated by the truck driver. The driver can activate either fuel tank's heater for a closed, single

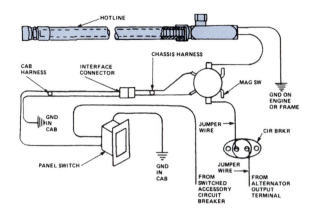

FIGURE 14–12 *Example of a single hot line fuel heater arrangement used on a heavy-duty class 8 truck/tractor. (Courtesy of Racor Division, Parker Hannifin Corporation.)*

draw/single-return system; however both tanks cannot be heated at the same time. Placing the dash switch in the center, or OFF position, turns off all power to both hot line heaters.

Cold-Weather Operation

The properties of diesel fuel and its contaminants, especially water, may be altered drastically in cold weather. Depending on the quality of the diesel fuel, its cloud point (the point at which paraffin crystals precipitate) may be 0 to 45°F (−17 to 7.2°C). Paraffin crystals (which are found in most diesel fuels) quickly coat filter elements and prevent fuel flow and vehicle operation. In addition, water contamination in the form of icy slush compounds the problem by slowing fuel flow even more quickly. It is desirable, therefore, to heat diesel fuel as close to the filter element as possible to reliquify wax and ice crystals.

Several methods are available to heat diesel fuel to maintain operation in cold weather. The two most common are electric heaters and coolant heaters. Both are inline units built into the diesel fuel filter/water separator.

For most low-flow applications [under 1.89 lpm (liters per minute), 0.5 gpm (gallons per minute)], an efficient 150- to 200-W electrical heater that is thermostatically controlled will economically provide immediate heat and maintain equipment operation. For higher-flow applications, the problem is more challenging. To ensure operation in cold conditions, a large amount of energy is required (for example, 1.5-gpm flow for a Cummins 350 to maintain operation.) Several options are available: an efficient 350- to 500-W electrical heater; a 150- to 300-W startup heater in conjunction with a coolant heater; and a combination

coolant heater with an electrical heater. These options will prevent paraffin crystals from coating the filter medium and will assist in providing diesel fuel flow to the injection system in most cold-weather conditions. In extreme cold conditions (−76°C, −60°F) additional measures are required.

In a diesel engine, only a small percentage of the fuel that is delivered to the unit injectors is actually used for combustion purposes. As much as 80% is used for cooling and lubricating the injection pump and injector component parts. The high rate of return fuel has been filtered of its wax precipitants and has been warmed by the heat from the engine. On high-pressure inline injection pumps, most of the fuel is returned from the pump, not from the nozzles.

SUMMARY

This chapter has described diesel fuel grades, filter design and operation, fuel filter/water separators, thermostatically controlled heaters, and the maintenance/service of these items. This knowledge will help in troubleshooting the engine fuel system. For greater details on specific fuel systems and their operation, refer to the respective chapters within this textbook for a specific type of fuel system.

SELF-TEST QUESTIONS

1. Technician A says that material used in primary fuel filters generally consists of resin pleated paper, whereas technician B says that the primary filter is usually composed of cotton material. Who is correct?

2. Technician A says that a micron is one-ten-thousandth of a meter. Technician B says that a micron is equivalent to one-millionth of a meter. Who is right?

3. After the discussion in question 2, technician A says that a micron can be written as 0.003937 in., whereas technician B disagrees, saying that a micron is shown as 0.00003937 in. With whom do you agree?

4. Technician A says that the filtering capability of most primary filters used in regular service is rated as 30 μm. Technician B says that it is closer to 12 μm. Who is right?

5. Technician A says that secondary fuel filters used in what is classified as severe-duty service are generally rated at between 3 and 5 μm. Technician B disagrees, saying that this would cause too great a fuel flow restriction. Who is correct?

6. Technician A says that it is not necessary to use a separate primary filter when a good fuel filter/water separator assembly is used in the fuel system. Technician B disagrees, saying that you should always use a primary fuel filter, regardless of whatever else is used in the system. Who is correct?

7. Technician A says that water in the fuel will simply cause rusting of injection components. Technician B says that a slug of water can blow the tip off an injector. Who is correct?

8. Technician A says that water in a fuel tank can be caused by allowing the warm return fuel from the engine to cool in the tank. Technician B says that the only way that water can get into the tank is through improper handling of bulk fuel during fill-up. Who is right?

9. To minimize condensation in a fuel tank, you should
   a. always park the truck inside at night in a warm shop
   b. plug in a cylinder block coolant heater at night
   c. use a fuel tank heater
   d. instruct drivers to fill up the fuel tank at the end of each shift or at the end of the day if no shift work is performed

10. A truck fleet supervisor instructs a mechanic that if a fuel filter/water separator is not used on an engine fuel system, to prevent fuel line freeze-up add
    a. methyl carbitol or butyl cellosolve
    b. liquid starting fluid as required
    c. kerosene to cut the fuel's specific gravity
    d. antifreeze in the ratio of 1 pint to every 125 gallons of diesel fuel

11. Fuel filter water separators generally operate on the principle of coalescence. This simply means
    a. droplets of water entering the fuel/water filter form into large globules or droplets, where they settle in the reservoir
    b. water is broken down into tiny droplets to make it easier to spin them loose by gravitational forces
    c. preheating the water to make it easier to trap in the filter

12. Technician A says that fuel filters must be changed every 300 hours or 9000 miles. Technician B says that the filter change period can be determined by the truck fleet operating conditions. Who is correct?

13. Technician A says that fuel filters should be replaced when they become plugged. This can be determined when the engine loses horsepower. Technician B disagrees, saying that they should be changed at regular intervals to suit the operating conditions of the equipment. Who is correct?

14. Technician A says that to determine if the primary fuel filter is plugged you can make a fuel system restriction (vacuum) check. Technician B says that you should insert a fuel pressure gauge and determine the pressure drop through the filter assembly. What procedure would be acceptable?

15. True or False: A shell-and-element filter assembly is a throwaway type of unit.

16. A truck fleet mechanic says that after replacing diesel fuel filters you should always
    a. ensure that the filters have been filled up with clean filtered fuel
    b. fill the filters with unfiltered fuel since any dirt will be filtered out as it passes through the filter
    c. bleed (prime) the fuel system of all entrapped air
    d. fill up the fuel tank and crank the engine over until it starts

17. Technician A says that spin-on types of fuel filters should be tightened between one-half and two-thirds of a turn after the gasket contacts the base. Technician B says that the spin-on filter should be tightened securely with a strap wrench. Who is right?

18. Technician A says that if the engine runs rough or fails to run after changing the fuel filter assemblies, the most probable cause is a lack of fuel in the tank. Technician B says that it is more likely to be due to air trapped in the system. Who is correct?

19. True or False: Fuel filter/water separators contain internal heater units that must be switched ON/OFF in cold weather to prevent fuel line freeze-up.

20. Technician A says that water accumulation in a fuel filter/water separator must be drained off every day to prevent fuel filter damage. Technician B says that water accumulation has to be drained off only when the reservoir bowl is full or when the warning light on the vehicle instrument panel comes on. Who is correct?

21. The reason for using a fuel heater in winter is to
    a. increase the engine horsepower
    b. prevent waxing of the fuel filters, which would cause plugging
    c. stop any water in the fuel from freezing
    d. allow the engine to idle overnight without damage

22. Technician A says that fuel heaters are operated by warm coolant from the engine, whereas technician B says that only electrically operated fuel heaters are used. Who is correct?

15

Types of Fuel Systems

Overview

The fuel injection system is the heart of the diesel engine. Slow-, medium-, and high-speed engines rely upon high-pressure fuel delivered to the combustion chambers in the proper quantity, and at the exact number of crankshaft degrees BTDC (before top dead center) for the highest thermal efficiency, with a minimum of exhaust emissions. To ensure that high-speed on- and off-highway diesel engines can comply with the mandated and stringent U.S. EPA, the CEPA, and the EEC exhaust emissions limits, major technological advancements in engine design and controls now rely heavily on electronic fuel injection and governor systems. Although a large number of diesel engines worldwide are still equipped with mechanical fuel systems, these types will eventually be superceded by full electronic controls. This chapter highlights the main types of fuel systems, both mechanical and electronic, and will serve as an introduction and familiarization to the varying designs of fuel injection systems. Basic fuel injection concepts discussed here can be studied in greater detail in respective OEM chapters throughout this book.

ASE OR TQ CERTIFICATION

The information provided in this chapter has no specific ASE or TQ test area; however, this background knowledge will serve you well when you review information relative to the ASE medium/heavy truck tests, diesel engines tasks list test T2, Part F, dealing with fuel system diagnosis and repair. This section addresses both mechanical components and electronic components. Additionally, a solid foundation in the different designs of the various types of fuel injection systems,

and how they function and operate, will be of value when you choose to challenge the ASE electronic diesel engine diagnosis specialist test L2. Details of the content areas for the L2 ASE test can be found by referring to the material contained in Chapter 18 of this book.

BASIC FUEL INJECTION SYSTEMS

Development History

Although Rudolph Diesel is credited with the internal combustion engine that bears his name, from his first designs and engine tests in 1895, many individuals before him laid the foundational concepts of injecting fuel into the cylinder of an internal combustion engine. Fuel injection was first used in Otto cycle (gasoline) engines before the invention of the diesel engine. The objective was to obtain sufficient atomization of the pressurized fuel through spray nozzles. This idea proved superior to the available carburetors of the day. Design improvements to carburetors in the 1900s were cheaper to manufacture, and thus superceded gasoline fuel injection. Not until the mid-1970s did gasoline fuel injection with electronic controls begin to resurface in mass-production automobiles.

In Diesel's original design, he employed high-pressure air to force fine coal dust into the cylinder as fuel. This was followed by the use of liquid fuel and compressed air that flowed into the engine cylinder, carrying with it the previously mechanically metered diesel fuel as a finely atomized spray. In 1900, Diesel was granted a U.S. patent for his method of fuel metering control; however, several other engineers preceded his specific patent for other types of liquid fuel injection control.

An American, John F. Holland, was granted a patent in 1886 for a mechanical method of injecting fuel into a cylinder. The originator of plunger pumps to force a metered quantity of fuel at high pressure into the cylinders can be traced to Richard Hornsby, and Sons of England, who used this concept in 1891. Today the well-known method of mechanical fuel metering control by means of a helix on the pumping plunger was actually patented to the German inventor Carl Pieper in 1892. In 1895, a patent was granted to William H. Scott, an Englishman, for his double port helix control design to vary both the beginning and end of injection. This design concept was subsequently utilized by the Robert Bosch Corporation.

Prior to 1922, when the Robert Bosch Company of Stuttgart, Germany, decided to manufacture and mass-produce fuel injection equipment, many other patents were granted to several individuals who worked with injector nozzle and unit injector designs, as well as mechanical governors and controls. In 1927, the well-known jerk pump with helix control, in both single engine cylinder and multiple plunger types for multiple cylinder engines, was introduced by Bosch. U.S. Patent No. 1,831,649 was granted to Ottmar Bauer in 1931 for the design of this system. With the availability of this injection equipment in mass production, the high-speed diesel engine as we know it today came into existence. Today, the Robert Bosch Corporation and their licensees produce approximately 60% of the required global diesel fuel injection equipment.

The Bosch high-pressure pump-line-nozzle (PLN) fuel injection system, although extremely popular then and now, requires steel tubing to transfer the fuel from the pump to the nozzle. Certain problems with leakage at the tube flared ends may occur with this type of system if the ends become twisted or bent, or are over-tightened and damaged. In addition, every fuel line to the respective nozzles in the cylinder head must be the exact same length to ensure that delivery of fuel to the cylinders occurs at the same time.

Elimination of high-pressure fuel lines (tubing) was developed by the adoption of low fuel pressure supplied to the unit injector that combined both the pump and nozzle into one common body. Hence the term 'low pressure design.' A patent was granted in 1905 to Carl Weidman of Germany, for an air injection type of system. In 1911, a British patent was granted to Frederick Lamplough for a mechanical unit injector (MUI) resembling those in use today. Commercial acceptance of the unit injector in the United States was first adopted in 1931, on Winton engines with a design by C. D. Salisbury; and in 1934, Arthur Fielden was granted a U.S. patent on the unit injector design adopted for use on the General Motors two-cycle engine, the forerunner of today's Detroit Diesel Corporation. The MUI was used by DDC in all of their two-stroke-cycle engines beginning in 1937 until they introduced their electronic unit injector (EUI) in 1985. Caterpillar later adopted the MUI in several of their engine models, namely the 3400, 3500, and 3600 engines series, later updated to EUI and HEUI systems on some models of the 3400 series.

Today EUIs are widely used by many major engine OEMs. Examples include Detroit Diesel, Caterpillar, John Deere, Cummins, MTU, and Volvo. Unit injectors today can obtain fuel spray-in pressures into the combustion chambers between 28,000 and 30,000 psi (1931 to 2068 bar). Each EUI electric solenoid is controlled by a pulsing electrical signal initiated from the ECM to determine the fueling rate, timing, duration, and end of injection.

Many engine OEMs other than those listed here now use electronic unit pumps (EUPs), where an individual pump is used for each engine cylinder. Mercedes-Benz, Volvo/Renault VI/Mack, MTU/DDC are major users of this design concept, in which each pump is engine camshaft actuated. A short high-pressure line delivers fuel to the nozzle in the cylinder head. Each EUP electric solenoid is controlled by a pulsing signal from the engine ECM to determine the fueling rate, timing, duration, and end of injection.

Today, hundreds of diesel engine OEMs worldwide employ the basic fuel injection pump and governor design that was mass produced by Bosch in 1927. Of course, today's injection pumps and injectors are now equipped with electronic controls, although many are still mechanically actuated from a camshaft and pushrod or an overhead camshaft design to raise the fuel pressure to a high enough level to open the spring-loaded valve within the nozzle/injector. The hydraulically actuated electronic unit injector (HEUI), co-designed by both International and Caterpillar and widely employed on their respective engine products, does not require mechanical activation, but relies upon high-pressure engine lube oil for actuation. See the HEUI system concept of operation described in later chapters of this book.

The four basic types of mechanical and electronically controlled fuel injection systems that have been and still are in use in diesel engines are:

- Constant pressure or common rail
- Spring pressure or accumulator type
- Jerk pump system following the existing Bosch design
- Distributor pump system

Common Rail Design

The stringent federal exhaust emission controls regulated by the U.S. EPA and by the regulating authorities in Europe and Japan have been addressed in several ways. One idea is to employ a fuel injection system that permits equal fuel atomization injected into the combustion chambers regardless of the load and speed variation of the engine. One of the most widely adopted fuel injection systems in use today is the electronically controlled common rail design (see Chapters 19, 22, and 23). Many major global engine manufacturers have now adopted this design concept.

The term *common rail* has been around since the inception of the diesel engine. Basically it means that fuel under high pressure is supplied to all nozzles/injectors from a common manifold or rail. In Diesel's original design, he employed high-pressure air that flowed into the engine cylinder carrying with it the previously mechanically metered diesel fuel as a finely atomized spray. The first American engine with a mechanical common rail injection system was built by the Atlas Imperial Diesel Company of Oakland, California, in 1919. A multiplunger pump delivered fuel to an accumulator, where the common rail fuel pressure was maintained at approximately 5000 psi (34,475 kPa) by a relief valve.

Similar rail-type systems have been in use for many years, in which both an inlet and return fuel manifold supply and return diesel fuel from the injector assembly. Early engines attached both fuel manifolds parallel to the outside of the cylinder head(s). Later-model engines cast the fuel manifolds internally within the length of the cylinder head(s). Fuel pressure in the inlet fuel manifold varied based upon the engine speed, because the gear-driven pump volume would change proportional to engine rpm. Maximum fuel pressure is controlled by a relief valve located in the fuel pump to bypass high-pressure fuel back to the suction side. Maximum fuel pressures typically run between 50 to 110 psi (345 to 758 kPa) based on the specific system; therefore, they are commonly referred to as low-pressure fuel systems. The high injection pressures are developed within the injector as it is actuated by a rocker arm assembly. MUI models typically are capable of injection pressures ranging between 19,000 to 23,000 psi (1293 to 1565 bar). These common types of systems have been used for many years by Detroit Diesel Corporation and Caterpillar.

Another low-pressure mechanical fuel system that is unique to some Cummins Engine Company models is the pressure time (PT) system which operates somewhat similar to the rail system. A gear pump supplies fuel flow to a rotating plunger. The mechanical governor positions the plunger based on engine speed and load. The fuel under pressure is delivered to a fuel rail in the cylinder heads to feed the injectors. The engine speed determines the fuel pressure, which is relief valve controlled; and the time available for fuel metering at the injector determines the quantity of injected fuel and its timing. The fuel pressure in the PT system can be altered by changing the size of a fuel pump button to determine when fuel bypass occurs. This in turn controls the system fuel rail operating pressure which typically can range between 150 and 300 psi (1034 and 2068 kPa) under full-load governed speed. Typical injection pressures with the PT system range between 19,000 and 22,000 psi (1293 and 1496 bar). The PT system has now been superceded in most Cummins engines by the use of newer electronically controlled fuel systems. See Chapter 22.

Accumulator Pump System

Today Cummins Engine Company employs the Cummins accumulator pump system (CAPS) which is widely used on their ISC, QSC8.3, and ISL engine models (see Chapter 22). This electronically controlled pump system delivers fuel at pressures ranging between 5000 and 15,000 psi (340 and 1020 bar). The major function of this system is to control fueling (quantity) and timing control (start, duration, and end). The system also controls governed speed between the low and high idle set points. A number of engine sensors are employed with the system that interface with the Cummins electronic control module (ECM).

Jerk Pump System

The jerk pump system is the design concept used in pump-line-nozzle (PLN) systems which are typically manufactured by the Robert Bosch Corporation and their licensees since 1927 (see Chapter 19). These mechanical or electronically controlled systems employ an engine-gear-driven horizontal rotating camshaft. The camshaft is located within the base of the injection pump housing where the cam lobes lift a series of vertical pumping plungers in multiple-cylinder engines up and down to raise the fuel pressure high enough to be delivered to the nozzles and then into the combustion chamber. Over the many years of its use, the jerk pump system has been capable of injection pressures in the range of 15,000 to 20,000 psi (1034 to 1379 bar). Equipped with a variety of mechanical governor types, or Bosch's own electronic diesel control (EDC), these popular types of systems have been and still are widely employed on literally millions of diesel engines globally.

Distributor Pump System

Smaller and more compact injection pumps, known as distributor pumps, were awarded a British patent in 1914 to Francois Feyens of Belgium for an injection system using a rotary distributor to deliver metered fuel to the cylinders (see also Chapter 19). The design concept was adapted from the spinning distributor rotor used in gasoline engines, but rather than distributing a high-tension spark, high-pressure diesel fuel is sent to each cylinder injector in firing order sequence. Some pumps use two or more pumping plungers to create the high fuel pressures required for injection. Others employ a single pumping plunger that strokes and rotates to deliver fuel to the nozzles. Employed today in lighter-duty, lower-horsepower, smaller-displacement diesel automotive and light to midrange industrial engines, these pumps (due to their much smaller size) are limited to how much fuel can be metered and delivered. Injection pressures are about half of that which are obtainable from electronically controlled unit injectors. Newer models of distributor pumps are equipped with electronic controls and injection pressures of approximately 14,000 psi (96.5 MPa).

Two-Stage Injection

To comply with the stringent EPA Tier 11 exhaust emissions beginning in 2001, and applicable to all engines by 2006, engine OEMs are using a variety of technological improvements. See the exhaust emissions section in Chapter 4 for examples of possible changes to reduce tailpipe exhaust emissions.

These mandated global exhaust emission reductions may very well mean the end of mechanically controlled injection systems. However, even with the use of electronically controlled fuel injection systems, the final component in reducing exhaust emissions remains with the quantity, timing, duration, and ending of actual delivery of the fuel into the combustion chamber via the nozzle or unit injector. This precombustion control is the preferred way to reduce emissions by direct improvement of the combustion phase. In the interim, some engine OEMs have been forced to adopt postcombustion controls via the adoption of particulate traps and various other catalytic-type systems. Engineers currently employ the latest computer-based finite element modeling techniques and predictive mathematical tools to minimize engine noise and emissions. From this empirical engineering data and information, many engines are now designed to use two-stage injection to help reduce exhaust emissions.

Electronic and HEUI fuel injection systems are controlled by decisions made within the ECM based upon preprogrammed sensor operating parameters fed back to the ECM during fixed and variable engine operating conditions. Pump-line-nozzle type electronic fuel injection systems also employ various engine sensors that interface with the engine ECM, but must use a purpose-designed fuel pump with integral timing control to soften combustion noise. At the nozzle, combustion takes place by initially injecting a small quantity of fuel slowly to establish a soft flame front within the combustion chamber. This lowers peak cylinder pressure and temperature rise common to one-shot injection systems and, therefore, lowers the combustion noise. With a flame front now established, the continual opening nozzle is now designed to permit a greater rate of fuel delivery at a more rapid rate into the reentrant combustion chamber. The reentrant combustion chamber is usually formed by the piston crown bowl shape (see Figure 8–6), which assists the turbulence of the burning air and fuel. Once again this concept lowers the rate of pressure rise within the cylinder to reduce combustion noise.

One typical example of two-stage combustion in a current engine lineup is Isuzu's new three-cylinder 3LD2 and 4LE2 four-cylinder models, both of which are direct-injected (DI) engines that use individual unit pump injectors for each cylinder with a short high-pressure line running to each nozzle. The engines use two-stage injection for very quiet operation. An Isuzu-designed high-swirl Cobra combustion system reduces peak temperature in the premixed combustion stage to lower both combustion noise and NO_x (nitric oxide) emissions, in addition to promoting vigorous fast mixing in the diffusion combustion stage for lower smoke and particulate matter (PM) exhaust emissions. A more complete and efficient burn is achieved through a lower initial injection rate in the premix stage, and a higher rate in the diffusion stage. The injected fuel during the combustion diffusion phase occurs with the high-pressure nozzle that employs small orifices (holes) to minimize fuel particle micron size. This design concept reduces the length of the combustion cycle, but ensures a relatively higher swirl in the later stages. The improved combustion efficiency of this engine results in a waste heat rejection rate that is typically 20 to 25% lower than that of comparable IDI engine designs.

DISTRIBUTOR PUMP SYSTEM

The distributor pump system is found on small to medium-size diesel engines and is often referred to as a rotary pump, because its concept of operation is similar to that of the ignition distributor found on gasoline engines. A rotating member called a rotor within the pump distributes fuel at high pressure to the individual

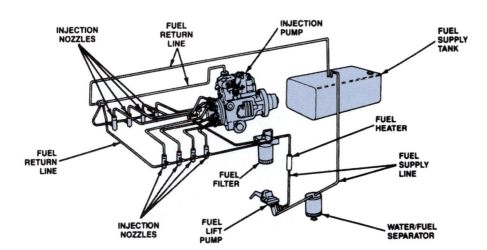

FIGURE 15–1 *Schematic of a distributor pump fuel system.* (Courtesy of Stanadyne Fuel Systems.)

injectors in engine firing-order sequence. It is classified as a high-pressure system and is limited to engine sizes up to about 1.3 L per cylinder. Distributor pumps do not have the capability to deliver sufficient fuel volume or to create high-enough fuel injection pressures and delivery rates for heavy-duty large-displacement high-speed diesel engines used in trucks. The distributor pump concept draws fuel from the tank through a primary filter or fuel filter/water separator as shown in Figure 15–1, which illustrates the fuel system for a V8 engine.

The fuel lift pump pressurizes the fuel to between 3 and 5 psi (21 to 34 kPa) and delivers it through a secondary fuel filter and on into the distributor pump housing, where the fuel pressure is increased by the use of a vane-type transfer or charging pump mounted inside the end plate of the injection pump assembly (opposite the drive end). Fuel under pressure from the vane pump is delivered to a charging passage inside the injection pump at a maximum regulated pressure of approximately 130 psi (896 kPa). The fuel is then metered and timed for delivery to the individual injection nozzles at pump pressures of from 3000 to 4000 psi (136 to 272 atm) on average. Each injection nozzle is directly connected to the pump hydraulic head by a high-pressure line. The adjustable nozzle release spring setting determines the actual injector opening pressure. A fuel return or leak-back line is used to by-pass fuel from the nozzles and injection pump to the secondary fuel filter assembly and the fuel tank.

Distributor pumps are manufactured by Stanadyne Diesel Systems; Robert Bosch, whose VE model is widely used; Lucas-Varity, now Delphi Automotive, with their legendary DPA (distributor pump assembly). Both Bosch and Delphi have a number of licensees worldwide who manufacture these distributor pumps for use in small lightweight and medium-duty diesel

engines, one being Zexel (Diesel Kiki) in Japan, and the United States.

Fuel Flow

Figure 15–2a illustrates the model DB2 Stanadyne mechanical injection pump and its major component parts. Flow through the injection pump is as follows: Fuel at lift pump pressure from the secondary fuel filter enters the injection pump at the hydraulic head end (injection line end). This fuel passes into the vane-type transfer pump (2) through a filter screen (1). To control maximum delivery pressure of the shaft-driven transfer pump, a spring-loaded pressure regulating valve will bypass fuel back to the inlet side of the transfer pump. This fuel pressure is set with the injection pump mounted on a fuel pump test stand and is usually limited to a maximum of 130 psi (896 kPa).

Transfer pump fuel flows through the center of the rotor and past the retainers (4) and into the hydraulic head of the injection pump. Fuel then flows up to the fuel metering valve (8), which is controlled by throttle position and governor action through connecting passage (5) in the hydraulic head to the automatic timing advance (6) and continues on through the radial passage (9) to this valve.

The pump rotor, which is turning at injection pump speed (one-half engine speed), allows the rotor fuel inlet passages (10) to align with the hydraulic head fuel charging ports. Fuel flows into the pumping chamber, where two rotor plungers are moved toward each other by their rollers (11), contacting a cam ring lobe. The rollers force the plungers inward to increase the pressure of the trapped fuel, which is directed out of the rotor discharge passage to the single spring-loaded delivery valve and then to the injection nozzle fuel delivery line. This occurs in firing-order sequence as the rotor revolves.

FIGURE 15–2 (a) Features of a Stanadyne model DB2 mechanical distributor injection pump; (b) fuel flow during the pump charging cycle; (c) fuel flow during the pump discharge cycle. (Courtesy of Stanadyne Diesel Systems.)

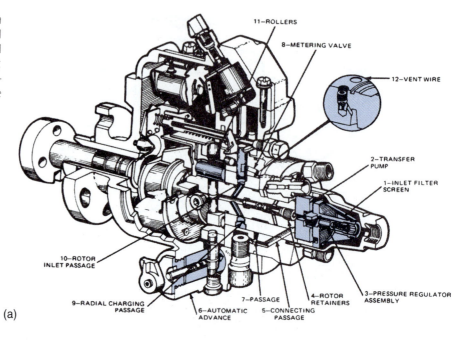

(a)

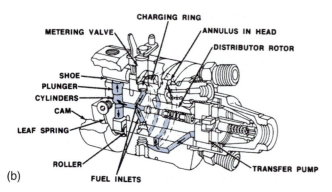

(b)

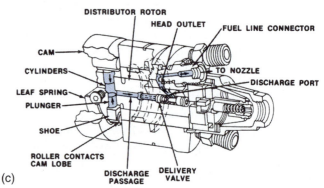

(c)

The purpose of the air vent passage (12) in the hydraulic head is to allow a percentage of fuel from the transfer pump to flow into the injection pump housing. This fuel is used to vent air from the system and also to cool and lubricate the internal pump components. This fuel flows back to the fuel tank via a return line.

Charging and Discharging Cycle

Charging Cycle

Rotation of the rotor allows both inlet passages drilled within it to register with the circular charging passage ports. The position of the fuel metering valve connected to the governor linkage controls the flow of transfer pump fuel into the pumping chamber and therefore how far apart the two plungers will be. The maximum plunger travel is controlled by the single leaf spring, which contacts the edge of the roller shoes. Maximum outward movement of the plungers will therefore occur only under full-load conditions. Figure

15–2b shows the fuel flow during the charging cycle. Any time that the angled inlet fuel passages of the rotor are in alignment with the ports in the circular passage, the rotor discharge port is not in registry with a hydraulic head outlet and the rollers are also off the cam lobes.

Discharging Cycle

The actual start of injection will vary with engine speed since the cam ring is automatically advanced by fuel pressure acting through linkage against it. Therefore, as the rotor turns, the angled inlet passages of the rotor move away from the charging ports. As this happens, the discharge port of the rotor opens to one of the hydraulic head outlets (see Figure 15–2c).

Also at this time, the rollers make contact with the lobes of the cam ring, forcing the shoes and plungers inward and thus creating high fuel pressure in the rotor discharge passage. The fuel flows through the axial discharge passage of the rotor and opens the spring-loaded delivery valve. Fuel then flows through the discharge port to the injection line and injector. This fuel delivery will continue until the rollers pass the innermost point of the cam lobe, after which they start to move outward, thereby rapidly reducing the fuel pressure in the rotor's axial discharge passage and simultaneously allowing spring pressure inside the injection nozzle to close the valve.

Delivery Valve Operation

To prevent after-dribble, and therefore unburned fuel with some possible smoke at the exhaust, the end of injection, as with any high-speed diesel, must occur crisply and rapidly. To ensure that the nozzle valve does in fact return to its seat as rapidly as possible, the delivery valve within the axial discharge passage of the pump rotor will act to reduce injection line pressure after fuel injection to a value lower than that of the injector nozzle closing pressure.

From some of the views shown so far you will recollect that the delivery valve is located within the rotor's axial passageway. To understand its function more readily, refer to Figure 15–3. The delivery valve requires only a stop to control the amount that it can move within the rotor bore. No seals as such are required, owing to the close fit of the valve within its bore. With a distributor pump such as the DB2, each injector is supplied in firing-order sequence from the axial passage of the rotor; therefore, the delivery valve operates for all the injectors during the period approaching the end of injection.

In Figure 15–3 pressurized fuel will move the valve gently out of its bore, thereby adding the volume of its

displacement to the delivery valve chamber, which is under high pressure. As the cam rollers start to run down the lobe of the cam ring, pressure on the delivery valve's plunger side is rapidly reduced and spring pressure forces the valve cuff to close the fuel passage off, thereby ending fuel injection at that cylinder.

Immediately thereafter, the rotor discharge port closes totally and a residual injection line pressure of 500 to 600 psi (3447 to 4137 kPa) is maintained. In summation, the delivery valve will seal only while the discharge port is open because the instant the port closes, residual line pressures are maintained by the seal existing between the close-fitting hydraulic head and rotor.

Fuel Return Circuit

A small amount of fuel under pressure is vented into the governor linkage compartment. Flow into this area is controlled by a small vent wire that controls the volume of fuel returning to the fuel tank, thereby avoiding any undue fuel pressure loss. The vent passage is behind the metering valve bore and leads to the governor compartment via a short vertical passage. The vent wire assembly is available in several sizes to control the amount of vented fuel being returned to the tank, its size being controlled by the pump's particular application. In normal operation, this vent wire should not be tampered with because it can be altered only by removal of the governor cover. The correct wire size would be installed when the pump assembly is being flow tested on a pump calibration stand.

The vent wire passage, then, allows any air and a small amount of fuel to return to the fuel tank. Governor housing fuel pressure is maintained by a spring-loaded ballcheck return fitting in the governor cover of the pump.

STANADYNE DS PUMP

Major manufacturers of distributor pump systems such as Delphi Automotive with its DPA, Robert Bosch with its automotive VE model, and Stanadyne with its well-known DB and DS distributor pumps are three of the major OEMs that have switched to electronic control for various models. One example of such an arrangement is illustrated in Figure 15–4 for the Stanadyne DS model, which is widely used on the General Motors turbocharged 6.5 L V8 pickup truck application.

The Stanadyne Model DS diesel fuel injection system offers electronic control of both fuel quantity and the start of injection timing. The mechanical governor and mechanical metering control system used on the DB2 automotive pump, for example, is replaced by a

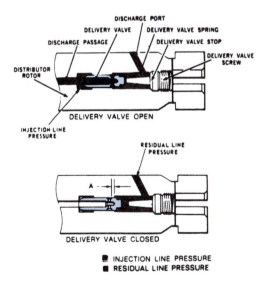

FIGURE 15–3 Mechanical distributor pump delivery valve action. (Courtesy of Stanadyne Diesel Systems.)

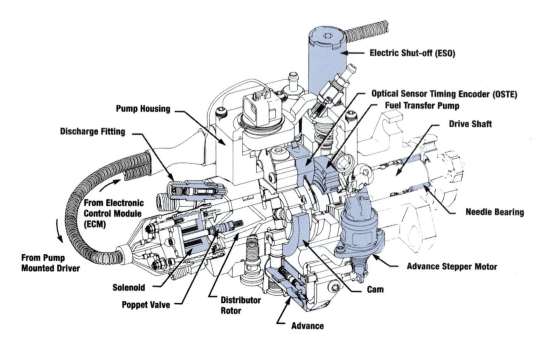

FIGURE 15–4   Major features of the Stanadyne electronic model DS distributor pump used on a number of diesel-powered pickup and light-duty truck applications. (Courtesy of Stanadyne Diesel Systems.)

FIGURE 15–5   Basic operation of the model DS distributor injection pump, ECM, and system sensors to send up-to-date engine information to the ECM. Pump speed and the angular pulse train data from the DS pump are also sent to the ECM where customized algorithms process this information and send appropriate injection command signals to the PMD. (Courtesy of Stanadyne Diesel Systems.)

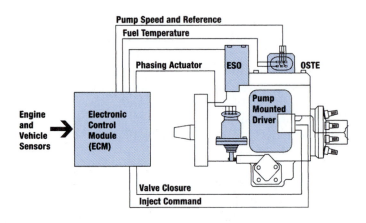

high-speed electrical actuator as shown in Figure 15–5. The DS pump is capable of handling up to 25 bhp (19 kW) per engine cylinder, with peak injection pressures to 14,500 psi (1000 bar).

As with all electronic engines, a number of electrical sensors send real-time engine operation information to the ECM. In addition, the injection pump speed and angular pulse train data are transmitted to the ECM. Custom algorithms process this information and send pulse-width-modulated (PWM) inject command signals to the pump-mounted solenoid driver. Additional input/output signals for other engine functions, such as glow plug control and EGR valves, are also initiated from the ECM. Figure 15–5 shows an electronic

control system schematic used with the DS model pumps. Each injection is directly controlled by a solenoid instead of an intermediate analog mechanism. This type of system permits precise control of both injection timing and fuel quantity to optimize engine performance and emissions.

This DS pump model features a single high-speed solenoid to control both fuel and injection timing. A solenoid spill valve mounted in the hydraulic head area of the pump rotor, to minimize high-pressure volume, is a key to the higher injection pressures available from this pump model over its mechanical counterpart. The geometry of the internal pump cam ring has been designed to ensure higher injection pressures as well as the desired control characteristics relative to the start, duration, and end of injection. The higher injection pressure has been enhanced through a new drive design that features a larger-diameter zero-backlash driveshaft containing the cam rollers and four plunger tappets. In this way, the driving loads are isolated from the spinning distributor rotor. A higher gear-drive torque, as well as a belt-drive capability if desired, are accommodated with the larger-diameter driveshaft.

This DS pump model was the first to be offered in the U.S. light-truck consumer market; it was introduced in 1994 Chevrolet and General Motors light trucks. The pump provides electronic control of both the fuel quantity and start of injection timing. The governor mechanism and fuel metering commonly used on the DB2 mechanical pump models have been replaced with a high-speed electrical actuator. Sensors provide information to an ECM, which then computes the actual time in milliseconds that the fuel delivery and timing should be for any given condition of engine operation. Signals from the ECM instruct the pump-mounted driver electronics to supply the correct fuel injection PWM signals.

Features of this electronic system can be seen in Figure 15–6; note the DS pump, the ECM, and the system sensors. These engine-mounted sensors send up-to-date operational data to the ECM. The pump speed

and the angular pulse train data from the pump are also sent to the ECM. The programmed algorithms within the ECM process this information and send an appropriate inject command PWM signal to the PMD (pump-mounted driver). Some of the features of the DS pump are listed next:

- Shot-to-shot modification of fuel delivery and timing
- Complete governing flexibility with enhanced idle speed control
- Flexible controls for cold-engine operation
- Transient adaptation of fuel delivery and timing
- Complete flexibility of fuel metering and injection timing control
- Electronic spill control with a single 12-V solenoid actuator for timing and fuel control
- Pump-mounted solenoid driver with poppet valve closure detection
- High-resolution pump-mounted angular encoder
- Four pumping plungers driven by the lobes on the internal pump cam ring
- Headless rotor drive to isolate torque loads from the rotor
- Fuel oil lubricated
- Fuel inlet at the top of the pump housing for V-engine configuration and accessibility

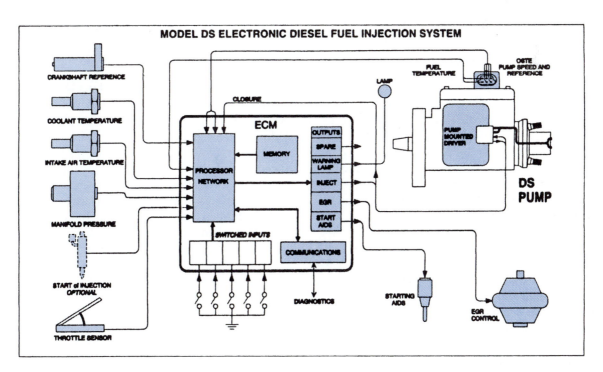

FIGURE 15–6 Model DS electronic distributor fuel injection system control schematic. (Courtesy of Stanadyne Diesel Systems.)

FIGURE 15–7 Model DS distributor injection pump mounted on a fuel pump test stand and connected to a special diagnostic test equipment package which includes a handheld diagnostic data reader (DDR), or scan tool. (Courtesy of Stanadyne Diesel Systems.)

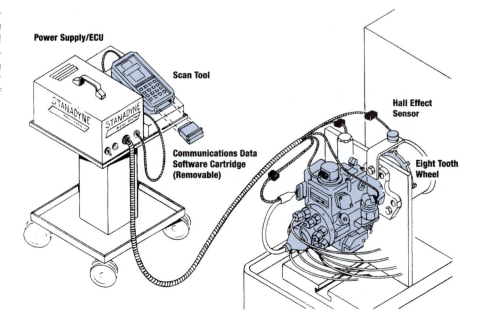

Servicing of this DS model pump requires approximately 20 new service tools. Figure 15–7 is an example of a DS pump mounted on a fuel injection pump test stand; the pump is connected to a power supply/ECU. A conventional-type handheld scan tool can also be used with the correct software data cartridge to monitor fault codes, and so on. Such a tool would be similar to that used on automotive gasoline engines and heavy-duty diesel engines with electronic unit injector systems.

DELPHI AUTOMOTIVE SYSTEMS

Delphi Automotive Systems headquartered in the United States recently purchased the Lucas fuel injection systems group from Lucas/Varity PLC. Lucas/Varity Industries PLC was the parent organization of Bryce, Simms, and CAV, all of which have been recognized fuel injection pump OEMs for many years. All three are now incorporated under the Delphi name. CAV began producing inline injection pumps under license from REF-Apparatebau in the late 1920s. A contract was signed in October 1931 whereby Robert Bosch became a 49% participant in CAV. This agreement was terminated due to World War II and the companies went their separate ways.

Today, Delphi is one of the world's leading suppliers of both electronic and mechanical diesel and gasoline fuel injection systems and components, supplying one-third of the growing European diesel car, van, and light-truck market with fuel injection systems. In the multiple-plunger inline fuel injection pump range, the Minimec, Majormec, and Maximec are very well known. In the smaller diesel engine line, the legendary CAV DPA (distributor pump assembly) has enjoyed unparalleled success for many years, with 30 million of these and the DPS-version pumps having been sold to date. Latest versions of the original DPA are now equipped with electronic controls, some of which are discussed in this section. In addition, Delphi produces small flange-mounted unit pumps for industrial, generator, and marine applications of 4 to 50 hp (3 to 37 kW), in one-, two-, three-, and four-cylinder configurations. Delphi injection pump products, nozzles, and injectors are produced throughout the world by a number of licensee companies. Caterpillar electronic injector systems were developed in conjunction with Delphi Automotive Systems.

The Bryce division of Delphi has for years produced single-cylinder plunger-type injection pumps for large-bore slow-speed engines. Today, Bryce continues in this field, now offering electronically controlled plunger pumps, or alternatively, an electronically controlled unit injector system. These single-cylinder heavy-duty jerk pumps range from a nominal stroke of 0.78 in. (20 mm) to 1.968 in. (50 mm), with a maximum pump plunger diameter from 0.866 in. (22 mm) to 1.968 in. (50 mm). The maximum fuel delivery output for these heavy-duty very-large-bore slow-speed industrial and marine engines can range from 2740 mm^3 per plunger stroke, to 39,250 mm^3 per stroke. Compare the delivery of 39,250 mm^3 [39.25 cm^3 (where 1000 cm^3 equals 1 liter)] to the injection quantity of approximately 205 mm^3 per stroke from an electronic unit

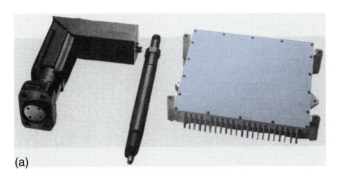

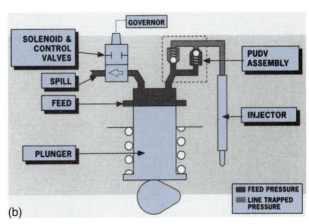

(a)   (b)

FIGURE 15–8   (a) Lucas Bryce electronically controlled fuel system. (b) electronic unit pump; injector nozzle; ECU. (Courtesy of Delphi Automotive Systems.)

injector typically used on a 400- to 450-hp (298- to 336-kW) high-speed heavy-duty truck engine, and you can readily appreciate the physical size difference and fuel requirements of these two engine systems.

Figure 15–8 illustrates an example of the electronic control system used by Lucas Bryce. In this system an electronically controlled plunger pump driven directly from the engine camshaft supplies fuel to the injector via a high-pressure pipe. The electric solenoids are operated by a heavy-duty electronic drive unit that is designed as an integral part of the system. Complementary electronic governors are available to suit specific applications.

Delphi also owns Hartridge Test Products, one of the leaders in the manufacture of diesel fuel injection test and servicing equipment. This division, resulted from combining the U.K. business of Lucas Hartridge Ltd. with U.S.-based Allen Automated Systems to form one of the world's largest assembly and test system specialists.

DELPHI DISTRIBUTOR PUMPS OVERVIEW

The current model range of Delphi distributor pumps are all based upon the original DPA (distributor pump assembly) design from Lucas CAV in England. The DPA pump was a result of an agreement with RoosaMaster (now Stanadyne Fuel Systems) in the United States signed in 1956, that enabled CAV (now Delphi) to manufacture their own version of Vernon Roosa's distributor pump system. There are still many millions of DPA pumps in existence around the world. Details on the operation of the DPA pump is described first as a base unit, since the newer Delphi distributor

pumps operation are easier to understand from the DPA concept of operation. Today the original DPA distributor pump is available in the following newer models; DP200, DPC, DPCN and EPIC versions. An overview of each one of these pump models follows the DPA pump description.

DPA Fuel Injection Pump

The pump derives its name from the fact that its main shaft is driven and runs through the center of the pump housing lengthwise. Fuel is in turn distributed from a single-cylinder opposed plunger control somewhat similar to a rotating distributor rotor in a gasoline engine. The pump can be hub mounted or gear driven because its shaft is very stiff to eliminate torsional oscillation and ensure constant accuracy of injection.

Figure 15–9 shows a cutaway view of a typical DPA fuel injection pump with a mechanical governor. Figure 15–10 shows a DPA pump with a hydraulic governor. All internal parts are lubricated by fuel oil under pressure from the delivery pump. The pump can be fitted with either a mechanical or hydraulic governor, depending on the application; a hydraulically operated automatic advance mechanism controls the start of injection in relation to engine speed. The operation of the fuel distribution is similar to that found in Stanadyne distributor pumps in that a central rotating member forms the pumping and distributing rotor driven from the main drive shaft on which is mounted the governor assembly.

Fuel Flow

Mounted on the outer end of the pumping and distributing rotor is a sliding vane-type transfer pump that receives fuel under low pressure from a lift pump

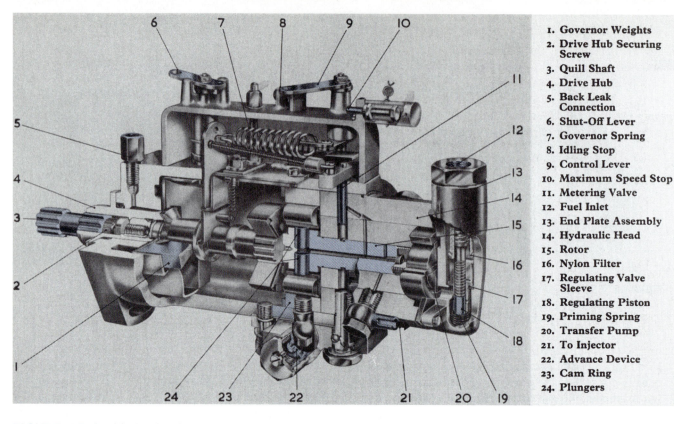

1. Governor Weights
2. Drive Hub Securing Screw
3. Quill Shaft
4. Drive Hub
5. Back Leak Connection
6. Shut-Off Lever
7. Governor Spring
8. Idling Stop
9. Control Lever
10. Maximum Speed Stop
11. Metering Valve
12. Fuel Inlet
13. End Plate Assembly
14. Hydraulic Head
15. Rotor
16. Nylon Filter
17. Regulating Valve Sleeve
18. Regulating Piston
19. Priming Spring
20. Transfer Pump
21. To Injector
22. Advance Device
23. Cam Ring
24. Plungers

FIGURE 15–9 Mechanical DPA (distributor pump assembly) equipped with a mechanical governor. (Courtesy of Delphi Automotive Systems.)

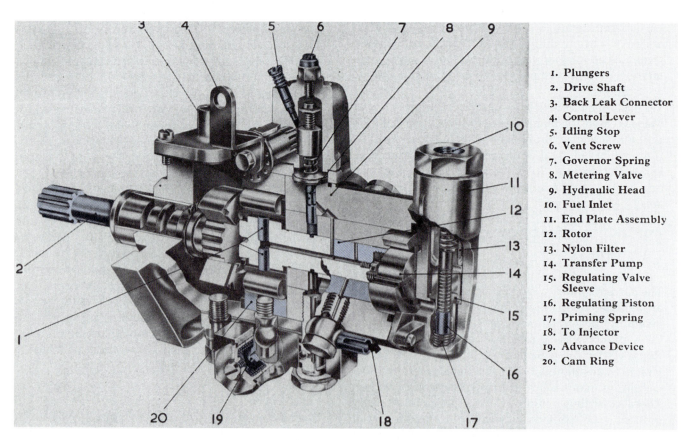

1. Plungers
2. Drive Shaft
3. Back Leak Connector
4. Control Lever
5. Idling Stop
6. Vent Screw
7. Governor Spring
8. Metering Valve
9. Hydraulic Head
10. Fuel Inlet
11. End Plate Assembly
12. Rotor
13. Nylon Filter
14. Transfer Pump
15. Regulating Valve Sleeve
16. Regulating Piston
17. Priming Spring
18. To Injector
19. Advance Device
20. Cam Ring

FIGURE 15–10 DPA (distributor pump assembly) pump equipped with a hydraulic governor. (Courtesy of Delphi Automotive Systems.)

mounted and driven from the engine. This lift pump pressure enters the vane-type pump through the fitting on the injection pump end plate opposite the drive end and passes through a fine nylon gauze filter.

The vane-type pump has the capability of delivering more fuel than the injection pump will need; therefore, a pressure-regulating valve housed in the injection pump end plate allows excess fuel to be bypassed back to the suction side of the vane transfer pump. This valve is shown in Figure 15–9, Item 18.

In addition to regulating fuel flow, the pressure-regulating valve also provides a means of bypassing fuel through the outlet of the transfer pump on into the injection pump for priming purposes. As seen in Figure 15–9 the regulating valve is round and contains a small free piston whose travel is controlled by two light springs. During priming of the injection pump, fuel at lift pump pressure enters the central port of the regulating valve sleeve and causes the free piston to move against the retaining spring pressure, thereby uncovering the priming port at the lower end of the sleeve, which connects by a passage in the end plate to the delivery side of the vane-type transfer pump, which leads to the injection pump itself.

Once the engine starts, we now have the vane-type transfer pump producing fuel under pressure, which enters the lower port of the regulating valve and causes the free piston to move up against the spring.

As the engine is accelerated, fuel pressure increases, allowing the free piston to progressively uncover the regulating port, thereby bypassing fuel from the outlet side of the vane pump. This action automatically controls the fuel requirements of the injection pump.

Let us study the action of the fuel under pressure once it leaves the vane-type pump and flows to the injection pump. The pumping and distributor rotor, which is driven from the drive on the engine, rotates within the stationary hydraulic head, which contains the ports leading to the individual injectors. The number of ports varies with the number of engine cylinders. Figure 15–11 shows the rotor during the charging cycle and delivery cycle. In Figure 15–11, fuel from the vane-type transfer pump passes through a passage in the hydraulic head to an annular groove surrounding the rotor and then to a metering valve (see Figure 15–9), which is controlled by the throttle position.

The flow of fuel into the rotor (volume) is controlled by the vane-type pump's pressure, which depends on the speed of the engine and hence throttle or governor position. Fuel flowing into the rotor [Figure 15–11(a)] comes from the inlet or metering port in the hydraulic head. These inlet ports are equally spaced around the rotor; therefore, as the rotor turns, these are aligned successively with the hydraulic head inlet port.

The distributor part of the rotor has a centrally drilled axial passage that connects the pumping space between the plungers with the inlet ports (the number depending on the number of engine cylinders) and single distributing port drilled radially in the rotor. As the rotor turns around, the single outlet port will successfully distribute fuel to the outlet ports of the hydraulic head and on to its respective injector. See Figure 15–11(b).

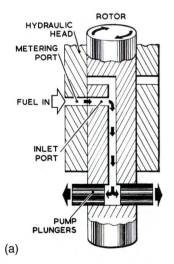

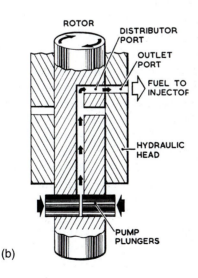

(a)   (b)

FIGURE 15–11 DPA injection pump. (a) Fuel inlet or charging; (b) Injection stroke or fuel delivery to nozzle. (Courtesy of Delphi Automotive Systems.)

The pumping section of the rotor has a cross-drilled bore that contains the twin opposed plungers, which are operated by means of a cam ring (internal) carried in the pump housing, through rollers and shoes that slide in the rotor. The internal cam ring has as many lobes as there are engine cylinders. For example, a 4-cylinder engine would have four internal lobes operating in diagonally opposite pairs.

The opposed plungers have no return springs and are moved outward by fuel pressure, the amount being controlled by throttle position, metering valve, and the time during which an inlet port in the rotor is exposed to the inlet port of the hydraulic head. As a result, the rollers that operate the plungers do not follow the contour of the internal cam ring entirely, but they will contact the cam lobes at points that will vary according to the amount of plunger displacement. The maximum amount of fuel delivered to an injector is therefore controlled by limiting the maximum outward movement of the plungers.

DP200

Applications

Designed for both on- and off-highway applications, the DP200 range of pumps is suitable for 3, 4, and 6 cylinder engines, up to 79 cu. in. or 1.3 liters per cylinder. It can be applied to both naturally aspirated and turbocharged engines.

- **Progressive Light Load Advance** A new hydraulic control mechanism has been introduced to regulate the pump's timing schedule. This enables closer matching of injection timing to that needed to meet the emissions regulations. A total of up to 8° pump advance range is available.
- **Torque Curve Shaping** The option of a Torque Trimmer means it is no longer necessary to compromise a pump's hydraulic performance and timing plan to produce a required delivery curve shape. Once the pump's hydraulics and timing plan have been developed to meet performance and emissions targets the Torque Trimmer is designed to deliver the required torque curve shape.
- **Enhanced Mechanical Governor** An improved mechanical governor offers close control and greater repeatability of governor performance which is maintained throughout the pump's life.
- **Control in Cold Conditions** A waxmotor actuated cold advance device is available to improve cold start performance, eliminate misfire, and reduce white smoke under cold conditions.

Operating Principle

The basic principle of the DP200 series of pumps is the same as for the DPA and DPS ranges. Fuel enters the pump and is raised to an intermediate pressure of around 72.5 to 87 psi, or 5 to 6 bar which is used for power and control of the pump's mechanisms which regulate fuel quantity and injection timing.

During the period between injections fuel is fed into the center of the distributor rotor through a control (metering) valve. At full fuel this is held wide open and the pump delivers a maximum fuel quantity which is regulated by the maximum displacement that is allowed for the pumping elements. This maximum displacement is a variable in the case of a torque trimmer specification giving control over the delivery (torque) curve shape. At lower loads the fuel delivery is controlled by the mechanical governor which acts on the metering valve to throttle the flow into the pump.

During the pumping phase the plungers are forced inwards by the internal cam ring causing an injection pulse to travel from the pump, through the outlet connections (usually delivery valves for secondary injection suppression), to the high pressure pipes and thence to the fuel injector in the engine's cylinder head. The timing of the injection event is controlled by rotating the cam relative to the driveshaft and thus the engine.

DPC

Applications

The DPC pump was developed for indirect injection diesel engines fitted in both passenger cars and light vans. There are DPC pumps available to suit NA or TC four cylinder engines up to 152.5 cu. in. or 2.5 liter capacity.

DPC Advantages

- **Proven Design** The DPC range uses the internal cam pumping mechanism employed on all the Delphi DP pumps, and proven in the 20 million pumps which incorporate this principle sold to date.
- **Improved Driveability** A two speed fuel governor fitted as standard improves driveability. At full load the mechanical governor regulates maximum engine speed by closing the metering valve. At idle the governor regulates speed at a constant value. A throttle lever damper, or dash-pot can be fitted as an option which controls the speed of operation of the throttle lever so reducing engine "judder."

- **Improved Operability** A Fast Idle enables the idle speed to be increased, and can be used either to improve operability, or to increase engine load.
- **Reduced Emissions** Using an electronic control unit to accurately control the exhaust gas recirculation valve position, a 40% reduction on NO_x is achieved.
- **Improved Engine Starting** Excess fuel delivery and start retard systems are used to assist engine starting.
- **Improved Cold Starting** A number of different cold advance devices are available which reduce smoke and engine speed instability:
  –Mechanical cold advance
  –Hydraulic cold advance
  –Solenoid cold advance
  –Electrical valve cold advance
- **Vehicle Security** A security mechanism has been developed and is being fitted to the DPC; this consists of an electronic anti-start device, which can have a number of security interfaces including keypad.
- **Choice of Timing Control Options to Meet Emissions Regulations** As emissions regulations become increasingly stringent, the accuracy of injection must improve; the DPC range offers three options:
  1. **Light Load Advance** Offering two options for the cam position, this minimizes engine emissions.
  2. **Progressive Advance** This ensures a smooth transition between the two cam positions, further minimizing engine emissions.
- **Improved Idling Performance** Due to the use of a pre- and post-heating device.
- **Turbocharger Boost Control** The boost controller adjusts the maximum fuel delivery versus turbocharger pressure. This ensures maximum engine torque while maintaining the smoke level within emissions regulations.
- **Altitude Compensation** This device reduces the maximum fuel delivery at altitude; the air mass reduction requires a fuel delivery reduction in order to prevent smoke being produced.

Operating Principle

- A built-in transfer pump draws fuel from the tank via a filter.
- The fuel then passes through a metering valve into the pumping element. This pumping element consists of two opposed plungers connected to a roller assembly which rotates in a cam ring.

- The rate of injection and the end of injection are defined by the cam profile.
- The beginning of injection is defined by the cam position. The cam is connected to an advance device.
- The fuel is distributed to each cylinder at high pressure via passages in the hydraulic head.
- Back leaks in the high pressure pipes are prevented by the delivery valves.

DPCN

Description

The DPCN range offers an advancement in emissions control and passenger comfort. Developed specifically for indirect injection diesel engines, and for use on cars and light vans, the DPCN range is based on the mechanical DPC, but operated via an electronic control unit (ECU).

Product Design

The DPCN uses the well-proven internal cam pumping mechanism used on all Delphi DPC pumps, which requires no external lubrication. A built-in transfer pump is used to draw fuel from the tank via the filter. The fuel then passes into the pumping element via a metering valve which is linked to the throttle lever and mechanical governor. The pumping element consists of two opposed plungers and forms part of the distributor rotor. These are connected to a roller and shoes assembly which rotates in a cam ring.

Applications

The DPCN range of rotary pumps are available for cars and light vans, for 4 cylinder engines up to a capacity of 152.5 cu. in. or 2.5 liters.

DPCN Advantages

- **Proven Technology** The DPCN is based on the proven DPC rotary pump, but fitted with an ECU, offering the benefits of advanced technology.
- **Reduced Emissions** The precision fuel injection offered by the ECU results in a reduction in emissions, and will enable engines to meet emissions legislation.
- **EGR Control** In addition to controlling the pump, the ECU can also control a wide range of EGR systems, including closed loop control.
- **Vehicle Security** DPCN pumps can assist vehicle security; all the pumps in the range can be fitted with an electronic anti-start device, operated via a dash-mounted keypad.

- **Fast Idle Control** With the DPCN pumps it is possible to increase idle speed using the fast idle device; controlled by the ECU, this device can be used to improve acceleration from a standing start. This device can be used to improve:
  - –cold operation
  - –acceleration from a standing start
  - –engine behavior on vehicles with air conditioning
- **ECU Control** The ECU enables a range of other features to be included on the DPCN pumps, these include: anti-theft device, air conditioning, automatic transmission, pre-post heating, and exhaust gas recirculation.

Operating Principle

- The fuel injection process is initiated when a transfer pump draws fuel from the tank via a filter.
- The fuel then passes into the pumping element. The rate at which the fuel is introduced is controlled by the cam profile, with the optimum cam position being determined by the ECU. The start of injection is detected by a needle lift sensor. The signal is given to the ECU to drive the actuator which rotates the cam ring.
- Fuel is then delivered at high pressure to each of the injectors at the optimum timing and in the correct firing order.

EPIC

Applications

EPIC is currently available for indirect injection engines where injection pressures are up to 5075 psi, or 350 bar, and direct injection engines where injection pressures of up to 13,775 psi, or 950 bar are necessary.

FIGURE 15–12 EPIC (electronic pump injection control) system. (Courtesy of Delphi Automotive Systems.)

Operating Principle

The principle component of the EPIC (electronic pump injection control) system shown in Figure 15–12, is the fuel injection pump which uses the proven cam pumping mechanism. The brain which operates the system is the ECU (electronic control unit); this receives signals from sensors positioned in various points in the vehicle, engine and pump, and in turn sends signals to the pump actuator to operate at the chosen timing and fuel delivery.

- Fuel enters the pumping chamber via a transfer pump.
- The ECU sends signals to the drain and feed solenoids in the pump to open or close; this enables precise control of the axial displacement of the rotor using a position sensor in a feedback loop, thereby providing accurate control of the fuel quantity injected.
- Timing is controlled by a solenoid actuator which regulates the position of the cam by varying hydraulic pressure.

EPIC Advantages

- **Emissions Reduction** The EPIC system enables accurate timing of fuel delivery and control of exhaust gas recirculation; this results in a substantial reduction in emissions.
- **Improved Driveability** EPIC minimizes engine speed oscillations during acceleration; this is achieved by using both the transient response characteristics of the pump and the sophisticated ECU.

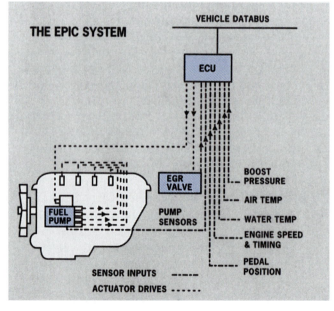

- **Smoother Idling** Engine idle speed is tightly controlled with EPIC by modulating shot to shot fuel delivery, thus reducing noise and vibration.
- **Integration With Other Vehicle Systems** EPIC can be integrated into a modern vehicle database; this then enables the system to communicate with other vehicle systems such as traction control, ABS, and automatic transmission. Other vehicle systems can also be incorporated.
- **Self Diagnostic and Performance Check** The system carries out an extensive range of self diagnostic and performance checks using two microprocessors: one carries out the data processing while the other acts as a back-up, checking correct operation of the first unit. The driver is alerted of any major faults by a light situated in the dashboard.
- **Optional Extra Features** The ECU enables the system to be linked to an extensive range of optional extra equipment including cruise control, anti-theft devices, and air conditioning.

Distributor Pump Timing

Timing of a distributor pump is not unlike that for a PLN fuel system, in that generally the No. 1 cylinder piston should be placed at TDC on its compression stroke. Minor variations exist between the makes and models of pumps used, and also the specific make and model of engine to which it is fitted. Information on Bosch VE distributor pumps can be found by referring to Chapter 19. In this chapter we will look at how to time a Stanadyne DB2 and DB4 and a Delphi-Lucas DPA model when fitted to Cummins midrange engines, namely the B-series models.

Stanadyne DB2 and DB4 Pumps

The procedure for both the DB2 and DB4 models is as follows:

1. Rotate the crankshaft to place No. 1 cylinder piston near its TDC-compression position. This can be confirmed by looking at the timing marks located on the flywheel via the flywheel housing inspection window. The number of degrees for a specific engine can be found on the engine CPL/dataplate. On engines with a front timing indicator, the notch in the pulley must align with the center of the timing indicator.

2. TDC can be determined by viewing the position of the valves for No. 1 cylinder, or you can manually stroke the fuel transfer pump priming lever. When the No. 1 piston is on the correct stroke, the lever will have free travel.

3. Refer to Figure 15–13 and, with the pump timing window removed, check the timing marks which

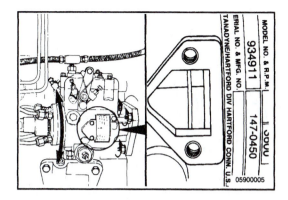

FIGURE 15–13 *Checking the injection pump mating timing line marks through the removed timing cover plate on a model DB2/DB4. (Courtesy of Cummins Engine Company, Inc.)*

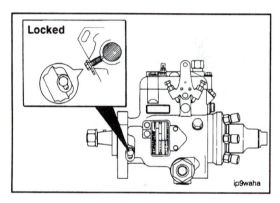

FIGURE 15–14 *Location of the DB2/DB4 injection pump driveshaft locking screw. (Courtesy of Cummins Engine Company, Inc.)*

should be aligned. If not, loosen off the three pump mounting nuts and manually rotate the injection pump until the marks are in alignment. Tighten the nuts and repeat the timing procedure to ensure that the marks are in fact aligned. Install the gasket and timing cover back onto the injection pump.

4. For the DB4 pump typically used on Cummins B gen-set applications, the procedure differs as follows:

- Rotate the injection pump driveshaft in the direction of rotation to align the timing line on the weight retainer (timing cover removed as per the DB2) hub with the line on the pump camshaft ring.
- Position the driveshaft locking key plate in the locked position as per Figure 15–14. Turn the locking screw until it contacts the pump driveshaft.

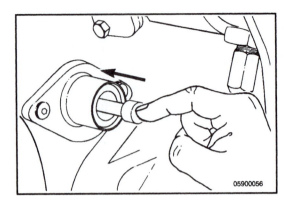

FIGURE 15–15 *Pushing in the timing pin on the backside of the engine front timing cover to locate TDC for No. 1 cylinder. (Courtesy of Cummins Engine Company, Inc.)*

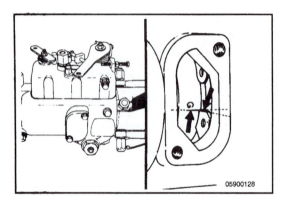

FIGURE 15–16 *With the injection pump timing inspection window cover removed, align the specified alphabetical letter scribe mark line with the flat side of the large internal snap-ring. (Courtesy of Cummins Engine Company, Inc.)*

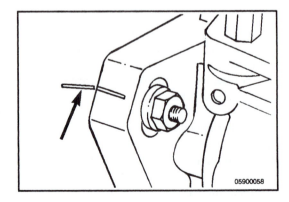

FIGURE 15–17 *Example of the matching timing scribe line between the injection pump and the engine mounting flange. (Courtesy of Cummins Engine Company, Inc.)*

Lucas CAV Pump Timing

The procedure for timing the DPA pump, somewhat similar to that for the Stanadyne, is as follows:

1. Rotate the engine crankshaft to place No. 1 piston at TDC compression. On some Cummins engines a timing pin can be inserted through the backside of the front timing cover as shown in Figure 15–15. This will confirm that No. 1 piston is at TDC-compression.

2. Remove the injection pump inspection window on the side as shown in Figure 15–16.

3. Locate the correct alphabetical letter on the engine data plate.

4. Look inside the injection pump window. For example, if the timing letter was *G*, this letter scribe mark should be aligned with the flat edge of the large internal snap-ring. If it is not aligned, loosen off the injection pump retaining nuts and rotate the pump housing until timing is correct. After tightening the nuts, repeat the timing procedure to check that the pump is in fact correctly timed.

5. Typically when the injection pump is correctly timed, the alignment marks on the injection pump flange and gear housing should be aligned as shown in Figure 15–17.

DCR (DELPHI DIESEL COMMON RAIL SYSTEM)

Description

To meet the future stringent emissions requirements, and offering further improvements in fuel economy, Delphi Diesel Systems, one of the world's largest producers of fuel injection equipment, has developed a new, high pressure fuel injection system—the Delphi Diesel Common Rail system (DCR). See Figure 15–18.

Fuel Injection Equipment with the capability of operating at very high pressures will be required to achieve the ultra low emissions challenges and low noise demands of the coming years, and this latest addition to the Delphi diesel portfolio, the Delphi Common Rail system extends the Delphi fuel injection product range for future High Speed Direct Injection (HSDI) engines.

Product Features

- Injection pressure, independent of speed.
- High pressure injection.
- Reduced NO_x emissions and engine noise.
- Modular system, easily adapted to different engine types.

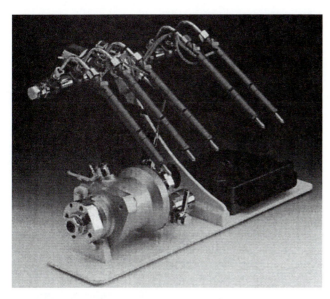

FIGURE 15–18 Components for a common rail fuel system. (Courtesy of Delphi Automotive Systems.)

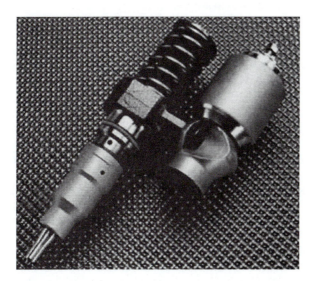

FIGURE 15–19 View of an electronic unit injector (EUI). (Courtesy of Delphi Automotive Systems.)

- Compact design.
- Full electronic control and interface with other vehicle functions.

Operating Principle
- A feed pump delivers the fuel through a filter unit to the high pressure pump.
- The high pressure pump delivers fuel to the high pressure accumulator (the Rail).
- The injectors, inject fuel into the combustion chamber when the solenoid valve is actuated.

- Because the injection pressure is independent of engine speed and load, the actual start of injection, the injection pressure, and the duration of injection can be freely chosen from a wide range.
- The introduction of pilot injection which is adjusted depending on engine needs, results in significant engine noise reduction, together with a reduction in NO_x emissions.
- The pressure in the system is controlled by the actuator.

EUI (ELECTRONIC UNIT INJECTOR)

Product Design
In the EUI system the fuel injection pump, the injector, and a solenoid valve are combined in one, single unit; these unit injectors are located in the cylinder head, above the combustion chamber. The EUI in Figure 15–19 is driven by a rocker arm which is in turn driven by the engine camshaft. This is the most efficient hydraulic and mechanical layout, giving lowest parasitic losses.

The fuel feed and spill pass through passages integrated in the cylinder head. The EUI uses sensors and an electronic control unit (ECU) to achieve precise injection timing and fuel quantities. Sensors located on the engine pass information to the ECU on all the relevant engine functions; this evaluates the information and compares it with optimum values stored in the ECU to decide on the exact injection timing and fuel quantity required to realize optimum performance; signals are then sent to the unit injector's solenoid-actuated spill valve system to deliver fuel at the timing required to achieve this performance.

Injection is actuated by switching the integrated solenoid valve; the closing point of the valve marks the beginning of fuel delivery, and the duration of closing determines the fuel quantity.

Product Features
- High injection pressure—up to 29,000 psi, or 2,000 bar.
- Near ideal rising rate injection diagram.
- Additional injection rate shaping using two stage lift and pilot injection.
- Fully flexible electronic fuel quantity and timing control.
- Control of all engine functions.
- 'Shot to shot' fuel adjustment.
  Ability to communicate with other vehicle functions.
- Full diagnostics capability.
- An integrated fuel injection system to help engine designers meet the needs of the 21st century.

Operating Principle

- Each plunger moves through a fixed stroke, actuated by the engine camshaft.
- On the upward (filling) stroke, fuel passes from the cylinder head, through a series of integrated passages and the open spill valve into a chamber below the plunger.
- The ECU then sends a signal to the solenoid stator which results in the closure of the spill control valve.
- The plunger continues its downward stroke causing pressure to build in the high pressure passages. At a preset pressure the nozzle opens and fuel injection begins.
- When the solenoid stator is de-energized the spill control valve opens, causing the pressure to collapse, which allows the nozzle to close, resulting in a very rapid termination of injection.
- More specific details on the complete operation of EUI's can be found in Chapters 18, 21, 22, and 23.

Delphi Diesel Systems expects that by 2005, diesel engines will account for more than 40% of European new car sales. Delphi supplies second generation common-rail diesel systems to Ford, Renault, and PSA Peugeot Citroen. This is the first closed-loop control system for diesel engines incorporating Accelerometer Pilot Control (APC) which allows injection to be adjusted as conditions change. This system provides lower noise levels and lower CO2 emissions. Although Delphi is No. 2 behind Bosch in overall diesel fuel injection systems for light, medium, and heavy-duty vehicles, Delphi is the only technology supplier worldwide with the capability to provide a complete solution, including injection systems, engine management systems, emissions control, and fuel handling systems. Expand your knowledge by accessing Delphi's excellent website at www.delphiauto.com; go to Engine Management Systems, then scroll-down to Diesel Systems and click on a chosen item where you can download PDF format files dealing with a wide variety of their diesel products discussed in this chapter.

SUMMARY

Having reviewed this chapter, you should be conversant with the various types of mechanical and electronic fuel injection systems, and the names of the major engine OEMs that use these different systems. Test your knowledge of these different systems by visually determining what type of fuel injection system is being used on a variety of available engines/equipment.

SELF-TEST QUESTIONS

1. Technician A says that the person credited with mass producing a high-pressure fuel injection system for diesel engines was
   a. Street
   b. Carnot
   c. Diesel
   d. Bosch

2. Technician A says that fuel injection systems are generally classified as being either a high-pressure or a low-pressure design. Technician B says that all fuel systems operate on a high-pressure design. Which technician understands this difference best?

3. Technician A says that all fuel systems operate on the distributor pump concept. Technician B disagrees and says that a distributor pump system is just one type of fuel system. Who is correct?

4. Technician A says that with the exception of distributor pumps and Cummins PT systems, all pump-line-nozzle and unit injector fuel systems operate on the jerk pump concept. Technician B disagrees. Who knows their basic operational theory best?

5. Technician A says that as well as being more compact than PLN systems, distributor pump systems are capable of delivering higher injection pressures. Technician B disagrees and says that PLN systems can produce higher injection pressures. Who is right?

6. Technician A says that unit injector fuel systems are capable of delivering higher injection pressures than are PLN systems. Technician B says that they deliver the same pressure. Who is right?

7. True or False: The letters PT in Cummins mechanical fuel systems stand for "pressure time."

8. True or False: Electronic controls permit closer regulation over the start and end of injection and, along with the various sensor inputs to the ECU/ECM, reduce exhaust emissions levels.

9. Technician A says that Detroit Diesel has been using unit injectors in their engines longer than any other engine OEM. Technician B says that Caterpillar has always used unit injectors in their engines. Who is correct?

10. Technician A says that PLN systems are classified as low-pressure fuel system: Technician B says that PLN systems are high-pressure fuel systems. Who is right?

11. True or False: Cummins PT fuel systems are classified as low-pressure fuel systems.

12. The letters HEUI mean
    a. hydrostatic engine unit injectors
    b. hydraulically actuated electronic unit injectors
    c. high-output engine unit injectors

16

Mechanical and Electronic Governor Operation

Overview

Although no ASE tasks list test deals specifically with mechanical and electronic governors, today's diesel technician needs to understand fully the purpose, function, and operation of both mechanical and electronic governor systems, because each controls fuel flow to the engine cylinders, and consequently can affect the vehicle, equipment, or vessel performance. The various tasks lists in the ASE medium/heavy truck tests preparation guide, test T2 diesel engines Part F, fuel system diagnosis and repair, which deals with both mechanical and electronic components, require that you understand these systems to be able to effectively and efficiently perform the diversified inspections, checks, and adjustments to fuel injection pumps and governors. Review the T2 tasks list for item F, Parts 1 and 2, as follows. Part 1, item 5—the inspection, adjustment, repair/replace throttle, and linkage/cable and controls—is a control part of the mechanical governor assembly. Items 7 and 13 also deal with mechanical governors, and are as follows:

7. Perform on-engine inspections, tests, adjustments, and time, or replace and time inline type injection pumps, governors, and drives.

13. Inspect, test, adjust, repair/replace engine fuel shutdown devices and controls, including engine protection shutdown devices, circuits, and sensors.

Also in the T2 tasks list, Part A, general engine diagnosis, items 11 and 12 can be related to mechanical or electronic governor controls, as follows:

11. Diagnose problems of no cranking, crank but fails to start, hard starting, and starts but does not continue to run; determine needed repairs.

TIP An engine that cranks but fails to start, hard starts, or does not continue to run can be traced to possible mechanical linkage/governor causes.

12. Diagnose surging, rough operation, misfiring, low power, slow deceleration, slow acceleration, and shutdown problems; determine needed repairs.

A speed surge invariably occurs when the engine is running at low idle speed. Engines equipped with Bosch PLN (pump-line-nozzle) systems, Zexel Corporation, and Nippondenso PLN injection pumps, and mechanical governors, offer a bumper screw located on the governor housing. This screw can be adjusted with the engine running at idle speed to eliminate surging or engine rolling. Refer to Chapter 19, which deals with Bosch fuel systems, for more specifics on this important adjustment. Detroit Diesel Corporation two-stroke-cycle mechanical engine models, and their earlier 8.2 L four-stroke models, employ a buffer screw which is located on the governor housing. This screw is also designed to eliminate engine surge at low idle rpm. Refer to Chapter 21 and DDC fuel systems for more specifics on this adjustment. Rough operation, engine misfiring and low power, acceleration and deceleration, and engine shutdown problems can be related to mechanical governor misadjustments or linkage faults.

Woodward hydramechanical governor models, such as the PSG and UG8 models, both offer a needle valve screw that can be adjusted when the engine/governor is at normal operating temperature. Typically this needle valve screw is adjusted in or out (CW or CCW) until hunting stops. If the screw is set to between one-half to three-fourths of a turn out from being lightly bottomed, the engine should run stable. On the UG8 model, an additional adjustment, the compensating lever adjusting pointer, may also require adjustment toward the maximum compensation position on the governor face plate to provide engine speed stability.

Electronic governors used on industrial engine applications such as gen-sets have various external screw pot (potentiometer) adjustments located on the control module. These typically provide correction to low idle and rated speed, as well as to engine gain and speed droop. On heavy-duty truck engines equipped with electronic governors (see Figure 18-1), an engine speed and position sensor is used to send informational data to the ECM, which in turn controls engine fueling, power, speed, and droop. Refer to the various OEM diesel engine fuel systems electronic engine control chapters in this book. The index can also help to locate specifics on exactly how the electronic governor interacts with the fueling system to control the various operating characteristics. Later in this chapter we provide a description of how an electronic governor operates in conjunction with a circuit schematic.

GOVERNOR FUNCTION

Since the speed of the engine is directly related to its power, speed must be maintained during operation. This is the job of the governor, which is considered the brain of the engine. The diesel engine governor controls the engine speed under various load conditions by changing the amount of fuel delivered to the engine cylinders. Governors, like engines, may be of many types and designs, but all will be designed to accomplish engine speed control under low-idle, high-speed, and full-load conditions.

If, for example, a truck engine did not have a governor, the operator would have to control the engine speed at idle manually, since the engine would not idle unattended. On the other end of the speed range, the top speed of the engine would have to be limited by the operator or the engine would overspeed and could cause engine damage. It is obvious that a governor on a truck engine is a much-needed component. Without it, the operator would have difficulty in controlling the engine properly.

This speed may be anywhere in the speed range from idle to high speed; then as the machine is operated, it may encounter a change in load many times a minute, causing the governor to change the fuel delivery accordingly. This fuel delivery change, in turn, maintains steady engine speed with sufficient power to pull the load. The operator could not possibly antici-

pate the rapid load change encountered by the engine to maintain a steady engine speed as well as sufficient power to pull the load.

WHY A GOVERNOR IS REQUIRED

The speed and horsepower capability of any internal combustion engine is regulated by the volume of air that can be retained within the engine cylinders and the volume of fuel that can be delivered and consumed during the engine power stroke. More than likely you have a driver's license, so you are aware of the fact that when you drive a car or truck equipped with a gasoline engine, *you* determine the rate of fuel supplied to the engine by manipulation of the gas or throttle pedal. Regardless of whether the engine is carbureted or fuel injected, throttle movement controls the flow of air into the engine cylinders and thus the desired fuel flow.

Therefore, a mechanical or electronic governor assembly is not necessary on a gasoline engine. Nevertheless, some gasoline engines in industrial and truck applications are equipped with a governor to control the maximum speed and power of the engine/vehicle. In addition, some models of passenger cars are equipped with an electronic ignition cutoff system to control the maximum speed of the vehicle. Remember, a governor is not a "must" with a gasoline engine as it is with a diesel engine.

Why then does a diesel engine require a governor assembly? The main reason is the throttle pedal controlled by the operator does not regulate the airflow into the diesel engine but controls the fuel flow. Current gasoline engines in passenger cars have electronic controls for both the ignition and fuel systems and are designed to operate at air/fuel ratios that allow the engine to comply with existing U.S. EPA exhaust emissions standards. Through the use of an exhaust gas oxygen sensor, the air/fuel ratio is in *closed-loop* operation (oxygen sensor receives an input reference voltage signal from the ECM and returns a system operating condition signal back to the ECM to complete the circuit). The oxygen sensor monitors the percentage of oxygen in the exhaust gases leaving the engine. The ECM then either leans out or enriches the air/fuel mixture to try and maintain a *stoichiometric* air/fuel ratio, which is between 14.6 and 14.7 parts of air to 1 part of fuel (gasoline).

Due to the unthrottled air supply condition, a diesel engine at an idle speed runs very lean, with air/fuel ratios being between 90 and 120:1, depending on the specific model of engine in question. Under full-load conditions, this air/fuel ratio is approximately 25–30:1.

Let us assume for instructional purposes that a given four-stroke-cycle diesel engine is designed to produce 400 bhp (298 kW) at 2100 rpm full-load speed. If we also assume that to produce this power, each fuel injector is designed to deliver 185 mm^3 of fuel into each cylinder for each power stroke, then by manual operation of the throttle we might assume that at an idle speed of 600 rpm, the fuel delivery rate to each cylinder might be only 18.5 mm^3 with the engine producing possibly 40 bhp (30 kW). A similarly rated two-stroke-cycle engine would inject approximately half as much fuel per power stroke, but since there are two power strokes for every one in the four-cycle engine, both engines will consume approximately the same amount of fuel.

If the vehicle is stationary and the throttle is placed into a WOT (wide-open throttle) position, the engine does not need to receive full fuel (185 mm^3) to accelerate to its maximum no-load speed. The engine can be accelerated with very little additional fuel being supplied to the cylinders, because with no load on the engine, we have to overcome only the resistance to motion from the engine components, as well as any accessory driven items that need more horsepower to drive them at this higher speed. In addition, if the engine has very little additional load from what it had at an idle rpm, the faster rotating flywheel will store enough inertia (centrifugal force generated at the higher speed) to keep the engine turning over smoothly at this higher no-load speed.

Once the engine obtains this higher no-load speed, in this example, say, 2250 rpm, the same amount of fuel (or slightly more) that was supplied at idle will basically maintain this higher speed. However, on a diesel engine, remember that manual operation of the throttle controls the fuel flow and *not* the airflow as happens on a gasoline engine. Therefore, by opening the throttle to a WOT position in this engine, we actually deliver 185 mm^3 of fuel to the engine cylinders, or 10 times more than we did at idle speed; but all we need to maintain this higher no-load rpm is basically the same volume of fuel that we used at idle (18.5 mm^3) at 600 rpm, or slightly more. If we generated 40 bhp (30 kW) at 600 rpm, at WOT we might develop an additional 10 to 15 hp (7.5 to 11 kW) to handle the increased power requirements of the various accessory items such as a fan, air compressor, or generator. We certainly do not require the 400 bhp (298 kW) rated power output of the engine under this operating condition.

Without a governor assembly, a WOT position grossly *overfuels* the engine in this high-idle no-load example by about 10 times its needs. Since we know from earlier discussions that the diesel engine always operates with an excess air supply, we have sufficient air to burn this full-fuel delivery rate. The result will be that with 10 times more fuel than necessary, the engine rpm will continue to climb in excess of a safe operating speed. Under such a nongoverned overfueled condition, most diesels will quickly self-destruct as a result of valves striking piston crowns and connecting rods punching through the engine block as well as possible crankshaft breakage.

When a load is applied to a diesel engine, more fuel delivery is obviously required to generate the extra heat energy to produce the higher horsepower required. In our simplified example, this engine can produce 400 bhp (298 kW) at 2100 rpm WOT full-load operating conditions. It is only under such a condition that this engine needs its 185 mm^3 of fuel delivery to each cylinder. Refer to the engine performance curve charts illustrated in Chapter 3; you can see that the power produced by the engine increases with speed, since horsepower is considered as being the rate or speed at which work is done by the engine. To prevent the engine from over-revving and running away, we must have some type of control mechanism that will limit the amount of fuel injected to the engine cylinders under all operating conditions. In other words, we need either a mechanical or electronic governor assembly on the engine.

MECHANICAL GOVERNOR OPERATION

Regardless of governor type, most governors operate with many of the same basic components. These components should be understood before further governor study can take place. The basic mechanical governor (Figure 16–1) is a speed-sensing device that uses two main components: a set of engine-driven flyweights and a spring. Each of these components serves a purpose in *all* mechanical governors. The force of the spring is designed to move the fuel control linkage to an *increased* setting under all operating conditions. The centrifugal force generated by the engine-driven flyweights is designed to *decrease* the fuel control linkage setting under all operating conditions.

When the engine is stopped, the force of the governor spring is therefore attempting to place the fuel control racks into a full-fuel position. On some engines, the governor is arranged so as to provide excess fuel for startup purposes, whereas on some turbocharged engine models, a mechanical adjustment device limits startup fuel to half-throttle to minimize exhaust smoke. In these simplified governor diagrams, we show the manual throttle control as being connected directly above the governor spring; in reality, seldom is this the case. Instead, additional linkage is used to transfer the manual operation of the throttle to the governor spring assembly.

Increasing the force of the governor spring through the throttle linkage when the engine is running manually increases the fuel rack setting, resulting in an increase in engine speed and power. As the engine accelerates, the centrifugal force generated by the

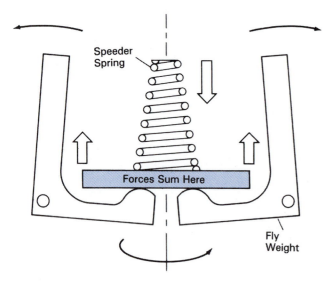

FIGURE 16–1 *Mechanical governor operating concept; weight force versus spring force to achieve governor speed balance—often referred to as a state of balance; weights always attempt to decrease the fuel rack setting, while the spring always attempts to increase it.*

rotating flyweights becomes stronger and the flyweights oppose the force of the spring. For a given throttle setting, the force applied to the spring will cause the weights to generate an equal and opposing force. When the spring force and weight forces become equal for a given engine load and speed, the governor is said to be in a *state of balance*, and the fuel racks will be held in a stationary position with the engine producing a specific horsepower at a given rpm.

Since the governor weights are engine driven, the governor assembly is said to be *speed sensitive*. An engine speed change due to a load increase or a load decrease will affect the rotational speed of the flyweights and, therefore, the state-of-balance condition that exists between the weights and the governor spring for any throttle setting position.

The only problem with the oversimplified governor assembly shown in Figure 16–1 is that we have no means by which we can change the engine speed setting by manipulation of a throttle. The simplified diagram in Figure 16–2 shows a method by which we can vary the compressive force of the governor spring assembly, but the speed regulation of the engine would be limited by the force required to balance out this spring by the rotating governor flyweights and this system would not allow an engine speed change by a speed control lever when the engine is running.

To be able to change the fuel delivery to the engine manually, we have to introduce linkage that allows the truck driver to accelerate and decelerate the engine at will due to changing road, load, and speed conditions. Figures 16–3 and 16–4 illustrate simple examples of

FIGURE 16–2 *Three examples of the mechanical governor action: (a) state of balance condition where the centrifugal force of the weights balances the spring force (b) an engine load decrease causes a speed increase, resulting in a decrease in the fuel rack setting; (c) an engine load increase causes a speed decrease resulting in an increase in the fuel rack setting.*

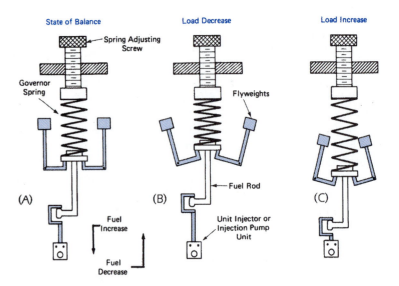

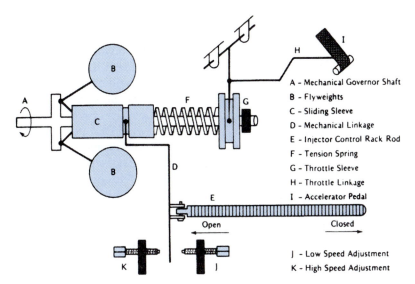

FIGURE 16–3 *Governor linkage connections from the throttle (either hand or foot) to the governor assembly for a port/helix multiple plunger inline injection pump assembly.*

A - Mechanical Governor Shaft
B - Flyweights
C - Sliding Sleeve
D - Mechanical Linkage
E - Injector Control Rack Rod
F - Tension Spring
G - Throttle Sleeve
H - Throttle Linkage
I - Accelerator Pedal

J - Low Speed Adjustment
K - High Speed Adjustment

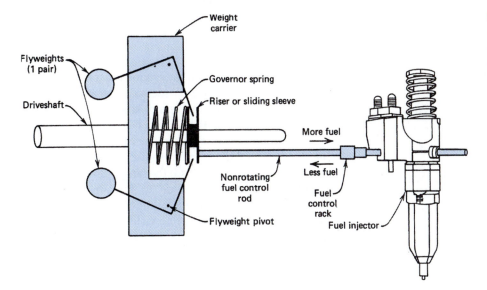

FIGURE 16–4 *Basic mechanical governor linkage connections used with a MUI (mechanical unit injector) type fuel system.*

how we might achieve this with a single-spring all-range or variable-speed mechanical governor. This governor is capable of controlling the idle speed, the maximum speed, and all ranges in between. Take careful note of the connections between the components of this governor assembly. To increase the fuel injection pump rack setting, the following events must take place in Figure 16–3:

1. Press down on the accelerator pedal, shown as item I.

2. Throttle linkage H will move to the left-hand side of the diagram.

3. The vertical throttle linkage that extends down from the support bracket is supported above in two bushings, to allow the linkage to rotate each time the pedal is moved.

4. The lower end of the vertical throttle linkage is engaged with a sliding throttle sleeve, shown as item G. Any throttle depression will therefore cause this sliding sleeve to move to the left against the compressive force of the governor spring F.

5. The mechanical linkage D will therefore move to the left-hand side of the diagram. As D moves, it will pull the injector control rack rod or inline multiple-plunger pump control rack E to an increased or "open" fuel position.

6. The maximum fuel rack position is limited by the fact that linkage D will eventually butt up against the adjustable high-speed stop bolt K.

7. The position of the throttle pedal is determined by the truck driver or operator. When the sliding sleeve G is moved to the left, the governor tension

spring F is placed under compression and the sliding sleeve C applies pressure to the toes of the flyweights, causing them to move inward slightly.

8.   The operator has manually caused the fuel rack to move to an increased setting which allows the engine to accelerate, and it starts to develop additional horse-power due to the additional fuel supply to the combustion chambers.

9.   When the operator halts throttle pedal movement, the now-faster rotating governor flyweights will reach a point where they attain a state of balance with the stronger governor spring. When this state of balance exists between the weight and spring forces, the engine will run at a steady speed.

10.   The simplified governor shown in Figure 16–3 is capable of controlling the engine speed throughout the complete speed range and is therefore known as an all-range or variable-speed type. The idle speed is set by the position of the adjustable low-speed adjustment screw shown as item J. Turning the screw clockwise will increase the speed, while rotating it counterclockwise will decrease the speed.

Starting and Idling the Engine

In Figure 16–3 the following sequence of events would occur during the initial cranking and starting procedures. With the engine stopped and the throttle linkage held in the idle position by the force of an external return spring, the tension spring F would expand and move the governor fuel control linkage D and E (rack) into a full-fuel position against the stationary flyweights. The throttle pedal would not move, since a yield link or telescopic link assembled into the throttle linkage can be used to prevent this from occurring. The expansion of the governor spring F allows the spring to give up some of its stored energy in moving the rack control linkage. When the engine is cranked over on the starter motor, shaft A will rotate and the weights B will attempt to move out against the tension spring F. As soon as the engine fires and runs, the accelerating flyweight force will start to compress the tension spring and push it to the right-hand side of the diagram. This action forces the linkage D and the rack E to move to a decreased fuel setting. The linkage movement D toward the closed fuel position will be limited by the setting of the low-speed adjustment screw J. As the weights compress the tension spring F, the spring force becomes stronger until the centrifugal force of the rotating flyweights is equal to that in the spring. When this position is obtained, the governor is said to be in a state of balance and the engine will run at a steady idle speed. To change the idle speed, the low-speed adjusting screw J is turned CW or CCW.

Load Increase at Idle

In Figure 16–3, when a load is applied to the engine at an idle speed, the state of balance between the weights and the tension spring F is disturbed in favor of the spring, because the engine speed will decrease with a load increase, causing the weights to move inward. The spring expands, giving up some of its energy in moving the fuel control linkage toward an open or fuel-increase position. The engine now receives additional fuel in order to develop additional horsepower to handle the increased load. The sensitivity of the governor mechanism determines just how quickly the engine will respond. As the engine develops more power, the weights will attempt to move outward again; however, since the spring is now longer and weaker than it was before the load was applied (expanded to increase fuel setting), the weights will obtain a new state of balance at a lower engine speed. This is known as the droop factor, because the engine will not return again to the same speed.

Load Decrease at Idle

If a load is removed from the engine at an idle rpm, the engine speed will tend to increase, causing the flyweights to move outward against the tension spring F. This action will push the sliding sleeve C and the linkage D, which is connected to the rack E, to the right-hand side of the diagram. Less fuel is delivered to the combustion chambers and the engine will now develop less horsepower. Due to the stronger initial weight force caused by the load decrease, the weights and tension spring obtain a new state of balance, but at a slightly higher speed, due to the force that was applied to the spring, which made it stronger. Again this is part of the governor's inherent droop factor.

Governor Action at the High-Speed End

The maximum speed of the engine is limited by the compressive force that can be applied to the tension spring F. Throttle pedal movement at I will force the throttle sleeve G to move the spring F, the linkage D, the rack E, and the sliding sleeve C to the left-hand side of the diagram. The maximum distance that the linkage D can move is limited by the high-speed adjustment screw K. This positive stop therefore limits the applied force to spring F from the throttle pedal. Regardless of where the truck driver places the governor linkage D between idle and maximum, the rotating governor flyweights B will be able to obtain a state of balance. Starting the engine under a no-load condition and then moving the throttle to its maximum (high idle) speed setting position will result in the engine obtaining a higher speed than it would under a full-load (rated) speed condition. The maximum no-load (high idle) speed of the engine is limited by the fact that the weights will start to compress the tension spring F, due to their higher rotative speed. Consider that if the engine were adjusted to produce a maximum no-load speed of 2310 rpm with a 10% sensitive governor, this means that the full-load or rated speed would be 2100 rpm. The initial placement of the throttle pedal into its maximum speed position compresses the tension spring F, which moves the fuel rack E to an increased fuel setting. As the engine accelerates, the weights are trying to develop enough force to oppose the spring. Since the weights are speed sensitive, as they reach a speed of 2100 rpm, they have enough force to start compressing the spring, which will move the rack E to a decreased fuel position. As they start to compress the spring, it becomes stronger, until a state of balance is obtained and the engine speed is limited in this case to no more than 2310 rpm no-load. If a load is now applied to the engine, its speed will decrease and the state of balance will be upset in favor of the tension spring F. The governor linkage D and the rack E will now be moved into an increased fuel position. If a full load is applied to the engine, it will settle at a rated speed of 2100 rpm. However, if less than full load is applied to the engine, the speed will settle down somewhere between the maximum no-load (high-idle) and the maximum full-load (rated) speeds. Therefore, the governor automatically compensates for changes in load and/or speed as a consequence of throttle movement or road terrain in a heavy-duty truck application.

GOVERNOR TERMS

All diesel engines must operate with a governor mechanism to control the speed and response of the engine under varying load and throttle opening conditions. As a foundation for our discussion of governor types and their operation, study the following governor terms; they are commonly used in reference to engine speed regulation.

Although most engine and fuel injection equipment manufacturers use the same general terms, phraseology fluctuates between specific engine manufacturers. Common meanings, and the different terms, will be discussed where applicable.

1. *Maximum no-load speed* or *high-idle* is a term used to describe the highest engine rpm obtainable when the throttle linkage is moved to its maximum position with no load applied to the engine. This rpm can be adjusted to suit changing conditions or applications according to the engine manufacturer's limits and recommendations.

2. *Maximum full-load speed* or *rated speed* indicates the engine rpm at which a particular engine will produce its maximum designed horsepower setting as stated by the manufacturer.

3. *Idle* or *low idle speed* is the term used to indicate the normal speed at which the engine will rotate with the throttle linkage in the released or closed position. Normally, truck idle speed settings range between 500 and 700 rpm and are adjustable.

4. *Work capacity* describes the amount of available work energy that can be produced at the governor's terminal or output shaft. Each specific mechanical or hydromechanical governor assembly is designed to have enough work output to ensure that it can move the associated linkage that is connected to it. The work capacity is generally expressed in inch-pounds or foot-pounds.

5. *Stability* refers to the condition of the governor linkage after a load or speed setting change. The governor must be able to return the engine to a new speed/load setting without any tendency for the engine speed to drift up or down (fluctuate) before settling down at the new setting. Stability of a governor is usually indicated by the number of corrective movements it makes and the time required to correct fuel flow for any given load change.

6. *Speed droop.* An engine operating at WOT with no load on it will run at a higher speed than it does at WOT under full load. Why will the engine not run at the same speed loaded or unloaded? The answer has to do with the term *governor droop*, or how "sensitive" the governor assembly is to an engine speed change. How much speed will be lost or gained depends on the governor reaction. The difference between the engine MNL (maximum no-load) speed (high idle) and the MFL (maximum full-load) speed (rated) is known as governor droop. This can be determined as follows:

$$\text{droop} = \frac{\text{MNL} - \text{MFL}}{\text{MFL}} \times 100\%$$

$$= \frac{2250 - 2100}{2100} \times 100\% = 7.14\%$$

In this example, the droop is actually 150 rpm, which is a full-load droop speed. Regardless of the speed at which the engine is running, this droop percentage will remain constant; however, the rpm will change. Seven percent of 2250 rpm versus 7% of 1200 rpm results in droop readings of 150 and 85 rpm, respectively. An engine idling at 600 rpm with no load would result in a speed loss of 42 rpm when fully loaded.

What causes droop? To describe this condition, we refer to the three simplified diagrams illustrated in Figure 16–2. When the engine is stopped, the weights are collapsed and the spring force pushes the fuel rack to the maximum position for startup purposes. When the engine is cranked and fires, the centrifugal force generated at the weights starts to compress the spring, while at the same time pulling the fuel rack to a decreased fuel setting. When the weight and spring forces are equal, the governor is said to be in a state of balance (SOB) condition. The position of the fuel rack is held at a position corresponding to this SOB. For example, with the throttle held at an idle position, the engine would run at this speed setting, which can be adjusted by a screw to change the spring force.

If in Figure 16–2a the weights and spring are at a SOB condition and the spring is compressed to 4 in. (102 mm), let us assume the spring has a stored energy (force) of 10 lb (4.5 kg). If we now apply a load to the engine at this fixed throttle position as shown in Figure 16–2c, the engine requires more power to maintain this SOB condition. The additional load will cause the engine speed to drop, which will upset the SOB condition between the weights and spring. This allows the spring to expand and give up some of its stored energy in moving the fuel racks to an increased position. Let us assume that the spring is now 4.25 in. (108 mm) long, with a stored energy of only 9 lb (4 kg); the centrifugal force generated by the rotating flyweights will be able to obtain a new SOB with this longer and weaker spring at a lower engine speed. The engine will now be running at a slower rpm, but with more fuel being delivered to the cylinders it will produce more horsepower to handle the additional load. The difference in engine speed due to this rebalancing between the weights and spring is what causes the "droop."

With the engine running at a fixed throttle position and a SOB condition similar to that shown in Figure 16–2a, we are now going to decrease the load as shown in Figure 16–2b. Once again we upset the SOB between the weights and spring in favor of the weights because the engine would now tend to pick up speed. As the weights fly outward due to the higher engine rpm, the spring is compressed as the fuel rack is pulled to a decreased fuel setting. Let us assume that the spring is now 3.75 in. (95.25 mm) long and has a stored energy of 11 lb (5 kg); with a shorter and stronger spring, the weights will have to rotate faster to maintain a new governor SOB condition. However, with the fuel rack at a decreased setting due to a lighter load, the engine now runs slightly faster but produces less horsepower. Once again, droop has entered the speed change picture.

In a variable-speed (all-range) governor, the weights and spring can control any speed setting selected by the operator. In a limiting-speed (minimum/maximum) governor, however, the speed control is designed to operate only at the lower and higher ends of the speed zones. Between these speeds, the operator controls engine speed by manual operation of the throttle. Regardless of the type of governor employed on an engine and the speed at which it is running, a load increase or a load decrease situation results in governor reactions similar to those illustrated in Figure 16–2.

7. *Sensitivity* is an expression of how quickly the governor responds to a speed change. For example, a governor that responds to a speed change of 5% is more sensitive than a governor that responds with a 10% speed change. Once the governor has sensed a speed change, it must produce a corrective movement of the fuel control mechanism.

8. *Response time* is tied closely to the governor's sensitivity and is normally the time taken in seconds for the fuel linkage to be moved from a no-load to a full-load position.

9. *Isochronous* is the term used to indicate zero-droop capability. In other words, the full-load (rated) and no-load (high idle) speeds are the same.

10. *Speed drift* is usually most noticeable at an idle speed and more commonly referred to as *hunting* or *surging*, where the set speed tends to rise above or below the initial governed setting. Speed drift is usually easily adjustable by means of a buffer screw or a bumper spring on the governor housing.

11. *Overrun* is a term used to express the action of the governor when the engine tends to exceed its maximum governed speed. Generally, overrun occurs when the engine is driven by the vehicle road wheels, such as when descending a steep hill.

12. *Underrun* is simply a term used to describe the governor's inability to prevent the engine speed from dropping below a set idle, particularly when the throttle has been moved rapidly to a decreased fuel setting from a high idle or maximum full-load position. This can generally result in the engine stalling.

13. *Deadband* is the term used to describe a very narrow speed range during which no measurable correction is made by the governor.

14. *State of balance* is the common term used to describe the speed at which the centrifugal force of the rotating governor flyweights matches and balances the governor speeder spring force. This can occur at any speed in an all-range governor as long as the speed of the engine can develop sufficient horsepower to carry the load applied.

TYPES OF GOVERNORS

There are a number of different types or styles of governors used on diesel engines. Some of these are common to industrial, marine, and power gen-set applications. Basic types of governors can be classified in the following six categories:

1. Mechanical centrifugal flyweight style, which relies on a set of rotating flyweights and a control spring; used since the inception of the diesel engine to control its speed. Millions of these are still used in one form or another on mechanically operated and controlled diesel fuel injection systems.

2. Power-assisted servomechanical style, which operates similarly to that described in category 1 but also employs engine oil under pressure to move the operating linkage. Used on many engines, such as Caterpillar PLN products, in a variety of applications.

3. Hydraulic governor, which relies on the movement of a pilot valve plunger to control pressurized oil flow to a power piston, which in turn moves the fuel control mechanism. Commonly used on industrial, marine, and power gen-set engine applications.

4. Pneumatic governor, which is responsive to the airflow (vacuum) in the intake manifold of the engine. A diaphragm within the governor housing is connected to the fuel control linkage, which changes its setting with increases or decreases in the vacuum.

5. Electromechanical governor assembly, which uses a magnetic speed pickup sensor on an engine-driven component to monitor the rpm. The sensor sends a voltage signal to an electronic control unit, which in turn controls the current flow to a mechanical actuator connected to the fuel linkage. Commonly used on stationary power plants and generator sets.

6. Electronic governor assembly, which uses a magnetic speed sensor to monitor the engine rpm. The sensor continuously feeds a signal back to an ECM (electronic control module). The ECM then computes this signal with information from other engine/vehicle sensors, such as the throttle position sensor, turbocharger boost sensor, engine oil pressure and temperature, engine coolant level or temperature, and fuel temperature, to limit the engine speed. The ECM actually alters the PWM (pulse-width-modulated) electrical signal to the electronically controlled injectors to control how long fuel is injected over a given amount of crankshaft degrees. This type of governor is typical of that now in use on Detroit Diesel, Caterpillar, Cummins, Mack, Volvo, and Mercedes-Benz engines.

The governors used on highway truck applications fall into one of two basic categories:

1. *Limiting-speed governors,* sometimes referred to as *minimum/maximum* models since they are intended to control the idle and maximum speed settings of the engine. Generally, there is no governor control in the intermediate range, which is regulated by the position of the throttle linkage by the driver/operator.

2. *Variable-speed* or *all-range governors,* which are designed to control the speed of the engine regardless of the throttle setting.

NOTE A constant-speed-range governor assembly is another type of governor that allows the engine to go immediately to a fixed-speed setting after startup and stays there minus the droop unless it is capable of isochronous control. This type is used for industrial applications only.

ZERO-DROOP GOVERNORS

A *zero-droop governor,* or isochronous (single time) governor, is capable of maintaining the same engine speed—loaded or unloaded. This governor assembly is designed for adjustable droop through either an internal or external adjustment screw mechanism. The adjustable-droop feature may range from 0 to 10%, depending on the model of governor used. A zero-droop condition is one in which the engine runs at the same rpm loaded or unloaded. The adjustable-droop feature allows the internal governor linkage fulcrum point to be adjusted, so that after a load change the spring force is returned to the same length and strength. This ensures that the engine will continue to rotate at the same rpm.

A governor with adjustable droop is commonly used on a diesel power gen-set. It is needed to ensure that when one or more engines are electrically tied together in a parallel arrangement, each engine can handle its share of the load in proportion to its gen-set rating. Generally, one engine governor is adjusted for zero droop to monitor the system, and the other engine governors are set to allow equal load sharing. Even if we select two identical model engines set at the same horsepower and driving equal sized gen-sets, mass production of parts prevents every engine from being able to produce the exact same horsepower at the same rpm. Variations in cylinder pressures and fuel delivery rates account for characteristic changes in both horsepower and acceleration. Adjustable-droop governors allow us to set up each engine for equal-load sharing capabilities.

ADJUSTABLE-DROOP GOVERNORS

In diesel engine applications that require closer speed regulation than that which can normally be achieved from the use of a mechanical governor assembly, a hydramechanical (oil pressure to move a power piston connected to the rack linkage is often used) or electronic governor can be selected.

It is often an advantage to employ a governor assembly that offers an adjustable-droop feature. This design allows the technician to tailor the desired droop rpm of the engine to suit many different engine and equipment applications.

One widely used example of a hydramechanical governor assembly is shown in Figure 16–5a, which illustrates a Woodward pressure-compensated simple governor (PSG) model. Manufactured by the Woodward Governor Company, one of the longest-established and best known prime mover governor control companies, Woodward products are used by every major engine OEM worldwide. In addition to hydramechanical models, Woodward also offers a wide range of electro-hydraulic and electronic models for engines and gas turbines of all shapes, sizes, and power outputs, including jet aircraft engines.

PSG Model

The governor shown in Figure 16–6 uses engine lube oil or an oil supply from a separate pump whose lift should not exceed 12 in. (0.3048 m), and a foot valve should be furnished. Use a 20-μm filter with a minimum capacity of 2 gallons (7.57 L). If the governor is mounted horizontally, the needle valve must be on the bottom and a 0.25 in. (6.35 mm) pipe tapped hole provided in the upper part of the governor case to drain oil away to the sump. Four check valves contained within the base plate of the governor permit rotation in either direction. Two of the passages can be plugged if rotation is only required in one direction. The oil pump within the governor is capable of producing either 75, 175, or 225 psi above inlet pressure and is controlled by the relief valve spring setting (517.12, 1206.62, or 1551.37 kPa oil pressure).

The PSG is normally isochronous (zero droop will be maintained as long as the engine is not overloaded). On power generator applications, when ac generating sets are tied in with other units, one governor can be set to zero droop by the droop adjusting bracket, which will regulate the frequency of the entire system. If speed droop is required, however, to permit load division between two or more engines driving generators

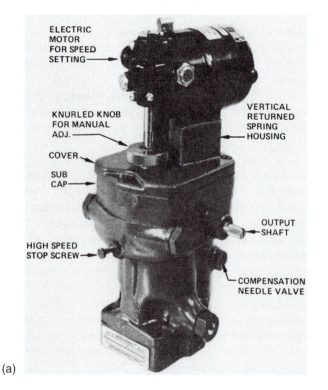

(a)

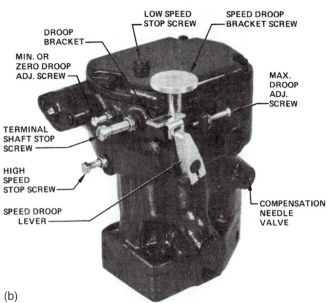

(b)

FIGURE 16–5   (a) PSG (pressure-compensated simple governor) hydraulic model equipped with a vertical return spring and an electric speed setting motor to permit remote speed setting of the engine such as on parallel gen-sets (b) PSG governor with an externally adjustable speed droop setting knob/bracket. (Courtesy of Woodward Governor Company.)

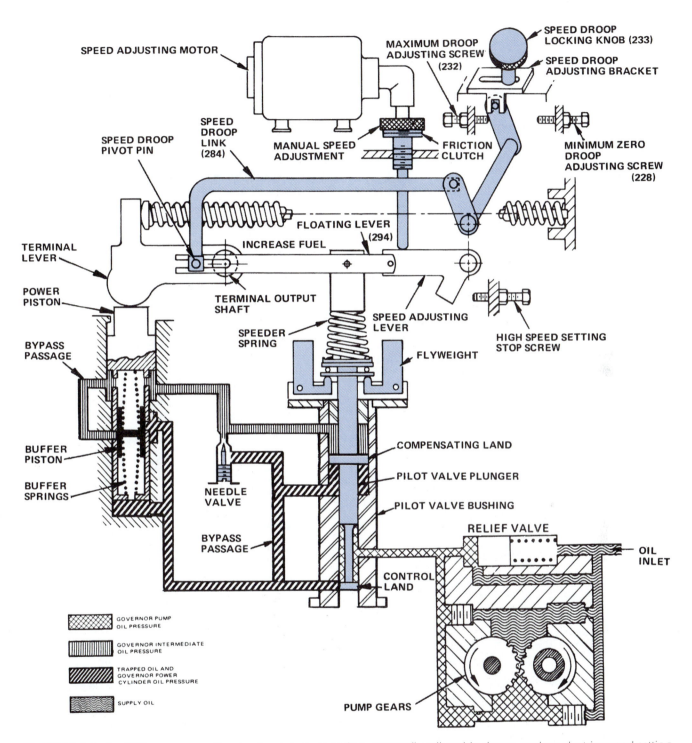

FIGURE 16–6 PSG governor with a horizontal return spring, externally adjustable droop, and an electric speed setting motor. (Courtesy of Woodward Governor Company.)

in parallel, the PSG can be adjusted between 0 and 7% droop.

The compensation system within the governor (see Figure 16–6), consists of an H-shaped buffer piston with a buffer spring located on either side of it, a needle valve, and a compensating land on the pilot valve plunger. This compensation system, then, is the major difference between the PSG and the SG.

Since the speeder spring force can be adjusted, it is the initial force of this spring that will determine at what rpm the engine will attain a state of balance between the weights and speeder spring.

Engine Stopped

As with the SG governor, the PSG would have the pilot valve plunger pushed all the way down owing to the force of the speeder spring. To shorten the cranking time, place the speed control or hand throttle lever connected to the terminal shaft in the full-fuel position, which takes control away from the governor for initial starting purposes. Once the engine starts, move the control lever back to the desired rpm until the engine warms up.

Engine Cranking

During cranking, the centrifugal force of the flyweights will oppose the speeder spring tension, and the instant the engine starts (depending on throttle position), the weights will attain a speed proportional to the amount of force within the speeder spring. In other words, if the throttle (terminal shaft) were left in the idle position, then the rotating flyweights would only have to produce enough centrifugal force to balance out the speeder spring force at this low speed. If, however, the

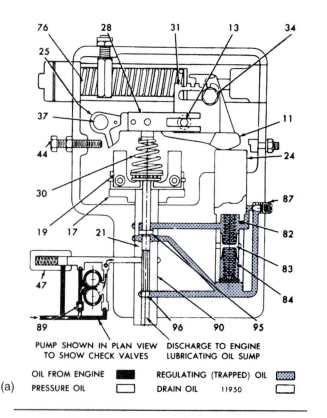

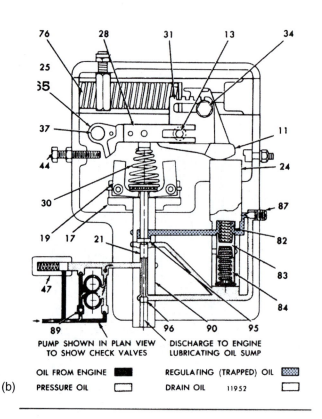

11.	Lever—Terminal	47.	Valve—Relief
13.	Shaft—Terminal (long)	76.	Spring—Terminal Lever
17.	Ball Head Assy.		Return
19.	Flyweight	82.	Spring—Buffer (upper)
21.	Plunger—Pilot Valve	83.	Piston—Buffer
24.	Piston—Servo-Motor	84.	Spring—Buffer (lower)
25.	Lever—Speed Adjusting	87.	Valve—Compensating
28.	Lever—Floating		Needle
30.	Spring—Speeder	89.	Valve—Check
31.	Bracket—Droop	90.	Bushing—Pilot Valve
	Adjusting	95.	Land—Receiving
34.	Bolt—Droop Adjusting		Compensating
37.	Shaft—Speed Adjusting	96.	Land—Pilot Valve
44.	Screw—Maximum		Control
	Speed Adjusting		

11.	Lever—Terminal	47.	Valve—Relief
13.	Shaft—Terminal (long)	76.	Spring—Terminal Lever
17.	Ball Head Assy.		Return
19.	Flyweight	82.	Spring—Buffer (upper)
21.	Plunger—Pilot Valve	83.	Piston—Buffer
24.	Piston—Servo-Motor	84.	Spring—Buffer (lower)
25.	Lever—Speed Adjusting	87.	Valve—Compensating
28.	Lever—Floating		Needle
30.	Spring—Speeder	89.	Valve—Check
31.	Bracket—Droop	90.	Bushing—Pilot Valve
	Adjusting	95.	Land—Receiving
34.	Bolt—Droop Adjusting		Compensating
37.	Shaft—Speed Adjusting	96.	Land—Pilot Valve
44.	Screw—Maximum Speed		Control
	Adjusting		

FIGURE 16–7 (a) PSG governor model mechanism shown in a state of balance (load and speed constant); (b) PSG governor model mechanism position when the engine load increases, and the engine speed tends to decrease; (c) PSG governor mechanism as engine load decreases and engine speed increases. (Courtesy of Woodward Governor Company.)

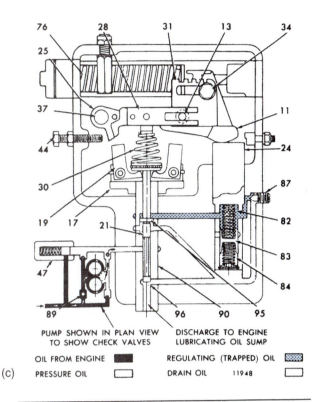

PUMP SHOWN IN PLAN VIEW TO SHOW CHECK VALVES

DISCHARGE TO ENGINE LUBRICATING OIL SUMP

OIL FROM ENGINE ▮

REGULATING (TRAPPED) OIL ▨

(c) PRESSURE OIL ☐

DRAIN OIL 11948 ☐

11.	Lever—Terminal	47.	Valve—Relief
13.	Shaft—Terminal (long)	76.	Spring—Terminal Lever Return
17.	Ball Head Assy.		
19.	Flyweight	82.	Spring—Buffer (upper)
21.	Plunger—Pilot Valve	83.	Piston—Buffer
24.	Piston—Servo–Motor	84.	Spring—Buffer (lower)
25.	Lever—Speed Adjusting	87.	Valve—Compensating Needle
28.	Lever—Floating		
30.	Spring—Speeder	89.	Valve—Check
31.	Bracket—Droop Adjusting	90.	Bushing—Pilot Valve
		95.	Land—Receiving Compensating
34.	Bolt—Droop Adjusting		
37.	Shaft—Speed Adjusting	96.	Land—Pilot Valve Control
44.	Screw—Maximum Speed Adjusting		

FIGURE 16–7 (continued).

terminal shaft were placed in the full-fuel position, the speeder spring force, being much greater, would require a greater weight force; this would only happen at the maximum engine rpm (state of balance).

As the engine is cranking, oil pressure would flow to the base of the piston toward the underside of the pilot valve plunger compensating land, and slowly bleed past the compensating needle valve to the upper area of both the buffer piston and pilot valve plunger land. This oil pressure due to the compensating needle valve would initially be higher on the underside of both the buffer piston and pilot valve plunger land.

As the buffer piston moves up, it would compress the upper buffer piston spring, which would in turn force up the power piston. The terminal and floating levers would move to the increased fuel position, their movement being determined by the initial terminal (throttle) lever position, which would control how fast the weights would have to rotate to balance out the preset speeder spring force.

As the buffer piston is moving up, the oil pressure on the underside of the pilot valve plunger (PVP) would be pushing up the pilot valve, thereby assisting the rotating flyweights to attain their state-of-balance position. As the oil pressure on the upper area of both the buffer piston and land of the PVP attains the same pressure as that on the bottom, the buffer piston and PVP will center, which will tie in with the state of balance being reached between the weights and springs. When this occurs, the engine will run at a steady-state speed. Figure 16–7a shows the position of the internal governor linkage anytime that a state of balance exists.

Load Increase

How quickly the governor responds to a load change is dependent on the droop bracket adjustment, and whether it responds without over or under corrections is tied into the compensating needle valve adjustment. Figure 16–7b shows the reaction within the governor during any load increase.

Refer to Figure 16–7b; with a load increase on the engine, the flyweights will tend to drop inward as the engine speed decreases. With the state of balance between the weights and speeder spring upset in favor of the spring, the pilot valve plunger will be forced down, which will allow pressurized oil from the pump to be directed to the underside of both the buffer piston and the receiving compensating land of the pilot valve plunger. The power piston has two diameters that are exposed to this pressurized oil from the base of the pilot valve plunger. The lower, smaller diameter is acted upon directly, and the upper annulus is connected through the bore in the power piston in which the buffer piston is carried.

The oil pressure will force the power piston up against the force of the terminal lever return spring, which can also be external if used with rotary motion of the terminal shaft instead of linear motion, such as would be used on some engines.

As the power piston moves up, it causes the terminal lever (11) to pivot around its support shaft (13) and compress the fuel rod return spring (76). This action causes the fuel rod to move the rack linkage toward an increased fuel setting. The movement of the terminal lever (11) will lift the droop-adjusting bracket

(31) with it, since the droop bracket is connected to the terminal lever by bolt (34). Part of the droop bracket contains a pin that pivots in the slotted end of the speed-adjusting floating lever (28). Therefore, terminal lever rotation by power piston upward movement will lift the slotted end of the floating lever. This action will cause the force on the speeder spring (30) to be decreased, and this action will permit the rotating flyweights to move outward faster in an attempt to assist the PVP to recenter.

The fuel racks will therefore be moved to an increased fuel position. The pressurized oil, due to the compensating needle valve, will initially be greater on the underside of the buffer piston; therefore, it forces the buffer piston up, which compresses the upper buffer spring and relieves the pressure on the lower one. Since there is a higher initial oil pressure on the underside of the compensating land of the PVP, the PVP will be pushed up, thereby recentering the flyweights and closing off the supply port. This will stop the upward movement of the power piston, which has now made the necessary fuel correction.

If the droop bracket has been set for zero droop, the engine speed will remain constant regardless of load change; however, if the droop bracket were set to its maximum of 7%, the engine speed would drop 7% when a load is applied before the governor corrected.

The speed loss of the engine when a load is applied is dependent on the position of the speed droop adjusting bracket pin, which pivots within the slotted floating lever (28). By loosening off the bolt (34), or the speed droop locking knob bracket screw shown in Figure 16–5b, the technician can push the droop bracket and pin toward or away from the speeder spring (30). With the droop pin closer toward the speeder spring, the governor reaction will be more sensitive (less droop, therefore less speed loss). Moving the droop bracket and pin away from the speeder spring results in a slower governor reaction, and therefore we have a greater speed loss when a load is applied or removed from the engine under a fixed throttle condition. This reaction is caused by the fact that each time the power piston (24) moves up or down, the rotative action of the terminal lever (11) causes the slotted floating lever (28) to move with it. During upward movement of the power piston (increasing fuel) or downward movement (decreasing fuel), the speeder spring (30) force will be decreased or increased, respectively, due to the floating lever action. With the droop bracket pin position being adjustable, the closer the pin is to the center of the spring, the quicker the reaction on the spring will be for a given power piston movement. Moving the pin away from the speeder spring will require a longer power piston stroke to cause a reaction at the speeder spring. Consequently, the engine speed droop is proportional to the droop bracket pin placement within the slotted end of the speed-adjusting floating lever (28). Droop adjustment is strictly a trial-and-error setting; therefore, the technician must make an adjustment, then load and unload the engine fully to determine the governor response.

A simple method to understand how adjustable droop works is to refer to Figures 16–8a and b. In both cases we show a fulcrum lever as being centered on the seesaw or teeter-totter, as well as in the center of the ship. If both kids weigh the same amount and sit equal distances from the fulcrum point, both will travel through the same arc of movement as they move up and down. If, however, one kid moves inward toward the center of the fulcrum point, they will move through a smaller arc of travel as they move up and down. Similarly, if the ship is moving through heavy seas and one deckhand stands an equal distance from the centerline of the ship (fulcrum point) at the bow while another deckhand stands an equal distance from the centerline but toward the stern of the vessel, both will move through the same arc of travel as the ship plows forward through the waves. If, however, one crew member moves closer to the centerline of the ship, they will move through a smaller arc of travel. Using this analogy, you can see why moving the governor droop bracket pin toward the centerline of the speeder spring will cause a reaction at the spring sooner (shorter power piston stroke equals less rack movement and less speed loss before the governor reacts).

Load Decrease

Figure 16–7c shows the governor linkage position when an engine load is removed. For a given (fixed) throttle setting, if a load is removed from the engine, engine speed will increase, which causes the flyweights to fly out farther, thereby overcoming the speeder spring force. This causes the PVP to lift, which opens the control port at its base, allowing trapped oil to drain from the base of the buffer piston and PVP compensating land. Terminal shaft return spring force will push the power piston in the decreased fuel direction, therefore reducing engine rpm. This reduced oil pressure on the underside of the buffer piston and receiving compensating land of the PVP will cause the higher (temporarily) oil pressure above to recenter the PVP, followed by recentering of the buffer piston as the oil bleeds through the compensating needle valve, and pressures above and below equalize. With a reduction in fuel input to the engine, a state-of-balance condition will again exist after the correction sequence.

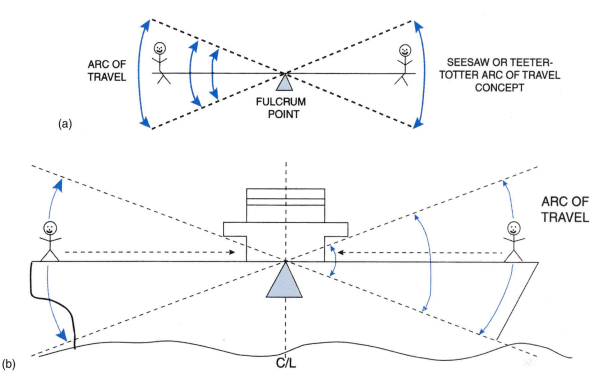

FIGURE 16–8 (a) How the arc of travel changes as children shift their seating position toward or away from the center of the fulcrum point on a seesaw; (b) how the individuals can change their arc of travel at the bow or stern of a ship as they move toward or away from the centerline (C/L) of the vessel as it pitches in rough seas. Relate both of these concepts to an adjustable-droop pivot pin shown in Figure 16–6.

PSG Adjustments

Figure 16–5 shows all the available external adjustments. To adjust the droop setting on an external droop governor, refer to Figure 16–5b. On an internal droop model the top cover must be removed to get at the internal adjustment bolt (see Figure 16–7a, item 34). By moving the bracket in toward the center of the governor, the droop pin pivot point is changed, which will decrease the droop. Moving the droop bracket away from the center of the governor will increase the droop. This is effected by the reasons explained in the description of the PSG model governor. All droop adjustments are done on a trial-and-error basis. Make sure that the engine is at normal operating temperature prior to any final adjustments.

Compensating Needle Valve Adjustment

With the engine at operating temperature, adjust the governor for no-load-rated speed by manually moving the terminal shaft to its maximum position; then adjust the high-speed stop on the side of the governor housing to obtain the speed desired. Open the compensation needle valve between two and three turns until the engine or turbine begins to hunt or surge. With a recently installed rebuilt governor, this will be more no-

ticeable than on a unit that has been in service, since you are bleeding the system of any entrapped air. Allow the unit to surge for at least 30 seconds. Gently close the needle valve until the hunting just stops; then manually disturb the engine or turbine speed to check that the engine will return to its original steady-state speed with only a small overshoot.

Closing the needle valve farther than necessary will slow down the oil bleed back between both sides of the buffer piston and PVP compensating land, resulting in a slow return to speed following a load change, whereas overcorrection can result if it is turned out too far.

Options

The PSG is available with a temperature-compensated needle valve that adjusts the compensated oil flow with the use of bimetal strips and a spring-loaded needle valve. Adjust it in the same manner as for the non-temperature-compensated valve.

Auxiliary Equipment (PSG)

In addition to those options available on the PSG, such as an external electric motor for remote speed setting, the PSG can have the external droop adjustment, the temperature-compensated needle valve, spring-driven oil-damped ballhead, a torsion spring, and a pneumatic speed setting. Figure 16–9 shows such a setup, whereby remote speed adjustment is provided through a pneumatic speed setting assembly consisting of a diaphragm, housing, oil reservoir, adjusting screws, and pushrod that extends down through the governor cover and makes contact with the floating lever.

An internal return spring is also available as an option. Air signal pressure to the speed setting assembly is applied to an oil reservoir to dampen out oscillations of air compression. Oil pressure acting upon the diaphragm is transmitted to the floating lever by the pushrod, which will increase or decrease governor speeder spring force to produce a change in the speed setting.

ELECTRONIC GOVERNORS

The introduction of electronically controlled diesel fuel injection systems on Detroit Diesel, Caterpillar, Cummins, Volvo, Mack, and Mercedes-Benz heavy-duty high-speed truck engines has allowed the speed of the diesel engine to be controlled electronically rather than mechanically. In an electronic governor, the same type of balanced condition to that shown in Figure 16–1 for a mechanical governor occurs. The major difference is that in the electronic governor, electric currents (amperes) and voltages (pressure) are summed together instead of mechanical weight and spring forces. This is possible through the use of a magnetic pickup sensor (MPS), which is in effect a permanent-magnet single-pole device. This magnetic pickup concept is being

FIGURE 16–9 *Governor pneumatic remote speed setting, where the control air pressure may originate from a speed setting/throttle lever located, for example, in the wheelhouse of a marine vessel or industrial control panel. (Courtesy of Woodward Governor Company.)*

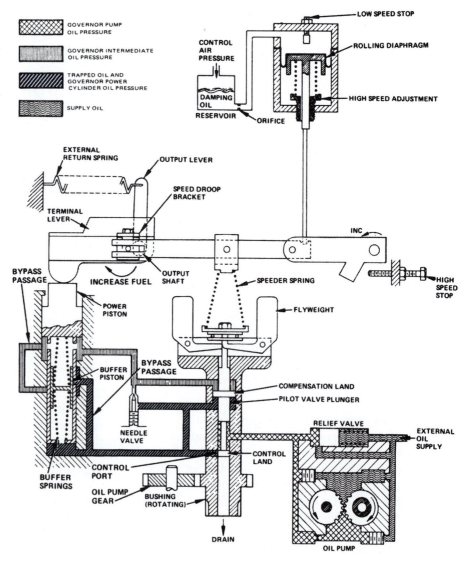

used on all existing electronic systems; therefore, its operation can be considered common to all of them. MPSs are a vital communicating link between the engine crankshaft speed and the on-board computer, known as the ECM. The MPS is installed next to a driveshaft gear made of material that reacts to a magnetic field. As each gear tooth passes the MPS, the gear interrupts the MPS's magnetic field. This, in turn, produces an alternating-current signal that corresponds to engine rpm. This signal is then sent to the ECM.

Figure 16–10 illustrates a simplified wiring diagram for a timing reference sensor (TRS) which is located on the engine block. Refer to Chapters 21 through 23 to see where this sensor is mounted on specific engines; usually this sensor picks up cylinder positions from a raised pin attached to either the crankshaft or camshaft gear. The sensor is installed so that a small air gap exists between the end of the sensor and the gear teeth or pickup pin.

The TRS generally receives a 5-V timing reference signal from the ECM and then returns a signal based on engine speed to the ECM, which then converts this signal to determine the speed of engine rotation. The rotation of the ferrous (metal) gear teeth past the end of the sensor causes the magnetic field or magnetic flux level to change every time a gear tooth passes through this electrically generated signal field since the air gap space is reduced. This action induces a voltage signal that is transmitted through the TRS return wire to the ECM. The shape and spacing of the gear teeth determine the electrical waveform of the sensor output voltage. The number of teeth on the gear determines the number of pulses per revolution of the gear. An 80-tooth gear, for example, rotating at 2100 rpm would produce 168,000 pulses per minute or 2800 pulses per second. This 2800 pulses per second in electronics terminology would be referred to as 2800 Hz (hertz), which is the frequency of the generated TRS signal. This TRS signal is used by the ECM to establish the

amount of fuel that should be injected into combustion chambers of the engine.

The components as described compose a closed-loop system of measurement, which is illustrated in Figure 16–11 in a simple line diagram. The output of the magnetic speed pickup sensor is connected to a speed sensor circuit inside the ECM. This circuit converts the ac magnetic pickup signal to a dc voltage whose level is proportional to the speed of the engine. An analog-to-digital converter within the speed control circuit provides this dc signal since the ECM circuitry is designed to operate only on dc signals. The dc voltage signal is compared with the speed reference voltage; therefore, if a difference or an error exists, the ECM output signal from the built-in amplifier causes the injector PWM signal to lengthen or shorten. This change to the PWM signal causes the injector fuel delivery cycle to last for a greater or shorter duration of crankshaft degrees, thereby changing the engine speed and fuel setting.

For the electronic governor system within the ECM to control the speed and fueling of the engine, it must know the following conditions:

- Speed of the engine
- Percentage of throttle depression
- Turbo boost/load on the engine
- Intake manifold temperature

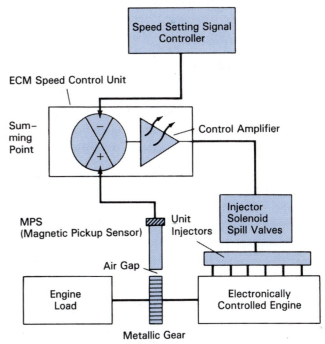

FIGURE 16–11 *Simplified electrical schematic showing the concept of operation for a closed-loop control electronic rack control governor assembly.*

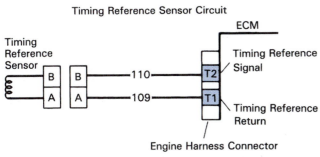

FIGURE 16–10 *Simplified schematic of a TRS (timing reference sensor) circuit for an electronically governed DDEC engine. (Courtesy of Detroit Diesel Corporation.)*

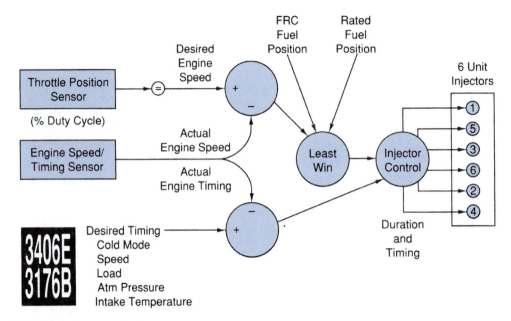

FIGURE 16–12 Typical concept employed with an EUI (electronic unit injector) governor timing and injection control circuit arrangement for the 3176B/C10/C12, 3406E, and 3408E/3412E engine models. FRC, fuel ratio control. (Reprinted courtesy of Caterpillar, Inc.)

An example of how an electronic governor control system operates on a heavy-duty high-speed truck engine is shown in Figure 16–12. The truck operator depresses the throttle pedal to the degree of fueling that he or she desires. The TPS relays a voltage signal to the ECM relative to the percentage of throttle pedal depression. Normally with a closed throttle, the TPS output signal will be in the range of 0.5 V, rising to a maximum value of approximately 4.5 V with a WOT (wide-open throttle). This desired engine speed signal is routed to the positive side of an ECM summing point. The actual engine speed obtained from the throttle input is determined from the engine timing sensor. This actual speed is relayed to the negative side of the summing point, where it is compared with the desired speed asked for by the operator. The ECM computes a corrected signal through its ALU chip and feeds this signal on to the least-win area. Two other signals are also fed into the least-win chip area: the fuel-ratio control (FRC) fuel position, which is tied into the engine turbocharger boost sensor, and the rated fuel position requirements needed to maintain the correct FRC position. The desired and actual engine speeds, FRC fuel, and rated fuel positions create a least-win signal, which dominates. In other words, the actual speed, turbo boost, and rated fuel position parameters are compared to determine if the speed asked for can be supported by sufficient turbo boost pressure versus that for the rated fuel position. This least-win signal is fed

on to the unit injector electric solenoid. In addition, the injector solenoid PWM (pulse-width modulation) signal is also factored in by other signals, based on desired engine timing, the coolant and oil temperatures of the engine, speed, engine load, atmospheric pressure, and intake manifold temperature. These signals are fed to another summing point, where a computed signal is generated and also sent to the unit injector solenoid control system. The injector PWM signal then determines the duration and required timing of each injector. In Chapters 21 through 23 we describe in greater detail the specific operation of electronically controlled fuel injection systems.

SUMMARY

A thorough understanding of this chapter, including commonly used governor terms, will broaden your perspective of the various governor functions, and prepare you with the knowledge and skills to effectively trace, diagnose, analyze, and troubleshoot mechanical and electronic engine control problems.

SELF-TEST QUESTIONS

1. Technician A says that a diesel engine requires the use of a governor because the air is not throttled into the engine. Technician B says that the governor is required to stop the diesel engine from stalling at an idle speed. Who is correct?

2. Technician A says that mechanical and hydraulically assisted governors are speed-sensitive devices. Technician B says that they are load-sensitive devices. Who is correct?

3. Technician A says that at an idle speed, the air/fuel ratio in a diesel engine can be as high as 30:1, whereas technician B says that it is much higher, being as lean as 130:1. Who is correct?

4. Technician A says that the recommended idle speed of an engine can usually be found stamped on the exhaust emissions decal on the engine, whereas technician B says it will always be found on the governor ID tag itself. Who is correct?

5. *High idle speed* is a term used by some manufacturers to indicate
   a. a higher-than-normal idle rpm used in cold-weather operation only
   b. the maximum no-load speed setting of the engine
   c. the maximum full-load speed setting of the engine
   d. the speed setting when the vehicle is stationary and a PTO (power takeoff) is being used.

6. Technician A says that the engine will use less fuel when running at a maximum no-load speed of, say, 2100 rpm than it will at a full-load speed of 1950 rpm. Technician B believes that it will use more fuel at the higher speed. Which mechanic knows the basic governor operation?

7. When the engine is running under full load (say, 1950 rpm) and its speed is slowly reduced to its peak torque speed of, say, 1200 rpm, why is the horsepower not constant if the engine is still receiving full-load fuel from the governor?

8. Why does the engine produce more torque under load at a lower engine speed (for example, at 1200 rpm) than it does at its full-load speed of, say, 1950 rpm, if the governor is still supplying maximum fuel to the fuel injectors?

9. Technician A says that as the engine speed increases from its maximum full-load rpm to its no-load rpm, the governor will decrease the fuel delivered to the injectors. Technician B disagrees, saying that the governor would have to increase the fuel delivery rate to allow an increase in speed. Who is correct?

10. Technician A says that a state of balance condition in a mechanical governor can exist only when the engine is running at an idle speed. Technician B says that a state of balance condition can exist at any speed throughout the governor control range as long as the weight and spring forces are equal. Who is correct?

11. In a limiting-speed mechanical governor, the governor controls
    a. the idle speed
    b. the maximum speed
    c. all speed ranges between idle and maximum
    d. both a and b

12. Technician A says that governor droop is the difference in speed between the maximum no-load and maximum full-load engine rpm. Technician B says that it is the difference between high idle and rated speed. Who is correct?

13. Technician A says that governor droop is generally expressed as a percentage figure. Technician B says that droop is expressed as an rpm. Who is correct?

14. Technician A says that the term *governor sensitivity* is generally expressed as an rpm value, whereas technician B says that it is expressed as a percentage value. Who is correct?

15. Technician A says that in a mechanical governor assembly, the force of the governor spring is always trying to increase the fuel delivery rate to the injectors. Technician B says that this is incorrect, and that the centrifugal force of the rotating flyweights are always attempting to increase the fuel to the engine. Who is correct?

16. A minimum/maximum governor is designed to control
    a. the idle and maximum speed of the engine
    b. the idle, intermediate, and maximum speed settings of the engine
    c. the idle and intermediate speed settings only
    d. the idle speed setting only

17. A variable-speed governor is designed to control
    a. idle speed
    b. idle, intermediate, and maximum speeds
    c. idle and intermediate speeds
    d. idle and maximum speed settings

18. Technician A says that when an engine using a mechanical minimum/maximum or limiting-speed mechanical governor is stopped and the engine is ready to start, the fuel control mechanism will be held in the full-fuel position. Technician B says that when the engine is stopped, the fuel control mechanism must be in the no-fuel position. Who is right?

19. True or False: The maximum engine speed settings are usually found stamped on the engine compliance/exhaust emissions label.

20. Technician A says that if an engine lacks power, the reason should be investigated. Technician B says that if an engine lacks power, the maximum speed setting of the engine should be increased until it performs according to specification. Who is correct?

21. Technician A says that if an engine was governed at a maximum full-load speed setting of 2100 rpm, then during operation, if the speed were allowed to increase to 2175 rpm, the engine would develop more horsepower. Technician B disagrees, saying that the horsepower would be less due to the action of the governor. Who is correct here?

22. Technician A says that if a truck running down a long steep incline is not slowed by use of an engine brake, retarder, or service brakes, engine overspeed can occur, causing damage to the engine. Technician B says that this cannot happen since the governor will automatically regulate the engine speed. Who is correct here?

23. Technician A says that to increase the truck road speed setting, the mechanical governor can be opened up and adjusted to raise the maximum no-load speed engine rpm setting. Technician B says that this should never be done. Who is correct here?

24. Supply the missing words in the following statement: When a load is applied to an engine, the speed will _____ and the governor will _____ the fuel setting.

25. Supply the missing words in the following statement: When a load is decreased on an engine, the speed will _____ and the governor will _____ the fuel setting.

26. Technician A says that the term *isochronous* means that the governor is capable of a zero-droop setting, which means that the no-load and full-load speeds are the same. Technician B says that no engine can operate at the same speed loaded and unloaded; since it has to work harder under load, it will run slower. Who is correct?

27. The letters MPS stand for
    a. magnetic pickup sensor
    b. mean position sensor
    c. motor point system
    d. motor position sensor

28. Technician A says that a rotating fiber gear tooth is used to interrupt the MPS field on a regular basis. Technician B disagrees, saying that the gear must be a metallic gear to operate. Who is correct?

29. Technician A says that the signal generated from the MPS is a dc signal, whereas technician B says that it is an ac signal. Who is correct?

30. Technician A says that most sensors used on truck electronic governor systems receive a 5-V reference signal from the ECM to operate. Technician B says that they operate on the 12-V battery supply power source. Who understands the system best?

31. Technician A says that the frequency of electrical sensor signals is determined by the engine speed and number of teeth on the pickup gear. Technician B says that the ECM determines the frequency of sensor signal output. Who is correct here?

32. Technician A says that the maximum no-load engine speed on a mechanical governor can be altered. Technician B says that the engine maximum no-load speed should never be tampered with. Who is correct?

33. Technician A says that the amount of droop (rpm loss) on all engines equipped with mechanical governors can be offset by setting the maximum no-load rpm higher than the full-load speed desired. Technician B says that both the full-load and no-load speeds are one and the same since the governor will compensate for any speed loss as the engine load is applied. Who is correct?

34. A state of balance in a mechanical governor means that
    a. the force of the weights and springs is equal
    b. the operator is controlling the engine speed
    c. the correct gear in the transmission has been selected to keep the engine at a steady speed
    d. the turbocharger boost and fuel delivery pressures are equal

35. Technician A says that the term *high idle* means the same as *maximum no-load* engine speed. Technician B says that it means the same as *rated* engine speed. Who understands the meaning of this terminology?

36. Technician A says that on a mechanical or hydramechanical governor, the fuel rack will be pushed into an increased fuel delivery position with a drop in engine speed from high idle to rated rpm. Technician B says that there will be less fuel delivered under such an operating condition. Who knows governor theory best?

17 Injection Nozzles

Overview

Fuel injection nozzles are key components in the successful delivery and combustion of fuel. Nozzles are basically closed valves that are opened by high-pressure fuel delivered from the injection pump assembly. Pump-line-nozzle (PLN) designs such as Bosch, Lucas/Varity/CAV, now owned by Delphi Automotive, Caterpillar, and electronic unit pumps, as well as distributor pump type systems, are coupled to nozzles. Within these systems, timing, high fuel pressurization, and metering (fuel quantity) are performed in the injection pump, while fuel atomization occurs at the nozzle spray tip. The high-pressure fuel is delivered through a small bore steel line from the injection pump to each nozzle. Conversely, the term injector is normally applied to both MUIs (mechanical unit injectors) and EUIs (electronic unit injectors), where the timing, atomization, metering, and high fuel pressure are created within the body of the injector.

This chapter describes various types of nozzles, their function and operation, and the necessary checks, tests, inspection, and adjustments needed to ensure a smooth-running engine, and one that complies with mandated EPA, CEPA, and EEC engine exhaust emissions regulations.

ASE CERTIFICATION

Within the ASE medium/heavy truck tests preparation guide, diesel engines, test T2 tasks lists, Part A, general engine diagnosis; B, cylinder head and valve train diagnosis and repair; F, fuel system diagnosis and repair, mechanical components, a number of tasks lists are shown that relate to injection nozzles. Refer to these various subsections to determine the areas and items that require you to become familiar with the hands-on tasks, so that you can demonstrate your accumulated theoretical and practical knowledge to enable you to challenge either the appropriate ASE or TQ tests.

The following ASE tasks lists indicate the skills and knowledge required for nozzle troubleshooting, diagnosis, and possible service. They are listed by the ASE tasks list number under their respective subheading in the ASE preparation guide.

A. General Engine Diagnosis

5. Check engine exhaust emissions, odor, smoke color, denseness (opacity), and signs of wet stacking.

TIP Determine if nozzles are at fault by loosening each high-pressure fuel line to one nozzle at a time while the engine is running at idle (see Figure 25–6). If the nozzle is firing, then there should be a loss of engine rpm and a positive sound change (misfire) in the engine as you do this. Repeat for each cylinder nozzle. If there is no loss of engine rpm and no sound change, then the nozzle is faulty (not firing). Remove this nozzle and perform a pop pressure test. Refer to the information in this chapter for appropriate checks and tests.

---

6. Perform fuel system tests for signs of restricted fuel filters, water in fuel, air in the fuel system, contamination, or a crimped/restricted high-pressure line; determine needed repairs.

12. Diagnose engine surging at idle, rough operation, misfiring, low power, and slow

acceleration, all of which could be due to faulty nozzles. Check for slow deceleration and/or engine shutdown problems which could be due to governor linkage problems.

TIP   Ensure that all high-pressure fuel lines are exactly the same length. Shorter or longer lines will change the time for the pressure rise within the line, thereby affecting timing at the nozzle. This can cause a misfire and hesitation when the throttle is opened.

F. Fuel System Diagnosis and Repair, Mechanical and Electronic Components

One or more of the following skill tasks are specific to, and could affect, nozzle operation, including mechanical components, items 1 through 4 and items 10 and 12. Items 1 through 13 would affect the injection pump function and operation. In the tasks list for electronic components, only item 8 is specific to nozzles, whereas all others would affect fuel system operation.

Mechanical Components (9 ASE questions)

1. Inspect, repair/replace fuel tanks, vents, cap(s), mounts, valves, screens, crossover system, supply and return lines and fittings.

2. Inspect, clean, test, repair/replace fuel transfer (lift) pump, pump drives, screens, fuel/water separators/indicators, filters, heaters, coolers, ECM cooling plates, and mounting hardware.

3. Check fuel system for air; determine needed repairs; prime and bleed fuel system; check, repair/replace primer pump.

4. Inspect, test, repair/replace low-pressure regulator systems (check valves, pressure regulator valves and restrictive fittings).

5. Inspect, adjust, repair/replace throttle and linkage/cable and controls.

6. Perform on-engine inspections, tests, adjustments, and time, or replace and time, distributor-type injection pumps.

7. Perform on-engine inspections, tests, adjustments and time, or replace and time, inline type injection pumps, governors, and drives.

8. Perform on-engine inspections, tests, and adjustments, or replace PT-type injection pumps, drives, and injectors.

9. Perform on-engine inspections, tests, and adjustments, or replace mechanical unit injectors.

10. Inspect, test, repair/replace fuel injection nozzles.

11. Inspect, adjust, repair/replace smoke limiters (air/fuel ratio controls).

12. Inspect, reinstall/replace high pressure injection lines, fittings, and seals.

13. Inspect, test, adjust, repair/replace engine fuel shutdown devices and controls, including engine protection shutdown devices, circuits, and sensors.

Electronic Components (11 ASE questions)

1. Check and record engine electronic diagnostic codes and trip/operational data; clear codes; determine needed repairs.

2. Inspect, adjust, repair/replace electronic throttle and PTO control devices, circuits, and sensors.

3. Perform on-engine inspections, tests, and adjustments on distributor-type injection pump electronic controls.

4. Perform on-engine inspections, tests, and adjustments on inline-type injection pump electronic controls.

5. Perform on-engine inspections, tests, and adjustments on PT-type injection pump electronic controls.

6. Perform on-engine inspections, tests, and adjustments on hydraulic electronic unit injectors (HEUI) and electronic controls (rail pressure control).

7. Perform on-engine inspections, tests, and adjustments on electronic unit injectors (EUI) and electronic controls.

8. Perform on-engine inspections, tests, and adjustments on pump-line-nozzle electronic systems (PLN-E) and electronic controls.

9. Inspect, test, adjust, repair/replace engine electronic fuel shutdown devices, circuits, and sensors, including engine protection systems.

10. Inspect and test power, ignition, and ground circuits and connections for electrical/electronic components; determine needed repairs.

11. Inspect and replace electrical connector terminals, pins, harnesses, seals, and locks.

12. Connect diagnostic tool to vehicle/engine; access and change customer parameters; determine needed repairs.

INJECTORS

The injectors described here are for pump line nozzle systems, including those for mechanical or electronically controlled systems. Now including injectors for electronic controlled systems, and with a new range of low emissions injectors, the Delphi and Bosch range comprises a variety of holder and nozzle combinations to allow application to all major engine configurations.

Injector Construction

The injector is made up of two main parts: a nozzle holder and a nozzle, as shown in Figure 17–1. The nozzle holder contains the valve spring, a spindle and/or, spring seat to transfer spring force to the nozzle valve, a means of adjusting the spring load (either by a shim or an adjusting cap), plus the fuel inlet and backleak connections, a nozzle capnut (which retains the nozzle) and a means to secure and position the injector and nozzle within the engine. The nozzle consists of a body and a needle valve. See Figure 17–2.

Injector Operation

Before the injection pump begins fuel delivery, the nozzle valve is closed and held by a spring. The injection pump begins its pumping stroke, and fuel enters the injector via an inlet connection, and travels down the fuel passages to the fuel gallery which surrounds the needle valve. Fuel pressure rises forcing the needle valve to open at the pre-set pressure. Fuel then passes through a small space called the "sac" to the injection hole or holes. The fuel comes out of these holes in the form of a fine spray. As pumping pressure falls, the valve spring closes the needle valve and fuel injection is ended. The valve then forms a seal against combustion pressure to prevent exhaust gas being forced back through the injector and into the fuel lines.

Injector Options

The two main types of injectors are High Spring and Low Spring.

- **High Spring**   In this traditional type of injector, the valve spring is positioned at the top of the

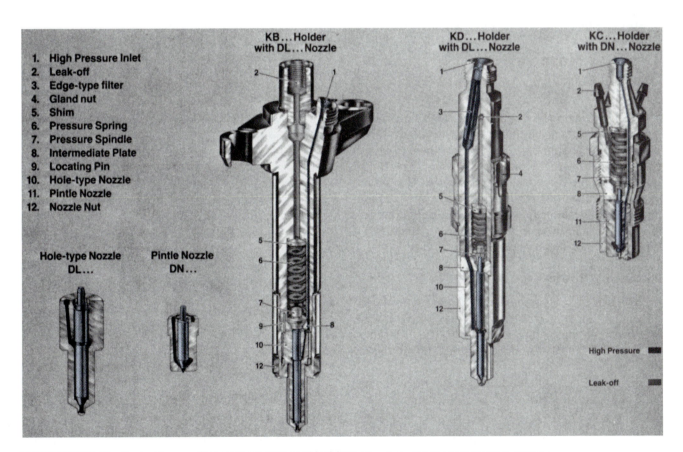

FIGURE 17–1   Typical types of injector nozzles and holders. (Courtesy of Robert Bosch Corporation.)

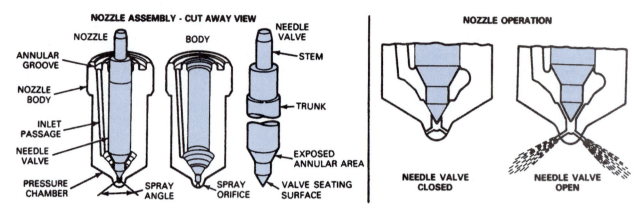

FIGURE 17–2 Cutaway view of the parts of a direct-injection multiple-hole nozzle; nozzle-closed and nozzle-open positions. (Courtesy of Robert Bosch Corporation.)

injector body. The opening pressure of this type of injector is set by means of an adjustable spring cap. The holder body is typically a forging with integral clamping flange, and has a range of inlet and backleak connection possibilities. Versions to accommodate both direct injection (DI) and indirect injection (IDI) engines are available.

- **Low Spring**   In the Low Spring Injector the valve spring is positioned much lower in the body of the injector. Because the spring is so low the need for an operating spindle is eliminated. As a consequence of the reduction in moving mass, better performance is achieved with a more precise cut off at the end of injection. The holder body is more typically of a bar type construction although forged construction is also available. The profile of the injector is generally compact, and ideally suited to modern engine application where space is at a premium. Both DI and IDI versions are available, and also a range of inlet and backleak configurations to suit individual installations. The more popular holder sizes have outside diameters of ∅17 mm and ∅21 mm. (0.670 and 0.827 in.)
- **Screw Fitted Injectors**   A range of injectors has been developed for suitable applications to allow ease of engine production fitment and design by allowing direct screw fitting without the need for additional clamping.
- **Screw-in Injectors**   These are a range of low spring injectors developed specifically for the small high speed IDI engine market typically fitted to car and light van applications. The capnut of these injectors is threaded and allows direct fitment to the threaded injector pocket of the cylinder head. These injectors are fitted with pintle nozzles where radial orientation is not required.
- **Screw-mounted Injectors**   Similar to the above, these injectors are available for DI engines to cover

a range of popular engine and injector sizes. The screw fitting usually takes the form of a gland nut, which acts against a shoulder or a snap-ring on the injector, to apply the clamping load. As these are fitted with hole type nozzles, where radial orientation is required, a separate location arrangement has to be provided. This typically takes the form of a location ball or dowel, aligning with a groove in the engine cylinder head.

- **Two Stage Injectors**   The Two Stage injector has been designed to combat the problem of engine noise and gaseous emissions, which can occur in some DI engines. These injectors provide an initial low rate of fuel injection by restricting the opening of the injector during the first stage of operation. During the second stage the injector is allowed to open fully, and injection occurs at a higher pressure and at a higher rate. This operating sequence lowers engine noise by reducing combustion pressure rise and peak cylinder pressure, without loss of power. Typically this injector is used in small High Speed Direct Injection engines found in modern car and light van applications. These injectors incorporate an additional spring and thrust component to achieve the second opening operation. The opening pressures and lifts are adjustable to enable the injector to be tailored to meet individual customer requirements.

NOZZLES

Delphi Diesel Systems and Robert Bosch Corporation both offer a wide range of injector nozzles; these fall into two groups:

- Multi-hole type
- Pintle type

Multi-Hole Nozzles

Designed for use with direct injection engines, these are divided into two further categories: long stem and short stem. These nozzles inject the fuel directly into the cylinder, with a combustion chamber formed in the top of the piston. The range of Multi-Hole nozzles includes:

- **Short-Stem Multi-Hole** Traditional nozzle construction. Mainly used with high spring holders.

- **Long-Stem Multi-Hole** These are used on current engine constructions and allow more flexibility in cylinder head design because of the small tip diameter. Low emission types have been introduced to meet future requirements.

- **Valve-Covered Orifice Nozzle (VCO)** This is a version of the low emission long-stem nozzle where the needle valve covers the injection holes when it closes, rapidly stopping the fuel flow. The "sac" in previous designs is also eliminated, so preventing the retention of fuel between the closed needle valve and the injection holes, further reducing exhaust emissions. See Figure 17–3.

Pintle-Type Nozzles

These are designed for use on indirect injection engines. See Figure 17–4. They produce a single spray plume that is tailored to match the required character-

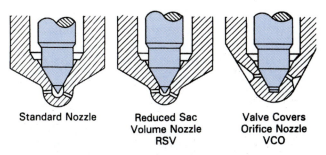

Standard Nozzle   Reduced Sac Volume Nozzle RSV   Valve Covers Orifice Nozzle VCO

FIGURE 17–3 *Various nozzle designs used to reduce hydrocarbon emissions from DI (direct-injection) diesel engines. (Reprinted with permission of the Society of Automotive Engineers, Inc., International, copyright 2001).*

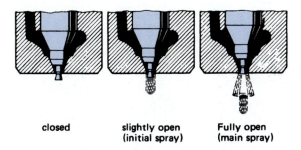

closed   slightly open (initial spray)   Fully open (main spray)

FIGURE 17–4 *Action of a throttling pintle nozzle. (Courtesy of Robert Bosch Corporation.)*

istics of the pre or swirl chamber of the engine. There are long and short stem types to suit the particular engine cylinder head construction. Throttling pintle nozzles provide two-stage injection.

- **Pintaux Nozzle** This has a small auxiliary hole which produces a high velocity spray at low injection rates to improve cold starting. This nozzle type also reduces engine knock when idling.

NOZZLE STRUCTURE AND FUNCTION

All diesel engines require an injector for each cylinder to permit high-pressure fuel to be sprayed into the combustion chamber. PLN (pump-line-nozzle) inline and V-configuration injection pumps as well as distributor pump systems are equipped with injection nozzles, which are sometimes referred to simply as an injector. They are called nozzles because in both of these types of fuel systems, the timing, metering, and fuel pressurization is accomplished within the injection pump. The high-pressure fuel is then directed through a steel-backed fuel line to the nozzle, which is encapsulated within the body of the injector. The nozzle is simply a valve that opens to permit atomized fuel to enter the combustion chamber. The valve closes when the fuel pressure is no longer high enough to hold the nozzle needle valve open against an internal spring.

Engines equipped with unit injectors, such as Detroit Diesel, Caterpillar, Cummins, Volvo, and John Deere etc., are designed to time, atomize, meter, and pressurize the fuel within the body of the injector rather than within an injection pump housing. Details on the function and operation of unit injectors are given in Chapters 21 to 23. Nozzles and unit injectors both provide atomization of the fuel as it leaves the holes in the spray tip.

In Figure 17–2, a needle valve is held on its seat at the base of the nozzle by spring pressure. The force of the spring can be altered either by rotating an internal adjusting nut or by the addition or removal of spring shims (5) see Figure 17–1. This adjustment determines the required fuel pressure acting against the tapered face of the nozzle needle valve required to lift the needle against the force of the spring. For example, if a nozzle has been adjusted so that it requires 4200 psi (28,959 kPa or 290 atm) fuel pressure to lift the needle valve, this is referred to as the opening or popping pressure of the nozzle. Once the needle valve is opened, fuel under high pressure from the injection pump can flow through a single hole or a series of small orifices within the tip of the nozzle body and into the combustion chamber. Direct-injection (DI) engines commonly used on larger-bore heavy-duty engines use nozzles with multiple holes or orifices (Figure 17–2) where the fuel is injected directly into the open combustion chamber formed by the piston crown shape. The spray-in pattern covers a much wider angle than in a IDI engine; DI is much more widely used in today's engines.

The popping pressure created within the nozzle is not high enough to permit successful atomization of the injected fuel; therefore, to increase the pressure of the injected fuel, and to break the fuel down into tiny droplets (atomization), one or more small holes or orifices are contained within the nozzle tip. Since a restriction to fuel flow is created by the size of the single or multiple holes in the nozzle tip, the fuel spray-in pressure into the combustion chamber is increased substantially. A simple method that can be used to understand this process is to consider a garden hose. If no nozzle is contained on the end of the hose, once the water is turned on, there is lots of flow, but at a reasonably low pressure. If, however, we place our thumb over the end of the hose, the result is an increase in water velocity (speed and direction of the fluid). This same process occurs at the tip of the nozzle.

The final atomized fuel spray-in pressure is dependent on the popping pressure, and the number and size of the holes used. In addition, the engine compression ratio, turbo boost, engine load and rpm, injection pump capability, and the cylinder bmep (brake mean effective pressure) all factor into the actual nozzle spray-in pressure. For example, typical spray-in pressures for nozzles can range from as low as 9000 psi (62,055 kPa/621 bar) to as high as 19,575 psi (134,969 kPa or 1350 bar) in Bosch's P8500 model pump and matching nozzle in Mack's E7 engines. Later-model EUP (electronic unit pump) fuel systems (see Chapter 21) offer spray-in pressures from the nozzle tip as high as 25,000 psi (172,375 kPa or 1724 bar); EUIs (electronic unit injectors) as high as 30,000 psi (206,850 kPa/2068 bar). Higher spray-in pressures result in finer fuel atomization, better penetration of the compressed air mass, cleaner burning and lower exhaust emissions, and overall fuel economy improvement.

In a multiple-hole nozzle, each orifice is usually equally spaced around the circumference of the spray tip. Generally there are never fewer than 4 holes and there may be as many as 12 holes. Hole sizes vary on high-speed engines between 0.006 and 0.010 in. (0.15 to 0.25 mm). A five-hole nozzle is shown in Figure 17–5, where each atomized jet of fuel (1 through 5 in this example, spaced 72° apart) carries the atomized high-pressure fuel into the combustion chamber. The high-pressure air within the direct injected cylinder is subjected to a swirling action by the shape of the contoured piston crown as it moves up the cylinder on its compression stroke. This swirling air assists in rapid mixing of the atomized fuel with the hot air to initiate combustion of the fuel (see Chapter 4 for more details on the combustion phase).

In addition, the spray-in angle is chosen to provide optimum fuel penetration into the compressed air mass within the combustion chamber. Some OEMs quote their spray-in angle from the horizontal deck surface of the cylinder head, while others quote this angle from a vertical centerline passing through the noz-

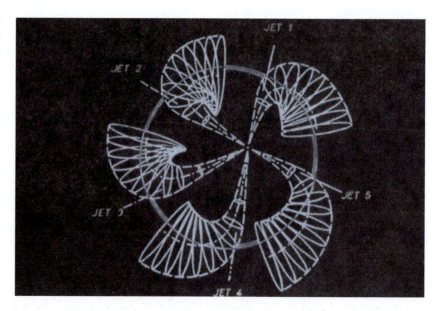

FIGURE 17–5 *Typical computer tracing of the fuel spray from a five-hole nozzle clearly showing the air/fuel turbulence effect. (Courtesy of Robert Bosch Corporation.)*

zle body. Figure 17–2 shows one example of an included spray-in angle as the fuel leaves the orifices of a multiple-hole nozzle.

NOZZLE FLOW

Injection nozzles are simply hydraulic valves operated by fuel pressure. Fuel flow generated by the injection pump enters the nozzle holder at the fuel inlet and proceeds down the fuel inlet and into the annular area of the valve (see Figure 17–1). When the pressure of the fuel against the annular area of the needle valve exceeds the preset pressure of the pressure spring, the needle valve is raised from its seat. Then a metered amount of fuel is injected through the orifices on a hole-type nozzle or by the pintle on a pintle-type nozzle and into the combustion chamber.

During operation a small amount of fuel will leak through the needle valve to help lubricate and cool the valve. This fuel accumulates in the pressure spring area and is returned to the supply tank by a fuel return line.

NOZZLE COMPONENTS

1. *Nozzle holder.* The nozzle holder (Figure 17–1) is the main structural part of the injection nozzle. It provides a means of holding the nozzle to the engine cylinder head; it routes fuel from the injection pump to the nozzle; and it sometimes contains passageways for leakoff fuel coming from the nozzle and going back to the fuel tank or injection pump. Excluding occasional breakage or thread damage due to poor handling, the nozzle holder is very reliable. Information listed directly on the holder includes:

   a. Holder type number (varies with engine application)
   b. Holder part number (manufacturer's part number)
   c. Application part number (on some types)
   d. Nozzle opening pressure (on some types)

2. *Pressure spring.* The pressure spring determines the opening pressure of the nozzle valve. Tension of the pressure spring can be adjusted in most cases by an adjusting screw located above it, or by a shim pack.

3. *Cap nut.* The cap nut provides a dust seal for the nozzle holder and usually incorporates a connection for leakoff fuel. Some nozzles using a shim pack to set nozzle opening pressure do not require a cap nut.

4. *Retaining nut.* The retaining nut connects the nozzle body to the nozzle holder and also serves as a compression seal in the cylinder head.

5. *Pressure spindle.* The pressure spindle is a metal rod that transfers the force of the pressure spring to the nozzle valve.

6. Nozzle valve assembly. The nozzle is the heart of the injection nozzle assembly. The valve and body of the nozzle are lapped together and are not interchangeable. The valve has a special tapered seat that effectively seals off nozzle fuel pressure and does not allow any fuel to dribble into the combustion chamber.

In Figure 17–1, the nozzle employs a tapered face type of needle valve, which is held on a lapped nozzle seat in the spray tip by the action of a coil spring. Fuel under high pressure from the injection pump delivered to the nozzle through an internal fuel passage acts on the tapered needle valve face, causing the valve to lift upward in a multiple-hole design (see Figure 17–2), or move downward, depending on whether the nozzle is an inward- or outward-opening type (Figure 17–6).

When the fuel pressure from the injection pump decreases, the needle valve is returned rapidly to its

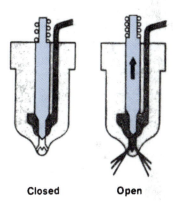

Closed   **Open**

INWARD-OPENING NOZZLE

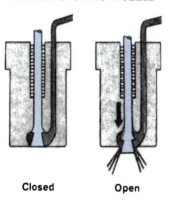

Closed   **Open**

OUTWARD-OPENING NOZZLE

FIGURE 17–6 *Operating concept of an inward-opening, versus an outward-opening, nozzle assembly. (Courtesy of Robert Bosch Corporation.)*

seat by the action of the coil spring above the needle valve. This action effectively ends fuel injection to that cylinder. The action of the fuel pressure on the needle valve causes the term *closed differential hydraulically operated type* to be used in describing these types of nozzles.

Inward-opening nozzles are used with DI (direct-injection) engines, and the nozzle tip contains multiple holes or orifices. The outward-opening nozzle is common to IDI (indirect-injection) engines that use glow plugs to facilitate starting in cold-weather operation. The outward-opening nozzle used with some IDI engines employs a pintle or single-hole design. The nozzle and its spray tip are matched to one another at the time of manufacture and should not be intermixed when overhauling or repairing the injector.

The conical area at the base of the nozzle needle valve is ground to a slightly different angle with respect to the valve seat, which results in line contact seating, thereby creating a high-pressure sealing area to prevent leakage that could cause an increase in fuel consumption, unburned fuel, and thus smoke at the exhaust pipe, as well as carbon buildup around the nozzle tip, which can cause the nozzle to hang up or stay open. Plugging of the tip is also a possibility.

Similar nozzles can be used with various types of nozzle holders, depending on the application and make of engine. Examples of the coding used to identify Bosch fuel injection nozzles are given below, and are typical of the type of coding employed by most nozzle manufacturers. The nozzle code number is stamped or etched on the body of the injector, or in some cases can be found on a tag riveted to the body.

BOSCH NOZZLES

The Robert Bosch Corporation manufactures a wide variety of nozzles and holders for use with its various injection pumps. The nozzle is the actual part of the complete injector that contains the holes where the fuel sprays into the combustion chamber, while the nozzle holder is the actual body of the injector that houses the nozzle itself. Figure 17–1 illustrates the basic types of nozzle holders produced by Bosch for trucks.

The nozzle holder is identified by a series of letters and numbers on the body. KBAL100SC2/13 would mean:

  KB: type of nozzle holder (flange type)

   A: spring location

   L: long nozzle

  100: installation length, in millimeters

   S: shoulder diameter, which must match the shoulder diameter of the nozzle

   C: nozzle locating pin placement when used

2/13: application information

DDLA150S633 would mean:

  DL: hole-type nozzle

   L: long nozzle

   A: engineering information

  150: spray-in angle in degrees (this is an included angle)

   S: shoulder diameter, which must match the shoulder diameter of the nozzle holder

  633: application information

A major user of both Bosch and Delphi injection nozzles is Cummins Engine Company, for use in the B and C series engine models. Figure 17–7 shows four different nozzle types used in these engines. Figure 17–8 illustrates that the Bosch injectors are identified with the nozzle opening pressure (E) commonly referred to as the nozzle popping pressure, stamped on the nozzle-holder assembly in bar (14.5 psi/bar); therefore, in this example, the bar is shown as 245 bar (3552 psi). The four digits (F) represent the last four numbers of the Cummins part number. Delphi injectors can be identified by noting the numbers stamped on the nozzle in the same general area (E) as shown for the Bosch models.

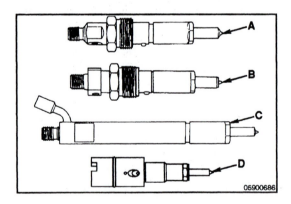

Fuel System - Overview
General Information
Injector Identification
   A. Bosch® used in B Series engines
   B. Lucas CAV used in B Series engines
   C. Bosch® used in C Series engines
   D. Bosch® used in ISB engines.

FIGURE 17–7 Example of fuel injector identification for various midrange Cummins engine models. (Courtesy of Cummins Engine Company, Inc.)

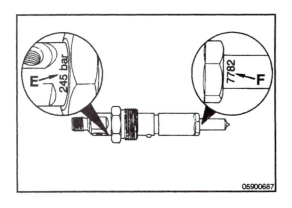

Bosch® Injectors

Bosch® injectors are identified with the opening pressure (E) (stamped on the nozzle-holder assembly in bar) and the last four digits of the Cummins part number (F) (stamped on the nozzle). These two identifiers can be cross-referenced to the assembly number required for each CPL.

FIGURE 17–8 *Bosch versus Cummins injector identification numbering system. (Courtesy of Cummins Engine Company, Inc.)*

INJECTOR NOZZLE SAC VOLUME

Sac volume is the small percentage of diesel fuel that collects below the tapered needle tip in its holder, which tends to drop into the combustion chamber at the end of injection. Because it is in an unatomized state, it causes incomplete combustion and therefore some smoke or unburned hydrocarbons at the exhaust. To meet the stringent exhaust emissions regulations now in effect in both the United States and Europe, most hole nozzles are now manufactured with no sac volume below the tip.

Still further improvement in the reduced sac volume (RSV) nozzle and injection is being obtained through the use of a valve covers orifice (VCO) type of design. Both the RSV and VCO injection nozzles, together with a standard type of nozzle arrangement, are shown in Figure 17–3.

NOZZLE PROBLEMS

The service life of injection nozzles is directly attributable to the following conditions:

- Proper control of engine operating temperature to ensure complete combustion of injected fuel
- Water- and dirt-free fuel supply
- Correct grade of fuel for ambient temperature conditions encountered.

Injection nozzle problems are usually indicated when one of the following conditions exists:

- Black smoke at the exhaust
- Poor performance and a lack of power
- Hard starting
- Rough idle and misfire
- Increased fuel consumption
- Combustion knock
- Engine overheating

A quick check of the nozzle operation when it is still in the engine can normally be performed by running the engine at the speed at which the problem is most noticeable. Loosen a high-pressure fuel line on inline Bosch pumps at each nozzle one at a time between one-half to one full turn (see Figure 25–6). Cover the fuel line with a rag to prevent fuel spraying onto you or the engine compartment. With the fuel line loose, the injector will not be able to inject because insufficient fuel pressure will be present to lift the internal nozzle valve against the return spring. Under such conditions the cylinder will receive no fuel. The engine speed should decrease, and its sound should change, indicating that it is running on one less cylinder.

If one nozzle is found where loosening the high-pressure fuel line makes little or no difference either in the misfiring condition or visible black smoke concentrations at the exhaust pipe, that nozzle should be removed and checked on a pop tester for release or popping pressure, chatter, spray pattern, holding pressure, and leakage. If the nozzle passes these tests, the problem is either in the injection pump itself or there is low compression in that cylinder.

NOZZLE REMOVAL

The nozzle removal procedure will vary slightly between different engine makes depending on the type of nozzle design used. Some nozzles are retained in the cylinder head by being rotated into a screw thread. Others use a clamp and bolt, while others may use a retaining bracket and two bolts. Each nozzle has a fuel leakoff line on top (see item 16 in Figure 17–9), that routes the internal fuel leakage past the needle valve stem back to the fuel tank. On some nozzles, a special puller clamp must be used to withdraw the nozzle and holder assembly from the cylinder head.

NOTE   Always obtain a suitable supply of plastic protective shipping caps, both male and female, prior to nozzle removal so that all open fuel lines or other lines can be plugged off during

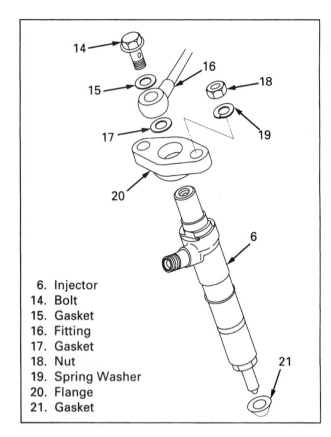

6. Injector
14. Bolt
15. Gasket
16. Fitting
17. Gasket
18. Nut
19. Spring Washer
20. Flange
21. Gasket

FIGURE 17–9 *Parts stackup of components to attach the fuel lines and retain the fuel injector in the cylinder head. (Courtesy of Cummins Engine Company, Inc.)*

servicing to prevent any dirt or foreign material from entering either the fuel system or the cylinder bore once the nozzle has been removed.

Removal Procedure

1. Wash or steam clean the valve rocker cover area. (Do not apply direct steam pressure to the injection pump housing since as it is an aluminum alloy, its expansion rate is approximately twice that of the steel components within the pump, and severe damage to the pump can result, especially if the engine is running while you steam clean it.)

2. Disconnect all high-pressure injection lines at the nozzles.

NOTE   If individual lines are to be replaced, remove the support clamp from the set of lines containing the line to be replaced.

a. Disconnect the line(s) from the injectors.
b. Disconnect the line(s) from the fuel pump.

CAUTION   If removed, reinstall the support clamp in the original position and make sure the lines do not contact each other or another component.

c. Install the lines in the reverse order of removal.

3. Disconnect all fuel return lines leading to the nozzles.

4. Remove the nozzle clamping nuts, studs, or special gland nuts.

5. Remove the nozzle from the cylinder head carefully (Figure 17–10). A pry bar or puller may be necessary in some cases.

The copper washer shown at the base of the nozzle in Figure 17–11 acts as a heat shield and should be replaced any time that the nozzle has been removed for any reason. The O-ring shown in this figure also seals the bore of the cylinder head to the nozzle body diameter. It should also be replaced after a nozzle has been removed.

NOTE   Ensure that nozzle sealing washers come out with the nozzle. If not, remove them with a tapered, serrated tool, or form a hook-shaped tool from a piece of welding rod or other suitable material.

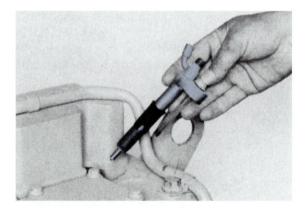

FIGURE 17–10 *Removing an injector/nozzle from the bore in the cylinder head. (Courtesy of Cummins Engine Company, Inc.)*

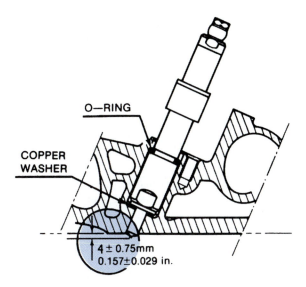

FIGURE 17–11 Injector O-ring and copper seating washer location as well as identification of the injector spray-tip protrusion specified for one engine model. *(Courtesy of Robert Bosch Corporation.)*

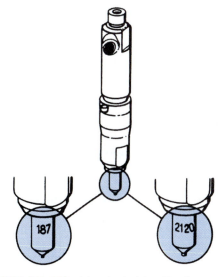

FIGURE 17–12 Nozzle tip identification number location. *(Courtesy of Robert Bosch Corporation.)*

At this time all connections and openings should be covered with plastic caps or aluminum foil. Do not use tape or rags because of the danger of lint or gummy residue getting into the lines.

Place the nozzles in an area where they will not be damaged or take them immediately to a shop specializing in this work.

Bosch Nozzle Testing and Repair

The nozzle body holder or injector may differ slightly in outward appearance and the injector installation torque to the cylinder head may also differ; however, testing, inspection, and overhaul of these nozzles can be considered common for all engines that use a Bosch holder and nozzle, such as is shown in Figure 17–1. Figure 17–12 illustrates how nozzle tips can be identified by an etched part number.

Each manufacturer specifies that a particular injector nozzle pop tester be used with specific fittings for checking their engines' nozzles; however, there are a variety of nozzle pop testers available on the market that can be used to check any number of different nozzles, since all that is required is to adapt the correct fitting to the injector body for the various tests.

Before testing nozzles, *do not* clean them, especially at the spray tip, because if you remove any carbon that was affecting the nozzle spray pattern or release pressure, you will have removed the evidence. Test the nozzle just as it was when it was removed from the engine.

TESTING NOZZLES FOR PERFORMANCE

The nozzles should be removed from the engine and checked for correct opening pressure and spray pattern. Testing of Bosch nozzles follows the same basic routine as that for other manufacturers' nozzles. Tests that would be conducted to the nozzles with a pop tester are as follows:

1. Nozzle release pressure (popping pressure)
2. Nozzle spray pattern
3. Nozzle chatter
4. Nozzle tip leakage
5. Nozzle fuel leak-off

If the injection nozzle fails to pass any of these tests, it should be sent to the local fuel injection repair shop in your area for repair or exchanged for a new or rebuilt one. Use calibrating fluid rather than diesel fuel for testing the nozzles for the reasons given in this chapter for other nozzles. The same safety precautions should be exercised regarding eye protection and hand protection as for other nozzle test procedures.

CAUTION The fuel pressure buildup required to cause the injector nozzle to release fuel is commonly known as the popping pressure or release pressure. This fuel is forced out of the nozzle tip in a finely atomized spray due to the high-pressure buildup within the injector body and at the nozzle tip. This fuel pressure is high enough to cause penetration of the skin, leading to blood poisoning. Therefore, *never* place your hands or fingers into this spray area.

Pop testing machines come equipped with a protective receptacle, usually manufactured from a heavy transparent plastic that protects you from the high-pressure spray while still allowing you to see the spray pattern of the fuel. Most pop testers such as that shown in Figure 17–13 come equipped with a variety of fittings and lines to allow a number of different nozzles to be tested.

NOTE   Use only calibrating fluid that meets ISO specifications ISO 4113, SAE 1968D, or SAE 208629 specs when checking a nozzle because it is more stable than diesel fuel, which can contain traces of water and sediment. Do not smoke or allow an open flame when testing nozzles, and always wear safety goggles.

Popping Pressure Test

1.   Connect the nozzle and holder to a suitable pop tester as shown in Figure 17–13 and place clear plastic tubes to the injector overflow connections (fuel return lines) so that return fuel is not confused with injector leakage.

FIGURE 17–13   *Testing the spray pattern of an injection nozzle assembly while mounted in a pop testing tool.* (Courtesy of Robert Bosch Corporation.)

2.   Leave the tester-to-nozzle holder fuel line loose and manually pump the tester handle until clear fuel free of air flows from the nozzle end of the tester fuel line; then tighten this fuel line nut.

3.   Open the tester gauge shutoff valve if it is closed, and pump the tester handle fairly rapidly (about 45 to 55 strokes per minute) and note at what pressure the nozzle pops or releases fuel. Compare the nozzle opening or release pressure with the engine manufacturer's specifications.

4.   Low popping/release pressure necessitates injector replacement or disassembly and repair. Nozzle opening pressure can be adjusted by adding or removing shims from above the internal nozzle valve spring, or by loosening a nut under the nozzle holder cap and turning an adjusting screw. Figure 17–1 shows the location of the spring and shims. Shim thicknesses can vary between different Bosch nozzles and the make of engine that it is used with.

Nozzle Chatter Test

The nozzle needle valve will open and close as you pump the tester handle up and down. Some nozzles may chatter more than others, due to minor variations in seating angles, carbon deposits, and gum from combustion blowby. Lack of a nozzle chatter is no positive indication in itself that the nozzle is faulty, as long as it passes the other tests. While checking the release pressure of the nozzle, listen for a chatter or hissing sound, which is an indication that the internal nozzle valve is in fact free and moving within the nozzle bore. No chatter is generally accompanied by a poor spray pattern and/or low release pressure.

Lack of good chatter is usually caused by carbon or varnish buildup within the nozzle, which can restrict flow and act as a cushioning effect on the moving nozzle valve. Test for chatters as follows:

1.   Close the shutoff valve to the pressure gauge to protect it.
2.   Pump the handle quickly up and down until a chatter, hiss, or squeal is detected.

Nozzle Spray Pattern Test

Spray patterns for Bosch pintle nozzles are very similar regardless of the make of engine the nozzle is used in. Generally, pintle nozzles are designed to provide a concentrated spray angle that is fairly narrow or cone shaped. To determine accurately if the nozzle is spraying fuel as recommended, you can place a piece of paper toweling under the nozzle tip (about 12 in. or 30 cm below it) and when you pop the nozzle, look at the mark left on the paper. It should be circular in shape because of the concentrated spray angle. A wide or poorly dispersed spray pattern over the paper requires that the nozzle be disassembled and serviced or replaced. With a multiple-hole nozzle, pop the tester handle once and count the number of drops on the paper to confirm that there are no plugged holes. Check also that all drops on the paper are evenly spaced and at the same height.

NOTE Some pop testers will not deliver fuel at a great enough velocity to obtain the correct spray pattern for proper analysis. Therefore, if the nozzle cannot be properly tested for spray pattern, yet passes the other tests, it should be considered acceptable unless performance problems occur with it in the engine.

Nozzle Holding Pressure Test

Although the nozzle may open at the correct pressure and have a suitable spray pattern, it must also be capable of preventing fuel dribble when it is not injecting fuel. Fuel dribble at the spray tip will result in nonato-mized fuel dribbling into the combustion chamber, resulting in unburned fuel and smoke appearing at the exhaust. Using a lint-free rag or an air pressure nozzle, wipe or blow dry the complete nozzle tip and its holder (injector body).

This condition is best checked by bringing the nozzle pop tester up to a point usually 150 to 200 psi (1034 to 1379 kPa) below the nozzle popping or release pressure and while keeping pressure on the pump handle, inspecting the condition of the spray tip for signs of raw fuel leakage or a bubble/dribble of fuel at the spray tip, although a slight sweat is acceptable at the tip after 5 seconds as long as no fuel droplets appear. Inspect the other sealing surfaces on the nozzle holder (injector body) for signs of external leakage.

To check for fuel leak-off (internal leakage past internal parts), quickly operate the tester handle while looking at the nozzle return fuel outlet—which can be a single outlet at the top center of the nozzle holder, or the nozzle may have two separate fuel return lines. A few drips per pump handle stroke is acceptable, but a steady flow of return fuel indicates that there is wear between the internal injector parts and that the nozzle should be replaced. Table 17–1 lists typical nozzle problems.

TABLE 17–1 Troubleshooting faulty nozzles

Fault	Possible cause	Remedy
Excessive leak-off	Dirt between pressure face of nozzle, spring retainer, or plate and nozzle holder	Clean nozzle
	Loose nozzle retainer nut	Inspect lapped faces and tighten retainer nut
	Defective nozzle	Replace nozzle
Nozzle bluing	Faulty installation or tightening	Replace nozzle
	Insufficient cooling	Correct cooling system
Nozzle opening pressure too high	Incorrect shim adjustment	Replace nozzle
	Nozzle valve dirty or sticky or opening clogged	Clean nozzle
	Seized nozzle	Replace nozzle
Nozzle opening pressure too low	Incorrect shim adjustment	Readjust nozzle
	Nozzle valve spring broken	Replace spring and readjust pressure
	Nozzle seat worn	Install new or reconditioned nozzle
Nozzle drip	Nozzle leaks because of carbon deposit or sticking nozzle valve	Clean nozzle
	Defective nozzle	Replace nozzle
Spray pattern distorted	Carbon deposit on tip of nozzle valve	Clean nozzle
	Nozzle hole partially blocked	Clean nozzle
	Defective nozzle	Replace nozzle

Source: Robert Bosch Corporation.

NOZZLE DISASSEMBLY AND CLEANING

Extreme cleanliness must be exercised when repairing fuel injection nozzles as well as having access to the special tools and equipment necessary for successful completion of a repair procedure. To clean and decarbonize nozzles/holders properly, place them into a parts tray or basket. Both cold and hot cleaning solutions are available for cleaning purposes. Handle these with care; always wear eye protection. If special cleaners are unavailable, clean solvent or diesel fuel can be used with a small brass bristle brush. Do *not* use a handheld steel wire brush or a bench grinder wire buffing wheel to clean up the injector components.

The cleaning of injection nozzles should be done in an area that is absolutely clean. Dirt and dust in the air, filings on benches, and greasy rags will contribute to faulty nozzle operation and early failure. Tools and equipment necessary for the cleaning of nozzles are:

- Parts cleaner (solvent or ultrasonic type)
- Clean pans
- Lint-free towels
- Nozzle cleaning kit
- Nozzle holder
- Hand tools
- Clean diesel fuel

Shown in Figure 17–14 are the items included in most nozzle cleaning kits.

Cleaning Injection Nozzles

After nozzles are received for cleaning, clean the exterior with solvent to remove loose dirt and grease.

FIGURE 17–15 *Loosening a nozzle retaining nut with the nozzle held in a special holding fixture.*

Loosen the cap nut and nozzle retaining nut (Figure 17–15). Place nozzles in a suitable parts cleaner to loosen carbon and remove varnish. After soaking for a minimum of 30 minutes, the nozzles should be rinsed in solvent.

Ultrasonic Nozzle Cleaner

Although loose carbon accumulations can be removed from the tips of injector nozzles by the use of a small brass bristle brush while soaking the part in calibrating fluid or solvent, often hard carbon cannot be removed successfully in this manner. To facilitate removal of hard carbon and varnish accumulations that tend to collect on nozzle components, it is best to use an ultrasonic cleaner, such as the one shown in Figure 17–16.

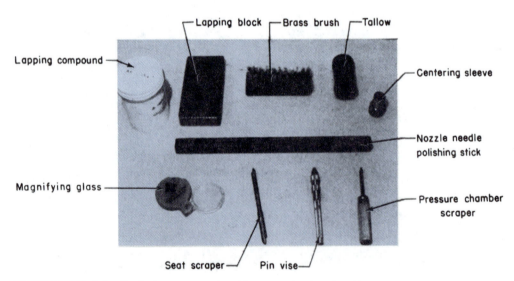

Labeled: Lapping block — Brass brush — Tallow — Lapping compound — Centering sleeve — Nozzle needle polishing stick — Magnifying glass — Pressure chamber scraper — Seat scraper — Pin vise

FIGURE 17–14 *Typical parts contained in a nozzle cleaning kit.*

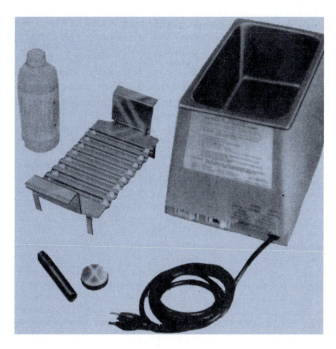

FIGURE 17–16 *Example of an ultrasonic injection nozzle parts cleaner. Cleaning solution is heated and ultrasonically agitated for fast results. (Courtesy of Kent-Moore division, SPX Corporation.)*

Ultrasonic Cleaning Method

Ultrasonic cleaning units use sound waves or mechanical vibrations that are above the human hearing range. Bransonic cleaners operate at frequencies around 55,000 cycles per second, or Hz. The sound waves are generated by the transducer, which changes high-frequency electrical energy into mechanical energy. This mechanical energy or vibration is then coupled into the liquid. This action forms millions of microscopic bubbles, which expand during the low-pressure wave and form small cavities. During the high-pressure waves these cavities collapse or implode, creating a mechanical "scrubbing" action that loosens solution. This action takes place approximately 55,000 times per second, making it seem as if dirt is blasted off the part.

Ultrasonic Cleaner Operating Checklist

- The tank should always be filled to about 1 in. from the top.
- Avoid contact with solutions and provide adequate ventilation.
- Ensure that the unit is grounded.
- When filling or emptying tank, unplug the line cord.
- The cleaner must not be overloaded.

- In the case of items containing working parts, parts should be cleaned individually and should be oiled immediately after cleaning.
- The ultrasonic cleaner should never be immersed in water. After use, rinse tank with warm tap water and wipe dry.
- To avoid discomfort, do not place fingers in the machine when in operation.
- A certain amount of heat is generated during the ultrasonic cleaning process. Do not become alarmed if the bottom surface of the cleaner becomes warm.

Setup and Operation

The ultrasonic nozzle cleaner, J29653-A, is featured in Figure 17–16. This unit consists of:

J29653-1	Cleaning tank and generator unit
J29653-2	1-lb container of cleaning powder
J29653-3	Nozzle disassembly tool
J29653-4	Parts tray

WARNING Protect yourself from injury. Wear protective gloves and safety glasses, or other suitable face and eye protection, when mixing chemicals. Avoid contact with solutions and provide adequate ventilation.

1. Mix the cleaning powder, Kent-Moore P/n J-29653-2 with warm tap water to make the solution (4 teaspoons to 3/4 gallon). The tank should always be filled to about 1 in. from the top.

2. Plug the unit into a grounded outlet and turn on both switches.

NOTE Allow the liquid to degas for a few minutes. Also, the cleaner will perform most effectively when the solution is between 120 and 140°F (49 to 60°C).

3. Position the tips and pintles in the tray; do not mix. The specially designed stainless steel tray holds nozzles in matched sets.

4. Install the tray into the tank and place the lid on during the cleaning process. Do not place objects to be cleaned directly on the bottom of the cleaning tank.

5. Remove the tips and pintles when clean (approximately 15 to 30 minutes). Cleaning times may vary, refer to the operator's manual for additional information.

Cleaning Procedure

1. Always obtain a suitable container(s) prior to disassembly so that each nozzle and its components can be kept together. Do not intermix components between nozzles and holders.

2. Wash the exterior of the injector body first to remove all dirt and loose carbon formation.

3. Place the injector nozzle holder in a soft-jaw vise if the manufacturer's special tools are not available. Do not overtighten the vise; otherwise, nozzle damage can result.

   a. Release pressure on the nozzle spring by removing the cap nut and loosening the pressure-adjusting screw (Figure 17–17).

CAUTION Failure to remove spring pressure may result in dowel pin breakage when the retaining nut is loosened.

---

   b. Invert the nozzle in the holder and remove the nozzle retaining nut and nozzle assembly. Be careful not to drop the nozzle needle!

4. Disassemble the injector/nozzle components and lay them out in a tray or individual container per injector.

5. Clean all disassembled parts in a cleaning solution.

6. Inspect all components under a lighted magnifying glass or a lighted microscope. Check for signs of discoloration (overheated), nicks, scratches, and scuffing on the polished surfaces.

7. To check the needle valve for freeness in its body after inspection, lightly dip the valve in calibrating fluid or clean filtered diesel fuel, and while holding the nozzle tip at a slight angle, insert the nozzle into its tip holder. Pull the nozzle out about halfway and let it go. It should drop under its own weight. Repeat this check by turning the needle valve to different positions. If it does not drop under its own weight, replace the nozzle and tip (sleeve) assembly.

NOTE Be certain that the nozzle needle is kept with the nozzle body from which it was removed, because nozzle needles are a selective fit in the nozzle body and cannot be interchanged from one nozzle body to another.

---

8. Examine the needle carefully for scoring, blue spots, excessive wear, and corrosion. If any are found, discard the nozzle.

CAUTION Never use steel wire bristle brush on precision nozzle parts. Always use brass wire brushes.

---

9. Using the pintle cleaning block, polish the tapered end of the needle with mutton tallow (Figure 17–18). Place tallow on needle, insert needle in cleaning block, and rotate gently to polish the needle seat. Rinse off excess tallow in clean diesel fuel or calibrating oil.

CAUTION Never use abrasives such as lapping compound, crocus cloth, or jewelers' rouge to polish the needle. Always use tallow.

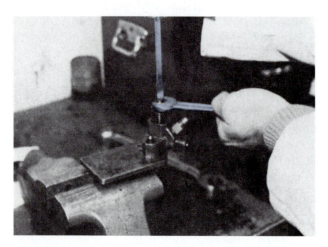

FIGURE 17–17 Loosening the injector popping pressure adjusting screw.

FIGURE 17–18 Polishing the end of the nozzle needle.

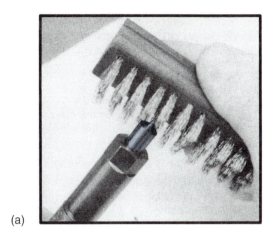
(a)

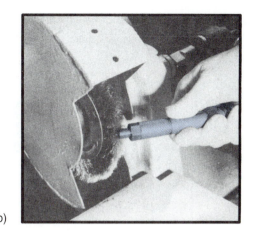
(b)

FIGURE 17–19 (a) Using a handheld brass bristle brush to clean any carbon accumulations from the end of the nozzle spray tip. (b) Carefully cleaning the carbon (use only a brass brush on the bench grinder) from the end of a nozzle spray tip.

10. Using the brass brush, clean the nozzle body to remove loose carbon deposits (Figure 17–19).

11. When cleaning orifice nozzles, clean the holes with the proper-size cleaning wire.

> **NOTE** Most nozzle valves will have the hole size stamped or etched on them. If the hole size is not stamped on the nozzle valve, refer to the manufacturer's specifications.

The cleaning wire should be fitted in a pin vise as shown in Figure 17–20, letting the wire protrude approximately 1/16 in. (1.5 mm). This lessens the danger of breaking wires off in the holes, since they are extremely hard to remove when broken. Most popular-size wires are contained in the nozzle cleaning kits.

12. Using the special pressure chamber scraper shown in Figure 17–21, clean the chamber by rotating and exerting an upward pressure on the tool. Five or six turns are usually sufficient.

13. The nozzle valve seat scraper (Figure 17–22) is used to clean carbon from the valve seat. Two sizes are contained on the same tool for varying nozzle sizes. Rotate the tool to clean the seat.

FIGURE 17–21 Cutaway view of a nozzle spray tip to indicate how the pressure chamber can be decarbonized using a special scraper tool.

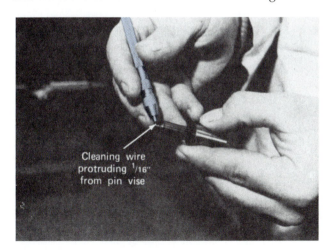

Cleaning wire protruding 1/16" from pin vise

FIGURE 17–20 Using a pin vise and cleaning wire to clean the orifice holes in the nozzle spray tip.

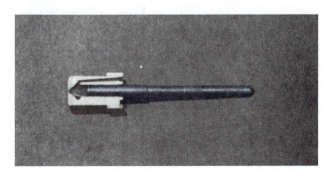

FIGURE 17–22 Cleaning the nozzle valve seat with a special tool (cutaway for clarity only).

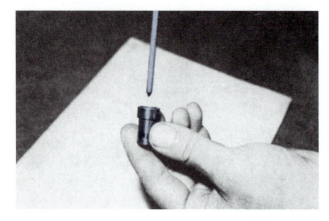

FIGURE 17–23 *Using a special tool to polish the nozzle spray tip valve seat.*

14. Apply a small amount of tallow to a polishing stick and thoroughly clean and polish the valve seat in the nozzle body (Figure 17–23).

15. The surface of the nozzle body that contacts the nozzle holder as well as the holder surface must be lapped before reassembly.

CAUTION Nozzles using dowel pins are not always lapped. If lapping is required, the dowels can be removed using diagonal pliers.

a. Place a small amount of nozzle lapping compound on the lapping plate. Hold the nozzle so that pressure will be exerted evenly on the entire surface. Move the nozzle smoothly and steadily in a figure eight motion (Figure 17–24).

FIGURE 17–24 *Lapping the nozzle spray-tip upper machined flat surface on a lapping block using a special lapping compound.*

CAUTION Do not rock the nozzle from side to side.

b. Lap only until the nozzle mating surfaces are clean and flat. Rinse the nozzle completely in clean diesel fuel to remove all traces of lapping compound.

c. Lap the nozzle holder in the same manner. Steady the holder near the lower end to prevent it from rocking.

16. Using a small screwdriver, scrape all loose carbon from the nozzle retaining nut and check for cracks and damaged threads. The sealing surface for the nozzle retaining nut may be cleaned up by rubbing it on the emery cloth.

INJECTION NOZZLE REASSEMBLY

1. Start reassembly by rinsing the nozzle needle and the body in clean diesel fuel and checking the valve fit (Figure 17–25). This can be done by holding the nozzle at a 45° angle and pulling the needle one-third of the way up. It should fall freely back to its seat. If it does not, remove the needle, rinse the parts, and try again.

2. Rinse the sealing surfaces of the nozzle holder and nozzle body in diesel fuel and assemble.

CAUTION Since no sealing rings of any type are used at this point, the mating surfaces must be absolutely clean. Do not use compressed air to clean the surfaces, as lint and dust will remain.

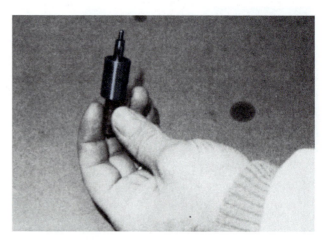

FIGURE 17–25 *Checking that the nozzle needle valve is free within the bore of the spray tip assembly.*

FIGURE 17–26 *Ensuring that the nozzle spray-tip dowel pins when used are correctly installed and aligned with the injector body.*

Make certain when assembling that locating dowels (if used) are in alignment with holes in the holder (Figure 17–26). On some nozzle types the spray tip is separate from the nozzle body and must be aligned by means of timing lines (Figure 17–27). Hold the tip with a small wrench while snugging up the retaining nut.

3. On pintle nozzles, before final torquing of the retaining nut, the nozzle must be centered in the nut to ensure proper operation.

NOTE   Do not center nozzles used with Bosch holders and retaining nuts, as they are self-centering.

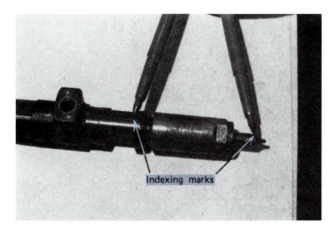

FIGURE 17–27 *Pen tip indicates that when index marks are used they must be aligned to correctly position the nozzle spray orifices (holes).*

To center the nozzle, a special sleeve (Figure 17–14) is used (supplied with nozzle cleaning kits). Carefully fit the centering sleeve over the nozzle body. The tapered end of the sleeve centers the nozzle within the retaining nut bore and on the holder. With the sleeve in place, tighten the nut finger tight. Make sure that the sleeve turns freely. Torque the nut to the manufacturer's specifications using a deep well socket.

NOTE   On orifice nozzle valves, centering is not required. Simply torque the nut to specifications.

---

4. When all parts have been cleaned, inspected, and checked, reassemble the parts. Torque the components and retest the injector as in the tests discussed earlier.

5. To adjust the opening pressure, attach nozzle to the test stand and flush thoroughly by operating the handle. Adjust the opening pressure with the pressure adjusting screw or shims as required (Figure 17–28).

CAUTION   Close the gauge isolating valve (Figure 17–13) before operating the tester handle to prevent damage to the pressure gauge.

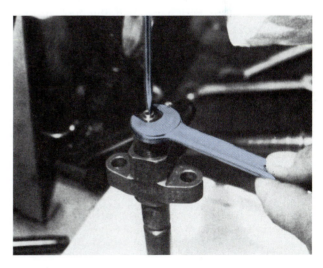

FIGURE 17–28 *Adjusting the injector nozzle spring for the correct release (popping) pressure with a screwdriver and wrench to tighten the locknut. Keep in mind that some nozzles require the use of selective shims within the spring cavity to adjust the popping pressure.*

NOZZLE INSTALLATION

Nozzle and holder installation requires that you clean the bore in the cylinder head of any carbon or debris prior to installation. This can be done using a small round brush or, if necessary, use a carbon reaming tool or hard wooden round stick to remove accumulated carbon. To retain the copper washer in position on the nozzle, a small quantity of clean 15W-40 engine oil can be applied, or alternatively, drop the washer into the bore, ensuring that it is installed correctly, then gently lower the nozzle and holder into position.

NOTE Copper washers are available in different thicknesses; therefore, always check their thickness with a micrometer to ensure that the same-thickness washer is installed; otherwise, severe piston/cylinder damage and poor engine performance can result by the nozzle tip being either too far in or too far out. These washers should be replaced each time the nozzle is removed, then reinstalled.

Some manufacturers suggest that you coat the nozzle holder/sleeve with antiseize compound to prevent sticking/freezing in the bore. This will make it easier to remove at any future time. Torque the nozzle holder retaining nuts to the manufacturer's specifications. Attach the fuel leakoff line, then insert the high-pressure inlet fuel line into position, but leave it loose until you have bled the fuel system of all entrapped air. Once you have bled the fuel system, torque all nozzle fuel lines and check for any signs of leakage.

SUMMARY

If the procedures outlined in this chapter are followed, injection nozzle servicing is an easy task. When working with any type of nozzle not listed in this chapter, always refer to the manufacturer's technical manual. It will give the correct torques, opening pressures, operation, and any other pertinent data. If a question still exists, consult your instructor or contact your nearest fuel injection service shop for information.

SELF-TEST QUESTIONS

1. Name the two basic types of nozzles.
2. What is the purpose of the Pintaux nozzle?
3. Explain the difference between a standard pintle nozzle and the throttling pintle.
4. What does each of the following numbers and letters stand for: KBAL100SC2/13?
5. State the difference between a nozzle and an injector.
6. Why do most pintle nozzles require centering on the nozzle body?
7. Explain in detail the procedures for removing and installing nozzles in the engine.
8. Why are orifice nozzles used with direct-injection engines?
9. List several reasons why nozzles should be cleaned regularly.
10. Why are retaining nut torque and nozzle holddown torque so critical?
11. What is the purpose of dowel pins and timing lines in reference to nozzles?
12. What five tests are made on the nozzle test stand?
13. List the steps required in the cleaning of a nozzle.
14. Explain how a faulty nozzle can be located in the engine.

18 Theory of Electronic Fuel Systems

Overview

This chapter introduces the electronically controlled high-speed heavy-duty diesel fuel injection systems. We describe their purpose, function, and operation. Today's electronic engines as manufactured by the major OEMs are more similar than they are different. If you understand the basic operation of one electronic engine, then you will be able to quickly transfer this data and information to Cummins, Caterpillar, Detroit Diesel, Volvo, John Deere, Mack/RVI, Mercedes-Benz, MAN, MTU, and Bosch systems, whether installed in a heavy-duty truck or in an industrial, off-highway, marine, or one of the other approximately 5000 diesel engine applications used globally.

We provide generic details on how analog and digital signals are used, signal processing, sensor function and operation, electronic control module (ECM) operation, waveforms, duty cycle, pulse-width-modulation signals, computer binary notation, standardized SAE diagnostic trouble/fault codes, and access instructions. To successfully challenge and pass either the appropriate Trade Qualification InterProvincial Red Seal Test in Canada, or the ASE L2 test of the National Institute for Automotive Service Excellence (NIASE) in the United States, you need to be familiar with not only how electronic fuel systems function and operate, but also be capable of performing the necessary hands-on skills to effectively and efficiently diagnose and troubleshoot faults with these types of fuel injection systems. To further assist and prepare you for these tasks, refer to and complete the various OEM chapters in this book dealing with their specific electronic fuel systems. The goals and objectives of this and other related chapters in this book are to provide a broad, yet specific overview of how each engine OEM's mechanical and electronic fuel systems operate. At the completion of your individual chapter studies, supported by the required hands-on skills in a shop environment, you will be able to perform the necessary technician-level diagnostic and troubleshooting tasks which will prepare you to challenge the ASE L2 test. The following information provides greater details on the ASE L2 test to guide you in your studies.

ASE L2 TEST

In preparation for the ASE electronic diesel engine diagnosis specialist test (L2), study the various chapters in this book dealing with electronic fuel systems and review the content areas of the ASE test specification that indicates the question test areas. Always read the tasks list to determine your strengths and weaknesses. If you are uncertain about specific test areas, study the questions at the end of this and the other respective chapters on specific makes of electronic fuel systems.

In addition, you can download from the ASE website (*www.asecert.org*) the internet version for the medium/heavy composite vehicle preparation/reference booklet. This booklet provides a general description of a medium/heavy-duty truck equipped with a generic four-stroke-cycle, inline six-cylinder engine, turbocharged and aftercooled, using EUIs (electronic unit injectors). It explains the general components required with this type of a fuel system, and briefly describes the various engine/vehicle sensors and how they interact with the ECM to control the fueling and operation of the engine. The booklet also discusses how the engine protection system functions and operates to protect the engine, and reviews the SAE-standardized trouble/fault codes stored in ECM memory when a sensor or system fault is detected.

Test Specifications for the Medium/Heavy Vehicle Electronic Diesel Engine Diagnosis Specialist Test (L2)

Content Area		Questions in Test	Percentage of Test
A. General Diesel Engine Diagnosis		7	16%
B. Electronic Diesel Engine Controls Diagnosis		23	51%
C. Diesel Engine Air Induction and Exhaust Diagnosis		5	11%
D. Diesel Fuel Systems Diagnosis		4	9%
E. Specific Fuel Systems Diagnosis		6	13%
1. Electronic Unit Injector	(2)		
2. Pump Line Nozzle—Electronic	(2)		
3. Hydraulic Electronic Unit Injector	(2)		
Total		45*	100%

*Note: The test could contain up to fifteen questions that are included for statistical research purposes only. Your answers to these questions will not affect your score, but since you do not know which ones they are, you should answer all questions in the test.

To support this ASE preparation booklet, and to provide you with more specific details about the various engine manufacturers' EUI fuel systems, refer to Chapters 19 through 23 in this textbook. Knowledge of both the theory and hands-on practical aspects of the minor variations that exist between the various makes of engine fuel systems will broaden your knowledge spectrum and provide you with a comfort zone in which to prepare you to successfully challenge and certify as an electronic diesel engine diagnosis specialist.

ASE L2 Content Area

To prepare for a course of study prior to challenging the ASE L2 test, you must be fully aware of the content area of knowledge and hands-on skills required. The chart on this page identifies the ASE content area, number of questions in the L2 test for each area, and the percentage split of the individual test questions.

ASE L2 Task List

A detailed listing of the individual content area tasks lists A through E follows.

Electronic Diesel Engine Diagnosis Specialist Task List

A. General Diesel Engine Diagnosis (7 Questions)

1. Inspect and test for missing, modified, damaged, or engine mechanical components.
2. Locate and utilize relevant service information, vehicle information, and diagnostic tools.
3. Verify operational complaint.
4. Determine appropriate diagnostic procedures based on operational complaint, engine/vehicle data, and service information.
5. Establish relative importance of observed vehicle data.
6. Determine if problem is electrical/electronic or engine mechanical.
7. Evaluate engine mechanical condition based on visual inspection of exhaust output.
8. Diagnose performance complaints caused by engine mechanical problems.
9. Diagnose performance complaints caused by cooling system problems.
10. Diagnose performance complaints caused by engine lubrication system problems.
11. Evaluate integrity of air induction system.
12. Evaluate integrity of exhaust system.
13. Diagnose performance complaints caused by problems or modifications to the transmission, drive axle ratio, or by incorrect tire specifications.
14. Diagnose performance complaints caused by vehicle operation and configuration.
15. Determine root cause of failures.
16. Determine root cause of multiple component failures.
17. Determine root cause of repeated component failures.

B. Electronic Diesel Engine Controls Diagnosis (23 Questions)

1. Inspect and test for missing, modified, or damaged, engine control components and programmed parameters (factory and customer).

2. Interpret diagnostic tool data to determine control system condition.

3. Establish relative importance of displayed data.

4. Determine if the control system problem is electrical/electronic or mechanical.

5. Locate and utilize relevant service information, vehicle information and diagnostic tools.

6. Determine appropriate electronic engine control diagnostic procedures based on vehicle data, operational complaint, and service information.

7. Perform digital multimeter tests on circuits.

8. Test input sensors/circuits using displayed data.

9. Test control system operation.

10. Test output actuators/circuits using displayed data.

11. Evaluate accuracy of displayed data.

12. Test and confirm operation of electrical/electronic circuits not displayed on diagnostic tools.

13. Research system operation using technical information to determine diagnostic procedures.

14. Diagnose performance complaints caused by non-engine electronic control system problems.

15. Determine root cause of failures.

16. Determine root cause of multiple component failures.

17. Determine root cause of repeated component failures.

C. Diesel Engine Air Induction and Exhaust Diagnosis (5 Questions)

1. Inspect and test for missing, modified, or damaged components.

2. Locate and utilize relevant service information and diagnostic tools.

3. Determine appropriate air induction and exhaust system diagnostic procedures based on vehicle data, operational complaint, and service information.

4. Establish relative importance of displayed data.

5. Diagnose performance complaints caused by air induction system problems.

6. Diagnose performance complaints caused by exhaust system problems.

7. Diagnose performance complaints caused by engine brakes, exhaust brakes, backpressure devices, and mechanically and electronically actuated wastegates.

8. Determine root cause of failures.

9. Determine root cause of multiple component failures.

10. Determine root cause of repeated component failures.

D. Diesel Fuel Systems Diagnosis (4 Questions)

1. Inspect and test for missing, modified, or damaged components.

2. Locate and utilize relevant service information, vehicle information, and diagnostic tools.

3. Determine appropriate fuel system diagnostic procedures based on available vehicle data, operational complaint and service information.

4. Establish relative importance of displayed data.

5. Determine if the fuel system problem is electrical/electronic or mechanical.

6. Diagnose performance complaints caused by fuel system problems.

7. Test and/or analyze fuel, fuel system pressure, temperature, and delivery rates.

8. Determine the need for fuel injector performance testing.

9. Determine root cause of failures.

10. Determine root cause of multiple component failures.

11. Determine root cause of repeated component failures.

E. Specific Fuel Systems Diagnosis (6 Questions)

Note: Each task in this section applies to the following types of fuel injection systems: E1-Electronic Unit Injector (EUI), E2-Pump Line Nozzle-Electronic (PLN-E), and E3-Hydraulic Electronic Unit Injector (HEUI). There will be two questions on each fuel system.

1. Inspect and test for missing, modified, or damaged engine control components and programmed parameters (factory and customer).

2. Determine if the control system problem is electrical/electronic or mechanical.

3. Research system operation, and determine appropriate electronic engine control/fuel system control diagnostic procedures based on vehicle data, operational complaint, and service information.

4. Test input sensors/circuits using displayed data.

5. Test control system operation.

6. Test output actuators/circuits using displayed data.

7. Test and confirm operation of electrical/electronic circuits not displayed on diagnostic tools.

8. Diagnose performance complaints caused by non-engine electronic control system problems.

9. Diagnose performance complaints caused by engine brakes, exhaust brakes, backpressure devices, and mechanically and electronically actuated wastegates.

10. Diagnose performance complaints caused by fuel system problems.

11. Test and/or analyze fuel, fuel system pressure, temperature, and delivery rates.

12. Determine the need for fuel injector performance testing.

ASE Medium/Heavy Truck Tests (T2)

Contained within the ASE preparation guide for medium/heavy trucks, diesel engines test T2, fuel system diagnosis and repair, is a tasks list dealing with parts 1 and 2, mechanical components and electronic components, respectively. There are 12 tasks listed for the electronic engine fuel systems that you must understand. These tasks plus the L2 tasks listed for the electronic diesel engine diagnosis specialist, which follow, will prepare you to successfully challenge both of these ASE tests, or to pass the TQ test.

T2 Electronic Components Tasks (11 questions)

1. Check and record engine electronic diagnostic codes and trip/operational data; clear codes; determine needed repairs.

2. Inspect, adjust, repair/replace electronic throttle and PTO control devices, circuits, and sensors.

3. Perform on-engine inspections, tests, and adjustments on distributor-type injection pump electronic controls.

4. Perform on-engine inspections, tests, and adjustments on inline-type injection pump electronic controls.

5. Perform on-engine inspections, tests, and adjustments on PT-type injection pump electronic controls.

6. Perform on-engine inspections, tests, and adjustments on hydraulic electronic unit injectors (HEUIs) and electronic controls (rail pressure control).

7. Perform on-engine inspections, tests, and adjustments on electronic unit injectors (EUIs) and electronic controls.

8. Perform on-engine inspections, tests, and adjustments on pump-line-nozzle electronic systems (PLN-E) and electronic controls.

9. Inspect, test, adjust, repair/replace engine electronic fuel shutdown devices, circuits, and sensors, including engine protection systems.

10. Inspect and test power, ignition, and ground circuits and connections for electrical/electronic components; determine needed repairs.

11. Inspect and replace electrical connector terminals, pins, harnesses, seals, and locks.

12. Connect diagnostic tool to vehicle/engine; access and change customer parameters; determine needed repairs.

ELECTRONIC FUEL SYSTEM BACKGROUND

Environmental concerns about exhaust emissions from the internal combustion engine were the force that motivated diesel engine manufacturers to adopt *electronic engine control systems*.

Mechanically governed and controlled fuel injection systems on diesel engines had reached their limit of efficiency. The next logical technological move was to adopt a series of electrical engine sensors, an electronic foot pedal assembly (EFPA), and an on-board ECM (electronic control module) programmed to extract the optimum fuel economy and engine performance.

Initially, heavy-duty high-speed diesel engine electronic fuel injection systems were add-on items attached to existing PLN (pump-line-nozzle) systems such as those manufactured by Robert Bosch, Zexel, Nippondenso, Lucas, and Caterpillar. The first major OEM to release full-authority electronic controls was Detroit Diesel, who introduced their DDEC 1 system in September 1985 on their two-stroke-cycle 92 series engines. This was followed by DDEC 11 in September

1987, the same year that the four-cycle series 60 engine was released to the marketplace. DDEC 111 was introduced in April 1993, and went into full production in January 1994, followed by DDEC 1 V's initial release in August 1997, and into full production by January 1998. DDEC V is due in late 2001, or sometime in 2002.

Caterpillar introduced its programmable electronic engine control (PEEC) system on its PLN fuel system for its 3406B truck engine in 1987. This was followed in 1988 by the release of its EUI system on the 3176 truck engine. The PEEC system on the 3406B and C engine models was superseded by the EUI system beginning in late 1993 and early 1994 with the introduction of the 3406E engine model. Both the 3500 and 3600 Caterpillar engines also employ EUI systems. Cummins introduced its first-generation ECI (electronically controlled injection) system in 1988. This was followed in 1990 by its Celect (Cummins Electronics) fuel system, which was then followed by the later-model Celect Plus system. The Celect system is widely used on the L10, M11, N14, and K-series engines. A similar electronic system is used on the Interact System (IS) engines such as the ISB, ISC, ISL, ISM, and ISX and Signature engines described in Chapter 22 for Cummins fuel systems.

In 1994 Volvo introduced its VE D12 overhead camshaft 12 L truck engine equipped with VE, for Vectro (Volvo electronics) controlled unit injectors, which are similar to the DDEC system.

Mack has used a system known by the acronym VMAC (vehicle management and controls) on its PLN Bosch electronic fuel injection pumps for several years. Robert Bosch, who is a major PLN OEM, recently purchased 49% of the Diesel Technology Equipment Division, Inc., of Detroit Diesel and now produces EUPs (electronic unit pumps) in addition to EUIs now used by Bosch's many engine OEMs in place of the long-used PLN fuel systems. Mercedes-Benz, the parent of Freightliner, and Detroit Diesel codesigned the stock engine used in the Century Class 8 trucks. This engine, known as the DDC series 55 (four cycle), is a 12 L engine that incorporates EUPs controlled by the DDEC electronic system. John Deere also employ EUIs in their 10.5 and 12.5 L Power Tech engine models using an overhead camshaft for actuation. Another unique system is the HEUI system, which was codesigned by Caterpillar and Navistar engineers. OEMs employing the HEUI system include Caterpillar, on their 3126, 3408E, and 3412E models, and International, on their 444, 466, and 530 models. The Navistar 444 engine is used by Ford in a broad cross section of their vehicles.

Engine OEMs are now committed to using electronically controlled diesel fuel injection systems. The trend at this time is to replace PLN systems with electronic unit injectors or EUP's. Electronic diesel control means an advanced technology electronic fuel injection and control system that offers significant operating advantages over traditional mechanically governed engines. Electronic systems optimize control of critical engine functions that affect fuel economy, exhaust smoke, and emissions. These electronic systems provide the capability to protect the engine from serious damage resulting from conditions such as high engine coolant temperatures, high oil temperatures, and low engine oil pressure conditions.

ADVANTAGES OF ELECTRONIC ENGINES

Before we study the electronic engine fuel system basic structure and function, let us consider the advantages of an electronically controlled diesel engine over its mechanical counterpart. The electronic engine has the following major advantages:

1. An *automated engine protection system* provides a warning to the driver/operator, ramps down the engine power, or shuts down the engine when specific sensors indicate to the ECM that a system is operating outside of normal safe parameters. See the detailed description later in this chapter.

2. *Engine diagnostics* provide continuous monitoring of all engine/vehicle sensors, fuel injectors, connectors, and wiring circuits by the ECM, so arranged that when a fault occurs in a sensor or circuit, the ECM will store a diagnostic trouble code (DTC), or fault code. When the technician is diagnosing/troubleshooting an engine, they can access these codes for assistance as to what caused the condition and where the problem may be. This results in faster troubleshooting times with more effective and efficient diagnosis.

3. *Reduced maintenance* is a plus due to tighter control of fuel injection and improved combustion. In addition, there is no mechanical governor linkage or fuel racks which reduce tune-up adjustments and repair times.

4. *Improved engine governing* through the use of electronics rather than a set of rotating flyweights results in more precise speed control. Electronics can be programmed for normal droop when driving, or zero droop when using a PTO and the vehicle is parked.

5. *Fuel economy* is *optimized* when operating conditions are programmed, then monitored by the ECM during engine operation, particularly the fuel injection process with variable timing, plus temperature, load, speed, and turbo boost.

6. *Cold starting is enhanced.* Some systems use a coolant temperature sensor whereas others employ the oil temperature sensor to determine engine coldness. From this sensor information, the ECM can optimize the injection timing and fuel input to minimize white smoke on startup. In addition, the ECM will raise the engine cold idle speed to as high as 800 to 850 rpm, and the ECM can be programmed to ignore any throttle inputs until the engine coolant or oil temperature has obtained a minimum operating point.

7. To comply with mandated EPA exhaust emissions, *steady-state and transient smoke are limited* by having the ECM control the actual fuel injection timing and quantity delivered as a direct function of throttle position, engine oil temperature, and turbocharger boost pressure.

8. *Reduced exhaust emissions levels* comply with EPA regulations. Each engine OEM has redesigned the following items:

- Every fuel injector is manufactured to very tight tolerances with some OEMs offering the capability to correct cylinder balance. This is achieved by a calibration code stamped on the EUI solenoid plate. The service technician can employ a handheld diagnostic tool or a PC or laptop computer to tell the ECM what code each injector has, thus reducing horsepower variability.
- Injector spray-tip design has been changed.
- Injection pressures are higher.
- Injector camshaft lobe lift is greater.

9. *Horsepower reprogrammability* allows a given engine model to be set for three independent horsepower settings, with one dependent cruise-control power rating.

FUEL SYSTEM STRUCTURE AND FUNCTION

Although there are unique differences in the electronic fuel systems employed by each OEM, overall there are more similarities than differences. Electronically controlled unit fuel injectors, with the exception of HEUI systems, are mechanically actuated. Each system employs a series of engine and vehicle sensors that are continually fed an electrical *input* signal from the ECM. Most sensors are designed to accept a 5.0-volt dc (direct-current) input signal from the ECM. Depending on the operating condition at the sensor, it will *output* a signal back to the ECM ranging between 0.5 and 5.0 V dc, although some systems can range as high as 5.25 to 5.5 V dc. The ECM then determines and computes a

digital PWM (pulse-width-modulated) electrical signal based on predetermined calibration tables in its memory to control the time that each injector actually delivers fuel to the combustion chamber. This type of system allows tailoring of the start, duration, and end of fuel injection to ensure optimum engine performance at any load and speed. Fuel is delivered to the cylinders by the EUIs, which are driven by an overhead camshaft on Detroit Diesel series 50 and 60 engines, Cummins ISX and Signature, Caterpillar 3406E, Volvo VE D12, John Deere 10.5 L and 12.5 L Power Tech models, and Isuzu 12 L 6WA1TC, or by an in-block camshaft and pushrod on Caterpillar's 3176B, C10, C12, 3408E, and 3412E models; and Cummins N14, M11, L10, and K models, to provide the mechanical input for sufficient pressurization of the fuel, resulting in injector spray-in pressures as high as 28,000 psi (193,060 kPa).

Figure 18–1 is a simplified schematic of an electronically controlled unit injector fuel system common to Caterpillar, Cummins, Detroit Diesel, and Volvo high-speed diesel engines. This line diagram of an electronic unit injector fuel system arrangement shows the engine crankshaft timing reference sensor (TRS), the gear train synchronous reference sensor (SRS), the basic layout of the ECM components, the electronically controlled unit injector solenoid, most of the sensors used, and the operator interfaces, which indicate to the ECM when a function is desired. The number of engine/vehicle sensors and their location varies in makes and models of engines; in all, however, the ECM continually monitors each sensor for an *out-of-range condition.* When this occurs, a dash-mounted warning light system is activated and a trouble code is stored in ECM memory. This code can be extracted by the technician by means of a diagnostic data reader (DDR).

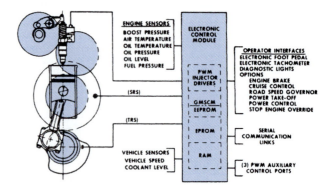

FIGURE 18–1 *Various electrical inputs and outputs between the engine, sensors, and ECM (electronic control module) of a DDEC system. (Courtesy of Detroit Diesel Corporation.)*

Electronic Fuel System Basics

Regardless of the make and model of electronic diesel engine in use today, we can refer to it as a complete integrated engine management and control system. Figure 18–2 illustrates the three main component parts of a basic electronically controlled fuel injection system. These are the inputs (switches and sensors), the ECM which analyzes the input data, and the actuators which operate the outputs (electronic unit injectors).

The system consists of an ECM that contains memory elements, a series of microprocessors (the brains of the system), and output drivers to handle the current load in amps required to actuate the EUIs, EUPs (electronic unit pumps), HEUIs (hydraulically actuated EUIs), a Bosch EDI (electronic diesel control) PLN (pump-line-nozzle) system, or an EDP (electronic distributor pump) system. As shown in Figure 18–1, the ECM receives and processes data and information from all engine/vehicle sensors and switches by com-

paring each sensor return voltage to information that has been preprogrammed in the ECM memory. The memory can be compared with a library of data and information. Within the library are shelves of filing cabinets containing specific information related to a given subject, in this case, to each specific switch and sensor. Therefore, on a running engine when the individual sensors input a signal to the ECM (if an analog signal is used from a sensor), this signal must first pass through an analog/digital (A/D) converter as shown in Figure 18–3. This process is necessary because the ECM can only recognize digital signals. The read-only memory (ROM) contains hardwired or fixed memory and with that the values for a particular engine or vehicle.

Different types of memory can be employed by using different types of chips. A basic layout of these memory devices is shown in Figure 18–3. Note that the ROM, RAM, and PROM chips are linked with the microprocessor (MP). Both RAM and PROM can talk back

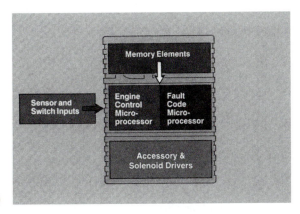

(a)

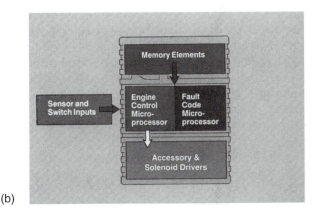

(b)

(c)

FIGURE 18–2   (a) Simplified flow of the engine/vehicle sensor inputs into the ECM engine control MPU (microprocessor unit); (b) how the sensor inputs interact with the preprogrammed memory elements, the control MPU, and the accessory and solenoid drivers section of the ECM; (c) the solenoid drivers function to handle the amperage requirements needed to actuate the injector solenoid drivers to permit fuel injection. (Courtesy of Cummins Engine Company, Inc.)

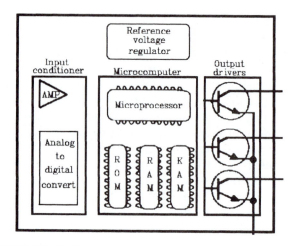

FIGURE 18–3 *Basic layout of the internal components of a microprocessor, plus its memory, form a microcomputer or engine ECM.*

and forward with the MP, but the ROM can only be read by the MP. The ROM chip is used for permanent storage and is hardwired by the engine manufacturer with operating data and information for engine speed, power setting, governor-droop features, type of governor (limiting versus variable), road speed governing, geardown protection, engine protection, and so forth. Such data are permanent and thus cannot be changed. A programmable read-only memory (PROM) chip is also hardwired and programmed at the end of the factory assembly line with fixed operating data and cannot be changed without physically removing the PROM chip and replacing it with another that is programmed for different operating values or parameters. An EPROM chip is an electrically erasable read-only memory chip that is capable of being programmed at the end of the assembly line in the factory. An EEPROM or "double E" PROM chip is an electrically erasable read-only memory that can be altered and reprogrammed in the field using a laptop computer and modem connected to the factory mainframe computer by telephone lines. The EEPROM memory is used to store customer calibrations, smoke control, cold-start fueling, and timing. When the ECM is reprogrammed, the system erases this area of memory and programs the updated customer calibrations back into the ECM. The term *flash memory* is used to store ECM software such as engine governing, cold-start logic, engine diagnostic, and engine protection features.

The microprocessor consists of thousands of chips, including logic gates, and an arithmetic logic unit which actually is designed to add, subtract, multiply, and divide all input data originating from the sensor and switch inputs. By referring to the various look-up

tables within the computer, technicians can decide to respond to changing input signals from the operator commands (throttle), changing engine speed due to load, vehicle speed, turbocharger boost pressure, oil pressure and temperature, coolant temperature and intake manifold temperature, coolant level, and so forth. Injector feedback from the EUIs is also used by the computer to determine when to fire the next injector in sequence, and to determine if a fault exists in an injector solenoid.

The random-access memory (RAM) functions as a working scratch pad as it is continually erased and updated when sensor signals change. The keep-alive memory (KAM) stores more permanent information that must be retained even when the ignition key is turned off. This memory is however lost if vehicle battery power is disconnected. The KAM is where diagnostic trouble codes (DTCs), or fault codes, are stored. In addition, some operational strategies to permit the vehicle to adapt to certain driving conditions and changing requirements are retained.

The inputs (sensors and switches) shown in Figure 18–2a consist of a variety of engine and vehicle sensors as well as driver/operator input. These individual inputs are sent to the engine-mounted ECM, which is a simple, yet powerful, computer. Note the location of the memory elements, the engine control microprocessor, the fault code MP, and the accessory and solenoid drivers for the EUIs. Figure 18–2b shows that the engine control MP sends fueling and timing commands to the solenoid driver circuitry. The ECM analyzes the inputs and compares this data with programmed operating parameters stored in the MP. The ECM then sends an output signal, as shown in Figure 18–2c, to each solenoid located on each EUI, EUP, or fuel rack solenoid on a PLN system. The ECM drivers signal to the EUI or EUP solenoids by a PWM voltage signal, which we describe in greater detail later in this chapter when we discuss injectors. The duty cycle of this signal determines the start, duration, and end of injection, and therefore controls the quantity of fuel metered for a given engine speed and load, and subsequently the power developed.

ECM/Engine Wiring Diagram Example

Figure 18–4 illustrates a typical example of the kind of wiring diagram that can be used by the service technician when diagnosing and troubleshooting an electronically controlled engine. This particular diagram is available from any Cummins dealer in laminated brochure form for each specific make/model of electronic engine that they offer. This publication is an invaluable diagnostic aid for use in the workshop and on the vehicle when tracing circuits because the plastic

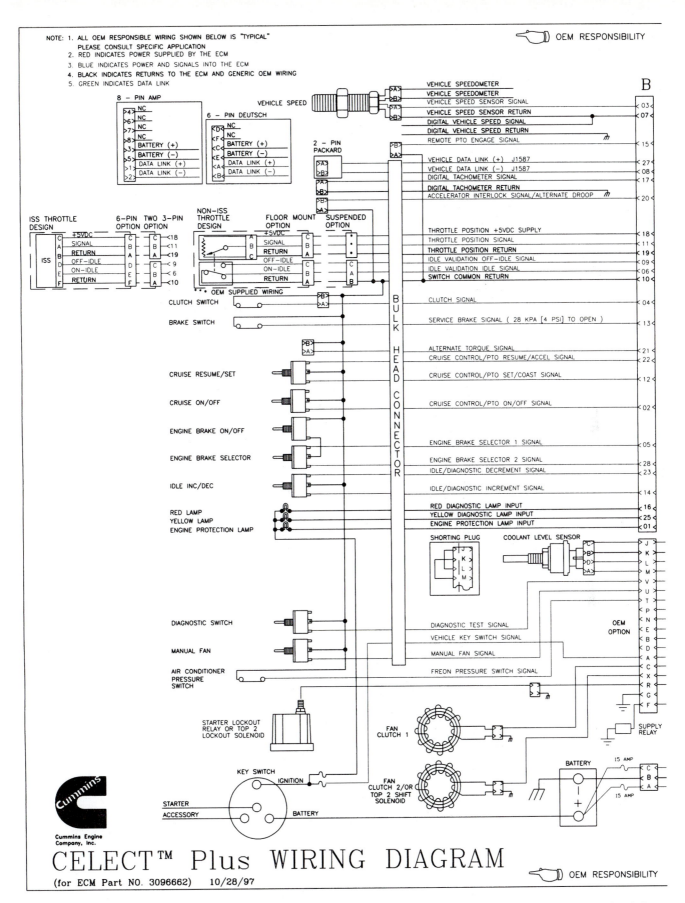

FIGURE 18–4 Example of an electronic engine wiring system schematic; in this case, we illustrate a circuit for a Cummins Celect (Cummins electronics) engine model. (Courtesy of Cummins Engine Company, Inc.)

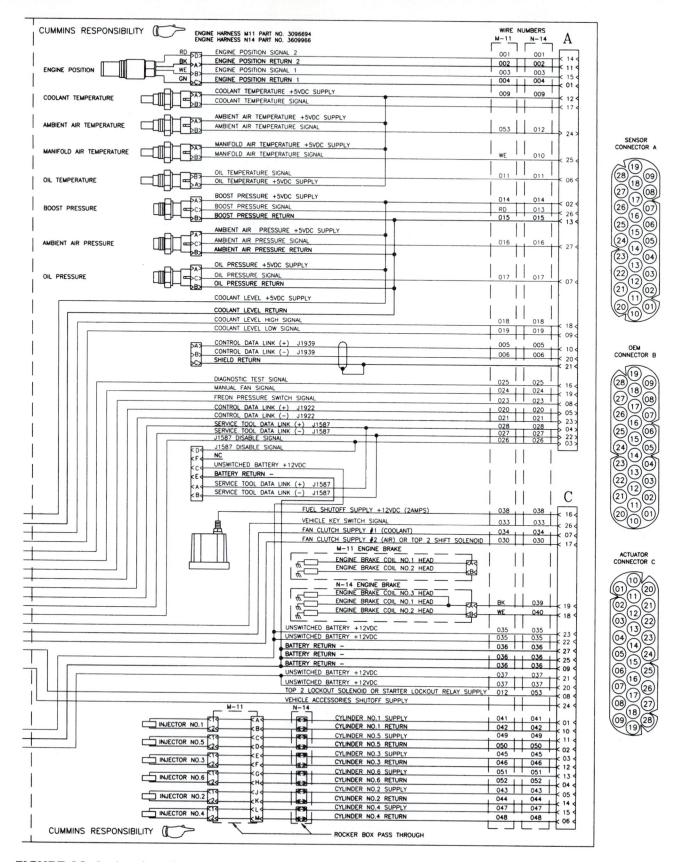

FIGURE 18–4 (continued). (Courtesy of Cummins Engine Company, Inc.)

cover protects it from getting oil soaked or damaged. Always refer to the appropriate electronic circuit wiring diagram when attempting to diagnose and troubleshoot a short, open, or ground, or when an intermittent or active diagnostic fault code is indicated. Refer to the appropriate engine OEM troubleshooting and repair manual for step-by-step details in solving a specific fault code problem.

Engine Sensors and Location

Regardless of the make of the electronically controlled heavy-duty diesel engine in use, they all employ engine sensors which are very similar in operation and even use identical sensors in some cases to monitor operating conditions using common technology. The various engine OEM sensors are located on the engine in similar positions. The exact location of these sensors can be seen in Figure 21–34 for Detroit Diesel, Figure 23–17 and Figure 23–18 for Caterpillar, and Figure 22–29 for Cummins. The sensors and engine protective features employed by each engine OEM normally have the following elements (see Figure 21–34 for DDEC):

1. *TRS* (timing reference sensor): provides a '36 per crankshaft revolution signal to the DDEC-ECM for optimum injection timing and low emissions. Cummins refer to this sensor as an EPS (engine position sensor; see Figure 22–29). Caterpillar employs an engine speed timing sensor (Figure 23–17 and Figure 23–18) that provides a PWM signal to the ECM, which the ECM interprets as a crankshaft position and engine speed reference.

2. *SRS* (synchronous reference sensor): provides a 'once per cam revolution' to the ECM to determine which cylinder is at TDC-compression on DDEC.

3. *TBS* (turbocharger boost sensor): provides information on intake manifold air pressure to the ECM and is used for control of the percentage of fueling requested by the operator from the throttle position sensor (TPS). For example, if the operator requests 75% fueling, the ECM always checks first to see if there is adequate turbo boost available to properly consume the quantity of fuel requested. If not, then the ECM will only provide a fuel setting that is proportional to the turbo-boost pressure to prevent overfueling and incomplete combustion that would lead to exhaust smoke and additional emissions. This sensor is also used in conjunction with the oil temperature and intake manifold air temperature sensor by the ECM to protect against white smoke particularly during cold-weather startup conditions.

4. *OPS* (oil pressure sensor): advises the ECM of the engine main oil gallery pressure. Engine protective features programmed into the ECM are calibrated to trigger an engine speed and power reduction feature when the oil pressure drops to a point lower than desired. If a dangerous oil pressure is sensed, the ECM warns the operator by flashing a dash-mounted red light; on some engine/vehicles it may be accompanied by an audible buzzer. If the ECM is so programmed, automatic engine shutdown will occur after 30 seconds of low oil pressure. In some cases the system may be equipped with a manual override button to provide an extra 30 seconds of running time to allow the operator to pull a vehicle over to the side of the road safely.

5. *OTS* (oil temperature sensor): indicates the engine oil temperature at all times to the ECM. Normally, the ECM and engine protective features can be programmed to provide the same safety features as those described for a low oil pressure condition. However, a yellow dash-mounted warning light is triggered first when the oil temperature exceeds a safe, normal limit. Continued oil temperature increase to a preset maximum limit results in an engine power-down feature, followed by engine shutdown similar to that for the OPS. Many electronic engines employ this sensor at engine startup to advise the ECM to provide a fast idle speed, particularly during cold ambient conditions. In some engines the coolant temperature sensor provides the input signal to the ECM for this operating condition. This signal causes the ECM to vary the fuel injection PWM time to control white smoke on a cold engine. Normal idle speed is automatically resumed when the oil or coolant temperature reaches a predetermined limit or after a programmed engine running time.

6. *OLS* (oil level sensor): mounts in front sump nonmetal oil pan, utilizes optical technology to "see" oil level. Engine must be off (zero RPM) for *X* minutes (based on oil temp.) to drain oil back to the pan. Switches at 4 qt low level, and has OEM impact such as order maintenance alert and system on the engine.

7. *CTS* (coolant temperature sensor): used to advise the ECM of the engine coolant temperature. This sensor can be used to trigger an engine protection response; it has an automatic power-down feature and shutdown similar to that for the OPS and OTS. In addition, many heavy-duty trucks now employ this sensor to activate thermatic fan controls.

8. *CLS* (coolant level sensor): monitors the level of coolant in the radiator top tank or in a remote surge tank. Normally, this sensor is tied into the ECM engine protection system and initiates an automatic engine shutdown sequence at a low coolant level. In addition, the engine will fail to start when this sensor senses a low coolant level, and it will trigger a dash-mounted warning light.

9. *ACLS* (auxiliary coolant level sensor): indicates when the coolant level requires topping up. Positioned within the top radiator tank or remote surge tank, this sensor is located above the CLS.

10. *CPS* (coolant pressure sensor): normally employed on larger-displacement engines to closely monitor water pump/engine block pressure.

11. *CPS* (crankcase pressure sensor): usually found on larger-displacement engines in mining, stationary, and marine engine applications. This sensor can be profiled to monitor crankcase pressure direct; on two-stroke-cycle engines, it monitors air pressure inside the airbox of the two-stroke-cycle engine block. Caterpillar refers to this sensor as an *atmospheric pressure sensor,* which measures the atmospheric air pressure in the crankcase and sends a signal to the ECM.

12. *FPS* (fuel pressure sensor): usually monitors the fuel pressure on the outlet side of the secondary fuel filter. This sensor is used for diagnostics purposes.

13. *FTS* (fuel temperature sensor): provides fuel temperature information to the ECM and is normally located on the secondary fuel filter head. Changes in fuel temperature allow the ECM to adjust the PWM signal to the unit injectors, since warmer fuel expands, resulting in less horsepower.

14. *FRS* (fuel restriction sensor): measures fuel system and restriction at fuel pump inlet. Sensor measures actual inlet restriction. OEM impact involves order maintenance alert system on the engine.

15. *ATS* (air-temperature sensor): indicates intake manifold temperature to the ECM to allow the ECM to alter the injector PWM signal for emissions control.

16. *BARO* (barometric pressure sensor): is sometimes called an atmospheric ambient air pressure sensor, and is used by the ECM to adjust the EUI PWM signal to adjust timing and fuel metering (quantity) based on engine operating altitude (power derate).

17. *EFPA* (electronic foot pedal assembly): is often referred to as a TPS or throttle position sensor because it incorporates a potentiometer or variable resistor located below the pedal. This sensor is the main input to the ECM to tell it how much fueling the operator is requesting. The TPS receives a 5 V dc input reference voltage from the ECM. When the operator depresses the throttle pedal, it indicates to the ECM the percentage of throttle pedal depression and therefore how much fuel is being requested. An idle validation switch (IVS) is attached to the EFPA. This switch ensures that the engine will remain at an idle speed in the event of a TPS circuit failure. With the throttle pedal in the idle position, the 5-volt ECM input is directed through the TPS potentiometer. The position of the pot

wiper forces the input voltage to be directed through all windings in the pot resulting in a return voltage to the ECM of approximately 0.5 volt. This TPS signal is directed to, and compared with, a microprocessor look-up table in which the voltage value indicates a closed throttle (idle) fueling request. A WOT (wide-open-throttle) position permits approximately 4.5 volts from the pot to be returned to the ECM; this voltage when compared with its look-up table indicates that WOT is being requested. For any throttle pedal position between idle and WOT, the voltage generated from the pot wiper position allows the voltage value return signal to be proportional to the fueling as requested by the operator. Therefore, the TPS is outputting a voltage signal between 0.5 and 4.5 volts for a given operator request. See more data and information on the EFPA later in this chapter.

18. *VSS* (vehicle speed sensor): usually mounted over the vehicle transmission output shaft to provide the ECM with the speed of the vehicle. This signal is used for cruise control, vehicle speed limiting, and automatic progressive application of the engine Jake brakes to maintain a preprogrammed maximum vehicle speed. In addition, engine fan braking engages the cooling fan clutch automatically when the engine brakes are on *high.* This feature adds 20 to 45 bhp (15 to 33.5 kW) to the engine retardation for slowing down the vehicle.

19. *SLS* (starter lockout sensor): indicates the engine condition to the ECM once the engine is running. This sensor prevents starter engagement to prevent grinding of the flywheel and starter pinion gears.

ECM SERIAL DATA/SENSOR COMMUNICATIONS

A serial communications link is used to transmit sensor and engine data to other vehicle modules. The number of times per second that an individual sensor signal is monitored by the ECM diagnostic circuit is commonly referred to as its *update rate.* The importance of a specific sensor to the overall ECM decision-making process and to the engine protection system establishes its desired update rate. For example, the following data indicate how often some sensor data need updating.

1. *Engine oil pressure sensor.* Update rate is once per second with a resolution of 0.5 psi (3.44 kPa) per bit (Uns/SI). The sensor range is normally rated between 0 and 65 psi (0 and 448 kPa).

2. *Turbocharger boost pressure sensor.* Updated twice per second with a resolution of 0.125

psi/bit (0.861 kPa/bit, Uns/SI). The sensor range is usually between 0 and 30 psi (0 and 207 kPa).

3. *Barometric pressure sensor.* Updated once per second at a resolution of 0.0625 psi (0.43 kPa) per bit (Uns/SI).

4. *Air inlet temperature sensor.* Updated once per second at a resolution of 0.25°F per bit (SI). Sensor range is usually between –40° and 175°F (–40° and 79.4°C).

5. *Engine oil temperature sensor.* Updated once per second at a resolution of 0.25°F/bit (S/I). Sensor range is usually between –40° and 300°F (–40° and 149°C).

6. *Fuel temperature sensor.* Updated the same as the air inlet temperature sensor.

7. *Engine speed sensor.* Updated 10 times/second with a resolution of 0.25 rpm/bit (Uns/I). Range is ECM calculated.

Basic Sensor Operation

Figure 18–5 is a simplified diagram of the basic sensor measurement system, where the sensor itself absorbs either a heat or pressure signal from a monitored engine condition. The sensor converts this signal into an electrical output and relays it to the signal processor. Within the signal processor, the sensor signal is amplified so that it can be sent to an analog or digital display; or alternatively, it may be used to activate a specific actuator on the engine or vehicle.

Signal processing can be accomplished with either analog devices or digital devices. Analog signals resemble the human voice and have a continuous waveform signal, whereas a digital signal forms a series of boxes to indicate an ON or OFF voltage condition. Analog signal processing involves amplifiers, filters, adders, multipliers, and other components; digital signal processing uses logic gates. In addition, digital processing requires the use of counters, binary adders, and microcomputers.

The IC (integrated circuit) can be analog or digital. The analog IC is one that handles or processes a wavelike analog electrical signal, such as that produced by the human voice; it is also similar to that shown on an ignition oscilloscope. An analog signal changes continuously and smoothly with time as shown in Figure 18–6. Its output signal is proportionate to its input signal.

Digital signals, on the other hand, show a more rectangular wavelength, as shown in Figure 18–7. These signals change intermittently with time, which means that, simply put, they are either on or off. This, of course, is quite different from the analog operating mode. The general characteristic of operation of the digital circuit can best be explained as follows: When the input voltage signal rises to a predetermined level, the output signal is then triggered into action. For example, assume that a sensor is feeding a varying 5-volt (V) maximum reference signal to a source such as a diode. In this condition the output signal remains at zero until the actual input signal has climbed to its maximum of 5 V.

This is why digital signals are classified as being either on or off. ON means that a signal is being sent, and OFF means that a signal is not being sent. For convenience sake, in electronics terminology, when a voltage signal is being sent (ON), the numeral 1 is used. When no voltage signal is being sent (OFF), this is indicated by the numeral 0. These numerals are used so that the computer program can distinguish between an ON and OFF signal and its voltage value.

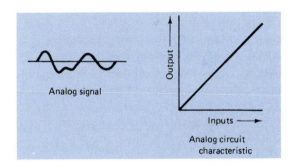

FIGURE 18–6 *Example of an analog-wave signal shape.*

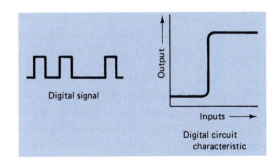

FIGURE 18–7 *Example of a digital-wave signal shape.*

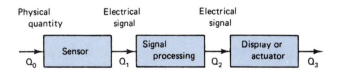

FIGURE 18–5 *Simplified sensor measurement operational system schematic.*

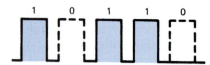

FIGURE 18–8 *Digital voltage signal in an on/off mode, in which a 5-V reference or trigger maximum signal value is used.*

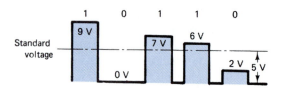

FIGURE 18–9 *Example of a digital wave signal when the voltage values are either above or below the standard maximum 5-V references.*

Figures 18–8 and 18–9 show how this numeric system operates. Most sensors in use today in automotive applications are designed to operate on a 5-V reference signal. Anything above this level is considered as being in an ON, or numeral 1, condition; and any voltage below this value is considered as OFF, or 0 numeral, since the voltage signal is too low to trigger a diode response. Digital systems consist of many numbers of identical *logic gates* and *flip-flops* to perform the necessary computations.

A simplified example of an analog signal is that generated from a speedometer sensor that changes continuously as the vehicle speed increases or decreases. An example of an applied digital signal that is either on or off can be related to the opening and closing of a car door. When open, the interior light comes on; therefore, the signal is at its maximum of 12 V. If, on the other hand, the door is closed, the signal is at 0 V.

Digital Inputs

Earlier-model electronic engines used sensors that generated analog voltage signals fed to a digital ECM. Therefore, the analog signal had to be converted through an ECM-located A/D (analog/digital) converter so that the ECM could understand it. Newer-model electronic engines employ digital sensors where these digital inputs function through an external switch request from the ECM, with the number of digital circuit options selectable by the engine/vehicle manufacturer. Typically, a number of input pins are available on the vehicle ECM wire harness connector for input functions. These functions are assignable to any of these pins through the use of a special diagnostic tool usually known as a re-

programming station. Examples of various digital inputs are listed below.

Digital Inputs	
Air Compressor Controls	Engine Protection
Air Compressor Load	Auxiliary Input Protection #1
Switch	Auxiliary Input Protection #2
Cruise Control (Uses up to	Diagnostic Request Switch
Five Inputs)	SEO/Diagnostic Request
Cruise Enable	Switch
Clutch Released	Engine Ratings
Service Brake Released	Limiting Torque Curve
Set/Coast On (Decrease)	Rating Switch #1
Resume/Acceleration On	Rating Switch #2
(Increase)	Fan Control
Engine Brake	Transmission Retarder Status
Engine Brake Disable	(Release 2.00 or Later only)
Engine Brake Low	Air Conditioner Status
Engine Brake Medium	Fan Control Override
Throttle Control	Pressure Governor System (PGS)
Alternate Minimum	(Uses Five Inputs)
VSG/Fast Idle (Release	Pressure Governor System En-
2.00 or Later Only)	able
Dual Throttle (LSG)	Pressure/RPM Mode Switch
Idle Validation Switch	Set/Coast On (Decrease)
Throttle Inhibit	Resume/Acceleration On (In-
VSG Station Change	crease)
VSG Station Complement	Additional Functions
	Auxiliary Coolant Level
	Sensor
	Parking Brake Interlock

Digital Outputs

Digital outputs are activated from the ECM which commands (internal switches/grounds) action of some external device, for example, a fan clutch control. The number of available digital outputs will vary between OEMs; however, approximately 20 to 25 options are usually available, with six pins available: three on the 30-pin vehicle connector and three on the 30-pin engine harness connector (auxiliary outputs). These outputs can be configured by a service technician using the reprogramming station tooling. An example of typical digital outputs are listed below.

Digital Outputs	
Coolant Level Low Light	VSG Active Indication
Cruise Control Active Light	(Release 2.00 or Later only)
(PGS Active Light)	Low Oil Pressure Light
Deceleration Light	High Oil Temperature Light
Engine Brake Active	High Coolant Temp. Light
Fan Control #1	(Release 3.00 or Later Only)
Fan Control #2	Ether Injection
Low DDEC Voltage	Low Coolant Pressure Light
Pressure Governor System	High Crankcase Pressure Light
Pressure Mode Light	(Release 4.00 or Later Only)
Starter Lockout	Optimized Idle Active Light
Transmission Retarder	Gas Solenoid Shutdown
Vehicle Power Shutdown	Air Compressor Load Switch

Types of Sensors

Various engine/vehicle sensors are described in this chapter. The physical operating characteristics of each unit depend on the following design types: two-wire design, three-wire design, and pulse-counter design. Each of these operating types is illustrated and explained next to show how various sensors operate.

Two-Wire Design

Figure 18–10 illustrates the two-wire design type of sensor, which is basically a variable resistor in series with a known-fixed resistor contained within the ECM. Sensors that use the two-wire type of design are the CTS, OTS, FTS, MAT (manifold air temperature), and OAT (outside air temperature) units. All of these sensors operate on a varying resistance; their resistance varies inversely with temperature (thermistor principle).

Since most sensors in use in automotive applications use a base voltage input of 5 V (some use 8 V), the value of the variable resistor can be determined from the base voltage along with the known voltage drop across the fixed resistor.

The coolant and oil temperature sensors are mounted on the engine, while the fuel sensor is mounted on the fuel filter. Each sensor relays temperature information to the ECM. The ECM monitors a 5-V reference signal, which it applied to the sensor signal circuit through a resistor in the ECM. Note that these sensors are in reality a thermistor, which means that they change their internal resistance as the temperature changes. Specifically, when the sensor is cold, such as when starting up an engine that has been sitting for some time, the sensor resistance is high, and the ECM monitors a high signal voltage. As the engine warms up, however, the internal resistance of the sensor de-

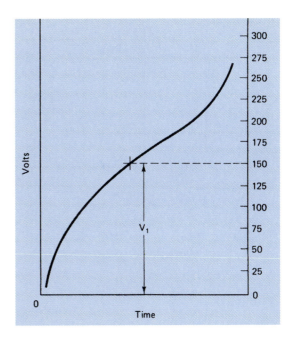

FIGURE 18–11 *Coolant temperature sensor versus its analog output voltage signal.*

creases and causes a similar decrease in the reference voltage signal. Therefore, the ECM interprets this reduced voltage signal as signifying a warm engine. The range of the coolant and oil temperature sensors varies with various engine/vehicle manufacturers, but normally it is between −10° and 300°F. At the low-temperature end of the scale, the resistance of the sensor tends to be about 100,000 ohm (Ω), while at the high range its internal resistance would have dropped to only 70 Ω. Figure 18–11 illustrates how a temperature of 150°F (65.5°C), which is an analog signal, is converted from analog to digital within the A/D (analog/digital) converter. In Figure 18–11 we see a typical upward-moving sine wave which is representative of the changing voltage output signal from the oil or coolant sensor as the engine temperature increases because of the decreasing resistance value of the sensor. At a temperature of 150°F, the sensor analog output voltage is sampled by the A/D converter, which converts values into a *binary number value* or code.

Three-Wire Design

Figure 18–12 illustrates the three-wire design type of sensor arrangement, which is commonly in use in TPS (throttle position sensors), MAP (manifold absolute pressure), and BARO (barometric pressure sensors). These types of sensors have a reference voltage, a ground, and a variable wiper, with the lead coming off the wiper being the actual signal feed to the ECM. A change in the wiper's position automatically changes the signal voltage being sent back to the ECM.

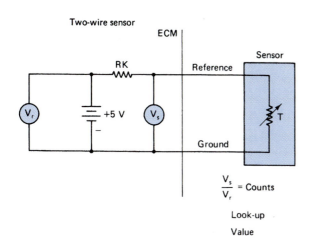

FIGURE 18–10 *Basic arrangement of a two-wire design sensor.*

Three-wire sensor

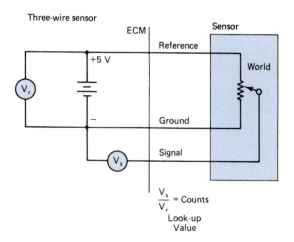

$$\frac{V_s}{V_r} = \text{Counts}$$

Look-up Value

FIGURE 18-12 *Basic arrangement of a three-wire design sensor.*

Pulse Counters

Figure 18–13 illustrates the basic operation of a pulse counter. Sensors relying on this type of counting system are typically the VSS, the rpm or engine speed sensor, which could be a crankshaft- or camshaft-sensed Hall-effect type on various makes of vehicles, and also the distributor reference sensor on gasoline vehicles employing this style of ignition system.

Consider, for example, that many gasoline-powered cars and light-duty trucks today have a distributorless ignition system. These systems rely on a crankshaft- or camshaft-mounted sensor, or both, to pick up a gear position, usually through the use of a raised tooth on the gear wheel. The resultant voltage signal produced is relayed by the sensor to the ECM, which then determines when to trigger the ignition pulse signal to the respective spark plug. On heavy-duty truck engines such as those employing the Detroit Diesel series 60 four-stroke-cycle DDEC engines, an electronic TRS (timing reference sensor) extends through an opening in the engine gear case and is positioned to provide a small air gap between it and the teeth of the crankshaft timing gear. The TRS sends a voltage signal to the ECM, which uses it to determine fuel injector solenoid operation/timing. This same engine employs an SRS (synchronous reference sensor) that is mounted to the rear of the engine gear case, where it is positioned to provide a small air gap between it and the rear of a bull gear driven from the crankshaft gear. The SRS sends a voltage signal to the ECM, which uses this information to determine engine speed.

The speed at which sensor signals are transmitted and monitored by the ECM microprocessor are usually updated a given amount of times in a second.

For those on request sensor values, the nominal response time in current ECMs used in heavy-duty trucks is 100 milliseconds.

Important Circuit Definitions

When sensor problems occur, many times it can be traced to a faulty connection at the sensor connector or wiring harness at the ECM connector. Often this can be traced to either an open, short, or grounded condition. The following descriptions will clarify what these terms mean.

Open circuit: This condition exists when a complete break in the path of current occurs at some point in the circuit. This will result in one or more loads in that circuit not operating.

FIGURE 18-13 *Digital pulse counter mode of operation.*

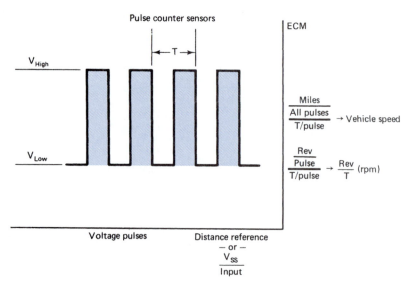

Short circuit: This condition exists when a load in the circuit is accidentally bypassed. Since electricity will always take the path of least resistance, the result of a short is that higher current will flow and cause excessive heat or action from a device protecting the circuit such as a blown fuse or circuit breaker activation.

Grounded circuit: A ground is similar to a short when current accidentally bypasses a load in the circuit. The difference is that the bypass connects directly to the negative terminal of the power source by way of the chassis ground path.

TIP   An open in a two-wire sensor circuit will show as a high voltage, whereas a short will show as a low voltage, when checking the circuit with a multimeter. An open or a short in a three-wire sensor circuit can create several variables when measured with a multimeter. Typically the following situations will occur:

Open supply = low voltage
Open signal = low voltage
Open return = high voltage

Supply short to Signal = high voltage
Supply short to Return = low voltage
Signal short to Return = low voltage

Oil Pressure Sensor Operation

To understand just how a typical sensor operates in a heavy-duty electronically controlled diesel truck engine, let us consider the oil pressure sensor as one example. The sensor outputs an analog signal, with the sensor resistance changing as a result of engine oil pressure changes. This oil pressure and sensor resistance change, in turn, creates changes in the sensor–resistor–battery circuit current flow. Any current in-crease will similarly create an increase in the voltage value across the resistor. Consequently, during engine operation, any oil pressure change is reflected by a sensor voltage output that the analog-to-digital subsystem will process accordingly.

Consider an oil pressure sensor with a sensor range between 0 and 65 psi (0 to 448 kPa) with a sensor output update rate of once per second and a resolution of 0.5 psi per bit. During engine operation, if the sensor failed, the check engine light would illuminate on the dash; if low oil pressure at the current engine speed is sensed, the check engine light will illuminate and the ECM would power down the engine. Unsafe oil pressure would result in the stop engine light (SEL) illuminating, followed 30 seconds later by an ECM-actuated engine shutdown procedure. If the engine is equipped with a stop engine override (SEO), the shutdown sequence can be delayed by holding the SEO button in for a couple more times only, after which the ECM shuts the engine off.

For ease of instruction, let us assume that the voltage across the oil pressure sensor is converted from an analog to a digital signal by an A/D converter in the form of a voltage-controlled oscillator (VCO), where the sensor voltage varies from 0 to 10 V. As you know from earlier information, the digital system is a square-wave signal typical of that shown in Figure 18–13. The amplitude (voltage strength) changes of the digital signals would have very fast ON/OFF reactions, varying from 0 to 5 V, with 0 V representing a logic number 0 and the 5 V amplitude representing a logic number 1.

Figure 18–14 illustrates a simplified system that represents this oil pressure sensor function. If a scale is selected to represent a change of engine oil pressure of from 0 to 65 psi (0 to 448 kPa), a change in voltage from 0 to 10 V can be used to duplicate/scale this change in oil pressure. If we assume that the VCO's output oscillates back and forth between 0 and 10 V based on changing engine oil pressure, the frequency of the

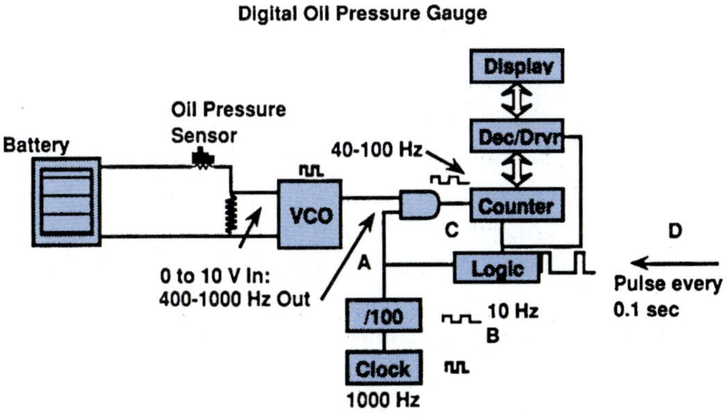

Digital Oil Pressure Gauge

FIGURE 18–14 *Simplified electronic oil pressure sensor system. (Reprinted with permission, copyright 2001, Society of Automotive Engineers International, Inc.)*

voltage signal (how often it happens) in our scaled example would vary between 400 and 1000 hertz (Hz), or 400 to 1000 times a second, based on the 0 to 10 V input signal to the VCO. A change in voltage from 0 to 10 V would cause a change in frequency of 600 (= 1000 − 400) Hz in our example. The voltage output of the VCO is connected to one input of an AND logic gate. (For a description of an AND gate and its truth table combination refer to Automotive Electronics and Computer Systems ISBN-0-13-744327-7 by Robert N. Brady published in 2001 by Prentice Hall, Upper Saddle River, NJ.)

Due to the operation of the AND logic gate shown to the immediate right of the VCO in Figure 18–14, the output of the VCO is connected to one input of the AND gate, while the other input is held to a logic level 1. This results in the output of the AND gate being a reproduction of the VCO's output; but when the second input from the VCO is at logic 0, the output of the AND gate would be a steady logic 0. Therefore, by actively controlling the logic levels on the second input, the VCO's output pulse can be gated through for a given amount of time, then blocked, then gated through again, with the process being repeated over and over.

For scaling purposes, let us consider that when a zero engine oil pressure exists, we will also have zero volts across the oil pressure sensor resistor. At 0 lb oil pressure, we will equate this to a frequency of 400 Hz. With the engine running and the oil pump creating 65 psi (448 kPa) of pressure, the voltage value is 10 V and the frequency is equivalent to a VCO output of 1000 Hz. If we also assume that the engine oil pressure rises linearly (gradual straight-line increase), there is a direct relationship created between the oil pressure, the voltage, and the frequency. Since our scale runs between 400 and 1000 Hz to represent 0 to 65 psi (0 to 448 kPa), this means that over the 600-Hz range between these two numbers, we can scale the VCO's output frequency to represent any given oil pressure. For example, based on our graduated scale, a 32.5 psi (224 kPa) oil pressure would correspond to a signal of 5 V and a frequency halfway between 400 and 1000, which would be 700 Hz. Therefore, as you can see, it is quite easy to convert a given oil pressure at the sensor into a voltage input at the VCO, along with a frequency output from the VCO. The engine oil pressure sensor used on the DDEC system on Detroit Diesel's 71, 92, series 50, 55, and 60 heavy-duty truck diesel engines has an update rate of once per second; therefore, when the oil pressure is 65 psi (448 kPa), the VCO will be outputting a signal every second that is representative of this pressure. In our descriptive example, this would be equivalent to the VCO outputting 1000 square-wave pulses

(digitally shaped) per second. For better resolution or monitoring of the changing oil pressure system, we could choose to set the logic gate up so that it is open for 0.1 second. This can be achieved by directing a signal to the second AND gate input, which has a logic 1 period equal to 0.1 second.

We can ensure this operating condition by employing a square-wave oscillating clock with a fixed frequency of 1000 Hz. The output can then be directed through a series of logic ICs (integrated circuits) that effectively divide the input count by 10, then by a further 10. Reference to Figure 18–14 indicates this clock system is identified as /100 above the 1000-Hz clock. This means that the 1000-Hz signal is divided by 100 to produce a square output wave with a 10-Hz frequency. Consequently, the signal would have a time period of 1/10 or 0.1 second.

If the logic gate pulses open for 0.1 second, it is closed, then opened once again on a continuing basis; then every time the logic gate is opened, 100 square waves will pass through as long as the oil pressure remains at 65 psi (448 kPa). If the engine speed is reduced, or the oil pressure were to drop to 32.5 psi (224 kPa), the VCO frequency would be reduced from 1000 to 700 Hz. This means that in a 0.1-second period, only 70 square-wave pulses will pass through the logic gate. When the 10-Hz signal is a logic 1 input, the VCO's output will pass through the AND gate. When the 10-Hz signal is logic 0, the AND gate's output is logic 0. Therefore, when the oil pressure is 65 psi (448 kPa), the internal digital clock counter will count 100 pulses in 0.1 second. At a pressure of 32.5 psi (224 kPa), it will count 70 pulses every 0.1 second. With zero oil pressure, the counter will register 40 pulses every 0.1 second. The clock counter's output is then input to a decoder/driver IC to drive a digital display that allows the truck driver to visually determine the engine oil pressure condition at a glance. Generally, the output of the decoder/driver is a latched output. This means that the output value changes only when a latch pulse, shown as item D in Figure 18–14, is input to a latch input.

Electronic Foot Pedal Assembly

A unique feature of the electronic fuel system is that the foot throttle pedal assembly consists of a small potentiometer (variable resistor) rather than a direct mechanical linkage as is found on mechanical engines. This throttle arrangement is often referred to as a *drive by wire system*, since no mechanical linkage is used; only electrical wires transmit the position of the throttle to the ECM. The potentiometer is electrically connected to the ECM.

The throttle position sensor (TPS) shown in Figure 18–15 is a simple potentiometer, or variable resistor, designed to output a voltage signal in direct response to the depression of the pedal. When the foot pedal or hand throttle is moved by an operator, the small rotary wiper, which is in contact with the TPS windings, moves through an arc of travel. The TPS receives a constant 5 V dc input reference voltage from the ECM. At a closed throttle (idle speed), the wiper forces the reference voltage to be impressed through the complete range of the resistance windings; the result is an output signal returned back to the ECM of approximately 0.5 volt. At a WOT, the position of the wiper is such that the reference input voltage travels through a smaller range of the resistance material; the result is an output voltage signal returned back to the ECM of approximately 4.5 volts. Positioning the throttle between idle and WOT will result in a return voltage back to the ECM which is proportional to where the wiper is on the resistance material. Since the ECM is programmed to recognize any return voltage signal by going to its look-up memory (file) for comparison,

it can determine the percentage of throttle that the operator is requesting.

As the operator pushes the throttle pedal down, the voltage signal from the sensor increases, and when the ECM recognizes this voltage change, it sends out a signal to activate the solenoid on each fuel injector for a longer pulse width period. This results in a greater amount of fuel being delivered to the cylinders and therefore a higher speed. The actual quantity of fuel delivered and therefore the horsepower produced by the engine also depend on the engine coolant temperature, the turbocharger boost pressure, and both the oil pressure and temperature sensor readings. Each one of these sensors is continually relaying a voltage signal back to the ECM, which then computes the injector pulse width signal.

Newer models of the EFPA (electronic foot pedal assembly) feature an integrated idle validation switch/sensor that combines two electrical signal generators: the accelerator position sensor (APS) and the idle validation switch (IVS) in a single housing. The two components are isolated electrically but are

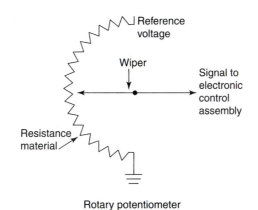

Rotary potentiometer

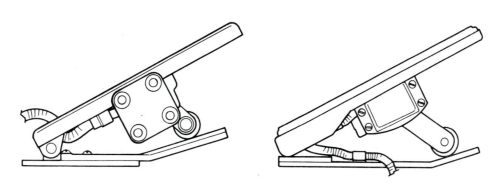

Bendix

Williams

FIGURE 18–15 Simple design concept of how a rotary potentiometer (variable resistor) functions; view of two commonly used EFPAs (electronic foot pedal assemblies) manufactured by Bendix and Williams which incorporate a rotary potentiometer encapsulated within/behind an access plate to determine the percentage of fueling demanded when the driver moves the throttle pedal. (Courtesy of Detroit Diesel Corporation.)

actuated by a common mechanical link to the accelerator pedal. The calibration between the two signals is set at the factory and will maintain uninterrupted adjustment throughout the life of the unit. The IVS provides verification independent of throttle pot movement that the pedal is, or is not, in the idle position. This scheme allows the ECM to detect potential throttle assembly problems. The IVS can be a separate mechanical or an integrated switch with the potentiometer.

Detroit Diesel, Caterpillar, and Cummins employ the same basic EFPA assembly, although the installation angle of the EFPA on its mounting plate varies to suit different truck floor pan installations. The pedal moves through approximately 20° from idle to WOT (wide-open throttle), thereby varying the voltage signal back to the ECM. The EFPA receives a 5-V input reference voltage signal from the ECM, and the return voltage signal is based on the percentage of throttle depression. Another feature of this EFPA with IVS and APS is that the automatic transmission shift point-control can be regulated by the integrated sensor. At a specified voltage, the transmission can be downshifted to a lower gear range. An engine retarder signal may be utilized to invoke an exhaust brake or other engine transmission retarder device through the idle validation setting within the EFPA.

Switches

1. *Engine cooling fan override manual switch.* This instrument panel–located switch permits the operator to manually engage the cooling fan if a problem exists in the automatic control circuit. Because this switch is a normally open (NO) design, when the operator toggles the switch, a request signal is sent to the ECM to allow it to deenergize the engine cooling fan solenoid.

2. *Air-conditioning high-pressure switch.* This normally closed (NC) type of switch is designed to open when the A/C high-side pressure rises to a preset maximum; it will signal the ECM to engage the engine cooling fan.

3. *Cruise-control (CC) ON/OFF switch.* This NO switch, when activated by the operator, will close the circuit and allow CC engagement.

4. *Cruise set/resume switch.* This switch is arranged with two momentary positions to provide set/coast and resume/accelerate. It permits the driver/operator to set a desired cruise speed, or to resume a cruise speed after breaking the circuit by brake or clutch pedal activation.

5. *Clutch switch.* This NC design switch is opened when the driver depresses the clutch pedal to disengage the clutch drive. When this occurs, the ECM will cancel cruise control, the PTO, engine exhaust or compression braking, and will also override the idle shut-down timer.

6. *Service brake* (hydraulic or air). This NC switch design will open any time the brake pedal is applied. This action will signal the ECM to allow engine braking, while simultaneously canceling cruise control, PTO operation, and the engine idle shut-down timer.

7. *Engine brake ON/OFF switch.* This NO switch design enables engine brake operation when closed manually by the operator/driver.

8. *Engine compression or driveline electric retarder brake selector switch.* This switch is generally arranged to permit manual selection by the driver of the degree of braking desired. Low, medium, and high on a six-cylinder engine allows two-, four-, or six-cylinder braking.

9. *Power takeoff (PTO) switch.* This NO design switch, when activated to the ON position by the driver/operator, will close. While closed, the cruise-control switches can be used to set and hold the rpm at the point you want the PTO to hold the engine speed. Typically in the PTO mode, the electronic governor will be switched to an isochronous (zero-droop) setting. A remote PTO switch located at a convenient external location on a truck (e.g., to control a hydraulic hoist, or garbage packer), allows convenient control by the operator.

10. *Diagnostic ON/OFF switch.* This switch is located on the instrument subpanel, and is a NO momentary switch that can be activated by an operator or service technician to illuminate (flash) the yellow and red warning/stop lamps to withdraw stored diagnostic fault codes from ECM memory when troubleshooting. See Chapter 22 for more details. This same switch can be used on some systems to override the engine protection system shutdown by depressing and holding the switch on.

11. Idle adjust switch (IAS). This switch is located on the instrument panel and can be toggled to alter the hot idle rpm to eliminate shaky mirrors. Usually provides +100 and −25 rpm.

12. Pressure governor system (PGS). This switch is used on fire trucks to maintain a set water pressure by varying the engine rpm.

13. Vehicle deceleration light (VDL). This switch is located on the rear of a truck or bus and illuminates when the driver takes a foot off the accelerator pedal, indicating that the vehicle is slowing down.

14. Top2 cruise-control ON/OFF feature switch. This switch signals the ECM when it is ON or OFF. When in the ON position, and during the vehicle cruise mode, both cruise control and Top2 transmission features are activated. The Top2 feature performs automated shifts into the top gear or first geardown, as well

as assisted shifts from second geardown to first geardown. An assisted shift is an automated shift that requires a clutch event and/or transmission shift lever movement. Top2 is factory programmed and is therefore not customer selectable.

Engine Warm-Up Protection

To protect the engine from high rpm operation after startup in cold ambient temperature conditions, the ECM will rely upon either the coolant or oil temperature sensors to advise it when this temperature has reached a predetermined value. Normally until this temperature is obtained, the ECM will permit the engine to run at a fast idle speed, typically between 800 and 850 rpm for faster warmup than would occur at a 600 to 650 rpm idle speed. This feature protects the conrod and turbocharger bearings from a lack of oil circulation. During this warmup period, the EFPA (throttle sensor) input will be ignored by the ECM. In addition, the engine compression brakes will not operate until the oil temperature has reached approximately 90° to 92°F (32.2° to 33.3°C). This is not a customer adjustable feature.

Actuators

Actuators used on electronically controlled engines are activated either by the ECM or by an operator toggling a switch. Typical actuators would include the following items:

1. The EIUs, EUPs, or rack solenoid on PLN systems are the most prominent actuators controlled from the ECM by a PWM signal. The PWM signal controls the number of crankshaft degrees for which the fuel is actually injected. An injector solenoid driver circuit within the ECM handles the current that is required to energize the solenoid and therefore close the EUI/EUP poppet valve to initiate the start of injection. In current-model engines, the poppet valve is responsive enough to open and close twice in milliseconds (thousandths of a second). This makes "pilot injection" possible where a small quantity of fuel is injected, followed by the main charge. This action improves engine startup and also reduces noise.

2. An ECM-controlled actuator is the engine cooling fan solenoid, which is an NC unit. When actuated, the solenoid energizes and opens to permit compressed air pressure to disengage the engine cooling fan clutch.

3. Engine compression brakes (Jake, Pac-Brake, Mack, Volvo, Mercedes-Benz, MAN, etc.) usually offer a three-position dash-mounted switch to provide selected braking or vehicle retarding. Position 1 on the switch offers two-cylinder braking; position 2 offers four-cylinder braking; position 3 offers six-cylinder braking on an inline six-cylinder engine. The ECM can be programmed to offer automatic engine braking in position 1, 2, or 3 during cruise control, plus engage the fan clutch when selected road speed has been exceeded.

4. Both the yellow and red instrument panel warning/stop lamps are illuminated from the ECM when a sensor signal operates outside of the designed parameters. Both of these lamps can be activated manually by a service technician to read either inactive or active diagnostic fault (flash) codes for troubleshooting purposes.

5. *ITS* (idle timer shutdown): a programmable engine idle shutdown feature ranging from as low as 5 minutes to 24 hours on some vehicles, depending on the make of engine. For example, on a Caterpillar 3176B/3406E engine, 90 seconds before the programmed idle time is reached, the dash-mounted diagnostic lamp starts to flash rapidly. For the idle shutdown timer to function, the following operating conditions must be met:

- Idle shutdown timer feature has been programmed into the ECM.
- Vehicle parking brake must be activated/set.
- Engine must be at normal operating temperature.
- Vehicle speed must be at zero mph (km/h).
- Engine is running under a no-load condition.
- Parking brake switch has been installed to alert the ECM and the idle timer when to start the idle time-down feature.
- If the engine speed is increased by 100 rpm during the last 90 seconds on the timer, the check engine light (yellow) will flash.
- If an optional vehicle power shutdown relay is used, it will turn off electrical power to the vehicle and stop the engine.

On some Cummins electronic engines, the idle shutdown system will not be active at coolant temperatures below 110°F (43.3°C).

Ambient Air Temperature Idle Shutdown Override

The Cummins Celect/Plus engines are equipped with this feature which determines when to override idle shutdown. This feature employs data from the ambient air temperature sensor plus the following three customer-programmed air temperature values:

- cold temperature setting (original factory setting is 5°F or –15°C)
- medium temperature setting (original factory setting is 45°F or 7.2°C)
- temperature setting (original factory setting is 80°F or 27°C)

ENGINE PROTECTION SYSTEM

All electronically controlled diesel engines offer an engine protection system to protect the engine from serious damage when one or more sensors indicate to the ECM that they are operating outside of the normal voltage operating parameters. The *out-of-range voltage parameter* is usually set for between 0.25 and 4.75 V, although minor variations in this range will exist for specific engine makes. Low or high sensor signal return voltages, either a short, open, or ground circuit, can be detected by the ECM monitoring circuit, and a DTC (diagnostic trouble code) or fault code will be logged in ECM memory, along with illumination of a yellow warning or red stop engine light located on the instrument panel. Figure 18–2 illustrates that the fault code microprocessor within the ECM performs the self-diagnostic functions of fault code information. Typically each engine OEM offers three levels of protection which include a visual and audible warning system, an engine power derate system, and an engine shutdown system feature.

Not all sensors will trigger the engine protection system. Typically most engines will use the following sensors for protection with the trigger temperature or pressure set point programmed into the ECM by the engine manufacturer.

- engine coolant temperature
- engine coolant level
- engine oil temperature
- engine oil pressure
- intake manifold air temperature
- engine overspeed

Therefore not all engines will be set for the same temperature or pressure out-of-range set point. In addition, the percentage of engine power derate depends on the engine make or model. Review Chapters 21 through 23 for more information on specific power-down conditions.

The engine protection system is also offered for industrial, off-highway, and marine applications. If the ECM has not been programmed for automatic shutdown, then the operator must quickly check the various gauges to determine the cause of the problem and make a conscious decision to either continue operating the engine or to shut it off before serious damage occurs.

Examples of the temperatures and pressures at which the engine protection system will trigger a fault lamp and engine powerdown/derate for Cummins Celect/Plus, series 60 Detroit Diesel, and Caterpillar 3406E/3176B engines are listed below. In each of these engines, the ECM compares oil pressure with both engine speed and load before initiating an engine shutdown procedure. For example, oil pressure at idle speed is lower than it is at higher engine speed, and the ECM has been programmed to recognize this difference.

Cummins Celect/Plus

- Coolant temperature is 220°F (104°C). Power derate is followed by a speed derate after 239°F (115°C).
- Coolant level is installation dependent, and will cause a power derate.
- Low oil pressure is speed dependent and will always cause a power derate.
- Very low oil pressure is also speed dependent, resulting in a speed derate since a power derate would have already occurred with the low oil pressure condition.
- High boost air temperature is 183°F (84°C) and will cause a power derate followed by a speed derate after 231°F (111°C).
- High oil temperature of 255°F (124°C) causes a power derate.

Detroit Diesel Series 60

DDC uses both a yellow (check engine) and a red (stop) light to advise the operator of detected faults. Each sensor can be programmed for warning, rampdown, or shutdown. Warning simply alerts the driver by illumination of the yellow and then the red light (optional truck OEM buzzer). Rampdown alerts the driver by illuminating the yellow light, reducing the engine power from 100% to 70%, illuminating the red light, and reducing engine power to 40%. Shutdown functions the same as rampdown, except that 30 seconds after the red light is illuminated, the engine will be shut off. If a stop engine override (STEO) switch is installed, it allows the engine to return to 70% power when toggled in the rampdown or shutdown mode every 30 seconds while the engine is running. This is the same as the diagnostic request switch on the dash.

- Oil gallery temperature is 239°F (115°C), yellow check engine light is illuminated, and engine powerdown is initiated.
- Oil gallery temperature is 250°F (121°C), red stop engine light is illuminated, and is followed by the initiation of the engine shutdown procedure.

Caterpillar 3406E/3176B

The ECM can be programmed for three conditions: warning, derate, or shutdown. The following are some examples used for engine protection:

- Coolant temperature is 217°F (103°C) and triggers ECM action. When the ECM is programmed for power derate for every 1.8°F (1°C) temperature change, the power and speed are reduced at a rate of 10% per second maximum.

- Coolant temperature at 223°F (106°C) reduces engine power to 160 hp (119 kW), and vehicle speed is limited to 45 mph (72.4 km/h). If the coolant continues at or above 223°F (106°C), the engine will shut down in 20 seconds if programmed for shutdown. The minimum time to shut down is 30 seconds if the engine has been running for at least that long.
- Intake manifold air temperature of 194°F (90°C) triggers Cat engine ECM action. The warning lamp will come on, and if the temperature rises to 230°F (110°C), a very high intake manifold air temperature DTC is logged, but the ECM will take no further action.
- The oil pressure protection system can function when low or very low oil pressure is detected, with a specific graph setup for each engine model and power rating. When the ECM has been programmed for derate, at very low oil pressure the ECM will begin to derate available power, vehicle speed, and engine speed. Power will eventually be limited to 160 hp (119kW), vehicle speed to 45 mph (72.4 km/h), and engine speed to 1350 rpm. If shutdown has been programmed, the engine is shut down after 30 seconds.

Engine Maintenance Monitor

Todays heavy-duty trucks are equipped with an ECM-controlled maintenance monitor (MM) or maintenance alert feature that advises the operator or service technician when it is time to perform one or more vehicle maintenance conditions. The system relies upon the vehicle speed sensor (VSS) to determine mileage/kilometers traveled and the amount of fuel consumed and the engine's accumulated running time. The system can be programmed for one of three alert conditions:

- automatic mode
- distance mode
- time mode

In the *automatic mode*, the system alerts the operator when it is time to change the engine oil and filter. In this mode, however, the severe oil drain interval duty cycle is normally in default. In the *distance mode*, the operator can select a desired mileage/kilometer interval distance for the MM to advise of the fact. The *time mode* of the MM allows the operator to select a desired time period before the MM will advise of the fact. The MM alerts the operator by flashing the engine protection lamp (fluids lamp) through approximately five cycles in a 10- to 12-second period after a key ON condition. If the instrument panel is equipped with a ProDriver module, then when service operation is due, it can alert

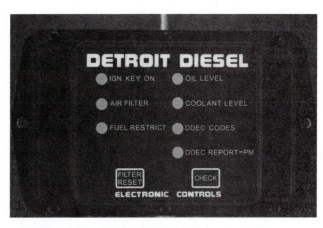

FIGURE 18–16 *Example of an instrument panel–mounted maintenance alert system to alert the driver or service technician when a monitored component requires servicing. (Courtesy of Detroit Diesel Corporation.)*

the driver by flashing a message on the facia/window of the unit.

Green and red lights indicate systems are running in or out of specified tolerances. When filters begin to clog or fluid levels drop, the maintenance alert system as shown in Figure 18–16 for DDEC, illuminates a light indicating exactly what the maintenance department must check.

Dual Horsepower Settings

The majority of heavy-duty truck/tractors today can be purchased with a dual power setting feature regardless of the engine make by programming the ECM accordingly. For example, an engine may be offered as a 430/470 hp (321/351 kW) model. What this means is that the engine will provide 430 hp (321 kW) under normal level road operating conditions, but during cruise control (CC) or when operating in hilly or mountainous terrain, it will produce 470 hp (351 kW) to produce higher torque. This feature provides for improved driveability performance for more consistent road speed, faster trip times, less down-shifting, and overall improvement of driver satisfaction. Keep in mind that you can multiply torque through the transmission and axle gearing, but you cannot multiply horsepower. Horsepower is the speed at which the work is done; therefore, at a higher engine speed, horsepower will be higher. Reduce the engine speed, and the horsepower will decrease. It is the torque (twisting and turning effort) that pulls a truck up a grade, not horsepower. If you increase engine speed, you decrease the torque; if you decrease the engine speed, you increase the torque, because the pistons are turning slower which allows a longer time for the expanding high-pressure cylinder gases to work on the piston. In addition, a slower-running engine allows the intake valves to remain open longer for an increase in volumetric efficiency (VE), or the weight of air retained in the cylinder. Let us consider an engine running at the same speed, but programmed for a different power setting as in our 430/470 hp (321/351 kw) example. If we use the formula for torque:

$$\text{Torque} = \frac{5252 \times \text{hp}}{\text{rpm}}$$

Therefore, in this example with the engine running at 1800 rpm and producing 430 hp (321 kW), we would develop 1254.6 lb-ft of torque. At a 470 hp (351 kW) setting at the same engine speed, we would develop 1371.3 lb-ft of torque. As you can see, the torque is what provides the vehicle with the ability to climb a hill under CC mode and not the horsepower. Also remember that when the engine speed is reduced to its peak torque rpm (typically 1200 to 1300 in most electronic heavy-duty engines), the torque will always increase while the hp/kW will decrease. Consider in this

same example that if the peak torque speed was 1200 rpm, and the horsepower was now 380, our torque from the above formula would be 1663 lb-ft.

This increase in pulling power with an increase in road grade percentage feature is achieved by loading a preselected calibration program into the ECM. For example, let us look briefly at Cummins electronic smart power (ESP) system. When the vehicle is operating on flat or near level terrain as shown in Figure 18–17a, the ECM will continually monitor the average vehicle road speed and will store this data as its "learned speed." The ECM will automatically switch the injector solenoid PWM signals (duty cycle) to the high torque mode when all conditions that have been learned are met, including the engine operating in CC or between 90 and 100% throttle (normal gear shift sequences will not disable ESP). The transmission must be in a gear where the overall drive ratio is less than 15:1. The ESP mode will not function if the vehicle road speed is above the ECM-programmed maximum CC speed.

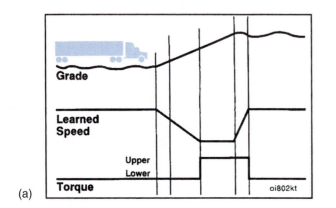

(a)

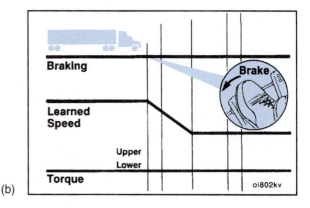

(b)

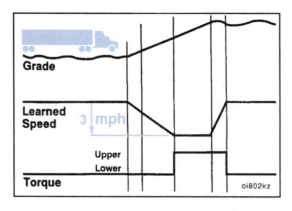

(c)

FIGURE 18–17 *Cummins ESP (electronic smart power) system: (a) monitoring of average vehicle road speed when operating on a flat or near level road; (b) steady application of the air brake pedal to reduce vehicle road speed prevents activation of the high-torque ESP mode; (c) when vehicle drops below its "learned speed," the ECM switches into the high-torque ESP setting. (Courtesy of Cummins Engine Company, Inc.)*

Figure 18–17b illustrates that applying the service foot brake to reduce vehicle speed will prevent activation of the high-torque ESP mode; however, momentary brake pedal activation will not disable ESP. Keep in mind that active diagnostic fault codes stored in the ECM related to the throttle pedal position, VSS, or ESP system will prevent ESP operation. Figure 18–17c illustrates that, should the vehicle road speed drop below its learned speed by more than a calculated value such as 3 mph (5 km/h) when running up a hill, the engine will be switched by the ECM into the high-torque ESP setting if all other calibration conditions are met. Once the vehicle obtains the learned speed and the road conditions level off (reducing the load), the engine power rating will return to the lower setting.

Media Signal and Baud Rate

Communication between the ECM, sensors, and actuators is constructed to comply with SAE ground vehicle "J" standards. The three main vehicle/engine electronics standards are identified as J1587, J1922, and J1939. Each is described as follows:

- J1587—Operating at 9600 baud rate (9600 bits of electronic data per second), this standard is used to transmit sensor and engine data for such items as electronic dash display, vehicle management systems, electronic transmissions, handheld diagnostic readers/scan tools for DTC code access, and the diagnostic datalink tooling.
- J1922—Operating at 9600 baud rate, this standard controls transmissions, ABS braking systems, anti-slip retard (ASR) traction devices, and vehicle retarders such as automatic compression brake controls when in the cruise-control mode.
- J1939—Operating at 250K (250,000) baud rate, this standard controls transmissions, braking systems, and retarders and is also used as the proprietary datalink in multi ECM engines of V12, V16, V20 configurations.

SAE J1939 Multiplexing

All electronically controlled engines are designed and configured so that their systems meet SAE (Society of Automotive Engineers) International technical "J" ground vehicle standards. For example, the J1939 standard permits the ECM to communicate with OEM service tools (scan tools, DDRs, PCs, laptops) and some other vehicle controllers such as transmissions, ABS (antilock braking systems), and ASR (automatic slip reduction), and throttles. Vehicle control devices can temporarily command engine speed or torque to perform one of its functions, such as transmission shifting.

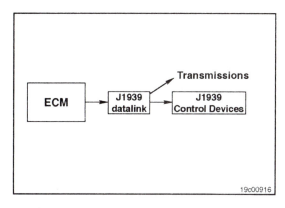

FIGURE 18–18 *Common connection between the ECM and the SAE standard J1939 datalink.*

Figure 18–18 illustrates the simplified connection between the ECM and the J1939 datalink.

Some later-model electronic engines/vehicles employ multiplexing which provides the ability to send and receive messages simultaneously over a J1939 datalink instead of using hardwired connections. This is accomplished by utilizing a vehicle electronic control unit (VECU). Inputs from switches, status parameters, and sensors can be hardwired into the VECU. The VECU can then broadcast this information throughout a vehicle system. A number of Cummins engines such as the ISX, QSX15, and Signature model engines employ multiplexing features. By employing Cummins own INSITE diagnostic tooling, the service technician can control/adjust individual devices. Once enabled, the ECM will ignore the input from the ECM input pins and will receive information over the J1939 datalink. Available inputs for multiplexing include the following items:

- Accelerator Interlock Switch
- Air Conditioner Pressure Switch
- Service Brake Switch
- Clutch Switch
- Cruise Control On/Off Switch
- Cruise Control Resume Switch
- Cruise Control Set Switch
- PTO On/Off Switch
- PTO Resume Switch
- PTO Set Switch
- Remote PTO Switch
- Idle Increment/Idle Decrement
- Diagnostic Switch/User Activated Datalogger
- Torque Derate Switch
- Manual Fan Switch
- Engine Brake Switch

- Electronic Air Compressor Switch
- Accelerator Pedal Position
- Idle Validation Status—On Idle
- Idle Validation Status—Off Idle
- Remote Accelerator Switch
- Remote Accelerator Position
- Stop Lamp Status
- Warning Lamp Status
- Maintenance Lamp Status

ECM Programmable Features

All engine OEMs provide special tooling that can be connected to the ECM diagnostic link to allow a service technician to reprogram options within the ECM. To prevent unauthorized entry into the ECM memory, every ECM/engine is assigned a *password* which must be entered before any changes can be made to the programmed options. This password is selected by the owner/operator or fleet, and it is retained in records at the factory level. Distributor/dealers have access to the factory mainframe computer should they need to know the password. Engine-governed rpm, horsepower setting, governed vehicle road speed, idle shutdown timer, cruise control, PTO operation, tire size, axle ratio, and so forth, can all be reprogrammed. Basically the diagnostic tooling, PC, or laptop permits you to enter a menu card on which it will list the various components that can be reconfigured for either an ON or OFF mode, as well as changing programming operating parameters to a desired specification level to control operating functions. Each of these parameters is stored within the ECM in what is commonly referred to as *non-volatile memory*. Thus the parameters are not lost or altered when the ignition key switch is turned off or battery power is disconnected. One example of typical parameter changes and selected settings for a heavy-duty on-highway Class 8 truck/tractor is shown below.

ELECTRONIC UNIT INJECTORS

In this section we describe briefly the operation of an electronically controlled unit injector. At this time, the high-speed heavy-duty electronic unit injectors employed by Detroit Diesel, Caterpillar, Cummins, Volvo, and Robert Bosch depend on an engine camshaft rocker arm activation system. The exception is the HEUI (hydraulically actuated electronic unit injector) codesigned by Caterpillar and International Trucks (Navistar) for use on their T444E (7.3 L) medium-duty truck engine. See Chapter 23 for more details.

The electronic unit injector has an electric solenoid that receives a command signal from an ECM, which determines the start of injection as well as the amount of fuel metered. As we discussed earlier, a series of electronic engine and vehicle sensors are used to advise the ECM of the various operating conditions, much the same as those now in wide use on passenger cars.

System Operation

Figure 18–19 illustrates the basic arrangement of an EUI (electronic unit injector) system on a heavy-duty truck engine. There is no direct connection between the throttle pedal and the injectors, since the position of the pedal sends out a signal to the ECM to let it know the percentage of throttle opening. In addition to the pedal position, the ECM receives input signals from a number of sensors, such as the engine turbo boost, intake manifold air temperature, fuel temperature, oil pressure, oil temperature, coolant level or coolant temperature, engine speed, and vehicle road speed. Prior to startup, the engine receives signals from both a timing reference sensor and a synchronous reference sensor, so that the ECM knows the relative piston positions and can then initiate fuel delivery to the injectors. Some unit injectors, such as the Detroit Diesel two-stroke-

Feature	Range	Setting	Feature	Range	Setting
Max Vehicle Speed in Top Gear	35–99 mph	60 mph	One Gear Down Ratio	.5–1.5	1.0
Cruise Control Set Speed	35–99 mph	60 mph	Min. Engine Cooling Fan On Time	0–999 sec.	240 sec.
Max Engine Speed with VSS Signal	1600–2500 rpm	2100 rpm	PTO/Remote PTO:		
Max Engine Speed w/o VSS Signal	1200–2500 rpm	1800 rpm	max PTO speed	600–2500 rpm	1000 rpm
Idle Set Speed	600–850 rpm	700 rpm	min PTO speed	600–2500 rpm	700 rpm
Gear Down Max Vehicle Speed:	35–99 mph	58 mph	set PTO speed	600–2500 rpm	900 rpm
Cruise Control and Engine Brakes:	mph above cruise set speed		resume PTO speed	600–2500 rpm	900 rpm
engine brake low	1–20 mph	6 mph	remote PTO speed	600–2500 rpm	1000 rpm
engine brake medium	1–20 mph	6 mph	Idle Shutdown Timer	3–60 min.	5 min.
engine brake high	1–20 mph	8 mph	Tire Revolutions per Mile	400–700	501
Road Speed Governor Droop	0–4 mph	2 mph	Rear Axle Ratio	2.50–12.0	4.10
Max Progressive Shift Speed	1500–2500 rpm	1800 rpm	# of VSS Wheel Teeth	5–16	16
Mph at Max Progressive Shift Speed	6–99 mph	18 mph			

FIGURE 18–19 (a) EUI (electronic injector) cam-in-block actuation mechanism; (b) EUI overhead cam actuation mechanism for a 3406E engine model: 1, EUI; 2, adjusting nut; 3, rocker arm assembly; 4, camshaft. (Reprinted courtesy of Caterpillar, Inc.)

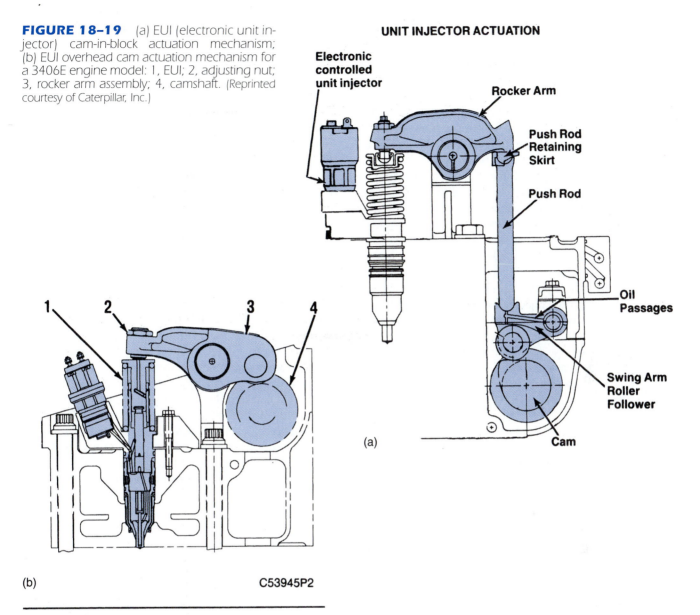

UNIT INJECTOR ACTUATION

Electronic controlled unit injector

Rocker Arm

Push Rod Retaining Skirt

Push Rod

Oil Passages

Swing Arm Roller Follower

Cam

(a)

(b)   C53945P2

Unit Injector Mechanism
(1) Electronically controlled unit injector. (2) Adjusting nut.
(3) Rocker arm assembly. (4) Camshaft.

cycle 71 and 92 models, the Caterpillar 3176, C10, C12, and 3116 engine models, and the Cummins Celect system are operated through an engine-camshaft-actuated pushrod and rocker arm assembly. On Detroit Diesel's series 50 and 60, the Caterpillar 3406E, the Volvo VE D12, and Deere's 10.5 L and 12.5 L Power Techmodels, an overhead camshaft operates the unit injector rocker arm (Figure 18–19b). Each injector is controlled by an injector-mounted electric solenoid.

There is no mechanically operated fuel rack on any electronically controlled unit injector; therefore, the amount of fuel metered and the timing are controlled by the signal generated at the ECM, based on the various sensor outputs and the throttle position. This ECM signal to the injector, or PWM signal, lasts for a given amount of crankshaft degrees. For a given speed, the longer the solenoid is energized, the greater the amount of fuel injected. Conversely, the shorter the PWM signal, the lower the volume of fuel injected into the combustion chamber. Generation of high-enough fuel pressure for injection purposes requires the action of the rocker arm assembly. Figure 18–20 illustrates the internal injector plunger, which is forced down by the rocker arm inside its barrel/bushing. Note that a small spill valve is shown to the right-hand side of the diagram; this spill valve is held open by a spring that will prevent any fuel pressure increase beyond that created by the fuel system's fuel supply pump. As the injector plunger moves down, fuel will simply flow or spill from this valve and return to the fuel tank. For injection to begin, this spill valve must be closed by a signal from the ECM energizing the small electric solenoid, which sits on top of the injector. Once the solenoid is energized by the PWM signal from the ECM, the downward-moving injector plunger will create a rapid increase in the trapped fuel pressure below it. Once this pressure is high enough, the needle valve in the injector spray tip will be opened against its return spring, allowing fuel to be injected into the combustion chamber. Any time that the injector solenoid is deenergized, the small spill valve is opened by its spring, and fuel injection comes to an immediate end.

The four step operation of a typical EUI (electronic unit injector) for a Caterpillar 3176B, C10, C12 and 3406E engine model is illustrated and described in Figure 18–20b. Minor design changes and variations exist between individual EUI equipped engines, however we can consider the EUI operation as common to all systems. Specific details of the individual OEM's (Original Equipment Manufacturers) EUI's can be found in the respective chapters within this book.

The basic difference between a mechanically operated and rack-controlled unit injector plunger, and the injector used on electronic-equipped engines, is that there is no helix on the electronic injector plunger; it is simply a solid plunger (Figure 18–21). Each one of the electronic unit injector systems is equipped with an electronic speed control system, which is a part of the solid-state circuitry contained within the ECM housing. On some systems, the ECM is cooled by routing diesel fuel through a cooling plate attached to the ECM mounting bracket to maintain the electronic components at an acceptable operating temperature.

Fuel Injector Operation

In the DDEC injector used with Detroit Diesel's series 50 and 60 engines, the fuel feed to the injector is similar to that found on other electronic engines. The fuel enters the injector through two fuel inlet filter screens around the circumference of the body between the third and fourth O-rings (seals) (Figure 18–22). All the injectors receive this fuel in the same manner, through the inlet manifold fitting. Fuel not required for combustion purposes, but which is used for cooling and lubrication of internal injector parts, exits the injector at the small fuel return hole located between the second and third O-rings and flows out of a restricted fitting connection shown in Figure 21–3, where it returns directly to the fuel tank.

The actual identification of component parts is clearly shown in Figure 18–22 for the series 60 electronically controlled injector. The functions of the injector are the same as those for a non-DDEC-equipped unit:

- Creates the high pressure required for efficient injection. This is achieved by the action of the overhead camshaft pivoting the rocker arm through its roller follower to force the injector follower down against its external return spring. Therefore, a mechanical means is still required to force the internal injector plunger down to raise the trapped fuel to a high enough pressure to lift the needle valve at the bottom of the injector off its seat.
- Meters and injects the precise amount of fuel required to handle the load. This quantity of fuel is determined by the ECM, which in turn continually receives input signals from the various engine sensors. The ECM sends out a pulse-width signal to close a small internal poppet valve. This action allows the downward-moving plunger to increase

FIGURE 18–20 (a) Basic concept of operation for a rocker arm–activated and solenoid-controlled fuel poppet valve for an EUI (electronic unit injector) assembly. (Reprinted courtesy of Caterpillar, Inc.)

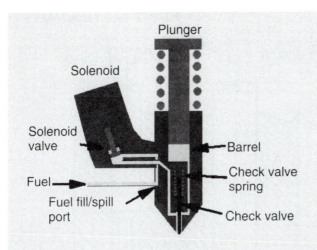

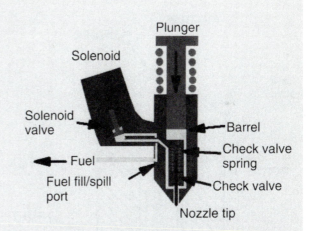

Without pressure applied to the plunger from the cam, a spring keeps the plunger retracted. Propelled by the new low pressure fuel transfer pump, fuel flows into the injector through the fill/spill port. From there it flows past the solenoid valve, down through the internal injector passages to the spring loaded check valve at the injector's tip and back up into the barrel. The pressure from the transfer pump is too low to unseat the spring loaded check valve at the injector's tip.

As the cam rotates, it starts to drive the plunger downward. Injection of the fuel may occur at any time after the plunger starts its downward travel. Until the ECM signals the start of injection, the displaced fuel is forced back out through the solenoid valve to the fill/spill port.

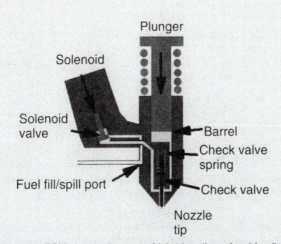

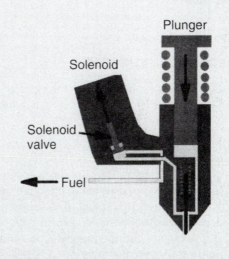

When the ECM signals the start of injection, the solenoid pulls the fuel valve closed, blocking the fuel's path to the fill/spill port. With this valve closed, pressure elevates at the injector tip to the 37 931 kPa (5500 psi) needed to unseat the spring loaded check valve. Once this valve is overcome, fuel is injected into the cylinder.

Fuel will continue to be injected until the ECM signals the solenoid to open the valve, allowing fuel to exit through the open valve and out the fill/spill port. The pressure at the injector tip immediately drops and the check valve snaps shut ending the injection cycle. The plunger will continue on its downward path however, displacing fuel through the open valve to the fuel manifold and back to the tank. This flow of fuel helps to cool the injector.

(b)

FIGURE 18–20 (continued). (b) Four-step operational schematic/description of how an EUI functions. (Reprinted courtesy of Caterpillar, Inc.)

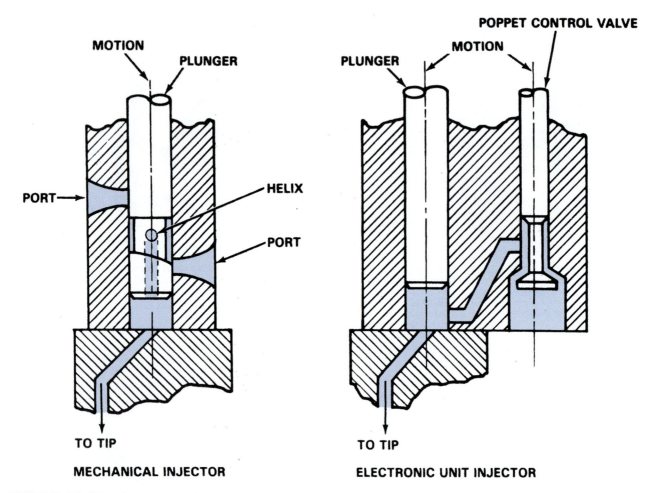

MECHANICAL INJECTOR

ELECTRONIC UNIT INJECTOR

FIGURE 18–21 Comparison of a MUI (mechanical unit injector) plunger design which uses a helix, and a no-helix design used with an EUI (electronic unit injector). (Courtesy of Detroit Diesel Corporation.)

the pressure of the fuel to lift the needle valve from its seat and injection begins. Injection lasts as long as the ECM is sending out a signal to energize the EUI (electronic unit injector) solenoid. As soon as the ECM deenergizes the solenoid, a spring opens the small poppet valve and the high fuel pressure that was holding the needle valve open is lost to the return line; therefore, injection ends. The longer the pulse width time, the greater the volume of fuel that will be injected.

■ Atomizes the fuel so that it will penetrate the air mass within the cylinder and initiate combustion. This atomization is achieved by the downward-moving plunger, which has to increase the fuel pressure to approximately 5000 psi (34,475 kPa) to lift the needle valve from its seat. The fuel is then forced through the multiple small holes (orifices) in the spray tip, which causes the fuel droplets to break down into a finely atomized

state as they approach injection pressures of 28,000 psi (193,060 kPa).

■ Permits continuous fuel flow in excess of that required for combustion purposes to ensure cooling and lubrication of all injector components.

The injection timing (start of injection) and metering (quantity) are controlled by the pulse width signal from the ECM through to the EUI. The longer the EUI solenoid is energized, the longer the small poppet valve will remain closed and the greater the amount of fuel that will be injected. In effect, by holding the poppet valve closed longer, we are lengthening the effective stroke of the downward-moving plunger, since it will always move down the same distance regardless of the pulse width time. This is so because the lift of the camshaft lobe will always be the same.

When the poppet valve is closed by the EUI solenoid activation, which is called *response-time feedback*,

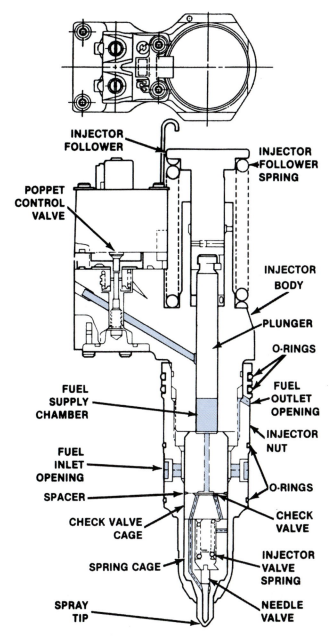

FIGURE 18–22 *Cross-sectional view and identification of the major parts for a series 60 EUI assembly. (Courtesy of Detroit Diesel Corporation.)*

Labels on figure:
INJECTOR FOLLOWER
INJECTOR FOLLOWER SPRING
POPPET CONTROL VALVE
INJECTOR BODY
PLUNGER
O-RINGS
FUEL OUTLET OPENING
FUEL SUPPLY CHAMBER
INJECTOR NUT
FUEL INLET OPENING
O-RINGS
SPACER
CHECK VALVE CAGE
CHECK VALVE
SPRING CAGE
INJECTOR VALVE SPRING
SPRAY TIP
NEEDLE VALVE

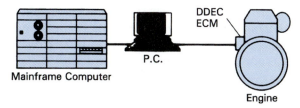

Labels: Mainframe Computer   P.C.   DDEC ECM   Engine

EEPROM CALIBRATION

Basic Rating
- BHP/RPM
- Governor Features
  - Low & High Idle
  - Droop

Customer Options
- Engine Protection (Warning or Shutdown)
- Road Speed/Cruise Control
  - Max Speed
  - Axle Ratio
  - Tires Rev./Mile
  - Transmission Data
  - Vehicle Speed Sensor
- Power Control
- Special Application Features

FIGURE 18–23 *Basic schematic of EEPROM (electrically erasable read-only memory) end-of-line factory engine ECM program calibration procedure. (Courtesy of Detroit Diesel Corporation.)*

ELECTRONIC CONTROL MODULES

All electronically controlled engines incorporate an engine-mounted ECM or ECU (electronic control module or unit). Illustrations in this chapter indicate the location of various ECMs in different engine makes. The wiring harness connections to and from the ECM differ slightly in engine makes; however, all systems generally incorporate several types of wire harness:

- The engine harness connector to connect all of the sensors and switches to the ECM. This harness is supplied by the engine manufacturer to allow the engine to run.
- The injector harness to allow unit injector operation.
- The power harness to carry battery power to the ECM.
- An OEM harness to interface with all of the cab controls and ECM-controlled instrumentation.

Each engine manufacturer uses a generic ECM across its line of engines. Thus when the engine reaches the end of the assembly line, it is a simple matter to program it according to the end user's requirements and desired options as indicated on the sales order data sheet. Figure 18–23 illustrates how this is accomplished by connecting a PC (personal computer) to the engine ECM. Information stored in the factory mainframe computer downloads specific engine operating parameters through the PC and into the engine ECM's

the ECM uses the information to monitor and adjust fuel injection timing. This action ensures that there will be no injector-to-injector variation in the start of injection timing. The EEPROM (electrically erasable programmable read-only memory) chip set within the ECM is programmed with a pulse width program for each particular engine and application; therefore, the maximum amount of fuel injected depends on this EEPROM information.

EEPROM chip. This information contains the engine calibration configurations such as maximum engine-governed speed, governor-droop characteristics, cruise-control features, maximum vehicle road speed, transmission geardown protection, PTO (power take-off) operating features, idle shutdown timer, fuel injector information, horsepower rating, engine data list, diagnostic trouble codes, and engine/trip data. Once the vehicle or equipment is placed into service, a number of ECM operating parameters can be changed by an authorized OEM through use of a portable *programming station* similar to the one featured in Figure 21–32. This suitcase-mounted system includes a laptop computer and special telephone modem and engine hookup harnesses to allow connection to the factory mainframe computer when it is necessary to change engine horsepower settings, and so on. If an engine horsepower setting is altered, or if major alterations to the engine parameters are required while the engine is still under warranty, the OEM needs to know what changes are being made. This reprogramming feature can cost the engine user from several hundred to several thousand dollars, particularly if a higher horsepower setting is desired, because experience proves that higher horsepower engines tend to cost more because of service failures than do lower power-rated engines. The user pays extra dollars to cover the anticipated possible failure costs charged back to the OEM while the engine is under an extended warranty period.

A field service technician can access ECM information with the use of a handheld diagnostic data reader (DDR) similar to the Microprocessor Systems, Inc. (MPSI) ProLink 9000 model. Access is controlled by the adoption of an electronic password, which is usually selected by the end user at the time of ordering the engine. Thousands of passwords are available and can be chosen by the owner or fleet management personnel. Without knowledge of the specific password (name or numbers), no changes can be made to the system operating parameters; therefore, system security is maintained. System security is usually offered to users in three forms:

1. *No password.* This option allows anyone to change selected options within a given range using a handheld DDR connected to the DDL (diagnostic datalink) of the engine ECM.

2. *Changeable password.* Only individual people with access to the password can make selected changes utilizing the DDR.

3. *System lockout.* A specific password is provided that allows only an authorized representative of the engine dealer to make changes to various options such as the horsepower or major engine settings.

ECM Operation

The ECM is the brains of the system. It continually receives input voltage signals from the various engine and vehicle sensors and computes these signals to determine the length of the EUI pulse-width-modulated signal. The longer the injector solenoid is energized, the greater will be the fuel delivered to the combustion chamber. Because of the high current switching requirements necessary for operation of the individual electronic unit injectors, the voltage signal from the ECM is sent to a series of drivers contained within the single ECM housing.

Introduction to Pulse-Width Modulation

Pulse-width modulation (PWM) is the term used to describe the duration of time that the injector solenoid is energized and fuel is being delivered to the engine. Timed in milliseconds, or thousandths of a second, PWM is measured in degrees of rotation of the engine crankshaft. Frequency is defined as the number of times in 1 second that a modulated electrical signal (voltage in this case) completes a cycle. Frequency is measured in units of hertz (Hz). *Cycles per second* and *hertz* are synonymous. For example, a signal modulating at a frequency of 10 Hz completes 10 cycles every second. An example of a modulated digital signal is illustrated in Figure 18–24.

In the case of engine controls, the electrical signal to the injection solenoids might have a frequency of 50 Hz during operation. This means that each second is divided into 50 segments or cycles during which the voltage will be ON for a period of time. The percentage of time the voltage is present inside each 1/50 second is called the solenoid's duty cycle. A 100% duty cycle indicates a maximum signal to the solenoid. A 0% duty cycle indicates a minimum or zero signal to the solenoid.

Pulse-width modulation is the ability of the ECU to vary the width (%) of the voltage ON time during a cycle. As the pulse width (or duty cycle) is increased, the solenoid is ON longer (see Figure 18–24).

Computer Programming

Although each computer contains the same major basic components for successful operation, the system must be programmed with a set of instructions that, in effect, tell the computer what it must do.

With its diodes, transistors, and resistors, the computer cannot accept a program that has been written in the normal everyday form of letters and numbers. Therefore, one function of a computer program is to transform data into a recognizable computer language so that the computer's solid-state devices can react to

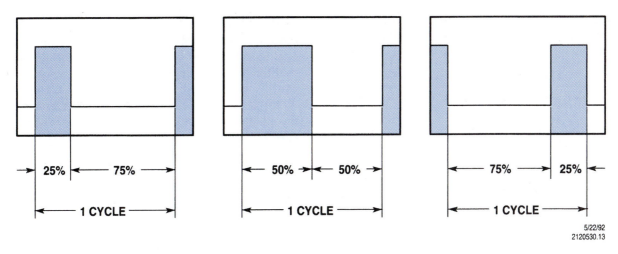

25% | 75% | 50% | 50% | 75% | 25%

1 CYCLE   1 CYCLE   1 CYCLE

5/22/92
2120530.13

FIGURE 18–24 *Sample digital waveforms showing various duty-cycle conditions.*

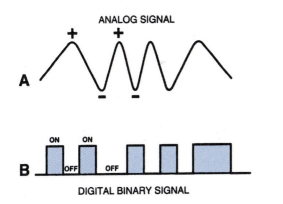

ANALOG SIGNAL

A

DIGITAL BINARY SIGNAL

FIGURE 18–25 *(a) Analog signal wave shape; (b) digital signal wave shape.*

various commands. This requires that the input analog-voltage signals from the various sensor devices be converted into digital form (1s for ON and 0s for OFF).

Figure 18–25 illustrates, in simplified form, the wave sine for an analog signal and the rectangular box shape of the digital sine wave.

Although we could take the regular digital numbers of 1 and 0 and program the computer, it would be very difficult to understand and use strings of 1s and 0s, particularly when we would need to use thousands of numbers. Therefore, to simplify this bulky system into a more manageable state, a special programming language has been developed.

Minicomputers in use in automobiles and trucks perform a limited number of calculations when compared with that of a large mainframe computer in an office or factory. Therefore, their programs are fairly simple to construct. A fixed program is built directly into the computer at the factory and is commonly re-

ferred to as hard wiring, because it is burned into the PROM (programmable read-only memory) or ROM (read-only memory) unit integrated chip by a laser beam in the latest systems. The PROM unit cannot be altered unless it is removed and replaced with another memory chip. EPROM or EEPROMs can be altered.

Binary Notation

Since the computer is constructed to understand only digital voltage signals, which are either in the ON (1) or OFF (0) mode, the many combinations of these numbers are represented in what is called *binary form*. What this means is that only the numerals 1 or 0 are used rather than the numbers from 0 through 9, which would represent 10 possible numbers.

To convert the decimal numbers into binary notation or form, a device within the minicomputer known as an *encoder* is required. In addition, to convert digital data (that is, binary numbers) into decimal form at any time, the computer also contains a *decoder.* Table 18–1 illustrates the system of numbers used with the binary system of notation. This is the system of numbers used to tell the computer what is going on at any time.

The binary system of numbers used with a computer is commonly called a *base 2 system,* while the conventional decimal system using 10 digits is known as a *base 10 system.* The word *decimal* is derived from the Latin word for *ten.*

The computer can interpret numbers only in the base 2 system. Since only zeros or ones (0s = OFF and 1s = ON) are continually produced by the various input sensors (analog-to-digital conversion done through an analog-to-digital converter within the computer unit), some form of equitable conversion system must be employed. Table 18–1 illustrates a

TABLE 18–1 *Minicomputer binary notation (base 2) system of numbering versus the normal base 10 decimal system*

Decimal base 10 system	Binary base 2 system
0	0000
1	0001
2	0010
3	0011
4	0100
5	0101
6	0110
7	0111
8	1000
9	1001
10	1010
11	1011
12	1100
13	1101
14	1110
15	1111
16	10000
255	11111111
256	100000000

comparison between a base 2 and a base 10 system. Note, for example, that the binary number 0011 is read and interpreted as the number "zero-zero-one-one," not as the number eleven.

Bits and Bytes

The digital signals created and interpreted in the computer are, as we now know, identified by binary numbers of 1 or 0, with 1 being an ON signal and with 0 representing an OFF signal (see Figure 18–25). These 1s and 0s are commonly referred to as *bits,* which is a word combination form contrived from the two words *binary digits.* A *bit* indicates one unit of data or information and is indicated to the computer by the numeral 1 or 0. Each one of these digital numbers contains a very small unit of information. Therefore, to handle large amounts of usable information, the computer is designed to combine and handle these separate bits into words of different lengths known as *bytes* (Figure 18–26). Various computers are designed to handle information data in word lengths of 4, 8, 16, 32, or 64 bits.

The term *kilobyte* or the letter *K* indicates that the memory storage unit of the CPU can hold 1000 bytes.

Logic Circuits

Since microprocessors operate on digital signals, any analog signal must be converted to a digital signal so that the feedback information from any sensor can be readily understood and acted upon. Components within the computer are designed and programmed to recognize voltage signals by a number assigned to a specific input signal. Because of the many functions that the computer is asked to do, the various input signals are converted to a specific binary digit number through the use of logic gates, briefly discussed below. Operating conditions that are sensed by specific sensors attached to the engine/vehicle, output voltage signals that are fed into the on-board electronic control module (minicomputer), where the various solid-state devices, assisted by the different logic gates, are able to interpret these input data's binary digit (bit) representation of the analog sensor's amplitude. The electronic control module then outputs a voltage signal to the diesel fuel injectors, for example, to control how long they operate. In this way the amount of fuel delivered to the engine cylinders becomes proportional to the throttle position. Similarly, an output voltage signal from the computer controls the injection timing and any other sensed components.

Paramount to the importance of ICs is the operation of the transistors. The converted digital voltage signals or circuits are known as *logic circuits,* and they consist of a series or combinations of varying types of systems and numbers, and interconnection patterns that are commonly referred to as *gates.* These gates are designed to accept voltage signals and logically make sense of them. In effect, they process two or more voltage signals. This is why they are called *logic gates.* They have the ability to make some sense out of all the various voltage feedback signals that are fed to the computer from the numerous sensors on the vehicle.

Sensors continually input voltage signals to the ECM when the engine is first cranked and is running. The idle rpm, fuel input, and therefore the horsepower developed at a given load/speed are determined by the injector solenoid pulse width signal, based on the various inputs from all the sensors used with the system.

The timers used are the basis for the fuel delivery system and have the following major functions:

- Time between cylinders (measured as crank degrees)
- Time from reference signal to injector solenoid turn on
- Solenoid response time
- Solenoid ON time
- Real-time program events

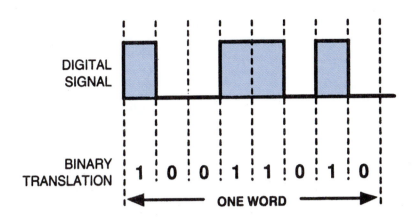

For each cylinder, a timer requests the beginning of injection (BOI), and the pulse width (PW) time (effective injector plunger stroke) is converted from degrees of crankshaft angle to a time reference.

Initiation of a cylinder injection sequence is started with the time delay between the beginning of the timing reference signal to actually turning the solenoid on. This time delay is estimated from the time between the last two sets of timing signals and subsequently reduced by the previously measured solenoid response time. Pulse-width or injector solenoid ON time (fuel being injected) is determined by converting the requested crank angle degrees sensor signal to an equivalent time period plus the solenoid response time.

ECM Control Functions

The ECM receives the various sensor voltage signals and sends out a command pulse to the unit injector based on throttle position and engine speed. The peak torque rpm and actual torque shaping are determined by scheduling fuel pulse width (injector plunger effective stroke) based on engine speed at full throttle. The speed governor is designed to maintain a precise speed setting for all engine loads from the information stored in the calibration EEPROM. (See Chapter 16 for details on the electronic governor.) From this information, the governor has the ability to calibrate droop, which is the difference between maximum full-load and maximum no-load speeds. The system is designed for closed-loop control, whereby all sensors are providing input signals to the ECM so that the desired idle speed can be set for accessory performance and fuel economy; therefore, PTO (power takeoff) functions can be handled by establishing a new set speed when a load is applied to the engine.

On each system there is a built-in flexibility feature for calibrating droop from 0 to 150 rpm, to provide the best performance from engine speed/vehicle gearing. Zero droop can be programmed into the system to limit

vehicle speed by setting the maximum full-load engine speed to match the maximum vehicle road speed. In addition, the system can be programmed for two-speed logic, whereby the maximum full-load rpm of the engine can be reduced any time that the transmission is in top gear. One or more switches can be used to indicate what gear the transmission is in, to limit vehicle speed or allow an extended rpm operating range in one or more gears for better fuel economy or performance improvement. The rated speed is determined by a switch input to the ECM. Improved cold starting of the engine is established by using a voltage signal from the engine oil temperature sensor to provide a 15% improvement over a nonelectronic engine.

Another feature of the electronic system is reducing white smoke on startup of a cold engine by increasing the idle-speed setting, along with advanced injection timing to allow faster engine warm-up. The idle speed is reduced and the injection timing is retarded as the engine warms up to ensure lower fuel consumption, reduced exhaust emissions, and lower combustion noise. If the ECM has been programmed to do so, a 3- to 100-minute idle shutdown can be incorporated into the electronic system. This shutdown timer starts its count once the engine is idling and the vehicle spring parking brakes are activated. An engine airflow turbocharged discharge pressure transducer sensor set for approximately 2 atm (29.4 psi) absolute, along with an engine speed sensor, provides improved engine acceleration as well as an improvement in engine torque because of the faster response of the electronic system. An air temperature sensor is also used to provide optimum timing for best fuel consumption based on changing air temperatures.

The electronic drivers contained within the ECM functions as the high-current switching unit for actuation of the unit injector solenoids as well as monitoring the solenoid voltage waveform to sense valve closure. Average 12V current draw for a 6 cylinder heavy duty engine is between 1 and 1.5 amperes (A) at idle speed, to 3 and 4A at full load engine rpm. Power draw at idle: V8 is 2A, V12 is 3A, V16 is 4A, V20 is 8A. Power draw at full load: V8 is 5A, V12 is 8A, V16 is 10A, V20 is 13A. 24V current draw is about 65% of a 12V system. A cold plate using the engine fuel flow as the cooling medium provides a heat sink for the ECM.

The cruise control interface system can use either the vehicle or the engine speed as the control input, while vehicle brake, set/coast, and resume/acceleration switch inputs provide drive commands. The engine brake operates when the ECM senses that the engine is in an unfueled state so that the engine brake can be applied. Output from the ECM is provided to interface with the engine braking system.

Each ECM contains two types of memory.

1. The EEPROM (electronically erasable programmable read-only memory) unit, which has been designed for use with a particular engine speed and horsepower setting, and coded for use in a particular truck based on its transmission and axle ratios as well as tire size, and so on. The EEPROM chip allows any engine to have its speed and horsepower settings changed without completely replacing the ECM.

2. The RAM (random-access memory) unit, which continually receives updated information from all the various engine/vehicle sensors to allow the ECM to be advised of any changes to the operating parameters for the engine vehicle during operation. In effect, the RAM unit becomes the working scratch pad of the ECM during engine operation.

ECM Safety Precautions

When working around electronic engines, major safety precautions must be observed.

Welding

Disconnect the vehicle batteries and the plug-in harnesses to the ECM to prevent any possibility of ECM damage during welding.

Electrical Shock

Never disconnect or connect any wires or harness connectors, particularly at the ECM, when the engine is running or when the ignition key switch is turned on. Also, remember that electronic unit injectors receive a PWM signal from the ECM that can range as high as 90 V and 105 V when the engine is running. *Do not* come in contact with the injector terminals while the engine is running!

When handling an electronic part that has an electrostatic-discharge-sensitive sticker (Figure 18–27), follow these guidelines to reduce any possible electrostatic charge buildup on your body and the electronic part:

FIGURE 18–27 *Typical industry standard warning label/decal to indicate that the contents are sensitive to static electricity.*

- Do not open the package until it is time to install the part.
- Avoid touching electrical terminals of the part.
- Before removing the part from its package, ground the package to a known good ground on the vehicle.
- Always touch a known good ground before handling the part. This should be repeated while handling the part and more frequently after sliding across the seat, sitting down from a standing position, or walking a distance.

Turbocharger Shield

It is sometimes necessary to operate an engine with the ducting to the intake side of the turbocharger disconnected. Never operate any engine without first installing a turbo "guard."

TROUBLESHOOTING OPTIONS

Troubleshooting an electronic engine can be done using one or more of the following approaches:

1. *Self-diagnosis.* Visually and physically inspecting suspected areas and/or components; performing manometer checks of the air, exhaust, and fuel systems; refer to Chapter 13 and 25 for information.

2. *OEM troubleshooting guide/manual.* Refer to the book index to quickly locate the information/data that you need and follow the step-by-step recommended troubleshooting/diagnosis procedure.

3. *Handheld reader (scan tool).* Shown in Figure 18–28, the 9000 or ProLink Plus has the appropriate diagnostic cartridge. Refer to the desired engine OEM chapters in this book for more details. The data that can be typically displayed on the screen of a scan tool are given in Table 18–2.

TABLE 18–2　*Example of typical displayed data that can be accessed from an electronic engine or power train when using a DDR handheld scan tool or PC*

Displayed Data			
Engine Coolant Temperature (ECT)	°F	Cruise Control Set Speed	mph
Intake Manifold Temperature (IMT)	°F	Cruise Control Switch	On/Off
Engine Oil Temperature (EOT)	°F	PTO Switch	On/Off
Fuel Temperature (FT)	°F	Remote PTO Switch	On/Off
Engine Oil Pressure (EOP)	psi	Engine Cooling Fan Switch	On/Off
Boost Pressure (BP)	psi	A/C High Pressure Switch	Open/Closed
Barometric Pressure (BARO)	In.Hg.	Clutch Switch	Depressed/Released
Throttle Position (TPS)	%	Service Brake Switch	Depressed/Released
Idle Validation Switch (IVS)	On/Off	Engine Brake Switch	On/Off
Engine Position (EPS)	rpm	Engine Brake Selector	Low/Med/High
Vehicle Speed (VSS)	mph	Diagnostic Lamp—Yellow	On/Off
Battery Voltage (B+)	Volts	—Red	On/Off
Coolant Level (CL)	Normal/Low	**Diagnostic Trouble Codes**	
		Active:	
		Inactive:	

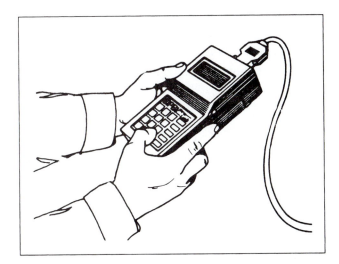

FIGURE 18–28　*Typical handheld scan tool or DDR (diagnostic data reader). MPSI ProLink 9000 J38500. (Courtesy of Kent-Moore Tool Division, SPX Corporation.)*

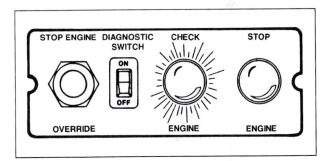

FIGURE 18–29　Portion of an instrument panel showing a typical electronic engine shutdown override switch, and the yellow (check) and red (stop) engine warning lights. (Courtesy of Detroit Diesel Corporation.)

4. *Breakout box.* Using this approach permits you to safely employ a digital multimeter (refer to Figure 21–38) when checking circuits for voltage, current, and resistance values, as well as for signs of shorts, opens, or grounds.

5. *Diagnostic datalink.* Combined with a jumper wire where recommended, you can obtain stored ECM flash codes; or you can activate the instrument panel diagnostic switch or shorting plug (see Figure 18–29) used to withdraw stored flash codes. (Cummins is one example.) OEMs also offer a software program known as *diagnostic link* (Detroit Diesel is one example); it includes a built-in service manual and the ability to view or change engine configurations and extract information into an easy-to-use report.

6. *OEM advanced software program.* When more sophisticated troubleshooting is required, this program (PC or laptop computer) is available to help you work through a fault/problem. By entering a brief description of the problem and then answering questions prompted by the software menu, the program will systematically guide you through a *case-based reasoning*

TABLE 18–3 *Example of how computer-based use of case-based reasoning CD-ROM programs can assist the service technician in effectively and efficiently diagnosing and troubleshooting an electronic engine*

PC Based Troubleshooting

Description:

low power, high rpm, not temperature related

Questions:	**Answers (list):**
Has the check engine light come on?	No
Does the problem only occur at certain outside temperatures?	No
When does the engine performance problem occur?	High Speeds
What type of engine performance problem is occurring?	Low power
What type of engine problem is occurring?	Performance

Actions:

97	Check turbo boost pressure.
97	Check air intake system for restrictions.
97	Check air intake system for low boost pressure.

Probability of this being the problem in %:

(Courtesy of Detroit Diesel Corporation.)

procedure. An example of a PC-based troubleshooting case-based reasoning software menu (courtesy of Detroit Diesel) is shown in Table 18–3. Cummins INSITE and Cat's ET (Electronic Technician) software programs are similar.

Public Datalink

The public datalink circuit is used for an electronic service tool connection such as a handheld DDR (diagnostic data reader) or common scan tool, a palm-type reader, or a PC. The link is used to communicate with the ECM, and can also be used to electronically communicate information with other on-board electronic devices such as electronic dash boards and other equipment. Some engines employ two public datalinks, one being attached to the entire wire harness (engine-side datalink) and the other datalink, which detaches from the OEM harness, is usually located in the vehicle cab (see Chapter 22 for an example).

Figure 18–30 illustrates a datalink used on earlier-model electronic engines, which used a rectangular 12-pin connector; the diagram also shows three special wire harnesses for different types of diagnostic datalink connectors. These allow the service technician to plug in appropriate diagnostic tooling to download fault/diagnostic trouble codes stored in ECM memory when troubleshooting. Later-model electronic engines all use a standardized SAE datalink connector, which uses a Deutsch-type 6-pin connector as illustrated in Figure 18–30b. (See also Figure 21–30.) The wiring positions are as follows for the 6-pin con-

nector and typical voltages that would be measured at each pin with a digital multimeter when checking this datalink pin for problems of failure to communicate with diagnostic tools.

A—data link (+); voltage spec is usually between 2.5 to 5 volts.

B—data link (−); voltage is usually between 0 to 2.5 volts.

C—battery (12/24 volts); voltage is usually between 10 to 27 volts based on either a 12- or 24-volt battery system.

D—open; voltage usually 4 to 5 volts.

E—block ground; 0 volt

F—not used

ECM Diagnostics

All electronically controlled engines are designed to store or log a trouble code in ECM memory when a sensor is operating in an out-of-range condition. When a problem is sensed and relayed back to the ECM, the severity of the problem will cause either the yellow or red diagnostic instrument panel light to illuminate. When the yellow light is illuminated, there may be a rampdown (power reduction) of both engine power and speed. If the red light is illuminated, the sensed operating problem is serious enough to trigger an engine shutdown condition if the ECM has been programmed to do so. Some electronic systems are equipped with a *diagnostic toggle switch* that can be activated to cause the dash-mounted CEL to illuminate and flash rapidly,

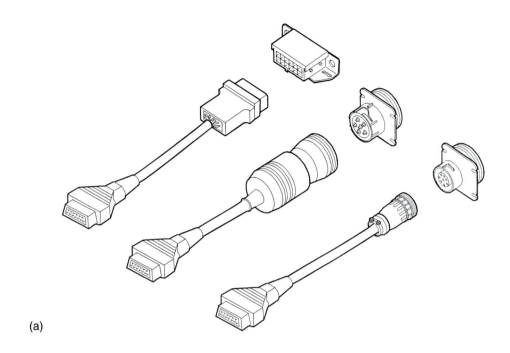

(a)

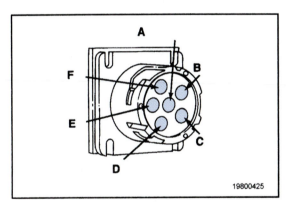

(b)

19800425

FIGURE 18–30

(a) Examples of three types of DDEC diagnostic datalink connectors used between the engine/vehicle plug-in, and either a handheld DDR, scan tool, or PC: a rectangular 12-pin DDEC I/II model; a 6-pin Deutsch, and a 9-pin Deutsch for the DDEC III/IV model. (Courtesy of Detroit Diesel Corporation.); (b) Identification of the individual pin-outs for a standard SAE 6-pin Deutsch connector. (Courtesy of Cummins Engine Company, Inc.)

thereby allowing the driver or technician to determine the *flash code number.*

In some electronic systems, the technician can use a *jumper wire* across two diagnostic connector terminals to cause any stored ECM trouble codes to "flash" the dash-mounted vehicle diagnostic light. See Figure 18–31a for one such example of a 12-pin DDL (diagnostic datalink) connector generally located within the truck cab area (placement varies by OEM). This particular example is for a DDEC I or DDEC II Detroit Diesel system. Note that this procedure cannot be used on the DDEC III or IV System! See Chapter 21 for information dealing with the DDEC system. To extract a flash trouble code, with the ignition key switch off, insert a jumper wire between terminals A and M, which are clearly marked on the connector. When the ignition switch is turned back on, closely watch the dash-mounted yellow diagnostic light. An example of how to interpret stored flash trouble codes is illustrated in

Figure 18–31b. A flash code 13, for example, on a DDEC system (I or II) indicates that a coolant level sensor has detected low coolant. A code 21 on this system indicates that the TPS (throttle position sensor) has detected a high circuit voltage reading.

Some vehicles with electronic dashboards can provide a direct readout of engine diagnostic codes. This system, known as a ProDriver unit, can continually update the driver on engine and vehicle operating conditions, for example, an instant mpg/km per liter fuel consumption reading.

Although flash codes are helpful, a more thorough analysis of system trouble codes and problem areas can be performed by the service technician using a handheld diagnostic reader, which is more commonly referred to as a DDR (diagnostic data reader). The type of diagnostic reader used to withdraw stored trouble codes varies in design among engine manufacturers; however, some major OEMs of diag-

FIGURE 18–31 (a) 12-pin diagnostic connector used by DDC on their DDEC 1/11 models to allow plug-in of a DDR (scan tool) to withdraw stored trouble codes, or to perform specific tests. On this system, if no scan tool is available, with the ignition key switch OFF, a technician can insert a jumper wire between terminals A and M; then turn the key switch ON and activate a download of stored trouble codes as shown in part b of this figure; (b) yellow warning light flash interpretation to identify stored diagnostic trouble codes. (Courtesy of Detroit Diesel Corporation.)

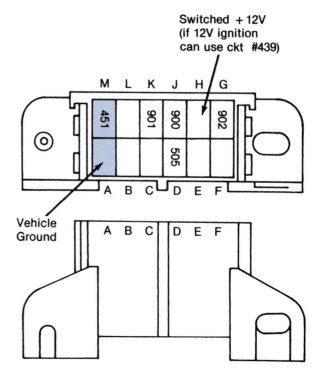

(a)   12 Pin DDL Connector P/N 12020043

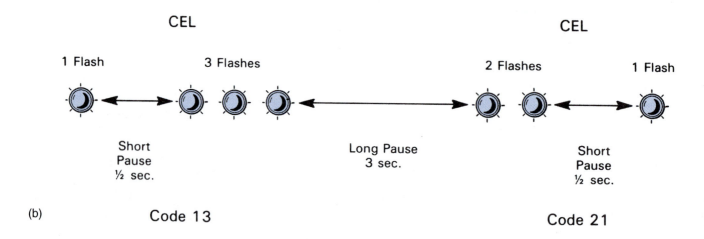

(b)   Code 13   Code 21

nostic tools now offer a generic tool that can handle any make of engine, in addition to transmission and anti-skid brake electronic controls, simply by removing and inserting an electronic cartridge assembly into the handheld DDR.

DIAGNOSTIC TOOLING

MPSI Diagnostic Tooling

MPSI (Micro Processor Systems, Inc.) is a supplier of diagnostic tooling and equipment to the majority of engine OEMs. The MPSI ProLink 9000 in Figure 18–28 can

be connected to a printer. For more information on MPSI contact the www.mpsilink.com website.

Diagnostic Tooling Principles

All electronic engine OEMs now offer dedicated software to facilitate diagnostic and programming information with their products using a laptop computer. Windows-based programs are available from each engine OEM which provide a point-and-click graphical interface for the technician.

The DDR, which is connected to a DDL (diagnostic datalink) connector located on the vehicle, see Figure

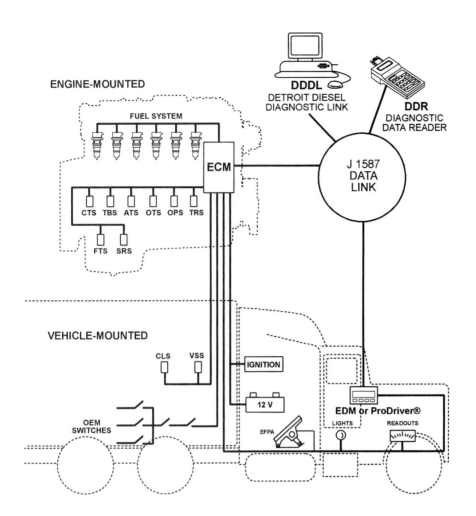

ENGINE-MOUNTED

FUEL SYSTEM

ECM

CTS TBS ATS OTS OPS TRS

FTS SRS

DDDL
DETROIT DIESEL
DIAGNOSTIC LINK

DDR
DIAGNOSTIC
DATA READER

J 1587
DATA
LINK

VEHICLE-MOUNTED

CLS   VSS

IGNITION

12 V

OEM
SWITCHES

EFPA

EDM or ProDriver®

LIGHTS   READOUTS

FIGURE 18–32 *Special tooling required to diagnose and troubleshoot a Class 8 heavy-duty truck electronic engine.*

18–32, can be used for troubleshooting and diagnostic purposes. It also can be used to provide unique capabilities such as these: running engine cylinder cutout, injector solenoid response times, injector calibration update, engine trip data, engine/vehicle speed calibration changes, cruise-control speed setting changes, idle shutdown and transmission progressive shift changes, engine and engine protection configuration changes, parameter versus engine speed (or time), engine snapshot data, and limited ECM reprogramming when customer changes are desired and/or required within the operating conditions/parameters of the engine OEM.

By using any of the readily available DDRs from one of the major suppliers, the technician can access the ECM memory storage bank and monitor the sensor outputs and the diagnostic trouble codes. The technician can also confirm what ECM options have been programmed into the system, such as cruise control, automatic engine shutdown in the event of a major engine system problem, idle control time limit, and so on.

The DDR can be operated from the vehicle battery power supply, as can a mini-printer (plug into the cigarette lighter). A 110-V power supply is also available

to run the printer and is preferable when the DDR and printer are to be used for any length of time.

ECM SAE Trouble Codes

The trouble code numbering system and interpretation stored in ECM memory are not the same in engines from different OEMs. For example, flash code 35 does not have the same meaning on Caterpillar, Cummins, Detroit Diesel, Mack, and Volvo engines. The SAE (Society of Automotive Engineers), through its technical standards committees, has been working with engine OEMs to arrive at a standard system of electronic coding and meaning. To encourage industry-wide acceptance of electronic serial data communication links between engines, SAE has created SAE-J reference standards, which are now in use.

- *SAEJ1587.* This standard enables the ECM to "talk" with diagnostic service tools, trip recorder and vehicle management information systems, electronic dash displays, and satellite communication systems. In other words, the J1587/J1708 data link provides sensor(s) and engine data to other vehicle modules.

- *SAEJ1922 and J1939.* These two standards give the ECM the capability to communicate with and provide control data to other vehicle systems such as antilock braking systems, electronic transmissions, and antislip ASR systems (traction control devices). The on-vehicle communications harness assembly connects the ECM's J1922 and J1939 control data ports to other vehicle systems. The J1939 datalink uses the controller area network (CAN) protocol.

- *SAEJ1924.* This is a PC-software-compatible standard to allow the PC to interface with and translate the datalink signal from the ECM. The software is installed as a terminate and stay resident (TSR) program.

When a technician uses a handheld DDR similar to the one shown in Figure 18–28 to interpret stored ECM trouble codes, these codes are now displayed in the SAE technical standard format. Previously, stored trouble codes appeared on the DDR screen as a two- or three-digit number. The technician then referred to a flash code listing in the engine service manual or on a small plastic card provided by the OEM that allowed him or her to interpret the specific trouble code. The technician then referred the trouble code number in the engine service manual and followed a step-by-step procedure to locate and correct the source of the problem. Although the technician can still follow this procedure, flash codes no longer appear on the screen of the DDR in newer electronic engine systems.

The flash codes have been replaced by parameter and system identification descriptions known as PID (parameter identifier) and SID (subsystem identifier) numbers. After the PID and SID numbers is a failure mode identifier (FMI), which defines the area where the fault has occurred. The following are summary descriptions of these acronyms:

- *PID:* appears on the screen of the DDR as a single- or double-byte character to identify data of varying length, for example, the ECM data list of engine operating parameters, which would include items related to oil pressure, oil and coolant temperature, TPS (throttle position sensor), and so on.
- *SID:* appears only as a single-byte character to identify field-repairable or field-replaceable subsystems for which failures can be detected or isolated. Such a code could identify an injector problem.
- *FMI:* describes the type of failure detected in a subsystem and identified by the PID or SID. The FMI and either the PID or SID combine to form a given diagnostic code as identified by the SAE J1587 technical standard.

SAE Code Message Descriptions

All electronic systems now in use on heavy-duty trucks include SAE codes that can be extracted by using a DDR similar to that shown in Figure 18–32. In addition to their use on electronic engines, message identifier codes are also used with ABS (antibrake skid) and TCS (traction control systems), transmissions, vehicle navigation, and driver information systems. When a DDR is connected to any of these systems, message types by SAE code can appear from the serial data line when these aftermarket devices are used. Examples of the standard MIDs (message identifiers), PIDs (parameter identifiers), SIDs (subsystem identifiers), and FMIs (failure mode indicators) are given in this chapter for Caterpillar, Cummins, Detroit Diesel, and Mack engines. Listed below are standardized SAE codes in various key areas.

When illuminated on a DDR or laptop screen, the first set of SAE codes, identified as MIDs (message identifiers), indicate to the technician the vehicle system to which it refers. Once the system is identified, the technician can then use the DDR to access/enter that system to monitor trouble codes, perform a functional test, or reprogram the system. Once this has been done, the various SAE trouble codes that appear on the DDR screen (PIDs, SIDs, and FMIs) help in determining the area and cause of the problem.

Message Identifiers (MIDs)

128	Engine controller (used in V-MAC system)
130	Transmission
136	Brakes: antilock traction control
137–139	Brakes: antilock, trailers 1, 2, 3
140	Instrument cluster
141	Trip recorder
142	Vehicle management system (V-MAC MID)
143	Fuel system (FIC MID)
162	Vehicle navigation
163	Vehicle security
165	Communication unit: ground
171	Driver information system
178	Vehicle sensors to data converter
181	Communication unit: satellite

Parameter Identifiers (PIDs)

65	Service brake switch
70	Parking brake switch
83	Road speed limit status
84	Road speed
85	Speed control status
91	Percent accelerator pedal position
92	Percent engine load
100	Engine oil pressure
105	Intake manifold temperature

110 Engine coolant temperature
111 Coolant level
175 Engine oil temperature
182 Trip fuel
183 Fuel rate
184 Instantaneous MPG
185 Average MPG
190 Engine speed

Subsystem Identifiers (SIDs) Common to all MIDs

242 Cruise control resume switch
243 Cruise control set switch
244 Cruise control enable switch
245 Clutch pedal switch
248 Proprietary datalink
250 SAEJ1708 (J1587) data link

Subsystem Identifiers for MIDs 128 and 143

20 Timing actuator
21 Engine position sensor
22 Timing sensor
23 Rack actuator
24 Rack position sensor
29 External fuel command input

Subsystem Identifiers for MID 130

1–6 C1–C6 solenoid valves
7 Lockup solenoid valve
8 Forward solenoid valve
9 Low-Signal solenoid valve
10 Retarder enable solenoid valve
11 Retarder modulation solenoid valve
12 Retarder response solenoid valve
13 Differential lockout solenoid valve
14 Engine transmission match
15 Retarder modulation request sensor
16 Neutral start output
17 Turbine speed sensor
18 Primary shift selector
19 Secondary shift selector
20 Special function inputs
21–26 C1–C6 clutch pressure indicators
27 Lockup clutch pressure indicator
28 Forward range pressure indicator
29 Neutral range pressure indicator
30 Reverse range pressure indicator
31 Retarder response system pressure indicator
32 Differential lock clutch pressure indicator
33 Multiple pressure indicators

Subsystem Identifiers for MIDs 136–139

1 Wheel sensor ABS axle 1 left
2 Wheel sensor ABS axle 1 right

3 Wheel sensor ABS axle 2 left
4 Wheel sensor ABS axle 2 right
5 Wheel sensor ABS axle 3 left
6 Wheel sensor ABS axle 3 right
7 Pressure modulation valve ABS axle 1 left
8 Pressure modulation valve ABS axle 1 right
9 Pressure modulation valve ABS axle 2 left
10 Pressure modulation valve ABS axle 2 right
11 Pressure modulation valve ABS axle 3 left
12 Pressure modulation valve ABS axle 3 right
13 Retarder control relay
14 Relay diagonal 1
15 Relay diagonal 2
16 Mode switch: ABS
17 Mode Switch: traction control
18 DIF 1: traction control valve
19 DIF 2: traction control valve
22 Speed signal input
23 Warning light bulb
24 Traction control light bulb
25 Wheel sensor, ABS axle 1 average
26 Wheel sensor, ABS axle 2 average
27 Wheel sensor, ABS axle 3 average
28 Pressure modulator, drive axle relay valve
29 Pressure transducer, drive axle relay valve
30 Master control relay

Subsystem Identifiers for MID 162

1 Dead reckoning unit
2 Loran receiver
3 Global positioning system (GPS)
4 Integrated navigation unit

Currently, SAE FMIs list 15 numbers that are used in conjunction with either PIDs or SIDs. All of these numbers appear on the DDR screen used by the service technician to recall stored trouble codes from the ECM. Most of the FMIs that accompany either a PID or SID tend to be either a 3 or a 4, and they are included in the following list of the SAE numbers currently in use.

Failure Mode Identifiers (FMIs)

0 Data valid but above normal operational range (that is, engine overheating)
1 Data valid but below normal operational range (that is, engine oil pressure too low)
2 Data erratic, intermittent, or incorrect
3 Voltage above normal or shorted high
4 Voltage below normal or shorted low
5 Current below normal or open circuit
6 Current above normal or grounded circuit
7 Mechanical system not responding properly
8 Abnormal frequency, pulse width, or period
9 Abnormal update rate

10   Abnormal rate of change
11   Failure mode not identifiable
12   Bad intelligent device or component
13   Out of calibration
14   Special instructions
15   Reserved for future assignment by the SAE data format subcommittee

For example, the DDR illustrated in Figure 18–32, when connected to a DDEC III system, may display on its screen the following sequence:

Code p 91 3 = EFPA circuit failed high
3 = high voltage
4 = low voltage

When using the DDR, the screen will display (when prompted) whether there are *active* and *inactive* trouble codes stored in the ECM memory. Such a diagnostic request might display the following sequence for a DDEC III system:

[The engine serial number]
Diagnostic code list
NO ACTIVE CODES
INACTIVE CODES
Engine throttle sensor input voltage low
    PID:91 FMI:4 (flash code 22)
Engine oil pressure sensor input voltage low
    PID:100 FMI:4 (flash code 36)
Engine turbo boost sensor input voltage low
    PID:102 FMI:4 (flash code 34)
Coolant level sensor input voltage high
    PID:111 FMI:3 (flash code 16)

The foregoing information indicates to the technician that there are no active codes and four inactive codes. Note, however, that the flash codes would show on a DDEC II system DDR screen but not on a DDEC III or IV system DDR screen. A dash-mounted flash code diagnostic request toggle switch can be activated on DDEC III/IV system to extract these types of codes.

Even though all engine manufacturers conform to the SAE technical standards, the flash codes are still different. Assume we are using a DDR and we uncover a PID/FMI number 10/01 on a Cummins, Caterpillar, or Detroit Diesel engine. This SAE code means that the engine ECMs have detected from the sensor input that a low oil pressure condition has been logged. The flash code on the Caterpillar would be a No. 46; on the Detroit Diesel, it would be No. 45; and on the Cummins it would be No. 143. The PID/FMI number 110/00 means a high coolant temperature warning; it would exhibit a flash code No. 61 on the Caterpillar, a No. 44 on Detroit Diesel, and a No. 151 on the Cummins. The adoption of the standardized SAE fault codes ensures that all engine manufacturers using electronic fuel injection systems will display the same PIDs and FMIs regardless of individual flash code numbering systems.

Active/Inactive Codes

When an engine or vehicle speed sensor detects an out-of-range operating condition, the ECM receives a high or low signal based on the failure mode detected. The ECM then logs a trouble code into its memory bank for extraction by the technician at a later date. For example, say the ECM was programmed to record a high engine oil temperature condition beginning at 250°F (121°C). When this condition is noted by the OTS (oil temperature sensor), the signal to the ECM will cause a yellow dash-mounted warning light to illuminate. This condition is known as an *active code* situation. If the ECM has been programmed for engine protection, the engine will usually start to lose speed and power to a level that was the average power occurring prior to the fault condition. If, however, the oil temperature continues to increase, at a preprogrammed point, the red SEL (stop engine light) on the dash will illuminate. Then a 30-second automatic rampdown (power reduction) will begin, followed by engine shutdown if the system has been programmed to do so. In some situations, if the fleet management or owners/operators have previously selected a temporary override option, the driver may push an STEO (stop-engine override) button on the dash, see Figure 18–29, to provide another 30 seconds of engine operation, so the vehicle can be pulled safely to the side of the highway.

In this same condition of high engine oil temperature, let us assume that the ECM is programmed to illuminate the dash-mounted yellow warning light at 251°F (122°C) and to shut the engine down at 261°F (127°C). The yellow light illuminates when the low-end temperature of the lube oil is reached, and a trouble code is stored in ECM memory. If the vehicle operating condition triggered this light when moving up a long hill and while heavily loaded, it is possible that once the hill is crested, the engine oil temperature condition would drop back into a normal operating range. This would cause the yellow light to go out; nevertheless, the trouble code would remain stored in ECM memory. This type of a condition is referred to as an *in-*

active code (sometimes called a "historic" code). An active code indicates to the vehicle driver that an out-of-range condition has been detected, and an inactive code indicates to the service technician that a problem was detected by a sensor/ECM at some time during engine/vehicle operation. Most current ECMs are programmed not only to log and retain trouble codes, but also to record how many times they occurred and at what hours or miles.

Examples of the various trouble codes—PIDs, SIDs, and FMIs—are listed for Detroit Diesel, Caterpillar, and Cummins engines in their respective chapters.

Clearing Codes

After trouble codes have been stored in ECM memory and you want to remove them, you must select the menu option from the DDR that indicates to the technician whether you wish to erase all stored codes. All current electronic systems require this method. In some first-generation systems the stored trouble codes could be erased either by using the DDR or simply by removing the power supply fuses to the ECM for 10 second, then reinserting them. The disadvantage of these systems is that after an operator removes the codes, any record of troubles that may have occurred on the trip would be lost, and the service technician or fleet maintenance manager would have no knowledge of any engine or vehicle problems.

For a complete list of all current SAE codes used throughout the automotive and heavy-duty trucking industry, contact SAE (Society of Automotive Engineers) at 400 Commonwealth Drive, Warrendale, PA 15096-0001; tel: 412-776-4841, fax: 412-776-5760. (www.sae.org).

Electrical/Sensor Specifications

Although standardized SAE diagnostic trouble codes or fault codes described earlier in this chapter provide effective information to direct you to a specific sensor or system problem area, they may not be able to indicate exactly where the fault lies. For this, you can use a *breakout box* (see Figure 21–38), and a multimeter to check specific circuits for voltage, current, and resistance as well as to determine if a short, open, or ground condition exists. Always refer to the engine/vehicle wiring diagram to guide you to the various circuit numbers when performing any of these checks/tests.

Each engine/vehicle OEM supplies all electrical and sensor specifications in their appropriate engine model service/troubleshooting and repair manuals, as well as in their appropriate software programs that can be used with a PC or laptop computer. Many sensors that are employed by different engine OEMs are often sourced from the same supplier(s), but will of course have a different part number from a Cat, Cummins, DDC, Volvo, or other dealer. In addition, often the exact same sensor can be used in more than one system. For example, the air inlet temperature, the oil temperature, the fuel temperature, and sometimes the coolant temperature sensors will be the same model and part number; therefore, their voltage, current, and resistance values are identical. Table 18–4 lists the following information for Cummins Signature/ISX engines and provides an example of the type of data that would appear for these various systems and components.

ECM Connector Maintenance

Each ECM uses seals around each connector which plug into the module to prevent/minimize moisture or dirt from being ingested. *Intermittent fault codes* can sometimes be caused by failure of a seal or by poor contact between male/female connections. Symptoms can include intermittent stumble or rough running and a logged fault code. Anytime that it is necessary to disconnect the ECM connectors such as when using a breakout box, checking pin contacts, or repairing one or more wire connectors, it is extremely important to ensure that the ECM ports/pins, or connectors, are completely dry. The use of pressurized air to blow connectors dry is not a good idea, as compressed air can contain moisture due to condensation. As shown in Figure 18–33a, the preferred method is to use a recommended quick-dry spray. This diagram shows the Cummins part no. 3824510 quick-dry electrical contact cleaner which can be used on the ECM connector ports and the harness connectors. Once done, it is also important to apply a dielectric grease, as shown in Figure 18–33b. Avoid using lube oil or regular grease in the connectors because it can cause ECM damage, poor engine performance, and/or premature connector wear. Always refer to the engine OEM's service literature to determine the recommended grease to use. Cummins recommends using a DS-ES lubricant, part no. 3822934 on their ECMs. Apply a thin coating of lubricant to the nosepiece of each connector, then spread the lubricant across the nosepiece with your finger making sure that the lubricant penetrates *every* pin cavity of the connector(s). Always reapply dielectric grease when reconnecting any electrical connection. This also applies to the various engine and vehicle sensor connections.

TABLE 18–4   *Cummins Signature/ISX engine models electrical specifications*

ELECTRICAL SPECIFICATIONS
Signature/ISX Engines

DATALINK

Positive wire to chassis ground (J1587 only)
- 4.0 to 5.0 VDC

Negative wire to chassis ground (J1587 only)
- 0.0 to 2.5 VDC

J1939 BACKBONE RESISTANCE

Positive wire to return wire
- 50 to 70 Ω

J1939 Termination Resistance
- 110 to 130 Ω

ALL CONTINUITY CHECKS
- OK (no open circuit) if < 10 Ω

ALL SHORTS TO GROUND

All other circuits
- OK (no short circuit) if > 10 MΩ

SHORT CIRCUIT TO EXTERNAL VOLTAGE
- OK if < 1.5 VDC

5 V POWER SUPPLY

@ ECM
- 4.75 to 5.25 VDC

ECM CONNECTOR

Retaining Cap Screw Torque = 3 N · m [25 in-lb]

SOLENOIDS

Fuel Shutoff Valve and Wastegate Controller Actuator Solenoids
- Coil Resistance = 7 to 8 Ω

Fueling Actuator Temperature
- Resistance =

0.54 to 1.07 Ω = −17°C (0°F) to 54°C (130°F)
0.67 to 1.20 Ω = 38°C (100°F) to 93°C (200°F).

Timing Actuator Temperature
- Resistance =

0.87 to 1.73 Ω = −17°C (0°F) to 54°C (130°F)
1.10 to 1.97 Ω = 38°C (100°F) to 93°C (200°F).

Engine Brake Solenoids
- Resistance = 9.5 to 11 Ω (cold) 11.5 to 14.5 Ω (hot).

Air Compressor Solenoids
- Resistance = 11.0 to 20.0 Ω.

SENSOR SPECIFICATIONS

OIL PRESSURE SENSOR

Torque (Threaded style) = 14 N · m [10 ft-lb]

Pressure (kPa)	Pressure [psia]	Voltage (VDC)
0	0	0.70 to 1.20
172.37	25	2.10 to 2.70
344.74	50	3.50 to 4.20
414.11	60	4.00 to 4.70

INTAKE MANIFOLD PRESSURE SENSOR

Torque (Threaded style) = 14 N · m [10 ft-lb]

Pressure (mmHg)	Pressure [inHg]	Pressure (psig)	Voltage (VDC)
0	0	0	0.75 to 1.20
646.48	25.45	12.5	1.60 to 2.10
1292.88	50.90	25	2.40 to 3.00
1939.36	76.35	37.5	3.25 to 3.85
2585.76	101.80	50	4.10 to 4.70

AMBIENT AIR PRESSURE SENSOR

Torque (Threaded style) = 14 N · m [10 ft-lb]

Altitude (m)	Altitude [ft]	Pressure (psia)	Voltage (VDC)
0 (sea level)	0	14.7	3.40 to 4.50
915	3000	13.2	2.80 to 3.80
1830	6000	11.8	2.20 to 3.25
2744	9000	10.5	1.70 to 2.70
3659	12000	9.35	1.20 to 2.20

RAIL PRESSURE SENSORS, FRONT AND REAR

Torque = 14 N · m [10 ft-lb]

Pressure (kPa)	Pressure [psig]	Voltage (VDC)
0	0	0.50 to 0.70
345	50	1.20 to 1.50
690	100	1.95 to 2.30
1380	200	3.40 to 3.80
2070	300	4.20 to 4.70

FUEL PRESSURE SENSOR

Torque = 14 N · m [10 ft-lb]

Pressure (kPa)	Pressure [psig]	Voltage (VDC)
0	0	0.60 to 0.75
345	50	1.20 to 1.50
690	100	1.90 to 2.15
1380	200	3.15 to 3.50
1970	285	4.20 to 4.70

FUEL INLET RESTRICTION SENSOR

Torque (Threaded style) = 14 N · m [10 ft-lb]

Pressure (inttg)	Pressure [psia]	Voltage (VDC)
21.8	4	0.34 to 0.66
17.7	6	1.00 to 1.33
13.7	8	1.67 to 2.00
9.6	10	2.34 to 2.66
5.5	12	3.00 to 3.33

TABLE 18-4 (continued).

AMBIENT AIR TEMPERATURE SENSORS

Temperature	Temperature	Resistance
(°C)	(°F)	(Ω)
0	32	29k to 36k
25	77	9k to 11k
50	122	3k to 4k
75	167	1300 to 1600
100	212	600 to 750

ALL TEMPERATURE SENSORS

Torque (Threaded style) = 14 N · m [10 ft-lb]

Temperature	Temperature	Resistance
(°C)	(°F)	(Ω)
0	32	30k to 36k
25	77	9k to 11k
50	122	3k to 4k
75	167	1350 to 1500
100	212	600 to 675

VEHICLE SPEED SENSOR

Torque = 47 N · m [35 ft-lb]
First Coil Resistance = 750 to 1100 Ω
Second Coil Resistance = 11090 to 1500 Ω

ENGINE POSITION SENSORS (CRANKSHAFT & CAMSHAFT)

Torque = 25 N · m [18 ft-lb]
On Metal = 3.5 to 5 VDC
Off Metal = 0.0 to 2.2 VDC

ACCELERATOR PEDAL (IVS, ISS, & APS)

Idle Validation Circuit Resistance:
For ON and OFF-IDLE states
IVS - MAX Closed Circuit Resistance < 10 Ω
ISS - MAX Closed Circuit Resistance < 125 Ω

IVS, ISS - MIN Open Circuit Resistance > 100 kΩ

Accelerator Position Sensor coil Resistance:
Between supply and return wires
  • 2000 to 3000 ohms
Between supply and signal wires (released pedal)
  • 1500 to 3000 ohms
Between supply and signal wires (depressed pedal)
  • 200 to 1500 ohms

NOTE: Released resistance minus depressed resistance **must** be 1000 ohms.

(Courtesy of Cummins Engine Company, Inc.)

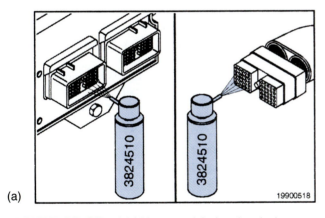

(a)

(b)

FIGURE 18-33 (a) Using a quick-dry electrical contact cleaner spray to remove moisture/condensation from the ECM harness plugs. (b) Apply a thin coating of dielectric grease to the nosepiece of each connector, then spread the lubricant until it penetrates every pin cavity of the connector. (Courtesy of Cummins Engine Company, Inc.)

SUMMARY

The informational data in this chapter will provide you with a sound working knowledge that you can transfer to the more detailed chapters contained within this book dealing with Caterpillar, Cummins, Detroit Diesel, Mack, and Bosch electronic fuel injection systems.

SELF-TEST QUESTIONS

1. Technician A says that the first major engine OEM to release electronic controls on their diesel engines was Caterpillar in 1987. Technician B says that Detroit Diesel was the first OEM to employ electronically controlled unit injectors in their two-stroke-cycle on-highway truck 92 series engines in September 1985. Which technician knows their electronics background best?

2. Technician A says that Caterpillar's first venture into electronic engine controls was with the introduction of the PEEC system on their 3406B truck engine. Technician B says that this occurred in 1985. Who is right?

3. Technician A says that EUIs (electronic unit injectors) are now being used by Detroit Diesel, Caterpillar, Cummins, Volvo, John Deere, and Mack. Technician B agrees, with the exception of Mack, which uses a Bosch electronic PLN system, while later engines use a EUP (electronic unit pump). Who is right?

4. Technician A says that the HEUI (hydraulically actuated EUI) fuel system is now in use by International and Caterpillar on selected engine models (3126, 3408E, and 3412E). Technician B says that only Caterpillar uses the HEUI system. Who is correct?

5. Technician A says that users of Bosch EUP fuel systems include Mercedes-Benz/Detroit Diesel series 55 engines offered in the Freightliner Century Class heavy-duty trucks. Technician B agrees, but also says that Mack uses EUPs on their later-model E7 engines. Are both technicians right in their statements?

6. True or False: The term *Celect* refers to "Cummins electronics."

7. True or False: The term *DDEC* refers to "Detroit Diesel electronic controls."

8. True or False: The term *Vectro* refers to "Volvo electronics."

9. True or False: The term *VMAC* refers to "Vehicle management and control" and is a Mack-designed system.

10. Technician A says that most engine sensors receive an input signal from the ECM rated at 5 V. Technician B agrees but states that some engine OEMs also use 8 V, and in some cases, 12 V sensor supply voltages. Are both technicians correct?

11. Identify the names of the components to match the following letters with respect to engine vehicle sensors:

    a. EFPA
    b. TRS
    c. SRS
    d. TBS
    e. ATS
    f. FPS
    g. FTS
    h. OPS
    i. OTS
    j. CTS
    k. CLS
    l. ACLS
    m. CPS
    n. CPS
    o. ITS
    p. IAS
    q. EBC
    r. PGS
    s. SLS
    t. VSG
    u. CEL
    v. SEL
    w. EPS
    x. VDL
    y. PWM
    z. EEPROM
    aa. DDR
    bb. RAM
    cc. CPU

12. Technician A says that some sensors operate on an analog signal, while others operate on a digital signal; however, analog signals must be converted to digital through a signal processor for the ECM to function. Technician B says that an engine and vehicle sensors operate as digital output signal processors. Which technician knows the theory best?

13. Technician A says that an analog signal varies in intensity over time, while a digital signal is either ON or OFF. Technician B says that digital signals vary in intensity over time. Who is right?

14. With the exception of a speed sensor signal or MPU (magnetic pickup unit), or TPS, Technician A says that sensors are designed to vary their voltage output based upon either a changing pressure or temperature signal. Technician B says that all sensors operate on temperature changes only. Who is correct?

15. True or False: Sensor output values depend on a changing resistance power over time, generally ranging from 0.5 V to 4.5 V on 5 V types.

16. True or False: An A/D convertor is an analog/digital converter.

17. When the TPS within the EFPA is at a closed throttle (idle) position, the voltage signal return to the ECM is at its maximum value according to technician A. Technician B disagrees, saying that at a closed throttle, the voltage return signal to the ECM is at its minimum value. Who is right?

18. Technician A says that an oil pressure sensor is usually monitored for a changing value once per second. Technician B says that the OPS is monitored 10 times per second. Who is right?

19. True or False: A voltage rheostat and/or a potentiometer are basically used to control the voltage output of the TPS between idle and maximum position.

20. True or False: The percentage of throttle pedal depression, and therefore the fueling demand by the operator, is sensed by a changing output voltage to the ECM as the pedal is depressed.

21. Technician A says that EUIs still require mechanical actuation by a rocker arm assembly to raise the fuel pressure to a high-enough level to open the spray tip needle valve. Technician B disagrees, saying that an electronic signal to a solenoid does this job. Which technician knows the system operation best?

22. Technician A says that the PWM signal to the injector solenoid is used to close a small poppet valve to initiate the beginning of injection. Technician B says that a rocker arm determines the start of injection. Who is correct?

23. True or False: The quantity of fuel injected is determined by the duty-cycle time of the signal sent from the ECM to the injector solenoid.

24. Technician A says that EUIs still require a plunger helix to allow variation of the start and end of injection. Technician B says that no plunger helix is necessary in an EUI. Who is right?

25. True or False: A DDR can be used to access the ECM, withdraw stored trouble codes, and reprogram certain ECM parameters.

26. Engine and vehicle computers operate on a binary system of measurement according to technician A. Technician B says that a base 10 system is used. Who is correct?

27. True or False: A *bit* is one unit of data or information.

28. True or False: A *byte* combines a series of bits into word lengths.

29. True or False: Within the CPU, a series of logic gates are used to add, multiply, subtract, divide, and compute the various sensor input signals to control engine and vehicle operation.

30. True or False: The RAM within the ECM is actually a working scratch pad when the engine is operating, to allow the ECM to be informed of changing sensor conditions which it can compare to preprogrammed operating parameters.

31. Technician A says that EUIs can create voltage signals between 90 and 105 V when the engine is running. Technician B says that the EUI voltage cannot exceed system voltage, being either 12 or 24 V. Who is correct?

32. True or False: Diagnostic access to stored ECM trouble or flash codes can only be extracted using a laptop computer.

33. Technician A says that each major engine OEM offers diagnostic programs based upon Windows for ease of troubleshooting. Technician B says that only a DDR can be used for troubleshooting. Which technician is correct?

34. True or False: Regardless of the different flash codes used by engine OEMs, SAE standardized code message descriptions are now in wide use.

35. Technician A says that the three standardized SAE trouble codes now in use for electronic systems include
    a. PID, FID, SMI
    b. PID, SID, FMI
    c. PID, FID, FMI

36. From your answer in question 35, describe what each of the three SAE code letters mean.

37. Technician A says that the two most common numbers appearing after an FMI code are 3 and 4. Technician B disagrees and says that numbers 1 and 7 are more commonly flashed. Who is correct?

38. Technician A says that an FMI 3 indicates that voltage is above normal or shorted high. Technician B says that it means that voltage is below normal or shorted low for that circuit. Who is correct?

39. Technician A says that an "active" code is an out-of-range sensor/wiring condition that is currently affecting the engine operation. Technician B says that only "historic" (inactive) codes will affect engine performance. Which technician is right?

40. Technician A says that when a fault code is detected by the ECM, the yellow dash warning light will be illuminated and the engine may lose power based on the severity of the out-of-range condition detected. Technician B says that when any fault is detected, the red dash light will always illuminate. Who is right?

41. Technician A says that if the system has been programmed for automatic engine shutdown, once the red light illuminates, the engine will start to depower, and normally 30 seconds later, it will shut down. Technician B says that you can program the ECM to vary the shutdown time between 3 and 100 minutes. Which technician is correct?

42. Technician A says that to activate the idle shutdown on a heavy-duty truck, the spring parking brakes must be applied in order to permit the idle timer to start its count. Technician B says that the idle timer will function at any time regardless of whether the spring brakes are on or off. Who is right?

43. Technician A says that an operator can continue to drive a truck with the yellow warning light illuminated but may do so at reduced speed and power from ECM control. Technician B says that the vehicle should be pulled over as soon as possible, the engine shut off, and checked. Who is correct?

44. Technician A says that system trouble codes logged in ECM memory of current electronic systems can be erased by temporarily disconnecting the battery. Technician B says that codes can only be erased through connecting up the DDR. Which technician is right?

19

Robert Bosch Corporation Fuel Systems

Overview

In this chapter we introduce the wide product diversification of diesel fuel injection equipment manufactured by Robert Bosch Corporation. Bosch produces both mechanical and electronic fuel systems and provides approximately 60% of the fuel injection systems to the global diesel engine market OEMs. A major manufacturer of pump-line-nozzle (PLN) systems with electronic diesel controls (EDCs), radial distributor pumps with EDC, electronic unit pumps (EUPs), electronic unit injectors (EUIs), common-rail fuel systems (CRFS), mechanical and electronic injectors/nozzles, their product offerings are employed by many of the major diesel engine OEMs.

Data and information herein describes both mechanical and electronic fuel systems (transfer pumps, injection pumps, nozzles, and governors). We also describe pump-to-engine timing, servicing/adjustment of pumps on a test stand, diagnosis, troubleshooting, and repair/replacement of various fuel system components.

End-of-chapter questions will permit you to review the knowledge gained, and in conjunction with performance of the ASE hands-on tasks, you should be prepared to challenge either the ASE or TQ tests.

ASE CERTIFICATION

Information in this chapter will permit you to focus upon the appropriate ASE test areas dealing with these types of fuel systems. If you refer to the ASE medium/heavy truck tests preparation guide, test T2, diesel engines, the following content areas deal with required knowledge for material described within this chapter.

A. General Engine Diagnosis (15 questions for 21% of the T2 test)

Skills areas related to the fuel system, and that you need to acquire, are listed by ASE number.

1. Verify the complaint, and road/dyno test vehicle; review driver/customer interview and past maintenance records/documents; determine further diagnosis.

2. Inspect the engine and compartment for signs of liquid leaks—oil, coolant, fuel—and determine needed repairs.

3. Inspect engine compartment wiring harness, connectors, seals, and locks; determine needed repairs.

4. Listen and determine engine noises that might be due to the fuel system: pump, nozzles, governor, misfire, air-in-the-fuel system, and so on.

5. Check engine exhaust smoke color/odor/density; determine necessary repairs.

6. Perform fuel system test/diagnosis, fuel contamination, consumption, and so on.

12. Diagnose engine surging, rough operation, air-in-the-fuel system, misfire, low power, slow acceleration/deceleration, and so on.

16. Check, record, and clear electronic diagnostic codes; monitor electronic data; determine needed repairs.

Skills areas related to Part F, Fuel System Diagnosis and Repair, are listed by ASE number as follows:

F. Fuel System Diagnosis and Repair (20 questions for 29% of the T2 test)

1. Mechanical Components (9 questions)

1. Inspect, repair/replace fuel tanks, vents, cap(s), mounts, valves, screens, crossover system, supply and return lines and fittings.

2. Inspect, clean, test, repair/replace fuel transfer (lift) pump, pump drives, screens, fuel/water separators/indicators, filters, heaters, coolers, ECM cooling plates, and mounting hardware.

3. Check fuel system for air; determine needed repairs; prime and bleed fuel system; check, repair/replace primer pump.

4. Inspect, test, repair/replace low pressure regulator systems (check valves, pressure regulator valves and restrictive fittings).

5. Inspect, adjust, repair/replace throttle and linkage/cable and controls.

6. Perform on-engine inspections, tests, adjustments, and time, or replace and time, distributor-type injection pumps.

7. Perform on-engine inspections, tests, adjustments and time, or replace and time, in-line type injection pumps, governors, and drives.

8. Perform on-engine inspections, tests, and adjustments, or replace PT-type injection pumps, drives, and injectors.

9. Perform on-engine inspections, tests, and adjustments, or replace mechanical unit injectors.

10. Inspect, test, repair/replace fuel injection nozzles.

11. Inspect, adjust, repair/replace smoke limiters (air/fuel ratio controls).

12. Inspect, reinstall/replace high pressure injection lines, fittings, and seals.

13. Inspect, test, adjust, repair/replace engine fuel shut-down devices and controls, including engine protection shut-down devices, circuits and sensors.

2. **Electronic Components (11 questions)**

1. Check and record engine electronic diagnostic codes and trip/operational data; clear codes; determine needed repairs.

2. Inspect, adjust, repair/replace electronic throttle and PTO control devices, circuits, and sensors.

3. Perform on-engine inspections, tests, and adjustments on distributor-type injection pump electronic controls.

4. Perform on-engine inspections, tests, and adjustments on in-line type injection pump electronic controls.

5. Perform on-engine inspections, tests, and adjustments on PT-type injection pump electronic controls.

6. Perform on-engine inspections, tests, and adjustments on hydraulic electronic unit injectors (HEUI) and electronic controls (rail pressure control).

7. Perform on-engine inspections, tests, and adjustments on electronic unit injectors (EUI) and electronic controls.

8. Perform on-engine inspections, tests, and adjustments on pump line nozzle electronic systems (PLN-E) and electronic controls.

9. Inspect, test, adjust, repair/replace engine electronic fuel shut-down devices, circuits, and sensors, including engine protection systems.

10. Inspect and test power, ignition, and ground circuits and connections for electrical/electronic components; determine needed repairs.

11. Inspect and replace electrical connector terminals, pins, harnesses, seals, and locks.

12. Connect diagnostic tool to vehicle/engine; access and change customer parameters; determine needed repairs.

COMPANY BACKGROUND

The name of Robert Bosch has been synonymous with fuel injection systems, both gasoline and diesel, for many, many years. After Robert Bosch had finished his apprenticeship with Thomas Edison in the United States, he opened his own precision mechanics shop in 1886. In 1892, Rudolph Diesel invented the diesel engine, but due to its size and weight, it was used mainly in stationary and marine applications. Not until Robert Bosch successfully designed and began mass producing diesel fuel injection systems in 1927 did use of this popular powerplant actually start to spread into all areas of the globe and into over 4200 different applications.

Today, the Robert Bosch Corporation is the largest manufacturer of fuel injection systems (both gasoline and diesel), with representatives in over 130 countries. Over 50% of all diesel fuel injection equipment sold in the free world is manufactured by Robert Bosch and its licensees. The original American Bosch Company, now part of Ambac International, was initially the American affiliate of Robert Bosch Corporation. Many companies worldwide now manufacture Bosch fuel injection equipment and products under a licensing agreement. Two examples are Zexel (Diesel Kiki) and Nippondenso in Japan, both of which supply fuel injection equipment to a wide range of OEMs. However, there is no longer any connection between Ambac and Bosch.

OVERVIEW

Robert Bosch Corporation is a leader worldwide in the manufacture of gasoline and diesel fuel injection systems. This chapter discusses the company's background and the vital role that Robert Bosch played in the success of the high-speed diesel engine that we use today. Details are provided on the main types of Bosch injection pumps used by major engine OEMs, along with the function, operation, testing, inspection, adjustment, service, and troubleshooting requirements. After reading this chapter you will be able to identify a

number of Bosch fuel injection products, and describe how each fuel injection pump operates, as well as how to adjust, service, and maintain it.

Bosch went to court in the United States and won a decision preventing any other company from using the name. There are many major diesel engine manufacturers worldwide who use Bosch fuel injection equipment and governor assemblies. Other injection pump manufacturers, such as Lucas CAV, now Delphi, were also licensees of Bosch but no longer have any tie-in with them. However, the CAV inline pumps do operate on the same basic concept as those produced by Bosch, as do the pumps manufactured by Ambac International. The name "Robert Bosch" is synonymous with success in diesel fuel injection equipment.

With the wide variety of inline pumps available from Bosch, almost every major engine manufacturer

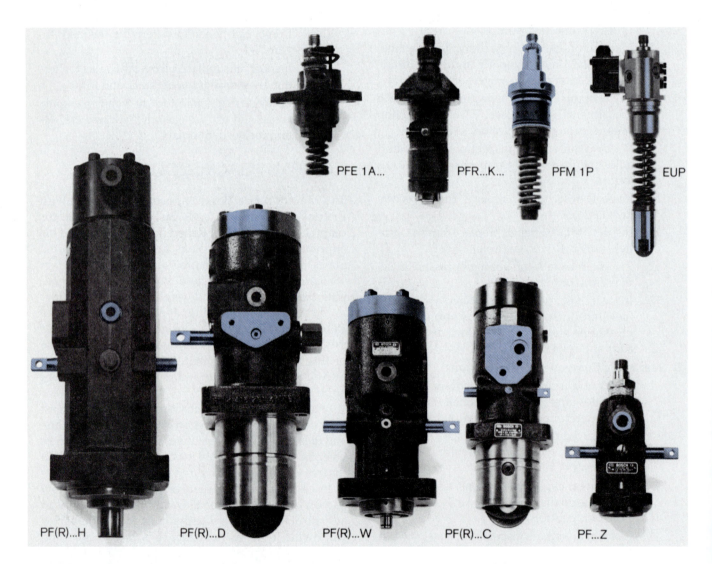

PFE 1A...   PFR...K...   PFM 1P   EUP

PF(R)...H   PF(R)...D   PF(R)...W   PF(R)...C   PF...Z

FIGURE 19–1 *Various models of individual jerk pumps, model PF (pump camshaft foreign) injection pumps.* (Courtesy of Robert Bosch Corporation.)

in existence that uses four-stroke-cycle engines in their product line, employ a Robert Bosch injection pump/governor. Well-known manufacturers such as Mack, Saab-Scania, Volvo, DAF, Hino, Isuzu, UD (Nissan), Mitsubishi Fuso, Navistar International, Ford, MAN, Mercedes-Benz, and Cummins are just some of the more prominent makes that use these Bosch fuel injection systems. Today, Bosch owns 49% of the Diesel Equipment Division of Detroit Diesel Corporation, allowing them access to DDC's DDEC technology.

PRODUCT OVERVIEW

Robert Bosch Corporation manufactures single-cylinder pumps, multiple-plunger inline and V-configuration pumps, and distributor pumps, nozzles, and mechanical governors for diesel engines, as well as electronic diesel control systems.

PF Jerk Pumps

Figure 19–1 illustrates a series of different-size single-cylinder PF jerk pumps. Some pumps are designed for use on small and medium-size engines, while other pumps are designed for use with large-bore slow-speed, high-horsepower engines. These types of single-cylinder jerk pumps are mounted and timed to the engine. Some pumps employ a flat tappet at their base and are driven from a camshaft drive in the engine. Figure 19–2 illustrates a cross-sectional view of a small PFE 1Q pump, and Figure 19–3 shows a view of a larger PF 1D model.

Since the camshaft is foreign to these pumps, being contained within the engine, they are designated as

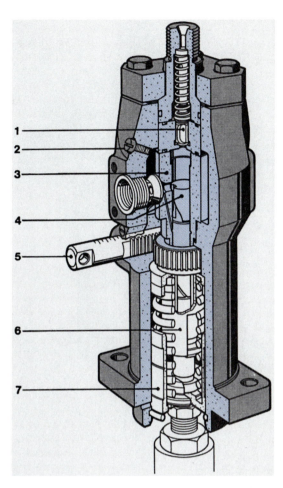

FIGURE 19–3 Section through a model PF 1D pump: 1, delivery valve; 2, bleeder screw; 3, pump barrel; 4, pump plunger; 5, control rod; 6, control sleeve; 7, guide bushing. (Courtesy of Robert Bosch Corporation.)

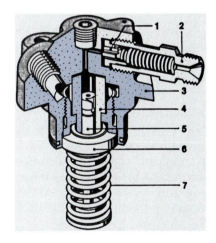

FIGURE 19–2 Section through a type PFE 1Q compact individual jerk pump used on small-bore displacement diesel engines: 1, delivery valve; 2, delivery valve holder; 3, housing; 4, pump barrel; 5, pump plunger; 6, control sleeve to rotate plunger; 7, plunger return spring. (Courtesy of Robert Bosch Corporation.)

PF models (the P stands for "pump" and the F for "foreign"). Some pumps in Figure 19–1 are known as PFR models (pump foreign with a roller tappet). A cross section of a PFR pump is shown in Figure 19–4. Based on the actual pump model, typically these pumps are capable of peak injection pressures ranging between 500 and 1000 bar (7252 to 14,504 psi).

The physical size of PF pumps can range from very small plunger sizes to suit single-cylinder portable diesel engines, to extremely large plunger diameters to suit very-large-displacement slow-speed diesel engines up to 60,000 hp (44,760 kW) in output.

The PF pumps can have their tappet adjusting screw adjusted to set the lift to port closure (LTPC) dimension, while the PFR models can use either over-sized rollers or shims placed below their mounting flange to set the correct LTPC specification. Later in the chapter we discuss timing of PF and PFR pumps to the engine, as well as how to set/adjust the individual fuel

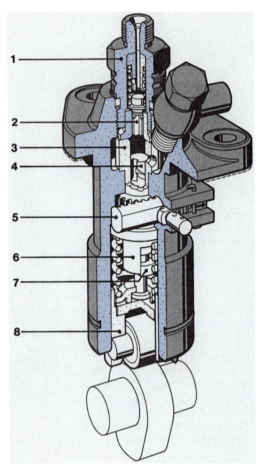

FIGURE 19–4 *Section through a type PFR (roller tappet) 1K single-cylinder injection pump: 1, delivery valve holder; 2, delivery valve; 3, pump barrel; 4, pump plunger; 5, fuel control rod (rack); 6, rack control sleeve; 7, plunger control arm; 8, roller tappet. (Courtesy of Robert Bosch Corporation.)*

rod/rack linkage. Each pump functions to pressurize, meter, time, and atomize the fuel delivered to the injection nozzle.

When the engine camshaft drive lifts the flat tappet or roller (8) in Figure 19–4, the plunger (4) moves up in its mated barrel to close off the inlet fuel port. Trapped fuel above the plunger is then placed under increasing pressure as the plunger continues to move up. When the fuel pressure reaches approximately 100 to 150 psi (690 to 1034 kPa), the delivery valve (2) is opened against its return spring to allow fuel to exit the delivery valve holder (1), which is connected to the steel tubing leading to the injection nozzle. When the fuel pressure is raised to a high-enough level, the nozzle needle valve is lifted against the return force of its spring to permit high-pressure fuel to flow through the small orifices (holes) in the spray tip and into the com-

bustion chamber. When the upward-moving plunger uncovers the spill port in the barrel, fuel pressure is released, and the nozzle return spring quickly closes the needle valve, ending injection. As the fuel in the nozzle line decreases, the delivery valve (2) is pushed back into the bore of the delivery valve holder. This action allows a volume of fuel equal to the retraction volume under the delivery valve to escape out of the fuel delivery line from the nozzle. Consequently, this lowers the fuel pressure in the delivery line to the nozzle, yet allows a residual pressure to be retained in the line (lower than the nozzle opening pressure) so that during the next injection cycle, the fuel within the line does not have to be repressurized from the very low transfer pump pressure level.

Inline Injection Pumps

When the individual pumps are contained in a single housing with their high-pressure fuel outlets arranged in a straight line, the assembly is referred to as a PLN (pump-line-nozzle) system. Bosch and other pump OEMs call these pumps PE models (the P for "pump" and the E for "enclosed camshaft"), since they are mounted lengthwise within the base of the pump housing and driven from the engine gear train. As shown in Figure 19–5, these pumps can be mounted in one of three ways: base, cradle, or flange. The type of mounting is determined by looking at the drive end of the pump. When an inline pump is flange mounted, a third letter, S, is added to the designation, with the pump designated as a PES unit.

Inline pumps are referred to by their physical size, which relates to pumping plunger diameter, how much fuel they can deliver (quantity), and the pressure they can deliver to the nozzle. These pump sizes are M, A, MW, and P. Therefore, PES-A, PES-M, PES-MW, and PES-P indicate pumps with an enclosed camshaft of the size represented by the letter. Pump size examples are included in Figure 19–6.

Pump Designation

Identification of inline pumps can be done visually once you are familiar with the basic differences in design and component layout. Specific information can, however, be obtained from the pump nameplate, riveted to the housing as shown in Figure 19–6. In this example, the pump is listed as PE6P100A320LS825, which can be interpreted as follows:

PE: pump with an enclosed camshaft

  6: number of pumping plungers (six-cylinder engine application)

  P: pump size

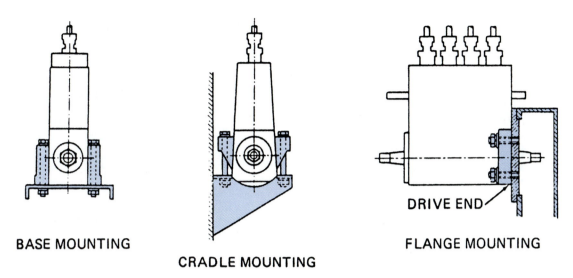

BASE MOUNTING

CRADLE MOUNTING

FLANGE MOUNTING

DRIVE END

FIGURE 19–5 *Examples of the common three types of mounting designs for inline PLN (pump-line-nozzle) injection pumps. (Courtesy of Robert Bosch Corporation.)*

Pump size	
M	= 7 mm plunger stroke
A	= 8 mm
MW	= 8 mm, 10 mmm
P	= 10 mm, 11 mm, 12 mm
Z	= 12 mm
C	= 15 mm
· · M	Multi-fuel operation
· · W	Heavy-duty version
· · WM	Heavy-duty version for multi-fuel operation

FIGURE 19–6 *Example of an inline PLN injection pump identification plate location on the pump housing. (Courtesy of Robert Bosch Corporation.)*

100: pump plunger diameter (multiply times 1/10 mm = 10 mm)

A: execution/original; A, first change; B, second change; C, third change

320: construction information

L: direction of pump rotation L, left-hand or counterclockwise; R, right-hand or clockwise

S825: application information

In this example the pump can be either base mounted onto a support on the engine or can be bolted to a cradle on the engine. In a PES designation, the S indicates that the pump is flange mounted.

PUMP FEATURES

The following material describes the basic function and operation of the models M, A, MW, and P multiple-plunger inline pumps, which all operate on the same basic fundamental principle—that of a jerk pump.

The following four inline Bosch pumps are commonly used:

1.   The M pump, the smallest inline pump that Bosch manufactures, which is designed for use on small passenger car and light-duty engines. We do not deal in detail with this pump in this book.

2.   The A model pump which was the original design concept created by Robert Bosch in 1923. This pump has undergone many product improvement changes and is still widely used on midrange to mid-heavy-duty high-speed diesel engines. This pump is limited to engines with an approximate cylinder horsepower not exceeding 36 hp (27kW).

3.   The MW model pump, which operates on the same basic principle as the A unit; however, the MW employs an integrated flange element at the top of each pumping plunger. The MW pump can handle engines up to approximately 48 hp (36 kW) per cylinder.

4.   The P model pump, which is the largest pump offered for use on high-speed heavy-duty truck engines, with a capability of handling up to approximately 98 hp (73 kW) per cylinder. This pump also employs an integrated barrel flange element similar to that for the MW model. The P pump is used extensively on diesel engines manufactured by such companies as Mack, DAF, MAN, Mercedes-Benz, Volvo, Ford, Scania, Hino, Isuzu, Mitsubishi, and Navistar International for use in their heavy-duty truck engines.

A-Size Pump

The A-size pump is illustrated in Figure 19–7 with its special features and major components shown. Still in wide use on a number of truck diesel engines, this pump is found on lighter-duty and mid- to midheavy-duty applications. An inspection plate on the side of the A pump housing can be removed to gain access to the individual pumping plunger and barrel elements when adjustments are required. Adjustments on the A model injection pump can best be established by referring to Figure 19–7 and reading the following description.

Adjusting the Pump

1.   Individual pump plunger prestroke (lift to port closure) is set on the A pump by loosening off a tappet locking screw immediately above item 7 and rotating the hex nut. A depth micrometer or dial gauge can be used on the top of the pumping plunger to determine that all pump plungers have the same lift and clearance at the top of their stroke.

2.   Fuel delivery for each pumping plunger is established by loosening a toothed clamp ring which is engaged with the fuel control rod (4) or rack. The

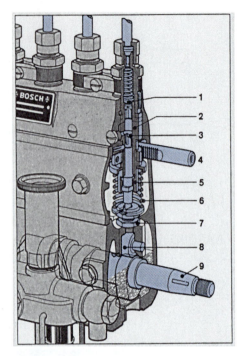

FIGURE 19–7   *Bosch model A injection pump assembly: 1, delivery valve; 2, pump barrel; 3, pump plunger; 4, control rod/rack; 5, control sleeve; 6, plunger return spring; 7, tappet adjusting nut; 8, roller tappet; 9, camshaft. (Courtesy of Robert Bosch Corporation.)*

clamping ring is assembled around the outside diameter of the control sleeve (5). By loosening the lock screw and moving this clamp ring and retightening its screw, its position in relation to the fuel rod/rack and the control sleeve (5) shown in Figure 19–7 can be changed. When the injector rod/rack (4) in Figure 19–7 is moved back and forward, the teeth on the rack, which are in mesh with the clamping ring, will also cause the control sleeve to rotate. At the base of the control sleeve (about halfway between 5 and 6) in Figure 19–7, you will notice that there is a projection on the pumping plunger which engages with slots on the control sleeve. Movement of the control sleeve (5) in Figure 19–7 will cause the plunger to be rotated and its "effective stroke" will be determined so that the amount of fuel delivered for a given rack setting can be adjusted to the manufacturer's specifications. The maximum amount of fuel is therefore adjusted by changing the setting of the individual clamping rings at each pump plunger. These adjustments for fuel delivery should be done only when the injection pump is on a test stand.

Both the M- and A-size pumps are pressure lubricated from the engine. The A-size pump contains a separate governor-housing that is bolted to the end of the injection pump housing.

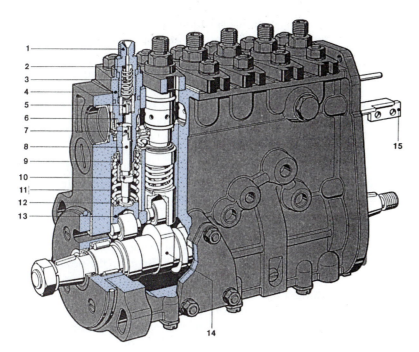

FIGURE 19–8 *Bosch model PES (pump enclosed camshaft, and flange mounted to the engine): 1, delivery valve holder; 2, filler piece; 3, delivery valve spring; 4, pump barrel; 5, delivery valve; 6, inlet and spill port; 7, plunger helix; 8, pump plunger; 9, rack control sleeve; 10, plunger control arm; 11, plunger return spring; 12, spring seat; 13, roller tappet; 14, camshaft; 15, control rod/rack. (Courtesy of Robert Bosch Corporation.)*

MW-Size Pump

The MW injection pump differs considerably from that of the M and A shown so far; however, the MW is very similar in design to the larger inline pump, the P-size unit. The MW pump was designed for higher injection pressures than the M and A units and is found on many automotive high-performance/high-output turbocharged engines produced by such manufacturers as Mercedes-Benz in its 300D and SD passenger cars, as well as by Volvo truck and marine engines, Navistar International, Mack Trucks, and Perkins diesel engines. Figures 19–8 and 19–9 illustrate the external and internal features of the MW model pump.

The MW pump uses a bolted flange/bushing installed into the top of the injection pump housing and does not have an access plate on the side of the pump housing that can be removed for individual pump adjustment as is the case with both the M and A pumps shown earlier. The bolted flange on top of the MW pump is slotted so that when loosened, the barrel and valve assembly can be rotated to ensure equal fuel delivery from each individual plunger and barrel assembly. In addition, each pump plunger prestroke can be set by the use of shims of varying thickness which are installed or removed from under each bolted flange on top of the pump housing.

The fuel control rod or rack, connected as shown in Figure 19–9, controls the rotation of each pumping plunger and therefore the start of the effective stroke (port closure) and the quantity of fuel delivered for a

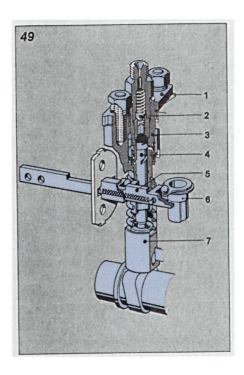

FIGURE 19–9 *Partial section through a MW (heavy-duty version) inline injection pump: 1, bolted retaining flange for the plunger and barrel assembly; 2, delivery valve; 3, pump barrel; 4, pump plunger; 5, control rod/rack; 6, control sleeve; 7, roller tappet. (Courtesy of Robert Bosch Corporation.)*

given throttle/rack setting. The rotation of the individual pump plungers is similar to the M model pump in that it employs a connection known as lever regulation, since the ball ends of the individual control levers engage with slots in the fuel control rod/rack.

Unlike the M and A model injection pumps, the MW model pump barrel (item 4 in Figure 19–8) extends above the top of the injection pump housing and is held in place by two retaining nuts and washers. The delivery valve and its holder (1) are screwed into the pump barrel (4) to form a compact, easy-to-service assembly. The pump is pressure lubricated from the engine's oil system. The MW pump has a separate governor assembly bolted onto the end of the injection pump housing.

P-Size Pump

The P-size injection pump, although not physically the largest unit manufactured by Robert Bosch, is the biggest pump that is used on high-speed heavy-duty type truck and industrial engine applications. Figure 19–10 illustrates the model P injection pump in a cutaway view so that you can familiarize yourself with its features. Note that it contains a sheet-metal protection cover held in place by screws, mounted on top of the pump to keep dirt and debris away from the barrel flanges. It is this cover that will allow you to quickly identify the model P injection pump from other Bosch models. The model P pump uses a separate governor housing, bolted onto the end of the pump housing.

The P pump is similar in construction to the MW model pump illustrated in Figure 19–8, in that both pumps employ shims underneath the barrel flanges to adjust the individual plunger lift to port closure, which is commonly known as *prestroke* on Bosch pumps. Prestroke is when the upward-moving pump plunger moves from BDC to the point where it covers the inlet ports in the barrel. The start of fuel injection would begin shortly thereafter once the trapped fuel reaches a high enough pressure to open the delivery valve.

Current model P pumps are capable of very high injection pressures. For example, the P7100 model can produce 1050 bar (15,225 psi) on the pump side and 1250 bar (18,125 psi) on the nozzle side. The uprated P8500 model can produce 1150 bar (16,675 psi) on the pump side and 1350 bar (19,575 psi) on the nozzle side. Both pumps use a 12-mm-diameter plunger with a plunger lift of 12 mm and 14 mm, respectively.

In addition, both the model MW and P pumps use bolted barrel flanges on the top of the pump housing that can be rotated CW or CCW in order to alter the delivery rate of fuel from each pumping element. However, both adjustments should be performed only when the pump is mounted onto a fuel pump test stand where the necessary special tooling and equipment is readily available. Figure 19–11 shows the actual

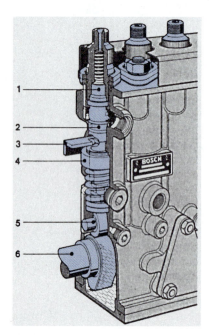

FIGURE 19–10 *Sectional view through a heavy-duty engine model P inline injection pump: 1, delivery valve; 2, pump barrel; 3, control rod/rack; 4, control rack sleeve; 5, roller tappet; 6, camshaft. (Courtesy of Robert Bosch Corporation.)*

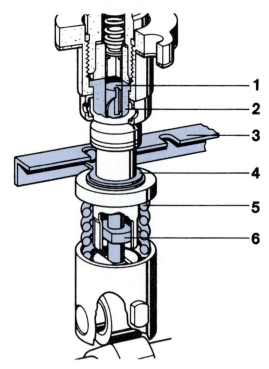

FIGURE 19–11 *Close-up view of the model P injection pump components: 1, plunger; 2, barrel; 3, control rod/rack; 4, rack control sleeve; 5, plunger return spring; 6, plunger control arm. (Courtesy of Robert Bosch Corporation.)*

adjusting mechanism that alters the pumping element fuel delivery through the control rod (rack), which is connected to the throttle pedal through the governor assembly.

INLINE PUMP FUEL SYSTEM

The general fuel system arrangement employed with all inline multiple-plunger pumps can be considered common regardless of the make of engine on which it

is employed. Figure 19–12 illustrates typical fuel injection pump external components, while the flow path of fuel from the tank to the supply pump is shown in Figure 19–13. The supply pump is referred to as a transfer or lift pump by some manufacturers. It is equipped with a small priming plunger that can have the plastic or metal handwheel on the top rotated CCW to loosen it, then by manually pulling/pushing the knob up and down, fuel can be drawn from the fuel tank to prime the filters or the injection pump. Some systems may use

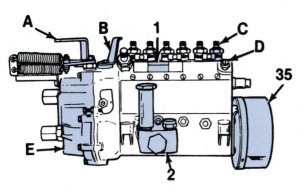

A. Accelerator Lever
B. Fuel Shut Off Lever
C. Number One Cylinder Delivery Valve Holder
D. Pump Bleed Screw
E. Governor
1. Identification Tag
2. Transfer Pump
35. Automatic Timer

FIGURE 19–12 Major external component parts identification of an inline injection pump. (Courtesy of ZEXEL USA Corp.)

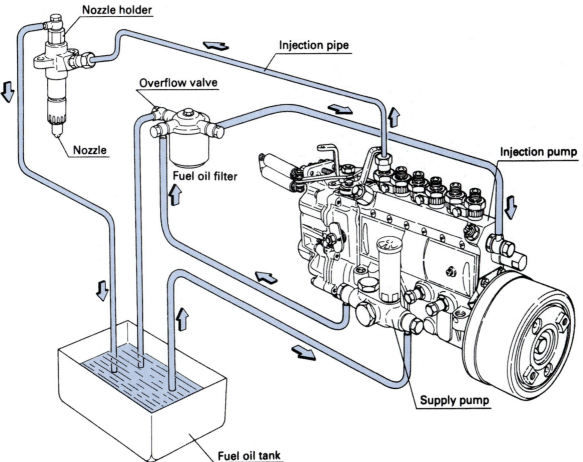

FIGURE 19–13 Typical fuel system schematic for a six-cylinder PLN-inline multiple-plunger injection pump system. (Courtesy of ZEXEL USA Corporation.)

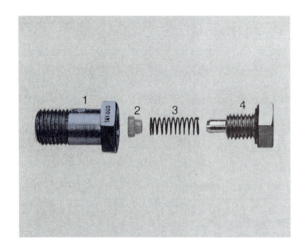

FIGURE 19–14 *Exploded view of an injection pump pressure relief valve: 1, valve body; 2, valve; 3, spring; 4, plug and seal ring. (Courtesy of Robert Bosch Corporation.)*

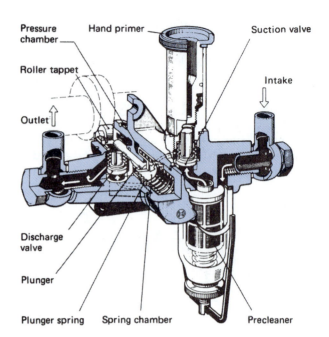

FIGURE 19–15 *FP/K fuel supply/transfer pump. (Courtesy of Robert Bosch Corporation.)*

a primary fuel filter or combination fuel filter/water separator between the fuel tank and the supply pump. The supply pump typically delivers fuel at low pressure, usually in the region 19 to 44 psi (131 to 303 kPa) maximum. This fuel is pushed through the secondary fuel filter, where it passes to the inlet fitting on the injection pump. Many injection pumps employ a spring-loaded pressure relief valve (see Figures 19–13 and 19–14) to maintain a set operating pressure within the pump fuel gallery. When the relief valve opens, fuel is routed back to the fuel tank. In this way warm fuel, used for cooling and lubrication purposes within the injection pump, is continuously recirculated back to the tank. A small spring-loaded overflow valve can also be used, which is shown in Figure 19–13 connected to the secondary fuel filter. Each injection nozzle also has a fuel return line connected to it to route regulated internal fuel leakage, which is also used for lubrication purposes, to return to the tank.

FUEL SUPPLY PUMP OPERATION

To ensure complete filling of the barrel assembly above the pumping plunger, the fuel gallery of the injection pump must be pressurized. A fuel supply pump is used to pump fuel from the fuel tank to the pump gallery (Figure 19–15).

FP/K Series Fuel Supply Pump

This is a single-acting plunger pump usually mounted on the side of the main injection pump and driven off the pump camshaft. The pump can be equipped with a preliminary filter enclosed in a sediment bowl and also

a hand primer as shown in Figure 19–15. The hand primer is used to purge (bleed) air from the system if it has run dry or if the fuel filters have been changed.

Suction/Discharge Stroke of Fuel Supply Pump

On the suction stroke, the roller of the supply pump follows the camshaft inward, because of the force of the plunger spring (Figure 19–16a). As the plunger is moved inward, a low-pressure area is created. Atmospheric pressure then pushes fuel through the preliminary filter, past the suction valve, and into the suction chamber. At the same time, the opposite side of the plunger pushes fuel from the pressure chamber into the outlet line. The pressure in this line, varying from 14 to 28 psi (1 to 2 kg/cm^2), depending on engine application, will close the pressure valve.

Intermediate Stroke Position

As the injection pump camshaft continues to revolve, it forces the roller tappet of the supply pump outward, away from the injection pump, also pushing the plunger out (Figure 19–16b). Fuel trapped in the suction chamber will open the pressure valve and enter the pressure chamber. This fuel will also close the suction valve on the inlet line. This stroke completely fills the pressure chamber so that it can empty on the discharge stroke.

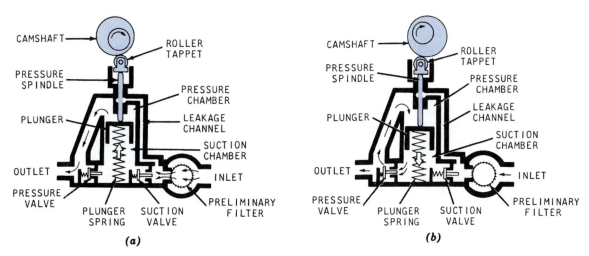

FIGURE 19-16 (a) FP/K transfer pump during the inlet stroke; (b) FP/K transfer pump during the intermediate stroke position. (Courtesy of Robert Bosch Corporation.)

Double-Acting Supply Pump

In the double-acting supply pump shown in Figure 19–17, two additional nonreturn valves make the suction chamber and the pressure chamber of the single-acting supply pump into two combined suction and pressure chambers. The pump does not execute an intermediate stroke. On each stroke of the double-acting supply pump the fuel is drawn into one chamber and simultaneously delivered from the other chamber of the injection pump. Each stroke is, therefore, a delivery and suction stroke. In contrast to the single-acting supply pump, the fuel delivery can never be reduced to zero. For this reason, the delivery line or the fuel filter must be provided with an overflow valve through which the excess fuel can flow back to the fuel tank.

INJECTION PUMP OPERATION

All of the different models of Bosch inline multiple-plunger injection pumps operate on the fundamental principles described in Figure 19–18. This operating principle is commonly known as the *jerk pump* concept, since each pump plunger is moved up and down by the action of a gear-driven pump camshaft. For injection to begin, the pumping plunger must be lifted by the pump camshaft until it closes off the inlet fuel ports of the barrel. This term is commonly known in Bosch pumps as *lift to port closure* and refers to how far the plunger must move or lift to effectively close off both fuel inlet ports within the barrel. Figure 19–18 illustrates the action of the plunger to create an injection cycle for one pumping element. The lift to port closure dimension can be found in the Robert Bosch pump technical specifications for all models and applications.

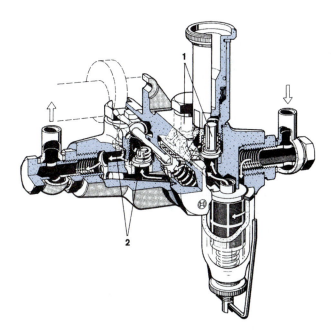

FIGURE 19-17 Double-acting fuel supply pump: 1, nonreturn valve (suction side); 2, nonreturn valve (pressure side). (Courtesy of Robert Bosch Corporation.)

When setting this specification, the injection pump is normally mounted onto a pump test stand, where all of the other checks and tests can be accurately performed.

FUEL METERING (MEASUREMENT)

The key to a good fuel system is the method by which the fuel is controlled. Some common methods are the port and helix, inlet metering, and sleeve control types.

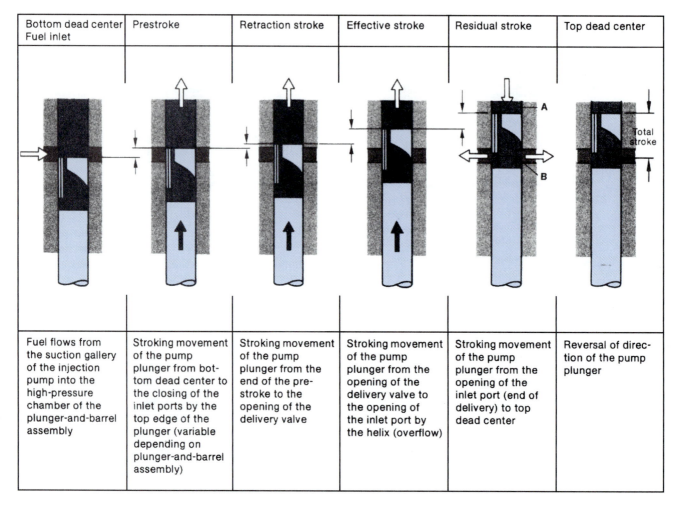

Bottom dead center Fuel inlet	Prestroke	Retraction stroke	Effective stroke	Residual stroke	Top dead center
Fuel flows from the suction gallery of the injection pump into the high-pressure chamber of the plunger-and-barrel assembly	Stroking movement of the pump plunger from bottom dead center to the closing of the inlet ports by the top edge of the plunger (variable depending on plunger-and-barrel assembly)	Stroking movement of the pump plunger from the end of the prestroke to the opening of the delivery valve	Stroking movement of the pump plunger from the opening of the delivery valve to the opening of the inlet port by the helix (overflow)	Stroking movement of the pump plunger from the opening of the inlet port (end of delivery) to top dead center	Reversal of direction of the pump plunger

FIGURE 19–18 Individual pumping phases of the injection pump plunger stroke to deliver fuel under high pressure to the injectors/nozzles. (Courtesy of Robert Bosch Corporation.)

The port and helix (Figure 19–18) is probably one of the most common types of fuel control systems in use today. It is called spill port metering because it controls the amount of fuel pumped by opening a port and by spilling off high-pressure fuel.

Components

The port and helix pumping unit is composed of:

1. Barrel-and-plunger unit fitted or lapped together with a very small clearance between them to allow enough fuel to enter between the mating parts for lubrication.

2. Helix and vertical groove. If the pumping plunger unit did not have a helix or control groove machined on it, the pumping element would pump the same amount of fuel at all times, giving the operator no control over the engine.

Fuel Flow and Operation

1. With the helix and vertical groove, the pump output can be easily varied by turning the pumping plunger in relation to the barrel.

2. As the pumping plunger is forced upward and covers the inlet and outlet ports in the barrel, fuel is trapped above the pumping plunger.

3. The chamber and the vertical groove in the plunger are filled with pressurized fuel.

4. As the pumping plunger moves farther upward, the pressurized fuel opens the delivery valve that is mounted directly above the pumping element (Figure 19–18).

5. Fuel is then delivered to the injection nozzle via the fuel injection line.

6. End of delivery occurs when the helix uncovers an inlet port, allowing high-pressure fuel to rush

down the vertical groove cut in the plunger. This lowers the pressure in the pumping chamber. Delivery to the cylinder stops, since the injection nozzle and delivery valve both close via spring pressure.

Metering Principle

The amount or volume of the fuel charge is regulated by rotating the plunger in the barrel as shown in Figure 19–19 to effectively alter the relationship of the control port and the control helix on the plunger. This is done by means of a rack and a control collar, or control sleeve as shown in Figure 19–20. The *rack* is basically a rod with teeth on one side, which is supported and operates in bores in the housing. The rack is in turn connected to a governor. The geared segment or control collar is clamped to the top of the control sleeve with teeth that engage the rack. The control sleeve is a loose fit over the barrel and is slotted at the bottom to engage the wings on the plunger so that as the rack is moved it will cause rotation of the collar, sleeve, and plunger.

The operation of Robert Bosch inline pumps is basically the same as that for CAV and Ambac inline pumps; however, let us quickly review the pumping plunger's operation and excess fuel device so that we thoroughly understand the principle.

The plunger within the barrel is moved up and down by the action of the rotating camshaft within the injection pump housing; it can also be rotated by the

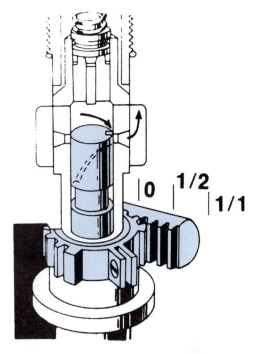

FIGURE 19–20 Rotating the pump plunger by action of the control rack/rod engaged with a gear segment to change the volume of fuel delivered per pump plunger stroke. (Courtesy of Robert Bosch Corporation.)

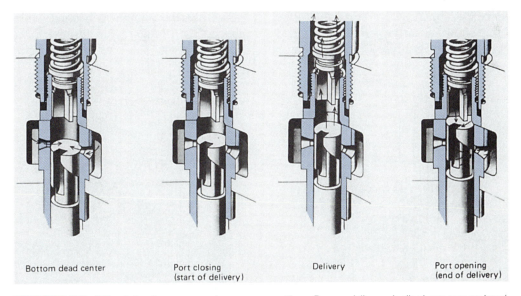

Bottom dead center   Port closing (start of delivery)   Delivery   Port opening (end of delivery)

FIGURE 19–19 Injection pump plunger operation. By providing a helical groove or land machined onto the plunger diameter and arranging to rotate it, the "effective stroke" of the upward-moving plunger can be varied to control the quantity of fuel delivered per stroke. (Courtesy of Robert Bosch Corporation.)

movement of the fuel control rack connected to the throttle and governor linkage. Anytime that the stop control is moved to the engine shutdown position, the plunger is rotated as shown in Figure 19–20, whereby the vertical slot machined in the plunger will always be in alignment with the supply or control port. Therefore, regardless of the plunger's vertical position within the barrel, fuel pressure can never exceed that delivered by the fuel-transfer pump. This pressure will never be able to overcome the force of the delivery valve spring, so no fuel can be sent to the injector nozzles.

During any partial fuel delivery situation, the amount of fuel supplied to the injector will be in proportion to the *effective stroke* of the plunger, which simply means that the instant the supply port is covered by the upward-moving plunger, fuel will start to flow to the injector. This will continue as long as the control port is covered; however, as soon as the upward-moving plunger helix uncovers this port, fuel pressure to the injector is lost and injection ceases. Therefore, we only effectively deliver fuel to the injector as long as the control port is covered; this is shown in Figure 19–21a for any partial throttle position. This will vary in proportion to the throttle and rack position from idle to maximum fuel.

When the operator or driver moves the throttle to its maximum limit of travel, the effective stroke of the plunger, due to the rotation of the plunger helix, will allow greater fuel delivery because of the longer period that the control port is closed during the upward movement of the plunger by the pump camshaft. This is shown in Figure 19–21b.

Figure 19–22c shows a starting groove machined into the plunger; whereas Figure 19–23 shows a lower

helix plunger with a retard notch. This groove is also referred to as an *excess fuel delivery and retard* notch. Excess fuel is possible only during starting, since while the engine is stopped the speed control lever is moved to the *slow idle* position, thereby moving the fuel rack to place the plunger in such a position that excess fuel can be delivered. The instant the engine starts, however, the governor will move the fuel rack to a position corresponding to the position of the throttle lever. The retard notch, also in alignment with the control port, delays port closing and therefore retards timing during starting.

HELIX SHAPES AND DELIVERY VALVES

Helixes

Plungers are manufactured with metering lands having lower or upper helixes (see Figure 19–22) or both to give constant port closing with a variable ending, variable port closing with a constant ending, or both a variable beginning and ending. With ported pumps, good control of injection characteristics is possible due to the minimum fuel volume that is under compression. However, a disadvantage of conventional port control pumps is the rising delivery characteristics as speed increases. This is caused by the fuel throttling process through the ports, resulting in less fuel being bypassed before port closing and after port opening as the speed of the pump increases.

When the plunger is rotated so that the vertical slot on the plunger is in line with the control port (locating screw side), all the fuel will be bypassed;

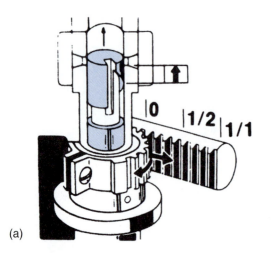

(a)

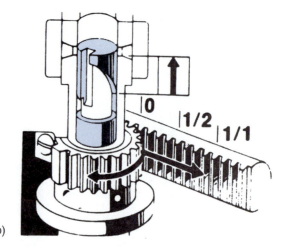

(b)

FIGURE 19–21   (a) Pumping plunger partial fuel delivery position; (b) plunger maximum fuel delivery position. (Courtesy of Robert Bosch Corporation.)

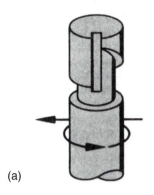

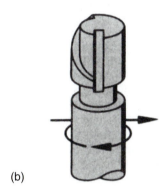

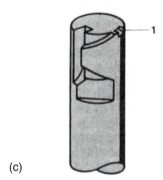

FIGURE 19–22 *Examples of typical inline injection pump plunger helix designs. (a) Lower helix; (b) upper helix; (c) upper and lower helix; 1. starting groove. (Courtesy of Robert Bosch Corporation.)*

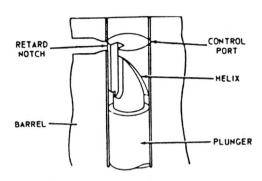

FIGURE 19–23 *Excess fuel delivery and retard notch. (Courtesy of Robert Bosch Corporation.)*

cations it is advantageous to advance timing as the fuel rate is increased. This is achieved by the use of an upper helix, which gives a variable beginning and a constant ending. The helix may be cut on the left- or right-hand side of the plunger. It does not alter the injection characteristic except that the rack must be moved in opposite directions to increase or decrease fuel. There are other special adaptions, such as a short, shallow helix on top to give a slight retarding effect to the injection timing on engines that operate in the idle range for extended periods, and a double helix used by some manufacturers to provide rapid response with minimum rack movement.

With a lower helix design, the beginning of delivery is constant and the ending of delivery is variable. The reason for the helix being on opposite sides is that the one on the left would be employed when the governor is on the left or when the fuel rack is in front of the plunger. Figure 19–22b shows an upper helix design; the delivery has a variable beginning but a constant ending. Figure 19–22c shows plungers with both upper and lower helixes; both the beginning and ending of delivery are variable.

Delivery Valves

The main function of any delivery valve in the injection pump is twofold:

1. At the end of the plunger's upward fuel delivery stroke, the delivery valve prevents a reverse flow of fuel from the injection line.

2. Figure 19–24 illustrates the sucking action that occurs at the delivery valve piston portion which controls the residual pressure in the injection line so as to effectively improve the injected spray pattern of the fuel without fuel dribble and possible secondary injection. The sucking action that does occur at the delivery valve therefore effectively reduces the fuel pressure in the injection tube at the end of injection.

therefore, there will be no injection. With the rack in the full-fuel position, the plunger is able to complete almost its entire stroke before the helix will uncover the control port. Remember, as the plunger is rotated, it will uncover the port earlier or later in the stroke (Figure 19–21).

Some plungers employ a lower-right-hand helix, where the start of injection is constant with regard to timing; however, the ending is variable. In some appli-

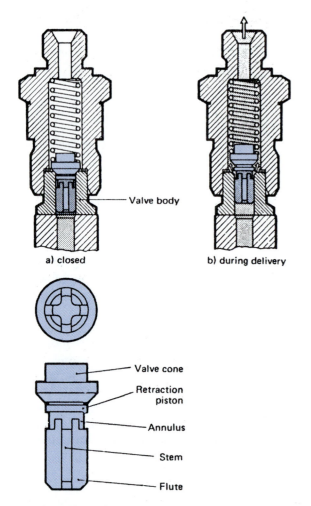

a) closed   b) during delivery

— Valve body

— Valve cone

— Retraction piston

— Annulus

— Stem

— Flute

FIGURE 19–24 *Pump plunger delivery valve nomenclature, and the cycle of operation. (Courtesy of Robert Bosch Corporation.)*

The delivery valve, or what is sometimes referred to as a discharge valve, is specially designed to assist in providing a clean, positive end to injection. Below the valve face is a collar that is a precision fit in the valve bore. When pressure is created in the pump above the plunger by the closing of the ports, the valve must be raised far enough off its seat for the collar to clear the bore.

At the end of injection when pressure in the pump chamber is relieved by the opening of the control port, the valve drops down on its seat assisted by spring pressure. A volume of fuel equal to the displacement volume of the valve is added to the line and nozzle, reducing this pressure and allowing the nozzle valve to snap shut without the cushioning effect of pressure retained in the line and nozzle, such as with the closing of an ordinary valve. This is commonly called *line retraction*, which lessens the possibility of secondary in-

jection or after-dribble at the spray nozzle. It is accomplished by an antidribble collar (accurately fitted relief or displacement piston) located at the upper end of the valve stem just below the seat.

INLINE PUMP-TO-ENGINE TIMING

The purpose of this book is not to provide detailed information on the removal, installation, timing, repair, and troubleshooting of inline pumps for every model of engine. Due to similarity of design and application, the methods required to service and time these fuel injection pumps to typical industrial, marine, midrange, midheavy, and heavy-duty on-highway trucks can be considered as being fairly similar to each other. Your guide when preparing to time an injection pump to the engine should always be the EPA exhaust emissions plate/label and tune-up specs decal. This decal is generally attached to the engine valve rocker cover and contains all the information you need.

Installation of an inline multiple-plunger fuel injection pump to an engine is a fairly straightforward procedure as far as actually mounting and bolting the pump into position is concerned. Prior to actual installation, however, it is necessary on some pumps to align a gear timing mark on the engine gear train with a matching mark on the fuel injection pump-driven gear. On other models of engine an external reference timing mark, provided by the engine manufacturer, may be located on either the flywheel itself or on the crankshaft vibration damper or pulley located at the front of the engine. On some engines timing marks can be found on both the flywheel and vibration damper pulley, as illustrated in Figure 19–25a; OT stands for "overtop" and FB stands for "fuel begins." Figure 19–25b shows the pump to drive coupling alignment marks.

Generally, piston 1 is used as the reference cylinder on the compression stroke to align the marks with the stationary pointer, which is attached to either the engine gear timing cover at the front or at an accessory inspection plate cover on the flywheel. This is the procedure recommended by the majority of diesel engine manufacturers, with cylinder 1 being determined from the vibration damper/pulley end of the engine. Note, however, that the specific make of engine determines what cylinder to use while on its compression stroke. On some engines cylinder 1 is determined from the flywheel end (rear) of the engine; others may use cylinder 6 on its compression stroke as the reference point to align the injection pump-to-engine timing marks. Similarly, when timing an engine to an injection pump, pump 1 in the housing is always located at the end closest to the drive coupling.

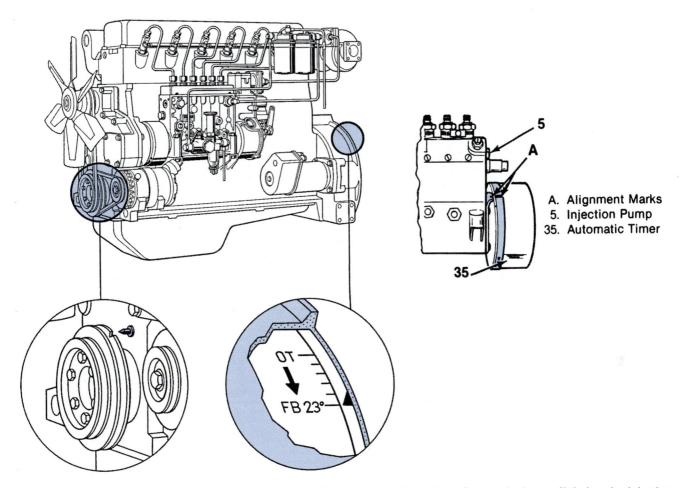

A. Alignment Marks
5. Injection Pump
35. Automatic Timer

FIGURE 19–25   (a) Example of engine-to-pump timing marks which can be referenced when spill timing the injection pump to the No. 1 cylinder (some engines use No. 6 cylinder). (b) Example of the actual timing reference marks between the injection pump to engine drive coupling. (Courtesy of Robert Bosch Corporation.)

The timing marks on the flywheel or vibration damper pulley may indicate TDC for both cylinders 1 and 6, or possibly for all engine cylinders. Remember the TDC mark on a four-stroke-cycle engine can occur once every 360°. Since the timing mark must be aligned only on the compression stroke, always remove the valve rocker cover to determine if free play exists at the valve operating mechanism on the cylinder being used as the reference point. Failure to do this can result in the piston being at TDC; however, it may be at TDC on the end of its exhaust stroke, which means that in fact the timing mark between the engine and injection pump would be 360° out of phase. This can be confirmed by checking for valve lash on the reference cylinder. If there is no valve lash, it is not on its compression stroke. Rotate the crankshaft manually another 360° to place the piston on its compression stroke.

Although we have discussed TDC for a particular cylinder, the static (engine stopped) pump-to-engine timing mark is always found on the engine exhaust emissions regulation plate or decal, which is usually attached to the valve rocker cover although on some engines it may be located elsewhere. Most engines have the static pump timing set for a number of degrees BTDC on the reference cylinder (No. 1); however, some engines use TDC as the actual pump-to-engine timing mark. On engines that have a BTDC timing mark, say 26° BTDC, then while rotating the engine over manually in its normal direction of rotation from the front, the pump-to-engine timing mark of 26° BTDC would appear before the TDC mark. If the TDC mark appears before the 26° marking, you are turning the engine over backwards. On some engines this timing mark may also have the letters BT or BTC, meaning before top or before top dead center, to assist you in aligning the correct marks. The letters OT, meaning "over top," also indicate that it is after TDC as shown in Figure 19–25.

OVERVIEW: STATIC SPILL TIMING

When an injection pump is suspected of being out of time, or after the pump has been reinstalled onto an engine, a pump-to-engine timing procedure must be followed. A commonly employed procedure is known as *spill timing*. During this procedure the engine is stopped (static) and the pump-to-engine timing is per-formed by determining when the fuel is just starting to be delivered to cylinder 1. A small gooseneck-shaped line is attached to the top of the delivery valve holder so that the fuel flow can be monitored visually. An example of a gooseneck line or drip spout can be seen in Figure 19–26a.

Engine-to-pump timing can be determined by either a low- or high-pressure spill timing procedure.

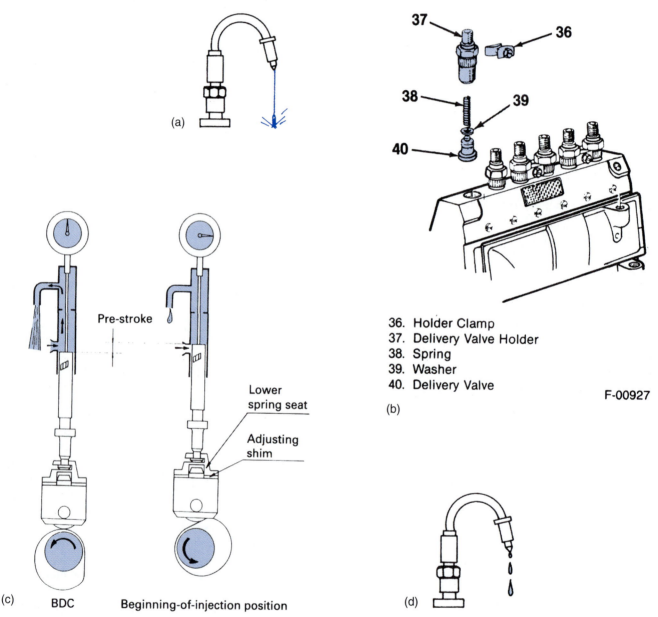

36. Holder Clamp
37. Delivery Valve Holder
38. Spring
39. Washer
40. Delivery Valve

F-00927

FIGURE 19–26 (a) Performing a low-pressure spill timing check using an old fuel line bent into a gooseneck shape and attached to the No. 1 cylinder injection pump delivery valve holder (internal delivery valve spring removed). Actuate the fuel priming pump handle until a steady stream of fuel pours from the gooseneck as shown into a suitable container; (b) delivery valve holder components; (c) sequence to determine injection pump prestroke, or lift-to-port-closure (LTPC) dimension using a dial indicator gauge and gooseneck to determine when the fuel flow stops; (d) stop engine crank-shaft manual rotation when the fuel flow changes from a solid stream to the formation of drops until they stop completely. (Courtesy of ZEXEL USA Corporation).

The low-pressure timing procedure involves using the hand priming pump attached to the transfer/lift pump shown in Figure 19–15, which supplies fuel to the No. 1 pumping plunger of the injection pump. Another low-pressure method uses regulated shop air to force the fuel through the injection pump. Both of these low-pressure spill timing procedures are commonly used and are reasonably accurate. The drawback of the low-pressure procedure is that the technician must first remove the pumping plunger spring-loaded delivery valve. The delivery valve components can be seen in Figure 19–26b. Removal is necessary because the low fuel pressure created is insufficient to lift the delivery valve against the spring force. For more precise pump-to-engine timing, a high-pressure spill timing procedure is recommended. The high-pressure procedure uses an electric-motor-driven fuel pump system that creates fuel pressure high enough to open the spring-loaded delivery valve in the top of each pumping plunger assembly.

Regardless of what spill timing method is used, when the engine-to-pump timing marks are not in alignment, and the piston in cylinder 1 is just starting its compression stroke, fuel will flow freely from the small gooseneck-shaped line attached to the No. 1 pumping plunger delivery valve holder shown in Figure 19–26a. This fuel flow occurs because the plunger is at the BDC (bottom dead center) position, which can be seen on the left-hand side of Figure 19–26c. This allows fuel under pressure from the injection pump gallery to flow in over the top of the plunger and exit out of the delivery valve holder at the top. As the engine is manually rotated in its normal direction of rotation, the injection pump camshaft will raise the pumping plunger (prestroke) until it closes off the fuel ports within the barrel. When this point is reached, fuel stops flowing out of the delivery valve holder, or the gooseneck-shaped fuel line if attached to the delivery valve holder. When the fuel from this line is reduced to 1 to 2 drops a minute (Figure 19–26d), this is the start of the static pump injection for that cylinder. The next step is to check the position of the engine flywheel or pulley timing marks to determine if the pump is correctly timed to the engine. If not, the pump or its drive coupling must be rotated to bring the engine and pump timing marks into proper alignment.

Method 1: Using High-Pressure Port Closing

Manually rotate the engine over in its normal direction of rotation, which is CW from the front, to place piston 1 on its compression stroke. The exhaust emission label on the engine valve rocker cover lists the number of degrees BTDC that the static timing should be. Slowly rotate the engine over until the timing marks on the vibration damper are in alignment with the stationary pointer on the engine gear case. Refer to Figure 19–27a and connect the tooling from the high-pressure timer shown in Figure 19–27b to the injection pump as shown, then proceed through the sequence given below.

1.   Cap or connect the injection lines on all injection pumping outlets other than the No. 1 cylinder, since this will be the reference unit for the spill timing procedure.

2.   Cap the valve return and bleed fitting from the nozzle drip line if it is connected to the injection pump overflow valve.

3.   Connect the No. 6 Aeroquip high-pressure line from the portable PC stand to the injection pump gallery inlet (fuel supply).

4.   Connect the No. 4 Aeroquip hose from the PC stand to the No. 1 cylinder injection pump delivery valve holder.

5.   Ensure that the injection pump stop lever is placed and held in the normal running position; otherwise, no fuel will be able to flow from the No. 1 delivery valve assembly.

6.   Activate the high-pressure PC stand so that fuel will flow into the injection pump fuel gallery.

7.   Slowly turn the engine opposite to its normal direction of rotation, which is usually CCW from the front. This should cause fuel to spill from the end of the No. 1 delivery valve holder on the injection pump out of the gooseneck as shown in Figure 19–26a from the end of the test line running back to the fuel reservoir.

8.   Slowly rotate the engine in its normal direction of rotation, which is CW from the front, until the fuel flow from the end of the gooseneck line or from the test line connected to the No. 1 delivery valve holder is reduced as shown in Figure 19–26d to 1 to 2 drops per minute. This action confirms port closure for No. 1 pumping plunger.

9.   Inspect the flywheel timing marks and pointer, or the marks on the crankshaft pulley/damper and stationary timing bracket located on the engine front cover. Compare these marks with the engine manufacturer's specs.

10.   If the injection pump is timed incorrectly, you can loosen the pump external flange mounting nuts and rotate the pump housing manually either CW or CCW until the fuel spilling from the No. 1 delivery valve holder occurs at the specified degrees BTDC. Tighten the external retaining nuts. On some pumps, timing must be adjusted by removing an access plate on the engine timing case cover to expose a series of internal retaining bolts on the pump drive gear. These bolts are installed through slotted holes to the pump drive hub. It is then necessary to loosen these bolts and

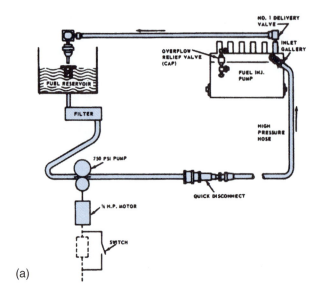

(a)

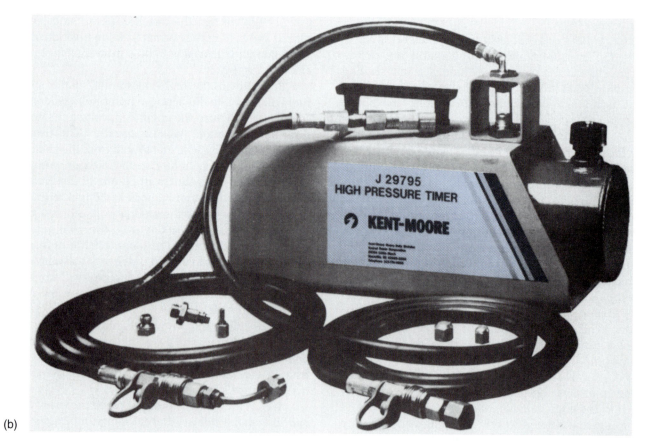

(b)

FIGURE 19–27 (a) Inline injection pump high-pressure port closing fuel system schematic showing hookup connections for spill timing purposes. (b) Model J29795 high-pressure injection pump timer. (Courtesy of Kent-Moore Tool Division, SPX Corporation.)

rotate the engine over to change the timing, then retighten the bolts.

11. Always recheck the pump-to-engine timing after making any necessary adjustments.

12. Disconnect the special high-pressure spill timing components and reconnect all fuel lines, then bleed all air from the fuel system.

Method 2: Using Low Air Pressure

1. Remove the No. 1 delivery valve holder from the injection pump and take out the delivery valve and spring.

2. Install a suitable air line onto the IN fitting of the pump gallery.

CAUTION Ensure that the air line is equipped with a separator and pressure regulator. Moisture-laden air can cause serious damage to injection pump parts.

---

3. Attach a locally fabricated fixture to the delivery valve holder similar to that shown in Figure 19–28.

4. Secure the stop lever in the running position.

5. Activate the throttle lever several times and secure it in the full-load position.

6. Turn on the air supply and just crack the regulator so that a steady flow of air bubbles is seen in the fixture jar without excessive turbulence.

7. Rotate the crankshaft slowly in its normal direction of rotation. Observe the flow of air bubbles in the fixture jar, and the instant the bubbles stop, discontinue rotating the crankshaft.

8. Check the position of the flywheel or vibration damper timing indicator. If properly timed, the indicator must register the recommended number of degrees as BTDC stamped on the valve rocker cover escutcheon plate.

9. If the timing checks out, repeat steps 7 and 8 to ensure accuracy.

10. If the timing does not check out, bar the engine over in its normal direction of rotation until cylinder 1 is on the compression stroke and the timing mark indicates the correct number of degrees BTDC as recommended on the valve rocker cover escutcheon plate.

11. Loosen the pump flange or gear retaining bolts and rotate the pump housing manually either CW or CCW until the flow of fuel from the gooseneck or test line slows from a steady stream to 1 to 2 drops per minute (Figure 19–26d). Tighten the retaining nuts or bolts.

12. Perform the spill timing procedure once more to confirm that pump-to-engine timing is in fact correct.

13. Remove the test equipment from the pump.

14. Carefully reinstall the No. 1 pumping plunger delivery valve and components (Figure 19–26b), and torque the holder nut to specs.

15. Bleed all air from the fuel system as shown in Figure 19–29a and b; start the engine and individually loosen and then tighten all high-pressure fuel lines at each nozzle, as shown in Figure 19–29c, to confirm that the engine is running correctly.

AIR-IN-THE-FUEL SYSTEM

Once spill timing is complete and the fuel lines have been reinstalled, bleed the fuel system. Basically, bleeding of the system involves removing all entrapped air, which can be done by opening up the various bleeder screws on the fuel filter housing and the injection pump housing, then using the hand priming pump (Figure 19–15) or the lift pump handle in Figure 19–29b to push fuel through the system. The pressure relief valve arrangement in the supply side of the fuel circuit creates a self-bleeding system for air introduced during replacement of the supply-side components (Figure 19–29b).

Once the injection pump is free of air, confirmed by the fact that no air bubbles are evident in the spilling fuel, each one of the fuel injector high-pressure lines can be left loose about one-half to one-full turn. The engine priming pump can be used again to push fuel

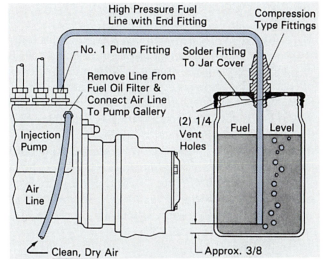

FIGURE 19–28 Spill timing an injection pump by using the airflow checking method. (Courtesy of Robert Bosch Corporation.)

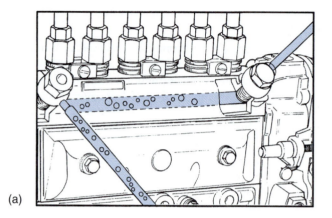

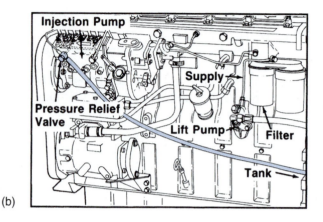

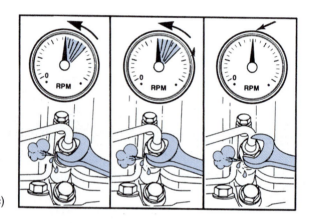

FIGURE 19–29   (a) Clear fuel return line from the injection pump showing air bubbles; (b) basic component plumbing for an inline injection pump; (c) on a running engine you can loosen off one high-pressure injector fuel line at a time to determine if the fuel injector is firing correctly, or if air is trapped in the system. (Courtesy of Cummins Engine Company, Inc.)

through the lines; however, it is usually better to crank the engine over until fuel free of air flows from each line at the injector, after which time each line can be tightened up. Start the engine and check for any fuel leaks. If the engine still runs rough, rebleed the system. You can, however, loosen each fuel injector line one at a time to see if any air escapes as you hold a rag around the line nut; then retighten it when you are sure that there is no air left in the system (Figure 19–29c).

Air from uncorrected leaks in the supply circuit will make the engine: hard to start, run rough, misfire, produce low power, and can cause excessive smoke and a fuel knock.

A source, which is often overlooked, for air to enter the fuel system is between the inlet of the prefilter and the suction tube in the tank. Fuel tanks that have the outlet fitting at the top will have a suction tube that extends down in the tank. Cracks or pinholes in the weld that joins the tube to the fitting can let air enter the fuel system.

CUMMINS C MODEL TIMING CHECK

The Cummins C model engine is a six-cylinder four-stroke-cycle unit with a displacement of 8.27 L (504.5 in^3) and is very widely used in a large number of applications. The engine is equipped with either a Bosch PES6A or PES6MW PLN system, as shown in Figure 19–29. The model of injection pump is determined by the particular engine power rating used. The engine-to-injection pump timing check is achieved using both an engine gear train timing pin and an injection pump camshaft timing pin (Figure 19–30) to confirm that the pump is timed to the engine correctly. To remove and replace the injection pump, follow the procedure described below.

Pump Removal

1.   Locate TDC for cylinder 1. This can be done by barring the engine over slowly with the special fly-

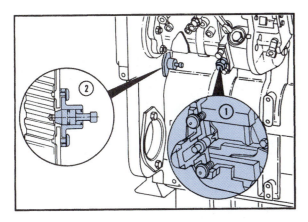

FIGURE 19–30 *Location of injection pump to engine timing pin on Cummins B and C model midrange engines. (Courtesy of Cummins Engine Company, Inc.)*

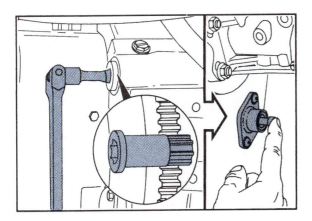

FIGURE 19–31 *Using a special tool to bar the engine flywheel over in order to install the engine timing pin into the backside of the pump drive gear on either a B or C model midrange engine. (Courtesy of Cummins Engine Company, Inc.)*

FIGURE 19–32 *Loosening the injection pump drive gear retaining nut for a Cummins B or C model midrange engine. (Courtesy of Cummins Engine Company, Inc.)*

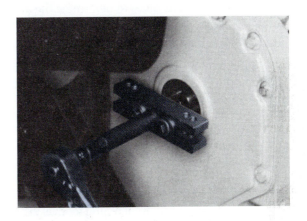

FIGURE 19–33 *Using a puller to loosen the injection pump drive gear from the camshaft end of the injection pump. (Courtesy of Cummins Engine Company, Inc.)*

wheel ring gear turning tool, then pushing the TDC pin into the hole in the camshaft gear as shown in Figure 19–31.

2. Remove the engine front gear cover access cap as shown in Figure 19–32; then, using a socket and breaker bar, remove the nut and washer from the front end of the fuel pump camshaft.

3. Attach a suitable gear puller as shown in Figure 19–33 and pull the fuel pump drive gear loose from the shaft.

4. Refer to Figure 19–34 and loosen/disconnect all the pump fuel lines as well as throttle linkage. If turbocharged, remove the AFC line between the pump and engine intake manifold. Remove the four 15-mm mounting nuts which secure the front end of the pump to the back side of the engine timing cover.

FIGURE 19–34 *Preparing to remove the injection pump from the engine. (Courtesy of Cummins Engine Company, Inc.)*

5. Grasp the injection pump and carefully remove it from the engine.

Pump Installation and Timing

1. Make sure that piston 1 is at TDC on its compression stroke. Refer to Figure 19–35 and bar the engine over until the timing pin engages with the hole in the back side of the camshaft gear, as shown in the figure.

SERVICE TIP   Although the injection pump is timed to piston 1 at TDC, the actual static timing will usually result in the pump being anywhere between 9 and 11.5° BTDC. The year of engine manufacture determines the actual pump-to-engine timing spec. Refer to the engine CPL plate and exhaust emissions decal to determine the actual timing spec.

---

2. Refer to Figure 19–36. The injection pump also has a timing pin (1) located in the governor housing in order to position the pump camshaft so that it will correspond to TDC for cylinder 1.

3. To access the pump timing pin, remove the 24-mm plug shown in Figure 19–37.

4. Remove the nylon timing pin as shown in Figure 19–38.

5. Carefully look into the access hole on the injection pump and note if the internal timing tooth is visible, as shown in Figure 19–39. If the timing tooth is not centered as shown, manually rotate the injection pump camshaft until the timing tooth is aligned as shown.

6. Reverse the position of the timing pin (see Figure 19–40) so that the slot in the pin will slide over the

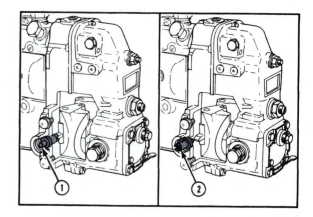

FIGURE 19–36   1, Injection pump camshaft timing pin in the "engaged" position; 2, timing pin in the "disengaged" position. (Courtesy of Cummins Engine Company, Inc.)

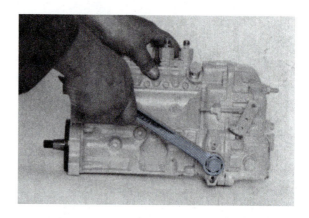

FIGURE 19–37   Loosening or tightening the injection pump timing pin retaining nut. (Courtesy of Cummins Engine Company, Inc.)

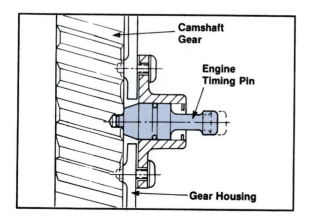

FIGURE 19–35   Closeup view of the engine-to-injection pump timing pin. (Courtesy of Cummins Engine Company, Inc.)

Camshaft Gear

Engine Timing Pin

Gear Housing

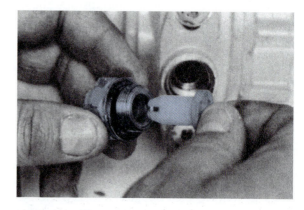

FIGURE 19–38   Removing captive injection pump camshaft timing pin from its location in the pump retaining nut. (Courtesy of Cummins Engine Company, Inc.)

FIGURE 19–39 Injection pump inspection hole showing the slotted camshaft timing location. (Courtesy of Cummins Engine Company, Inc.)

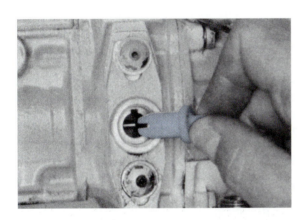

FIGURE 19–40 Installing the injection pump camshaft timing pin into the access hole within the pump housing. (Courtesy of Cummins Engine Company, Inc.)

timing tooth in the pump as shown. Temporarily install the access plug over the pin to retain it in position.

7.   Refer to Figure 19–41 and ensure that the O-ring seals at the drive end of the pump for the fill orifice and pilot are installed correctly and are not damaged. Lubricate the mounting flange with clean engine oil.

8.   Carefully lift the injection pump into position as shown in Figure 19–34 so that the end of the pump camshaft slides through the central hole in the pump drive gear; then locate the pump flange over the four mounting studs on the engine cover.

9.   Install the four 15-mm nuts over the flange studs and tighten these to a torque value of 32 lb-ft (43 N · m).

10.   Refer to Figure 19–32 under step 2 for pump removal, and install the retaining nut and washer which were removed earlier. Using a socket and torque

FIGURE 19–41 Carefully inspect the O-ring seals at both the fill-orifice and pilot. (Courtesy of Cummins Engine Company, Inc.)

wrench, tighten this nut to 7 to 11 lb-ft (10 to 15 N · m). Be careful not to exceed this torque value at this time; otherwise, timing pin damage can result!

11.   Disengage the engine timing pin as shown in Figure 19–35.

12.   Remove the fuel pump timing pin plug and reverse the nylon timing pin as shown in Figure 19–38. Install the pin, plug, and sealing washer, and torque the plug to 11 lb-ft (15 N · m).

13.   Repeat step 10 using a torque wrench and final-tighten the pump camshaft retaining gear nut to 60 lb-ft (82 N · m) for a Bosch model PES6A pump, and to 66 lb-ft (90 N · m) for a Bosch PES6MW pump model.

14.   Bleed the air from the fuel system as described in this chapter. Note that on later-model PES6MW pumps, to facilitate bleeding, loosen the vent screw shown in Figure 19–42, which is located close to the front of the pump on the side closest to the engine

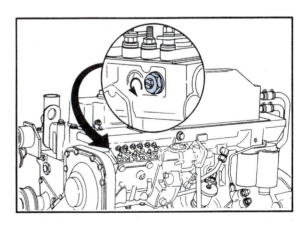

FIGURE 19–42 Injection pump vent-screw location; open when bleeding entrapped air from the pump. (Courtesy of Cummins Engine Company, Inc.)

block. Place the governor speed control lever in the run position and crank the engine over until all signs of air have been vented (steady fuel flow). Tighten the vent screw. PES6A pumps equipped with a pressure relief valve as shown in Figure 19–29b are self-venting; however, each individual nozzle will still have to be bled of air as shown in Figure 19–29c.

Adjusting the Idle Speed

The idle adjustment screw location will vary based on the type of governor being used. Refer to the section dealing with Bosch mechanical governors to determine the actual idle screw location.

Once the engine is started, adjust the idle speed on industrial engines using an RSV governor by loosening the locknut and turning the screw (1), shown in Figure 19–43. CW rotation will increase the idle speed, and CCW rotation will decrease the idle speed. On automotive engines equipped with an RQV governor, refer to Figure 19–44 and using a 10-mm wrench and screwdriver, rotate the screw CCW to raise the engine speed and CW to decrease the idle speed.

1. Start and run the engine at its idle speed. Use a tach and note the idle rpm. Compare this with the spec stamped on the engine CPL plate.

2. If idle adjustment is required, loosen the locknut and back out the bumper spring screw until there is no change in the idle speed.

3. Adjust the idle screw to obtain an idle speed approximately 20 to 30 rpm lower than that recommended and lock the retaining nut.

4. Slowly turn the bumper spring screw (2) shown in Figure 19–43 CW only enough to bring the desired idle rpm to a stable speed, then lock the retaining nut.

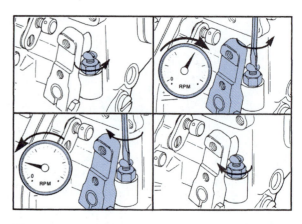

FIGURE 19–44 Bosch RQV governor idle adjustment screw location. (Courtesy of Cummins Engine Company, Inc.)

TIMING PF JERK PUMPS

Individual jerk pumps of the PF style similar to those shown in Figure 19–1 are found extensively on small, single, two- and three-cylinder diesel engines, as well as on very-large-displacement slow-speed heavy-duty deep-sea marine, railroad, and stationary applications. Timing of the individual pumps to the engine is done in the same basic procedure regardless of the OEM model. Use the following procedure as a general guide.

1. Refer to the flywheel markings on the engine to establish the base circle of the camshaft for the particular pump being installed.

2. Place the pump unit onto its mounting base, and bolt it down.

3. Check plunger movement through the inspection window, as shown in Figure 19–45. With the proper flywheel timing mark aligned with the stationary pointer on the engine, the timing line on the pump plunger and inspection window should be as shown in Figure 19–45c.

4. If the pump timing lines do not appear as in Figure 19–45c, double-check to ensure that the engine flywheel marks correspond to the pump cylinder.

5. To correct the timing, some pumps employ a tappet adjusting screw to effectively raise or lower the plunger; however, some units require the use of selective shims under the pump base to correct this condition. Once adjusted, with the pump at the bottom and top of its stroke, the timing line on the plunger should stay in view, as shown in Figures 19–45a and b.

PF Rack Setting

Engines equipped with individual PF pumps usually have their fuel racks (control rods) interconnected by adjustable mechanical linkage to permit balancing the fuel flow to each nozzle and the combustion chamber.

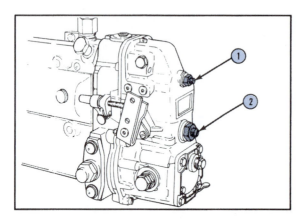

FIGURE 19–43 Bosch RSV governor; 1, idle screw; 2, bumper spring screw. (Courtesy of Cummins Engine Company, Inc.)

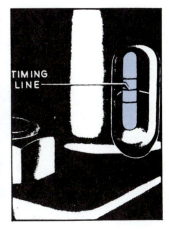

FIGURE 19–45 (a) PF/PFR type injection pump plunger timing line retarded; (b) injection pump timing line advanced; (c) injection pump timing line correctly aligned. (Courtesy of Robert Bosch Corporation.)

Some larger engines employ a micrometer-type knurled knob adjusting screw that the technician can rotate manually to obtain very fine adjustment of fuel delivery. On large, slow-speed engines, fuel delivery and cylinder balance are best achieved by monitoring the individual cylinder exhaust temperatures by looking at the pyrometer gauge(s) and adjusting the individual fuel rack adjustment knobs.

AUTOMATIC TIMING ADVANCE DEVICE

In the combustion process, diesel fuel takes a certain amount of time to ignite and burn. As the engine runs faster, the burn time remains the same, and much of the burning takes place after TDC (top dead center). This is called ignition lag and almost always results in lowered performance. To offset this ignition lag, fuel must be injected sometime before TDC to give good performance at rated speed. However, with this fixed advance of injection, engine performance is optimum at rated speed only. Engines that vary speeds over a wide range, that is, automotive vehicles, need injection timed correctly at all speeds. This is the function of the timing device.

The Bosch automatic timing device is used on in-line camshaft driven pumps (Figure 19–46), and is classified as a flyweight-operated device. Mounted at the front of the injection pump on the camshaft, the timing device is connected to the driving gear of the engine (Figure 19–46). Through the action of centrifugal force,

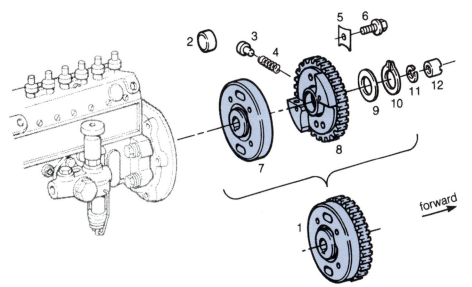

FIGURE 19–46 Component parts of a pump-mounted (1) automatic timing advance unit; 2, governor weight; 3, pin; 4, spring; 5, locktab; 6, capscrew; 7, segment plate; 8, injection pump gear; 9, spacer; 10, snap ring; 11, lockwasher; 12, round nut. (Courtesy of Robert Bosch Corporation.)

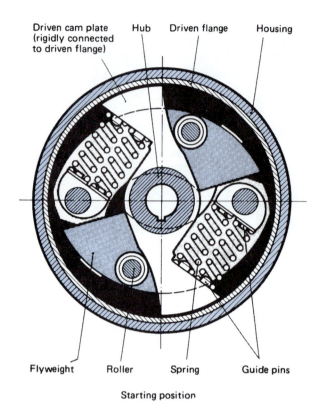

Driven cam plate (rigidly connected to driven flange)   Hub   Driven flange   Housing

Flyweight   Roller   Spring   Guide pins

Starting position

FIGURE 19–47 *Assembled view of an automatic timing device. (Courtesy of Robert Bosch Corporation.)*

the flyweights swing outward with increasing speed. Rollers mounted on the flyweights push against the cam plate (Figure 19–47), which is connected to the pump camshaft. This causes the camshaft to rotate a maximum of 8°, providing proper timing in relation to engine speed.

Stop pins limit the maximum amount of advance that can be obtained from any timing advance assembly. As with any automatic timing advance device, should the unit become worn or damaged, fuel injection timing will not be controlled correctly, resulting in poor engine performance and possible engine damage. Generally, if the timing advance unit were to stick in the full-advance position, the start of fuel injection would be too early at an idle speed, and severe combustion knock would result, together with a tendency for white smoke to appear at the exhaust stack. On the other hand, a timing advance unit that will not advance past the idle setting would result in late injection and the engine would be very sluggish, together with black smoke appearing at the exhaust stack through incomplete combustion.

BASIC FUEL SYSTEM TROUBLESHOOTING

Information contained in this chapter deals with identification of the various models of Bosch pumps, governors, and nozzles, the general operation and function of each component, and the procedure required to check and correct the injection pump-to-engine timing. Regardless of what make of engine a Bosch inline pump is used on, there are common procedural steps that are required to systematically pinpoint trouble areas in the fuel system. Figure 19–48 lists some of these typical problem symptoms, causes, and suggested remedies. In addition to this troubleshooting chart, the following information can be considered common to any make of engine employing the models A, MW, or P Bosch inline multiple-plunger injection pumps. When low power, rough idle, or stalling is reported on an engine with no unusual exhaust smoke color, the problem can most likely be traced to fuel starvation or low transfer pump delivery. To pinpoint the cause quickly, the following checks and tests should be performed:

1. Check the relief valve opening pressure. This relief valve is usually incorporated into the injection pump housing and return fuel line (Figures 19–14 and 19–29b).
2. Check the delivery pressure of the transfer pump.

SERVICE TIP   Checks 1 and 2 above can be performed simultaneously.

---

3. Check the restriction to fuel flow at the suction side of the transfer pump (vacuum test).
4. Check the fuel delivery pressure to the injection pump inlet from the secondary fuel filters.

To perform the four tests listed above, several special tools are required, which can be found in most service shops:

- A fuel pressure gauge
- A vacuum gauge or mercury manometer
- Assorted fittings and lines to tap into the existing fuel system
- A length of clear plastic hose to note the presence of air bubbles

Symptom

- Starting Problems
- Engine Surges at Idle
- Rough Idle
- Engine Misses When Under Load
- Low Power or Low Speed
- Engine Fuel Consumption Off
- Excessive Black Smoke
- Poor Performance Cannot Be Shut Off at Full-Load Speed
- Fog-Like Exhaust or Low (White or Blue) Smoke Range
- Incorrect Idle or Not Rev Up in Maximum Speed
- Engine Injection Does Pump Not Runs Hot / Engine Is Warm

Cause	Remedy
Tank empty or tank vent blocked	Fill tank/bleed system, check tank vent
Air in the fuel system	Bleed fuel system, eliminate air leaks
Shut off/start device defective	Repair or replace
Fuel filter blocked	Replace fuel filter
Injection lines blocked/restricted	Drill to nominal I.D. or replace
Fuel-supply lines blocked/restricted	Test all fuel supply lines—flush or replace
Loose connections, injection lines leak or broken	Tighten the connection, eliminate the leak
Paraffin deposit in fuel filter	Replace filter, use winter fuel
Pump-to-engine timing incorrect	Readjust timing
Injection nozzle defective	Repair or replace
Engine air filter blocked	Replace air filter element
Pre-heating system defective	Test the glow plugs, replace as necessary
Injection sequence does not correspond to firing order	Install fuel injection lines in the correct order
Low idle misadjusted	Readjust idle stop screw
Maximum speed misadjusted	Readjust maximum speed screw
Overflow valve defective or blocked	Clean the orifice or replace fitting
Delivery valve leakage	Replace delivery valve (max. of 1 on 4 cyl., 2 on 6 cyl.)
Bumper spring misadjusted (RS . . . governors)	Readjust bumper spring
Timing device defective	Repair or replace timing device
Low or uneven engine compression	Repair as necessary
Governor misadjusted or defective	Readjust or repair
Fuel injection pump defective or cannot be adjusted	Remove pump and service

Source: Robert Bosch Corporation.
ªIt is assumed that the engine is in good working order and properly tuned, and that the electrical system has been checked and repaired if necessary.

FIGURE 19–48 Troubleshooting guide for Bosch inline injection pumps. (Courtesy of Robert Bosch Corporation.)

Many engine manufacturers supply special tool kits with all the necessary gauges and fittings to perform these tests. In addition, these special tools and fittings can be obtained from most reputable tool suppliers.

Test 1: Relief Valve and Pump Pressure Check

This test is a check to ensure that the injection pump relief valve is, in fact, opening at the correct pressure and that the transfer pump is performing correctly. If the relief valve is stuck open or is opening at too low a pressure, the fuel delivery pressure within the injection pump housing will be too low to sustain sufficient flow to the plunger and barrel of the individual pumping assemblies. On the other hand, if the relief valve is stuck closed or opens at too high a pressure setting, the fuel within the injection pump housing, which is also used for cooling and lubricating purposes, will run hot. This can result in a loss of horsepower due to the expansion of the fuel, since a less dense fuel charge will be delivered to the injectors and combustion chamber. In addition, fuel that is too hot can cause internal pump plunger damage due to its inability to properly cool and lubricate the component parts. Note that only 25 to 30% of the fuel delivered to the injection pump housing is actually used for combustion purposes. The remainder cools and lubricates the injection pump components.

Procedure

1. Refer to Figure 19–49 and disconnect the fuel line between the outlet side of the transfer pump which leads to the secondary fuel filters.

2. Connect a fuel pressure gauge tester similar to the one shown in Figure 19–49 into the fuel system between the transfer pump and secondary fuel filters. Use suitable fittings to ensure that there will be no fuel leaks. The special tester gauge shown in Figure 19–49 is equipped with a clear fuel line to allow you to check for any signs of air bubbles in the fuel system. If you do not have a gauge similar to this one, insert a clear plastic fuel line into the system to allow you to monitor this condition.

3. Start and run the engine. Carefully note and record the fuel pressure reading on the gauge, which is an indication of the relief valve opening pressure. On most Bosch inline pumps this will run between 19 to 44 psi (131 and 303 kPa) at maximum no-load speed. Check the engine manufacturer's service manual for this specification.

NOTE   If the engine runs rough or misfires, you may have to open the bleed screw on the filter and injection pump housing to vent any entrapped air from the fuel system.

---

4. While the engine is running, take careful note of the fuel running through the special gauge or clear plastic line. If there is any sign of air bubbles, check the fuel-line connections for looseness or possible damage, including the fuel lines themselves.

5. Pinch the fuel line hose in the area indicated in Figure 19–49 and carefully note the reading on the test gauge. This value actually indicates the transfer pump

FIGURE 19–49 *Fuel pressure gauge connected between the transfer pump outlet and secondary fuel filters: 1, fuel filter housing; 2, transfer pump; 3, tester. (Courtesy of Robert Bosch Corporation.)*

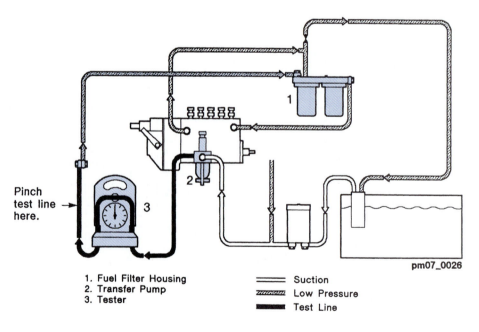

pm07_0026

Pinch test line here.

1. Fuel Filter Housing
2. Transfer Pump
3. Tester

— Suction
— Low Pressure
— Test Line

pressure, which should be at least equal to the OEM's minimum speed.

6. When this test has been completed, stop the engine, disconnect the gauge tester, and reconnect the fuel system lines.

Test 2: Pump Vacuum Restriction Check

This test allows the mechanic/technician to determine if there is a high restriction to fuel flow to the suction side of the fuel transfer pump. If there is, the injection pump will not receive enough fuel. This will be accompanied by lack of power as well as possible rough idling and stalling. Either a vacuum gauge or a mercury manometer can be used to check the restriction to fuel flow. However, if a mercury manometer is teed into the fuel system in place of the special gauge (Figure 19–50), make sure that you hold or mount the manometer higher than the engine. Failure to do this can result in diesel fuel running back into the manometer when the engine is stopped. A low reading is what we are looking for here, since this indicates that the fuel lines and connections are offering a minimum restriction to flow at the suction side of the fuel transfer pump.

Procedure

1. Refer to Figure 19–50 and connect the special gauge fixture or mercury manometer into the fuel system as shown between the suction (inlet) side of the fuel transfer pump and the fuel line from the primary fuel filter or fuel filter/water separator assembly.

2. Start and run the engine at an idle speed and note the gauge or mercury manometer reading. Accelerate the engine up through the speed range and record the maximum gauge reading. Pinch the fuel line hose in the area indicated in Figure 19–50 and carefully note the reading on the gauge or mercury manometer. The value obtained indicates the fuel transfer pump vacuum, which should be between 7 to 12 psi (50 and 80 kPa). If using a mercury manometer, this value is equivalent to 14.25 to 24.4 in. on the scale. Refer to the metric conversion chart in Chapter 3 if using a metric-scale manometer.

SERVICE TIP   If the vacuum reading is too high, carefully inspect the fuel lines between the fuel tank and the transfer pump for signs of crimping, crushing, or physical damage. Also keep in mind that a plugged primary filter can cause a restriction to fuel flow.

---

3. Disconnect the gauge or manometer and reconnect the fuel-line fittings firmly. If either the transfer pump delivery pressure or vacuum (restriction) check is not within the engine manufacturer's specifications, proceed to remove and disassemble the transfer pump in order to carefully check the condition of the check valves inside the pump. If signs of wear or damage are evident, replace the valves or install a new exchange transfer pump assembly. If the fuel transfer pump and relief valve pressures as well as the vacuum

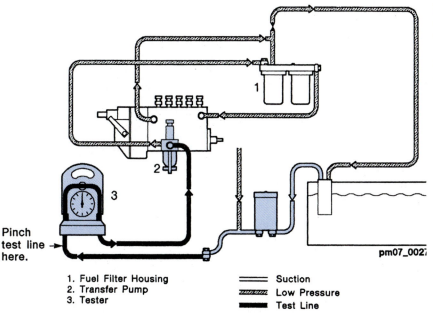

FIGURE 19–50 Vacuum tester connected between the fuel transfer pump inlet side and the primary filter/fuel-water separator: 1, fuel filter housing; 2, transfer pump; 3, tester. (Courtesy of Robert Bosch Corporation.)

Pinch test line here.

1. Fuel Filter Housing
2. Transfer Pump
3. Tester

═══ Suction
▨▨▨ Low Pressure
━━━ Test Line

pm07_0027

check valves are within the manufacturer's specifications, proceed to Test 3, described below.

Test 3: Secondary Fuel Filter Pressure Check

Refer to Figure 19–51 and disconnect the fuel line between the outlet side of the secondary fuel filter(s) and the inlet side of the fuel injection pump. Insert a special pressure gauge or, alternatively, a fuel pressure gauge and clear plastic line between the filters and injection pump as shown in Figure 19–51.

Procedure

1. Start and run the engine while carefully looking for any signs of air bubbles in the special gauge window or clear test fuel line. Remember, however, that there may be some air bubbles initially, due to the introduction of air into the fuel system while installing the test gauge. If the air bubbles do not disappear within a short period, try opening the bleeder screw on the fuel injection pump until all signs of aerated fuel disappears. If after bleeding the fuel system air bubbles still appear in the clear test fuel line, check the fuel filter seals for leakage, the fuel-line connections for tightness, and the fuel lines for damage.

> **Service Tip:** Keep in mind that all fuel lines and fittings on the outlet side of the transfer pump up to the injection pump and nozzles are under pressure; therefore, a fuel leak will be evident. Air introduced into the fuel system will generally be drawn into the fuel system between the suction side of the transfer pump and the fuel tank connections.

2. Normal fuel pressure on the test gauge should be between the minimum and maximum listed specs. If the earlier tests confirmed that the relief valve, transfer pump, and restriction check were within specifications, a low fuel pressure gauge reading at this time would indicate that the secondary fuel filters are plugged and require changing. If after changing the fuel filters, the fuel pressure is still low, double-check the operating condition of the pressure relief valve.

3. If the fuel pressure reading is within specifications, stop the engine, remove the test gauge and lines, and reconnect and tighten the service fuel lines and fittings. Start and run the engine and bleed any air from the system. Check and correct any signs of fuel leakage. Similarly, if the fuel filters have to be changed, bleed the fuel system and make certain that there are no fuel leaks.

ROBERT BOSCH GOVERNORS

Robert Bosch governors used with inline pumps (M, A, MW, and P) can look the same externally; however, they are designed for different types of engine applications, and therefore engine speed control can be governed at different settings of the throttle. Types of governors manufactured by Robert Bosch Corporation and used on their inline injection pumps in truck applications are described below.

The letter designations used for these mechanical governors take the following forms:

R: flyweight governor
S: swivel lever action
V: variable-speed (all-range) governor
Q: fulcrum lever action

FIGURE 19–51 Pressure tester gauge connected between the secondary fuel filters and the injection pump inlet: 1, fuel filter housing; 2, transfer pump; 3, tester. (Courtesy of Robert Bosch Corporation.)

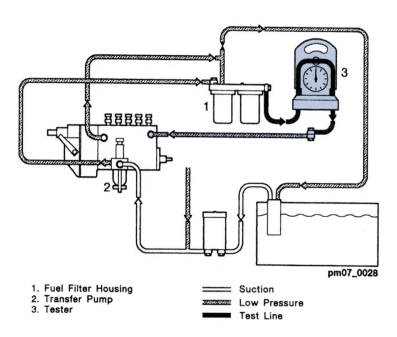

pm07_0028

1. Fuel Filter Housing
2. Transfer Pump
3. Tester

▬▬▬ Suction
〜〜〜 Low Pressure
▬▬▬ Test Line

K: torque cam control

W: leaf spring action

For example, if the nameplate on a governor read EP/RS275/1400AOB478DL, this would mean:

EP: found on older governors, no longer used

RS: R/flyweight governor with swivel lever action, minimum/maximum (limiting speed) type of governor

275: low-idle pump speed (this would be 550 rpm engine speed, four cycle)

/: also indicates min/max (limiting speed) governor

1400: full-load-rated speed (this would be 2800 rpm engine speed, four cycle)

A: fits on A-size inline injection pump

O: amount of speed regulation (droop percentage)

B: execution—not used to indicate the original design on governors; A, first change; B, second change; and so on

478DL: application and engineering information only

Types of Bosch Governors

Prior to studying the various types of truck governors manufactured by Robert Bosch in this section, it would be helpful to consider that although there are a variety of governor models, basically they fall into one of two main types and designs. The types are:

1. *Minimum–maximum governor:* often referred to as a limiting-speed unit since it governs only the low-idle and high-idle (maximum no-load speed) ranges.

2. *Variable-speed governor:* an all-range governor that controls not only the low-idle and maximum speed ranges, but will maintain any speed range selected between these two ranges by the operator as long as the engine is not overloaded for a specific setting of the throttle.

The concept of operation of the RSV and RQV governors is discussed in detail in this section; however, their design characteristics differ as follows:

1. The governor weights in the RQ and RQV models act directly against a coil spring which is assembled into the weights as shown in Figure 19–52.

2. The governor weights in the RS and RSV models act through mechanical linkage to transfer their motion to the coiled governor spring as shown in Figure 19–53.

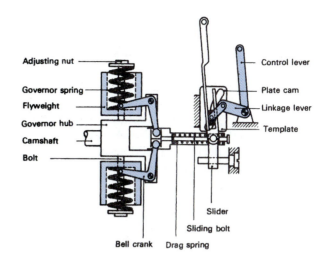

FIGURE 19–52 *Governor weight and spring arrangement in the Bosch RQ/RQV models. (Courtesy of Robert Bosch Corporation.)*

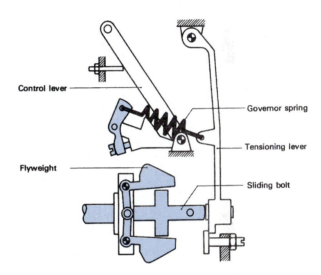

FIGURE 19–53 *Governor weight and spring arrangement in the RS/RSV models. (Courtesy of Robert Bosch Corporation.)*

Regardless of the type of governor used, all rely on the centrifugal force generated by the rotating flyweights acting through mechanical linkage to change the injection pump fuel rack position (see Chapter 16). Remember that weight forces are always trying to decrease the fuel rack position (less fuel), while the spring forces are attempting to increase (more fuel) the fuel rack position. If you remember this fact when you are studying the various governor models, you will soon be able to understand the various linkage differences between them and how they operate. The weight forces are nonadjustable; however, the spring tension can be altered in the RQ/RQV models by the adjusting nut shown in Figure 19–52 which is accessible through a plug in the governor housing. Similarly, the spring tension is adjustable in the RS/RSV models by a screw adjustment. Maximum engine speed is controlled by the tension on the governor springs, since the faster the engine rotates, the greater will be the force created by the rotating governor flyweights, which will reach a state of balance with the spring at a predetermined speed. If this speed is exceeded, the stronger weight forces will pull the fuel rack to a decreased speed position, thereby limiting the maximum speed of the engine.

RSV Governor Model

The RSV governor assembly is designed as an all-range (variable) governor which functions to control the engine idle and maximum speeds, in addition to allowing the operator to place the throttle at any position between idle and maximum where the governor will control the speed setting minus the droop (see Chapter 16 for a description of governor droop). The RSV governor is widely used on combination on- and off-highway truck applications, as well as farm tractors and industrial and marine units employing the M, A, MW, or P Bosch model inline multiple-plunger injection pumps. Although similar in external appearance to the RS limiting-speed (minimum/maximum) governor described in this section, the RSV does allow several adjustments at points outside the housing that are not available on the RS unit. Figure 19–54 illustrates an ex-

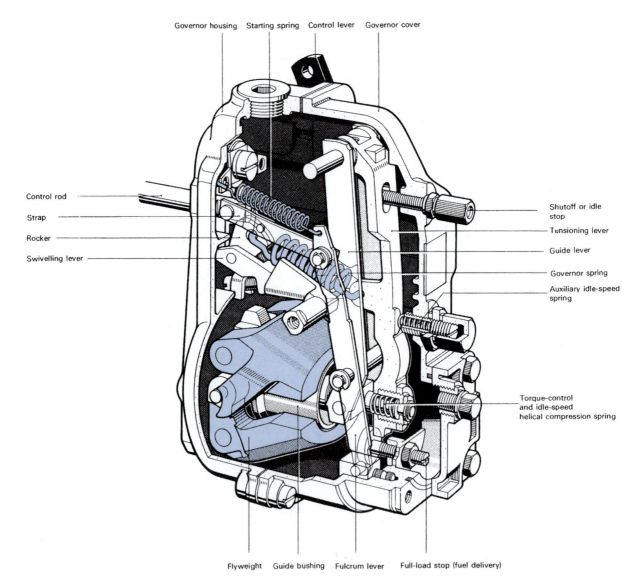

FIGURE 19–54 *Schematic view of an RSV variable-speed governor model showing the major components.* (Courtesy of Robert Bosch Corporation.)

ternal view of the RSV governor housing with the various external adjustments shown. These include:

- The idle-speed screw
- The auxiliary idle-speed spring or bumper screw
- The throttle lever linkage maximum speed adjusting screw

Components

Prior to describing the operation of the RSV governor, refer to Figure 19–54 which illustrates the major component parts and the associated linkage used with this governor model. Note that within the governor housing there are four springs used with this governor assembly:

- A starting aid spring
- The governor main spring
- An idle spring, sometimes referred to as a bumper spring
- A torque control spring

All of these springs are opposed by the rotating flyweights and act to provide governor control under various operating conditions. Figure 19–55 illustrates in simplified schematic form the various linkage component hookups within the governor.

RSV Governor Operation

Engine Startup. When the engine is stopped, the weights are collapsed and with the throttle linkage in the idle position, the fuel control rack is placed into its maximum (overfueling) position by the force of the

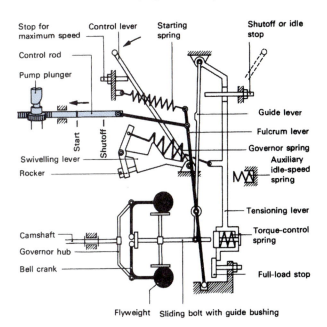

FIGURE 19–55 *RSV mechanical governor linkage schematic. (Courtesy of Robert Bosch Corporation.)*

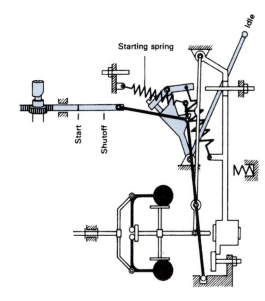

FIGURE 19–56 *RSV governor linkage/rack position during engine startup with the throttle in the idle-speed position. (Courtesy of Robert Bosch Corporation.)*

starting spring pulling the linkage as shown in Figure 19–56. The main governor spring at this time adds almost no energy to the position of the fuel control rack because of the position of the control lever against the idle stop. When the engine is cranked over, the weights are attempting to move outward against the force of the idle spring and the starting spring in order to pull the control rack to a decreased fuel position to return the engine to an idle speed.

Engine Idling. When the engine fires, the centrifugal force of the rotating governor flyweights increases rapidly, with the engine in a temporary overfueling condition. As the weights transfer their motion through the sliding bolt, the guide lever moves to the right, causing the fulcrum lever to move in the same direction. If the throttle linkage has been moved by the operator to the maximum speed setting position before the engine starts, the speed will not return to idle unless the operator physically moves the speed control lever to the idle position. However, if the throttle was placed into its normal low-idle position, then once the engine starts, it will return to the idle speed. Regardless of the throttle position, through governor linkage, the fuel control rack is pulled to the right and the fuel delivery rate is reduced. At an idle speed, the tensioning lever now starts to bear against the auxiliary idle speed (bumper) spring. When the weight force and idle spring forces are equal, a state of balance occurs and the engine runs at a reduced fuel setting sufficient to keep the engine running at an idle speed. The idle speed can be adjusted through the screw adjustment shown in Figure 19–54.

Load On/Load Off at Idle.   With the engine running at an idle speed, if a load is applied, the rpm will drop and the centrifugal force of the flyweights is reduced. This upsets the previous state of balance between the weights and the idle spring, and the stronger idle and main governor spring forces will move the governor linkage and control rack to an increased fuel setting to produce additional crankshaft torque to prevent engine stalling. During this load increase, the action of the main governor spring holds the tensioning lever and fuel control rack away from the idle (bumper) spring. The engine will run at a slower rpm rate under this increased load, due to the governor droop characteristic of the spring, giving up some of its stored energy in moving the control rack to its new fuel setting. Therefore, the weights rebalance at a lower speed against a weaker spring.

If the load at idle is reduced, the weight forces increase as the engine picks up speed at this fixed throttle setting. The weights will force the sliding bolt and with it the guide lever to the right to cause a pivoting action at the fulcrum lever, which results in the fuel control rack being pulled to a decreased fuel setting. The tensioning lever is again forced against the idle (bumper) spring and the engine will run at a new state of balance speed which is higher than it was while the load was applied because of the droop characteristic of the governor spring.

High-Speed Governor Reaction.   When the operator moves the speed control lever to the maximum position as shown in Figure 19–55, the internal swiveling lever attached to both this speed control lever and the main governor spring causes the main spring to add its greatest force to the tensioning lever. When the speed control lever butts against the full-load stop screw, the engine will receive its maximum fuel to produce its rated horsepower. In Figure 19–55 on a governor without a torque capsule spring, maximum fuel is controlled by weight action and spring forces; once the operator places the speed control lever in the full-fuel position, the engine accelerates. The difference is that when a torque control spring is used, as the engine speed increases the weight forces will start to compress the torque spring and the fuel rack would be pulled out of fuel. This results in a lower fuel delivery and therefore an engine with less rated horsepower at its governed speed than that of one without a torque capsule spring.

If the engine speed due to less than full-load conditions were to exceed the maximum full-load speed setting, the increased centrifugal force of the faster-rotating flyweights would pull the fuel rack to a decreased position. In this way the maximum engine speed is controlled and the fuel delivery is decreased in proportion to the decrease in load. If the engine were running at its full-load rpm, developing its rated horsepower, and the vehicle encountered a hill without the operator attempting to downshift the transmission, the engine speed would drop as a result of increasing load at the full throttle setting. On an engine with no torque spring, the horsepower would drop as the speed decreased and the rate of torque rise would be dependent on the volumetric efficiency of the engine at this full-fuel setting with a decreasing engine rpm. On an engine governor equipped with a torque spring, as the engine speed drops, the weight forces decrease and the tension of the torque spring adds its force to that of the main governor spring. The result would be that the engine would receive a further increase in fuel as the speed drops. This action would result in a flatter horsepower curve and a higher torque curve in the engine.

Stopping the Engine.   RSV governor-equipped engines can be stopped in one of two ways, depending on whether they have a governor control lever stop or a shutoff mechanism. Figure 19–54 illustrates an RSV governor with a governor control lever shutdown system. To stop the engine, this lever is moved all the way back to the right in the diagram, which causes lugs on the swiveling lever (connected to the main governor spring) to come into contact with the guide lever. As the guide lever is forced to the right, it pulls both the fulcrum lever and the fuel control rack with it and shutdown occurs. At the same time, the release of spring tension from the governor springs allows the weights to fly outward to further ensure a no-fuel situation, and the engine is now in the shutdown mode.

In some models engine shutdown is accomplished by the use of a special shutoff lever located at the top end of the housing. See Figure 19–12. Movement of this lever to the shutoff position causes the upper part of the fulcrum lever to move to the right as it pivots around the fulcrum point of the guide lever in Figure 19–54. This action forces the control rack to be pulled back by the strap to the shutoff position. When the shutdown lever is released, a return spring (not shown) would snap the lever back to the running position for the next engine startup procedure.

RQV Governor Model

The RQV governor is a variable-speed mechanical unit that employs the governor springs assembled into the weights in the same manner as that for other RQ models. As such, it controls idle speed, maximum speed, and any speed range in between at which the operator places the throttle linkage. Figure 19–57 illustrates the pear-shaped housing of the RQV governor, which is also found on all other RQ models.

The RQV governor is used with the models M, A, MW, and P Bosch inline multiple-plunger pumps, as well as on the VA and VE models of Bosch distributor pumps. Major truck engine manufacturers that use the RQV variable-speed governor are Deutz, Fiat-Allis, Navistar (International Harvester), Mack, Mercedes-Benz, and Volvo. The RQV is employed on vehicles with auxiliary drive, such as garbage compactor trucks, tanker trucks, and cement mixer trucks, to control the PTO (power takeoff) applications. Since

the RQV is a variable-speed (all-range) governor, it operates on the same basic principle as the RSV shown and discussed earlier in this chapter, the only difference being in the internal linkage arrangement. The RSV uses a starting and main governor spring, while the RQV has the springs assembled inside the weight carrier.

The difference between the RQ governor model and the RQV is that since the RQV is an all-range variable-speed unit, and the RQ is a minimum/maximum (limiting-speed) unit, the weights in the RQV will move out throughout the complete speed range, and will not lose control between the end of the idle speed range and the start of high-speed governing such as occurs within the RQ model.

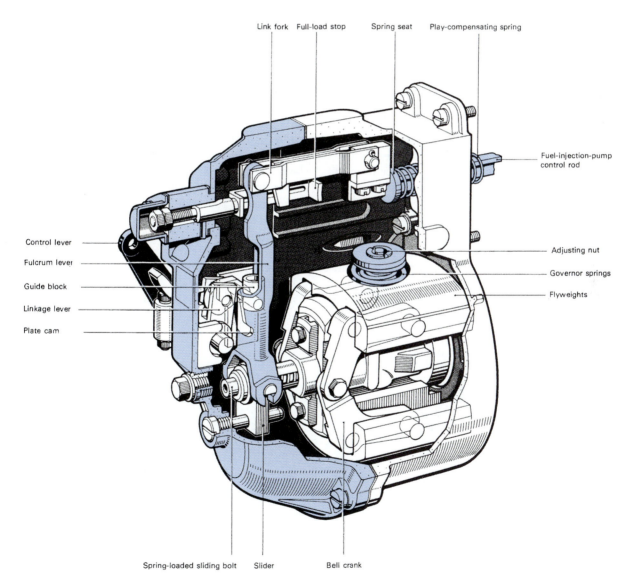

FIGURE 19–57 *Schematic view of an RQV mechanical governor assembly. (Courtesy of Robert Bosch Corporation.)*

Prior to discussing the RQV governor action, refer to Figure 19–57 which illustrates the RQV governor differences from those of the RQ model. These differences, which should be noted in Figure 19–57, are:

- Spring-loaded sliding bolt
- Full-load stop
- Plate cam

Governing action is affected by adjustment of the flyweight springs, which are accessible through the pear-shaped housing access nut, and the leverage provided by the changing position of the pivot pin (piston within the bored and slotted fulcrum lever) which is itself connected through the linkage lever and shaft to the external control lever connected to the accelerator pedal or hand throttle linkage. The operating characteristic curve for the RQV governor is almost identical to that for the RSV governor model; therefore, refer to the description for the basic rack position under different operating conditions. In addition, the earlier discussion relating to the RSV governor characteristic curve can be applied to that of the RQV model.

RQV Governor Operation

The governor reaction of the RQV is similar to that for the RSV since both are all-range variable-speed models. Any load applied to the engine, whether it be at low-idle, maximum rpm, or part-throttle position, will cause an upset in the state of balance between the weights and springs, with the spring giving more rack under load, and the weights giving less rack when a load is removed. A new state of balance is reached when the weight and spring forces are once again equal. The difference being that when a load is taken off the engine for a fixed throttle position, the new state of balance will be at a slightly higher engine speed, and when a load is applied, the new state of balance will be at a slightly lower speed because of the governor droop characteristic caused by the change in spring compression. A detailed description of droop is given in Chapter 16. Figure 19–58 illustrates the weight travel of the RQ governor at an idle speed. As you can see, the outer spring becomes the low-speed control, while all three springs would come into play as the engine is accelerated and the centrifugal force of the rotating governor flyweights increases.

The position of the governor linkage when the engine is operating at part-load speed is shown in Figure 19–59. Note carefully the position of the plunger helix. In these diagrams the governor rack movement will rotate the plunger CCW (right to left) to expose more of the helix, which in effect lengthens the effective stroke of the plunger as it moves up within the barrel of the injection pump. Full rotation of the plunger would occur only when the engine throttle is placed into the maximum position with the engine running under full-load conditions. If the throttle were placed into its maximum position but there was no load on the engine, the engine would run faster, causing the stronger centrifugal force of the rotating governor flyweights to pull the sliding bolt in toward them. This in turn would move the slider and the pivoting lower end of the fulcrum lever toward the right, while the upper end pivoting around the guide pin would pull the rack to the left to decrease the fuel delivery. In this way the maximum no-load speed of the engine is controlled.

Engine overspeed, such as when a truck runs down a hill, can occur because of the direct mechanical connection between the drive wheels and the engine. However, the faster the engine rotated, the greater the weight forces developed, and they succeed in pulling the rack out of fuel. If a piston were to strike a valve

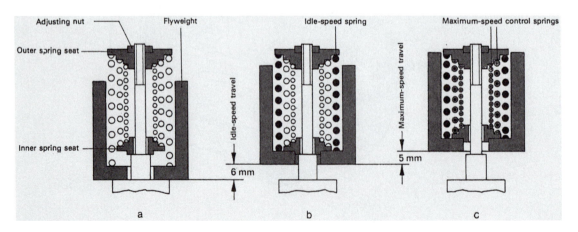

FIGURE 19–58 Flyweight travel and governor spring positions in the RQ mechanical governor assembly. (Courtesy of Robert Bosch Corporation.)

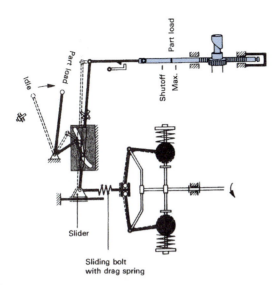

FIGURE 19–59 *RQ governor linkage positions during part-load engine operation. (Courtesy of Robert Bosch Corporation.)*

during such an overspeed, the governor has still done its job. The problem is poor driver control.

Torque Control

In all engines used in highway vehicles, some form of torque control is desired to increase rack position during a decrease in engine speed under full-load control, such as when the truck climbs a hill. Earlier discussions of the RSV and RQ model governors described how this is accomplished. The system used in the RQV governor model is shown in Figures 19–57 and 19–59 with the torque control travel adjustment being accessible through a plug located at the top rear of the governor housing. Torque control occurs as a result of the interaction between the sliding bolt drag spring and the torque control spring. The position of the throttle lever will directly affect the control lever on the side of the governor housing. Therefore, if the throttle is placed at a high-speed position for starting, the drag spring is tensioned for the duration of the acceleration mode of the engine. As a result, the torque control spring is also compressed as the fuel rack strap connected to it pulls the torque spring control rod with it as the fuel rack moves to maximum fuel for starting. Once the rotating governor flyweights move out to this higher rpm range, however, the force on the sliding bolt drag spring is reduced and the compressive force of the torque spring is now strong enough to pull the fuel control rack back to lower fuel delivery after startup. Torque control adjustment can only be done with the pump/governor combination mounted on a test stand. The start of torque control is set by varying the tension

adjustment screw of the torque control spring. In addition, the use of shims of different thicknesses will set the torque control travel.

RQV-K Governor Model

The RQV-K governor model has the same pear-shaped housing as both the RQ and RQV, but its control mechanism differs slightly. It also includes access to fine adjustments, which can be reached through the metal cover on top of the housing as well as behind a plate on the governor cover at the rear as shown in Figure 19–60. However, major adjustments to the RQV-K governor should be made only with the pump and governor combination on a test stand.

The RQV-K governor is mated to the P model Bosch inline multiple-plunger pump, with major users of this combination pump/governor being Navistar (International Harvester) and Mack trucks. The RQV-K is a mechanical variable-speed governor that can be fitted with any type of engine torque control arrangement to suit a wide range of desirable conditions. This flexibility of torque control allows the RQV-K to fill the different fuel injection requirements of the various engine users. Since the RQV-K uses the same basic flyweight assembly with three springs enclosed within the weight carrier as that in the RQV model, and operates in the same manner as described in this chapter for the RQV, you should have little trouble in systematically following the governor actions during startup, idle, part-load, and maximum speed/full-fuel control conditions. What we do need to consider, however, is the unique method employed in the RQV-K governor to maintain torque control.

If you are already familiar with the governor linkage arrangement from the weight carrier through the fulcrum lever to the fuel control rack in the RQV models, reference to Figure 19–60 will allow you to identify the major component parts difference in the RQV-K model. Additional components used on the RQV-K that are not used on the RQV are listed below.

- A strap (spring loaded for tension), connected between the fuel control rod (rack) and the fulcrum lever
- An adjusting screw (spindle) for full-load delivery
- A full-load stop with a rocker guide
- An adjusting screw to change the slope (angle) of the rocker guide
- A rocker

Review Figure 19–60 and familiarize yourself with each of these five components and their relationship to other governor parts before proceeding, since the RQV-K rocker action becomes critical to your

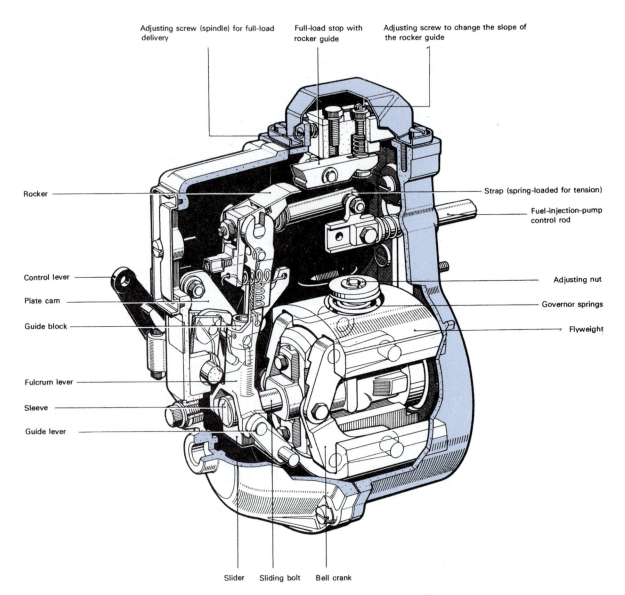

Adjusting screw (spindle) for full-load delivery

Full-load stop with rocker guide

Adjusting screw to change the slope of the rocker guide

Rocker

Strap (spring-loaded for tension)

Fuel-injection-pump control rod

Control lever

Plate cam

Guide block

Adjusting nut

Governor springs

Flyweight

Fulcrum lever

Sleeve

Guide lever

Slider   Sliding bolt   Bell crank

FIGURE 19–60   Schematic diagram of a model RQV-K mechanical governor assembly. (Courtesy of Robert Bosch Corporation.)

understanding of just how this torque control system functions with this type of governor.

RQV-K Governor Operation

With the engine stopped the weights are collapsed and the speed control lever, which is connected through external linkage to the throttle pedal on a truck, would be in the shutoff position. Refer to Figure 19–61 and note the control lever position, the guide block position within the slot of the plate cam, and the position of the rocker in relation to the rocker guide. Also note the fuel control rack identification mark, which is opposite the fuel shutoff indicator.

When the governor speed control lever is placed into the starting position, as with other Bosch governors, excess fuel delivery for ease of starting under all operating environments is desired. The fuel control rack would be moved 21 mm to the position shown in Figure 19–61. In this example, the rack movement at idle would sit between about 7 and 10 mm, depending on the load at initial startup. The rack position at full-load speed in this example is about 11 mm, which is about half of what is delivered during starting (excess fuel) and approximately 4 mm greater than at low-idle speed. If the engine load were increased beyond the horsepower capability of the engine such as when a ve-

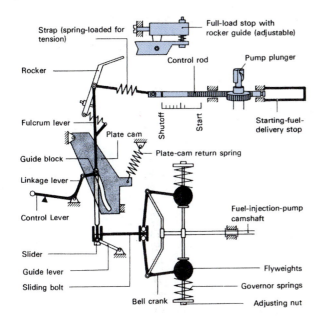

FIGURE 19-61 *RQV-K governor linkage schematic with the engine stopped. (Courtesy of Robert Bosch Corporation.)*

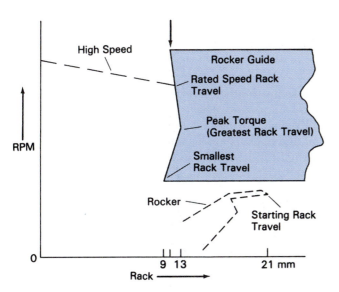

FIGURE 19-62 *Rocker guide cam shape for an RQV-K mechanical governor. (Courtesy of Robert Bosch Corporation.)*

hicle climbs a hill, the engine speed would start to decrease without a transmission downshift. Consequently, the loss of speed would cause a reduction in the centrifugal force of the rotating flyweights and the three governor springs would start to expand against the governor linkage to move the rack to an increased position. The rocker would now sit in the base of the V-shaped rocker guide, which means that the rack has been advanced as shown in Figure 19-62 to a position

corresponding to about 13 mm of travel, which is about 2 mm greater than it was under full-load-rated speed conditions. This additional fuel delivery would provide a fairly flat (constant) horsepower curve plus a high rate of torque rise, with a reduction in speed from the no-load rpm position.

ANEROID/BOOST COMPENSATOR CONTROL

On engines using Robert Bosch injection pumps with a turbocharged engine, an aneroid/boost compensator control is used to prevent overfueling of the engine and hence black smoke during acceleration. This device controls the amount of fuel that can be injected until the exhaust-gas-driven turbocharger can overcome its initial speed lag and supply enough air boost to the engine cylinders. Such a device is used extensively by all four-stroke-cycle engine manufacturers today to comply with U.S. EPA smoke emission standards.

The aneroid is mounted on either the end or the top of the injection pump governor housing, with its linkage connected to the fuel control mechanism and a supply line running from the pressure side of the intake manifold (turbocharger outlet) to the top of the aneroid housing. Such a device is shown in Figure 19-63.

Figure 19-63a shows the position of the aneroid control linkage when the engine stop lever is actuated, which moves the aneroid fuel control link out of contact with the arm on the fuel injection pump control rack. Figure 19-63b shows the aneroid linkage position when the throttle control lever is moved to the slow idle position. This causes the starter spring to move the fuel control rack to the excess fuel position. Only during the cranking period is excess fuel supplied to the engine. This is because the instant the engine starts, we have the centrifugal force of the governor flyweights overcoming the starter spring tension, thereby moving the fuel control rack to a decreased fuel position. As this is occurring, the aneroid fuel control lever shaft spring will move the control link back into its original position. In Figure 19-63, the fuel control rack arm will contact the aneroid fuel control link, thereby limiting the amount of fuel that can be injected to approximately half-throttle and preventing excessive black smoke upon starting. The same lever will control the rack position at any time that the engine is accelerated, preventing any further increase in fuel delivery until the turbocharger has accelerated to supply enough boost air for complete combustion.

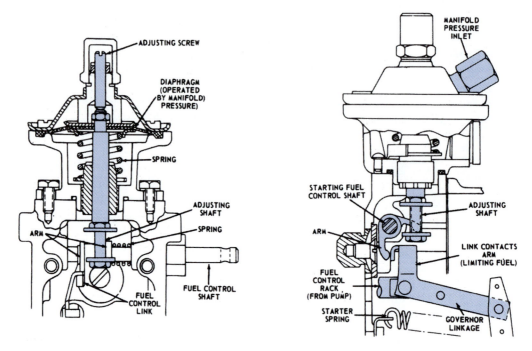

FIGURE 19–63 *Mechanical governor aneroid (without liquid) control linkage component parts on an inline fuel injection pump. (Courtesy of Robert Bosch Corporation.)*

Boost Compensator Operation

Basically, the boost compensator ensures that the amount of injected fuel is in direct proportion to the quantity of air within the engine cylinder to sustain correct combustion of the fuel and therefore increase the horsepower of the engine. With the engine running, pressurized air from the cold end of the turbocharger passes through the (Figure 19–63b) connecting tube from the engine air inlet manifold to the boost compensator chamber. Inside this chamber is a diaphragm (Figure 19–63a) which is connected to a pushrod, which is in turn coupled to the compensator lever. Movement of the diaphragm is opposed by a spring, therefore for any movement to take place at the linkage, the air pressure on the diaphragm must be higher than spring tension. As the engine rpm and load increase and the air pressure within the connecting tube becomes high enough to overcome the tension of the diaphragm spring, the diaphragm and pushrod will be pushed down.

This movement causes the compensator lever to pivot, forcing the fuel control rack toward an increased fuel position. The boost compensator will therefore react to engine inlet manifold air pressure regardless of the action of the governor. When the turbocharger boost air pressure reaches its maximum, the quantity of additional fuel injected will be equal to the stroke of the aneroid boost compensator linkage, in addition to the normal full-load injection amount that is determined by the governor full-load stop bolt.

ALTITUDE PRESSURE COMPENSATOR

In naturally aspirated (nonturbocharged) diesel engines such as cars or trucks that can travel through varying terrain and altitudes, a means by which the fuel delivery rate can be altered is an important function of the governor and altitude pressure compensator. Since atmospheric pressure decreases with an increase in altitude, the volumetric efficiency of the engine will be less at higher elevations than it will be at sea level. On turbocharged engines, a boost compensator performs a function similar to that of the altitude compensator on nonturbocharged engines. Bosch refers to the altitude compensator as an ADA mechanism, and it is used in conjunction with either the RQ or RQV mechanical governor models. The ADA is located on the governor cover.

ROBERT BOSCH ELECTRONIC DIESEL CONTROL

Within the various chapters of this book are featured a number of high-technology diesel fuel injection control systems, with DDC's DDEC system (late 1985), Caterpillar's PEEC system (early 1987), and Cummins ECI system (1989) being mass-produced designs that have gained prominence since late 1985. The Robert Bosch Corporation offers electronic sensing and control of both its heavy-duty inline multiple-plunger pumps and its smaller model VE distributor pump assemblies used in automotive applications. As with the DDC and Cat systems, the high pressures necessary for injection purposes are still created mechanically by a reciprocating plunger within a barrel; however, control of the fuel rack position, and therefore of the quantity of fuel injected for a given throttle position and load, is determined by an ECU (electronic control unit) which has been programmed to output specific control signals to the governor/rack in relation to the accelerator position, turbocharger boost pressure, mass airflow rate, engine oil pressure, and temperature and coolant level.

The upgraded version of the Bosch P electronic model inline multiple-plunger injection pump, designated as the PDE, which is now in use in Europe on such OEM trucks as Mercedes-Benz, Volvo, and Saab-Scania, is also now in use in the United States. This pump incorporates several new design features for exhaust emissions–sensitive engines that need to comply with the EPA regulations. Newly developed pump plunger control-sleeve elements permit tighter control of prestroke regulation resulting in higher injection pressures of 1500 bar (21,796 psi) and precise control of injected fuel quantity and start of injection. Mack Trucks has already adapted the electronic pump to its heavy-duty line of E6 and E7 (electronic controlled) diesel engines. Robert Bosch continues to offer mechanically controlled governors and electronically controlled systems for monitoring and controlling engine performance.

Figure 19–64 illustrates an electronically controlled PLN system for a high-speed heavy-duty diesel engine. Modifications to the mechanical injection pump assembly are best viewed by reference to Figure 19–65. Note that although the pumping plunger (8) still operates within a barrel (2), it also moves through a control sleeve (3). The sleeve can be moved to allow an adjustable prestroke to change the port closing, or to start injection. Compare this lift to port closure shown as *h* in Figure 19–65. By moving the control sleeve upward in the direction of fuel delivery—closer toward TDC as per Figure 19–65—the plunger has to lift through a greater distance (longer prestroke) before it is able to close the control bore (6); therefore, injection starts later. If the sleeve is closer to BDC, injection starts earlier, since the control bore enters the sleeve earlier.

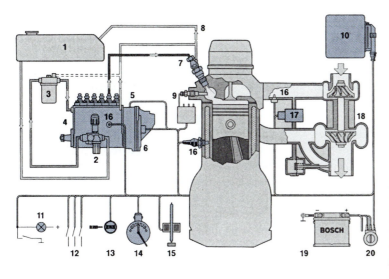

1 Fuel tank, 2 Supply pump, 3 Fuel filter, 4 In-line fuel-injection pump, 5 Timing device, 6 Governor, 7 Nozzle-and-holder assembly, 8 Fuel return line, 9 Sheathed-element glow plug with glow control unit, 10 Electronic control unit, 11 Diagnosis indicator, 12 Switches for clutch, brake, exhaust brake, 13 Speed selector lever, 14 Pedal position sensor, 15 Engine-speed sensor, 16 Temperature sensor (water, air, fuel), 17 Charge-pressure sensor, 18 Turbocharger, 19 Battery, 20 Glow-plug and starter switch.

FIGURE 19–64 Major components of an inline fuel injection pump equipped with EDC (electronic diesel control). Courtesy of Robert Bosch Corporation.)

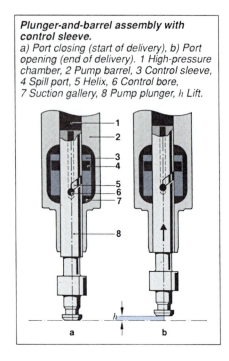

Plunger-and-barrel assembly with control sleeve.
a) Port closing (start of delivery), b) Port opening (end of delivery). 1 High-pressure chamber, 2 Pump barrel, 3 Control sleeve, 4 Spill port, 5 Helix, 6 Control bore, 7 Suction gallery, 8 Pump plunger, h Lift.

FIGURE 19–65 *Components of an electronically controlled fuel injection pump plunger-and-barrel assembly. (Courtesy of Robert Bosch Corporation.)*

The actual fuel delivery rate can be altered by the design of the injection pump camshaft lobe.

The cutaway view of a six-cylinder engine injection pump in Figure 19–66 highlights the control sleeve design on the pumping plunger. Both the injected fuel quantity and the start of injection are electronically controlled by means of linear solenoid actuators. The injection sequence is controlled from an ECU (electronic control unit) which receives electrical inputs from a number of engine sensors (see Figure 19–64). Each sensor is fed a voltage input from the ECU in the region of 5 V, although this may be higher depending on the OEM using the system. Each sensor completes the electrical loop back to the ECU by sending an output signal based on its existing operating condition. Each temperature sensor, for example, is designed to have a fixed resistance value when cold; as it warms up, the resistance value decreases. An oil, fuel, or coolant temperature sensor may be designed to have 115,000 ohms (Ω) when cold and drop to 70 ohms (Ω) when it is at normal operating temperature. What this means is that if the ECU outputs a 5 V reference value to the sensor, the high resistance value will restrict the return signal to the ECU and the voltage value will be lower, usually in the region of 0.5 V. For any operating temperature, therefore, the return voltage signal value to the ECU will vary between 0.5 and 5 V. A pressure

sensor, such as an oil or turbocharger boost, operates similarly to that described for the temperature sensors.

An inductive position sensor tells the ECU the position of the injection pump control rod/rack. An engine speed sensor (Figure 19–64, item 15) scans a pulse ring located to monitor the camshaft speed. A fuel temperature sensor monitors the fuel in the supply line to the injection pump. The accelerator pedal incorporates a variable resistor (potentiometer) so that the percentage of pedal opening can be relayed to the ECU. The throttle pedal is designed to show a high resistance value with a closed throttle at idle speed; consequently, the input voltage value of 5 V is reduced to approximately 0.5 V back to the ECU. At a WOT (wide-open throttle) position, the return voltage back to the ECU is close to 5 V, or the same as the input value. In addition, an intake manifold air-temperature sensor indicates to the ECU the denseness of the air flowing into the engine cylinders based on temperature. If a turbocharger is used, a turbo boost sensor functions to tell the ECU basically the load under which the engine is operating. A high boost pressure means greater load, while low boost pressure indicates a lower load level. An alternator speed signal can also be employed to drive an electronic tachograph. This signal, in turn, can be used to indicate to the ECU the vehicle's road speed. The clutch pedal position is indicated by a switch, and the stop-lamp switch provides information relative to the brake pedal position.

From all of the various sensor inputs, the ECU calculates and adjusts the electrical current to the rack actuator system of the fuel injection pump. Figure 19–67 illustrates the sequence of events involved in the EDC (electronic diesel control) system. The ECU compares the actual plunger/barrel port closing signal for the start of injection from a needle-motion sensor installed in one of the injector nozzle holders with an operating value that has been programmed into the computer map. The port closing actuator system is then adjusted by varying the control current so that the actual requested throttle/fuel demands are met. The travel of the injection pump rack electromagnet is directly proportional to the current demands of injection. The end of injection caused by port opening is varied on the electronically controlled pump in the same way it is for the mechanical system; that is, the pump plunger is rotated through rack movement.

DISTRIBUTOR PUMPS

Distributor pumps manufactured by Bosch include the VA and VE models (the V is from the German word *Verteiler*, and the second letter, A or E, indicates the

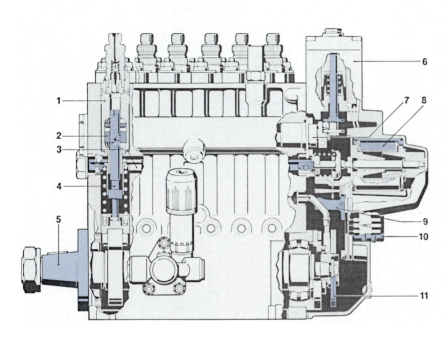

1 Pump cylinder, 2 Control sleeve,
3 Control rod, 4 Pump plunger, 5 Camshaft,
6 Port-closing actuator solenoid, 7 Control-
sleeve setting shaft, 8 Rod-travel actuator
solenoid, 9 Inductive rod-travel sensor,
10 Connector, 11 Inductive speed sensor.

FIGURE 19–66 Cutaway view of an electronically controlled inline injection pump illustrating the main components. (Courtesy of Robert Bosch Corporation.)

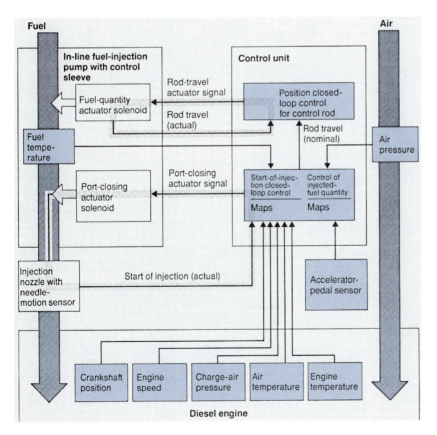

FIGURE 19–67 EDC electronic open-loop and closed-loop control of the inline fuel injection pump with a control sleeve. (Courtesy of Robert Bosch Corporation.)

BOSCH Distributor-type fuel-injection pump type VE

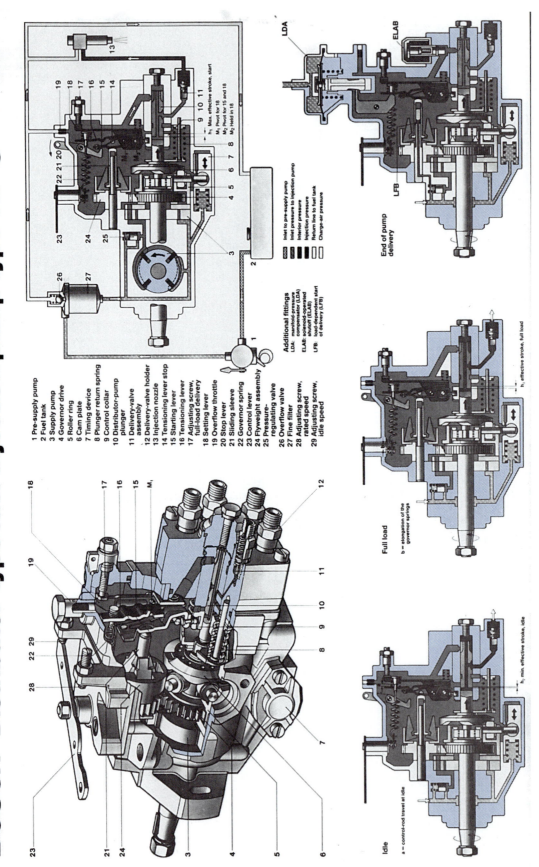

Robert Bosch GmbH © 1980
Training Publication VDT-T 2/7-4 En

1 Pre-supply pump
2 Fuel tank
3 Supply pump
4 Governor drive
5 Roller ring
6 Cam plate
7 Timing device
8 Plunger return spring
9 Control collar
10 Distributor-pump plunger
11 Delivery-valve assembly
12 Delivery-valve holder
13 Injection nozzle
14 Tensioning lever stop
15 Starting lever
16 Tensioning lever
17 Adjusting screw, full-load delivery
18 Setting lever
19 Overflow throttle
20 Stop lever
21 Sliding sleeve
22 Governor spring
23 Control lever
24 Flyweight assembly
25 Pressure-regulating valve
26 Overflow valve
27 Fine filter
28 Adjusting screw, rated speed
29 Adjusting screw, idle speed

Inlet to pre-supply pump
Inlet pressure to injection pump
Interior pressure
Injection pressure
Return line to fuel tank
Charge-air pressure

Additional fittings
LDA: manifold-pressure compensator (LDA)
ELAB: solenoid-operated shutoff (ELAB)
LFB: load-dependent start of delivery (LFB)

h₁ Max. effective stroke, start
M₁ Pivot for 18
M₂ Pivot for 15 and 18
M₃ Held in 18

End of pump delivery

Full load
b = elongation of the governor springs

h₁ effective stroke, full load

Idle
a = control-rod travel at idle

h₂ min. effective stroke, idle

FIGURE 19–68 Bosch model VE-F distributor injection pump operational diagram.

specific model). The distributor pumps are used, for example, in Volkswagen cars and light trucks, Volvo and Peugeot cars, and International Harvester and Deutz farm tractors. Figure 19–68 illustrates that the VE pump has a horizontal control lever (throttle) and the timing piston (advance) cover is located near the bottom of the pump. The VA pump has two vertical control levers, with the timing advance piston cover located near the top of the pump.

ROBERT BOSCH MODEL VE INJECTION PUMP

The model VE fuel injection pump (Figure 19–68), takes its name from the German word *Verteiler,* which means distributor pump, although it is also commonly referred to as a rotary-type design that operates upon the same basic principle as that of a gasoline engine ignition distributor. Rather than employing high-tension pickup points inside a distributor cap, we have high-pressure fuel outlet lines to carry diesel fuel to each cylinder. On a gasoline engine, the ignition distributor feeds the high-tension spark via wire leads to each spark plug in engine firing-order sequence. In the diesel engine, the fuel injection pump delivers high-pressure fuel through steel-backed fuel lines to each cylinder's injector in firing-order sequence.

The E designation in the pump model refers to the particular model of rotary injection pump produced by Robert Bosch Corporation. The pump is available in two-, three-, four-, five-, six-, and eight-cylinder engine configurations to suit a variety of engines and applications. The VE injection pump is used widely on both passenger car and light-truck applications worldwide. The pump, although of Robert Bosch design and manufacture, is also manufactured under license by both Diesel Kiki and Nippondenso in Japan.

The product designation for VE pumps is similar to VA pumps with two notable exceptions. First, the plunger diameter is generally given in whole millimeters; and second, no execution letter is used. Let us break down a typical VE pump product designation—VE4/9F2500R16-2:

    V: distributor pump type

    E: pump capacity

    4: number of high-pressure outlets

    9: plunger diameter, in whole millimeters

    F: flyweight governing

 2500: full-load-rated speed

    R: direction of rotation (R, right; L, left)

 16-2: engineering and application information

Let us look at just the letters and numbers that are important to us now: VE6/11F1800L19. This will be much simpler because there are fewer important letters and numbers to remember.

    V: Distributor pump

    E: Capacity

    6: High-pressure outlets

  11: Plunger diameter, 11 mm

    L: Left-hand rotation

It is one of the most widely used distributor-type fuel injection pumps on the market today in automotive industrial and marine applications. Because of the various engine/vehicle manufacturers using this injection pump, minor differences or options may be found on one pump/engine that is not used on another; however, the design and operation of the VE pump regardless of what engine it is installed on can be considered common to all vehicles. The major differences would be:

1. The engine to injection pump timing.

2. The injection pump lift or prestroke (discussed later in this chapter).

3. The use of an altitude/boost compensator found on engines operating in varying altitudes and or equipped with a turbocharger. This device limits the amount of fuel that can be injected in order to comply with EPA exhaust emissions standards.

4. All VE pumps contain a vane transfer pump built within the housing of the injection pump assembly to transfer diesel fuel under pressures of from approximately 36 psi (250 kPa) at an idle rpm up to about 116 psi (800 kPa) at speeds of 4500 rpm into the hydraulic head of the injection pump. Some vehicles rely on this pump alone to pull fuel from the vehicle fuel tank; however, some vehicles employ an additional lift pump, usually electric-driven, between the fuel filter and the vane transfer pump to pull fuel from the tank and supply it to the vane transfer pump.

5. The VE pump is much more compact than the inline fuel injection pump used extensively on larger midrange and heavy-duty truck applications. The distributor pump uses approximately half as many component parts and usually weighs less than half that of an inline pump. Contained within the housing of the distributor pump are both a fuel transfer pump (vane type) and a governor mechanism.

Fuel Flow: Operation

Although minor differences may exist between the actual layout and fuel flow path from the vehicle fuel tank to the injection pump, Figure 19–68 illustrates a typical fuel flow arrangement used with the VE model pump as it applies to its use in passenger car and light pickup truck engines.

To start the engine, the operator must turn the ignition key on, which will electrically energize a fuel shutoff solenoid located on the injection pump housing just above the fuel outlet lines from the hydraulic head of the injection pump.

This solenoid is shown in Figures 19–68 and 19–69 and when energized is designed to allow fuel under pressure from the vane transfer pump to pass into the injection pump plunger pumping chamber. When the ignition key is turned OFF, the fuel solenoid is deenergized and fuel can no longer be supplied to the plunger pumping chamber; therefore, the engine will starve for fuel and stop immediately.

Some vehicles use only the vane transfer pump, which is contained within the injection pump housing to draw fuel from the tank to the injection pump, while others may employ either a mechanical diaphragm or an electrically operated lift pump to draw fuel from the tank and deliver it to the vane transfer pump.

Also, most vehicles today employ a fuel filter/water separator plus a secondary fuel filter in the system between the fuel tank and the vane transfer pump.

The vane transfer pump is shown as item 3 in Figure 19–68. This pump is capable of producing fuel delivery pressures of about 36 psi (248 kPa) at an engine idle speed up to as high as 120 psi (827 kPa), although maximum pressures are generally maintained at around 100 psi (689.5 kPa). This fuel under pressure is then delivered through internal injection pump drillings to the distributor pump plunger shown as item 10 in Figure 19–68. All internal parts of the fuel injection pump are lubricated by this fuel under pressure; there is no separate lube oil reservoir.

Maximum fuel pressure created by the vane transfer pump, which is located within the injection pump body, is controlled by an adjustable fuel pressure regulator screw.

On four-stroke engines, the injection pump is driven at one-half engine speed and is capable of delivering up to 2800 psi (approximately 200 bar) to the injection nozzles; however, the adjusted release pressure of the nozzle establishes at what specific pressure the nozzle will open.

An overflow line from the top of the injection pump housing allows excess fuel that is used for cooling and lubrication purposes to return to the fuel tank through a restricted bolt readily identifiable by the word OUT stamped on the top of it.

Since the vane transfer pump is capable of either left- or right-hand rotation, take care when servicing this unit that you assemble it correctly. Take careful note of the various holes in Figure 19–68. Hole 1 in the eccentric ring is farthest from its inner wall compared to hole 2. When looking at the eccentric ring, this hole must be in position 1 for right-hand rotation pumps and to the left for left-hand rotation fuel injection pumps. Hole 3 should be on the governor side when the transfer pump is installed. Also the pump vanes should always be fitted with the circular or crowned ends contacting the walls of the eccentric ring.

Fuel under pressure from the vane transfer pump is then delivered to the pumping plunger shown in Figure 19–68 and also in Figure 19–70, where it is then sent to the fuel injectors (nozzles). Let us study the action of the plunger more closely, since it is this unit that is responsible for the distribution of the high-pressure fuel within the system. Figure 19–71 shows the actual connection between the cam rollers and the pump plunger, which is also visible in Figures 19–68 and 19–70.

Notice that the plunger is capable of two motions: (1) circular or rotational (driven from the drive shaft), and (2) reciprocating (back and forth by cam plate and roller action).

Reference to Figures 19–68 and 19–71 shows that the cam plate is designed with as many lobes or projections on it as there are engine cylinders. Unlike Delphi/Lucas CAV and Stanadyne distributor injection pumps, the

Electric shutoff (with pull solenoid).

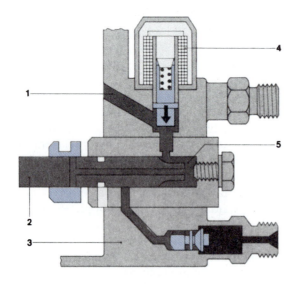

1 Inlet bore,
2 Distributor plunger,
3 Distributor head,
4 Pull (or push) solenoid,
5 High-pressure chamber.

FIGURE 19–69 VE injection pump plunger-and-barrel unit showing an electric fuel solenoid shutoff device. (Courtesy of Robert Bosch Corporation.)

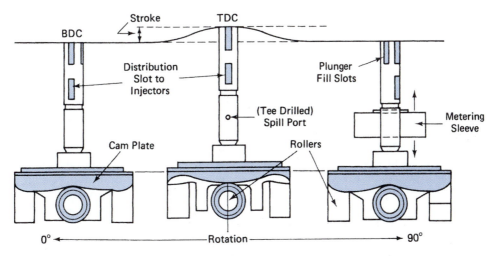

FIGURE 19–70 VE injection pump distributor plunger location and design. (Courtesy of Robert Bosch Corporation.)

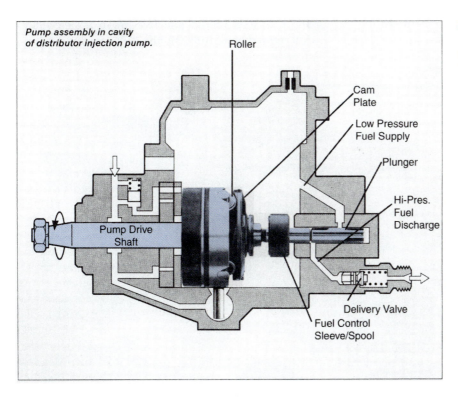

FIGURE 19–71 High-pressure fuel delivery passage within the VE model pump. (Courtesy of Robert Bosch Corporation.)

rollers on the VE pump are not actuated by an internal cam ring with lobes on it, but instead the cam ring is circular and attached to a round cam plate. As the cam ring rotates with the injection pump driveshaft and plunger, the rollers (which are fixed), cause the cam lobe to lift every 90° (for example) in a four-cylinder engine, or every 60° in a six-cylinder engine.

In other words, the rollers do not lift on the cam as in a conventional system, but it is the cam ring that is solidly attached to the rotating plunger that actually lifts as each lobe comes into contact with each positioned roller spaced apart in relation to the number of engine cylinders. With such a system then, the plunger stroke will remain constant regardless of engine rpm. At the end of each plunger stroke, a spring ensures a return of the cam ring to its former position as shown in Figure 19–68 (item 8). Therefore, the back-and-forth motion of the single pumping plunger is positive.

Anytime that the roller is at its lowest point on the rotating cam ring lobe, the pumping plunger will be at a position commonly known as BDC (bottom dead center); and with the rotating cam ring lobe in contact with the roller, the pumping plunger will be at TDC (top dead center) position, as shown in Figure 19–70. Distribution of fuel to the injector nozzles is via plunger rotation, and metering (quantity) is controlled by the metering sleeve position, which varies the effective stroke of the plunger.

If we consider the plunger movement, that is, *stroke* and *rotation*, Figure 19–72 depicts the action in a 90° movement such as would be found on a four-cylinder four-cycle engine pump. Even though there is a period of dwell at the start and end of one 90° rotation (one cylinder firing), the plunger movement during this time continues.

The sequence of events shown in Figure 19–72 is as follows:

1.   The fill slot of the rotating plunger is aligned with the fill port, which is receiving fuel at transfer pump pressure as high as 100 psi (7 bar approximately), one cylinder only.

2.   The rotating plunger has reached the *port closing* position. The plunger rotates a control spool regulating collar (see Figures 19–72, item 8, and 19–68, item 9). The position of the regulating collar is controlled by the operator or driver though linkage connected to and through the governor spring and flyweights. Because the plunger rotates as well as moving back and forth, the plunger must lift for port closure to occur; then delivery will commence. Because the rotating plunger does stroke through the metering sleeve in the VE pump, this pump is classed as the *port closing* type. Therefore, even though the roller may be causing the cam–ring–plunger to lift, the position of the regulating collar determines the amount of travel of the plunger or *prestroke*, so the actual effective stroke of the plunger is determined at all times by the collar position.

FIGURE 19–72 VE model distributor pump single plunger movement in a four-cylinder four-stroke-cycle engine through 90° of pump rotation. (Courtesy of Robert Bosch Corporation.)

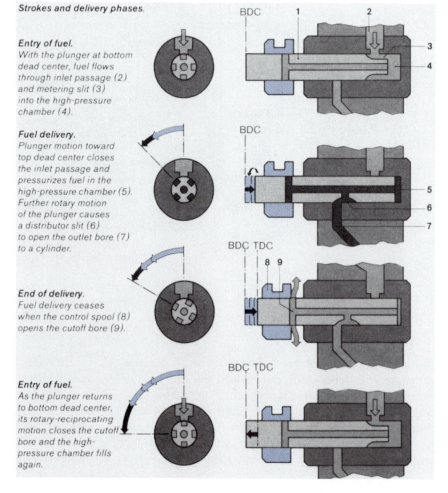

Strokes and delivery phases.

Entry of fuel.
With the plunger at bottom dead center, fuel flows through inlet passage (2) and metering slit (3) into the high-pressure chamber (4).

Fuel delivery.
Plunger motion toward top dead center closes the inlet passage and pressurizes fuel in the high-pressure chamber (5). Further rotary motion of the plunger causes a distributor slit (6) to open the outlet bore (7) to a cylinder.

End of delivery.
Fuel delivery ceases when the control spool (8) opens the cutoff bore (9).

Entry of fuel.
As the plunger returns to bottom dead center, its rotary-reciprocating motion closes the cutoff bore and the high-pressure chamber fills again.

3. At the point of plunger lift (start of effective stroke), fuel delivery to the hydraulic head and injector line will begin in the engine firing order sequence.

4. The effective stroke is always less than the total plunger stroke. As the plunger moves through the regulating collar, it uncovers a *spill port*, opening the high-pressure circuit and allowing the remaining fuel to spill into the interior of the injection pump housing. This then is *port opening* or spill, which ends the effective stroke of the plunger; however, the plunger stroke continues.

5. With the sudden decrease in fuel delivery pressure, the spring within the injector nozzle rapidly seats the needle valve, stopping injection and preventing after-dribble, unburned fuel, and therefore engine exhaust smoke. At the same time, the delivery valve for that nozzle located in the hydraulic head is snapped back on its seat by spring pressure.

In a four-cylinder four-stroke engine, we would have four strokes within 360° of pump plunger rotation, which is of course equal to 720° of engine rotation. In summation, the volume of fuel delivered is controlled by the regulating collar position, which alters the (*effective stroke*) time that the ports are closed.

If there is an annulus or circular slot located on the plunger, all distributor slits are tied together; this is the reason that the plunger must lift for port closure to occur. Only after the annulus lifts beyond the fill port do we have port closure. Port closing occurs only after a specified lift from BDC.

Delivery Valve Operation

Contained within the hydraulic head (outlets) of the injection pump where the high-pressure fuel lines are connected to the injection pump are delivery valves (one per cylinder) (Figure 19–73), which are designed to open at a fixed pressure and deliver fuel to the injectors in firing-order sequence.

These valves function to ensure that there will always be a predetermined fuel pressure in the fuel lines leading to the fuel injectors. Another major function of these individual delivery valves is to ensure that at the end of the injection period for that cylinder there is no possibility of secondary injection and also that any pressure waves during the injection period will not be transferred back into the injection pump.

If secondary injection were to occur, the engine would tend to misfire and run rough. The delivery valves ensure a crisp cutoff to the end of injection when the fuel pressure drops off in the line and also maintains fuel in the injection line so that there is no possibility of air being trapped inside the line.

Pressure valve.

a closed,	4 Valve body,
b open.	5 Shaft,
1 Valve holder,	6 Relief piston,
2 Valve seat,	7 Ring groove,
3 Valve spring,	8 Longitudinal groove.

a) closed.

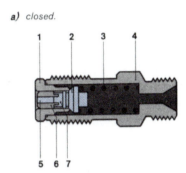

b) open.

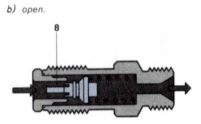

FIGURE 19–73 VE injection pump delivery valve operation. (Courtesy of Robert Bosch Corporation.)

Fuel Return Line

All model VE pumps use a percentage of the fuel delivered to the injection pump housing to cool and lubricate the internal pump components. Since the diesel fuel will pick up some heat through this action, a bleed off or fuel return from the injection pump housing is achieved through the use of a hollow bolt with an orifice drilled into it as shown in Figure 19–74.

FIGURE 19–74 VE injection pump fuel return bolt with a restricted orifice. (Do not confuse with the inlet bolt.) (Courtesy of Robert Bosch Corporation.)

This bolt is readily identifiable by the word OUT stamped on the hex head, and if substituted with an ordinary bolt, no fuel will be able to return to the fuel tank from the injection pump.

Emergency Stop Lever

Should the fuel shutoff solenoid fail to operate when the ignition key is turned OFF, an emergency stop lever is connected to the injection pump housing and accessible underhood. This lever can be pulled to cut off fuel in the event of electric fuel solenoid failure. This lever is shown in Figure 19–68 as item 20.

Minimum/Maximum Speed Settings

The idle rpm and the maximum engine speed is controlled by adjusting two screws located on the top of the injection pump housing and shown as items 28 and 29 in Figure 19–68. Both of these adjustments should always be done with the engine at normal operating temperature.

Turning the idle-speed adjusting screw clockwise will increase idle rpm. Turning the high-speed adjusting screw counterclockwise will increase the maximum speed setting of the engine. The minimum and maximum engine speed settings are listed on the ve-

hicle emissions label/decal that is generally affixed under the hood in the engine compartment or at the front end of the engine compartment close to the radiator end.

Cold-Start Device or KSB

All vehicles equipped with the VE fuel injection pump are equipped with either a manually operated or automatic cold-start device (CSD). The year of vehicle manufacture and make establishes whether it has the former or the latter.

The main purpose of a cold-start device is to provide easier engine starting and warm-up properties by controlling pump housing fuel pressure which acts upon the injection timing piston, item 8 shown in Figure 19–76a for the automatic KSB model. When the cold-start device is activated, the beginning of fuel injection is advanced through the movement of the injection pump cam roller ring in relation to the cam disc.

With a manually operated CSD such as shown in Figure 19–75, a control cable, which is mounted inside the vehicle, is pulled out by the operator and turned clockwise to lock it in place. This action causes a lever connected to a cam (Figure 19–76a) to butt up against the injection pump advance piston and push it for-

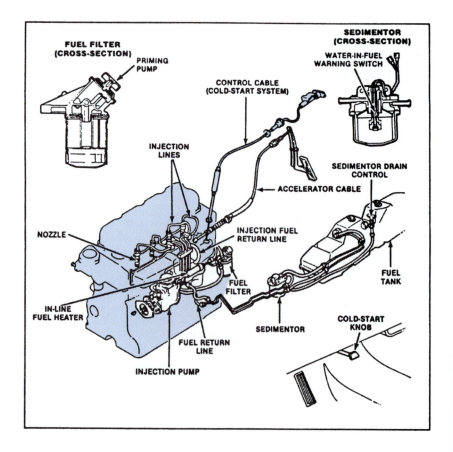

FIGURE 19–75 Manual cold-start device components used on earlier model VE pumps. (Courtesy of Robert Bosch Corporation.)

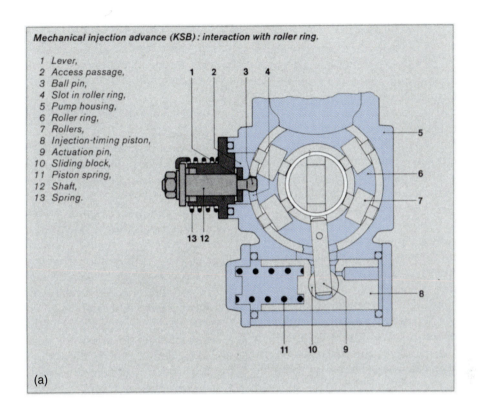

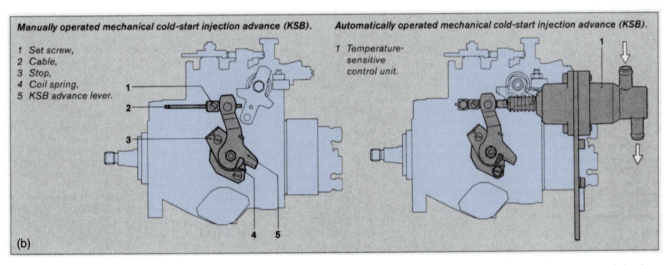

FIGURE 19–76 (a) KSB mechanical injection advance device. (b) KSB cold-start mechanical and automatic injection advance devices and linkage. (Courtesy of Robert Bosch Corporation.)

ward. Movement of the advance piston rotates the cam roller ring as shown in Figure 19–76a so that fuel injection will occur earlier in the cylinder BTDC. The manual CSD uses a ball pin shown as item 3 in Figure 19–76a to rotate the roller ring (6).

The automatic CSD operates on the basis of engine coolant temperature in contact with a thermovalve that contains a wax element similar to a ther-mostat. Therefore this device shown in Figure 19–76b controls the linkage in both an engine-cold and engine-warm mode. Rotation of this linkage operates upon the timing control piston that will rotate the cam roller ring similar to the manually controlled system. The degree of timing advancement will vary between makes of engines and is determined by the engine manufacturer.

Governors for the VE Pump

The Robert Bosch VE distributor/rotary injection pump is available with one of two mechanical governors to control the speed and response of the engine. These two types of governors and their functions are:

1. *Variable-speed governor:* controls all engine speed ranges from idle up to maximum rated rpm. With this governor, when the throttle lever is placed at any position, the governor will maintain this speed within the droop characteristics of the governor. The variable-speed governor and its operation are illustrated in Figures 19–77a and 19–77b with its actual location in relation to the other injection pump components being clearly shown in Figure 19–68.

2. *Limiting-speed governor:* sometimes known as an idle and maximum speed governor since it is designed to control only the low- and high-idle speeds (maximum rpm) of the engine. When the throttle lever is placed into any position between idle and maximum, there is no governor control. Any change to the engine speed must be determined by the driver/operator moving the throttle pedal. This governor is shown in Figure 19–77c.

The variable-speed governor can be used on any application where all-range speed control is desired such as on a stationary engine or on a vehicle that drives an auxiliary power takeoff (PTO).

Operation of the Variable-Speed Governor

If you are not already familiar with the basic operation of a mechanical governor, it may be advantageous to you to review the description of operation given in Chapter 16.

The thing to always remember is that the force of the governor spring is always attempting to increase the fuel delivery rate to the engine, while the centrifugal force of the governor flyweights is always attempting to decrease the fuel to the engine.

Anytime that the centrifugal force of the rotating governor flyweights and the governor spring forces are equal, the governor is said to be in a *state of balance* and the engine will run at a fixed/steady speed. You should also be familiar with the operation of the injection pump and how the *effective stroke* of the rotating pump plunger operates.

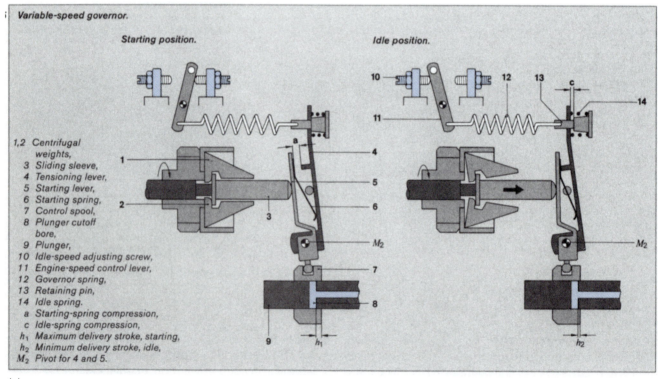

Variable-speed governor.

Starting position.   Idle position.

1,2 Centrifugal weights,
  3 Sliding sleeve,
  4 Tensioning lever,
  5 Starting lever,
  6 Starting spring,
  7 Control spool,
  8 Plunger cutoff bore,
  9 Plunger,
 10 Idle-speed adjusting screw,
 11 Engine-speed control lever,
 12 Governor spring,
 13 Retaining pin,
 14 Idle spring.
  a Starting-spring compression,
  c Idle-spring compression,
 h_1 Maximum delivery stroke, starting,
 h_2 Minimum delivery stroke, idle,
 M_2 Pivot for 4 and 5.

(a)

FIGURE 19–77 VE injection pump mechanical governor components arrangement: (a) variable-speed governor—starting/idle position of control spool/sleeve item 7; (b) speed increase/decrease position, notice control spool/sleeve item 10 position; (c) idle/maximum-speed governor, idle/full-load position—see control spool/sleeve item 12 position. (Courtesy of Robert Bosch Corporation.)

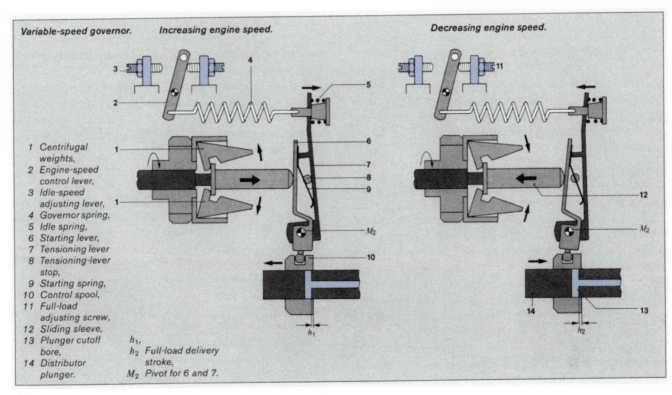

Variable-speed governor.   Increasing engine speed.   Decreasing engine speed.

1 Centrifugal
   weights,
2 Engine-speed
   control lever,
3 Idle-speed
   adjusting lever,
4 Governor spring,
5 Idle spring,
6 Starting lever,
7 Tensioning lever
8 Tensioning-lever
   stop,
9 Starting spring,
10 Control spool,
11 Full-load
   adjusting screw,
12 Sliding sleeve,
13 Plunger cutoff
   bore,
14 Distributor
   plunger.

h_1,
h_2 Full-load delivery
   stroke,
M_2 Pivot for 6 and 7.

(b)

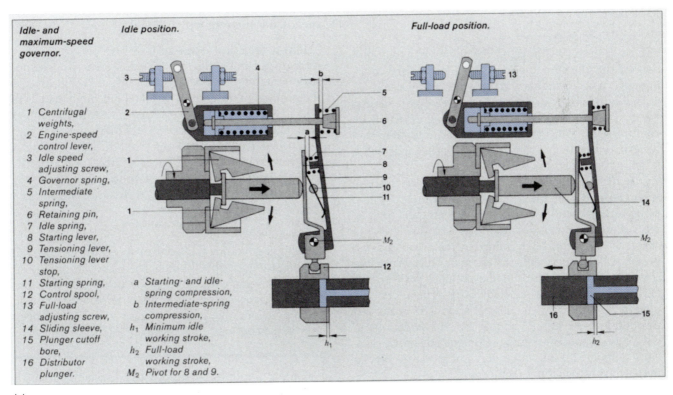

Idle- and
maximum-speed
governor.   Idle position.   Full-load position.

1 Centrifugal
   weights,
2 Engine-speed
   control lever,
3 Idle speed
   adjusting screw,
4 Governor spring,
5 Intermediate
   spring,
6 Retaining pin,
7 Idle spring,
8 Starting lever,
9 Tensioning lever,
10 Tensioning lever
   stop,
11 Starting spring,
12 Control spool,
13 Full-load
   adjusting screw,
14 Sliding sleeve,
15 Plunger cutoff
   bore,
16 Distributor
   plunger.

a Starting- and idle-
   spring compression,
b Intermediate-spring
   compression,
h_1 Minimum idle
   working stroke,
h_2 Full-load
   working stroke,
M_2 Pivot for 8 and 9.

(c)

FIGURE 19–77 (continued).

543

Engine Stopped

Refer to Figure 19–77a. With the engine stopped there is no governor weight force and consequently the force of the idle spring (14) and the starting spring (6) force the governor linkage attached to the control spool (7) to a position whereby the effective stroke of the rotating pump plunger (9) will be at its maximum; therefore, during engine cranking, maximum fuel will be delivered to the cylinders.

Engine Cranking and Starting

As the engine is cranked over, the centrifugal force developed by the rotating governor flyweights (1 and 2) will force the sliding sleeve (3) to the right in Figure 19–77a against the starting lever (5) and its spring (6). When the spring (6) is compressed, the lever (5) will butt up against a stop on the tensioning lever (4), which will now act directly against the force of the idle spring (14). Movement of the tensioning lever (4) will pull the speed control lever on top of the governor back until it bottoms on the idle speed adjusting screw (10).

Once the centrifugal force of the flyweights equals the preset tension of the idle spring (14), the engine will run at a steady speed. A state-of-balance condition exists between the weights and the idle spring. If the throttle lever is moved above the idle speed, the spring will be collapsed by the distance c shown on the right-hand side of Figure 19–77a.

Engine Acceleration

Refer to Figure 19–77a. When the engine is accelerated beyond the idle rpm, the centrifugal force of the rotating governor flyweights will force the sliding sleeve (3) to the right, and with the starting lever (5) up against the tensioning lever (4), the idle spring (14) will be compressed. Additional engine speed and therefore weight force will now cause lever (4) to pull against the larger governor spring (12).

Refer to Figure 19–77b. Movement of the throttle lever causes the engine speed control lever (2) to move away from the idle speed adjusting screw and toward the full-load adjusting screw (11). The travel of the speed control lever is determined by the driver and just how fast he or she wants the engine to run. When the driver steps on the throttle, the previous state-of-balance condition that existed at idle is upset in favor of the governor spring (4). The control spool (10) is moved through lever (6) and (7) so that the effective stroke of the rotating pump plunger is lengthened by moving the control spool (10) initially to its right in Figure 19–77b under the heading "increasing engine speed."

As the engine receives more fuel and accelerates, the centrifugal force of the rotating flyweights (1) will push the sliding sleeve (12) to its right as shown in Figure 19–77b causing levers (6) and (7) to stretch the governor spring (4). When a state-of-balance condition exists once again between the rotating weights (1) and the spring (4), the engine will run at a steady speed with the throttle in a fixed position.

If the throttle is placed in full fuel, the speed control lever (2) will butt up against the full-load adjusting screw (11), which will limit the maximum speed of the engine. Weight force at this point is greater than spring force; therefore, the sliding sleeve (12) will cause the starting (6) and tensioning lever (7) to pivot around the support pin M2.

The control spool (10) will be moved to the left as shown in Figure 19–77b under the heading "increasing engine speed," which will reduce the effective stroke of the rotating pump plunger. As a result, the engine will receive less fuel, thereby automatically limiting the maximum speed of the engine.

When the centrifugal force of the rotating governor flyweights (1) are equal to the governor spring force (4), the engine will run at a fixed rpm at maximum speed. If the engine was started and accelerated to its maximum rpm with the vehicle in a stationary position, the action of the governor weights would limit the maximum amount of fuel that the engine could receive by moving the control spool to decrease the pump plunger's effective stroke. When the engine is running under such a condition (maximum no-load speed), it is not receiving full fuel.

Decreasing Engine Speed

If the driver moves the throttle to a decreased speed position, the engine speed control lever (2) will reverse the position of the control spool (10) through the levers (6) and (7). As the effective stroke of the pump plunger is reduced, the engine receives less fuel and therefore it will run at a lower rpm. For a fixed throttle position at this lower speed, once the centrifugal force of the weights equals that of the governor spring (4), a new state of balance will occur and the engine will run at a steady speed.

Load Increase

Since this governor will control speed throughout the complete engine speed range, for a fixed throttle position, the engine will deliver a specific horsepower rating. As long as the engine is not overloaded at a given rpm position, the governor can control the speed within the confines of its droop characteristic.

Note: Droop is the difference between the maximum no-load rpm and the full-load rpm. Obviously, the engine speed will be lower under full load than it will be at no load. Similarly, when a load is applied to the engine for a given speed setting, it will tend to slow down since it now has to work harder to overcome the resistance to rotation. A detailed explanation of droop can be found under the basic governor description in Chapter 16.

The reaction of the governor when a load is applied to the engine will be the same at any speed setting. A simplified description is as follows (Figure 19–77b):

1. Load applied at a given speed setting of the throttle, and engine slows down such as when going up a hill.

2. Upsets state of balance between weights (1) and spring (4) when above idle speed; if at idle, spring (5) in favor of the spring force.

3. Spring pressure is greater and therefore lever (6) and (7) acting through pivot point M2 moves the control spool (10) to its right to lengthen the effective stroke of the rotating pump plunger and supply the engine with more fuel to develop additional horsepower.

4. If the load on the engine continues to increase, the engine will receive more fuel to try to offset the load, but it will run at a slower rpm.

5. As long as the engine can produce enough additional horsepower, the governor will once again reach a state of balance between the weights and the spring, but at a slower speed than before the load was applied.

6. When the load was applied, the spring expanded (lengthened) to increase the fuel to the engine and in so doing lost some of its compression; therefore the weights do not have to increase their speed/force to what existed before to reestablish a new state of balance. The engine will produce more horsepower with more fuel but will be running at a slower rpm.

7. Regardless of the governor's reaction to increase fuel to the engine, if the load requirements exceed the power capability of the engine, the rpm will continue to drop. In an automotive application, the only way that the speed can now be increased is for the driver to select a lower gear by downshifting.

8. If the engine was running at an idle rpm and an air conditioner pump was turned on, the engine would tend to slow down (load increase). The governor through the spring force/less weight force would increase the fuel to the engine to prevent it from stalling.

Load Decrease

When the load is decreased at a fixed throttle position, we have the following situation:

1. Engine speed increases; weights fly out with more force and they will cause the sliding sleeve (12) in Figure 19–77b to move levers (6) and (7) against the force of the spring (4).

2. The reaction is the same as shown under the heading "increasing engine speed," where the control spool (10) will move to its left to decrease (shorten) the effective stroke of the pump plunger and reduce fuel to the engine until a new corrected state-of-balance condition exists.

3. With less load on the engine, it requires less horsepower and therefore less fuel and as the engine slows down, so do the weights until the state of balance is reestablished.

4. If a vehicle goes down a hill, the load is reduced. If the drive does not check the speed of the vehicle with the brakes, it is possible for the driving wheels to run faster than the engine. If the drive wheels start to rotate the engine, the governor weights will also gain speed and in so doing they will reduce the effective stroke of the pump plunger and the engine's fuel will automatically be reduced.

Limiting-Speed Governor Operation

The reaction in this governor is illustrated in Figure 19–77c and is the same as that described for the variable-speed governor above with the exception that there is no governor control in the intermediate speed range, which is the speed range between idle and maximum rpm.

Engine Stopped

The engine will receive maximum fuel for startup since the force of the starting spring (11) and the idle spring (7) will move the control spool (12) to a position where the pump plunger will obtain its maximum effective stroke.

Engine Cranking and Starting

As the engine is cranked, the centrifugal force of the governor weights (1) will force the sliding sleeve (14) to its right against the force of the starting spring (11) and the idle spring (7). As the starting levers (8) and (9) are moved to the right, the control spool (12) will be pulled back (left) to reduce the effective stroke of the pump plunger.

How far the spool (12) will be pulled back is established by the setting of the idle spring. When a state of balance exists between the weights (1) and the idle spring (7), the control spool (12) is held at a fixed position and the engine receives a fixed amount of fuel suitable for an idle rpm which is set by the adjusting screw (3).

Engine Acceleration

When the throttle is moved initially beyond the idle range, the weights will compress the idle spring (7), and the weight force will now act upon the force of the intermediate spring (5) for a short time. This spring

(5) allows a reasonably wide idle-speed range, a large speed droop, and a soft or gradual transition from the low idle-speed range (governor control) to the point where the driver has complete control over the engine speed.

The intermediate spring (5) will be completely compressed (collapsed) shortly after the engine is accelerated from idle, and the throttle pedal now acts directly through the linkage to the sliding sleeve (14). There is not enough weight force to act upon the high-speed spring (4) until the engine speed approaches the high end. Engine speed is now directly controlled by the driver.

High-Speed Control

When the engine speed and therefore governor weight force is great enough, the centrifugal force of the weights will oppose the high-speed spring (4) until a state of balance occurs. When the weights and spring (4) come into play at the higher speed range, the maximum speed of the engine is limited by the fact that the weights as they fly out cause the sliding sleeve (14) to transfer motion through lever (8) and (9), which will compress the spring (4) and therefore move the control spool (12) to its left to shorten the effective stroke of the pump plunger. In this way, the engine receives less fuel and the maximum speed of the engine is therefore limited when the weights and spring (4) are in a state of balance. As load is applied and released from the engine (up hill) and (down hill), the governor will react in the same way that it did for the variable-speed governor described in detail earlier.

Automatic Timing Advance

The automatic advance mechanism employs the same principle of operation as that of CAV and Roosa Master Stanadyne distributor injection pumps. Fuel pressure from the transfer pump is delivered to a timing piston whose movement is opposed by spring pressure. At low engine speeds, the relatively low supply pump pressure has little to no effect on the timing piston travel. As engine speed increases, the rising fuel pressure will force the timing piston to overcome the resistance of the spring at its opposite end. At the center of the piston, as shown in Figure 19–76a, is a connecting pin extending up into the roller ring. The movement of the piston transmits this motion through the pin, which in turn rotates the roller ring in the opposite direction to drive shaft rotation, thereby advancing the timing of the cam plate lift from BDC to begin the plunger stroke. The timing piston travel should not be toyed with, but should be checked while the injection pump is mounted on a test bench.

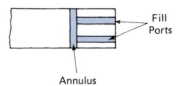

FIGURE 19–78 VE injection pump single rotating and stroking plunger with a machined annulus groove to interconnect the individual fill ports requiring a LTPC (lift to port closure) of the pumping plunger. (Courtesy of Robert Bosch Corporation.)

Prestroke Compared with Nonprestroke Pumps

Some VE injection pumps use a plunger whereby all the fill ports are interconnected by an annulus, or circular passage, running around the circumference of the plunger as shown in Figures 19–71 and 19–78. With this type of plunger containing the annulus, the unit is known as a *prestroke* pump. With this type, the fill ports cannot close by plunger rotation alone. The plunger must lift for port closure to occur. Only after the annulus lifts beyond the fill port do we have port closure. The plunger must be adjusted for a specific lift from BDC for port closure to happen. With this type, fuel pressure buildup within the Tee-drilled plunger takes a few degrees longer than for the zero prestroke type, which does not have the annulus and wherein port closure occurs by plunger rotation alone: the plunger lifts from BDC after rotation from port closure.

Overhaul of the Injection Pump

Repair and major overhaul of any injection pump should only be undertaken by personnel trained in the diversified and intricate work of fuel injection equipment. Since special tools and equipment are required, which are not always readily available to everyone, refer to the Robert Bosch publication 46, VDT-W-460/100 B, Edition 1, *Repair of Distributor-type Fuel Injection Pump 04604-VE-F.* This is obtainable through your local Robert Bosch dealer or from one of the Robert Bosch licensees.

Bleeding the Fuel System

Anytime that fuel lines have been opened/loosened or the fuel system has been serviced, it will be necessary to vent all air from the fuel system in order to start the engine.

1. On engines equipped with an electric fuel lift pump, this procedure is relatively easy. However, if the fuel system does not have a separate lift pump, it will take a little longer because the vane transfer pump in-

side the drive end of the injection pump will have to pull the fuel from the tank to the pump on its own.

2.   If the engine is equipped with an electric lift pump, make sure that all filter and injection pump vent screws are tight.

3.   Turn the ignition key switch to the ON position to energize the fuel cutoff solenoid and allow the electric lift pump to operate for 1 to 2 minutes.

4.   Crank the engine over, and if it starts and runs correctly without misfire or stumble, the system is properly bled of all air.

5.   If the engine does not start, loosen the individual fuel line nuts (place a rag around the nut to absorb the spilled fuel) at the injectors and crank the engine over until air-free fuel appears at each line, then tighten them up.

6.   If the engine is not equipped with an electric lift pump and only has a vane injection transfer pump, perform the sequence in step 5 while cranking the engine.

7.   If the vehicle is equipped with a hand priming pump on the fuel filter/water separator, use this pump to bleed the filter first after opening the vent screw on top of the filter until air-free fuel appears. The inlet fuel stud on top of the injection pump housing can also be loosened off to vent air from the system right up to the injection pump. Place a drain tray underneath the fuel filter and pump to catch any leaking fuel. Step 5 can then be performed to bleed fuel up to the individual fuel injectors.

8.   Once the engine starts and runs, if it is running rough, loosen each injector fuel line nut one at a time (engine idling) to bleed each unit with a rag placed around it then tighten the nut.

9.   Wipe all spilled or bled fuel from the engine and compartment.

SPECIAL NOTE   On a fuel system that has been emptied completely by running the engine out of fuel, it may be necessary to perform additional bleeding of the system by cranking or attempting to run the engine as follows:

1.   Loosen the fuel return fitting on the injection pump that is stamped OUT on the head of the hollow bolt (Figure 19–74).

2.   Loosen the timing plug located in the center of the injection pump distributor head (Figure 19–79).

3.   Loosen the fuel shutoff solenoid.

4.   Loosen the injector pressure outlet valves.

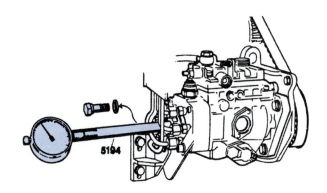

FIGURE 19–79 Checking VE injection pump plunger lift/timing with a dial gauge installed into the hydraulic head of the pump. (Courtesy of Robert Bosch Corporation.)

CHECKING INJECTION PUMP STATIC TIMING

Contained within each engine chapter is a description of the various adjustments and timing checks for that particular engine. The following static timing check can be considered common to all model VE injection pumps with the major difference being in the dimension given by the manufacturer for a particular model engine. Several engines using the model VE pump will have the same setting while others will differ slightly.

Generally, a static timing check is required only when a new pump is being installed or when an engine has been rebuilt or the pump has been removed for one reason or another. A dynamic timing check (engine running) can be done with the use of special test equipment.

1.   Manually rotate the engine over to place piston 1 at TDC on its compression stroke (both intake and exhaust valve closed). Align the timing mark on the crankshaft front pulley with the stationary pointer timing reference mark on the engine front cover.

2.   Refer to Figure 19–79 and remove the center bolt from the injection pump hydraulic head along with its sealing washer. A dial indicator adapter is available for use with the particular engine that you are checking to allow the dial gauge to be held in position during the static timing check. One example of the timing gauge adapter is shown in Figure 19–80.

3.   The adapter and dial gauge are installed onto the injection pump so that the plunger portion of the adapter projects into the injection pump. This will allow the dial gauge plunger to be in contact with the fuel injection pump plunger when installed. To do this correctly, ensure that the dial gauge shows at least 0.100 in. (2.54 mm) of preload on its face. Note, however, that

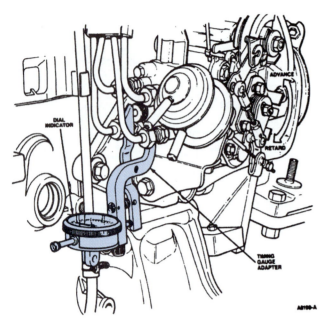

FIGURE 19–80 *Using a dial gauge and a support bracket installed into a VE injection pump to check the pump-to-engine timing specifications. (Courtesy of Robert Bosch Corporation.)*

VW recommends a preload of only 0.040 in. (1 mm), while Volvo on their D24 engine recommends 0.080 in. (2 mm) of gauge preload. The key here is that adequate preload be applied to the dial gauge to ensure that the pump plunger movement as you rotate the engine over during the static timing check will be felt/registered by the dial gauge plunger—otherwise a false reading will be obtained.

4.   Manually rotate the engine in its normal direction of rotation until the dial gauge registers its lowest reading, then set the dial gauge to zero by rotating the face bezel to place the needle at zero.

5.   Continue to rotate the engine manually in its normal direction of rotation smoothly until piston 1 is at TDC on its compression stroke. Some engine manufacturers supply a TDC aligning pin that is installed through a hole in the block to index with a hole in the flywheel so that the engine cannot be moved during this timing check (one example is the BMW 2.4 L six-cylinder turbocharged engine). If such a device is not available, ensure that either the timing marks between the crankshaft pulley/damper and stationary timing pointer are in correct alignment or that the flywheel timing marks such as found on the VW and Volvo diesel engines are in alignment.

6.   The measurement on the dial gauge face should be noted and compared with the engine manufacturer's specification. For example, if the static timing was given as 0.03937 in. (1 mm), the gauge should

register this specification. If it doesn't, the injection pump-to-engine timing needs adjustment.

7.   To change the injection pump-to-engine timing, loosen the injection pump housing retaining bolts and move the pump toward the engine if the measurement on the gauge is too small (this will advance the timing); move the pump housing away from the engine if the gauge reading is too large (this will retard the timing).

SPECIAL NOTE   What you are actually doing when you move the injection pump toward or away from the engine is adjusting the pump plunger lift from the BDC position to the point of port closure by turning the cam ring away from or toward the rollers.

ADDITIONAL NOTE   Certain engine manufacturers supply a special adjusting bracket that can be bolted onto the injection pump housing to facilitate accurate adjustment of the timing. This allows the pump to be held in position as you tighten the retaining bolts.

---

8.   A specified tightening sequence is also given by various engine manufacturers to ensure proper seating of the pump-to-engine block.

9.   Always rotate the engine over manually at least twice when you have completed your adjustment to double-check that the setting is in fact correct. If the setting is incorrect, repeat steps 1 to 8.

ROBERT BOSCH VE INJECTION PUMP TROUBLESHOOTING

Problems related to the VE injection pump are basically similar regardless of the type of engine and vehicle that it is installed on. Figure 19–81 lists the typical types of problems that might be encountered on the engine when using a VE injection pump.

When an engine exhibits heavy smoke after a cold start, the cold-start device should be checked by monitoring the engine idle rpm. The cold-start device used with the VE pump is controlled by a wax-type thermostat arrangement shown in Figure 19–76 that responds to engine coolant as it warms up. When the vehicle attains its normal operating temperature, the cold-start device (CSD) does not operate.

Actual testing of the CSD can only be done properly with the injection pump mounted on a test bench

It is assumed that the engine is in good working order and properly tuned, and that the electrical system has been checked and repaired if necessary.

SYMPTOM
- Starting Problem
- Engine surges at idle
- Rough idle when engine is warm
- Engine misses under load
- Low power
- Excessive Fuel Consumption
- Engine cannot be shut off
- Fog-like exhaust in full-load range (white or blue)
- Poor performance or low power
- Incorrect idle or maximum speed
- Engine does not rev up
- Injection pump runs hot

CAUSE	REMEDY
Improper fuel (gasoline) in tank	Drain tank, flush system, fill with proper fuel
Tank empty or tank vent blocked	Fill tank/bleed system, check tank vent
Air in the fuel system	Bleed fuel system, eliminate air leaks
Pump rear support bracket loose	Replace as necessary
Low voltage, no voltage or stop solenoid defective	Correct electrical faults/replace stop solenoid
Fuel filter blocked	Replace fuel filter
Injection lines blocked/restricted	Drill to nominal I.D. or replace
Fuel-supply lines blocked/restricted	Test all fuel supply lines — flush or replace
Loose connections, injection lines leak or broken	Tighten the connection, eliminate the leak
Paraffin deposit in fuel filter	Replace filter, use Diesel Fuel no. 1
Pump-to-engine timing incorrect	Readjust timing
Injection nozzle defective	Repair or replace
Engine air filter blocked	Replace air filter element
Pre-heating system defective	Test the glow plugs, replace as necessary
Injection sequence does not correspond to firing order	Install fuel injection lines in the correct order
Low idle misadjusted	Readjust idle stop screw
Maximum speed misadjusted	Readjust maximum speed screw
Overflow fitting interchanged with inlet fitting	Install fittings in their proper positions
Overflow blocked	Clean the orifice or replace fitting
Cold-start device not operating	Check bowden cable and lever movement
Low or uneven engine compression	Repair as necessary
Fuel injection pump defective or cannot be adjusted	Replace

FIGURE 19-81 Troubleshooting guide for VE mechanical distributor pumps. (Courtesy of Robert Bosch Corporation.)

549

(stand). However, a simple test of the CSD can be made on the engine as follows. Engine idle rpm should usually be about 200 rpm higher when the engine is cold compared with when it is at operating temperature. In addition, when the engine is at operating temperature, the cold-start device lever should not contact the lever on the injection pump as shown in Figure 19–76b. On vehicles equipped with an automatic transmission, an emergency stop lever is fitted to the side of the injection pump as shown in Figure 19–68. If the engine fails to shut off when the ignition key is turned OFF, there is a fault with the fuel solenoid located on the injection pump housing.

On a standard transmission equipped vehicle, the engine can be stopped by placing the transmission in gear with the engine idling and with your foot on the brakes, engaging the clutch to stall the engine.

On automatic transmission–equipped vehicles, refer to Figure 19–68, item 20, and pull the emergency stop lever. If the engine fails to start, the cause may well be the fuel solenoid on the injection pump as illustrated in Figure 19–68 (item ELAB) and Figure 19–69. Check the fuel solenoid valve by placing a voltmeter across its terminal and ground. A voltage of less than 10 V will fail to open (energize) this valve, while at least 8 V is required to keep the valve in an open state while the starter motor is cranking the engine.

ELECTRONIC DISTRIBUTOR PUMP

As early as 1985, Robert Bosch Corporation applied electronic controls to its mechanical VE distributor pump. Figure 19–82 illustrates a cross section of an electronically controlled distributor-type pump. As with any electronic system (see details in Chapter 18), a variety of sensors input a signal to an ECU (electronic control unit), which computes an output signal to the pump to manage fuel metering and/or timing. Metering is achieved by an electromagnetic actuator, timing by modulation of internal pump pressure via a solenoid. Figure 19–83 shows the arrangement required for the electronically controlled distributor pump system. To monitor and control the system effectively, the ECU electronic system is shown in graphic form in Figure 19–84. The distributor pump system produces a maximum injection pressure at the nozzles of approximately 14,600 psi (1000 bar) for high-speed automotive engine applications.

System Operation

The ECU receives continuous signals from the various engine sensors, based on changing operating conditions. The ECU then processes these signals and electronically controls the injected fuel quantity, start of injection, time-on of the glow plugs in IDI engine models, and exhaust gas recirculation rate. After initial start of a cold engine, the ECU operates the engine in an open-loop mode until the fuel temperature has reached a certain level. During open-loop mode, the ECU allows the engine to function from a preselected PROM (programmable read-only memory) chip. Switchover to the closed-loop control system occurs only after a given engine speed has been obtained. All sensor signals are now used by the ECU to closely control metering and timing.

Adjustment of the start of injection is determined by the ECU after consulting the input signal from the throttle pedal potentiometer, engine rpm, and intake

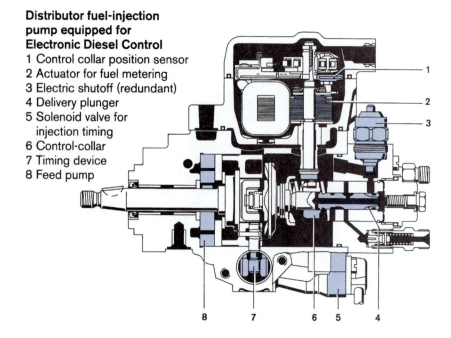

FIGURE 19–82 VE distributor pump equipped for electronic diesel control: 1, control collar position sensor; 2, actuator for fuel metering; 3, electric shutoff; 4, delivery plunger; 5, solenoid valve for injection timing; 6, control collar; 7, timing device; 8, feed pump. (Courtesy of Robert Bosch Corporation.)

Distributor fuel-injection pump equipped for Electronic Diesel Control
1 Control collar position sensor
2 Actuator for fuel metering
3 Electric shutoff (redundant)
4 Delivery plunger
5 Solenoid valve for injection timing
6 Control-collar
7 Timing device
8 Feed pump

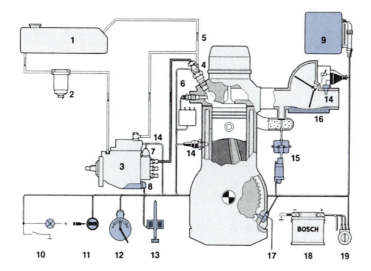

FIGURE 19–83 Fuel system schematic for an electronically controlled distributor injection pump: 1, fuel tank; 2, fuel filter; 3, VE pump; 4, injection nozzle with a needle motion sensor; 5, solenoid valve for injection timing; 6, control collar; 7, timing device; 8, feed pump. (Courtesy of Robert Bosch Corporation.)

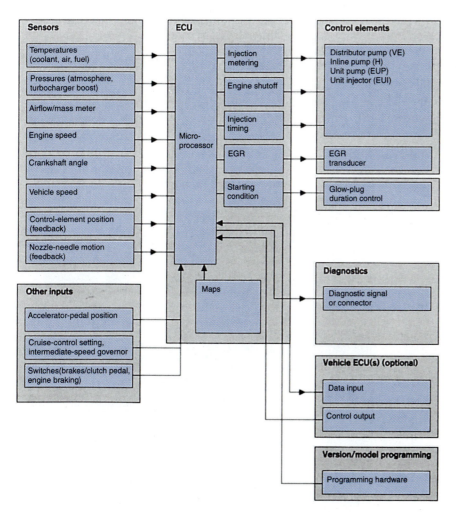

FIGURE 19–84 Electronic control unit (ECU) operational schematic. (Courtesy of Robert Bosch Corporation.)

manifold pressure. The ECU compares the actual start of injection measured by the small nozzle needle-motion sensor shown in Figure 19–85. Timing adjustment is performed within the ECU circuitry by using a clocked solenoid valve to modulate the fuel pressure on the inlet side of the timing-device piston until the start of injection has been reached.

To control exhaust emissions from the engine, an ECU signal to an exhaust gas valve permits graduation of recirculated exhaust gases to mix with the intake air

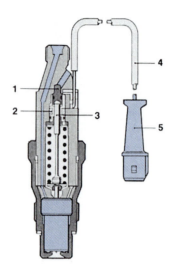

FIGURE 19–85 *Nozzle and holder assembly with needle motion sensor: 1, adjusting pin; 2, sensor winding; 3, thrust pin; 4, cable; 5, connector. (Courtesy of Robert Bosch Corporation.)*

to reduce NO_X (nitrogen oxide) emissions. Signals from an intake manifold airflow sensor to the ECU are used to control the exhaust gas recirculation rate. On turbocharged engine models, the boost pressure sensor

signal also indicates to the ECU the percentage of engine load and torque so that timing and metering can be adjusted accordingly. On IDI engine models, glow plug ON time is controlled as a function of engine operating temperature, speed, and injected fuel quantity in order to reduce HC (hydrocarbon) exhaust emissions shortly after engine startup. The service technician can access the ECU to withdraw stored trouble codes using a handheld DDR (diagnostic data reader) similar to the one shown in Figure 18–28.

TESTING/SETTING INJECTION PUMPS

Introduction

Details on the testing and overhaul of all types of fuel injection pumps requires more space than can be provided in this textbook, consequently this section will deal very briefly with the two major settings of a Bosch PLN injection pump, models A, MW and P. Prior to fuel injection pumps leaving the factory, or after a pump overhaul procedure has been performed, it is necessary to mount the injection pump onto a test stand similar to the one shown in Figure 19–86.

FIGURE 19–86 *Example of a VDM (video display metering) fuel injection pump test stand. (Courtesy of Delphi Automotive Systems.)*

Both injection pump overhaul and the testing and adjustment procedure requires special tools, equipment and knowledge. Fuel injection technician specialists perform these tasks every day, therefore a regular heavy-duty equipment technician, commercial transport technician, or diesel engine tech is not expected to perform this type of repair and testing. Local fuel injection specialist repair shops who are generally members of the Association of Diesel Specialists (ADS) are best equipped with trained technicians to conduct these types of repairs and adjustments.

CAUTION DO NOT attempt to perform fuel injection pump LTPC (lift to port closure), or calibration adjustments, on any fuel injection pump while it is mounted on the engine. Both injection pump and engine damage can result from untrained personnel performing either one of these adjustments.

Basic Sequence of Adjustment

The following information is provided to give you a brief overview of the two most important adjustments required on Bosch models A, MW, and P PLN systems.

The two most important checks and settings on a PLN fuel system involves:

Step 1: Timing

Initial pump timing which generally involves adjusting each individual pumping plunger for a specified LTPC (lift to port closure) or prestroke shown in Figure 19–18. This adjustment ensures that as the injection pump camshaft rotates, that the plunger tappet or roller will be lifted at the correct number of degrees BTDC to establish initial injection timing. Adjustment of LTPC will depend upon the model of injection pump being used. For example on a Bosch A model pump, LTPC is achieved by loosening off a tappet locknut, then rotating the adjustment nut CW or CCW to obtain the correct setting. This is illustrated in Figure 19–87. The LTPC dimension can be checked by using the dial indicator shown in Figure 19–88, or in Figure 19–89. The LTPC setting for Bosch MW and P model pumps requires that split timing shims or one-piece timing shims be added or removed from below the pumping plunger barrel flange. These shims can be seen in Figure 19–90.

For example, on a six-cylinder PLN system, the service technician would first begin by setting No. 1 pumping plunger LTPC. This can be achieved by using

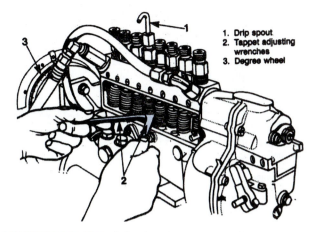

1. Drip spout
2. Tappet adjusting wrenches
3. Degree wheel

FIGURE 19–87 *Adjusting the tappet setting to correct for LTPC (lift to port closure) on a Bosch model A injection pump. (Courtesy of Robert Bosch Corporation.)*

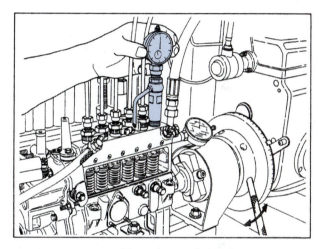

FIGURE 19–88 *Mounting a dial indicator onto the injection pump to measure the pump plunger lift. (Courtesy of ZEXEL USA Corporation.)*

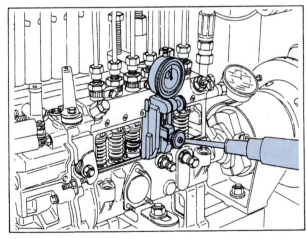

FIGURE 19–89 *Injection pump plunger stroke measuring tool installed on the No. 1 pump plunger to determine plunger bumping clearance. (Courtesy of ZEXEL USA Corporation.)*

1. Delivery Valve Holder
2. Fill Piece
3. Delivery Valve Spring
4. Delivery Valve
5. Delivery Valve Gasket
6. Timing Shims
7. Spacer
8. O-rings
9. Delivery Valve Body
10. Flange Bushing
11. Barrel
12. Baffle Ring
13. Plunger
14. O-rings
15. Control Rack
16. Upper Spring Seat
17. Control Sleeve
18. Plunger Vane
19. Plunger Spring
20. Lower Spring Seat
21. Plunger Foot
22. Roller Tappet
23. Camshaft
24. Bearing End Plate
25. End Play Shim
26. O-ring
27. Bearing

One-Piece Timing Shims

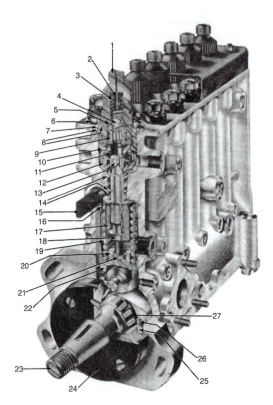

Split Timing Shims

ROBERT BOSCH CORPORATION   AUTOMOTIVE SERVICE

FIGURE 19–90 Model P injection pump one-piece and split timing shims concept used to alter lift to port closure dimension. (Courtesy of Robert Bosch Corporation.)

either a dial indicator mounted as shown in Figure 19–88 that is also equipped with a gooseneck (short bent fuel line), or a gooseneck line alone mounted on top of the pumping plunger delivery valve holder. High-pressure test stand fuel can be used; if low-pressure fuel is employed you need to remove the pumping plunger delivery valve spring. This test illustrated in Figure 19–91 allows the technician to determine when LTPC has occurred, since the fuel will stop flowing from the end of the drip spout or gooseneck line. Note in Figure 19–91 that in this particular pump example, shims within the tappet can be added or removed to achieve the correct LTPC dimension. Once this has been performed, the technician would manually rotate and then align a degree wheel mounted on the test stand and attached to the injection pump camshaft drive to the "zero degrees" position. The degree wheel can be seen in Figure 19–88 on the lower right-hand side, where a small bar is used to rotate the degree wheel CW or CCW as desired. The remaining pumping plungers LTPC on a six-cylinder pump would then be set at succeeding 60° intervals; for example with a firing order of 1–5–3–6–2–4, number 5 would be set for LTPC at 60°; 3 at 120°; 6 at 180°; 2 at

240°; 4 at 300°; which would then bring us back to 360 or zero degrees for No. 1. This process is commonly referred to as "phasing." A four-cylinder pump would be set at 90° intervals.

Step 2: Calibration

Calibration of each pumping plunger is done to ensure that every cylinder receives the same quantity of metered and delivered fuel by lengthening or shortening the pump plungers effective stroke. This is obtained by loosening off the injection pump rack lock collar screw (see Figure 19–21) for A model pumps, and then physically rotating this small collar by inserting a small pin punch into the holes drilled around the rack collar as shown in Figure 19–92. To change the fuel setting on both MW and P model Bosch pumps requires that the technician loosen off the barrel locating screws and then turn the barrel flange CW or CCW to obtain the desired fuel delivery. See Figure 19–93. Each pump manufacturer lists the allowable tolerance between cylinders in fuel delivery CCs while running the pump on the test stand over a specified number of strokes (typically 1000), with the fuel control rack set for a specified amount of travel. The rack travel is checked with the

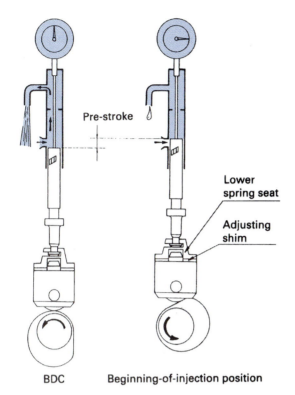

Pre-stroke

Lower
spring seat

Adjusting
shim

BDC   Beginning-of-injection position

FIGURE 19–91   *Noting position where fuel flow stops, then recording the dial indicator reading. (Courtesy of ZEXEL USA Corporation.)*

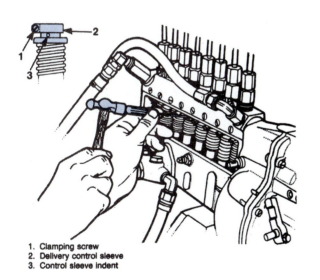

1. Clamping screw
2. Delivery control sleeve
3. Control sleeve indent

FIGURE 19–92   *Procedure used to adjust each pumping plunger for the same fuel delivery rate on an A model pump. (Courtesy of Robert Bosch Corporation.)*

use of a dial gauge shown in Figure 19–88 and Figure 19–89 located on the side of the injection pump closest to the test stand drive end. Always refer to the pump test specification sheet for all dimensions and settings.

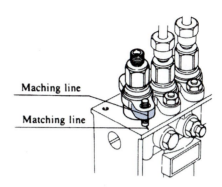

Maching line

Matching line

FIGURE 19–93   *Aligning the plunger block (barrel-and-flange assembly) to the match mark on the injection pump housing. (Courtesy of Robert Bosch Corporation.)*

There are a variety of other injection pump and governor adjustments that must be performed on the test stand, however, space within this textbook does not permit us going into detail on how to perform these. Have your instructor cover this with you, or arrange a tour of a local fuel injection repair shop for more details.

BOSCH COMMON-RAIL FUEL SYSTEMS

Introduction

Rudolph Diesel's original engines (1897) were designed to function and operate with a common-rail blast-air fuel system; however, it was many years before technology permitted actual successful adoption of a truly functional common-rail fuel system (CRFS) using this design. Today, both gasoline and diesel engines are in production, using direct injection of fuel into the combustion chamber.

Cummins Engine Company uses the CRFS design on their ISC model engines where it is referred to as Cummins accumulator pump system (CAPS). Common-rail-designed fuel systems typically create injection pressures of approximately 19,580 psi (1350 bar). This results in improved combustion leading to a reduction in both visible black exhaust smoke density and reduced exhaust emissions levels. These reductions in exhaust emissions are obtained by using a small amount of pilot-injected fuel ahead of the main injected fuel quantity. In addition, multiple injections throughout the fuel delivery period further improve combustion efficiency and reduce engine noise.

The difference between common-rail and regular-type fuel injection systems of the PLN (pump-line-nozzle), radial distributor pump, EUP (electronic unit pump), or EUI (electronic unit injector) systems is that the fuel pressure varies with a change in engine speed and load. In the CRFS design, however, the injection pressure can be maintained/selected independent of the engine speed or load operating conditions. A major advantage of the CRFS design is that the engine crankshaft torque (twisting and turning force) can be increased at the lower engine operating speed ranges to thus improve engine response or snap throttle reaction.

With the use of electronics, the CRFS system (see Figure 19–94) provides a cost-productive advantage over the long-used types/models of fuel systems. Therefore, we can summarize the advantages of the CRFS as follows:

1. Reduced exhaust emissions
2. Lower combustion noise through pilot and multiple injection
3. Reduced fuel consumption
4. Reliable, long life, and of high quality

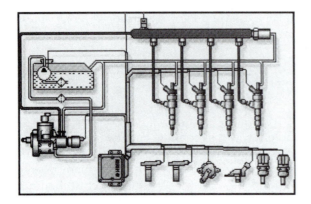

FIGURE 19–94 *Schematic of an electronic common-rail fuel system showing the fuel tank, high-pressure pump, ECU, sensors, high-pressure accumulator (rail), and the injectors. (Courtesy of Robert Bosch Corporation.)*

We can further simplify the CRFS design by viewing its individual components, as shown in Figure 19–95. The main components are as follows:

1. Presupply low-pressure pump (electric or mechanical)
2. High-pressure pump
3. High-pressure accumulator (rail)
4. Pressure control valve
5. Rail pressure sensor
6. Injectors
7. EDC (electronic diesel control) unit, ECU (electronic control unit), and required engine/vehicle sensors. In North America, the term ECU is often referred to as an ECM (electronic control module).

Closed- and Open-Loop Operation

In electronically controlled gasoline or diesel engines, in order to efficiently and effectively control systems operation, a series of engine/vehicle sensors are used. Typically each sensor receives an input supply voltage of between 0.5 and 5.0 V dc from the ECM. Sensors are designed to have a changing resistance value based on temperature or pressure changes, while position sensors function on magnetic fields that affect both the amplitude and frequency changes. Consequently, each sensor's output voltage will vary with changes to one of its operating conditions. Therefore, each sensor is designed for what is known as an *operating parameter* (range of operation). The processes used for this range of control are typically described as sensor set points, or desired values. We can therefore say that the sensor variables (signal responses) are measured quantities. The range within each individual sensor would normally operate is commonly referred to as a set point or

FIGURE 19–95 *Major components of an electronic common-rail fuel system. (Courtesy of Robert Bosch Corporation.)*

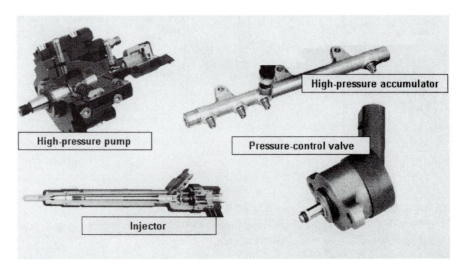

High-pressure pump

High-pressure accumulator

Pressure-control valve

Injector

desired value, for example, between 0.5 and 5.0 volts. This could also include variables related to speed, resistance, quantity, and position.

The ECM monitoring circuitry constantly receives return signals from each sensor as the engine is operating to advise it if in fact one or more sensors is operating within the designed parameter range. Sensor values falling outside the set point values, and the action taken by the ECM, are programmed into the ECM at the time of manufacture.

In its simplified description, these terms refer to the operation of an electronically controlled system, gasoline or diesel, where the following conditions occur.

Open Loop

In gasoline engines the various sensors feed changing operating conditions signals back to the ECM where it can make a decision as to proper fueling/timing as well as ignition spark advance/retard, and so forth. One important sensor in gasoline engines is the HO_2S (heated exhaust gas oxygen sensor) that is used to monitor and determine the excess oxygen remaining in the exhaust gases. In this way, an ideal air/fuel ratio known as stoichiometric (14.7 to 1 air-to-fuel) mixture can be maintained to minimize exhaust gas emissions. In earlier-model gasoline engines, a nonelectrically heated HO_2S was used. Consequently it took several minutes after cold engine startup to raise the exhaust sensor probe to a high enough operating temperature to permit it to start sending a rich or lean air/fuel ratio signal back to the ECM. During this time, the engine is said to be operating in the open-loop mode and the ECM will control the engine based on preprogrammed algorithms or operating conditions. The ECM will also take into account the operating signals being returned from the various other engine/vehicle sensors.

Also keep in mind that the ECM with the key ON typically sends out a 5 V dc reference signal to *every* sensor used; and based upon the return signal sent back from each sensor, the ECM can determine the operating condition of the engine systems. Until such time as the oxygen sensor returns a signal to the ECM, the engine operates in this open-loop mode, which will be at less than or greater than stoichiometric (14.7 parts of air to 1 part of fuel). However, once the oxygen sensor is at normal operating temperature, the return signal back to the ECM indicates if the air/fuel ratio is rich or lean. This places the system into its closed-loop operating mode. The ECM can then vary the injector solenoid signal known as PWM (pulse-width modulation, or duty cycle) to lean-out or enrichen the air/fuel ratio to bring it as close to stoichiometric as possible.

In a diesel engine that always operates with an unthrottled or excess air supply (lean), no oxygen sensor is required, but since the ECM still relies upon individual sensor signals to monitor the successful operation of the engine, should any given sensor signal fall out of the normal operating parameter (range), typically between 0.5 and 5 volts, then the ECM diagnostic circuit would log a diagnostic trouble code (DTC) in ECM memory along with the operating conditions. A service technician can then access the fault with special diagnostic tooling and determine the reasons. If one of these sensor faults is a part of the engine protective system, then the ECM can automatically power down the engine to protect it from damage. The ECM will also illuminate either a yellow dash-mounted lamp, or a red lamp (which is a serious situation). If the ECM system has been programmed for automatic engine shutdown protection features, normally within 30 seconds of the red lamp being illuminated, the engine will be shut off. It is also possible that when the yellow warning lamp is triggered, the engine may operate at less than ideal conditions of speed and power. The ECM makes this decision based upon sensor feedback and comparison with preprogrammed lookup tables/maps within the ECM memory system. For every engine operating status, these maps contain the correct values for the corresponding injected fuel quantity and the start of injection.

CRFS Operation

A description of the various sensors used with the CRFS can be found in Chapter 18, dealing with electronic engine controls.

In the latest automotive and light-truck applications, the use of a mass air-flow sensor is installed between the air filter and turbocharger (when used). Either a hot-wire or a hot-film air mass unit is used. This unit measures the air mass entering the engine cylinders, and is used by the ECM to establish the fuel setting, timing, and duration of injection. The common-rail actuators are the pressure control valve and the injectors. The electronic exchange of information takes place through the CAN-bus; therefore, the ECM instructs the actuators to align the measured sensor values to the set point or desired value.

Accumulator System

The term *common-rail fuel system* is also referred to as an *accumulator injection system,* hence Cummins use of the acronym CAPS for Cummins accumulator pump system used on their ISC engine models. (See Chapter 22.) The CRFS meets the following objectives:

1. Provides fuel to the engine.
2. Generates the high fuel pressures required for efficient fuel injection.
3. Distributes the high-pressure fuel to the individual cylinders.

4. Injects the precise quantity of fuel at the exact number of crankshaft grees BTDC (before top dead center) on the compression stroke.

CRFS Functions

If you refer to Figure 19–95, which illustrates a basic CRFS, we can describe more easily the three main functional groups of the system, categorized as follows:

1. *Low-pressure circuit.* This consists of either an in-tank modular fuel cell containing an electric low-pressure fuel pump, generally of the roller-cell design, or in some automotive applications this pump is located in the line between the fuel tank and the filter to the high-pressure system. Note that a gear-type pump is available as an option to the electric-pump model.

2. *High-pressure circuit.* This consists of the lines and an injection pump similar in shape to a conventional distributor-type pump. This pump is shown in Figure 19–96. The high-pressure fuel generated by this pump is directed to the fuel accumulator or rail which can be seen in Figure 19–95. The high-pressure pump is driven from the engine at half-engine speed via a coupling, gearwheel, chain, or toothed belt. A series of three pumping plungers within this pump assembly are moved out and in by a rotating driveshaft with camlike lobes on them as shown in Figure 19–96. Each plunger is spring loaded to prevent bounce and to keep them in positive contact with the driveshaft cams. When the pumping plungers move downward on what is commonly referred to as the *suction stroke*, an inlet check valve opens to permit fuel at low pressure to enter the pumping chamber. At BDC (bottom dead center), the inlet valve closes and the fuel in the pumping chamber is now pressurized by the upward moving plunger and delivered into the accumulator rail. The high-pressure fuel is stored here and used for injection purposes. Figure 19–95 illustrates the high-pressure accumulator/rail which is a forged-steel tube. The internal diameter of the rail is approximately 0.400 in. (10 mm), and varies in length based on the engine fueling requirements. This rail length can range between 11 and 24 in. (280 and 600 mm). Each injector is connected by its own line to the rail.

The pressure control valve, which can be mounted on the high-pressure pump or attached to the accumulator rail, is actuated by the ECU/ECM to accurately maintain the fuel rail pressure. Figure 19–97 illustrates the PCV (pressure control valve) in cross-sectional view. The PCV contains an electric armature, an electromagnet, and a ball-type seat valve. The ball is forced against the high-pressure input by a spring. The electromagnet is also capable of exerting a force against the ball. A support ring incorporating an O-seal ring functions as a seal at the connection point to the high-pressure pump assembly. Note that the ball seat valve is acted upon by the high-pressure fuel within the accumulator rail. This force is opposed by the sum of the forces exerted against the ball from the spring and the electromagnet. The electromagnet strength is dependent upon the PWM current applied to it from the ECM; therefore, a variation of this applied current will determine the fuel pressure retained within the accumulator rail. Should the rail pressure exceed the desired setting for the engine operating status, the valve opens and permits rail

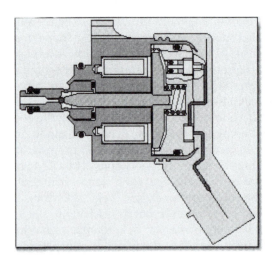

FIGURE 19–97 Pressure control valve (DRV) maintains the pressure in the common rail at a constant level. (Courtesy of Robert Bosch Corporation.)

FIGURE 19–96 High-pressure electronic common-rail pump schematic. (Courtesy of Robert Bosch Corporation.)

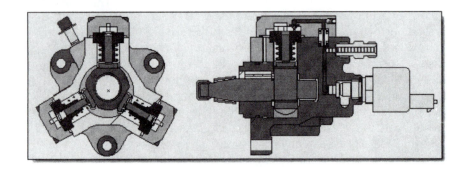

pressure to flow back to the tank via a return line. If rail pressure drops too low, then the valve closes, allowing the high-pressure pump to increase the fuel pressure in the rail. Therefore, in reality, the ECM control of this valve ensures that a closed-loop pressure control system is maintained.

The electronic RPS (rail pressure sensor) mounted on the rail (see Figures 19–94 and 95) functions to detect the fuel pressure within the rail. This sensor returns a pressure equivalent voltage signal back to the ECU/ECM. The ECU uses this value for the closed-loop pressure control in the CRFS.

3. *ECU (electronic control unit)*. With sensors, these key elements determine fuel quantity and timing. The low-pressure circuit fuel in the tank is circulated via an in-tank electric fuel pump with its own prefilter, and low-pressure fuel is sent to the high-pressure circuit where the fuel is further filtered to prevent premature wear of injection components. The fuel is then sent to the high-pressure pump which forces it into the high-pressure accumulator (rail), where the fuel pressure is held at a maximum pressure of 19,580 psi (1350 bar). For each injection, fuel is drawn from the rail. The rail pressure is held constant due to the fact that the pressurized fuel retains an accumulator effect. In addition, a pressure control valve ensures that the rail pressure does not exceed, or drop below, the preset desired value. The rail pressure control valve is activated by a signal from the ECU. When this valve is open, high-pressure fuel will bleed off and return to the fuel tank through the return lines, therefore lowering rail pressure to its precalibrated pressure value. The ECU receives a signal from the rail pressure sensor at all times so that it can determine when to open/close the rail pressure control valve.

The CRFS injector is externally similar to mechanical Bosch nozzles. Figure 19–98 shows the injector. Note that the injector valve, the nozzle, and the electromagnet solenoid are all located within the injector body. Major injector components consist of:

- the nozzle spring
- the valve spring
- electromagnet (solenoid)

High-pressure fuel from the rail passes through an input throttle and into the valve control chamber, so this fuel pressure is equal to what is inside the accumulator rail. When the injector electromagnet solenoid valve is activated by a PWM signal from the ECU, a magnetic field permits the valve to open against spring pressure. High-pressure fuel enters the nozzle chamber and fuel enters the combustion chamber through the spray-tip orifice holes. The duty-cycle time of the injector solenoid from the ECU/ECM determines the start,

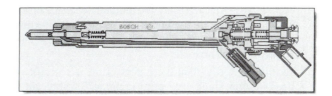

FIGURE 19–98 *Sectional view of an electronic common-rail injector assembly. (Courtesy of Robert Bosch Corporation.)*

duration, and end of injection. As with all electronically controlled diesel engine fuel systems, this PWM duty-cycle signal is determined by calculations completed by the various logic gates within the arithmetic logic unit (ALU) within the ECM-CPU. These in turn rely upon all various sensor input signals as discussed in Chapter 18. The preprogrammed maps stored in the ECM contain the appropriate injection data necessary for all possible variables of each sensor measured value. Consequently, the CRFS can implement pilot injection before the introduction of the full injector flow rate. Pilot injection allows a small quantity of fuel to be delivered into the combustion chamber before the main injector flow. This action will initiate a flame front in the combustion chamber with a minimum pressure rise. Consequently, the ignition delay period is reduced, creating a quieter running engine. (Injected liquid atomized micron-sized fuel droplets can quickly vaporize to start the combustion process.) Once the main fuel delivery begins, the established flame front instantly ignites the main fuel charge. The result is smoother and quieter combustion, along with improved fuel economy and lower exhaust emissions. At the end of injection, excess fuel is routed back to the fuel tank via the return line.

SUMMARY

With between 55 and 60% of fuel injection systems being of Bosch manufacture, this chapter has prepared you to understand the various models of Bosch fuel pumps; how to service, maintain, adjust, diagnose, and troubleshoot these different models; and to appreciate the detailed function and purpose of a correctly adjusted and operating high-pressure fuel system.

SELF-TEST QUESTIONS

1. The first successfully mass-produced diesel fuel injection pump system as we know it today was developed by
   a. Thomas Edison in 1886
   b. Rudolph Diesel in 1892
   c. Robert Bosch in 1927
   d. Charles A. Vandervell in 1938

2. Technician A says that only the model MW and P Bosch injection pumps are used on truck applications. Technician B disagrees, saying that the A model pump is also widely used. Who is right?

3. Technician A says that the letters PE in reference to a Bosch pump stand for "pump engine." Technician B says that they stand for "pump with an enclosed camshaft." Who is correct?

4. Technician A says that the letter S in a pump model, such as PES, means that the injection pump can either be base mounted or bolted to a cradle on the engine. Technician B says that the letter S in a pump ID implies that the pump is flange mounted. Who is right?

5. The four basic models of Bosch inline multiple-plunger pumps used in automotive or truck applications are the
   a. A, PE, S, and P
   b. M, A, MW, and P
   c. MW, PE, PES, and CW
   d. A, B, S, and MW

6. A P-size inline pump that is base mounted would be identified by the model coding
   a. PES4A
   b. PFR6A
   c. PF5R
   d. PE6P

7. Technician A says that the largest inline Bosch pump used in truck applications is the model P. Technician B disagrees, saying that it is the model PE. Who is correct?

8. Technician A says that the pump plunger lift in all Bosch inline pump models is determined by the pump camshaft. Technician B disagrees and says that the engine camshaft drives the pump and determines the plunger lift. Who is correct?

9. The term *prestroke* means
   a. The plunger stroke needed to supply excess fuel for startup
   b. The amount of lift required to reach port closure
   c. The amount of plunger rotation required to expose the retard notch for a cold-start condition
   d. The small lift designed into the camshaft for initial injection

10. Technician A says that fuel delivery begins when the plunger starts its lift. Technician B disagrees, saying that fuel delivery can begin only at port closure. Who is correct?

11. Technician A says that the amount of fuel delivered to the injectors can be altered by changing the effective stroke of the plunger. Technician B says that to do this, you would have to alter the camshaft lift. Who is correct?

12. Technician A says that in Bosch inline multiple-plunger pumps, injection ends when the barrel inlet port is uncovered. Technician B says that fuel injection ends when the pressure is relieved through the fuel return line. Who is right?

13. Technician A says that the fuel feed pump delivers fuel to the injectors. Technician B says that this is incorrect—that the fuel feed pump simply transfers fuel at low pressure to the injection pump. Who is right?

14. Technician A says that the basic function of the injection pump is to pressurize and deliver fuel to the injectors. Technician B says that the pump pressurizes, times, and meters fuel to the injectors. Who is correct in his statement?

15. Technician A says that the term *phasing* is the term used to describe port closing at correct intervals by all pump plungers. Technician B says that it means equal delivery of fuel to all injectors. Who is correct here?

16. Technician A says that fuel metering depends on the speed of the engine and the camshaft lift. Technician B says that metering depends on the effective stroke of the plunger. Who is right?

17. Technician A says that with an upper helix plunger, prestroke is shorter to port closure. Not so, says technician B; prestroke would be longer to port closure. Who is correct?

18. Technician A says that fuel delivery on a Bosch A model pump is balanced by adjusting the position of each control sleeve. Technician B says that fuel delivery is balanced by adjustment of the plunger lift. Who is right?

19. Technician A says that pump plunger prestroke on an A model pump is adjusted by installing tappet rollers of different diameters. Technician B says that a tappet adjustment screw is used for this purpose. Who knows the correct procedure?

20. Technician A says that pump plunger prestroke on the MW and P model pumps is done by rotating the barrel flange on top of the injection pump housing. Technician B says that it is obtained by removing or inserting shims underneath the barrel flange. Who is aware of the correct procedure here?

21. Technician A says that the MW pump is similar to construction and adjustment to the P model pump. Technician B says that the MW and A model pumps are basically the same. Who knows his or her Bosch pumps in this instance?

22. The P-8500 model injection pump is capable of injection pressures as high as
   a. 15,287 psi (1054 bar)
   b. 16,375 psi (1129 bar)
   c. 17,404 psi (1200 bar)
   d. 19,580 psi (1350 bar)

23. The two major checks and adjustments on an inline multiple-plunger fuel injection pump are
   a. phasing and calibration
   b. phasing and maximum speed adjustment
   c. calibration and governor overrun
   d. low- and high-speed fuel delivery rates

24. Technician A says that to alter the fuel delivery rate on Bosch model MW and P pumps, the barrel flange re-

taining nuts must be loosened and the barrel rotated either CW or CCW to suit. Technician B says that to change the fuel delivery rate, the rack flange collar screw must be loosened and the collar rotated. Who knows the correct procedure here?

25. Technician A says that when lift to port closure is done on a pump mounted on a test stand, to determine the degrees between individual cylinders, you simply divide 360° by the number of cylinders. Technician B says that regardless of the number of cylinders used, they are always set 60° apart. Who is correct?

26. Technician A says that when setting a pump for lift to port closure on a test stand, you should follow the firing-order sequence for best results. Technician B says that you can simply start with number 1 and proceed systematically through each additional cylinder number, such as 1–2–3–4–5–6. Who is correct?

27. Technician A says that the effective stroke of the pumping plunger is simply the lift from BDC to TDC established by the pump camshaft. Technician B says that effective stroke is the period of time during which the fuel inlet ports in the barrel are closed. Who is right?

28. Technician A says that the maximum amount of fuel rack movement is set by installing an adjustable fuel rod stop mechanism in the end of the fuel injection pump housing. Technician B says that rack movement is controlled by the governor. Who is right?

29. Technician A says that the delivery valve is located inside the injector, while technician B says that it is located above the plunger and barrel within the injection pump. Who is correct?

30. Technician A says that the function of a delivery valve is to allow relief of the high fuel pressure in the fuel line at the end of injection. Technician B says that the delivery valve prevents a loss of fuel line prime between injection periods. Who is right?

31. Technician A says that a rough idle when the engine is warm could be caused by a leaking delivery valve. Technician B says that a rough idle could be caused by air in the fuel system. Who is right?

32. Technician A says that if the engine surges at idle, it could be caused by air in the fuel system or a misadjusted bumper spring. Technician B says that it could be due to pump-to-engine timing being incorrect. Who is the most analytical here?

33. Technician A says that failure of the engine to accelerate from an idle speed could be due to a defective timing device. Technician B says that it could be due to a plugged fuel filter. Who is right?

34. Technician A says that a low-power problem could be associated with a leaking delivery valve. Technician B says it is more likely to be a plugged fuel filter or loose connections in the fuel lines. Who is right?

35. Technician A says that an overheating injection pump can be caused by a defective or blocked overflow valve.

Technician B says that the problem is a defective pump and that the pump should be removed for inspection. Who is correct?

36. Technician A says that poor engine performance, associated with low power and black smoke at the exhaust, can be attributed to a plugged engine air filter. Technician B says that the cause could be a defective injection nozzle. Who is correct?

37. Technician A says that white smoke at the exhaust under full load can be caused by incorrect pump-to-engine timing. Technician B says that the cause is more likely to be air in the fuel system. Who is right?

38. Technician A says that excessive fuel consumption can be caused by incorrect pump-to-engine timing. Technician B says that a plugged fuel filter is more likely to be the cause. Who is right?

39. Technician A says that low or uneven cylinder compression can cause white smoke under load, whereas technician B says that low compression would cause black smoke and a lack of power. Who is right?

40. Technician A says that failure of the engine to shut off can be caused by a misadjusted or defective governor, whereas technician B says that it can only be caused by a defective shutoff/start device. Who is right?

41. Technician A says that the best method to employ to check injection pump to engine timing is to spill time it. Technician B says that it is best first to remove the pump and check the timing marks on the engine gear train to pump drive. Who is correct?

42. Technician A says that a Bosch RS governor is a minimum/maximum unit, whereas technician B says that it is a variable-speed design. Who is right?

43. Technician A says that mechanical governors use the force of springs to increase fuel delivery. Technician B says that this is achieved by the centrifugal force developed by the rotating governor flyweights. Who is correct?

44. Technician A says that the greatest amount of fuel is delivered during initial startup. Technician B disagrees, saying that the greatest fuel delivery occurs at the full-load speed. Who is correct?

45. Technician A says that in Bosch governors at breakaway, high-speed regulation pulls the rack to prevent engine stalling. Technician B says that breakaway prevents overspeed. Who is correct?

46. Technician A says that in an RQV-K governor, breakaway can occur at full load or part load. Technician B says that breakaway can occur only under a no-load condition. Who is correct?

47. In an RSV governor model at idle speed, the flyweights force the tensioning lever against the

    a. torque spring
    b. shutoff lever
    c. high-speed spring
    d. bumper spring

48. Technician A says that in an RSV governor, torque control increases rack travel with an increase in engine speed. Technician B disagrees, saying that rack travel is decreased. Who is right?

49. True or False: The function of the starting spring in Bosch governors is to assist the slow rotative speed of the flyweights to move the rack into a decreased fuel position to prevent overfueling.

50. Technician A says that the springs in an RQV governor model are contained inside the weight assemblies. Technician B says that he is confused—that it is the RS/RSV models which have this feature. Who is right?

51. Technician A says that in an RQV-K governor, there are three springs used for speed regulation. Technician B says that there are only two. Who is correct?

52. The aneroid boost compensator control used on some Bosch injection pumps/governors is connected to the
    a. cold-start device
    b. turbocharger/intake manifold line
    c. altitude-sensing device
    d. overspeed governor linkage

53. True or False: When checking the individual condition of the nozzles while still in a running engine, if you loosen a high-pressure fuel line to an injector and there is no change to the engine speed/sound, the injector is good.

54. Technician A says that if an injector is suspected of being faulty after testing it in the engine by opening the high-pressure line, it should be replaced. Technician B says that the injector should be checked in a pop tester first to determine its spray pattern and opening pressure. Who is correct?

55. Technician A says that a fuel system vacuum restriction check can be performed by installing a fuel pressure gauge into the secondary fuel filter assembly. Technician B says that you should use a mercury manometer or a vacuum gauge teed into the system between the fuel tank and fuel transfer pump for this test. Who is correct?

56. Port closing of the injection pump is accomplished by tappet screw adjustment on the
    a. M pump
    b. A pump
    c. MW pump
    d. P pump

57. Port closing of the injection pump is accomplished by shim adjustment on the
    a. M pump
    b. A pump
    c. MW pump
    d. P pump

58. Calibration on an injection pump is accomplished by loosening the bolted flange and rotating the bushing on the
    a. M pump
    b. A pump

c. MW pump
d. P pump

59. Technician A says that prior to removing the fuel injection pump from the engine you should align the FB (fuel begins) timing mark on the crankshaft damper and marked tooth on the injection pump drive gear. Technician B says that you should align the FB mark with the stationary pointer on the front timing gear cover. Who is right?

60. Technician A says that a spill timing check is used to determine exactly when port closure occurs in the No. 1 pumping unit. Technician B says that spill timing determines the metering position of the rack. Who is correct?

61. Technician A says that it requires approximately 25 to 30 psi (172 to 207 kPa) of fuel pressure to lift the delivery valve from its seat in the injection pump. Technician B says that it is much higher, being about 150 psi (1034 kPa). Who is right?

62. Technician A says that manipulation of the fuel transfer pump priming handle can be used to create high-enough pressure to lift the delivery valve from its seat when spill timing. Technician B disagrees, saying that a special spill timing kit pump is required. Who is right?

63. Technician A says that the two common methods used to spill-time an injection pump to the engine is by removing the delivery valve from its holder or by using a high pressure pump kit. Technician B says that only a high-pressure pump kit can be used. Who knows the correct procedure?

64. Technician A says that to determine if cylinder 1 is at TDC on its compression stroke, you can check to see if both the intake and exhaust valve rocker arm have clearance. Technician B says that only the exhaust valve should have clearance; otherwise, you have cylinder 6 at TDC. Who is right?

65. Technician A says that when performing a spill timing check you should always rotate the engine CW from the front at least 90° to remove all gear backlash, then slowly, without jerking, rotate it CCW to align the FB mark with the stationary pointer. Technician B says that he agrees with the procedure, except that the engine should be rotated CCW from the front first, followed by CW rotation to align the timing marks. Who is right?

66. Technician A says that typical mechanical timing advance units employed on Bosch fuel injection pumps operate on the principle of weight advance. Technician B says that they operate on a spring advance principle. Who is right?

67. Technician A says that a timing advance unit that fails to operate would result in early injection and white smoke, whereas Technician B says that it would result in late injection, sluggish performance, and black smoke at the exhaust stack. Who is correct?

68. Technician A says that a timing advance unit stuck in the full advance position would result in early fuel injection at the lower engine speeds, associated with severe com-

bustion knock and a tendency for white smoke. Technician B disagrees, saying that there would simply be a lack of power and excessive fuel consumption. Who is correct?

69. Technician A says that on Bosch injection pumps that employ a pressure relief valve on the pump housing, bleeding of the fuel system becomes unnecessary, due to the fact that the valve will open and expel all air from the system back to the fuel tank. Technician B disagrees, saying that you must bleed all air from the fuel system by opening the individual bleeder screws on the secondary fuel filter(s) and injection pump as well as the individual high-pressure fuel lines at each injector. Who is right?

70. Technician A says that the injection pump-to-engine timing specification can be found on the exhaust emission label attached to the engine. Technician B says that this contains only basic engine information and that you have to refer to the service manual. Who is correct?

71. Technician A says that when checking the static injection pump-to-engine timing specification, you have to employ a portable high-pressure port closing timer tool. Technician B says that you should use a low-air-pressure port closing method tool. Who is right?

72. Technician A says that a common rail fuel system uses a manifold containing high-pressure fuel to feed all of the injectors from a common source. Technician B says that each individual injector is connected to its own separate high pressure fuel rail source. Who is correct?

73. The Bosch common rail fuel system is capable of creating injection pressures in the region of:
    a. 15,000 psi (1035 bar)
    b. 19,580 psi (1350 bar)
    c. 23,000 psi (1586 bar)
    d. 26,500 psi (1828 bar)

74. Technician A says that Cummins Engine Company employs a common rail fuel system in their ISX/Signature series engines. Technician B says that the CAPS, or Cummins Accumulator Pump Systems is used in their ISC engine models. Who is correct?

75. Technician A says that a common rail fuel system can maintain injection pressure independent of engine speed or load. Technician B says that the fuel pressure will vary with any change in engine speed or load. Who is correct?

76. Which one of the following advantages does a common rail electronically controlled fuel system offer?

a. Reduced exhaust emissions
b. Lower combustion noise through pilot and multiple injection
c. Reduced fuel consumption
d. Reliable, long life and high quality
e. All of the above

77. Sensors used with the common rail fuel system will generally output a return voltage signal back to the ECU in the range of:
    a. 0.5 to 5 volts
    b. 2 to 4 volts
    c. 3 to 5 volts
    d. 5 to 8 volts

78. Technician A says that the ECU in the common rail fuel system controls the actual injector needle valve lift to control fuel volume delivery into the combustion chamber. Technician B says that the duty-cycle of the PWM (pulse width modulated) signal from the ECU to the injector solenoid is what controls actual fuel delivery volume. Who is correct?

79. Technician A says that all common rail systems must employ a heated exhaust gas oxygen sensor to operate correctly. Technician B disagrees saying that no oxygen sensor is required. Which technician is correct?

80. Technician A says that the low pressure fuel circuit of the common rail system uses a gear-type pump. Technician B says that either an in-tank roller-cell type electric pump, or an external gear pump can be used. Who is correct?

81. Technician A says that a high-pressure pump delivers fuel to an accumulator manifold or rail to feed the individual injectors. Technician B says that the electric in-tank roller cell pump does this. Who is correct?

82. Technician A says that the fuel pressure control valve (PCV) is always mounted within the high-pressure pump. Technician B says that the PCV can be mounted on the high-pressure pump, or attached to the accumulator rail. Who is correct?

83. Technician A says that the PCV valve is controlled by a signal from the ECU/ECM. Technician B says that a spring loaded relief valve controls the maximum pressure. Who is correct?

84. Technician A says that when the PCV valve pressure is too high, the fuel is bypassed back to the suction side of the high pressure pump. Technician B says that the high pressure fuel is rerouted back to the fuel tank. Who is correct?

20 Mack Electronic Fuel Systems

Overview

In this short introduction to Mack fuel injection systems, you should be aware that Mack does not manufacture a fuel system of its own, but sources these components as a package from Robert Bosch Corporation. Earlier Mack engines used American Bosch sourced components for many years, switching to Robert Bosch when this company was forced to change its name, and was eventually taken over. For many years now, Mack's parent company has been RVI (Renault Vehicles Industriels) in France, a major truck and engine OEM in its own right. More recently Mack/RVI and Volvo of Sweden formed a partnership through a share exchange with each other to form a Mack/RVI/Volvo consortium. Volvo of course have for years been a major world player in the mid-range and heavy duty truck line, with Volvo also being very successful with both their industrial and marine diesel engine applications. All of these OEM's diesel engines are equipped with Robert Bosch Corporation PLN fuel injection pumps and nozzles, details of which are available in Chapter 17 and Chapter 19. Later model engines of all of these truck, industrial and marine engines are available with either Bosch's PLN-EDC (electronic diesel control) system. Mack's latest vehicles employ an electronic system known as VMAC (Vehicle Management and Control) now into the third version of this system. Volvo uses its own VECTRO (Volvo Electronics) fuel injection system employing EUI's (electronic unit injectors). The operating characteristics and details of this system are very similar to those used by both Detroit Diesel Corporation (Daimler-Chrysler), and Caterpillar in their range of heavy-duty high speed engines. More specifics on EUI systems is described in Chapters 18, 21, 22, and 23. Mack engines that are equipped with Bosch EUP's (electronic unit pumps) are similar to the system that was used in the mid 90's by Freightliner (Daimler-Chrysler) when they offered the Series 55 Detroit Diesel six-cylinder engine which was a Mercedes-Benz European engine product known as the M.B. OM457 and identified for North America as the OM447LA. The EUP system is also used on the MTU/DDC 4000 series heavy-duty engines. A description and diagrams of the operation of a EUP system can be found in Chapter 21, see Figures 21–46 and Figure 21–47.

Since all electronic fuel injection systems function and operates as described in detail in Chapters 18, 19, 21, 22, and 23, we will not repeat this same information here. Each one of these chapters will provide you with the details you require to understand Mack/RVI/Volvo fuel systems. Diagnostics and troubleshooting features for these engines is also described in detail in these same chapters. We therefore provide a simple overview of the VMAC system here to enable you to have a frame of reference when working with, or troubleshooting the VMAC system.

The VMAC system and components utilizes two microprocessors: the VMAC module supplied to Mack by Motorola, and a fuel injection control module manufactured by Robert Bosch Corporation. A variety of engine and vehicle sensors relay operating parameters and changing conditions to the microprocessors. The VMAC module and the FIC module are both mounted on a panel underneath the vehicle dashboard in front of the passenger seat. Access to both control modules is easily achieved by removing the panel retaining screws and carefully dropping the panel toward the passenger seat.

Performance Advantages

The VMAC electronic system gives the driver more control over the engine's power, improves fuel economy, and is generally more reliable than the mechanical system.

VMAC SYSTEM TROUBLESHOOTING

The design of the VMAC system will prevent the extraction of inactive fault codes from the dash-mounted malfunction lamp. This lamp will provide only "active" fault code readout (blink). To access all fault codes and perform other diagnostic functions, the VMAC system can be accessed in the same general way as that shown for other electronically controlled fuel systems shown in this chapter (Caterpillar, Cummins, Detroit Diesel) by using a ProLink 9000 DDR (diagnostic data reader) and printer as shown in Figure 21–31. Alternatively, a laptop computer similar to the concept shown can be used along with VMAC software.

If a ProLink 9000 system is not available or the technician wants to save some time in determining if any fault codes exist in the system, when active fault codes are detected by the ECM, these codes can be displayed on the electronic malfunction lamp on the vehicle dashboard by activating the system to create "blink" or "flash" codes similar to that shown in Figure 18–31b. To activate the blink code lamp, proceed as follows:

1. Turn the ignition key ON and wait about 2 seconds until the system bulb check is completed.

2. If the electronic malfunction lamp does not illuminate after the check lamp goes out, there are no stored fault codes stored in computer memory.

3. With the speed control ON/OFF switch in the OFF position, press and hold the SET/DECEL or the RESUME/ACCEL switch until the fault lamp goes OFF.

4. The fault lamp will remain OFF for about 1 second.

5. The VMAC module will begin to flash a two-digit blink code. The two digits of the code will be separated by a 1-second idle time (lamp OFF) condition.

6. Each digit of the blink code may consist of up to eight ON/OFF flashes. The ON and OFF time for each flash will be 0.25 second, so be prepared to write down each code as it appears.

7. Only one active fault code is flashed per request. There must be a separate request for each active fault code when multiple codes are stored. To request another fault code, hold in the SET/DECEL or RESUME/ACCEL switch until the fault lamp goes OFF. The blinking sequence will begin again after a 1-second delay.

8. If the fault blinking request is repeated while VMAC is in the process of blinking an active fault, that sequence will stop and the next active fault will be blinked.

9. If an active fault is cleared while VMAC is blinking that fault, the procedure will not stop.

10. After every complete blinking sequence, the fault lamp will return to normal functions. It will remain ON for active faults and OFF for inactive faults.

NOTE When more than one active fault code is present, continue the blink code sequence until the first active fault is deployed to be certain that all faults have been recovered.

Mack Troubleshooting Connections

Although the technician can withdraw the active fault blink codes as described earlier, to utilize the diagnostic capabilities of the VMAC system, greater information retrieval can be obtained by using the MPSI (Microprocessor Systems Incorporated) ProLink 9000 diagnostic tool or any IBM PC–compatible computer that will perform all the functions of the DDR (diagnostic data reader) ProLink 9000. The PC also allows for enhanced diagnostics of the system and reprogramming of Mack propietary data.

The various ProLink connections where the DDR is connected to an ATA (American Trucking Association) serial link adapter which is available from Kent-Moore/SPX as part J38351. The adapter is in turn connected to a quick-connect wiring adapter at one end and to the VMAC 9-pin serial cable to the communication port located under the vehicle dash to the left of the steering column. See typical examples in Figures 18–28, 18–30, 18–32, and Figure 21–33.

Although blink codes can be extracted as described, if using the ProLink 9000 or a laptop computer with Mack software, standardized SAE (Society of Automotive Engineers) trouble codes will provide the technician with enhanced diagnostics capability of the VMAC system. These SAE codes are the PID (parameter identifier), the SID (system identifier), and the FMI (failure mode indicator). Greater detail on these SAE codes is provided in Chapter 18 on page 479. Codes that would appear in the VMAC system when activated would include the items listed in Table 20–1.

VMAC 111 Systems Diagnostics

A number of Mack truck (RVI) models, such as the CL, LE, and MR model chassis equipped with Cummins engines, have an interface between the Mack vehicle electronic unit (VMAC 111) and the Cummins ECM. Both the vehicle electronic control unit and the ECM detect faults. When an ECM active fault code is flashed, the red fault lamp will flash once to signify the beginning of the ECM fault code sequence. The amber fault

TABLE 20–1 SAE/ATA J1708 serial line standard terminology

Active blink	Fault code	Protocol identification	Assignment listing	Failure
1	1	PID 100/FMI 4	Engine oil pressure	Voltage below normal or shorted low
1	2	PID 100/FMI 3	Engine oil pressure	Voltage above normal or shorted high
1[a]	7	PID 111/FMI 3	Coolant level	Voltage above normal or shorted high
2	1	PID 110/FMI 4	Engine coolant temperature	Voltage below normal or shorted low
2	2	PID 110/FMI 3	Engine coolant temperature	Voltage above normal or shorted high
2	3	PID 105/FMI 4	Intake manifold air temperature	Voltage below normal or shorted low
2	4	PID 105/FMI 3	Intake manifold air temperature	Voltage above normal or shorted high
3	1	SID 21/FMI 8 (active)	Engine position (buffered rpm)	Abnormal frequency, pulse width, or period
		SID 31/FMI 8 (inactive)	Tachometer drive output (buffered rpm)	Abnormal frequency, pulse width, or period
3	2	SID 21/FMI 2	Engine position sensor (rpm/TDC)	Data erratic, intermittent, or incorrect
3	3	PID 190/FMI 2	Engine speed (injection, pump rpm)	Data erratic, intermittent, or incorrect
3	4	SID 22/FMI 2	Timing sensor (TEM)	Data erratic, intermittent, or incorrect
3	5	SID 20/FMI 7	Timing actuator	Mechanical system not responding properly, or out of adjustment
4	1	PID84/FMI 4	Road speed (mph)	Voltage below normal or shorted low
4	2	PID 84/FMI 3	Road speed (mph)	Voltage above normal or shorted high
4	3	PID 84/FMI 8	Road speed (mph)	Abnormal frequency, pulse width, or period
4	4	SID 24/FMI 4	Rack position sensor	Voltage below normal or shorted low
4	5	SID 24/FMI 3	Rack position sensor	Voltage above normal or shorted high
5	1	PID 91/FMI 4	Percent accelerator pedal position	Voltage below normal or shorted low
5	2	PID 91/FMI 3	Percent accelerator pedal position	Voltage above normal or shorted high
5	3	SID 23/FMI 5	Rack actuator	Current below normal or open circuit
5	4	SID 23/FMI 7	Rack actuator	Mechanical system not responding properly, or out of adjustment
6	1	PID 183/FMI 8	Fuel rate	Abnormal frequency, pulse width, or period
		SID 29/FMI 8 (future)	External fuel command input	Abnormal frequency, pulse width, or period
6	2	SID 248/FMI 8	Proprietary data link	Abnormal frequency pulse width, or period
6	3	SID 250/FMI 8	J1708 (J1587) data link	Abnormal frequency, pulse width, or period
7	2	PID 118/FMI 7	Parking brake switch	Mechanical system not responding properly, or out of adjustment
7	4	SID 25/FMI 7	Shutdown override switch	Mechanical system not responding properly, or out of adjustment
N/A	N/A	PID 190/FMI 0	Engine speed (injection pump rpm)	Data valid but above normal operating range
Red and amber light and alarm		PID 110/FMI 0	Engine coolant temperature	Data valid but above normal operating range
Red and amber light and alarm		PID 100/FMI 1	Engine oil pressure	Data valid but below normal operating range
Red and amber light and alarm		PID111/FMI 3	Engine coolant level	Voltage above normal or shorted high

[a]Red light and amber light and alarm.

566

TABLE 20–2 Mack Fault Codes

Fault Code	Circuit	Failure
16	Starter input	High voltage
46	Tachometer output	Low/high voltage
47	Speedometer output	Low/high voltage
51	Accelerator pedal position	Low/open/high voltage
	Idle validation switch	Special instructions, switch indicated **not** idle, pedal indicates idle
52	V ref out of range	Low/high voltage
53	Engine shutdown lamp	Low/high voltage
54	Driver alarm	Low/high voltage
55	Electronic malfunction lamp	Low/high voltage
63	J1708/J1587 link	Abnormal frequency, PW or time
64	J1939 link	Abnormal frequency, PW or time
68	J1939 link	Lost contact with transmission

lamp will then flash the numeric fault code followed by a single flash of the red fault lamp to signify the end of the sequence. All Mack fault codes use a two-digit number, and activate only the amber lamp, whereas Cummins fault codes use a three-digit code flashing the amber fault lamp preceded and followed by one flash of the red fault lamp. Table 20–2 lists the Mack fault codes, and Cummins fault codes can be found in Chapter 22, Tables 22–1, 22–2, and 22–3.

At this time, Mack has one calibration for their vehicle electronic control unit which multiplexes the features that it supports. When active fault codes are present with either the VMAC unit or the Cummins ECM, the yellow/amber fault lamp illuminates. These fault codes can be determined by flashing out the codes by counting the number of flashes of the fault lamp. To extract these flashing fault codes on Mack CL, LE, and MR model chassis, the key switch must be ON with the engine stopped. With the speed control switch (cruise/PTO ON/OFF switch) turned OFF, press the speed control set switch (cruise-control/PTO set/resume switch) to SET, to begin the fault code cycle. Count the number of amber lamp flashes to determine the first code. Repeat the same procedure of pressing the speed control SET switch to access each remaining active fault code. Note that all active vehicle electronic control unit fault codes are flashed first, followed by all active Cummins ECM active fault codes.

Valve Lash Adjustment

To set the valves use either the flywheel marks or the vibration damper. The vibration damper at the front of the crankshaft is marked in 120° increments on six-cylinder Mack engine models; the paired cylinders are

1 and 6, 5 and 2, and 3 and 4 for the firing order of 1–5–3–6–2–4. On the V8 models, the vibration damper is marked in 90° increments; the paired cylinders are 1 and 6, 5 and 3, 4 and 7, and 8 and 2 for a firing order of 1–5–4–8–6–3–7–2. On the six-cylinder engines when the cylinder markings are aligned with a stationary pointer marked "valve" above the damper, they provide the 30° ATDC damper relationship for valve lash adjustment. On the V8 models the cylinder markings, when aligned with the stationary pointer, indicate TDC for each cylinder piston. When a paired cylinder damper mark is aligned with the stationary pointer, check the rocker arms of both numbered cylinders to determine which one has free play. Adjust the valves on this cylinder only. Rotate the engine CW to bring up the next numbered pair of cylinders and repeat the process until all intake and exhaust valves have been adjusted to the correct clearance.

SUMMARY

The basic information and diagnostics procedures described in this chapter can be used when diagnosing and troubleshooting either a Mack, RVI, or Volvo diesel engine equipped with Robert Bosch PLN fuel systems, EUP's, or EUI's. There are more similarities in place today between different OEM electronically controlled engines than there are differences, consequently familiarization with one system will make it relatively easy to transfer this knowledge to other engines and trucks. A review of Chapters 18, 19, 21, 22, and 23 will prepare you with the information required to successfully understand how to effectively diagnose and troubleshoot these systems.

SELF-TEST QUESTIONS

1. Technician A says that Mack Trucks is owned by Freightliner, while Technician B says that they have been owned for some time by RVI (Renault Vehicles Industriels) in France who recently signed a working agreement with Volvo. Who is correct?

2. Technician A says that Mack manufactures all of the components used in their trucks. Technician B says that Mack sources the fuel injection system from Robert Bosch Corporation. Who is correct?

3. Technician A says that Mack trucks employ PLN or EUP fuel systems. Technician B disagrees saying that all current Mack products use EUI fuel systems.

4. Technician A says that VMAC means, 'Vehicle Management and Control' Technician B says that it means, 'Vehicle Mack Accessory Controls'. Who is correct?

5. Technician A says that the VMAC system employs one ECM or electronic control module. Technician B says that it employs two microprocessors; the VMAC module supplied to Mack from Motorola, and the fuel injection control module manufactured by Robert Bosch Corporation. Who is correct?

6. Technician A says that the VMAC module is located underneath the vehicle instrument panel in front of the passenger seat. Technician B says it is located in the engine compartment. Who is correct?

7. Technician A says that you can access system fault codes in the VMAC system by toggling the vehicle cruise control switches. Technician B says that the only way you can access fault codes in the system is to use a laptop computer. Who is correct?

8. Technician A says that you can access fault codes in the VMAC system by employing an MPSI Pro-Link handheld diagnostic tool. Technician B still insists that you must use a laptop computer. Who is correct?

9. A VMAC trouble code identified as an SAE standardized SID 22/FMI 2 indicates a problem in the following system:
   a. Coolant level sensor
   b. Rack position sensor
   c. Intake manifold air temperature sensor
   d. Timing sensor fault

10. An accelerator position sensor which has either a low, open, or high voltage condition is indicated by the following two-digit fault code:
    a. 68
    b. 54
    c. 52
    d. 51

11. Technician A says that to check/adjust the valve lash on a six-cylinder Mack E7 engine, you rotate the engine crankshaft over until the appropriate mark on the engine vibration damper is correctly aligned for the cylinder that you wish to check. Technician B says that these valve set marks are only located on the engine flywheel circumference. Who is correct?

21

Detroit Diesel Corporation Fuel Systems

Overview

Within this chapter we offer data and information dealing with both the "mechanical" and "electronic" fuel systems used by Detroit Diesel Corporation (DDC) in their line of both two- and four-stroke-cycle diesel engines. We describe the purpose, function, operation, adjustment, diagnosis, and troubleshooting of these systems. At the completion of this chapter, if you apply this theoretical knowledge to the various hands-on skills tasks listed in ASE's diesel engine or electronic diesel engine diagnosis specialist test areas, you will be prepared to challenge either the ASE or TQ (Trade Qualification) tests successfully.

Today DDC's major product lineup includes four-stroke-cycle EUI (electronic unit injector) controlled engines represented by the series 50 and 60 models. Although they still manufacture two-stroke-cycle engine models, these EUI-equipped engines represent approximately only 5 to 8% of their total product production per year. However, DDC estimates that there are still about 800,000 two-stroke-cycle engines globally still in service, some equipped with MUI (mechanical unit injector) fuel systems and others with EUI systems. In addition, DDC and Motoren-und Turbinen-Union (Friedrichshafen GMBH) (MTU) have a joint venture agreement allowing them to manufacture both 2000 and 4000 series EUI/EUP large-bore engines for use in industrial, off-highway, and marine applications. They also have an agreement with International Truck Engines to distribute their DTC-466 engine, known as a series 40 in DDC's product category. The prerequisite needed to assist you in gaining maximum knowledge on DDC engine electronic fuel systems is to complete Chapter 18 dealing with the theory and diagnosis of electronic engines. DDC was the first major heavy-duty high-speed diesel engine OEM to adopt electronic fuel injection controls, when in 1985 they released EUIs on their two-cycle 92 series engine models.

ASE CERTIFICATION

Within the ASE medium/heavy truck tests preparation guides, diesel engines, test T2, see page 4 in this book, as well as ASE's electronic diesel engine diagnosis specialist test (L2), see Chapter 18, are a number of tasks lists areas that describe the knowledge required to challenge these test content certification modules. Tasks lists for "mechanical" fuel systems are listed in the diesel engines content, see subheading F, Fuel System Diagnosis and Repair, Part 1, Mechanical Components, see page 4. For "electronic" fuel systems, see diesel engines (T2 preparation guide), subheading Fuel System Diagnosis and Repair, Part 2, Electronic Components.

Aspiring technicians who wish to specialize/certify as an electronic diesel engine diagnosis specialist should obtain the ASE L2 preparation guide which provides all of the necessary information and content areas that you will need to master. The content tasks list for the L2 area is shown on pages 440–442 in Chapter 18. The complete L2 preparation guide can be downloaded from the ASE website at *www.asecert.com*.

ENGINE LABELS

All DDC engines are equipped with an option plate on the rocker cover of older-model units. On engines manufactured since August 1985, a new paper-laminate engine option and emissions label is used. These labels provide the mechanic/technician with general engine information as well as detailed information regarding the horsepower setting of the engine, its fuel rate, maximum rpm, and valve and injector settings.

Bar code labels on the engine are printed in computer-readable form, with one bar identifying the engine serial number and the other listing the

569

customer specification number when the engine was ordered initially. This allows a check at any time with the factory or DDC distributor/dealer as to what special options were originally ordered on that engine. The disclaimer label indicates that when the engine was manufactured, it complied with all government emission regulations and that DDC will not be held responsible for alterations to engine fuel settings, and so on; that would affect engine horsepower and/or emission certification. Items listed on an option plate or a paper-laminate label indicate that each of these items has been specially ordered for the particular model and application of that engine. It is in reality a built-in parts book. When parts are required, the mechanic/technician simply refers to the type number on the label, along with the engine model and serial number, and you can then order parts through any DDC distributor/dealer worldwide, and along with the engine model number, you will be guaranteed the correct component part. The parts person simply cross-references the type number with a part number listing through a PC program.

BASIC FUEL SYSTEM FUNCTIONS

Both the mechanical and electronic fuel systems employed by Detroit Diesel are commonly known as low-pressure fuel systems, owing to the fact that fuel delivered to the unit injectors averages 50 to 70 psi (345 to 482.6 kPa), compared with the average 2500 to 4000 psi (17,237 to 27,580 kPa) PLN (pump-line-nozzle) that passes through the fuel lines from the injection pump to the nozzles on fuel systems such as Ambac, Robert Bosch, ZEXEL–Diesel Kiki, Delphi (Lucas/CAV), Caterpillar, Nippondenso, and others.

The five main functions of the fuel system employed by Detroit Diesel are as follows:

1. To supply clean, cool fuel to the system by passing it through at least a primary and secondary filter before the pump and injectors
2. To cool the injectors as the fuel flows through them and returns to the tank (recirculatory system)
3. To lubricate the injector's moving parts, through the inherent lubricity of diesel fuel, which is basically a very light oil
4. To maintain sufficient pressure at all times through the action of the positive-displacement gear pump and the use of a restricted fitting located at the cylinder head return fuel manifold
5. To purge the fuel system of any air; the system is recirculatory in operation, therefore allowing any air to be returned to the fuel tank

MECHANICAL FUEL SYSTEM COMPONENTS

Figure 21–1 shows a schematic view of a typical VEE fuel system used on a 6 V two-cycle MUI (mechanical unit injector) engine. Since the basic fuel system employed on all two- and four-cycle Detroit Diesel engines is identical as far as components used, the description of operation for one can be readily related to any other series of DD engine. An inline engine, for example, would use only one cylinder head, whereas a V-engine using two would have a fuel system as shown in this diagram.

The basic fuel system shown consists mainly of the following:

- Fuel injectors.
- Fuel pipes or jumper lines to and from the injectors (inlet and outlet).
- Fuel manifolds, which are cast internally within the cylinder head (older engines used external fuel manifolds running lengthwise along the head). Either way, the upper manifold is the *inlet* and the lower is the outlet or *return* on two-cycle models. To prevent confusion, the words *in* and *out* are cast in several places on the side of the head.
- Fuel pump (supply pump, not an injection pump).
- Fuel strainer or primary filter.
- Fuel filter (secondary).
- Fuel lines.
- One-way check valve.
- Restricted fitting on inline engines or a restricted T on V-type engines to maintain a minimum fuel pressure of 30 psi in the return fuel manifold.

FUEL PUMP

Figure 21–2 shows the typical fuel pump used on all series 53, series 71, series 92, 8.2 L, and series 50 and 60 engines.

Fuel Flow: Two-Cycle MUI Models

The fuel pump draws fuel from the tank past the one-way nonreturn check valve into the primary filter, where the fuel passes through a 30-μm-filtering-capacity cotton-wound sock-type element. From the primary filter it passes up to the suction side of the fuel pump, where the fuel is then forced out at between 65 and 75 psi (448.2 and 517.1 kPa) to the secondary filter, which is a pleated paper element of 10-μm filtering capacity. Fuel then passes up to the inlet fuel manifold (upper) of the cylinder head, where it is distributed through the fuel jumper lines into each injector. All surplus fuel (not injected) returns from the injectors through the return

that in fact the proper restricted fitting, and not just any fitting, is installed into the return line. Use of too large a fitting can lead to low fuel pressure within the head manifolds and poor engine performance, whereas too small a fitting can lead to increased fuel temperatures and some restriction against the fuel flow. The one-way check valve is used to prevent fuel from draining back to the tank from the primary filter and line when the engine is stopped.

The fuel pump is a positive-displacement gear-type unit that transfers fuel from the tank to the injectors at 65 to 75 psi (448.2 to 517.1 kPa). The standard pump has the ability to deliver 1.5 U.S. gallons/minute (5.67 L) or 90 U.S. gallons/hour (340.68 L), approximately at 1800 engine rpm.

Since the pump constantly circulates an excess supply of fuel to and through the injectors, the unused portion, which also cools and lubricates the injectors and purges the system of any air, returns to the fuel tank via the restricted fitting and fuel return line.

Series 50 and 60 Fuel System

Let us briefly look at the fuel system layout for the Detroit Diesel series 50 and 60 EUI (electronic unit injectors) engine models. Figure 21–3a illustrates that the fuel system is similar to that used with the MUI (mechanical unit injector) engines in that a gear-type fuel transfer pump driven from the rear of the air compressor assembly on truck applications creates the flow requirements for the system. Fuel leaves the fuel tank and passes through either a primary fuel filter or fuel/water separator assembly to the inlet side of the fuel pump. This is the suction side of the fuel system; therefore, any loose fittings or connections will allow air to be drawn into the system, resulting in a rough-running engine and a lack of power. From the outlet side of the pump, fuel under pressure flows through a cooling plate bolted to the ECM (electronic control module) on certain applications to maintain the internal operating temperature of the electronics components within the ECM at an acceptable level. This fuel cooler is not normally required on heavy-duty highway truck series 60 engines unless fuel temperatures are consistently above 140°F (60°C), although it is used on series 50 models in transit bus applications. Fuel now enters the secondary fuel filter and exits to the rear of the cylinder head, where it flows through an internally cast manifold to feed each EUI. Fuel that is not required for injection purposes is used to cool and lubricate the internal components of the injector. Return fuel leaves the injector where it flows through an internal fuel return manifold cast within the cylinder head. Fuel leaves the head at the rear through a restricted fitting as shown in Figure 21–3b and returns to the fuel tank.

Identification of Fuel Pump Rotation

If you are in doubt as to a fuel pump's rotation, it can be identified as follows:

1. Stamped on the pump cover are the letters LH or RH, plus an arrow indicating the direction of rotation.

2. On inline engines, the fuel pump rotation can be determined by its location on the engine. When viewed from the flywheel end: left-hand-side location, LH pump rotation; right-hand-side location, RH pump rotation. All V71 and V92 engines use LH rotation pumps only; 149 engines use only RH rotation pumps.

3. A similar method would be to grasp the pump in your left or right hand as it mounts on the engine with an overhand grip. Whichever thumb covers the relief valve indicates the pump's rotation.

The letters I/L (inlet) are also stamped on the pump cover; however, if not visible, the inlet side is the hole on the pump cover closest to the relief valve plug. The fuel pump body and cover are aligned by means of two dowels, and the body and cover are ground surfaces that contain no gasket between them, although a thin coat of sealant applied to these surfaces is recommended at installation. The relief valve bypasses fuel back to the inlet side of the pump when pressure reaches 65 to 75 psi (448.2 to 517.1 kPa).

Fuel drawn into the suction side of the pump fills the space between the gear teeth and the pump body, where it is carried around and discharged to the outlet cavity under an average pressure of 45 to 70 psi (310.2 to 482.6 kPa). Closer study of Figure 21–2 will indicate the characteristics of the pump shown.

Figure 21–2 shows an exploded view of the pump; the stackup of the component parts is clearly visible. The standard fuel pump gears are 0.25 in. wide and contain 10 teeth, whereas the high-capacity pump that is available has gear teeth 0.375 in. or 0.50 in. wide, with this size stamped on the pump cover. The output of the 0.375 in. gear pump is approximately 135 gph, and the 0.50 in. unit is 175 to 180 gph U.S. Engine injector size, application, and rpm determine pump size. The drive gear is a 0.001 in. (0.0254 mm) press fit onto the shaft, and a gear retaining ball locates it on its shaft.

As shown in Figure 21–2, two oil seals are pressed into the pump bore from the flanged end for the following purposes:

- The seal closest to the drive fork prevents lube oil from entering the fuel pump.
- The inner seal closest to the pump gears prevents fuel oil leakage.

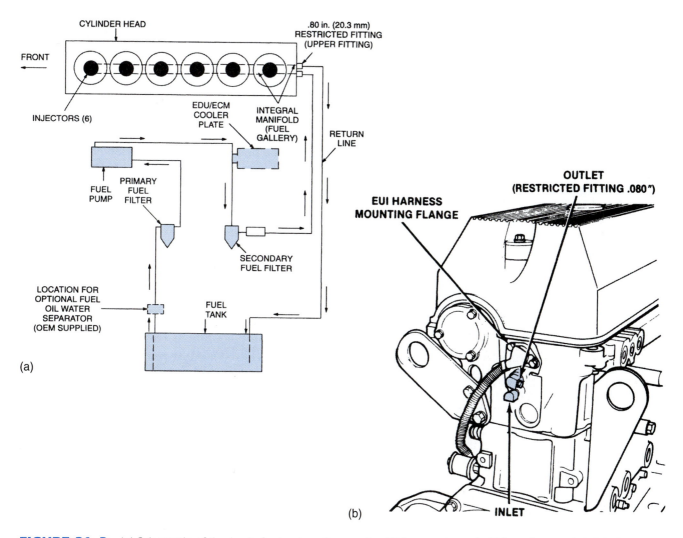

FIGURE 21–3   (a) Schematic of the basic fuel system for a series 60 four-stroke-cycle EUI engine model. (b) Closeup of the series 50/60 fuel gallery inlet and outlet fittings located at the rear of the engine cylinder head. Note the 0.080 in. restricted fitting at the outlet line. (Courtesy of Detroit Diesel Corporation.)

The installed seals do not butt up against each other but have a small space between them. Drilled and tapped into this cavity in the fuel pump body are two small holes, one of which is usually plugged; the other is open to allow any fuel or lube oil leakage to drain, thereby indicating damaged seals. Sometimes a small fitting and tube extend from one of these holes to direct any leakage to a noticeable spot. Acceptable leakage should not exceed one drop per minute.

A fuel pump with a star or the word *day* stamped on its cover indicates that the inner seal is reversed, and is used on *gravity feed* installations where the fuel tank is above the level of the fuel pump. The reversed inner seal (seal closest to the pump gears) prevents fuel seepage down the pump shaft and out the drain cavity hole, especially when the engine is shut down. *Never* plug both drain holes in the pump body be-

tween the oil seals; otherwise, any fuel leakage will cause crankcase oil dilution.

MINIMUM FUEL-LINE SIZES VERSUS RESTRICTION

All diesel engines, regardless of the make of manufacture, require a minimum size (diameter) of fuel line in order to keep the restriction to the suction side of the fuel transfer pump as low as possible. This minimum resistance to flow will ensure that the engine will not be subjected to periods of fuel starvation and lack-of-power complaints. The suction side of the fuel system extends from the fuel tank up to the inlet side of the fuel transfer pump. Refer to Figures 21–1 and 21–3, which illustrate the basic fuel system. Therefore, any

fittings, connections, or fuel lines that are too small on the suction side of the system will create problems. The greatest amount of restriction to the system is generally caused by such items as fittings, one-way check valves, and the actual piping size itself.

A properly designed fuel system should have a maximum restriction with a clean primary filter installed of 6 in. Hg (mercury). This restriction can be checked by removing the small pipe plug from the left- or right-hand outlet side of the primary filter fuel strainer housing as shown in Figure 21–4. To connect the mercury manometer, remove the left-hand or right-hand filter outlet pipe plug, and install a suitable brass fitting. To this fitting would be connected a piece of rubber hose/tubing, with the other end attached to a mercury manometer. How to use manometers is discussed in detail in Chapter 13, Figs. 13–38 through 13–41.

The restriction check, if possible, should be taken by connecting a suitable tee fitting to the inlet fitting of the fuel pump. However, it is often not convenient to access the pump on many applications; therefore, the primary filter, which is generally within 2 ft of the pump inlet, is acceptable (Figure 21–3). In addition, any loose fittings or connections on the suction side of the system will allow the pump to suck air into the system, resulting in low delivery. The engine will idle rough and stumble badly as you accelerate it and attempt to load it. See Fuel Spill Back Check section in this chapter.

Another condition that can cause an increase in fuel system restriction is the height that the fuel pump is above the fuel tank, with every foot of lift causing a restriction increase of 0.8 in. Hg. Maximum allowable restriction in the fuel system with a dirty fuel filter should not exceed 12 in. Hg (mercury). The best guide for fuel-line size on any engine is to determine the size of the inlet to the transfer pump, then select the largest size fitting and fuel line that will fit this connection.

PRIMING THE FUEL SYSTEM

There are several ways in which to prime the fuel system. The degree of priming required depends on what caused the fuel loss in the first place. However, the priming of the fuel system on a Detroit Diesel engine is usually not as involved or as hard as it can be on some high-pressure fuel systems, owing to the fact that since it is a low-pressure recirculatory type of fuel system, it will purge itself of air more readily than the conventional high-pressure type of system.

FILTER REPLACEMENT

Replace the primary and secondary fuel filters at the normal preventive maintenance change period.

Shell and Element Type Filters

1.   With the engine stopped and the drain tray under the filter canister, open the drain cock and lightly loosen the cover nut or bolt to facilitate free drainage of the fuel, then close the drain cock.

2.   Be sure to protect wiring harnesses or electrical equipment from fuel oil during the change period.

3.   Remove the shell and element, and remove and discard the cover nut retaining ring if used; discard the filter element and shell gasket or seal ring, the cover nut or bolt gasket, and cover bolt snap ring, if used.

4.   Wash out the shell in clean fuel oil and blow it dry with compressed air. Carefully examine the element seal and retaining ring to make sure that they are in position, since they cannot be replaced; if damaged or if the seat is not against the retaining ring, the shell assembly must be replaced.

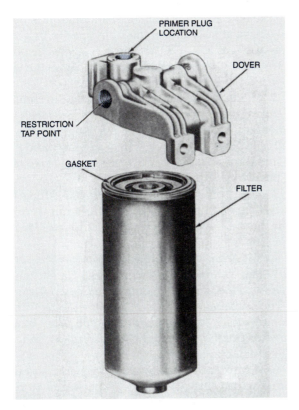

FIGURE 21–4 *Identification of a primary fuel filter showing the filter restriction tap point to connect to a Hg (mercury) manometer, and the filter primer plug location. On a secondary filter, the restriction tap point is used to measure fuel "pressure" on the outlet side of the filter, while the primer plug location can also be used to measure the fuel pump inlet pressure to the secondary filter. (Courtesy of Detroit Diesel Corporation.)*

5. Thoroughly soak the element in clean fuel before installation, which helps to expel entrapped air and therefore makes for an easier initial engine start. Place the new element into the shell and push it down against its seat; then fill the shell two-thirds full with clean, filtered fuel.

6. Place a new gasket or seal ring in the shell recess and a new gasket on the cover nut or bolt, and thread the nut or bolt into the shell. With the shell gasket in place, tighten the cover bolt or nut to prevent leakage. Remove the pipe plug at the top of the shell cover (Figure 21–4) and complete filling of the shell with clean fuel.

Spin-on Filters

1. With spin-on types of filters (Figure 21–4), if no drain cocks are provided and water is a problem, a fuel–water separator should be employed. Unscrew the filter via the 1 in. (25.4 mm) 12-point nut at its base, discard it, fill the new unit two-thirds full with clean, filtered fuel, coat the seal gasket lightly with clean fuel oil, and after the filter contacts the gasket, tighten it two-thirds of a turn.

2. The pipe plug on the inlet side of the filter cover in Figure 21–4 can be removed and using a suitable hand-operated pump the entire fuel system can be primed.

3. Start the engine and check for fuel leaks.

ENGINE RUNS OUT OF FUEL

If an engine runs out of fuel, it is due strictly to carelessness on the part of either the equipment operator or the maintenance personnel. Downtime caused by this situation can be expensive, especially if it happens on the road or in a remote off-highway location. If you have to restart an engine due to this condition, check the sequence given earlier in this chapter on priming the fuel system.

Figure 21–4 shows the filler plug location employed in both the primary and secondary fuel filters that can be removed for the purpose of priming the fuel system when necessary. The problem in restarting an engine after it has run out of fuel stems from the fact that after the fuel is exhausted from the fuel tank, fuel is then pumped from the primary fuel strainer and is often partially removed from the secondary fuel filter before the fuel supply becomes insufficient to sustain engine operation. Therefore, these components must be refilled with fuel and the fuel lines rid of air in order for the system to provide adequate fuel for the injectors. This situation is not only avoidable, but expensive in terms of equipment downtime. On an engine that has run out of fuel, attempting to crank the engine over on the starter will not sustain engine firing. It will have to be primed.

NOTE   To facilitate starting after running out of fuel, do *not* spray ether (starting fluid) into the air intake to try to keep the engine running without adequate fuel. Severe damage to the injector plunger and bushing, as well as the spray tips, will result because they are running dry during this time. In addition, excess ether can cause cracked cylinder heads due to the high volatility of ether. Severe pressures can be created inside the combustion chamber.

Restarting Procedure

1. It may not always be possible to fill the fuel tank completely, particularly if the vehicle/equipment is in a remote location; therefore, although it is desirable to have at least 25% of the tank capacity, or a minimum of 10 gallons in it, this may not always be possible. Obviously, the more fuel that is added to the tank, the easier it will be to prime the system.

2. If clean, filtered fuel is available to you, remove both the primary and secondary fuel filters and fill them up. If nonfiltered fuel is available, remove the small pipe plug on top of each filter assembly and pour fuel into the assembly, or use a priming pump to force fuel positively through the system.

3. The priming pump will allow you to force fuel through the fuel lines up to the injectors and therefore prime the complete system before attempting to restart the engine.

4. It is helpful when the injectors have run completely dry to remove the No. 1 injector inlet jumper line, and prime the system with a prefiltered fuel supply. The inlet manifold and all injectors can be primed to assure quick startup of the engine after having poured or primed fuel into both the primary and secondary fuel filter assemblies.

5. Crank the engine over until it starts, and with the fuel return line disconnected, allow fuel to pour into a container until all the air has disappeared and a steady flow of fuel is visible. If the air bubbles do not disappear, there is an air leak on the suction side of the fuel system (between the inlet on the pump and the fuel tank).

6. Reconnect the fuel return line and run the engine to check for any signs of fuel leakage.

FUEL INJECTORS—MUI

Fuel Injector Mounting

The two-stroke DDC engine unit fuel injector is located in the cylinder head. The injector sits in a copper tube in the head, which is surrounded by water in all the two-stroke-cycle DDC engines for cooling purposes. The injector is located by a dowel pin on the underside of the body, and it is held in the head by a single bolt and clamp arrangement. The injector shown in Figure 21–5 is known as an *offset* body since the fuel inlet and outlet studs are offset to one another rather than being parallel or straight. This feature of the offset body is to allow sufficient clearance between the valves on four-valve-head engines.

The injector is actuated by a roller-type cam follower and pushrod threaded into the rear of the rocker arm. This threaded pushrod and locknut arrangement allows adjustment of the injector follower to body height (see the section "Tune-Up Sequence"). Two fuel jumper lines supply fuel to the injector, with one being connected to an inlet fuel stud that is fed from the upper manifold in the cylinder head on 53, 71, and 92 engines, while the return fuel line is connected to a return fuel stud which directs fuel to the lower cylinder head manifold, through the restricted fitting, and back to the fuel tank. On the 8.2 L and series 60 four-stroke-cycle

engines, the injectors are fed from an internal fuel manifold in the cylinder head. These injectors can be seen in the section dealing with these two engines.

> NOTE: The inlet fuel stud on the unit injector is always the one directly above the fuel rack, or the one on the right-hand side of the injector body when viewed from the rack control end. This is very important because only the inlet fuel stud contains a filter underneath it; therefore, if these fuel jumper lines are reversed, dirty fuel could enter the injector, creating serious damage.

Clearly visible in Figure 21–5 is the injector fuel control rack connected to a control lever. A fuel control tube is connected to the governor by a fuel rod so that the speed of the engine can be changed by either manual operation of the throttle or by governor action. When the rack is moved in toward the injector body, fuel is increased, and when it is pulled out all the way, this is the fuel shutoff position.

Non-DDEC Unit Fuel Injector Function

The fuel injector, or what is often referred to as a *unit injector*, used by Detroit Diesel Corporation has some variations in basic injector model design and in the actual testing procedures used; however, the function and operation are the same for all.

These injectors were designed with simplicity in mind from both a control and an adjustment outlook. They are used on direct-injection, open-type, two- and four-cycle combustion chamber engines manufactured by DDC. No high-pressure fuel lines are required with these injectors, since the fuel from the fuel pump is delivered to the inlet fuel manifold cast internally within the cylinder head at a pressure of 50 to 70 psi (345 to 482.6 kPa), and then to the injectors through fuel pipes.

Figure 21–5 shows a typical MUI (mechanical unit injector) employed by Detroit Diesel Corporation in their non-DDEC engines. Once the fuel from the pump reaches the injector, it performs the following functions:

1. *Times the injection.* Timing of the injector is accomplished by movement of the injector control rack, which causes rotation of the plunger within the injector bushing. Since the plunger is manufactured with a helical chamber area, this rotation will either advance or retard the closing of the ports in the injector bushing, and therefore the start and end of the actual injection period. Pushrod adjustment establishes the height

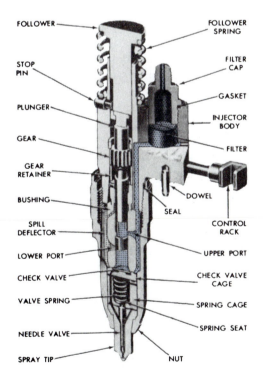

FIGURE 21–5   Cutaway view of a MUI (mechanical unit injector) assembly. (Courtesy of Detroit Diesel Corporation.)

of the injector follower above the body. This in turn establishes the point or "time" that the descending plunger will close the bushings' ports and therefore the start of the injection.

2. *Meters the fuel.* The rotation of the plunger by movement of the injector control rack will advance or retard the start and end of injection. If the length of time that the fuel can be injected is then varied, so will the amount of fuel be varied.

3. *Pressurizes the fuel.* Fuel that is trapped underneath the plunger on its downward stroke will develop enough pressure to force its way past the check valve and needle valve, as the case may be, and therefore enter the combustion chamber.

4. *Atomizes the fuel.* Fuel under pressure that forces its way past the check or needle valve must then pass through small holes or orifices in the injector spray tip. This breaks down the fuel into a finely atomized spray as it enters the combustion chamber.

Horsepower Change—MUI Engines

When the horsepower of a DDC engine is to be changed, this is generally done by increasing or decreasing the injector size in the engine as long as the maximum recommended injector size for that engine and application is not exceeded. Changing an injector from one size, say an N60 to an N65, would result in an increase in horsepower, depending on the size and model of engine that it is in at the same governed rpm. Each successive move up the scale in multiples of 5 mm^3 will continue to increase the horsepower setting in a similar fashion.

The maximum no-load governed rpm for any engine is always stamped on either the engine rocker cover option plate and/or paper-laminate label on the newer engines. The tolerance on this speed setting is ±25 rpm and should not be exceeded under any circumstances, unless an engine is to be overhauled or placed into a different type of application.

Injector Removal: Two-Cycle Engines

1. Steam clean the valve rocker cover area and adjacent surroundings to prevent the entrance of dirt into the engine.

2. Remove the valve rocker covers; loosen and remove the injector fuel pipes. Immediately install plastic shipping caps over all injector fuel cap studs and all other fuel connectors, and open fuel lines to prevent the entrance of any dirt.

3. Crank the engine over, or bar it over, until the flats across the rocker arms (at the pushrod) are all in line or horizontal (53, 71, and 92 series only).

FIGURE 21–6 *Using a small heel bar to carefully pry the unit injector from the cylinder head. (Courtesy of Detroit Diesel Corporation.)*

4. Install plastic shipping caps over all fuel inlet and outlet holes.

5. On 53, 71, and 92 engines, loosen and remove the two rocker shaft hold-down bolts; tip back the rocker assemblies clear of the valves and injector (see Figure 21–6).

6. On four-valve cylinder heads, remove the two exhaust valve bridges by lifting them from their guides (reinstall them on the same guide).

7. Remove the injector clamp hold-down bolt and clamp; then loosen both the inner and outer adjusting screws (earlier engines) on the injector rack control lever tube far enough to allow you to slide the lever away from the injector. Current engines have only one screw held by a locknut.

8. Insert a small heel bar or injector removal tool under the injector body, taking care not to exert any pressure directly on the control rack, and gently pry the injector from the cylinder head (Figure 21–6).

9. At this time, cover the injector hole in the cylinder head to prevent the entrance of foreign material. If you are removing the injector from a four-valve-head 53 series engine, there is no separate bridge mechanism. It is attached to the end of the rocker arm by a pin and is self-centering when in contact with the valve stems.

10. The exterior of the injector should now be cleaned with clean fuel oil and dried with compressed air prior to any additional tests.

Injector Installation: Two-Cycle Engines

If the cylinder head is off the engine, do not install the injector until the head has been replaced on the engine; however, the injector tube can be cleaned of carbon while the head is off, which will minimize the possibility of carbon particles dropping into the cylinder. If the cylinder head has been removed for any reason other than injector replacement, the injector copper tubes in the head may be replaced if necessary; however, refer to the section on injector tube replacement for this function in all DDC service manuals.

If the cylinder head is on the engine, check the beveled seat on the injector tube where the injector nut seats for any signs of carbon deposits, which would prevent proper seating of the injector. To remove carbon deposits from 53, 71, and 92 injector tubes, use injector tube bevel reamer J5286-9. When using these reamers, be very careful to remove only the carbon and not the copper from the tube itself; otherwise, the clearance between the injector and the cylinder head will be altered, with possibly disastrous results.

NOTE It is advisable to pack the flutes of the reamer with grease to retain the carbon removed from the tube and to prevent any carbon from dropping into the cylinder.

The injector should be filled with fuel oil through the inlet filter cap until it runs out of the outlet cap prior to installation into the cylinder head.

Installation Procedure

1. Insert the injector into the injector tube, making sure that the dowel pin on the underside of the injector body fits into the mating hole in the cylinder head.

2. Slide the injector rack control lever on the control tube on the head over until it sits into the injector control rack end.

3. Install the injector clamp and special washer (with the curved side toward the injector clamp), and bolt and tighten to 20 to 25 lb-ft (27 to 34 N · m) maximum on 53, 71, and 92 injectors.

CAUTION Check to make sure that the injector clamp is centered over the follower spring prior to tightening; otherwise, the spring may contact the clamp during injector operation. In addition, overtorquing of the injector clamp bolt can cause the injector control rack to stick or bind.

4. On four-valve-head engines (71, 92) install the exhaust valve bridges over their guides and onto the valve stem tips (53 series four-valve-head engines have the bridge mechanism attached to the end of the rocker arms).

5. Move the rocker arm assemblies into position and tighten the hold-down bolts to the spec.

NOTE Extreme care must be used so as not to bend the fuel pipes during installation; also, overtightening of the fuel pipe nuts can twist or fracture the flared end of the fuel pipe, resulting in leaks that cause lube oil dilution and damage to engine bearings.

FUEL SYSTEM TROUBLESHOOTING

One of the most common complaints received by the mechanic/technician is that the engine runs rough or lacks power. When this complaint is received, it can be caused by a number of conditions that often have nothing at all to do with the fuel system itself, but more often than not, it is the fuel system that receives the blame. Prior to condemning the fuel system as the cause of the complaint, you should always gather as much information as possible from the operator of the vehicle or equipment to assist you in systematically tracing the probable cause, or causes. However, it is always advisable to run the engine and closely monitor the color of the exhaust smoke, both at a no-load and a full-load condition, if possible.

The color of the exhaust smoke will quickly lead you to one or more of the engine systems. For example, gray-to-black smoke is usually an indication of air starvation, although it can also be caused by overfueling, which is not too common on today's engines. Blue smoke indicates oil being burned in the combustion chamber. This could be an internal engine problem, or even blower or turbocharger seal leakage. White smoke is generally associated with low compression or water in the cylinder; however, do not be misled on cold-weather startup, particularly on MUI engines when white smoke is evident. This is caused by the lower cylinder temperature due to the cold air which affects the ignition delay characteristic of the fuel. The unburned fuel particles quickly cool on entering the atmosphere and white smoke is created. If the white smoke is evident on startup but clears up within a short period of time (2 to 3 minutes or so on MUI engines), this is not the reason for the lack-of-power complaint.

NOTE: Electronically controlled engines tend to clear white smoke 20 to 30 seconds after cold-weather startup.

If the white smoke fails to clear after the engine warms up, possible causes could be:

- Low cylinder compression
- The use of low-cetane diesel fuel
- Water in the combustion chamber from a leaking head gasket or a cracked cylinder head (can result in severe piston and con-rod damage due to the hydrostatic lock that will occur as the piston attempts to compress the trapped water)

DDC has determined that white smoke or misfire at an engine idle speed can be attributed in some cases to the idle fuel output being substantially higher or lower on one or more injectors than on the others. Cylinders receiving too little or too much idle fuel tend to white smoke, and idle quality suffers greatly due to these unbalanced firing impulses. On non-DDEC-equipped two-cycle engines only, it may be necessary after a tune-up and injector rack adjustment procedure to short out each individual injector by pushing and holding down the injector follower with a screwdriver to determine what cylinders are in effect firing with the engine idling. On those cylinders that are not firing, no change will be noticed in the engine rpm and sound when the nonfiring cylinder injector follower is depressed. It may therefore be necessary to adjust these particular injector racks while the engine is idling by turning the rack screw lightly to increase the fuel delivery to that cylinder. Series 92 engine racks should not be adjusted more than one-quarter turn (90°), while series 53 and 71 engine injector racks should not be adjusted more than one-eighth turn (45°).

NOTE   On older engines employing two rack adjustment screws, the screw closest to the rack (inner) is the adjuster; the outer screw is a lock screw. On newer engines, only one rack screw is used on the injector control tube to rack.

After any such adjustment, slowly accelerate the engine a number of times, then allow it to settle down at the normal idle speed to determine if the idle is now smoother and the white smoke or roughness has disappeared. Should a rough idle or white smoke persist, further checks would be required to determine the cause.

With a lack-of-power complaint, black smoke is common and can generally be traced back to a high AIR (air inlet restriction) condition, or a combination high AIR and low blower or turbocharger boost condition. If a lack-of-power complaint is received with no visible smoke at the exhaust, this generally indicates that the engine is not receiving adequate fuel delivery. A check of throttle linkage travel should be made to determine whether the engine is actually receiving full-rack travel when the pedal is in its maximum fuel position.

Fuel Flow or Fuel Spill-Back Check

Checking Procedure

1.   Check first that you have the correct size of restricted fitting for your model and engine series. This can be found listed in section 13.2 in all DDC service manuals.

2.   The amount of fuel spill-back varies with the restricted fitting size. A general rule of thumb average for fuel spill-back on engines employing a standard fuel pump is approximately related to the restricted fitting size. For example, an engine using a 0.055 in. (1.397 mm) restricted fitting should return 0.5 U.S. gallon (1.892 L) per minute minimum. An 0.080 in. (2.032 mm) fitting should return 0.8 U.S. gallon (3.028 L) per minute minimum at 1200 rpm or 0.9 U.S. gallon (3.406 L) per minute minimum at 1800 to 2300 rpm. In other words, if for some reason you did not have specifications readily at hand, by using the basic rules stated above you will be able to establish whether or not sufficient fuel is being circulated.

3.   Disconnect the fuel return line at a convenient place that will readily allow you to run the fuel into a clean, adequately sized container (Figure 21–7).

4.   You will need a watch with a second hand; if in a shop, a large wall clock with a second hand will do.

On turbocharged engines, the fuel spill-back is normally taken at 1800 rpm, but it can also be taken at the higher rpm ranges as specified under fuel spill-back to ensure continuity of fuel flow.

5.   Start and run the engine at the specified speed for 1 minute, after which you can determine whether the system is receiving an adequate supply of fuel. While you are doing this check, immerse the fuel return line into the container to check for any sign of air bubbles rising to the surface. This would indicate that air is being drawn into the fuel system on the suction side of the fuel pump. Check all fuel line connections from the suction side of the pump back to the fuel tank, including the seal ring at the primary filter and at the strainer or fuel water separator if used. Remember, from the

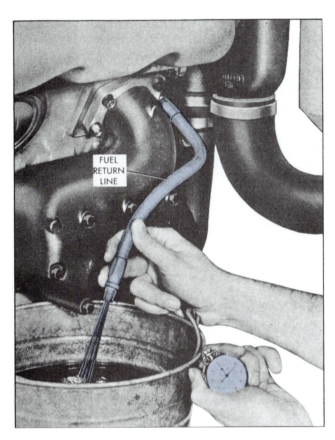

FIGURE 21–7 *Performing a fuel spill-back check/test for 1 minute while running the engine at 1800 rpm. Use on either DDC two- or four-stroke-cycle engine models. (Courtesy of Detroit Diesel Corporation.)*

outlet or discharge side of the pump the fuel is under pressure; therefore, a fuel leak would occur from here on up to the cylinder head fuel manifold rather than sucking in air. When checking for air bubbles at the container during a fuel spill-back test, ensure that the fuel line is in fact submerged totally. Otherwise, agitation and aeration on the surface of the fuel may lead you to believe that the system is sucking air.

6. If the amount of fuel returned is less than specified in DDC manuals, replace the primary fuel filter, remove the pipe plug from the top of the secondary filter, and install a fuel pressure gauge. Start and run the engine again at 1800 rpm, and measure the amount of fuel returned to the container. Also note what fuel pressure registers on the gauge at the secondary filter. Normal fuel pressure should be between 50 and 70 psi (345 to 483 kPa).

7. If the fuel return and pressure are still low, replace the secondary filter element and repeat the previous procedure.

8. If, after replacing the secondary filter, low fuel flow persists, then tee-in a vacuum gauge or mercury manometer at the primary filter outlet line or restriction tap point (Figure 21–4). Start and run the engine and note what the maximum restriction to fuel flow is. The maximum allowable on a system with new filters is 6 in. Hg (mercury), or 12 in. Hg on a dirty system. Check that the fuel line size is as recommended for your engine as stated by DDC. In addition, if the fuel tank is in excess of 20 ft (6.096 m) away from the pump, the next size of line should be used. Also, if the fuel is lifted vertically more than 4 ft (1.219 m), you will have to go to a high-lift fuel system.

9. If low fuel pressure and return still exist, tee-in to the fuel pump outlet; start and run the engine to establish what pressure the pump is producing. If it is suspected that the pump is faulty, temporarily replace it with a new or rebuilt unit and again perform the spill-back check to determine if the original pump was faulty. If an alternative pump is unavailable, loosen the pump relief valve plug and remove the bypass relief valve components to check that the valve is not stuck in the open position. If it is, attempt to remove the valve and clean the piston. You may also have to remove the pump from the engine and disassemble and clean it in order to free the stuck relief valve. If the gears are scored or damaged, a new pump will be required.

10. Another area that should be checked with a continued low spill-back is the ECM (DDEC) for possible internal plugging or restriction within the cooler plate. To isolate the cooler plate, bypass it by simply connecting the inlet and outlet lines from the cooler plate and run the engine at its maximum no-load speed to determine if the fuel spill-back volume is within minimum acceptable rates. If it is, replace the cooler plate.

CAUTION If step 10 is performed, do *not* run the engine for longer than 5 minutes, since overheating of the electronics components within the ECM/DDEC can result.

NOTE To check if the pump driveshaft is rotating, insert a piece of small wire up through the pump flange drain hole, crank the engine momentarily, and note if the wire vibrates. If it does not, remove the pump and check the condition of the drive hub and coupling.

11. Although not a common problem, do *not* neglect checking out the fuel tank for foreign objects that may be blocking the fuel flow. There have been several instances in my own experience, especially around logging equipment, where an engine will run fine until the level in the tank drops low enough to allow a piece of wood chip or bark to be held against the fuel suction line and suddenly create a lack-of-power complaint, rough running, and even stalling.

12. Another possible problem area can be a plugged injector inlet filter. This is not common since most equipment owners usually change their primary and secondary fuel filters on a reasonably steady basis. If it is found that the injector filter is in fact plugged, it is advisable to remove the injectors for service and replace them with a matched rebuilt set.

13. A quick check for plugged filters is to remove the fuel return jumper line from the injector. Install an old line onto the injector, which is bent to take fuel away from the head area. Crank the engine with the starter and note if a steady gush of fuel emanates from the fuel line. If not, the injector filter is probably plugged.

Checking Cylinder Compression Pressure: DDC Two- and Four-Cycle Engines

Because a certain amount of time is required to do a compression check on the engine, you should first analyze the color of the smoke coming out of the exhaust stack.

Checking Procedure—Two Cycle

1. Refer to Figure 21–8. Remove the hand hole cover inspection plate from the side of the cylinder block. This allows free access into the airbox area and the cylinder liner port area. Select a blunt (nonpointed) tool and push against the compression rings to check for free spring or tension. If there is no sign of this, the piston ring is stuck in its groove. An additional check would be to carefully note whether the compression rings have a visible groove all the way around the center circumference. This groove is placed there at the time of manufacture: If it is not visible, the rings are very badly worn. If it is visible in some spots but not others, irregular ring wear is evident. You can also check for damage to the piston ring lands and skirt area at this time.

2. If piston rings are badly worn in one or more cylinders, this would be noticeable as high crankcase pressure when using a water manometer. All rings badly worn would be reflected by blue exhaust smoke, lack of power, hard starting, and rough running.

3. Prior to taking a compression check, it is imperative that the engine be at normal operating tem-

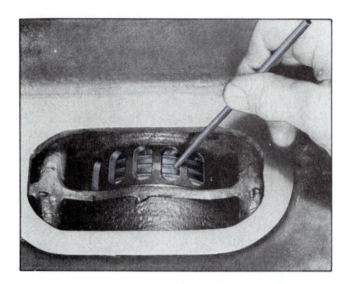

FIGURE 21–8 *Inspecting the condition of the piston rings through the cylinder liner ports of a two-stroke-cycle engine model after removal of the airbox inspection cover. (Courtesy of Detroit Diesel Corporation.)*

perature. If only one cylinder is suspected of having low compression, start with it. If doing them all, start with cylinder 1.

4. A cylinder compression check is taken on all DDC two-cycle engines at a speed of 600 rpm; therefore, you cannot hope to use a typical handheld automotive-type gauge. Several suitable test gauges are readily available from well-known tool suppliers, or an old injector nut and body can easily be adapted for this purpose. A good machinist can easily make up a dummy-type injector for this also. Figure 21–9 shows the gauge installed ready for the compression check.

FIGURE 21–9 *Compression gauge and dummy injector in position for conducting a running compression check. (Courtesy of Detroit Diesel Corporation.)*

5. To install the dummy injector and pressure gauge unit, it is first necessary to remove the fuel jumper pipes from the inlet and outlet of the injector. Place plastic shipping caps over the injector fuel holes. Remove the rocker arm hold-down bolts, and tip the assembly back. Loosen the injector clamp bolt and remove the injector.

6. Install the proper adapter (dummy injector), and clamp it in place with the hose and gauge attached. Using an old fuel pipe, connect it between the fuel inlet and return manifold connections (all engines).

7. It is advisable, if at all possible, especially on the larger-model engines, to use an old rocker cover that has suitable sections cut out of it to facilitate running the engine during the compression test. This will minimize oil throw-off.

8. Start the engine and run it at 600 rpm until the pressure on the test gauge reaches its maximum point. Note and record the cylinder pressure. The pressure variation should not exceed 25 psi (172.37 kPa) between cylinders. To determine what the minimum acceptable pressure is for your engine, check the DDC service manual for your particular engine under section 13, operating conditions. There are quite a variety of minimum acceptable standards, which vary with altitude.

9. In addition to stuck or broken rings, compression leakage can occur at the cylinder head gasket, valve seats, injector tube, and in extreme cases through a cracked or holed piston.

DDC TWO-STROKE-CYCLE ENGINE TUNE-UP: NON-DDEC ENGINES

When performing a necessary tune-up on an engine, do *not* back off all the necessary adjustments. It is only necessary to *check* these for a possible change in the settings. If, however, a cylinder head or the governor or injectors have been removed and overhauled or replaced, several initial adjustments are necessary before the engine can be started. These adjustments would consist of the first four items in the DDC tune-up sequence, the only exception being that the valve clearance is greater on a cold engine.

TUNE-UP SEQUENCE

The tune-up sequence *must* be followed exactly as given; otherwise, you can affect other adjustments which have already been performed.

Tune-up Procedure

1. Check and adjust the exhaust valve bridge adjustment.
2. Check and adjust the exhaust valve clearances.
3. Check and adjust the injector follower timing height above the injector body.
4. Check and adjust the governor gap.
5. Position/adjust the injector rack control levers.
6. Check and adjust the maximum no-load speed.
7. Adjust the engine idle speed.
8. Adjust the buffer screw.

Exhaust Valve Bridge Adjustment

Procedural Check

1. Rotate the engine over to place the injector follower all the way down on the cylinder to be checked.
2. Obtain two pieces of 0.0015 in. (0.038 mm) brass shim stock or feeler gauge material that have been cut to approximately 0.19 in. (4.75 mm) in width.
3. Lift up on the bridge slightly to allow you to slip each 0.0015 in. strip of feeler gauge between the bridge and both exhaust valve stem tips.
4. Apply light, even pressure to the bridge assembly in the center and check the drag on both feeler gauge strips between the bridge and each valve.
5. If both feeler gauges have the same drag, the bridge is properly adjusted. However, if they do not have the same drag, the fuel jumper lines have to be removed along with the rocker arm bracket hold-down bolts to gain access to the individual cylinder bridges.

Once the individual rocker arms have been removed, adjust the individual bridges.

Bridge Adjustment Procedure

1. Place the valve bridge in a *soft-jaw* vise or, if available, bridge holding fixture J21772, and loosen the locknut on the bridge adjusting screw. Back out the adjusting screw several turns.

NOTE Failure to follow the sequence noted above can result in damage. If the locknut is loosened or tightened with the bridge in place, the twisting action involved can result in either a bent bridge guide or a bent rear valve stem.

---

2. Install the bridge back onto its respective bridge guide.
3. While firmly applying pressure to the bridge, as shown in Figure 21–10, turn the adjusting screw clockwise until it lightly contacts the valve stem. Carefully turn the screw an additional one-eighth to one-quarter turn and run the locknut up finger-tight.
4. Install the bridge in a soft-jaw vise and, while using a screwdriver to hold the adjustment screw, tighten the locknut to 20 to 25 lb-ft (27.1 to 33.87 N · m) torque.

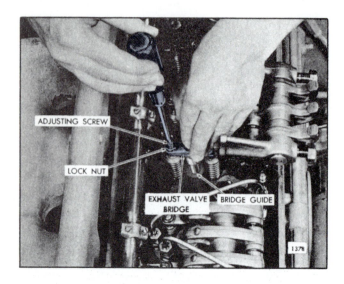

FIGURE 21–10 *Valve bridge adjustment procedure on a four-valve-head, two-stroke-cycle 71/92 engine model. (Courtesy of Detroit Diesel Corporation.)*

FIGURE 21–11 *Checking/adjusting the valve lash (clearance) by rotation of the square shoulder located on the threaded pushrod of a 71/92 two-stroke-cycle engine model. (Courtesy of Detroit Diesel Corporation.)*

5. Using engine oil, lubricate the bridge and guide, and reinstall it in its original position.

6. Select two 0.0015 in. (0.0381 mm) feeler gauges (pointed-finger type), or cut two thin strips that will fit under the bridge at each valve stem tip. Apply finger pressure to the pallet (center) surface of the valve bridge, and check to see that both feeler gauges are in fact tight. If they are not tight, readjust the screw as outlined previously.

7. Adjust the remaining valve bridges in the same manner.

8. Ensure that when the rocker arm assemblies are swung into position, the valve bridges are properly positioned on the rear valve stems; otherwise, damage to the valve and bridge mechanism is a possibility.

Exhaust Valve Clearance Adjustment

CAUTION When using either a barring tool or socket on the crankshaft bolt at the front of the engine, do *not* turn the crankshaft opposite its normal direction of rotation as this may loosen the bolt.

1. To determine which valves or injector is in a position to be adjusted, do the following: To set the valves on any given cylinder, the center rocker arm, which is the injector arm, must be all the way up when viewing the rocker assembly from the pushrod side.

2. Loosen the exhaust valve rocker arm pushrod locknut (53, 71, 92); on 149 series engines, loosen the locknut on the top of the rocker arm. Select the proper feeler gauge for the particular engine that you are working on (see engine emissions label).

NOTE It is advisable to use go-no-go feeler gauges for this purpose, which will ensure that all the valves are in fact set to the same clearance (see Figure 21–11).

3. Place the correct gauge between the valve bridge pallet on four-valve heads or between the valve stem and rocker arm on two-valve heads. Assume that you were setting a four-valve-head 71 series engine *cold.* You would require a 0.015 to 0.017 in. (0.381 to 0.431 mm) go-no-go feeler gauge for this purpose. Adjust the pushrod with a 0.31 in. (7.93 mm) wrench on the square shoulder until the 0.017 in. (0.431 mm) portion of the gauge can be withdrawn with a smooth pull, and tighten the locknut with a 0.50 in. (12.7 mm) wrench.

4. If the adjustment is correct, you should now be able to push the 0.015 in. (0.381 mm) part of the feeler gauge through the rocker arm area freely, but the 0.017 in. (0.431 mm) portion should not pass through. You should feel the shoulder of the feeler between the two sizes actually butt up against the rocker arm pallet. If necessary, readjust the pushrod.

Fuel Injector Timing

TECH TIP   This dimension is given in section 14, engine tune-up, in all DDC service manuals; current timing pin dimensions can also be found stamped on the valve rocker cover emissions decal. Be certain that you select the proper timing pin gauge; otherwise, serious damage could result to the engine, not to mention poor performance.

All the injectors can be timed in firing-order sequence during one full revolution of the crankshaft similar to the valves on all two-cycle DDC engines. Four-cycle engines would require two revolutions of the crankshaft.

The sequence for injector timing is as follows:

1.   The governor speed control lever should be in the *idle* position. If a stop lever is provided, secure it in the *stop* position.

2.   The crankshaft can be rotated as explained in step 4 for exhaust valve adjustment.

3.   To determine which injector is in a position to be checked or adjusted, do the following: Turn the engine over until the exhaust valves are fully depressed (completely open) on the cylinder on which you wish to set the injector.

4.   Insert the small end of the timing pin (gauge) into the hole provided in the top of the injector body, with the flat portion of the gauge facing the injector follower as shown in Figure 21–12. An optional dial gauge is also available for setting injector timing height.

5.   Gently push the shoulder of the gauge by holding the knurled stem with the thumb and forefinger (see Figure 21–12) toward the follower; there should be a slight drag between the gauge and follower. You can also turn the gauge around in a circular motion to determine this same feel.

6.   If this cannot be done, loosen the injector pushrod locknut and adjust it until the drag of the gauge (slight feel) has been determined; then hold the pushrod and tighten the locknut.

7.   Recheck the feel, and if necessary, readjust.

8.   When hot setting this adjustment, wipe off the top of the injector follower and place a clean drop of oil on it. When properly adjusted, the gauge should just wipe the oil film from the follower when the slight drag is felt and the pin gauge is rotated.

9.   Time the remaining injectors in the same fashion.

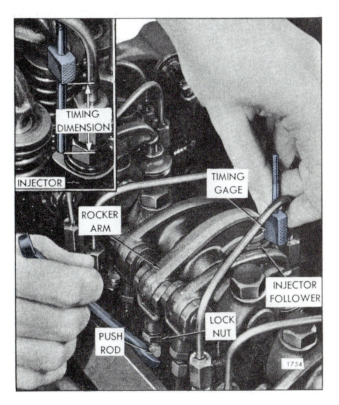

FIGURE 21–12 *Inserting the unit injector timing height pin between the injector follower and body pin hole to check/adjust the correct distance as per specs on a two-stroke-cycle engine model. Adjustment is achieved by rotating the threaded pushrod. (Courtesy of Detroit Diesel Corporation.)*

Governor Gap Adjustment

Figures 21–13 to 21–15 illustrate where to check this gap on all double- and single-weight limiting-speed governors. However, prior to performing a governor gap adjustment, make sure that the following conditions are met:

1.   Adjust the idle speed to the normal idle rpm that the engine will run at when it is operating.

2.   Clean and remove the governor cover and gasket.

3.   Back out the buffer screw prior to checking/adjusting the gap. (0.63 in. from the locknut).

4.   Back out the starting aid screw on turbocharged engines.

5.   It is necessary to bar the engine over manually on double-weight limiting speed (DWLS) V governors in order to insert the wedge spreading tool J35516 (Figure 21–14) between the larger low-speed weights and the riser shaft. On DWLS governors the gap should

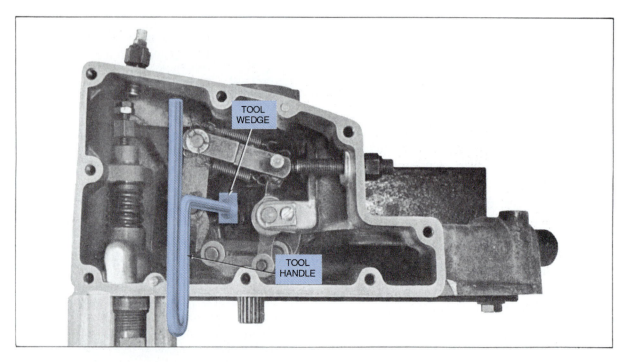

FIGURE 21–13 *Installation of the special DWLS (double-weight limiting-speed) mechanical governor wedge setting tool J35516. (Courtesy of Detroit Diesel Corporation.)*

FIGURE 21–14 *Closeup view of the special DWLS mechanical governor wedge setting tool J35516 between the larger low-speed weight and riser shaft. Insert the tapered side of the tool against the riser shaft. (Courtesy of Detroit Diesel Corporation.)*

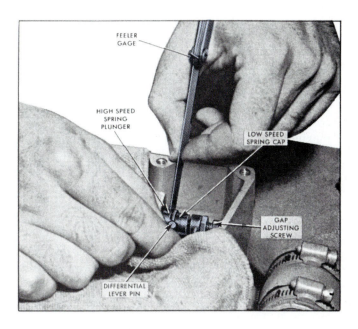

FIGURE 21–15 *Using a feeler gauge to check the DWLS governor gap. Insert the gauge between the low-speed spring cap, and the high-speed spring plunger. Allowable spec is between 0.003 and 0.019 in. (0.076 and 0.48 mm), otherwise adjust the gap to 0.008 in (0.20 mm). (Courtesy of Detroit Diesel Corporation.)*

be between 0.003 and 0.019 in. (0.076 to 0.48 mm); otherwise, set it to 0.008 in. (0.2 mm). On single weight limiting speed (SWLS) governors, the wedge tool is not necessary, since the weights are not touched. The gap is checked and set between the low-speed spring cap and the high-speed spring plunger to 0.170 in. (4.31 mm) on inline engines, and to 0.200 in. (5 mm) on V-engines with the engine stopped (Figure 21–15). On variable-speed governed models (SWVS):

a. Engine stopped; governor cover removed.
b. Place the speed control lever in the maximum speed position.
c. Insert a 0.006 in. feeler gauge between the governor spring plunger and the plunger guide (similar to that shown in Figure 21–15). If required, loosen the locknut and turn the adjusting screw until a slight drag is noted on the feeler gauge.

Injector Racks Setting and Adjustment

Since all the injector racks are connected to the fuel control tube and then to the governor via the fuel rod or rods, they must be set correctly to ensure that they are all equally related to the governor. Their positions determine the amount of fuel that will be injected into the

individual cylinders and therefore assure equal distribution of the load. Properly adjusted injector rack control levers with the engine at full load will ensure the following:

1. The speed control lever at the maximum speed position
2. The governor low-speed gap closed
3. The high-speed spring plunger on its seat in the governor control housing
4. The injector fuel control racks in the full-fuel position

Failure to set the racks properly will result in poor performance and a lack-of-power complaint.

The governor's location on the engine will control which injector rack is set first. On those engines with the governor located at the front, cylinder 1 injector rack would be set first, whereas with the governor mounted at the rear (flywheel end), the rear cylinder injector rack would be set first.

For V-design engines, the right and left banks are determined from the rear, and the cylinder numbering sequence is determined from the front. Therefore, all V-engines with the governor located at the front have the No. 1 left bank injector rack set first, since it is the closest (shortest rack) to the governor. On those V-design engines (6V-53) with the governor located at the rear, the No. 3 left-bank injector rack would be set first.

With this in mind, prior to setting the first injector rack, do the following:

1. Disconnect any linkage attached to the governor speed control lever (hand or foot throttle cables or rods).

2. Back out the idle-speed adjusting screw until there is no tension on the low-speed spring (limiting-speed governors only). When approximately 0.50 in. (12.7 mm) or 12 to 14 threads are showing beyond the locknut when the nut is against the high-speed plunger, the tension of the low-speed spring will be low enough that it can be easily compressed. This allows closing of the low-speed gap without possible bending of the fuel rod or rods or causing the yield link (used with throttle delay engines) spring mechanism to yield or stretch.

NOTE   Failure to back out the idle speed adjusting screw as stated may result in a false fuel rack setting and the problems associated with this.

3. If the engine is equipped with a throttle delay mechanism, this would have been removed or the U-bolt clamp loosened prior to checking the governor gap.

4. Similarly, the buffer screw should *still be backed out* approximately 0.625 in. (15.875 mm) as it was prior to setting the governor gap.

5. Also, the governor belleville spring retainer nut on engines so equipped should have been backed off to provide a 0.06 in. (1.524 mm) clearance.

6. On turbocharged or fuel-squeezer engines employing a starting aid screw, *do not touch it* at this time. Leave it backed out.

NOTE: When the injector racks are adjusted properly, the effort expended in moving the throttle from an idle to maximum speed position should be uniform throughout its travel. Any increase in effort while doing this could be caused by the following: (a) injector racks adjusted too tight, causing the yield link to separate; (b) binding of the fuel rods; or (c) failure to back out the idle screw.

---

7. On earlier-model engines, loosen all the inner and outer adjusting screws of each injector rack control lever at the control tube (Figure 21–16). The newer engines employ only one adjusting screw (the inner one) with a locknut on it. On V-design engines, loosen the screws on both banks. Be sure that all the injector rack

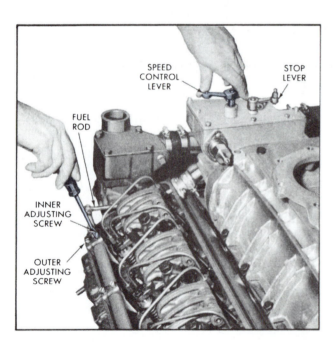

FIGURE 21–16 *Adjusting the No. 1 left-bank (LB) mechanical unit injector rack to full fuel while lightly holding the governor speed control lever (throttle) in the maximum speed setting position. Note that earlier engines contained two screws as shown. (Courtesy of Detroit Diesel Corporation.)*

control levers are free on the control tube. Make sure that the screws are backed off at least 0.19 in.

8. *V-design engines only.* Remove the clevis pin from the fuel rod at the right bank injector control tube lever (LB still connected to the governor).

9. On *limiting-speed* governors, move the speed control lever on top of the governor housing to the maximum speed position and hold it there with light finger pressure, as shown in Figure 21–16; on single-screw systems alternatively, hold the speed control lever in the full-fuel position with the aid of a light spring, as shown in Figure 21–17.

10. With the (throttle) speed control lever being held lightly in the full-fuel position, turn down the inner adjusting screw (two-screw type) or adjusting screw (one-screw type) until the No. 1 left bank injector rack is almost against the injector body and is observed to roll up (Figure 21–18) or an increase in effort to turn the screwdriver is noted. Tighten the screw approximately one-eighth turn more on the single-screw type; then lock it securely with the adjusting screw locknut. On the two-screw type, turn the inner adjusting screw down on the No. 1 LB of V-design engines, or the screws on the rack closest to the governor on inline engines, until a slight movement of the control tube lever is observed or a step up in effort to turn the screwdriver is noted. Turn down the outer adjusting screw until it bottoms lightly on the injector control tube; then alternately tighten both the inner and outer adjusting screws one-eighth turn each until snug. Finally, torque the screws to 24 to 36 in.-lb (3 to 4 N · m) to avoid damage to the injector control tube.

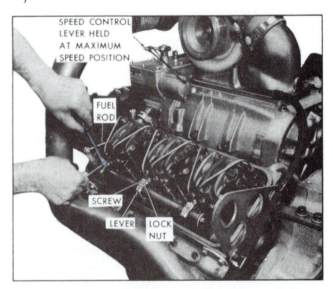

FIGURE 21–17 *Adjusting the No. 1 LB unit injector rack to full fuel for a later-model 71/92 engine equipped with only one screw and a locknut. (Courtesy of Detroit Diesel Corporation.)*

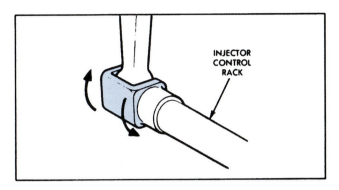

FIGURE 21–18 Location of where to check for visible bounce (no slop) between the ball end of the rack leg and the injector rack linkage. (Courtesy of Detroit Diesel Corporation.)

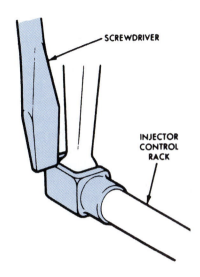

FIGURE 21–19 Using a flat-blade screwdriver to lightly push down on the injector rack after adjustment to determine if a good bounce (light springback) exists on a two-stroke 53/71/92 engine model. (Courtesy of Detroit Diesel Corporation.)

CAUTION While turning down the inner adjusting screw (one- or two-screw type), if you go too far, you will feel the speed control lever (limiting-speed governor) move. If this happens, you have gone too far, and the rack is being forced out of the full-fuel position. Therefore, adjust the screw until very slight movement can be felt at the speed control lever; then back the screw off slightly.

At this time the No. 1 LB rack on V-design engines, or the closest rack to the governor on inline engines, should be in the full-fuel position with the governor linkage and control tube assembly in the same position they will attain while the engine is operating at normal operating temperature under full load.

11.   To be sure that you have in fact adjusted the rack correctly, hold the speed control lever (limiting-speed governor) in the maximum fuel position. Refer to Figure 21–19 and press down on the injector rack clevis with a screwdriver blade, which should cause the rack to tilt downward; when the pressure of the screwdriver blade is released, the control rack should bounce or spring back upward. If the injector rack does not have a good bounce or spring, it is too loose; to overcome this condition, back off the outer adjusting screw very slightly and tighten the inner one an equal amount. On single-screw units, loosen the locknut, turn the adjusting screw clockwise slightly, and retighten the locknut. Recheck the rack condition for bounce.

To ensure that the rack is not set *too tight*, do the following. Move the speed control lever (limiting speed) from the idle to the maximum speed position. While doing this, if the injector rack becomes tight on the ball end of the rack leg (see Figure 21–18) before the end of the lever travel, the rack also needs readjusting.

To correct this condition, either loosen the screw locknut or the *inner* adjusting screw on the rack slightly and tighten the outer screw a similar distance, or back out the one-screw type and tighten the locknut. Recheck the rack bounce and movement. If an engine has been in service for a considerable period of time, the ball end of the rack leg sometimes becomes slightly scuffed. This can prevent a good bounce when setting the racks; if you encounter this problem, loosen both rack screws and slide the rack leg lever to the side of the injector, swing it upward, and lightly rub the ball end with fine emery cloth.

12.   On all inline engines the first rack that has been set is the one closest to the governor. On V-design engines the No. 1 LB is the closest to the governor, with the exception of the 6V-53, which has the No. 3 LB closest. In either case, once the first rack has been adjusted, this now becomes the *master rack,* since it has been set to the governor. To adjust the remaining injector rack control levers on the engine, proceed as follows:

a. *Inline engines.* Remove the clevis pin from the fuel rod at the injector control tube lever; hold the injector control racks in the full-fuel position by means of the lever on the end of the control tube.

b. *V-design engines.* Remove the clevis pin from the fuel rod at the LB injector control tube lever. Install the clevis pin in the fuel rod at the right-bank injector control tube lever and adjust the No. 1 RB rack the same way as for the No. 1 LB in step 10. To verify that both No. 1

racks are adjusted the same, insert the clevis pin at the LB fuel rod. Move the speed control lever (LSG) to the maximum speed position and check the drag on the clevis pin at each bank. In addition, check the bounce on each No. 1 rack. If they are not the same, the No. 1 RB rack has to be readjusted, since the No. 1 LB was the first one set to the governor and is therefore the master rack. To increase drag or bounce on the No. 1 RB rack, turn the rack adjusting screw clockwise on the one-screw setup, or the *inner* screw clockwise on the two-screw setup, after slightly loosening the *outer* screw. Turn the screws counterclockwise to decrease pin drag or bounce.

13. To adjust the remaining injector racks on each bank, you can remove both clevis pins from each bank and:

a. Hold the LB injector control racks in the full-fuel position by means of the lever on the end of the control tube (same setup as for the inline engines); or

b. Hold the governor speed control lever lightly in full-fuel by hand or leave the spring shown in Figure 21–17 attached; then

c. Tighten or run down the adjusting screw (inner) of the No. 2 LB injector rack control lever until the rack clevis rolls up or a step up in effort to turn the screwdriver is noted. If you feel the control tube lever move, back off on the adjusting screw slightly and turn it clockwise gently until you are satisfied that the rack is positioned correctly. While holding the control tube in the full-fuel position, compare the bounce on the No. 2 LB rack with that of the No. 1 LB rack. They should be the same; if not, readjust No. 2.

CAUTION Do not alter the adjustment of the No. 1 LB rack at any time. Remember that it is the master rack and has already been set to the governor.

---

d. Adjust the remaining racks on the LB in the same fashion, checking the bounce of each rack with the No. 1 setting every time. They should all have the same bounce when you are finished. Repeat the same procedure for the RB injector rack adjustments, always bearing in mind that the racks on each bank are set to the No. 1 rack on that bank. Therefore, do not alter the No. 1 LB or RB setting to suit the others.

14. When all the injector control racks have been adjusted, install the clevis pins in each fuel control tube to fuel rod if step 13a was used. Move the governor speed control lever to the maximum fuel position. Check each injector control rack for the same bounce or spring condition and also the drag on each clevis pin at each bank. If they are not the same, further checks and adjustments will be required. If one clevis is tight and the other not, one bank will invariably run hotter than the other, indicating that it is doing most of the work.

15. Once you are satisfied that you have adjusted each bank equally, secure the clevis pin with a cotter pin at each bank.

16. On limiting-speed governors, turn in the idle screw adjustment until the screw projects approximately 0.19 in. (4.762 mm) from the locknut, which will permit starting of the engine.

17. On inline engines the injector racks are adjusted in the same fashion as for those on the V-design engines, the only difference being that you do not have two separate banks to adjust. Also, once the first rack has been set to the governor, do not readjust it to suit another rack's bounce.

18. Replace the valve rocker cover or covers if the engine is going to be run for any reason, after making sure that the racks will move to the no-fuel position when the stop lever is activated.

Maximum No-Load Engine Speed Adjustment: Limiting-Speed Governors

The type of engine application determines the maximum governed speed of the engine, and this is set on the engine prior to leaving the factory. For a variety of reasons, and to ensure that the engine speed will not exceed its recommended no-load speed, which is stamped on the engine's *option plate* or emissions paper-laminate label on the valve rocker cover, it is necessary to check and set the maximum no-load engine speed.

Adjustment Procedure

1. Make sure that the buffer screw is still backed out 0.625 in. (15.875 mm) from the governor housing and locknut. If not, interference can occur while adjusting the maximum no-load speed.

2. On limiting-speed governors (Figure 21–20), loosen the spring retainer locknut and back off the high-speed spring retainer nut approximately five full turns. With the engine operating at normal operating temperature of 160 to 185°F (71 to 85°C), and with no load on the engine, place the speed control lever in the full-fuel position. Turn the high-speed spring retainer nut clockwise until the engine is running at the recommended no-load rpm.

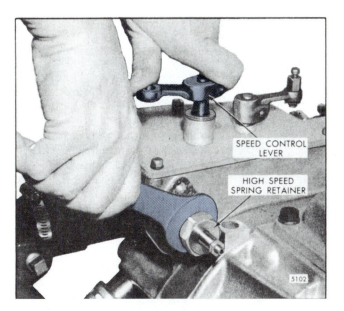

FIGURE 21–20 *Engine running and speed control lever held in full fuel to determine maximum no-load engine rpm. Rotate the high-speed spring retainer adjusting nut CW to increase, or CCW to decrease the engine speed setting on a two-cycle engine model. (Courtesy of Detroit Diesel Corporation.)*

NOTE Hold the high-speed spring retainer nut and tighten the locknut. Limiting-speed governors used on industrial engines, and some 53 engines, use shims at the bellcrank end of the governor spring to vary the speed, similar to a variable-speed governor.

Idle Speed Adjustment

See Figure 21–20. The idle screw is in front of the high-speed spring retainer (nut). The idle speed for an engine will vary with its particular application; therefore, always check the governor ID plate or emissions label for the recommended idle range. The recommended idle speed for non-EPA-certified engines with limiting-speed governors is 400 to 450 rpm on the majority of these units, but may vary with special engine applications. EPA-certified minimum idle speeds are 500 rpm for trucks and highway coaches and 400 rpm for city coaches. After the maximum no-load speed has been adjusted properly, the idle speed can be set.

Adjustment Procedure

1.   Ensure that the engine is operating at the normal operating temperature of 160 to 185°F (71 to 85°C) and that the buffer screw is still backed out, to avoid contact with the differential lever.

2.   On earlier engines, the idle screw had a slotted end for screwdriver adjustment; however, later engines use a 0.125 in. Allen head screw for idle adjustment. Loosen the idle screw locknut, and turn the idle speed adjusting screw either CW to increase the rpm or CCW to reduce the rpm until the engine operates at approximately 15 rpm below the recommended idle speed.

NOTE: You may find it necessary to use the buffer screw (turn it in) to eliminate engine roll or surge so that you can establish what the engine idle speed is at this time. Once this is established, *back out the buffer screw* to its previous setting, which should be 0.625 in. (15.875 mm).

3.   Hold the idle screw and tighten the locknut.

Buffer Screw Adjustment

Buffer screw adjustment on DDC engines must be done carefully to avoid any unnecessary increase to the normal engine idle range and to the maximum no-load speed. Prior to buffer screw adjustment, the specified engine idling speed must be properly set to within 15 rpm of that desired. Use an accurate electronic digital tachometer for this purpose.

CAUTION   Running the buffer screw in too far can cause a runaway engine.

With the idle speed properly set, adjust the buffer screw as follows:

1.   With the engine having been adjusted to its recommended idle speed and running at normal operating temperature, refer to Figure 21–21 and turn the buffer screw in so that it lightly contacts the differential lever inside the governor housing. This is easily determined by the fact that the engine speed will pick up slightly, and the roll or surge in the engine will level out.

NOTE: Be very careful that you do not increase the engine idle speed more than 15 rpm with the buffer screw adjustment. This is why an accurate tachometer must be used.

2.   Move the speed control lever to the maximum fuel position to check the no-load speed. If it has increased more than 25 rpm, you have gone too far on the initial adjustment; back off the buffer screw until this increase in the no-load rpm is less than 25 rpm.

3.   Hold the buffer screw with a screwdriver and tighten the locknut.

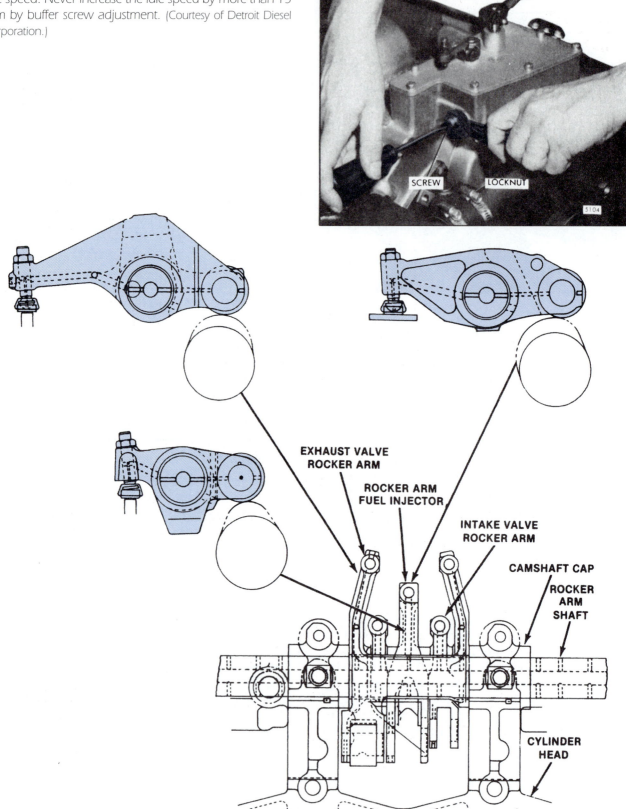

FIGURE 21–21 Adjusting the buffer screw on a two-cycle engine model to remove the engine roll or hunt at an idle speed. Never increase the idle speed by more than 15 rpm by buffer screw adjustment. (Courtesy of Detroit Diesel Corporation.)

SPEED CONTROL LEVER

SCREW   LOCKNUT

EXHAUST VALVE ROCKER ARM

ROCKER ARM FUEL INJECTOR

INTAKE VALVE ROCKER ARM

CAMSHAFT CAP

ROCKER ARM SHAFT

CYLINDER HEAD

FIGURE 21–22 Unique design of the rocker arm assemblies used with the four-cycle series 50 and 60 electronic engine models eliminates the necessity for a valve bridge on a four-valve-head engine. (Courtesy of Detroit Diesel Corporation.)

DETROIT DIESEL SERIES 50/60 FOUR-STROKE-CYCLE ENGINES— TUNE-UP

Detroit Diesel employs a rather unique rocker arm mechanism arrangement in its series 50 and 60 engines (Figure 21–22). The arrangement allows for two long and two short rocker arm assemblies without having to resort to a valve bridge mechanism to open the two intake and two exhaust valves per cylinder. Note the internal oil holes to lubricate the self-centering adjusting screw button, rocker shaft, and roller follower, as well as the various profiles of the camshaft lobes for the intake, exhaust, and unit injector. As you can see, the actual cam lobe profiles are quite different for each system.

Since the engine has a firing order of 1–5–3–6–2–4, refer to Figure 21–23. Bar the engine over manually until one of the injector followers has just started to move down. This procedure allows all of the valves and injectors to be set in two complete crank rotations (720°). Refer to Figure 21–24 and adjust all four valves (two intake and two exhaust) on this cylinder using the procedure illustrated. From the information provided in Figure 21–23a, set the fuel injector height on the mating (companion) cylinder. For example, if we had just set the valve lash on cylinder 1, we would now set the injector on the cylinder 6. The unit injector is adjusted for a listed dimensional height (indicated on the engine decal) from the top machined surface of the follower to the injector body by using a *timing pin* which fits into a drilled hole in the injector body as shown in Figure 21–25. Adjust the injector height as illustrated in Figure 21–26 until a slight drag is felt on the flag of the gauge as it passes

over the top of the injector follower. Tighten the locknut when done and recheck the injector height.

SERVICE TIP   Some experienced technicians like to place a small amount of clean engine oil onto the injector follower. When the timing height gauge is rotated over the follower, a small half-circle shape, which is visible as the oil is wiped off, confirms that the injector is correctly set. Other technicians simply rely on feel as the gauge is moved backward and forward over the follower, which is machined with a small chamfer on its circumference.

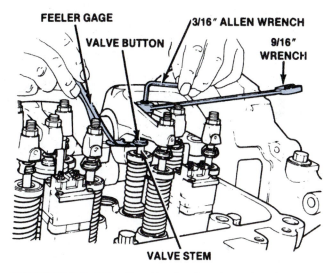

FIGURE 21–24   Checking/setting the valve clearance adjustment on a series 50/60 four-stroke-cycle engine model. Valve clearance specs can be found on the rocker cover decal. (Courtesy of Detroit Diesel Corporation.)

Overlap Series 60

Cylinder Overlap	Valves	Injector
6	1	5
2	5	3
4	3	6
1	6	2
5	2	4
3	4	1

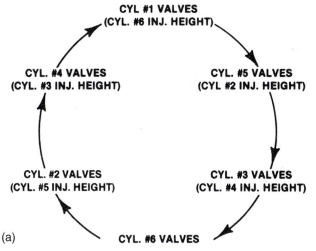

(a)

(b)

FIGURE 21–23   (a) Timing circle chart that can be followed to correctly adjust the valve lash and injector height on earlier-model series 50 and 60 engines. (b) Chart for adjusting both the valves and injectors on later-model series 50 and 60 engines employing a valve overlap procedure. (Courtesy of Detroit Diesel Corporation.)

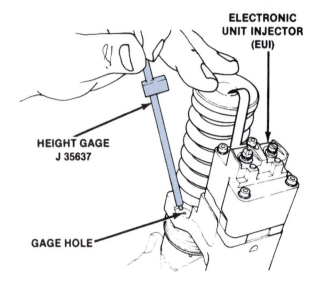

FIGURE 21–25 *Inserting the injector timing height pin gauge J 35637 into the body of the injector to adjust the follower height as per the dimension listed on the rocker cover decal. (Courtesy of Detroit Diesel Corporation.)*

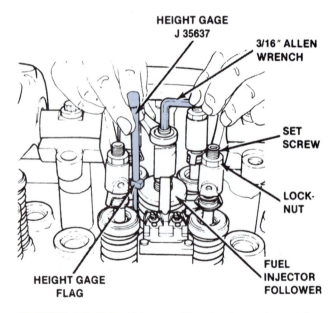

FIGURE 21–26 *Using an Allen key/wrench to adjust the injector timing height by screw rotation. Tighten the locknut when finished and recheck the height. (Courtesy of Detroit Diesel Corporation.)*

MODEL 790 JAKE BRAKES— FLATBRAKE

Introduction

A new model of Jacobs compression brake is used on all 2000 model year build series 60 engines requiring engine brakes. Known as a model 790, its design is commonly referred to as a flatbrake, because the spacer bars between the cylinder head and the Jake brake housings have been eliminated, resulting in a lower height above the cylinder head. The model 790 Jake differs from the former Jake models (see Figure 13–52), in that two brake housings are used in place of the three former housings. The 790 model mounts to the rocker shaft instead of to the overhead camshaft caps. More bolts are used to retain the Jake housings to the engine, and tube spacers are employed in place of the former spacer bars. The 790 brakes have dual slave pistons and coil springs in place of the torsion springs to retract the slave pistons. Figure 21–27 illustrates the components of a model 790 Jake brake.

Adjustment

Model 790 Jake brakes must have the slave piston lash set after the brake housings have been removed or require adjustment during a tune-up. Adjustments should always be made with the engine stopped and cold (engine oil temperature at or lower than 140°F, 60°C). The exhaust valves for each cylinder to be adjusted must be in the closed position. This can best be determined by viewing the position of the overhead camshaft lobes for a specific cylinder. The rocker arm roller follower should be on the base circle of the camshaft. See Chapter 10, Figure 10–11, for base circle identification. To accurately adjust the 790 Jake model slave piston clearance, proceed as follows:

Procedure

1. Refer to Figure 21–28, which shows the component parts of the adjusting mechanism, and loosen the locknut. Using a 0.31 in. Allen wrench, rotate the J-Lash (Jake-Lash) adjusting screw counter clockwise until a 0.026 in. (0.660 mm) feeler gauge can be inserted between the slave piston and the exhaust rocker adjusting screw.

2. Using the 0.31 in. Allen wrench, turn the J-Lash screw clockwise until you just feel the slave piston make contact with the feeler gauge and exhaust rocker adjusting screw. Take careful note of the point at which the valve spring just begins to compress, then rotate the Allen wrench one additional turn or 360°. Be sure to wait at least 30 seconds for any oil to be purged

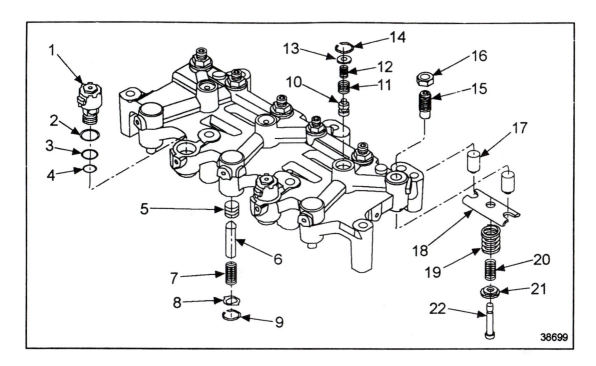

1. Solenoid Valve
2. Upper Seal
3. Center Seal
4. Lower Seal
5. Master Piston
6. Master Piston Pushrod
7. Master Piston Spring
8. Washer
9. Retaining Ring
10. Control Valve
11. Outer Control Valve Spring

12. Inner Control Valve Spring
13. Washer
14. Retaining Ring
15. J-Lash® Screw
16. Locknut
17. Slave Piston
18. Slave Piston Bridge
19. Outer Slave Piston Spring
20. Inner Slave Piston Spring
21. Slave Piston Spring Seat
22. Shoulder Bolt

FIGURE 21–27   Series 60 engine model 790 (flatbrake) Jake brake components identification. (Courtesy of Detroit Diesel Corporation.)

from the J-Lash adjusting screw. *Take careful note that if the engine oil temperature is lower than 60°F (16°C), you must allow at least 2 minutes for oil to be purged from the J-Lash adjusting screw. Failure to allow the oil to purge will cause inaccurate clearance adjustment and result in damage to either the engine or brake.*

3. After the required time interval to permit oil to purge from the J-Lash adjusting screw, gently back out the adjusting screw (CCW) until you feel a slight drag on the feeler gauge; if using a go-no-go feeler gauge,

make sure that the 0.025 in. part moves through with no drag and you can feel the 0.027 in. side butt up against the screw.

4. Securely hold the Allen wrench and proceed to torque the locknut to 25 lb-ft (35 N · m). Double-check the clearance again with the feeler gauge and reset if necessary.

5. Repeat this same procedure for the second lash adjusting screw on the same cylinder (uses two slave pistons/cylinder), and for the other cylinders.

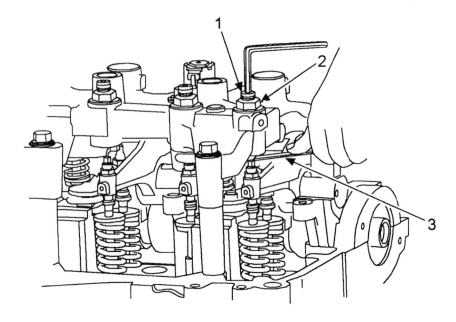

FIGURE 21–28 *Using a feeler gauge (3) to check the Jake brake slave piston-to-valve clearance dimension; 1, Jake brake adjusting screw; 2, locknut. (Courtesy of Detroit Diesel Corporation.)*

DETROIT DIESEL ELECTRONIC SYSTEMS

In September 1985 Detroit Diesel Corporation was the first major engine OEM in the world to release electronic unit fuel injection controls in a high-speed diesel engine. This system was known as DDEC I (Detroit Diesel Electronic Controls) and was followed in September 1987 by the more advanced DDEC II system, then III and IV.

SPECIAL NOTE The information contained within this section dealing with the DDEC (Detroit Diesel Electronic Controls) systems is designed to provide an overview of the system operation and the special diagnostic tools that can be used to troubleshoot the system. It is not intended to supplant the excellent printed literature and audiovisual materials readily available from Detroit Diesel. If you intend to perform service diagnostics on DDEC systems, you should acquire the appropriate service publications from your local Detroit Diesel service dealer for the *DDEC III and IV systems. Also see 7SA742 DDEC III/IV Application and Installation Manual*, and *DDEC III/IV Troubleshooting Guide* 6SE497, which contains all of the system trouble codes, wiring diagrams, and step-by-step diagnostic troubleshooting procedures to quickly and effectively analyze system problems; and an engine service manual related to the particular Detroit Diesel engine that you will be working on, for example, the series 60 service manual.

DDEC III/IV Systems

As a result of a unique set of events such as requests from truck OEMs and customers for additional electronic engine features and more information-gathering capability, plus the need to meet increasingly stringent air-quality standards, improvements in microprocessor capabilities were able to be adopted to existing ECMs due to the significant strides in the electronics industry.

DDEC ECMs are manufactured by Motorola Incorporated and use a two-layer poly-rigidizer circuit board mounted in an aluminum case. The ECM utilizes a single microprocessor operating at 16 MHz with a 16-bit-wide data bus. Software is contained in a 128K × 16-bit flash memory. DDEC III was introduced in April 1993, and entered full production in January 1994. The DDEC IV system was initially released in August 1997, and entered full production in January 1998. Therefore, we concentrate on these two systems because they will be the two most common DDC models that you will diagnose, service, or troubleshoot. Briefly, the DDEC III system computing capability was eight times faster and memory capacity is seven times larger than the earlier DDEC II model (1987). The DDEC IV ECM has 57% more memory and 50% more speed than the DDEC III ECM. In addition, the DDEC IV ECM has a built-in clock and calendar with a battery-backed real-

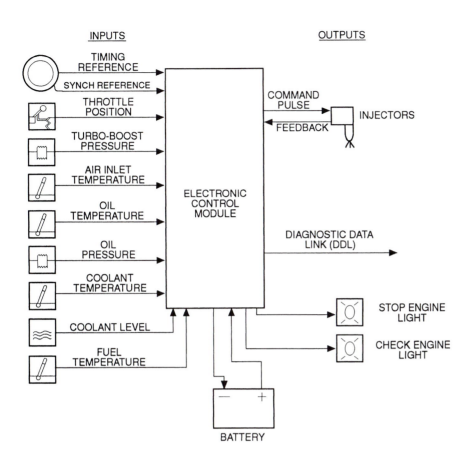

INPUTS   OUTPUTS

TIMING
REFERENCE
SYNCH REFERENCE
THROTTLE
POSITION
TURBO-BOOST
PRESSURE
AIR INLET
TEMPERATURE
OIL
TEMPERATURE
OIL
PRESSURE
COOLANT
TEMPERATURE
COOLANT LEVEL
FUEL
TEMPERATURE

ELECTRONIC
CONTROL
MODULE

COMMAND
PULSE
FEEDBACK
INJECTORS

DIAGNOSTIC DATA
LINK (DDL)

STOP ENGINE
LIGHT

CHECK ENGINE
LIGHT

BATTERY

FIGURE 21–29 *Schematic diagram of the DDEC (Detroit Diesel Electronic Controls) III/IV system. (Courtesy of Detroit Diesel Corporation.)*

time clock, calendar, and data recorder system, as well as enhanced ECM data pages.

One of the benefits of extra ECM memory capacity is the ability to offer multiple horsepower (kW) ratings in one engine. These multiple ratings allow customers to order an engine with up to four ratings; three independent ratings, plus one dependent cruise-control power rating. The switch power options offer maximum power for fully loaded engines, and minimum power ratings for a lightly loaded engine. A schematic of both the DDEC III and the DDEC IV systems is illustrated in Figure 21–29. From information described earlier in Chapter 18 dealing with the theory of electronic fuel systems, you should be familiar with the basic operation of the system. As you can see in Figure 21–29, the ECM receives inputs from the various sensors, then analyzes each signal and compares it with the preprogrammed operating parameters and executes an output signal (PWM) to actuate the EUI solenoids, and so on. The injection timing and fuel quantity is based on predetermined calibration tables in ECM memory.

The power supply for DDEC II systems is 12 volts; for DDEC III/IV it can be either 12 or 24 volts, with nor-mal operating voltage between 11 and 32 volts measured at the ECM. Take careful note that the power source must be isolated from any other vehicle electrical accessory to prevent electrical interference which could affect the ECM. The ECM power source must be fused with the properly sized fuse(s). In addition, a small 5 amp fuse is normally used for the ignition switch on the wire circuit. Two 15 amp fuses also are wired into two parallel lines from the battery power supply on series 50 and 60 engines. Note that on DDEC-equipped two-stroke-cycle engines, a V8 model uses two 20 amp fuses; on a V12, there are four 15 amp fuses; and on V16s, there are four 20 amp fuses used.

The ECM can control the engine brakes, so a separate brake controller is not necessary. The fan can be engaged by the ECM based on a variety of input signals that could call for fan operation. The low coolant system no longer needs its own control module because it is managed by the DDEC III ECM.

Reprogramming of DDEC software is now much easier than it was in the older-model DDEC I or II systems. All software can now be reprogrammed using the in-cab six-pin connector, illustrated in Figure 21–30, through advances to DDEC memory chips. Connecting

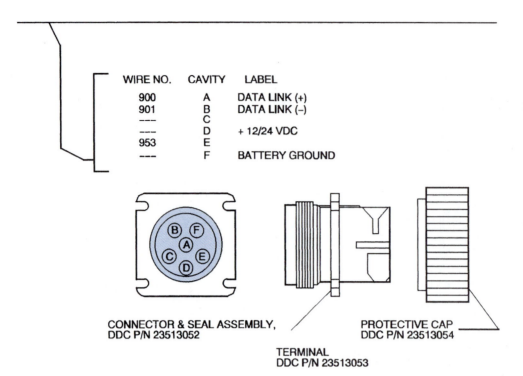

WIRE NO.	CAVITY	LABEL
900	A	DATA LINK (+)
901	B	DATA LINK (−)
---	C	
---	D	+ 12/24 VDC
953	E	
---	F	BATTERY GROUND

CONNECTOR & SEAL ASSEMBLY,
DDC P/N 23513052

TERMINAL
DDC P/N 23513053

PROTECTIVE CAP
DDC P/N 23513054

FIGURE 21–30   DDEC III/IV system ECM six-pin diagnostic connector used to connect a scan tool or PC to allow a service technician to access stored data and trouble codes, and to conduct various engine tests, or to reprogram the ECM. (Courtesy of Detroit Diesel Corporation.)

FIGURE 21–31   Handheld DDR (diagnostic data reader) scan tool ProLink 9000 or ProLink Plus connected to a small Ono-Soki portable printer to download a hard paper copy of engine operational data and logged trouble codes. (Courtesy of Detroit Diesel Corporation.)

either the DDR shown in Figure 21–31 or the reprogramming unit shown in Figure 21–32 reduces reprogramming time and improves reliability, because removal of the ECM or wire harness connector is no longer required.

Downloading ECM Data

When it is desirable to connect a desktop PC or a laptop computer to an electronic engine for diagnostic/troubleshooting purposes, or when reprogramming is necessary, each engine OEM offers special connectors/cables and an interface box to allow ease of attachment between the engine ECM and the downloading source. Figure 21–33 illustrates two examples of the connectors necessary for either a 25-pin serial port or a 9-pin serial port for Detroit Diesel electronic engines. These connectors, all identified with the J prefix, are sourced from Kent-Moore OE Tool and Equipment Group, SPX Corporation.

Media Signal and Baud Rate

A field service or shop technician can use a computer to reprogram the engine ECM, interface with the factory mainframe to change engine horsepower settings during the warranty period, or download information

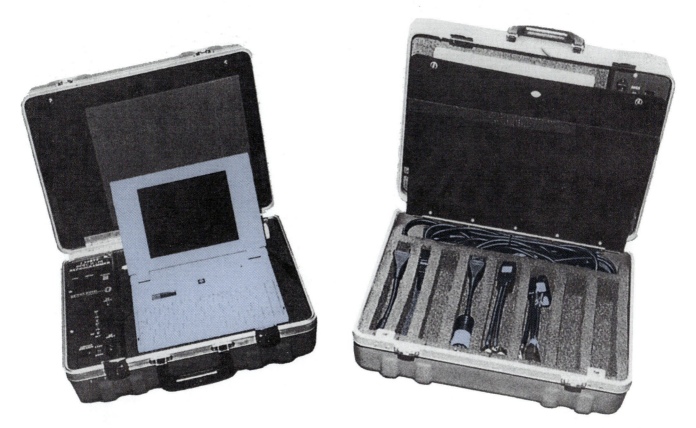

FIGURE 21–32 Portable technician briefcase equipped with a laptop computer, special adapters, and electronic controls to allow ease of ECM programming, diagnostics, testing, and troubleshooting. (Courtesy of Detroit Diesel Corporation.)

from the engine to a company office PC (see Figure 21–33). It is of value for the technician to understand just how this is done. From our discussion of data related to Figure 18–25, there are two possible ways to classify the signal sent on a line: analog and digital.

To interface with the factory mainframe computer, the technician requires the use of a modem to hook up the engine ECM and laptop computer through the telephone lines. Because digital impulses cannot be sent over the analog phone lines, conversion of the ECM digital signals to the continuous-wave form (analog) is called modulation. Translation from continuous waves back to digital impulses is termed demodulation. A single device called a modem (coined from the words *modulation* and *demodulation*) takes care of both operations. Therefore when a PC terminal sends a remote CPU (central processing unit) a message that must be carried over an analog line, a modem is needed at both the sending end to convert from digital to analog, and at the receiving end to convert from analog to digital. Modems that are not hardwired to specific equipment and that have an acoustic cradle to accept a phone headset are called acoustic couplers.

When using a modem, or sending data across phone lines, the speed of data communication is measured in bits per second (bps). The slowest rates of speed are referred to as narrowband transmission. Medium speed lines, which are commonly used in the telephone network, are capable of voice-grade transmission. The highest rates of speed, referred to as wideband transmission, are possible only with coaxial cable, fiber-optic cable, and microwaves. The *baud rate* is a term used to indicate the speed at which data travel between computers, and is measured in bits per second (bps). Therefore a long file which takes 10 minutes to travel from one computer to another at 1200 baud, will take 5 minutes at 2400 baud, 2.5 minutes at 4800 baud, and half-as-much again at 9600 baud. A 1200 baud modem cannot send or receive data at a faster rate, but a 2400 baud modem can work at the higher or lower speed. If you are familiar with using a PC on the internet, or when using the e-mail format, most modems today are set for a speed of transmission of 115,200 bps or faster. Therefore if long-distance phone charges are involved, speed of transmission may be a consideration.

Detroit DDL   DDDL ← J42384

Serial Link Adapter Kit ⟩ ✓ here also for some other adapters
J 38351-D

TYPICAL DESKTOP PC CONNECTION (25-PIN SERIAL PORT)

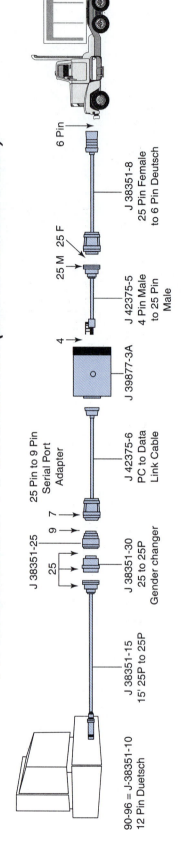

90-96 = J-38351-10
12 Pin Duetsch

J 38351-15
15' 25P to 25P

J 38351-30
25 to 25P
Gender changer

J 38351-25

J 42375-6
PC to Data
Link Cable

J 39877-3A

J 42375-6
25 Pin to 9 Pin
Serial Port
Adapter

J 42375-5
4 Pin Male
to 25 Pin
Male

J 38351-8
25 Pin Female
to 6 Pin Deutsch

6 Pin

TYPICAL LAPTOP PC CONNECTION (9-PIN SERIAL PORT)

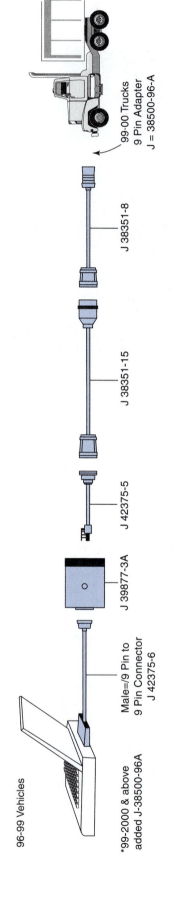

96-99 Vehicles

*99-2000 & above
added J-38500-96A

Male=/9 Pin to
9 Pin Connector
J 42375-6

J 39877-3A

J 42375-5

J 38351-15

J 38351-8

99-00 Trucks
9 Pin Adapter
J = 38500-96-A

Additional cables can be purchased separately to extend connections if needed

12 Pin to go with above
J 38351 - 10

FIGURE 21-33   Schematic showing the various part numbers of connectors required to interface between the engine ECM and a desktop PC, or to a laptop computer. (Courtesy of Kent-Moore Division, SPX Corporation.)

Engine Sensors and Location

Figure 21–34 illustrates the location of various DDEC engine sensors as they are described here:

1. Air temperature sensor located in the intake manifold allows the ECM to adjust engine timing to reduce white smoke on startup, improve cold starts, and provide engine protection should the intake manifold air become too hot.

2. The turbo boost sensor (TBS) monitors turbocharger compressor discharge pressure and provides data to the ECM for smoke control during engine acceleration while under load. This is a critical sensor

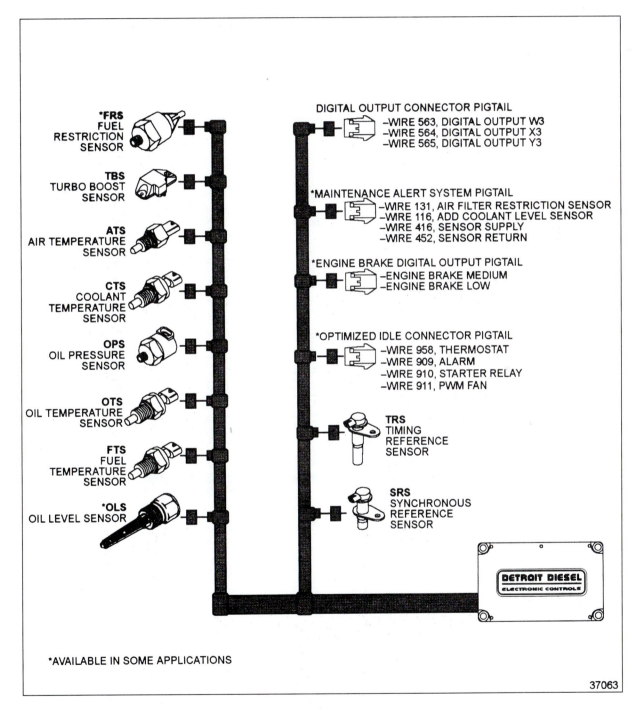

FIGURE 21–34a *Major components used with the DDEC system engine sensor harness. (Courtesy of Detroit Diesel Corporation.)*

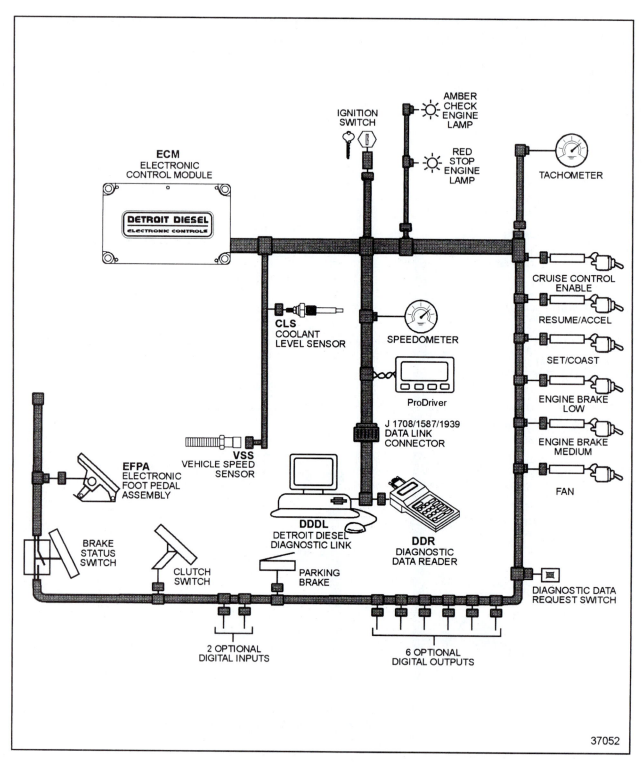

FIGURE 21–34b *(concluded). Major components used with the DDEC system vehicle interface harness. (Courtesy of Detroit Diesel Corporation.)*

in the successful operation of the engine. Consider that if an operator pushed the throttle pedal down requesting an 80% fueling rate, but the TBS indicated to the ECM that for the amount of fueling requested, there was insufficient turbo boost, then the least-win signal would dominate. In this case, let us assume that there was only sufficient boost to sustain a 77% fueling rate without creating incomplete combustion and smoke, then the ECM would only allow fueling at this rate. The TBS is known as a piezoresistive pressure sensor, which is a type of variable resistor. Basically it contains an internal diaphragm of silicon material. Turbo boost air pressure deflects the diaphragm to change its resistance value. The 5 V ECM input reference value is therefore changed by the resistance variation resulting in an output or return signal back to the ECM of between 0.5 and 4.5 V. The second function of the TBS is that when the ignition key is ON but the engine is stopped, it acts as a barometric pressure sensor from the TBS return signal. This can actually be read directly from a handheld DDR.

Minor variations exist between the DDEC II and the DDEC III/IV sensors, with both having a range of 0 to 3 atmospheres, or 45 psi. A new TBS for DDEC IV is set for between 10.2 and 58 psi (70 and 400 kPa) absolute. The reason for this higher-pressure value is to support the wastegated turbo used on series 50/60 engines should a high boost pressure condition occur possibly due to a failed wastegate, or someone tampers with the wastegate setting.

3. Oil pressure sensor activates the engine protection system when the oil pressure falls below a normal oil pressure at a given engine rpm. A dash-mounted warning light can be used to warn the driver of a low oil pressure condition.

4. Oil temperature sensor tells the ECM the engine operating temperature; oil temperature is a closer reflection of engine operation than is coolant. This information optimizes idle speed (fast idle at cold startup) and injection timing to improve cold startability and reduce white smoke. In addition, this sensor activates the engine protection system if the oil temperature is higher than normal. A dash-mounted warning light can be used to warn the driver of a high oil temperature condition.

5. Fuel temperature sensor, usually located at the secondary fuel filter, provides a signal to the ECM to calculate fuel consumption for instant readout at the push of a button on a truck instrument panel such as the Detroit Diesel ProDriver option. The ECM also utilizes the fuel temperature signal to adjust the unit injector PWM time for changes in the fuel density with a change in temperature.

6. Coolant level sensor, mounted on the radiator top tank, triggers the engine protection feature when a low coolant condition is sensed. An additional coolant level sensor located higher in the radiator top tank indicates, through either a dash-mounted warning lamp or the ProDriver readout module, that the engine coolant is low, but not enough to activate the DDEC engine protection feature.

7. Coolant temperature sensor, located on the right side of the engine, also triggers the engine protection system if the coolant temperature exceeds specified limits. A warning light can be provided on the dash to inform the driver when this situation occurs.

8. Both the synchronous reference sensor (SRS) and the timing reference sensor (TRS) are important to the starting and continual running of the engine. Working together, they indicate to the ECM which cylinder is at TDC for correct injector-cylinder firing. Precise monitoring of piston position allows for optimum injection timing, resulting in improved fuel economy, performance, and low emissions. The SRS/TRS sensors are located at the right-hand side of the engine block when viewed from the front of the engine. The SRS is mounted higher up on the block since it picks up its signal from a pin attached to the backside of the timing train bull gear. The SRS provides a once-per-cam revolution signal. Note that the SRS bull-gear pin protrudes approximately 0.120 in. (3 mm) above the face of the gear assembly to distinguish a DDEC II from a DDEC III/IV assembly. In addition, the SRS pin was moved approximately 10° to avoid the SRS and TRS signal being sent to the ECM at the same time. Therefore, DDEC II gear assemblies are not interchangeable with the DDEC III/IV model.

The TRS is mounted below the SRS; the TRS picks up a speed signal from a 36-tooth gear wheel attached behind the crankshaft gear and is therefore said to provide a 36-per-crankshaft rev signal (one tooth per 10°). Earlier DDEC I and II engines only used a 6-tooth gear wheel to generate a signal only 6 times per crankshaft rev, or every 60°.

9. Vehicle speed sensor is usually mounted over the vehicle transmission output shaft to provide the ECM with the speed of the vehicle. This signal is used for cruise control, vehicle speed limiting, and automatic progressive application of the engine Jake brakes to maintain a preprogrammed maximum vehicle speed. In addition, engine fan braking engages the cooling fan clutch automatically when the engine brakes are on *high*. This feature adds 20 to 45 bhp (15 to 33.5 kW) to the engine retardation for slowing down the vehicle.

10.   On fire truck applications, a fire pump water pressure sensor is used to monitor the pressure governor system. The signal back to the ECM changes engine rpm to allow the fire water pump to maintain a steady water pressure during pumping operation.

11.   Throttle position sensor is located within the body of the electronic foot pedal assembly (EFPA), as featured in Figure 18–15.

The EFPA return signal to the ECM is used by the microprocessor to control the EUI timing and fueling. This signal is in the form of a PWM (pulse-width-modulated) signal and establishes the injectors duty cycle to control engine power on a limiting-speed governor (LSG) electronic type, or engine speed on an electronic variable-speed governor (VSG) type. In both cases, the fueling request is proportional to the throttle position. The idle position for a LSG is established at the lowest position of the EFPA each time the ignition is switched ON. Full power will not be obtained unless the EFPA is cycled into the idle range (between 105 and 205 counts) on DDEC III/IV models. You may recall from your study of electronics that a *count* is a computer representation of voltage that the ECM reads at an input port. Total counts at WOT (wide-open throttle) on DDEC III/IV systems is normally between 717 and 871. Counts less than 48 indicate that the TPS sensor has failed low, while counts higher than 968 indicate a sensor failed high. DDEC I and II EFPAs were scaled for lower counts of approximately 25 to 30 at idle, and for 230 to 235 at WOT. Throttle counts can be checked using a ProLink or Pro-Link Plus handheld reader, or by using DDC's software with a laptop computer.

On EFPAs employing an idle validation switch (IVS), this unit is designed to provide redundancy to ensure that the engine will return to idle rpm anytime that the system fault diagnostics determines an out-of-range voltage condition, or detects an associated wiring fault at the TPS. The ECM will log a diagnostic fault code and warn the operator by lighting the warning lamp on the instrument panel.

On larger-model Detroit Diesel two-stroke-cycle 149 series engine models, a crankcase pressure sensor and a coolant pressure sensor are two additional sensors unique to these models. On the smaller model 71 and 92 two-cycle engines, the sensor locations vary from those on the series 50 and 60 engines but function in the same manner. In addition, the 71 and 92 engines usually mount the ECM above and in front of the engine blower assembly; the SRS and TRS sensors pick up their signals from the left front camshaft accessory drive pulley. On 149 engines two ECMs are used, a "master" and "slave" to handle the additional electrical loads on these larger displacement engine models.

The DDEC system has several additional features:

1.   Throttle inhibit system can disable the accelerator pedal on a passenger bus application when the doors are open or on a fire truck when the pressure governor fire pump is active.

2.   A deceleration light typically used on buses can be mounted on the dash and at the rear of the vehicle to indicate that the vehicle is slowing down when the operator takes his or her foot off of the throttle pedal.

3.   A starter motor lockout is commonly used on buses to prevent starter activation after the engine is already running.

4.   A green cruise-control light illuminates when "cruise" is selected to alert the driver of this condition.

5.   A fan clutch override switch can engage the cooling fan at any time when either the engine oil, coolant, or intake manifold temperatures exceed their preset values.

6.   A low DDEC voltage light illuminates on the dash when the ECM records a voltage less than 10 V on either a 12 or 24 V vehicle system. This light is typically used on fire truck applications.

Engine Protection System

An engine protection system is programmed into the ECM and operates based on out-of-range operating conditions from the individual engine and vehicle-mounted sensors. On the DDEC III and IV systems, the ECM initiates the protection procedure when it receives an out-of-range signal from the oil pressure, oil temperature, coolant temperature, coolant level, and intake manifold air temperature sensors. The system can be programmed for one of three protection features: shutdown, rampdown, or warning.

A warning feature alerts the driver by illuminating a yellow dash-mounted warning light with 100% engine power still available. For example, the oil temperature sensor may be programmed to illuminate the light at 250°F (121°C). If the oil temperature continues to increase, a gradual loss of engine power will occur down to approximately the 70% level, at which time the red dash light will illuminate, for example, at 260°F (127°C). The operator must then choose to pull the vehicle over and shut it down. If the vehicle or marine unit is equipped with a ProDriver feature such as the one illustrated in Figure 21–35, oil temperature can be monitored by the push of a button.

A rampdown condition alerts the driver also by illuminating the yellow dash warning light and reducing the engine power from 100% to 70%, at which time the red dash light will illuminate and the engine power will quickly be reduced to a 40% level.

A shutdown condition occurs similarly to the rampdown mode, except that 30 seconds after illumination

FIGURE 21–35 Example of an instrument panel–mounted ProDriver diagnostic readout access tool. (Courtesy of Detroit Diesel Corporation.)

of the red light, the ECM has been programmed to automatically shut the engine down.

When toggled or pushed, an STEO (stop engine override) switch located on the instrument panel will allow the engine to return to a 70% power level every 30 seconds while the engine is running. In other words, the operator must activate this switch manually after the red light is illuminated and before the 30-second time interval expires; otherwise, the engine will shut down and will not restart.

Maintenance Alert System

Two main methods are available to diagnose the operating condition of DDEC engines: either the DDR (diagnostic data reader) or the DDC diagnostic link. A fairly recent maintenance alert system (MAS) is now available for owner/operator or fleet maintenance conditions. The MAS unit shown in Figure 18–16 is an electronic display that receives input from DDEC sensors and is available for any type of engine application. The MAS system can be installed into the instrument control panel of any DDEC engine application. The system is designed to warn the operator or service technician of filter and fluid conditions on the engine. It is designed specifically to monitor oil level, coolant level, and pressure drop across both the fuel and air filters and thus provide on-time preventive maintenance and out-of-tolerance DDEC monitored engine systems. When fuel and air filter restriction climbs due to dirt accumulations, or fluid levels drop, DDEC will illuminate a light on the MAS panel indicating specifically what system is at fault.

Engine Diagnostics

The DDEC system provides an indication of engine and vehicle malfunctions by illuminating the yellow CEL (check engine light) or red SEL (stop engine light) at any time that a sensor or system fault is detected. When the yellow CEL is illuminated, it signifies that a fault has been detected; however, the fault is not serious enough to activate the automatic engine shutdown feature if it has been programmed within the ECM. The condition should be diagnosed as soon as possible; if the vehicle is equipped with a ProDriver diagnostic system similar to the one shown in Figure 21–35, the operator can determine what the fault condition is. This allows the operator to contact a service facility or the home service base and report the problem to the service/maintenance personnel.

Any faults that are stored in ECM memory can be accessed in one of three ways:

1.   Connect a DDR (diagnostic data reader) such as the model shown in Figure 21–31 to the DDL connector of the vehicle (see Figure 21–30 for DDEC systems). Depending on the vehicle or equipment in which the engine is installed, the diagnostic connector shown in Figure 21–30 for DDEC III and IV models may be located in several areas; therefore, refer to the vehicle/equipment service manual for the exact location. On heavy-duty trucks, this connector is usually within the cab area and located under the dash or behind a side kick panel.

2.   On DDEC II systems use a DDR, or install a jumper wire, see Figure 18–31a, across terminals A to M on the 12-pin connector to activate the yellow CEL flash codes. On DDEC III and IV systems, flash codes *cannot* be activated in this manner; instead, a diagnostic request switch mounted on the dash must be toggled. See Figure 18–29.

3.   Connect a PC or a laptop to the ECM vehicle diagnostic connector on either a DDEC II or a DDEC III and IV system as illustrated in Figure 21–33. The use of a DDEC translator device converts the SAE J1708 standard to an RS232 serial output protocol. Refer to Figure 21–31, where the small printer shown is connected to the RS232 serial port on the side of the DDR. This same PC hookup can be employed with Detroit Diesel software called TRAC (Trip Record Access) which is a programmed package that extracts operational data stored in the ECM. This data can be used to automate fleet record keeping or analyzed to evaluate fleet performance in key areas such as miles (kilometers) driven, engine hours, fuel consumed, total idle/PTO time, total idle fuel used. Fault codes and ECM setup parameters can also be reviewed by using DDEC Case Based Reasoning software CD-ROM.

There are two types of trouble codes that can be stored and extracted from the ECM. Active codes flash the red light; inactive or hi-toxic codes flash the yellow light. Inactive codes in ECM memory are "time stamped" with: (1) the first occurrence of each code in engine hours; (2) the last time each code occurred in engine hours; (3) the number of STEO actions when a code occurred; and (4) total time in seconds that a code was active.

ECM Connectors

The ECM wire harness connectors differ between the DDEC II and the DDEC III/IV models. In the DDEC II ECM, all of the wire harness connectors are located at one end. Figure 21–36 shows that the connectors for the DDEC III/IV ECMs are located at both ends of the module housing; the DDC engine connectors are located at one end, while at the opposite end are all of the OEM vehicle harness connections.

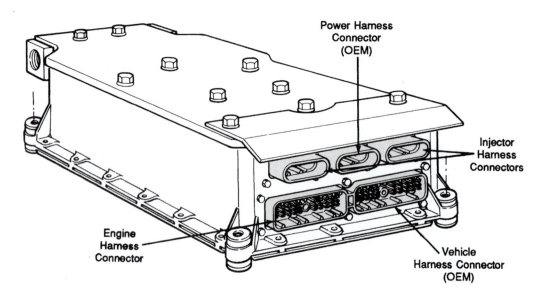

Electronic Control Module (ECM)

FIGURE 21–36   DDEC III/IV ECM harness connector identification. (Courtesy of Detroit Diesel Corporation.)

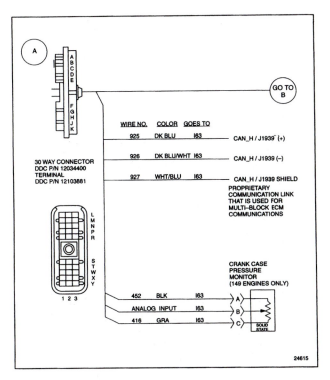

(a)

LABEL	WIRE NO	CAVITY	COLOR
TRS (–)	109	T–1	PPL
TRS (+)	110	T–2	DK GRN
SRS (+)	111	S–2	LT BLU
SRS (–)	112	S–1	WHT
OIL TEMPERATURE	120	R–2	TAN
AIR TEMPERATURE	132	N–2	YEL/RED
COOLANT TEMP	133	P–3	PNK
SENSOR SUPPLY (5VDC)	416	W–1	GRA
TURBO BOOST	432	P–1	ORN
SENSOR RETURN (ENGINE)	452	Y–2	BLACK
FUEL TEMP	472	R–3	ORN
OIL PRESSURE	530	P–2	BRN
ENGINE BRAKE MED	561	S–3	LT BLU
ENGINE BRAKE LO	562	T–3	LT GRN
DIGITAL OUTPUT W–3	563	W–3	YEL
DIGITAL OUTPUT X–3	564	X–3	TAN/BLK
DIGITAL OUTPUT Y–3	565	Y–3	RED
TIMED INPUT	573	X–1	BRN
BARO PRESSURE	904	L–1	PPL/WHT
FUEL PRESSURE	905	M–1	YEL
ANALOG INPUT #3	906	N–1	ORN
ANALOG INPUT #6	907	R–1	DK GRN
PWM OUT #2	909	Y–1	LT GRN/YEL
PWM OUT #3	910	W–2	ORN
PWM OUT #4	911	X–2	PNK
J1939 (+)	925	L–3	DK BLU
J1939 (–)	926	M–3	DK BLU/WHT
J1939 SHIELD	927	N–3	WHT/BLU
ANALOG INPUT #5	958	M–2	BLU
ANALOG INPUT #4	976	L–2	DK GRN

(b)

FIGURE 21–37 DDEC III/IV ECM 30 pin engine harness electrical connections identifications. (Courtesy of Detroit Diesel Corporation.)

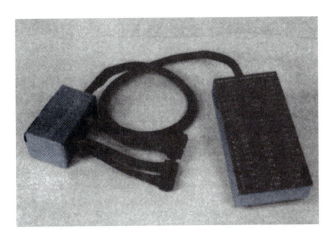

FIGURE 21–38 ECM breakout box J35634 for use in testing and troubleshooting possible DDEC system circuit problems. (Courtesy of Kent-Moore Division, SPX Corporation.)

SPECIAL NOTE: When disconnecting or connecting ECM or sensor wire harnesses, the ignition switch power must always be in the OFF position to prevent serious damage to the various circuits. The ignition system is fuse protected; nevertheless, make certain that no power is on when connecting or disconnecting diagnostic equipment or special tester tools.

ECM and Special Tools

If it becomes necessary to trace a wiring circuit fault in a DDEC system, open up the alligator-style wiring harness protective cover by prying it apart with your hands. Each wire is identified by an ink-stamped number corresponding to the system wiring diagram. ECM connector pins, are identified in the DDEC engine harness wiring diagram shown in Figure 21–37. Thus it is a reasonably easy task for the service technician to trace all wires for possible faults. However, *never* attempt to pierce the insulation on any wire to probe for a reading with a multimeter. Breaking the insulation causes serious problems from corrosion and/or short circuits. When it becomes necessary to trace the wiring circuits and/or possible faults in wire harness connectors, or within the ECM, refer to Figure 21–38, which illustrates a BB (breakout box) designed specifically for this purpose. When connected into the system, the probes of a multimeter can be inserted into the lettered and numbered BB sockets that correspond to the engine wiring diagram connections. Readings can then be safely taken according to the BB directions or diagnostic step-by-step procedure for tracing a specific trouble code in the engine service manual.

What Is a Breakout Box?

A breakout box is a handheld device that allows the technician to "break out" or access electronic circuits so they can be checked for proper voltage, resistance, and continuity.

Why Use the Breakout Box?

- The Breakout box allows complete interrogation of any DDEC circuit (engine or vehicle) from one convenient device at a comfortable position away from the engine compartment.
- No need to probe the back of the harness connectors or pierce wire insulation to pick-readings.
- All testing is done after "one" initial hookup of the breakout box. No individual jumper wires to install in male and female connectors. No chance of error in locating the proper circuit.

How Is the Breakout Box Used?

- Simply disconnect the vehicle and engine harness at the electronic control module (ECM) and connect to the breakout junction box. The vehicle and engine connectors from the junction box are then connected to the ECM.
- The probes from a volt/ohm meter (such as Kent-Moore J 34039-A) are then inserted into the proper sockets to take readings with ignition ON and with or without engine running.

Specifications

- Uses same connectors as found in DDEC.
- Six-foot cable between junction box and probe panel.
- Sixty socket probe panel with connector cavities marked to correspond with vehicle and engine connectors J1A and J1B.

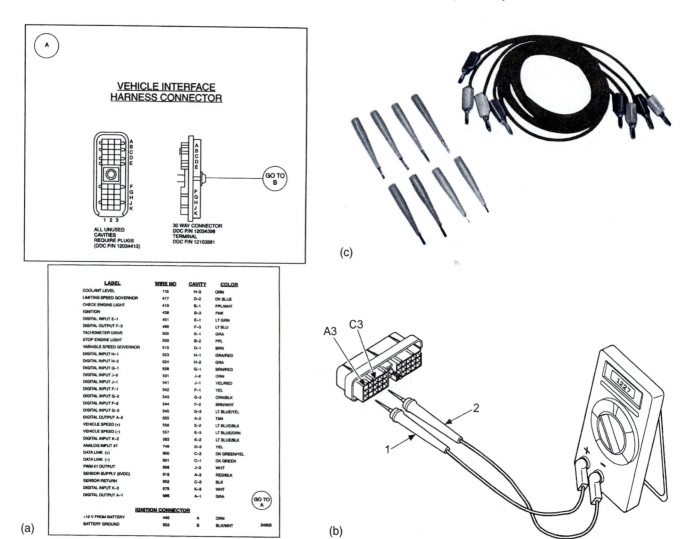

(a)   (b)   (c)

FIGURE 21–39 (a) OEM vehicle interface 30 pin connector, wires, and pin number indentification. (b) Measuring voltage at a 30 pin connector. (c) Special jumper wire set required when checking for amperage, voltage, or resistance checks with a DMM (digital multimeter). (Courtesy of Detroit Diesel Corporation.)

- Includes handy reference card to identify connector cavities.

A Kent-Moore special DDEC jumper wire set Part Number I-35751 with its various probe connectors are designed for insertion into either the ECM female or male connection points and harness connectors. Multimeter leads can then be inserted into the opposite ends of these special probe connectors to safely determine a voltage or resistance value. This reading can then be compared to the service manual specs. Figure 21–39a shows and identifies the various ECM 30 pin vehicle interface (DEM) harness connector pins and wiring.

Voltage Measurements
Perform the following steps to measure voltage.

1. Connect the red test lead to the ΔVOM V-Ω connector and the black lead to the com input on the meter. If a DC-AC switch is present, ensure it is switched to the DC position.

2. Set the function range/switch to the desired volts position. If the magnitude of the voltage is not known, set the switch to a range that will be able to read most voltages seen on a vehicle. Typically, a 20V range will do. Then, reduce the range until a satisfactory reading is obtained.

3. Connect the test leads to the circuit being measured. In the DDEC system diagnostic procedures, voltage measurements are always given as being taken at pins, sockets, battery +, or ground. Following the voltage measurement point, the color test lead to be used is

FIGURE 21–40 DDEC engine sensor tester tool used to isolate possible faulty sensors or wire harness faults. Tester requires the use of a 12 V battery power source and a digital multimeter. (Courtesy of Kent-Moore Division, SPX Corporation.)

given in parenthess (red is the V-Ω connection, and black is the com connection). Example: If the procedure says, "Take voltage reading at socket A3 (red lead) to socket C3 (black lead)", see Figure 21–39b for the hook-up.

DDEC Sensors Tester
Should it become desirable to check the various DDEC system sensors individually, refer to Figure 21–40 which illustrates a special Kent-Moore sensor tester. Simply disconnect the snap wire harness connector from one or more sensors and attach the correct mating sensor tester harness. Rotate the sensor tester dial knob to the sensor that you want to check; then insert the multimeter test leads into the two probe holes on the tester to read the sensor value and compare it with service manual specs.

DIAGNOSTIC TOOLING

All electronic engine OEMs now offer dedicated software to facilitate diagnostic and programming information with their products. Using a laptop computer, Windows-based programs are available from each specific engine OEM, which offers a point-and-click graphical interface for the technician. These software programs require an IBM-compatible PC. All OEMs offer similar functions to fleets that want to implement an interactive maintenance system.

Diagnostic Codes
In accordance with SAE industrywide technical standardization trouble codes, all engine OEMs now employ the same PIDs, SIDs, and FMIs to indicate the same problem area with their systems. Refer back to the section in Chapter 18 titled, "ECM SAE Trouble Codes" for a description of these on pages 479–483.

ECM flash codes, which were described and shown in Figure 18–31b, are listed in Figure 21–41 along with the equivalent SAE Fault Code for DDEC systems. Keep in mind that these flash codes appear on the DDR screen in DDEC I and DDEC II systems but not on DDEC III or IV systems, which reveal only the SAE PIDs, SIDs, and FMIs fault codes. Flash codes can be extracted from DDEC III and IV systems only if a diagnostic request switch has been wired into the ECM system. See Figure 18–29.

Using the MPSI DDR
The MPSI ProLink 9000 DDR illustrated in Figure 21–31 and later ProLink Plus is designed to provide the service technician with a number of functions. It contains an operational soft-touch *keypad* (with 16 keys) similar to that illustrated in Figure 21–42. The MPSI reader can be used with all current heavy-duty diesel electronic

DDEC® III/IV System Diagnostic Codes and MPSI Reader Functions

SAE Faults	Flash Code	DDEC System Description
s053 4	62	Aux. Output #5 open circuit
s053 7	62	Aux. Output #5 Mech. System not responding properly
s054 3	62	Aux. Output #6 short to battery (+)
s054 4	62	Aux. Output #6 open circuit
s054 7	62	Aux. Output #6 Mech. System not responding properly
s055 3	62	Aux. Output #7 short to battery (+)
s055 4	62	Aux. Output #7 open circuit
s055 7	62	Aux. Output #7 Mech. System not responding properly
s056 3	62	Aux. Output #8 short to battery (+)
s056 4	62	Aux. Output #8 open circuit
s056 7	62	Aux. Output #8 Mech. System not responding properly
s057 3	63	PWM driver #1 short to battery (+)
s057 4	63	PWM driver #1 open circuit
s058 3	63	PWM driver #2 short to battery (+)
s058 4	63	PWM driver #2 open circuit
s059 3	63	PWM driver #3 short to battery (+)
s059 4	63	PWM driver #3 open circuit
s060 3	63	PWM driver #4 short to battery (+)
s060 4	63	PWM driver #4 open circuit
s061 11	26	Aux. engine shutdown #2 input active
s072 0	61	#21 Injector response time long
s072 1	71	#21 Injector response time short
s073 0	61	#22 Injector response time long
s073 1	71	#22 Injector response time short
s074 0	61	#23 Injector response time long
s074 1	71	#23 Injector response time short
s075 0	61	#24 Injector response time long
s075 1	71	#24 Injector response time short
s076 0	66	Engine knock level above normal range
s076 3	66	Engine knock sensor input voltage high
s076 4	66	Engine knock sensor input voltage low
s076 7	66	Engine knock sensor torque reduction
s077 0	73	Gas valve position above normal range
s077 1	73	Gas valve position below normal range
s077 3	73	Gas valve position input voltage high
s077 4	73	Gas valve position input voltage low
s151 14	73	System Diagnostic Code #1 (ESS)
s226 11	73	Transmission Neutral Switch (ESS)
s227 4	73	Aux. Analog Input #1 voltage low (ESS)
s227 3	73	Aux. Analog Input #1 voltage high (ESS)
s227 2	73	Aux. Analog Input #1 data erratic, intermittent, or incorrect (ESS)
s230 5	68	TPS idle validation switch open circuit
s230 6	68	TPS idle validation switch short to ground
s231 12	55	J1939 data link fault
s238 3	32	SEL short to battery (+)
s238 4	32	SEL open circuit
s239 3	32	CEL short to battery (+)
s239 4	32	CEL open circuit
s240 2	—	Fram checksum incorrect
s248 8	55	Proprietary data link fault (master)
s248 9	55	Proprietary data link fault (slave)
s249 12	57	J1922 data link fault
s250 12	56	J1587 data link fault
s253 2	53	Non volatile memory data incorrect
s253 12	53	Non volatile memory fault
s253 13	—	Incompatible calibration version
s254 0	—	External failed RAM
s254 1	—	Internal failed RAM
s254 6	—	Entered boot via switches
s254 12	52	ECM A/D Conversion fail

DEFINITIONS

ATS	Air Temp. Sensor	MID	Message Identification
CEL	Check Engine Light	OLS	Oil Level Sensor
CLS	Coolant Level Sensor	OPS	Oil Pressure Sensor
CTS	Coolant Temp. Sensor	OTS	Oil Temp. Sensor
ESS	Engine Synchronous Shift	SEL	Stop Engine Light
		TBS	Turbo. Boost Sensor
FPS	Fuel Pressure Sensor	TPS	Throttle Position Sensor
FTS	Fuel Temp. Sensor	VSG	Variable Speed Governor
IVS	Idle Validation Switch	VSS	Vehicle Speed Sensor

DDEC System MPSI Reader Functions

Engine Selections

ENGINE DATA LIST

DIAGNOSTIC CODES
Active Codes
Inactive Codes
Clear Codes
J1587 Code Disc.

FUEL INJ. INFO.
Cylinder Cutout
Response Times
Calibration Update
Change Injector Password

CALIBRATION CONFIGURATION
Engine & Engine Protection Configuration
VSG & Cruise Control Configuration
Idle Shutdown & Progressive Shift Configuration
ECM input & output
Air compressor Config.
Function lockout Config.

ENGINE/TRIP DATA
Fuel used
Engine Hours
Miles
Idle Hours
Idle Fuel used
Engine Brake Hours
VSG Fuel used
Optimized Idle® Savings Time & Fuel
VSG Hours
Cruise Hours
Fuel Economy (MPG - km/L)

CALIBRATION CHANGES
Reprogram Options
Changes Password

RESET COMPONENTS
ACTIVATE OUTPUTS

SWITCH/LIGHT STATUS
MID'S RECEIVED
ESS TRANSMISSION

Pro-Link Selections

RS-232 SERIAL PORT
CUSTOM DATA LIST

CONTRAST ADJUST
ENGLISH/METRIC
RESTART
SNAPSHOT

FIGURE 21-41 Listing of DDEC III/IV SAE fault codes, definitions, and MPSI (Microprocessor Systems Inc.) ProLink 9000/ProLink Plus diagnostic data reader functions and engine selections.

TO READ CODES: Use the diagnostic data reader or depress and hold the diagnostic request switch with the ignition on, engine at idle or not running. Press and hold the switch. Active codes will be flashed on the stop engine light, followed by the inactive codes being flashed on the check engine light. The cycle will repeat until the operator releases the diagnostic request switch.

Flash Codes	DDEC System Description
11	VSG sensor input voltage low
12	VSG sensor input voltage high
13	Coolant level sensor input voltage low
14	Oil, coolant, or intercooler, temp. sensor input voltage high
15	Oil, coolant, or intercooler, temp. sensor input voltage low
16	Coolant level sensor input voltage high
17	Bypass or throttle, valve position sensor input voltage high
18	Bypass or throttle, valve position sensor input voltage low
21	TPS input voltage high
22	TPS input voltage low
23	Fuel temp. sensor input voltage high
24	Fuel temp. sensor input voltage low
25	No active codes
26	Aux. engine shutdown #1, or #2, input active
27	Air inlet or intake air, temp. sensor input voltage high
28	Air inlet or intake air, temp. sensor input voltage low
31	Aux. high side output open circuit or short to ground
32	CEL or SEL short to battery (+) or open circuit
33	Turbo boost sensor input voltage high
34	Turbo boost sensor input voltage low
35	Oil pressure sensor input voltage high
36	Oil pressure sensor input voltage low
37	Fuel pressure sensor input voltage high
38	Fuel pressure sensor input voltage low
41	Too many SRS (missing TRS)
42	Too few SRS (missing SRS)
43	Coolant level low
44	Oil, coolant, intercooler or intake air, temp. high
45	Oil pressure low
46	ECM battery voltage low
47	Fuel, air inlet, or turbo boost, pressure high
48	Fuel or air inlet pressure low
52	ECM A/D conversion fault
53	ECM non volatile memory fault
54	Vehicle speed sensor fault
55	J1939 data link fault
56	J1587 data link fault
57	J1922 data link fault
58	Torque overload
61	Injector response time long
62	Aux. output short to battery (+) or open circuit, or mech. fault
63	PWM drive short to battery (+) or open circuit
64	Turbo speed sensor input fault
65	Throttle valve position input fault
66	Engine knock sensor input fault
67	Coolant or air inlet, pressure sensor input voltage fault
68	TPS idle validation switch open circuit or short to ground
71	Injector response time short
72	Vehicle overspeed
73	Gas valve position input fault or ESS fault
74	Optimized Idle² safety loop short to ground
75	ECM Battery voltage high
76	Engine overspeed with engine brake
77	Fuel temperature high
81	Oil level, crankcase prs, dual fuel BOI, or exh. temp. volt. high
82	Oil level, crankcase prs, dual fuel BOI, or exh. temp. volt low
83	Oil level, crankcase prs. exhaust temp.. or external pump prs.. high
84	Oil level or crankcase pressure, low
85	Engine overspeed
86	External pump or barometer, pressure sensor input voltage high
87	External pump or barometer, pressure sensor input voltage low
88	Coolant pressure low

SAE Faults	Flash Code	DDEC System Description
p0510	65	Throttle valve position above normal range
p0511	65	Throttle valve position below normal range
p0513	17	Throttle valve input voltage high
p0514	18	Throttle valve input voltage low
p0517	65	Throttle valve not responding
p0520	44	Intercooler temp. high
p0523	14	Intercooler sensor input voltage high
p0524	15	Intercooler sensor input voltage low
p0704	74	Optimized idle safety loop short to ground
p0723	17	Bypass position sensor input voltage high
p0724	18	Bypass position sensor input voltage low
p0730	83	External pump pressure high
p0733	86	Pump pressure sensor input voltage high
p0734	87	Pump pressure sensor input voltage low
p0840 11	72	Vehicle overspeed (fueled)
p0841 12	72	Vehicle overspeed (absolute)
p0914	21	Throttle position sensor input voltage high
p0915	22	Throttle position sensor input voltage low
p0920	58	Torque overload
p0940	47	Fuel pressure high
p0941	48	Fuel pressure low
p0943	37	Fuel pressure sensor input voltage high
p0944	38	Fuel pressure sensor input voltage low
p0980	83	Oil level high
p0981	84	Oil level low
p0983	81	Oil level sensor input voltage high
p0984	82	Oil level sensor input voltage low
p1000	45	Oil pressure low
p1003	35	Oil pressure sensor input voltage high
p1004	36	Oil pressure sensor input voltage low
p1010	83	Crankcase pressure high
p1011	84	Crankcase pressure low
p1013	81	Crankcase pressure sensor input voltage high
p1014	82	Crankcase pressure sensor input voltage low
p1020	47	Turbo boost pressure high
p1023	33	Turbo boost pressure sensor input voltage high
p1024	34	Turbo boost pressure sensor input voltage low
p1038	64	Turbo speed sensor input failure
p1050	44	Intake air temp. high
p1053	27	Intake air. sensor input voltage high
p1054	28	Intake air. sensor input voltage low
p1060	47	Air inlet pressure high
p1061	48	Air inlet pressure low
p1064	67	Air inlet pressure sensor input voltage high
p1064	67	Air inlet pressure sensor input voltage low
p1083	86	Baro. pressure sensor input voltage high
p1084	87	Baro. pressure sensor input voltage low
p1091	88	Coolant pressure low
p1094	67	Coolant pressure sensor input voltage high
p1094	67	Coolant pressure sensor input voltage low
p1103	44	Coolant temp. high
p1104	15	Coolant temp. sensor input voltage high
p1110	16	Coolant temp. sensor input voltage low
p1110	43	Coolant level low
p1111	16	Coolant level sensor input voltage high
p1114	13	Coolant level sensor input voltage low
p1210	76	Engine overspeed with engine brake
p1680	75	ECM battery voltage high
p1681	46	ECM battery voltage low
p1724	27	Air temp. sensor input voltage high
p1724	28	Air temp. sensor input voltage low
p1730	83	Exhaust temperature high
p1733	83	Exh. temp. sensor input voltage high
p1734	83	Exh. temp. sensor input voltage low
p1740	77	Fuel temperature high
p1743	23	Fuel temp. sensor input voltage high
p1744	24	Fuel temp. sensor input voltage low

SAE Faults	Flash Code	DDEC System Description
p175 0	44	Oil temp. high
p175 3	14	Oil temp. sensor input voltage high
p175 4	15	Oil temp. sensor input voltage low
p187 3	12	VSG sensor input voltage high
p187 4	11	VSG sensor input voltage low
p187 7	11	VSG switch system not responding
p190 0	85	Engine overspeed
p251 10	—	Clock module abnormal rate
p251 13	—	Clock module fault
s001 0	61	Injector #1 response time long
s001 1	71	Injector #1 response time short
s002 0	61	Injector #2 response time long
s002 1	71	Injector #2 response time short
s003 0	61	Injector #3 response time long
s003 1	71	Injector #3 response time short
s004 0	61	Injector #4 response time long
s004 1	71	Injector #4 response time short
s005 0	61	Injector #5 response time long
s005 1	71	Injector #5 response time short
s006 0	61	Injector #6 response time long
s006 1	71	Injector #6 response time short
s007 0	61	Injector #7 response time long
s007 1	71	Injector #7 response time short
s008 0	61	Injector #8 response time long
s008 1	71	Injector #8 response time short
s009 0	61	Injector #9 response time long
s009 1	71	Injector #9 response time short
s010 0	61	Injector #10 response time long
s010 1	71	Injector #10 response time short
s011 0	61	Injector #11 response time long
s011 1	71	Injector #11 response time short
s012 0	61	Injector #12 response time long
s012 1	71	Injector #12 response time short
s013 0	61	Injector #13 response time long
s013 1	71	Injector #13 response time short
s014 0	61	Injector #14 response time long
s014 1	71	Injector #14 response time short
s015 0	61	Injector #15 response time long
s015 1	71	Injector #15 response time short
s016 0	61	Injector #16 response time long
s016 1	71	Injector #16 response time short
s020 3	81	Duel fuel BOI input voltage high
s020 4	82	Duel fuel BOI input voltage low
s021 0	41	Too many SRS (missing TRS)
s021 1	42	Too few SRS (missing SRS)
s025 11	26	Aux. engine shutdown #1 input active
s026 3	62	Aux. Output #1 short to battery (+)
s026 4	62	Aux. Output #1 open circuit
s026 7	62	Aux. Output #1 Mech. System not responding properly
s040 3	62	Aux. Output #2 short to battery (+)
s040 4	62	Aux. Output #2 open circuit
s040 7	62	Aux. Output #2 Mech. System not responding properly
s047 0	61	Injector #17 response time long
s047 1	71	Injector #17 response time short
s048 0	61	Injector #18 response time long
s048 1	71	Injector #18 response time short
s049 0	61	Injector #19 response time long
s049 1	71	Injector #19 response time short
s050 0	61	Injector #20 response time long
s050 1	71	Injector #20 response time short
s051 3	31	Aux. Output #3 open circuit
s051 4	31	Aux. Output #3 short to ground
s052 3	31	Aux. Output #4 open circuit
s052 4	31	Aux. Output #4 short to ground
s053 3	62	Aux. Output #5 short to battery (+)

FIGURE 21–41 Listing of DDEC III/IV SAE fault codes, definitions, and MPSI (Microprocessor Systems Inc.) ProLink 9000/ProLink Plus diagnostic data reader functions and engine selections.

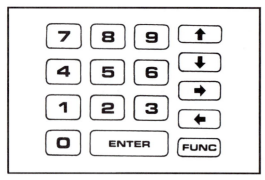

FIGURE 21–42 *MPSI ProLink 9000 DDR tests/checks are available/selected by using the various function keys on the handheld diagnostic tool. (Courtesy of Detroit Diesel Corporation.)*

systems. However, since each engine and vehicle manufacturer has chosen its own computer operating system, the ProLink 9000 DDR can have its software cartridge changed to suit the engine or transmission type. The slip-in cartridge can be easily removed or installed from the rear of the DDR with light pressure.

Figure 21–42 lists the MPSI DDR reader functions that can be used to access the engine ECM. The DDR shown in Figure 21–31 contains 10 numeric keys and 4 arrow keys. See closeup in Figure 21–42. The up and down arrow keys can be used to scroll through the digital screen readout displays, while the right and left arrow keys can be used to toggle back and forth between choices on the display. The Function key is used to choose one of the functions listed in Figure 21–42. The Enter key must be pressed once you have selected a function from the readout window screen to confirm your choice or instruct the DDR to continue to the next step.

NOTE   Within the DDR ProLink is a 2-A fuse; failure of the unit to power up and display information on the window screen may indicate a blown fuse.

DDR operation requires connection of a special cable with a 15-pin terminal to the top of the housing, as shown in Figure 21–31. Once installed, lightly tighten the two captive plastic thumbscrews to secure the cable connection. If a printer is being used, connect it as shown in Figure 21–31.

Troubleshooting with the DDR

Always make sure that the ignition switch/key is OFF before connecting or disconnecting the DDR connectors. When the DDR is connected to the ECM diagnostic data link connector, the technician can select any of the items listed in Figure 21–42. Scroll through the se-

lections illuminated on the DDR screen with the up and down arrows. When you see the function you want, you may have to use the left and right arrow keys to place the brackets [ ] around your selection when prompted to do so on the screen. Then you have to press the Enter key. As you select a given function, the DDR screen prompts you about what to do next. If you want to extract stored trouble codes, or short out engine cylinders automatically or by cylinder selection, you can do so using the Function and Enter keys. After a short practice period with the DDR, you will become relatively comfortable using it.

Injector Calibration with the DDR

Injectors in the 1994 and later-production DDEC engines have performance *bar codes* and are individually programmed into the ECM after installation. This feature is shown in Figure 21–43, where the injector load plate has a bar code label on it plus a calibration code number that can range from 00 to 99. This number must be entered into the ECM using the DDR when injectors are replaced. By doing so, we can ensure a cylinder balancing feature to help control engine horsepower vari-

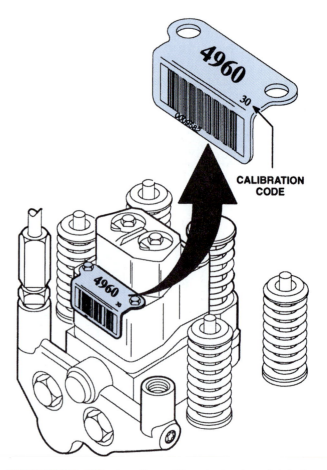

FIGURE 21–43 *Location of the electronic unit injector calibration code for DDEC III/IV engines. (Courtesy of Detroit Diesel Corporation.)*

ability in each cylinder. This variability occurs due to mass production tolerances that result in variations in cylinder compression pressures, fuel injector delivery volume, and so on. Use of the calibration number results in improved engine response and fuel efficiency because the ECM is able to accurately compute many

factors, including each injector's performance, and meter an exact fuel quantity into each cylinder.

Figure 21–44 illustrates the procedure required when the DDR is used to recalibrate injectors; the following description explains the procedure in more detail. When using the DDR to calibrate injectors, select

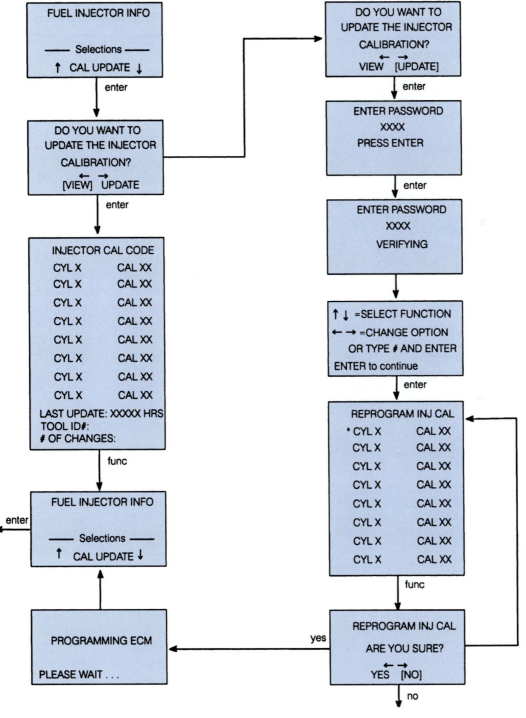

FIGURE 21–44 *Sample step-by-step procedure that would be followed on the ProLink DDR tool screen when installing and recalibrating new or rebuilt DDEC injectors so that the ECM can accurately control fuel delivery and timing. (Courtesy of Detroit Diesel Corporation.)*

ENGINE from the screen and hit the Enter key. Using the arrow keys, scroll to FUEL INJECTOR INFO on the screen and press the Enter key. Scroll with the arrow keys again until CAL-UPDATE appears on the DDR screen and press the Enter key. From DO YOU WANT TO UP-DATE THE CALIBRATION select [VIEW] and hit the Enter key. The DDR screen will display the various injector calibration codes. Compare the two-digit calibration numbers shown on the injectors (see Figure 21–43) with the numbers shown on the DDR screen. If no changes are required, press the Function key and turn off the ignition; then disconnect the DDR.

If some of the injector codes differ from those shown on the DDR screen, press the Function key to return to the FUEL INJECTOR INFO menu. Select UPDATE and press the Enter key. Type in the four-digit update injector calibration password for the DDR and press Enter. If this feature is not password protected, type 0000 and press the Enter key. A message will appear telling you to use the up and down arrow keys to SE-LECT FUNCTION (in this case the cylinder number), and TYPE # (the injector calibration code). An asterisk (*) will highlight the first cylinder number in the list. Using the arrow keys, scroll to the cylinder requiring the code change and type in the new two-digit injector calibration code number; then press the Enter key. Repeat the same procedure for each cylinder that requires a change to the injector code number. Note, however, that the Enter key must be pressed before the DDR will allow selection of another cylinder number.

When all cylinders have been updated with the required new injector calibration code numbers, press the Function key. Select YES from the display and press Enter to reprogram the ECM with the revised injector calibration codes. Turn the ignition key to the OFF position and wait a minimum of 5 seconds before starting the engine.

NOTE Always replace removed injectors back into the same cylinder after a service operation; otherwise, correct cylinder balance will not occur. If you have placed injectors back into a different cylinder from which they were removed, they will have to be rechecked with the DDR as just described and updated.

OPTIMIZED IDLE

Introduction

On long-haul trucks with sleeper cabs, it is advantageous for the operator to be able to have the engine electronic controls automatically stop and restart the en-

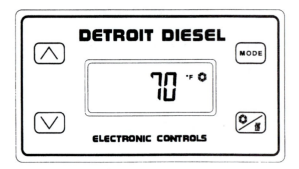

FIGURE 21–45 *Schematic of the control panel for the optimized idle (OI) feature. (Courtesy of Detroit Diesel Corporation.)*

gine, particularly in cold weather operation for heater operation and in hot weather for air conditioning operation. Figure 21–45 illustrates the OI (optimized idle) dash-mounted electronic controls panel. The OI system when engaged is designed to automatically stop and restart the engine to maintain oil temperature, battery voltage, and cab temperature. The DDEC system will stop the engine when the oil temperature reaches 104°F (40°C), and restart the engine when the oil temperature drops to 60°F (15°C). The system will also start the engine when the battery voltage drops to 12.2 volts with the minimum run time for a low battery condition being programmed in for 20 minutes. In cold weather the programmed idle speed is set for 1100 rpm, while in hotter weather the idle is set for 1000 rpm.

Advantages

The OI feature has the following advantages:

1. Maintains the engine oil temperature at factory set limits.

2. Ensures a fully charged battery. A plus at anytime, but even more so in cold-weather operation.

3. Maintains the cab and sleeper compartment at a preselected operator temperature from an optional thermostat.

4. Idle time reduction; improved fuel economy and engine reliability resulting in longer life to overhaul.

5. No cold starts thereby providing maintenance savings.

6. It eliminates warm-up time and fuel usage.

7. Increased driver satisfaction through use of the in-cab thermostat.

8. The optimized idle system is more cost/weight effective than existing pony packs (small auxiliary engine and heating system mounted behind the cab).

9. Reduces both air and noise pollution.

10. Can be added to existing DDEC III equipped engines.

OI On/Off Conditions

When the operator desires to use the OI (optimized idle) feature, the following conditions must be met:

- Engine running at an idle with the ignition switch ON.
- Hood or cab closed.
- Transmission in neutral and in high-range (if so equipped).
- If a vehicle cruise-control switch is used, it must be in the ON position "after" the vehicle is idling.
- When OI is ON, a dash-mounted active light will illuminate.

To disable optimized idle, turn off the ignition switch or use the drive-away feature which will automatically disable the system. This simply involves releasing the parking brake(s) and/or placing the transmission lever into gear. When the engine returns to base idle, the system OI active light will turn off. During OI operation, the variable speed engine governor, cruise VSG, and the foot pedal will not function, therefore if operation of these features is desired, OI must be disabled.

The system operates in the engine mode until the in-cab thermostat is turned on by the operator pressing any button. The thermostat may be turned off by pressing and holding the MODE button for three seconds. The in-cab thermostat set point range for OI activation is between 60 and 85°F (15 and 29°C), with comfort zone choices being adjustable between 4, 7, and 10°F (2, 4, and 6°C). The OI system will provide continuous run temperatures when the ambient temperature is less than 25°F (−4°C), and in hot weather when ambient temperatures are higher than 100°F (38°C), and an air conditioning fan is desired. The heater or A/C fan will cut in 30 seconds after engine start. An extended idle system operation will occur for 45 minutes, then cycle for 15 minutes on/15 minutes off until the cab thermostat is satisfied, or the system is disabled.

If the OI system fails to start the engine, a CEL (check engine light) and logged ECM trouble code will be set. The maximum start attempts are limited to two, and the maximum cranking time to 8 seconds. The time between automatic start attempts is 45 seconds.

ELECTRONIC UNIT PUMP SYSTEM

A derivative of the basic Bosch PLN (pump-line-nozzle) system is the recently introduced camshaft-driven and electronically controlled EUP (electronic unit pump) used on the MTU/DDC 4000 engines and DD/Mercedes-Benz series 55 used in the mid-1990s Freightliner Century models as an optional engine. The

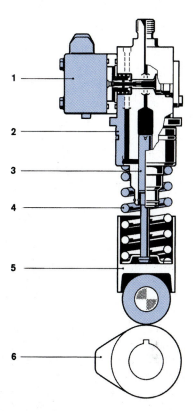

FIGURE 21–46 *Schematic of the component parts of an EUP fuel system previously used on the DDC series 55 engine of the Freightliner (Daimler-Benz) trucks, and now in use on the MTU/DDC 4000 series large-bore engine models. (Courtesy of Detroit Diesel Corporation.)*

camshaft roller follower within the unit pump body raises a plunger within a barrel to create the high pressures necessary for injection. The basic parts of the unit pump are shown in Figure 21–46, where item 1 is the electric solenoid which receives a PWM signal from the DDEC ECM. Operating in the same way as a DDEC EUI, the actual time of one cam revolution is about 60 ms.

Injection can occur only when the solenoid valve is closed and the camshaft is lifting the internal plunger within the EUP body. Low-pressure fuel spill occurs when the solenoid valve is open and the plunger is moving downward by the force of the spring (item 4). Fuel delivered from the EUP flows through a small-bore high-pressure fuel line and into the nozzle shown in Figure 21–47. The nozzle tip contains eight holes (orifices) and requires approximately 4500 to 5000 psi (31,027 to 34,475 kPa) to open it against spring pressure, resulting in a spray-in pressure around 26,000 psi (1769 atm).

Troubleshooting and diagnosis of the EUP system can be done in a manner similar to the DDEC system by using a DDR or laptop to withdraw stored trouble

FIGURE 21–47 *Schematic of a DDEC IV electronic unit pump (EUP) system for a DDC/MTU 2000 series engine used in construction and industrial applications. (Courtesy of Detroit Diesel Corporation.)*

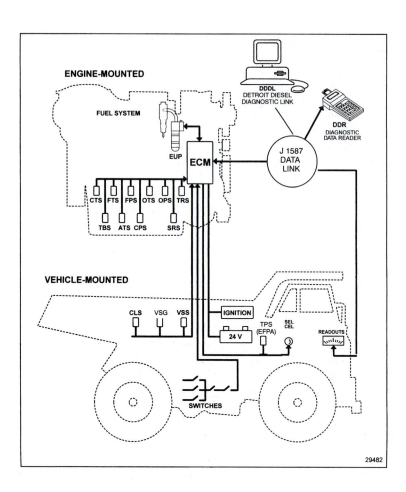

codes within the ECM and to perform a cylinder cutout sequence automatically or by selected cylinder.

SPECIAL NOTE: Mack's (late 1997 and later) six-cylinder engines are equipped with Robert Bosch EUP systems on the 500 hp (373 kW) model E7 engines.

SUMMARY

A detailed description and analysis of how DDC fuel injection systems—both mechanical and electronic—function and operate, along with information of how to service, maintain, diagnose, analyze, and effectively use special diagnostic tooling, has provided you with expanded knowledge and capabilities to understand fuel system operation, and will permit you to function as an effective fuel system troubleshooter and diagnostic technician.

SELF-TEST QUESTIONS

1. DDC engines use a fuel system known as a
   a. high-pressure system
   b. low-pressure recirculatory system
   c. common-rail system
   d. distributor pump system
2. Identify the basic functions of a DD fuel system:
   a. supplies clean fuel, and cools and lubricates the injectors
   b. purges the system of air and maintains adequate pressure
   c. self-primes, lubricates, and supplies pressure
   d. both a and b are correct
3. Technician A says that installing too small a fuel inlet/suction line from the fuel tank can result in a high fuel system restriction to the suction side of the fuel transfer pump. Technician B says that too small a line can cause lack of power under load. Who is right?
4. Technician A says that he would perform a fuel system restriction check by performing a fuel spill-back check. Technician B says that he would use a mercury

manometer at the primary filter. Who knows the correct procedure?

5. Technician A says that if air is drawn into the fuel system, it can occur only between the fuel tank and inlet side of the fuel pump. Technician B says that you could also suck air at the secondary fuel filter if the gasket is not sealing properly. Who is right?

6. Technician A says that normal fuel system pressure on a DDC engine is between 30 and 45 psi (207 to 310 kPa). Technician B says that this is too low and that it should be between 50 and 70 psi (345 to 483 kPa). Who is right?

7. Technician A says that the fuel system restricted fitting is installed at the fuel inlet manifold. Technician B disagrees, saying that it is located at the fuel outlet/return fuel manifold. Who is correct?

8. Technician A says that the purpose of the fuel system restricted fitting in all DDC engines is to maintain a minimum pressure of 35 psi (241 kPa) at the inlet fuel manifold. Technician B says that the restricted fitting is to limit the fuel flow to the injectors to limit the engine horsepower. Who understands the purpose of this fitting?

9. Technician A says that the size of the restricted fitting orifice is stamped on the brass fitting. Technician B says that all restricted fittings on DDC engines are the same. Who is correct here?

10. Technician A says that a fuel spill-back check is used to confirm that the fuel pump pressure is up to specs. Technician B says that this check can confirm whether there is air in the system and if the fuel filters are plugged. Who is right?

11. Technician A says that an RO8 or R8O stamping on a fuel system restricted fitting indicates that the orifice size is 0.080 in. Technician B says that it means that the orifice size is 0.8 mm. Who is correct in this instance?

12. Technician A says that the fuel inlet manifold on two-stroke 71 and 92 series engines is always the upper fuel manifold on the cylinder head. Technician B says that the inlet manifold is the lower one. Who is correct?

13. Technician A says that the fuel inlet manifold on the series 60 four-stroke-cycle engine is always the lower manifold on the cylinder head. Technician B says that the inlet is always the upper manifold. Who knows their basic fuel system knowledge?

14. Fuel pump rotation can be identified by
    a. an arrow etched on the pump housing
    b. an arrow stamped on the pump cover
    c. both an arrow and LH or RH stamped on the pump cover
    d. the letters LH or RH stamped on the pump cover

15. Technician A says that to quickly determine if the fuel pump drive has sheared or broken, you can perform a fuel spill-back check to establish how much fuel is being circulated. Technician B says that you can gently insert a small piece of wire up through the seal drain hole and feel for movement as the engine is cranked over. Who is right?

16. Technician A says that the fuel pump relief valve will open and bypass fuel between 45 and 65 psi (310 to 448 kPa). Technician B says that the bypass relief valve opens between 65 and 75 psi (448 to 517 kPa). Who is correct?

17. Technician A says that if the fuel pump relief valve was stuck open, low fuel pressure would exist and a lack of horsepower would occur, particularly under heavy load. Technician B says that the engine would tend to stall at idle. Who is right?

18. Technician A says that spin-on fuel filters should be tightened one full turn after the gasket contacts the filter base. Technician B says that they should only be turned approximately two-thirds of a full turn. Who is correct?

19. Technician A says that the four functions of the unit injector used in DDC engines is to time, atomize, meter, and pressurize the fuel. Technician B says that the four functions are to time, meter, inject, and atomize the fuel. Who is correct?

20. Technician A says that the basic horsepower on DDC mechanical engines (non-DDEC) can be changed by installing a larger or smaller injector size. Technician B says that to change the horsepower setting, you have to increase the maximum full-load engine speed. Who is right?

21. Technician A says that to change the horsepower setting on a DDC electronically controlled fuel injection system engine (DDEC), you would have to alter the EEPROM (electrically erasable programmable read-only memory) in the ECM. Technician B says that you would have to physically remove the existing PROM chip and install a new one that has been recalibrated for a new setting. Who is correct?

22. Technician A says that overtorquing a mechanically controlled unit injector (non-DDEC) can result in a binding rack condition. Technician B says that it could cause injector misfire. Who is right?

23. Technician A says that metering of the fuel inside a mechanical (non-DDEC) unit injector is accomplished by the position of the rack, which alters the helix position and therefore the fuel delivery rate. Technician B says that the length of the plunger effective stroke does this function. Who is right?

24. Technician A says that the fuel delivery rate in DDEC-equipped engines is controlled by rocker arm movement and the governor linkage connection. Technician B says that the ECM regulates the fuel delivery by a PWM (pulse-width-modulated) electrical signal. Who is correct?

25. Technician A says that to time the injector on both non-DDEC- and DDEC-equipped engines, you have to set the height between the injector body and the top of the injector follower to a given specification. Technician B says that you have to do this only on non-DDEC engines,

since the DDEC injectors are electronically controlled. Who is right?

26. Technician A says that a governor gap must be set into the governor assembly. Technician B says that this is not necessary since the injector rack adjustment will establish this gap. Who is correct?

27. Technician A says that the maximum no-load engine speed should be set according to the engine option plate/decal and can be altered by rotating the high-speed governor spring nut CW or CCW. Technician B says that the engine maximum no-load speed should never be tampered with. Who is right?

28. Technician A says that the amount of droop (rpm loss) on all DDC engines equipped with mechanical governors can be offset by setting the maximum no-load rpm approximately 7% higher than the full-load speed desired. Technician B says that both the full-load and no-load speeds are one and the same since the governor will compensate for any speed loss as the engine load is applied. Who is right here?

29. Technician A says that when adjusting a buffer screw on a non-DDEC-equipped engine, you can rotate the screw until a steady idle speed is obtained. Technician B says that you should never increase the idle speed more than 15 rpm; otherwise, the maximum no-load speed can be altered. Who is aware of the function of the buffer screw?

30. Technician A says that to increase the idle speed on a non-DDEC-equipped engine, you have to rotate the adjusting screw CW to increase the compressive force on the internal spring. Technician B says that you must back the screw out CCW to raise the idle speed. Who is right?

31. Technician A says that engine tune-up must be performed every 50,000 miles (80,465 km) to ensure that the engine exhaust emissions comply with EPA regulations. Technician B says that tune-up is required only when a low-power complaint is received and the air and fuel systems are mechanically sound. Who is correct?

32. Technician A says that when performing a tune-up on a V71 or V92 engine, the first injector rack to be adjusted should always be the No. 1 left bank. Technician B says that it does not make any difference whether you start with No. 1 on the left bank or No. 1 on the right bank. Which mechanic knows his tune-up procedure correctly?

33. Technician A says that when timing an injector on a two-stroke-cycle DDC engine, the exhaust valves should be fully closed. Technician B says that the exhaust valves should be fully open. Who is correct?

34. Technician A says that when setting the injector on a series 60 four-stroke-cycle engine, the valves and injector cannot be set at the same time on the same cylinder. Technician B says that the injector can only be set when the intake and exhaust valves are in position to be set on its companion cylinder. Who is right here?

35. Technician A says that to clear the ECM trouble codes from DDEC II or DDEC III memory, you simply have to pull the inline system fuses for 10 seconds. Technician B says that you have to employ an electronic DDR (diagnostic data reader). Who is correct?

36. Technician A says that if a DDEC-equipped engine shuts down repeatedly after idling for 5 minutes, this is a normal condition controlled by the ECM. Technician B says that this indicates a plugged primary fuel filter and the engine is simply using the fuel volume contained within the secondary filter assembly. Who is right?

37. A bus driver with a DDEC-equipped coach complains that the engine fails to rev up when the coach is parked and idling with the passenger door open. Technician A says that this is a normal condition. Technician B says that this is an abnormal condition. Who is correct?

38. Technician A says that the throttle pedal on a DDEC system uses a sensor which is basically a variable potentiometer that changes the voltage output signal proportional to throttle depression. Technician B says that the throttle pedal is connected to mechanical linkage running to a TPS sensor and then to the electronic governor in front of the blower on two-stroke-cycle engines. Who is correct?

39. Technician A says that when the CEL (check engine light) on the dash illuminates, a trouble code has been logged into ECM memory and that the driver should have the DDEC system checked at the first available opportunity. Technician B says that when the CEL illuminates, within 30 seconds the engine/ECM will initiate an engine shutdown sequence. Who is correct here?

40. Technician A says that the EUI (electronic unit injectors) used on the DDEC systems can be effectively cut out in the engine by using a DDR tester. Technician B says that you have to use a large screwdriver and hold the injector follower down while the engine is running in order to check their operation. Who is right?

41. Technician A says that when checking the DDEC system wiring for either a resistance or voltage value, it is acceptable to puncture the wiring to gain a good connection. Technician B says that you should never do this since this will expose the weatherproof connections to the elements. Who is correct?

42. Technician A says that the DDR (diagnostic data reader) can be used to reprogram part of the engine calibration in the ECM. Technician B says that this can be done only by connecting the DDR to a factory computer interface hookup. Who is correct?

43. A fuel system problem is generally indicated when
    a. black smoke emanates from the exhaust stack
    b. white smoke emanates from the exhaust stack
    c. the engine loses power with no abnormal exhaust smoke
    d. high crankcase pressure is apparent

44. Technician A says that high fuel system operating temperatures will result in high horsepower. Technician B

says that this will result in a loss of horsepower. Who is correct?

45. Technician A says that a low fuel spill-back rate with normal fuel pressure would indicate air in the fuel system. Technician B says that this is probably due to too small a restricted fitting. Who is right?

46. Technician A says that to check an injector for a misfiring condition in a non-DDEC 71 or 92 engine, you can run the engine at idle and simply depress the injector follower (hold it down). Technician B says that you should individually push each injector rack into the full-fuel position and see if the engine picks up speed. Who knows the correct procedure?

47. Technician A says that the DDL connection for the DDR on the DDEC III system incorporates a six-pin Deutsch connector. Technician B says that it is a 12-pin connector, the same as DDEC II systems. Who is right?

48. True or False: A portable laptop computer (see Figure 21–32) must be used to reprogram the ECM.

49. Technician A says that the DDEC III and IV system employs an ATS (air temperature sensor) which was not used on DDEC I and DDEC II systems. Technician B says that all DDEC systems, I, II, III, and IV all used the ATS. Who is right?

50. True or False: Automatic engine shutdown of a DDEC-equipped engine will usually be tied into an out-of-range operating condition in either the oil pressure, oil temperature, and coolant level sensors.

51. Technician A says that the ProDriver permits the operator to detect problems with the engine and DDEC system. Technician B says that only the DDR can tell you this. Who is right?

52. Technician A says that if any injectors are changed in a DDEC III system, the DDR should be used to recalibrate the ECM information to provide a proper cylinder balance. Technician B says that this is not necessary. Who is right?

53. Technician A says that only the DDEC III/IV system is programmed to illuminate standardized SAE trouble codes to the DDR. Technician B says that all DDEC systems will send SAE codes to the DDR. Who is right?

54. Describe the meaning of the following SAE code letters:
    a. PID
    b. SID
    c. FMI

55. Technician A says that the most common FMI codes are the numbers 3 and 4. Technician B says that codes 7 and 10 are more common. Who is right?

56. Technician A says that an active code can cause the engine to shut down. Technician B says that only a historic code can initiate this action. Who is right?

57. Technician A says that if it is suspected that a problem exists within the ECM, a breakout box can be used. Technician B says that only the DDR can detect this problem. Who is right?

58. Technician A says that the DDEC III and IV system can be programmed to allow automatic progressive engine compression braking (Jacobs or PacBrake) when in the cruise mode to maintain the set cruise speed, particularly when descending an incline. Technician B says that the compression brake needs to be manually activated by the operator to cause this to happen. Who is right?

59. Technician A says that automatic engine fan engagement during cruise control on a DDEC III–equipped vehicle would indicate a fan relay problem. Technician B says that this is a normal occurrence and is tied in with automatic compression brake engagement. Who is correct?

60. True or False: The SRS provides a once-per-cylinder signal to the ECM.

61. True or False: The TRS provides a 36-per-crankshaft revolution signal from a toothed wheel bolted behind the crankshaft gear.

Cummins Fuel Systems

Overview

In this chapter we describe the purpose, function, and operation of the various Cummins Engine Company fuel systems, which include the following models. The mechanical PT (pressure-time) system, Celect (Cummins Electronics) and Celect Plus, Cummins accumulator pump system (CAPS) electronic system used on the ISC engine models, the ISX/Signature system, the Bosch VP44 used on the B model engines, and the Bosch mechanical PLN and VE distributor pump systems used on earlier-model B and C Series engines. Diagnostic tooling required for electronic engine maintenance, diagnosis, analysis, and troubleshooting is also provided, as are certain adjustments and checks for mechanical fuel systems. Keep in mind, however, that greater detail for Bosch-equipped Cummins engines fitted with these products is best found in Chapter 19 of this book. Note also that the Cummins CAPS electronic fuel system is actually a Bosch CRFS (common-rail fuel system), and is described in detail in Chapter 19, although the diagnosis of the Cummins CAPS electronic system is described in this chapter.

An overview and prerequisites for Cummins electronic fuel systems study should begin with a review of Chapter 18. End-of-chapter questions are provided to assist you in self-checking your progress and in ensuring that after performing the various ASE hands-on content area tasks lists, you are prepared to challenge either the ASE or TQ test areas.

ASE CERTIFICATION

Within the ASE medium/heavy truck tests, diesel engines, preparation guide, test T2, subsection F, Fuel System Diagnosis and Repair, Parts 1 and 2, Mechanical and Electronic Components, the various content task lists are provided. In addition, the ASE electronic diesel engine diagnosis specialist test, L2, deals with the knowledge and hands-on skills required to successfully challenge and certify in this specialist area. Chapter 18 provides an overview of the theory and diagnosis of electronic engines, as well as a display of the required content area tasks lists. Refer also to Chapter 19, subsection F, Fuel System Diagnosis and Repair, Mechanical and Electronic Components tasks lists. You must be knowledgeable and capable of performing these tasks in order to prepare yourself for challenging either the ASE or TQ test areas. Detailed copies of both the ASE T2 and L2 test content area preparation guides can be downloaded from the Internet (*www.asecert.org*).

COMPANY BACKGROUND

The incorporation of Cummins Engine Company on February 3, 1919, brought together the company's namesake, Clessie Lyle Cummins, a self-taught mechanic-inventor, and William Glanton "W. G." Irwin, a successful Columbus, Indiana, banker-investor who supplied the starting capital. Cummins first engines were 6 hp, four-stroke-cycle models used for stationary power. In those early years when getting established was a tough task, Clessie's creativity averted bankruptcy. For example, he mounted a diesel engine in a used Packard limousine, and on Christmas Day, 1929, he took W. G. Irwin for a ride in America's first diesel-powered automobile. He set a diesel speed record with a Duesenberg at Daytona Beach, then piloted a Cummins-powered truck coast-to-coast on a mere $11.22 worth of fuel. In 1931, a Cummins team set a new endurance record, a grueling 13,535 miles (21,782 km), at the Indianapolis Motor Speedway. In the 1950s, Cummins-powered race cars entered a number of Indy Motor Speedway events. Cummins did not earn a profit until 1937; then, in 1940 he offered an unheard of 100,000 mile (160,930 km) warranty for his on-highway truck engines. In the early 1990s, Cummins Engine Company's international efforts moved ahead with manufacturing ventures in Japan, China, and India. Now a truly global enterprise, the name Cummins is associated with technological leadership in its field.

Today, in addition to their success in midrange and heavy-duty highway trucks, Cummins engines are widely used in off-highway, industrial, logging, mining, and marine applications, and are the power of choice for the world's leading farm equipment manufacturers, including AGCO/Massey-Ferguson, AgChem, Case, Hesston, New Holland, and many others. In 1988, Cummins and Dodge revolutionized the pickup truck market with the introduction of their first Cummins-powered Ram. In 2000, the turbocharged Dodge Ram engine is rated at 245 hp (183 kW), has a 24-valve head, and employs a Bosch electronically controlled high-pressure common-rail fuel injection system and an exhaust brake.

At this time, Cummins Engine Co. Inc., is the world's largest producer of 200+ hp (149.2 kW) diesel engines, and is a leading manufacturer of midrange and heavy-duty high-speed engines. In 2000, Cummins was selected by the U.S. Department of Energy to participate in a project designed to develop heavy-duty diesel engines with improved fuel efficiency and marked exhaust emissions reductions. The department will award up to $5 million to Cummins during the first year of the project, which is expected to continue through January 2006.

Engine Model Identification

Identification of Cummins engine models is an important part of a service technician's job, both when ordering parts and when locating appropriate service information data. Cummins engines use a data plate affixed to the side of the engine front timing cover known as a control parts list (CPL).

Cummins Fuel Systems

Since its inception, Cummins Engine Company has employed a diverse number of fuel injection systems, from its first single-disk fuel system to the unique Cummins PT or "pressure-time" fuel system introduced in 1954, and only recently completely superceded by electronically controlled fuel systems designs. Based upon the year of manufacture, and their horsepower rating, earlier Cummins midrange B models were equipped with mechanical distributor injec-

tion pumps, and used either a Robert Bosch VE (German word *verteiler* for "rotary"), Lucas (now Delphi-Automotive) (CAV) DPA (distributor pump assembly), or Lucas (CAV—a DPS electronic for European automotive engines), or a Stanadyne DB4 model. PLN (pump-line-nozzle) injection pumps used with the B six-cylinder 5.9 L models are represented by Bosch model A, P7100, P3000, or Nippondenso EP-9 models. The six-cylinder 8.3 L Cummins C models are equipped with PLN Bosch models A, MW, P7100, P3000, or the Nippondenso EP-9 model. Earlier A model Cummins midrange engines were equipped with the Bosch VE or Stanadyne DB2 distributor pump models. Mechanical governors used with these various midrange engine PLN injection pumps were Bosch RSV, RQV, or RQV-K models based upon the specific year of engine and its application. A description of the operation of Bosch injection pumps and governor assemblies is best described in Chapter 19.

Cummins engines have also stayed abreast of technological advancements. Their first electronic fuel system known as the Celect (Cummins Electronics) appeared in November 1989, and is still in use today but now known as the Celect Plus. A number of Cummins engines including the B, C, L, M, and ISX/Signature models are now equipped with an electronic system commonly referred to as the *Interact System*. Consequently, engine models with the prefix letters IS followed by the alphabetical model letter (for example, ISB) indicates that the engine model is equipped with an interact system. This innovative engineering platform combines electronic engine controls with high-pressure fuel injection and high-strength components. The features and concept of electronic operation of the Interact Systems are similar to that described for the Celect systems. The mechanical PT and the various electronic systems are described in this chapter.

PT FUEL SYSTEM

The PT (pressure-time) fuel system illustrated in Figure 22–1 is exclusive to Cummins diesel engines, being introduced in 1951; it employs injectors that meter and inject the fuel, with this metering based on a pressure-time principle. Fuel pressure is supplied by a gear-driven positive-displacement low-pressure fuel pump, and the time for metering is determined by the interval that the metering orifice in the injector remains open. This interval is established and controlled by the engine speed, which therefore determines the rate of camshaft rotation and consequently the injector plunger movement, which is pushrod and rocker arm actuated.

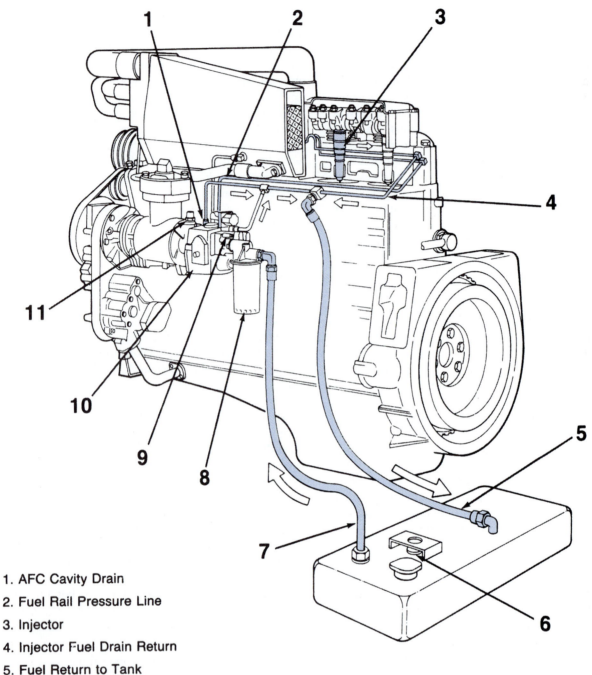

1. AFC Cavity Drain
2. Fuel Rail Pressure Line
3. Injector
4. Injector Fuel Drain Return
5. Fuel Return to Tank
6. Fuel Tank Breather
7. Fuel Inlet Supply
8. Fuel Filter
9. Gear Pump Coolant Drain
10. Fuel Pump
11. Tachometer Drive

FIGURE 22–1 Basic mechanical PT (pressure-time) fuel system schematic and identification of major components. (Courtesy of Cummins Engine Company, Inc.)

The flyball type of mechanical governor controls fuel pressure and engine torque throughout the entire operating range. It also controls the engine's idling speed and prevents engine overspeeding in the high-speed range. The throttle is simply a shaft with a hole; therefore, the alignment of this hole with the fuel passages determines pressure at the injectors.

A single low-pressure fuel line from the fuel pump serves all injectors; therefore, the pressure and the amount of metered fuel to each cylinder are equal.

The main components of the PT fuel system that control the pressure at the injectors are shown in Figure 22–1. The PT fuel pump assembly is coupled to the air compressor drive on the engine, which is driven from the engine gear train. The fuel pump main shaft in turn drives the gear pump, governor, and tachometer shaft assemblies.

System Operation

Figure 22–2 describes the PT system flow and injector function and operation. The fuel metering process in the PT system has three main advantages:

1. The injector accomplishes all metering and injection functions.

2. The injector injects a finely atomized fuel spray into the combustion chamber at spray-in pressures exceeding 20,000 psi (1360 atm).

3. A low-pressure common-rail system is used, with the pressure being developed in a gear-type pump. This eliminates the necessity for high-pressure fuel lines running from the fuel pump to each injector, similar to that found in a multiple-plunger inline injection pump system.

To understand the sequence of events pertaining to actual injection of fuel by the injector, a study of the injector operating mechanism is necessary.

Downward movement of the injector plunger forces metered fuel into the cylinder as shown in Figure 22–2. Since the shape of the camshaft lobes is directly related to the start and end of injection, let us take a look at this first. Figure 22–2 shows a cross-sectional view of the camshaft. The injector cam shape is based on two circles, an inner and an outer circle.

To follow this a stage further, let us return to basics for a minute. Using a circle to represent 720°, as when using a polar valve timing diagram, the 720° circle can represent two rotations of the engine crankshaft. We can then place or superimpose one cam lobe shape in the center of this circle and illustrate injector push tube and injector plunger travel.

Figure 22–2 actually shows the motion transfer from the camshaft lobe, to the push tube and rocker arm, then the injector plunger.

Having studied Figure 22–2 you should now be familiar with the basic camshaft positions; during the *intake* stroke, the follower roller moves from the outer cam base circle across the retraction ramp to the inner or lower base circle, which will allow the injector push tube to follow it down. Injector plunger return spring pressure lifts the plunger as the lowered push tube permits the rocker arm lever to tilt backward. As the injector plunger lifts (start upstroke) it allows fuel at low pressure to enter the injector at part 6 and flow through the inlet orifice (7), internal drillings, around the annular groove in the injector cup, and up passage 16 to return to the fuel tank. The amount of fuel flowing through the injector is determined by the fuel pressure before the inlet orifice (7). Fuel pressure is determined by engine speed, governor, and throttle.

As the injector plunger continues its upward movement, metering orifice 20 is uncovered and a charge of fuel is metered to the cup, the amount being controlled by fuel pressure. Passage 16 is blocked, momentarily stopping fuel circulation and isolating the metering orifice from any fuel pressure pulsations (upstroke complete).

As the camshaft continues to rotate and the cylinder's piston is coming up on *compression,* the follower roller crosses the inner base circle, thereby holding the plunger up for metering. As it reaches the camshaft lobe injection ramp, the upward-moving push tube working through the rocker arm assembly forces the injector plunger toward injection (downstroke). You will notice that the downward-moving plunger closes off the metering orifice, thereby cutting off fuel entry into the cup. At this instant, the drain outlet (16) is uncovered; fuel that was not metered to the cup can now leave the injector and fresh fuel enters the balance orifice 7. As the plunger continues down into its seating position in the cup, it forces the fuel under great hydraulic pressure through tiny holes (for example, eight holes 0.007 in. or 0.177 mm in diameter), creating a fine fuel spray for penetration of the air mass to ensure complete combustion of fuel in the cylinder.

At the completion of the plunger downstroke after injection has ceased, the plunger remains seated until the next metering and injection cycle. The end of injection occurs as the roller follower reaches the nose of the cam; this ensures that the plunger remains seated in the cup because the follower is riding evenly around the concentric outer base circle of the cam lobe. During this time, however, as the downstroke is completed, fuel is allowed to flow freely through the injector and lubricate and cool internal parts. The fuel picks up some heat during this time, which warms the fuel in the tank, which is helpful during cold-weather operation.

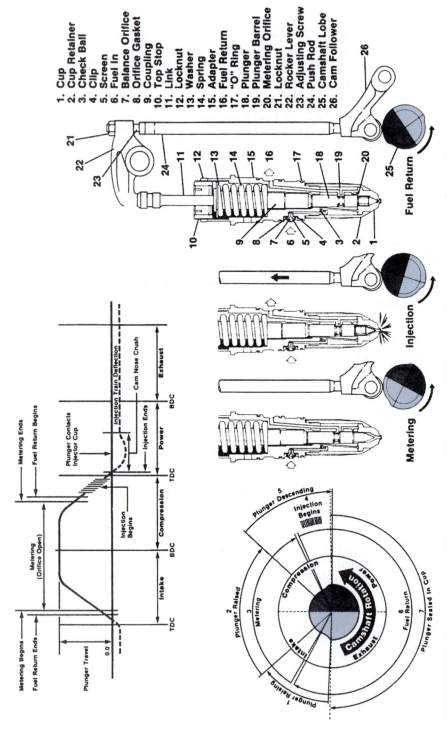

1. Cup
2. Cup Retainer
3. Check Ball
4. Clip
5. Screen
6. Fuel In
7. Balance Orifice
8. Orifice Gasket
9. Coupling
10. Top Stop
11. Link
12. Locknut
13. Washer
14. Spring
15. Adapter
16. Fuel Return
17. "O" Ring
18. Plunger
19. Plunger Barrel
20. Metering Orifice
21. Locknut
22. Rocker Lever
23. Adjusting Screw
24. Push Rod
25. Camshaft Lobe
26. Cam Follower

FIGURE 22–2 Mechanical PT (pressure-time) fuel system, PT-D top-stop injector sequence of operation. (Courtesy of Cummins Engine Company, Inc.)

PT FUEL PUMPS

Figure 22–3 illustrates a typical PTG-AFC fuel pump, which is normally equipped with a limiting-speed governor assembly. A PTG-AFC/VS designation indicates that the pump is equipped with a variable-speed governor assembly. The P in the name "PT fuel system" refers to the actual fuel pressure that is produced by the gear pump and maintained at the inlet to the fuel injectors. The T is obtained from the fact that the actual time available for fuel to flow into the injector assembly (cup) is determined by the engine speed as a function of the engine camshaft and injection train components. Actual flow into the combustion chamber from an injector is therefore not only a function of both pressure and time, but is also the actual flow area within the injector. For this reason, injectors are calibrated for a given flow at rated engine speed where the maximum horsepower will be obtained.

Within the pump assembly a fuel pump idle spring plunger (bypass button) of varying size can be installed to control the actual maximum fuel delivery pressure of the gear pump before it opens and bypasses fuel back to the inlet side of the pump. In this way, the actual horsepower setting of the engine can be altered fairly easily (more on this later).

A major feature of the PT pump system is that there is no necessity to time the pump to the engine, since the pump is designed simply to generate and supply a given flow rate at a specified pressure setting to the rail (common fuel line passage) to all injectors. The injectors themselves are timed to ensure that the start of injection will occur at the right time for each cylinder.

Fuel delivery between idle and maximum speed ranges to the injectors is normally controlled by manual operation of the throttle by the operator. Fuel under pressure (see Figure 22–4) is then allowed to flow through the idle passage at low engine speed as well as through the throttle shaft. At higher engine speeds, the idle passage is blocked off and fuel flows through the main supply passage to the throttle shaft, then on to the injectors in a PTG pump, or in a PTG-AFC pump, the fuel from the throttle shaft first flows to and through the AFC unit, and then onto the injectors. Manipulation of the throttle by the operator will vary the rail pressure to the injectors. At wide-open throttle the rail pressure will be higher than at half-throttle or at an idle speed.

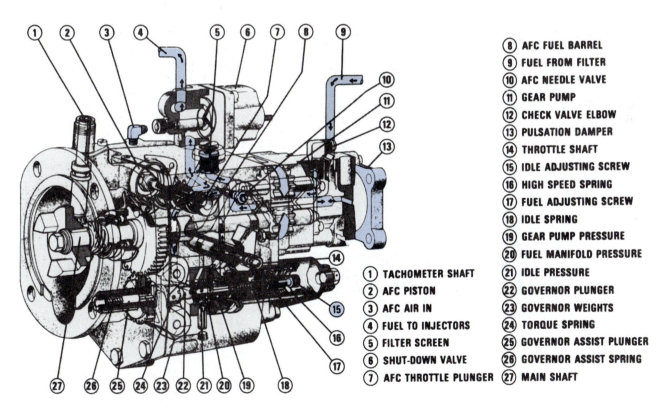

① TACHOMETER SHAFT
② AFC PISTON
③ AFC AIR IN
④ FUEL TO INJECTORS
⑤ FILTER SCREEN
⑥ SHUT-DOWN VALVE
⑦ AFC THROTTLE PLUNGER
⑧ AFC FUEL BARREL
⑨ FUEL FROM FILTER
⑩ AFC NEEDLE VALVE
⑪ GEAR PUMP
⑫ CHECK VALVE ELBOW
⑬ PULSATION DAMPER
⑭ THROTTLE SHAFT
⑮ IDLE ADJUSTING SCREW
⑯ HIGH SPEED SPRING
⑰ FUEL ADJUSTING SCREW
⑱ IDLE SPRING
⑲ GEAR PUMP PRESSURE
⑳ FUEL MANIFOLD PRESSURE
㉑ IDLE PRESSURE
㉒ GOVERNOR PLUNGER
㉓ GOVERNOR WEIGHTS
㉔ TORQUE SPRING
㉕ GOVERNOR ASSIST PLUNGER
㉖ GOVERNOR ASSIST SPRING
㉗ MAIN SHAFT

FIGURE 22–3 *Schematic of a PTG-AFC (pressure-time-governor, air fuel control) fuel pump equipped with a standard automotive mechanical governor, and identification of major components. (Courtesy of Cummins Engine Company, Inc.)*

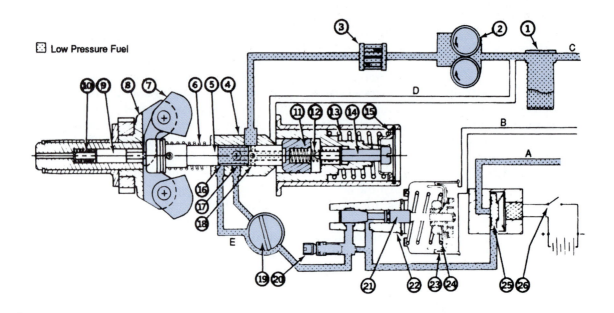

1	PRIMARY FUEL FILTER	17	MAIN GOVERNOR PORT
2	GEAR PUMP	18	GOVERNOR DUMP PORTS
3	FILTER SCREEN	19	THROTTLE
4	GOVERNOR SLEEVE	20	AFC NEEDLE VALVE
5	GOVERNOR PLUNGER	21	AFC CONTROL PLUNGER
6	TORQUE CONTROL SPRING	22	AFC BARREL
7	GOVERNOR WEIGHTS	23	DIAPHRAGM (BELLOWS)
8	GOVERNOR WEIGHT CARRIER	24	AFC SPRING
9	WEIGHT ASSIST PLUNGER	25	SOLENOID VALVE
10	WEIGHT ASSIST SPRING	26	IGNITION SWITCH
11	IDLE SPRING PLUNGER	A	FUEL TO INJECTORS
12	IDLE SPEED SPRING	B	AIR FROM INTAKE MANIFOLD
13	MAXIMUM SPEED GOVERNOR SPRING	C	FUEL FROM TANK
14	IDLE SPEED ADJUSTING SCREW	D	BY-PASSED FUEL
15	MAXIMUM SPEED GOVERNOR SHIMS	E	IDLE FUEL PASSAGE
16	IDLE SPEED GOVERNOR PORT		

(a)

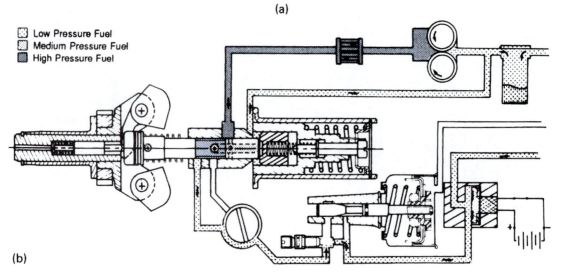

(b)

FIGURE 22–4 Fuel flow through a mechanical PTG-AFC fuel pump: (a) engine stopped; (b) starting and idling; (c) normal driving; (d) beginning of high-speed governing; (e) complete high-speed governing. (Courtesy of Cummins Engine Company, Inc.)

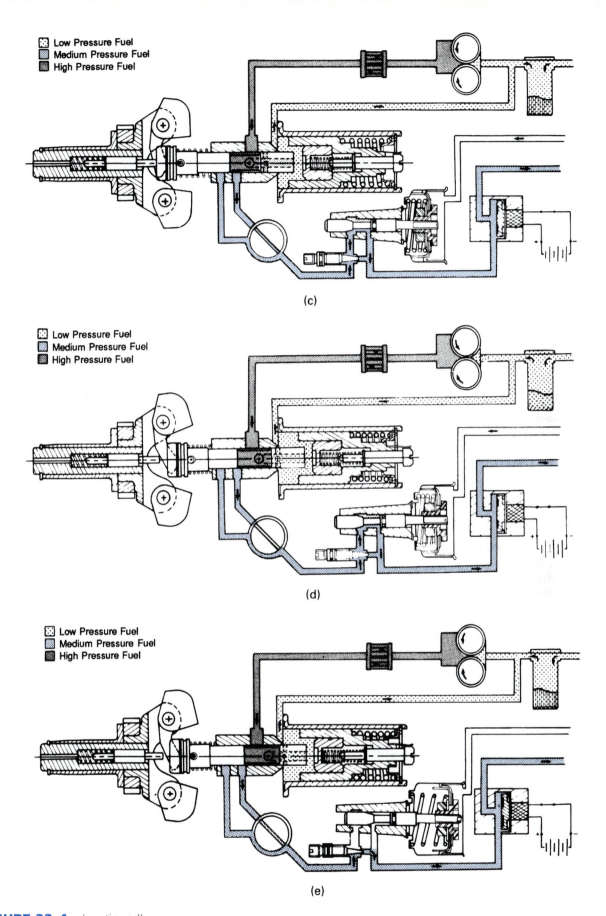

(c)

(d)

(e)

FIGURE 22–4 (continued).

627

The throttle shaft illustrated in Figure 22–5 is cylindrical in shape and is hollow throughout approximately half its overall length in order that a fuel adjusting screw can be screwed into this bore horizontally. This screw in turn will restrict the flow of fuel leaking through the vertical hole drilled through the throttle shaft, and therefore the maximum flow area of the throttle shaft passage when the throttle is in its wide-open position.

When the operator rotates the throttle shaft through mechanical linkage, this fuel rate setting acts as a variable-area orifice since the vertical hole within the shaft indexes with the outlet passage to the injectors, as shown, for example, in Figure 22–5 at an engine idle speed. When the operator accelerates the engine, the throttle shaft will rotate CCW (item 19 in Figure 22–4) to expose more of the outlet passage to this fuel flow.

Fuel entering the PT pump's governor plunger and barrel assembly flows around and into the plunger area, where the plunger rides freely in the carrier and sleeve, which is being lubricated by this fuel. Fuel flowing into the plunger travels in both directions and will therefore follow the route of least resistance. Figure 22–5 shows that spring pressure on the right-hand side holds the idle plunger (11) against the end of the governor plunger (5) until fuel begins to flow, at which time they are pushed apart enough for some fuel to escape.

In the cutaway section shown in Figure 22–5 the amount of fuel being bypassed depends on resistance to its flowing out in other directions through the idle and throttle openings in the plunger and barrel assembly. To simplify this action of how the fuel flow is controlled, the fuel pressure as it reaches the governor plunger is caused by the restriction to this flow by placing the surface of the idle plunger against the end of the governor plunger. Such a condition can be likened to that created when you place a thumb over the end of a garden hose minus the nozzle. Water pressure builds up in the water behind your thumb owing to restriction caused by your thumb over the end of the hose; therefore, water that does escape has an increased velocity or greater force and direction.

Under this condition, fuel is held in the governor plunger by the surface of the idle plunger, which is under spring pressure; therefore, as the volume of fuel flow increases, fuel will eventually push the idle plunger back if no other outlet is found. There are, however, two other outlets for governor plunger fuel, which are shown in Figure 22–5.

Figure 22–5 shows the *idle* port (or drilling), which allows fuel to escape during *low* speeds, and the *throttle* port, through which fuel escapes during times of higher speeds or loads. Whether fuel is routed through these two other passages is controlled by just how they are aligned with fuel from the governor plunger (5), and how hard it is for the fuel volume to push the idle plunger surface (11) away from the end of the governor plunger.

In all truck engine PT fuel pumps the fuel delivered to the injectors (rail pressure) is controlled by use of a selected idle spring plunger button such as those illustrated in Figure 22–6. In Figure 22–6, for example, a No. 7 button (part 141624) has a counterbore diameter of between 0.2135 and 0.2165 in. (5.42 to 5.50 mm), while the No. 45 button (part 138862) has a

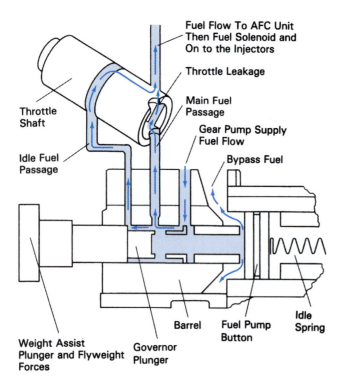

FIGURE 22–5 PTG-AFC fuel pump idle fuel flow and throttle leakage paths. (Courtesy of Cummins Engine Company, Inc.)

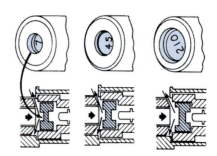

FIGURE 22–6 Different sizes of PTG fuel pump idle spring plungers used to control the amount of fuel and therefore the horsepower setting of the engine. (Courtesy of Cummins Engine Company, Inc.)

counterbore size of 0.2885 to 0.2915 in. (7.33 to 7.40 mm). The largest button shown in this figure is No. 210 (part 145963) with a counterbore dimension between 0.4185 and 0.4215 in. (10.63 to 10.70 mm). The smallest button is a size No. 5 (part 141623), with a dimension between 0.2085 and 0.2115 in. (5.30 to 5.36 mm), and the largest is a No. 237 (part 145974), with a counterbore size between 0.4735 and 0.4765 in. (12.03 to 12.10 mm). Button sizes increase in increments of 0.005 in. (0.127 mm) from the smallest to the highest. Therefore, when an engine seems to be lacking power, and all possible areas have been checked out to satisfaction, be certain that the correct idle spring plunger button size is being used, since either too small or too large a fuel pump button can drastically alter the fuel rail pressure, and therefore the power output of the engine.

Basic Governor Plunger Control

Since what happens to the fuel flow is dependent on the forces that change the amount of restriction to flow, we have to look at how these forces are created and consequently controlled. The governor weight assembly applies force to push the governor plunger back toward the idle plunger surface. The weight assembly is driven through gears from the engine via the engine's gear train and fuel pump mainshaft, as shown in Figure 22–4. The weights are supported and pivot on pins contained in the weight carrier assembly shown in Figure 22–4.

The combined forces of the weight-assist plunger spring (10) and the centrifugal force being developed by the rotating governor flyweights at an idle speed are opposed by the idle spring (12) located at the opposite end of the pump plunger. When a state of balance exists between these opposing forces, the engine will run at a predetermined idle rpm. Therefore, the forces developed by the rotating governor flyweights and the weight-assist plunger (5) spring are attempting to force the fuel plunger (5) to a position that will close off the idle fuel passage, while the force of the idle spring at the opposite end of the plunger is attempting to push it to open the idle fuel flow passage.

It should be noted that when the engine speed approaches either high-idle (no-load rpm) or rated (full-load) speed, the weight-assist plunger and spring no longer affect the position of the governor fuel plunger, since the rotating flyweights have moved away from them. The idle fuel passage will have been closed by the centrifugal weight force pushing the fuel plunger forward in the barrel, and the idle spring no longer affects the operation, since the fuel pump button has also bottomed in the idle plunger guide.

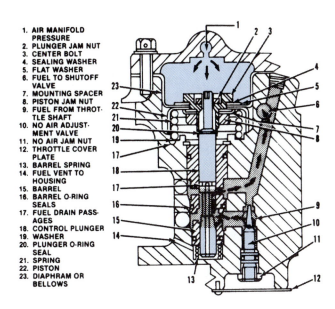

1. AIR MANIFOLD PRESSURE
2. PLUNGER JAM NUT
3. CENTER BOLT
4. SEALING WASHER
5. FLAT WASHER
6. FUEL TO SHUTOFF VALVE
7. MOUNTING SPACER
8. PISTON JAM NUT
9. FUEL FROM THROTTLE SHAFT
10. NO AIR ADJUSTMENT VALVE
11. NO AIR JAM NUT
12. THROTTLE COVER PLATE
13. BARREL SPRING
14. FUEL VENT TO HOUSING
15. BARREL
16. BARREL O-RING SEALS
17. FUEL DRAIN PASSAGES
18. CONTROL PLUNGER
19. WASHER
20. PLUNGER O-RING SEAL
21. SPRING
22. PISTON
23. DIAPHRAM OR BELLOWS

FIGURE 22–7 Cross section of the AFC (air/fuel control) unit used with the PTG fuel pump identifying the major components. (Courtesy of Cummins Engine Company, Inc.)

AFC PUMPS

The PTG-AFC fuel pump is an acceleration exhaust smoke control device built internally into the pump body. The AFC (air/fuel control) assembly is shown in Figure 22–7 with the major components identified. The AFC (air/fuel control) unit is designed to restrict fuel flow in direct proportion to engine air intake manifold pressure during engine acceleration, under load, and during lug-down conditions. Both parts (a) and (b) of Figure 22–8 are plan views (top) of the AFC unit. View (a) is a cross section of the control plunger in the *no-air* position; view (b) shows the control plunger in the *full-air* position.

Fuel enters the AFC control after leaving the governor and passing through the throttle shaft. When no air pressure is supplied from the turbocharger, the AFC plunger closes off the primary fuel flow circuit (see Figure 22–8). A secondary passage controlled by the position of the no-air needle valve supplies fuel for this condition, such as engine cranking, or at initial acceleration of the engine. The no-air needle valve is located directly above the throttle shaft under the throttle cover plate.

As intake manifold pressure increases or decreases, the AFC throttling plunger reacts to deliver a proportional increase or decrease in fuel, which prevents the air/fuel mixture from getting overrich and causing excessive exhaust smoke. The AFC plunger is positioned by action of the intake manifold air pressure

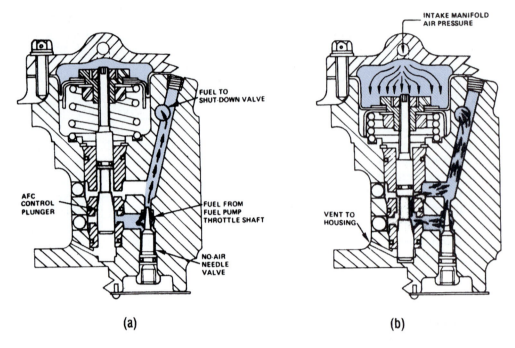

(a)   **(b)**

FIGURE 22–8 AFC (air/fuel control) pump flow; (a) with no turbocharger boost; (b) with turbocharger boost. (Courtesy of Cummins Engine Company, Inc.)

acting against a piston and diaphragm opposed by a spring to a proportionate amount of travel (see Figure 22–8).

MANUAL FUEL SHUTOFF

All Cummins PT engines are equipped with an electric fuel shutoff solenoid valve, which is mounted on top of the fuel pump body. See item 6 in Figure 22–3. A closer view of this solenoid shutdown illustrates a knurled thumbscrew (not numbered) just to the right of item 3. The thumbscrew allows manual control of the fuel flow/shutoff at any time a problem may exist in the normal electric fuel control solenoid assembly. Rotating this knurled thumbscrew clockwise (into the solenoid) will allow the flow control valve to be placed in an open position, therefore allowing fuel to flow to the injectors. If, at any time, the engine fails to shut down in the normal manner, the knurled thumbscrew can be manually rotated in a counterclockwise direction, which will close off the fuel supply to the injectors, and engine shutdown is therefore assured.

PT PUMP CHECKS AND ADJUSTMENTS

There is no ASE task that requires the technician to perform major disassembly overhaul and testing of the PT

pump. This job is best left to a fuel injection specialist employed at a local Association of Diesel Specialist (ADS) certified shop where they have the high-tech equipment and fuel pump test stands to accurately perform these tasks. Therefore, we will not deal with this particular task in this book. Some Cummins dealers, however, have a portable PT fuel pump test stand that can be connected to an engine while in a vehicle to permit a series of checks and tests, including a fuel flow rate measuring device. Vehicles can be taken to your local Cummins dealer for this task if and when required.

A diesel service technician will be expected to perform the necessary checks and adjustments listed in the ASE medium/heavy truck tests preparation guide T2 tasks list, subsection F, Fuel System Diagnosis and Repair, Mechanical Components, and Electronic Components. Listed in this ASE tasks list content area are two tasks specific only to Cummins engine fuel systems—one in the mechanical and one in the electronic area. In the mechanical content area, task 8 is specific to Cummins PT fuel systems, which states:

8. Perform on-engine inspections, tests, and adjustments, or replace PT-type injection pumps, drives, and injectors.

In the electronic area, task 5 states:

5. Perform on-engine inspections, tests, and adjustments on PT-type injection pump electronic controls.

NOTE   Task 5 in the tasks list refers to Cummins engines equipped with the Celect systems, industrial and off-highway engines with CENTRY, and ISB, ISC, ISL, and ISX/Signature models. However, some N14 (855 in^3) model engines were equipped with the PT-PACE and PACER system, a simple electronic design that employs an electronically activated fuel control valve, sensors, and a PT control module for operation/monitoring of the mechanical PT fuel pump. It differs from the mechanical PT system in that it employs electronic governing features with some minor changes to the actual PT pump fuel flow controls. It offers road speed governing, cruise, C-brake and PTO control, and built-in diagnostics capability through the use of Cummins own Compulink tooling. This system will not be described here because it was the forerunner of the Cummins first ECM-controlled fuel system, known as ECI (electronically controlled injection). This was followed by the Cummins-Celect system. Details on how the Celect system functions and operates are provided later in this chapter.

Idle Adjustment: PTG-AFC

1.   Refer to Figure 22–9 and with the engine already at operating temperature, remove the access plug at the bottom of the pump housing.

2.   Install special idle adjusting tool 3375981 into the access hole by threading its fitting into position. This tool is equipped with a small sealing ring to prevent air from being drawn into the pump during this adjustment with the engine running.

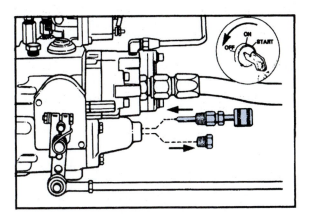

FIGURE 22–9 Idle-speed adjustment screw special tool and access plug to the actual screw. (Courtesy of Cummins Engine Company, Inc.)

3.   Start and run the engine at high idle for about 30 seconds to ensure that all air has been removed from the fuel system.

4.   Allow the engine to return to a low idle speed and ensure that the pump throttle lever is at its normal low-speed position.

5.   With the special idle adjusting tool engaged with the internal idle screw, turn the tool CW to increase the tension on the idle spring and therefore raise engine idle rpm, or CCW to decrease idle spring tension and lower engine idle rpm.

6.   When the correct idle adjustment has been obtained, stop the engine and remove the special adjusting tool.

7.   Install the small pipe plug into the hole in the pump body.

8.   Start and run the engine until it operates smoothly, which will ensure that all air has been removed from the system, and recheck the idle speed.

High-Idle Adjustment: PTG-AFC Pump

Adjustment of the high-speed spring on the PTG and PTG-AFC fuel pumps is done by removing the four bolts that retain the spring pack assembly cover to the bottom rear of the fuel pump housing. Figure 22–4 illustrates the high-speed spring assembly location (item 13). The spring cover is the one shown in Figure 22–9 through which you can adjust the idle screw. The engine's maximum speed can be changed by adding or removing shims from behind the spring. Generally, each 0.001 in. (0.0254 mm) shim added to the spring will increase the engine speed by approximately 2 rpm, while removal of these same shims will decrease the speed accordingly.

ENGINE-TO-INJECTOR TIMING

Once a mechanical or electronic N14, L10, or M11 engine has been assembled, basic piston-to-camshaft timing is established through alignment of the timing marks between the crankshaft and camshaft gearing. Injector timing must be checked and set if any of the following are changed: camshaft, timing gears, cam follower box gaskets, cam followers, or cam follower box. However, we now have to ensure that the actual start of injection occurs at a specific amount of degrees BTDC, therefore, this involves a series of checks and adjustments and if the actual injection timing does not match that specified on the CPL (control parts list) data plate located on the side of the engine front engine timing cover. Once the injection timing code has been noted on the CPL data plate, it is necessary to refer to the Cummins *CPL Manual*, part 3379133, which lists all the various codes and respective injector push tube travel specifications for all engine models and CPL codes.

> NOTE   The injection timing check confirms that the distance existing between the injector plunger and the injector cup when measured with a dial indicator is correct when the piston is 19° BTDC, which is equal to a measurement of 0.2032 in. (5.161 mm) BTDC. The timing is correct when the reading on the piston travel dial indicator and the push tube dial indicator are as in the specs listed in the Cummins *CPL Manual* 3379133. The injection timing code on the CPL engine data plate can be cross-referenced to the specs in this manual for all Cummins engines. Therefore, the injection timing relates to the amount of push tube travel remaining before the plunger bottoms in its cup when the engine piston is 19° BTDC on its compression stroke.

Engine-to-PT-Injector Timing Example

To remove any confusion about why injection timing is so important to the successful operation of the engine, Figures 22–10 and 22–11 illustrate graphically just how the piston position and injector push tube movement relate to one another. If we were to assume for discussion purposes that the engine injector push tube specification was listed as 0.066 in. (1.67 mm) in the CPL manual for a particular engine when the piston was 0.2032 in. (5.161 mm) from TDC on its compression stroke, which is equal to 19° BTDC, any reading less than this 0.066 in. would indicate that timing is advanced or "fast," since it would place the injector plunger closer to bottoming in its cup with the piston

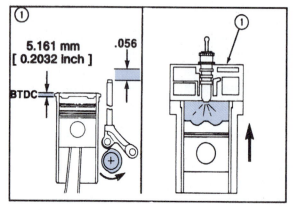

FIGURE 22–10   *Schematic of early fuel injection as a result of too small a push tube lift BTDC (before top dead center). (Courtesy of Cummins Engine Company, Inc.)*

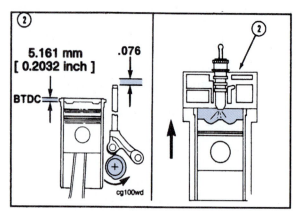

FIGURE 22–11   *Schematic of late fuel injection as a result of too large a push tube lift BTDC. (Courtesy of Cummins Engine Company, Inc.)*

in its correct position of 19° BTDC. In effect, fuel would be injected too early, as shown in Figure 22–10 with an example reading of 0.056 in. (1.42 mm).

Figure 22–11 illustrates the result of "slow" or retarded timing with an example push tube reading on the dial indicator of 0.076 in. (1.93 mm) instead of the correct 0.066 in. (1.67 mm). In this situation, the start of injection would occur too late (piston closer to TDC).

Changing Injection Timing

CPL codes on the engine data plate for injection timing are either a single or double alphabetical letter that relates to a specification numeral listed in the CPL manual. Injection timing can be changed on the NT 855 series of engines by removing the cam follower housing and increasing or decreasing the thickness of the gasket used. On V-type, K series, and L10 and M11 engine models, injection timing is changed by removing the camshaft gear and installing an "offset key" to alter the timing dimension. Advancement or retardation of injection timing is accomplished by altering the position of the injector cam follower roller in relation to its position on the camshaft lobe when the piston is 19° BTDC on its compression stroke.

Figure 22–12 illustrates how a thicker or thinner cam follower housing gasket on an NT 855 engine would alter the push tube lift in relation to the piston position. In addition an offset key can be installed into the slotted keyway on the engine camshaft to change the timing. Figure 22–13 represents two different offset keys for an 855 (14 L) model engine; if the arrow on the key is pointing toward the engine, the injection timing is retarded, while if the arrow is pointing away from the engine, the timing is advanced. Figure 22–14 lists the timing change for the different camshaft keys used.

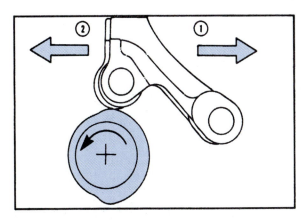

FIGURE 22–12 Result of adding cam follower housing gaskets (1) to advance, or removing gaskets (2) to retard the injection timing by shifting the pivoting roller follower toward or away from the rotating engine camshaft lobe which affects the pushtube lift on an N14 engine model when the piston is 0.2032 in. (5.16 mm), or 19° BTDC on the compression stroke. (Courtesy of Cummins Engine Company, Inc.)

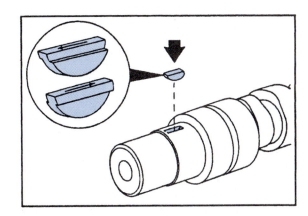

FIGURE 22–13 Altering injector push tube/rod lift to alter the start of injection timing by using an offset camshaft key. (Courtesy of Cummins Engine Company, Inc.)

NOTE On 855 model engines, since three cylinder heads are used to cover the six cylinders, we also have three cam follower housings. This means that the injection timing check must be done for all three cam follower housings by performing the timing check on one cylinder for each housing. Therefore, prior to performing the injection timing check, remove the fuel injectors from cylinders 1, 3, and 5.

To establish that the injector will in fact inject fuel into the combustion chamber at the proper number of degrees BTDC during the compression stroke, two dial indicators are required. One dial indicator measures the relative piston position in the cylinder, and the other establishes the actual injector push tube lift and duration. Cummins timing fixture, 3375522 (Figure 22–15), is required on the engine for this purpose, or a suitable alternative.

FIGURE 22–14 Examples of engine camshaft keys that can be used to change the initial engine/injection timing value on an N14 engine model.

3/4-in. Key part no.	Offset in	mm	Timing change	Change in pushrod travel at 19° BTDC in	mm
3021601	None		None	None	
3021595	0.0060	0.15	Retard	0.0030	0.07
3021593	0.0075	0.19	Retard	0.0037	0.09
3021592	0.0115	0.29	Retard	0.0057	0.14
3021594	0.0185	0.47	Retard	0.0092	0.23
3021596	0.0255	0.65	Retard	0.0127	0.32
3021598	0.0310	0.79	Retard	0.0155	0.39
3021597	0.0390	0.99	Retard	0.0195	0.49
3021600	0.0510	1.30	Retard	0.0255	0.65
3021599	0.0115	0.29	Advance	0.0057	0.14
3022352[a]	0.0185	0.47	Advance	0.0092	0.23
3022353[a]	0.0310	0.79	Advance	0.0155	0.39

[a]For mechanical variable timing (MVT) engines.
Source: Cummins Engine Company, Inc.

FIGURE 22–15 *Part number 3375522 injection timing fixture special tools. (Courtesy of Cummins Engine Company, Inc.)*

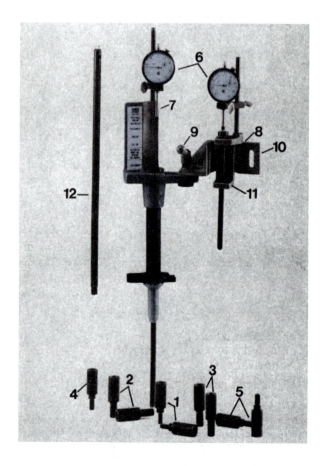

Ref. No.	Detail No.	Description	Qty.
1	3376212	Adapter (K-6, KV, NH 5-1/2 bore)	2*
2	3376213	Adapter (NH 5-1/8) 1/2 X 13 thread	2*
3	3376214	Adapter (NH 5-1/8) 1/2 X 20 thread	2*
4	3376215	Adapter (V6-V8)	1*
5	3376216	Adapter (J & C)	2*
6	3376408	Dial Indicator	2
7	3376409	Spindle Extension	1
8	3376451	Knob	1
9	3376452	Handle Assembly	1
10	3376453	Bracket	1
11	336454	Support Assembly	1
12	3376611	Extension Assembly	1

* Adapters are used by pairs; however are sold by the piece when ordered separately.

Part No. 3376625 Kit must also be purchased to time 10 Litre engines. 3376625 Kit includes 3376217 Adapter, 3376218 Adapter and 3376180 Setting Gauge.

The Timing Fixture is designed to determine the injector push tube travel in relation to the piston travel.

SERVICE TIP   To prevent a possible false reading of the dial indicator setup shown in Figure 22–15, it is always advisable to check the cam follower housing capscrews located on the side of the engine block on 14 L six-cylinder engines. These bolts should be tightened to between 30 and 35 lb-ft (41 to 48 N; pd m), starting from diagonally opposite corners, moving to the two diagonally opposite corners then finishing in the middle of the six-bolt pattern.

Injector Timing Fixture Installation

1.   Select the proper injector timing fixture adapters for the engine to be checked, from the special tool kit (see Figure 22–15).

2.   Attach the correct adapters to the fixture hold-down screws.

3.   Tighten the jam nuts against the adapters to lock them in place.

4.   If your engine does not require adapters, simply remove the jam nuts from the hold-down screws, which will allow the hold-down screw threads to be screwed into the rocker housing. Note that rocker-box removal is not necessary.

5.   Slide both dial indicators to the upper end of their support brackets, which will prevent possible indicator damage when you install the timing fixture onto the cylinder head.

6.   Carefully install the timing fixture over the cylinder to be checked. (The injector has, of course, been removed from the cylinder previously.) Position

the timing tool so that the extension rod attached to the main fixture dial indicator passes through the injector tube hole on into the cylinder.

7. Screw the hold-down screws into the tapped hole or studs of the cylinder head to secure it in place. (Make sure that the timing tool is straight.)

8. Refer to Figure 22–15. Rotate the swivel bracket so that the plunger assembly of the other dial indicator can be located into the injector push tube socket and tighten the capscrew.

9. Engage the dial-indicator plunger rod into the push tube socket and slide the plunger rod bracket down until the spring is compressed approximately 0.050 in. (1.27 mm). Align the edge of the pushrod plunger bracket with the vertical scribe mark on the fixture.

10. With the timing fixture in position, rotate the crankshaft in the normal direction of engine rotation, which is CW from the front. If both dial indicator plunger rods on the timing fixture move together in the upper direction, this will confirm that the piston is moving up the cylinder on its compression stroke.

11. Continue to rotate the engine crankshaft CW slowly until the dial indicator piston plunger rod stops moving.

12. Carefully position the piston dial indicator over the plunger rod in its fully compressed or bottomed state. Slowly allow the dial gauge plunger rod to move up until a reading of 0.025 in. (0.63 mm) is obtained and lock the gauge assembly in position.

13. Slowly rotate the engine from the front in a backward and forward motion until you have determined the rock point of the dial gauge needle pointer. Gently turn the crankshaft CW until the pointer stops moving. Loosen the dial indicator bezel retaining screw and rotate the gauge to place the pointer at the zero position (see Figure 22–16).

14. Rotate the engine over CW from the TDC position until it is 90° ATDC. Position the injector dial indicator over its plunger rod until it is fully compressed, then gently allow it to rise until a reading of 0.025 in. (0.63 mm) registers on the dial gauge and lock it in place. Zero the indicator pointer by loosening the gauge bezel retaining screw, then rotate the bezel until the pointer is opposite the zero reading. Lock it in this position (see Figure 22–17).

15. Refer to Figure 22–18 and rotate the engine CCW from the front until the piston dial gauge registers between 0.425 and 0.450 in. (10.8 to 11.4 mm). This dimension represents a piston position approximately 45 crankshaft degrees BTDC. The reason for this action is to ensure that all gear backlash will be removed when we go to the next procedural step.

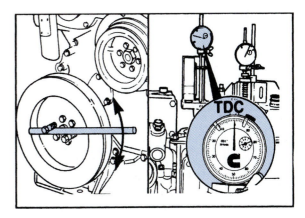

FIGURE 22–16 Placing the No. 1 piston at TDC and zeroing-in the dial indicator above the piston. (Courtesy of Cummins Engine Company, Inc.)

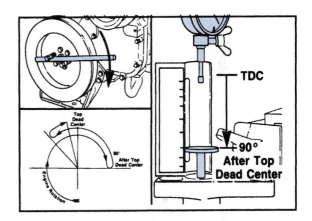

FIGURE 22–17 No. 1 piston at 90° ATDC (after top dead center) to position the injector push tube and dial indicator rod at zero. (Courtesy of Cummins Engine Company, Inc.)

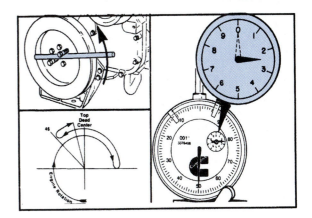

FIGURE 22–18 Rotating the engine crankshaft to place No. 1 piston at 45° BTDC. (Courtesy of Cummins Engine Company, Inc.)

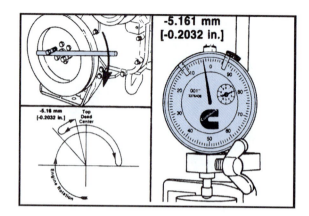

FIGURE 22–19 *Rotate the engine crankshaft to place No. 1 piston at 19° BTDC; piston dial gauge should read 0.2032 in. (5.161 mm) if the engine/injection timing is correct on an N14 PT or Celect engine. (Courtesy of Cummins Engine Company, Inc.)*

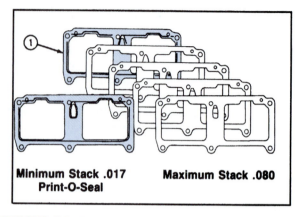

FIGURE 22–20 *Minimum and maximum acceptable cam follower housing gasket thickness stackup for a 2.5 in. (63.5 mm) Big Cam model N14 engine. (Courtesy of Cummins Engine Company, Inc.)*

16. Slowly rotate the engine CW and stop at a position equal to about 30° BTDC. Very gently nudge the engine CW until the piston dial indicator registers 0.2032 in. (5.161 mm) (see Figure 22–19).

17. Look now at the pointer needle value registered on the injector push tube dial indicator assembly. This value is read from zero in a counterclockwise direction. Compare the injector dial indicator value with the specification for your engine, which can be found in:

    a. An engine shop manual

    b. Engine CPL (control parts list) publications

    c. The timing code for your engine, listed on the CPL data plate located at the side on the gear train cover at the front of the engine

18. If the reading you obtain on the injector push tube dial indicator is greater than specified, the engine/injector timing is said to be "slow." If the reading is less than specs, the timing is said to be "fast."

19. To alter an incorrect injector dial indicator reading, we must add or remove gaskets as shown in Figure 22–20 from behind the pivoted cam follower roller boxes located on the side of the engine block. This action changes the lift of the injector push tube, which is basically a pivoted roller follower. With this in mind, the following conditions will hold true:

    a. To decrease the dial indicator reading value, we would add cam follower housing gaskets which would advance the injection timing in relation to the piston position.

    b. To increase the dial indicator reading value, we would remove gaskets from behind the cam follower housing. This would have the effect of retarding the injection timing in relation to the piston position.

20. Each 0.007 in. (0.18 mm) of gasket thickness will affect injection timing by approximately 0.002 in. (0.05 mm) of dial indicator travel on all 2.5 in. (63.5 mm) cam models. Gaskets for the NH/NT 855 2.5 in. cam model engines are available in the following nominal thicknesses:

    a. 0.007 in. (0.18 mm)

    b. 0.017 in. (0.43 mm)

    c. 0.017 in. (0.43 mm), Print-O-Seal gasket

    d. 0.022 in. (0.56 mm)

    e. 0.030 in. (0.76 mm)

SPECIAL NOTE   One Print-O-Seal gasket *must* be used on each cam follower housing. Increasing the gasket thickness will *advance* injection timing, while decreasing gasket thickness will *retard* injection timing.

CAUTION   On 2 in. (50.8 mm) cam model engines, each 0.007 in. (0.18 mm) of gasket thickness will alter the reading on the dial indicator gauge by approximately 0.001 in. (0.025 mm). Gasket selection sizes for the 2 in. cam model engines are 0.007, 0.015, 0.022, 0.030, and 0.037 in. or 0.18, 0.38, 0.56, 0.76, and 0.76 mm.

21. Figure 22–21 lists the various cam follower housing gaskets available for the NH/NT type 855 engines along with the approximate change to the dial

FIGURE 22–21
Cam follower housing gasket thickness and part numbers that will change the initial engine/injection timing value for a model N14 engine.

Gasket part no.	Thickness		Change in pushrod travel at 19° BTDC	
	mm	in.	mm	in.
3020000 (Print-O-Seal)	0.36–0.51	0.014–0.020	0.09–0.13	0.0035–0.005
3020001	0.15–0.20	0.006–0.008	0.04–0.05	0.0015–0.002
3020002	0.36–0.51	0.014–0.020	0.09–0.13	0.0035–0.005
3020003	0.51–0.61	0.020–0.024	0.13–0.15	0.005–0.006
3020004	0.69–0.84	0.027–0.033	0.18–0.20	0.007–0.008

Source: Cummins Engine Company, Inc.

indicator (push tube) travel with the piston 19° BTDC on its compression stroke.

22. Figure 22–20 illustrates that the minimum thickness of gasket stackup that can be used on 2.5 in. (63.5 mm) cam models should never be less than 0.017 in. (0.43 mm), while the maximum stackup should never exceed 0.080 in. (2.03 mm). With a Print-O-Seal gasket (item 1), the sealing bead should always be toward the cam follower housing for effective sealing.

NOTE   On 2 in. (50.8 mm) cam models, the minimum amount of gasket thickness stackup is 0.015 in. (0.38 mm), while the maximum amount is 0.125 in. (3.175 mm).

CAUTION   If injection timing cannot be achieved according to the specification listed in the *CPL Manual* 3379133 with either the minimum or maximum recommended gasket thickness stackup, an offset camshaft key similar to that shown in Figure 22–13 *must* be installed, then the injection timing procedure repeated to determine what cam follower housing gaskets are now required.

NOTE   Use of an offset key will allow the camshaft lobe profile to be rotated slightly while ensuring that the engine gear train timing remains stationary. Cam keys on the NH/NT 855 engines are available in 0.75 in. (19 mm) and 1 in.

(25.4 mm) sizes, with the 0.75 in. offset keys interchangeable with the 1 in. straight keys; however, 0.75 in. straight keys cannot be interchanged for 1 in. offset keys. To retard injection timing, the top of the offset key *always* points in the direction of camshaft rotation. The greater the amount of key offset, the greater the degree of injection timing retardation. This rule can be applied to all Cummins engine models.

STEP TIMING CONTROL SYSTEM

The STC (step timing control) system introduced in 1986 is used on NH/NT 855-14 L engines with the PT fuel system and is designed to allow the engine to operate in advanced injection timing during startup or light-load conditions, and return to normal injection timing for medium- or high-load conditions. The STC system performs the following functions:

During Advanced Timing

- Reduces cold-weather white smoke (hydrocarbons)
- Improves cold-weather idling characteristics
- Improves light-load fuel economy
- Reduces injector tip/cup carboning

During Normal Timing

- Increases engine durability
- Reduces nitrous oxide emissions

The STC system injector is a top stop design which uses two plunger springs and a hydraulic top stop

FIGURE 22–22   *STC (step timing control) top stop injector components. (Courtesy of Cummins Engine Company, Inc.)*

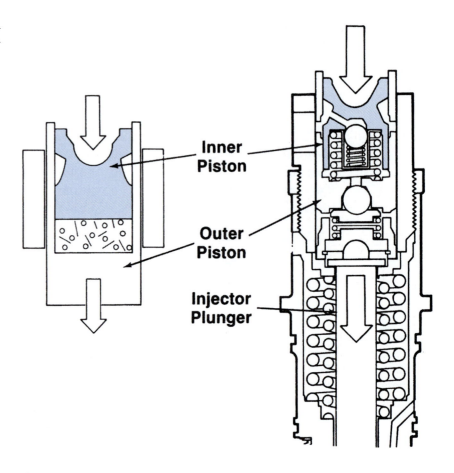

tappet. The tappet assembly illustrated in Figure 22–22 is dependent on engine oil for its operation.

Advanced injection timing occurs when the STC tappet is filled with engine oil. This action lengthens the tappet in the same basic way as that for a gasoline engine hydraulic valve lifter, and therefore effectively increases the injector plunger length for each degree of rotation of the camshaft lobe. Simply put, this means that the injector plunger will be advanced in its effective stroke; therefore, fuel is pressurized and injected earlier than normal into the combustion chamber. This earlier start, or advancement of injection, will create higher-than-normal cylinder pressures and temperatures, with the result being that there will be less white smoke and improved engine performance. The STC tappet operation is similar to that used for the HVT tappet assembly. In the STC system during normal timing, no oil is allowed into the injector tappets; therefore, the tappet piston will collapse before the injector plunger starts to inject fuel because the injector lobe profile on an STC engine camshaft is designed with a greater lift than a conventional engine camshaft.

During advanced camshaft timing, when the tappets are filled with pressurized engine oil, the start of injection will occur earlier, as the injector plunger is lifted sooner per degree of camshaft rotation by the longer tappet assembly (filled with oil). This action causes the plunger to bottom in the injector cup before the cam lobe obtains peak lift. The result of this action is that the added pressure on the tappet will unseat the internal load-cell check ball and permit oil to escape; therefore, the tappet collapses. In summation, in the STC system the tappet collapses before the plunger begins to move when in normal timing, but the tappet collapses after the plunger is finished moving (bottomed in the cup) when in the advanced timing mode of operation.

Tappet Assembly Oil Flow

When the injector cam follower roller is on the inner base circle of the engine camshaft, the injector plunger is at the top of its stroke/travel, and the metering orifice is uncovered inside the injector body to allow fuel to flow into the injector cup. As the injector follower rides up on the camshaft lobe (outer base circle), the metering orifice will close as the plunger descends, and the plunger will seat in the cup forcing fuel into the combustion chamber. During this same period, the drain port in the injector body is open to allow fuel to flow from the drain groove back to the fuel tank to carry heat away from the injector.

Figure 22–22 shows a sectional diagram of the STC tappet assembly. When fuel pump pressure is less than a predetermined value such as during startup and light loads, the system oil control valve is open to allow engine lube oil to flow to an oil manifold which supplies the STC injector tappets. When oil pressure exceeds approximately 10 psi (69 kPa), it moves the tappet inlet check ball off its seat, and oil flows between the inner and outer pistons of the tappet. As the injector cam rotates, the rocker arm will force the inner piston of the tappet down, causing oil pressure trapped below it to increase and force the outer piston (tappet) down as shown in Figure 22–23. This tappet movement also causes the injector plunger to move down. Therefore,

any time that the tappet is filled with oil, the injector plunger will move down earlier, causing fuel injection timing to be "advanced." During advanced timing, oil is trapped in the tappet by the inlet check valve ball and the load-cell check ball.

At the end of the injection cycle, injector force will increase the oil pressure inside the tappet to hold the injector plunger firmly seated in the cup. This causes the tappet oil pressure to rise to between 1100 and 1500 psi (7585 to 10,343 kPa), which unseats the load-cell check ball (lower one in Figure 22–23) in the tappet, and oil drains through holes in the injector adapter and returns to the oil pan through drain passages in the cylinder head and engine block as shown in Figure 22–23. Meanwhile, with the continuing camshaft lift, the plunger makes contact with the socket and sleeve assembly (tappet) and maintains injector plunger seating force.

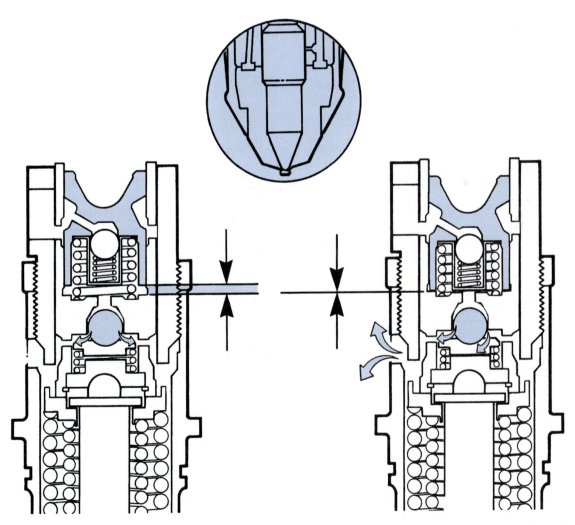

FIGURE 22–23 STC top stop injector tappet assembly components during loaded and unloaded engine positions for an N14 engine. (Courtesy of Cummins Engine Company, Inc.)

When the engine fuel pressure exceeds a predetermined value, the oil flow control valve is closed to prevent any pressurized engine lube oil from entering the tappet and altering the timing. During this condition, static oil will remain in the oil supply manifold and oil lines without affecting operation of the STC tappets. With this oil pressure being lower than 10 psi (69 kPa), no STC can occur. Since no oil is trapped within the tappets inner and outer pistons, injection timing returns to a "normal" mode. With tappet oil removed, the camshaft lift must be greater to force the tappet's inner piston against the outer piston, which results in a later start to fuel injection for both an increase in engine durability and the reduction of nitrous oxide emissions.

M11 Electronic STC

In the Cummins M11 PT equipped engines using STC (step timing control) systems, later production models started in mid-March 2000, use an electronic STC design. In engine applications that encounter high-speed and rapidly varying duty cycles such as excavators (severe-duty cycles), injector cup cavitation can result over many hours of operation. This can create excessive black smoke and/or poor fuel economy. This condition is caused by a slow rail pressure decay rate that corresponds to a slow response time of the hydromechanical STC switch. Under engine operating conditions other than at STC normal timing, the injector metering chamber fuel temperature rises, leading to an increase in the vapor pressure of the diesel fuel. This will result in vapor bubble formation and cavitation damage when the bubbles collapse at the bottom of the injector cup.

This electronic STC kit can also be used on existing M11 engines in the field to improve/fix injector cup cavitation problems. The electronic STC valve allows for a much faster transitional timing response time in the high-speed varying load applications such as an excavator by utilizing two switch points based on fuel rail pressure and engine speed.

Setting the STC Overhead—OBC Method

The setting procedure for the PT-D STC injector has been changed to a camshaft OBC (outer base circle) method, where the crush of the injector plunger to cup is set by tightening the injector rocker lever adjusting screw to a prescribed in.-lb (N · m) torque value. The early method required that the technician use a special STC tappet clearance tool; however, this procedure resulted in engine performance degradation as internal and external wear caused a loss of injector plunger to cup crush, which led to plunger carboning, decreased injector fuel flow, and more retarded injection timing. Therefore, this procedure is no longer valid.

NOTE   Do not attempt to use the IBC (inner base circle) camshaft method on early-model engines, since doing so will result in engine damage and bent pushrods. Figure 22–24a and b lists both the IBC and OBC method.

The procedure required for N14 engines follows.

1. Refer to Figure 22–25 which illustrates the accessory drive pulley VS (valve set) timing marks. When any of these VS marks are aligned with the stationary pointer on the engine front cover, the coupled pistons are actually 90° ATDC. One piston would be on its power stroke, while the other would be on its intake stroke.

Signature / ISX
Injector and Valve Adjustment Sequence

Bar Engine in Direction of Rotation	Pulley Position	Set Cylinder Injector	Valve
Start	A	1	1
Advance to	B	5	5
Advance to	C	3	3
Advance to	A	6	6
Advance to	B	2	2
Advance to	C	4	4
Firing Order: 1-5-3-6-2-4			17c00094

(a)

Injector and Valve Adjustment Sequence

Bar Engine in Direction of Rotation	Pulley Position	Set Cylinder Injector	Valve
Start	A	3	5
Advance to	B	6	3
Advance to	C	2	6
Advance to	A	4	2
Advance to	B	1	4
Advance to	C	5	1
Firing Order: 1-5-3-6-2-4			oi100vd

(b)

FIGURE 22–24   (a) OBC (outer base circle) camshaft position method for adjusting the valve and injector settings for all Cummins six-cylinder 14 L STC, Celect, ISX, and Signature series engine models. (b) IBC (inner base circle) camshaft position method for adjusting the valve and injector settings for earlier-model six-cylinder 14 L engine models. (Courtesy of Cummins Engine Company, Inc.)

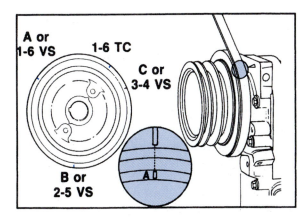

FIGURE 22–25 Engine accessory drive pulley VS (valve set) markings and stationary pointer location on the engine front gear cover of a CW rotating 14 L (855 in³) engine model. (Courtesy of Cummins Engine Company, Inc.)

2. Figure 22–25 shows the position at which the accessory drive pulley should be placed to set both the injector and valves for a given cylinder using the OBC method.

3. To determine what cylinder valves and injector can be set, let us assume that the A mark is aligned. Since the engine is a four-stroke-cycle model, two complete revolutions of the crankshaft are required to set and adjust all valves and injectors. Manually grasp the intake and exhaust valve rocker arms for both cylinders 1 and 6. Whatever rocker arms are loose when you move them confirms that this cylinder is on its power stroke and therefore in the OBC camshaft position. Prepare to adjust both the injector and valves for this cylinder. Let's assume that it is No. 6.

SERVICE TIP If the engine or cylinder heads have been removed for overhaul, the injector and valve adjusting screws will be loose. Therefore, the easiest method to determine which cylinder is on its power stroke is to watch the intake and exhaust valve push tubes carefully (or lightly place two fingers on the top of each tube). When both the intake and exhaust valve push tubes move downward, this confirms that the valves are closed and that the piston is on its power stroke. You can also look visually to see if both push tubes are level when viewed from the side.

4. Refer to Figure 22–26, which lists the N14 engine model, engine CPL number, and the specifications for both the injector and valve adjustments, as well as for the C-brake. Let us assume that the CPL stamped on the CPL plate on the side of the engine front timing cover indicates a CPL No. 805. We will therefore set the No. 6 STC injector to 105 in.-lb (12 N · m).

5. Select an accurate inch-pound (N · m) torque wrench and loosen the No. 6 injector rocker arm locknut.

NOTE The injector adjusting screw may be a slotted type on non-C-brake engines, or employ a hex-head screw on C-brake engines. Therefore, obtain the correct type of torque wrench socket prior to adjustment.

6. Use a screwdriver and lightly run the injector adjusting screw down until a slight step up in effort is felt. Do this three or four times to settle down the linkage and to squeeze any oil out. Then back the screw off until it is loose.

FIGURE 22–26 Sample valve adjustment specifications. Can also be found on the engine CPL (control parts list) plate. (Courtesy of Cummins Engine Company, Inc.)

Engine model	Engine CPL	Injector adjusting screw torque		Intake valve lash	Exhaust valve lash	C-brake lash
		in.-lb	N · m			
NBCIV	621.633, 903, 904, 805	105	12	0.014	0.027	0.016
86BCIV	910, 827, 1185, 1188, 1210, 1211, 1256, 1280	90	10	0.014	0.027	0.016
N14	1374, 1380, 1395 1405, 1507	125	14	0.014	0.027	0.023

FIGURE 22–27 *Using an inch-pound torque wrench to set/adjust the injector preload to the correct specifications. (Courtesy of Cummins Engine Company, Inc.)*

7. Refer to Figure 22–27 and place the torque wrench into position over the injector adjusting screw. Carefully tighten the injector adjusting screw until the torque wrench clicks, or if using a dial-type wrench, watch the torque wrench. Tighten the screw until 105 in.-lb (12 N · m) is obtained.

8. Hold the adjusting screw and tighten the locknut to 40 lb-ft (54 N · m) on New Big Cam IV engines, or to 50 lb-ft (68 N · m) on 1988 Big Cam IVs.

9. Proceed to set the intake and exhaust valves on the same cylinder as that for the injector just completed. Refer to Figure 22–26 for the correct valve set clearance. Torque the valve rocker arm locknuts to the same spec as for the injector described in step 8.

10. If the engine is equipped with a C-brake, check and adjust the slave piston to exhaust valve crosshead with the VS pulley mark in the same position as that used for the valve adjustment. The C-brake clearance can be found on the C-brake data plate or Jacobs brake label. On Big Cam 14 L engine models, this is usually 0.018 in. (0.46 mm). Use either a feeler gauge or a dial indicator for this procedure.

Celect-Valve and Injector Adjustment

The procedure required to set and adjust the valves and injectors on the Celect-equipped L10 and N14 L engines is similar to that for a PT-equipped Cummins engine. Refer to Figure 22–25, which illustrates the position of the accessory drive pulley markings at the front of the engine. Manually rotate the crankshaft over CW from the front to align the A or 1–6 VS (valve set) mark on the accessory drive pulley with the stationary pointer on the engine gear cover.

The Celect engines can have both the valves and injectors set at the same time on any one cylinder (OBC method). With the A or 1–6 VS mark aligned

with the gear case pointer, check to see if both the intake and exhaust valves are closed on cylinder 1 or 6. This can be confirmed by the fact that when you manually pull up and push down on the valve rocker arms, they should both rattle or indicate that free play exists between the end of the rocker arm and valve crosshead assembly. At the same time the injector plunger should be at the bottom of its stroke. Once you have determined whether the cylinder 1 or 6 injector and valves are ready to be adjusted, refer to Figure 22–24a, which illustrates the respective accessory drive pulley location to perform both valve and injector adjustments.

NOTE The engine should be at a temperature not higher than 140°F (60°C) when performing injector and valve adjustments.

Adjustment Procedure

1. If we assume that you are starting with the No. 1 cylinder, the A or 1–6 VS mark on the accessory drive pulley will be aligned with the stationary pointer.

2. Bottom the injector plunger three to four times by installing an inch-pound (N · m) torque wrench with a slotted screwdriver adapter in the adjusting screw slot. Turn the torque wrench until it obtains a value of 25 in.-lb (2.82 N · m). This action will remove all fuel from below the plunger so that we can obtain an accurate setting.

3. Gently turn the injector rocker arm adjusting screw down until it just bottoms.

4. Carefully back out the injector adjusting screw 120°, which is the equivalent of two flats on the locknut.

5. Hold the screw and tighten the locknut to between 40 and 45 lb-ft (54 to 61 N · m).

SPECIAL NOTE On N14 engines, two flats (120°) on the locknut will be equivalent to 0.020 in. (0.51 mm) of clearance, while on the L10 engines, two flats are equal to 0.023 in. (0.58 mm). Cummins specifies that this lash must be between 0.018 and 0.025 in. (0.46 to 0.64 mm). This adjustment can be performed as stated above, or a dial indicator can be used if desired.

6. Once you have adjusted the injector, set the valve lash on that same cylinder to the specifications listed on the engine CPL data plate, which is located on the side of the engine gear case cover.

CUMMINS CELECT SYSTEM

The information in this section describes an overview of the function, purpose, and operation of the Cummins Celect (Cummins Electronics) system, the generic concept applied to all Cummins electronically controlled engines. For broader and much more detailed coverage, or if you intend to perform service/diagnostics/troubleshooting on Cummins Celect, Celect Plus, ISB, ISC, ISL, ISM, and ISX/Signature engine models, it is necessary that you obtain from your local Cummins dealer the appropriate service, troubleshooting, and repair manuals which contain data, information, and procedures required to safely and effectively withdraw ECM fault codes, perform snapshots of engine operation, short-out individual injectors, or conduct an automated cylinder performance test. Some of the more appropriate manuals are listed below.

- Troubleshooting and Repair Manual, CELECT Plus System, Volume 1 and 11, Bulletin No. 3666130-01.
- INSITE Celect User's Manual, Bulletin No. 3885785.
- Bulletin No. 3666018-04. Plasticized Celect Colored Wiring Diagram (great for in-shop use when tracing circuits). Also contains electrical and sensor specs, plus fault code information.
- INSITE Celect Plus User's Manual, Bulletin No. 3666147-01.
- Operation and Maintenance Manual, Signature and ISX Engines, Bulletin No. 3666251-01.
- Features Manual, Signature, ISX, and ISM Engines. Bulletin No. 3666320-01.
- Troubleshooting and Repair Manual, Electronic Control System, Signature, ISX, and QSX15 Engines, Volume 1 and 11, Bulletin No. 3666259-01.
- Troubleshooting and Repair Manual, Signature, ISX, and QSX15 Engines, Bulletin No. 3666239-01.
- Bulletin No. 3666268-01. Plasticized Signature/ISX Colored Wiring Diagram (great for in-shop use when tracing circuits). Also contains electrical and sensor specs, plus fault code information.
- INSITE Signature User's manual, Bulletin No. 3397063.
- Troubleshooting and Repair Manual, ISB Light-Duty Fuel System, ISB Engines, Bulletin No. 3666288-00.
- Troubleshooting and Repair Manual, Electronic Control System, ISB and QSB5.9 Engines, Volume 1 and 11, Bulletin No. 3666194-01.
- Bulletin No. 3666195-02. Plasticized ISB Colored Wiring Diagram (great for in-shop use when trac-

ing circuits). Also contains electrical and sensor specs, plus fault code information. Order Bulletin No. 3666325-01 for the ISB 23-Pin Wiring Diagram.
- Operation and Maintenance Manual, ISC Engine. Bulletin No. 3666262-000.
- Troubleshooting and Repair Manual, Electronic Control System, ISC, QSC8.3, and ISL Engines, Volume 1 and 11, Bulletin No. 3666271-01.
- Bulletin No. 3666267-01. Plasticized ISC Colored Wiring Diagram (great for in-shop use when tracing circuits). Also contains electrical and sensor specs, plus fault code information.

Celect Fuel System Flow

The fuel pump shown in Figure 22–28 is driven from the rear of the air compressor on an N14 engine. Refer to Figure 22–29 to see more clearly the location of the fuel system components. The fuel pump is a gear type

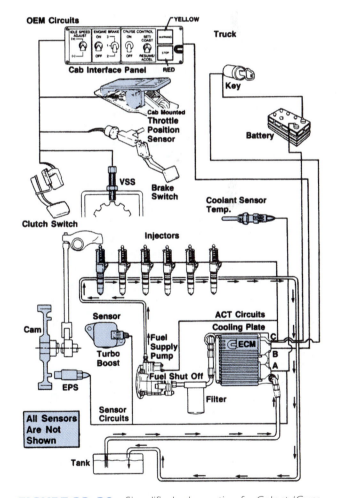

FIGURE 22–28 Simplified schematic of a Celect (Cummins Electronics) system for a six-cylinder engine. (Courtesy of Cummins Engine Company, Inc.)

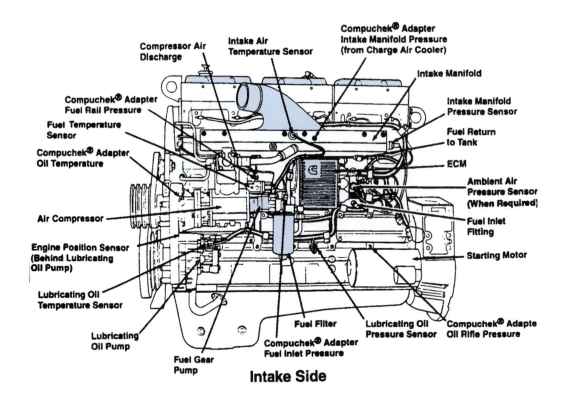

Intake Side

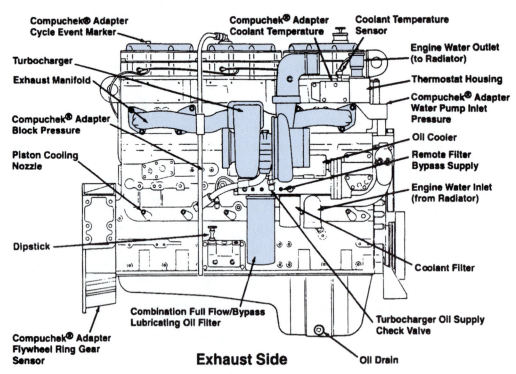

Exhaust Side

FIGURE 22–29 Intake and exhaust side views of component locations of a six-cylinder N14 Celect engine model. (Courtesy of Cummins Engine Company, Inc.)

644

and operates similarly to the gear transfer pump that was used on earlier PT (pressure-time) fuel systems. Figure 22–30 is a cross-sectional view of the fuel pump and the flow through the housing, and Figure 22–30 illustrates the basic fuel flow into and through the electronically controlled injector. Fuel is drawn from the tank by the pump where it can pass through a primary fuel filter or fuel/water separator filter assembly before it flows into and through a cooler plate bolted to the rear of the ECM assembly. The purpose of directing fuel through the cooling plate is to ensure that the electronics package components are maintained at an acceptable operating temperature level during engine operation. Fuel then flows through a filter and on to the inlet side of the gear transfer pump. The system pressure and flow rate will vary proportionally to engine speed; the maximum system operating pressure ranges between 140–150 psi (965–1034 kPa) at rated engine speed. Within the fuel pump, a spring-loaded bypass valve opens to bypass fuel back to the suction side of the pump to regulate fuel pressure. Fuel under pressure is directed through the electric solenoid on top of the fuel pump, which is similar to that used in the earlier PT fuel systems. When the ignition key is switched ON, this solenoid is energized. Turning the key switch OFF deenergizes the fuel pump solenoid to allow engine shutdown by blocking further fuel flow out of the pump assembly.

ECI Injector

Fuel Supply Pump

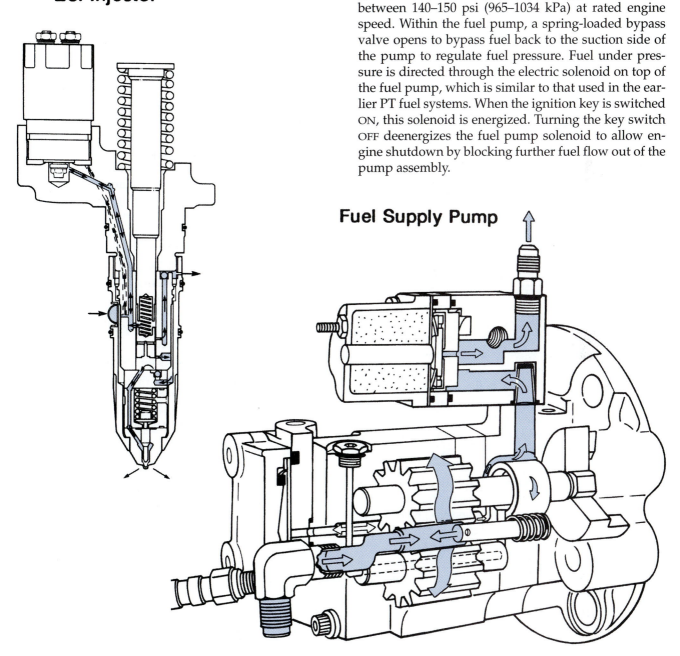

FIGURE 22–30 *Typical schematic showing the fuel injector and gear pump flow for a Celect model engine.* (Courtesy of Cummins Engine Company, Inc.)

Fuel from the gear pump flows into the rear of the
cylinder head on N14 engines, where a common rail allows all injectors to receive fuel through the cast manifold within the cylinder head. The pump is designed to
circulate an excess amount of fuel to and through the
injectors, so that fuel not used for injection purposes is
used to cool and lubricate the internal components, as
well as to purge any air from the fuel system and injectors. Fuel from the inlet manifold enters the injector as
shown in Figure 22–30 at the left center of the body
through a small circular filter screen similar to that for
the PT injector systems. Fuel is then directed up to and
around a small poppet valve. This poppet valve is electronically controlled by a signal from the ECM. Injection can occur only when this PWM signal closes this
small internal poppet valve as the injector pushrod is
activating the injector rocker arm assembly. Rocker
arm motion is required to raise the trapped fuel pressure within the injector body to a high enough level to
lift the needle valve from its seat in the spray tip (cup).
Therefore, the start of injection, the quantity of fuel metered, and the duration of injection are electronically
controlled by the ECM.

The injector is mechanically operated by a rocker
arm and pushrod assembly. The injector contains three
O-rings for fuel sealing purposes and it is held in the
cylinder head by use of a hold-down clamp and bolt.
The injector requires rocker arm actuation of the
plunger to create the high fuel pressures necessary for
injection purposes. To control both the start of injection
timing and the quantity of fuel metered, the ECM sends
out a PWM (pulse-width-modulated) electrical signal
to each injector. The initial PWM signal determines the
start of the injection. The duration of this signal determines how long the injector can effectively continue to
spray fuel into the combustion chamber as the plunger

is forced down by the rocker arm assembly. A shorter
PWM signal means that the effective stroke of the injector plunger will be decreased, while a longer PWM signal means that the effective stroke will be increased.
Simply put, this means that the longer the duration of
the PWM signal, the greater the amount of metered fuel
that will be delivered to the combustion chamber. The
greater the fuel rate, the greater will be the developed
horsepower. The start of injection and the duration of
the PWM signal is determined by the ECM based on the
various input sensor signals and the preprogrammed
PROM information within the ECM. Each PROM is designed for a specific engine/truck combination based
on the desired horsepower setting and rpm, the tire
size, and gear ratios used in the vehicle.

Figure 22–31 illustrates a typical electronic injector
circuit arrangement. To control fuel metering (quantity)
and timing, the injector solenoid valves are actuated by
a PWM signal from the ECM. Each injector solenoid is
connected to the ECM by both a supply and a return
wire shown as wire 1 and wire 10 in this example for an
ISM engine from ECM harness connector C. Note that
each solenoid valve within the fuel injector is normally
open, and is closed by an electrical pulse from the ECM
when fuel injection is required. Typical injector fault
codes can be found in the fault code listing shown in
Table 22–1 in this section. For example, a Cummins fault
flash code 311 for an M11 engine would show as an
SAE–SID (S) system identifier S001 accompanied by a
failure mode identifier (FMI) 6 to trigger the yellow
warning light on the instrument panel. This fault code
is set when current is detected at the No. 1 injector
return pin 10 of the actuator harness when the voltage
supply at pin 1 of the actuator harness is OFF. This fault
code would cause an engine speed derate condition.

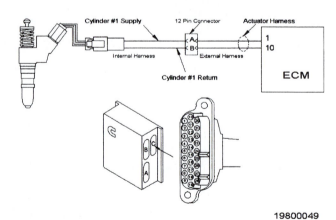

19800049

FIGURE 22–31   Example Celect engine injector solenoid wire connections to the ECM. (Courtesy of Cummins
Engine Company, Inc.)

TABLE 22–1   *Some examples of Celect engine model fault codes*

Fault Code Lamp	PID(P) SID(S) FMI	Reason	Effect
311 Y	S001 6	Current detected at No. 1 injector return pin No. 10 of AH when voltage supply at pin No. 01 of AH is off.	Speed derate to 1400 to 1600 RPM. Current to injector is shut off.
312 Y	S005 6	Current detected at No. 5 injector return pin No. 02 of AH when voltage supply at pin No. 11 of AH is off.	Speed derate to 1400 to 1600 RPM. Current to injector is shut off.
313 Y	S003 6	Current detected at No. 3 injector return pin No. 12 of AH when voltage supply at pin No. 03 of AH is off.	Speed derate to 1400 to 1600 RPM. Current to injector is shut off.
314 Y	S006 6	Current detected at No. 6 injector return pin No. 04 of AH when voltage supply at pin No. 13 of AH is off.	Speed derate to 1400 to 1600 RPM. Current to injector is shut off.
315 Y	S002 6	Current detected at No. 2 injector return pin No. 14 of AH when voltage supply at pin No. 05 of AH is off.	Speed derate to 1400 to 1600 RPM. Current to injector is shut off.
321 Y	S004 6	Current detected at No. 4 injector return pin No. 06 of AH when voltage supply at pin No. 15 of AH is off.	Speed derate to 1400 to 1600 RPM. Current to injector is shut off.
322 Y	S001 5	No current detected at No. 1 injector return pin No. 10 of AH when voltage supply at pin No. 01 of AH is on.	Speed derate to 1400 to 1600 RPM. Current to injector is shut off.
323 Y	S005 5	No current detected at No. 5 injector return pin No. 02 of AH when voltage supply at pin No. 11 of AH is on.	Speed derate to 1400 to 1600 RPM. Current to injector is shut off.
324 Y	S003 5	No current detected at No. 3 injector return pin No. 12 of AH when voltage supply at pin No. 03 of AH is on.	Speed derate to 1400 to 1600 RPM. Current to injector is shut off.
325 Y	S006 5	No current detected at No. 6 injector return pin No. 04 of AH when voltage supply at pin No. 13 of AH is on.	Speed derate to 1400 to 1600 RPM. Current to injector is shut off.
331 Y	S002 5	No current detected at No. 2 injector return pin No. 14 of AH when voltage supply at pin No. 05 of AH is on.	Speed derate to 1400 to 1600 RPM. Current to injector is shut off.
332 Y	S004 5	No current detected at No. 4 injector return pin No. 06 of AH when voltage supply at pin No. 15 of AH is on.	Speed derate to 1400 to 1600 RPM. Current to injector is shut off.
333 Y	S254 12	No voltage detected on one or more of the injector supply pins No. 01, 03, 05, 11, 13, or 15 of AH when power is commanded.	Speed derate to 1400 to 1600 RPM.
335 R	S254 12	RAM memory read/write error inside ECM.	Unpredictable—possible no start (no power to either fuel solenoid or injectors).
341 R	S254 12	ROM memory checksum error inside ECM.	Unpredictable—possible no start (no power to either fuel solenoid or injectors).
342 R	S253 12	ECM not calibrated with ESDN or internal EEPROM memory checksum error.	Engine will not start (no power to fuel solenoid).
343 Y	S254 12	Micro-processor communication error inside ECM.	None on performance.
351 Y	S254 12	Injector power supply below specifications inside ECM.	Possible no noticeable effects. Possible reduced performance.

Source: Cummins Engine Company, Inc.

Figure 22–32 illustrates the basic design arrangement of the injector assembly in schematic form. Contained within the injector is a timing plunger, a return spring, and an injector control valve, which is the key to the operation, since this electrically operated valve receives an energize/deenergize voltage control signal from the ECM, which determines the actual start of injection. The length of time that this solenoid is energized determines the quantity of metered fuel which will actually be injected to the combustion chamber. Also within the injector body is a metering spill port which must be closed to allow injection, a metering check valve, fuel supply passages, the closed nozzle subassembly, the metering piston, the bias spring, and the spill-timing port. When the injector receives a signal from the ECM, the small injector control valve will close and the metering phase begins while the metering piston and timing plunger are bottomed in the injector.

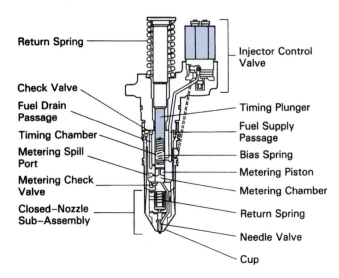

FIGURE 22–32 Basic component identification of a Celect electronically controlled fuel injector assembly. (Courtesy of Cummins Engine Company, Inc.)

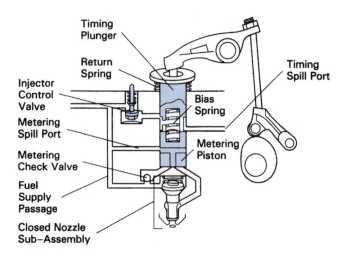

FIGURE 22–33 Basic engine camshaft and mechanical operating mechanism to actuate a Celect injector. (Courtesy of Cummins Engine Company, Inc.)

Study Figure 22–32 first so that you can associate the differences between the Celect injector and the standard PTD injector. Once you know these differences, it will make it easier for you to understand the operation since pushrod and rocker arm actuation are still necessary to create the high pressures necessary for injection purposes.

Injector Operation

Figure 22–33 illustrates in a much more simplified version the major operating components required to effectively meter and time the fuel delivery rate to the combustion chamber. The same components that were shown earlier in Figure 22–32 are laid out slightly different in this diagram; however, this simplified diagram will allow you to better understand the system's operation. The following sequence of events occur as described:

1. In Figure 22–33, both the metering piston and timing plunger are bottomed in the injector. Note carefully that the injector solenoid-operated control valve is held closed by the action of a small spring. This is the *start* of the metering action.

2. As the engine camshaft rotates, the injector pushrod cam follower roller will ride down the cam ramp, thereby allowing the rocker arm and pushrod to be forced up and down by the energy of the timing plunger return spring as shown in Figure 22–34. Fuel at gear pump pressure of approximately 150 psi (1034 kPa) can now flow into the fuel supply passage and unseat the small lower check valve. This action allows the metering chamber to be charged with pressurized fuel as long as the timing plunger is being pulled upward by the force of the large external return spring. This

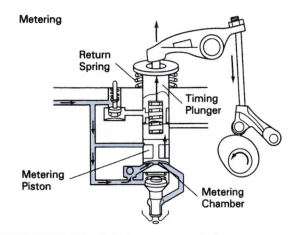

FIGURE 22–34 Initial engine camshaft rotation to provide charging of the Celect injector with pressurized fuel. (Courtesy of Cummins Engine Company, Inc.)

fuel pressure acting on the bottom of the metering piston forces it to maintain contact with the timing plunger within the bore of the injector body.

3. Metering ends when the ECM energizes the injector control valve, thereby causing it to open. Pressurized fuel can now flow through the open injector control valve into the upper timing chamber, which will effectively stop any further upward travel of the metering piston. This action is shown in Figure 22–35. To ensure that the metering piston remains stationary, the small bias spring in the timing chamber holds it stationary while the timing plunger continues to move upward due to camshaft rotation. The fuel and bias spring forces acting on the metering piston will ensure that adequate fuel pressure is maintained below the piston to keep the small lower metering check ball (valve) closed. This sequence of events will allow a precisely metered quantity

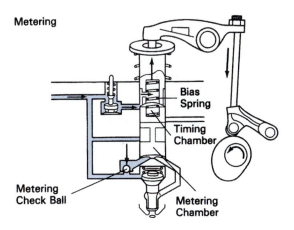

FIGURE 22–35 End of Celect injector metering; ECM controls the small injector control valve by a PWM (pulse-width-modulated) electrical signal. (Courtesy of Cummins Engine Company, Inc.)

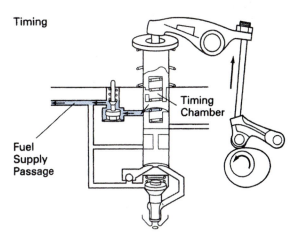

FIGURE 22–36 Celect injector timing action. (Courtesy of Cummins Engine Company, Inc.)

of fuel to be trapped in the metering chamber. Note that this quantity of trapped fuel is what will actually be injected into the combustion chamber.

4. As long as the timing plunger moves upward due to the rotating camshaft lobe action and the force of the external return spring on the injector, the upper timing chamber will continue to fill with pressurized fuel.

5. When the engine camshaft lobe starts to lift the injector cam follower roller, the pushrod moves up and the rocker arm reverses this motion to push the timing plunger downward. On the initial downward movement the injector control valve remains open and fuel flows from the timing chamber and through the control valve to the fuel supply passage. In other words, a small amount of fuel spills from the timing chamber. Figure 22–36 illustrates the action. When the ECM closes the control valve, fuel is trapped in the timing chamber; this fuel will act as a solid hydraulic link between the timing plunger and metering piston; therefore, the metering piston is forced to move downward with the descending timing plunger being moved by rocker arm action. The downward movement of the timing plunger therefore causes a rapid increase in the trapped fuel within the metering chamber. At approximately 5000 psi (34,475 kPa) the tapered needle valve in the tip of the injector will be lifted up against the force of its return spring and injection begins.

6. Injection will continue until the spill passage of the downward-moving metering piston uncovers the spill port as shown in Figure 22–37. Fuel pressure within the metering chamber is lost and the needle valve will be forced back on its seat by its return spring. This in effect terminates injection. Immediately after the metering spill port has been uncovered, the upper edge of the metering piston also passes the timing spill port (Figure 22–38) to allow fuel within the upper

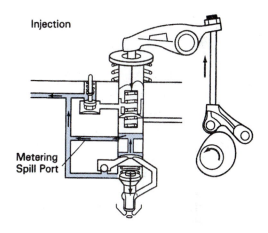

FIGURE 22–37 Start of Celect injection; injection ends when the metering spill port is opened. (Courtesy of Cummins Engine Company, Inc.)

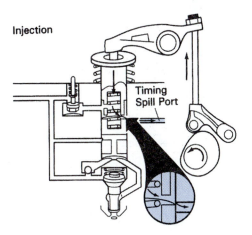

FIGURE 22–38 Spilling fuel from the timing spill port after injection ends. (Courtesy of Cummins Engine Company, Inc.)

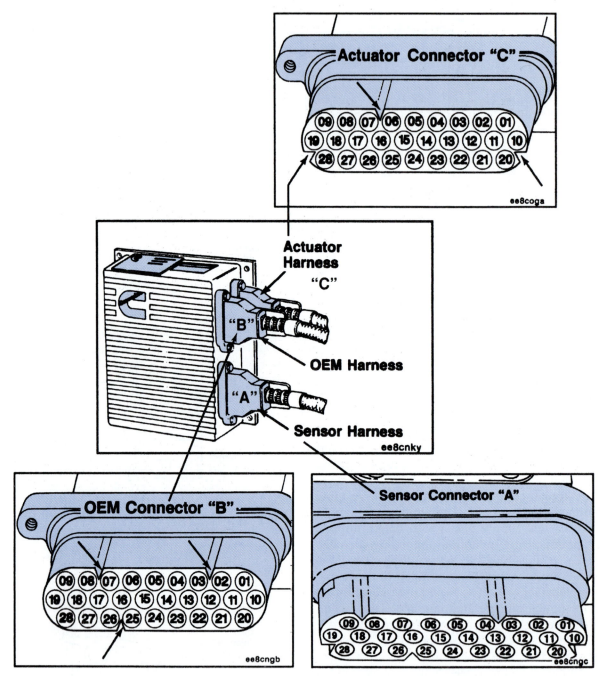

FIGURE 22-39 Location and identification of the three ECM wire harness connectors and individual pin numbers of a Celect (non-plus) system. (Courtesy of Cummins Engine Company, Inc.)

timing chamber to be spilled back to the fuel drain as the timing plunger completes its downward movement. The injection cycle has now been completed.

You can now appreciate that the start of injection is controlled by the ECM closing the small injector control valve. The point in the compression-cycle when the control valve closes thereby varies the actual start of injection timing. Opening of the small injector control valve terminates metering and therefore controls just how much fuel will be trapped and injected. In this manner the Celect system through ECM action allows the engine power to be closely tailored to changing demands. Both fuel economy and exhaust emissions can be improved substantially.

ECM Connectors

The ECM has three wire harnesses plugged into it to control the Celect and Celect Plus systems. Figure 22–39 illustrates these three individual wire harnesses:

1. The sensor harness identified as A receives electrical signals from all of the engine-mounted sensors, which are shown in Figure 22–29. The sensors tell the ECM the current state of the engine operation regarding throttle position, air intake manifold temperature, ambient pressure, turbocharger boost temperature, engine piston position from a sensor located to monitor a pin attached to the engine camshaft gear, engine coolant and oil temperature, and oil pressure. Some engines are equipped with a fuel pressure and fuel temperature sensor.

2. The OEM (original equipment manufacturer such as a truck builder) harness identified as item B is wired to all of the vehicle instrument panel control switches. These include the cruise-control switch and the vehicle speed sensor which monitors the transmission output shaft rpm, an instant readout of fuel consumption, engine compression brake controls, and the cab interface panel. This harness is not supplied by Cummins but by the truck or equipment manufacturer.

3. The actuator harness identified as item C controls the injector solenoids.

The three ECM harness connectors cannot be inadvertently installed into the wrong position. This is ensured by the fact that each connector has a different *key design feature* as illustrated in Figure 22–39, so that each connector is readily identifiable by the letter A, B, or C. Note also that each connector pin is identified by a number that can be traced back through the system wiring diagram. Figure 22–40a illustrates the wires that are connected to the oil temperature sensor ECM connector A. This example shows wires 3 and 6. If this sensor and wires were operating outside a designed limit, the ECM would log a fault code 215 (SAE-PID = parameter identifier 175, and FMI = failure mode identifier 1).

Figure 22–40b illustrates the OEM-ECM connector B. This example shows wires 17 and 26, which are the two wires connected to the engine tachometer. Figure 22–40c illustrates the ECM actuator harness C. This example shows how the battery is connected into

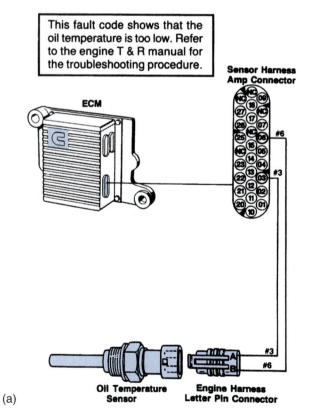

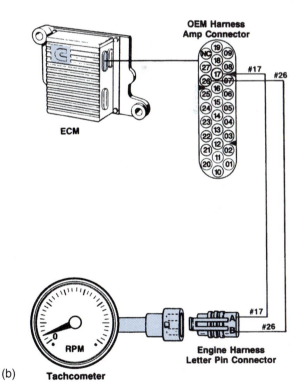

(a)

(b)

FIGURE 22–40 (a) Celect engine sensor wire harness example showing the oil temperature sensor wiring—fault code 215 (PID 175, FMI 1); [PID = parameter identifier, FMI = failure mode identifier]. (b) OEM wiring harness connection showing the wiring to the electronic engine tachometer—fault code 234 (PID 190, FMI 0). (Courtesy of Cummins Engine Company, Inc.)

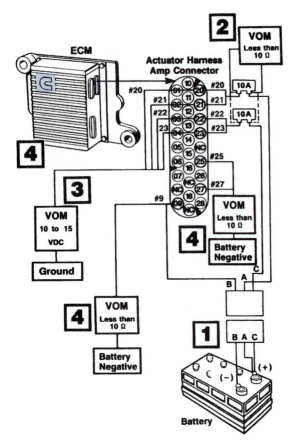

FIGURE 22–40 (continued). (c) Actuator harness connector illustrating typical wire connections—fault code 434 (SID 251, FMI 4). (Courtesy of Cummins Engine Company, Inc.)

the system, some of the fuses used, and some of the typical multimeter readings that might be obtained when checking the system. By using these wiring diagrams and a *breakout box* similar to that shown for the DDEC system in Figure 21–38, or by using special pin-out jumper wires inserted into specific numbered connector holes, a multimeter can be employed to check any wire system for a voltage or resistance value. Then compare the values with Cummins' specs.

Celect Plus

To many people the word *electronics* simply encompasses household conveniences and various forms of entertainment. In the trucking industry, however, the word takes on a whole new meaning. Where Cummins products are concerned, the catch phrase is *Celect Plus*. The C in *Celect* stands for "Cummins," the *elect* stands for "electronics," and the *Plus* means that you get everything that you need plus more.

Behind the Celect Plus name tag the engines have been vastly improved.

The Celect Plus ECM requires three 28-pin AMP connectors with modified keying on each connector to ensure that older Celect engine models/ECMs are not installed mistakenly on Celect Plus engines. Figure 22–41 illustrates the A (sensor), B (OEM), and C (actuator) harness connectors used on the Celect Plus ECMs. The sensor harness and actuator harness have been combined to form the engine harness with a sensor connector and an actuator connector.

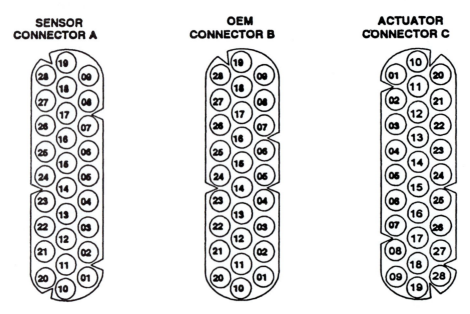

FIGURE 22–41 Celect Plus ECM 28-pin AMP connectors identification. (Courtesy of Cummins Engine Company, Inc.)

FIGURE 22–42 *Using the idle-speed adjust toggle switch to move forward or back to the next or previous fault code. (Courtesy of Cummins Engine Company, Inc.)*

The Celect Plus system employs an intake manifold temperature sensor known as an ETAT (exposed thermistor air temperature) sensor, which has a faster response time to air-temperature changes and can only be used on Celect Plus engines and specified transit bus calibrations. The ETAT sensor is exposed to airflow through the caged plastic housing. In addition, Celect Plus engines employ a factory-installed AAP (ambient air pressure) sensor, which is a flange-mounted design mounted to the engine with two capscrews.

Vehicle Cab Interface Panel

The dash-mounted cab interface panel illustrated in Figure 22–42 can be activated by the driver through a series of small toggle switches. This panel contains several elements:

1. An idle-speed adjust switch can be used to adjust the engine idle speed between 550 and 800 rpm. Each time the switch is moved briefly to either the + or − position, the idle speed changes by approximately 25 rpm.

2. The engine compression brake control switch has an ON/OFF position to activate either a Jacobs or Cummins C-brake system. The other toggle switch used with the engine brake control can be placed into position 1, 2, or 3. In position 1, on NT (14 L) engines, only two cylinders are activated; position 2 activates the compression brake on four cylinders, and position 3 allows all six engine cylinders to provide compression braking.

3. The cruise control panel has two toggle switches; one of these is simply the ON/OFF switch. The second one is actually the cruise-control position select switch that the truck driver actually uses to set and adjust the cruise control speed while driving. This toggle switch can be used to set and adjust the engine

speed while the PTO is in operation. Take careful note that some truck manufacturers may choose to employ a labeling system with a cruise-control system that reads SET/ACCEL and RESUME/COAST instead of what is shown in the example of Figure 22–42 which is SET/COAST and RESUME/ACCEL. The cruise-control switch operates in the same manner as that found on most passenger cars equipped with a cruise-control feature. The cruise control will not operate if the brake pedal has been depressed. In addition, the cruise control will not operate below 30 mph (48 km/h).

To adjust the cruise-control set speed up, move the control select switch briefly to the ACCEL position once for 1-mph increments, or twice to this same position for 2-mph increments. To reduce the speed, use the COAST select switch in the same manner just described. The engine PTO is controlled from the cruise-control switches while the vehicle is in a parked position, although there are certain Cummins-approved applications that allow the vehicle to move up to 6 mph (10 km/h) during PTO operation.

Trip Information

The Cummins RoadRelay (Figure 22–43) feature gives you access to vital operational data. Celect Plus via RoadRelay provides information about how an engine is being operated under various conditions such as idling, PTO, and when pulling a load. You can use the in-depth information about vehicle operation, including areas such as fuel, braking, and shifting, to improve your productivity and efficiency. The RoadRelay and Detroit Diesel's Pro-Driver shown in Figure 21–35 are similar. You can also access this information through a variety of Cummins electronic products and download directly to a PC.

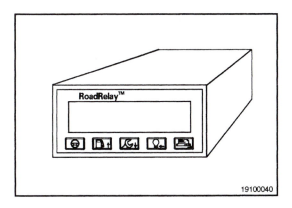

FIGURE 22–43 *Schematic of an instrument panel–mounted RoadRelay unit used to advise the driver of fault codes and engine/vehicle operating conditions. (Courtesy of Cummins Engine Company, Inc.)*

A security feature, *antitheft*, prevents the engine from starting until the driver enters a unique password into the RoadRelay (as many as six unique passwords may be entered into the RoadRelay). The password is sent from the RoadRelay to the ECM. If the password is valid, the ECM will deactivate antitheft. The customer may then start the engine.

IMPORTANT INFORMATION   Do not forget your password! When protected by the antitheft feature, the engine will not start without entering the password. Do not write your password where it can be found by a thief. Keep it someplace safe where you can find it easily.

In temperatures above 140°F (60°C) or below −4°F (−20°C) the RoadRelay display may not be visible. The antitheft feature will still operate. Enter the password as usual after the keyswitch has been turned ON and RoadRelay has powered up.

Troubleshooting Symptoms

Approach *electronic* engine troubleshooting in a systematic manner just as you would for a mechanically equipped and governed engine. Plugged fuel filters or air filters will result in the same basic complaints on either engine type, namely, a lack of power and visible exhaust smoke. This book cannot provide the test sequences that should be followed to successfully troubleshoot all of the various trouble codes for a Cummins engine. Refer to the Cummins Celect troubleshooting manual and follow closely the *troubleshooting trees* in the performance of each repair; these will guide you through a sequence of possible causes and symptoms. Refer to Chapter 25 for more details on troubleshooting.

DIAGNOSTIC FAULT CODES

Overview

All electronic engines are designed with features that permit the ECM sensor monitoring system to continually review each and every sensor during engine operation. Basically this feature checks if the sensor operating parameters are within the predesigned range for operating voltage and current. There are two warning systems used. One monitors the electronic fuel system, while the second monitors an engine protection system. If a sensor signal to the ECM is detected as being out of range, then the ECM can warn the equipment operator of this condition by turning on a circuit to illuminate a yellow and red light located on the instrument panel as shown in Figure 22–44. The yellow or red

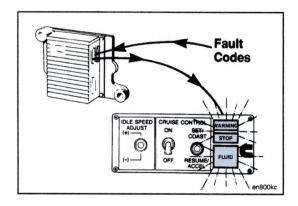

FIGURE 22–44   *Monitored systems and fault codes will trigger/illuminate either the low fluid, warning, or stop engine lamps. (Courtesy of Cummins Engine Company, Inc.)*

light when illuminated indicates that a system fault has been detected, and the ECM will log a three-digit diagnostic fault code (DFC) in memory for withdrawal at a later time by a service technician using special diagnostic equipment.

Illumination of the yellow warning light signifies that a fault has occurred, but the vehicle can continue to be operated. Based upon the severity of the fault condition, the ECM may cause an engine derate condition between 1400 and 1600 rpm. The operator should have the fault code condition checked at the first available opportunity. When the red stop light signifies a much more serious condition, the engine protection system will activate a warning device (either a lamp or buzzer, or both) in the cab when a system fault occurs. Note that the lamp labels and colors can vary by OEM. If the ECM has been programmed to do so (option), when the red stop light illuminates indicating a serious fault, a timed automatic engine shutdown will follow. The operator should pull over to the side of the highway as soon as possible and shut off the engine. This automatic shutdown feature is typically programmed for 30 seconds, although a temporary override switch is an option to permit the vehicle to be safely pulled over to the side of the road. In addition, a progressive power-down of engine speed and power will occur when the red light is illuminated.

Engine Protection System

The engine protection system is programmed to monitor specific systems that when out of range could create serious engine problems. This system monitors the following sensors and conditions:

- coolant temperature
- coolant level
- oil temperature

- oil pressure
- intake manifold temperature

Active/Inactive Fault Codes

There are two types of electronic fuel system fault codes that are referred to as being either *active* or *inactive*. The active code means that the fault is occurring during engine operation, whereas an inactive code is a fault that is not happening during engine operation. For example, during hot weather and heavy uphill hauling in low gear, it is possible that the engine oil temperature may exceed the maximum allowable safe level. If this occurs, then a warning lamp will be illuminated. The ECM will derate the engine during this condition. Once the hill has been crested, the engine oil may once again drop below the fault lamp/code temperature level causing the warning lamp to go out; however, the logged DTC will remain in ECM memory. This code(s) can be accessed by the service technician. Repeated same-number codes may indicate a problem in a particular system that requires further investigation and correction.

Accessing Fault Codes/DTCs

To assist the service technician in diagnosis and troubleshooting an electronic engine, withdrawal of the logged/stored three-digit fault codes can be done using Cummins special tooling. The four methods available to do this are as follows:

1. Activate the diagnostic trouble lights shown in Figure 22–45. Activation of the red and yellow dash-mounted fault lamps is the simplest of the four methods available, and can be performed by shutting the engine OFF, then moving the diagnostic switch shown in Figure 22–46 to the ON position, or connect the shorting plug into the ECM diagnostic connector.

a. Refer to Figure 22–46 and turn the ignition key switch ON.

b. If no active codes are registered, both the yellow and red lamps will illuminate and remain ON.

c. If there are active fault codes in ECM memory, after several seconds both lamps will begin to flash indicating that there are stored codes.

d. Figure 22–47 illustrates an example of two active codes. These can be interpreted as follows: The yellow warning light flashes first followed several seconds later by the red stop lamp. Carefully note how many times the red lamp flashes. There is a slight pause between each number as shown in the diagram. The lights continue to flash until you choose to activate something else in the diagnostic sequence.

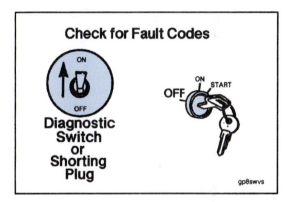

FIGURE 22–46 Using the ignition key switch, diagnostic switch, or shorting plug to check for stored fault codes. (Courtesy of Cummins Engine Company, Inc.)

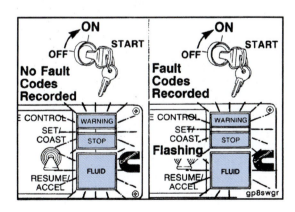

FIGURE 22–45 Key switch ON to determine if any fault codes are inactive or active. (Courtesy of Cummins Engine Company, Inc.)

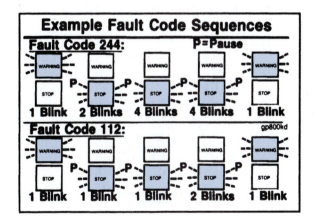

FIGURE 22–47 Example fault code number detection sequence indicating a fault code 244 and 112 by monitoring the flashing warning/stop lamps flash codes. (Courtesy of Cummins Engine Company, Inc.)

e. To move to another stored fault code, refer to Figure 22–44 and toggle the idle-speed adjust switch once to the (+) position. If no other fault code(s) is stored in ECM memory, the same code will appear again.

f. If you want to backtrack to a previous stored code, toggle the idle-speed adjust switch once to the (−) position.

2. Use Cummins Echek handheld scan tool, part number (PN) 3823474, connected to the vehicle datalink shown in Figure 22–48. When the Echek connector is coupled/attached to the vehicle datalink shown in Figure 22–49, and the ignition key is turned ON with the engine OFF, the backlit display on the Echek is illuminated. The user can select the function required by pressing one or more soft-touch buttons shown on the unit in Figure 22–48. A series of menus will appear on the screen, and by using the up, down, and across (back and forward) arrow-head buttons you command the ECM to perform a specific test. You can access DFCs, perform individual cylinder cutout tests, or perform an automated cylinder performance test, in addition to fault code snapshot data recovery information, and so forth.

3. Use Cummins Compulink part number 3823549, so this tooling can be connected to the ECM as shown in Figure 22–49. This special diagnostic equipment can perform all tests that the Echek will, plus provide greater flexibility and substantially greater data/information.

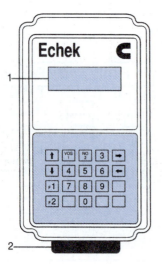

FIGURE 22–48 *Handheld Echek diagnostic reader (scan tool): 1, digital data messages/characters; 2, software cartridge installation location. (Courtesy of Cummins Engine Company, Inc.)*

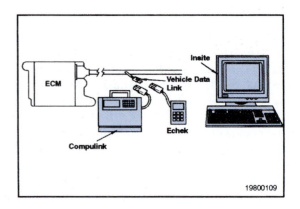

FIGURE 22–49 *Interacting with the Celect/Plus engine ECM diagnostic link by hooking up either a Cummins Compulink tool, handheld Echek scan tool, or a PC or laptop. (Courtesy of Cummins Engine Company, Inc.)*

4. Use a PC or laptop containing Cummins Insite software, part number 3824638, which is also shown in Figure 22–49. The Insite software not only allows the service technician to perform all tests available with both the Echek and Compulink systems, but also contains menus and programs containing all troubleshooting and repair information and diagrams found in hard copy manuals.

Injector Fault Codes

Figure 22–31 illustrates a typical injector circuit where each injector solenoid is connected to the ECM by both a supply and return wire sourced from the C connector at the ECM. Therefore, the PWM (pulse-width-modulated) electrical signal enters via the supply wire, activates the solenoid, and then flows through the return wire back to the ECM to complete the circuit. Remember that normally each solenoid valve is open; it can only be closed by the signal from the ECM during fuel injection and metering. To provide for quick-acting solenoids and to reduce heat buildup, the solenoids have a very low resistance value, typically between 0.5 to 1.5 ohms after subtracting the volt-ohmmeter (VOM) resistance.

CAUTION The injector solenoids receive high voltage on a running engine; therefore, do not touch the solenoids or the wires because this can cause a severe shock.

Each injector solenoid is monitored by the ECM diagnostic circuit to determine if and when a circuit current or voltage falls outside of the normal operating parameter, or no signal is detected. A fault code lamp will be illuminated and an automatic engine speed derate to between 1400 and 1600 rpm will occur, and is usually accompanied by the ECM cutting off the current to the injector solenoid. If, on the other hand, the injector power supply is below specs inside the ECM, then possible reduced engine performance will occur. The specific fault code logged in ECM memory when an injector fault is detected will be dependent on the cause and what specific injector is at fault. These fault codes can be detected by using the Cummins Compuchek, the handheld Echek scan tool, or a laptop computer loaded with the Cummins Insite software program.

Typical M11 and N14 engine injector fault codes would be 311 through 315, which refers to injector 1, 5, 3, 6, and 2, thus indicating that current has been detected at each injector return pin of the actuator harness when voltage at the supply pin of the actuator harness is OFF. Injector No. 4 would log a fault code 321 when these same conditions are detected by the ECM.

Fault codes 322 through 332 are for injectors 1, 5, 3, 6, 2, and 4 would and will appear when no current is detected at the injector return pin of the actuator harness when the voltage at the supply pin of the actuator harness is ON. See Table 22–1. A fault code 333 indicates that no voltage is detected on one or more of the injector supply pins of the actuator harness when power is commanded by the ECM. Remember also that each one of these three-digit Cummins fault codes will also be shown in SAE standard fault code format. Chapter 18 describes the meaning and interpretation of the SID (subsystem identifier or indicator), PID (parameter identifier), and FMI (failure mode indicator) codes adopted by SAE and now in use by all electronic engine OEMs.

Cylinder Cutout Test

When a Celect engine misses or runs poorly, and it is suspected that the fault lies with the fuel system or injectors, use of the Echek handheld scan tool, Compulink, or Cummins Insite program will permit you to retrieve specific fault codes and take a "snapshot" of running engine data. You can also enter the audit trail menu to help you determine where and what is causing a specific fault code. To perform a cylinder cutout (CCO) test, you can use either one of these diagnostic tools and enter the menu that permits activation of the CCO feature while the engine is running at idle speed.

When you enter the CCO menu on the diagnostic tooling screen, you can select the single-cylinder cutout test. This permits you to remove individual cylinders from the engine firing cycle. You can then listen for a sound change from the engine and look at the diagnostic tooling tachometer to monitor speed changes as well as the increase in the PWM time of the other five cylinders on a six-cylinder engine model. The system will display the percentage of load and rpm values during this CCO test. A hard copy can be downloaded after any CCO test to allow you to study the changes.

Automated Cylinder Performance Test

With the aid of Cummins special diagnostic tools as described, and when connected to the engine ECM, the service technician can choose to activate from the appropriate screen menu an automated cylinder performance test (ACPT). Once the ACPT has been started, the service tool controls the injectors that are enabled (injecting fuel), or that are disabled (not injecting fuel), what ECM values are recorded, and what information displays as a result of the test. The ACPT will produce either a *pass* or *fail* message for each cylinder. When a cylinder fails, its percent contribution value will also be displayed on the diagnostic tool screen. Prior to performing this test, make sure that the engine oil temperature is at 170°F (77°C); lock the fan clutch in the ON position; shut off the air-conditioning; disengage any accessory load devices that could come on, and so affect the engine during this test; and engage the PTO feature (this test cannot be performed unless the PTO feature is available in the ECM). An example of a typical ACPT could appear as follows:

Cylinder no.	Percentage of contribution	Pass/fail
1	68	Fail, Not OK
2	101	Pass OK
3	97	Pass OK
4	101	Pass OK
5	101	Pass OK
6	101	Pass OK

Fault Code Information Table

Table 22–1 lists some fault codes for a Celect engine, while Table 22–2 lists fault codes relevant to a Cummins ISX/Signature Series 15 L engine. Not all of these codes will appear in other Cummins engine series electronic models. The number of codes employed will depend upon the fuel system and options used for a specific engine application. However, all codes that are employed correspond to the SAE (Society of Automotive Engineers) International fault code standards. SAE fault codes are shown and identified as a four-digit alphanumeric number such as P129, or S043, where P (PID—parameter identifier) and S (SID—system identifier) can be followed by a single- or double-digit

TABLE 22–2 Signature/ISX engine fault code information data

SIGNATURE/ISX FAULT CODE INFORMATION

FAULT CODE LAMP	PID(P) SID(S) FMI	SPN(S) FMI	REASON	EFFECT
111 Red	S254 12	629 12	Error Internal to the ECM related to memory hardware failures or internal ECM voltage supply circuits.	Engine will **not** start.
115 Red	P190 2	190 2	No engine speed signal detected from the camshaft engine position sensor.	Engine may take longer to start.
121 Yellow	P190 10	190 10	No engine speed signal detected from the crankshaft engine position sensor.	Hard starting, low power, rough idle; or possible white smoke.
122 Yellow	P102 3	102 3	High voltage detected at the intake manifold pressure circuit.	Derate in power output of the engine.
123 Yellow	P102 4	102 4	Low voltage detected at intake manifold pressure circuit.	Derate in power output of the engine.
131 Red	P091 3	91 3	High voltage detected at throttle position signal circuit.	Severe derate (power and speed). Limp home power **only**.
132 Red	P091 4	91 4	Low voltage detected at throttle position signal circuit.	Severe derate (power and speed). Limp home power **only**.
133 Red	P029 3	974 3	High voltage detected at remote throttle position signal circuit.	None on performance if remote throttle is **not** used.
134 Red	P029 4	974 4	Low voltage detected at remote throttle position signal circuit.	None on performance if remote throttle is **not** used.
135 Yellow	P100 3	100 3	High voltage detected at oil pressure circuit.	No engine protection for oil pressure.
141 Yellow	P100 4	100 4	Low voltage detected at oil pressure circuit.	No engine protection for oil pressure.
143 Yellow	P100 1	100 18	Oil pressure signal indicates oil pressure below the low engine protection limit.	Progressive power and speed derate with increasing time after alert. If Engine Protection Shutdown feature is enabled, engine will shut down 30 seconds after the red lamp starts flashing.
144 Yellow	P110 3	110 3	High voltage detected at coolant temperature circuit.	Possible white smoke. Fan will stay on by ECM. No engine protection for coolant temperature.
145 Yellow	P110 4	110 4	Low voltage detected at coolant temperature circuit.	Possible white smoke. Fan will stay on by ECM. No engine protection for coolant temperature.
151 Red	P110 0	110 0	Coolant temperature signal indicates coolant temperature is above 104°C. (220°F).	Progressive power derate with increasing time after alert. If Engine Protection Shutdown feature is enabled, engine will shut down 30 seconds after the red lamp starts flashing.
153 Yellow	P105 3	105 3	High voltage detected at intake manifold temperature circuit.	Possible white smoke. Fan will stay on by ECM. No engine protection for manifold temperature.
154 Yellow	P105 4	105 4	Low voltage detected at intake manifold temperature circuit.	Possible white smoke. Fan will stay on by ECM. No engine protection for manifold temperature.
155 Red	P105 0	105 0	Intake manifold air temperature signal indicates intake manifold temperature is above 93.3°C. (200°F).	Progressive power derate with increasing time from alert. If Engine Protection Shutdown feature is enabled, engine will shut down 30 seconds after the red lamp starts flashing.
187 Yellow	S232 4	620 4	Low voltage detected on the ECM voltage supply line to some sensors (VSEN2 supply).	Engine will run derated. No engine protection for oil pressure and coolant level.
198 Yellow	S122 3	612 3	High voltage detected at the ICON™ lamp circuit when low voltage was expected by the ECM.	The ICON™ idle control system will be disabled. **Only** mandatory shutdown will be enabled.
199 Yellow	S122 4	612 4	Less than 6 VDC detected at the ICON™ lamp circuit when high voltage was expected by the ECM.	The ICON™ idle control system will be disabled. **Only** mandatory shutdown will be enabled.
212 Yellow	P175 3	175 3	High voltage detected at oil temperature circuit.	No engine protection for oil temperature.
213 Yellow	P175 4	175 4	Low voltage detected at oil temperature circuit.	No engine protection for oil temperature.
214 Red	P175 0	175 0	Oil temperature signal indicates oil temperature above 123.9°C. (255°F).	Progressive power derate with increasing time after alert. If Engine Protection Shutdown feature is enabled, engine will shut down 30 seconds after the red lamp starts flashing.
216 Yellow	P046 3	46 3	High voltage detected at air compressor tank pressure signal circuit.	Air compressor will run continuously.
217 Yellow	P046 4	46 4	Low voltage detected at air compressor tank pressure signal circuit.	Air compressor will run continuously.
218 Yellow	P046 2	46 2	Voltage at air compressor tank pressure signal indicates air compressor tank pressure is too high or too low.	Air compressor will run continuously.
219 Maintenance	P017 1	1380 17	Low oil level was detected in the Centinel™ makeup oil tank.	None on performance. Centinel™ deactivated.
221 Yellow	P108 3	108 3	High voltage detected at ambient air pressure circuit.	Derate in power output of the engine.
222 Yellow	P108 4	108 4	Low voltage detected at ambient air pressure circuit.	Derate in power output of the engine.
223 Yellow	S085 4	1265 4	Incorrect voltage detected on the Centinel™ actuator circuit by the ECM.	None on performance. Centinel™ deactivated.
227 Yellow	S232 3	620 3	High voltage detected on the ECM voltage supply line to some sensors (VSEN2 supply).	Engine will run derated. No engine protection for oil pressure and coolant level.
234 Red	P190 0	190 0	Engine speed signal indicates engine speed greater than 2650 rpm.	Fuel shutoff valve closed until engine speed falls to 2000 rpm.
235 Red	P111 1	111 1	Coolant level signal indicates coolant level is below normal range.	Progressive power derate with increasing time after alert. If Engine Protection Shutdown feature is enabled, engine will shut down 30 seconds after the red lamp starts flashing.
241 Yellow	P084 2	84 2	The ECM lost the vehicle speed signal.	Engine speed limited to ''Max. Engine Speed without VSS'' parameter value. Cruise control, gear-down protection, and the road speed governor will **not** work (automotive **only**).
242 Yellow	P084 10	84 10	Invalid or inappropriate vehicle speed signal detected. Signal indicates an intermittent connection or VSS tampering.	Engine speed limited to ''Max. Engine Speed without VSS'' parameter value. Cruise control, gear-down protection, and the road speed governor will **not** work (automotive **only**).
245 Yellow	S033 4	647 4	Less than 6 VDC detected at fan clutch circuit when on indicates an excessive current draw from the ECM or faulty ECM output circuit.	The fan may stay on at all times.
249 Yellow	P171 3	171 3	High voltage detected on the ambient air temperature circuit.	None on performance. The idle shutdown ambient air temperature override feature will use the intake air temperature sensor value to determine idle shutdown and availability of override (automotive **only**).

TABLE 22–2 (continued).

FAULT CODE LAMP	PID(P) SID(S) FMI	SPN(S) FMI	REASON	EFFECT
254 Red	S017 4	632 4	Less than 6 VDC detected at FSO circuit when on indicates an excessive current draw from the ECM or faulty ECM output circuit.	The ECM turns off FSO supply voltage. The engine will shut down.
255 Yellow	S017 3	632 3	Externally supplied voltage detected going to the Fuel Shutoff supply circuit.	None on performance. Fuel shutoff valve stays on.
256 Yellow	P171 4	171 4	Low voltage detected on the ambient air temperature circuit.	None on performance. The idle shutdown ambient air temperature override feature will use the intake air temperature sensor value to determine idle shutdown and availability of override.
259 Yellow	S017 7	632 7	Fuel shutoff valve is stuck open mechanically or leaking.	Engine will run derated.
284 Yellow	S221 4	1043 4	Incorrect voltage detected on the ECM voltage supply line to the crankshaft engine position sensor.	Engine may **not** run or will run derated. Possible hard starting, low power, or white smoke.
285 Yellow	S231 9	639 9	The ECM expected information from a multiplexed device but did **not** receive it soon enough or did not receive it at all.	At least one multiplexed device will **not** operate properly.
286 Yellow	S231 13	639 13	The ECM expected information from a multiplexed device but only received a portion of the necessary information.	At least one multiplexed device will **not** operate properly.
287 Red	S091 2	91 19	The OEM vehicle electronic control unit (VECU) detected a fault with its throttle pedal.	The engine will **only** idle.
288 Red	S029 2	974 19	The OEM vehicle electronic control unit (VECU) detected a fault with its remote throttle.	The engine will **not** respond to the remote throttle.
295 Yellow	P108 2	108 2	An error in the ambient air pressure sensor signal was detected by the ECM.	Engine is derated to no air setting.
319 Maintenance	P251 2	251 2	Real-time clock lost power.	None on performance. Data in the ECM will **not** have accurate time and date information.
338 Yellow	S087 3	1267 3	Voltage detected on the idle shutdown vehicle accessory/ignition bus relay circuit when no voltage was being supplied by the ECM or open circuit detected.	Vehicle accessories or ignition bus controlled by the idle shutdown vehicle accessory relay will **not** power up.
339 Yellow	S087 4	1267 4	Less than 6 VDC detected at the idle shutdown vehicle accessory/ignition bus relay circuit when on indicates an excessive current draw from the ECM or faulty ECM output circuit.	Vehicle accessories or ignition bus controlled by the idle shutdown vehicle accessory relay will **not** power down.
341 Yellow	S253 2	630 2	Severe loss of data from the ECM.	Possible no noticeable performance effects OR engine dying OR hard starting. Fault information, trip information, and maintenance monitor data may be inaccurate.
343 Yellow	S254 12	629 12	Internal ECM error.	Possible none on performance or severe derate.
352 Yellow	S232 4	1079 4	Low voltage detected on the ECM voltage supply line to some sensors (VSEN1 supply).	Engine is derated to no air setting.
359 Yellow	S124 11	613 31	ICON™ has failed to start the engine automatically.	ICON™ will be disabled. **Only** mandatory shutdown will be enabled. May be able to start engine normally.
378 Yellow	S018 5	633 5	Low current or open circuit detected at front fueling actuator circuit.	Engine will **only** run using the rear three cylinders.
379 Yellow	S018 6	633 6	High current detected at front fueling actuator circuit.	Engine will **only** run using the rear three cylinders.
386 Yellow	S232 3	1079 3	High voltage detected on the ECM voltage supply line to some sensors (VSEN1 supply).	Engine is derated to no air setting.
387 Yellow	P221 3	1043 3	High voltage detected on the ECM voltage supply line to the throttle(s) (VTP supply).	Engine will **only** idle.
388 Yellow	S028 11	1072 11	Less than 6 VDC detected at engine brake circuit 1 when on indicates an excessive current draw from the ECM or faulty ECM output circuit.	Engine brake on cylinder 1 can **not** be activated.
392 Yellow	S029 11	1073 11	Less than 6 VDC detected at engine brake circuit 2 when on indicates an excessive current draw from the ECM or faulty ECM output circuit.	Engine brakes on cylinders 2 and 3 can **not** be activated.
393 Yellow	S082 11	1112 11	Less than 6 VDC detected at engine brake circuit 3 when on indicates an excessive current draw from the ECM or faulty ECM output circuit.	Engine Brakes on cylinders 4, 5, and 6 can **not** be activated for 6-level engine brake harness OR engine brakes can **not** be activated on cylinders 1, 4, 5, and 6 for 3-level engine brake harness.
394 Yellow	S020 5	635 5	Low current or open circuit detected at front timing actuator circuit.	Engine will **only** run using the rear three cylinders.
395 Yellow	S020 6	635 6	High current detected at front timing actuator circuit.	Engine will **only** run using the rear three cylinders.
396 Yellow	S083 5	1244 5	Low current or open circuit detected at rear fueling actuator circuit.	Engine will **only** run using the front three cylinders.
397 Yellow	S083 6	1244 6	High current detected at the rear fueling actuator circuit.	Engine will **only** run using the front three cylinders.
398 Yellow	S084 5	1245 5	Low current or open circuit detected at rear timing actuator circuit.	Engine will **only** run using the front three cylinders.
399 Yellow	S084 6	1245 6	High current detected at rear timing actuator circuit.	Engine will **only** run using the front three cylinders.
415 Red	P100 1	100 1	Oil pressure signal indicates oil pressure below the very low engine protection limit.	Progressive power derate with increasing time after alert. If Engine Protection Shutdown feature is enabled, engine will shut down 30 seconds after the red lamp starts flashing.
418 Maintenance	P097 0	97 15	Water has been detected in the fuel filter.	Possible white smoke, loss of power, or hard starting.
419 Yellow	P102 2	1319 2	An error in the intake manifold pressure sensor signal was detected by the ECM.	Engine is derated to no air setting.
422 Yellow	P111 2	111 2	Voltage detected simultaneously on both the coolant level high and low signal circuits OR no voltage detected on both circuits.	No engine protection for coolant level.
426 None	S231 2	639 2	Communication between the ECM and the J1939 datalink has been lost.	None on performance. J1939 devices may **not** operate.
428 Yellow	P097 3	97 3	High voltage detected at water-in-fuel sensor circuit.	None on performance.
429 Yellow	P097 4	97 4	Low voltage detected at water-in-fuel sensor circuit.	None on performance.
431 Yellow	S230 2	558 2	Voltage detected simultaneously on both the idle validation off-idle and on-idle circuits	None on performance.

(continued)

FAULT CODE LAMP	PID(P) SID(S) FMI	SPN(S) FMI	REASON	EFFECT
432 Red	S230 13	558 13	Voltage detected at idle validation on-idle circuit when voltage at throttle position circuit indicates the pedal is **not** at idle OR voltage detected at idle validation off-idle circuit when voltage at throttle position circuit indicates the pedal is at idle.	Engine will **only** idle.
433 Yellow	P102 2	102 2	Voltage signal at intake manifold pressure circuit indicates high intake manifold pressure but other engine characteristics indicate intake manifold pressure **must** be low.	Derate to no air setting.
434 Yellow	S251 2	627 2	Supply voltage to the ECM fell below 6.2 VDC for a fraction of a second OR the ECM was **not** allowed to power down correctly (retain battery voltage for 30 seconds after key off).	Possible no noticeable performance effects OR engine dying OR hard starting. Fault information, trip information, and maintenance monitor data may be inaccurate.
435 Yellow	P100 2	100 2	An error in the oil pressure sensor signal was detected by the ECM.	None on performance. No engine protection for oil pressure.
441 Yellow	P168 1	168 18	Battery voltage below normal operating level.	Possible no noticeable performance effects OR possibility of rough idle.
442 Yellow	P168 0	168 16	Battery voltage above normal operation level.	None on performance.
443 Yellow	S221 4	1043 4	Low voltage detected on the ECM voltage supply line to the throttle(s) (VTP supply).	Engine will **only** idle.
449 Yellow	P094 0	94 16	Excessive fuel supply pressure was detected at the fuel pressure sensor.	Engine may have black smoke and will run derated.
451 Yellow	P157 3	157 3	High voltage detected on the front rail pressure sensor circuit.	Engine will run derated.
452 Yellow	P157 4	157 4	Low voltage detected on the front rail pressure sensor circuit.	Engine will run derated.
465 Yellow	S032 3	1188 3	High voltage detected at the wastegate actuator #1 circuit when no voltage was being supplied by the ECM.	Engine will run derated.
466 Yellow	S032 4	1188 4	Less than 6 VDC detected at the wastegate actuator #1 circuit when on indicates an excessive current draw from the ECM or faulty ECM output circuit.	Engine will run derated.
469 Yellow	S215 2	614 2	The ICON™ cab thermostat has logged a fault (E3 on the cab thermostat) OR the cab thermostat signal to the ECM is lost.	E3 will cycle the engine between 20 minutes run and 15 minutes off or **not** autostart the engine for Cab Comfort Mode. ICON™ will **not** be disabled. Engine mode will remain active.
471 Yellow	P098 1	98 17	Low crankcase oil lelvel was detected by the ECM.	None on performance. Centinel™ system deactivated.
472 Maintenance	P017 2	1380 2	Either high or low voltage was detected on the crankcase oil level sensor circuit by the ECM.	None on performance. Centinel™ system deactivated.
474 Yellow	S237 2	1321 2	Either low voltage detected on the starter lockout relay circuit when 12 VDC are commanded or voltage detected when no voltage is commanded.	Either engine will **not** start or engine will **not** have starter lockout protection.
475 Yellow	S089 4	1351 4	Low voltage detected at the electronic air compressor governor circuit when high voltage was expected.	Air compressor will **not** shutoff.
476 Yellow	S089 3	1351 3	High voltage or open circuit detected at the electronic air compressor governor actuator circuit.	Air compressor may run continuously or **not** at all.
482 Yellow	P094 1	94 18	Low fuel supply pressure was detected at the fuel pressure sensor.	Engine may **not** start, may have low power, may have white smoke, or run rough.
483 Yellow	P129 3	1349 3	High voltage detected on the rear rail pressure sensor circuit.	Engine will run derated.
484 Yellow	P129 4	1349 4	Low voltage detected on the rear rail pressure sensor circuit.	Engine will run derated.
485 Yellow	P129 0	1349 16	Unexpectedly high rail pressure was detected on the rear three cylinders.	Engine will return to idle speed then, may **only** idle or shut down.
486 Yellow	P129 1	1349 18	Unexpectedly low rail pressure was detected on the rear three cylinders.	Low power or rough idle.
491 Yellow	S088 3	1189 3	High voltage detected at the wastegate actuator #2 circuit when no voltage was being supplied by the ECM.	Engine will run derated.
492 Yellow	S088 4	1189 4	Less than 6 VDC detected at the wastegate actuator #2 circuit when on indicates an excessive current draw from the ECM or faulty ECM output circuit.	Engine will run derated.
496 Yellow	S221 11	1043 11	Incorrect voltage detected on the ECM voltage supply line to the camshaft engine position sensor.	Engine may **not** run, be hard to start, or will run derated.
536 Yellow	S044 11	718 11	Either low voltage detected on autoshift low gear actuator circuit when 12 VDC are commanded or voltage detected when no voltage is commanded.	Top2 shift solenoid will **not** function properly. Transmission will **not** shift properly.
537 Yellow	S043 11	717 11	Either low voltage detected on autoshift high gear actuator circuit when 12 VDC are commanded or voltage detected when no voltage is commanded.	Top2 shift solenoid will **not** function properly. Transmission will **not** shift properly.
538 Yellow	S045 11	719 11	Either low voltage detected on autoshift neutral actuator circuit when 12 VDC are commanded or voltage detected when no voltage is commanded.	Top2 shift solenoid will **not** function properly. Transmission will **not** shift properly.
541 Yellow	S123 11	615 31	Incorrect voltage detected at the ICON™ starter relay/interlock circuit by the ECM.	The ICON™ idle control system will be disabled. **Only** mandatory shutdown will be enabled. Engine can be started normally.
544 Yellow	S151 7	611 7	Autoshift failure; at least three shift attempts were missed.	Top2 transmission will **not** be controlled correctly. Transmission remains in manual mode.
546 Yellow	P094 3	94 3	High voltage detected at the fuel pressure sensor circuit.	Engine will run derated.
547 Yellow	P094 4	94 4	Low voltage detected at the fuel pressure sensor circuit.	Engine will run derated.
551 Yellow	S230 4	558 4	No voltage detected simultaneously on both the idle validation off-idle and on-idle circuits.	Engine will **only** idle.
553 Yellow	P157 0	157 16	Unexpectedly high rail pressure was detected on the front three cylinders.	Engine will return to idle speed then may **only** idle or shut down.
559 Yellow	P157 1	157 18	Unexpectedly low rail pressure was detected on the front three cylinders.	Low power or rough idle.
581 Yellow	P015 3	1381 3	High voltage detected at the fuel inlet restriction sensor signal pin.	Fuel inlet resriction monitor deactivated.
582 Yellow	P015 4	1381 4	Low voltage detected at the fuel inlet restriction sensor signal pin.	Fuel inlet resriciton monitor deactivated.
583 Yellow	P015 1	1381 18	Restriction has been detected at the fuel pump inlet.	Fuel inlet resriciton monitor warning is set.

TABLE 22–2   (continued).

FAULT CODE LAMP	PID(P) SID(S) FMI	SPN(S) FMI	REASON	EFFECT
588 Yellow	S121 3	611 3	High voltage detected at the alarm circuit when low voltage was expected by the ECM.	The ICON™ system will be disabled. Only mandatory shutdown will be enabled. The engine start alarm may sound continuously.
589 Yellow	S121 4	611 4	Less than 6 VDC detected at the alarm circuit when high voltage was expected by the ECM.	The ICON™ system will be disabled. **Only** mandatory shutdown will be enabled. The engine start alarm may sound continuously.
595 Yellow	P103 0	103 16	Turbocharger overspeed protection fault.	Engine will run derated.
596 Yellow	P167 0	167 16	High battery voltage detected by the battery voltage monitor feature.	Yellow lamp will be lit until high battery voltage condition is corrected.
597 Yellow	P167 1	167 18	ICON™ has restarted the engine 3 times within 3 hours due to low battery voltage (automotive **only**) OR low battery voltage detected by the battery voltage monitor feature.	Yellow lamp will be lit until low battery voltage condition is corrected. The ECM may increase idle speed and deactivate idle decrement switch if idle speedup is enabled. The engine will run continuously if ICON™ is active (automotive only).
598 Red	P167 1	167 1	Very low battery voltage detected by the battery voltage monitor feature.	Red lamp lit until very low battery voltage condition is corrected.
753 Yellow	P064 2	723 2	Engine position signal from the camshaft and crankshaft engine position sensors do **not** match up.	Low power, rough idle, or possible white smoke.
755 Yellow	P157 7	157 7	Incorrect fueling was detected on the front three cylinders.	Engine will misfire.
758 Yellow	P129 7	1349 7	Incorrect fueling was detected on the rear three cylinders.	Engine will misfire.
774 Yellow	P046 5	46 5	Open circuit detected at the electronic air compressor governor actuator circuit by the ECM.	Air compressor may **not** operate.
775 Maintenance	P046 1	46 17	A slow leak has been detected in the air system.	None on performance.
776 Yellow	P046 1	46 18	A fast leak has been detected in the air system.	None on performance.
951 None	P166 2	166 2	A power imbalance between cylinders was detected by the ECM.	Engine may have rough idle or misfire.

Bulletin No. 3666268-01

number known as a failure mode identifier (FMI). Greater detail on these SAE codes is found in Chapter 18. Table 22–3 lists examples of fault code information for switch positions, audit trail explanations and engine protection used with Cummins electronic engine systems. Fault codes can be extracted from the ECM memory by a service technician using either the instrument panel–mounted diagnostic switch and shorting plug, the handheld Echek, Compulink, or Cummins Insite software program loaded into a PC or laptop computer. (See Figures 22–46 and 22–49.)

Cummins QuickCheck Diagnostics

A fairly recent method that can be used by service technicians when diagnosing Cummins electronic engines is to use a Palm Pilot, an example of which is illustrated in Figure 22–50. Cummins refers to this diagnostic tool as the QuickCheck, because it is designed to read and capture SAE J1587 engine data from any Cummins electronic diesel engine. This Palm Pilot tool can also be used with any make of electronic diesel engine. The QuickCheck kit for use with the Palm Pilot consists of a custom datalink adapter to communicate through the vehicle or equipment 6-pin or 9-pin J1587 datalink connector, an interface cable and connector, and the diagnostic software application. By adding the Cummins QuickCheck system, you simply plug it into the appropriate vehicle harness to view engine data real time, or save it to download into a PC. By choosing the fault screen you can quickly determine if any problems exist. Specifically, you can check:

- Equipment ID
- Engine speed
- Coolant temperature
- Boost pressure
- Oil pressure
- Fuel rate
- Percentage of engine load
- Engine hours
- Throttle
- Output torque
- Fault codes
- Intake manifold temperature

You can also download both engine and trip data which includes the following:

- Maximum vehicle speed
- Cruise set speed
- Idle time
- Idle fuel consumed
- Vehicle distance
- Engine hours
- PTO hours
- Fuel used

TABLE 22–3 *Celect and Celect Plus engines fault code information, switch positions, and audit trail information/explanation*

FAULT CODE INFORMATION

Engine operating conditions are recorded in the ECM at the time a fault code is first recorded. The following data fields are reported by Compulink™ and Echek™ under the Fault Code menu:

COMPULINK™	ECHEK™	DESCRIPTION
Code	Code	Cummins code in Compulink™ and Echek™
—	PID or SID, FMI	Optional SAE J1587 code in Echek™
Stat	Status	Active or inactive status of fault codes
Spd	MPH	Vehicle speed in MPH or KPH
Th	% Throttle	Percent that throttle pedal was depressed
RPM	RPM	Engine speed
Count	Count	Number of occurrences of a fault code
—	x/y (e.g., 1/3)	Sequence/Total (e.g., first of three fault codes)
Switch position	SW	Switch position at first occurrence of fault

ENGINE PROTECTION FAULT CODE INFORMATION

FAULT CODE	FLUID SYSTEM	LIMIT	COMMENTS
143	Low Oil Pressure	Speed Dependent	Power Derate
151	High Coolant Temp	104°C [220°F]	Power Derate, Speed Derate after 115°C [239°F]
155	High Boost Air Temp	84°C [183°F]	Power Derate, Speed Derate after 111°C [231°F]
214	High Oil Temp	124°C [255°F]	Power Derate
235	Low Coolant Level	Installation Dependent	Power Derate
415	Very Low Oil Pressure	Speed Dependent	Speed Derate, Power is already derated with Fault Code 143

SWITCH POSITIONS*

1 2 3 4 5 6 7 8 9 10 11 12 13 14 15 16

POSITION	EXPLANATION
1	Clutch
2	Service brake
3	Cruise/Resume
4	Cruise/Set
5	Cruise/PTO
6	Test diagnostic switch
7	Radiator coolant level high
8	Radiator coolant level low
9	Not used
10	Key switch
11	Idle validation switch on idle
12	Remote PTO
13	Engine brake
14	Idle validation switch off idle
15	Idle decrement
16	Idle increment
TMP:	Coolant Temperature (Deg. C or F)
BO:	Boost Pressure (in Hg or mm Hg)
FUEL:	Percent Fuel (%)
Note: (*)	If value = 1, Switch Activated when fault was recorded. If value = Ø, Switch Not Activated when fault was recorded.

AUDIT TRAIL

CODE	EXPLANATION
C1	New calibration
C2	Accelerate/Coast Flag
D1	Vehicle information (make, model ID, year)
E1	Max engine speed without VSS
F1	Low idle adjust feature switch
F2	PTO feature switch
F3	Cruise control feature switch
F4	Progressive shift feature switch
F5	All speed governor feature switch
F6	Idle shut down feature switch
F7	Gear-Down Protection feature switch
F8	Engine protection shutdown switch
I1	Low idle RPM
I2	Idle shutdown time
I3	Idle shut down override
I4	Idle shut down in PTO
M1	Maximum vehicle speed in top gear
M2	Maximum cruise control speed
M3	Maximum vehicle speed in lower gear (light and heavy engine loads)
M4	MPH at maximum progressive shift RPM

AUDIT TRAIL (Continued)

CODE	EXPLANATION
P1	Maximum PTO RPM
	Minimum PTO speed
	Remote PTO speed
P2	Resume PTO RMP
P3	Set PTO RPM
	Light load PTO % Fuel
P4	CELECT™ password
P5	New parameter file
S1	Maximum progressive shift RPM
S2	Maximum progressive shift RPM at zero MPH
T1	Overdrive Transmission/Top Transmission Gear Ratio
V1	Tire Revolutions Per Mile Application Type
V2	Rear Axle Ratio, Engine Distance Offset, Engine Time Offset VSS Anti-Tampering (Fault Code 242)
V3	VSS type, VSS(Y/N) MM Feature Switch, MM Mode Selection, MM Distance, MM Time, MM Interval Factor
V4	Number of tailshaft gear teeth Automatic Transmission

To repair CELECT™/PT Pacer™/Pace™ wire harnesses, use Wiring Repair Kit, Part No. 3822926, which is a collection of connectors, seals, wires, test leads, tools and miscellaneous accessories. Distributed by: Cummins Service Products Company, Order Desk 1-800-433-9341.

FIGURE 22–50   Using a Palm Pilot to perform a series of QuickCheck functions, tests, or fault code analysis. (Courtesy of Cummins Engine Company, Inc.)

ISB ENGINE ELECTRONIC FUEL SYSTEM

Introduction

The ISB engine model was the first Cummins entry in the Interact System (IS) of products. The Cummins IS light-duty fuel system equipped B series engines use a Robert Bosch VP44 electronically controlled common-rail injection pump. Figure 22–51 illustrates the location of the 24-valve engine components on the fuel pump side. The B series engines are very popular and are used globally in a wide variety of applications being offered in a four-cylinder 3.9 L, or a six-cylinder 5.9 L displacement.

The ISB electronic system follows the same basic arrangement of function and operation as do other Cummins IS series electronically equipped engines, and also the Celect models, being equipped with a variety of engine/vehicle sensors and an ECM. Information in this section and in other chapters of this textbook describe in detail how electronically controlled fuel injection systems operate. Refer to these areas for more details on this type of system. The B engine speed sensor (ESS) is located on the intake side of the engine block at crankshaft level between cylinders 4 and 5 on the six-cylinder models. The sensor generates its signal of speed and position by sensing movement of target teeth machined into a tone wheel mounted on the crankshaft. This wheel has 35 teeth, then a gap. This missing tooth indicates to the ECM when both piston 1 and 6 are at TDC. All engine sensors receive a 5 VDC input reference signal from the ECM.

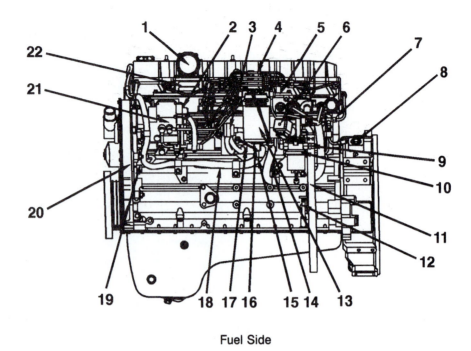

Fuel Side

1. Engine Air Inlet
2. VP44 Connector
3. 23-pin OEM Connector
4. High-Pressure Fuel Lines
5. Intake Manifold
6. VP44 Relay-OEM Mounted
7. 3/4 NPTF (in) Water Heater (optional)
8. Magnetic Pickup Location 3/4 to 16 UNF
9. Fuel Inlet Connection
10. Fuel Lift Pump
11. WIF Sensor
12. Crankcase Breather

13. Engine Speed Sensor
14. Fuel Filter/Water Separator
15. Oil Pressure Sensor
16. Fuel Water Drain
17. Electronic Control Module (ECM)
18. 1/8 NPTF (in) Oil Pressure
19. Engine Position Sensor
20. Engine Dataplate
21. Fuel Injection Pump (Bosch VP44)
22. Intake Air Preheater (optional)

FIGURE 22–51 Identification of external components on an ISB model engine equipped with a Bosch electronically sensed and controlled VP44 distributor-type injection pump. (Courtesy of Cummins Engine Company, Inc.)

ISB Fuel System Layout

The fuel system employs an ECM-controlled electric lift pump shown as item 10 in Figure 22–51. When the key switch is turned on, the lift pump is energized for a short time to prime the low-pressure fuel lines. Similar to the ISC engines water-in-fuel (WIF) sensor, it is located in the fuel filter housing, item 14 in Figure 22–51. When the sensor detects water in the fuel it will illuminate an instrument panel warning lamp.

The VP44 distributor-type fuel injection pump employs an internal vane pump to create the required flow and pressure to keep the internal components filled with fuel. A timing solenoid is used to vary injection timing. An electronic internal check is used to determine if the fuel injection pump can reach the commanded timing for the speed and load of the engine. If the pump fails to reach the ECM commanded timing value necessary for a given operating condition, possi-

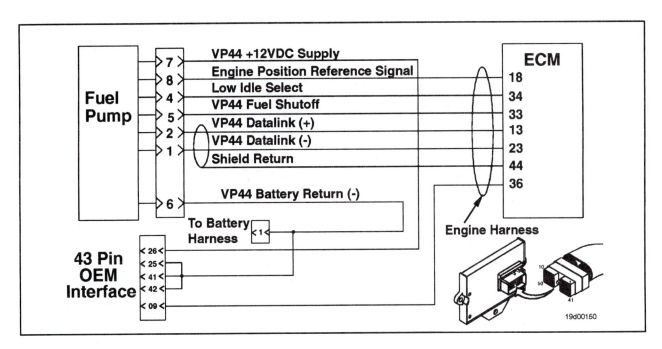

FIGURE 22–52 ISB model engine VP44 electronic pump wiring system schematic. (Courtesy of Cummins Engine Company, Inc.)

ble white smoke will be visible at the exhaust stack. A diagnostic fault code will be logged during this condition. A restriction to either the vane pump inlet or outlet can cause injection timing problems. This may be due to a plugged filter, crushed or collapsed fuel lines, and so forth. The maximum allowable pump inlet restriction measured at the fuel filter outlet is 5 psi minimum.

The VP44 model Bosch distributor pump contains its own fuel pump control module (FPCM). When system faults are detected, certain actions are initiated by the Cummins engine ECM, while others are taken by the Bosch FPCM. For example, an active pump fault code can result in deactivation of the fuel lift pump by the engine ECM. A schematic of the connections between the Bosch VP44 pump FPCM electronic control and the Cummins ECM is shown in Figure 22–52. The VP44 pump employs a relay to supply voltage to the engine shutdown relay circuit. This power is controlled from the engine ECM. The Bosch FPCM controls the quantity of fuel being delivered to each cylinder. The single fuel metering valve inside the VP44 pump is located in the center of the hydraulic head, or in the center of the six delivery valve holders to each nozzle. Low or no current to this delivery valve will result in a rough-running engine or engine shutdown. The Cummins ECM also monitors the engine and detects when a cylinder is misfiring and will log a fault code.

Figure 22–49 shows a PC connected into the ECM diagnostic datalink when troubleshooting and diagnosis is required using Cummins Insite software.

BOSCH VP44 DISTRIBUTOR PUMP

Introduction

All Cummins ISB (Interact B model engines) use the Bosch VP44 electronically controlled fuel system which is equipped with a Cummins designed ECM programmed for specific horsepower ratings. The ISB engine's automotive ratings meet all 1998 and later emissions regulations. A side view of the 24-valve ISB engine is shown in Figure 22–51, in which the fuel injection pump is identified as item 21, while the ECM is shown as item 17, and is located on the left-hand side of the block below the fuel filter. The ECM monitors all of the various engine sensors to control the Bosch VP44 pump by issuing commands based on engine load and speed, as well as the throttle/accelerator position. The operator can access cruise control on a truck, the power takeoff, and adjustable idle speed. The ECM, as with other Cummins ECMs, is programmed to recognize generated diagnostic fault/trouble codes, and those generated by the Bosch VP44 fuel pump.

The Bosch VP44 electronically controlled radial distributor injection pump used by Cummins on the ISB model engines is referred to as a time-controlled

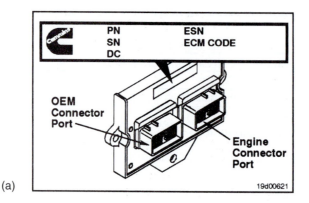

(a)

19d00621

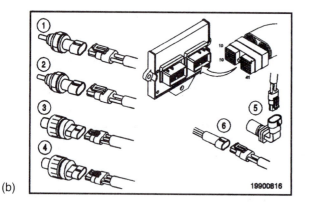

(b)   19900816

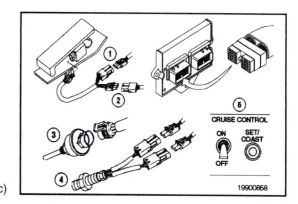

(c)   19900858

FIGURE 22–53 (a) ECM data plate for a ISB model engine identifies the ECM part number (PN), the ECM serial number (SN), the manufacturing date code (DC), the engine serial number (ESN), and the ECM code. (b) Sensor identification: 1, coolant temperature; 2, intake air temperature; 3, intake manifold pressure; 4, oil pressure; 5, engine speed/position; 6, water-in-fuel. (c) OEM inputs: 1, accelerator pedal position; 2, idle validation switch; 3, coolant level sensor; 4, vehicle speed sensors; 5, feature control switches such as cruise control. (Courtesy of Cummins Engine Company, Inc.)

model, because the injection process is controlled by a solenoid valve. Therefore, the duration of injection and the quantity depend on the time that this solenoid valve is open.

An engine harness connects all engine sensors to the Cummins ECM, while the OEM harness allows the OEMs access to the ISB's electronic features which include a datalink to exchange information between the ECM and other electronic components. Figure 22–53 illustrates the features of the ECM and its various inputs.

Mechanical Service Tools

Numerous special service tools are required to effectively and efficiently perform service repairs to the VP44 pump and to the ISB engine. These tools are available from any Cummins dealer.

Electronic Diagnostic Tool

When a no-start condition, or problems are suspected on an engine equipped with a Bosch VP44 distributor injection pump, the service technician can use a VP44

diagnostic tool to check the pump operation prior to removal from the engine. Before using this diagnostic tool, you should always check to ensure that the problem is not being caused by the following:

1. Low fuel level or a lack of fuel supply
2. Aerated fuel (air in the fuel)
3. Low battery voltage

The diagnostic tool illustrated in Figure 22–54, permits the technician to isolate the engine fault to either the fuel pump, the wiring harness, or the ECM. If fault codes are present, follow the engine OEM's suggested fault code troubleshooting procedure in the respective service literature.

Diagnostic Tool Usage

An example of the use of this diagnostic tool is best described by considering its use on a Bosch VP44 pump on a Cummins ISB (interact system model B engine), or on a QSB 5.9 L inline six-cylinder engine.

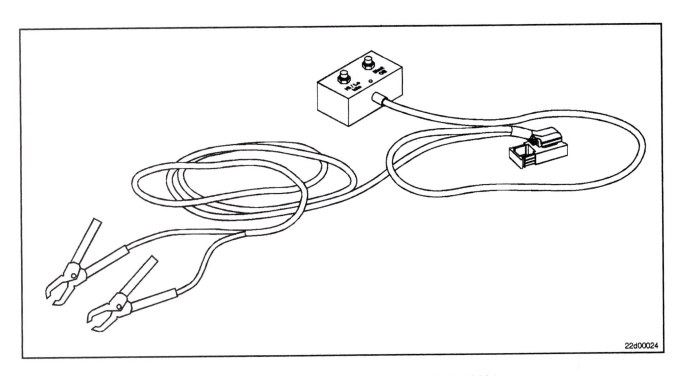

FIGURE 22–54   ISB model engine VP44 injection pump diagnostic tool, PN 3163834. (Courtesy of Cummins Engine Company, Inc.)

Procedure

1. Refer to Figure 22–55 and disengage the injection pump clamp (item 1) to allow removal of the 9-pin electrical connector from the fuel pump control module.

2. Carefully inspect the 9-pin connector for any signs of loose, corroded, or damaged pins. Replace the connector if damage is found.

3. Connect the diagnostic tool 9-pin harness connector (item 2) onto the fuel pump module and lock the clamp (1) in place.

4. With the engine stopped and the ignition key switch OFF connect the diagnostic tool battery leads as shown in Figure 22–56. *Always* remove the negative battery cable first to avoid possible arcing. As shown in the diagnostic tool diagram, connect the fuel pump diagnostic + tool clamp to the + side of the battery. Connect the fuel pump diagnostic − tool tool clamp to the − battery terminal. The diagnostic tool power ON lamp will illuminate at this time.

5. Start the engine.

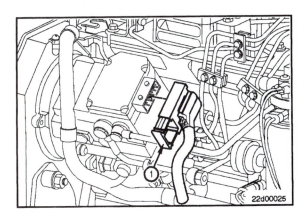

FIGURE 22–55   ISB engine; disengage the pump clamp (1) to allow removal of the 9-pin connector (2) from the fuel pump control module. (Courtesy of Cummins Engine Company, Inc.)

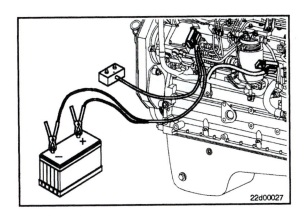

FIGURE 22–56   ISB engine stopped—key switch OFF; connect battery power cables as shown. (Courtesy of Cummins Engine Company, Inc.)

　Take careful note that if you start the engine while voltage is applied to the pump independent of the ECM with the pump harness connector disconnected, on these Cummins engines a fault code 364 (no communication or invalid data transfer between the VP44 pump and the ECM) will log. Clear the fault code from the ECM after the fuel pump test has been completed. If the engine will not start, replace the VP44 pump.

6.　When the engine is running, depress the test tool "Hi/Lo Idle" button to check the engine idle speed. Lo idle = 700–875 rpm; limp home hi idle = 1400–1500 rpm (see Figure 22–57).

7.　Should no change occur to the idle speed, or if the idle rpm registers less than or greater than the range listed in item 6 above, refer to the ISB base engine troubleshooting and repair manual for possible causes.

8.　When the engine is running, depress the diagnostic tool "Shut Off" button to stop the engine.

9.　If the engine starts and passes the performance tests, the VP44 injection pump is functioning correctly; therefore, fault causes may be due to a faulty wiring harness or ECM problem/failure.

10.　If the VP44 pump module passes the test sequence, disconnect the diagnostic tool connector by removing the negative tool clamp from the negative battery terminal first. Disconnect the positive side next.

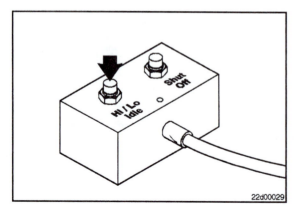

FIGURE 22–57　*ISB engine test tool; press the "Hi/Lo Idle" button with the engine idling to check the actual idle rpm. (Courtesy of Cummins Engine Company, Inc.)*

11.　Use a Cummins service diagnostic tool to clear a false fault code 364 from the electronic control module.

ISB Static Timing

When a hard start, visible exhaust smoke, or engine power derate occurs due to the ISB 24-valve engine Bosch VP44 pump's inability to achieve proper dynamic (engine running) timing, this can be traced back in many cases to use of the incorrect pump woodruff key. Figure 22–58a illustrates an example of such a key. Every VP44 pump key is marked with the last three digits of its Bosch part number along with an installation arrow, as shown, which must always point toward the pump housing. To confirm that the proper key is used, Figures 22–58b and c illustrate the location on both the Bosch and Cummins ReCon dataplates where the last three digits of the Bosch part number are indicated. To cross-reference from the Bosch part number to the Cummins part number, refer to Cummins parts information data.

CUMMINS—ISC ENGINES

Overview

The Cummins B and C series mechanically governed, and the later model ISB and ISC electronic engines, are midrange engines that are used globally by a number of major OEMs (original equipment manufacturers) in a variety of applications. These include buses, trucks, industrial, marine, agricultural, and a number of other diesel applications. The Cummins IS (Interact System) is found on a variety of its engine models, including models B, C, L, M, and ISX/Signature series engines. Therefore, the letters ISC indicate that this fuel system is used on the C model engines. The ISC engine is a six-cylinder four-stroke-cycle model with a displacement of 8.3 L (504.5 in³), employing four valves per cylinder for increased power and response over the previous two-valve-head C models. In addition vertically mounted fuel injectors are centered over the piston for improved combustion and low-end torque. The single-piece cylinder head contains an integral fuel intake manifold and fuel return. The cylinder block has been improved for a stiffer design to minimize vibration with all fluid lines contained within the block. Increased cooling and lube oil flows provide cooler operation and longer life to overhaul. Mid-stop design cylinder liners are used for enhanced durability and ease of replacement. Widely used in on- and off-highway applications, the ISC engine delivers an optimum balance of performance and fuel efficiency when operating in the 2000 to 2300 rpm range. The Interact System in-

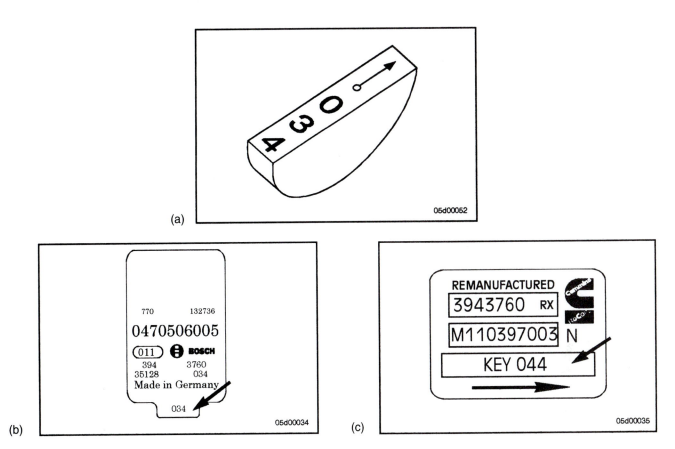

FIGURE 22–58   (a) ISB engine VP44 injection pump keys can be changed to provide correct dynamic timing when hard start, visible exhaust smoke, or engine power derate problems occur. (b) Correct ISB VP44 pump key is identified on the Bosch dataplate. (c) Correct VP44 injection pump key is also shown on the Cummins dataplate. (Courtesy of Cummins Engine Company, Inc.)

cludes full-authority electronics with features of diagnostics, asset protection, road speed governing, PTO, trip information, duty cycle monitor, and a real-time clock. The system is also equipped for the SAE industry standard J1587 and J1939 datalinks.

CAPS FUEL SYSTEM

Overview

The Cummins accumulator pump system (CAPS), shown in Figure 22–59 is an electronically controlled system that uses an ECM similar to that found on other Cummins engine models. The CAPS system and electronic controls is similar for the ISC, QSC8.3, and ISL Cummins engines. The fuel system provides high-pressure fuel injection pressures independent of engine speed. This design results in improved transient (momentary) response and fuel economy along with reduced exhaust emissions. The fuel injectors used with this fuel system are Robert Bosch closed-nozzle types.

See Chapters 17 and 19 for information about a closed nozzle. The major function of the CAPS system is to control fueling (quantity) and timing (start, duration, and end). The system also controls governed engine speed between the low- and high-idle set points. The CAPS fuel system is a Bosch supplied CRFS (common-rail fuel system), complete details of which are described in Chapter 19. Operational information in this section is specific to the Cummins application of the CRFS to the ISC model engines.

CAPS Fuel System Flow/Injection

Figure 22–60a illustrates a schematic of the basic fuel flow for the CAPS system to and from the fuel tank. When the ignition key switch is turned ON, the ECM enables the lift pump by relaying an electrical signal to the pump which then cycles on for 30 seconds to ensure that the fuel system is fully primed. The lift pump location can be seen by referring to item 2 in Figure 22–59. The distributor-type CAPS injection

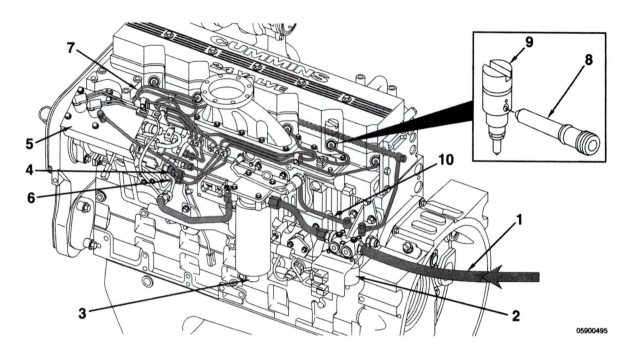

CAPS P11 Subsystems

05900495

1. Fuel from Supply Tank
2. Electronic Lift Pump
3. Fuel Filter and Water Separator
4. Fuel Drain Line
5. CAPS Injection Pump
6. Distributor Outlet Fitting
7. High-Pressure Supply Lines
8. Fuel Connector
9. Injectors
10. Fuel Return to Supply Tank.

Specifications

Fuel System

Maximum Lift Pump Inlet Restriction at Rated	102 mm Hg [4 in Hg]
Maximum Fuel Filter Outlet Restriction at Rated	254 mm Hg [10 in Hg]
Minimum Fuel Filter Inlet Pressure during Cranking (Lift Pump Operating)	508 mm Hg [20 in Hg]
Maximum Fuel Drain Line Pressure	254 mm Hg [10 in Hg]
Minimum Engine Cranking Speed	150 rpm

FIGURE 22–59 ISC engine model CAPS (Cummins accumulator pump system) fuel system flow diagram. (Courtesy of Cummins Engine Company, Inc.)

pump delivers high-pressure fuel to each individual closed nozzle injector from a hydraulic head somewhat similar to that for a Bosch VE, Lucas CAS-DPA, or a Stanadyne DB2/DB4 model. However, the high fuel system pressure is created by both a front and rear pumping control valve/solenoid arrangement, both of which are located on the top of the CAPS injection

pump. Figure 22–60b illustrates the two pumping control valves (1), the CAPS accumulator fuel pressure and temperature sensors (2), and the ICV (injection control valve), item 3, which determines fuel timing and delivery quantity (metering). Note that all these components are controlled from the ECM also shown in the diagram. The CAPS injection pump includes the major

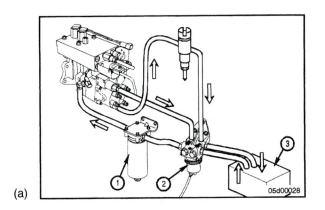

(a)

05d00028

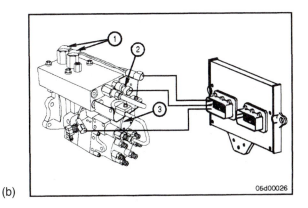

(b)

05d00026

FIGURE 22–60 (a) ISC engine CAPS pump fuel flow to and from the fuel tank. (b) CAPS pump: 1, two pumping control valves; 2, fuel pressure and temperature sensors; 3, injection control valve (ICV). (Courtesy of Cummins Engine Company, Inc.)

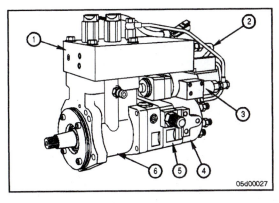

(a)

05d00027

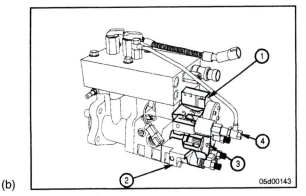

(b)

05d00143

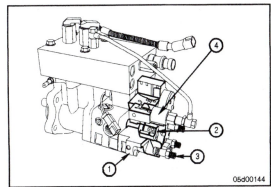

(c)

05d00144

FIGURE 22–61 ISC engine CAPS injection pump component identification; (a) 1, accumulator; 2, rate shape tube; 3, ICV (injector control valve); 4, distributor; 5, gear pump; 6, cam housing. (b) 1, injection control valves; 2, fuel pressure and temperature sensors; 3, ICV; (c) 1, distributor; 4, ICV pressure regulator. (Courtesy of Cummins Engine Company, Inc.)

subcomponents identified in Figure 22–61a. Each of these subcomponents functions as follows:

1. *Accumulator.* Functions to store energy. Within the accumulator a 0 to 24,000 psi (165,480 kPa) pressure sensor provides direct feedback to the ECM to monitor and maintain the desired accumulator fuel pressure.

Fuel flows from the accumulator to the distributor and through the rate shape tube.

2. *Rate shape tube.* Fuel is delivered to the injection control valve (1) shown in Figure 22–61b by the rate shape tube and through a drilling in the distributor (2).

3. *ICV (injector control valve).* The ICV controls both fueling and timing as its solenoid valve is controlled by a PWM signal from the ECM. Fuel under high pressure is directed from the ICV to the distributor rotor and then to the drain line back to the tank.

4. *Distributor.* The internal distributor rotor functions the same as any distributor pump assembly in that it directs the high-pressure fuel to each cylinder in firing-order sequence. Figure 22–61c illustrates the distributor (1), and the ICV pressure regulator (4) that routes drain fuel back to the fuel tank. Each distributor/injector outlet contains its own delivery valve.

5. *Gear pump.* Driven from the pump camshaft via an internal coupling, the gear pump functions to supply fuel at a regulated pressure of 160 psi (1103 kPa) at rated engine speed to and through drillings in the CAPS pump cam housing. The volume above each of the two pumping plungers is filled as the plungers travel downward on the base circle of the rotating pump camshaft. When the two pumping control valves, which are NO (normally open), are closed by an ECM signal, fuel is pushed into the accumulator where it is held by check valves. As the pump camshaft rotates, the trapped fuel above the two pumping plungers is raised to a very high pressure. Keep in mind, however, that the gear pump and injection pump camshaft both rotate at one-half engine speed.

6. *Cam housing.* Within the cam housing, its camshaft is driven at half-crankshaft speed from the engine camshaft through an internal coupling. Each of the two pumping plungers is driven by a three-lobed camshaft (3), as shown in Figure 22–62a. The camshaft, its bearings, and the two tappets are all lubricated by pressurized engine oil.

The CAPS front pumping element contains a front barrel and plunger, front pumping control valve, and a front check valve within the accumulator. The pumping element functions to pump fuel into the accumulator to maintain the desired operating pressure. The rear pumping valve circuit regulates the quantity of fuel pumped into the accumulator. The ECM commands the rear valve to close based upon various engine operating parameters. These typically include fuel pressure, engine load, and operator throttle position. An injection control valve located on the fuel injection pump on top of the distributor regulates both the quantity and timing of the fuel injection event. Figure 22–63 illustrates the pumping valve circuit arrangement for the CAPS system. Note that the ECM wire connection 25 is for the rear pumping control valve solenoid (+), while the ECM wire connection 15 is for the rear pumping control valve solenoid (−).

ISC Fuel System Specs

When faults such as hard starting, low power, and rough running are received with an ISC engine, remember that simple mechanical problems can be the reasons, and not necessarily an electronic condition. Possible causes to take into account would include a lack of fuel, fuel starvation, fuel pump suction side high restriction, a plugged fuel filter, crushed or crimped fuel lines or hoses, water in the fuel, a plugged or restricted fuel drain line, high air inlet restriction, restricted air-to-air charge aftercooler, low fuel pressure, high exhaust back pressure, low turbocharger boost, and so forth. Ensure that the following conditions are within Cummins published specifications:

1. Minimum lift pump inlet pressure at rated speed (vacuum)—4 in. Hg (102 mm Hg)

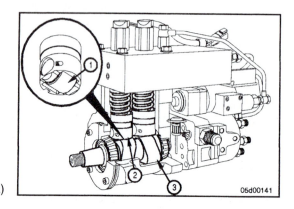
(a)

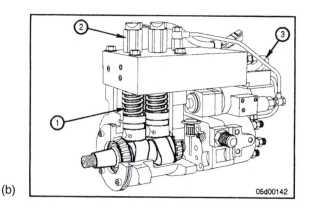
(b)

FIGURE 22–62 (a) 1, Roller tappet; 2, pumping plunger; 3, three-lobe camshaft. (b) 1, Pumping plunger follower spring; 2, pumping control valves; 3, fuel pressure/temperature sensor. (Courtesy of Cummins Engine Company, Inc.)

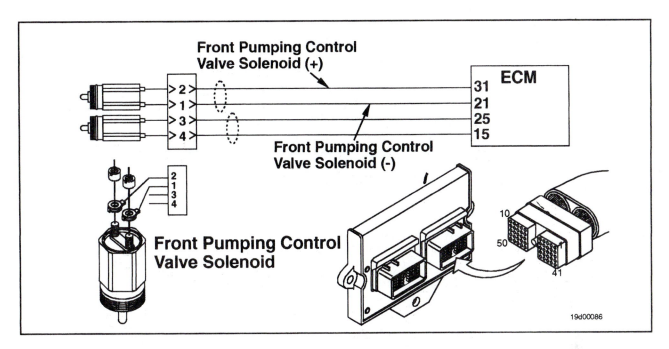

Front Pumping Control Valve Solenoid (+)

ECM

Front Pumping Control Valve Solenoid (-)

Front Pumping Control Valve Solenoid

19d00086

FIGURE 22–63 Schematic of the front pumping valve circuit for an ISC engine CAPS (Cummins accumulator pump system) injection pump. (Courtesy of Cummins Engine Company, Inc.)

2. Minimum fuel filter outlet pressure at rated speed (vacuum)—10 in. Hg (356 mm Hg)

3. Minimum fuel filter inlet pressure during cranking)—20 in. Hg (508 mm Hg)

4. Fuel drain line maximum pressure 10 in. Hg (356 mm Hg)

5. Fuel inlet maximum fuel temperature 160°F (71°C)

CAPS Fuel Filter

The spin-on fuel filter with this engine employs a combination fuel filter and water separator. A WIF (water-in-fuel) sensor screwed into the filter base will activate a dash-mounted lamp to warn the operator when excess water has collected in the filter assembly. Note in Figure 22–59 that the sensor assembly wiring harness must be disconnected prior to removing the filter. The filter drain valve knob located at the base can be opened (rotated) to drain water from the filter. Similarly, open this valve for about 5 seconds to lower the filter fuel level before spinning the filter loose during change-out periods. Since the CAPS system has an electric fuel transfer pump, it is not necessary to pour fuel into a new filter to assist priming. Simply turn the ignition key switch to the RUN position (not CRANK) for approximately 30 seconds to allow fuel flow to purge air from the fuel system.

CAPS Sensors

A variety of engine/vehicle/equipment and CAPS fuel pump sensors are employed with the ISC engines to provide optimum performance and fuel economy. These sensors are similar in both function and operation to those found on other electronically controlled Cummins engines. Figure 22–64 illustrates an engine fuel pump side view which also shows the location of the various sensors. Each sensor receives a 5 VDC reference input voltage from the engine ECM. The sensor output is based upon its internal resistance change due to engine operating conditions sensed. Conditions sensed include various temperatures, pressures, crankshaft rpm, and piston cylinder location. Each individual sensor returns a voltage signal to the ECM to advise it of all operator and engine inputs. The ECM computes the various signal return voltages and makes an appropriate decision of the required engine fueling and timing requirements to handle the load and speed conditions under which the engine is operating. Figure 22–65 shows how the various sensors receive an input voltage signal of approximately 5 V from the ECM.

CAPS Electronic Troubleshooting

Problems/corrections with the base engine CAPS fuel system can be found in Cummins publication, *Troubleshooting and Repair Manual, Electronic Control System,*

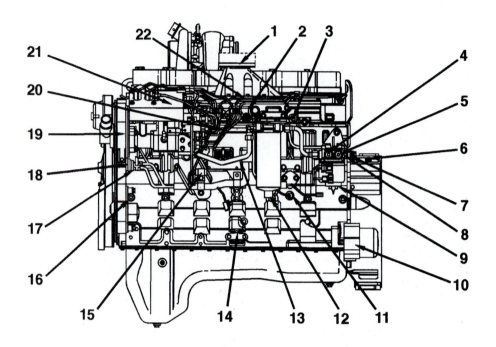

Fuel Pump Side View
1. Engine Air Inlet
2. Intake Manifold Pressure Sensor
3. Intake Manifold Temperature Sensor
4. M10 (STOR) Fuel Pressure After Lift Pump
5. M10 (STOR) Fuel Pressure Before Lift Pump
6. Magnetic Pickup Location 3/4-16 UNF
7. Fuel Return Connection
8. Fuel Inlet Connection
9. Fuel Lift Pump
10. Starter Mounting Flange
11. Oil Pressure Sensor
12. Fuel Filter/Water Separator
13. Engine Control Module (ECM)
14. Dipstick Location
15. Transient Suppressor
16. M10 (STOR) Oil Pressure Port
17. Engine Position Sensor (EPS) - (inboard)
18. Engine Speed Sensor (ESS) - (outboard)
19. Engine Dataplate
20. High Pressure Fuel Lines
21. Fuel Injection Pump
22. Intake Air Preheater

FIGURE 22–64   ISC CAPS equipped engine showing the major fuel pump side components identification. (Courtesy of Cummins Engine Company, Inc.)

ISC, QSC 8.3, and ISL Engines, Volumes 1 and 2, Bulletin 36666271-01. In addition, the use of Cummins Insite **software** and a laptop/PC to monitor fault/trouble **codes** will greatly assist the service technician when **problems** occur. Other training aids to assist in diagnosing and tracing system faults would be the ISC system wiring diagram contained in the front of the abovementioned manuals. A separate plasticized, colored foldout of this same wiring diagram is available from Cummins in Bulletin 3666267-01. This handy guide provides assistance when working around an ISC engine and piece of equipment.

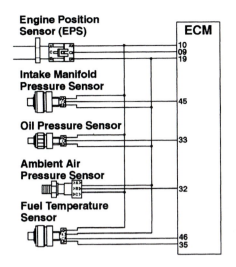

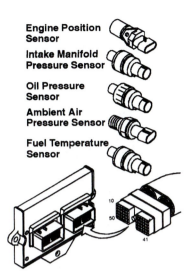

FIGURE 22–65 *Various ISC engine sensor connections to the ECM. (Courtesy of Cummins Engine Company, Inc.)*

Any sensor faults (outside of the normal operating voltage parameters) will cause the ECM diagnostic system to activate a fault code to permit the service technician to identify the system problem using a handheld diagnostic reader, Cummins Insite CD-ROM program, or by viewing the equipment/vehicle instrument panel fault lamps. The ECM will also take a snapshot of the engine operating parameters at this time, and store this data in memory for retrieval at a later date by the service technician to assist in effective and efficient trouble diagnosis.

NOTE When checking sensors and switches for a voltage value, the ECM input pin to the sensor for a specific sensor circuit should be between 4.75 to 5.25 VDC. At the sensor harness, voltage values should be between 4.50 to 5.25 VDC.

Typically when a system falls outside of the normal operating parameters, the yellow instrument panel warning lamp will blink or flash based on the severity of the problem detected by the ECM. The operator should have the fault condition checked at the first available opportunity, and the engine may perform at both a reduced speed and power condition. If the red warning lamp illuminates, the driver or equipment operator should either pull over to the side of the road or stop the machine when safe to do so, but as soon as possible to minimize potential serious engine damage. The red lamp will flash for 30 seconds before the ECM shuts the engine off.

The basic three types of electronic system codes that can be tripped/logged are as follows:

1. Engine electronic control system diagnostic fault codes, sometimes referred to in the industry as DTCs (diagnostic trouble codes).
2. Engine protection system fault codes. Fault codes mentioned in Item 1 and 2 above can be active or inactive. Refer to Chapter 18 for full details on these two types of fault codes.
3. Engine maintenance indicator codes (used to remind the owner/operator or fleet maintenance personnel that a specific service level is necessary).
   The ISC system ECM engine protection system monitors the following:
   - Coolant temperature
   - Coolant level (optional item)
   - Engine oil pressure
   - Intake manifold air temperature (boosted turbocharger air pressure)
   - Engine overspeed conditions
   - Fuel temperature

NOTE If any of the engine protection systems fall outside of normal operating parameters, the more severe the detected fault, then the engine power and speed will be reduced accordingly. If the vehicle/equipment owner/operator has had the ECM programmed for automatic engine shutdown, then this feature will be enabled when the preprogrammed out-of-limit level has been detected.

FIGURE 22–66 (a) ISC engine sensors and switches: 1, accelerator pedal position sensor; 2, idle validation switch; 3, coolant level sensor; 4, vehicle speed sensors. (b) ISC engine closeup of pressure and temperature sensor: 1, pressure sensor; 2, small seal washer; 3, pressure sensor adapter; 4, large seal washer; 5, temperature sensor adapter; 6, temperature sensor; 7, wiring harness. (Courtesy of Cummins Engine Company, Inc.)

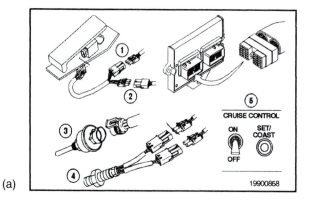

(a)

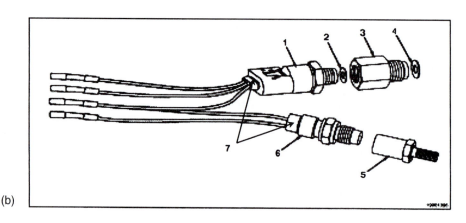

(b)

Additional sensor and switch inputs fed to the ECM, and provided by the vehicle OEM, include the items shown in Figure 22–66a. Based upon the specific OEM options offered, not all of these sensors and switches will be used. Note also that an accelerator interlock feature similar to that used on the larger Cummins engines series units is an option on the ISC engines. When the throttle is at an idle speed, or in the remote PTO speed zone, or for example on a bus/coach with any of the passenger doors open, the accelerator will disregard any input from the operator for safety reasons. Another heavy-duty engine feature is that when the engine is initially started up from cold, an engine warm-up protection system will inhibit any throttle response to permit the engine oil to be distributed to all moving parts and components before the engine speed can increase beyond the preset idle rpm. All other electronically controlled features used with heavy-duty Cummins engines is readily available on all ISC engines.

ISC CAPS Starting Precautions

The ISC CAPS engines are equipped with an ECM-controlled electric intake air heater grid element to facilitate ease of starting in cold ambient weather. DO NOT USE ETHER SPRAY CAN STARTING FLUID to assist cold-weather starting procedures. This highly combustible fluid will create a severe explosion leading to serious damage. The preheat time is determined by the ECM, which uses the intake manifold temperature sensor to determine how long to energize the internal heater before permitting the WAIT-TO-START lamp to go off.

Speed and Position Sensors

The CAPS fuel system requires an engine speed and piston position sensor to provide information to the ECM. See Figure 22–64, items 17 and 18. The sensor generates a return voltage signal to the ECM by detecting the rotation of target teeth cut into a steel ring bolted to the backface of the engine cam gear. The sensing ring has 71 teeth and a gap following this. When the sensor detects the missing tooth gap, it picks this up as an indication that pistons 1 and 6 are at TDC. The ESS (engine speed sensor) consists of two coils wound around its soft iron core. The resistance of the first coil is between 750 and 1000 ohms, while the second coil measures between 1100 and 1500 ohms. If for any reason the ESS signal is not detected at pin 17 of the engine harness, the ECM will cause an engine power derate along with possible white smoke.

Fuel Pressure/Temperature Sensors

The CAPS pump is also fitted with both a fuel pressure and a fuel temperature sensor. The fuel pressure/temperature sensor is used by the ECM to monitor the fuel temperature in the CAPS fuel system accumulator. Changes in pressure and temperature at the sensor will alter its resistance value. A change in resistance will allow the return voltage signal to the ECM to change accordingly. Examples of resistance changes versus temperature is as follows for all CAPS temperature sensors when using a multimeter.

CAPS Temperature Sensors

Sensor °C	Temperature °F	Resistance (Ohms) k = 1000 ohms
0	32	30k to 36k
25	77	9k to 11k
50	122	3k to 4k
75	167	1350 to 1500
100	212	600 to 675

NOTE Earlier-model ISC engines (prior to July 1999) employed a single combination fuel sensor (pressure and temperature), while ISC engines built starting in July 1999 use a two-sensor system similar to that illustrated in Figure 22–66b. A Cummins service kit PN 3800794 is available for updating the wiring harness and sensors.

The CAPS fuel pressure sensor will output a return signal voltage to the ECM to advise it of the accumulator system pressure. Examples of voltage values versus fuel pressure readings are listed in the following chart:

CAPS Fuel Pressure Sensor

Pressure		
MPa	PSI	Voltage Value
0	0	0.31 to 0.69
35.84	5000	1.19 to 1.47
57.34	8000	1.69 to 1.97
78.84	11000	2.19 to 2.47
107.51	15000	2.92 to 3.08

Intake Manifold Pressure Sensor

This sensor is located on the rear of the intake manifold in the second port on the side of the cylinder head to the right of the fuel filter, as shown in Figure 22–64,

item 2. Should the turbocharger boost pressure sensor fall outside of the normal high-voltage range parameters, the engine will usually derate to the no-boost fueling position, while with low voltage it may simply lack power. Typical turbocharger boost pressure sensor values and voltages will change throughout the load and speed range. The following chart shows pressure versus voltage.

Boost Pressure Sensor Chart

Pressure mm Hg	Pressure in. Hg	Voltage
0	0	0.44 to 0.56
646.48	25.45	1.44 to 1.56
1292.88	50.90	2.44 to 2.56
1939.36	75.35	3.44 to 3.56
2585.76	101.80	4.44 to 4.56

Note: One pound of boost pressure will displace Hg (mercury) 2.036 in., therefore, at a boost pressure of 101.80 in. Hg, it is equivalent to 50 psi. There are 25.4 mm in 1 inch. If we divide 2585.76 by 25.4, we have 101.8 in.

Fault Codes (DTCs)

The service technician should always be aware that operating and performance problems with a diesel engine, whether it is mechanically or electronically controlled, can often be created and traced to the same fault conditions. Fuel or air starvation on both types of engines can lead to a common complaint. Unless the electronic engine is equipped with an air inlet restriction and fuel pressure sensor, it will not log a fault code in ECM memory, although it would register low turbo boost, intake manifold temperature changes, and so forth. The fault code chart shown in Table 22–1 and Table 22–2 lists a variety of reasons for specific fault codes. Some fault codes specific to the CAPS system not shown in Table 22–1 and Table 22–2 would include:

Fault code 271—Low or no current detected at the front pumping valve pin 21 of the engine harness. Engine power will derate.

Fault code 272—High current detected at the front pumping valve pin 21 of the engine harness. Engine power will derate.

Fault code 493—The ECM detected a failure in the injection control valve identifier circuit. A 5% engine power derate will occur.

Fault code 268—High counts; fuel pressure in the accumulator is not changing with engine operating conditions (fuel pressure sensor fault).

Fault code 277—Intermittent; engine ECM has detected a failure in the injection control valve (ICV).

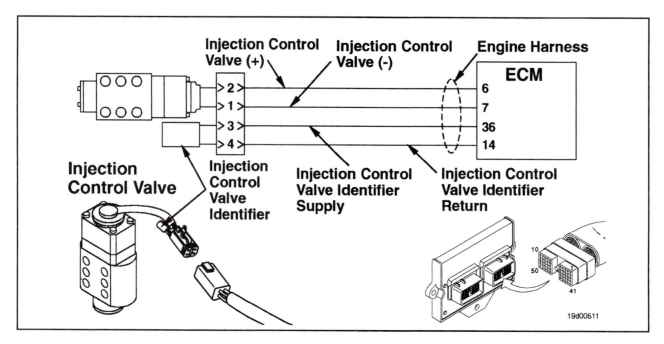

FIGURE 22–67   ISC engine CAPS injection control valve identifier circuit. (Courtesy of Cummins Engine Company, Inc.)

A failure in the ICV will log a fault code 277 and cause the engine to lose power or die. This fault can be caused by high circuit resistance and poor grounds. The service technician can check the snapshot data in memory. Look for battery voltage below + 9 VDC when the fault was actually logged into memory. Figure 22–67 illustrates the injection control valve circuit.

Low or no current detected at the rear pumping valve (pin 15 of the engine harness) will result in an engine power derate, and the service technician can detect this when a fault code 273 is logged. A fault code 274 indicates high current has been detected at the rear pumping valve pin 15 of the engine harness. (See Figure 22–63.) High resistance, shorts, or opens will cause problems with the CAPS fuel system. When checking the front, rear, or injection control valves, you should be able to hear a click when using the Cummins Insite diagnostic tooling.

Fault code 329—High counts with possible FC 277; the ECM has detected an overpumping failure in the CAPS pump possibly caused by the ICV, accumulator, air in the fuel system, or a fuel system restriction.

ISC Overhead

The ISC engines feature a no-adjust overhead (valve adjustment). The valve train adjustment is not neces-

sary during the first 150,000 miles (241,500 km), and requires reset at each 50,000 miles (81,000 km) succeeding intervals. The valve train operates within the valve lash limits of 0.006 to 0.022 in. (0.152 to 0.559 mm) on the intake valves, and 0.015 to 0.032 in. (0.381 to 0.813 mm) on the exhaust valves. Recommended engine valve lash can be found on the engine CPL plate/decal along with the minimum idle speed, high idle rpm, engine horsepower setting, and so on.

Should it become necessary at any time to reset the intake/exhaust valve lash on ISC engines, begin as follows:

Valve Lash Adjustment Procedure

1. For accurate valve lash measurements, the engine coolant temperature should be less than 140°F (60°C).

2. Refer to Figure 22–68a and remove the front timing cover plastic fuel pump drive cover as illustrated. It is screwed into place.

3. Install Cummins engine flywheel ring gear barring tool PN 3824591 into the access hole above the starter motor. See Figure 22–68b.

4. Use a 0.50 in. socket breaker bar inserted into the barring tool and manually rotate the flywheel over until the TDC marks on the gear cover and fuel pump drive gear are aligned as shown in Figure 22–68b.

5. Remove the valve rocker cover and gasket.

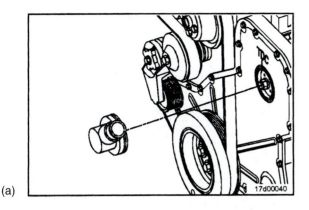

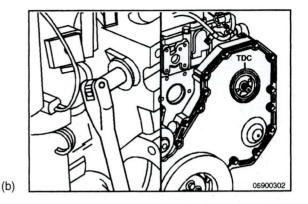

FIGURE 22–68 (a) Removal of the plastic fuel pump drive cover located on the front of both B and C model engines. (b) Use a manual barring tool, Cummins PN 3824591 to rotate the crankshaft to align the top dead center (TDC) marks on the gear cover and the fuel injection pump drive gear. (Courtesy of Cummins Engine Company, Inc.)

6. Check and set/adjust the valve lash for the following rocker arms: 1i, 1E, 2i, 3E, 4i, and 5E. Loosen the locknut and adjust the valve lash by checking the feeler gauge drag between the crosshead and the rocker lever ball insert and socket. Tighten the locknut and recheck the valve lash.

7. Using the barring mechanism rotate the engine crankshaft 360°. (Remember, because this is a four-cycle engine, the fuel pump drive gear will only rotate one-half of this, or 180°.)

8. Check the valve lash on the following rocker to valves: 2E, 3i, 4E, 5i, 6i, and 6E.

9. Replace the valve rocker cover gasket and cover and tighten the retaining bolts to 18 ft-lb (24 N · m).

10. Reinstall the fuel pump drive cover which was removed in step 2.

CUMMINS ISX/SIGNATURE SERIES ENGINES

Introduction

The ISX/Signature series engines are six-cylinder 15 L (912 in^3) displacement models. The crankshaft is CW rotating when viewed from the front and has a firing order of 1–5–3–6–2–4. All Cummins engines are equipped with an engine dataplate on the front side of the gear train housing, or on top of the rocker lever cover. The engine serial number, CPL (control parts list), model, and advertised horsepower and rpm are shown. In addition, the engine idle rpm, high idle, and valve lash specs are listed. Figures 22–69a and b illustrate the location of the ISX and Signature engine components from the intake side and from the exhaust side.

The IS (Interact System) is used across a number of engine models in the Cummins lineup, including the B, C, L, M, and ISX engines. Both the ISX and Signature engines are basically the same engine but with different horsepower ratings. The ISX Smart Torque models (two ratings), can be set between 400 and 500 hp (298 and 373 kW), whereas the ISX single ratings offer between 400 and 600 hp (298 and 448 kW). The Signature is rated only at the higher horsepower settings. The ISX and Signature models incorporate DOHC (dual overhead camshafts) where one camshaft drives the high-pressure fuel injection for clean, responsive power. The lobes on this camshaft are extra wide for longer life and higher-pressure capacity. The second camshaft includes a dedicated set of lobes for the specific operation of both the intake and exhaust valves as well as for the integrated (Intebrake) engine compression brake. The electronic controls are mounted on the cylinder head to the unique air-cooled ECM which coordinates all engine/transmission functions, ABS, engine brake, cooling fan, and the optional air compressor. The ICON (idle control) system operates similar to Detroit Diesel's optimized idle feature where the ECM minimizes the fuel consumed at idle by automatically starting and stopping the engine to maintain in-cab/sleeper temperature as well as maintaining battery state of charge.

Equipped with a variable output turbocharger, the need for a turbocharger wastegate to prevent overboost is avoided. The variable output turbocharger is electronically monitored from the ECM via the load on the engine (boost sensor), then delivers the exact amount of airflow needed for maximum engine

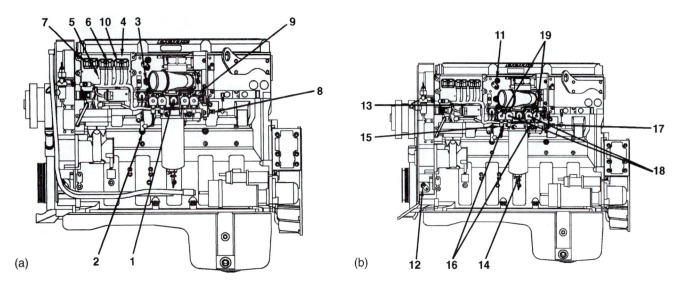

FIGURE 22–69 *Major components for the Signature, ISX, and QSX dual overhead camshaft engines fuel system. (a) 1, Fuel shutoff valve; 2, oil pressure/temperature sensor; 3, intake manifold pressure/temperature sensor; 4, cooling plate behind the ECM; 5, ECM; 6, ECM/engine harness port (actuator); 7, ECM/engine harness port (OEM); 8, fuel inlet; 9, fuel outlet; 10, ECM/sensor port. (b) 11, Camshaft position sensor; 12, crankshaft position sensor; 13, ambient air pressure sensor; 14, water-in-fuel sensor; 15, fuel pressure sensor; 16, front and rear rail sensors; 17, fuel inlet restriction sensor; 18, timing actuators; 19, fueling actuators; 20, coolant level sensor (in radiator)—optional. (Courtesy of Cummins Engine Company, Inc.)*

performance through the electronic wastegate. See Chapter 13 for wastegate information.

When a problem occurs with an electronic wastegate, typically a fault code 466 and 492 will log in ECM memory. See Table 22–2. In both fault cases the engine will run in a derated mode of operation. The resistance of the wastegate solenoids *must* be checked when these two codes are logged. As an example, in both the ISX and ISM engine models, the wastegate solenoid resistance values should measure as follows:

1. *12 V system*—7 to 8 ohms at room temperature (68 to 77°F/20 to 25°C). At other temperatures the resistance should read between 6 to 10 ohms.

2. *24 V system*—28 to 32 ohms resistance at room temperature. At other temperatures the resistance should read between 24 to 40 ohms.

Other features available with these engines includes Cummins Intellect family of software for selected information gathering, and Inform software for management reporting features which lets the driver download data from the ECM to a PC. The ISX system is compatible with Cummins new Inrange option for wireless "drive-through downloading" as trucks are refueling at company facilities. Cummins electronic engines are compatible with Cummins RoadRelay 4 in-dash system which is similar to Detroit Diesel's Pro-Driver system.

As with other electronically controlled diesel engine systems, when a problem occurs, the ECM immediately notifies the driver by illumination of a dash-mounted light, then the engine protection system automatically derates the engine until the fault is brought under control. If the ECM is programmed to do so, should the problem become serious enough, the engine protection system will shut down the engine to prevent serious mechanical damage. When a fault code is detected by the ECM monitoring system, the driver can activate a "snapshot feature" to record events that have led to the sensor-out-of-range conditions. This permits the service technician to download this data at a service facility. Combined with Cummins Intercept and Insite, the service technician can pinpoint the diagnostic trouble code and follow step-by-step instructions on how to repair the fault along with laptop screen–supplied diagrams and views. The diagnostics system will then confirm if the repairs have cured the problem.

Fuel System Description

The fuel system employed with the ISX/Signature engines is an ECM electronically controlled design. The general arrangement of the system is shown in Figure 22–70. In this system, fuel from the tank (1) is directed through a fuel filter/water separator (2) on its way up to the gear-type fuel pump (3). This pump supply pressure is regulated to between 245 to 320 psi

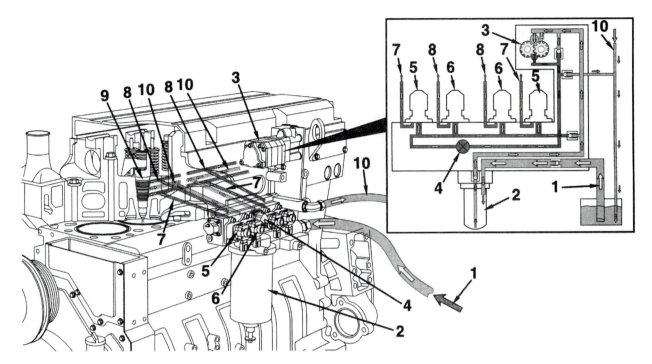

FIGURE 22–70 *Signature series engine fuel system flow diagram: 1, fuel supply from tank; 2, fuel filter; 3, gear pump; 4, fuel shutoff valve; 5, rail metering actuator; 6, timing actuator; 7, rail metering supply to injector; 8, timing fuel supply to injector; 9, injector; 10, fuel drain to tank. (Courtesy of Cummins Engine Company, Inc.)*

(1689 to 2206 kPa) at 2100 engine rpm. Fuel then passes through a 36 micron pressure side filter and through a rapid re-start type fuel shutoff valve (4) as it passes up to the fuel rail metering actuators (5) and timing actuators (6). Both of these actuators are opened by an electronically controlled signal from the ECM. Pressurized fuel leaving the actuators (5 and 6) is directed to the injectors (9). The timing of these events is tied to piston position, engine speed, and load. Fuel return from the injectors is routed back to the fuel tank through the drain line (10) for cooling purposes. The fuel injectors are of the open-nozzle design as shown in Figure 22–71. This is opposite to that of the closed-nozzle design used with the ISC engines.

The major components of the fuel system are illustrated in Figures 22–69 and 22–70. The ECM processes information from the various engine/vehicle sensors and controls the fuel pressure and timing via the actuators (items 5 and 6 shown in Figure 22–70). Therefore, the quantity of metered fuel to the injectors and combustion chambers determines the engine torque and horsepower accordingly.

The fuel system on the ISX/Signature and QSX15 engines is arranged so that the control system is split into two banks. The front bank controls cylinders 1–2–3, and the rear bank controls cylinders 4–5–6. This is why there are two rail metering and two timing ac-

tuators shown as items 5 and 6 in Figure 22–70. The ECM timing ensures that only one injector within the bank receives fuel at a given time.

The components of the fuel delivery housing are shown in Figures 22–72a and b to illustrate both the front and rear views.

Fuel System Specifications

When problems are traced to the fuel system, simple checks and diagnostics will often show that lack of power complaints, rough running, and hard starting are often the fault of the mechanical and not the electronic system. Basic quick checks in these instances would involve testing/monitoring the following areas:

1. Maximum allowable restriction to the pump with or without a fuel cooler:
   - Clean filter (new); 8 in. Hg (203 mm Hg)
   - Dirty filter (in use); 12 in. Hg (305 mm Hg)
2. Maximum allowable fuel return line restriction; 9 in. Hg (229 mm Hg)
3. Minimum allowable fuel tank vent capability 70 ft^3/h (2.0 m^3/h)
4. Maximum allowable fuel inlet temperature 160°F (71°C)
5. Fuel shutoff solenoid resistance; 7 to 8 ohms

FIGURE 22–71 *Signature/ISX engine injector external components. (Courtesy of Cummins Engine Company, Inc.)*

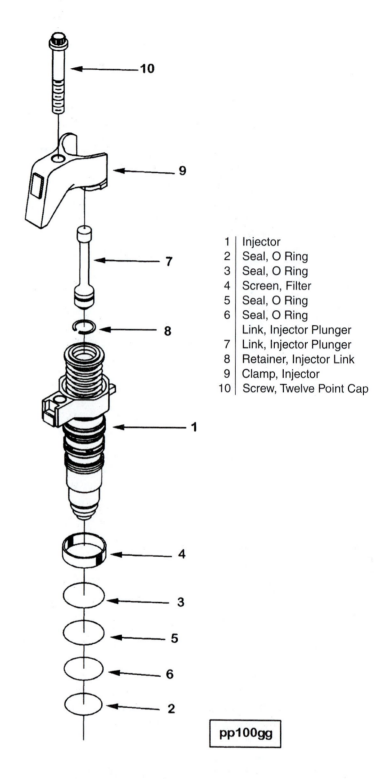

1	Injector
2	Seal, O Ring
3	Seal, O Ring
4	Screen, Filter
5	Seal, O Ring
6	Seal, O Ring
	Link, Injector Plunger
7	Link, Injector Plunger
8	Retainer, Injector Link
9	Clamp, Injector
10	Screw, Twelve Point Cap

pp100gg

ISX Engines—Hard Starting

Insite Software

When you encounter a problem with a difficult-to-start or a no-start condition on ISX model engines, use of the Cummins Insite diagnostic program can lead you to possible causes. However, in many instances, a difficult start or no-start condition can often be attributed to a lack or starvation of fuel. Typical causes may include, but are not limited to, air in the fuel system, low fuel level, fuel rail pressure malfunction, fuel shutoff valves closed in the electronic system, high fuel system restriction, integrated fuel system module (IFSM) inlet screen or fuel pump filter screen restricted, IFSM check valves malfunctioning, fuel pump pressure regulators malfunctioning, fuel leak-

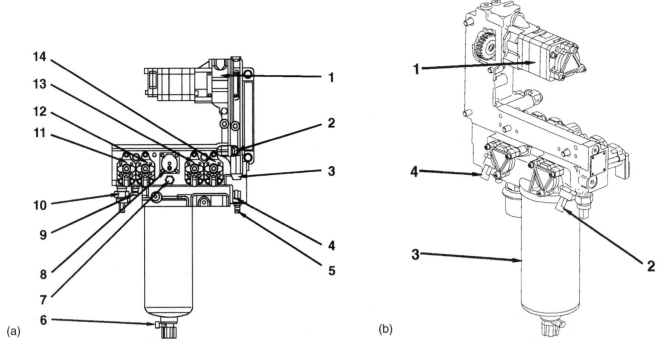

FIGURE 22–72 (a) Signature engine fuel filter and delivery housing front view: 1, internal priming bypass valve; 2, 320 psi (2206 kPa) pressure regulator; 3, 36 micron filter screen; 4, fuel inlet; 5, quick disconnect pressure tap—suction side; 6, water-in-fuel sensor; 7, 250 psi (1724 kPa) pressure regulator; 8, fuel shutoff valve; 9, quick disconnect pressure tap—pressure side; 10, fuel pressure sensor; 11, front rail actuator; 12, front timing actuator; 13, rear timing actuator; 14, rear rail actuator. (b) Rear view of fuel delivery housing: 1, fuel pump assembly; 2, front rail pressure sensor; 3, fuel filter; 4, rear rail pressure sensor. (Courtesy of Cummins Engine Company, Inc.)

age, restricted fuel drain line, fuel pump gear/shaft not rotating, or a malfunctioning injector.

Poor fuel filter maintenance is a common cause of a no-start or hard-start condition. Figure 22–73 illustrates that in the ISX fuel system should the 300 micron inlet filter screen identified as item 5 in the diagram become plugged or contaminated, either of these conditions as described with no visible exhaust smoke can occur.

ISX/Signature Fuel Pressure Control Problems

The fuel pressure regulator controls the normal range of fuel pressure in a running engine. Figure 22–73 shows the location of both the low- and high-end fuel pressure regulators located on the fuel delivery housing on the intake side of the engine block. The low-end (250 psi, 1724 kPa) and the high-end (320 psi, 2206 kPa) pressures are monitored by the ECM. Should the fuel pressure be outside of an acceptable limit, a fault code is activated. The fault code will log quickly for large differences in fuel pressure, and more slowly for smaller differences in fuel pressure. The acceptable range of fuel pressure can be viewed by using Cummins Insite software and a PC or laptop computer sim-

ilar to that shown in Figure 22–49. By selecting the appropriate Insite menu from the monitor screen, fuel pressure can be viewed as, "Fuel Pressure Lower Limit," and "Fuel Pressure Upper Limit." When a low fuel supply pressure is detected at the fuel pressure sensor, a fault code 482 described in Table 22–2 will log in ECM memory. Low fuel pressure will cause a no-start engine condition, or if it does start, low power will occur, and rough running possibly accompanied by white smoke.

Cylinder Performance Test

When conducting a cylinder misfire test on Cummins engines equipped with either Celect, Celect Plus, ISB, ISC, and ISM engine models using Insite while in the monitor mode, a definite sound change to the engine can be detected as you cut out an individual cylinder. with both the ISX and Signature series engines, if you select the Insite monitor mode, *no difference in engine sound will be heard*.

For best results of cylinder misfire, the ISX/Signature engines' ECM should be operated in the cylinder performance test mode. Ensure that Insite version 5.3 or later is used for this test. Also the engine ECM should

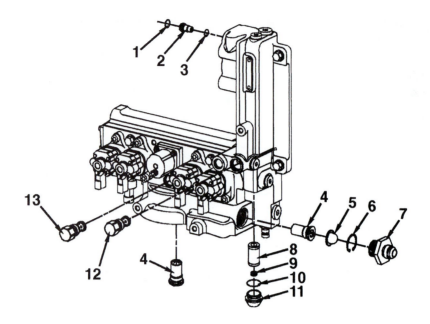

05c00108

Reference No.	Part No.	Part Name	Number Required
1	3042543	Seal, o-ring	1
2	3330056	Valve, check (priming bypass)	1
3	151900	Seal, rectangular ring	2
4	3347960	Valve, check	2
5	4010099	Filter screen, inlet	1
6	3072478	Clip, retainer	1
7	3417130	Union, male	1
8	3090769	Screen, filter	1
9	70700	Spring, compression	1
10	3021123	Seal, o-ring	1
11	3014575	Cap, fuel pump filter	1
12	3348706	Valve, pressure regulator (320 psi)	1
13	3348322	Valve, pressure regulator (250 psi)	1

FIGURE 22–73 Signature/ISX engine exploded view and parts identification for the fuel delivery housing. (Courtesy of Cummins Engine Company, Inc.)

be loaded with a calibration from the March 1999 CD-ROM or later. Prior to a cylinder misfire test, make certain that all air has been removed from the fuel system. This may require running the engine at high idle for several minutes or even road-testing the vehicle to ensure that all air has been purged. To provide further accuracy of the cylinder performance test, maintain the engine at a minimum 150°F (66°C) oil temperature and lock the thermatic fan in the ON position.

SPECIAL NOTE The Signature and ISX engine fuel system is a two-bank design where both the front and back three cylinders share a common fuel and timing rail. Diesel fuel is fed into the rails by electronically controlled pulsing actuators that receive their solenoid-controlled signals from the ECM. The ISX and Signature engines have a 1–5–3–6–2–4 firing order. The front bank fires 1–3–2, while the rear bank fires 5–6–4.

Due to variations in cylinder-to-cylinder interactions such as minor compression pressure differences, solenoid response times, and minute fuel delivery differences, cylinders contributing less than 70%, or greater than 125% will be considered out-of-normal range when the cylinder performance test is conducted. With the Insite diagnostic program connected to the engine ECM, select the cylinder performance

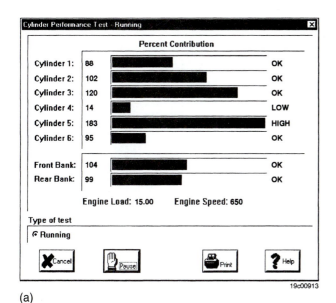

(a)

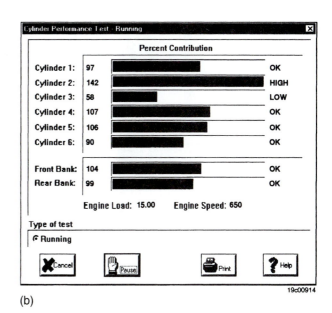

(b)

FIGURE 22–74   (a) Typical Insite screen capture from a PC indicating that both cylinders 4 and 5 of the rear bank are operating outside of the normal parameters of 70% and 125%. (b) Typical Insite screen capture from a PC indicating that cylinder No. 2 is overfueling (142%), while the bar graph indicates that cylinder No. 3 is delivering less than 70% fuel. (Courtesy of Cummins Engine Company, Inc.)

test from the appropriate Insite diagnostic menu. An example of how you might interpret the cylinder performance test results is illustrated in Figure 22–74a, which shows a typical Insite screen capture that indicates both cylinders 4 and 5 of the rear bank are operating outside of the normal parameters of 70% and 125% each. In this example, cylinder No. 4 contained an injector with a stuck lower plunger, while there was no fault with the injector in cylinder No. 5. In Figure 22–74b, cylinder No. 2 is overfueling (142%), while the bar graph indicates that cylinder No. 3 is delivering less than 70%. Checks indicated that No. 3 injector showed a broken lower return spring, while there was no apparent problems in cylinder No. 2. Typical examples for consideration might include the following operating conditions:

1.   If only one injector is contributing less than 70%, or greater than 125%, check the overhead setting on only the injector and valves for that particular cylinder.

2.   If checks indicate that the overhead is correctly adjusted, replace the injector in that cylinder.

3.   If two injectors in the same bank (either 1–3 or 2, or 5–6 or 4) are indicated as delivering less than 70% or greater than 125%, check the overhead (valves and injector) settings on both cylinders.

4.   If adjustments are okay on both cylinders, replace the out-of-range injector that fires first in that bank (1–3 or 2, or 5–6 or 4).

5.   If all three injectors in the same bank show less than 70% or greater than 125%, the service technician should swap the metering actuators from front to back in an attempt to determine if this action causes the problem to follow the swapped actuator. *If* the problem does in fact follow the swapped actuator, then it confirms that the actuator is the cause of the fault and it should be replaced.

Other Considerations

If an injector fails so that the operating condition prevents injection of the correct volume of fuel from actuator solenoid pulse energizing via the ECM, this could be caused by a stuck lower injector plunger, a broken lower return spring, and so on. Therefore, diesel fuel that is not actually injected as it should be will be retained in the fuel rail until the next injector in the engine firing order of that same bank (1–3 or 2 in the front bank, or 5–6 or 4 in the rear bank) is fired by activation of the actuator PWM ECM solenoid signal.

ISX/Signature Wiring Diagram

Figure 22–75 illustrates the wiring diagram used with ISX and Signature model 15 L electronically controlled engines. (This diagram, although similar to the one shown in Figure 18–4 for the Celect Plus 14 L engines, uses a different ECM.) The Celect Plus engines use three 28-pin plug-in connectors, while the ISX/Signature models employ three plug-in harness connectors,

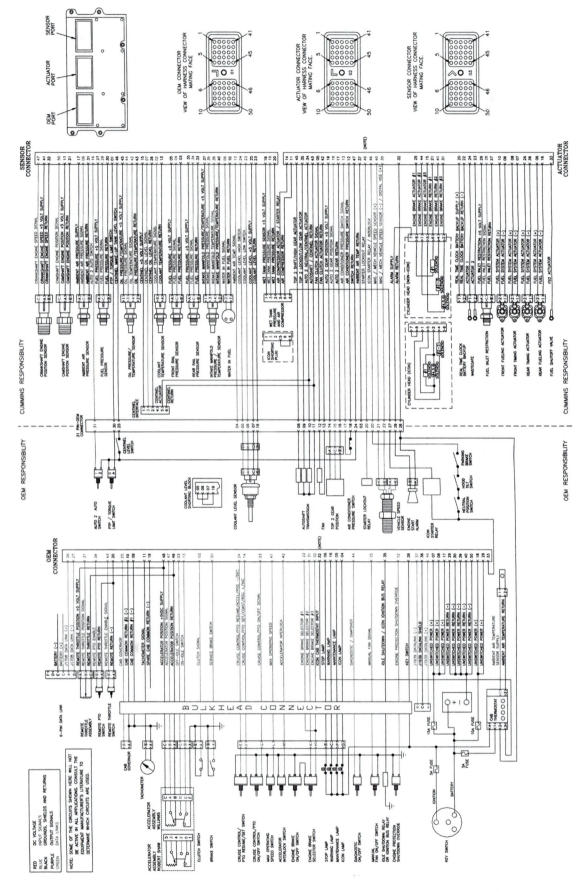

FIGURE 22-75 Signature/ISX engine wiring diagram system schematic. (Courtesy of Cummins Engine Company, Inc.)

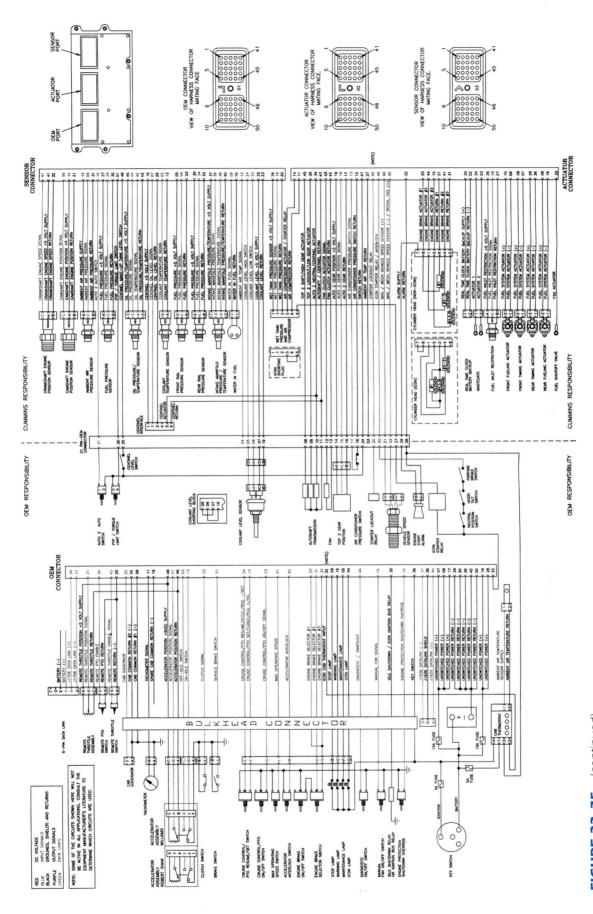

FIGURE 22-75 (continued).

but they are placed on the front face of the ECM rather than on the side. The three harness/ECM connectors used with the ISX/Signature engines are the OEM port shown at the top left of the ECM, the actuator port located in the center of the ECM, and the sensor port located on the top right of the ECM housing. These three plug-in connectors/ports each contain a 50-pin socket, made up of two 25-pin harness connectors. These can be seen in the wiring diagram.

When troubleshooting fault codes, particularly for opens, shorts, or grounds, or when directed to a specific connector by Insite or Compulink, *always* refer to this diagram. A plasticized version of this diagram can be obtained from your Cummins dealer under Bulletin 3666268-01. Note that slight variations exist between the ECM part number used; therefore, where possible, quote the ECM part number.

Both the ISB and ISC model engines use a similar-looking ECM to the ISX/Signature, but they only use two connectors, an engine, and an OEM connector each with a 50-pin arrangement similar to that shown for the ISX/Signature ECM models.

ISX/Signature Overhead Adjustment

Cummins recommends that the overhead (valves and injectors) be checked and set at intervals of 500,000 miles (800,000 km), 10,000 hours, or five years, whichever comes first. However, these adjustments are required after any major repair that requires the cylinder head or valve train to be removed.

The valve and injector settings on ISX and Signature engines are very similar to the OBC (outer base circle) method used for other Cummins engines described earlier in this chapter, in that both the valves and injectors are checked and adjusted on the same index mark on the vibration damper. Figure 22–24a indicates the injector and valve adjustment sequence used. To facilitate engine crankshaft rotation in a CW direction, remove the oil-fill connector located on the front of the engine timing cover above and to the right of the vibration damper. Use a 0.75 in. drive ratchet and short extension, as shown in Figure 22–76, inserted into the air compressor drive. The engine firing order is 1–5–3–6–2–4 with number 1 starting at the front of the engine. By following the sequence shown in Figure 22–24a, all valves and injectors can be set in two complete revolutions (720°) of crankshaft rotation. Both the valve clearances and injector setting values are listed on the CPL plate attached to the side of the engine timing cover. When using the sequence shown in Figure 22–24a, ensure that the valves are fully closed on the cylinder on which you are going to set the valve clearances. The A-B-C vibration damper

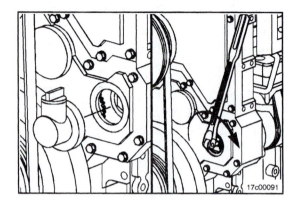

FIGURE 22–76 Using a 0.75 in. (19 mm) square drive ratchet and short extension inserted into the air compressor drive to manually rotate the crankshaft over to set/check the valves and injectors. (Courtesy of Cummins Engine Company, Inc.)

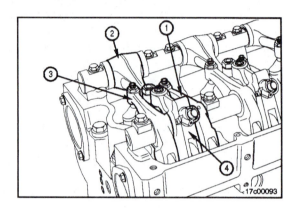

FIGURE 22–77 Identification of the Signature/ISX engine rocker levers: 1, exhaust valve rocker lever; 2, injector rocker lever; 3, intake valve rocker lever; 4, engine compression brake rocker lever. (Courtesy of Cummins Engine Company, Inc.)

markings are aligned with a static scribed line on the front of the timing cover at approximately the 9 o'clock position where the oil-fill cover is located.

Injector Setting

Figure 22–77 illustrates the four rocker levers for one cylinder and identifies their function. Begin by loosening the appropriate injector adjusting screw locknut and back it out between one to two full turns. Use a torque wrench and tighten the screw to 70 in-lb (6 N · m). Hold the screw and torque the locknut to 55 ft-lb (75 N · m).

Valve Lash Setting

Proceed to set the valve lash clearance on the same cylinder on which you set the injector. Back off the

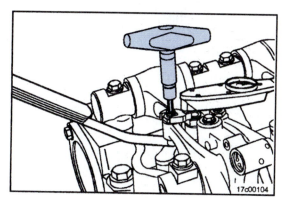

FIGURE 22–78 *Setting the Signature/ISX engine valve lash with a feeler gauge, Cummins special T-handle tool 3376592 and torque wrench. (Courtesy of Cummins Engine Company, Inc.)*

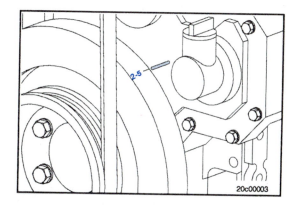

FIGURE 22–79 *Signature/ISX engine compression brake setting positions; example shows cylinders 2–5 on the crankshaft damper aligned with the stationary scribe line for earlier engines. Later models use the letters A, B, and C, where A = 1–6, B = 2–5, C = 3–4. (Courtesy of Cummins Engine Company, Inc.)*

valve rocker arm locknut and turn out the screws between one to two turns. Insert the correct feeler gauge (see CPL for spec) between the top of the crosshead and the rocker lever nose pad as shown in Figure 22–78. Tighten down the adjusting screw to 5 to 6 in-lb with a small torque wrench, or use the Cummins special T-handle tool, PN 3376592 shown in Figure 22–78. Always use a torque wrench with a crows-foot to tighten the locknut to 33 ft-lb (45 N · m). Be sure to hold the adjusting screw while torquing the retaining nut. Remove the feeler gauge. Set the remaining valve clearances in a similar manner.

Compression Brake Set

To set the engine compression brakes, follow the engine firing order of 1–5–3–6–2–4. On early-model engines, locate the brake-set marks shown on the circumference of the engine vibration damper as shown in Figure 22–79. Notice that there are two cylinder brake set marks side by side, which appear as follows:

Brake set 1–6—adjust cylinder 1 or 6
Brake set 2–5—adjust cylinder 2 or 5
Brake set 3–4—adjust cylinder 3 or 4

Newer engine model vibration dampers are marked with only A, B, or C, where A indicates that cylinder 1 or 6 can be adjusted, B means that cylinder 2 or 5 can be adjusted, and C means that cylinder 3 or 4 can be adjusted. With a firing order of 1–5–3–6–2–4, 1 and 6, 2 and 5, and 3 and 4 are mated cylinders, meaning only one of these brakes can be set at any one brake set or A-B-C position. Your guide is to check that both the intake and exhaust valves are fully closed (in the valve-set position). If not, rotate the

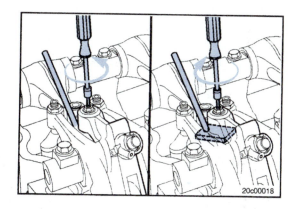

FIGURE 22–80 *Using a special feeler gauge tool to check/set the engine compression brake clearance for a Signature/ISX engine. (Courtesy of Cummins Engine Company, Inc.)*

crankshaft another 360° using the 0.75 in. bar concept shown in Figure 22–76. Loosen off the locknut on the brake-lever adjusting screw and back out the adjusting screw one full turn. Insert the correct feeler gauge (part number 3163530, which is 0.276 in. + or − 0.005 in./7.00 mm + or − 0.13 mm) between the bottom of the brake piston and the top of the exhaust pin on the crosshead assembly. Tighten the screw until the proper drag is felt at the feeler gauge indicated when there is no motion of the brake lever camshaft follower against the cam lobe. Hold the brake lever adjusting screw as shown in Figure 22–80 and tighten the locknut to 177 in-lb (20 N · m). Repeat for the other brake settings.

SUMMARY

In this chapter you have acquired technical information about Cummins mechanical and electronic engines. With their diversity of product offerings, Cummins Engine Company, Inc., use PLN fuel systems supplied by Robert Bosch Corporation, distributor pumps supplied by Stanadyne Diesel Systems, Robert Bosch Corporation, and Delphi Automotive Systems, the PT (Pressure-Time) fuel system in their earlier mechanically governed engines, and a variety of electronically controlled injection pumps supplied by each one of these major OEM's. The Cummins CELECT (Cummins Electronics), and CELECT Plus fuel systems are of their own design. The later model ISX and Signature series engines with their dual overhead camshaft design and electronics package is their most technologically advanced heavy-duty high speed heavy-duty truck, industrial and marine engine in its horsepower class within the Cummins engine family. Larger displacement and higher horsepower engines are available from Cummins for off-highway, mining, industrial and marine applications. Details of how to use diagnostic tooling and equipment should now be fairly familiar to you. Self-test your knowledge with the numerous end-of-chapter questions, and raise your expertise of the Cummins products by performing hands-on tasks of engine overhaul and repair, troubleshooting and diagnostics, as well as preventive maintenance procedures.

SELF-TEST QUESTIONS

1. Technician A says that the CPL dataplate indicates the control parts list for the engine. Technician B says that the CPL plate means "Cummins pump list." Who is correct?

2. Technician A says that the letters PT stand for "pressure timed" system. Technician B says that it stands for "pump timed." Who is right?

3. Technician A says that the amount of PT fuel flow at idle is controlled by the size of the idle spring plunger. Technician B says that fuel flow at idle is controlled by the throttle position. Who is correct?

4. Technician A states that fuel pressure in the PT system is produced by a gear-type pump. Technician B says that it is produced by a plunger-actuated pump from the injection pump housing. Who is correct?

5. Technician A states that fuel flow to the PT injectors is controlled by the idle spring. Technician B says that the throttle control shaft provides an external means of manually restricting or interrupting the fuel flow to the injectors. Who is right?

6. Technician A says that if the fuel solenoid was faulty, the engine could be started and stopped by manual rotation of the PT pump thumbscrew on the top of the pump. Technician B says that you would have to replace the solenoid. Who is correct?

7. Technician A says that to adjust the engine idle speed on a PT system, you would have to remove the pipe plug on the end of the pump spring housing, insert a screwdriver, and rotate the adjusting screw CW to increase the speed and CCW to decrease it. Technician B says that this is not necessary; you simply have to adjust the external throttle shaft lever stop screws to alter the idle speed. Who is right?

8. Technician A says that to manually stop the engine, you can rotate the PT pump thumbscrew outward. Technician B says that you should turn the thumbscrew inward. Who is correct?

9. Technician A says that the letters AFC following a PTG pump designation stands for "air fuel control." Technician B says that it stands for "aftercooler fuel control." Who is correct?

10. The injector supply pressure in a PTG-AFC fuel pump is determined or preset by
    a. the size of the injector supply orifice
    b. the relief valve pressure in the transfer pump
    c. the recess size of the idle plunger
    d. throttle leakage

11. Technician A says that the Cummins PT governor controls engine speed by controlling the fuel supply to the engine by regulating the fuel pressure. Technician B says that the governor mechanically limits the fuel flow. Who is correct?

12. At an idle speed, technician A says that the PT governor weights pull the idle-speed plunger backward to allow fuel flow. Technician B disagrees, saying that the weights push against the plunger in order to compress the idle spring and position the plunger recess. Who is right?

13. Technician A says that during high-speed governing in the PT fuel system, idle fuel flow is cut off completely and fuel flows through the main passage only. Technician B says that you still need idle passage fuel flow to supplement that from the main passage. Who is correct?

14. Technician A says that metering takes place in the PT injector when the plunger is held down. Technician B disagrees, saying that metering can occur only when the plunger is held up. Who is right?

15. Technician A says that the amount of fuel injected depends on the time that the metering orifice is uncovered and the pressure on the fuel. Technician B says that the amount of fuel injected is dependent on the size of the injector balance orifice. Who is right?

16. Technician A says that all of the valves and injectors can be adjusted in one complete revolution of the crankshaft. Technician B disagrees and says that two complete revolutions of the crankshaft are necessary. Who is correct?

17. The three VS (valve set) marks A, B, and C stamped on the accessory drive pulley on an L10 or 14 L engine relate to cylinder numbers:
    a. A = 1–6, B = 2–5, C = 3–4
    b. A = 1–3, B = 2–5, C = 4–6
    c. A = 2–5, B = 3–4, C = 1–6
    d. A = 3–4, B = 1–2, C = 5–6

18. Technician A says that injection timing relates to the amount of push tube travel remaining before the injector plunger bottoms in its cup with the piston BTDC on its compression stroke. Technician B says that injection timing relates to the alignment marks between the PT pump and the engine crankshaft. Who is right?

19. Technician A says that the injection timing specification can be found stamped on the engine CPL plate. Technician B says that you have to obtain the PT pump part number and then cross-reference the Cummins PT fuel pump specifications booklet. Who is right?

20. Technician A says that when checking injector push tube travel, if the dial indicator reading was less than that specified, the timing would be slow or retarded. Technician B says that this would be indicative of fast or advanced timing. Who is correct here?

21. Technician A says that on 14 L NT and L10 model engines, the injection timing can be changed by adding or subtracting cam follower housing gasket thickness. Technician B says that you would change the timing on an L10 by installing a different offset camshaft key. Who is right?

22. Technician A says that increasing the gasket thickness on the cam follower housing will advance injection. Technician B says that this action will retard the timing. Who is correct?

23. Technician A says that the Cummins Compuchek system is a vehicle cruise-control system. Technician B disagrees, stating that Compuchek is simply a diagnostic test tool to monitor engine operating conditions. Who is correct?

24. Technician A says that engine cylinder balance can be checked on a Cummins engine by using the Compulink system. Technician B disagrees and says that you have to perform an engine compression check in order to determine cylinder compression and therefore cylinder balance. Which technician understands the functions of the Compuchek or Compulink system?

25. Technician A says that a simple gear pump controls fuel system pressure in a Celect system. Technician B says that the Celect fuel system pressure is controlled by the size of the fuel pump button recess as in the PT system. Who is correct?

26. Technician A says that the Celect system operates at an approximate fuel pressure of 200 psi (1379 kPa). Technician B says that this is too high and that it is usually around 140 to 150 psi (965 to 1034 kPa). Who is correct?

27. Technician A says that diesel fuel routed through the ECM cooling plate functions to keep the internal solid-state components at a safe operating temperature. Technician B says that the purpose of the cooling plate is to allow ECM warm-up in cold ambient temperatures. Who is correct here?

28. Technician A says that the purpose of the EPS (engine position sensor) on a Celect system is to monitor engine rpm. Technician B disagrees and says that its function is to provide both a piston position and engine speed condition to the ECM. Who is right?

29. Technician A says that on a Celect-equipped engine, only the engine coolant temperature sensor signal to the ECM will determine the engine idle speed at startup. However, technician B states that it is the engine oil temperature sensor signal that determines the initial idle speed at startup. Who is correct?

30. Technician A says that when an oil or coolant sensor signal on the Celect system is outside normal operating parameters, the ECM will lower the engine's maximum speed automatically. Technician B says that only a low coolant level sensor will do this. Who knows the Celect system best?

31. Technician A says that the TSP (throttle position sensor) on the Celect system is mounted on the PT fuel pump housing, whereas technician B says that it is located within the throttle pedal in the vehicle cab. Who is correct?

32. On a Celect-equipped engine, technician A says that any time the throttle pedal is in any position but idle, both the PTO and engine brakes will be deactivated. Technician B says that depressing the throttle pedal past idle will allow the cruise control feature to be overridden. Are both technician correct, or only one of them?

33. The term PWM (pulse-width modulated) refers to the
    a. duration in crankshaft degrees that the injector actually delivers fuel
    b. length of signal duration from the engine position sensor
    c. percentage of throttle depression
    d. fuel pressure created in the fuel rail to the electronically controlled injectors.

34. Technician A says that each time the idle-speed adjust switch is toggled once on a Celect engine, the idle rpm will increase by approximately 50 rpm. Technician B says that the speed change is closer to 25 rpm. Who is right?

35. Technician A says that the maximum fuel system pressure in the Celect system is controlled by a spring-loaded bypass valve within the gear pump. Technician B says that a restricted fuel return fitting in the fuel rail to the injectors controls the fuel pressure. Who is right?

36. On a Celect-equipped engine, technician A says that the injector is manually operated by a rocker arm and pushrod similar to that used on a PT system to create the pressures necessary for injection. Technician B says not so, that the injector is operated by an electric solenoid to create the high fuel pressures necessary for injection

purposes. After all, he asks, isn't that what electronic fuel injection is all about? Which technician understands how the Celect system operates?

37. Technician A says that in order for injection to occur within the Celect injector, a metering spill port must be closed. Technician B says that there is no metering spill port and that injection begins and ends based on the PWM signal to the injector from the ECM. Who is correct?

38. Technician A says that metering ends in the Celect injector when the small electric control valve is opened by a signal from the ECM. Technician B says that fuel metering is controlled by gear pump pressure. Who is right?

39. Technician A says that fuel system performance checks of the Celect system can be performed only by using a handheld electronic diagnostic data reader. Technician B says that a fuel supply restriction check, fuel drain line restriction check, and cooling plate restriction check can be performed in a similar manner to that for a PT-equipped engine. Which mechanic/technician is correct?

40. Technician A says that removal of a Celect injector from the cylinder head should be done only after the rocker boxes have been removed, and then only by use of a special hydraulic puller. Technician B says that the injector can be removed in a similar manner to that for a PT injector by employing a similarly designed type of injector puller. Which technician is correct here?

41. Technician A says that the valves and injectors adjustments on a Celect-equipped engine follow the same basic procedure as that on a PT-equipped engine. Technician B says that no injector adjustment is required since the injector is electronically controlled. Which technician is correct?

42. Technician A says that the Celect injector can be checked for a misfire condition in the same manner as for a PT injector. Technician B says that an electronic diagnostic data reader is required to effectively short out the ECM signal to the injector solenoid. Who is right?

43. Technician A says that a fault code lamp 311 on a Celect engine model see Table 22–1, would indicate that current to an injector is shut off. Technician B says that it indicates a possible no start condition due to no power to the fuel solenoid. Who is right?

44. Technician A says that when using a Cummins ECHECK hand held diagnostic reader, an S before a fault code indicates it is an SAE code. Technician B says it is an SAE code, but is specific to a subsystem identifier fault. Who is correct?

45. Refer to Table 22–1, and Chapter 18, page 481. Technician A says that a FMI number 6 indicates that the cause of the failure is related to the current above normal or a grounded circuit. Technician B says that it indicates the cause as being too high a voltage. Who is correct?

46. Refer to Table 22–1 and Chapter 18, page 481. Technician A says that a FMI number 5 indicates that the cause of the fault code is related to current below normal, or an open circuit. Technician B says that it is an abnormal rate of change condition. Who is correct?

47. Refer to Table 22–1 and Chapter 18, page 481. Technician A says that a FMI number 12 indicates a fault code related to voltage below normal or shorted low. Technician B says it means a bad intelligent device or component. Who is correct?

48. Technician A says that the Cummins Road Relay is a device that provides access to vital operational data. Technician B says that the Road Relay is simply a cruise control device. Which tech is right?

49. Technician A says that there are two warning systems on Cummins electronic engines. One monitors the electronic fuel system, while the second one monitors the engine protection system. Technician B says that only one system is used, and that is the engine protection system. Who is correct?

50. The Cummins engine protection system monitors which one of the following sensors and conditions?
    a. coolant temperature and coolant level
    b. oil temperature and pressure
    c. intake manifold temperature
    d. all of the above

51. Technician A says that any fault code stored in ECM memory registers, is always "active". Technician B says that it could be historic or "inactive". Who is right?

52. Which one of the following methods can be used to access diagnostic fault codes in Cummins engines?
    a. Actuating the diagnostic switch or shorting plug on the dash
    b. Use the Cummins ECHECK handheld reader
    c. Use Cummins Compulink system
    d. Use a laptop computer with Cummins Insite
    e. Using a Palm Pilot
    f. All of the above

53. Technician A says that the injector solenoids will typically exhibit a resistance value when checked with an ohmmeter of between 5 and 15 ohms. Technician B says the value should range between 0.5 and 1.5 ohms. Who is correct?

54. Technician A says that injector fault codes will exhibit numbers from 311 through 333. Technician B says that these codes range from 400 through 415 series of numbers. Who is correct?

55. Technician A says that an 'audit trail' can be accessed to assist the technician in determining an explanation when attempting to find the cause of a fault code. Technician B says that the audit trail is only used when reprogramming the ECM. Who is correct?

56. Technician A says that a ACPT test is an active control PT fuel system test. Technician B says that it is an automated cylinder performance test. Who is right?

57. Which one of the following Cummins engines is equipped with a Robert Bosch VP44 electronically controlled injection pump?
    a. B engine
    b. C engine
    c. M11
    d. ISX and Signature models

58. Technician A says that the letters ISC mean Injection System Controls. Technician B says it means Interact System—C model engine. Who is correct?

59. Technician A says that the letters FPCM mean, fuel pump controls for a M series engine. Technician B says that it means fuel pump control module. Who is correct?

60. Technician A says that on an ISB 24 valve engine model, hard starting, visible exhaust smoke, or engine power derate could be due to use of the incorrect pump woodruff key. Technician B says this would not affect the engine performance, and that the cause is more likely to be due to fuel starvation. Who is correct?

61. Technician A says that the acronym CAPS means Cummins Accumulator Pump System. Technician B says it means Cummins Advanced Pressure System. Who is correct?

62. Technician A says that the ISC model engines are equipped with a CAPS fuel system. Technician B says only the Signature series engine models use this system. Who is correct?

63. The CAPS fuel system is capable of operating at pressures as high as:
    a. 18,000 psi (124.1 MPa)
    b. 20,000 psi (137.9 MPa)
    c. 22,000 psi (151.7 MPa)
    d. 24,000 psi (165.5 MPa)

64. Technician A says that when checking sensors and switches for a voltage value on Cummins engines, you should register between 4.25 and 5 VDC. Technician B says you should measure between 4.75 to 5.25 VDC. Who is correct?

65. Technician A says that when checking for voltage at a sensor harness you should register between 4.5 and 5.25 VDC. Technician B says it should be between 4.75 and 5.5 VDC. Who is correct?

66. ISC engines equipped with the CAPS fuel system employ an electrically heated intake air grid element to facilitate ease of cold weather starting. Technician A says that this heater will vaporize starting fluid easier to assist in a quick start. Technician B says that you should never use starting fluid with this system, otherwise serious engine damage can occur. Who is correct?

67. Technician A says that the Signature engines use a variable output turbocharger, therefore a wastegate is not required. Technician B says that all turbochargers require a wastegate to prevent overboost protection. Who is correct?

68. The fuel pump supply pressure on a Signature model engine runs between:
    a. 150 to 190 psi (1034 to 1310 kPa)
    b. 210 to 225 psi (1448 to 1551 kPa)
    c. 245 to 320 psi (1689 to 2206 kPa)
    d. 285 to 360 psi (1965 to 2482 kPa)

69. Technician A says that the fuel system on a Signature engine is split into two banks with the front bank controlling cylinders 1–2–3, while the rear bank controls cylinders 4–5–6. Technician B says that the front bank controls 1–5–3, while the rear bank controls 6–2–4. Who is correct?

70. Technician A says that a fault code on an ISX or Signature engine with a SID018 and a FMI of 6 would indicate low current detected at the rear fueling actuator circuit. Technician B says it would mean that high current has been detected at the front fueling actuator circuit and that the engine will only run using the rear three cylinders. Who is correct?

23

Caterpillar Fuel Systems

Overview

In this chapter we describe the purpose, function, and operation of the various Caterpillar pump-line-nozzle (PLN) fuel systems, as well as the MUI (mechanical unit injector), EUI (electronic unit injector), and HEUI (hydraulically actuated EUI) fuel systems. Diagnostic tooling required for electronic engine maintenance, diagnosis, analysis, and troubleshooting is also provided, as are certain adjustments and checks for mechanical fuel systems. An overview and prerequisites for Caterpillar electronic fuel systems study should begin with a review of Chapter 18. End-of-chapter questions are provided to assist you in self-checking your progress and in ensuring that after performing the various ASE hands-on content area tasks lists, that you are prepared to challenge either the ASE or TQ (Trade Qualification) test areas.

ASE CERTIFICATION

Within the ASE medium/heavy truck tests preparation guide, diesel engines, test T2, subsection F, Fuel System Diagnosis and Repair, Parts 1 and 2, Mechanical and Electronic Components, the various content tasks lists are provided. In addition, the ASE electronic diesel engine diagnosis specialist test (L2) deals with the knowledge and hands-on skills required to successfully challenge and certify in this specialist area. Chapter 18 provides an overview of the theory and diagnosis of electronic engines and the content area tasks lists knowledge that is required. Chapter 19 deals with Bosch fuel systems. It illustrates the ASE subsection F, Fuel System Diagnosis and Repair, Mechanical and Electronic Components tasks lists. You must be knowledgeable and capable of performing all of these tasks in order to prepare yourself for challenging either the ASE or

TQ test areas. Detailed copies of both the T2 and L2 ASE content areas preparation guides can be downloaded from the ASE website (*www.asecert.org*). Internet version.

COMPANY BACKGROUND

Caterpillar Tractor Company, now known as Caterpillar, Inc., was formed on April 15, 1925, as the result of a merger between two well-known U.S. west coast firms, the Holt Manufacturing Company and the C.L. Best Gas Traction Company. Both of these companies were formed in 1869. Caterpillar's Engine Division was started in 1931 as the Special Sales Group and was formed into the Engine Division of Caterpillar in 1953. Today "Caterpillar" and "Cat" are registered trademarks of this well-known company.

SYSTEM STRUCTURE AND FUNCTION

Caterpillar has used a variety of different styles of fuel systems over the years on its different engine series. These systems include the following:

1. *Forged body fuel system:* individual pumping plunger elements contained in a bolted and flanged body attached to the top of the fuel injection pump housing. Used on earlier-model Cat engines.

2. *Compact body fuel system:* similar in external appearance to some Bosch PLN systems where individual pumping plungers and barrels are contained within a common housing. Each pumping element can be removed individually from the main injection pump housing. Used across the line of Cat engine products for many years.

3. *New scroll fuel system* (NSFS): an update of the compact body system. The NSFS incorporates a more robust design to permit higher injection pressures; used initially on the 3406B and 3406C mechanical model engines.

4. *Sleeve metering fuel system* (SMFS): designed for use on the 3208 and earlier-model 3300 series engines. This design incorporates a sliding sleeve through which the pumping plunger strokes. The sleeve position determines the effective stroke and therefore the quantity and timing of the fuel delivered.

5. *Mechanical unit injector* (MUI) *system:* used on the 3116, 3500, and 3600 engines. The MUI operates similar to that described for a DDC unit injector. The major difference is that with the Cat MUI, the rack movement is opposite that for the DDC models.

6. *Electronic unit injector* (EUI) *system:* rocker arm activated, but controlled by energizing an electric solenoid which receives its signal from an ECM (electronic control module). This system is used on the 3176, C10, C12, 3406E, 3500, and 3600 engines.

7. *Hydraulically actuated electronic unit injector* (HEUI) *system:* currently in use on the 3126, 3408E, and 3412E engine models.

The general concept of operation of Cat's PLN fuel systems is similar to that described for Bosch injection pumps, while the MUI and EUI systems are similar to that described for DDC's unit injectors. In this chapter we discuss briefly the NSFS, EUI, and HEUI fuel systems.

NEW SCROLL FUEL SYSTEM: 3306 AND 3406 ENGINES

Injection Pump Operation

The *new scroll* fuel system was introduced in 1979 and was targeted initially for the 3300 series engines. Since that time Caterpillar has applied the new scroll system to the 3300 and 3406B truck engines. As mentioned earlier in the introductory comments dealing with the various types of fuel systems that have been and are now in use on Caterpillar diesel engines, the major reason for using the new scroll fuel system was to create higher injection pressures for use on direct-injection engines, which offer approximately 10% fuel economy improvement over precombustion-type engines. The ability to meet long-term EPA exhaust emission regulations and better overall engine performance, as well as the ability to provide greater parts commonality between different series of engines and lower overall heat rejection, allow new scroll engines to use smaller cooling systems than those of previous

engines. In addition, service personnel will be able to use the same special tooling and test procedures to tune up, adjust, and troubleshoot fuel systems on different engines.

A schematic of the new scroll fuel system flow is shown in Figure 23–1, which illustrates the injection nozzle mounted straight up and down in the cylinder since it is located underneath the rocker cover. This is common to the 3406 engine; however, the injection nozzle in the 3300 series engines is mounted outside the rocker cover and is installed at an angle of 15° to position the nozzle tip in the center of the piston. The new scroll injection pump is shown in Figure 23–2, while the actual flow through the pump barrel is illustrated by the arrows in Figure 23–3. In the new scroll system shown in Figure 23–3, two ports are used: the bypass closed port (4) and the spill port (1). Fuel is supplied from the transfer pump to an internal fuel manifold in the injection pump housing at approximately 35 psi (240 kPa). When the pump plunger is at the bottom of its stroke, fuel at transfer pump pressure flows around the pump barrel and to both the bypass closed port (4) and spill port (1), which are both open at this time to allow fuel flow into the barrel area above the pump plunger.

The major advantage of separate fill and spill ports to the plungers is that hot fuel (after the injection period) is not discharged on one stroke and reused on the next stroke such as is the case with the older forged body system and the compact body system. Pump plunger movement is similar to that used in Robert Bosch inline pump systems, in that it is moved up and down by the action of a roller lifter (9) riding on the injection pump camshaft (10), which rotates at one-half engine speed as shown in Figure 23–2. The plunger can also be rotated by the use of a rack (7) and gear (8). As the injection pump camshaft rotates and the plunger rises, some fuel will be pushed back out of the bypass closed port (4) until the top of the plunger eventually closes both the bypass port and the spill port.

NOTE When both ports are covered by the plunger, this is the start of the *effective stroke*, which means that fuel is effectively being placed under pressure and injection will begin. Further plunger movement will cause an increase in the trapped fuel pressure, and at approximately 100 psi (689.5 kPa) the check valve (2) will open and fuel will flow into the fuel injection line to the injection nozzle.

The fuel pressure of 100 psi (689.5 kPa) is insufficient to open the injection nozzle; a pressure of

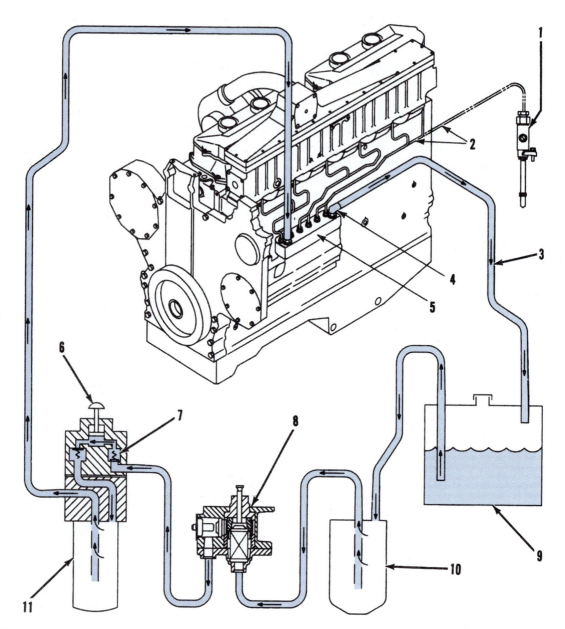

FIGURE 23–1   3406B mechanical fuel system flow schematic: 1, injection nozzle; 2, fuel injection lines; 3, fuel return line; 4, constant-bleed orifice; 5, fuel injection pump; 6, fuel priming pump; 7, check valves; 8, fuel transfer pump; 9, fuel tank; 10, primary fuel filter; 11, secondary fuel filter. (Reprinted courtesy of Caterpillar, Inc.)

between 1200 and 2350 psi (8300 to 16,200 kPa) is required to open it on 3304/3306 engines and between 2400 and 3100 psi (16,500 to 21,390 kPa) on 3406B engines. Fuel-line pressures of 15,000 psi (103,425 kPa) can be maintained with the scroll system, with an injection pump camshaft lift of 0.012 in. per camshaft degree. However, as the plunger continues to move up in its barrel, this fuel pressure is reached very quickly.

A high-pressure bleed-back passage and groove machined around the barrel are in alignment during the effective stroke to bleed off any fuel that leaks between the plunger and barrel for lubrication purposes;

otherwise, engine oil dilution would result. When the upward-moving plunger scroll (helix) (14 in Figure 23–3) uncovers spill port (1), the fuel above the plunger goes through the slot (15) between the solid part of the plunger and the scroll (helix), along the edge of the scroll and out the spill port (1) and a hollow dowel back into the fuel manifold within the injection pump housing. The instant that the scroll uncovers the spill port, injection ceases, and although the plunger can still travel up some more, this is simply to allow most of the warm fuel (due to being pressurized) to spill back out into the manifold.

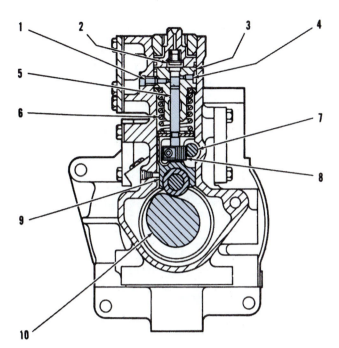

FIGURE 23–2   Cross-sectional view of a new scroll fuel injection pump: 1, spill port; 2, check valve; 3, pump barrel; 4, bypass port; 5, pump plunger; 6, spring; 7, fuel rack; 8, gear; 9, lifter; 10, cam. (Reprinted courtesy of Caterpillar, Inc.)

As the plunger travels down in the barrel, it will once again uncover the bypass closed port (4) and cool fuel will again fill the area above the plunger for the next injection stroke. When the pump spill port is opened as shown in Figure 23–3, pressure inside the barrel is released and the check valve (2) is seated by its spring (13). Within the check valve assembly is a reverse-flow check valve (11) which will be opened by the fuel pressure within the fuel injection line as long as this pressure remains above 1000 psi (6895 kPa). High-pressure fuel which returns through the pump barrel will flow out through the spill port (1) and a hollow steel dowel pin, which prevents erosion of the pump housing. This fuel deflects off a pulse deflector within the injection pump housing to protect the aluminum fuel manifold from erosion due to the high-pressure fuel spillage.

The return fuel from the fuel injection line will cease as soon as the fuel pressure drops to 1000 psi (6895 kPa), when the reverse-flow check valve spring (12) will seat the valve. This action will keep the injection line filled with fuel at 1000 psi approximately for the next injection period. The reverse-flow check valve controls the fuel-line hydraulics to provide a consistent, smooth engine power curve. If the engine is stopped, the fuel-line pressure will bleed down through the action of a small groove machined into the bottom face of the reverse-flow check valve. The amount of fuel delivered

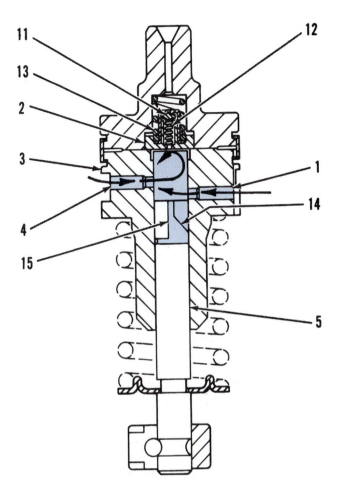

FIGURE 23–3   New scroll pump barrel-and-plunger assembly showing both the spill and bypass ports open: 1, spill port; 2, check valve; 3, pump barrel; 4, bypass port; 5, pump plunger; 11, orificed reverse-flow check valve; 12, spring; 13, spring; 14, scroll; 15, slot. (Reprinted courtesy of Caterpillar, Inc.)

to the injection nozzle is controlled by the length of the plunger's effective stroke.

The plunger stroke itself will not change since the injection pump camshaft always has a constant lift; however, *effective stroke* refers to the period of time that the bypass closed port remains closed, because as long as it stays closed, fuel trapped above the plunger can be pressurized. The effective stroke is controlled by closure of the bypass closed port and opening of the spill port; the longer the period of time that these ports are closed, the greater the amount of fuel injected (longer injection period in actual crankshaft degrees). This closure time is established by rotation of the pump plunger by the rack and gear arrangement. This rotation of the plunger causes the injection to start earlier or later by the fact that the helix or scroll on the plunger will uncover the spill port earlier or later in the upward-moving plunger's stroke, thereby "effectively" metering a given quantity of fuel for any particular rack position.

An orifice bleed valve allows approximately 10 U.S. gallons (40 L) of fuel per hour along with any air in the system to return to the fuel tank. This action allows a continual bleed-off of hot fuel from the fuel manifold that has spilled back from the end of injection, and which is also used for lubrication purposes, to carry this heat back to the tank and let cooler transfer pump fuel flow into the manifold. On engines equipped with this orifice bleed valve, it will not be necessary to bleed the fuel system or use the hand priming pump after changing the fuel filters, since any air in the system will be vented back to the fuel tank through this valve. However, if the system has been completely drained of fuel, it will be necessary to loosen the fuel injection lines at the injection nozzle on the 3300 engines (external) or the fuel line at the valve rocker cover on 3400 engines in order to bleed any entrapped air from the system. To stop the engine the pump plunger is simply rotated so that the slot on the pump plunger is always "inline" with the spill port regardless of the pump plunger's position (vertically) within the barrel. The scroll-metered plungers are driven through steel roller lifters by the action of the heat-treated steel pump camshaft.

Fuel Shutoff Solenoid

The engine can be equipped with an electrical solenoid which is usually mounted on the rear of the fuel injection pump below the air/fuel ratio control unit. This solenoid can be used to move the fuel rack to a no-fuel position and thereby effectively stop the engine when the ignition key is turned off. The solenoid is available in two modes: One mode offers *energize to run*; the other option is *energize to shutoff*. In the energize-to-shutoff solenoid, a special kill button is pressed and held until the engine stops, then it is released. In the energize-to-run solenoid, when the ignition key is turned ON, the solenoid is electronically energized to allow rack movement toward the fuel ON or OFF direction. When the ignition key is turned OFF, the solenoid is deactivated and rack movement toward the fuel-on direction is prevented, causing the engine to shut down. Generally, a diode is used between the two electric terminals of the energize to run a solenoid to eliminate electric spikes that could possibly damage other electronic circuitry in the vehicle electrical system.

FUEL TRANSFER PUMP

With the introduction of the new scroll fuel injection system to the 3406 B and C models, the gear-type fuel transfer pump that had been used for many years with the

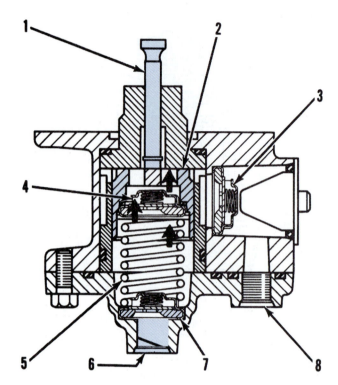

FIGURE 23–4 Fuel transfer pump—start of down-stroke (arrows indicate fuel flow direction): 1, pushrod; 2, piston; 3, outlet check valve; 4, pumping check valve; 5, pumping spring; 6, pump inlet port; 7, inlet check valve; 8, pump outlet port. (Reprinted courtesy of Caterpillar, Inc.)

compact body injection system was superseded by the use of a piston-type transfer pump for use on the new scroll system. Current new scroll fuel systems employ a single-piston, double-acting pump with three one-way check valves, as shown in Figures 23–4 and 23–5. The transfer pump is bolted onto the low side of the injection pump housing and is capable of delivering up to 51 U.S. gallons (192 L) per hour at 25 psi (172 kPa). There is no requirement for a pressure relief valve in this transfer pump, due to the fact that maximum pressure is controlled automatically by the force of the piston return spring (5), shown in the operating schematic.

Pushrod 1 in Figure 23–4 is activated by an eccentric on the injection pump camshaft which causes the pushrod to move in and out as the engine is running. Refer to Figure 23–4 which shows that pushrod 1 will also cause piston 2 to move down against the force of the piston return spring (5) as the eccentric on the injection pump camshaft forces the pushrod down inside the transfer pump housing. The downward-moving piston will cause the inlet check valve (7) and the outlet check valve (3) to close, while the pumping check valve (4) will open to allow fuel below the piston to flow into the area immediately above the downward-moving piston.

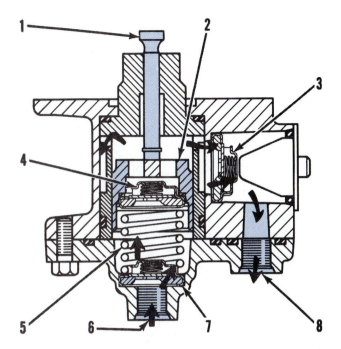

FIGURE 23–5 *Fuel transfer pump—start of upstroke (arrows indicate fuel flow direction): 1, pushrod; 2, piston; 3, outlet check valve; 4, pumping check valve; 5, pumping spring; 6, pump inlet port; 7, inlet check valve; 8, pump outlet port. (Reprinted courtesy of Caterpillar, Inc.)*

As the injection pump camshaft eccentric rotates around to its base circle or low point, the transfer pump spring (5) pushes the piston (2) up inside its bore, which causes check valve 4 to close; however, both the inlet check valve (7) and the outlet check valve (3) will be forced open. Fuel above the piston will now be forced through the outlet check valve (3) and flow through the pump outlet port (8) at approximately 35 psi (240 kPa), as shown in Figure 23–5. While this action is taking place, fuel will also flow through the pump inlet port (6) and the inlet check valve (7) to fill the area below the piston (2), and the pump will repeat the cycle described above.

GOVERNOR

The governor assembly used with the new scroll fuel system is a hydramechanical servo-type unit, illustrated in Figure 23–6. The reason for using a servo-valve with the new scroll governor assembly is that without this unit to provide a boost, both the governor spring and flyweights would have to be very large, heavy, and cumbersome to move the injection pump rack and overcome the resistance of the gear segments and plungers within the barrels. With the use of the servo assist, little force is required to move

both the accelerator and the governor control lever, and rapid rack movement and throttle response time can be achieved.

Basically, the governor assembly consists of three separate components:

1. The mechanical components of the governor, such as the weights, springs, and linkage (Figure 23–7).
2. The governor servo (Figure 23–6), which provides hydraulic assistance through the use of pressurized engine oil to provide rapid throttle response and to reduce the overall size requirements of the governor flyweights and springs.
3. The dashpot assembly, which is designed to provide stability to the governor during rapid load/throttle changes (Figure 23–6).

Prior to reading the explanation of the governor operation, take a minute to become familiar with the component parts and their arrangement to each other. If you are already familiar with the basic operation of a mechanical governor, you can proceed to the description of operation. If, on the other hand, you are not familiar with the operation of a basic mechanical governor, it may be of assistance to you at this time to study the description of operation in Chapter 16, where we discuss in detail how a basic mechanical governor operates.

SPECIAL NOTE   Bear in mind that the centrifugal force of the governor flyweights is always attempting to decrease fuel to the engine, while the force of the governor spring is always attempting to increase fuel to the engine.

Governor Oil Flow

Figure 23–6 illustrates the location of the governor in relation to the fuel injection pump assembly, as well as the oil flow path for both the injection pump and the governor. The governor mounting base contains both a small oil inlet hole and a larger oil drain port. Engine oil under pressure enters the governor end of the housing and flows up to the governor servo valve and to the hydraulic air/fuel control unit on turbocharged engines. A percentage of this oil drains down to the bottom of the governor housing for lubrication of governor components and to supply oil to the dashpot unit. Drain oil flowing over the governor weights allows the weights to throw oil up and around over the remaining governor components. The oil drain hole maintains the oil at a fixed level at all times.

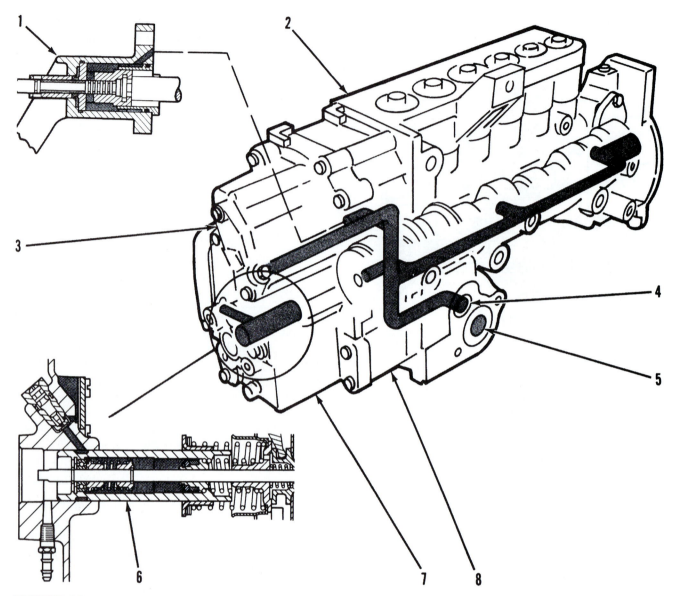

FIGURE 23–6   *New scroll fuel injection pump and governor oil flow passages: 1, servo; 2, injection pump housing; 3, oil supply from cylinder block; 5, oil drain into cylinder block; 6, dashpot; 7, governor rear housing; 8, governor center housing. (Reprinted courtesy of Caterpillar, Inc.)*

Pressurized oil also flows to and through the fuel injection pump camshaft via a centrally drilled oil hole where cross-drilled passages feed the camshaft journals as well as the front camshaft bearing. The oil drains out of the front of the pump housing and over the engine gear train on its way back to the engine crankcase.

AUTOMATIC TIMING ADVANCE UNIT

The automatic fuel injection timing advance unit used with the new scroll fuel system differs from that used with the earlier compact body fuel system. The timing unit used with the new scroll system is a combination of a hydraulic variable timing unit and a mechanical unit. The major difference is that the new scroll fuel system timing unit is adjustable by use of a setscrew that limits the degrees of allowable advance. Figure 23–8 shows the new scroll fuel system automatic timing advance unit.

Unit Operation

Before discussing its operation, refer to Figure 23–8, which illustrates the assembled automatic timing advance unit located at the front of the engine behind the timing gear cover. The fuel injection pump

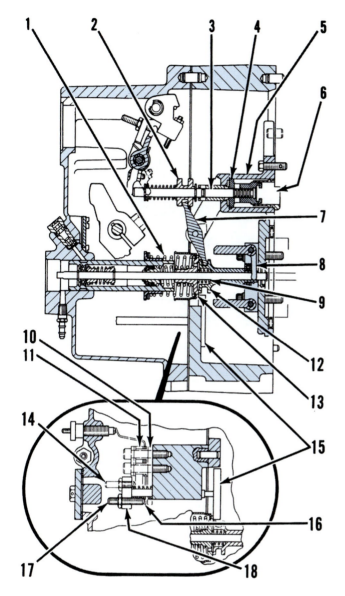

FIGURE 23-7 3406B mechanical governor: 1, governor spring; 2, sleeve; 3, valve; 4, piston; 5, governor servo; 6, fuel rack; 7, lever; 8, flyweights; 9, overfueling spring; 10, load stop bar; 11, stop bar; 12, riser; 13, spring seat; 14, torque rise setting screw; 15, stop bolt; 16, torque spring; 17, fuel setting screw; 18, stop collar. (Reprinted courtesy of Caterpillar, Inc.)

camshaft, has left-hand helical cut teeth machined onto it.

Figure 23–8 shows the carrier, which is illustrated as item 4. Note that the carrier is machined with external straight spur cut gear teeth, while the inner hub area contains helical splines (teeth) that will engage with the teeth on the forward end of the fuel injection pump camshaft.

The timing advance unit relies on the centrifugal force created by the four weights shown as item 2 and

on pressurized engine oil delivered through the centrally drilled camshaft, which will enter the timing advance unit at its right-hand side as shown in the diagram through a drilled hole shown in the center of the spool (12). The pressurized engine oil is used to force a carrier (4) back and forward within the confines of a ring (10) bolted to the timing gear (3), which is in mesh with the engine gear train at the front of the engine. To allow the pressurized engine oil to work on the carrier (4), a set of four flyweights opposed by a spring (8) moves a control spool back and forth within the bore of the body (13).

Advancement

When the engine speed becomes fast enough to create a strong enough centrifugal force at the flyweights (2), they will pull the spool valve (12) to the left while simultaneously compressing the small spring (8). The movement of the spool (12) allows pressurized engine oil to flow out of the centrally drilled pump camshaft and through the body (13). This oil will now act on both the body (13) and the carrier (4). When the oil pressure becomes greater than the force of the large spring (1), both the body and the carrier will move to the left in the diagram. This action will allow the carrier (4), with its straight-cut outer splines (gear teeth) and its helically cut inner splines, to exert a twisting force through the inner splines, which are in mesh with the helical cut teeth on the forward end of the pump camshaft (5). The pump camshaft will therefore be rotated in relation to the timing gear (3), which is driven from the engine gear train, thereby providing maximum injection timing advance in relation to the speed of the engine. For further clarification, the advancement takes place between the inner splines, and the teeth of the camshaft gear.

Timing advancement will continue as the engine speed increases until the moving parts, particularly the spool (12), butts up against the adjustable setscrew (7). The body (13) will stop moving when the oil pressure on the body and the carrier (4) is equal to the force of the large spring (1), which will take place as the oil ports begin to close. Adjustment of the setscrew (7) will determine and limit the amount of automatic timing advancement. This setting can vary for different Caterpillar engines and can be obtained by referring to the service supplement for the particular engine.

Deceleration

When the engine speed decreases, the centrifugal force of the flyweights (2) will allow the force of the smaller spring (8) to push the spool valve (12) to the right in the diagram, which will block the oil supply from the camshaft and simultaneously drain the previously trapped oil out of the automatic timing advance unit.

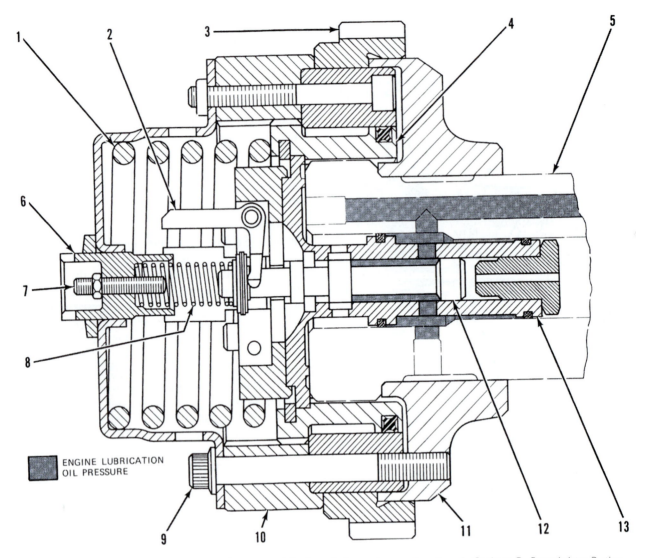

FIGURE 23–8 Automatic timing advance unit before timing advance begins. 1, Spring; 2, flyweights; 3, timing gear; 4, carrier; 5, injection pump camshaft; 6, screw; 7, setscrew; 8, spring; 9, bolt; 10, ring; 11, ring; 12, spool; 13, body. (Reprinted courtesy of Caterpillar, Inc.)

The force of the large spring (1) will now push the carrier (4), the body (13), and the spool valve (12) to the right, which will cause the inner splines on the carrier (4) to retard the injection timing as it rotates the camshaft in the opposite direction with a decrease in engine speed.

STATIC ENGINE TIMING

Locating Top Dead Center: 3406B Engine

It often becomes necessary to locate the No. 1 piston at its TDC compression position, such as when checking the static fuel injection pump-to-engine timing. Finding TDC on all 3400 series engines follows a similar pattern in that an injection pump timing pin and a flywheel timing bolt are used to check this condition. Pis-

ton 1 is the reference cylinder for checking injection pump-to-engine gear train timing.

Although the engine can be rotated over manually from the front of the crankshaft, Caterpillar offers an engine turning tool, 9S9082, which can be inserted into a hole in the forward side of the flywheel housing to facilitate turning the engine over during the timing check or when setting valves. (See Chapter 13, Figures 13–49 through 13–51.) This tool can be seen in Figure 13–50 along with the flywheel timing bolt in Figure 13–49, normally stored in the forward side of the flywheel housing on the left-hand side. An optional hole for installing the timing bolt during a No. 1 piston TDC check can be found on the forward side of the flywheel housing on the right-hand side of the engine.

To check the static timing of the injection pump to the engine, piston 1 must be placed at TDC on its compression stroke.

Location Procedure

1. Refer to Figure 13–49 and remove the timing bolt, access plug, and access plate from the forward side of the flywheel housing.

2. With the access plate removed, turning tool 9S9082 can be inserted through this hole to engage with the flywheel ring gear as shown in Figure 13–50.

3. Install the timing bolt (Figure 13–51) into the pipe plug hole.

4. Slowly rotate the engine with the turning tool and ratchet until the timing bolt slides into its mating threaded hole in the flywheel.

5. If you miss the hole and reverse the engine rotation, always come back at least 30° before coming forward again, to ensure that all gear train backlash will be eliminated.

6. To ensure that piston 1 is at TDC on its compression stroke, remove the front valve rocker cover and check that both the intake and exhaust valve rocker arms have free play. This confirms that all valves are closed and that the piston is on TDC compression.

NOTE If both rocker arms do not have clearance, the piston is at TDC but is 360° off. It is, in fact, just finishing the exhaust stroke and starting the intake with a valve overlap condition evident.

---

7. Remove the timing bolt from the flywheel, rotate it another 360°, and reinsert it into the threaded hole in the flywheel.

8. Piston 1 is now at TDC compression with all valves closed.

Static Timing Check

The static timing check is confirmed when piston 1 is at TDC compression, the timing bolt will screw into the threaded hole in the flywheel, and at the same time, the injection pump timing pin will slip into engagement with the injection pump camshaft slot.

1. With piston 1 at TDC compression, remove the flywheel timing bolt.

2. Using turning tool 9S9082, manually rotate the flywheel opposite its normal rotation, which is clockwise from the front. Therefore, pull the 0.5 in. drive ratchet upward when standing at the side of the engine to turn the flywheel CCW when viewed from the front. Turn the flywheel back between 30 and 45°.

3. Refer to Figure 23–9 and remove the plug (2) from the injection pump housing.

4. Refer to Figure 23–9 and install timing pin 6V4186 into the hole in the injection pump housing.

5. Slowly rotate the engine in its normal direction of rotation, which is CW from the front (CCW from the rear), until the injection pump timing pin 6V4186 drops into engagement with the machined slot in the pump camshaft. Gently rotate the engine until the pin is tight.

6. If you can now install the timing bolt into the threaded hole in the flywheel, the static pump timing is correct.

7. If you cannot install the bolt into the flywheel housing, the timing is incorrect and should be remedied by moving to step 8.

SPECIAL NOTE On 3406B truck engines starting with engine serial number 4MG3600 and up, a new timing advance holding tool, illustrated in Figure 23–10 is required to hold the timing advance at the bottom of its travel (retarded position) when pin timing the fuel injection pump to the engine. Failure to employ this special tool on engines with these serial numbers will result in an inability to perform pin timing correctly.

---

8. Remove the cover from the front right-hand side of the gear train timing housing to expose the automatic timing advance assembly.

9. Loosen the four bolts, and with the injection pump timing pin still in position, remove the flywheel timing bolt.

10. Rotate the flywheel with the 9S9082 turning tool and ratchet opposite its normal rotation (either CCW when viewed from the front, or CW when viewed from the flywheel end) approximately 45°.

11. Select two of the four bolts that were loosened in step 9 that are 180° apart, and tighten them carefully to a torque reading of 27 lb-in. (not lb-ft!) (which is 3 N · m), in order to apply a small degree of clamping force to the automatic timing advance unit.

12. Rotate the flywheel, now in its normal direction of rotation (CW from the front and CCW from the rear), until the flywheel timing bolt can just be installed into its mating threaded hole.

13. Tighten the four automatic timing advance unit bolts to a torque of 41 to 46 lb-ft (55 to 62 N · m).

14. Remove the flywheel timing bolt and the timing pin from the injection pump housing.

15. To double check the static timing, rotate the flywheel opposite its normal rotation about 45° (one-eighth turn).

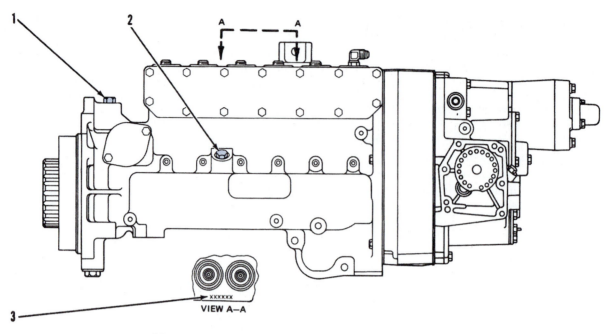

FIGURE 23-9   *View of injection pump showing location of rack centering pin (1) and timing pin (2). View A–A, location of stamped part number, and serial number for fuel injection and governor groups. Injection sequence firing order 1–5–3–6–2–4. Rotation of fuel pump camshaft when seen from drive end is CCW. (Reprinted courtesy of Caterpillar, Inc.)*

(1)   Location for rack centering pin.

(2)   Location for timing pin.

(3)   Location of stamped part number and serial number for FUEL INJECTION PUMP AND GOVERNOR GROUPS.

See FUEL SETTING AND RELATED INFORMATION FICHE for the correct fuel injection timing.

Injection sequence (firing order) 1,5,3,6,2,4

Rotation of Fuel Pump Camshaft
(when seen from pump drive end) .... counterclockwise

VIEW A–A

FIGURE 23-10   *Timing advance holding tool 1U8271 for use on 3406B engines from 4MG3600 and up. (Reprinted courtesy of Caterpillar, Inc.)*

16.   Slowly rotate the flywheel in its normal rotation until the timing pin drops into the camshaft slot of the injection pump.

17.   Carefully rotate the flywheel again in its normal rotation to ensure that there is no gear lash left in the gear train and see if the flywheel timing bolt will thread into position. If it does, the static timing is indeed correct.

18.   If it does not, repeat the procedure.

DYNAMIC ENGINE TIMING

Dynamic Timing Charts

The specific timing curve information for various models of Caterpillar truck engines is readily available, upon request, through any local Cat dealer. The static (engine stopped) and dynamic (engine running) timing characteristics for the same model of engine will be different for each horsepower setting and are also based on

CAT				3406B		
SER. NO.	7FB38516		DATE DELIVERED			
MODIFICATION NO.				DLR CODE		
AR NO.	4W4109	PERF SPEC	0T4953		MAX ALT	22550 M
OEM NO.	34A49PSI/051134B					
FULL LOAD STATIC FUEL	2.60 mm		FULL TORQ. STATIC FUEL	3.10 mm		
POWER	400 HP	0298.0 kw	A/F RATIO DYNAMIC	-02.00 mm		
BARE ENG. HI IDLE RPM	2339	FULL LOAD RPM	2100	FUEL TIMING	18.0 BTC	
					9L6531 13	

FIGURE 23–11 *Sample 3406B engine information plate. (Reprinted courtesy of Caterpillar, Inc.)*

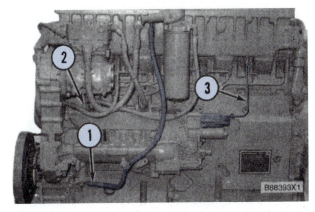

FIGURE 23–12 *Removal of fuel line (1); aftercooler (2); to the AFC housing (3). (Reprinted courtesy of Caterpillar, Inc.)*

whether the engine is JWAC (jacket water aftercooled) or ATAAC (air-to-air aftercooled). Figure 23–11 illustrates a sample engine information plate for a 3406B, 400 hp engine model with a static fuel timing specification of 18.0° BTC (before top dead center). Other information on this plate includes the full-load static fuel rack setting dimension, the full-torque static fuel dimension, and the A/F (air/fuel) ratio dynamic setting.

FUEL INJECTION PUMP 3406B ENGINE

Pump Removal

1. Steam clean the engine, particularly in the area of the engine front timing cover and around the air compressor and injection pump housing.

2. Disconnect the batteries to prevent any possibility of the engine being cranked over.

3. Make sure that the vehicle spring brakes are applied. Block the wheels to prevent possible movement forward or reverse.

4. Bleed all air from the vehicle's compressed-air tanks. Ensure that all compressed air from the air compressor governor air line has also been vented to zero.

5. Refer to Figure 23–8 and remove the automatic timing advance access cover from the front of the geartrain housing (upper right).

6. Refer to Figure 23–12 and remove:
   a. The fuel line from the fuel transfer pump
   b. The fuel line from the injection pump housing
   c. The intake manifold aftercooler air line to the air/fuel ratio control

7. Remove from the top of the injection pump housing all of the high-pressure fuel lines that connect to the injector nozzles.

8. Refer to Figure 23–13 and remove the air line (5) and the compressor coolant line (6). Use a suitable container to catch coolant that will vent from this hose.

FIGURE 23–13 *Removal of air line (5); compressor coolant line (6). (Reprinted courtesy of Caterpillar, Inc.)*

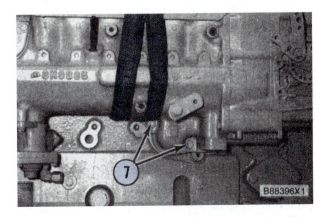

FIGURE 23–14 *Web sling supporting injection pump prior to removal of retaining bolts (item 7). (Reprinted courtesy of Caterpillar, Inc.)*

9. Since the 3406B injection pump and governor assembly weighs 125 lb (57 kg), sling the pump to an overhead hoist with a webbing harness as shown in Figure 23–14.

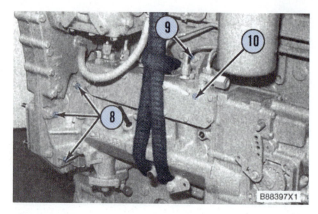

FIGURE 23–15 *Removal of nuts (8), bolts (9) to allow injection pump (10) removal. (Reprinted courtesy of Caterpillar, Inc.)*

10. Refer to Figure 23–14 and remove the retaining bolts (7).

11. Refer to Figure 23–15 and remove the two nuts and bolts (8 and 9). Check that the webbing sling is attached securely and carefully pull the injection pump and housing clear of the engine.

Pump Installation

Pump installation follows the reverse procedure as that described above for removal. However, once the pump has been reinstalled onto the engine, it will have to be timed.

VALVE ADJUSTMENT: 3406-ENGINE

Valve Bridge Adjustment

If an engine has been overhauled or the cylinder head has been worked on, the bridges can be set prior to installing the rocker arm assemblies; however, if the bridges are being checked on an engine already in service, it is not necessary to remove the rocker arm shaft to perform the bridge adjustment. With the valves closed for the cylinder being checked, simply push down on the top of the rocker arm immediately above the center of the bridge to check and perform the adjustment listed below.

1. Place the bridge assembly in a soft-jawed vise and loosen the adjusting screw locknut. This makes it easier than trying to do it while in place on its dowel.

2. To remove all friction, apply a small amount of oil on both the bridge support dowel on the cylinder head and in the actual bore of the bridge itself.

3. Place the bridge over its dowel, with the bridge adjusting screw facing toward the engine exhaust manifold.

4. Back out the bridge adjustment screw several turns.

5. Apply light pressure with your finger on top of the bridge pallet to keep it in contact with the valve stem tip.

6. Lightly turn down (CW) the bridge adjustment screw until it just makes contact with the valve stem tip.

7. Rotate the adjustment screw another 30° CW, which should cause the bridge to sit square on its dowel as well as allowing for any clearance that might exist in the adjustment screw threads.

8. Hold the adjustment screw firmly in this position and torque its locknut to 22 ± 3 lb-ft (30 ± 4 N · m).

NOTE   If the engine rocker arms are not in position, such as during reassembly of the head, it is easier to remove the bridge after lightly snugging the locknut up, place it in a soft-jaw vise, and perform the torque procedure on the locknut.

---

9. Apply clean engine oil between the bridge pallet and the end of the rocker arm assembly if reassembling a rebuilt head.

Valve Clearance Adjustment

Once the valve bridges have been set, the valve lash clearance can be checked and adjusted. The firing order for the 3406 engine is 1–5–3–6–2–4 with the No. 1 cylinder being at the front of the engine.

NOTE   When checking the valve clearance between the end of the rocker arm and the bridge pallet, adjustment is not necessary if the clearance falls within the following specifications:

Valve Clearance: Engine Stopped (Tolerance)

- Exhaust: 0.027 to 0.033 in. (0.69 to 0.84 mm)
- Intake: 0.012 to 0.018 in. (0.30 to 0.46 mm)

However, if the engine cylinder head has been removed for service work, the valve clearances should be set to the following specifications:

Valve Clearance: Engine Stopped and Resetting to Spec

- Exhaust: 0.030 in. (0.76 mm)
- Intake: 0.015 in. (0.38 mm)

If setting the valve clearance to spec, it can be checked using either a go-no-go feeler gauge or a straight feeler gauge, although go-no-go gauges are easier to use and generally result in a more accurate setting. Check the valve clearance between the rocker arm and bridge pallet.

Adjustment Procedure

1. Rotate the engine over manually in its normal direction of rotation from the front, which is CW, to place the No. 1 piston at TDC on its compression stroke. This ensures that both the intake and exhaust valves are closed. This can be confirmed by the fact that clearance will exist between the end of each rocker arm and the pallet of the valve bridge. TDC for piston 1 can be accomplished as described earlier in this chapter and shown in Chapter 13 (see Figures 13–49 through Figure 13–51). The engine can be rotated by the use of a 0.50 in. drive ratchet and special turning tool 9S9082, until the timing bolt will enter the hole in the engine flywheel.

2. With the piston 1 at TDC on its compression stroke, check and adjust the intake valve clearance on cylinders 1, 2, and 4, and the exhaust valve clearance on cylinders 1, 3, and 5, by loosening the rocker arm adjusting screw locknut, and rotating the screw until the correct feeler gauge clearance is obtained.

3. Torque the locknut to 22 ± 3 lb-ft (30 ± 4 N · m) after each adjustment setting and recheck that the clearance is still correct.

4. Remove the flywheel timing bolt, then manually rotate the engine one full turn or 360° until the bolt will again reenter the hole in the flywheel. The No. 6 piston is now at TDC on its compression stroke.

5. Adjust the intake valves for cylinders 3, 5, and 6, and the exhaust valve clearance for cylinders 2, 4, and 6.

CAUTION Be sure to remove the timing bolt from the flywheel when all adjustments have been performed, and install it back into position in the flywheel housing as shown in Figure 13–49.

NEW ADJUSTMENT PROCEDURE FOR JAKE BRAKE (MODELS 340/340A/340B) SLAVE PISTON LASH

3406E (5EK1-Up, 1MM1-Up, 5DS1-Up, 6TS1-Up, 2WS1-Up, 1LW1-Up) Truck Engines

The procedure for adjusting the slave piston lash has changed for Models 340/340A/340B Jake Brakes. Use the following procedure to adjust the slave piston lash on these models:

1. Loosen the slave piston adjustment locknuts. (See Chapter 13, Figure 13–48.) Back out the slave piston adjusting screws until the slave piston spring is no longer compressed.

2. Adjust the inlet valves and the exhaust valves.

3. Rotate the crankshaft to the correct position for setting the exhaust valve clearance on the cylinder to be adjusted.

4. Turn in the slave piston adjusting screw until the slave piston contacts the exhaust rocker arm and the exhaust valve springs begin to compress. Then, turn the adjustment screw in one additional turn. Allow a minimum of 30 seconds for the oil to be purged from the slave piston adjusting screw. If the oil is below 65°F (18°C), wait at least 2 minutes for the oil to be purged from the slave piston adjusting screw.

NOTICE All oil must be purged from the slave piston adjusting screw. Oil remaining in the slave piston adjusting screw will cause inaccurate clearance adjustment which may lead to engine damage.

---

5. After the time interval specified in step 4, turn the adjusting screw in ONLY until the correct size feeler gauge can be inserted between the slave piston and the exhaust rocker arm. Turn the adjusting screw so that a light drag is felt on the feeler gauge. Do not back out the adjusting screw more than required to obtain a light drag on the feeler gauge. Hold the adjusting screw in position with a screwdriver and tighten the adjustment locknut to a torque of 25 lb-ft (35 N · m). Refer to the rocker cover Jake Brake Decal or Installation Manual for the correct size feeler gauge.

NOTE If the slave piston adjusting screw is backed out until it no longer compresses the slave piston spring, oil will enter the adjusting screw and the adjustment will be incorrect. If this occurs, repeat Steps 4 and 5.

---

6. Recheck the slave piston lash settings. If the lash settings are incorrect, repeat steps 4 and 5.

7. Repeat steps 3 through 6 for the remaining cylinders.

NOTE Once the engine has been run, you will not be able to check the slave piston lash adjustment because of oil in the adjusting screw. If unsure of the adjustment, repeat steps 3 through 6.

CATERPILLAR ELECTRONIC FUEL SYSTEMS

Caterpillar introduced its first electronic control system in early 1987 on its 3406B model heavy-duty highway truck engine series, which was known by the acronym PEEC (programmable electronic engine control). This system retained the conventional PLN (pump-line-nozzle) system that had been in use by Caterpillar for many years. This first system was retained through the 3406C model until the introduction in late 1993 of the 3406E model, which uses an overhead cam design and EUIs similar to those used by Detroit Diesel. Caterpillar, however, first released its EUI system in 1988 on its on-highway truck 3176 model engine.

Caterpillar truck engine models that employ EUI controls are the 3176B, C10, C12, and 3406E. Cat's smaller 3116 and 3126 truck models, and the larger-displacement 3408E and 3412E industrial and marine engines, use a HEUI (hydraulically actuated electronic unit injector) system. The 3176B, C-10, and C-12 models share a common cylinder block, but with the elimination of the aluminum spacer deck that was used on the 3176 model. This lowers overhaul costs and eliminates a joint from the engine. There are a number of major components in common between the C-10 and C-12, but with major updates.

Both the C-10 and C-12 have a one-piece solid aluminum front housing versus the two-piece clamshell type used on the 3176B. The same fuel pump is used on the 3176B, C-10, and C-12; it has been relocated to the front of the engine from its rear mount on the 3176. The C-10 and C-12 electronic fuel system is basically the same as that for the 3176B engine, which is a Caterpillar/Lucas design, with the electronic control module being common to all Cat electronic truck engines. The ECM includes a full range of programmable options,

more data storage capacity, and rapid data retrieval using industry-available tools or via direct link to a PC.

The C-10 and C-12 engines use a redesigned front gear train with a new air compressor drive using a larger drive gear bolted to the air compressor driveshaft. The cylinder head remains largely the same on the 3176B, C-10 , and C-12 using a four-valve design. The C-10 and C-12 camshaft has been located into a midmount cylinder block position versus the earlier aluminum spacer deck location of the 3176 models. Other changes for the C-10 and C-12 models include 8% larger crank main bearings, and 4% wider con-rod journal bearings. A stainless steel versus copper (3176) injector sleeve and beefed-up valve train components appear in the C-10 and C-12 models. Other differences between the C-10 and C-12 are that the C-12 uses different pistons, liners, connecting rods, crankshaft, turbocharger, oil cooler, and injector tips, due primarily to the larger displacement. Both the C-10 and C-12 employ two-piece articulated Metal Leve pistons with a forged steel crown and cast aluminum skirt, similar to that shown in Figure 8–7 (Chapter 8).

EUI Operation

The EUI operates similar to that shown in Figures 18–19 and 18–20. The visual difference is that the 3406E unit has its solenoid mounted at an angle. The 1994 and later EUIs were manufactured with preradius nozzle orifices to eliminate erosion, reduce emissions, and decrease engine performance variability.

The operation of the EUI on engines is the same, except that the activation of the injector follower is different. On the 3176B, C-10, and C-12 engine, the camshaft is block mounted and employs a short pushrod, as shown in Figure 18–19a. On the 3406E engine, which uses an overhead camshaft located in the cylinder head, a roller follower attached to the rocker arm is actuated by the camshaft directly, as shown in Figure 18–19b. Keep in mind that all of the sensor inputs, as well as the position of the EFPA (electronic foot pedal assembly) sending signals to the ECM, are what determines the start, duration, and end of injection. The length of the PWM signal from the ECM to the injector solenoid controls the fuel delivery rate and the power developed by the engine.

EUI Electronics

For the 1994 and later-model years, all engines used new advanced diesel engine management (ADEM) electronic controls, which provide fleet managers with such information as tracking trip and lifetime data through stored data from the ECM. Figure 23–16 illustrates the ECM layout for the 3176B and 3406E with its

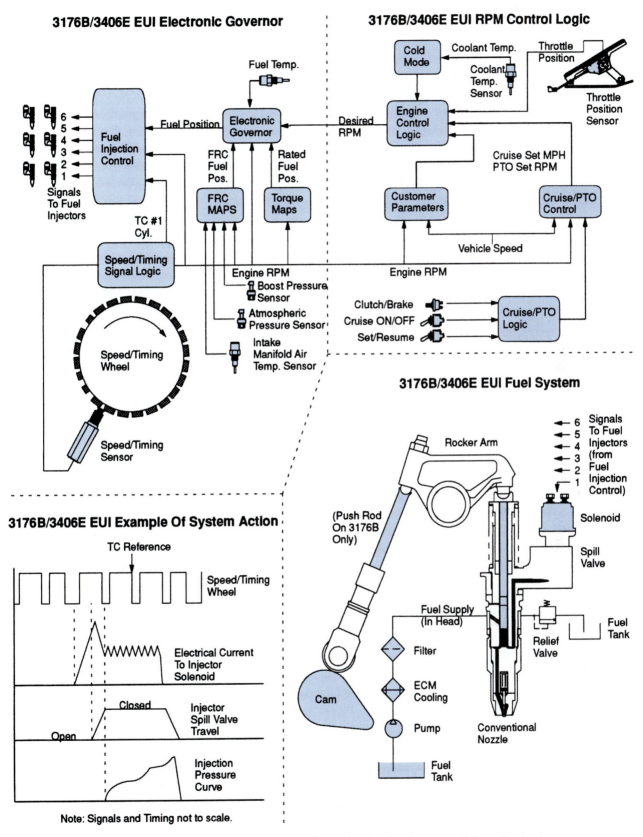

FIGURE 23–16 3176B/3406E EUI electronic system schematic. (Reprinted courtesy of Caterpillar, Inc.)

dual microprocessors, which have reduced calculation times for critical engine control parameters and improved engine efficiency and performance response. The same ECM is installed in the 3176B–3406E C-10 and C-12 series engines. The ECM continues to be diesel-fuel cooled to greatly reduce damaging thermal (heat) cycles and increase reliability/durability under the most extreme operating temperatures.

Information from the ECM can be displayed on a diagnostic data reader (DDR) (Figure 21–31) or downloaded to a PC (Figure 21–32). A generic ECM is used across all applicable engine lines so that the ECM can be programmed for the specific application of the engine. This new ECM has eight times the memory capacity, processes data from twice as many sensor inputs, and makes calculations four times faster. Engine/vehicle parameters that can be monitored are total miles, average fuel consumption, and speed and load factors. This information can be used for management software to help determine precise maintenance intervals. With dual microprocessors, engine performance, response, and fuel economy are improved. Fault codes are logged in memory, and the ECU also records engine parameters immediately before a fault and shortly after it has occurred. The ECM processes information supplied by a fuel temperature sensor located in the fuel manifold and makes adjustments to compensate for fuel warming, thereby avoiding the possibility of a power loss. If fuel temperature exceeds 150°F (65.5°C), the ECM logs a fault code.

For vehicle PTO operation, the rate of speed increase can be controlled. As an option, the Caterpillar "softcruise" speed control system modulates fuel delivery above and below the set speed, particularly when a truck is running over rolling terrain, to eliminate abrupt fuel cutoffs, and it helps to keep turbo boost spooled up for the next hill. The ECM is soft mounted to the engine and cooled by diesel fuel piped through a cooler plate to ensure that radiated engine heat does not affect the operation of the electronics components. Mounted within the ECM is the engine's *flash memory chip,* which contains the engine's control software. The flash memory technology enables software to be downloaded directly to the ECM and eliminates the need for the replaceable "personality module" for individual engine ratings as was the case with the earlier 3406B and C PEEC and 3176A engines. New software previously stored in 3176A personality modules can be downloaded directly to the ECM via a PC. All sensors are connected to the ECM by two Deutsch 40-pin connectors. One of the 40-pin connectors provides the electrical interface between the engine and vehicle.

Figures 23–17 and 23–18 show the sensor and component locations for both a 3406E/3176B electronic system that allows you to visually trace the system components and wiring arrangement. The sensors shown along the bottom row of Figure 23–18 receive a 5 V input signal from the ECM. Their output voltage value varies between 0.5 and 4.5 V based on the changing resistance value at the sensor, and whether it is a pressure or temperature type. The pedal-mounted throttle position sensor (PMTPS) shown in Figure 23–19 receives an 8 V input signal from the ECM. Other switches operate on a 12 V battery supply. Injector solenoids are pulsed on and off by ECM voltage signals. A good injector solenoid exhibits a resistance value between 0.5 and 2.0 Ω (20 kΩ), while the resistance value from either injector solenoid terminal to the injector case should always be greater than 20,000 Ω (20 kΩ). Other changes in the ECM include SAE J1922 power-train datalink to allow the engine to communicate with ABS (antibrake skid), new automatic transmissions, and traction control ASR systems. A PMTPS similar to that shown in Figure 18–15, which is basically the standard EFPA now used by all heavy-truck OEMs, replaces Caterpillar's own earlier and bulkier TPS system. The newer ECM system also provides either 12 or 24 V Jacobs brake control and speedometer and tachometer inputs to eliminate OEM sensors. The system also includes both an SAE J1708/J1587 satellite communications interface and improved diagnostics. As with other competitive systems, the Caterpillar system provides a programmable droop feature up to 150 rpm above the truck engine limit to provide fewer transmission shifts in rolling terrain, driver comfort, and improved fuel economy. Another improvement is the incorporation of the previously external truck speed buffer into the ECM to minimize the need for cleaning up the signal from the OEM-provided truck speed sensor. The ECM continuously monitors battery voltage and logs a diagnostic code if battery voltage decreases below an acceptable limit. This provides a continuous health check of the wiring and pinpoints system problems that may affect engine operation.

The previous transducer module used on the 3406B and 3406C engine PEEC systems has been eliminated, because new technology sensors allow remote mounting of these units, thereby doing away with needed hose connections. The radiator engage/disengage fan system is automatically turned on when the engine retarder *high mode* is applied to provide increased engine braking. The ECM continuously monitors coolant temperature, intake manifold air temperature, the engine compression brake position, and the

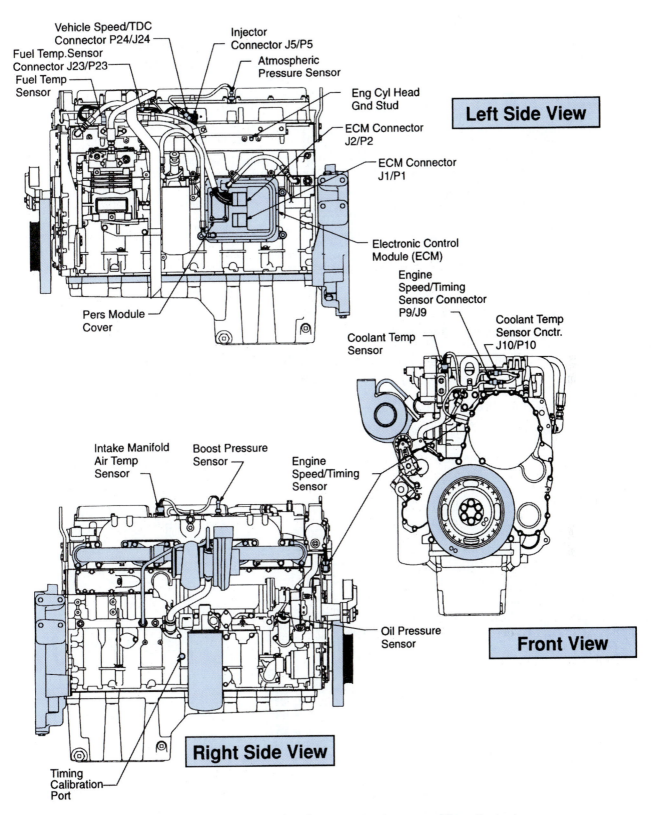

Vehicle Speed/TDC
Connector P24/J24

Fuel Temp.Sensor
Connector J23/P23

Fuel Temp
Sensor

Injector
Connector J5/P5

Atmospheric
Pressure Sensor

Eng Cyl Head
Gnd Stud

ECM Connector
J2/P2

ECM Connector
J1/P1

Left Side View

Electronic Control
Module (ECM)

Engine
Speed/Timing
Sensor Connector
P9/J9

Coolant Temp
Sensor Cnctr.
J10/P10

Coolant Temp
Sensor

Pers Module
Cover

Intake Manifold
Air Temp
Sensor

Boost Pressure
Sensor

Engine
Speed/Timing
Sensor

Front View

Oil Pressure
Sensor

Right Side View

Timing
Calibration
Port

FIGURE 23–17   3176B sensor and connector locations. (Reprinted courtesy of Caterpillar, Inc.)

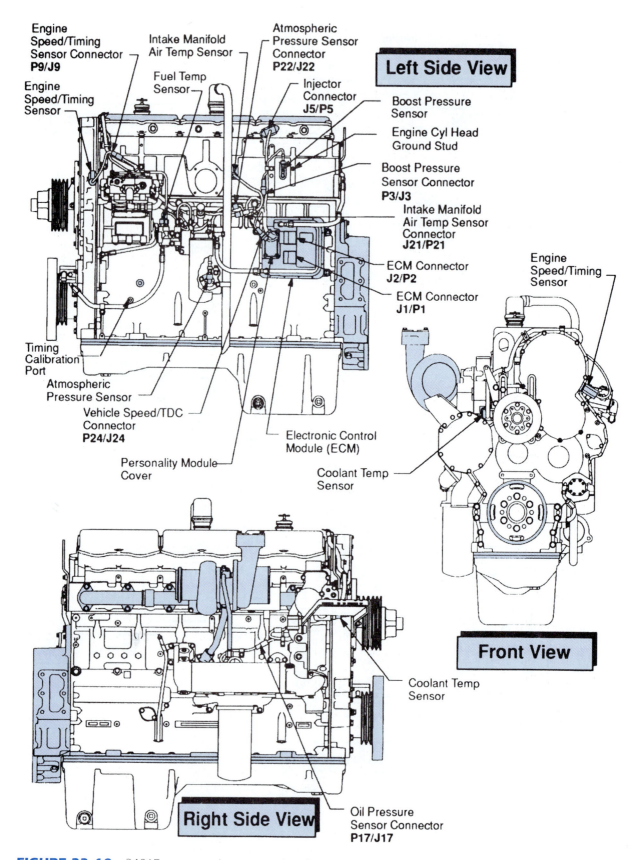

FIGURE 23–18 *3406E sensor and connector locations. (Reprinted courtesy of Caterpillar, Inc.)*

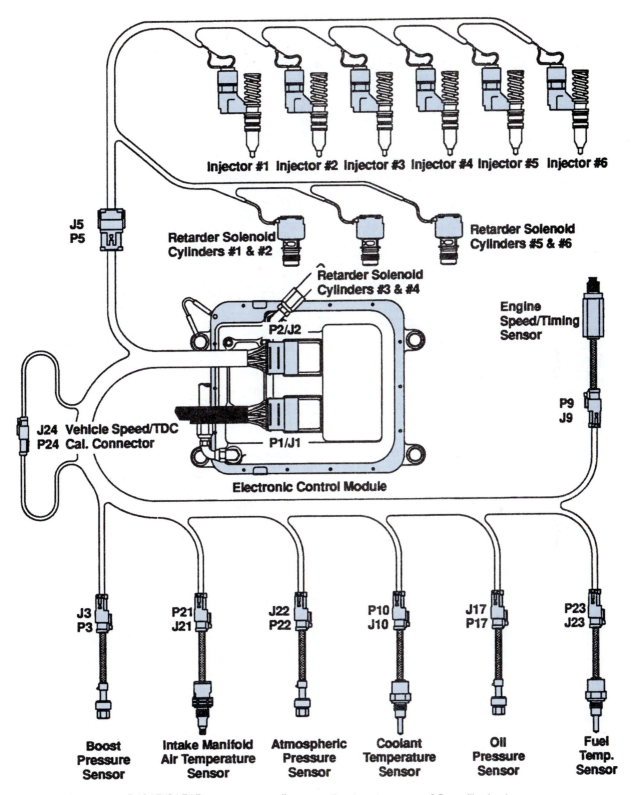

Injector #1 Injector #2 Injector #3 Injector #4 Injector #5 Injector #6

J5
P5

Retarder Solenoid
Cylinders #1 & #2

Retarder Solenoid
Cylinders #5 & #6

Retarder Solenoid
Cylinders #3 & #4

P2/J2

Engine
Speed/Timing
Sensor

P9
J9

J24 Vehicle Speed/TDC
P24 Cal. Connector

P1/J1

Electronic Control Module

J3   P21   J22   P10   J17   P23
P3   J21   P22   J10   P17   J23

Boost   Intake Manifold   Atmospheric   Coolant   Oil   Fuel
Pressure   Air Temperature   Pressure   Temperature   Pressure   Temp.
Sensor   Sensor   Sensor   Sensor   Sensor   Sensor

FIGURE 23–19   3406E/3176B components diagram. (Reprinted courtesy of Caterpillar, Inc.)

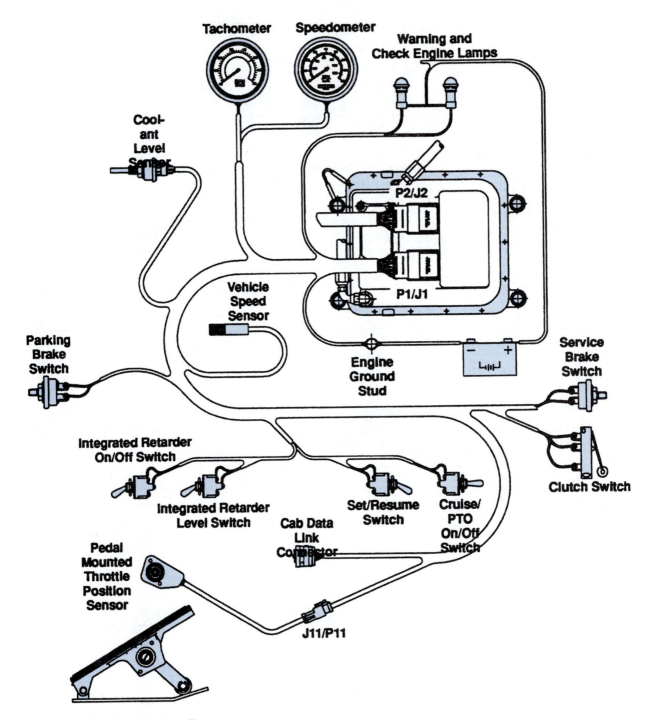

FIGURE 23–19 (continued).

air-conditioning system pressure to determine if and when the radiator fan should be activated.

An electronic full-range governor features a programmable low idle rpm (600 to 750 rpm), with a factory setting of 600 rpm and 20 rpm overrun. There is no need for a mechanical air/fuel ratio control system, since the intake manifold air temperature sensor, turbo boost pressure sensor, and atmospheric pressure sensor allow electronic control of engine fuel delivery.

Fuel System Layout

Although similar in function and operation, the fuel systems used on the 3176B, C-10 and C-12, and the 3406E EUI-equipped engines differ slightly in layout. Figures 23–20a and b illustrate the location of the major fuel system external components and the actual fuel flow through the system for the 3176B model. Figure 23–21a and b represent the fuel system arrangement and flow for the 3406E. In Figure 23–21b you can see

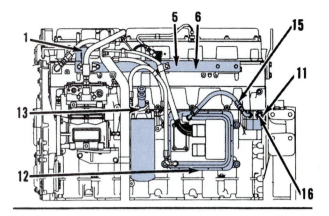

FIGURE 23–20 (a) Component location and identification for a model 3176B electronic engine external fuel system; (b) fuel system schematic and flow. (Reprinted courtesy of Caterpillar, Inc.)

Fuel System Components
(1) Adapter (siphon break). (5) Fuel return manifold. (6) Fuel supply manifold. (11) Fuel transfer pump. (12) Electronic control module (ECM). (13) Fuel priming pump. (14) Fuel filter. (15) Fuel outlet (to
(a)   ECM). (16) Fuel inlet (from tank).

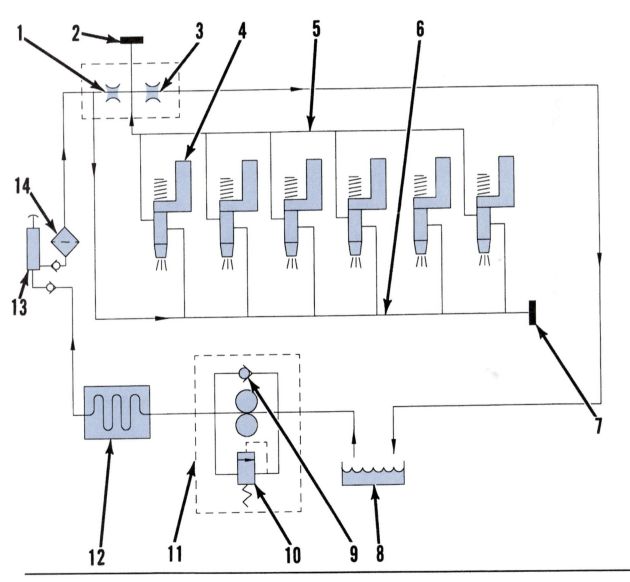

Fuel System Schematic
(1) Siphon break passage. (2) Vent plug. (3) Pressure regulating orifice. (4) Electronically controlled unit injectors. (5) Fuel manifold (return path). (6) Fuel manifold (supply path). (7) Drain plug. (8) Fuel tank. (9) Check valve. (10) Pressure regulating valve. (11) Fuel transfer pump.
(b)   (12) Electronic control module (ECM). (13) Fuel priming pump. (14) Fuel filter (secondary).

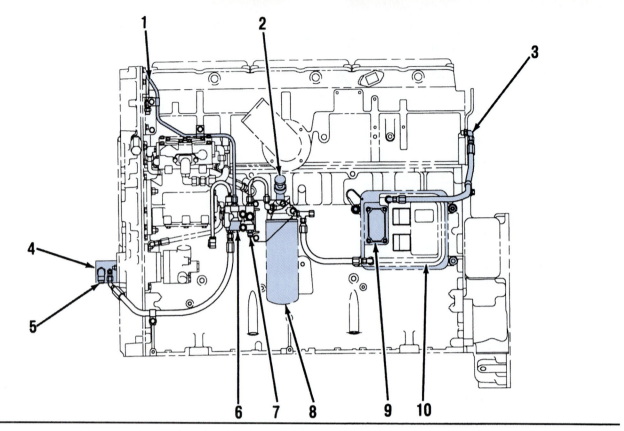

Component Locations

(a) (1) Fuel return line. (2) Fuel priming pump. (3) Fuel inlet line. (4) Fuel transfer pump. (5) Fuel inlet from fuel tank. (6) Distribution block. (7) Fuel return to tank. (8) Fuel filter. (9) Personality module. (10) Electronic control module (ECM).

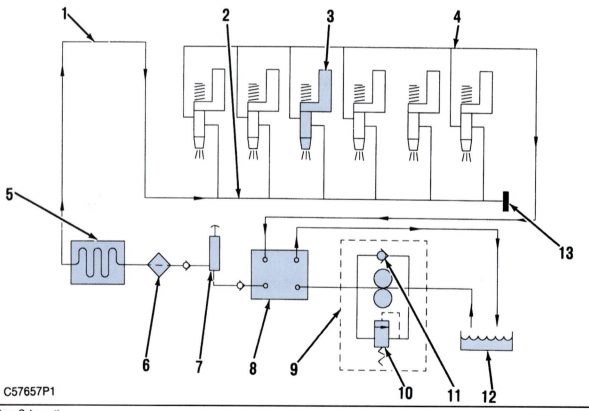

C57657P1

Fuel System Schematic

(b) (1) Fuel supply line. (2) Fuel gallery (supply path). (3) Electronically controlled unit injectors. (4) Fuel gallery (return path). (5) Electronically controlled module (ECM). (6) Fuel filter. (7) Fuel priming pump. (8) Distribution block. (9) Fuel transfer pump. (10) Pressurized regulating valve. (11) Check valve. (12) Fuel tank. (13) Drain plug.

FIGURE 23–21 (a) Component location and identification for a 3406E model engine, external fuel system; (b) fuel system schematic and flow path. (Reprinted courtesy of Caterpillar, Inc.)

that the fuel supply to the system's electronically controlled unit injectors (3) is provided by a gear fuel pump (9) which pulls fuel from the tank (12). Within the pump body, a check valve (11) allows fuel flow around the gears when the fuel priming pump (item 2 in Figure 23–21a) located on top of the filter housing is used, for example, when priming the fuel system after the filters have been changed or service work has been performed on the system.

Also within the fuel pump body is a pressure regulating valve (item 10 in Figure 23–21b) to limit and protect the system from extreme pressure. Fuel under pressure from the pump (91 psi, 630 kPa, at rated speed) is directed through cored passages in the distribution block (8), around the hand-priming pump (7), and into the fuel filter (6), which is rated at 5 μm (0.00020 in.). Fuel enters a cooler plate bolted to the ECM (5) to maintain the operating temperature of the electronics components within the ECM at an acceptable level. Fuel leaves the ECM and enters the fuel manifold (2) at the rear of the cylinder head, where it is distributed equally to all injectors from the common-rail design. An amount of fuel over and above that required for injection purposes is circulated through the EUIs. Fuel not required for injection purposes is used for cooling and lubrication of the EUIs (3) as well as purging any air from the system. Fuel then leaves the cylinder head through the fuel return manifold (4) and is directed back into the fuel distribution block (8), where a regulating valve is designed to maintain sufficient pressure within the fuel return manifold to ensure that the EUIs remain filled with fuel. This warm fuel then travels back to the fuel tank (12), where it cools before being recirculated through the system. Minimum fuel transfer pump flow for the 3176B engine is 3.5 L (0.93 U.S. gallon) per minute at 1800 engine rpm. On the 3406E, the minimum pump flow is quoted as being 3.2 L (0.83 U.S. gallon) per minute at a speed of 840 rpm with a delivery pressure of 45 psi (310 kPa).

The fuel pump for the 3176B engine is located as shown in Figure 23–20a at the left rear corner of the engine. It is mounted to a spacer block and is driven by the camshaft through a pair of helical gears. On the 3406E engine shown in Figure 23–21a, the fuel pump is located at the left front corner of the engine, where it is mounted to the timing gear cover (plate) and is driven from the engine gear train.

The 3176B and 3406E fuel systems are very similar; the normal fuel pressure for both engines is 91 psi (630 kPa). A low-fuel-pressure condition would be 75 psi (517 kPa); check the fuel filters for plugging. A high system pressure would be 100 psi (690 kPa) or higher; remove the fuel regulating valve from the adapter be-hind the return fuel line fitting and check for debris plugging the orifice holes. The injector popping pressure on the 3406E is 5003 ± 275 psi (34,474 ± 1896 kPa), while it is 5500 psi (37,931 kPa) for the 3176B. Both injector solenoids receive a 90 V signal from the ECM to determine the start of injection.

CATERPILLAR ELECTRONIC DIAGNOSTIC TOOLING

Caterpillar offers a variety of electronic engine diagnostic tooling for use on their engines. Some of these tools are shown in Figure 23–22. The main tool is an electronic control analyzer programmer (ECAP), which can be connected to the ECM Deutsch-type connector diagnostic datalink. In addition, a Microprocessor Systems Incorporated (MPSI) handheld scan tool or equivalent with the appropriate software plug-in module can also be used. In early 1997, Caterpillar announced the final sale of the ECAP hardware, although ECAP repair capability will be maintained until approximately the year 2002. The advance of technology in engine control systems was exceeding the capability of the technology within the ECAP tool hardware. The ECAP was replaced with a PC-based tool known as Cat ET (Caterpillar Electronic Technician), which is now the primary service tool used with Cat electronic engines. Figure 23–23 illustrates an example of the Cat datalink diagnostic tools arrangement showing ET, and the service tool connector. ECAP will support many, but not all, functions up through 1999 engines. ECAP version 2.3 is able to monitor the settings and perform the same special tests as ET version 2.3, except ECAP version 2.3 *cannot* perform the 3126B ADEM 111 (advanced electronic engine management system), automatic cylinder cutout test. All current on-highway truck engines are equipped with the ADEM 111 ECM system commonly referred to as ADEM2000 in on-highway truck applications. The first use of the ADEM 111 ECM along with the HEUI-B fuel system for non-truck use can be found in the 8.8L six-cylinder Model C9 engine. This engine model draws strongly on features from both the 3126 and the C-10, such as using the gear train and the rear PTO from the 3126. It also employs two-piece ferrous pistons similar to those in use on the high-rated 3126B, C-10 and C-12 applications.

The MPSI ProLink tool (see Chapter 21, Figure 21–31) will also have less capability relative to Cat ET over time. Table 23–1 lists an example of the compatibility of the ET version 2.3, ECAP version 2.3, and Pro-Link version 1.07 to work with the heavy-duty 1999

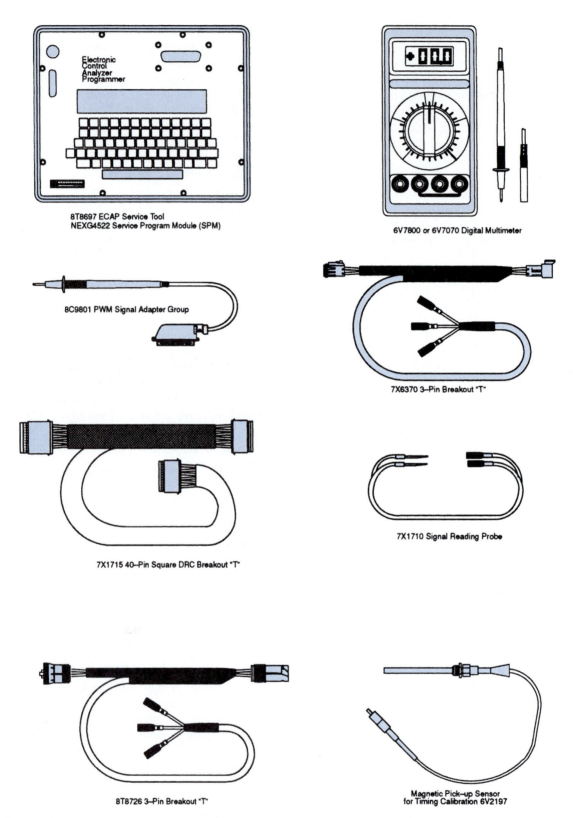

8T8697 ECAP Service Tool
NEXG4522 Service Program Module (SPM)

6V7800 or 6V7070 Digital Multimeter

8C9801 PWM Signal Adapter Group

7X6370 3–Pin Breakout "T"

7X1715 40–Pin Square DRC Breakout "T"

7X1710 Signal Reading Probe

8T8726 3–Pin Breakout "T"

Magnetic Pick–up Sensor
for Timing Calibration 6V2197

FIGURE 23–22 Electronic engine service diagnostic tools for use with the 3176B and earlier-model 3406E engine models. (Reprinted courtesy of Caterpillar, Inc.)

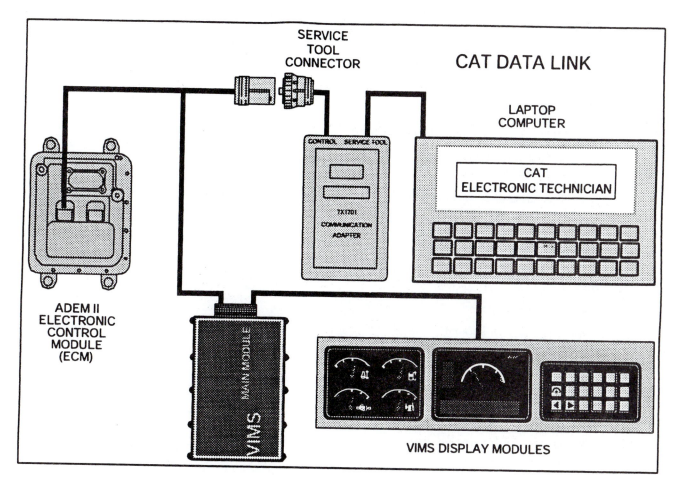

FIGURE 23–23 *Current Cat datalink diagnostic tools arrangement. (Reprinted courtesy of Caterpillar, Inc.)*

and later truck engines. Note that ProLink can be used as a communication adapter for flashing new software to the ECM. The 1999 model year Cat engines will experience significantly longer flash time with ProLink versus the Cat communications adapter.

DataView Portable Tech Station

Figure 23–24 illustrates the Caterpillar DataView tooling, which is a portable diagnostic unit that allows data, measured by sensors temporarily installed on Cat products, to be viewed on a PC. It permits many of the current handheld scan tools used by service techs to be replaced with a single unit. DataView also allows diagnostic data to be shared with other PC programs, such as the Car Service Information System (SIS), and with the Cat ET (Electronic Technician). This tool connects to a standard PC as shown in the diagram via the parallel printer port and a Windows-based software program (DataView Software) that runs on the PC. The software program provides setup, digital dis-

plays, graphs, and data logging of the measurements being taken. The hardware will accept up to nine standard Caterpillar sensors. A parallel port on DataView is provided for operating a printer. DataView operates from an internal battery pack, but can also be powered from an external power source (110 or 220 V ac). Power can also be taken directly from a vehicle or machine battery of from 11 to 40 V dc, or by using a vehicle 12 or 24 volt lighter socket in the cab. A schematic of a Caterpillar PC-based diagnostic tools capability diagram can be viewed in Figure 23–25. The DataView Portable TechStation Group is available from Caterpillar through Part No. 131-5051. Optional cables and sensors are available to allow diagnosis/testing of the following items:

- Pressure sensors for analog channels
- Probe-type RTD temperature sensors
- Exhaust RTD temperature sensor
- Blowby sensors for analog channels
- Position sensor for analog channels

TABLE 23–1 *Chart shows the electronic service tool capabilities/features.*

Feature	Cat ET	ECAP	Pro-Link
Read/Change Customer Parameters	Yes	Limited[1]	Limited[1][3]
Read/Change Factory Parameters	Yes	Yes	No
Display Engine Status	Yes	Yes	Limited[3]
Display/Clear Diagnostic Codes	Yes	Yes	Yes[2]
Calibrations and Calibrate Speed/Timing Sensor	Yes	Yes	Yes
Cylinder Cutout	Yes	Yes	Yes
Injection Signal Duration	Yes	Yes	No
Engine Retarder Special Test	Yes	Yes	Yes
Cooling Fan Driver Special Test	Yes	Yes	No[3]
View Fleet Trip Data Segment	Yes	Yes	No[3]
View Driver Trip Data Segment	Yes	Yes	No[3]
View Trip Histograms	Yes	Yes	No[3]
Custom Data	Yes	Yes	Read Only
View Maintenance Indicator Data	Yes	Yes	Yes
View/Trigger Snapshot Recorder	Yes	Yes	No
Special Service Tests	Yes	Yes	No[3]
ECM Replacement/Fleet Configuration	Yes	No	No
Guided Diagnostics (On-line Troubleshooting Guide)	No[4]	No	No
Totals and ECM Date and Time	Yes	Yes	Yes
Customer Parameter Lockout	Yes	Yes	Read Only
Rating/Date Tracking	Yes	No	No
Flash Programming	Yes	No	No
Improved Graphics and Other Enhancements	Yes	No	No

[1]"Read only" on input and output selection parameters. See Electronic Troubleshooting Guide for details.
[2]MPSI Pro-Link will not clear any critical event because it does not support factory passwords.
[3]Support available mid 1999.
[4]Available with E.T. 2.4 or on SIS by 1/99.

Reprinted Courtesy of Caterpillar, Inc.

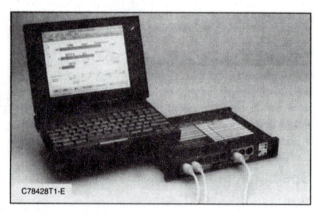

FIGURE 23–24 *View of the 131-5050 DataView Group; PC not included. (Courtesy of Caterpillar, Inc.)*

- Photo pickup speed sensor
- Injection line speed sensor
- Tach generator speed sensor
- Flywheel TDC magnetic speed sensors
- Magnetic speed sensors
- Fuel flowmeters and fuel flow communicator
- Hydraulic flowmeters for frequency channels

The *Tool Operating Manual; NEHS0662, Using the Caterpillar DataView System* is available from any Caterpillar dealer. This contains all the necessary information to effectively and efficiently apply the DataView tooling for diagnostic and troubleshooting purposes. In addition to the DataView operating manual, Cat also offers a guide entitled, "The Programming of Cat Electronic Truck Engines," available as Form LEXT8269 (updated regularly, so a new number will be used). These electronic troubleshooting guides should be the primary source for troubleshooting and programming.

Reprogramming a New ECM

If an ECM replacement is necessary, all customer-specified operating parameters and J1/P1 settings for optional input and output selections need to be programmed into the new ECM. Figure 23–23 illustrates an example of a communication adapter and harness cable to interface with the engine ECM and a desktop or laptop computer when reprogramming the ECM for a 3176B and 3406E, non-ADEM-equipped engines. If the failed ECM communicates with Cat Electronic Technician (Cat ET), you can use the "Copy Configuration" in ET to copy the parameters to program the new

Caterpillar PC Based Diagnostic Tools

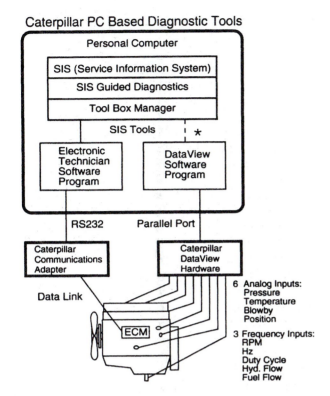

FIGURE 23–25 *Caterpillar PC-based diagnostic tools. A future version of DataView software will provide startup of DataView from the Tool Box Manager. (Reprinted courtesy of Caterpillar, Inc.)*

(7AS) truck engines starting in January 1998. ADEM 2000 ECM was introduced on 1999 and later-model year heavy-duty truck engines, and on the 2000 model year 3126B. ADEM 2000 ECM is now used on the 3126B (8YL, 7AS), C-10 (3CS), C-12 (2KS), and the 3406E (2WS, 1MM) truck engines. A single test ECM is available (through Caterpillar's Test Center, or inquire at any Cat dealer). This test ECM can determine if the engine ECM is in working order. This test ECM will function with both ADEM 111 and ADEM 2000 engines. Special instructions for using a test ECM are available through Caterpillar.

Download Flash Files

Flash files are used when it is necessary to change the ECM personality module. The personality module contains the software with all of the fuel setting information related to horsepower, torque rise, and air/fuel ratio rates for specific engines performance parameters. The personality module replaces the mechanical governor and controls the EUIs to deliver fuel for combustion. Speed timing and throttle position sensors determine when, at what pressure, and how much fuel to deliver to the cylinders (based on the actual and desired conditions) to optimize engine response. Earlier models of electronic engines required the actual physical removal and replacement of the personality module (PROM chip); however, later-model engines are manufactured with a EEPROM chip which allows "flash programming" when software updates are required or desired. Later-model truck engines are programmed to permit the selection of four different horsepower settings. This can be performed by flash programming. The flash file must be downloaded into a test ECM prior to changing the personality module (flash file). Failure to download the 188-9579 test ECM primer file into the test ECM prior to changing the personality module (flash file) will make the test ECM inoperable. After downloading the test ECM primer file, the test ECM will only communicate with Winflash until a standard personality module (flash file) is installed. The test ECM requires June 1999 or newer software. Failure to adhere may cause the test ECM to be inoperable.

Caterpillar's SIS (Service Information System) can be used to download flash files by using either SIS CD (compact disc), SIS DVD (digital video disc), or through the Cat SIS website available only to Cat dealers, truck engine parts and service (TEPS) dealers, and customers. This is a subscription offering that provides a new CD or DVD monthly with the CD or DVD containing all of the latest flash files needed to support Cat products. This data/information will interact with the Cat ET program.

ECM. If the ECM being replaced does not communicate with ET, the parameters will all need to be programmed manually. It is always a good idea to keep a current printout of the vehicle/equipment operating parameters in the vehicle cab glove box to be used as a quick reference or backup. A 16-page special instruction booklet, Part No. REHS0416, lists a complete breakdown of the required parts and tools, and the literature describes the electrical and programming requirements for installing Cat's ADEM 2000 software parameter programming into the ECM.

With the new ADEM system for Caterpillar's 3126B (7AS), C-10 (3CS), C-12 (2KS), and 3406E (2WS, 1MM) truck engines, there is now a new 70-pin breakout T-harness used with the new 70-pin ADEM 2000 ECM which has two 70-pin connectors. Previous engines used a 40-pin connector on the ECM. The 70-pin breakout harness is known as a "partial breakout T," rather than a full breakout T-harness. This 70-pin harness is intended for troubleshooting with the ignition switch in the ON position, but the engine not running. In addition, the 70-pin breakout T-harness offers decreased noise susceptibility, is easy to install, and is reasonably inexpensive. ADEM 111 was used on 3126B

TABLE 23–2 *Chart lists the diagnostic flash code/engine performance relationship for both a 3176B and a 3406E engine*

Diagnostic flash code	Effect on engine performance				Suggested driver action		
	Engine misfire	Low power	Engine speed reduced	Engine shutdown	Shut down vehicle[a]	Service ASAP[b]	Schedule service[c]
01—Idle shutdown override							
02—Event recorder data lost							✓
12—Coolant level sensor fault[d]							✓
13—Fuel temperature sensor fault							✓
14—Retarder solenoid fault							✓
19—A/C high-pressure switch open circuit							✓
21—Sensor supply voltage fault[d,e]		✓					✓
24—Oil pressure sensor fault[d]							✓
25—Boost pressure sensor fault[e]		✓					✓
26—Atmospheric pressure sensor fault[e]							✓
27—Coolant temperature sensor fault[d,e]							✓
28—Check throttle sensor adjustment							✓
31—Loss of vehicle speed signal			✓				✓
32—Throttle position sensor fault			✓			✓	
34—Engine rpm signal fault	✓		✓	✓		✓	
35—Engine overspeed warning							
36—Vehicle speed signal fault			✓				✓
38—Intake air temperature sensor fault[d,e]							✓
41—Vehicle overspeed warning							
42—Check sensor calibrations		✓					✓
46—Low oil pressure warning		✓	✓	✓	✓	✓	
47—Idle shutdown occurrence				✓			
51—Intermittent battery power to ECM	✓	✓		✓		✓	
53—ECM fault	✓	✓	✓	✓		✓	
55—No detected faults							
56—Check customer/system parameters		✓	✓				✓
58—Powertrain data link fault							✓
59—Incorrect engine software							✓
61—High coolant temperature warning		✓		✓		✓	
62—Low coolant level warning		✓		✓		✓	
64—High intake air temperature warning							✓
65—High fuel temperature warning							✓
72—Cylinder 1 or 2 fault	✓	✓				✓	
73—Cylinder 3 or 4 fault	✓	✓				✓	
74—Cylinder 5 or 6 fault	✓	✓				✓	

[a]Shut down vehicle: Drive the vehicle cautiously off the road and get immediate service. Severe engine damage may result.
[b]Service ASAP (as soon as possible): The driver should go to the nearest qualified service location.
[c]Schedule service: The driver should have the problem investigated when convenient.
[d]Reduces the effectiveness of the engine monitoring feature when active.
[e]May affect the system only under specific environmental conditions, such as engine startup at cold temperature, cold-weather operation at high altitudes, etc.

Reprinted Courtesy of Caterpillar, Inc.

Timing Sensor

The 1999 model year and later C-10 and C-12 ADEM-equipped truck engines have a 36-tooth timing wheel which is part of the crankshaft used for the timing sensor. The 2000 model year C-10 and C-12 engines have a 48-tooth timing wheel for the timing sensor. This allows tighter control of the engine speed and position to meet EPA exhaust emissions regulations.

System Troubleshooting

When an operator lodges an operational complaint on any electronic engine, always keep in mind that the engine fuel system or a mechanical problem may be the cause for the complaint. Consider that simple items such as a plugged air filter, plugged fuel filters, or high exhaust back pressure can be the reason for a low power complaint. To help a truck driver determine the cause on a 3176B or a 3406E engine, refer to the engine performance chart shown in Table 23–2.

This chart is also helpful for the service technician to use before performing a series of checks and tests to pinpoint the problem. By using the various special tools and diagnostic equipment illustrated in Figures 23–22, 23–23, and 23–24, then referring to the various SAE standard codes listed in Table 23–3, the service technician can systematically determine the cause of the performance complaint. For more details on the SAE standardized trouble codes, refer to Chapter 18 for information on "ECM-SAE Trouble Codes, page 479."

Both the 3176B and 3406E engines are equipped with an ECM that is programmed to offer three levels of engine protection during operation. These three situations are triggered by sensor values that change based on engine operating conditions. The ECM programming feature will initiate the following type of engine protection actions: a dash-mounted *warning* light, an engine *derate* or *shutdown,* and engine *shutdown.* Table 23–4 indicates the PID-FMI (parameter identifier–failure mode identifier) sensor-induced trouble code condition that will cause each one of these conditions to occur.

All electronic diesel engines today are password protected by factory-inserted alphanumeric (letter/number) codes. Factory passwords are calculated on a computer system available only to Caterpillar dealers to protect the customer-selected engine operating parameters. Passwords are selected by the end user or customer.

The Caterpillar electronic systems have some ability to self-diagnose. When a problem is detected, a diagnostic code is generated and the diagnostic *check engine lamp* is turned on, and in most cases the code is stored in permanent memory within the ECM for extraction by a service technician. Codes that present current faults are known as *active* because they indicate an existing problem. *Logged* codes stored in ECM memory may have been temporary conditions and record "events" rather than actual failures. By using the ECAP (electronic control analyzer programmer) diagnostic tool shown in Figure 23–22, Cat ET in Figure 23–23, or the DataView group in Figure 23–24, all stored trouble codes, engine operating parameters and conditions, shorting out of individual injectors, and fault tracing can be performed.

When using the ECAP, which is powered by vehicle 12 V supply, always ensure that the ignition key switch is off during connector hookup or when test wires are being disconnected. The ECAP is connected to the system through the DDL (dash datalink) connector by means of one of the adapters shown in Figure 23–22. The ignition key can be turned on to power up the ECAP, which will operate with the engine running or stopped as long as the key is on.

The ECAP window screen presents you with a choice of functions. Select one simply by pressing the desired control keys or scroll through the ECAP menu until you find the operating parameter or condition that you want to enter. You can reprogram the ECM personality module by connecting up a communication adapter and PC as illustrated in Figure 23–23. Figure 23–26 is an example of what a service technician may encounter on the information screen of the ECAP when it is powered up and he or she has selected "system configuration parameters." By pressing the up and down arrows on the ECAP keyboard pad, the technician can scroll through the information for that selected menu. As with the DDR used on the DDEC system, with continued exposure you will master the use of the ECAP tool and be able to diagnose performance complaints quickly.

The built-in maintenance indicator (MI) or maintenance alert system, see Figure 18–16, calculates service intervals for PM 1 (preventive maintenance 1), PM 2 (preventive maintenance 2), and coolant flush/fill maintenance procedures. The customer has the option of programming a specific number of hours or miles (kilometers) or even, based on engine oil sump quantity, the optimal PM 1 time interval. Note, however, that the PM 2 and coolant flush intervals are not programmable but are based on the recommended mileage or hours from the operation and maintenance manual. Within the ECM, the maintenance indicator sends a signal via the SAE J1587 datalink to a handheld service tool similar to that shown in Figure 21–31, to a

TABLE 23–3 *3176B and 3406E engine models SAE standard diagnostic troubleshooting code description and flash code numbers.*

PID-FMI	Flash code	Code description
1—11	72	Cylinder 1 fault
2—11	72	Cylinder 2 fault
3—11	73	Cylinder 3 fault
4—11	73	Cylinder 4 fault
5—11	74	Cylinder 5 fault
6—11	74	Cylinder 6 fault
22—13	42	Check timing sensor calibration
41—03	21	8-V supply above normal
41—04	21	8-V supply below normal
71—00	01	Idle shutdown override
71—01	47	Idle shutdown occurrence
84—00	41	Vehicle overspeed warning
84—01	31	Loss of vehicle speed signal
84—02	36	Invalid vehicle speed signal
84—08	36	Vehicle speed out of range
84—10	36	Vehicle speed rate of change
91—08	32	Invalid throttle signal
91—13	33	Throttle sensor calibration
100—01	46	Low oil pressure warning
100—03	24	Oil pressure sensor open circuit
100—04	24	Oil pressure sensor short circuit
100—11	46	Very low oil pressure
102—00	25	Boost pressure reading stuck high
102—03	25	Boost pressure sensor open circuit
102—04	25	Boost pressure sensor short circuit
102—13	42	Boost pressure sensor calibration
105—00	64	High intake manifold air temperature warning
105—03	38	Intake manifold air temperature sensor open circuit
105—04	38	Intake manifold air temperature sensor short circuit
105—11	64	Very high intake manifold air temperature
108—03	26	Atmospheric pressure sensor open circuit
108—04	26	Atmospheric pressure sensor short circuit
110—00	61	High coolant temperature warning
110—03	27	Coolant temperature sensor open circuit
110—04	27	Coolant temperature sensor short circuit
110—11	61	Very high coolant temperature
111—01	62	Low coolant level warning
111—02	12	Coolant level sensor fault
111—11	62	Very low coolant level
121—05	14	Retarder solenoid low/high open circuit
121—06	14	Retarder solenoid low/high short circuit
122—05	14	Retarder solenoid medium/high open circuit
122—06	14	Retarder solenoid medium/high short circuit
168—02	51	Low or intermittent battery power to ECM
174—00	65	High fuel temperature warning
174—03	13	Fuel temperature sensor open circuit
174—04	13	Fuel temperature sensor short circuit
190—00	35	Engine overspeed warning
190—02	34	Loss of engine rpm signal
228—03	19	A/C high-pressure switch open circuit
232—03	21	5-V supply above normal
232—04	21	5-V supply below normal
244—02	02	Event recorder data lost
249—11	58	Power train data link fault
252—11	59	Incorrect engine software
253—02	56	Check customer or system parameters
254—12	53	ECM fault

Source: Reprinted courtesy of Caterpillar, Inc.

724

TABLE 23–4 Engine ECM warning and protection system PID/FMI trouble codes that will initiate various operating parameters on a 3406E engine.

Programmed to Warning

PID—FMI	Flash code	Code description	Warning lamp	45 mph max.	160 hp max.	1350 rpm max.
100—01	46	Low oil pressure warning	Solid	No	No	No
100—11	46	Very low oil pressure	Solid	No	No	No
105—00	64	High intake manifold air temperature warning	Solid	No	No	No
105—11	64	Very high intake manifold air temperature	Solid	No	No	No
110—00	61	High coolant temperature warning	Solid	No	No	No
110—11	61	Very high coolant temperature	Solid	No	No	No
111—01	62	Low coolant level warming	Solid	No	No	No
111—11	62	Very low coolant level warming	Solid	No	No	No

Programmed to Derate or Shut Down

PID—FMI	Flash code	Code description	Warning lamp	45 mph max.	160 hp max.	1350 rpm max.
100—01	46	Low oil pressure warning	Solid	No	No	No
100—11	46	Very low oil pressure	Flash	Yes	Yes	Yes
105—00	64	High intake manifold air temperature warning	Solid	No	No	No
105—11	64	Very high intake manifold air temperature	Solid	No	No	No
110—00	61	High coolant temperature warning	Flash	Yes	Yes	No
110—11	62	Very high coolant temperature	Flash	Yes	Yes	No
111—01	62	Low coolant level warning	Solid	No	No	No
111—11	62	Very low coolant level warning	Flash	Yes	Yes	No

Programmed to Shut Down

PID—FMI	Flash code	Code description	Warning lamp	Time to shut down	Start time
100—01	46	Low oil pressure warning	Solid	No	No
100—11	46	Very low oil pressure	Flash	30 sec.	18 sec.
105—00	64	High intake manifold air temperature warning	Solid	No	No
105—11	64	Very high intake manifold air temperature	Solid	No	No
110—00	61	High coolant temperature warning	Flash	No	No
110—11	61	Very high coolant temperature	Flash	20 sec.	60 sec.
111—01	62	Low coolant level warning	Solid	No	No
111—11	62	Very low coolant level	Flash	30 sec.	80 sec.

Source: Reprinted courtesy of Caterpillar, Inc.

dash display (see Figure 21–35) or to the fleet management program and indicates that maintenance is due 3000 miles (4828 km) prior to the estimated service. Once the MI has been alerted, it can be reset using the handheld or ECAP service tool (see Figure 23–22) or the dash display controls.

Breakout Cable Assemblies

Figure 21–38 showed a *breakout box* that can be used on the DDEC systems to check system wiring and harness connections with the aid of a multimeter. Wiring and harness connections on Caterpillar's 3176B and 3406E engine models can be checked using the various wire harness breakout T's shown in Figure 23–22 to speed up electrical troubleshooting. These cables allow the probe tips of a multimeter to be safely inserted into the tip jacks to obtain a signal from any harness wire. The 7X6370 three-pin breakout T-harness is inserted in series between a 3176B/3406E harness jack and plug to permit voltage measurement on an operating system. The 8T8726 T-harness is only required to check a remote-mounted throttle position sensor, which receives a battery signal between 11 and 13.5 V.

```
                    Read System Configuration Parameters
Selected Engine Rating
    Rating #:                                          1            # 4
    Rating Type:                                Standard
    Rated Power:                                     445  HP
    Rated RPM:                                      1700  RPM
    Rated Peak Torque:                             1650  LB FT
more... Press  ↑ or ↓ to move through the rest of the parameters.

    Rated Peak Torque RPM:                          1200  RPM
    Top Engine Limit–RPM Range:                1620–2120  RPM
    Test Spec:                                     0T1234
         with BrakeSaver:                          0T5678
    Last Service tool to change system parameters:   TMCA1000
    Last Service tool to change customer parameters: TMCA1000
    Full Load Setting:                                10         # 0
    Full Torque Setting:                              10         # 0
    Personality Module Code:                           1         # 0
    Personality Module P/N:                      12T4321–02
    Personality Module Release Date:                OCT91
    Electronic Control Module S/N:              XXX–000000
    Vehicle ID:                                 1234509876       #2
    Engine Serial Number:                         XXX 01234
    Total  Tattletale:                                60
```

FIGURE 23–26 Sample ECAP information/data screen—system configuration parameters. (Reprinted courtesy of Caterpillar, Inc.)

Troubleshooting the 5 V Sensors
1900, 1906, 1917, 1921, 1922, 1923, 1924, 1928
3176B (9CK),
C-10 (2PN, 8YS),
C-12 (1YN, 9NS),
3406E (1LW, 5DS, 5EK, 6TS) Truck Engines

Cat References: Electronic Troubleshooting, C-10, C-12, and 3406E Truck Engine, RENR1328, "Troubleshooting with a Diagnostic Code."
Electronic Troubleshooting, 3176B, C-10, C-12, and 3406E Truck Engine, SENR5582, "Troubleshooting with a Diagnostic Code."
Schematic, C-10, C-12, and 3406E Truck Engine, RENR 1327.
Schematic, 3176B, C-10, C-12, and 3406E Truck Engine, SENR5574.

Analysis of returned sensors indicate that a significant percentage of the sensors did not need to be replaced. The sensors covered by the following two procedures are the boost pressure sensor, the atmospheric pressure sensor, the oil pressure sensor, the coolant temperature sensor, the fuel temperature sensor, the outside air temperature sensor, and the inlet manifold temperature sensor. In order to ensure that a proper diagnosis is performed, these two procedures should be used. The procedures are contained in the electronic troubleshooting manuals that are referenced above.

NOTE If a sensor has a single logged fault or even many logged faults it is not necessarily a bad sensor. A fault can be caused by an intermittent electrical connection anywhere from the ECM to the sensor. All steps in the electronic troubleshooting guide should be closely followed in order to find the root cause. An ECM snapshot can be manually triggered by toggling the cruise-control set/resume switch. An ECM snapshot can also be triggered with the ECAP service tool or the Electronic Technician service tool. If there is an intermittent operating problem that is difficult to reproduce in the shop, the driver can manually trigger an ECM snapshot when the problem occurs. This may help troubleshoot the problem when he or she returns to the shop.

1. **PC-34: +5V Sensor Voltage Supply Circuit Test.** This procedure is used to troubleshoot the system when there is an active, or an easily repeated "232-03" 5 V supply above normal or "232-04" 5 V supply below

normal diagnostic fault code. This procedure provides step-by-step instructions for checking the complete 5 V system, including the wiring harness. It is important to note, that if either the "232-03" or the "232-04" diagnostic fault code is active, then all the 5 V sensors will be set to default values. The diagnostics for these sensors will also be disabled.

2. **PC-35: Engine Sensor Open or Short Circuit Test.** This procedure is used when there is an active, or easily repeated open or short circuit diagnostic fault code associated with one of the 5 V sensors. The troubleshooting procedure for each sensor is the same and includes step-by-step instructions for checking connectors, pins, and sockets. The procedure also describes the process for checking the signal, common, and supply circuits.

HEUI FUEL SYSTEM

Existing EUI systems currently in use by Caterpillar, Cummins, Detroit Diesel, Volvo, and John Deere on their high-speed heavy-duty engine models utilize a camshaft-actuated rocker arm assembly to force the injector follower and fuel plunger downward. This action is required to raise the trapped fuel within the injector barrel to a high enough pressure to open the injector needle valve within the spray tip assembly.

However, a rather unique electronically controlled injection system now in use by both Caterpillar and (Navistar) International Truck Transportation Corporation on their diesel engine product line is HEUI (hydraulically actuated electronically controlled unit injection). The system is commonly referred to in the industry by the term HEUI, pronounced as in the name "Hughie." In this system, which was codesigned by Caterpillar and International, no camshaft-actuated rocker arm is needed to raise the fuel pressure within the injector to the high levels needed to open the needle valve within the spray tip assembly.

In place of a rocker arm, the HEUI system employs high-pressure lube oil acting on an intensifier piston designed into the top end of each injector. Figure 23–27 illustrates a schematic arrangement of the components required with the HEUI system used with the 3100 series Cat engines. The HEUI system is also used by International on their T444E V8 engine model. This engine is widely used by Ford in a number of their pickup and midrange truck models as well as by International in their own product lineup. In addition, International employs the HEUI system on their inline six-cylinder DT-466 model as well as in their 530E engine series. Caterpillar employs the HEUI system in their 3116, 3126, 3408E, and 3412E engine models.

The first application of the HEUI-B (2nd generation) fuel system is used on the recently developed six-cylinder 8.8L C9 engine model for industrial, construction and agricultural applications in the Challenger ag tractor, and Lexion combine. One of the keys to the HEUI-B system and its H1300B injector is that it allows for flexible injection rates, such as ramp, square and split injection to produce lower noise, improved exhaust emissions, lower fuel consumption, faster end to injection, and higher injection pressures. The C9 engine is the first application of the ADEM 111 ECM (3rd generation Advanced Electronic Engine Management ECM) in a non-truck application. Enhancements to ADEM 111 specific to the HEUI-B include additional sensing capability and prognostics.

System Operation

The design of the HEUI system permits enhanced performance through improved fuel economy and lower exhaust emissions by controlling the rate of injection hydraulically rather than mechanically, which depends on engine speed. Because the HEUI injector plunger does not move until the injector solenoid is energized by a signal from the ECM, plunger movement is not limited to the speed or duration of the engine cam lobe as it is in a mechanically actuated EUI system. Therefore, timing control is more precise.

In the HEUI system, other than using a hydraulically actuated unit injector, the system layout and arrangement is similar to Cat's own EUI system used on the 3176B, C-10, C-12, and 3406E engines. Figure 23–28 shows the system arrangement for a 3406E (EUI system), versus that for the 3408E/3412E engines using the HEUI system. As you can see, the main difference lies in the fact that the HEUI system employs both an injection actuation pressure sensor and an injector actuation pressure control valve. The electrical system power supplies used with the HEUI system on both the 3408E/3412E are as follows:

1. ECM—24 volts
2. Speed/timing sensors—12.5 volts
3. HEUI injector solenoids—105 to 110 volts
4. Analog sensors—5 volts; this includes the following sensors:
   - hydraulic pressure
   - coolant temperature
   - atmospheric pressure
   - turbocharger inlet pressure
   - turbocharger outlet pressure
   - lubrication oil pressure
   - hydraulic temperature
   - fuel temperature

FIGURE 23–27 Fuel system schematic for a 3100 HEUI engine fuel system and components. (Reprinted courtesy of Caterpillar, Inc.)

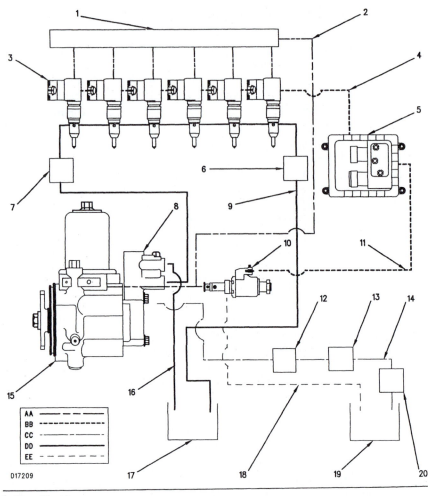

Fuel System Schematic
(AA) High pressure oil line. (BB) Unit injector wiring harness. (CC) Low pressure oil supply line. (DD) Fuel line. (EE) Low pressure oil return line. (1) High pressure oil manifold. (2) High pressure oil line. (3) Hydraulic electronic unit injector. (4) Unit injector wiring harness. (5) Electronic control module (ECM). (6) Fuel pressure regulator. (7) Fuel filter. (8) Fuel transfer pump. (9) Fuel return line. (10) Injection actuation pressure control valve (IAPCV). (11) Electrical signal from ECM to IAPCV (controls oil manifold pressure). (12) Oil cooler. (13) Secondary oil filter. (14) Low pressure oil supply line. (15) High pressure oil pump. (16) Fuel line. (17) Fuel tank. (18) Low pressure oil return line. (19) Oil sump. (20) Oil pump (engine lubrication).

5. Digital sensors—8 volts; this includes the following sensors:
   - throttle position
   - pump control valve signal
   - exhaust temperature
6. Pump control valve—0 to 24 volts

Low-Pressure Fuel System

The fuel system used with the HEUI system is a low-pressure system. On the 3408E/3412E engines, the fuel pressure of between 45 and 60 psi (310 and 415 kPa) is maintained by a gear-transfer pump and fuel pressure regulating valve. If you refer to Figure 23–29, fuel is drawn from the tank through a combination fuel filter/water separator to the pump where it is then directed through the cooler plate of the ECM to maintain the electronics package at an acceptable temperature during engine operation. A fuel temperature sensor installed in the fuel supply system compensates for power losses as the fuel temperature rises during engine operation. Fuel is then routed to and through the secondary fuel filter and is directed to the low-pressure supply galleries located in the manifolds on top of the cylinder heads. As with all unit injector systems, approximately four times more fuel than is required for injection purposes is used. This ensures that sufficient lubrication and cooling is provided for the injectors. Fuel that is not injected leaves the manifold and flows through a single pressure regulating valve and common line back to the fuel tank. The low-pressure fuel system on the

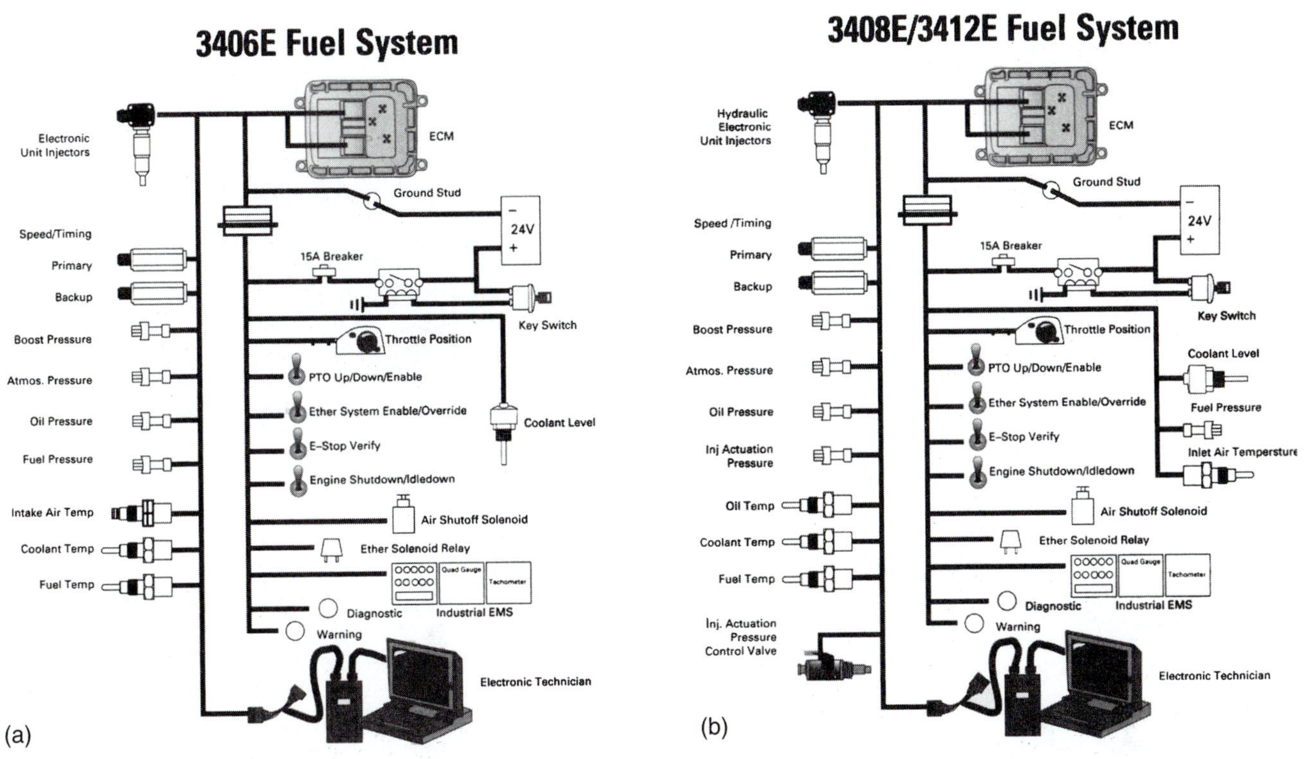

3406E Fuel System

3408E/3412E Fuel System

(a)

(b)

FIGURE 23–28   (a) Schematic diagram of a 3406E engine equipped with an EUI fuel system; (b) schematic diagram for a 3408E/3412 equipped with a HEUI fuel system. (Reprinted courtesy of Caterpillar, Inc.)

3116/3126 engine models typically operates at between 58 and 76 psi (400 and 525 kPa).

HIGH-PRESSURE OIL SYSTEM

Figure 23–29b illustrates a schematic of the high-pressure oil system used with the Cat 3408 engine model HEUI system. In the schematic, the high-pressure oil pump is gear driven and draws oil through both a filter and an oil cooler from the engine oil sump.

The oil circuit shown in simplified form in Figure 23–29 consists of both a low- and a high-pressure section: the low side from the engine oil pump and the high side, which provides the oil to the injector intensifier piston.

The high-pressure lube oil is controlled by the regulator pressure control valve (RPCV), which opens and dumps oil directly back to the engine oil pan. The RPCV is an electrically controlled dump valve that controls the pump output pressure. A variable signal current from the ECM determines pump output pressure. Figure 23–30 illustrates a cross section of the RPCV valve. With the engine stopped, the internal valve spool is held to the right by a return spring and the oil

drain ports are closed. At engine startup the ECM signal to the RPCV permits the solenoid to generate a magnetic field to allow the armature to exert a force on the push pin and poppet. The combination of spring force and oil pressure flowing into the spool chamber continues to hold the spool valve to the right to ensure that the drain ports are held closed. Therefore, all oil flow is directed to the pressure rail manifold or manifolds cast into each cylinder head until the desired oil pressure is obtained.

OPERATION—ENGINE START UP

Approximately 1,500 psi of oil pressure is required to start a relatively warm engine. If the engine is cold (coolant temperature below 32°F), 3,000 psi of oil pressure is commanded by the ECM.

Once the engine fires and runs, the ECM sends a signal to the RPCV, and the injection control pressure sensors monitor actual gallery pressure. The ECM then compares the actual rail pressure to the desired rail pressure and adjusts the electrical signal to the RPCV to obtain the desired rail pressure. Within the RPCV valve, the pressure in the spool chamber is controlled

FIGURE 23-29 (a) External components for a 3100 engine equipped with a HEUI fuel system; (b) 3408E/3412E HEUI system showing the flow of the high-pressure lube oil system. (Reprinted courtesy of Caterpillar, Inc.)

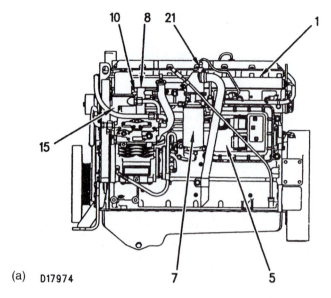

(a)   D17974

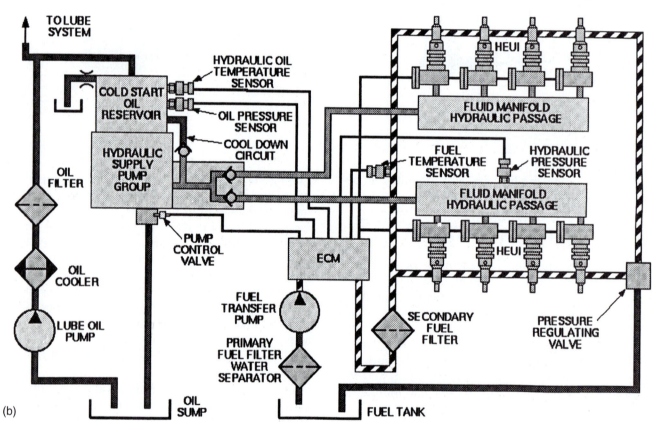

(b)

by adjusting the position on the poppet and allowing it to bleed off some of the oil in the spool chamber. The position of the poppet is controlled by the strength of the magnetic field based on the ECM signal. Therefore, the spool position determines how much area of the drain ports is open to control the rail pressure oil.

Injector Fuel Flow

Figure 23–31 illustrates the main components within the HEUI injector. During the fill cycle, the internal spring below the intensifier piston 8 returns all components to their nonactuated positions. Figure 23–32 shows that high-pressure hydraulic oil is provided to

ENGINE OFF

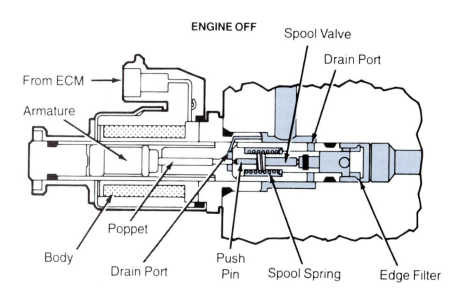

FIGURE 23–30 *Cross section of a HEUI fuel system RPCV (regulator pressure control valve) actuator. (Reprinted courtesy of Caterpillar, Inc.)*

the injector(s) from the passages cast within the cylinder head through individual jumper tubes. Fuel is supplied to the injector by the low-pressure supply passage located and drilled in the fluid manifolds as shown in Figure 23–33. This fuel pressure unseats the plunger fill check valve allowing the plunger cavity to fill with fuel. The fill cycle ends when the intensifier piston (item 8 in Figure 23–31) is pushed to the top of its bore, permitting the check valve to close. Since the injector solenoid is deenergized (no signal from the ECM), no high-pressure lube oil from the rail manifold can enter the injector.

> **CAUTION** The injector solenoids operate on 105 to 110 V dc electrical pulses from the fuel injection control circuits in the ECM. Always keep your hands clear of the injector solenoid area when the engine is running or severe electric shock can occur.

Figure 23–34 illustrates all of the components of the HEUI electronic control system. When the ECM determines from various input sensor signals to actuate a specific fuel injector, it sends a fuel delivery control signal to the injector driver module, and a PWM (pulse-width-modulated) duty signal activates the injector solenoid. The solenoid when actuated overcomes the spring pressure that is holding the poppet valve closed. When the poppet valve opens, it simultaneously closes off any path to drain for the oil and allows high-pressure oil to flow around the poppet valve and into the top of the intensifier piston (8) as shown in Figure 23–31.

If you refer to Figure 23–31, when the HEUI injector is not firing (at rest), the solenoid valve (5) is held on its lower seat (2) by the solenoid return spring (4). When the engine is running, but a specific injector is not firing, high-pressure inlet oil will be blocked, and the poppet cavity (9) is open to drain; the intensifier piston (8) and its plunger (7) are pushed to the top of the bore, and the intensifier piston cavity (12) is full. When the PWM signal from the ECM actuates the injector solenoid (5), the poppet valve (1) will move from its lower seat (2), and rest against the upper seat (6). This action now closes the path to the poppet valve cavity (9) and permits high-pressure oil to enter the unit injector via port (3) to act directly upon the top of the intensifier piston (8). The intensifier piston has approximately seven times the area to that of the fuel plunger; therefore, when the hydraulic circuit is supplying a pressure of 3000 psi (21,000 kPa), approximately 21,000 psi (145,000 kPa) will be generated below the fuel plunger. When this pressure is high enough, it will push both the intensifier (8) and plunger (7) down to pressurize the diesel fuel contained in the barrel (11) and piston cavity (12). When the fuel pressure exceeds the injector valve opening pressure (approximately 4500 psi or 31,000 kPa), the nozzle valve (17) will open and inject fuel directly into the engine combustion chamber through the small orifices drilled in the spray tip. Typically the 3408E and 3412E engines have six orifices each with a diameter of 0.010 in. (0.252 mm) arranged at an angle of 140°. The reverse flow check valve (14) prevents backflow of the fuel so that it can apply pressure on the nozzle (17). Injection will end when the solenoid (5) is deenergized. This allows the poppet valve (1), the intensifier piston (8), and the

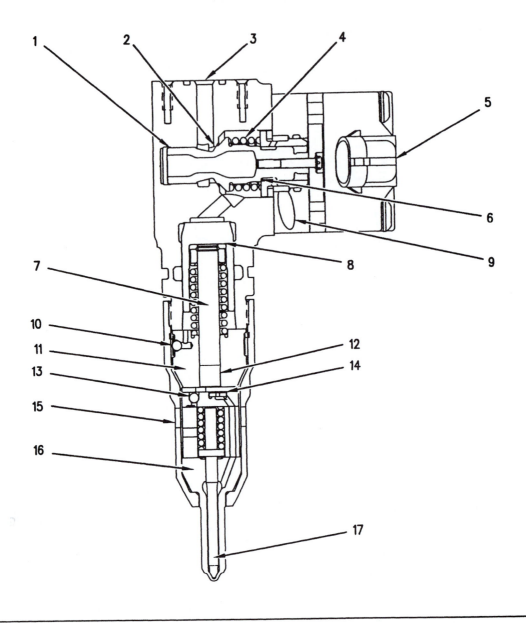

D17967

Hydraulic Electronic Unit Injector
(1) Poppet valve. (2) Lower seat (poppet valve). (3) Entry port (high pressure oil). (4) Solenoid return spring. (5) Solenoid. (6) Upper seat (poppet valve). (7) Plunger. (8) Intensifier piston. (9) Poppet cavity (oil). (10) Check ball (spring loaded). (11) Barrel. (12) Piston cavity (fuel). (13) Check ball (fuel inlet). (14) Reverse flow check. (15) Fill port(s) (Fuel). (16) Nozzle assembly. (17) Nozzle valve.

FIGURE 23–31   Component parts identification of a HEUI injector assembly. (Reprinted courtesy of Caterpillar, Inc.)

plunger (7) to return to its at-rest position. During the upward stroke of the plunger (7), it draws fuel into the piston cavity (12), through the fill ports (15), across the fuel inlet check ball (13), and then the injector is prepared for the next firing cycle.

Note that the nozzle assembly (16) is of conventional design other than the fuel inlet check ball (13) and the reverse flow check ball (14). Keep in mind that

the purpose of the inlet check ball (13) unseats and seals during the plunger (7) downstroke to ensure that the piston cavity (12) is filled with fuel. The one-way check valve (14) will only allow fuel flow in one direction (into the nozzle), but will prevent any backflow at the end of injection. This action of the reverse flow check is similar to that found in all unit injectors to prevent the possibility of combustion gases entering the

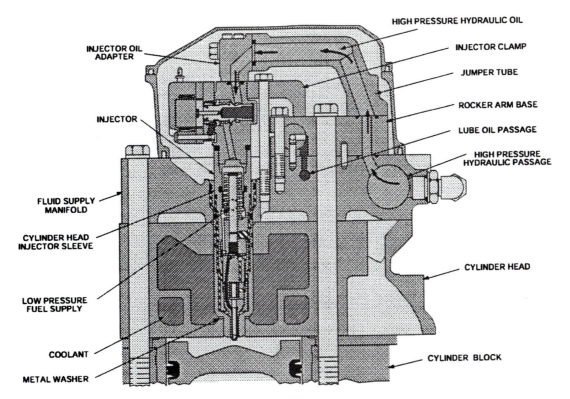

FIGURE 23–32 HEUI system showing that the high-pressure lube oil is provided to the injector(s) from passages cast within the cylinder head through individual jumper tubes. (Reprinted courtesy of Caterpillar, Inc.)

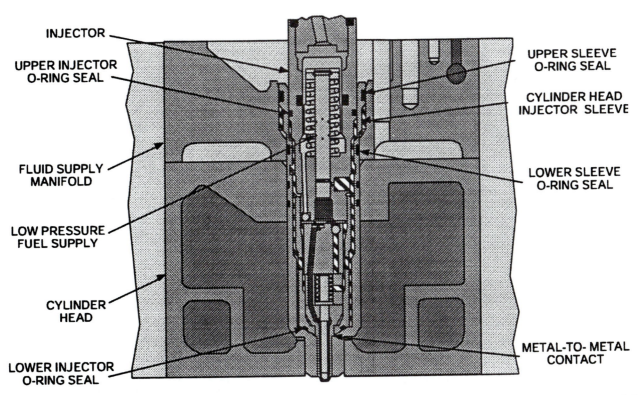

FIGURE 23–33 Fuel is supplied to the injector(s) by the low-pressure supply passage located and drilled in the fluid manifolds within the cylinder heads. (Reprinted courtesy of Caterpillar, Inc.)

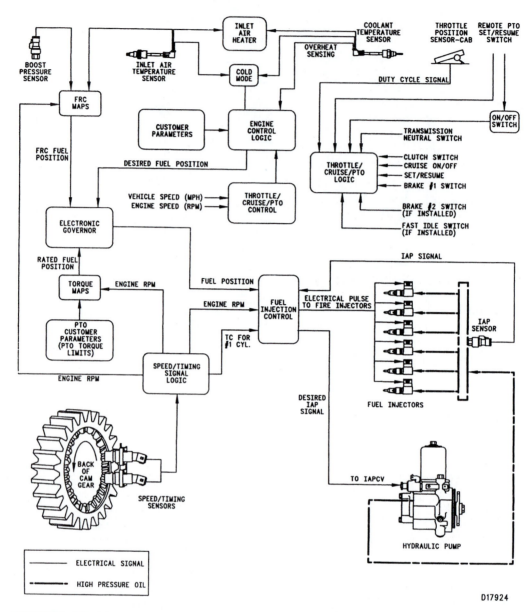

FIGURE 23–34 *3100 HEUI model engine showing the layout of the electronic control system. (Reprinted courtesy of Caterpillar, Inc.)*

nozzle when the needle valve seat of the nozzle is held closed by the pressure of the spring directly above it.

Logged Trouble Codes

When a sensor signal operates outside of the normal operating parameters, logged events will store a diagnostic trouble code in ECM memory, and trigger illumination of an instrument panel warning lamp similar to the sequence used in all electronically controlled engines. Items that would log a code include:

- High coolant temperature above 225°F (107°C)
- Loss of coolant flow
- Low lube oil pressure (according to the oil pressure map)
- Abnormal injection actuation hydraulic pressure (low or high)
- Injection actuation pressure system fault
- Air inlet restriction (if installed)
- Engine overspeed histogram
- Low fuel pressure (industrial engines only)

SUMMARY

The description of Caterpillar mechanical and electronic fuel injection systems in this chapter has rounded out your knowledge of the advantages of using electronic controls on today's diesel engines. Many similarities exist between the types of EUI systems used by Caterpillar, Cummins, Detroit Diesel, Volvo, and Mack. The diagnostic tooling employed by each major diesel engine OEM has more similarities than differences. A review of each of these major fuel systems can be readily applied to your maintenance and diagnostic capabilities as a diesel technician.

SELF-TEST QUESTIONS

1. Technician A says that the 3406B truck engine was the first Caterpillar vehicle engine to receive electronic controls. Technician B believes that it was the 3176 engine model. Who is correct?

2. Technician A says that the basic concept of design/operation of a Caterpillar multiple-plunger injection pump is similar to that for Robert Bosch systems. Technician B says that is not so. Who is correct?

3. The conventional term used by Caterpillar in their injection pumps for the *helix* is the word
   a. port
   b. plunger
   c. barrel
   d. scroll

4. Technician A says that Caterpillar now only uses direct-injection combustion chamber engines in their line of highway truck engines. Technician B disagrees, saying that for cold-weather operation, a PC (precombustion) engine is still available with glow plug controls. Who is correct?

5. Technician A says that mechanical governors used on Caterpillar truck engines are speed sensitive. Technician B says that they are load sensitive in order to be able to respond to highway operating conditions such as hills. Who is correct?

6. Technician A says that the AFC (air/fuel control) unit is designed to limit injection pump rack travel, thereby eliminating exhaust smoke. Technician B says that the AFC is designed to act as a wastegate for the turbocharger to limit boost under load. Who is correct?

7. Technician A says that the automatic timing advance unit used on 3406B engines is nonadjustable. Technician B says that you can adjust the automatic timing device on 3406B engines. Who is right?

8. Technician A says that the governor springs are always attempting to pull the fuel rack to a decreased fuel position. Technician B says that it is the centrifugal force of the rotating governor flyweights that pull the rack to a decreased fuel position. Who is right?

9. Technician A says that the term *high idle* means the same as *maximum no-load* engine speed. Technician B says that it means the same as *rated* engine speed. Who understands the meaning of this terminology?

10. Technician A says that if the engine lacks power with no unusual exhaust smoke color, the problem is probably due to fuel starvation. Technician B says that it is more likely a faulty injector. Who is right?

11. To determine if an injection nozzle is misfiring on an NSFS, you should
   a. loosen the high-pressure fuel line nut while the engine is running to check the engine sound and speed drop
   b. loosen the high-pressure fuel line nut while the engine is running to check the engine sound and speed pickup rate
   c. remove the nozzle from the engine and install it into a pop tester
   d. block off the fuel supply line from the injection pump and run the engine at an idle speed

12. On a 3406B engine the flywheel timing bolt
   a. is located in the forward side of the flywheel housing
   b. is located in the injection pump housing
   c. is located in the rocker cover recess
   d. is a special order bolt

13. Technician A says that the use of the electronic controls on both the 3176 and 3406B engines does away with the need for an AFC unit. Not so, says technician B; you still need the AFC unit. Who is right?

14. The letters PWM in reference to an electronic unit injector engine stand for
   a. power width module
   b. pulse-width modulated
   c. pressure working motor
   d. pneumatic with magnetic controls

15. Technician A says that the letters TPS stand for "throttle position sensor," while technician B says that they stand for "throttle power switch." Who is right?

16. The throttle pedal on an electronically controlled engine such as the 3406 and 3176 is basically a(n)
   a. variable potentiometer
   b. hydraulic/pneumatic cylinder
   c. on/off relay switch
   d. mechanical/electrical circuit breaker

17. Technician A says that the term *PROM* stands for "programmable read-only memory," whereas technician B says that it stands for "power road override module." Who is correct?

18. Technician A says that an EEPROM unit is an "electrically erasable programmable read-only memory," whereas technician B says that it is an "electric engine power road override module." Who is correct?

19. Technician A says that to prevent unauthorized adjustment of the engine power setting on electronic engines

models, an electronic password is required. Technician B says that you can alter the engine horsepower setting by removing and installing another PROM assembly. Who is right?

20. Technician A says that the control module determines injection timing, fuel delivery rate, and governor reaction/setting. Technician B says that this is done by manipulation of the TPS. Who is right?

21. TDC for No. 1 cylinder on a Cat 3406E engine is achieved by:
    a. installing a flywheel timing bolt
    b. installing a vibration damper bolt
    c. installing a crankshaft pulley bolt
    d. installing a fuel injection pump bolt

22. When setting the valve lash on a 3406E model engine, Technician A says that when No. 1 piston is at TDC on its compression stroke, you can check and adjust the intake valve clearances on cylinders 1, 2 and 4, and the exhaust valve clearances on cylinders 1, 3, and 5. Technician B says you would set the intake valves on cylinders 3, 5, and 6, and the exhaust valves on cylinders 2, 4, and 6. Who is correct?

23. Technician A says that to adjust the Jake Brake slave piston setting on a 3406E engine, rotate the engine over to place the cylinder to the correct position for setting the intake valve clearance. Technician B says you should rotate the engine over to the correct position for setting the cylinder exhaust valves. Who is correct?

24. Caterpillar introduced its first electronic engine in:
    a. 1980
    b. 1984
    c. 1987
    d. 1990

25. Technician A says that the 3406E engine model uses an in-block camshaft. Technician B says it uses an overhead camshaft design. Who is correct?

26. Technician A says that when the EUI equipped engines fuel temperature exceeds 150 degrees F (65.5 C) the ECM will log a fault code. Technician B says the fuel temperature needs to reach 180 F (82 C) before a fault code will log. Who is correct?

27. Technician A says that the term ADEM means advanced diesel engine management. Technician B says it means advanced diesel electronic modulation. Who is correct?

28. Technician A says that the term ECAP means engine controls with automated pressure. Technician B says it means electronic control analyzer programmer. Who is correct?

29. The first use of the ADEM 111 ECM along with the HEUI-B fuel system can be found on the following Caterpillar engine:
    a. C10 and C12 models
    b. C9 model
    c. 15.8L 3406E model
    d. 14L 3406E model

30. Technician A says that the primary service tool now used for electronic engine diagnostics is the Cat ET (electronic technician) tool group. Technician B says it is the ECAP (electronic control analyzer programmer). Who is correct?

31. Technician A says that Caterpillar's Data View tooling can be used with a PC or laptop. Technician B says only the ECAP can be used for this purpose. Who is correct?

32. Technician A says that 'flash files' are used when active fault codes need to be diagnosed. Technician B says that 'flash files' are used when it is necessary to change the ECM Personality Module. Who is correct?

33. Technician A says that 1999 model year C10 and C12 ADEM engines used a 48 tooth timing wheel on the crankshaft. Technician B says they used a 36 tooth wheel, while the 2000 and later engines used a 48 tooth crankshaft timing wheel. Who is correct?

34. Technician A says that if a sensor has a single logged fault, or even many logged faults it is not necessarily a bad sensor since the fault could be caused by an intermittent electrical connection. Technician B says that any logged fault is confirmation that the sensor is faulty. Who is correct?

35. Technician A says that a PID/FMI combination fault code such as a 232-03 indicates that the 5V sensor supply is below normal. Technician B says the sensor voltage is above normal. Who is correct?

36. Technician A says that a PID/FMI combination fault code such as a 100-01 indicates that there is a low oil pressure condition. Technician B says it means that there is a high oil temperature condition. Who is correct?

37. Technician A says that a low oil pressure warning will illuminate the dash warning lamp as a solid color. Technician B says the lamp will flash continuously. Who is correct?

38. Technician A says that a very low oil pressure condition will allow limp-home capability features. Technician B says that this condition will provide a flashing warning lamp followed 30 seconds later by engine shutdown. Who is correct?

39. The HEUI fuel system employs high oil pressure to actuate the injector plunger.
    True _____   False _____

40. Technician A says that the HEUI injector solenoids operate at voltages between 30 and 40 volts. Technician B says they operate with voltages between 105 and 110 volts. Who is correct?

41. The HEUI fuel system used on the 3408E and 3412E engines uses an ECM that operates on:
    a. 5 volts
    b. 8 volts
    c. 12 volts
    d. 24 volts

42. Technician A says that the speed and timing sensors on the 3408E and 3412E engines operates on 12.5 volts. Technician B says it operates on 5 volts. Who is correct?

43. Technician A says that the 3 digital sensors TPS, exhaust temperature and pump control valve signal on the 3406E and 3412E HEUI engines all operate on 5 volts. Technician B says that they operate on 8 volts. Who is correct?

44. Technician A says that on the HEUI fuel system approximately 1,500 psi (10.34 MPa) of oil pressure is required to start a relatively warm engine. Technician B says that it requires 3,000 psi to actuate the injector. Who is correct?

45. Technician A says that the popping pressure in a HEUI injector is approximately 31,000 psi (214 MPa). Technician B says it is 4500 psi (31,000 kPa). Who is correct?

24

Engine Run-In and Dyno Testing

Overview

This chapter describes the proper steps and presents guidelines for preparing to start, run, and test a rebuilt/overhauled engine with a dynamometer. Necessary adaptation hardware and safety checks and tests are also discussed. In many diesel engine, truck/bus, off-highway, industrial, and marine companies, engine dyno testing is often performed by a technician who specializes in this procedure. If the engine has been completely removed from its equipment prior to overhaul, it is ideal to "run it in" on a stationary shop dynamometer assembly. If, however, as is often the case with heavy-duty on-highway trucks, an in-frame overhaul using new cylinder kits, for example, is performed, then a chassis dynamometer is usually employed. Chassis dynos are used often with heavy-duty Class 8 truck/tractors when a lack of power complaint is received to confirm whether there actually is a lack of power, or to help isolate exactly where the problem lies. During a chassis dyno test, the following diagnostic tests can be performed and monitored:

- Engine oil pressure and temperature
- Engine/driveline vibrations
- Fuel pressure and temperature
- Crankcase blowby (pressure) test
- Coolant pressure and temperature
- Turbocharger boost pressure
- Air inlet restriction
- Aftercooler performance
- Exhaust back pressure
- Intake manifold air temperature
- Thermatic fan ON temperature
- Exhaust temperature

At the completion of this chapter, accompanied with an opportunity to actually perform an engine or chassis dyno test procedure, you will be familiar with the safety and sequential test procedures involved in this process. End-of-chapter questions will permit you to self-test your new knowledge in preparation for challenging either the ASE or TQ test areas.

ASE CERTIFICATION

Dyno testing is referenced in the ASE preparation guide for the medium/heavy truck test T2, subsection A, General Engine Diagnosis. Tasks list content area 1 states:

1. Verify the complaint, and road/dyno test vehicle; review driver/customer interview and past maintenance documents (if available); determine further diagnosis.

Problematic complaints that are discovered during a dyno test procedure can be systematically confirmed by noting all of the monitored systems as listed in this chapter's overview. In addition, if the engine being tested is an electronic model, a scan tool, laptop, PC, or specific engine OEM's diagnostic equipment can be hooked up during the test. Freeze-frame information and data and recall (snapshot) information can be used to determine what fault/trouble codes have occurred during testing. In addition, see Chapter 25 for help in determining specific engine fault causes.

GENERAL INFORMATION

The durability and service life of an overhauled engine is directly related to its initial *run-in* (testing) after repair. Ideally, testing should be performed on an engine dynamometer. When a dynamometer is not readily available, the engine can be run in correctly by following a procedure related to the type of equipment application in which the engine is used. On-highway trucks or mobile equipment can be run in on a *chassis dynamometer*. The advantage of using a dynamometer is that the engine can be loaded gradually at different speeds. In addition, the technician can observe and record the engine coolant temperature, oil pressure and temperature, fuel pressure, turbocharger boost, and crankcase pressure conditions as well as note any leakage of fluid or air.

The actual run-in routine varies slightly depending on the rpm, rating, and displacement of the engine; for our purposes here, the process can be considered common for all engines. Each engine manufacturer describes and explains the recommended run-in procedure, speeds, loads, and time under load for their particular model of engine. This information can be found in most service manuals or in special publications readily available from a local engine dealer or distributor.

ENGINE DYNAMOMETERS

Ideally, an engine dynamometer (dyno for short) should be placed in a soundproof room to minimize noise radiation throughout the shop area. A dyno room should be equipped with all of the necessary coolant, lube, fuel, air, and exhaust connections. The engine must be securely bolted to a frame that is itself secured to the floor of the dyno room. Portable dyno models such as the one shown in Figure 24–1 bolt directly to the engine flywheel. A splined driveshaft extending from the center of the dyno is attached to a drive plate hub that has been bolted to the engine flywheel; the dyno housing is secured by bolts to the flywheel housing. Fixed or stationary dynamometers which are mounted to a frame and bolted to the shop floor, require that a heavy-duty short-length driveshaft similar to that used in Class 8 trucks be bolted to the dyno-driven member at one end while the opposite end is bolted to the engine flywheel. When using the driveshaft system, make sure that both ends of the flanges are parallel to one another and that a small angle exists along the length of the driveshaft. Mounting the driveshaft so that it is perfectly flat will prevent the universal joints at each end from functioning. This will be noticeable by a vibration or rattling noise when the engine is running and can damage or shear the U-joints.

Although an engine can be dyno tested using its own radiator or heat exchanger system, it is preferable to employ the cooling tower system of the dyno manufacturer. (A large electric fan can be placed in front of the radiator and ATAAC core to keep the engine from overheating.) This tower contains an inlet and outlet connection as well as deaeration lines from the engine to vent all air from the cooling system. In addition, the cooling tower can use city water, and a built-in temperature regulator can be adjusted to maintain the flow of water in and out of the cooling tower to ensure that a preset engine coolant temperature is maintained. If a pressurized cooling system is preferred, two cooling tower options are available that allow the use of glycol for cooling the engine in a closed-loop system. Another option is a separate engine tubular-type oil cooler for use in high-horsepower engines or when performing

FIGURE 24–1 Portable engine dynamometer bolted to the engine flywheel. (Courtesy of Superflow Corporation.)

lengthy dyno or engine endurance testing. The oil cooler is cooled by city water plumbed through it.

The rate of water circulation through the engine should be sufficient to maintain the engine within the maximum recommended operating temperature under all loads and conditions during the test. Normally, the water outlet temperature from the thermostat housing should be maintained at no more than a 10°F (5.6°C) difference between the water inlet temperature back into the engine water pump. On some engines that are used in equipment with automatic (powershift type) transmissions, where the transmission oil cooler dissipates its heat to the engine jacket water, a 15°F (9.4°C) coolant temperature difference is allowable.

Dynamometer loads on modern engines are usually electronically monitored with a panel that indicates digitally the engine rpm, horsepower, and torque. More expensive models can be programmed to perform a detailed engine dyno run-in procedure on its own from a PC controlled by a technician in a separate soundproof room. The test cell is equipped with a safety glass window through which the technician can visibly monitor the engine during the test routine. All diesel engines are dyno tested at the factory and cycled through a series of speed and load profiles to check them for performance. In addition, exhaust emissions are checked to ensure that the engine complies with the U.S. EPA heavy-duty transient cycle. Figure 24–2 is a graph showing an automatic dyno test sequence that an engine manufacturer might program into its test routine. This test will start the engine, warm it up, loop through a sequence of stages two times, cool the engine down, and shut it off. Throughout the test procedure, the technician can specify emergency actions such as aborting the test or shutting off power, or a warning

can be flashed to the technician's screen. In addition, limits can be evaluated as a group and action taken only when certain combinations of limits are exceeded. During the test, engine sensor outputs are compared with programmed limits. These are checked and data are gathered and stored on a PC high-capacity fixed disk, diskettes, or CD-ROM R/W disks. The test information can be extracted to a printer or remote computer screens for the engine manufacturer's internal records and to satisfy government emissions agencies. Figure 24–3 lists the typical U.S. Federal Register specifications for a routine engine test sequence.

The power absorbed by the dyno is generally measured as a torque value (twisting and turning force). A calibrated scale then converts this value along with the known engine speed to an equivalent horsepower (kilowatt) readout. This is accomplished by the following formula:

$$bhp = \frac{T \times RPM}{5250}$$

where bhp = brake horsepower
          T = torque in lb-ft (N · m)
      rpm = engine speed
      5250 = constant number to determine power

This formula is generally not required on current dynamometers since they are calibrated to read both torque and horsepower at the push of a selector button. The formula does apply if an older-model dyno is being used that requires the technician to add weights to the end of a brake arm. If the technician wants to check that the instrumentation on a newer dyno is calibrated correctly, he or she can insert the engine rpm into the formula along with the torque gauge readout value and determine what the horsepower should be. The torque meter can also be checked by using this formula:

$$torque = \frac{5252 \times bhp}{rpm}$$

Some dynamometers operate on water pressure and others use electricity (eddy currents) to provide the rotating resistance to the engine flywheel. The water-type dyno can be connected to a city water supply, or it may have its own water reservoir and pump system. Both water inlet and outlet control valves are connected to the dyno control panel. Within the load cell of the dyno is a vaned impeller, which is similar to that found on a water pump and not unlike the impeller found in the Allison and Voith transmission hydraulic retarders or the Caterpillar 3406 engine Brakesaver.

If the water outlet valve is closed and the inlet valve is opened, the dyno load cell is filled with water

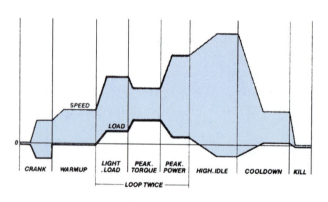

Speed, Load Profile of "TURBO.DIESEL.TEST."

FIGURE 24–2 *Sample automatic dyno test sequence showing the speed and load profile for a turbocharged diesel engine. (Courtesy of Superflow Corporation.)*

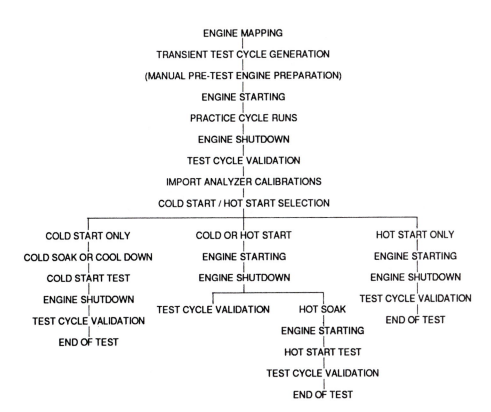

ENGINE MAPPING

TRANSIENT TEST CYCLE GENERATION

(MANUAL PRE-TEST ENGINE PREPARATION)

ENGINE STARTING

PRACTICE CYCLE RUNS

ENGINE SHUTDOWN

TEST CYCLE VALIDATION

IMPORT ANALYZER CALIBRATIONS

COLD START / HOT START SELECTION

COLD START ONLY	COLD OR HOT START	HOT START ONLY
COLD SOAK OR COOL DOWN	ENGINE STARTING	ENGINE STARTING
COLD START TEST	ENGINE SHUTDOWN	ENGINE SHUTDOWN
ENGINE SHUTDOWN		TEST CYCLE VALIDATION
TEST CYCLE VALIDATION	TEST CYCLE VALIDATION HOT SOAK	END OF TEST
END OF TEST	ENGINE STARTING	
	HOT START TEST	
	TEST CYCLE VALIDATION	
	END OF TEST	

FEDERAL REGISTER SPECIFICATIONS FOR TEST SEQUENCE

Note: This overview illustrates the typical sequence of steps followed by the dynamometer controller. The dynamometer controller enters and exits the major functions independently of the others. It is possible to map the engine only, generate test cycles only, do practice cycles only, do Cold Starts only, do Hot Starts only, perform cycle validation only, or any combination.

FIGURE 24–3 *Overview of typical U.S. Federal Register specifications for a heavy-duty diesel engine dyno test. (Courtesy of Superflow Corporation.)*

under pressure. By manipulation of the inlet and outlet valves, the technician can determine how much trapped water is allowed to remain in the dyno load cell. This controls the resistance to engine flywheel rotation as the dyno impeller is driven against the water within its housing. A hydraulic dyno uses fluid instead of water to apply the load. On electric dynamometers, a resistance control knob allows the technician to vary the current supplied to a series of electromagnets surrounding the dyno driveshaft. The stronger the magnetic force developed, the greater is the load applied to the engine flywheel.

Pre-Run-In Checks

Before you conduct a run-in, follow these preparatory steps:

1. Open the dyno coolant supply to fill and deaerate the system. If no deaeration lines are routed from the engine thermostat housings to the cooling tower, open up the petcock on the taps at the housings to completely vent the system of all entrapped air. Failure to properly deaerate the cooling system can lead to an air lock, and serious overheating may result.

2. Ensure that a fully charged battery (or batteries) is used. This is very important when testing elec-

tronically controlled diesel engines to be sure that the ECM will function properly.

3. Prelube the engine as described in Chapter 11 (see Figure 11–17).

4. Install all gauges required to monitor the following systems and conditions: lube oil pressure, lube oil temperature, coolant temperature, crankcase pressure (water manometer), turbocharger boost pressure (mercury manometer or pressure gauge), fuel temperature, fuel pressure, exhaust temperature (pyrometer), air inlet restriction (water manometer or vacuum gauge), air inlet temperature, exhaust back pressure, and fuel consumption check.

5. Install a fuel cooler if the fuel supply to the engine is from a fuel tank that allows the fuel temperature to exceed recommended maximums. Ideally, the fuel temperature should be maintained between 90° and 95°F (32° to 35°C) since a horsepower loss of approximately 1% will occur on non-turbo engines and of 1.5% on turbo engines for every 10°F (5.6°C) rise beyond this range. This occurs due to the expansion of the fuel—meaning that a less dense fuel charge is metered and injected. The maximum fuel temperature should never be allowed to exceed 150°F (66°C). Note also that on electronically controlled engines, fuel temperatures in

excess of 140°F (60°C) can damage the electronics within the ECM.

6. Ensure that a regular supply of cool air is available to the engine intake system. Usually this means that the air inlet ducting must be pulled from outside the building. Warm air also causes a reduction in engine horsepower, and on heavy-duty truck electronic engines that are designed for use with AAACs (air-to-air aftercoolers), some means must be provided to ensure that the air inlet temperature is cool enough. Most AAACs are designed to reduce the pressurized air temperature from the turbocharger from 300°F (149°C) to between 100° and 110°F (38° to 43°C). Engine operating temperature and piston and valve cooling can be adversely affected by hot air entering the engine.

7. Plumb the exhaust system to the outside to minimize heat radiation within the dyno room. Some systems use water-cooled exhaust manifolds. Another possibility is to heat wrap (insulate) the exhaust piping within the dyno room.

8. Make sure all engine adjustments such as valve and injector timing and initial governor controls (mechanical engines only) have been performed. Check that the *buffer screw* on DDC mechanical engine models has been backed out; otherwise, engine overspeed can occur.

DYNO RUN-IN PROCEDURES

Prior to actually starting the engine, obtain the recommended specs and operating conditions from the manufacturer. The recommended minimum idle speed, maximum no-load (high idle) and full-load (rated) speeds, as well as the engine horsepower, can be found on the engine decals attached to the rocker cover or engine block. The maximum peak torque value and engine speed are normally not listed on the engine decal, so obtain a sales brochure for your engine to review all of the specs.

Perform the following steps of the run-in procedure:

1. As soon as the engine is started at idle, check the oil pressure gauge. Continue to run the engine at an idle speed for at least 1 minute on all turbocharged engines to ensure that there is oil pressure to the turbo oil supply line.

2. With the engine running at 800 to 1000 rpm, inspect all systems for signs of leaks. Fix if necessary. If there are no leaks, allow the engine to run for a maximum of 5 to 8 minutes while you listen for any unusual rubbing noises, tapping or clacking (valves), hum,

deep base noises, knocking, scraping, and so forth. Make sure there is no significant oil pressure drop on the gauge.

3. Slowly increase the engine rpm to WOT and using an accurate tachometer, note and record the speed. On mechanical engines, adjust the governor assembly to obtain the recommended maximum no-load (high idle) rpm. This can be found on either the engine decal or in the engine service manual or sales literature spec sheet. Note and record the engine oil pressure.

4. Allow the engine to return to its low idle speed and check that this rpm is correct. On mechanical engines, adjust the idle speed to specs. On some engines such as DDC two-stroke-cycle models, you may also have to adjust the governor buffer screw to prevent engine surge (hunt). Engines using multiple-plunger in-line pumps may also require adjustment to the low idle speed and the bumper spring to prevent engine roll.

5. With the engine and dyno both operating correctly, refer to the engine manufacturer's dyno run-in spec sheet. An example is given in Figure 24–4 for a Detroit Diesel series 60 and a Cummins Signature four-stroke-cycle heavy-duty electronically controlled engine.

6. Increase the engine rpm to half speed and apply the load shown in the spec sheet of Figure 24–4 (under warm-up) for 5 minutes or longer to allow the coolant temperature to stabilize at its normal operating level. During this time, repeat the same checks that you did in step 2. On this engine, normal coolant temperature is controlled by a 180°F (82°C) thermostat system. Under full-load conditions, coolant operating temperatures will be maintained within a range of 180° to 197°F (82° to 92°C). Under certain ambient temperatures, grades and loads, however, coolant temperatures may approach higher levels than this. Under no circumstances should the coolant temperature be allowed to exceed 210°F (99°C) because serious engine damage could result.

7. Refer to the run-in spec sheet and proceed through the individual steps while applying the recommended percentage of full load. Note that the run-in times are minimum values, so the engine can be run or loaded for longer periods of time if necessary. During all speeds and load levels, record all of the information relative to the systems shown and any others listed under the engine pre-run-in checks. In addition, closely monitor the engine for any speed changes, fluid or air leaks, and unusual noises.

8. Excessive blowby indicated by steady fumes emanating from the breather cap, or by the water manometer displacement, indicates possible valve stem, piston ring, liner, or turbocharger malfunction.

SERIES 60 ENGINE TEST REPORT

Date: _____   Unit Number: _____
Repair Order Number: _____   Model Number: _____
PROM I.D.: _____   Max. N/L RPM: _____
Rated F/L RPM: _____
Idle RPM: _____

A. PRESTART

1. PRIME LUBE OIL SYSTEM	2. PRIME FUEL OIL SYSTEM	3. FILL COOLING SYSTEM

B. START-UP AND IDLE FOR 30 SECONDS

START_____ STOP _____ OIL PRESSURE _____ WATER TEMPERATURE _____

C. WARM-UP — 5 MINUTES   START _____ STOP _____

RPM MAX. SPEED	LOAD 50%	OIL PRESSURE	WATER TEMPERATURE
1. LUBE OIL LEAKS	2. FUEL OIL LEAKS	3. COOLANT LEAKS	4. LOOSE BOLTS

D. RUN-IN — 5 MINUTES   START _____ STOP _____

RPM MAX. SPEED	LOAD 75%	OIL PRESSURE	WATER TEMPERATURE

E. FINAL RUN-IN — 20 MINUTES   START _____ STOP _____

RPM MAX. SPEED	LOAD 100%	CRANKCASE PRESSURE AT F/L	EXHAUST BACK PRESSURE AT F/L
LUBE OIL PRESS. AT F/L	LUBE OIL TEMP. AT F/L	FUEL OIL TEMP. AT F/L	FUEL OIL PRESSURE AT F/L
WATER TEMP. AT F/L	TURBO BOOST PRESS. AT F/L	LUBE OIL PRESSURE AT IDLE	IDLE RPM

REMARKS: _____

OK _____ Reject _____ Dynamometer Operator _____ Date _____

20867

(a)

FIGURE 24–4 (a) Sample blank sheet which can be used during a heavy-duty diesel engine dyno test. (Courtesy of Detroit Diesel Corporation.)

Dynamometer Worksheet

Date:		Repair Order No.:		Operator:	
ESN:		CPL:		Fuel Pump Code:	
Complaint:				SC Code:	

PARAMETER	CODE SPECIFICATIONS	ACTUAL READING
Fuel Pressure (psi @ rpm)	Refer to Specifications - Engine Testing	
Fuel Rate (lb/hr)		
Intake Mfd. Pressure (in Hg)	See Fuel Pump Code	
Intake Mfd. Temperature		
*Intake Air Restriction	25 in H_2O, Maximum	
*Exhaust Air Restriction	3 in Hg, Maximum	
*Fuel Inlet Restriction	Refer to Specifications - Engine Testing	
*Fuel Drain Line Restriction	3.5 in Hg	
Engine Blowby	12 in H_2O New Engines, Max. 18 in H^2O Used Engines, Max.	
*Recorded at maximum horsepower speed and full load		

Road Speed Limit				Engine High Speed Limit		
Check Oil Level	Low	High	OK	Fuel Quality	OK	**Not** OK

Engine Speed	Fuel *Rate/ Press		Fuel Temp.	Turbo Inlet Air Temp.	Intake Manifold Temp./Press		Coolant Temp./ Press		Engine Blowby	Lube Oil Press	HP or Torque

*Be sure that the fuel rate is corrected for temperature.

Fuel Temperature	Correction for Flow Rate
Less than 7°C [45°F]	Flow meter **not** accurate
7 to 13°C [45 to 55°F]	Subtract 2% from flow rate reading
13 to 2°C [55 to 68°F]	Subtract 1% from flow rate reading
20 to 29°C [68 to 85°F]	No Correction
29 to 42°C [85 to 108°F]	Add 1% to flow rate reading
42 to 56°C [108 to 132°F]	Add 2% to flow rate reading
56°C above [132°F]	Flowmeter **not** accurate

Pressure Conversions

1 in H_2O = 0.074 in Hg = 0.036 psi

1 in Hg = 13.514 in H_2O = 0.491 psi

1 psi = 2.036 in Hg = 27.7 in H_2O

This Page Can Be Copied for Your Convenience.

(b)

FIGURE 24–4 (continued). (b) Sample dynamometer worksheet for a Cummins Signature series engine. (Courtesy of Cummins Engine Company, Inc.)

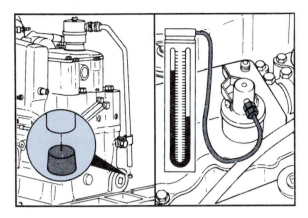

FIGURE 24–5 H₂O (water) manometer connections to monitor engine crankcase pressure during an engine dyno test. (Courtesy of Cummins Engine Company, Inc.)

Crankcase pressure can be checked as shown in Figure 24–5. A connection is made to the engine rocker cover breather, or a bottle-stopper type of plug can be inserted in place of the breather. A handle or knob can be tightened on the rubber stopper to expand it tightly. It also has a tap point for a rubber hose to connect to a water manometer. On some engines, crankcase pressure can be monitored through the dipstick tube or by removing an inspection plug alongside the engine block which sits above the oil pan rail. Check the service specs to determine the maximum allowable crankcase pressure. The engine may require slightly longer time under load to allow the piston rings to seat; however, failure of the blowby condition or engine crankcase pressure to stabilize might require engine component disassembly to correct the cause.

9.   When the engine has been cycled through the run-in procedure, gradually reduce the load from the dyno and allow it to remain at these reduced load (speed) levels for several minutes each. This allows the various components such as the cylinder head, valves, pistons, and turbocharger to dissipate their heat gradually.

10.   Once the engine has been reduced to an idle speed, let it run for at least 3 minutes to allow the turbocharger to cool off.

11.   Shut the engine off!

NOTE   Some engine manufacturers recommend that the cylinder head bolts be retorqued after a dyno run-in. Be sure to check the service manual for your specific engine to determine if this is necessary.

12.   Once the engine has cooled, if it is to be stored for any length of time, the fuel system should be rust-proofed, the cooling system filled with a rust inhibitor, and the crankcase filled with a lube oil preservative. All intake and exhaust openings should be plugged with plastic shipping caps and/or masked closed. The same procedure should be done for the coolant, fuel, and lube systems.

CHASSIS DYNO RUN-IN PROCEDURES

Although chassis dynamometers can be used to run in an engine after a major overhaul, most truck service dealers employ this type of load device to troubleshoot complaints of low engine power and/or possible driveline problems and horsepower losses. The OEM or truck manufacturer may use a chassis dyno to monitor and test new truck designs. Current microprocessor-controlled chassis dynamometers typically measure and calculate the items listed in Figure 24–6.

Vehicle wheel horsepower (kW) output on a chassis dyno will always be lower than that specified for the engine itself due to driveline efficiency and engine-driven accessories. The wheel horsepower will usually be reduced by approximately 20% for a single-axle vehicle and 25% for tandem-axle vehicles. These percentages are used in relation to engine run-in only and are not to be considered absolute figures. *Always* refer to

---

MEASURES AND CALCULATES:

1. Engine speed	26. Corrected BSFC
2. Vehicle power	27. Aftercooler temperature
3. Roll 1 speed	28. Air temperature
4. Roll 2 speed	29. Fuel temperature
5. Roll % difference	30. Exhaust temperature
6. Roll 1 power	31. Coolant out temperature
7. Roll 2 power	32. Coolant in temperature
8. Corrected Vehicle Speed	33. Oil out temperature
9. Corrected Vehicle Power	34. Oil in temperature
10. Caterpillar Balance Point	35. Extra temperature
11. Manifold pressure	36. Caterpillar rack switch %
12. Air inlet pressure	37. Current date and time
13. Fuel pressure	38. Test time
14. Exhaust back pressure	39. Voltage D.C.
15. Rail pressure	40. Engine blow-by*
16. Coolant pressure	41. Exhaust opacity*
17. Oil pressure	42. Engine dyno power*
18. Barometric pressure	43. Engine corrected power*
19. Extra pressure	44. Engine torque*
20. Fuel API	45. Current to 1000 amps*
21. Fuel mass flow	46. Airflow 1*
22. Fuel volume flow	47. Airflow 2*
23. Fuel economy	48. Air-fuel ratio*
24. Vehicle BSFC	49. Engine volumetric efficiency*
25. Engine BSFC	50. Coolant flow*

*Items 40-50 are extra cost options.
All items may be displayed and stored in English or Metric units.

FIGURE 24–6   Example of items that can be measured and calculated on a typical microprocessor controlled heavy-duty truck chassis dynamometer. (Courtesy of Super-flow Corporation.)

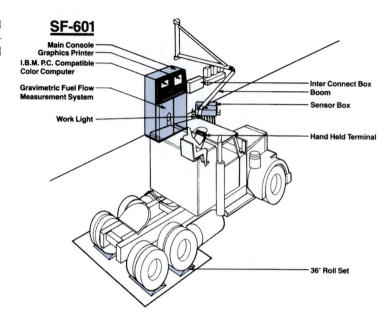

FIGURE 24–7 *Example of a heavy-duty Class 8 highway tractor mounted on a dual-roller chassis dynamometer. Also shown are the dyno and handheld terminal controls. (Courtesy of Superflow Corporation.)*

the vehicle service literature of the OEM to establish what these wheel horsepower (kW) figures should be for a given model of truck. Figure 24–7 illustrates a Class 8 heavy-duty tandem-axle truck sitting on a dual-roller system. The technician can sit in the vehicle cab during the dyno test to control the transmission gear selection. By using a handheld terminal, the technician can control the operation and load characteristics of the dyno assembly. A computer mounted inside or outside of the dyno test cell records all of the accumulated test data. Most computerized chassis and engine dynamometers today can maintain a selected roll speed to within ± 0.8 km/h (0.5 mph), engine speed to ± 5 rpm, and power to ± 1 hp (0.75 kW). At the end of the test period, printed copies can be extracted for the technician to study and for the customer to consult. In addition, the test data can be analyzed using a graphic plotting system to compare the test results with the engine or truck manufacturer's standards.

If the chassis dyno is being used to run in an overhauled engine, chassis dyno manufacturers caution against employing recapped or snow-tread tires mounted on the vehicle. They also issue some cautions against using radial-ply tires. Low-profile radial tires are more sensitive to heat than bias-ply tires. Excessive operating time at full load can damage tires as a result of overheating. Tire manufacturers can advise on the maximum allowable chassis dyno operating time. Recap tires can experience tread separation, while snow tires may upset and reduce dyno readings due to their different grip characteristics on the dyno rollers. Never operate with tires that have been used less than 100 miles (160 km). Some dyno manufacturers suggest that

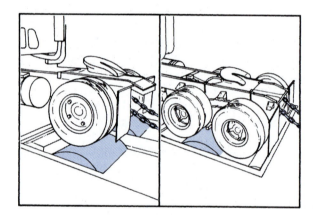

FIGURE 24–8 *Example of a heavy-duty tractor mounted on a large single-roll chassis dynamometer. Take careful note of the safety hold-down chains connected between the truck frame and the shop floor tie-downs. (Courtesy of Cummins Engine Company, Inc.)*

a set of *slave tires* with a cross-ply tread design of minimum depth be used during the chassis dyno test. Check the information for the specific dyno that you are using. Also be aware that the vehicle chassis power reading can be affected by heavy truck bodies and tanks and excessively loaded vehicles.

Figure 24–8 illustrates a heavy-duty truck sitting on a chassis dyno with a single set of rollers. Either a large single-roller or double-roller type can be used. During testing, the vehicle transmission is shifted into gear to allow the rear axle(s) tires to drive the dyno rollers. The load applied to the rollers is similar to that described for an engine dynamometer. When using the chassis the vehicle frame *must* be securely tied down.

FIGURE 24–9   Safety chain tie-downs and front wheel chocks to prevent vehicle movement during a chassis dyno test. Notice the overhead exhaust pipe connection. (Courtesy of Cummins Engine Company, Inc.)

This is usually done with safety chains connected to the rear of the vehicle, as shown in Figure 24–9, and anchored through shackles to hold-down eyes in the cement floor to prevent any possible truck breakaway under load testing. In addition, refer to Figure 24–9 and chock the front wheels; or, as shown in Figure 24–10, use chains to securely hold each front wheel to rails embedded in the concrete floor. Also connect the overhead exhaust stack(s) to the dyno ducting as indicated in Figure 24–9.

Most turbocharged trucks today employ AAACs mounted in front of the radiator core. The AAAC depends on forced air driven through its core when the vehicle is moving along the highway. Therefore, it is necessary to install a suitable electric-driven blower fan in front of the truck radiator to ensure adequate air-

flow through the AAAC as well as the radiator cores during chassis dyno testing.

All of the necessary engine checks and instrumentation discussed under the previous section on dyno run-in procedures can be applied to a chassis dyno test. In addition, the instrumentation and gauges on the truck can be used to monitor various systems. Prior to testing, all tires should be checked for equal pressures and for matched size. Use a matching stick, square, or string wound around the circumference of each tire. Mismatched tires can cause interaxle fight and one side of an axle to rotate through more revolutions per mile (km) than the other. Tire size differences vary by tire manufacturer; however the widely used standard is that dual tires should not differ more than 0.25 in. (6.35 mm) in diameter or more than 0.75 in. (19 mm) in circumference when mounted on the same dual wheel. If differences are unavoidable, place the larger or less worn tire on the outside. If the tires mounted on the forward-rear axle are larger than those on the rear-rear axle, a difference in speed between the two axles results. With the forward- and rear-rear axles connected, the rear-rear axle attempts to overrun the slower turning forward axle, and the forward axle attempts to slow down the rear axle; the result is wheel fight between the two axles. The propeller shaft tries to wind up, and the axle shafts try to do the same. The axle gear teeth are loaded to very high pressures, which causes overloading of the bearings and eventual failure of the bearings and possibly the axle gear teeth.

During testing, axle speed difference must not exceed 5 mph (8 km/h). With the engine at the speed to be tested and the dyno unloaded, the two load buttons for the dyno (*load* and *unload*) must be applied slowly

FIGURE 24–10   Closeup view of how to chain down the front wheels to securely anchor the vehicle to the rails embedded into the concrete floor. (Courtesy of Superflow Corporation.)

and evenly while observing the road speed meters to be sure that the allowable axle speed difference is not exceeded. On vehicles equipped with an interaxle *power divider* lockout control, the lockout should be engaged during testing. All-wheel drive vehicles should have the front propellor shaft disconnected, and the transfer case lockup clutch should be engaged.

SAFETY TIP Check that all safety chains are secured to both the truck frame and floor hooks. The tie-down chains *must* have some slack in them to avoid damage to the chassis dyno rollers. Check that all stones have been removed from the tire treads because they can fly out with destructive force.

Although the vehicle is securely chained down, never stand in front or behind a truck or bus during a chassis dyno test run! Make sure that there are no other vehicles or shop components parked in front of the test truck.

Perform the following steps in the chassis dyno run-in:

1. With all checks and conditions performed as just described, start the engine with the transmission in neutral and allow the engine to warm up until the air compressor has cut out at its maximum value. You can warm up the engine by operating the truck on the dyno in a gear range with about 25% of rated engine load between 1200 and 1500 rpm for about 15 minutes or until the coolant gauge indicates that normal operating temperature has been reached (at least 160°F, 71°C).
2. Release the spring parking brakes.
3. Place the transmission in *direct gear,* not overdrive to produce a road speed of 55 to 60 mph (90 to 95 km/h).

NOTE Depending on the engine model used, the actual time and loads applied to the vehicle will vary. The following steps refer to one example. The truck manufacturer's service manual and/or engine service manual will provide you with specific run-in details.

---

4. Select an engine speed and gear range that permits the engine to operate at or near the full-load governed speed for 15 to 30 minutes for run-in. Note and record all operating data

in a manner similar to that for an engine dyno test described earlier.

5. Starting at a high engine rpm, conduct a power test at each decreasing 200 rpm. One test should be made 100 rpm below engine-governed speed and continued down to the engine peak torque rpm. Hold full load for approximately 3 minutes with the transmission in direct drive in each speed range. Take careful note of all power levels and engine/vehicle operating conditions, particularly the axle oil temperatures.

ON-HIGHWAY ENGINE RUN-IN PROCEDURES

In an on-highway truck application in which either a new or rebuilt engine has been installed or an in-frame overhaul has been performed, the engine can be *on-road* dyno tested, in the absence of an engine or chassis dynamometer, to check for possible problem areas. Note that on electronically equipped diesel engines, a hand-held diagnostic data reader (see Figures 21–31, 21–32, 21–33, 22–49, and 23–23) or a portable PC can be connected to the on-board computer (ECM) of the vehicle, and a snapshot of the accumulated data can be stored for retrieval after the road test. A review of the stored data, operating parameters, and sensor performance can indicate the condition of the engine. Follow this procedure:

1. Check that all engine fluid levels are correct and that the maximum no-load and idle speeds have been adjusted properly.
2. Perform a vehicle *pre-trip* inspection to ensure that all components are operating correctly.
3. Load the vehicle to its usual maximum GVW (gross vehicle weight—straight truck body) or GCVW (gross combination vehicle weight—semitrailer).
4. Use a progressive shift technique and operate the vehicle through all gear ranges for at least 30 minutes. Take care that the engine speed does not exceed approximately 1800 rpm. Regularly check all of the gauges on the instrument panel.
5. With the vehicle on a suitable road surface, continue to operate it at or near its maximum governed speed for between 30 and 60 minutes. Regularly check all the gauges on the instrument panel.

6. When back at home base, recheck the engine maximum no-load (high-idle) speed as well as the idle rpm and reset if necessary.

7. Allow the engine to idle for 3 to 5 minutes after the run-in so the turbocharger can cool down.

8. Check all fluids and inspect the engine closely for any signs of leaks or unusual noises.

NOTE If the engine manufacturer specifies a cylinder head bolt retorque, perform it now.

OFF-HIGHWAY EQUIPMENT RUN-IN PROCEDURES

Off-highway engines can be operated in the equipment for at least 3 hours after overhaul, but avoid running the engine higher than 75% of throttle while loaded. Do not operate the engine at rated speed and full load for more than 5 minutes at any one time. Do not idle the engine for more than 5 minutes at any one time either. Take careful note of crankcase blowby or fumes, leaks, and any unusual noises during the run-in time.

MARINE ENGINE RUN-IN PROCEDURES

On many marine applications, overhaul of the engine must be performed inside the engine room, unless accessible deck plates can be removed to allow engine removal. In some situations (steel workboats and so on), the deck plates have to be cut out and rewelded into place after completion of the repairs.

After prelubrication of the engine as described and illustrated in Figure 11–17, start the engine(s). The governed speed of the engine will, of course, determine the specific test speeds to follow. Assume that we are preparing to run in a high-speed high-output engine(s) and follow this typical procedure:

1. Allow the engine(s) to idle with the marine gear in *neutral* for approximately 10 minutes. Carefully check all fluid levels; look for signs of fluid leakage at the engine and marine gear, exhaust system, air intake ducting, and so forth.

2. With the marine gear still in neutral, increase the engine(s) speed to 1200 rpm and operate here for 20 minutes. Monitor and record all pressure and temperature gauges for both the engine and marine gear.

3. Engage the marine gear in *forward*, and with the vessel underway, run the engine(s) at the following time intervals: 800 rpm for 20 minutes, 1000 rpm for 20 minutes, 1600 rpm for 20 minutes, 1800 rpm for 30 minutes, 2000 rpm for 30 minutes, 2100 rpm for 30 minutes, and maximum full-load speed for 30 minutes.

SUMMARY

We have described and recommended the correct procedures to use when preparing to run-in a rebuilt engine on either an engine dynamometer or a truck chassis dyno. It is critical that you pay careful attention to details during this phase of the engine run-in or testing procedure to ensure that your own and the safety of others is not put in jeopardy. Additionally, improper dyno-testing can result in damage to a rebuilt engine, or to other components on a truck by failure to follow correct speed and load recommended time periods. Follow carefully the dyno run-in example test sheets shown in Figure 24–4. During these tests take and record carefully all of the major items listed which will indicate quickly if problems are developing with the engine or truck. With machinery such as large off-highway equipment, or marine vessels, read and follow the recommendations described in this chapter. Diligence when testing expensive engines and equipment will be rewarded by an engine that will last for many hours or miles.

SELF-TEST QUESTIONS

1. How does the water dynamometer effectively load or unload an engine?

2. Technician A says that the power absorbed by a dyno is a direct horsepower (kW) value. Technician B says that it is a torque value that is then calibrated to an hp reading. Which technician knows dyno theory best?

3. Describe how you would prelubricate an engine after overhaul and prior to dyno testing.

4. Ideally, during dyno testing the diesel fuel temperature should be maintained between
   a. 65° and 70°F (18° to 21°C)
   b. 75° and 80°F (24° to 27°C)
   c. 85° and 90°F (29° to 32°C)
   d. 90° and 95°F (32° to 35°C)

5. True or False: On initial engine startup, run the engine at approximately 1500 rpm to quickly allow oil to circulate.

6. What check should be done on the turbocharger as soon as the engine starts?

7. What other checks should be performed as soon as the engine starts?

8. True or False: Oil pressures less than 30 psi at idle speed indicate a serious oil pressure condition.

9. Typical oil pressures on high-speed heavy-duty diesel engines at close to regulated speed usually range between
   a. 30 and 40 psi (207 to 276 kPa)
   b. 40 and 50 psi (276 to 345 kPa)
   c. 50 and 60 psi (345 to 414 kPa)
   d. 60 and 80 psi (414 to 552 kPa)

10. Under full-load engine operating conditions, what is a normal engine coolant temperature range?

11. What is the maximum allowable coolant temperature range for a typical high-speed heavy-duty engine under full load in a dyno test?

12. Describe the normal variation in engine oil temperature and engine coolant temperature for a high-speed heavy-duty diesel engine under load in a dyno test run.

13. Failure of an engine to show a reduction in crankcase pressure after several hours on a dyno would usually be indicative of
   a. failure of the piston rings to seat properly
   b. cracked piston
   c. cracked liner
   d. cracked cylinder head

14. The shortest run-in time on a dyno test should not be less than
   a. 15 minutes
   b. 30 minutes
   c. 60 minutes
   d. 2 hours

15. An engine in a dyno test should be capable of producing its rated power output within
   a. ± 5%
   b. ± 8%
   c. ± 10%
   d. ± 12%

16. Once an engine has been warmed up on a dyno, it should be loaded down to no more than what percentage of its rated output?
   a. 25%
   b. 35%
   c. 50%
   d. 60%

17. What systems and gauge readings should you monitor and record during an engine/vehicle dyno test? Make a list.

18. Technician A says that when running a truck or tractor on a chassis dyno, you should never use recap or snow-tread tires. Describe the reasoning behind this precaution.

19. What other checks must be done on truck or tractor tires prior to a chassis dyno test of the vehicle?

20. If testing a heavy-duty high-speed truck or tractor on a chassis dyno, or an engine on a dyno that is equipped with an ATAAC, what step must be employed to prevent damage to the engine valves, pistons, and cylinder head(s)?

21. To prevent a truck or tractor from moving on a chassis dyno test, what safety precautions should be employed?

22. List the engine speeds and times that you would employ to run in a rebuilt engine on a marine application.

Engine Troubleshooting

Overview

In this chapter we describe and provide a simplified analytical approach to engine troubleshooting. The nature of the diesel service/repair industry is similar to that found in automotive, in that technology has become so advanced that many certified technicians simply choose to qualify in a highly specific area. This can often create highly valuable personnel, but with a narrow focus. Consequently in many shops, sometimes there is only one or several out of a large dedicated group of service techs with such a focus. So when an apprentice or service tech is thrust into an engine performance complaint job, their background knowledge and experience makes it tough for them to effectively and efficiently diagnose where the problem is located, or it takes them substantially longer than the specialist to perform the job.

Today with the advancements in electronic engines and the availability of the diverse diagnostic test equipment, it has become much easier and simplified for a technician to quickly and accurately pinpoint an engine performance problem and cause(s). By using a scan tool, laptop, or specific OEM's special diagnostic equipment, running engine **snapshot data** and **fault/trouble code information** can lead you to a system or subsystem, and can often identify the SAE **failure mode indicator (FMI)**.

Even with this special diagnostic equipment, problems can often be traced to a simple mechanical problem, or to a basic system fault. This is where your thorough understanding of how and what makes a system function and operate will serve you well. If you do not have the knowledge, dedication, and commitment to fully grasp the hows and whys of the operation of each and every system and component, you will invariably find that basic problems can create lengthy troubleshooting and diagnostic times.

When you have completed reading this chapter, accompanied by exposure to and accumulated hands-on shop/field time troubleshooting and diagnosing diesel engines, you will develop and prepare a systematic approach as to how to quickly and effectively pinpoint the cause(s) of efficient problem solving. This bank of data and information will prepare you well to tackle and challenge either the ASE or TQ tests that will qualify you as a service tech with the highest standards of excellence.

ASE CERTIFICATION

Within the ASE medium/heavy truck tests preparation guide dealing with diesel engines (test T2), much of the content area skills tasks listed in subsections A through H deal with effective knowledge and hands-on data and information that aspiring service technicians must develop if they are to successfully challenge one or more ASE certification tests. Many of these skills tasks deal with troubleshooting and diagnosis. In addition, the ASE electronic diesel engine diagnosis specialist test L2 is heavily weighted toward troubleshooting and diagnosis concerns. An overview of the tasks lists for this area can be found in Chapter 18. Also access the ASE guides through its website (www.asecert.org).

GETTING STARTED

The introduction of electronically controlled diesel fuel injection systems has made pinpointing a problem area in the fuel control and engine systems easier for the technician. Plug-in diagnostic equipment is now readily available and recommended by the engine manufacturer (See Chapters 18, 21, 22, and 23 for details).

With this diagnostic equipment hooked into the microprocessor, the system performs a self-diagnostic run through and issues trouble codes from those stored in computer memory. The technician can then zero in on a specific area, conduct a series of tests, and pinpoint the exact problem fairly easily. In some cases, a particularly tough problem may require the technician to follow closely a step-by-step service manual procedure to pinpoint one or more problems in the system. The use of electronic diagnostic tools does not mean that the technician can simply plug in the unit and sit back. On the contrary, often the electronic components are blamed for a particular problem. Fully 50% of supposedly faulty computers are found by the manufacturers to be completely operational when they are returned under warranty. The technician did not check closely enough to determine if the problem could have been a simple mechanical one. So do not condemn the on-board computer system before making a number of basic system checks, examples of which are given in this chapter.

Effective troubleshooting is an art that can only be developed over a period of time. How quickly you become proficient at it depends on a number of factors, one of which is how often you have the opportunity to pursue this process which requires an active and quick mind. The ability to be able to diagnose an engine problem quickly and effectively is related to the following basic conditions:

- A thorough understanding of the fundamentals of what actually goes on within an internal combustion engine
- The amount of experience of the technician involved
- How familiar the technician is with a particular make of engine; also, how up to date he or she is
- The ability to be analytical
- The ability to control one's temper when an irate customer or operator is pushing for an answer
- The ability of the technician not to second-guess himself or herself (if in doubt, check it out)
- A willingness, if necessary, to refer to the manufacturer's specifications or troubleshooting charts in the appropriate engine service manual.

People often refer to someone as being a really good mechanic. How do you think that person achieved such respect? In many instances experience is gained through a series of mistakes in the apprenticeship stage. Nevertheless, one must have a genuine desire to succeed—to be the best in the field of diesel technology. Certainly, in this ever-changing technological era, especially with high labor costs and overhead, it is easy to become simply the "parts replacer" instead of a highly skilled and dedicated technician. In many instances, of course, a new part may be required. There are many, many instances, however, when a new component part is installed and within a short time, the same problem exists, leading you to scratch your head and ask why.

Unless a part shows particular excessive wear or damage, do not accept at face value that it is nonserviceable. Learn to accept, where possible, nothing less than the best; in every job think of the engine or equipment as your own. People will remember your abilities as a first-class technician only as long as you produce first-class work. Foul up once, and that is the job that stays in their minds, regardless of how many jobs you completed successfully for them at other times.

It is hard work to stay abreast of the many changes that occur constantly in the field of modern diesel technology. Accept the challenge as a person and as a skilled technician. Tackle a troubleshooting problem with an open and keen mind. Do not panic, take it easy, and eventually you will find that most problems are of a minor nature.

The problems that can relate to the fuel system of an engine are diversified in nature. The method chosen to pinpoint a particular problem will depend on how familiar you are with the make of engine. However, if you systematically collect all the information available regarding what led up to the problem, you should be able to analyze on a step-by-step basis the reason for the problem. Remember, satisfactory operation of the engine depends primarily on the following nine items:

1. Adequate supply of clean, relatively cool air, which once in the cylinder can be compressed to a high enough pressure to effect proper combustion.
2. Injection of the correct amount of fuel at the proper time during the compression stroke.
3. Use of the proper grade of fuel for the environment in which the engine operates.
4. Ability to maintain the fuel oil, if possible, at an optimum temperature range of 90° to 95°F (32° to 36°C) for high-speed diesel operation (maximum allowable of 150°F, 65°C).
5. Clean, sediment- and water-free filtered fuel.
6. Maintenance of the proper engine water temperature. Most high-speed diesel engines operate between 180° and 200°F (82° to 83°C). Satisfactory water treatment.
7. Maintenance of exhaust back pressure within specifications.

8. Use of the proper grade of oil with proper service intervals.

9. Proper selection and application of the engine for what it was intended.

When collecting information before analyzing a problem, keep an open mind. There will always be those who are ready to tell you what the problem is. Listen to their suggestions, but remember *you* are the trained and skilled technician. It is easy to become sidetracked into believing that what an operator says is in fact the cure for the problem. Maybe it is, but think before jumping to conclusions.

Suppose you find yourself in this situation: You are called to repair a heavy-duty truck. As you step out of the truck you see the contractor, loader operator, and a couple of truck drivers. The contractor has been "chewing out" the operator; the scene is tense. When you enter the area, the contractor starts in on you, much to the relief of the operator and the amusement of the truck drivers. You are drawn into the tension whether you like it or not. As the contractor vents frustration and anger, nothing constructive is learned. The regular toolbox is not much use at this point, but the two tools of self-control and reason are!

What should you do with the customer's opinions? Use your reasoning ability. Sift the answers to questions as they come. Some will be factual and pertinent to the problem. Others will be incidental or entirely unrelated. Sort out the facts and list them. Do not discard any related facts, even though they may seem unimportant. When everything is examined together, one seemingly unimportant fact may be the key to the problem.

Through questioning and testing, you gather all the facts. You can now make some decision concerning the cause of the problem and the procedure to use in correcting it. In examining the facts, look beyond the individual parts. Visualize the whole system and how it functions. (Like a jigsaw puzzle, you cannot get the picture from the individual parts.) Relate the facts to the whole system and the possible causes for the failure will be more evident.

Through testing, questioning, and analyzing answers, the technician lays the groundwork for the repairwork that follows. All this scrutiny and study often takes place in an atmosphere of tension and pressure. Each job experience will be different, but this only points out more strongly the need for self-control and reason.

In these days of high labor costs, it is more profitable in the long run to spend 5 or 10 minutes on basic checks and collecting your thoughts so you are able to arrive at a solution to the problem rather than going off haphazardly. Given the high costs involved in purchasing equipment, most companies have a reasonably good maintenance program that in most instances is reflected in minimum engine failures and downtime. When a problem occurs, then, you will find that many times it is of a minor nature. Do not automatically suspect a major reason for failure. Consider the procedure illustrated in Figure 25–1 to systematically determine the reasons and causes for a suspected problem.

TROUBLESHOOTING TIPS

When faced with a troubleshooting problem, learn to complement your mechanical expertise and knowledge with four faculties that are always at your disposal. Figure 25–2 illustrates the most important tools available to you when troubleshooting a complaint—faculties that if used correctly might pinpoint one or more problems without your having to pull out any tools or special diagnostic equipment. They often will lead you to the system that may be causing the problem, although they may not spell out the exact cause of the problem.

Consider item 1, your eyesight, which allows you to quickly view the color of the exhaust smoke, signs of fuel oil, lube oil or coolant system leaks, and any signs of damage—collapsed intake piping; damaged air cleaner assembly; crushed exhaust piping, muffler, stack exhaust pipe, or rain cap; signs of overheated components; loose or corroded wiring, particularly on electronically equipped fuel-injected engines such as those of DDC, Caterpillar, Cummins, Mack, and Volvo. Take a few minutes to look for telltale signs before jumping to any conclusions.

Item 2, your hearing, allows you to listen for unusual noises such as air or exhaust leaks, particularly on turbocharged engines, or for sounds that are not usually associated with a mechanically sound engine. A misfiring cylinder or cylinders or rough-running engine can be heard immediately. Complement your hearing by using a stethoscope to pinpoint and pick up the intensity of noises at each injector, fuel pump plunger, valve train mechanism, bearing noise, and so on. If a stethoscope is unavailable, use a metal rod or pipe, screwdriver, or similar object to intensify the sounds to your ear.

Item 3, your sense of smell, allows you to pick up the aroma of burning lube oil, fuel oil, coolant, wire insulation, hoses, and so on. In addition, your sense of touch can lead you to a possible problem area, such as a small vibration, particularly on engines with externally

The Diagnostic Process

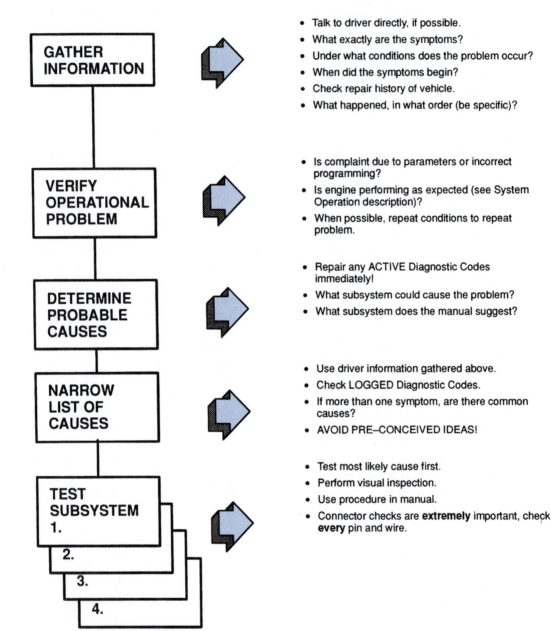

- Talk to driver directly, if possible.
- What exactly are the symptoms?
- Under what conditions does the problem occur?
- When did the symptoms begin?
- Check repair history of vehicle.
- What happened, in what order (be specific)?

- Is complaint due to parameters or incorrect programming?
- Is engine performing as expected (see System Operation description)?
- When possible, repeat conditions to repeat problem.

- Repair any ACTIVE Diagnostic Codes immediately!
- What subsystem could cause the problem?
- What subsystem does the manual suggest?

- Use driver information gathered above.
- Check LOGGED Diagnostic Codes.
- If more than one symptom, are there common causes?
- AVOID PRE–CONCEIVED IDEAS!

- Test most likely cause first.
- Perform visual inspection.
- Use procedure in manual.
- Connector checks are **extremely** important, check **every** pin and wire.

GATHER INFORMATION

VERIFY OPERATIONAL PROBLEM

DETERMINE PROBABLE CAUSES

NARROW LIST OF CAUSES

TEST SUBSYSTEM
1.
2.
3.
4.

FIGURE 25–1   Sequential procedure to use when troubleshooting any system. (Reprinted courtesy of Caterpillar, Inc.)

mounted injectors and high-pressure fuel lines. An injector or pumping plunger in the injection pump which is at fault will exhibit a different feel when you lightly place your fingers over a high-pressure fuel line. Placing your hand along the cylinder block to determine possible variations in operating temperature, or lightly touching an exhaust manifold on a cold engine immediately after startup, can let you feel if one cylinder is running cooler than another. A heat-indicating crayon can be used to make marks on the exhaust manifold opposite each cylinder; as the engine warms up, look to see if the crayon marks all melt together. If not, place a pyrometer on each manifold and check to ensure that each cylinder exhaust operating temperature is within 50°F (10°C) maximum of the others. Any spread greater than this indicates either lower compression in

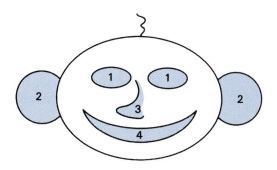

FIGURE 25-2 *Before attempting to trace a problem, stop and use the four most important troubleshooting tools at your disposal: 1, eyesight to look for visible telltale signs; 2, hearing to listen for unusual noises, squeals, grinding, rumble, etc.; 3, sense of smell to detect burning oil, fuel, coolant, etc.; 4, formulate questions in your mind from the input obtained from the first three inputs.*

that cylinder or less fuel being delivered through that injector.

Item 4 involves gathering as much information as you can through dialogue with the equipment operator.

Another helpful tool that can be used to check an engine internally (such as the condition of valves and cylinders, crankcase state, overheated bearings) is the *borescope*, a tool used for many years by aircraft mechanics on gas turbine engines. This tool comes in varying lengths with a flexible body that can bend in and around curves and irregular shapes. Complete with a small light and magnifying window, it allows you to peer into components and areas without having to remove major engine components.

Exhaust smoke meters are manufactured by a variety of companies, two of which are Hartridge Equipment and Robert Bosch. Expensive though they are, smoke meters are necessary tools of engine manufacturers, distributors/dealers, federal and state truck licensing agencies and police traffic organizations, and large fleets that need to know and maintain engines within the legislated U.S. EPA exhaust emissions regulations. Many additional special tools are available, such as fuel injection test equipment, fuel consumption testers, and electronic diagnostic equipment, particularly for use with electronic fuel injection control systems.

ENGINE IDLING

Sometime you may be considering a performance complaint on an engine that deals with a rough-idle situation or unusual exhaust smoke color at low speed. Keep in mind that excessive amounts of engine idling, particularly in cold-weather environments, will cause incom-

plete combustion, slobbering, or wet stacking at the exhaust stack (unburned raw fuel) and white smoke for up to 5 minutes or longer after initial engine startup, particularly on nonelectronic controlled engines. Idling an engine for long periods results in a rapid loss of heat from the cooling system because the small amount of fuel required to keep the engine running at an idle speed does not generate enough heat rejection to the surrounding water jackets. If an engine is to be idled for longer than 5 minutes, it should be shut off.

Tests on midrange and heavy-duty trucks that operate in a wide variety of applications in North America have shown that the average 1 year idling period for a typical over-the-road truck or tractor totals 800 hours, equivalent to 64,000 miles (103,000 km). Idling causes engine damage through rapid oil breakdown and increased combustion chamber deposits. Idling wastes fuel and tends to wash down the cylinder liner. The incomplete combustion can result in deposits forming not only in the combustion chamber, but also on exhaust valves and around piston rings. For this reason, current high-performance heavy-duty diesel truck engines equipped with electronic controls offer an optional 3 to 100 minute idle shutdown system. This system automatically stops the engine after this period should the operator leave the engine running unattended.

SEQUENTIAL TROUBLESHOOTING STEPS

It is not the intent of this chapter to include all the complaints you will come across when maintaining, servicing, or troubleshooting engines. The various troubleshooting charts within this chapter will provide you with a lengthy list of typical conditions that can result in a given symptom. Keep in mind, however, that problems associated with one make and type of engine (two stroke versus four stroke) may not occur exactly in the same way in another.

For example, particular features on one four-stroke-cycle engine may not appear on another because of the type of fuel system used and the optional features on that engine. Follow the basic troubleshooting steps listed next *prior to* rolling up your sleeves and trying to pinpoint a problem area:

1. Obtain as much information as possible concerning the complaint.
2. Analyze the problem in detail first, beginning with the smallest and simplest things.
3. Relate the problem symptoms to the basic engine systems and components.
4. Consider any recent maintenance or repair job that might relate to the problem.

5. Always double-check and think about the problem before disassembling anything.

6. Try to solve the problem by checking the easiest and simplest things first.

7. Refer to various troubleshooting charts in this chapter to assist you.

8. If possible, use the special tools and diagnostic equipment at your disposal to verify a complaint and pinpoint the general area.

9. Determine the cause(s) of the problem and carry out the repair.

10. Operate the engine and road test the vehicle to confirm that the problem has been corrected.

GENERAL PROCEDURE FOR CHECKING ENGINE AND VEHICLE

A general procedure is essential to effectively troubleshoot and isolate a cause for a lack of power complaint or an engine that runs rough under load. Follow these steps:

1. Determine from discussions with the operator if possible, just when the problem occurs. Possibly the operator's driving habits require modification and/or the horsepower setting for the engine is not suitable for the application.

2. On mobile equipment, always check to ensure that the brakes are not dragging, or that the axles are not misaligned (dog-legging), or that a problem does not exist in the driveline (bearings and so on).

3. Check the brakes by feeling all the brake drums. If the brakes of a wheel do not completely release, the brake drum for that wheel will be hotter than the brake drums for the other wheels. With the truck lifted with a jack, the wheels must have free rotation when turned by hand.

4. Check the color of the exhaust smoke at no load and full load. Perform an AIR check, turboboost check, EBP check, and crankcase pressure check with water and mercury manometers if unusual smoke is detected.

5. Air coming into the engine must be cool for the engine to have full horsepower. If the air inlet system is not of correct design or is not in good mechanical condition, hot air can come into the engine, causing a loss of horsepower. To check the inlet air temperature, install a thermistor-thermometer into the engine air inlet pipe.

6. Check that full throttle is being obtained, with an accurate tachometer, particularly if there is no visible or unusual smoke at the exhaust stack. Is the engine obtaining maximum no-load rpm in accord with the option plate or rocker cover decal (label)? Check the governor linkage as well, through to the injection pump, or injector control tube and racks. Is there any binding—particularly if the rocker covers have been improperly installed or if they have been dented or crushed?

7. Ask the operator if any repairs were performed recently. If the vehicle is fairly new, check that any related engine parts have been correctly installed at the OEM. Components such as fuel filters and lines, as well as intake and exhaust system components, are often installed by the OEM and not by the engine manufacturer.

8. It is possible for a transmission or rear axle to use extra horsepower because of these conditions: being damaged, not being in correct adjustment, having the wrong type of fluid or not enough fluid, or having an inside mechanical problem. If a part of the drive train unit operates at a higher temperature than normal, it may be the problem. Check this part of the unit before working on any other part of the unit. Power-shift or automatic transmissions can cause vehicle performance to be low if they are out of adjustment or not working correctly. See the transmission service manual for the correct adjustments.

9. The tire size, rear axle ratio, and transmission gear ratios must be correct to obtain maximum engine performance. If the transmission gear ratios are wrong, they can cause the engine rpm to go low enough during shifting that the engine does not have correct *acceleration* (increase in speed). A rear-axle gear ratio that supplies too high a vehicle speed with the engine at a low rpm during normal vehicle operation will cause the engine to be *lugging* (when the truck is used in a gear too high for engine rpm to go up as the accelerator pedal is pushed farther down, or when the truck is used in a gear where engine rpm goes down with the accelerator pedal at maximum travel). Application personnel can give you the correct tire sizes and gear ratios for your operation.

10. Perform a fuel spill-back check as shown in Figure 21–7. This test is a quick way to determine if the fuel system is, in fact, receiving sufficient fuel during engine operation. If an engine lacks power and the exhaust smoke is not an unusual color, it is probably starving for fuel. This may be due to a plugged primary fuel filter, a plugged secondary fuel filter, a fuel line restriction, or drawing air on the suction side of the fuel system. The spill-back test is a common procedure on all models of Detroit Diesel two- and four-stroke-cycle engines. It involves disconnecting the fuel return line between the engine and fuel tank, then running the en-

gine at rated speed (usually 1800 or 2100 rpm) for 1 minute to measure the quantity of fuel returned, or spilled back. This quantity can be compared with the specification in the service manual. For example, if an 0.080 in. (2.03 mm) restricted fitting (series 60 engine) is used in the fuel return line, the fuel spill back should be a minimum of 1.08 U.S. gallons per minute (4.1 L). While performing this test, the technician can also submerge the return line below the level of the spilling fuel within the container to look for signs of air bubbles, which would indicate that the fuel pump is drawing air on the suction side (between the fuel tank and the inlet side of the fuel pump). Signs of air would result in a low spill-back. Check all of the fuel lines and fittings between the fuel tank and fuel pump inlet for leakage (drawing air).

11. Perform a fuel system restriction check by removing the small pipe plug located on the outlet side of the primary fuel filter assembly. See Figure 21–4. Screw in a suitable small brass fitting at the filter that can have a small-bore rubber hose connected to it; connect the opposite end to a Hg (mercury) manometer or vacuum gauge. Start and run the engine at idle and slowly accelerate to a WOT position while carefully noting the fuel system restriction. Compare the reading with that in the engine service manual. A reading that exceeds the limits indicates either a plugged primary fuel filter or a restriction between the fuel tank and inlet side of the transfer pump, possibly caused by a kinked or collapsed fuel line. In addition, check to ensure that the fuel lines are of the correct size. For example, DDC recommends that this restriction should not exceed 6 in. (15.24 mm) of Hg when using a clean primary fuel filter and no more than 12 in. (30.48 mm) when a filter has been in service. Other engine manufacturers such as Cummins call for the following restrictions:

- 14L, L10, and M11 engine models: 4 in. (102 mm) Hg with a clean fuel filter; 8 in. (203 mm) Hg with a dirty filter. The fuel drain line maximum restriction without check valves is 2.5 in. (64 mm) Hg; with check valves, it is 6.5 in. (165 mm) Hg.
- C and B model engines: fuel lift pump maximum inlet restriction not exceeding 3.75 in. (95 mm); fuel return line maximum restriction not exceeding 20.4 in. (518 mm)

12. Check the fuel system operating pressure by installing a gauge on the inlet and outlet side of the secondary fuel filter assembly. This is accomplished easily by removing the small square or Allen-head access pipe plug located on the filter cover. Now check the fuel transfer pump delivery pressure and the pressure drop through the filter itself. Generally, the allowable pressure drop through a secondary fuel filter should not exceed 5 psi (34.5 kPa). Normal fuel system pressures for various engines running at rated speed (usually 1800 or 2100 rpm) are as follows:

- Detroit Diesel two-cycle engines: 50 to 70 psi (345 to 483 kPa); DDC series 50 and 60 four-stroke engines: 65 psi (450 kPa).
- Caterpillar 3176B and 3406E engines: 91 psi (630 kPa) at rated rpm
- Cummins Celect engines: 140 psi (965 kpa)

NOTE Keep in mind that warm fuel allows the fuel to expand. On mechanically governed engines, this will result in a power loss due to less fuel (denseness) being metered. On electronically controlled engines, a fuel temperature sensor continually sends a signal to the ECM to advise it of any change in fuel system operating temperature. The ECM then alters the PWM (pulse-width-modulation) signal to the electronically controlled unit injectors or pump injectors to maintain a steady horsepower (kilowatt) output for a given throttle position.

13. Check the API gravity of the fuel being used. Engines are set at the factory to produce rated power with a fuel of a specific API number. Fuel with higher API gravities (number) will produce less horsepower. For more information on API numbers, refer to Chapter 14.

14. Check the customer engine and vehicle order specification and vehicle road speeds.

15. Check the mechanical throttle delay, fuel modulator, or AFC (air/fuel control) setting and operation.

16. Check all adjustments; the engine may need a tune-up.

17. If the engine is fitted with a Jake brake, check it for proper operation and adjustment.

18. Check for hard starting which might indicate low compression, which is usually accompanied by white smoke. Check the piston rings through the airbox inspection covers on DDC two-stroke-cycle series engines (see Figure 21–8). If necessary, perform a compression check as shown in Figure 21–9. On four-cycle engines, you can also perform a cylinder leak-down test using special test tools.

19. Test the engine/truck with a dynamometer to confirm that the published horsepower is being obtained.

EXHAUST SMOKE COLOR

One of the easiest methods to use when troubleshooting an engine for a performance complaint is to visually monitor the color of the smoke emanating at the exhaust stack. This is particularly true when a low-power complaint is received, because the smoke color allows you to determine fairly quickly whether the engine is exhibiting an internal mechanical problem and leads you to the air intake, exhaust, or fuel system to find the reason for the complaint. Four basic colors may exit from the exhaust system at any time during engine operation—white, gray, black, or blue. Each is a clue to what the problem is and where the problem might be located.

In this section we discuss why one color of exhaust smoke may lead you to a specific problem area. To thoroughly understand the reasons behind exhaust smoke, refer to Chapter 4, where the theory and dynamics of the combustion phase in an internal combustion diesel engine are described.

White Smoke

White smoke is generally most noticeable at engine startup, particularly during conditions of low ambient temperatures when the air drawn into the engine is cold. Although more dense than warmer air, this cold air will result in lower temperatures and pressures at the end of the piston's compression stroke. Consequently, all of the fuel will not burn to completion in the cylinder; when the exhaust valves open, these fuel droplets are exhausted into the atmosphere as unburned hydrocarbons which cool, condense, and appear as white smoke. Recollect from the discussion in Chapter 4 that hydrocarbons are basically soot produced from the carbon in the diesel fuel. Operating an engine at 20°F (–7°C) in the winter months versus 80°F (27°C) in the summer results in a reduction in the intake air temperature of 100°F (38°C). At the end of the compression stroke, the temperature of this pressurized air can be anywhere between 230° and 300°F (110° to 149°C) lower, depending on the compression ratio of the engine and the shape of the piston crown, which controls the degree of air swirl within the cylinder and combustion chamber. This colder air results in a longer ignition delay period, which can be offset slightly by use of a more volatile higher-cetane-number diesel fuel. As the combustion and cylinder temperatures increase during the first few minutes of engine operation, this white smoke generally starts to disappear in a mechanically sound engine.

If the white smoke takes longer than 3 to 5 minutes to start to disappear, the problem may be caused by low cylinder compression from worn rings, scored piston or liner, or valve seating problems, as well as from faulty injectors or the use of a low-cetane diesel fuel. The time for the white smoke to disappear depends on how cold the outside air is, the design of the engine, and how quickly it warms up. White smoke on startup is much more predominant on high-horsepower fixed-injection timing engines, because the fuel and combustion systems have been optimized for maximum performance, reliability, and durability under high-load operating conditions.

Excessive white smoke at idle speed, or some sign of white smoke once the engine is up to operating temperature, could be associated with any one of the conditions listed in the troubleshooting chart (see Figure 25–3) for excessive white smoke. In addition to the conditions listed in the chart, keep in mind that white smoke at idle or when the engine is up to operating temperature can also be attributed to low cylinder compression or to coolant leakage into the combustion chamber from a leaking cylinder head gasket, injector copper tube, or cracked head or liner.

Black or Gray Smoke

Black or gray smoke should be checked with the engine at a minimum operating temperature of 160°F (71°C). Generally, either color of exhaust smoke is caused by the same conditions; the difference in color is due to the opacity or denseness of smoke. Less than 5% exhaust smoke opacity is hardly visible to the naked eye. Acceptable standards being set in North America by the U.S. EPA currently allow a maximum opacity of 20% during acceleration, 15% under engine lug, and 50% under peak-load operation. Each engine manufacturer must certify that its engines comply with the limits of maximum allowable exhaust smoke emissions under a variety of situations that include full-load acceleration, transient response under load, and lug-down conditions. Once an engine is certified to comply with legislated exhaust emissions, it becomes the maintenance technician's job to ensure that each engine continues to perform according to this certification. Heavy fines are levied by state and federal authorities on companies that allow their heavy-duty truck exhaust emissions to exceed regulated limits. In addition, abnormal amounts of exhaust smoke emission is an indication that the engine is not operating correctly, resulting in a lack of power as well as decreased fuel economy. Excessive black or gray exhaust smoke is generally caused by an improper grade of diesel fuel, air starvation, or high exhaust back pressure. See Figure 25–4.

Smoke, White-Excessive

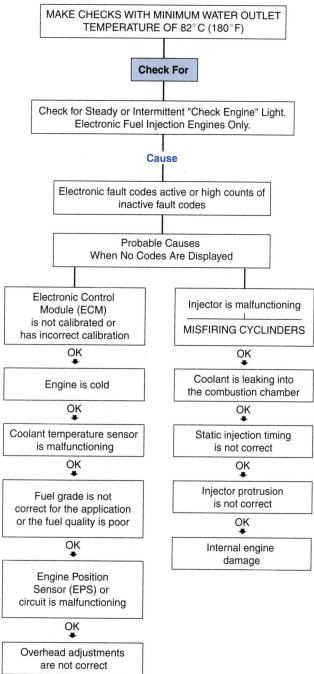

FIGURE 25–3 *Troubleshooting chart for causes of excessive white smoke.*

The grade of fuel must meet the engine manufacturer's specifications according to the service manual and special bulletin information. Anything that causes a high-AIR condition or aftercooler plugging, resulting in hot air entering the engine, is a typical reason for air starvation. In this chapter we describe how to check for high AIR. Similarly, a high-EBP condition can create problems in both the exhaust and air intake systems, particularly on two-stroke-cycle engines and turbocharged four-stroke-cycle models.

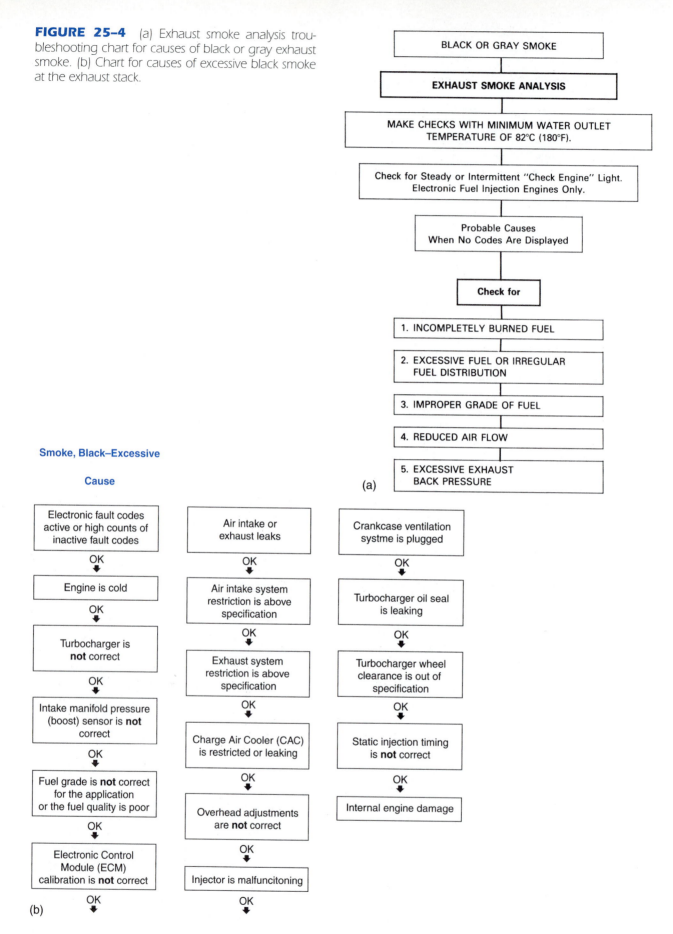

FIGURE 25–4 (a) Exhaust smoke analysis troubleshooting chart for causes of black or gray exhaust smoke. (b) Chart for causes of excessive black smoke at the exhaust stack.

BLACK OR GRAY SMOKE

EXHAUST SMOKE ANALYSIS

MAKE CHECKS WITH MINIMUM WATER OUTLET TEMPERATURE OF 82°C (180°F).

Check for Steady or Intermittent "Check Engine" Light. Electronic Fuel Injection Engines Only.

Probable Causes When No Codes Are Displayed

Check for

1. INCOMPLETELY BURNED FUEL

2. EXCESSIVE FUEL OR IRREGULAR FUEL DISTRIBUTION

3. IMPROPER GRADE OF FUEL

4. REDUCED AIR FLOW

5. EXCESSIVE EXHAUST BACK PRESSURE

(a)

Smoke, Black–Excessive

Cause

Electronic fault codes active or high counts of inactive fault codes
OK
Engine is cold
OK
Turbocharger is **not** correct
OK
Intake manifold pressure (boost) sensor is **not** correct
OK
Fuel grade is **not** correct for the application or the fuel quality is poor
OK
Electronic Control Module (ECM) calibration is **not** correct
OK

Air intake or exhaust leaks
OK
Air intake system restriction is above specification
OK
Exhaust system restriction is above specification
OK
Charge Air Cooler (CAC) is restricted or leaking
OK
Overhead adjustments are **not** correct
OK
Injector is malfuncitoning
OK

Crankcase ventilation systme is plugged
OK
Turbocharger oil seal is leaking
OK
Turbocharger wheel clearance is out of specification
OK
Static injection timing is **not** correct
OK
Internal engine damage

(b)

760

Other reasons for black or gray exhaust smoke include these:

- Incorrect fuel injection timing
- Incorrect fuel setting (delivery rate)
- Faulty nozzles or injectors
- Incorrect-thickness washer installed under the nozzle seat in the bore in the cylinder head, or two washers installed instead of one
- Incorrect valve adjustment clearances or valve seat leakage
- Faulty fuel injection pump
- Faulty automatic timing advance unit

Blue Smoke

Blue exhaust smoke is attributable to oil entering the combustion chamber and being burned or blown through the cylinder and burned in the exhaust manifold or turbocharger. Check the simplest things first, such as too much oil in the crankcase or a plugged crankcase ventilation system breather (or the two main items listed in Table 25–1).

More serious causes can be worn valve guides, piston rings, or cylinder walls; scored pistons or cylinder walls; broken rings; turbocharger seal ring leakage; glazed cylinder liner walls through use of the wrong type of oil; improper run-in procedures of a new or rebuilt engine; or excessive periods of idling and/or light-load conditions. A cylinder compression or leak-down check can be used to confirm whether the problem is in the valves or rings. If a cylinder leak-down kit is not available, perform a compression check on the engine. On two-stroke-cycle DDC engines, the condition of the pistons, rings, and liners can be checked visually, with the engine stopped, by removing an air box inspection cover on the side of the engine block and accessing the components through the cylinder liner ports (see Figure 21–8).

EXHAUST SMOKE DETECTION

Although smoke meters are readily available, not everyone has such a device. A Ringelmann-type smoke

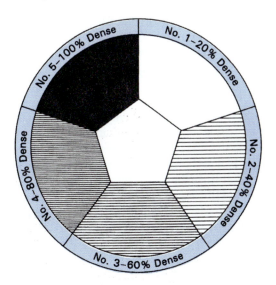

FIGURE 25–5 *Example of a Ringlemann-type exhaust smoke color chart that indicates the approximate percentage opacity (denseness) by color comparison and the varying degrees of incomplete combustion. Can be used when a smokemeter is not readily available.*

chart can be used to approximate the density of the exhaust smoke emanating from the stack (see Figure 25–5). A Ringelmann smoke scale enables you to observe conveniently the approximate density of the smoke coming out of the engine exhaust stack. The scale should be held at arm's length, at which distance the shaded areas on the chart can be compared with the shade or density of the smoke coming from the exhaust stack. Your line of observation should be at right angles to the direction of smoke travel and not be less than 100 ft (30.48 m) or more than a 0.25 mile (0.4 km) from the stack. The background directly beyond the top of the exhaust stack should be free of buildings or other dark objects and direct sunlight. By recording the changes in smoke density, the average *percentage of smoke density* for any period of time can be approximated.

Mechanical Engines— Causes of Exhaust Smoke

The causes for a particular color of exhaust smoke vary somewhat in mechanically governed engines and electronically controlled engines. In this section we discuss the causes for exhaust smoke in the mechanical engines. Reasons for unusual colored exhaust smoke in electronic engines are given in the next section. Although many of the causes for a particular color of exhaust smoke can be the same for both types of engines, electronic sensors and circuits are added variables that we normally do not have to deal with on mechanical engines.

TABLE 25–1   Blue exhaust smoke check chart

Blue Smoke

Check For

1. Lubricating oil not burned in cylinder (blown out of cylinder and burned in exhaust manifold or turbocharger)—four-cycle engine
2. Lubricating oil not burned in cylinder (blown through cylinder during scavenging period)—two-cycle engine

Black or Gray Smoke

The procedure to follow when black or gray smoke is detected is shown in Figure 25–4.

Possible Causes and Corrections

1. *Incompletely burned fuel.* High exhaust back pressure or a restricted air inlet causes insufficient air for combustion and results in incompletely burned fuel. Excessive exhaust back pressure may be caused by faulty exhaust piping or muffler obstruction and is measured at the exhaust manifold outlet from the turbocharger with a manometer or suitable gauge. Replace faulty parts. You can also check by removing the exhaust pipes from the exhaust manifolds. With the exhaust pipes removed, start and load the engine on a chassis dynamometer to see if the problem is corrected.

2. *Excessive fuel or irregular fuel distribution.* Check for the following conditions:

   a. *Misadjusted throttle delay mechanisms or fuel modulators.* This affects smoke at excessive acceleration but not smoke at constant speed.

   b. *Bad fuel nozzle(s).* Bad fuel nozzles normally cause the engine to misfire and run rough, but they can cause too much smoke with the engine still running smooth. Remove the fuel nozzles and test.

   c. *Wrong seal washer installed under nozzle(s).* The use of incorrect washers changes the location of the fuel injection nozzles in the combustion chamber. This affects smoke.

   d. *Fuel injection timing not correct.* Check and make the necessary adjustments. Check for improperly timed injectors and improperly positioned injector rack control levers. Time the fuel injectors and perform the appropriate governor tune-up. Replace faulty injectors if this condition persists after timing the injectors and performing the engine tune-up. Avoid lugging the engine, as this will cause incomplete combustion.

   e. *Fuel setting not correct.* Check and make necessary adjustments as described in the service manual.

   f. *Bad fuel injection pump.* An injection pump can have a good fuel flow coming from it but cause rough running because of slow timing caused by wear on the bottom end of the plunger. Fuel pumps that are severely scored from debris can cause rough running, but fuel dilution usually occurs before horsepower is affected. Low installation torque on the fuel pump retaining nut can cause misfire, rough running, and low power.

   g. *Automatic timing advance not operating correctly.* A timing advance that does not operate correctly on engines equipped with an inline pump can cause delays on the engine acceleration at some rpm before high idle, or possibly cause the engine to run rough and have exhaust noise (backfire) during acceleration. This condition is difficult to find if engine acceleration is slow or at a constant engine rpm.

   h. *Air in the fuel system.* With air in the fuel system, the engine will normally be difficult to start, particularly on inline-pump-equipped engines, run rough, and release a large amount of white smoke. If the engine does not start, loosen a fuel injection line nut and crank the engine until fuel comes out. Tighten the fuel line nut. If the engine still does not run smooth or releases a large amount of white smoke, loosen the fuel line nuts one at a time until the fuel that comes out is free of air. Tighten the fuel line nuts. If the air cannot be removed this way, put 5 psi (35 kPa) of air pressure to the fuel tank. Check for leakage at the connections between the fuel tank and the fuel transfer pump. If leaks are found, tighten the connections or replace the lines. If there are no visual leaks, remove the fuel supply line from the tank and connect it to an outside fuel supply. If this corrects the problem, the suction line (standpipe) inside the fuel tank has a leak.

3. *Low-quality fuel.* Check for use of an improper grade of fuel. The use of low-cetane fuel will cause exhaust smoke. Refer to the fuel specifications section of the engine service manual. See also Chapter 14 in this book.

4. *Reduced airflow.* Reduced airflow to the engine cylinders is caused by a restricted intercooler or air cleaner, an air leak in the piping between the air cleaner and the intake manifold, or a faulty turbocharger. Check, clean, and/or repair these items as necessary. Restricted air inlet to two-stroke-cycle engine cylinders is caused by clogged cylinder liner ports, air cleaner, or blower air inlet screen. Clean these items. Check the emergency stop to make sure that it is completely open and readjust it if necessary.

   a. *Air inlet piping damage or restriction.* Make a visual inspection of the air inlet system and check for damage to piping, rags in the inlet piping, or damage to the rain cap or the cap pushed too far on the inlet pipe. If no damage is seen, check inlet restriction with a clean air cleaner element.

b. *Dirty air cleaner.* Check if the air cleaner has a restriction indicator. See Figure 13–11. If there is no restriction indicator, restriction can be checked with a water manometer or a vacuum gauge (see Figure 13–39). Make a connection to the piping between the air cleaner and the inlet of the turbocharger. Check with the engine running at full-load rpm. Maximum restriction is usually between 20 and 25 in. (500 to 635 mm) of water. If a gauge is not available, visually check the air cleaner element for dirt. If the element is dirty, clean the element or install a new element.

c. *Valve adjustment not correct or valve leakage.* Check and make necessary adjustments. Valve leakage normally causes the engine to misfire and run rough.

5. *High or excessive exhaust back pressure.* Refer to Figure 13–41.

White Smoke

The procedure to follow when white smoke is detected is shown in Figure 25–3.

Possible Causes and Corrections

1. *Misfiring cylinders.* To check for a misfiring cylinder, you can short out the mechanical unit injector by running the engine at an idle rpm. To do this, manually depress and hold down the injector follower using a large screwdriver or a hooked adaptor under the rocker arm assembly, and force and hold down the injector follower. If there is no significant change in the operational sound of the engine when you do this, then the injector is not functioning correctly. On engines equipped with an inline pump system, loosen off each individual nozzle fuel line nut one at a time as shown in Figure 25–6 to determine the same situation. Keep in mind, however, that low cylinder compression can cause a cylinder misfire condition as well as low cetane fuel.

CAUTION: On the Detroit Diesel four-stroke-cycle 8.2 L V8 engine, which uses a unit injector, do *not* attempt to hold the injector follower down to short it out as you would do with the two-stroke-cycle model, since the injector pushrod on the four-stroke engine is not threaded into the rocker arm as it is on the two-stroke engine. Consequently, if you hold the injector follower down

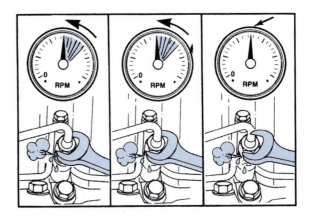

FIGURE 25–6 Loosening off a Bosch injection pump-type high-pressure fuel line at the injector to determine if the fuel injector is firing properly. No sound and/or engine speed change when this is done indicates that the nozzle is not firing. (Courtesy of Cummins Engine Company, Inc.)

with a large screwdriver while the engine is running, the pushrod will either fly out of the engine or drop off to the side and be bent. To short out the unit injector on the 8.2 L engine, individually push the injector fuel rack into its full-fuel position. This is known as flooding the cylinder. The engine should pick up speed when you do this to confirm that it is firing. If there is no change in speed, the injector is faulty.

2. *Miscellaneous causes*
    a. *Cold outside temperatures.* When the air outside is cold, the cylinder temperature is cooler. Not all the fuel will burn in the cylinders. The fuel that does not burn comes out the exhaust as white smoke. White smoke is normal in cold temperatures until the engine operates long enough to become warm. There will be less white smoke if No. 1 diesel fuel is used.
    b. *Long idle periods.* When an engine runs at idle speed for a long period of time, the cylinders cool and all of the fuel does not burn. Do not idle an engine for a long period of time. Stop an engine when it is not in use. If long idle periods are necessary, use No. 1 diesel fuel.
    c. *Engine operating temperature too low.* This can cause white smoke on startup. If the smoke is slow to clear from the exhaust, check and make a replacement of the thermostat if needed.

d. *Low-quality fuel.* Test the engine using fuel according to recommendations by the engine manufacturer. See Figure 14–1.

e. *Air-in-the-fuel system.* If there is air in the fuel system, the engine will normally be difficult to start, run rough, and release a large amount of white smoke. If the engine does not start, loosen a fuel injection line nut and crank the engine until fuel comes out. Tighten the fuel-line nut. Start the engine. If the engine still does not run smooth or releases a large amount of white smoke, loosen the fuel-line nuts one at a time until the fuel that comes out is free of air. Tighten the fuel-line nuts. If the air cannot be removed in this way, put 5 psi (35 kPa) of air pressure to the fuel tank. Check for leakage at the connections between the fuel tank and the fuel transfer pump. If leaks are found, tighten the connections or replace the lines. If there are no visual leaks, remove the fuel supply line from the tank and connect it to an outside fuel supply. If this corrects the problem, the suction line (standpipe) inside the fuel tank has a leak.

f. *Fuel injection timing not correct.* Check and make the necessary adjustments as described for Figures 21–25 and 21–26.

g. *Valve adjustment not correct.* Check and make the necessary adjustments as described in Chapters 13, 21, 22, and 23.

h. *Bad fuel nozzle(s).* Bad fuel nozzles normally cause the engine to *misfire* and run rough, but they can cause too much smoke with the engine still running smooth. Remove the fuel nozzles and test as described in testing and adjusting section of Chapter 17 in this book.

i. *Coolant leakage into combustion chamber.* Coolant in the combustion chamber can cause white smoke. A cracked cylinder head or liner, or a bad cylinder head gasket, is a possible cause for this condition.

j. *Low compression.* Worn piston rings and cylinder liners lower compression pressures, which can cause white exhaust smoke.

Blue Smoke

Possible Causes and Corrections

1. *Fuel or oil leaks.*
   a. *Engine oil level too high.* Do not put too much oil in the crankcase. If the oil level in the crankcase goes up as the engine is used, check for fuel in the crankcase.

   b. *Oil leaks.* Check for internal lubricating oil leaks and refer to the high lubricating oil consumption chart in this chapter.

   c. *Worn valve guides.* Consult the specifications section of the service manual for the maximum permissible wear of the valve guides.

   d. *Worn piston rings and/or cylinder walls.* Worn piston rings and/or cylinder walls can be the cause of blue smoke and can cause a loss of compression. Make a visual inspection of the cylinder walls and piston rings. If necessary, measure the cylinder walls and piston rings. For the cylinder and piston ring specifications, see the specifications section of the service manual.

NOTE   High wear at low mileage is normally caused by dirt coming into the engine with the inlet air. See 'dusting' in Chapter 13.

---

   e. *Wear or damage to pistons.* Check the piston ring grooves for wear. Most high-speed, heavy-duty engines have piston grooves and rings of the keystone (taper) design. A piston ring groove gauge is available to check the top two ring grooves in the piston. See Figure 8–14. Worn grooves and pistons with damage or defects can cause blue smoke and too much oil consumption. Make sure that the oil return holes under the oil ring are open.

Electronic Engines—Causes of Exhaust Smoke Color

Causes for a particular color of exhaust smoke are similar regardless of whether the engine is mechanically or electronically controlled. When an *electronically controlled* engine has been operating normally, and a performance complaint is registered that deals with either white or black exhaust smoke include the following checks.

White Smoke

1. Remember some white smoke is normal when an engine is started and running, particularly during cold outside temperatures.

2. Check and recalibrate the engine speed or timing sensor (for example, Cat 3176, C10, C12, and 3406E engines).

3. Check the fuel system for either low- or high-pressure combustion gas or air in the fuel (perform a fuel spill-back test as shown in Figure 21–7). Check for poor fuel quality.

4. Check the intake manifold air temperature sensor signal. If ambient air is cool while the engine is idling, or after extended idling, monitor the intake manifold air temperature. If the reading is significantly higher than ambient air temperature at idle, it could be because of intake manifold heat soak: there is insufficient airflow for the sensor to accurately measure the air temperature, and the sensor is detecting conducted heat from the manifold. This could be normal operation after an extended idle period. Drive the vehicle to see if the airflow eliminates the problem.

5. Use a DDR, ET, or ECAP (Cat), Insite (Cummins), and check for atmospheric pressure sensor diagnostic codes. Monitor atmospheric pressure sensor status and compare with known atmospheric pressure for your area and elevation. If atmospheric pressure is 1 psi (6.895 kPa) higher than the known atmospheric pressure for your area, inspect the crankcase breather for restrictions. Remove a valve cover and recheck the pressure reading. If removing the valve cover solves the problem, replace the breather assembly. If the breather is not restricted, check the operating condition of the atmospheric pressure sensor.

6. Using diagnostic tooling, check for any coolant temperature sensor diagnostic codes. Monitor the coolant temperature sensor status, and if a problem is detected, perform a coolant temperature sensor circuit test.

7. Check for security of the individual unit injector plug-in harness connections, and make sure they are free of corrosion. Inspect the ECM injector harness end connections. Perform a cylinder cutout test using diagnostic tooling to isolate a misfiring cylinder.

8. Use diagnostic tooling to make sure that the EEPROM or Personality Module (Cat) is programmed correctly for the engine hardware.

9. Use diagnostic tooling and check for a positive 5 V sensor supply from the ECM. If this check is OK, perform a sensor supply circuit test.

Black Smoke

1. Check for high air inlet restriction.
2. Check for restricted fuel supply.
3. Check for poor fuel quality.

4. Check for incorrect intake and exhaust valve adjustment.

5. Check for defective unit injector. Perform a cylinder cutout test using the diagnostic tooling.

6. Inspect the ECM connector for full connection and corrosion.

7. Check boost pressure or atmospheric pressure sensor signal. Check the ECM with the DDR to see if a logged trouble code has been stored in memory. You can also run the engine through a full-range speed test, and by using the DDR, program it to perform a boost pressure test; then compare the readings with test specs.

8. Connect the OEM's diagnostic tooling and check to make sure the correct Personality Module (CAT) is installed compared to the engine hardware.

CHECKING THE FUEL SYSTEM

If an engine is misfiring, running rough, and lacking power, refer to the appropriate troubleshooting charts in this chapter. They will guide you to the possible problem areas. Note whether the condition occurs only at an idle rpm, high idle (maximum no-load speed), or only under acceleration or at loaded conditions, since the troubleshooting charts will guide you through each general condition. A quick way to determine if the fuel system is the problem is to note whether there is an unusual smoke color at the exhaust stack and to compare this with the exhaust smoke analysis chart (see Figure 25–5). Generally speaking, if there is no unusual exhaust smoke color, but the engine lacks power, then the engine is not starving for airflow, does not have high EBP, and is mechanically sound. Suspect simple things such as plugged fuel filters or a restriction to fuel flow somewhere, since the engine can still run with a lack of fuel but will fail to accelerate properly, can run rough at idle, and will most likely have trouble reaching the maximum no-load rpm. If it does reach the no-load rpm, but dies when a load is applied to it, fuel starvation is more than likely the cause. Nevertheless consider all possible areas listed in the troubleshooting charts, start with the simplest possibilities first and move to the more complex. The first rule of effective troubleshooting is to walk before you run.

Fuel Temperature

On high-speed diesel engines, fuel temperature can adversely affect the horsepower output of the engine. The optimum fuel temperature should be kept between

90° and 95°F (32° to 35°C). With each 10°F temperature rise beyond these figures, there is approximately a 1% loss in horsepower due to expansion in the fuel on a conventional engine. On turbocharged-aftercooled engines, each 10°F fuel temperature rise beyond 95° to 100°F (32° to 38°C) results in approximately a 1.5% horsepower loss. Therefore, if you were running at a fuel temperature of 135° to 140°F (57° to 60°C), theoretically your engine would be producing approximately 4% less horsepower on a conventional engine and closer to 6% less on a turbocharged and aftercooled engine. On a 350 hp engine, this would amount to about 14 hp (10.4 kW) on a conventional engine and closer to 21 hp on the turbocharged and aftercooled engine. Maximum temperature should *never* be allowed to exceed 150°F (65°C). A reduction in engine horsepower can also result due to an increase in air temperature (ambient), since this causes the air to expand and therefore become less dense. On a turbocharged engine, this is offset by the increase in airflow and pressure increase and the use of an aftercooler or intercooler.

On most high-speed engines, a power decrease can be expected of between 0.15 and 0.5 hp (0.11 to 0.373 kW) per cylinder, depending on the delivery capability of the fuel injector or pump for each 10°F (5°C) air temperature rise above 90°F (32°C). Therefore, when investigating complaints of low horsepower, always check to ensure that these two temperatures are within specifications. If you don't, you could spend a lot of time trying to find the reason for the complaint, which is not directly related to the normal mechanical operation of the engine fuel or air inlet system.

If the engine fails to reach its maximum governed speed and generally seems to be starving for fuel, install a fuel pressure gauge into the secondary filter, run the engine, and check the fuel pressure with the engine manufacturer's specifications. On Detroit Diesel engines, perform a fuel spill-back check. Some engines have a small filter screen located just under the cover of the fuel transfer pump; check that this is not plugged.

If a fuel strainer or fuel water separator is used, check it for plugging and excessive amounts of water. Check that all fuel lines are free of sharp bends and kinks. Check the tightness of all fittings and connections from the suction side of the transfer pump back to the fuel tank. Install a clear test line connection into the suction line to check for air bubbles. You may have to undertake a restriction check to the fuel flow as discussed in Chapter 21, Figure 21–4.

Check the fuel transfer pump drive for security and proper engagement. Ensure that there are no external fuel leaks, especially at the pump or injectors. Also, if more than one fuel tank is employed, check to see that the balance-line valve is open between them; if

a three-way valve is employed, check that it is in the correct position. In certain instances you may also find that there is a restriction to fuel flow from inside the fuel tank caused by sediment or some foreign object that has dropped into the tank either during filling or maintenance checks.

One complaint that you may occasionally come across is that the engine runs well in the early part of a shift, but stalls and lacks power as the day wears on. This could be caused by debris, such as a piece of wood or bark, especially around logging equipment. A restriction to fuel flow is created as the level in the fuel tank drops and the debris is drawn over the suction line.

If the engine has been overhauled recently or the injection pump or injectors serviced, double-check the injection pump timing, injector release pressure, or injector timing.

If the engine has a considerable amount of hours or miles on it, it very well may be in need of a tune-up; however, this alone may not be the cause of the problem. Too many people immediately assume that if an engine is lacking power the answer is to tune it up. Although many large companies have developed a sequence of checks to be carried out at certain intervals of time, a tune-up should be done only if other checks show that everything else is according to specifications.

When conducting a tune-up, do not back off all adjustments and start from scratch. Check each adjustment first and if necessary, readjust. One of the first checks that should be made is to disconnect the throttle linkage and manually hold the speed control lever on the governor to the full-fuel position and accurately record the maximum governed engine rpm. Reconnect the throttle linkage, place it in the full-fuel position, and compare the readings. If they are not the same, adjust the linkage to correctly obtain the maximum engine rpm. Similarly, the maximum governor no-load speed setting may require adjustment. Ensure that there is no binding anywhere in the fuel control linkage.

Fuel Flow

When an engine is suspected of using too much fuel, a close check of daily fuel usage versus miles (km) covered can be made. In addition, fuel flow measurement systems are available from some major truck manufacturers. On board computer monitoring devices are now being widely used by many truck fleets to keep an accurate check of vehicle fuel mileage (Figure 21–35).

A bad speedometer does not give the correct speed or the correct indication of fuel consumption. An indication of low speed can cause the operator to think there is a power problem.

PRIMARY ENGINE CHECKS

Engine Timing

Improper engine timing, improper valve adjustment clearances, or an out-of-adjustment sequence can lead to physical, or mechanical damage, such as valves hitting pistons.

If the injection pump timing or injector timing is off, problems of smoking exhaust, low power, high fuel consumption, and internal engine damage can result. Always ensure that the engine is timed according to the manufacturer's specifications and that injection pump and injectors are timed for the particular application for which the engine is being employed. An engine timing indicator that operates off fuel pressure through a transducer pickup can be used on engines that employ a high-pressure fuel system.

Pyrometers

Exhaust temperature gauges, more commonly called *pyrometers,* are extremely helpful when checking an engine for a lack-of-power complaint. Most heavy-duty highway trucks with diesel engines are equipped with dash-mounted pyrometers, which can readily assist you in determining if both engine banks are running at the same temperature on V-type engines. On inline engines, the pyrometer can establish whether the engine is operating within the range specified by the engine manufacturer.

The most common form of pyrometer uses a pickup, or thermocouple, consisting of two wires of different metals welded together at their ends—a *hot junction.* The metals used in these wires are selected for their response to temperature and ability to withstand high heat. As the hot junction is exposed to a heat source, a small electric current is generated at the junction; it flows through the wires to the measuring instrument, which is a *millivoltmeter.* The amount of current flow is proportional to the heat created at the hot junction.

Many companies offer pyrometers that can be readily used by one person during troubleshooting. These are of the handheld type; they have a heat probe that registers temperature upon contact with the surface to be checked. The newer pyrometers that offer a digital readout are very helpful. Just point the infrared thermometer, pull the pistol trigger, and an instant reading is recorded on the face.

Engine exhaust temperatures vary in engine types based on fuel setting, horsepower, speed, and load conditions. Typical full-load exhaust temperatures can range as follows:

- Two-stroke-cycle diesel: 585° to 740°F (307° to 393°C)

- Four-stroke-cycle diesel: 647° to 1030°F (342° to 554°C)

Peak torque exhaust temperatures, which occur at a lower engine speed, will consistently show higher temperatures of 200°F (93°C) plus over those encountered under full-load engine speed conditions at the rated governed-engine rpm.

Two-stroke-cycle engines run cooler than four-stroke-cycle engines due to the shorter power stroke in crankshaft degrees, plus the fact that almost twice the airflow is pumped through the two-cycle engine. Approximately 30% of the cooling on a two-stroke-cycle diesel engine is achieved by airflow alone.

Engine Overspeed

The maximum speed of diesel engines is controlled either by a mechanical or electronic governor assembly (see Chapter 16). Causes of possible engine overspeed can usually be traced to the following conditions:

1. Maximum governed rpm adjustment improperly set. Use an accurate digital tachometer to determine engine speeds.

2. Internal governor problem.

3. Oil pullover from an oil bath air cleaner or other external fuel source such as blower or turbocharger seals.

4. Running a mechanical engine with the governor linkage disconnected.

5. Operator problem. This particular problem is not unusual on mobile equipment and highway truck operation. If an operator allows the engine rpm to climb beyond the maximum safe road speed for a particular gear, in effect, the vehicle's road wheels become the driving member. As there is a direct mechanical link from the road wheels to the differential and the driveline, this increased road wheel speed works through the transmission, causing the engine to be the driven member instead of the driving member. During this time, it matters not that the operator has his or her foot on the throttle, since the governor will react to pull the engine to a decreased fuel situation. Even if the operator has the throttle in the idle speed position, the road wheels as the driving member can spin the engine to a point that the valves strike the piston crown, leading to mechanical failure of the engine. Therefore, caution drivers and operators about excessive road speed when going down long inclines and steep hills.

Detonation

Do not confuse the normal combustion sound within the engine for this complaint. Some engines do run louder than others, and many of them have a peculiar sound common to that particular engine or application. Pressure pulsations within the engine cylinder create the condition often referred to as *diesel knock;* it is an inherent characteristic of all diesel engines.

Experience will tune your ear to pick up sounds other than the normal combustion pressure sounds. Often it is helpful, even to an experienced mechanic, to isolate any irregular noises with the use of an engine *stethoscope,* which amplifies sounds remarkably well. A piece of welding rod or even a lead pencil placed on the engine with the other end at your ear can magnify sounds reasonably well.

If detonation occurs, check for the following conditions:

- Lube oil picked up by the air intake stream to the engine; this also causes engine overspeed.
- Low coolant temperature caused by excessive periods of idling and light-load operation or cold-weather operation without proper attention to maintaining coolant operating temperatures.
- Faulty injectors: leaking fuel, fuel spray-in pressure low

High-Horsepower Complaint

Both mechanically governed and electronically controlled diesel engines are adjusted for a specific horsepower (kW) at a specific engine speed setting. If the mechanical governor settings are tampered with, or the ECM-EEPROM settings are reprogrammed, it is possible to increase the maximum rated power output of the engine for a given application. This can cause an increase in fuel consumption, higher noise levels, and shorter engine, clutch, transmission, and driveline life. If a complaint of this nature is made, carefully check the engine power setting by running the engine on a dyno, or if in a vehicle, on a chassis dyno, to confirm the settings. The ECM options and power settings on electronic engines can be checked by accessing the ECM programming with the aid of diagnostic tooling (see Figures 18–28, 18–32, and 22–49).

Crankcase Oil Dilution

This complaint is sometimes referred to by mechanics as "the engine is making oil," meaning that the engine oil level continually rises above the full mark on the dipstick. This is generally due to fuel oil leakage from under a rocker cover fuel line connection or from leaking injector O-ring seals. Crankcase dilution of DDC two-stroke 71 and 92 series engines can be caused by overtightening of the fuel pipe retaining nuts on the injector body fuel stud. Additional fuel leakage on these engines can occur from the fuel stud that is screwed into the cylinder head. On DDC four-stroke engines, fuel leakage can occur at the injector upper seal rings (see Figure 18–22). On Cummins 14L (855 in^3), L10, MII, 15X, and Signature engines, fuel leakage can occur from O-rings (see Figure 22–71). Caterpillar electronic unit injectors have several O-rings around the body (see Figure 18–19). On the Caterpillar 3116 engine mechanical injector assembly, there is an O-ring seal on the body. On Mack engines, check the injector nozzle holder O-ring seals for signs of leakage.

To check for fuel leaks under the rocker cover, start and run the engine with the cover off, if possible. If it is not possible to run the engine, simply seal off the fuel return line from the injection pump or engine return line and apply low pressure (not to exceed normal fuel system pressure) to the system with a small priming pump. Carefully check all fuel lines and the injectors for signs of fuel leakage and correct as necessary. In some cases it may be necessary to remove the injector or nozzle holder assembly and mount it in a pop-tester. The fuel pressure can then be raised to just below the nozzle/injector release pressure; then the pop-tester valve can be closed and an inspection made for signs of fuel leakage at the suspected areas.

Piston Scuffing, Scoring, and Possible Seizure

These problems are often caused by injectors either dribbling raw fuel into the combustion chamber, due to a faulty check valve, or by a combination of water and dirt entering the injector. On multihole fuel injectors, water can blow the tip off the end of the injector. With dirt passing through the small spray-tip holes, they can become enlarged, leading to a flattening out of the fuel spray-in angle. This can create what is commonly called *wall wash,* since the fuel tends to penetrate the outer periphery of the piston crown, causing burning of the outer circumference of the piston and leading to increased piston temperatures and seizure or breakup of the fire ring. If the fuel sprays onto the cylinder wall, this creates wall wash and lube oil dilution, leading to eventual scuffing and scoring of the cylinder and piston. See Figures 8–16 through 8–21.

Engine Vibration

Misfiring cylinders as a result of low compression or faulty injectors, improper timing of individual pumping units or injectors, valves set too tight, improperly balanced cylinder banks or individual injector racks, water in the fuel, or plugged fuel filters are some of the typical causes of engine vibration. However, vibration may be caused by accessory items on the engine; if so, conduct a more thorough analysis with a vibration meter.

Compression Checks

A compression check may be necessary to determine the condition of the valves and rings. On many engines this check is done with the use of a dummy injector and with the engine running (see Figure 21–9). Each make of engine will have some variation in the sequence of events required for the compression check. Check the engine manufacturer's service manual for the routine and specifications. A crankcase pressure check conducted using a water manometer can alert you to worn rings, as can an exhaust smoke analysis, hard starting, and low power.

Dynamometers

The quickest and most effective method of determining if an engine is producing its rated horsepower is through the use of a dynamometer. A variety of load-testing machines are available for any purpose and application. Basically, they are as follows:

- A truck or bus chassis dynamometer (see Figure 24–7). The rear driving wheels of the vehicle are forced to drive against either a single or double set of rollers connected to the dynamometer. This allows road wheel horsepower to be read directly from the dyno instrument cluster or a hard copy of test results to be printed out from a computerized interface system.
- A stationary dynamometer that can have an engine coupled to either end of it for convenience. Only one engine can be tested at a time.
- A portable, compact, relatively lightweight dynamometer that can be bolted to the engine flywheel housing and driven from the engine flywheel. This type can also be readily adapted to truck applications simply by disconnecting the driveline and coupling up the dynamometer unit.

Chassis dynamometers can be a great help in testing a vehicle for engine performance if they are in good condition and used correctly. When the dynamometer is not in good condition, or a bad operating procedure is used, the result will be incorrect readings. To achieve good comparison of horsepower readings from different vehicles, use the same dynamometer with the same operator.

Manometers

One of the most effective troubleshooting tools that you can use is a set of manometers, one a water type and the other a mercury type. These can be of a solid-tube fashion mounted on a stand or cabinet fixture, which is usually more common in a shop setup. Many mechanics prefer to use a *slack tube* manometer, which is a clear, heavy-plastic tube. It is less susceptible to breakage and can be easily packed in a toolbox or service truck. Both types perform the same function. Both are known as U-tube manometers because of their shape, and they are available in sizes from 12 to 48 in. (30.48 to 122 cm), with longer units available if required. Hand-held digital models are available.

Manometers measure either a pressure or vacuum reading on the engine. This is done through a sliding scale connected to the manometer, as shown in Figure 13–38, which can be adjusted before use to a zero position. The scale is calibrated in either English or metric units or a combination of both. The scale reflects water or mercury displacement within the U-shaped tube in either inches or millimeters. Most engine manufacturers list relative specifications in their service manuals for the particular test that you wish to conduct. A typical pressure conversion chart is given in Chapter 3 for converting from inches or millimeters to either pounds per square inch (kiloPascals) or back and forth between water and mercury.

Diesel Fuel Quality Tester

Often the cause of lack of power can be attributed directly to the quality of the fuel being used in the engine. Many hours can be spent in analyzing and troubleshooting performance complaints, only to find that there is nothing out of adjustment and that the engine is mechanically sound. Remember, the wrong grade of fuel can affect the horsepower developed by the engine. To determine if diesel fuel quality should be considered as a possible problem area when diagnosing a lack-of-power complaint in an engine, use a simple *diesel fuel quality tester*—basically a hydrometer (see Figure 14–1).

TROUBLESHOOTING CHARTS

The troubleshooting charts shown in Figures 25–7 through 25–13 deal with a variety of problems related to various diesel engines that do not necessarily use the same type of fuel injection system. Specific types of fuel injection systems will exhibit particular problems related to their design that may not necessarily be reflected in the same manner in another. Some commonality does exist, however, between engines and fuel systems regardless of whether the engine is a two-stroke or four-stroke-cycle model. When using these troubleshooting charts, keep in mind that a suggested cause may not apply directly to the type of fuel injection system or engine you are dealing with.

If the engine is equipped with an electronically controlled fuel injection system, the special diagnostic equipment that can be plugged into these systems will quickly direct you to a stored trouble code in computer memory, so you can go to the system or area in which the problem lies. Keep in mind, however, that although these engines may use electronic controls, the cause of a problem may be a simple mechanical condition that would also occur in a nonelectronically equipped engine. Accept the trouble code(s) output by the computer, but also use the faculties that were discussed earlier (see Figure 25–2), and you will solve the problem or problems. Good luck in your endeavors, and keep a high standard of excellence in all your efforts.

Hard Starting

Figure 25–7 is the troubleshooting chart for hard starting.

Possible Causes and Corrections.

1. *Engine cannot be rotated.* Bar the engine over at least two complete revolutions. If the engine cannot be rotated, internal damage is indicated and the engine must be disassembled to ascertain the extent of damage and the cause.
   a. *Transmission or power takeoff (if so equipped) problem prevents crankshaft from turning.* If the crankshaft cannot be turned by hand, disconnect the transmission and power takeoff. If crankshaft now turns, find the cause of the problem in the transmission or power takeoff and make necessary corrections.
   b. *Inside problem prevents engine crankshaft from turning.* If the crankshaft cannot be turned after disconnecting the transmission and power takeoff, remove the fuel nozzles and check for fluid in the cylinders while turning the crankshaft. If fluid in the cylinders is not the problem, the engine must be disassembled to check for other inside problems. Some of these inside problems are bearing seizure, piston seizure, and valves making contact with pistons.
2. *Oil too thick for free crankshaft rotation.* Use the correct SAE grade oils for the temperatures in which the engine is operated (refer to Chapter 11). At temperatures below 32°F (0°C), it may be necessary to warm the oil for free crankshaft rotation.
   a. *Cold outside temperatures.* It may be necessary to use starting aids or to heat engine oil or coolant at temperatures below 10°F (−12°C).
3. *Battery voltage is low or nonexistent.* Check battery voltage. If battery voltage is less than 8 volts for a 12 volt system, or 16 volts for a 24 volt system, put a charge to the batteries. Recharge the battery if a light-load test indicates low or no voltage. Replace the battery if it is damaged or will not hold a charge.
4. *Terminals are damaged or corroded.* Clean or replace terminals that are damaged or corroded.
5. *Cranking system has problems.*
   a. *Bad switch, bad wiring, or bad connection in switch circuit.* With ignition switch in the START position, check the voltage at the switch connection on the starter solenoid. If there is no voltage, or of if the voltage is low at this connection, check the wiring, connections, ignition switch, and magnetic switch (if used).
   b. *Bad cable or connection—battery to starter.* With the ignition switch in the START position, check voltage at the connection of the battery cable to the starter. If there is no voltage, or if the voltage is low at this connection and there is good voltage at the battery, check for a bad cable or connection between the battery and the starter.
   c. *Bad starter solenoid.* Remove and repair a solenoid that does not work when voltage is correct at both the battery and ignition switch connections.
   d. *Bad starter motor.* If the solenoid works and the starter motor does not turn the crankshaft, the starter motor is bad. Before removing the starter motor, turn the crankshaft by hand to be sure that a mechanical failure inside the engine, transmission, or power takeoff is not preventing the crankshaft from turning. If the crankshaft turns freely by hand, engage the starter motor again. If the starter motor still will not work, remove the starter motor and repair it, or install a new starter motor.

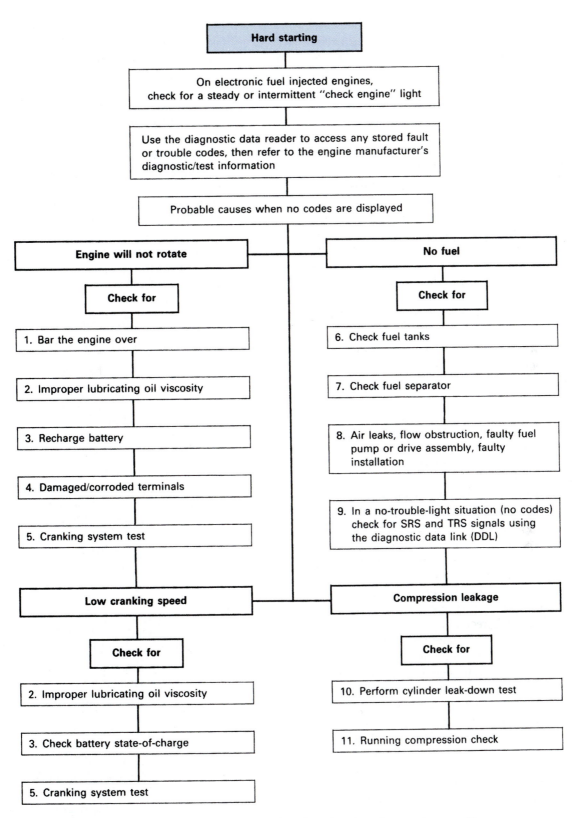

FIGURE 25–7 Sequential troubleshooting chart for a hard-starting engine condition.

e. *Extra outside loads.* Damage to the power takeoff equipment (if so equipped) and/or transmission can put extra load on the engine. This prevents free rotation of the crankshaft. To check, disconnect the transmission and power takeoff, and start the engine.

f. *Mechanical problem inside engine.* Take the engine apart and check all components for damage.

6. *Exhaust smoke cannot be seen while starting.*

a. *No fuel in tank(s).* Check fuel level visually (do not use the fuel gauge only). Be sure that the dual tank selection valve is open to the tank with fuel in it. Be sure that the valve in the fuel line between the tanks is open and/or the check valve is correctly installed.

7. *Fuel separator* (if equipped) *may have water in the bowl.*

a. *Low fuel pressure.* Change the primary and secondary fuel filters and check to make sure that the fuel lines are not plugged or damaged. If the filters or lines are not the cause, repair or replacement of the fuel transfer pump is needed.

8. *There may be air leaks, flow obstruction, faulty fuel pump, faulty fuel pump drive, or faulty installation.*

a. *Air in the fuel system.* If there is air in the fuel system, the engine will normally be difficult to start, run rough, and release a large amount of white smoke. If the engine does not start, loosen a fuel-injection-line nut at the through-the-head adapter and crank the engine until fuel comes out. Tighten the fuel-line nut. Start the engine. If the engine still does not run smooth or releases a large amount of white smoke, loosen the fuel-line nuts one at a time at the through-the-head adapters until the fuel that comes out is free of air. Tighten the fuel-line nuts. If the air cannot be removed in this way, put 5 psi (35 kPa) of air pressure to the fuel tank.

NOTE   Do not use more than 8 psi (55 kPa) of air pressure in the fuel tank, or damage to the tank may result.

Check for leakage at the connections between the fuel tank and the fuel transfer pump. If leaks are found, tighten the connections or replace the lines. If there are no visual leaks, remove the fuel supply line from the tank and connect it to an outside fuel supply. If this corrects the problem, the suction line (standpipe) inside the fuel tank has a leak.

b. *Low-quality fuel.* Remove a small amount of fuel from the tank and check for water in the fuel. If there is water in the fuel, remove fuel from the tank until it is free of water and fill with a good-quality fuel. Change the fuel filter and *prime* (remove the air and/or low-quality fuel from the fuel system) the fuel system with the fuel priming pump. If there is no water in the fuel, prime and start the engine by using an outside source of fuel. If the engine starts correctly using different fuel, remove all fuel from the tank and fill with good-quality fuel. Prime the fuel system, if necessary.

c. *No fuel from fuel injection pump.* Loosen a fuel-injection-line nut at the through-the-head adapter. With ignition switch in the ON position and accelerator in the FUEL ON position, turn the engine with the starter to be sure there is no fuel from the fuel injection pump. To find the cause for no fuel, perform the following steps—1 through 4—until the problem is corrected:

(1) Use the priming pump to make sure the fuel lines and fuel injection pump housing are full of fuel.

(2) Check the shutoff solenoid. With the ignition switch on, the plunger should be fully retracted to allow full-rack travel. Also, remove the rack position indicator cover and check to see if the fuel rack has moved to the FUEL ON position (toward the rear of the engine). This can be an indication of possible governor problems. If rack travel is restricted, replace the solenoid or repair the governor.

(3) If you are not using a good-quality fuel at temperatures below 10°F (−12°C), it is possible that the fuel in the system can *wax* (not have correct flow characteristics) and cause a restriction in the fuel system. Install a new fuel filter. It may be necessary to drain the complete fuel system and replace with a No. 1 grade of fuel.

(4) Check for fuel supply line restriction by removing the fuel supply line for the fuel filter base. Put 5 psi (35 kPa) of air pressure to the fuel tank. If there is no fuel, or only a weak flow of fuel from the fuel supply line, there is a restriction in the fuel supply line and/or the fuel tank.

d. *Check the air inlet and exhaust systems for restrictions.*

9. *Check for SRS and TRS signals using the diagnostic datalink reader on electronically equipped engines.* See Chapter 21.

10. *Perform a cylinder leak-down test* or an *engine compression check* as shown in Figure 21–9.

Abnormal Engine Operation

The troubleshooting chart for abnormal engine operation is shown in Figure 25–8.

Misfiring and Running Rough

Possible Causes and Corrections

1. *Perform a cylinder cutout test.* Refer to the engine manufacturer's diagnostic troubleshooting guide or to the information in this chapter dealing with mechanical and electronic unit injectors as well as inline pump and nozzle systems.

   a. *Air or water in fuel system.* If there is air in the fuel system, the engine will normally be difficult to start, run rough, and release a large amount of white smoke. If the engine does not start, loosen a fuel-injection-line nut at the through-the-head adapter and crank the engine until fuel comes out. Tighten the fuel-line nut. Start the engine. If the engine does not run smooth or releases a large amount of white smoke, loosen the fuel-line nuts one at a time at the through-the-head adaptors until the fuel that comes out is free of air. Tighten the fuel-line nuts. If the air cannot be removed in this way, put 5 psi (35 kPa) of air pressure to the fuel tank.

   NOTE Do not use more than 8 psi (55 kPa) of air pressure in the fuel tank, or damage to the tank may result.

   Check for leaks at the connections between the fuel tank and the fuel transfer pump. If leaks are found, tighten the connections or replace the lines. If there are no visual leaks, remove the fuel supply line from the tank and connect it to an outside fuel supply. If this corrects the problem, the suction line (standpipe) inside the fuel tank has a leak. Water in the fuel can cause rough running and possible fuel system damage.

   b. *Valve adjustment not correct.* Check and make necessary adjustments according to the engine service manual. Also check closely for a possible bent or broken pushrod.

   c. *Bad fuel nozzle(s).* Find a bad nozzle by running the engine at the rpm where it runs rough. Loosen the high-pressure fuel-line nut at the cylinder head enough to stop fuel supply to that cylinder (see Figure 25–6). Each cylinder must be checked this way. If a cylinder is found where loosening of the nut makes no difference in the rough running, remove and test the nozzle for that cylinder.

   d. *Fuel leakage from fuel-injection-line nut.* Tighten the nut to specs. Again check for leakage. Be sure to check the fuel injection lines inside the valve cover base.

   e. *Bad fuel injection pump.* An injection pump can have good fuel flow coming from it but cause rough running because of slow timing that is caused by wear on the bottom end of the plunger. Fuel pumps that are severely scored from debris can cause rough running, but fuel dilution usually occurs before horsepower is affected. Low installation torque on the fuel pump retaining nut can cause misfire, rough running, and low power.

   f. *Fuel with a high cloud point.* In cold-weather operation, this condition should be checked first. The fuel *cloud point* is the temperature at which wax begins to form in the fuel. If the atmospheric temperature is lower than the cloud point of the fuel, wax will form and plug the filter. Change the filter and drain the tank and the complete fuel system. The replacement fuel must be of a better grade with a lower cloud point.

   g. *Fuel injection timing not correct.* Check and make necessary adjustments.

   h. *Automatic timing advance not operating correctly.* Check with engine warm. Use the engine manufacturer's timing indicator

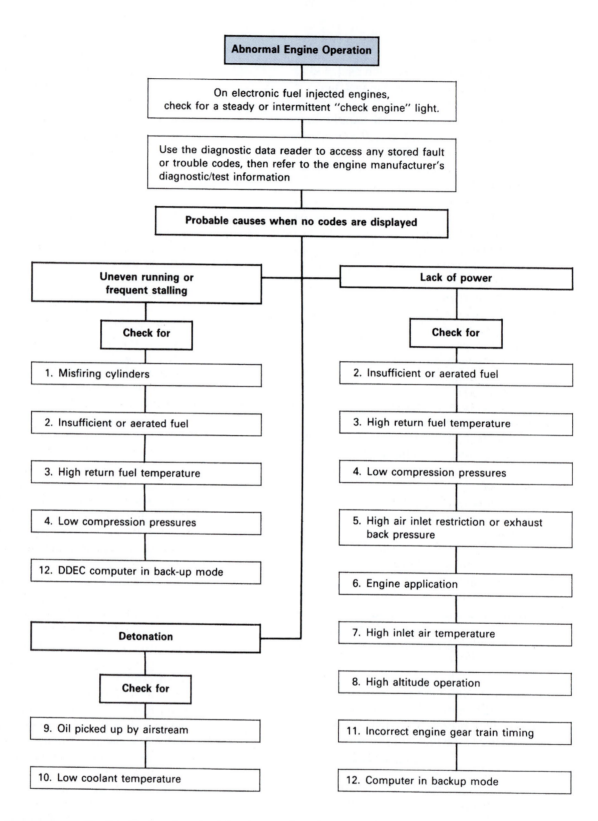

FIGURE 25–8 Troubleshooting chart for abnormal engine operation.

group. If not available, make a rapid *acceleration* (increase in speed) from low idle to high idle. Engine must have smooth acceleration. A timing advance that does not operate correctly can cause delays of the engine acceleration at some rpm before high idle, or possibly cause the engine to run rough and have exhaust noise (backfire) during acceleration. This condition is difficult to find if engine acceleration is slow or at a constant engine rpm.

i. *Fuel return line has restriction.* This condition blocks or slows the fuel flow back to the fuel tank. The result is higher fuel temperatures in the fuel injection pump housing. Also, the removal of air from the fuel is prevented. Make a visual inspection of the fuel lines and fittings for damage and make repairs or replacements as needed.

j. *Valve leakage; wear or damage to pistons and/or piston rings; wear or damage to cylinder walls.* The cylinder head will have to be removed to make a visual inspection of these inside problems.

k. *Cylinder head gasket leakage.* Leakage at the gasket of the cylinder head can show as an outside leak or can cause loss of coolant through the radiator overflow. Remove the radiator filler cap and, with the engine running, check for air bubbles in coolant caused by combustion gases.

WARNING Do *not* loosen the filler cap or pressure cap on a hot engine. Steam or hot coolant can cause severe burns.

1. *Check the throttle position sensor signal and circuit as well as the intake manifold air temperature sensor signal.*

2. *Perform a fuel flow test.* Determine if sufficient fuel quantity is being delivered. If less than the specified amount is returning, or if the fuel is aerated, check for a fuel system restriction using a mercury manometer connected to the primary fuel filter.

3. *Check the fuel spill-back temperature.* The relative fuel temperature should be less than 150°F (60°C) or a loss of horsepower may occur. Ideal fuel temperature should be between 90° and 95°F (32° to 35°C), since for every 10°F (6°C) rise in fuel temperature

above this, horsepower losses can run between 1% and 1.5%. Note that 150°F (60°C) is the allowable maximum. Continuing to operate an engine with temperatures higher than this will result in injection component damage as well as possible ECM damage.

4. *Perform a cylinder leak-down test, or perform an engine compression test (see Figure 21–9).*

5. *Check that the air inlet restriction and exhaust back pressures are within prescribed limits.* Repair or replace defective parts as necessary. Use a water manometer to check the air inlet restriction and a mercury manometer to check the exhaust back pressure.

Low-Power Complaint

When a low-power complaint is received, determine after discussions with the operator whether the lack of power is consistent or if intermittent power cutouts are the main problem. Using electronic diagnostic equipment, check that the ECM operating parameters are set according to the desired horsepower setting. On electronically controlled engines, poor electrical connections could be the cause, so check the vehicle harness and connectors, the ECM power, and ground connections. Select tooling from Figure 22–49 and check for active or historical codes in ECM memory. For either a consistent or intermittent low-power complaint, check the valve and injector settings, engine brake, fuel temperature, turbocharger boost sensor, throttle position sensor, and vehicle speed sensor signal. Perform a cylinder cutout procedure, check the fuel supply system for restrictions and correct delivery pressure, check fuel quality, perform an air-to-air aftercooler leakage test, check air inlet or exhaust restrictions.

If the low-power complaint is ongoing, and you have made all of the primary engine checks, use an engine or chassis dynamometer to save a lot of diagnostic time.

Possible Causes and Corrections

1. *High inlet air temperature.* Air coming into the engine must be cool for the engine to have full horsepower. If the air inlet system is not of correct design or is not in good mechanical condition, hot air can come into the engine, causing a loss of horsepower. Check the air inlet temperature to the engine. The engine should not be operated with a winter shield (radiator cover) in front of the intercooler. The nominal air inlet temperature should be 120°F (49°C). An approximate 1.5% power loss will be noted for each 100°F (38°C) the

inlet air temperature is above nominal. If high air inlet temperature is noted, check and clean the exterior intercooler and radiator cores. Check the fan, fan drive, and fan shroud to ensure maximum airflow is provided. To check the inlet air temperature, install a thermistor-thermometer into the engine air inlet pipe.

2. *High-altitude operation.* An engine loses horsepower with an increase in altitude. The percentage of power loss is governed by the altitude at which the engine is operated. On many current heavy-duty high-speed truck engines, there is no effect on the horsepower of the engine for the first 7500 ft (2280 m) above sea level of operation.

3. *Examine the air intake piping after the turbocharger for evidence of oil from a malfunctioning turbocharger.*

4. *Check the engine coolant temperature gauge for accuracy.* If the coolant temperature does not reach a minimum temperature of 180°F (82°C) while the engine is operating, consult the abnormal engine coolant temperature chart in this chapter.

5. *Check the engine gear train timing.* An improperly timed gear train results in a loss of power due to the valves and injectors being actuated at the wrong time in the engine operating cycle.

6. *Examine the check-engine light.* A steady check-engine light, with no codes, may indicate that the electronic control module is in the backup mode. Refer to the engine manufacturer's diagnostic troubleshooting guide.

No Fuel or Insufficient Fuel

The troubleshooting chart for no fuel or insufficient fuel is shown in Figure 25–9.

Possible Causes and Corrections

1. The fuel tank should be filled above the fuel suction (pickup) tube in the tank.

2. Perform a fuel flow test. If air is present, check all fuel lines and connections for cracks or damage. Tighten all connections. Check the fuel filters for cracks or damage, and be sure that they have been properly installed. Repair worn or broken components as necessary.

3. With all fuel lines, filters, and connections correctly installed and tightened, and air in the fuel system still present, check and/or replace questioned injectors. Faulty or incorrectly seated injectors are usually associated with a darkening of the fuel.

4. Check the restricted fitting on the fuel return line at the rear of the cylinder head for the correct size. See Figure 21–3.

5. Check the primary and secondary fuel filters for plugging. Replace as necessary.

6. Check the fuel lines for pinching, damage, obstruction, or incorrect routing. Be sure that the fuel lines are of adequate size.

7. Check for correct installation and operation of the fuel check valve or shutoff valve (if so equipped).

8. Check for fuel temperature being less than 10°F (6°C) above the pour point of the fuel.

9. Bypass the electronic control module cold plate to check for internal plugging.

10. Check the fuel pump and relief valve. Check the fuel pump drive and coupling. Repair or replace worn or damaged components as necessary.

11. In the event of a no-fuel/no-start situation and no check-engine light displayed, check for voltage at the electronic injector terminals while cranking the engine. If no voltage is present, consult the engine manufacturer's diagnostic troubleshooting guide.

High Fuel Consumption

A measurement of fuel consumption is used to check fuel system performance. If fuel consumption of an engine is within OEM specifications, the fuel system is performing correctly and no additional time should be spent checking fuel delivery.

■ *Fuel consumption.* If the specified amount of fuel is being injected into the engine, the fuel delivery specification is being met. Therefore, the basic fuel system (fuel pump and lines, transfer pump, filters, and primary fuel pressure) is within functional limits. Additional time spent troubleshooting these components is probably not justified.

■ *Fuel system timing.* Fuel cannot be burned efficiently if it is not injected into the cylinder at the correct time. Because engines develop horsepower only when they are running, timing must be measured when they are running. The static pin timing of the engine is not adequate. Timing must be measured throughout the speed range (this also checks the timing advance operation).

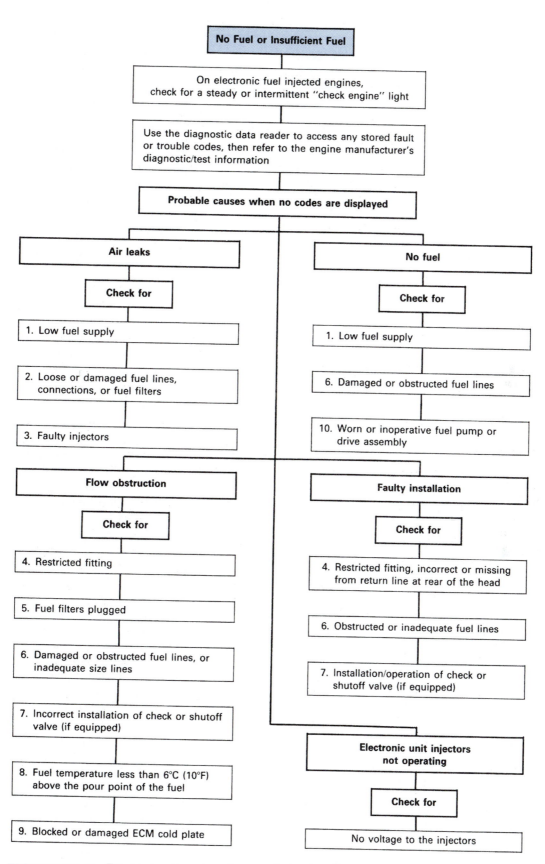

FIGURE 25–9 Troubleshooting chart for a no-fuel or insufficient-fuel condition.

- *Intake manifold pressure.* Manifold pressure is an indication of the overall health of the engine. Boost is affected by any one or all of the following: fuel consumption, compression (valve condition, piston ring condition), turbocharger performance, intake restriction (air filters), exhaust restriction (muffler), and timing.

Complaints about fuel consumption are related to engine owners' expectations. They may be related to the engine itself or causes other than the engine; in some cases, the fuel consumption may be normal for the application. Only a good discussion with the owner/operator, as described next, will guide you to a correct repair or prevent unnecessary repairs.

The following questions should be asked before beginning any diagnosis or repair for an engine performance complaint. *There are no hard and fast answers for these questions.* Many factors can cause poor fuel mileage, or make users believe they are getting poor fuel mileage. Customer expectations are also a factor. The answers to these questions will give you a better understanding and perspective on the complaint and may identify characteristics that will help pinpoint the cause of the complaint quickly.

1. *Are miles measured accurately?* A most common problem in determining mpg is errors in recording the number of miles traveled.
    a. *Is this vehicle hub or cab odometer accurate?* The easiest way to check an odometer is to install a hub odometer known to be accurate and appropriate for the tire size on the truck. Run the truck over several hundred miles and compare the reading with the reading of the original odometer. Odometers may also be checked by comparing them with interstate mile posts or by running over a course of known length—50 miles is required to get a good check.

2. *Is fuel measurement accurate?* There are a number of ways in which fuel measurement can be the source of mpg problems.
    a. *Are fuel pumps calibrated?* If fuel tickets come from company-owned fuel pumps, there can be errors because nonrevenue fuel pumps do not have calibration requirements in many states.
    b. *Are road fuel tickets accurate?* The only way to verify fuel additions when road fuel tickets are used is a laborious ticket-by-ticket audit ensuring that the correct amount of fuel has been entered for the vehicles in question and that there are no indications of incorrect entries.

NOTE   On-board vehicle computer recording devices are helpful in determining fuel consumption usage (see Figure 21–35).

3.
    a. *Is the wheel horsepower comparable?* When checking wheel horsepower, compare the horsepower ratings of competitive fleet engines; if one make of engine has more wheel horsepower or power at higher rpm, the competitive engine has an advantage.
    b. *Is the maximum vehicle speed comparable?* When you give the driver of the vehicle higher rpm and more power, it gives the vehicle the potential to go faster. The faster the truck goes, the more fuel it will burn.
    c. *Is wheel horsepower and vehicle speed higher than unit with better mpg?* If an engine is set to specifications and this does not equalize the wheel horsepower and vehicle speed, the use of an alternate lower-horsepower rating—when available for the same engine—should be considered.

4. *Are the tractor specifications comparable?* Often, a general discussion or questioning of a tractor's specifications will uncover a significant difference that leads to differences in mpg results.
    a. *Tires.* The difference in fuel efficiency between radial and bias-ply tires is well known. A vehicle or a fleet of vehicles that have bias-ply tires will have worse fuel consumption than those with radial tires. Also, tire size changes have the same effect as changes in rear end ratio.
    b. *Rear-end ratio.* One objective in choosing a rear-end (axle) ratio for optimum fuel consumption is to limit the engine rpm at the user's desired road speed. Normally, a higher ratio (lower number) will yield better fuel consumption at a given speed. In some situations, however, the higher ratio can give additional vehicle speed, which will hurt the fuel consumption if the higher potential vehicle speed is used.
    c. *Transmission ratios.* The transmission ratio difference that has the greatest effect is an overdrive transmission versus a direct transmission with the same rear end ratio. Obviously, the overdrive ratio allows the

vehicle to go faster, which can hurt mpg; but overdrives can be used to reduce average engine rpm at a low vehicle speed, which helps mpg. Therefore, the same situation exists as with rear end ratios. What can be good in one application can be bad in another. The number of gears in the transmissions can also be significant. The effect of the number of gears depends on the skill and motivation of the driver. Again, general rules do not always apply, but less skillful drivers would probably get better mpg results with 7- or 9-speed transmissions than with a 13-speed transmission. A very skillful driver may be able to get better mpg with a 13-speed transmission.

d. *Temperature-controlled fan.* A malfunctioning or poorly engineered temperature-controlled fan can be a very significant contributor to an mpg complaint. An appropriate question for all mpg complaints is, Does the temperature-controlled fan run often? If the answer to that question is yes, normally there is something wrong with the way the temperature-controlled fan is installed or engineered, or there has been a system malfunction. Normally the fan will operate about 10% of the time.

e. *Cab aerodynamics or cab style.* There can be significant differences in aerodynamics, and therefore, mpg between two cab designs. The effects are not always predictable. When cab designs of two vehicles are different, it is difficult to make comparisons or prove that engines are the source of mpg complaints.

f. *Air deflector and air deflector setting.* Use of wind screens or air deflectors is common today. Obviously, different brands of air deflectors perform differently. Also, some deflectors may be adjusted to various settings that affect their performance.

g. *Gap between back of cab and trailer.* The performance of air deflectors and the fuel consumption of tractors without deflectors are greatly influenced by the distance between the back of the cab and the front of the trailer. The wheelbase of the tractor, and therefore, distance between the back of the cab and the front of the trailer, significantly affect mpg. The closer the trailer is to the tractor, the better the mpg will be.

5. *Is the operation the same for all units?* For dump trucks, mixers, garbage trucks, and so on, variations in the operation that can be very difficult to find may have significant effects on mpg.

a. *Assigned or slip-seat drivers.* With assigned drivers, the driver's driving habits are applied to the vehicle directly. The assigned driver can be the total problem. In a slip-seat operation where different drivers drive the truck every trip, the effect of the driver on fuel consumption is essentially eliminated.

b. *Routes.* If vehicles consistently run different routes, there is an effect on mpg.

c. *Equal loads.* If one vehicle is consistently at a significantly higher gross weight than another vehicle, it will have poorer fuel consumption than the lighter unit.

d. *Assigned trailers, trailer aerodynamics, and trailer tires.* If one tractor always pulls a vertical rib trailer and another tractor always pulls a smooth-sided trailer, the tractor pulling the smooth-sided trailer has an advantage as far as fuel consumption is concerned. The same is true if one trailer has radial tires and another trailer has bias-ply tires; if one trailer is properly aligned and another is not; or if one trailer is higher than another.

e. *Operational changes and weather changes.* Some mpg complaints can result from operational changes. Moving trucks from one location to another can have a dramatic effect on fuel consumption. Changes in the weather also change fuel mileage dramatically. An industry rule of thumb of 10 to 15% loss in fuel mileage from summer to winter is a close approximation of actual results for fleets that run throughout the country.

Possible Cause and Corrections

1. *Check records used to determine fuel consumption.* Make sure that the records are accurate. The minimum period for accurate fuel records is 1 month or 10,000 miles (16,093 km). Check the tires (air pressure and size), the gap between the tractor and trailer, air deflectors, trailer width, trailer type, engine cooling fan, and driver habits.

2. *Determine minor operating faults.* To help identify a problem before a more involved troubleshooting procedure is started, follow the

procedure given in the section, "Primary Engine Checks."

3. *Fix an air/fuel ratio control that is out of adjustment or bad.*

4. *Check engine performance.* Be sure to make a record of the temperatures for inlet air, fuel (at filter base), lubricating oil, and coolant. Also, check for excessive exhaust smoke. At this point, the governor fuel settings should be verified.

5. *Replace worn fuel nozzles.* Check the horsepower on a dynamometer. Make a replacement of the fuel injection nozzles and check the horsepower output again. If there is more than 10 hp difference, the old nozzles had eroded orifices and were causing high fuel rate.

Fuel in Crankcase Oil

Possible Causes and Corrections

1. *Loose inner fuel-injection-line nut(s).* A loose fuel-injection-line nut or a bad O-ring seal on the end of the adapter inside the cylinder head can cause fuel leakage into the crankcase. Check for a bad O-ring seal and tighten nuts to specifications. On DDC engines (two-stroke models), distorted or bent fuel jumper lines or damaged pipe flared-end conditions can cause severe crankcase oil dilution.

2. *Fuel nozzle leaks.* A loose bleed screw (Cat 3406 model mechanical fuel systems) or leaking bleed screw washer will cause fuel dilution in the crankcase. Check for bad bleed screw washers or damaged bleed screw washer face. Make sure that the bleed screws are tightened to specifications.

3. On unit injectors, check for fuel leakage at the injector O-rings.

High Lubricating Oil Consumption

The troubleshooting chart for high lubricating oil consumption is shown in Figure 25–10.

NOTE   Lube oil consumption must be verified after each repair is made.

Possible Causes and Corrections

1. Check the oil dipstick, tube, and engine installation angle for proper oil level.

2. Check the air storage tanks for oil. If oil is found, check the air compressor or discharge line for oil. If oil is found, repair or replace as necessary.

3. Steam clean the engine. Start the engine and bring it to operating temperature (82°C, or 180°F). Check for oil leaks at lines, connections, mating joints, seals, and gaskets. Correct the source of the leak.

4. Check crankcase pressure. Clean the breather and recheck the pressure.

5. Check for indications of oil at the turbocharger compressor outlet and the turbine inlet to determine turbocharger oil seal leakage.

6. Remove the exhaust manifold and inspect the exhaust ports and manifolds for wetness or oil discharge. Determine if the oil appears to originate from the cylinder or around the valve stem. If the oil appears to originate from the cylinder, perform a cylinder leak-down or compression test (refer to Figure 21–9). If the oil appears to originate around the valve stem, check for worn or damaged valve stem seals or excessive clearance between the valve stem and valve guide.

7. Pressure test the cooling system. Inspect the coolant for lube oil contamination and the lubricating oil for coolant contamination. Pressure test the oil cooler core. If contamination is found, correct the source and clean the affected system.

8. Perform a cylinder leak-down test as outlined. If the cylinder pressure is below the recommended minimum, listen for air leakage at the oil filler tube, intake manifold, or turbocharger exhaust outlet. Also look for bubbles in the engine coolant. Excessive leakage heard at the oil filler tube indicates worn or damaged cylinder kit components. Removal of the cylinder head is necessary to determine and correct the cause.

9. If the cylinder kits are worn, check the engine air intake system for a possible source of contaminated air entrance.

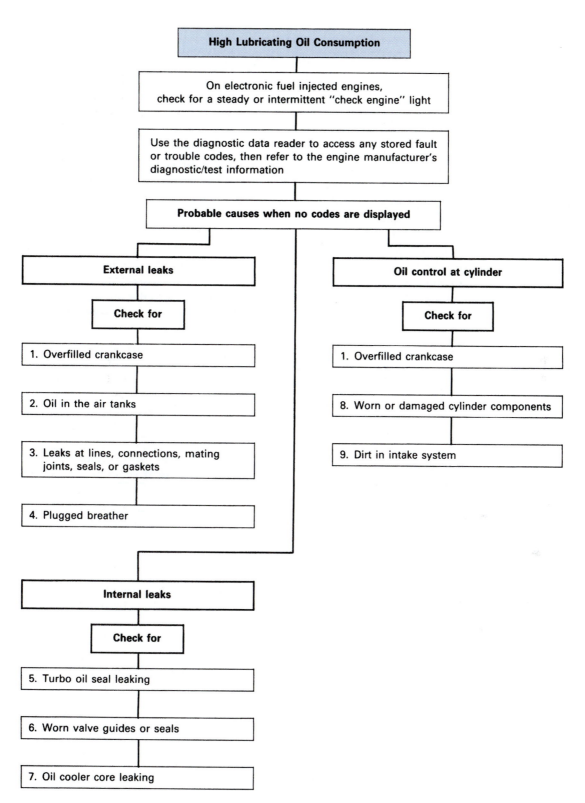

FIGURE 25–10 Troubleshooting chart for a high lube oil consumption condition.

Excessive Crankcase Pressure

The troubleshooting chart for excessive crankcase pressure is shown in Figure 25–11.

Possible Causes and Corrections

1. Clean and repair or replace breather assembly.

2. Perform a cylinder leak-down or compression test (see Figure 21–9). If the cylinder pressure is below recommended minimum, listen for air leakage at the oil fill tube, intake manifold, or the turbocharger exhaust outlet. Also look for bubbles in the engine coolant at the radiator. Leakage heard at the oil fill tube indicates worn or damaged cylinder kit components. Removal of the cylinder head is necessary to verify. Bubbles in the radiator coolant indicate a leaking head gasket or damaged cylinder head. Valve leakage could

be indicated by air leakage heard at the intake manifold or turbocharger exhaust outlet.

3. Check the exhaust back pressure. Repair or replace the muffler and/or piping if an obstruction is found or it is determined that the piping is too small, too long, or has too many bends.

Low Oil Pressure

The troubleshooting chart for low oil pressure is shown in Figure 25–12.

Possible Causes and Corrections

1. Check the engine oil level. Bring it to the proper level on the dipstick. Ensure the proper engine installation angle.

2. Be sure the correct lubricating oil is being used. Refer to the service manual for recommended grade and viscosity.

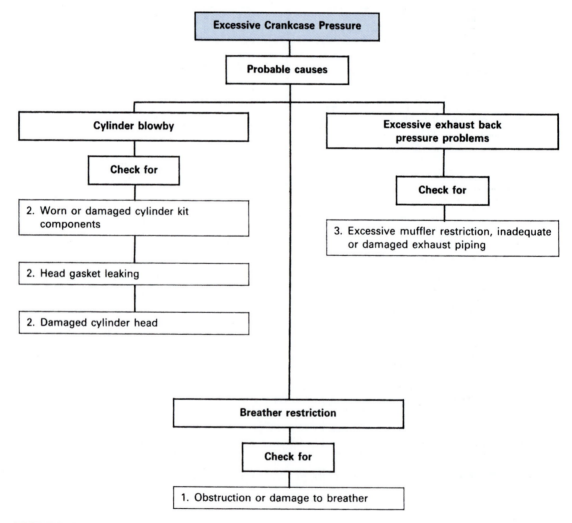

FIGURE 25–11   Troubleshooting chart for excessive crankcase pressure problem.

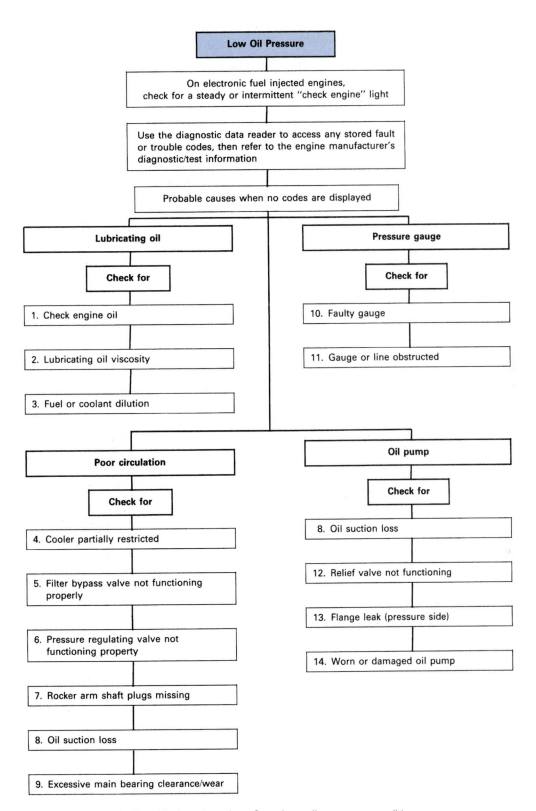

FIGURE 25–12 Troubleshooting chart for a low oil pressure condition.

783

3. Pressurize the appropriate system (fuel or coolant) and closely examine components for leakage. After completing the checks, bar the engine over at least two revolutions (by hand) to ensure against possible hydrostatic lock.

4. A plugged oil cooler is indicated by excessively high lubricating oil temperature. Remove and clean the oil cooler core.

5. Remove the bypass valve from the oil filter adapter. Clean and inspect the valve, valve spring, and bore. Replace worn or damaged parts. Always replace the copper washer whenever the adapter plug is removed.

6. Remove the pressure regulator valve. Clean and inspect the valve, valve body, and spring. Replace any worn or damaged parts.

7. Check for missing plugs at each end of the rocker shafts. Replace any missing plugs.

8. Remove, clean, and inspect the oil pickup tube and screen assembly. If cracked or damaged, repair or replace the assembly. Always use a new pickup tube flange-to-oil pump gasket upon reassembly.

9. Inspect the crankshaft main bearings for wear and/or correct clearance.

10. Check the oil pressure with a reliable gauge. Replace the oil pressure gauge if it is faulty.

11. Remove and clean the oil gauge line and gauge orifice.

12. Remove, clean, and inspect the pressure relief valve. Clean and inspect the valve, valve body, and spring. Replace any worn or damaged parts.

13. Remove the oil pump-to-cylinder block tube assembly. Clean and inspect the assembly for cracks or damage. Also inspect the flanges for flatness of the mating surface. Always use new gaskets upon reassembly.

14. Remove the oil pump assembly. Clean and inspect the pump for wear or damage. Replace all worn or damaged parts.

Cooling System

The troubleshooting chart for the cooling system is shown in Figure 25–13.

Overheating

Possible Causes and Corrections

1. *Low coolant level.* If the coolant level is too low, not enough coolant will go through the en-gine and radiator. This lack of coolant will not take enough heat from the engine, and there will not be enough flow of coolant through the radiator to release the heat into the cooling air. Low coolant level is caused by leaks or under filling of the radiator. With the engine cool, be sure that coolant can be seen at the low end of the fill neck on the radiator top tank. Check the coolant level. The coolant should be within 2 in. of the radiator filler neck (if coolant is low, and no fault or trouble code is logged, refer to the diagnostic troubleshooting guide for the particular make of engine).

   a. *Bad temperature gauge.* A temperature gauge that does not work correctly will not show the correct temperature. If the temperature gauge shows that the coolant temperature is too hot but other conditions are normal, either install a gauge that you know is functioning properly or check the cooling system with a thermistor-thermometer tool.

2. *Poor circulation*

   a. *Dirty radiator.* Check the radiator for debris between the fins of the radiator core, which prevents free airflow through the core. Check the radiator for debris, dirt, or deposits on the inside of the radiator core; this prevents free flow of coolant through the radiator. Clean the exterior of the radiator and intercooler to remove dirt and debris; this will permit complete airflow. If so equipped, remove the front winter shield (radiator cover). Some engines should not be operated with a winter shield in front of the intercooler. Check for damaged, incorrectly positioned, or inadequate shrouding. Check for an incorrectly sized radiator.

   b. *Shunt-line restriction.* A restriction of the shunt line from the radiator top tank to the engine front cover, or a shunt line not installed correctly, will cause a reduction in water pump efficiency. The result will be low coolant flow and overheating.

   c. *Air inlet restriction.* Restriction of the air coming into the engine causes high cylinder temperatures and more than normal amount of heat to pass to the cooling system. Check for a restriction with a water manometer or a vacuum gauge (which measures in inches of water). Connect the

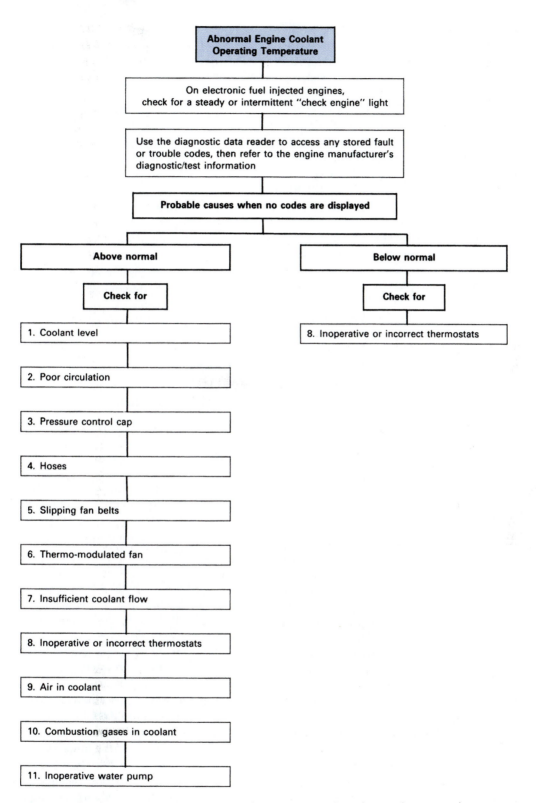

FIGURE 25–13 Troubleshooting chart for an abnormal engine coolant operating temperature condition.

gauge to the engine air inlet between the air cleaner and the inlet to the turbocharger. With the gauge installed, run the engine at full-load rpm and check the restriction. Maximum restriction of the air inlet varies between 20 and 30 in. of water. If the indication is higher than the maximum permissible restriction, remove the dirt from the filter element, or install a new filter element and check the restriction again. If the indication is still too high, there must be a restriction in the inlet piping.

d. *Exhaust restriction.* Restriction in the exhaust system causes high cylinder temperatures and a higher than normal amount of heat to pass to the cooling system. To see if there is an exhaust restriction, make a visual inspection of the system. Check for damage to piping or for a bad muffler. If no damage is found, check the system for back pressure from the exhaust (pressure difference measurement between exhaust outlet and atmosphere). The back pressure must not be more than the engine manufacturer's specs. You can also check the system by removing the exhaust pipes from the exhaust manifolds. With the exhaust pipes removed, start and run the engine to see if the problem is corrected.

e. *High outside temperature.* When outside temperatures are too high for the rating of the cooling system, there is not enough temperature difference between the outside air and coolant temperatures. To get better cooling, use the truck in a lower gear.

f. *Operating at high altitude.* The cooling capacity of the cooling system goes down as the truck is used at higher altitudes. A system, under pressure, large enough to keep the coolant from boiling must be used.

g. *Engine used in a lug condition. Lugging* (means the truck is used in a gear too high for engine rpm to go up as the accelerator pedal is pushed farther down, or the truck is used in a gear where engine rpm goes down with the accelerator pedal at maximum travel). Lugging the engine causes the engine rpm and fan rpm to be low.

This low rpm causes a reduction in airflow through the radiator and a reduction in the flow of coolant through the system. This combination of less air and less coolant flow during high input of fuel causes above normal heating.

h. *Fuel injection timing not correct.* Check and make necessary adjustments as described in the testing and adjusting section of the appropriate service manual.

i. *Transmission problems.* Powershift or automatic transmissions that are cooled by the engine cooling system can cause above normal heating if they are out of adjustment or not working correctly. See the transmission service manual for the correct adjustments.

j. *Radiator too small.* A radiator that is too small does not have enough area to release the heat to the cooling air. This causes the engine to run at higher than normal temperatures. Make sure that the radiator size is in accord with the recommendations of the truck manufacturer.

3. *Pressure control cap.* Check for an inoperative or incorrect pressure control cap.

4. *Bad hose(s).* Inspect the cooling system for any soft, deteriorated, or collapsed hoses. Replace any suspected hoses. Bad hoses with leaks normally can be seen. Hoses that have no visual leaks can "collapse" (pull together) during operation and cause a restriction in the flow of coolant. Hoses become soft and/or get cracks after a period of time, and they must be changed after specific miles or time. The inside can become loose, and the loose particles of the hose can cause a restriction in the flow of coolant.

5. *Loose belt(s).* Loose fan or water pump belts will cause a reduction in air or water flow. Adjust the fan drive belts to the correct tension to prevent slippage. Replace any damaged, frayed, glazed, or worn belts.

a. *A wrong fan, a fan or shroud not in correct position.* A wrong fan, or a fan or shroud in a wrong position, will cause a reduction or a loss of airflow through the radiator. The fan must be large enough to send air through most of the area of the radiator core. Make sure that the fan size, fan shroud, and position of fan and shroud are in accord with the recommendations of the truck manufacturer.

    b. *Not enough airflow through radiator because of restriction in engine compartment.* The airflow through the radiator comes into the engine compartment. Make sure that the filters, air conditioners, and similar items are not installed in a way that prevents free flow of air into and out of the engine compartment.

6. *Inoperative fan clutch.* Repair or replace an inoperative fan.

7. *Insufficient coolant flow.* Check the flow of coolant through the radiator. Clean the cooling system with a good cooling system cleaner and thoroughly flush the system to remove all scale deposits.

8. *Thermostats.* Remove, inspect, and test the thermostats for correct operation. Replace any thermostats that are not operating properly. Always replace the thermostat seals in the housing whenever the thermostats are removed. See Chapter 12.

    a. *Bad water temperature regulators.* A regulator that does not open, or opens only part of the way, can cause above normal heating.

    b. *Shutters not opening correctly.* Check the opening temperature of the shutters. The shutters must be completely closed at a temperature below the fully open temperature of the water temperature regulators. Also, verify that fan control switches on viscous fans are operating correctly.

9. *Air in the cooling system.* Air can get into the cooling system in different ways. The most common causes are not filling the cooling system correctly and combustion gas leaking into the system. Combustion gas can get into the system through inside cracks or bad cylinder head gaskets. Air in the cooling system causes a reduction in coolant flow and bubbles in the coolant. Air bubbles hold coolant away from engine parts, preventing heat flow. Check for the presence of air in the cooling system. The presence of air or gases in the cooling system may be detected by connecting a rubber hose from the overflow pipe and submerging the other end in a container of water. Another method is inserting a section of clear, thick-wall Pyrex tube between the thermostat housing and the top radiator hose and observing for bubbles. If bubbles are present, check for leaks on the suction side of the water pump.

    Air in the cooling system can also be found by the *bottle test.* The equipment needed to make this test is a pint bottle, a bucket of water, and a hose that fits the end of the overflow pipe of the radiator. Before testing, make sure that the cooling system is filled correctly. Use a wire to hold the relief valve in the radiator cap open. Install the radiator cap and tighten it. Put the hose over the end of the overflow pipe. Start the engine and operate it at high idle rpm for a minimum of 5 minutes after the engine is at normal operating temperature. Use a cover on the radiator core to keep the engine at operating temperature. After 5 or more minutes at operating temperature, place the loose end of the hose in the bottle filled with water. Put the bottle in the bucket of water with the top down. If the water gets out of the bottle in less than 40 seconds, there is too much exhaust gas leakage into the cooling system. Find the cause of the air or gas getting into the cooling system and correct as necessary.

10. *Gases in coolant.* If no leaks were detected in step 9, and bubbles remain present, perform a cylinder leak-down test.

11. *Bad water pump.* Check the water pump for a loose or damaged impeller. A water pump with a loose impeller does not pump enough coolant for correct engine cooling. A loose impeller can be found by removing the water pump and by pushing the shaft backward and pulling it forward. If the impeller has no damage, check the impeller clearance.

Overcooling

Possible Causes and Corrections

1. *Long idle periods.* When the engine is running with no load, only a small quantity of fuel is burned and engine heat is removed too quickly.

2. *Very light load.* Very light loads and a very slow speed or downhill travel can cause overcooling because of the low heat input of the

engine. The installation of shutters helps to correct this condition.

3. *Bad water temperature regulators.* A regulator that is stuck open (will not move to the closed position) will cause overcooling. A thermostat that is stuck between the open and closed positions, or opens only part of the way, can cause overcooling when the truck has a light load. Also, coolant leaks around the thermostat, such as vent lines, can cause overcooling.

Loss of Coolant

Outside Leaks

Possible Causes and Corrections

1. *Leaks in hoses or connections.* Check all hoses and connections for visual signs of leakage. If no leaks are seen, look for damage to hoses or loose clamps.
2. *Leaks in the radiator and/or expansion tank.* Put pressure to the radiator and/or expansion tank with the cooling system pressurizing pump and check for leaks.
3. *Leaks in the heater.* Put pressure to the cooling system with the cooling system pressurizing pump and check the heater for leaks.
4. *Leaks in the water pump.* Check the water pump for leaks before starting the engine; then start the engine and look for leaks. If there are leaks at the water pump, repair or install a new water pump.
5. *Cylinder head gasket leakage.* Look for leaks along the surface of the cylinder head gasket. If you see leaks, install a new head gasket.

Coolant Leaks at the Overflow Tube

Possible Causes and Corrections

1. *Bad pressure cap or relief valve.* Check the sealing surfaces of the pressure cap and the radiator to be sure that the cap is sealing correctly. Check the opening pressure and sealing ability of the pressure cap or relief valve with the cooling system pressurizing pump.
2. *Engine runs too hot.* If coolant temperature is too high, pressure will be high enough to move the cap off of the sealing surface in the radiator and cause coolant loss through the overflow tube.

3. *Expansion tank too small or installed incorrectly.* The expansion tank can be a part of the radiator or it can be installed separately from the radiator. The expansion tank must be large enough to hold the expansion of the coolant as it gets warm or has sudden changes in pressure. Make sure that the expansion tank is installed correctly and that the size is in accord with the recommendations of the truck manufacturer.
4. *Cylinder head gasket leakage or crack(s) in cylinder head or cylinder block.* Remove the radiator cap and, with the engine running, look for air bubbles in the coolant. Bubbles in the coolant are a sign of probable leakage at the head gasket. Remove the cylinder head from the engine. Check the cylinder head, cylinder walls, and head gasket surface of the cylinder block for cracks. When the head is installed, use a new head gasket, spacer plate gasket, water seals, and O-ring seals.

Inside Leakage

Possible Causes and Corrections

1. *Cylinder head gasket leakage.* If the cylinder head gasket leaks between a water passage and an opening into the crankcase, coolant will get into the crankcase.
2. *Crack(s) in the cylinder head.* Crack(s) in the upper surface of the cylinder head, or an area between a water passage and an opening into the crankcase, can allow coolant to get into the crankcase.
3. *Crack(s) in the cylinder block.* Crack(s) in the cylinder block between a water passage and the crankcase will let coolant get into the crankcase.

Inline Pumps

High-pressure inline multiple-plunger fuel injection pump systems can exhibit symptoms that are unique to their particular design characteristics. Much of the information contained in this chapter can be applied to general troubleshooting techniques for these types of pumps manufactured by companies such as Robert Bosch, Zexel USA, Nippondenso, Delphi Automotive, Lucas, and licensees of these manufacturers. Many light-, medium-, and heavy-duty diesel engines today employ inline pumps. Table 25–2 lists typical problems, possible causes, and corrections to consider when you are troubleshooting.

TABLE 25–2 Diagnostic troubleshooting of a PLN (pump-line-nozzle) system

Problem	Possible causes	Correction
Hard starting	1. Empty fuel tank 2. Blocked fuel vent 3. Air in the fuel system 4. Misadjusted stop cable 5. Plugged fuel filter 6. Broken or restricted injection lines 7. Incorrect injection timing 8. Low compression 9. Internal injection pump problem 10. Incorrect valve adjustment 11. Glow plugs not operating properly	1. Fill tank and prime the fuel system. 2. Clean the fuel vent. 3. Bleed the fuel system. 4. Adjust the cable. 5. Replace the filter. 6. Replace injection lines. 7. Time the injection pump. 8. Do a compression test. 9. Remove the injection pump and have it serviced by an authorized dealer. 10. Adjust valves. 11. Check for current flow.
Surge at idle	1. Blocked fuel vent 2. Air in the system from loose connections 3. Idle speed misadjusted 4. Governor defective or misadjusted 5. Injection pump not operating properly 6. Cold engine oil affecting the governor	1. Clean the fuel vent. 2. Repair the loose fittings. Bleed the fuel system. 3. Adjust the idle speed. 4. Remove the injection pump and have it serviced by an authorized dealer. 5. Remove the injection pump and have it serviced by an authorized dealer. 6. Run the engine until the oil warms up.
Rough idle	1. Air in the fuel system 2. Injector nozzle not working 3. Wrong firing order or misrouted injection line 4. Low or uneven engine compression 5. Misadjusted fuel injection pump	1. Bleed the fuel system. 2. Replace the nozzle. 3. Correct to the right firing order. 4. Perform a compression test. 5. Remove the injection pump and have it serviced by an authorized dealer.
Incorrect idle speed or no-load high idle	1. Low idle not adjusted 2. No-load high idle not adjusted 3. Governor not working properly 4. Accelerator linkage out of adjustment	1. Adjust the low idle. 2. Adjust no-load high idle. 3. Remove the injection pump and have it serviced by an authorized dealer. 4. Adjust the accelerator linkage.
Engine misses under load	1. Blocked fuel vent 2. Air in the fuel system 3. Plugged fuel filter 4. Plugged injection line 5. Incorrect injection timing 6. Injection nozzle not working 7. Injection pump not operating properly	1. Clean the fuel vent. 2. Bleed the fuel system. 3. Replace the fuel filter. 4. Replace the injection line. 5. Time the injection pump. 6. Replace the nozzle. 7. Remove the injection pump and have it serviced by an authorized dealer.
Low power	1. Plugged fuel filter 2. Leaking or restricted injection lines 3. Incorrect injection timing 4. Injection nozzle not working 5. Restricted air filter 6. Incorrect firing order 7. Fuel pump timing assembly gear not working 8. Incorrect valve adjustment 9. Injection pump not working properly 10. Accelerator linkage not adjusted properly	1. Replace the fuel filter. 2. Replace injection lines. 3. Time the injection pump. 4. Replace the nozzle. 5. Replace the air filter. 6. Correct to the proper firing order. 7. Replace the timing assembly. 8. Adjust valves. 9. Remove the injection pump and have it serviced by an authorized dealer. 10. Adjust linkage.
Excessive fuel consumption	1. Incorrect injection timing 2. Leaking injection lines 3. Restricted air filter 4. Low idle speed 5. Fuel pump timing assembly gear not working 6. Governor not working	1. Time the injection pump. 2. Replace the injection line and test the nozzle. 3. Replace the air filter. 4. Adjust the idle speed. 5. Replace the timing assembly. 6. Remove the injection pump and have it serviced by an authorized dealer.

(continued)

TABLE 25–2 (continued).

Problem	Possible causes	Correction
Black smoke	1. Air in the fuel system 2. Leaking or restricted injection line 3. Incorrect injection timing 4. Leaking injection nozzle 5. Restricted air filter 6. Incorrect firing order 7. Timing gear in full advance 8. Low compression 9. Injection pump or governor adjusted improperly 10. Incorrect valve adjustment	1. Bleed the fuel system. 2. Replace the injection line. 3. Time the injection pump. 4. Test and replace the nozzle if necessary. 5. Replace the air filter. 6. correct to the proper firing order. 7. Replace the time gear. 8. Do a compression test. 9. Remove the injection pump and have it serviced by an authorized dealer. 10. Adjust valves.
White or blue smoke	1. Air in the fuel system 2. Plugged fuel filter 3. Leaking or restricted injection lines 4. Incorrect injection timing 5. Incorrect firing order 6. Fuel pump timing gear assembled incorrectly 7. Injection pump or governor not adjusted properly 8. Incorrect valve adjustment	1. Bleed the fuel system 2. Replace the fuel filter. 3. Replace injection line. 4. Time the injection pump. 5. Correct to the proper firing order. 6. Replace the gear. 7. Remove the injection pump and have it serviced by an authorized dealer. 8. Adjust valves.

SUMMARY

The information and suggestions in this chapter are designed to provide you with the capability to logically trace and troubleshoot problems with internal combustion diesel engines. To become an effective troubleshooter, learn to begin with a systematic and analytical procedure as per the suggestions in Figure 25–1. Follow carefully your thought processes shown in Figure 25–2 before you open your tool box. Don't make rash decisions based on insufficient tell-tale signs. To be an effective diagnostic technician, you must understand completely how a system or component functions and operates, and how it interacts with other parts and components of a system. In electronically controlled engines, check all of the stored fault codes stored in ECM memory. Don't be embarrassed to use the OEM Service and troubleshooting manuals at your disposal. Equipment downtime is money lost, therefore an accurate and efficient diagnoses as to the cause or causes of an existing fault is your goal and objective as soon as possible. Once a fault has been corrected, double check that the repair conducted has in fact cured the specific problem. Failure to road test a vehicle or to put an engine and piece of equipment through a number of cycles, may result in an unhappy customer returning to your facility. Maintain standards of excellence in all that you do, but even more so when troubleshooting, diagnosing and repairing a fault condition.

SELF-TEST QUESTIONS

1. Technician A says that self-control and reason are two of the most important faculties to use when faced with an irate customer during a troubleshooting problem. Technician B says that your sense of vision, hearing, smell, and touch are the four most important faculties that you possess. Who is correct here?

2. Technician A says that a slobbering exhaust is usually caused by unburned raw fuel after initial engine startup from cold and that it will usually clear up within a 5 minute time period. Technician B feels that a slobbering exhaust is indicative of worn piston or turbocharger seal rings, allowing oil to enter the exhaust stream. Who is correct here?

3. If an engine is to be idled for longer than 5 minutes, technician A feels that it should be shut off. Technician B says that as long as there is no slobbering at the exhaust, the engine can be left idling for any length of time with no problems. Who is correct?

4. True or False: Electronically equipped engines can be fitted with automatic 3 to 100 minute idle shutdown timers.

5. Technician A says that a lack of power complaint can best be diagnosed by monitoring the exhaust smoke color for possible clues. Technician B says that you should first check the maximum no-load (high idle) engine speed setting. Who is right?

6. Technician A says that white smoke at the exhaust stack after starting a diesel truck engine, particularly in cold ambient conditions, may be due to a leaking cylinder

head gasket, which as the engine warms up will expand and seal. Technician B says that this is a natural phenomenon caused by unburned fuel droplet hydrocarbons. Who is correct?

7. Technician A says that exhaust smoke cannot exceed 5% capacity under any operating condition, whereas technician B says that the U.S. EPA stipulates acceptable smoke limits under a variety of conditions that include full-load acceleration, transient response under load, and lug-down conditions. Who is right?

8. Technician A says that black exhaust smoke is an indication of using the improper grade of diesel fuel. Technician B says that it can only be caused by air starvation (plugged air filter element). Who is correct here?

9. Technician A says that blue exhaust smoke indicates that the piston rings or intake valve guides are worn. Technician B says that this could be caused by leaking turbocharger seals. Who is right?

10. Technician A says that the best way in which to determine if the piston rings are worn on a two-stroke-cycle DDC engine is to remove the airbox inspection covers and check the condition of the rings. Technician B says that the type and design of the engine may require a leak-down check. Who is correct?

11. Technician A says that a compression check on all diesel engines should be performed with a dummy injector and the engine running at an idle speed. Technician B disagrees, saying that a compression check will differ between makes of engines. Who is correct?

12. Technician A feels that if an engine lacks power and there is no unusual color exhaust smoke, the problem is more than likely restriction of fuel flow. Technician B, on the other hand, believes that this condition could be due to misadjusted throttle linkage, which does not allow full-rack travel. Who might be right here?

13. Technician A says that when diesel fuel filter plugging occurs in cold weather, it is due to using a fuel with too low a pour point. Technician B disagrees, saying that the problem is caused by using fuel with not a low enough cloud point for the ambient temperature encountered. Who understands fuel theory?

14. Technician A says that an engine that reaches its maximum no-load (high idle) rpm but then dies when a load is applied to it is more than likely experiencing fuel starvation. Technician B says that this condition is due to a faulty governor. Who is correct?

15. An engine performs well until it has been working under load for some time; then starts to lose power, particularly in warm-weather operation. Technician A believes that this situation could be caused by the fuel becoming too hot. Technician B says that it is probably due to a sticking fuel rack when hot. Who do you think might be right here?

16. An engine performs well with a full tank of fuel, but it loses power toward the end of the daily shift as the fuel level drops in the tank. Technician A says that this could be caused by water vapor through condensation of the warm air in the tank. Technician B believes that it is more likely due to a piece of floating debris aligning itself with the fuel pickup tube as the fuel drops. Who do you think is correct?

17. Technician A says that failure of the engine to obtain its maximum no-load speed rpm is probably due to a fuel system restriction, whereas Technician B says that the throttle linkage may be in need of adjustment. Who is right?

18. Technician A says that if an engine fails to crank or cranks too slowly, the cause could be a low battery. Technician B says it could be a no-voltage condition at the starter solenoid. Who might be right here?

19. An engine cranks over satisfactorily on the starter motor but fails to start and there is no smoke from the exhaust stack. Technician A says that the problem is more than likely no fuel in the tank. Technician B feels that the problem is probably caused by a faulty electrical fuel solenoid assembly that does not allow the fuel to flow. Who is right?

20. The reason an engine is hard to start may be the intake and exhaust valves being adjusted incorrectly, according to technician A's theory, since exhaust smoke is present at the stack. Technician B says this theory is wrong. Who is right?

21. Air in the fuel system could result in an engine starting but not continuing to run according to Technician A. Technician B says that the engine would not start at all if air was present in the fuel system. Who is correct?

22. Technician A says that a rough idle on a warm engine could be the result of one or more cylinders losing compression. Technician B says that this could not be the cause; otherwise, the engine would fail to start. Who is correct here?

23. An engine that surges at idle could be due to an incorrectly adjusted buffer screw or bumper spring according to technician A. Not so says technician B, who thinks that this condition is more likely caused by air in the fuel system. Who is correct?

24. Engine misfire can be caused by low compression in one or more cylinders, according to technician A. Technician B says that it would be due to incorrect valve adjustment. Who is right?

25. Technician A says failure of an engine to reach rated speed under load could be caused by the throttle linkage being out of adjustment. Technician B says that this is not possible, since the governor will always ensure that full fuel is obtained. Who is correct?

26. Technician A says that a low-power complaint can be caused by an air leak between the turbocharger and exhaust manifold, whereas technician B says that an air leak between the turbocharger and intake manifold would result in low boost and therefore low power. Who is right?

27. Technician A says that a high intake air temperature will cause a low-power complaint in warm weather. Techni-

cian B says that low power will occur only when intake air temperatures are low, such as when operating below 32°F (0°C). Who understands theory of combustion?

28. Technician A says that excessive white smoke at idle can be caused by poor fuel quality and you can check it by using a portable fuel quality tester similar to a hydrometer. Technician B says that you should verify this possibility by operating the engine from a temporary fuel tank that contains a known, good-quality fuel. Whose advice will you follow?

29. Technician A says that excessive exhaust smoke that occurs only under load could be due to a plugged air cleaner. Technician B says that if the air cleaner were plugged, smoke would occur under both a no-load and a full-load condition. Who is correct in this instance?

30. True or False: Excessive black smoke under load could be caused by a faulty turbocharger (air leak).

31. An engine that fails to shut off when the ignition key switch is turned OFF could be caused by a faulty electric fuel shutdown solenoid, according to technician A. Technician B thinks that it could also be caused by an external source of fumes or oil pullover. Does technician B's statement have any validity here?

32. Technician A says that a compression or fuel knock in the engine can be caused by air in the fuel system. Technician B does not believe that air in the fuel system could cause such a condition. Who is correct?

33. Technician A says that air in the fuel system usually reflects itself as a rough-running engine, a stumble at idle, failure to accelerate smoothly, and a lack of power under load. Technician B says that air in the system creates nothing more than a fuel knock. Who is right?

34. Technician A says that low fuel delivery can be caused by plugged fuel filters or an air leak on the suction side of the system. Technician B says that this condition could only be caused by a fuel leak on the pressure side of the system. Is technician B totally correct?

35. Technician A says that to quickly determine the condition of a low-power complaint on a DDC engine with no unusual exhaust smoke color, you should monitor the fuel pressure at the secondary fuel filter. Technician B believes that a fuel spill-back check would be more appropriate. Whose advice will you take?

36. Technician A says that to conduct a fuel system restriction check, you should connect a mercury manometer to the suction side of the fuel system as close as possible to the transfer pump. Technician B says that you should connect it to the secondary fuel filter. Who is right here?

37. Technician A says that an engine that is out of time may result in higher exhaust temperatures. Technician B says that it is liable to cause possible preignition, uneven running, and a loss of power. Who is correct?

38. Technician A says that high exhaust back pressure can result in white exhaust smoke. Technician B says that it will cause a loss of engine power and a tendency for gray to black smoke. Who is right?

39. When setting the injector timing height on DDC engines, technician A says that using a longer pin than necessary will result in retarded ignition timing. Technician B says that it will result in advanced ignition timing. Who is correct?

40. Technician A says that a popping sound at the exhaust stack is most likely caused by a burned exhaust valve, whereas technician B leans more toward a burned intake valve. Who is right here?

41. Technician A says that air inlet restriction can be monitored and measured with a water manometer. Technician B says that you should use a mercury manometer. Whose advice will you follow?

42. Technician A says that turbocharger boost pressure should be monitored and checked by using a mercury manometer, whereas technician B says that you should use a water manometer. Who is right here?

43. Technician A says that you should always check exhaust back pressure by using a mercury manometer, but technician B says that you should use a water manometer. Who is right?

44. Technician A says to check crankcase pressure by using a water manometer. Technician B says to use a mercury manometer. Which manometer will you use?

26 Batteries, Alternators, and Starter Motors

Overview

Today's and tomorrow's service technicians must have a solid foundation in electrical concepts in addition to understanding the fundamentals of electronics systems. Space limitations within this book do not permit individual chapters dealing with the detailed fundamentals and operation of basic electricity and electronics. The intent here is to build upon your prerequisite knowledge of these two areas and to be capable of applying this information to the service and diagnosis of batteries, alternator charging systems, and electric starter motors. In this chapter we describe the purpose, function, operation, and testing/diagnosis of these three main interactive components of the diesel engine electrical system. Part A of this chapter will deal with the battery system which provides the power to crank the engine and also to handle the load draw of the various electrical components and accessories. In Part B, the alternator charging system generates the electricity required to maintain the battery in a full state of charge. In Part C, the electric starter motor functions to spin the crankshaft over at a high enough speed to initiate combustion in order to necessitate starting of the engine. After reading the information within this chapter, and performing the various hands-on tasks related to these three systems in conjunction with a review of the end-of-chapter questions, you should have developed and acquired the skills necessary to challenge either the ASE or TQ test areas.

> **NOTE** Within the introductory chapter of this book you will find a listing of the various content areas and skills tasks for the different ASE certification tests that ASE offers to improve the skills of technicians. You can also download copies of ASE's preparation guides from their own respective website (www.asecert.org).

PART A: BATTERIES

Within the ASE medium/heavy trucks tests preparation guide dealing with diesel engines, test T2, the various subheadings deal with a number of content tasks lists. In subheading G, Starting Systems Diagnosis and Repair, the tasks lists make reference to inspecting, testing, and charging of batteries. Successful operation of both the starter motor and electrical system loads depends upon maintaining the batteries in a full-state-of-charge condition.

BATTERIES

The electricity produced in the charging system must be stored for use during starting. This job is handled by the battery. Batteries used in diesel-powered equipment are lead acid batteries and may be of three different types: conventional, low maintenance, and maintenance free.

Battery Construction

Lead acid batteries are made up of cells that are separated from each other by compartments (Figure 26–1). Each individual cell contains negative and positive plates separated by porous separators and electrolyte (a mixture of water and acid). The negative and positive plates are connected by a molded strap across the top of the cells. This strap connects the cells in series, meaning that they are connected negative–positive through the entire battery.

Every battery contains a number of cells; 6V batteries contain three cells and 12V batteries contain six cells. Each cell has a voltage potential of 2V.

FIGURE 26–1 *Cross-sectional view of an 1100 series Delco heavy-duty 12V maintenance-free heavy-duty truck battery. (Courtesy of AC Delco.)*

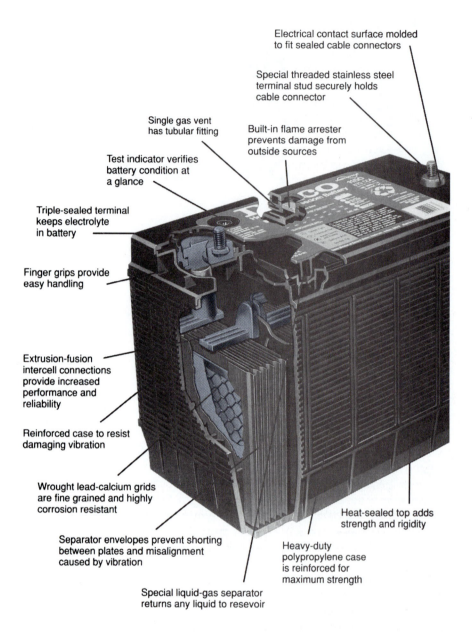

Electrical contact surface molded to fit sealed cable connectors

Special threaded stainless steel terminal stud securely holds cable connector

Single gas vent has tubular fitting

Built-in flame arrester prevents damage from outside sources

Test indicator verifies battery condition at a glance

Triple-sealed terminal keeps electrolyte in battery

Finger grips provide easy handling

Extrusion-fusion intercell connections provide increased performance and reliability

Reinforced case to resist damaging vibration

Wrought lead-calcium grids are fine grained and highly corrosion resistant

Separator envelopes prevent shorting between plates and misalignment caused by vibration

Heavy-duty polypropylene case is reinforced for maximum strength

Heat-sealed top adds strength and rigidity

Special liquid-gas separator returns any liquid to resevoir

Battery Testing

Testing batteries requires a certain degree of know-how and equipment. Work at becoming a proficient battery tester, since this is one place where many technicians have problems. It has been estimated that approximately 50% of the batteries that are replaced are replaced needlessly. This unnecessary replacement of batteries could be avoided if battery tests were taken with more accuracy and less guesswork. Unfortunately, batteries sometimes have to be tested in a short period of time because many customers will not or cannot allow their vehicle to stand idle while the battery is being charged at a slow charge rate to determine if it is usable or not. In situations like this a quick, accurate test applied in a systematic approach is needed. Battery testing becomes confusing, however, because of the many different recommended procedures. The following information attempts to sort out and clarify some of them:

Visual Inspection

Battery visual inspection plays an important part in making the decision of the battery's condition. Inspect the battery visually for the following:

1. Check the date the battery was put into service, since an old battery has a better chance of being worn out. The date the battery was put in service is usually stamped on the battery or indicated on a tag fastened to the top of the battery.

2. Check for cracks in the battery case and/or cover. A cracked battery case may have been caused by freezing of electrolyte, improper hold-down clamp or brackets, plugged vent caps that prevent venting of the hydrogen gas given off during charging, battery explosion, and excessive charging.

3. Check battery top for acid and dirt accumulation. This accumulation can allow the battery to discharge across the top by making a connection through the dirt from the positive to negative cell of the battery. Clean this accumulation from the battery by washing it with a mixture of baking soda and water.

4. Remove the vent caps and inspect the color of the electrolyte. Discolored electrolyte indicates cell problems. Note also the odor of the electrolyte. A very toxic odor indicates the cell is sulfated and will not take a charge.

5. Check electrolyte level. Electrolyte level is important if the battery is going to function normally, since cell capacity is reduced greatly when it is low on water.

6. Check battery posts for looseness and signs of abuse, such as partially melted posts caused by arching the battery from terminal to terminal.

NOTE   If the battery is installed in the vehicle when making the inspection, check the cables and cable clamps for corrosion and correct size. Most 12V applications will require a 4- or 6-gauge cable (Figure 26–2). Also check the cables for corrosion or fraying.

Battery Voltage and Specific Gravity Tests

The state of charge of the battery can be checked using a voltmeter across the positive and negative terminals, or on batteries with removable cell caps an SG (specific gravity) test of the electrolyte can be performed to determine if all cells are producing the same voltage. If one cell is low, it will tend to pull down the remaining cells, and battery failure will soon occur. On maintenance-free types of batteries similar to the one shown in Figure 26–1, an inspection test window can visually determine the state of battery charge as in Figure 26–3.

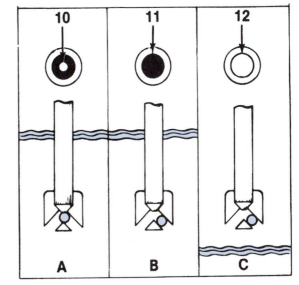

10. Green
11. Dark
12. Clear
A. 65% or Above State of Charge
B. Below 65% State of Charge
C. Low Level Electrolyte

FIGURE 26–3 How to interpret a built-in battery hydrometer for a maintenance-free battery. (Courtesy of AC Delco.)

SG can be checked by using either a squeeze bulb type of hydrometer shown in Figure 26–4, or by employing a refractometer tool, which is shown in Figure 26–5. Figure 26–6 describes how to use the refractometer in a safe and efficient manner. The hydrometer compares the SG of the battery electrolyte to that of water, which is assigned an SG value of 1.000, meaning that 1 Imperial gallon (4.546 L) weighs 10 lb (4.5 kg). A U.S. gallon (3.785 L) weighs only 3.746 kg. All hydrometers measure the SG between an expanded scale of 1.100 and 1.300.

Bulb-Type SG Test.
To test the battery electrolyte:
1. Wear safety glasses. Remove the cell cap and squeeze the bulb of the hydrometer, expelling the air.

FIGURE 26–2 Typical examples of battery cable sizes.

NO. 0 GAUGE   NO. 1 GAUGE   NO. 2 GAUGE   NO. 4 GAUGE   NO. 4 GAUGE   NO. 6 GAUGE   NO. 8 GAUGE

FIGURE 26–4 (a) A bulb-type battery hydrometer unit; (b) reading the battery electrolyte hydrometer.

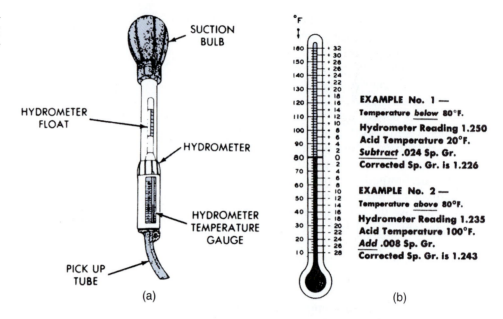

(a)

EXAMPLE No. 1 —
Temperature *below* 80°F.
Hydrometer Reading 1.250
Acid Temperature 20°F.
Subtract .024 Sp. Gr.
Corrected Sp. Gr. is 1.226

EXAMPLE No. 2 —
Temperature *above* 80°F.
Hydrometer Reading 1.235
Acid Temperature 100°F.
Add .008 Sp. Gr.
Corrected Sp. Gr. is 1.243

(b)

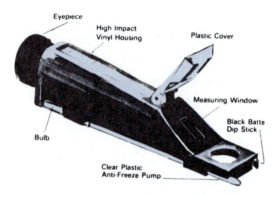

FIGURE 26–5 Refractometer battery electrolyte tester. (Courtesy of Kent-Moore Division, SPX Corporation.)

2. Insert the hydrometer pickup tube in the cell of electrolyte and release slowly, drawing electrolyte into the float bulb chamber.

3. Draw in only enough electrolyte to cause the float to rise.

4. Read the number or letter directly at the electrolyte level.

5. Correct this reading for temperature depending on the type of hydrometer you have.

6. Squeeze the bulb to force the electrolyte back into the cell and then flush the hydrometer with water.

CAUTION Be careful when handling a hydrometer filled with acid. Avoid splashing acid on your clothing or getting it into your eyes.

7. After determining what the cell's specific gravity is, make your decision about the cell, based on the following: If the specific gravity reading is 1.215 or more, the state of charge is satisfactory. Refer to Table 26–1, which lists the SG of battery electrolyte, compares it with an open-circuit voltage reading, and permits you to determine the actual equivalent state-of-charge condition.

NOTE To double-check the state of charge, make a capacity test, outlined later in this chapter.

If the reading is 1.215 or less, recharge the battery.

NOTE The difference in specific gravity between cells should not exceed 0.050. If it does, one or more cells are probably defective. Replace the battery.

Battery Load Tests (High-Rate Discharge Test)

One of the most accurate ways of performing a high-rate discharge test on a battery is to use the AVR tester.

NOTE Make sure that the battery temperature is between 60 and 100°F (16 and 38°C) when testing.

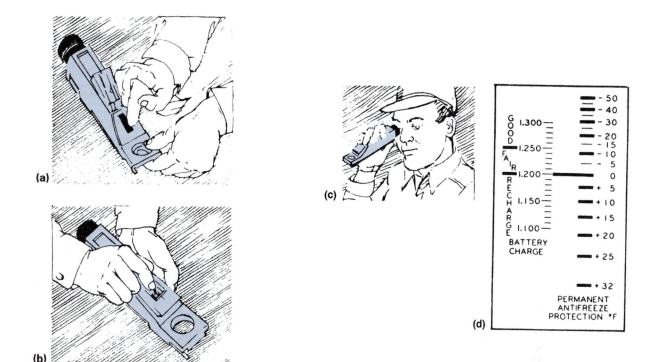

FIGURE 26–6 (a) Preparing the refractometer battery electrolyte tester to take a reading; (b) placing a drop of battery electrolyte (acid) onto the refractometer tester; (c) carefully viewing/reading the refractometer scale as per the example shown in view (d). (Courtesy of Kent-Moore Tool Division, SPX Corporation.)

TABLE 26–1 Comparison/conversion of battery electrolyte specific gravity value versus an equivalent voltage value.

Open-circuit voltage reading	Corresponding specific gravity	State of charge	
1.95	1.100	1.100 to 1.130	discharged
1.96	1.110		
1.97	1.120		
1.98	1.130		
1.99	1.140		
2.00	1.150		
2.01	1.160		
2.02	1.170	1.170 to 1.190	25% charged
2.03	1.180		
2.04	1.190		
2.05	1.200	1.200 to 1.220	50% charged
2.06	1.210		
2.07	1.220		
2.08	1.230	1.230 TO 1.250	75% charged
2.09	1.240		
2.10	1.250		
2.11	1.260	1.260 to 1.280	100% charged
2.12	1.270		
2.13	1.280		
2.14	1.290		
2.15	1.300		

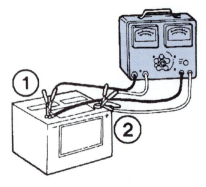

FIGURE 26–7   *Load testing a battery using a VAT (volt-amp tester); black to black and red to red.*

NOTE   If the battery has just been charged, remove the surface charge by loading the battery to 200 to 300 A for 15 seconds. Then wait 15 seconds for the battery to recover before testing.

1.   Connect the tester to the battery with respect to polarity, as shown in Figure 26–7.
2.   Operate the tester to obtain an ampere draw of half the cold cranking amperes.
3.   Maintain this load for approximately 15 seconds.
4.   If the battery is in good condition, the battery voltage should stay above 4.8V for a 6V battery and 9.6V for a 12V battery.
5.   If the battery voltage meets the recommended voltage after the discharge test, the battery is generally good and will perform satisfactorily. Charge the battery and put it back in service.
6.   If the battery fails the test on the basis of voltage, do not condemn the battery until it has been charged and rechecked.

NOTE   The procedure above is a common test in most shops. The danger in this test is that the technician may make a hasty decision and replace a perfectly good battery. Always recharge the battery and make a second test to ensure that you are getting an accurate test.

Three-Minute Charge Test

The 3-minute charge test is made on batteries to determine if cells are sulfated to the point where they will not accept a charge and the battery must be replaced.

NOTE   A sulfated battery means that the sulfate compound on the battery plates, which is normally returned to the electrolyte during charging, is not doing so and the battery will not accept a charge.

To make the 3-minute charge test, proceed as follows:

1.   Connect the battery charger to the battery with respect to polarity.
2.   Connect the voltmeter to the battery terminals.
3.   Set the charger for a 3-minute charge.

NOTE   Charge a 12V battery at approximately 40 A and a 6V battery at approximately 75 A.

4.   After charging for 3 minutes, with the charger operating read the voltmeter.
5.   The battery is acceptable if voltage is less than 15.5V on a 12V battery or less than 7.75V on a 6V battery. The battery can be recharged and put back in service.

NOTE   The voltages given are with the battery at 70°F (21°C).

6.   The battery is not acceptable if voltage is more than 15.5V for a 12V battery and more than 7.75V for a 6V battery.
7.   Depending on how much time is available, you may place the battery on a slow charge (1 A) for a 24-hour period; in many cases the battery will respond to this slow charge and be acceptable after charging. If this time is not available, replace the battery.

The 3-minute charge test, like all other battery tests, is not 100% fail safe, but after you have gained some experience in making these tests, you will be able to test a battery and make sound recommendations on its continued use or replacement.

NOTE   Manufacturers of freedom-type batteries do not consider the 3-minute charge test a valid test.

Battery Analyzer

On sealed-top or maintenance-free type batteries, use of a hydrometer or refractometer is not convenient, therefore the service technician has to rely upon a voltmeter. Newer test equipment however such as a digital power sensor meter illustrated in Figure 26–8 measures the battery's ability to produce current by using the battery itself to measure conductance. The tool does this by creating a small signal that is sent through the battery, then it measures a portion of the AC current response. This is more accurate than using a voltmeter! As the battery ages, the internal plate surfaces tend to sulfate, and can shed active material which adversely affects its ability to perform up to specs. Conductance can also be used to detect cell defects, shorts, and open circuits which reduce the ability of the battery to deliver current. Therefore conductance testing permits enhanced testing that accurately compensates for low battery charge, and effectively separates the battery's condition from the influence of the existing state of charge. The MidTronics tool shown provides a simple menu-driven test procedure and provides automatic temperature compensation.

Battery General Maintenance

The diesel technician will be called on to perform general maintenance on batteries. Some of these maintenance procedures are as follows:

Battery Charging

Slow Charge. To slow charge a battery properly, charge the battery at 1 A for approximately 12 to 16 hours. Slow charging is recommended if you think the battery is sulfated.

Quick Charge. To quick charge a battery properly, charge a 12V battery at 40 A and a 6V battery at 75 A for approximately 1 hour. This will not charge the battery completely, but it should be sufficiently charged so it can be put back in service. To charge the battery completely, the fast charge must be followed with a slow charge.

NOTE During fast charging do not charge the battery at a rate that will cause the battery cell temperature to rise beyond 125°F (52°C).

Charging More Than One Battery at a Time. A number of batteries of the same voltage can be charged at the same time by connecting them in parallel (Figure 26–9), positive to positive and negative to negative. Two batteries may be charged hooked in series if the

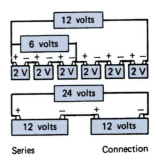

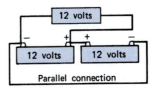

FIGURE 26–9   Example of how to hook up batteries in a series and a parallel arrangement.

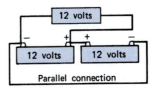

FIGURE 26–8   Digital battery tester. (Courtesy of Midtronics, Inc.)

charger has the capability. Two 6V batteries hooked in series can be charged the same way as one 12V, since two 6V batteries in series equal one 12V.

Filling Dry-Charged Batteries

Most batteries, with the exception of maintenance-free batteries (sealed), will need to be filled with acid before putting them in service. These batteries are dry charged at the factory and are shipped without electrolyte.

1. Carefully fill each cell with electrolyte.

CAUTION Make sure to wear protective goggles and gloves to prevent injury when filling the battery with electrolyte.

---

2. After filling, charge the battery at a rate of approximately 30 to 40 A until the electrolyte has a specific gravity reading of 1.240 or higher with an 80°F (27°C) temperature.

Installing the Battery into the Vehicle

Special care should be taken when installing a battery so that it will provide trouble-free power for a long period of time.

1. Check the battery box for rocks, corrosion, and foreign objects. Also make sure that the battery box or compartment is solid, since a loose battery compartment can ruin a battery in a short time.

2. Check all battery cables to make sure that they are free of corrosion. Replace any bolts that show signs of deterioration.

3. If you have two or more batteries in one vehicle, place the batteries in the compartment in a manner that will enable you to connect the cables. Install hold-down brackets or clamps.

4. Install and tighten cables on the batteries. Coat cables with a special battery cable preservative or a spray paint.

After installing the battery or batteries, check the starter operation to make sure all cables are connected correctly.

Battery Failure Causes

It is not enough to be able to determine what is wrong with a battery and whether it should be replaced; an effort must be made to determine why the battery failed. Some of the common reasons for battery failure are:

1. *Overcharging.* In many cases the voltage regulator in the charging system is not functioning correctly and the battery is continuously being overcharged. The first symptom of this condition is excessive use of water in the battery.

2. *Undercharging.* The voltage regulator may be set to cause the battery to be in a low undercharged condition at all times. Undercharging the battery can cause the battery to become sulfated.

3. *Battery too small for application.* A battery that does not have sufficient capacity for the vehicle load will fail quickly, since the battery will be discharged in large amounts and may not have time to charge adequately before it is again called on to deliver large amounts of current, such as during engine starting.

4. *Improper or lack of maintenance.* If the battery is not properly maintained as outlined in the battery maintenance section, the battery will age prematurely and fail much sooner than normal.

If you have any further questions concerning battery service and testing, consult your instructor or the information supplied with your battery tester.

SELF-TEST QUESTIONS—BATTERIES

1. Technician A says that the electrolyte in a fully charged battery at 80°F (27°C) has a specific gravity of approximately 1.240. Technician B says that it should be closer to 1.270. Who is right?

2. Technician A says that a specific gravity of 1.240 means that the battery electrolyte is heavier than water. Technician B says that it means the electrolyte is lighter than water. Who is right?

3. Technician A says that a fully charged battery would exhibit a voltage of approximately 2.1 to 2.2V per cell, providing a reading between 12.6 and 13V for a 12V battery. Technician B says since it is a 12V battery, each cell only can produce 2V. Which technician is correct?

4. Technician A says that a battery specific-gravity reading of 1.235 at 80°F (27°C) converted to voltage would be equivalent to approximately a 65% state of charge. Technician B says that it would be closer to a 75% charged state. Which technician is correct?

5. Technician A says that a battery specific-gravity reading of 1.150 at 80°F (27°C) corresponds to a voltage reading of approximately 2.0V per cell. Technician B says that it would represent 2.1V per cell. Which technician is right?

6. Technician A says that when using a hydrometer to check the specific gravity of battery electrolyte, you have to add or subtract 0.002 point to the scale for every 5° temperature change above or below 80°F (27°C). Technician B says that you need to add or subtract 0.004 point for each 10°F change above or below 80°F (27°C). Which technician is correct?

7. Technician A says that the reason you need to continually add water to a non-maintenance-free battery is due to spillage from the vent caps during handling. Technician B says it is due to gassing of the electrolyte during normal operation, a result of the normal chemical reaction. Who is right?

8. A good state of charge of a maintenance-free battery can be confirmed by viewing the built-in hydrometer, which should appear yellow in color according to technician A. Technician B says that it should appear green in color. Who is right?

9. Technician A says that to create 24V starting on a truck, the batteries must be connected in series. Technician B says that you should connect them in parallel. Who knows basic electricity better?

10. Technician A says that connecting batteries in parallel results in greater voltage. Technician B says it provides the same voltage but increases the amperage available. Who is right?

11. Technician A says that a series-parallel switch will provide 24 V starting and 12 V charging power. Technician B says it is the other way around. Who is correct?

12. Technician A says that the battery positive terminal is always red in color and the negative is blue. Technician B says that the positive terminal is red and the negative terminal is black. Who is right?

13. Technician A says that on post-type batteries the – terminal is physically larger than the + terminal. Technician B says that the + terminal is always the larger of the two. Who is right?

14. Technician A says that a battery should never be boost-charged if its specific gravity is higher than 1.225. Technician B says that you can boost-charge at any specific gravity level. Who is correct?

15. Technician A says that boost-charging results in applying a full charge to the weak cells. Technician B says that you simply provide a surface charge condition to each battery cell. Which technician is correct?

16. Technician A says that batteries can only be charged when they are connected in series. Technician B says that they can be connected either in series or in parallel depending upon the type of charger being used. Who is right?

17. Technician A says that when disconnecting a battery, you should always remove the negative grounded cable clamp first. Technician B says you should always remove the positive cable first. Which technician is correct?

18. Technician A says that when reconnecting battery cable clamps, you should always connect the positive cable last. Technician B says you should connect the negative ground cable last. Who is right?

19. Technician A says that the state of charge of a battery can only be determined by using a voltmeter. Technician B says that a hydrometer or a voltmeter can be used on a conventional screw-in cell connector. Who is right?

20. Technician A says that an open-circuit voltage reading is the voltage obtained across the battery terminals with no load on the battery. Technician B says that it is achieved when a light-load test is applied to the battery. Which technician is correct?

21. Technician A says that battery cable sizes for heavy-duty trucks using high-output starter motors are generally a No. 0 AWG size. Technician B says that you should select an AWG 00 size. Which technician is correct?

22. Technician A says that when jump-starting a vehicle, you should always connect the jumper cable clamps to the discharged battery first, and to the good battery last. Technician B says that you should connect to the good battery first, and then to the discharged battery. Which technician knows the procedure better?

23. Technician A says that it is a good idea during jump-starting to connect the ground cable to a solid connection on the engine block rather than to the negative discharged battery post. Technician B says that this would create a poor ground condition; attach the cable to the negative battery post. Which technician is correct?

PART B: ALTERNATOR CHARGING SYSTEMS

In order to maintain the battery or batteries in a proper full-state-of-charge condition and to avoid major electrical system problems, the alternator is a key component to trouble-free operation. In heavy-duty on- and off-highway equipment, it is imperative that a technician be capable of inspecting, testing, troubleshooting, analyzing, and replacing/repairing the alternator charging system. In Part B of this chapter we describe how to test, diagnose, troubleshoot, and analyze this important component. Both brush-type and brushless-type models are described. Within the ASE medium/heavy truck tests preparation guide dealing with diesel engines, test T2, the various sub-headings deal with a number of content tasks lists. Note that nowhere within the T2 test is there a sub-heading that addresses alternator charging systems; however, if you refer to the ASE automobile technician tests area, subsection D, Charging System Diagnosis and Repair, there are tasks lists that need to be learned in order to successfully challenge and certify in this important area.

ALTERNATOR FUNCTION

The name *alternator* originates from the fact that this engine-driven component (belt or gear) is designed to produce an alternating current that when rectified will supply the battery or batteries with a direct-current flow to maintain them in a full state of charge. Often referred to as a *generator*, the alternator is part of the charging system on any car or truck. The alternator forms part of the basic heavy-duty electrical system.

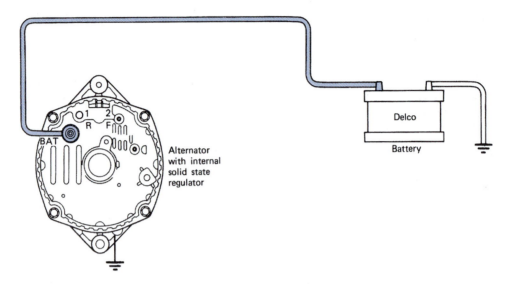

FIGURE 26–10 *Typical simplified alternator charging circuit. (Courtesy of Delco-Remy America.)*

Figure 26–10 shows a typical charging circuit used on a diesel engine. Every vehicle has different current requirements, so different-size alternators are required. The amperage rating of the alternator may be from 35 to 100 A. If the alternator had an amperage rating of 45 A and the system requirements were 55 A, the battery would quickly be discharged, since the additional 10 A would be supplied from the battery. When replacing an alternator, always make sure you have the correct amperage.

ELECTRICAL SYSTEM LOADS

Typical electrical loads placed on the batteries and charging system of a vehicle will vary depending on the classification of truck. A tractor/trailer will have more marker lights, parking lights, and stoplights than those on a straight-body medium-duty truck. The options specified for any given vehicle determine the maximum electrical load that the alternator/battery charging system must handle. In addition, even though medium- and heavy-duty trucks often use the same electrical accessories, the construction of the component is usually more rugged on a diesel powered Class 8 highway tractor than in a gasoline-powered midrange straight-body truck, which necessitates a heavier current (amperage) draw. Table 26–2 illustrates typical electrical accessories and their respective amperage ratings.

TYPES OF ALTERNATORS

In diesel-powered trucks and equipment, two main types of charging system alternators are used:

1. The slip-ring and brush type
2. The brushless type

Figure 26–11A illustrates a widely used Delco 21-SI (System Integral) heavy-duty brush generator and identification of the major component parts. The 21-SI offers high output to 160 A, a built-in integrated-circuit regulator designed for low parasitic draw, and it provides excellent RFI (radio-frequency interference) suppression. A specially designed bridge provides protection for other electronic devices on the vehicle by effectively clamping voltage surges up to 40V. The swivel brush holder design minimizes brush side wear, bounce, hang-up, and erosion. The 21-SI is available between 65 and 160 A in a 12V model or between 50 and 70 A on a 24V model.

Figure 26–11B illustrates a 26-SI heavy-duty brushless generator with a stationary field coil and no brushes or slip rings. This design features increased service life over brush units. The absence of moving electrical connections eliminates sparks from brush/slip ring contact. A special diode-trio/capacitor assembly provides superior RFI suppression. The 26-SI's electronics are protected in two ways. Standard load dump protection guards the generator against voltage-spikes caused by loose connections or interruptions in the charging line and total environmental sealing against dirt, road salt, and other corrosives. The 26-SI features either 85 A at a 12V rating or 50 or 75 A at a 24V rating. For larger amperage outputs, a Delco 30-SI model brushless generator rated at 105 A at 12V, 75 or 100 A at 24V, or 60 A at 32V is available. The SI Delco generators use a diode trio and rectifier bridge to change stator ac voltage to dc voltage at the alternator output.

TABLE 2 Typical amperage rating loads for vehicle accessories.

Device	Amperes	Hours used per 12-hour shift	Ampere-hours per 12-hour shift
Ignition, engine	0.4	12	4.8
Auxiliary heater fan	9.0	12	108
Air dryer, heated	5.0	12	60
CB radio	3.0	12	36
Defroster fans	8.8	12	105.6
Clearance lights	4.14	12	49.68
Headlights, single high	9.94	10	99.4
Heated mirrors	20	10	200
License plate lights	1.4	10	14
Marker lights	5.5	10	55
Panel and meter lights	3.63	10	36.3
Fuel filter, heated	30	12	360
Stop lights	9.09	0.5	4.5
Turn lights	13.9	0.5	6.9
		Subtotal	1140.18
		Plus 25% safety factor	285.05
		Total	1425.23[1]

[a]The truck in this example needs a total of 1,425 amps of power generated by the alternator during the 12-hour period to match the demand.

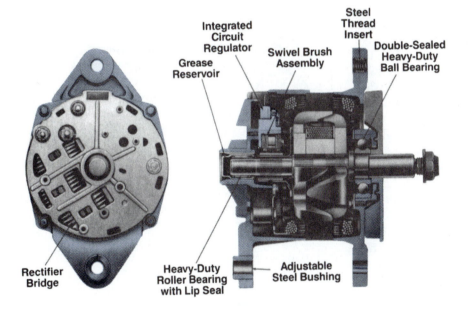

Integrated Circuit Regulator
Grease Reservoir
Swivel Brush Assembly
Steel Thread Insert
Double-Sealed Heavy-Duty Ball Bearing
Rectifier Bridge
Heavy-Duty Roller Bearing with Lip Seal
Adjustable Steel Bushing

FIGURE 26–11A Features of a Delco 21-SI (System Integral) heavy-duty brush-type generator. (Courtesy of Delco-Remy America.)

HEAVY-DUTY ALTERNATOR TEST: ON VEHICLE

When a problem is reflected in the starting/charging system through complaints of hard starting or low power to operate accessories, there are a couple of checks that can be performed fairly quickly to confirm whether the problem is actually in the batteries, starter motor, alternator, or associated wiring. Simple causes such as high circuit resistance in a number of wiring connections can lead the mechanic/technician to suspect either battery or starter problems, with some suspicion that the problem might also be in the alternator or voltage regulator. High circuit resistance will cause

FIGURE 26–11B Features of a Delco 26-SI model heavy-duty brushless generator assembly. (Courtesy of Delco-Remy America.)

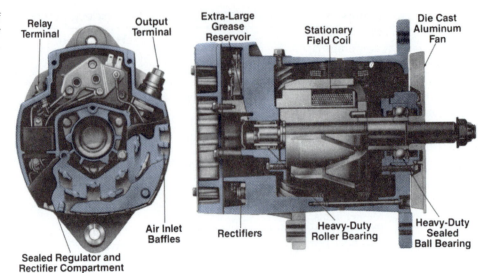

Relay Terminal

Output Terminal

Extra-Large Grease Reservoir

Stationary Field Coil

Die Cast Aluminum Fan

Air Inlet Baffles

Rectifiers

Heavy-Duty Roller Bearing

Heavy-Duty Sealed Ball Bearing

Sealed Regulator and Rectifier Compartment

a voltage loss to the batteries, and this can be caused by corrosion, loose or dirty terminals, or damaged wiring or connections.

The first step in pinpointing any starting/charging system problem is to note whether the lack of power occurs only during a cranking/starting attempt. If it does, you can refer to the section for batteries or for starting motors. Visually check and feel the battery connections and all other wire terminals and connections between the battery, starter, and alternator. If nothing unusual is noted, perform a load test on the batteries according to the instructions. Replace any faulty batteries and clean and tighten all battery connections. What we want to do now is to perform a charging circuit voltage drop and alternator output test.

For purposes of discussion, we select a heavy-duty truck equipped with four 12V batteries in parallel using a Delco 42MT starter motor and a Delco SI brushless generator.

1. With the engine stopped, connect a carbon pile load tester (make sure that the carbon pile control knob is in the OFF position) between the alternator output terminal and the ground of the alternator housing. The alternator output terminal is at battery voltage.

CAUTION Care must be exercised when connecting the carbon pile to the alternator output terminal to ensure that the pile clamp does not touch a ground circuit such as the alternator body or other metal bracket that may be in close proximity.

---

2. Battery voltage can be monitored simply by connecting the red voltmeter lead to the + battery post and the black lead to the − battery post, as shown in Figure 26–12 at position A.

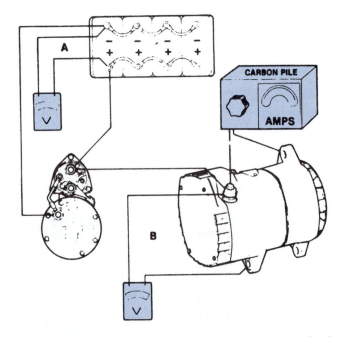

FIGURE 26–12 Step 1: electrical test hookup to check the charging circuit voltage drop condition with a voltmeter connected in position A, then in position B. (Courtesy of Detroit Diesel Corporation.)

NOTE Determine the alternator part number then refer to OEM test specs and pick out the rated output in amperes for the alternator model in question. Some alternators have the rated output stamped on the alternator housing or on a name tag attached to the housing.

---

3. Slowly rotate the control knob on the carbon pile until the built-in ammeter registers the alternator

rated output in amperes. If the carbon pile does not have an ammeter, connect a separate ammeter into the system so that amperage draw can be monitored.

4. Quickly note and record the battery voltage on the voltmeter while the carbon pile is drawing the recommended amperage, then turn the carbon pile control knob OFF.

5. Disconnect the voltmeter from position A in Figure 26–12 and reconnect it to position B. This requires that the red voltmeter lead (+) be attached to the alternator (BAT) output terminal and that the black lead (–) be attached to the alternator housing for ground purposes.

> **CAUTION** Do not connect the voltmeter leads to the carbon pile leads; otherwise, when the carbon pile is turned on, the high amperage will damage the voltmeter and its leads.

6. Slowly rotate the carbon pile control knob once again until the ammeter registers rated alternator output according to the note between steps 2 and 3 on the previous page.

7. Quickly note and record the voltage at the alternator (BAT) output terminal, then turn off the carbon pile by rotating the control knob OFF or to the MIN position.

8. The system voltage drop can now be determined simply by subtracting the voltage reading that was obtained at the alternator BAT terminal in step 7 from that recorded previously in step 4.

9. If the reading determined in step 8 is greater than 0.5V for a 12V system, or 1.0V for a 24V system, proceed to step 10. If, however, the voltage drop is within specifications, proceed directly to the alternator output test described after step 16.

10. With the carbon pile still connected but in the OFF position, connect a digital scale voltmeter, since we want to read precisely what the voltage drop is on either the + or – side of the charging circuit.

11. Refer to Figure 26–13 and connect the digital voltmeter red (+) lead to a battery positive terminal. Connect the black (–) lead of the voltmeter to the alternator (BAT) output terminal. If the batteries are too far away from the alternator, hook up a jumper wire to extend the voltmeter leads.

12. Slowly rotate the carbon pile load control knob until the ammeter registers rated alternator output once again.

13. Quickly note and record the voltmeter value, then turn the carbon pile load control knob OFF.

14. Refer to Figure 26–13 step 2, and connect the voltmeter leads to the negative side of the charging cir-

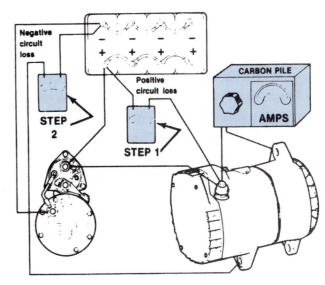

FIGURE 26–13 Step 2: electrical test hookup to check the charging circuit voltage drop condition. (Courtesy of Detroit Diesel Corporation.)

cuit, which involves placing the red (+) lead to the alternator housing and the black (–) lead to the battery negative terminal.

15. Rotate the carbon pile load control knob slowly until the ammeter registers the alternator rated output in amperes, then quickly read and record the voltmeter reading. Turn off the carbon pile by rotating the control knob.

16. Add the positive circuit voltage loss to that for the negative circuit loss. This combined value should not exceed 0.5V for a 12V system, or 1.0V for a 24V system.

Once you have determined where the voltage loss is, correct by removing the necessary connections and cleaning and tightening them again. Recheck the system voltage drop again, then proceed to the alternator output test.

ON-VEHICLE ALTERNATOR OUTPUT TEST

This check will quickly confirm if the problem is in either the alternator or voltage regulator.

1. Make sure that the engine is at shop ambient temperature prior to conducting this test.

2. Refer to Figure 26–14 and select a starting/charging system analyzer, such as a Sun Electric VAT tester model, that contains both an ammeter and a voltmeter and, usually, a built-in carbon pile.

3. Connect the voltmeter leads to one of the 12V batteries, making sure that the red lead goes to a + connection and that the black lead goes to a – connection.

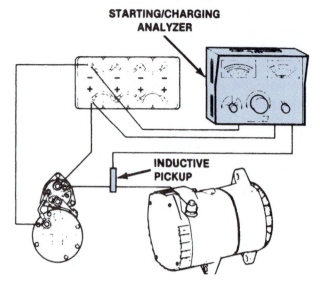

FIGURE 26–14 Using a VAT tester inductive pickup to monitor the alternator rated output value. (Courtesy of Detroit Diesel Corporation.)

FIGURE 26–15 Model J35590 current clamp. (Courtesy of Kent-Moore Tool Division, SPX Corporation.)

4.   Place the tester inductive pickup plastic clamp around the alternator output wire (Figure 26–15).

5.   Connect the carbon pile leads or a separate carbon pile if the tester is not equipped with one so that it spans one battery on a 12V parallel-connected system. If the system is a 24V arrangement, connect the carbon pile leads across one 12V battery and the voltmeter across the normal 24V battery connection.

6.   Make sure that all vehicle electrical accessory load switches are off.

7.   Make sure that the carbon pile load control knob is off.

8.   Start the engine and accelerate it to a fast idle, between 1000 and 1200 rpm maximum.

9.   Turn the carbon pile on and slowly rotate the control knob to cause the alternator to produce its

rated amperage output. Read and record the voltage value.

10.   The voltage value should not exceed 15V on a 12V system, or 30V on a 24V system, although 28V is usually stated and accepted as maximum. If the voltage exceeds these limits by more than 1V, and the alternator output is not within 10 A, a voltage adjustment can be attempted on Delco 26-S1 and 30-S1 models by removing the alternator rear cover and accessing the voltage potentiometer adjusting screw.

11.   Failure of the alternator to function to rated amperage and voltage after any voltage adjustment would require that the voltage regulator be replaced.

12.   Voltage that exceeds the limit by more than 1V and that cannot be lowered by adjustment would require that the generator be removed for inspection and repair.

TROUBLESHOOTING LEECE-NEVILLE ALTERNATORS

To effectively troubleshoot Leece-Neville alternators, refer to Figure 26–16 and systematically test the charging system in the steps listed. To check battery overcharge, undercharge, and wiring and belt tension is a simple procedure (check the batteries as per this Chapter). To check the diode trio on alternators so equipped, refer to Figure 26–17, and after removing the diode trio from the alternator, connect the ohmmeter test leads as shown. The diode trio is okay when a LOW resistance reading is observed in one direction and a HIGH resistance is observed in the other; otherwise, replace it.

Full Field Test

1.   Start and run the engine at about 1000 rpm with all electrical accessories OFF. Measure the output voltage across the alternator terminals and write it down for reference.

2.   Refer to Figure 26–18 and attach a short jumper wire to the alternator as illustrated; use a piece of 2 in. (50 mm) stiff wire such as a paper clip. Insert the wire in the full field access hole and hold it firmly against the brush terminal inside the housing (this action also flashes the field).

3.   With the jumper in place as shown, connect a "digital" voltmeter across the alternator terminals and run the engine at approximately 1000 rpm. Compare the reading with that obtained in step 1.

4.   With the jumper still connected and the wire in place, connect an ac voltmeter across terminals 1 and 2, 1 and 3, and 2 and 3 to be able to read the voltages. If

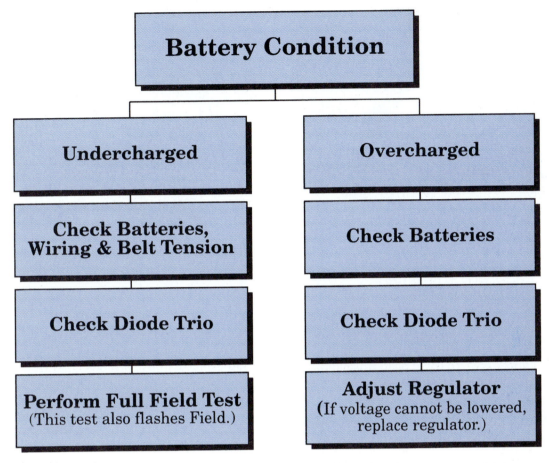

FIGURE 26–16   Self-check chart to systematically determine a charging system complaint.

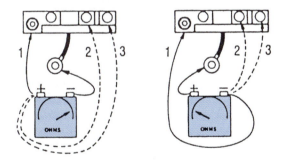

FIGURE 26–17   Checking alternator diode-trio. (Courtesy of Leece-Neville, PEI.)

FIGURE 26–18   Performing a field test. (Courtesy of Leece-Neville, PEI.)

they are all the same, they are considered to be "balanced."

5.   Remove the jumper wire. If the voltage in step 3 is higher than in step 1, and the voltages measured in step 4 are balanced, the stator and alternator are okay; therefore, move to the voltage regulator adjustment procedure.

6.   However, if the voltage in step 3 is higher than that in step 1 and the voltages measured in step 4 are not balanced, the alternator stator or rectifier is defective.

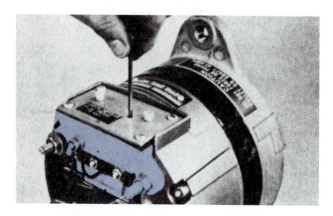

FIGURE 26–19 *Voltage regulator adjustment.* (Courtesy of Leece-Neville, PEI.)

Voltage Regulator Adjustment

Inspect the alternator to determine if it has:

A. A flat cover plate similar to that shown in Figure 26–19 which indicates that it is a fully adjustable regulator

B. A finned, curved cover plate which indicates that a three-step regulator is used

Type A Procedure

1. Ensure that the battery is at least 95% charged and that all wire connections and the drive belt tension is correct.

2. With all electrical accessories OFF, start and run the engine at 1000 rpm.

3. Connect a digital voltmeter to the alternator outputs.

4. Remove the plastic screw from the regulator as illustrated in Figure 26–19 and insert a small slotted screwdriver into the access hole until it engages with the adjustment screw.

5. Exercise care during this adjustment process so as not to place undue force on the adjustment screw.

6. Rotate the screwdriver CW to raise the voltage and CCW to lower the voltage setting, which should be set between 14.0 and 14.2V (28.0 to 28.4V on a 24V charging system). Replace the small plastic screw back into the cover plate.

Type B Procedure

1. With the engine stopped, disconnect the battery ground cable.

2. Refer to Figure 26–20 and remove the No. 10-32 nuts and lockwasher from the voltage regulator terminal and disconnect the diode trio if so equipped.

3. Remove the four regulator cover retaining screws.

4. If dirt or corrosion is evident, clean the brush contact pads with No. 600 or finer sandpaper.

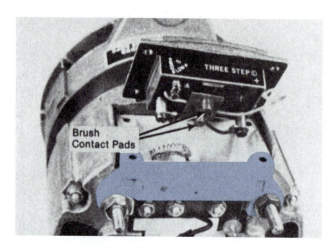

FIGURE 26–20 *Inspecting voltage regulator brush contact pads in preparation for voltage adjustment.* (Courtesy of Leece-Neville, PEI.)

5. Inspect and reinstall the brushes.

6. If voltage regulator adjustment is required after pad cleaning, remove and reinstall the adjustment strap in one of three positions:

- Between terminals A and B (low)
- Between terminals A and C (medium)
- Between terminals B and C (high)

Each strap change within these three settings will alter the voltage output by approximately 0.4V.

SELF-TEST QUESTIONS— ALTERNATOR CHARGING SYSTEMS

1. Technician A says that the word *alternator* is derived from the alternating electrical current produced within the windings. Technician B says that the alternator produces DC current in its winding, which is then rectified to AC to charge the battery. Which technician is right?

2. Technician A says that connecting the battery cables backwards (reverse polarity) can result in alternator diode damage. Technician B says that the alternator is immune to reverse-polarity hookup. Which technician is correct?

3. Technician A says that a reverse-polarity diode is usually located between the hot side of the circuit and the isolation diode. Technician B says that it is located between the ground circuit and the isolation diode, with a fuse installed between the two. Who is right?

4. Technician A says that the purpose of a diode is to allow current flow in one direction only. Technician B says that it functions to permit current flow in both directions. Who is right?

5. Technician A says that disconnecting the batteries while the engine is running allows you to determine if the alternator output is sufficient to handle the loads. Technician B says you should never disconnect the batteries on

a running engine, since this can lead to diode damage. Which technician is correct?

6. Technician A says that grounding the generator field circuit on a running engine can cause diode burnout. Technician B says that it will cause increased generator output. Which technician is correct?

7. Technician A says that if an uninsulated starting motor is used, a ground strap must be used, otherwise faulty alternator operation can occur. Technician B says that a ground strap must be used on an insulated starter motor. Which technician is correct?

8. Technician A says you should always disconnect the batteries and isolate the alternator if arc welding is to be performed on the vehicle frame. Technician B says this is not necessary since the alternator is insulated and fuse protected. Who is right?

9. Technician A says that a carbon pile tester is used to apply a variable load to the battery and starter motor. Technician B says it is used to apply a variable load to the battery and alternator charging system. Which technician is correct?

10. Technician A says that the most important precaution prior to hooking up a carbon pile tester is to ensure that the control knob is in the OFF position. Technician B says that it can be full on as long as the ignition switch is off. Which technician is right?

11. Technician A says that you should always adjust drive belt tension with a belt tension gauge. Technician B says that as long as you set the belt deflection to between 0.38 and 0.50 in. (9.5 and 12.7 mm) there should not be any problems. Which technician is correct?

PART C: STARTER MOTORS

In Part C we describe the purpose, function, and operation of the heavy-duty 12 and 24V starter motors commonly used on heavy-duty high-speed diesel engines. Within the ASE medium/heavy truck tests preparation guide, diesel engines (test T2), subsection A, General Engine Diagnosis, refer to the following:

3. Inspect the engine compartment wiring harness, connectors, seals, and locks.

11. Diagnose no-cranking, cranks but fails to start, hard starting, and starts but does not continue to run problems; determine needed repairs.

Also refer to diesel engines (test T2) subsection G, Starting System Diagnosis and Repair, for additional task lists.

STARTER MOTOR FUNCTION

The purpose of an engine starter motor is to rotate the engine flywheel ring gear by the use of either an electric or compressed air-driven starter assembly. The starter drive gear must be rotated fast enough to permit the engine to fire and initiate combustion. After the engine starts, the motor must disengage automatically to prevent damage to the drive pinion assembly.

Because of the higher compression ratio and heavier components used with a heavy-duty high-speed diesel engine, the electric starter motor can be designed to operate on either 12 or 24V. However, if a 24V starter motor is used along with a 12V alternator charging system, then either a series–parallel switch or a battery equalizer system must be used to permit the electrical system to function at these two different voltages. Most heavy-duty truck diesel engines are now equipped with high-torque 12V starters; however, many buses/coaches, industrial, and marine applications operate with 24/32V starter motors and generator charging systems.

ELECTRIC STARTER SYSTEM STRUCTURE

Figure 26–21 illustrates two external views of a heavy-duty truck high-speed diesel engine starter motor assembly, while Figure 26–22 shows a cross-sectional view of the internal components for the starter motor shown in Figure 26–21.

To support engagement of a heavy-duty starter motor, an electrical system similar to that shown in Figure 26–23a using an external magnetic switch is required. However, newer models may employ a system similar to that shown in Figure 26–23b, where an IMS (integral magnetic switch) is used.

The purpose of the individual system components are as follows:

1. *Starting motor.* A dc electric motor that converts electrical energy into cranking power to rotate the engine for starting.

2. *Solenoid switches.* An electrical magnetic switch that makes and breaks the circuit between the starter and battery. It also shifts the starter drive in and out of the flywheel ring gear.

3. *Cables.* Large cables are required to transmit the huge amount of current needed by the starter motor to crank the engine.

4. *Battery.* The battery provides the source of power to operate the starter motor. In many systems more than one battery is required, since one battery does not contain sufficient amperage to turn the starter.

5. *Thermostatic connector.* Both systems shown in Figure 26–23 feature the use of a thermostatic connector which is designed to open the electrical circuit to prevent cranking when the temperature of the starter motor windings reach a predetermined temperature. This action will inhibit cranking for between 1 to 6 minutes, after which time the thermostat will close and allow cranking action once again. This lengthens starter motor life substantially.

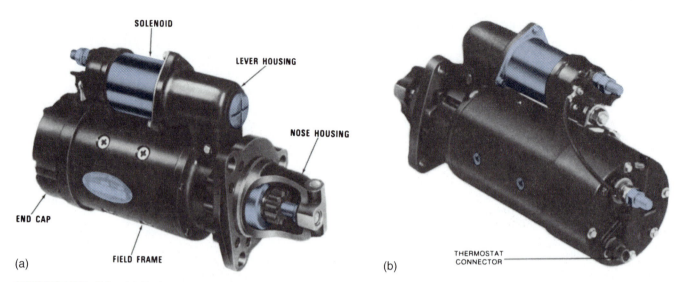

FIGURE 26–21   (a) Typical model 37-MT starter motor features; (b) end view of a model 42-MT starter motor showing the thermostat connector. (Courtesy of Delco-Remy America.)

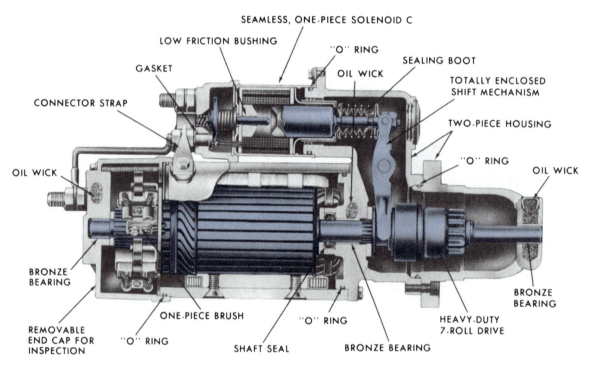

FIGURE 26–22   Cross-sectional view of a heavy-duty model 42-MT starter. (Courtesy of Delco-Remy America.)

12 AND 24 VOLT CIRCUITS

Heavy trucks and equipment can be equipped with either a 12 or 24V high-torque starter motor. Figure 26–24a illustrates the typical hookup required when more than one battery is employed in an electrical system. In a parallel hookup, all the positive terminals are connected together and all the negative terminals are connected together as shown in the diagram. This wiring arrangement results in the amperage of all batteries being added together; however, the voltage is the sum of only one battery, or 12V.

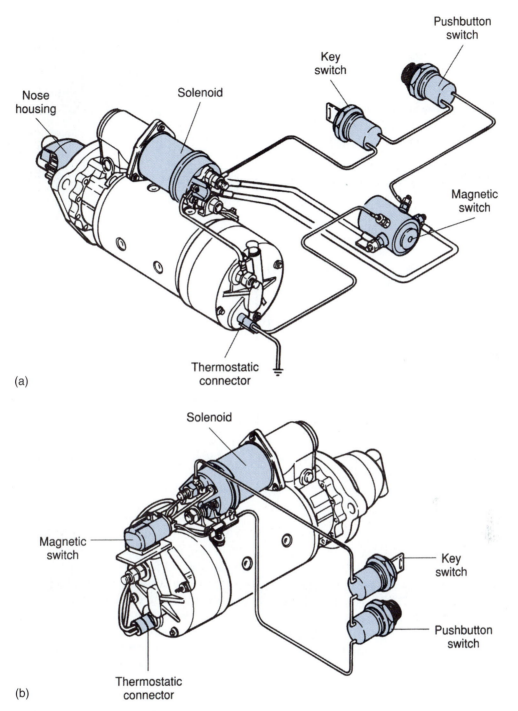

(a)

(b)

FIGURE 26-23   *(a) Heavy-duty starter motor electrical circuit employing a remote mounted magnetic switch; (b) starter electrical system using an integral magnetic switch. (Courtesy of Delco-Remy America.)*

When a 24V starter motor is used, the batteries must be connected in a series hookup as shown in Figure 26–24b. The positive terminals are connected to the negative terminal of the opposite battery. This wiring arrangement results in 24V, with the amper-age being the sum of only one battery. When a 24V starter motor is used along with a 12V charging system, it is necessary to employ a series–parallel switch arrangement similar to that shown in Figure 26–24c.

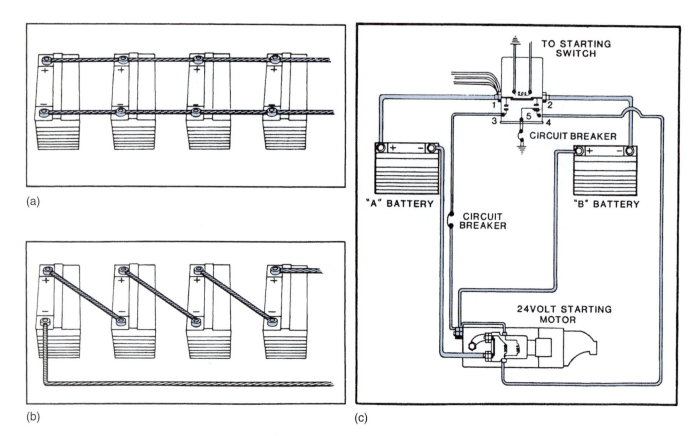

FIGURE 26–24 (a) Starter motor multiple 12V battery parallel hookup arrangement to provide the same voltage, but greater amperage. (b) Starter motor 12V battery series hookup to provide higher 24V voltage, but the same amperage. (c) Starter motor/battery series/parallel hookup to provide 24V cranking, but 12V charging once the engine fires and runs.

ELECTRIC STARTER MOTOR COMPONENTS

An exploded view of a heavy-duty Delco 42-MT starter motor is shown in Figure 26–25. The major components shown function as follows:

1. *Field frame.* The field frame provides a place to mount the fields and also the front and rear bearing housing.

2. *Brush end bearing housing.* This housing provides a place for the commutator end bushing or bearing. See items 118, 198, and 206.

3. *Armature assembly.* This assembly is composed of many conductors (heavy copper ribbons) mounted between iron laminations on an iron shaft. On one end of the armature is the commutator, and on the other end is the starter drive. See items 237 and 241.

4. *Starter drive.* It is mounted onto the armature shaft and transmits the power of the starting motor to the flywheel. On all drives is a pinion that engages the flywheel ring gear when the starter motor is operating.

To allow the starter motor to turn faster than the flywheel ring gear, a gear reduction of approximately 15 to 1 is utilized to increase torque. The pinion mechanism must be designed to disengage from the flywheel or overrun after the engine starts; otherwise, the starting motor would be rotated by the engine at too fast a speed and cause damage to the starter. Many different types of starter drives are used today; some of the most common ones are listed here:

a. *Posi-torque.* As the name implies the posi-torque drive is designed to eliminate slippage. Designed like a ratchet, it will not slip under load but will ratchet if engaged when the engine starts (Figure 26–26A).

b. *Sprag clutch drive* (Figure 26–26B). The sprag clutch is an overrunning clutch that locks the pinion to the armature shaft in one direction and allows it to rotate freely in the other direction. It is composed of inner and outer shells that are locked to-

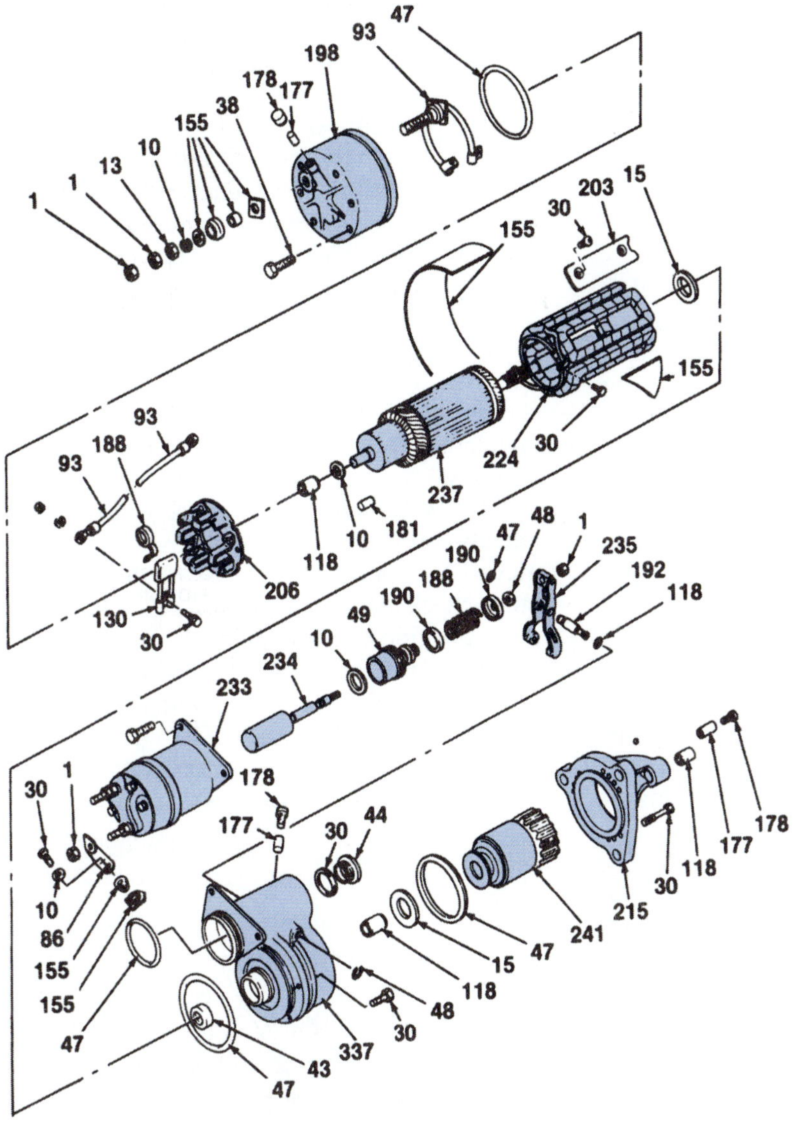

FIGURE 26–25 Exploded view of a Delco heavy-duty 42-MT model starter motor assembly. (Courtesy of Delco-Remy America.)

1. Nut
10. Washer
15. Spacer washer
30. Retaining screws
30. Inspection plug washer (mated to item 44)
38. Screw and washer
43. Oil seal
44. Inspection plug
47. O-ring
48. Retainer ring
49. Rubber boot
86. Connector
93. Lead
118. Bushing
130. Brush
155. Insulator
177. Oil wick
178. Oil reservoir
181. Pin
188. Spring
190. Spring retainer
192. Shift lever shaft
198. End frame
203. Pole shoe
206. Brush plate
215. Drive housing
224. Coil
233. Solenoid
234. Plunger
235. Shift lever
237. Armature
241. Drive assembly
337. Shift lever housing

gether by sprags. It is engaged by the starter solenoid through a shift lever. Figure 26–26C shows two widely used starter motor drives.

5. *Brushes.* They are made from a carbon and graphite mixture, are square or oblong in shape, and connect the starter commutator segments to the gener-ator terminals. They are called brushes because they brush the commutator segments to make contact.

6. *Drive end housing.* The starter housing that provides a means of mounting the starter onto the engine. See item 215.

7. *Bearings and bushings.* The starter armature is supported in the field frame by bushings or bearings.

SOLENOID SWITCH COMPONENTS AND OPERATING PRINCIPLES

Components

A starter solenoid (Figure 26–27) is made up of the following component parts:

1. *Terminal studs.* Items 70 and 71 to which the battery cable and motor terminal are connected.

2. *Contact plate.* The plate, item 204, that makes the contact between the terminal studs.

3. *Pull-in coil.* A coil within the solenoid that helps engage the solenoid shift lever (grounded in the starting motor).

4. *Hold-in coil.* A coil within the solenoid that holds the solenoid in the engaged position (grounded to solenoid case). Or solenoid insulated ground terminal.

5. *Plunger.* The iron core of the solenoid, which is connected to the starter shift lever.

Switch Operation

The solenoid switch is used to engage the starter pinion and close the circuit between the starter and the battery. When the starter switch on the vehicle instrument panel is closed, the solenoid operates as follows:

1. The hold-in and pull-in coils work together to pull the solenoid plunger into the solenoid.

2. As the plunger is pulled into the solenoid housing, the contact plate shorts the pull-in coil and the hold-in coil holds the switch engaged (Figure 26–28).

NOTE   The pull-in coil circuit during engagement is from switch to coil to starter motor for ground. After engagement the solenoid plate contacts the solenoid inner terminals. This circuit has much less resistance than the pull-in coil circuit. As a result the pull-in coil is shut off.

---

3. In addition to closing the circuit between the battery and starter with the contact plate, the solenoid operates the drive shift lever, which moves the drive into the flywheel.

4. The switch remains in this position until the starter switch on the instrument panel is released, causing the solenoid to disengage the shift lever and break the contact between the battery and starter. When this happens, the starter stops turning and the pinion is disengaged from the flywheel (Figure 26–29).

ELECTRIC STARTER TROUBLESHOOTING

When a problem exists with the starter motor, the fault may lie either in the motor itself or in the wiring circuit. Figure 26–30 lists problems associated with slow cranking or a clicking or chattering solenoid. Figure 26–31 lists possible causes for no cranking and/or no sound from the solenoid when the starter switch is engaged. Often a low-voltage supply to the starter is one of the main causes of failure to crank. Figure 26–32 illustrates the use of a voltmeter connected into the starter motor circuit to determine the voltage drop (available cranking voltage). Perform the voltage check as follows:

1. A starter motor voltage drop check can quickly confirm whether or not the starter should be removed for service. Figure 26–32 illustrates a typical quick check that can be performed with the starter motor in position on the engine.

2. Place the positive (red) lead of a voltmeter against the solenoid BAT terminal and the negative (black) voltmeter lead against the starter motor ground terminal.

3. Close the starter switch (key or button) to crank the engine while noting the voltage reading on the face of the meter.

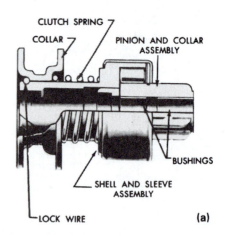

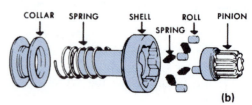

FIGURE 26–26   A: Starter motor roller clutch drive: (a) cutaway view. (Courtesy of Delco-Remy America.)

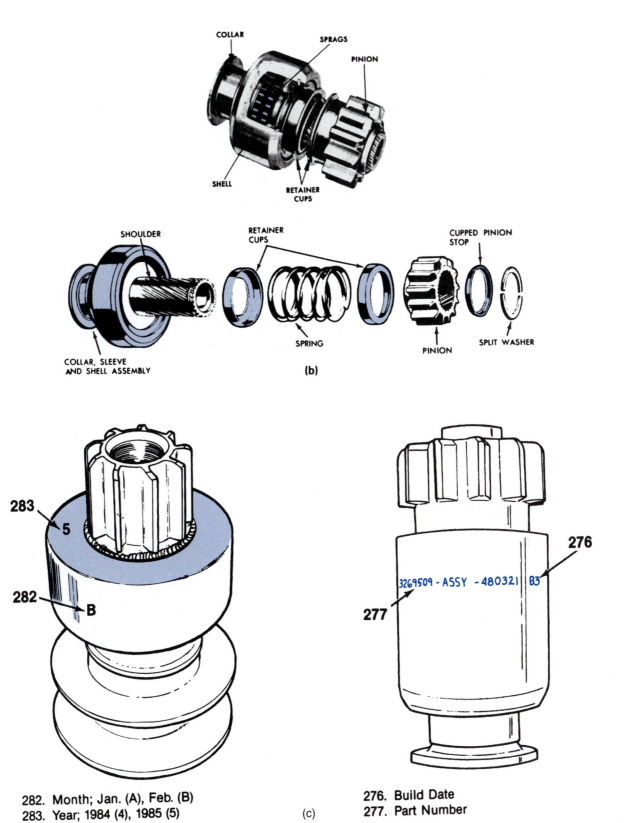

COLLAR SPRAGS PINION

SHELL RETAINER CUPS

SHOULDER RETAINER CUPS CUPPED PINION STOP

COLLAR, SLEEVE AND SHELL ASSEMBLY SPRING PINION SPLIT WASHER

(b)

283
5

282
B

3269509 - ASSY - 480321 B3

276

277

282. Month; Jan. (A), Feb. (B)
283. Year; 1984 (4), 1985 (5)

(c)

276. **Build Date**
277. **Part Number**

FIGURE 26–26 (continued). A: Starter motor roller clutch drive: (b) exploded view. B: (a) sprag clutch assembly; (b) disassembled view of a heavy-duty sprag clutch drive assembly. C: (a) intermediate-duty drive clutch identification; (b) heavy-duty drive clutch identification. (Courtesy of Delco-Remy America.)

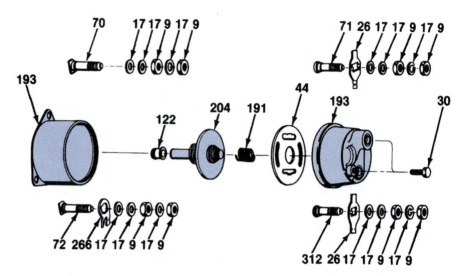

FIGURE 26–27 Exploded view of a Delco heavy-duty 42-MT starter motor model solenoid components. (Courtesy of Delco-Remy America.)

9. Terminal Nut
17. Terminal Washer
30. Screw
44. Gasket
70. "BAT" Terminal Stud

71. Solenoid Terminal Stud
72. Motor Stud
122. Plunger Rod Bushing
191. Contact Spring
193. Solenoid Housing

204. Contact
266. Clip
312. Terminal Stud

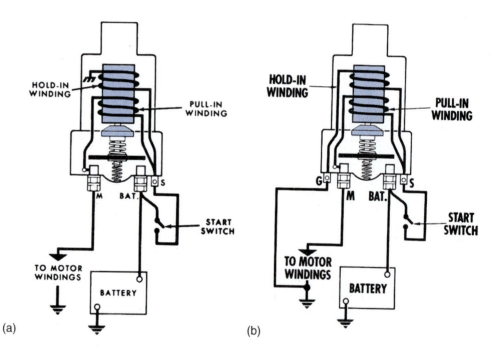

FIGURE 26–28 (a) Solenoid circuit (hold-in winding grounded internally); (b) solenoid circuit with ground return terminals. (Courtesy of Delco-Remy America.)

(a)

(b)

4. If the voltage is 9V or less on a 12V starter system while cranking at normal room temperature of 60 to 70°F (15 to 21°C), check the resistance and voltage loss between the interconnecting cables of the batteries.

5. While cranking the engine, touch the voltmeter leads to the positive and negative posts or stud nut of each battery. There should not be more than 0.5V difference between any two battery readings; otherwise, there is high resistance level between con-nections. A starting circuit resistance check procedure is listed below.

Typical starter circuit voltage drops are established by the use of a voltmeter connected across sections of the circuit in parallel, then isolating the problem area.

Starter Motor Bench Check

If a starter motor problem cannot be traced while on the engine, remove the starter and perform a bench

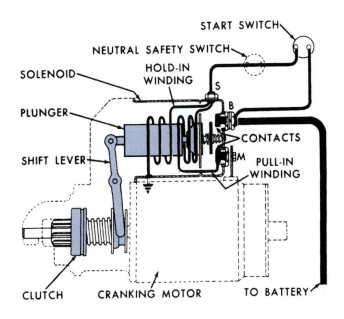

FIGURE 26–29 Operation of the hold-in and pull-in winding coil within the starter motor solenoid assembly. (Courtesy of Delco-Remy America.)

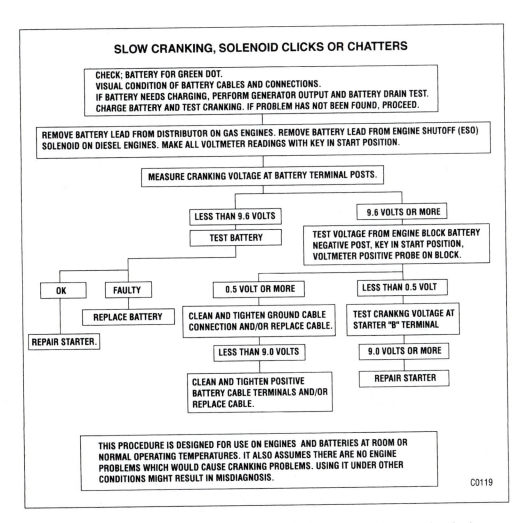

SLOW CRANKING, SOLENOID CLICKS OR CHATTERS

CHECK; BATTERY FOR GREEN DOT.
VISUAL CONDITION OF BATTERY CABLES AND CONNECTIONS.
IF BATTERY NEEDS CHARGING, PERFORM GENERATOR OUTPUT AND BATTERY DRAIN TEST.
CHARGE BATTERY AND TEST CRANKING. IF PROBLEM HAS NOT BEEN FOUND, PROCEED.

REMOVE BATTERY LEAD FROM DISTRIBUTOR ON GAS ENGINES. REMOVE BATTERY LEAD FROM ENGINE SHUTOFF (ESO) SOLENOID ON DIESEL ENGINES. MAKE ALL VOLTMETER READINGS WITH KEY IN START POSITION.

MEASURE CRANKING VOLTAGE AT BATTERY TERMINAL POSTS.

LESS THAN 9.6 VOLTS

TEST BATTERY

9.6 VOLTS OR MORE

TEST VOLTAGE FROM ENGINE BLOCK BATTERY NEGATIVE POST, KEY IN START POSITION, VOLTMETER POSITIVE PROBE ON BLOCK.

OK   FAULTY

REPLACE BATTERY

REPAIR STARTER.

0.5 VOLT OR MORE

CLEAN AND TIGHTEN GROUND CABLE CONNECTION AND/OR REPLACE CABLE.

LESS THAN 9.0 VOLTS

CLEAN AND TIGHTEN POSITIVE BATTERY CABLE TERMINALS AND/OR REPLACE CABLE.

LESS THAN 0.5 VOLT

TEST CRANKNG VOLTAGE AT STARTER "B" TERMINAL

9.0 VOLTS OR MORE

REPAIR STARTER

THIS PROCEDURE IS DESIGNED FOR USE ON ENGINES AND BATTERIES AT ROOM OR NORMAL OPERATING TEMPERATURES. IT ALSO ASSUMES THERE ARE NO ENGINE PROBLEMS WHICH WOULD CAUSE CRANKING PROBLEMS. USING IT UNDER OTHER CONDITIONS MIGHT RESULT IN MISDIAGNOSIS.

C0119

FIGURE 26–30 Slow cranking system diagnosis. (Courtesy of Delco-Remy America.)

FIGURE 26–31 *Starter motor fails to crank, with no sound from the solenoid. (Courtesy of Delco-Remy America.)*

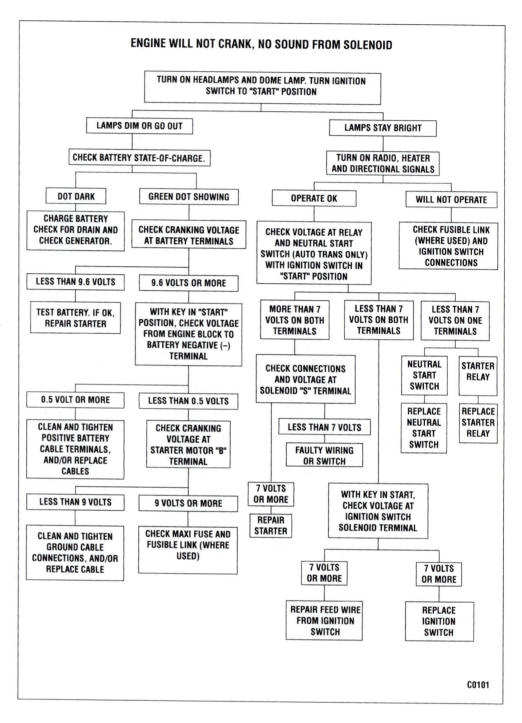

check according to the hookup shown in Figure 26–33. During this bench check, mount the motor into a starter motor holder or clamp it tightly into a vise. Tests that can be performed include voltage and amperage draws, resistance checks, solenoid operation, cranking speed, and breakaway torque using a special pinion drive torquemeter.

Solenoid Disassembly and Testing

The starter motor solenoid handles the battery power required to energize the enclosed shift mechanism connected to the starter motor pinion. Figure 26–22 shows the connection, while Figure 26–27 illustrates the typical component parts for a heavy-duty solenoid assembly. Often when a starter motor problem exists, the

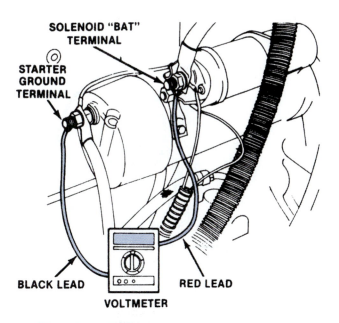

FIGURE 26–32 *Voltmeter connections at the starter motor to determine the available cranking voltage. (Courtesy of Detroit Diesel Corporation.)*

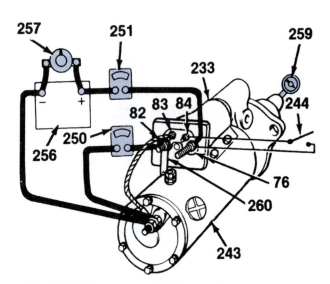

76. "BAT" Terminal	251. Ammeter
82. "MTR"	256. Battery
83. "GRD"	257. Carbon Pile
84. "SW"	259. RPM Indicator
233. Solenoid	260. Connector Strap
243. Starting Motor	
244. Switch	
250. Voltmeter	

FIGURE 26–33 *No-load test hookup on a heavy-duty truck starter motor with ground terminals. (Courtesy of Delco-Remy America.)*

cause may lie within the solenoid unit. The solenoid can be tested for internal shorts or open circuits using a multimeter or test lamp across the windings. An example of how to perform a solenoid check is illustrated in Figure 26–34a and b for both three- and four-terminal models.

Checking Procedure

1. To check the solenoid for grounds, connect a test lamp between the solenoid case and each terminal one at a time.

2. There should be no test light illumination if the solenoid is operating correctly. However, if the test light does illuminate, the terminal is grounded and the solenoid should be replaced.

3. To check the solenoid hold-in and pull-in windings, disconnect all of the wire leads from the solenoid and make the test connections as shown in Figure 26–34.

SPECIAL PRECAUTION   Serious damage to the solenoid pull-in winding can occur if during this test you allow current to flow for longer than 15 seconds. The carbon pile must be used to limit the voltage to that specified in the manufacturer's printed data. Note also that the current draw to the winding will decrease as the winding temperature increases.

---

4. Turn the load switch on and adjust the carbon pile to lower the battery voltage to the value shown in test specs for the solenoid switch.

5. Carefully note the amperage reading; a higher reading than specified is indicative of a shorted or grounded winding, a low-amperage reading indicates excessive resistance.

6. The winding resistance value can be read directly by using a digital ohmmeter capable of measuring in tenths of an ohm, since typical values for the pull-in winding will be between 0.14 and 0.16 Ω. Values for the hold-in winding on heavy-duty Delco starters is usually between 0.65 and 0.70 Ω. A low resistance value reading usually indicates that there is an internal short circuit, while no reading indicates an open circuit. If a coil resistance value is not available, you can determine this by using Ohm's law, divide the voltage by the current (ampere) value.

If the solenoid fails any of the tests above, disassemble it and inspect all components for signs of overheating, burning, and damage to the internal contacts, such as the disk plate.

FIGURE 26–34 (a) Testing three-terminal type solenoid windings; (b) testing the pull-in windings on three- and four-terminal solenoids. (Courtesy of Delco-Remy America.)

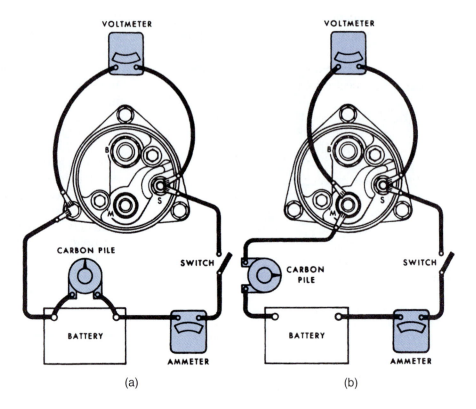

(a)   (b)

Cranking with a low-battery condition will cause the solenoid to overheat, resulting in possible welding (closing) of the contacts, which will result in the starter circuit being continuously energized and the engine attempting to crank steadily. Alternatively, the pinion may not engage with the ring gear, but the starter will continue to motor without cranking the engine. Disassembly of the solenoid is straightforward, usually requiring only the removal of the cover screws and attachments to expose the internal components. An example of a disassembled solenoid for a heavy-duty starter is shown in Figure 26–27.

Generally, the part that requires the most attention is the circular solenoid contact disk, identified as item 204. This circular disk comes into contact with the terminal stud that is connected to the battery power when energized. If the contact disk and terminals are not badly burned, the disk and terminals can be cleaned up. The disk can be turned over and the terminals rotated 180° to provide an unworn surface. First you have to remove the contact disk.

Removing the Contact Disk

1. Remove the small spring from the end of the disk, then carefully compress the contact cushion spring.

2. Remove the small roll pin from the plunger pin.

3. Remove the spring retainer, spring, and plunger pin from the disk.

4. Replace or turn the disk over to expose a new clean surface, and reinsert the small pin.

5. Install the spring, retainer, small roll pin, and spring in front of the disk.

Typical damage occurs to the disk due to attempting to crank the engine over with batteries that are in a state of low charge. This results in serious damage to the solenoid contact disk as a result of repeated attempts to start the engine with low battery power.

Pinion Clearance Check

Once the starter has been completely reassembled, it is necessary to check and adjust the solenoid plunger and shift lever movement so that the pinion drive mechanism will shift the gear drive into proper engagement with the flywheel ring gear once the starter switch has been closed.

SPECIAL NOTE Heavy-duty starter motor drives have a provision to adjust the pinion clearance if it is incorrect; however, there are no provisions for adjusting the pinion clearance on starter motors using an intermediate-duty clutch.

To check and adjust the solenoid plunger and shift lever movement, clamp the starter field frame into a vise.

1.   To check the pinion clearance, disconnect the motor field coil connector from the solenoid motor terminal.

2.   Connect the necessary battery voltage to match the solenoid rating (either 12 or 24V) from the solenoid switch terminal to the solenoid frame or ground terminal (Figure 26–35).

3.   To minimize power flow through the solenoid, momentarily flash a jumper lead from the solenoid motor terminal to the solenoid frame or ground terminal. This will immediately energize the solenoid and shift the pinion gear and clutch drive into the cranking position, where it will remain as long as the jumper wire is held in place.

4.   Manually push the pinion or drive back toward the commutator end to eliminate all free play.

5.   Using a feeler gauge, measure the distance between the drive gear pinion and the nose cone retainer (Figure 26–36). Note that the clearance limits for different starter drive types will vary.

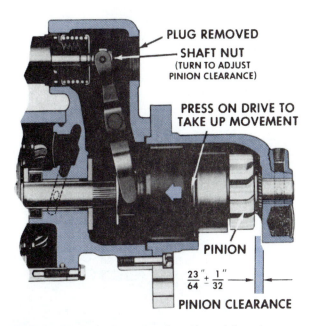

FIGURE 26–36 Checking the drive pinion clearance for a heavy-duty 42-MT model starter motor (shown earlier in Figure 26–22). (Courtesy of Delco-Remy America.)

6.   After any starter rebuild, solenoid lever adjustment is invariably required; therefore, disconnect the battery power temporarily if you have not already removed the shift lever housing access plug (Figure 26–36).

7.   To adjust the pinion clearance to within the published limits, use a socket, short extension, and ratchet drive to access the solenoid plunger adjustment nut.

8.   Using the jumper wire again, energize the starter pinion drive and with hand pressure against the pinion, recheck the pinion-to-nose cone clearance as shown in Figure 26–36. Rotate the shaft adjusting nut clockwise or counterclockwise until an acceptable clearance value is obtained.

9.   Always recheck the clearance at least once more to confirm that there is sufficient free play between the pinion gear and nose cone.

10.   Reinstall the access plug from the shift lever housing and tighten it securely.

SPECIAL NOTE   Always perform a no-load test on the starter after assembly and after completing the pinion clearance check. Details of this test were discussed and shown earlier in this chapter.

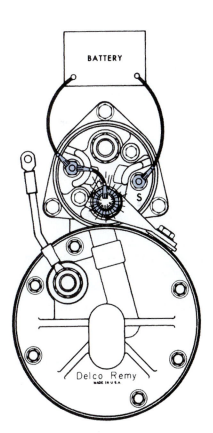

FIGURE 26–35 Connections for checking starter motor drive pinion clearance (seven-roller drive model shown). (Courtesy of Delco-Remy America.)

FIGURE   26–37 (a) Basic plumbing arrangement for an air starter motor; (b) details of a Turbostart design heavy-duty air starter motor assembly. (Part b: Courtesy of TDI-Tech Development Inc.)

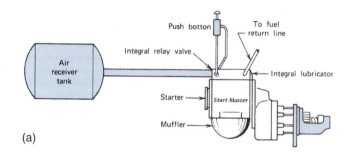

(a)

Ultra Low Pressure Starts

T100-V (Pre-Engaged)

(b)

AIR STARTER SYSTEM

Another popular starting system is an air starter powered by compressed air from the vehicle or equipment reservoirs, which in turn are charged from an engine-driven air compressor assembly. Figure 26–37A illustrates the basic components required for an air starter motor system.

Shown in Figure 26–37b is a turbo-twin compressed air starter motor widely used on modern engines. Features of this design are it produces up to 25% more horsepower and superior torque to vane-type models for faster cranking speed. Weighing between 43 and 54 lbs (19.5 and 24.5 KG's) it is lighter and more compact than other starters in its class. Additional features include:

T100 Turbine Air Motor has large air passages . . . won't clog or break

Clean Exhaust . . . no oily exhaust mist means emissions compliance

Aerodynamic Speed Control . . . prevents starter over-speed

Robust steel & aluminum alloy construction . . . no plastic or fragile parts

Vaneless Air Motor requires no lubrication of the air/gas supply

Grease-Packed Gearbox Design . . . no oil sump to check, change or fill

Pre-engaged Pinion Gear . . . ideal for multiple starter applications (T100-V)

Offset, Overhung Pinion Gear offers fit, flexibility and more pinion options (T100-V)

All TurboTwin Engine Air Starters feature grease-packed gears and bearings, and aerodynamic speed control, to provide long, trouble-free operation.

Lightweight rotating elements provide "soft engagement" . . . extending the life of both ring and pinion gears

SUMMARY

This chapter, and performing hands-on tasks, has provided you with the skills required to effectively maintain, service, and troubleshoot batteries, alternators, the electric and air starter motor systems. Coupled with your knowledge of these 3 systems, you should be capable of effectively maintaining the electrical system.

SELF-TEST QUESTIONS— STARTER MOTORS

1. Technician A says that starter motors for heavy-duty trucks can be driven by either electricity or compressed air. Technician B says that air starters are only used on off-highway and industrial equipment. Which technician is correct?

2. Technician A says that all heavy-duty on-highway trucks operate with 12V starter motors. Technician B says that some are equipped with 24V starter motors. Which technician is correct?

3. Technician A says that when a 24V starter motor is used, the batteries must be connected in parallel. Technician B says they must be connected in series and use a series–parallel switch arrangement. Who is right?

4. Technician A says that all starter motor circuits must use a magnetic switch. Technician B disagrees, saying that some systems use a magnetic switch, but others use a heavy-duty solenoid. Which technician is correct?

5. Technician A says that the starter motor drive pinion is engaged or pulled into engagement with the flywheel ring gear by centrifugal force as it is rotated. Technician B says that shift linkage connected to the solenoid assembly performs this function. Which technician is correct?

6. Technician A says that when the starter switch is closed, a set of magnetic switch contacts closes and the solenoid pull-in windings are connected to the battery source. Technician B says that once the switch is closed, the solenoid hold-in windings connect the motor to the batteries. Who is right?

7. Technician A says that once the starter drive pinion engages with the flywheel ring gear, the hold-in windings allow full battery power to flow to the brushes and through the armature windings, and then to rotate the drive pinion. Technician B says that it is the pull-in windings of the solenoid that provide this action. Which technician understands the motor operation better?

8. Technician A says that once the engine fires, centrifugal force will cause drive pinion disengagement. Technician B says that positive drive pinion disengagement is provided by the heavy-duty roller clutch used with the drive pinion. Who is right?

9. Technician A says that you should never engage the starter motor for periods longer than 15 seconds. Technician B says that you should not exceed a 30-second cranking time without allowing a cool-down period. Which technician is correct?

10. Technician A says that if a starter motor fails to operate or engage the flywheel ring gear after several cranking attempts, but will operate once again after a cool-down period, you should remove and overhaul it. Technician B says it is probably equipped with a thermostatic switch to avoid overheating. Which technician do you think is right here?

11. Technician B says that starter motor cool-down time after attempting to start the engine for a 30-second crank time should be 2 minutes. Technician B says that a 30-second cool-down time is sufficient. Who is right?

12. Technician A says that a starter motor that fails to engage unless the clutch pedal is depressed indicates that the electrical system is fitted with a neutral safety switch. Technician B believes it indicates that a short exists in the electrical system to the starter motor through the battery cable contacting the clutch linkage. Which technician do you think is correct in this case?

13. Technician A says that the solenoid mounted on top of the starter motor assembly functions to open and close the circuit between the batteries and the starter motor. Technician B says that the solenoid functions both to open and close this circuit and to shift the internal plunger to move the drive pinion into engagement

with the flywheel ring gear. Which technician do you think is right?

14. Technician A says that the motor solenoid terminal marked *S* connects the battery power to one side, then through the pull-in winding to ground on the other side to complete the circuit. Technician B says that the battery power flows to the hold-in winding instead. Who is right?

15. Technician A says that on a heavy-duty starter motor circuit, once the drive pinion is fully engaged, the solenoid disc in contact with the B and M terminals now requires less magnetism, and the pull-in winding is shorted to stop current flow through it. Technician B says that the pull-in winding must stay energized to keep the starter motor turning. Which technician understands the system operation better?

16. Technician A says that a chattering noise from the starter and failure to crank the engine is probably due to low voltage at the solenoid from undercharged batteries. Technician B says that high circuit resistance or a faulty solenoid could also be the cause. Are both technicians correct, or is only one?

17. Technician A says that if a starter motor continues to motor after the engine has started and the key switch or push button has been released, the problem is probably due to failure of the solenoid or wiring to open the circuit. Technician B says that this problem would be due to the drive pinion overrunning clutch not disengaging. Which technician do you think is correct?

18. Technician A says that voltage readings across the solenoid coil terminals of a heavy-duty 12V starter motor should be at least 11V. Technician B says that 10.5V would be acceptable. Who is correct?

19. Technician A says that voltage readings across the solenoid coil terminals of a 24V starter motor should be at least 21V. Technician B says it should be nothing less than 22V. Which technician is right?

20. Technician A says that a starter motor that exhibits a low rotative speed and a low current draw probably has shorted field coils. Technician B says that it probably has high internal circuit resistance. Who is correct?

21. Technician A says that the starter motor pinion clearance can be adjusted by shims on a heavy-duty model. Technician B says that this adjustment is obtained by a nut located inside the solenoid assembly. Which technician is correct?

Index

DATE DUE

May 5/05					
Oct 25/06					